Berlitz®

Complete Guide to

CRUISING
& CRUISE SHIPS

2012

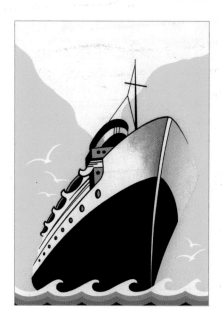

BY DOUGLAS WARD
President
The Maritime Evaluations Group

Editorial

Written by
Douglas Ward
Edited by
Brian Bell
Managing Editor
Tom Le Bas

Editorial address
Berlitz Publishing
PO Box 7910, London SE1 1WE
United Kingdom
berlitz@apaguide.co.uk

Distribution

North America
Ingram Publisher Services
1 Ingram Boulevard, PO Box 3006
La Vergne, TN 37086-1986
customer.service@ingrampublisherservices.com

UK & Ireland
GeoCenter International Ltd
Meridian House, Churchill Way West
Basingstoke, Hants RG21 6YR
sales@geocenter.co.uk

Worldwide
**Apa Publications GmbH & Co.
Verlag KG (Singapore branch)**
7030 Ang Mo Kio Avenue 5
08–65 Northstar @ AMK
Singapore 569880
apasin@singnet.com.sg

©2011 Apa Publications (UK) Ltd
All Rights Reserved

Printed by CTPS-China

*Berlitz Trademark Reg. U.S. Patent Office
and other countries. Marca Registrada.
Used under licence from the Berlitz
Investment Corporation*

First Edition 1985
Twentieth Edition 2012

CONTACTING THE AUTHOR
Although every effort is made to
provide accurate information, we live
in a fast-changing world and would
appreciate it if readers would call our
attention to any outdated information by
writing to Douglas Ward at:

**The Maritime Evaluations Group
Canada House, 1 Carrick Way
New Milton, Hants BH25 6UD
United Kingdom**
shipratings@hotmail.com

www.berlitzpublishing.com

HOW TO PICK THE RIGHT SHIP

Douglas Ward introduces the "bible" of the cruising world

The cruise industry is a fiercely competitive business, and one within which any marketing opportunity is seized upon and hyped to the nth degree. Travel industry awards – often in the form of magazine readers' polls – provide a perfect such opportunity and are extremely valuable to the cruise lines.

Yet these polls are only ever as good as the number of people who vote in them, the number of ships included and the criteria established for measuring quality. For example, if a magazine in the United States initiates a readers' poll and no readers have cruised aboard a Spanish-speaking cruise ship, that ship will get no votes. It stands to reason that the votes will go to the most traveled ships. The magazines never state the criteria for their decisions.

At Berlitz, we do. That's why *Berlitz Complete Guide to Cruising and Cruise Ships 2012* is the most authoritative guide you can buy. What's more, it is totally independent and in no way subsidized by advertising or sponsorship.

Value for money

The international cruise industry consists of more than 70 ocean-going cruise ship operators carrying over 21 million passengers a year. It can provide safe and hassle-free

vacations but offers an almost overwhelming choice. So how do you identify the "X-factor," that special quality that makes a ship stand out from the rest? What this book will do is help you choose the right ship, for the right reasons, and will leave you as well informed as most specialists in the industry.

An uncertain economic outlook has led to much innovative marketing activity in the industry. Although standards suffered from cost-cutting as the major cruise lines tried to counter the industry's deep discounting (mostly in North America), the lines have since been adding new items to woo

Douglas Ward aboard *Nippon Maru*.

WHAT THIS BOOK GIVES YOU

This book is divided into two main parts, followed by a short section of practical information and useful addresses. The first part helps you define what you are looking for in a cruise vacation and advises you on how to find it. It provides a wealth of information, including a look at life aboard ship and how to get the best from it. Specialist cruises are discussed, too, culminating with that ultimate travel experience: the around-the-world cruise.

The book's main section profiles 285 ocean-going cruise vessels. From large to small, from unabashed luxury and exclusivity to ships for the budget-minded, new and old, they are all here.

The ratings and evaluations are a painstaking documentation of the author's personal work. He travels constantly throughout the world, and is at sea for up to 200 days each year. All evaluations have been made objectively, without bias, partiality, or prejudice.

Chicago goes to sea: staging well-known Broadway shows aboard large resort ships is a growing trend.

passengers. Examples include premium mattresses and bed linen, shipwide wi-fi access, and larger spa and sports facilities. Whatever the compromises, it remains true that cruise companies can provide vacation experiences seldom matched in product delivery, cleanliness, and friendliness by land-based resorts.

Some things once included in the basic fare now cost extra. The resulting "onboard revenue" helps to compensate the industry for the fact that basic prices are still extremely low, while the newest ships have far more novel features than even a few years ago, and many more dining choices. Discounted pricing has done one thing, however, and that is to open up cruising to a much wider range of

customers, including younger people and more families with children.

All the above changes have affected the ratings of some cruise ships and are reflected in this book.

My 5,700 days at sea

In welcoming new readers to this edition, I should mention my qualifications for assessing cruise ships on your behalf. I first fell in love with ships when, in 1965, I worked Cunard Line's 83,673-ton ocean liner RMS *Queen Elizabeth* – then the world's largest passenger ship. Over the next 17 years, I worked for eight companies in various roles.

To date, I have completed over 5,700 days at sea, participating in more than 1,000 cruises, 157 trans-

atlantic crossings and countless Panama Canal transits, plus many shipyard visits, ship-naming ceremonies and maiden voyages.

The first edition of this book, reviewing, testing, and evaluating 120 ships, appeared in 1985, when cruising seemed to most people an expensive, rarefied experience. Today, the book is the most highly regarded source of comparative information not only for cruise purchasers, but also for cruise industry executives, crew members, and travel agents.

This book is a tribute to everyone who has made my seafaring experiences possible, and I thank the cruise lines for their assistance during the complex scheduling, sailing, inspection, evaluation, and rating processes.

In almost all instances, the ships have been visited recently by the author or one of his team in order to assess current status. Passenger comments are taken into account in the final evaluations *(see form on page 688)*.

Please note that, although price indicators are supplied for such things as alternative restaurants, spa treatments and other items, prices may have changed since this book went to press.

Most of the statistical informa-

tion contained in the ship profiles was supplied and checked by the cruise lines and ship owners. Any errors or updated information should be sent to the author at the address shown on the facing page.

Please note that the author's constant ship inspection schedule means he is infrequently on land, and is no longer able to answer letters. However, every comment received will be studied and will help maintain the authority of the next edition for the benefit of all.

CONTENTS

Practical Information

Maps

Tables and Charts

Introduction

WHAT TO LOOK FOR IN 2012

More than 21 million people took a cruise in 2011, and new ships on the horizon will offer attractions aimed at expanding the market despite tough economic conditions

The cruise industry has in service more than 50 ships measuring over 100,000 gross tons *(see page 157)*, and more are coming. As this book went to press, 16 new ships of various sizes were scheduled for delivery between January 2012 and the end of 2015. Cruise lines need to build new tonnage in order to stay ahead of the competition – or so the shipyards hope. There's also the consideration that new ships benefit from the latest in fuel-efficient technology and environmentally friendly engines.

But there's a problem. After the recent credit crunch, the cost of newbuilds – and the cost of borrowing to finance them – went north. Banks have been less willing to lend the huge sums needed to secure loans and guarantees to shipyards. In addition, there's the higher price of steel, the higher cost of labor, and the higher fees demanded by banks, private finance groups, and others lending money for construction and shipbuilding guarantees. As a result, there are fewer new ships on the horizon than there might have been.

Most cruise lines earn their money in US dollars, but ships are built in Europe, where the relatively weak dollar buys fewer euros than it used to. While 2011 was a year when some cruise lines just managed to stay afloat due to challenging marketing conditions and ever-rising fuel, crew and operating costs, 2012 promises to be better.

In 2012, the new ships are all mid-size or large resort ships, varying in capacity from the 1,260-passenger *Regatta* to the 3,690-passenger *Carnival Breeze*. In 2013, just five new cruise ships will be delivered, from the 516-passenger *Europa 2* to a 4,000-passenger yet unnamed ship for Norwegian Cruise Line.

Some of the new ships are clones of a similar series in terms of size, layout and configuration, although there are exceptions. All are being built by the specialist shipyards in France, Finland, Germany, and Italy (Fincantieri and STX Europe). Here's a preview of what the cruise lines plan to unveil.

PRECEDING PAGES: a trio of large resort ships in port at Old San Juan, Puerto Rico.
LEFT: *Carnival Destiny* continues the cruise line's ceaseless fight against monochrome.
RIGHT: AIDA Cruises appeals to families who like an über-casual approach to cruising.

NEW IN 2012

AIDA Cruises

The 2,192-passenger über-casual *AIDAmar* will be one of only a few ships to have its own micro-brewery – the others are *AIDAblu* and *AIDAsol*. As aboard all its ships, self-serve buffet eateries are the standard, tablecloth-less way of family feeding. The spa facilities are excellent, and AIDA Cruises offers an urban lifestyle. The sport bikes will be on board. *AIDAmar* promises to be a trendy, well-packaged ship for youngsters.

Carnival Cruise Lines

In 2010 the new *Carnival Dream* started a trend to include more facilities and gathering areas for its youthful audience, including the first outdoor promenade aboard a Carnival ship. The company's newest ship, the 3,646-passenger *Carnival Breeze*, continues that trend. The ship will have its very own brew, ThirstyRedFrog, a beer first offered aboard *Carnival Magic*.

Celebrity Cruises

The 3,030-passenger *Celebrity Reflection* is the fifth ship in the Solstice class, following *Celebrity Eclipse*

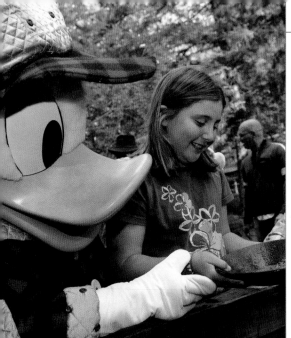

Panning for gold – but Disney Cruise Line has already found it.

and showlounge. Replacing the Hot Glass Blowing Show of some earlier ships in the series, *Celebrity Reflection*, like *Celebrity Silhouette*, has a Lawn Club and Grill on its top deck, with "interactive" hot stone cooking.

Costa Cruises

The 3,012-passenger *Costa Fascinosa* is a continuation of the *Costa Fortuna*-class series. Facilities include a Formula One race car simulator experience where you sit in and drive – just like the real thing – at high speed on one of the world's great racing tracks. A huge nine-deck high glass-domed atrium has a lifestyle bar/lounge at its base, and a retractable glass dome covering the pool area.

Disney Cruise Line

Early in 2012, family-friendly Disney Cruise Line will introduce the 2,500-passenger *Disney Fantasy* (sister to *Disney Dream*, which debuted in 2011). The whimsical ship will feature its superb AquaDuck thrill ride for young and not-so-young passengers. The water coaster flume ride stretches 765ft (about 233 meters), and goes

(2010), *Celebrity Equinox* (2009), *Celebrity Silhouette* (2011) and *Celebrity Solstice* (2008). But there's a difference – although it's the same size, *Celebrity Reflection* carries more passengers because an additional deck housing more suites and cabins has been incorporated, and extra seating has been provided in the dining rooms

between, through, and around the ship's two funnels, over the main pool, and drops through four decks during the ride. High above the water, it provides a superb view from the sections of the ride that are open (some are covered, so it's like going through a tunnel with some snatches of light from the outside world). Inside

---

BE PREPARED: SIX CRUISE LINE RIP-OFFS TO AVOID

❶ Currency conversion
Currency conversion is a game where cruise lines win from total control over your onboard account. Using a foreign credit card to pay this account means you could incur currency conversion charges, known in the trade as dynamic currency conversion (DCC). This is because cruise lines may have a "guaranteed exchange rate." When you pay your bill, the price quoted is recalculated into a "guaranteed" price, which can be higher than the rate quoted by banks or other credit card companies. For example, if your onboard bill is in euros and you pay with a US dollar-based credit card, the cruise line will convert the amount at its convenience – not necessarily on the day of the transaction, but later in the month when conversion rates could change to your disadvantage. Many passengers are annoyed by this tactic, which they learn about only when they receive

Beware of double-tipping for spa treatments.

their credit card statements at home, weeks after their cruise.

❷ Extra gratuities
The major cruise lines typically imprint an *additional* gratuity line on signable receipts for such things as spa treatments or extra-cost coffees or other bar charges, *despite* a 15% gratuity having already been added to the actual cost of the item. Example: for an espresso coffee costing $1.50, a 15% gratuity of 23 cents is added, thus making the total cost $1.73. You are then asked to sign the receipt, but one line *above* the signature line says

"Additional Gratuity" – thus inviting you to pay a *double* gratuity. What a rip-off!

❸ Transfer buses
The cost of airport transfer buses in some ports, such as Athens, Barcelona, and Civitavecchia (the port for Rome).

❹ Mineral water
The cost of bottled mineral water for shore excursions. Example: Celebrity Cruises charges $4.50, but then adds another 15% gratuity "for your convenience."

❺ Navigation bridge tours
You'd like to see the view from the bridge? Princess Cruises charges $150 per person to be entered into a "raffle" to compete for just six available tickets to visit the ship's bridge. Still want to see it?

❻ Bingo cards
The cost of cards for a simple game of bingo is rising dramatically. One extreme example: NCL charges $40 for a block of four cards.

the ship, look out for the "enchanted artwork" on some walls – it incorporates movement. One thing you won't find, of course, is a casino.
See feature on Disney Cruise Line, pages 14–15.

MSC Cruises

The 3,502-passenger *MSC Divina* will have a dedicated restaurant for its "Yacht Club" accommodation occupants only. The new restaurant will be located within the exclusive Yacht Club, and linked to the expansive Yacht Club Lounge, with direct access to the suite-grade accommodation. After check-in and embarkation, passengers are escorted by their own butler directly to their accommodation. So you really can feel a little exclusive – even aboard a large resort ship. A shimmering infinity pool represents the latest in illusion-provoking design and experiences.

Oceania Cruises

Oceania Cruises' 1,258-passenger *Riviera* continues with the elegant, traditional grand hotel/ocean liner decor theme aboard its latest ship, scheduled to launch in April 2012. (It's sister to *Marina*, which debuted in 2011.) Having been designed by new blood in the world of cruise ship interior design, such as Dakota Jackson, some of the largest suites are typical of the decor and quality in *Architectural Digest* magazine's home features. The horseshoe-shaped staircase in the foyer is a beauty – a mix of black wrought iron and large Lalique crystal plates. With its wide choice of restaurants and dining venues, this will be a great ship if you like really good food.

Oceania Cruises is known for the high quality of its food.

NEW IN 2013

Hapag-Lloyd Cruises

The 516-passenger *Europa 2*, due to debut in spring 2013, promises to be a shining example of evolution in design and functionality in a beautifully designed small ship format, for a more exclusive yet upbeat style of cruising. The ship will have more space per passenger than any other cruise ship, at more than 75 (gross tonnage divided by the number of passengers carried).

The focus will be on the finest quality dining experiences – there are seven dining venues – and wellness

---

Europa 2 will be more family-friendly than *Europa*.

facilities. But there's a twist, as the new ship will also be family-friendly in order to cater to the increasing trend of affluent, well-behaved families taking a vacation together.

Princess Cruises

The SeaWalk aboard Princess Cruises' 3,600-passenger *Royal Princess*, set to debut in May 2013, will be new and exciting. It will be a cantilevered, half-moon-shaped walkway extending over both sides of the ship. One side will be just a walkway, while the other will include a bar. In both, you look straight down through the glass bottom of the walkway, which extends about 28ft (8.5 meters) from the side of the ship to the ocean, 128ft (39 meters) beneath your feet. It promises to be a dramatic feature for this class of ship – the ultimate glass bottom boat? – and will give you a chance to pretend you're walking on water. The ship itself looks more streamlined than the previous Grand-class ships.

All outside-view suites/cabins aboard the new ship will have a balcony – a first for any Princess Cruises ship. The vessel, many will be pleased to learn, does not have the shopping-cart look of the previous Grand-class ships, but rather resembles the more rounded, Vista-class ships favoured by several other cruise lines.

Maybe coming later...

Although ocean-going residences have thus far been limited to *The World*, another company, Utopia Residences, may become the second company to offer a ship where the accommodation is strictly for purchase by the wealthy. Although a Letter of Intent between Utopia Residences and Korea's Samsung Shipyards was signed in December 2009, the construction has yet to start. One of the hopeful future occupants of the £1.1 billion ship is the entertainer Pat Boone, who signed in December 2010 for one of the floating apartments aboard the 105,000 gross ton ship.

However, other similar projects have come to naught. *The Four Seasons*, *The Magellan*, and *The Orphalese* were all scheduled to launch between 2008 and 2010. While the names sound enticing, they have yet to assume a reality beyond the drawing board.

Refurbishment as an alternative

For cruise operators and companies that are small or lack substantial financial resources, refitting and revitalizing older ships will become increasingly popular. This option makes sense in light of the enormous cost of a new ship and the two-year time frame needed for completion and delivery. Even so, refits are expensive, at approximately $2 million a day – and the figure is being pushed up by material, equipment and labor costs.

A positive aspect of refits is that the latest green technology can often be incorporated, or existing equipment modified, to make the ships more eco-friendly. Logis-

Berthing space is tight in some regions.

tics are key, and the aim is to put the ships back in service as quickly as possible.

Choppy economic waters

Although more than 21 million people took a cruise in 2011, the cruise companies found the economic waters unpleasantly choppy. Enacting cost-efficiencies was the order of the day. Head offices further reduced management and staff, squeezed suppliers and port costs, and tried to make their ships more efficient.

Cruise lines moved ships away from low-profit regions such as Alaska and the Caribbean, and sent them to Europe and Southeast Asia, or Australasia. Europe has become awash with cruise ships – so much so that getting berthing space has become a difficult task for the itinerary planners. Australasia, too, has seen dramatic growth recently.

But there is pressure from the regulatory bodies, too, such as the cost of implementing the latest requirements of SOLAS (Safety of Life at Sea) in 2010, and the cost of compliance of imminent emissions regulations and the use of certain fuels.

As a result of the looming low-sulphur fuel regulations, you can expect ships to slow down, and for itineraries to be changed accordingly. So, expect to spend less time in ports of call and more time at sea – a better scenario for onboard revenue.

After the credit crunch

One way of making fares seem more attractive was to charge less for the basics but then push hard to earn more onboard revenue from all the "extras" that many passengers don't really want in the first place. Put another way, cruising aboard the large resort ships is now like buying a new car, with so-called "cruise enhancements" being the equivalent of optional extras.

Sadly, "two for one" pricing has almost become an industry standard in some mar-

---

AT A GLANCE: THE LATEST TRENDS

More passengers are looking for active pursuits on shore excursions.

- More charging for "extras."
- More multi-generational cruising aboard the large resort ships.
- More single-parent cruising.
- More adults-only ships, for those who have matured beyond noise and games.
- Small ship cruising, for those seeking to avoid large resort ships and crowds.
- More themed dining venues.
- More sophisticated spas and wellbeing treatment options.
- More "healthy eating" and "spa" menu choices.
- More variety of active adventures ashore.
- More demand for smoking-free ships.
- More demand for longer cruises.
- More demand for short "getaway" cruises.

Is cruising still good value?

It's never been better, thanks in part to the fact that the economic downturn has forced cruise lines to offer more incentives – such as onboard credit, cabin upgrades, and other perks – in an effort to keep their companies afloat and their ships full.

The price of your vacation is protected by advance pricing, so you know before you go that your major outgoings have already been set. A fuel surcharge is the only additional cost that may change at the last minute, although recently introduced laws in Australia and the European Union require all add-on port charges, charged gratuities, taxes, and fuel surcharges to be included in the advertised price ("single figure advertising").

How to get the best deal

● Find out what's available by reading newspaper advertising and checking the internet. Then identify a travel agency that *specializes* in cruises. In some countries, such as the UK, they'll be bonded if they belong to a shipping association. A good agent will get you the best price, as well as upgrades and other benefits you won't be able to get on your own.

● Big travel agency groups and consortiums often

kets. But such pricing is really a marketing gimmick used by people who don't understand the wonderful product that a cruise vacation delivers to so many people. It's better to concentrate on your vacation – where you want to go, what size of ship you want to sail aboard, and what kind of food and service you are willing to pay for (or prepared to accept).

The truth about low fares

Although bargains still exist, it's important to read the small print. A highly discounted fare may apply only to certain dates and itineraries – for example, the eastern Caribbean instead of the more popular western Caribbean. It may be subject to a booking deadline or, typically, is "cruise-only," which means you must arrange your own air transportation separately. This can prove expensive (to Alaska or Europe, for example). If air transportation *is* included, deviations may not be possible.

Your cabin choice, grade and location may not be available. You could be limited to first seating at dinner aboard a ship that operates two seatings, and some highly discounted fares may not apply to children. Port charges, handling fees, fuel surcharges, or other taxes may cost extra.

As with low-cost airlines, add-ons such as government taxes and perhaps a non-refundable processing fee take the glow off an apparent give-away price. The cruise lines have copied outfits such as the Irish airline Ryanair, which charges extra for making a reservation (handling charge), airport check-in, checked baggage, priority boarding, carry-on duty-free items, carrying sports equipment, and changing a flight. There are so many *potential* extra charges, in fact, that it's probably cheaper to book a scheduled airline.

Once you strip all the "free" extras away and obtain the final per-person, per-day cost, you'll have a better idea of what's included, what's not, and how good the "price deal" really is.

HOW CRUISE LINES CUT COSTS TO STAY AFLOAT

The trick is to save costs while still offering value for money. But of course there'll always be people who buy rock-bottom fares and then complain when they don't get lobster every night. Cruise lines have also trimmed costs by increasing efficiency – the latest ships have more efficient powerplants, for example – and some have reduced staff.

Food is a target for cost-cutting.

15 cost-cutting ploys:
● Reducing menu selections.
● Reducing food portions in main dining venues.
● Providing cheaper types of meat (pork, not beef or lamb).
● Reducing the strength of "free" coffee.
● Reducing the variety of green vegetables.
● Removing trays from self-serve buffets (some lines) so you can't carry as much food.
● Reducing service levels and giving minimal training.
● Charging for ship postcards that used to be free.
● Replacing live flowers with silk flowers.
● Reducing in-cabin toiletries.
● Cutting speed between ports.
● Switching to lower-cost suppliers.
● Removing free writing paper and postcards.
● Taking advantage of bulk buying (across several brands).
● "Squeezing" port agents, berthing and handling charges.

Adding "value"
Some major cruise lines are desperately trying to put back some of the things that the accountants did away with in the past few years and then boasting that they're "adding value."

Twin titans: *Allure of the Seas* and *Oasis of the Seas* can each carry 6,360 passengers and 2,164 crew.

reserve large blocks of cabins, and smaller independent agencies can access extensive discounts not available on the internet. Because the cruise lines consider travel agents as their principal distribution system, they provide special discounts and value-added amenities that are not provided to internet sites.

● Cruise lines offer their best prices to those who book early. It's worth taking the bait to get the best choice of cabin and location, and the best chance of any upgrades, in case any are offered closer to your sailing date. Booking late may sometimes get you cheaper prices, too, but you *won't* get a choice of cabins and locations, so you could end up with a tiny cupboard above the galley.

● Choose an older ship – the newest, much publicized ships command a premium.

● If you're on a tight budget, book an interior (no view) cabin on one of the best ships, instead of an outside cabin on a less fancy ship. This buys you better food and entertainment for the same money.

● A number of ships offer drinks-inclusive pricing, saving you a bundle in extra onboard costs. It works well for families with children.

● Savvy passengers join frequent passenger clubs to get maximum benefits. These offer additional perks (onboard credit, free wi-fi service, private cocktail parties), and further discounts for booking your next cruise while on board (at prices not available on the internet).

● Check to make sure that all port charges, government fees, and any fuel surcharges are included in an advertised price quote.

● If you find a highly discounted cruise rate on the internet, fine. But, if a cruise line suddenly offers special discounts for your sailing, or cabin upgrades, or things go wrong with your booking, your internet booking service may prove quite unfriendly – many are not licensed or bonded. Your specialist travel agent, however, can probably work magic in making those special discounts and upgrades benefit you. And there's a bonus: travel agents don't charge for their service.

● **...and a deal to avoid:** Don't fall for one of those automated telemarketing scams, operated mainly from the United States, which tell you "Congratulations! You've won a free two-night cruise," or, "If you just answer our 10-question survey we'll send you two boarding passes for a two-night Bahamas cruise." These are scams – nothing more – and are *not* connected to genuine cruise lines. Don't even *think* about giving your credit card details "for port taxes."

E-cruising is in

The major cruise lines have changed to online bookings and check-in. This makes life difficult for anyone with arthritis or typing problems, or for households without a computer, and bad luck if there's a power outage, your router or computer gives up the ghost, or you run out of printer paper. There's a lot to be said for letting your travel agent do it all for you.

Inevitably, though, there is more reliance on e-technology, and this means the reduction of the number of paper tickets issued by the cruise lines – but you'll have to spend more money to print out your tickets, boarding pass, and other documents. So, in effect, the cruise lines are passing the carbon footprint buck to you, the consumer.

Only the really exclusive, upscale cruise lines, expedition companies, and tall ship lines will provide boxes or wallets packed with documents, cruise tickets, leather (or faux-leather) luggage tags, and colourful destination booklets – cruise lines operating large resort ships have all but abandoned such niceties already. Aboard ship, e-technology is increasingly prominent. Today, we are seeing the disappearance of printed news sheets and sports results, with news available only on in-cabin "interactive" television systems.

Getting on the brandwagon

Image-conscious cruise lines are jockeying to become the "greenest" brand. Size is a major factor, and so each line touts the benefits of its particular size of ship. For that reason, choosing the right sized ship for your vacation is now more important than ever.

Rebranding sometimes involves a change of name. Azamara Cruises, for example, restyled itself more intimately as Azamara Club Cruises, while The Yachts of Seabourn sounds much more elegant as, simply, Seabourn. On an upbeat note, Quail Cruises became Happy Cruises.

The growth of shopping malls

Onboard "enhancement" items – such as luggage and tote bags, bed linen, personal amenities, wooden deck lounge (steamer) chairs, coffee tables and chairs, ship posters, cruise line memorabilia and collectibles, wine glasses, chocolate, flowers, and even mattresses – can now be purchased online from the major cruise lines (examples: www.carnivalcomfortbed.com; www.shop-hollandamerica.com). But such online shopping usually only works if you have a US address and credit card.

The floating playgrounds

The world's "largest ever" cruise ships, Royal Caribbean International's *Allure of the Seas* and *Oasis of the Seas*, have redefined large resort ship cruising. With a capacity of 6,000-plus passengers, they are innovative and exciting – which means they are not quiet or relaxing.

Being aboard such a floating playground can mean waiting for elevators, and disembarkation is a bit like getting out of a sports stadium at the end of a big game. After which, of course, you'll need to locate your luggage.

Mid-size ships benefit from the introduction of so many large resort ships because more and more experienced cruisegoers are downsizing to avoid the big ships' sanitized cruise experience and long lines.

Dining and service

"Alternative" restaurants are fashionable, particularly aboard the large resort ships, and are ideal for escaping from huge dining halls full of noise and singing, table-dancing waiters. These are typically à la carte restaurants serving superior food. But a couple each having two glasses of palatable wine could, with the cover charge, easily end up paying $100 for dinner.

Cruise lines stuck with traditional two-seating dining are looking for ways to be more flexible. More ships offer flexible dining and 24-hour casual (get-your-own-food) eateries, so you can eat or snack when you want. Although the concept is good, the delivery often is not; it is typically rather soulless, self-service eating. ❏

EXTRA-COST ITEMS ARE COSTING EVEN MORE

Cruise lines have been offering some appealingly low fares, but most have been making strenuous efforts to maintain revenues by increasing the cost of onboard facilities. Some examples are quoted throughout this book to indicate the cost of, for example, massages, internet access, cover charges for "alternative" restaurants, and gratuities added to your onboard account, and the most common extra-cost items are listed below. But please note that these are provided only as guidelines, and may have changed since this book was completed. Always check with the cruise line, onboard concession, or your travel provider for the latest prices.

An internet connection is usually an extra cost.

Item	Cost
"Alternative" dining (cover charge)	$15–$100 each
Baby-sitting (per hour)	$5
Bottled water	$2.50–$7 (per bottle)
Cappuccino/espresso	$2–$3
Cartoon character bedtime "tuck-in" service	$20
Wash one shirt	$2–$3
Dry-clean dress	$4–$7.50
Dry-clean jacket	$4–$8
Golf simulator	$20 (30 minutes)
Group bicycling class	$10 per class
Hair wash/set	$30–$50
Haircut (men)	$25
Ice cream	$2–$3.75
In-cabin movies	$6.95–$12.95
Internet connection	$0.50 per minute
Kick-boxing class	$11 per class
Laundry soap	$1–$1.50
Massage	$2-plus a minute (plus tip)
Satellite phone/fax	$4.95–$15 per minute
Send/receive emails	$0.50–$0.75 per minute
Shuttle bus in ports of call	$3–$6
Sodas (soft drinks)	$2–$3
Souvenir photograph (8" by 6")	$10–$12
Souvenir photograph (10" by 8")	$20–$30
Tuxedo rental (7-day cruise)	$85
Use of Aqua Spa	$30 per day
Video postcard	$4.95–$6.95
Wine/cheese tasting	$10–$20
Wine with dinner	$7–$500
Yoga class	$11 per class

WHY THEY'RE CHASING A CARTOON MOUSE

Spurred on by Disney Cruise Line's success, other operators are recruiting a menagerie of comic characters to win a share of the growing family market

In 1932, a Disney cartoon, *Steamboat Willy*, depicted Mickey Mouse at the wooden wheel of a ship. But it took another six decades until Disney decided to get into the family cruise market, creating Disney Cruise Line as an extension of its resort hotel business, offering a "seamless vacation package."

Now it has three large resort ships catering to families with children, with a fourth joining them in 2012. The casino-free ships have ambitious entertainment programs, as well as the longest water slide at sea, and everything is centred around Disney and its superb stable of famous characters. Cruises vary between three and seven days. Disney also has its own Art Deco passenger terminal and facilities at Port Canaveral, Florida, plus a fleet of motorcoaches.

There has been tremendous growth in family cruising, and not only in the English-language market. AIDA Cruises sells family cruises for German-speakers, Costa Cruises for Italian-speakers, and Pullmantur Cruises for Spanish-speakers. Even the upscale Hapag-Lloyd Cruises, which is building a new *Europa*, has included children's facilities in the belief that well-behaved children are part of today's affluent young family environment.

Disney's four ships may not constitute a lethal commercial threat to the giant cruise lines that dominate the industry – there's more money to be made from bar sales and giant casinos – but the Disney theme-park approach has been hugely influential. Norwegian Cruise Line, for example, has forged strong links with Nickleodeon, the television channel with fun characters like Sponge Bob and Dora the Explorer. Royal Caribbean International has developed its Royal Promenade "Move On! Move On!" parade, a 15-minute circus-like extravaganza featuring characters from DreamWorks Animation's *Madagascar*. And Princess Fiona, Shrek's girlfriend, named RCI's *Allure of the Seas* in the cruise industry's first animated ship-naming ceremony by breaking a bottle of bubbly with a karate chop. Carnival Cruise Lines promotes its mascot, Fun Ship Freddy, and is to unveil a 6-ft (1.8-meter) tall towel elephant.

TOP: Disney characters star in the ships' big production shows.
ABOVE AND LEFT: there's no escaping Mickey – or Donald Duck.
BELOW: DreamWorks characters prowl *Allure of the Seas*.

ABOVE: even the funnels prominently display Mickey Mouse ears.

WHAT MAKES DISNEY SO HARD TO BEAT

Disney Cruise Line's ships are cleverly designed to handle both children and adults well. Each vessel has three distinct areas: one for families with young children, one for families with older children and teens, and one for adults only. Each group has its own swimming pool and deck facilities. The cabin bathrooms are practical and have a separate toilet.

As in the company's theme parks, Disney characters are much in evidence. Children can book a breakfast with their favorite – or be tucked up in bed by one. Each ship has three identically sized main restaurants, with different Disney themes and decor, enabling passengers to change restaurants daily, keeping the same table number and accompanied by their regular waiters. It's an ingenious arrangement, and very popular.

Facilities are highly organized for specific age groups, and each group has its own daily program, Personal Navigator. Flounders Reef Nursery is for children between three months and three years old. Those from three to eight years old get to play in the Oceaneer Club, a playroom themed on Captain Hook, with lots of crawling and climbing-centered activities. The Oceaneer Lab is an interactive area for eight- to 12-year-olds, where kids find out about science, get to use microscopes, build things, act and direct their own TV commercials, and learn how animation works.

Pre-teens and teens have their own chill-out spaces and teen counselors. Each ship carries more than 40 children's and youth counselors.

Disney even has its own private island, Castaway Cay, conveniently situated on one of its standard routes from Port Canaveral to the Bahamas. Here young children can have fun with pirate themes and water slides, while adults have their own stretch of beach plus facilities such as snorkeling. Free strollers are provided, and a tram takes tired passengers back to the ship. It's clear that Disney has applied many of its theme-park skills to Castaway Cay.

Rival cruise companies can't hope to beat The Mouse at its own game. But they can copy some of its smart ideas, and most have the advantage of much lower fares.

ABOVE: Captain Hook confronts a Disney passenger.
RIGHT: P&O Cruises takes Enid Blyton's Noddy on board.

CRUISING'S UNSTOPPABLE GROWTH

When the first jet aircraft made many of the old passenger liners redundant, some were scrapped but others gave birth to the modern cruise industry

Twenty-seven years ago, the first edition of this book listed 120 ships, about 30 of which are still operating in one form or another. Today, that number has grown to more than 280 (around 350 including the list of ships operating coastal cruises). Throughout the period, the cruise industry has maintained a global growth rate of over 7% each year. But many well-known cruise lines have also gone to the deep blue seabed in the past 25 years. Indeed, since 1990 more than 65 cruise companies have either merged, or been taken over, or simply gone out of business, including such well-liked companies as Royal Cruise Lines, Royal Viking Line, and Sun Line Cruises.

Some start-up lines, using older ships and aimed at specific markets, also came and went – operations such as American Family Cruises, Fiesta Marina Cruises, Premier Cruise Lines, and Regency Cruises. In came new shiny tonnage, complete with vanity logos and adornments painted on all-white

A classic Holland America Line poster.

hulls – the attributes of the industry's emerging giants. Fresh thinking transformed the design of accommodation, the use of public spaces, and more food and entertainment venues.

Yield management, a term purloined from the airline industry, was introduced. These days company executives think of little else, because running a cruise company is all about economics.

Modern cruising is born

In the early 1960s, passenger-shipping directories listed over 100 passenger lines. Until the mid-1960s, it was cheaper to cross the Atlantic by ship than by plane, but the appearance of the jet aircraft changed that rapidly, particularly with the introduction of the Boeing 747 in the early 1970s. In 1962, more than 1 million people crossed the North Atlantic by ship; in 1970, that number was down to 250,000.

The success of the jumbo jets created a fleet of unprofitable and out-of-work passenger liners that appeared doomed for the scrap heap. Even the famous big "Queens," noted for their regular weekly transatlantic service, were at risk. Cunard White Star Line's *Queen Mary* (81,237 gross tonnage) was withdrawn in September 1967.

Cunard Line's sister ship *Queen Elizabeth*, at 83,673 gross tonnage the largest-ever passenger liner (until 1996), made its final crossing in November 1968.

Ships were sold for a fraction of their value. Many lines went out of business and ships were scrapped. Those that survived attempted to mix transatlantic crossings with voyages south to the sun. The Caribbean (including the Bahamas) became appealing, cruising became an alternative, and an entire new industry was born, with new lines being formed exclusively for cruising.

Then smaller, more specialized ships arrived, capable of getting into the tiny ports of developing Caribbean islands; there were no commercial airlines taking vacationers to the Caribbean then, and

WHO GOES CRUISING

The Maritime Evaluations Group has analyzed by nationality the breakdown of cruise line passengers:

United States	13,500,000
Europe (excluding UK)	3,900,000
UK	1,600,000
Canada	770,000
Asia (excluding Japan)	600,000
Australia/New Zealand	330,000
Scandinavia	200,000
Japan	180,000
Cyprus *	75,000
Cargo ship passengers	3,000
Total	**21,158,000**

* Local Cyprus market only.

Note: The above numbers include the approximately 1 million passengers who took a river/inland waterway cruise, but not the 300,000 passengers who took a coastal voyage aboard the Hurtigruten (Norwegian Coastal Voyages) ships. All figures are for 2010.

few hotels. Instead of cruising long distances south from more northerly ports such as New York, companies established their headquarters in Florida. This avoided the cold weather, choppy seas, and expense of the northern ports and saved fuel costs with shorter runs to the Caribbean.

Cruising was reborn. California became the base for cruises to the Mexican Riviera, and Vancouver on Canada's west coast was the focus for summer cruises to Alaska.

Flying passengers to embarkation ports was the next logical step, and soon a working relationship emerged between the cruise lines and the airlines. Air/sea and "sail and stay" packages thrived – joint cruise and hotel vacations with inclusive pricing. Some of the old liners came out of mothballs, purchased by emerging cruise lines and refurbished for warm-weather cruising operations, often with their interiors redesigned and refitted. During the late 1970s, the modern cruise industry grew at a rapid rate.

Cruising today

Today's cruise concept hasn't changed much from that of earlier days, although it has been improved,

Caribbean cruising as depicted in a 1947 advertisement.

refined, expanded, and packaged for ease of consumption. No longer the domain of affluent, retired people, cruising today attracts passengers of *every* age and socio-economic background. It's no longer the shipping business, but the hospitality industry – although it has to be said that some cruise ship personnel appear to be in the hostility industry.

New ships are generally larger than their predecessors, yet cabin size is "standardized" to provide more space for entertainment and other public facilities. Today's ships boast air conditioning to keep out heat and humidity; stabilizers to keep the ship on an even keel; a high level of maintenance, safety, and hygiene; and more emphasis on health and fitness facilities.

Although ships have long been devoted to eating and relaxation in comfort, ships today offer more activities, and more learning and life-enriching experiences than before. For the same prices as a quarter of a century ago, you can cruise aboard the latest large resort ships that offer ice skating, rock climbing, golfing, rollerblading, wave surfing, bowling, and so on while dining at fine restaurants that offer varied cuisines, being pampered in luxurious spas, and being entertained by high-quality production shows. And there are many more places you can visit on a cruise: from Antarctica to Acapulco, Bermuda to Bergen, Dakar to Dominica, Shanghai to St Thomas.

Cruising tomorrow

Current ship design follows two quite distinct paths: large resort ships or smaller niche-market ships.

● Large resort ships, where "economy of scale" helps the operator to keep down the cost per passenger. The first, *Carnival Destiny*, debuted in 1996, and today seven companies have ships measuring over 100,000 gross tons *(see page 157)*. Some

---

WHAT'S NEW IN THE MODERN CRUISE INDUSTRY – BUT NOT ALWAYS AN IMPROVEMENT

- Cruise-only travel agents
- Pay-extra dining venues
- Vacuum (barking-dog) toilets
- "Art" auctions, jewelry shops
- Vibration-less "pod" propulsion systems
- Online check-in for some of the major cruise lines
- Balcony- and French-balcony, loft and lobby cabins
- Adults-only ships
- Child-only playrooms and teen clubs
- More active and adventurous shore excursions
- Medivac helicopter lift for medical treatment
- Cashless cruising ("just sign here!")
- Electronic cabin key cards
- Pay-extra adult-only sanctuaries
- Pay-extra spa and wellness facilities
- Pay-extra tours to view the "Back of House"

Email facilities are widespread.

- Personal safes
- Exclusive private accommodation areas (effectively gated communities)

- Multi-room suites for multi-generational families or friends
- Satellite-linked telephones in cabins
- Interactive touch- and flat-screen cabin television sets
- Gratuities charged automatically to your onboard account or online pre-pay
- Much wider choice of dining venues, eateries, and food
- High-tech production shows, click-tracks
- Internet-connect centers, wi-fi, and email facilities
- Large casinos, themed lounges and bars
- Huge self-serve stuff-your-face buffets (camping at sea)
- Better facilities for the frail and physically challenged
- "Private island" beach days
- Cruises for gays, singles, and themed groups
- More sports facilities (rock-

- climbing walls, ice-skating rinks, golf simulators, bowling alleys, boxing rings, race-car simulators, surf-riders)
- Deluge of sales flyers under cabin door
- Digital photographs and personal videos
- Lack of dress code
- Passengers with tattoos, and tracksuits
- A crew that can't speak your language
- Security personnel aboard ship who don't understand hospitality (but they're worse in the cruise terminals)
- Obnoxious port security staff for embarkation
- Sunbed hoggers
- Roll-over lifeboats
- Headline-making attacks of norovirus
- Overboards (whether for crime, accident, "assisted" suicide, or insurance money)

THE BIGGEST OF THE BIG

Oasis of the Seas and *Allure of the Seas* are floating cities, complete with parks and boulevards. Each ship can accommodate 6,296 passengers and 2,164 crew.

accommodate more than 6,000 passengers, with the "bigger is better" principle being pursued for all it's worth. Many are, however, too wide to transit the Panama Canal and so are designated non-Panamax.
● Small ships, where the "small is beautiful" concept has taken hold, particularly in the exclusive and luxury categories. Cruise lines offer high-quality ships of low capacity, which can provide a highly personalized range of quality services. This means better-trained, more experienced staff (and more of them to serve fewer passengers), higher-quality food, and more meals cooked to order. Small ships can also visit the less overcrowded ports.

Other cruise lines have expanded by "stretching" their ships. This is accomplished literally by cutting a ship in half, and inserting a newly constructed mid-section, thus instantly adding more accommodation and public rooms, while maintaining the same draft.

Ships that have been "stretched" (with year and length of "stretch") include: *Albatros* (1983, 27.7 meters), *Aquamarine* (1980, 26 meters), *Balmoral* (2007, 30 meters), *Black Watch* (1981, 27.7 meters), *Boudicca* (1982, 27.7 meters), *Braemar* (2008, 31.2 meters), *Enchantment of the Seas* (2005, 22.2 meters), *Louis Majesty* (1999, 30 meters), *Norwegian Dream* (1998, 40 meters), *Spirit of Adventure* (1986, 20 meters), *SuperStar Aquarius* (1998, 40 meters), and *Thomson Dream* (1990, 40 meters).

More exclusivity

Gated communities at sea are likely to proliferate. These areas are accessible only to those willing to pay extra to "live" in one of the larger suites, and gain access to "private" facilities, concierge lounges, and private sunbathing areas. Ships that have them: *MSC Fantasia, MSC Splendida, Norwegian Epic, Norwegian Gem, Norwegian Jade, Norwegian Pearl*. So two-class cruising (in some cases, three-class cruising) is back.   ❏

HIGHLIGHTS OF THE PAST 25 YEARS

1986 Direct-dial satellite calls were introduced. Cunard acquired Sea Goddess Cruises.
1987 *Queen Elizabeth 2* was converted from steam turbine to diesel-electric power.
1988 Royal Caribbean Cruise Line merged with Admiral Cruises to form Royal Admiral Cruises (later Royal Caribbean Cruises). Carnival Cruise Lines acquired Holland America Line. Seabourn Cruise Line's first ship, *Seabourn Pride*, entered service.
1989 The Chandris Group of Companies created Celebrity Cruises. The Panama Canal celebrated its 75th birthday.
1990 At the start of the Gulf War, the US government chartered *Cunard Princess* for six months as a rest and relaxation center for US service personnel in Bahrain.
1991 Carnival Cruise Lines acquired a 25 percent stake in Seabourn Cruise Line.
1992 Chargeurs and Accor, the French property and leisure industries group, bought 23% of Costa Crociere, parent of Costa Cruises.
1993 Star Cruises was founded by Malaysia's Genting Group.
1994 Radisson Diamond Cruises and Seven Seas Cruise Line merged to become Radisson Seven Seas Cruises.
1995 British company Airtours purchased *Southward* from Norwegian Cruise Line and *Nordic Prince* from Royal Caribbean Cruises.
1996 Cunard (and parent company Trafalgar House) were bought by Kvaerner.
1997 Carnival Corporation, jointly with Airtours, purchased Costa Cruises. Royal Caribbean International bought Celebrity Cruises.
1998 Kvaerner sold Cunard to Carnival Corporation. Norwegian Cruise Line bought Orient Lines.
1999 Crown Cruise Line was reintroduced as an upscale part of Commodore Cruise Line.
2000 Star Cruises took full control of Norwegian Cruise Line (including Orient Lines) after buying the outstanding shares held by Carnival Corporation. P&O Group separated its cruising activities from the rest of the group. Costa Cruises became 100% owned by Carnival Corporation.
2001 Renaissance Cruises (10 ships) ceased operations after the September 11 terrorist attacks on the US – one of several casualties.
2002 SeaDream Yacht Club began with *SeaDream I* and *SeaDream II*.
2003 NCL America launched its US-flag operation.
2004 Carnival Corporation and P&O Princess plc merged to become the world's largest cruise company, with 60-plus ships and 13 brands.
2005 Orion Expedition Cruises launched with one ship, *Orion*.
2006 Radisson Seven Seas Cruises became Regent Seven Seas Cruises. Royal Caribbean International bought Pullmantur.
2007 Celebrity Cruises created a sub-brand, Azamara Cruises. *Queen Elizabeth 2* was sold for £50 million ($100 million) to a state investment company in Dubai, to be refitted and become a floating hotel and museum alongside the Palm Jumeirah.
2008 Fred Olsen Cruise Lines "stretched" its *Braemar* by 102ft (31.2 meters). Almost all cruise lines increased fuel surcharges the face of rising oil prices. Most paddlewheel riverboats ceased operations in the USA.
2009 Island Cruises was acquired by TUI Travel's Thomson Cruises division. TUI Cruises started cruising with one ship. Imperial Majesty Cruise Line ceased operations, replaced by Celebration Cruise Line. Azamara Cruises was renamed Azamara Club Cruises. Seabourn Cruise Line changed its name (temporarily, it turned out) to The Yachts of Seabourn.
2010 The Ocean Village brand disappeared; its two ships joined the P&O Cruises (Australia) fleet. Island Cruises became a sub-brand of Thomson Cruises. NCL America was merged into Norwegian Cruise Line (NCL). Cruise West and Delfin Cruises ceased operations. India's Blue Ocean Cruises began operations.
2011 Middle East conflicts forced cruise lines to cancel port calls in Egypt, Libya, and Tunisia. Some cruise lines changed their around-the-world itineraries to avoid Somalia's pirates. Disney Cruise Line introduced the first real water coaster at sea, AquaDuck.

WHAT THE BROCHURES DON'T ALWAYS TELL YOU

We answer frankly the questions about ocean cruising most frequently asked both by those new to this type of vacation and by experienced passengers

GENERAL DEFINITIONS

What exactly *is* a cruise?

A cruise is a vacation, an escape from the stress and strain of life ashore, a floating hotel where you have to unpack only once. It offers you a chance to relax and unwind in comfortable surroundings, with attentive service, good food, and a ship that changes the scenery for you. It can be a hassle-free, and, more importantly, a crime-free vacation. Everything's close to hand, and there are always polite people to help you. A cruise provides great value for money, variety (in ship size, destinations, facilities, cuisine, entertainment, activities, and shore excursions), a chance to explore new places, meet new people, make friends, and, above all, provides the ingredients for a wonderful vacation.

More than 350 ocean-going cruise ships carrying from 50 to more than 6,000 passengers visit almost 2,000 destinations throughout the world, and new ships are being constantly introduced. They range from under 200ft (60 meters) to over 1,100ft (330 meters) in length, and their shapes vary enormously. Facilities, food, and service vary from company to company, and according to the size of the ship.

Ambience ranges from ultra-casual to very formal (starchy and reserved). Entertainment ranges from amateur dramatics to full-fledged high-tech production shows and circus-like theatrics, from the corner cabaret to a world-famous headliner.

How long does a cruise last?

The popular standard length is seven days, although cruises can vary from two-day party cruises to a slow exotic voyage around the world of up to 180 days. There are even passengers who stay aboard some ships all year round, and disembark only when the ship has to go into dry dock for refits. If you are new to cruising and want to "get your feet wet," try a short cruise first. Its length will depend on the time and money at your disposal and the degree of comfort you are seeking, but more leisurely cruises can last 14 days or more. To operate long, low-density voyages, cruise lines must charge high rates to cover the extensive preparations, high food and transportation costs, port operations, fuel, and so on.

WHO GOES CRUISING

Isn't cruising really meant for old people?

The average age of passengers gets younger each year, with the average age of first-timers now well under 40. But retirees find cruising a safe and comfortable way to travel and many have plenty of get-up-and-go.

On a typical cruise you're likely to meet singles, couples, families with

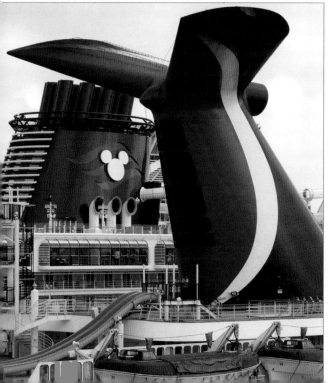

Big brands: Disney aims at the family market, Carnival promises fun.

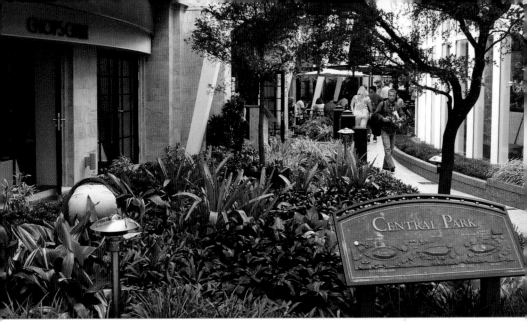

Today's biggest ships are like cities with propellers.

children of all ages (including single parents and grand-parents), honeymooners (some second- or third-time around), groups of friends, and college buddies. You may even run across your next-door neighbors.

Won't I get bored?

Usually, it's the men who ask this question, but get them aboard and often there's not enough time in the day to try all the things they want to do – as long as you choose the right ship, for the right reasons.

There are more things to do aboard today's ships than there is on almost any Caribbean island. So, whether you want to lie back and be pampered, or be active non-stop, you can do it on a cruise, and you will have to pack and unpack only once.

Just being at sea provides an intoxicating sense of freedom that few places on dry land can offer. And, in case you think you may feel cut off without contact, almost all large resort ships (those carrying over 1,600 passengers) offer internet access, pay-per-view movies, digital music libraries, and ship-wide wi-fi access.

Isn't it all very regimented?

Some cruises simply aren't relaxing, despite cruise brochure claims that "you can do as much or as little as you want to." For example, the large resort ships carrying more than 1,600 passengers, and particularly those with 5,000-plus, cram lots of people into small cabins and provide nonstop activities that insult the intelligence and assault the wallet. The purpose of this book is to help you identify the cruise that's right for you.

Are there facilities for singles?

Some. A cruise vacation is good for those traveling alone (over 25% of all passengers are solo travelers – world-wide, that's over 4 million a year), because it is easy to meet other people in a non-competitive environment. Many ships have dedicated cabins for singles and special add-on rates for single occupancy of double cabins. Some cruise lines will even find a cabin mate for you to share with, if you so desire.

However, in cabins with three or four berths (two beds plus upper berths), personal privacy doesn't exist. Some companies sell two-bed cabins at a special single rate, forgetting that many people who cruise solo do so

---

I'M NEW TO THIS. WHERE DO I START?

First, think about where you want to go, how long a cruise you would like, and how much money you want to spend. How large a ship would you like to cruise aboard? Then, find a good travel agent who specializes in cruises and can match your needs, requirements, lifestyle, and personality. Ask the following questions:

❶ What size cruise ship would you recommend?
❷ What should I budget for the cruise?
❸ What is included in the cruise price?
❹ What extra costs can I expect to pay?
❺ Which destinations are included?
❻ What kind of accom-modation would suit my tastes and budget?
❼ What is the ship's onboard ambience like?
❽ What facilities does the ship have?
❾ What kind of food and service does it provide?
❿ What kind of entertainment should I expect?
You can also research the internet, although you won't be able to ask those all-important questions.

because their partner has died, and the last thing they want is to be in a cabin with two beds.

Why is it so expensive for singles?

Because it's a couples' world in most of the travel industry. Almost all cruise lines base their rates on double occupancy, as do hotels. Thus, when you travel alone, the cabin portion of your fare reflects an additional supplement. While almost all new ships are built with cabins for double occupancy, older ships have more single-occupancy cabins. Cruise line special offers are nearly always aimed at double-occupancy passengers.

Is there enough to keep kids busy?

A cruise provides families with more quality time than any other type of vacation, and family cruising is the industry's largest growth segment, with activities tailored to various age groups. Responding to this trend, Disney Cruise Line is doubling, from two to four, its family-friendly fleet, with the introduction of *Disney Dream* in 2011 and *Disney Fantasy* in 2012.

The Serenity adults-only retreat aboard *Carnival Dream*.

A cruise is also educational, allows children to interact in a crime-free environment, and takes them to destinations in comfortable, familiar surroundings. In fact, children have such a good time aboard ship and ashore, you may have difficulty getting them home after the cruise – as long as you have chosen the right ship.

If you cruise aboard one of the major cruise lines, you may find gratuities for your children automatically added to your onboard account – or you may be able to pre-pay online. NCL, for example, requests $6 per day from each child of 3–12 years, while those over 13 pay the adult rate of $10 or more per day.

● *See also Cruising for Families, pages 73–83.*

Are there adults-only ships?

If you don't like crowds, noise, and long lines, try a small ship – a sail-cruise vessel or a river or barge cruise could also provide the right escape. Companies that operate adults-only ships include P&O Cruises (*Adonia, Arcadia, Oriana*) and Saga Cruises (*Spirit of Adventure, Saga Pearl II, Saga Ruby, Saga Sapphire*).

HEALTH ISSUES

Will I get seasick?

Today's ships have stabilizers – large underwater "fins" on each side of the hull – to counteract any rolling motion, and most cruises are in warm, calm waters. As a result, fewer than 3% of passengers become seasick. Yet it's possible to develop some symptoms – anything from slight nausea to vomiting.

Both old-time sailors and modern physicians have their own remedies, and you can take your choice or try them all (but not at the same time):

● When you notice the first movement of a ship, walk back and forth on the deck. You will find that your knees, which are our own form of stabilizer, will start getting their feel of balance and counteraction. This is known as "getting your sea legs."

● Get the sea breeze into your face (arguably the best antidote) and, if nauseous, suck an orange or a lemon.

● Eat lightly. Don't make the mistake of thinking a heavy meal will keep your stomach anchored. It won't.

● When on deck, focus on a steady point, such as the horizon.

Drugs: Dramamine (dimenhydrinate, an antihistamine and sedative introduced just after World War II) will be available aboard in tablet (chewable) form. A stronger version (Meclazine) is available on prescription (brand names: Antivert, Antrizine, Bonine, Meni-D). Ciba-Geigy's Scopoderm (or Transderm Scop), known as "The Patch," contains scopolamine and has proven effective. Possible side effects are dry mouth, blurred vision, drowsiness, and problems with urinating.

If you are really distressed, the ship's doctor can give

DO CRUISES SUIT HONEYMOONERS?

Absolutely. A cruise is the ideal setting for romance, for shipboard weddings aboard ships with the right registry (they can also be arranged in some ports, depending on local regulations), receptions, and honeymoons. Most decisions are already made for you, so all you have to do is show up. Many ships have double, queen- or king-sized beds, too. And for those on a second honeymoon, many ships can perform a "renewal of vows" ceremony; some will make a charge for this service.

you, at extra cost, an injection to alleviate discomfort. It may make you drowsy, but the last thing on your mind will be staying awake during the movie.

A natural preventive is ginger in powder form. Mix half a teaspoon in a glass of warm water or milk, and drink it before sailing. This is said to settle any stomach for up to eight hours.

"Sea Bands" are a drug-free method of controlling motion sickness. These are slim bands (in varying colors) that are wrapped around the wrist, with a circular "button" that presses against the acupressure point Pericardium 6 (nei kuan) on the lower arm. Attach them a few minutes before you step aboard and wear on both wrists throughout the cruise.

Another drug-free remedy can be found in Reletex, a watch-like device worn on the wrist. First used for patients undergoing chemotherapy, it emits a small neuromodulating current that stops peristaltic waves in the stomach causing nausea and vomiting.

Is having hay fever a problem?

People who suffer from hay fever and pollen allergies benefit greatly from a cruise. Most sufferers I have talked to say that their problems simply disappear on a ship – particularly when it is at sea.

Are hygiene standards high enough?

News reports often focus on hygiene and sanitation aboard cruise ships. In the 1980s, the North American cruise industry agreed with the Centers for Disease Control (CDC) that hygiene and sanitation inspections should be carried out once or twice yearly aboard all cruise ships carrying American passengers, and the Vessel Sanitation Program (VSP) was born. The original intention of the VSP was to achieve and maintain a level of sanitation that would lower the risk of gastro-intestinal disease outbreaks and assist the cruise industry to provide a healthy environment for passengers and crew.

It is a voluntary inspection, and cruise lines pay handsomely for each inspection. For a ship the size of *Queen Mary 2*, for example, the cost would be about $15,000; for a ship the size of *Azamara Journey*, it would be about $7,800. However, the 42 inspection points are accepted by the international cruise industry as a good system. Inspections cover two main areas:

● Water sanitation, including free chlorine residuals in the potable water system, swimming pool, and hot tub filters.

● Food sanitation: food storage, preparation and serving areas, including bars and passenger service pantries.

The ships score extremely well – the ones that undergo inspections, that is. Some ships that don't call on US ports would possibly not pass the inspections every time. Older ships with outdated galley equipment and poor food storage facilities would have a harder time complying with the USPH inspection standards. Some other countries also have strict health inspection standards. However, if the same USPH inspection standards were applied to restaurants and hotels ashore, it is estimated that at least 90% or more would fail, consistently.

Anyone concerned about personal hygiene should note that some ships have fixed shower heads. A removable shower and hose are better for reaching those parts that fixed head showers can't. Check with your cruise provider *before* you book.

What about the norovirus?

This temporary but highly contagious condition occurs worldwide. Humans are the only known hosts, and only the common cold is reported more frequently than viral gastroenteritis as a cause of illness in the USA. About 23 million Americans each year are diagnosed with the effects of the Norwalk-like virus (NLV gastroenteritis, sometimes known as winter vomiting virus or norovirus). It is more prevalent in adults and older children than in the very young.

Norovirus is part of the "calicivirus" family. The

Modern stabilizers help counteract any swelling motion.

name derives from the chalice or calyx, meaning cuplike; this refers to the indentations of the surface of the virus. The condition itself is self-limiting, is mild, and is characterized by nausea, vomiting, diarrhea, and abdominal pain. Although it can be transmitted by person-to-person contact, it is more likely to arrive via contaminated foods and water.

Shellfish (most notably clams and oysters), salad ingredients (particular salad dressings) and fruits are the foods most often implicated in noroviral outbreaks.

Water can also be a common source of outbreaks – water aboard cruise ships stored in tanks, etc. A mild and brief illness typically occurs 24 to 48 hours after contaminated food or water has been consumed, and lasts for 24 to 72 hours. The virus can also be brought on board when passengers are ashore in foreign ports with poor hygiene standards. If you board a large resort ship after norovirus has struck, bread and bread rolls, butter, and salt and pepper shakers may not be placed on tables, but will be available on request during meals.

All restaurants and showlounges prohibit smoking.

Note that only cruise ships are required to report every incidence of gastrointestinal illness. Nowhere else in the health system of the US are such viruses a reportable illness.

How can you avoid them? Don't drink from aircraft water dispensers on the way to join your cruise – they are seldom cleaned thoroughly. Always wash your hands after using the toilet.

Where is smoking allowed?

Some cruise lines allow smoking in cabins, while others permit it only in cabins with balconies. Some, such as P&O Cruises (Australia), place a notice in each cabin advising passengers: "A $300 cleaning fee will be added to your onboard account if we find evidence of smoking in your cabin." But it does allow smoking on balconies.

Almost all cruise lines prohibit smoking in restaurants and food service areas; almost no ships have smoking sections in dining rooms. If you are concerned, check

with the cruise line or your travel agent before booking. Most ships now allow smoking only on the open decks. But that means when non-smokers are sunbathing on an open deck the person next to them can light up.

What about cigars?

Cigar-smoking lounges are found aboard *Adventure of the Seas, Amadea, Asuka II, Bleu de France, Brilliance of the Seas, Crystal Serenity, Crystal Symphony, Europa, Explorer of the Seas, Freedom of the Seas, Grand Mistral, Independence of the Seas, Liberty of the Seas, Mariner of the Seas, MSC Armonia, MSC Davina, MSC Fantasia, MSC Lirica, MSC Magnifica, MSC Musica, MSC Opera, MSC Orchestra, MSC Poesia, MSC Sinfonia, MSC Splendida, Navigator of the Seas, Norwegian Dawn, Norwegian Epic, Norwegian Gem, Norwegian Jewel, Norwegian Pearl, Norwegian Star, Norwegian Sun, Queen Elizabeth, Queen Mary 2, Queen Victoria, Radiance of the Seas, Seabourn Odyssey, Seabourn Quest, Seabourn Sojourn, Serenade of the Seas, Seven Seas Mariner, Seven Seas Voyager, Silver Shadow, Silver Spirit, Silver Whisper, SuperStar Virgo,* and *Voyager of the Seas.*

Note, however, that ships starting or ending their cruises in a United States port are not permitted to carry genuine Cuban cigars. Instead, most cigars will be made in the Dominican Republic.

Remember that, if you smoke a cigar in a ship's dedicated cigar lounge, the air purification system will often not be effective enough if someone comes in to smoke a cigarette, and you may suffer the consequences of inhaling second-hand cigarette smoke.

Only a few cruise lines provide a purgatory area for smokers.

Have there been murders during a cruise?

Violent crime is much less common on a cruise than during land-based vacations, but there have been a few suspicious deaths, and a number of passengers have gone missing, mainly in the Caribbean and on Mexican Riviera cruises. A small number have been thrown over a balcony by another passenger, typically after an alcohol-fueled argument.

Murder is hard to prove if no actual body is found (did he jump or was he pushed?). Another headache is that, if the alleged crime happens at sea, the jurisdiction responsible for investigating it will depend on the ship's registry, perhaps in Panama, Liberia or Malta.

WHAT CRUISING COSTS

Isn't cruising expensive?

Compare what it would cost on land to have all your meals and entertainment provided, as well as transportation, fitness and sports facilities, social activities, educational talks, parties, and other functions, and you can see the remarkable value of a cruise.

Cost provides a useful guideline to a ship's ambience, type of passengers, and degree of luxury, food, and service. What you pay determines the size, location, and style of accommodation. Be wary of huge discounts – it either means that the product was unrealistically priced or that quality will be reduced somewhere. Ships are as individual as fingerprints: each can change its "personality" from cruise to cruise, depending on the mix of passengers (and crew). The choice ranges from basic to luxury, so give yourself a budget, and ask your professional travel supplier how to make the best use of it.

Will a repositioning cruise be cheaper?

When ships move from one cruise region to another, it is termed repositioning. When ships move between the Caribbean and Europe, typically in April/May, or between Europe and the Caribbean (typically in October/November), for example, the cruise fares are usually discounted. The ships rarely sail full, and offer excellent value for money.

I've found a seven-day cruise advertised at a very cheap price. Is there a catch?

As a rule, yes. If the price is a fraction of what you might pay for a decent hotel room in London or New York without meals or entertainment, something is not quite as it seems. Before booking, read the fine print. Look at all the extra costs such as tips to cabin and dining room stewards, shore excursions, drinks, plus getting to and from the ship. The price per person adver-

CAN I BRING MY PET?

Pets are not allowed aboard cruise ships, with one exception: the regular transatlantic crossings aboard Cunard Line's ocean liner *Queen Mary 2*, which has carried more than 500 pet animals since its debut in 2004. It provides air-conditioned kennels, plus a genuine British lamppost and New York fire hydrant for dogs' convenience, and cat containers.

tised could well be for a four-berth cabin adjacent to the laundry or above the disco, but in any event, not in a desirable location – in fact, just like a dirt-cheap hotel room in London or New York.

Is the brochure price firm?

No. A cruise's brochure price is set by the sales and marketing departments of cruise lines, rather as the "recommended retail price" of a new car is set by the manufacturer. It's the price they would like to achieve to cover themselves against currency fluctuations, international bonding schemes and the like. But, in the real world, discounts attract business, and so there is always some leeway. Also, travel agents receive a commission (typically 10–15%, plus special overrides for volume bookings). So, as a consumer, always ask for the "best price," watch for special offers in newspapers and magazines, and talk to your specialist travel agent.

European cruises cost more than in the Caribbean. Why?

There are several reasons. Almost all aspects of operations, including fuel costs, port charges, air transportation, and supplying food to the ships, are higher.

European destinations such as Venice cost more.

Cruising in style: *Allure of the Seas*' Royal Loft Suite.

European-sourced food has more taste – eggs with real yellow yolks, and food free from chemical additives, coloring and flavoring – than is found in the processed foods that cruise lines often buy from US-based suppliers.

Companies can make more money than in the cut-price Caribbean, where sun, sea, and sand are the main attractions, whereas sightseeing, architecture, culture, and other things are part of a more enriching cruise experience in other parts of the world. Many services cost more in Europe than in the US, so the price of shore excursions in Europe is higher. Admission prices to some historic sites and museums have risen recently.

10 SMART WAYS TO SAVE MONEY

- Research online, but book through a real cruise-travel agency.
- Cut through the sales hype and get to the bottom line.
- Make sure that all taxes are included.
- Book early – the most desirable itineraries go soonest. If air travel is involved, remember that air fares tend to rise in peak seasons.
- Book early – the best cabins and locations go sooner rather than later.
- Book a cabin on a lower deck – the higher the deck, the more expensive will it be.
- An interior (no view) cabin is cheaper, if you can live without natural light.
- Be flexible with your dates – go off-season, when fares will be lower.
- Book an older (pre-1980) ship – the newest ships are more expensive.
- Do purchase travel cancelation insurance – your cruise is an investment, after all.

How inclusive is "all-inclusive"?

That's like asking how much sand is on the beach. It usually means that transportation (often including flights), accommodation, food, and entertainment are wrapped up in one neat package. Today on land, however, "super clubs" offer everything "all-in," including drinks, although mostly low-quality brands are provided, with a much smaller selection than aboard most cruise ships.

While that concept works better aboard small ships (those carrying fewer than 600 passengers), large cruise ships (those carrying more than 1,600 passengers) provide more facilities and more reasons for you to spend money on board. So "mostly inclusive" might be a better term to use. Check the panel on facing page.

Should I take a back-to-back cruise?

If you're considering two seven-day back-to-back cruises (for example: eastern Caribbean/western Caribbean), bear in mind that many aspects of the cruise – the seven-day menu cycle, one or more ports, all shows and cabaret entertainment, even the cruise director's jokes and spiel – may be duplicated.

Do cruise lines have their own credit cards?

Most don't. Among those that do: Carnival Cruise Lines, Celebrity Cruises, Disney Cruise Line, Holland America Line, Princess Cruises, Saga Cruises, Seabourn. You'll earn credits for any spending charged to the card. If you accrue enough points, you can exchange them for cruises, onboard credit, or discounted airfare.

Do ships have different classes?

Yes and no. Gone are the class distinctions and the pretensions of formality of the past. Differences are now found mainly in the type of accommodation chosen, in the price you pay for a larger cabin (or suite), the location of your cabin (or suite), and whether or not you have butler service.

Some cruise lines, including Holland America Line, MSC Cruises (*MSC Davina, MSC Fantasia,* and *MSC Splendida* only) and Royal Caribbean International (except *Sovereign-* and *Vision-*class ships), provide a "concierge lounge" which can be used only by occupants of accommodation designated as suites (thus reviving the old two-class system).

Private areas have been created by MSC Cruises (Yacht Club) and Norwegian Cruise Line (The Courtyard) for occupants of the top suites, in an effort to insulate them from the masses. The result is like a "ship within a ship."

Celebrity Cruises has, in essence, created three classes: 1) Suites; 2) Concierge Class (middle-level) mini-suites/cabins; 3) Standard cabins (either exterior view or interior – no view). Perhaps it's less complicated to think in general terms of "Balcony Class" and "Non-Balcony Class."

Cunard Line has always had several classes for transatlantic travel, but today's ships *(Queen Elizabeth, Queen Mary 2, Queen Victoria)* are classed according to the restaurant and accommodation grade chosen.

Cabins advertised in newspapers aren't always available. Why not?

Newspaper advertisements are written way ahead of publication. Meanwhile, some cabin price grades may

15 THINGS AN "ALL-INCLUSIVE" PRICE DOESN'T INCLUDE

- Dining in extra-cost restaurants
- Premium (vintage) wines
- Specialty ice creams
- Specialty teas and coffees
- Wine tastings/seminars
- Internet access (extra charge)
- Spa treatments
- Some fitness classes
- Personal training instruction
- Use of steam room/saunas
- Laundry, pressing and dry-cleaning
- Babysitting services
- Professional souvenir photographs
- Casino gaming
- Medical services

have sold out. Often, the cheapest "lead-in" price is for a cabin that is small, or has obstructed views, or is in an "inconvenient" or "noisy" location.

What does a category guarantee mean?

It means you have purchased a specific grade of accommodation (just as in a hotel), although the actual cabin may not have been assigned to your booking yet. Your cabin may be assigned before you go, or when you arrive for embarkation.

What are port charges?

These are levied by various ports visited, rather like city taxes imposed on hotel guests. They help pay for the infrastructure required to provide facilities including docks, linesmen, security and operations personnel, and porters at embarkation and disembarkation ports.

FACILITIES ABOARD

Can I eat when I want to?

Yes, you can – well, almost. If you're hungry when you get aboard on the day of embarkation, you may want to head to the self-serve buffet – but, be warned that aboard the large resort ships, it'll probably be a bit of a free-for-all, with the frustrations of lining up for food, and then trying to find a place to sit and eat. And those buffets are only really good when they first open. It's more civilized aboard mid-size and small ships.

A casual eatery aboard *Carnival Destiny*.

Several major cruise lines offer "flexible dining" which allows you to choose (with some limitations) when you want to eat, and with whom you dine, during your cruise. Just like going out to restaurants ashore, reservations may be required, you may also have to wait in line at busy periods, and occupants of the most expensive suites get priority.

Aboard large resort ships (1,600-plus passengers) the big evening entertainment shows typically are staged twice each evening, so you end up with the equivalent of two-seating dining anyway.

What is "alternative" dining?

Mass-market dining isn't to everyone's taste, so some ships now have alternative dining spots other than the main restaurant. These à la carte restaurants usually cost extra – typically between $15 and $75 a person – but the food quality, preparation, and presentation are decidedly better, as is service and ambience.

Most alternative dining spots are also more intimate, and much quieter than the main dining rooms and are suitable for a special occasion. You may need to make a reservation. *For more details, see pages 56–7.*

What's the difference between an "outside" and an "interior" cabin?

An "outside" (or "exterior") cabin doesn't mean it's outside the ship; it simply means that it has a window (or porthole) with a view of the outside, or there is a private balcony for you physically to be – or look – outside. An "interior" (or "inside") cabin means that it does not have a view of the outside, but it will have artwork or curtains on one wall instead of a window or patio-like

Tee time: a golf lesson aboard *Crystal Symphony*.

(balcony) door. Naturally, an outside cabin costs more than an interior cabin of the same size.

Should I tip for room service?

No. It's part of the normal onboard duties that the hotel staff are paid to carry out. For more on tipping other staff, see page 53.

Is it hard to find one's way around large resort ships?

Well, it can take at least a few hours in a ship such as *Oasis of the Seas*, which is more than one-fifth of a mile long, so wear good walking shoes. However, in general, remember that decks are horizontal, while stairs are vertical. The rest comes naturally, with practice. If you're arranging to meet one of the thousands of other passengers, be very specific indeed about the rendezvous point.

Hi-tech: the engine room aboard *Allure of the Seas*.

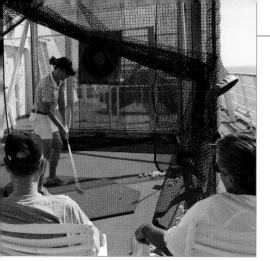

"all-in" packages allowing participants to play on some of the world's most desirable courses. Hapag-Lloyd Cruises and Silversea Cruises, for example, operate a number of golf-themed sailings each year, and if you take your own clubs, they will provide storage space and arrange everything.

What about my bicycle?

Most cruise lines will let you take your bike – preferably the folding variety because of lack of storage space. If you use a flight case, however, it may not be easy to find storage space for it.

Airlines will also charge you to transport your bike. Ask your travel provider to contact the cruise line for its rules.

Note that very few ships provide bicycles for free. Those that do include *Europa, Hanseatic,* and *Hebridean Princess.*

Do cellular phones work on board?

Cruise passengers use cell phones on open decks, in cabins, and, sadly, even in restaurants. Most cruise lines have contracts with land-based phone service companies – rates for usage vary, but you will typically pay international roaming rates. Mobile phone signals piggyback off systems that transmit internet data via satellite.

When your ship is in port, the ship's network may be switched off and you will pay the going local (country-specific) rate for mobile calls if you can manage to access a local network.

Keeping in touch with children's whereabouts on a big resort ship can be expensive using mobile phones. It's permissible to use two-way radio transceivers

Isn't it very noisy aboard these giants?

It can be, because of the constant activities and music, and many announcements. Since some cruise lines and staff seem to think that high volume enhances ambience, anyone averse to loud noise should consider taking earplugs, just in case.

Do cruise ships vibrate?

Many ships built before 1990 suffer from vibration, usually at the stern. It is usually worse when the vessel is maneuvering at slow speed. So anyone occupying a cabin on the lowest decks at the stern is likely to be affected most. Vibration-free cruising is more possible aboard ships that have the latest "pod" propulsion system fitted (to check whether a particular ship has it, see the "Propulsion" entry in the ship's alphabetical listing in the ratings section of this book).

Can I visit the bridge?

Usually not, for insurance and security reasons. But some companies, such as NCL and Princess Cruises, run extra-cost "Behind the Scenes" tours, and a background video on how the ship is run may be shown on your cabin TV.

Are there any ships with walk-in pools (instead of steps)?

Not many, because of space considerations, although they can often be useful for older passengers. Some examples: *Aurora, Crystal Serenity, Crystal Symphony,* and *Oriana.*

Can I bring golf clubs?

Yes, you can. However, although cruise lines do not charge for carrying them, some airlines do – worth checking if you have to fly to join your cruise because the "budget" airlines charge a fortune. Some ships cater for golfers with mini-golf courses on deck and electronically monitored practice areas.

Golf-themed cruises are popular, with

Hanseatic is one of the few ships that provides free bicycles.

Big-screen entertainment aboard *Carnival Freedom*.

(walkie-talkies) for this purpose; at sea they won't interfere with any public-service radio frequency.

Can I send and receive emails?

Aboard most ships, email facilities have now been added to some degree. Many ships have wi-fi, for a fee, allowing you to connect your own laptop. Several ships have an internet café, or internet-connect center, where you can log on for about 50 cents a minute. Note that connections and downloads are often very slow compared to land-based services (shipboard emails link through satellite systems, and are therefore more expensive than land-based connections). Attachments are not generally allowed. For many cruise companies, email has now become an important revenue generator.

Where can I watch movies?

Some – but not many – ships have a dedicated movie theater. The movies are provided by a licensed film distribution or leasing service. Many newer ships have replaced or supplemented the movie theater with TV sets and DVD players in cabins, or with giant poolside screens for 24-hour viewing.

Do all cabins have flat-screen TV sets?

No. Many older cruise ships still have bulky CRT sets, but all the latest ships have flat-screen TVs. So, if you think you'll spend time in your cabin relaxing and watching movies, it's best to choose a ship that is less than five years old.

DESTINATIONS

Where can I go on a cruise?

As the saying goes: the world is your oyster! There are over 30,000 different cruises to choose from each year, and about 2,000 cruise destinations in the world. A cruise can also take you to places inaccessible by almost any other means, such as Antarctica, the North Cape, the South Sea islands, and so on. In fact, if you close your eyes and think of almost anywhere in the world where there's water, there's probably a cruise ship or rivership to take you there. To get an idea of the choice available, see pages 33–45 and 93–100.

What is "homeland" cruising?

The term stems from cruise ships sailing out of an increased number of ports in the United States (more than 20 at last count, with over 4,000 cruises a year). While some, like Miami and Fort Lauderdale, have good facilities for checking in, many do not, and long lines are the result, particularly when 50 motorcoaches arrive at virtually the same time *(see page 17 for rating of ports)*.

"Homeland" cruising has great appeal for people who can drive themselves to a local (regional) port of embarkation. The result, however, is that one ship sailing out of, say, Baltimore, will attract many other people from the surrounding area, and that could mean you'll bump into any of your neighbors who've had the same idea as you. It also makes for particularly strong regional dialects aboard any given ship, and can even change the ways that cruise consumers act and dress.

What is expedition cruising?

Expedition cruises are operated by specialists such as Quark Expeditions *(see page 168)*, using small ships that have ice-strengthened hulls or with specially constructed ice-breakers that enable them to reach areas totally inaccessible to "normal" cruise ships. The ships are usually converted to carry passengers in some degree of basic comfort, with comfortable accommodation and a relaxed, informal atmosphere, with expert lecturers and expedition leaders accompanying every cruise.

These cruises really are for small groups, and much care and attention is placed on minimizing the impact on the environment. *More information: pages 93–6.*

What is a Panamax ship?

This is one that conforms to the maximum dimensions possible for passage through the Panama Canal – useful particularly for around-the-world voyages. These dimensions are: 294 meters (964.56ft) long, with a beam of 32.3 meters (105.97ft); or below approximately 90,000 gross tonnage. Because of the locks, the 50-mile (80-km) journey takes from eight to nine hours. Most large resort cruise ships (examples: *Carnival Dream, Celebrity Solstice, MSC Fantasia, Queen Mary 2, Ruby Princess*) are too big to go through the Panama Canal, and are thus classed as "post-Panamax" ships.

Is there a cruise that skips ports?

Yes, but it isn't really a cruise. It's a trans-atlantic crossing, from New York to South-ampton, England (or vice versa), aboard *Queen Mary 2. More details: page 101.*

Can I shop in ports of call?

Yes, you can. Many passengers embrace retail therapy when visiting ports of call such as Dubai, Hong Kong, Singapore, St Maarten, and St Thomas, among many others. However, it's prudent to exercise self-control. Remember that you'll have to carry all those purchases home at the end of your cruise; duty-free liquor – a favorite, for example – is heavy.

Do I have to go ashore in each port?

Absolutely not. In fact, many passengers enjoy being aboard "their" ships when there are virtually no other passengers aboard. Also, if you have a spa treatment, it could be less expensive during this period than when the ship is at sea; some ships, such as *Queen Mary 2*, have price differentials for sea days and port days.

MAKING BOOKINGS

Can I fly in the day before or stay an extra day after the cruise?

Cruise lines often offer pre- and post-cruise stay packages at an additional cost. The advantage is that you don't have to do anything else. All will be taken care of,

Zodiacs from *Hanseatic* on an expedition up the Amazon.

as they say. If you book a hotel on your own, however, you may have to pay an "air deviation" fee if you don't take the cruise line's air arrangements or you want to change them.

Can I pre-book seats on flights?

With packaged vacations such as cruises, it is normally not possible to reserve airline seats prior to check-in, and, although the cruise line will typically forward your requests for preferred seating, these may not be guaranteed. However, most airlines allow you to check-in online, access the seating plan, and select a seat.

Should I book early?

The further ahead you book, the greater will be any discount available. You'll get the cabin you want, in the location you want, and you may even be upgraded. When you book close to the sailing date, you may get a low price, but you probably won't get the cabin or location you'd like, or – worse still – in ships with two seatings for dinner, you won't be able to choose early or late seating.

What legal rights do I have?

Very few. After reading a cruise line's Passenger Ticket Contract, you'll see why. A 189-word sentence in one contract begins "The Carrier shall not be liable for..." and goes on to cover the legal waterfront *(see page 677).*

AND FINALLY...

What are cruising's downsides?

Much-anticipated ports of call can be aborted or changed due to poor weather or other conditions. Some popular ports (particularly in the Caribbean) can become extremely crowded – there can be up to 12 ships in St Thomas, or six

Most people go ashore at ports of call, but they don't have to.

in St Maarten at the same time, disgorging 20,000 people. Fellow passengers, and those lacking social manners, can be irritating, notably in the dining room where you may have to share a table with strangers.

Many frequent irritations could be fixed if the cruise lines really tried. Entertainment, for instance, whether production shows or cabaret acts, is always linked to dinner times. Also, many aggressive, young, so-called "cruise directors" insist on interposing themselves into every part of your cruise, day and night, military-style through the public address system. Some of these cruise directors may make good cheerleaders, but seem unable to communicate with anyone over 25.

Where did all the money go?

Apart from the cruise fare itself, incidentals could include government taxes, port charges, air ticket tax, and fuel surcharges. On board, extra costs may include drinks, mini-bar items, cappuccino and espresso coffees, shore excursions (especially those involving flight-seeing tours), internet access, sending or receiving email, beauty treatments, casino gaming, photographs, laundry and dry-cleaning, babysitting services, wine tasting, bottled water placed in your cabin, and medical services.

A cruise aboard a ship belonging to a major cruise line could be compared to buying a car, whereby motor manufacturers offer a basic model at a set price, and then tempt you with optional extras to inflate the cost. Cruise lines say income generated on board helps to keep the basic cost of a cruise reasonable. In the end, it's up to your self-restraint to stop those little extras mounting up to a very large sum.

How are ships weighed?

They aren't. They are measured. Gross tonnage is a measurement of the enclosed space within a ship's hull and superstructure (1 gross ton = 100 cubic feet).

Where does all the money go? It can all too easily end up in the casino.

10 WAYS TO MANAGE ONBOARD SPENDING

- Plan spa treatments *(above)* for days when the ship is in port – when prices are usually lower.
- Buy a soda package only if you drink a lot of sodas, but buy individually if you have only one or two a day.
- Check and re-check anything you sign for on board.
- Say no to "souvenir" glasses that come with your cocktail.
- Say "no" to extra-cost name-brand ice creams at the pool.
- Don't use your cell phone (which can incur excessive roaming charges) except for emergencies.
- Forget the extra costs of internet and email access – you're on vacation.
- Don't use the ship's (extra charge) laundry services – wait until you get home.
- Be really selective about hiring water-sports gear at "private island" beach calls.
- Use a debit card for payment of your onboard account (using a credit card could mean you pay more in interest if you don't pay off your card in full each month).

How long do cruise ships last?

In general, a long time. For example, during the *QE2*'s almost 40-year service for Cunard Line, the ship sailed more than 5½ million nautical miles, carried 2½ million passengers, completed 25 full world cruises, and crossed the Atlantic more than 800 times. But *QE2* was built with a very thick hull, whereas today's thin-hulled cruise ships probably won't last so long. Even so, the life expectancy is typically a healthy 30 years.

Where do old cruise ships go when they're scrapped?

They go to the beach. Actually, they are driven at speed onto a not very nice beach at Alang in India, or to Chittagong in Bangladesh, or to Pan Yo in China – the main shipbreaking places. Greenpeace has claimed that workers, including children, at some sites have to work under primitive conditions without adequate equipment to protect them against the toxic materials that can be released into the environment. In 2009, a new IMO guideline – "International Convention for the Safe and Environmentally Sound Recycling of Ships" – was adopted. ❑

WHERE TO?

Cruise lines currently visit around 2,000 destinations, from the Caribbean to Antarctica, from the Mediterranean to the Baltic, from Northern Europe to the South Pacific

Because itineraries vary widely, it is wise to make as many comparisons as you can by reading the cruise brochures for descriptions of the ports of call. Several ships may offer the same or similar itineraries simply because these have been tried and tested. Narrow the choice by noting the time spent at each port (few ships stay overnight in port) and whether the ship docks in port or lies at anchor – it can take time to get ashore by the tender. Compare the size of each vessel and its facilities.

Caribbean cruises

There are over 7,000 islands in the Caribbean Sea, although many are small or uninhabited. Caribbean cruises are usually destination-intensive, cramming between four and eight ports into one week, depending on whether you sail from a Florida port or from a port already in the Caribbean, such as Barbados or San Juan. This means you could be visiting at least one port a day, with little time at sea for relaxation. This kind of island-hopping leaves little time to explore a destination – but you'd probably get bored after a few days on one island. Although you may see several places in a week, by the end of the cruise you might need another week to unwind.

June 10 to November 30 is the official hurricane season in the Caribbean (including Bermuda and the Bahamas) and Florida. Cruise ships can change course quickly to avoid weather problems, which can also mean a change of ports or itinerary. When that happens, cruise lines will generally not offer compensation, nor will travel insurance providers.
● **Eastern Caribbean** cruises sail to the Leeward and Windward Islands, and might include calls at Antigua, Barbados, Dominica, Martinique, Puerto Rico, St Croix, St Kitts, St Maarten, St Lucia, and St Thomas.
● **Western Caribbean** cruises sail to the Cayman Islands, Mexico, and Jamaica, and might call at Calica, Cozumel, Grand Cayman, Grand Turk, Playa del Carmen, Ocho Rios, and Roatan Island.
● **Southern Caribbean** cruises might call at Antigua, The Netherlands Antilles (Aruba, Bonaire, Curaçao), Barbados, La Guaira (Venezuela), Tortola, and San Juan.

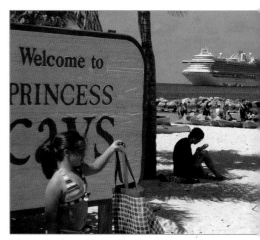

Princess Cruises visits its own island in the Bahamas.

Cuba, the Caribbean's largest island, holds a fascination for many. Although several cruise lines have called there during the past 25 years (examples include Fred Olsen Cruise Lines, Hapag-Lloyd Cruises, Phoenix Cruises, Thomson Cruises, Transocean Cruises), no American cruise passengers can visit the island because of a Kennedy-era US trade embargo which severely restricted trade with Cuba, including tourism. It's time it was eased.

Private islands

Several cruise lines with Bahamas/Caribbean itineraries feature a "private island" (also called an "outisland"). NCL pioneered the trend when it bought a former military outpost in 1977, and it is currently

THE CRUISE LINES THAT OWN PRIVATE ISLANDS

Cruise Line	Name of Island	Location	First Used	Rating (out of 10)
Celebrity Cruises	Catalina Island	Dominican Republic	1995	5.7
Costa Cruises	Serena Cay	Dominican Republic	1996	5.7
Disney Cruise Line	Castaway Cay	Bahamas	1998	8.6
Holland America Line	Half Moon Cay	Bahamas	1997	8.4
MSC Cruises	Cayo Lecantado*	Dominican Republic	2005	6.8
Norwegian Cruise Line	Great Stirrup Cay	Bahamas	1977	7.5
Princess Cruises	Princess Cays	Eleuthera, Bahamas	1992	7.8
Royal Caribbean Int.	Coco Cay	Bahamas	1990	6.4
Royal Caribbean Int.	Labadee	Haiti	1986	7.2

Not exactly private, but a fine beach and palm tree island.

Caribbean

spending $22 million to upgrade its facilities. Disney Cruise Line recently spent $13 million on upgrading and expanding its facilities – Disney's Castaway Cay has separate areas for adults and families with children.

These islands, usually leased from the owning governments, have all that's needed for an all-day beach party – water sports, scuba, snorkeling, crystal-clear waters, warm sands, even a hammock or two, and, possibly, massage in a beach cabana. There are no reservations to make, no tickets to buy, no hassles with taxis. But you may be sharing your private island with more than 5,000 others from a single large resort ship anchored for a "beach day."

Such beach days are not all-inclusive, however, and command premium prices for things like snorkel gear and mandatory swim vest, rental pleasure craft, "banana" boat fun rides, floating beach mats, private waterfront cabanas for the day, sunfish sailboat rental, floating foam mattresses, and hammock rental. Rent a cabana with deck and sunbeds for the day (around $300), and you even get "butler" service, with lunch and drinks.

Such charges have become yet another way for cruise lines to increase revenue – but then it does cost a lot of money to develop a "private" island.

One bonus is that such an island will not be cluttered with hawkers and hustlers, as are so many Caribbean beaches. And, because they *are* private, there is security, and no fear of being mugged, as occurs in some islands. Reality can intrude, though, as it did in Royal Caribbean International's private resort of Labadee in Haiti when it narrowly escaped the devastating 2010 earthquake.

Alaska cruises

These are especially popular because:
● Alaska is a vast, relatively unexplored region.
● They offer the best way to see the state's magnificent shoreline and glaciers.
● There is a wide range of shore excursions, including many floatplane and helicopter tours, some going to glaciers and salmon fisheries.
● There are many excursions, including "dome car" rail journeys to Denali National Park to see North America's highest peak, Mt McKinley.
● Pre- and post-cruise journeys to Banff and Jasper National Parks can be made from Vancouver.

There are two popular cruise routes:

The Inside Passage Route, a 1,000-mile (1,600-km) stretch of protected waterways carved by Ice Age glaciers. This usually includes visits to tidewater glaciers, such as those in Glacier Bay's Hubbard Glacier

or Tracy Arm (just two of the 15 active glaciers along the bay's 60-mile/100-km coastline). Glacier Bay was established in 1986 as a biosphere reserve, and in 1992 the 3.3-million-acre (1.3-million-hectare) park became a World Heritage Site. Typical ports of call might include Juneau, Ketchikan, Skagway, and Haines.

The Glacier Route usually includes the Gulf of Alaska during a one-way cruise between Vancouver and Anchorage. Typical ports of call might include Seward, Sitka, and Valdez.

Holland America Line and Princess Cruises own many facilities in Alaska (hotels, tour buses, even trains), and between them have invested more than $300 million in the state. Indeed, Holland America Line-Westours is Alaska's largest private employer. Both companies take in excess of 250,000 passengers to

Aleutian Islands

0		100 miles
0	100 km	

BERING SEA

Near Islands
Rat Is
Andreanof Islands
Islands of the Four Mountains
Fox Islands
Unimak Island

ARCTIC OCEAN

RUSSIA
Arctic Circle
Bering Strait

Barrow
Prudhoe Bay

Uelen
Providenija
Kotzebue
USA
Alaska

Nome
Porcupine
Fort McPherson
Fort Good Hope
Great Bear Lake

St Lawrence Island
Norton Sound
Yukon
Fairbanks
Yukon
Dawson
CANADA
Mackenzie

St Matthew Island

Nunivak Island
Bethel
Denali National Park & Preserve
Mt McKinley
▲ 20320
Anchorage
Whitehorse
Watson Lake

Whittier ● Prince William Sound
Valdez

Alaska

0	200 miles
0	200 km

King Salmon
Homer
Seward
Skagway/Haines
Juneau

Chicagof I.
Baranof I.
Sitka

Kodiak Island
Gulf
of Alaska

Aleutian
Islands
Alaska Peninsula
Unimak Island

Prince of Wales I.
Ketchikan
Prince Rupert

Vancouver, Seattle

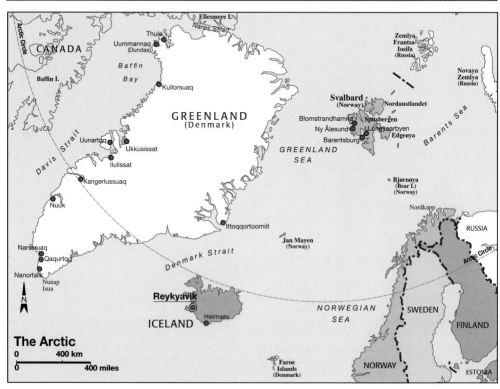

Arctic Circle

CANADA

Ellesmere I.
Nares Strait

Thule
Uummannaq (Dundas)

Baffin Bay

Baffin I.
Kullorsuaq

GREENLAND
(Denmark)

Zemlya Frantsa Iosifa (Russia)

Novaya Zemlya (Russia)

Svalbard (Norway)
Nordaustlandet

Blomstrandhamna
Ny Ålesund
Barentsburg
Spitsbergen
Longyearbyen
Edgeøya

Barents Sea

GREENLAND SEA

Davis Strait

Uunartoq
Ukkusissat
Ilulissat
Kangerlussuaq

Nuuk

Ittoqqortoormiit

Bjørnøya (Bear I.) (Norway)

Nordkapp

RUSSIA

Narsarsuaq
Qaqurtoq
Nanortalik
Nunap Isua

Jan Mayen (Norway)

Arctic Circle

Denmark Strait

Reykyavik
Heimaey
ICELAND

NORWEGIAN SEA

SWEDEN
FINLAND

NORWAY
ESTONIA

Faroe Islands (Denmark)

The Arctic

0	400 km
0	400 miles

Alaska each year. Other lines depend on what's left of the local transportation for their land tours.

In ports where docking space is limited, some ships anchor rather than dock. Many cruise brochures do not indicate which ports are known to be anchor (tender) ports.

With around 930,000 cruise passengers visiting Alaska in 2010 and several large resort ships likely to be in port on any given day, there's so much congestion in many of the small ports that avoiding crowded streets can be difficult. Even nature is retreating; with more people around, wildlife is harder to spot. And many of the same shops are now found in Alaska as well as in the Caribbean.

The more adventurous might consider one of the more unusual Alaska cruises to the far north, around the Pribilof Islands (superb for bird watching) and into the Bering Sea.

Alaska isn't always good-weather cruising – it can be wet and windy and excursions may be canceled or changed. Even if it's sunny in port, glaciers have their own weather systems and helicopter flightseeing excursions are vulnerable.

European and Mediterranean cruises

Traveling within Europe (including the Aegean, Baltic, Black Sea, Mediterranean, and Norwegian fjord areas) by cruise ship makes economic sense. Although no single cruise covers every port, cruise ships do offer a comfortable way of exploring a rich mix of destinations, cultures, history, architecture, lifestyles, and cuisines – and without having to pack and unpack each day.

European cruises have become increasingly popular because:

● So many of Europe's major cities – Amsterdam, Athens, Barcelona, Copenhagen, Genoa, Helsinki, Lisbon, London, Monte Carlo, Nice, Oslo, St Petersburg, Stockholm, and Venice – are on the water. It is far less expensive to take a cruise than to fly and stay in decent hotels, paying extra for food and transport.

● You will not have to try to speak or understand different languages when you are aboard ship as you would ashore – if you choose the right ship.

● Aboard ship you use a single currency – typically US dollars, British pounds, or euros.

● A wide variety of shore excursions are offered.

● Lecture programs provide insights into a culture before you step ashore.

Small ships are arguably better than large resort ships, as they can obtain berthing space – the large resort ships may have to anchor in more of the smaller ports, so it can take time to get to and from shore, and you'll probably have to wait for shore tender tickets. Many Greek islands are accessible only by shore tender. Some companies allow more time ashore than others, so compare itineraries in the brochures; it's probably best to choose a regional cruise line (such as Louis Cruises) for these destination-intensive cruises, for example.

Canada/New England cruises

These typically sail between New York or Boston and Montreal (northbound and southbound). Ports of call may include Boston; Quebec City, Quebec; Charlottetown, Prince Edward Island; Sydney and Halifax, Nova Scotia; Bar Harbor, Maine; and Saguenay, Quebec. The ideal time to sail is during the fall, when the leaves dramatically change color.

Middle East cruises

These include the Arab countries bordering the Arabian and Red seas, and the south-eastern Mediterranean. Countries with cruise facilities and places of historic interest are: Bahrain, Egypt, Iran, Jordan, Oman, Yemen, and the seven sheikdoms of the United Arab Emirates (UAE). Different visas may be required for each of the emirates.

Abu Dhabi and Dubai are fast becoming cruise bases, although cruise terminal and handling facilities are still quite limited. If you visit Dubai – which, incidentally, has the world's largest carbon footprint – note that displays of affection such as hand-holding or kissing are not permitted in public, and you can't drink alcohol in a public place.

If you fly into Dubai with prescription medicines, make sure you have the appropriate, signed prescription. The authorities are extremely strict with drugs and medication.

South Africa and Indian Ocean

Attractions include cosmopolitan cities, wine tours, wildlife safaris, unspoiled landscapes, and uninhabited beaches. Itineraries (usually 10–14 days) include sailings starting and finishing in Cape Town (in the same time zone as the UK), or from Cape Town to East African ports such as Port Elizabeth, Richards Bay, Durban, Zanzibar and Mombasa (Kenya). Longer itineraries, of 21 days or more, could include Madagascar, Mozambique, and the Seychelles.

The Mexican Riviera

These typically sail from Los Angeles or San Diego, along Mexico's west coast, calling at ports such as Cabo San Lucas, Mazatlan, Puerto Vallarta, Ixtapa/Zihuatanejo, Manzanillo, and Acapulco. These cruises also typically include a call in the Baja Peninsula, Mexico's northernmost state.

Route Canal (Transcanal cruises)

These take you through the Panama Canal, constructed by the United States after the failure of a French effort which began in 1882 with a labor force of over 10,000 but was plagued by disease and financial prob-

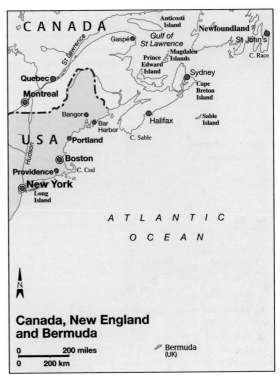

Canada, New England and Bermuda

0   200 miles

0   200 km

The Middle East

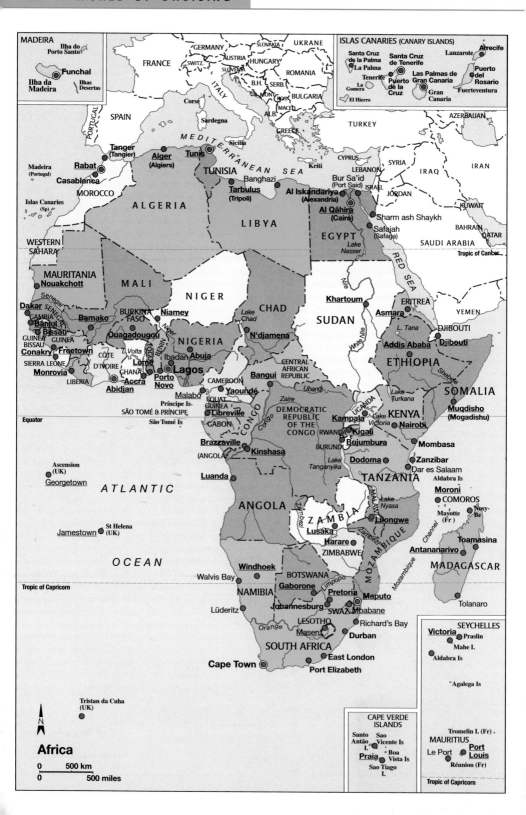

MADEIRA

Ilha do Porto Santo

Funchal

Ilha da Madeira

Ilhas Desertas

ISLAS CANARIES (CANARY ISLANDS)

Santa Cruz de la Palma
La Palma

Santa Cruz de Tenerife

Lanzarote
Arrecife

La Gomera
Tenerife

Puerto de la Cruz

Las Palmas de Gran Canaria

Puerto del Rosario

El Hierro

Gran Canaria

Fuerteventura

GERMANY

SLOVAKIA

UKRANE

FRANCE

SWITZ.

AUSTRIA

SLOVENIA

HUNGARY

ROMANIA

B.H.

SERB.

MONT.

KOS.

MACED.

BULGARIA

ITALY

Corse

GREECE

ALB.

Sardegna

Kríti

TURKEY

AZERBAIJAN

SPAIN

Corse

MEDITERRANEAN SEA

Sicília

CYPRUS

SYRIA

LEBANON

IRAQ

IRAN

Madeira (Portugal)

Tanger (Tangier)

Alger (Algiers)

Tunis

TUNISIA

Banghazi

Bur Sa'id (Port Said)

ISRAEL

JORDAN

KUWAIT

Rabat

Casablanca

Tarbulus (Tripoli)

Al Iskandariya (Alexandria)

Al Qâhira (Cairo)

Sharm ash Shaykh

BAHRAIN

QATAR

Islas Canaries (Sp.)

MOROCCO

Safajah (Safaga)

SAUDI ARABIA

WESTERN SAHARA

ALGERIA

LIBYA

EGYPT

Lake Nasser

Tropic of Cancer

MAURITANIA

Nouakchott

MALI

NIGER

CHAD

Khartoum

ERITREA

Asmara

YEMEN

RED SEA

Nile

Dakar

Senegal

GAMBIA

Banjul

Bamako

BURKINA FASO

Niamey

Lake Chad

N'djamena

SUDAN

L. Tana

DJIBOUTI

Djibouti

Bissau

GUINEA BISSAU

Conakry

GUINEA

Freetown

Ouagadougou

NIGERIA

Ibadan

Abuja

CENTRAL AFRICAN REPUBLIC

Addis Ababa

ETHIOPIA

SIERRA LEONE

Monrovia

LIBERIA

CÔTE D'IVOIRE

GHANA

Lomé

Porto Novo

Lagos

CAMEROON

Bangui

White Nile

Shebele

SOMALIA

Accra

Abidjan

Malabo

Yaoundé

EQUAT. GUINEA

Ubangi

Lake Turkana

Muqdisho (Mogadishu)

Equator

Príncipe Is.

SÃO TOMÉ & PRÍNCIPE

São Tomé Is

Libreville

GABON

CONGO

DEMOCRATIC REPUBLIC OF THE CONGO

Zaire

UGANDA

Kampala

Lake Victoria

KENYA

Nairobi

Ascension (UK)

Georgetown

ATLANTIC

Brazzaville

Kinshasa

Congo

RWANDA

Kigali

BURUNDI

Bujumbura

Dodoma

Lake Tanganyika

Mombasa

Zanzibar

Dar es Salaam

Aldabra Is

Luanda

TANZANIA

Moroni

COMOROS

St Helena (UK)

Jamestown

ANGOLA

ZAMBIA

Lake Nyasa

MALAWI

Lilongwe

Mayotte (Fr.)

Nosy-Be

OCEAN

Lusaka

Harare

ZIMBABWE

Zambezi

MOZAMBIQUE

Toamasina

Antananarivo

MADAGASCAR

Tropic of Capricorn

Windhoek

Walvis Bay

BOTSWANA

Gaborone

Limpopo

NAMIBIA

Lüderitz

Johannesburg

Pretoria

Maputo

SWAZ. Mbabane

Tolanaro

Orange

LESOTHO

Maseru

Richard's Bay

Durban

SOUTH AFRICA

Cape Town

East London

Port Elizabeth

Port Elizabeth

SEYCHELLES

Victoria

Praslin

Mahé I.

Aldabra Is

Agalega Is

Tristan da Cuha (UK)

N

Africa

0 ——— 500 km

0 ——— 500 miles

CAPE VERDE ISLANDS

Santo Antão I.

Sao Vicente Is

Praia

Boa Vista Is

Sao Tiago I.

Tromelin I. (Fr.)

MAURITIUS

Le Port

Port Louis

Réunion (Fr.)

Tropic of Capricorn

lems (over 22,000 people died). The US took over the building effort in 1904 and the waterway opened on August 15, 1914, shaving over 7,900 nautical miles off the distance between New York and San Francisco. The Panama Canal runs from *northwest* to *southeast* (not west to east), covering 51 miles (82 km) of locks and gates and dams.

Control of the canal passed from the US to Panama in 2000. The $6 billion widening of the canal and new locks, to be built by 2014, will double its capacity, enabling the latest large resort ships to use it.

Between the Caribbean and the Pacific, a ship is lifted 85ft (26 meters) in a continuous flight of three steps at Gatun Locks to Gatun Lake through which it travels to Gaillard Cut where the Canal slices through the Continental Divide. It is lowered at Pedro Miguel Locks 31ft (9.4 meters) in one step to Miraflores Lake, then the remaining two steps to sea level at Miraflores Locks before passing into the Pacific.

Ships move through the locks under their own power, guided by towing locomotives. The 50-mile (80-km) trip takes eight to nine hours. What does it cost? Well, *Disney Magic* paid a record $331,200 for one transit of the canal in 2008.

Most Panama Canal cruises depart from Fort Lauderdale or San Juan, calling at islands such as Aruba or Curaçao before entering the canal and ending in Acapulco, Los Angeles, or San Francisco. In 2008, the Inter-American Development Bank's (IDB) board of directors approved a $400 million loan to help finance the historic Panama Canal Expansion Program.

South America cruises

Cruises around Cape Horn between Santiago or Valpariso in Chile and Buenos Aires in Argentina are increasingly popular. The optimum season is November to March and most cruises last 14 days.

Sailing southbound, ports of call might include Puerto Montt (Chile), the magnificent Chilean fjords, Punta Arenas (Chile), and Ushuaia (Argentina), the world's southernmost city (pop. 64,000) and the starting point for many cruises to the Antarctic Peninsula.

Coming up the continent's east coast, ports of call might include Puerto Madryn (Argentina) and Montevideo (Uruguay). Slightly longer itineraries may include a call at Port Stanley in the Falkland Islands. Do watch for pickpockets in the major cities of South America.

A number of cruise lines also operate seven-day cruises from Rio de Janeiro, Brazil, mainly for Brazilians (who love to dance the night away and don't arise until nearly afternoon). Called "eat late, sleep late" cruises, these are typically aboard large resort ships chartered to local companies such as CVC.

Australia, New Zealand, and Asia cruises

If you live in Europe or North America, be aware that the flight to your port of embarkation will be long. It's advisable to arrive at least two days before the cruise, as time changes and jet lag can be severe. Economic constraints have depressed bookings recently, which is a shame because the region has so much to offer that it's worth taking a cruise of at least 14 days. Australia, New Zealand, the islands of the South Pacific, Hong Kong, China, Japan, Indonesia, Malaysia, Singapore, Thailand, and Vietnam are all fascinating destinations. ❑

Crystal Serenity squeezes through the Panama Canal.

South America

0   500 km
0   500 miles

CARIBBEAN SEA

Lesser Antilles

Isla de Margarita

TRINIDAD AND TOBAGO
Trinidad

Barranquilla
Maracaibo
Caracas

PANAMÁ

Panama

Llanos
Orinoco

VENEZUELA

Georgetown

Paramaribo

GUYANA

Cayenne

Medellín

GUIANA HIGHLANDS

SURINAME

French Guiana (France)

Bogotá

COLOMBIA

Macapa

ATLANTIC

OCEAN

Equator

Manta
Quito
ECUADOR

Amazon

Manaus

Amazonas

Santarém

Belém

Guayaquil

Iquitos

Basin

Alter do Chão

Fortaleza

Galápagos Is

Marañón

Madeira

Ucayali

Trujillo

PERU

B R A Z I L

São Francisco

Xingu

Recife

Callao
Lima

Cusco

Salvador (Bahia)

Arequipa

Altiplano

BOLIVIA
La Paz

Brasilia

not to same scale

Sucre

Pantanal

Belo Horizonte

Equator ECUADOR
Quito
Galápagos
Guayaquil

PACIFIC OCEAN

Gran Chaco

Paraguay

PARAGUAY

Paraná

Rio de Janeiro

Antofagasta

Asunción

Foz do Iguaçu

São Paulo

Tucumán

CHILE

Atacama

Salado

Uruguay

ARGENTINA

Falkland Islands (UK)

Isla Grande de Tierra del Fuego

CHILE

Valparaíso

Mendoza

URUGUAY

Porto Alegre

Cabo de Hornos

Santiago

Montevideo

Punta del Este

Drake Passage

Concepción

Buenos Aires

Rio de la Plata

South Shetland Islands (UK)

South Orkney Islands (UK)

Pampas

ARGENTINA

Mar del Plata

Graham Land

Bellinghausen Sea

Weddell Sea

Puerto Montt

Bahía Blanca

Puerto Madryn

Charcot Island

Palmer Land

Isla Grande de Chiloé

PATAGONIA

ATLANTIC

Alexander Island

PACIFIC

Gulf of San Jorge

OCEAN

ANTARCTICA

Ronne Ice Shelf

OCEAN

Laguna san Rapheal

Falkland Islands (UK)
Stanley

Punta Arenas

Isla Grande de Tierra del Fuego

South Georgia Island (UK)

Ushuaia

Grytviken

Cabo de Hornos

WHO GOES WHERE: THE PRINCIPAL CRUISE LINES SERVING EACH REGION

This is a selection of just some of the cruise companies that operate cruises regularly in the world's most popular cruise regions. These are not recommendations but rather suggestions to help you research what's right for you.

● **Caribbean**
Carnival Cruise Lines, Disney Cruise Line, Holland America Line, Norwegian Cruise Line, Oceania Cruises, Princess Cruises, Royal Caribbean International, SeaDream Yacht Club, Star Clippers, Windstar Cruises

● **Alaska**
American Safari Cruises, Celebrity Cruises, Crystal Cruises, Holland America Line, Norwegian Cruise Line, Oceania Cruises, Princess Cruises, Regent Seven Seas Cruises, Royal Caribbean International, Silversea Cruises

● **Baltic/Northern Europe**
Azamara Cruises, Crystal Cruises, Cunard Line, Fred Olsen Cruise Lines, Hapag-Lloyd Cruises, Oceania Cruises, P&O Cruises, Phoenix Reisen, Saga Cruises, Swan Hellenic Cruises

● **Mediterranean**
AIDA Cruises, Azamara Cruises, Celebrity Cruises, Costa Cruises, Cunard Line, MSC Cruises, Oceania Cruises, P&O Cruises, Princess Cruises, Pullmantur Cruises, Regent Seven Seas Cruises, Saga Cruises, SeaDream Yacht Club, Seabourn, Silversea Cruises, Star Clippers, Thomson Cruises, TUI Cruises, Voyages of Discovery, Windstar Cruises

● **Greek Islands**
Louis Cruises, Oceania Cruises, Swan Hellenic Cruises, Voyages of Discovery, Voyages to Antiquity

● **Canary Islands**
Fred Olsen Cruise Lines, P&O Cruises, TUI Cruises

● **Middle East**
AIDA Cruises, Hapag-Lloyd Cruises, MSC Cruises, Noble Caledonia, Phoenix Reisen, Swan Hellenic Cruises, TUI Cruises

● **Indian Ocean**
Hapag-Lloyd Cruises, Phoenix Reisen, Ponant Cruises

● **South America**
Celebrity Cruises, Costa Cruises, Crystal Cruises, Holland America Line, MSC Cruises, Oceania Cruises, Princess Cruises, Regent seven Seas Cruises, Silversea Cruises

● **Great Lakes (USA)**
Noble Caledonia, Ponant Cruises

● **New England/Canada**
Celebrity Cruises, Crystal Cruises, Holland America Line, Oceania Cruises, Princess Cruises, Regent Seven Seas Cruises,

● **Australia/New Zealand**
Classic International Cruises, Celebrity Cruises, P&O Cruises (Australia), Orion Expedition Cruises, Princess Cruises

● **Southeast Asia**
Crystal Cruises, Oceania Cruises, Seabourn, Silversea Cruises, Star Cruises

● **South Pacific**
Paul Gauguin Cruises, P&O Cruises (Australia), Princess Cruises

● **South Africa**
MSC Cruises, plus several cruise lines operating around-the-world cruises

● **Transatlantic Crossings**
Cunard Line

Australasia

0   500 km

0   500 miles

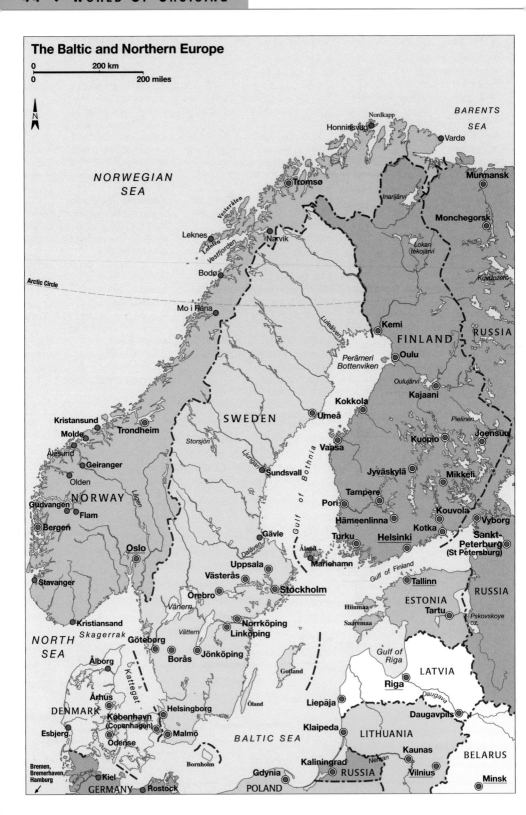

The Baltic and Northern Europe

Japan

Wakkanai / Kyushir
Kushiro
Hokkaido
Hakodate
Aomori
Sapporo
Sendai
Honshu
Niigata
Yokohama Tokyo
Fuji-san 3776
Nagoya
Kyoto
JAPAN
Kobe Osaka
Hiroshima Shikoku
Kitakyushu Kyushu
Fukuoka
Nagasaki
Kagoshima
Naha, Okinawa

RUSSIA
Vladivostok
Nakhodka
Sea of Japan
Ch'ŏngjin
Kimch'aek
NORTH KOREA
Kangnang
SOUTH KOREA
Busan
Korea Strait
CHINA

Southeast Asia

PACIFIC OCEAN

Rabaul
Admiralty Islands
Bismarck Sea
Jayapura
New Guinea
PAPUA NEW GUINEA
Port Moresby
Torres Strait
AUSTRALIA
Equator

Pulau Biak
Pulau Yapen
Kepulauan Aru
Pulau Dolak
Pulau Yamdena

Halmahera
Pulau Waigeo
Maluku (Moluccas)
Pulau Misool
Seram
Seram Sea
Ambon
Banda Sea
Buru
Pulau Sula
Kepulauan Sula
Wetar
EAST TIMOR
Arafura Sea

Manado
Celebes Sea
Sulawesi
Samarinda
Ujung Padang
Pulau Muna
Flores Sea
Bali
Lombok
Sumbawa
Sumba
Flores

PHILIPPINE SEA

Mindanao
Davao
Cebu City
Legazpi
Samar
Luzon
PHILIPPINES
Manila
Baguio
Mindoro
Panay
Negros
Palawan
Sulu Sea

Naha, Okinawa
Nansei-shoto (Japan)
Taiwan
Taipei
Kaohsiung
Xiamen
Hong Kong
Guangzhou (Canton)
Macau
Liuzhou
Nanning
Hainan Dao
Haikou
CHINA

SOUTH CHINA SEA

Batam Islands
Babuyan Islands

Kota Kinabalu
Sandakan
Bandar Seri Begawan
BRUNEI
Kuching
MALAYSIA
Borneo
Banjarmasin
Java Sea
Semarang
Surabaya
Denpasar
Java
Bandung
Pontianak
Pulau Belitung
P. Bangka
Pulau Natuna (Indonesia)
Jakarta
Teluk Betung
Palembang
Sumatra

Da Nang
Nha Trang
Ho Chi Minh (Saigon)
VIETNAM
Hai Phong
Ha Noi (Hanoi)
Yuan Jiang
CAMBODIA
Phnum Penh (Phnom Penh)
Mekong
Viangchan (Vientiane)
Chiang Mai
THAILAND
Nakhon Ratchasima
Bangkok (Krung Thep)
Gulf of Thailand
Songkhla
Kota Bharu
Johor Bahru
Singapore
SINGAPORE
Kuala Lumpur
Ipoh
George Town
MALAYSIA
Strait of Malacca
Medan
Pematangsiantar

Mandalay
Naypyidaw
Chittagong
BURMA (MYANMAR)
Yangon
Irrawaddy
Salween
Gulf of Martaban
Mergui
Ko Phangan
Ko Samui
Pulau Langkawi
ANDAMAN SEA
Ko Phuket
Kep. Mentawai
Pulau Siberut
Pulau Nias
Pulau Simeulue
Padang
INDIAN OCEAN
Equator

500 miles
500 km

LIFE ABOARD

This A to Z survey covers the astonishing range of facilities that modern cruise ships offer and tells you how to make the most of them

Air conditioning

Cabin temperature can be regulated by an individually controlled thermostat, so you can adjust it to suit yourself. Public room temperatures are controlled automatically. Air temperatures are often kept cooler than you may be used to. In some cases, the air conditioning can't be turned off (e.g. "Vista"-class ships *Arcadia, Carnival Legend, Carnival Miracle, Carnival Pride, Carnival Spirit, Costa Atlantica, Costa Deliziosa, Costa Luminosa, Costa Mediterranea, Eurodam, Nieuw Amsterdam, Noordam, Oosterdam, Queen Elizabeth, Queen Victoria, Westerdam, Zuiderdam*).

Art auctions

Beware of these. Aboard most large resort ships, intrusive art auctions form part of the "entertainment" program, with flyers, brochures, and forceful announcements that almost demand that you attend. They may be fun participation events – though the "free champagne" given to entice you is mostly sparkling wine and *not* champagne – but don't expect to purchase an heirloom, as most of the art pieces (lithographs and seriographs) are rubbish. It's funny how so many identical pieces can be found aboard so many ships.

Note that art "appraisal prices" are done in-house by the art provider, a company that *pays* a cruise line to be onboard. Watch out for the words: "retail replacement value". Also, listen for phrases such as "signed in the stone" – it means that the artists did not sign the work – or "pochoire" (a stencil print less valuable than an original etching or lithograph). If the auctioneer tries to sell a piece of art (particularly a "block" print or woodcut/engraving) with an "authenticated signature," don't buy it – when it's delivered to your home and you have it appraised, you'll probably find it's not genuine. Forged signatures are not uncommon.

If you do buy something, do so because it will look good on your wall, not as an investment. Read the fine print, and buy with caution. Remember that the cruise line takes absolutely no responsibility for artwork that's worthless – it acts only as the carrier, and the art auction house is just a concession.

LEFT: *Allure of the Seas* has 16 decks.
RIGHT: an art auction aboard *Noordam*.

Babysitting

In some ships, stewards, stewardesses, and other staff may be available as babysitters for an hourly fee. Make arrangements at the reception desk. Aboard some ships, evening babysitting services may not start until late; check times and availability before you book a cruise.

Beauty salon/Barber shop

Make appointments as soon after boarding as possible, particularly on short cruises. Appointment times fill up rapidly, especially before social events such as a captain's cocktail party. Charges are comparable to city prices ashore. Typical services: haircut for men and women, styling, permanent waving, coloring, manicure, pedicure, leg waxing. *See Spas, pages 66–71.*

Cashless cruising

You simply settle your account with one payment (by cash or credit card) before disembarking on the last day. An imprint of your credit card is taken at embarkation or when you register online, permitting you to sign for everything. Before the end of the cruise, a detailed statement is delivered to your cabin.

Some cruise lines, irritatingly, discontinue their "cashless" system for the last day of the cruise. Some may add a "currency conversion service charge" to your credit

Celebrity Cruises and Royal Caribbean International, abide by Nevada Gaming Control Board regulations. Most table games have a $5 minimum and $200 maximum – but, for serious players, Carnival Cruise Lines' casinos have blackjack tables with a $25 minimum and $500 maximum.

Some cruise lines have "private gaming club" memberships, with regular newsletters, rebates, and special offers (example: Star Cruises/Genting Hong Kong). Slot machines are also in evidence and make more than half a casino's profits.

Note that, for American citizens and resident aliens in the US, slot machine winnings may be subject to WG-2 tax withholding.

Comment cards

On the last day of the cruise you will be asked to fill out a company "comment card." Some lines offer "incentives" such as a bottle of champagne. Be truthful, as the form serves as a means of communication between you and the cruise line. Pressure from staff to write "excellent" for everything is rampant but, unless you highlight problems you have encountered, things are unlikely to improve.

Daily program

This contains a useful list of the day's activities, entertainment, and social events. It is normally delivered to your cabin the evening before the day that it covers.

Relax upstairs, gamble downstairs aboard *Norwegian Epic*.

card account if it is not in the currency of the cruise line.

Ships visiting a "private island" on a Bahamas or general Caribbean itinerary may ask you to pay cash for beverages, water sports and scuba diving gear, and other items that you purchase ashore.

Casino gaming

Many cruise ships have casinos, where the range of table games includes blackjack or 21, Caribbean stud poker, roulette, craps, and baccarat. Under-18s are not allowed in casinos, and photography is usually banned inside them. Customs regulations mean that casinos generally don't open when the ship is in port.

Gaming casino operations aboard cruise ships are unregulated. However, some companies, such as

Disembarkation

This can be the most trying part of any cruise. The cruise director will already have given an informal talk on customs, immigration, and disembarkation procedures. The night before the ship reaches its destination, you will be given a customs form. Include any duty-free items, whether purchased aboard or ashore. Save the receipts in case a customs officer asks for them.

The night before arrival, place your main baggage outside your cabin on retiring, or before 2am. It will be collected and offloaded on arrival. Leave out fragile items and the clothes you intend to wear for disembarkation and onward travel – it is amazing just how many people pack absolutely everything. Anything left in your cabin will be considered hand luggage to be hand-carried off when you leave.

On disembarkation day, breakfast will probably be early. It might be better to miss breakfast and sleep later, providing announcements on the ship's public address system do not wake you (it may be possible to turn off such announcements). Even worse than early breakfast is the fact that aboard many ships you will be commanded – requested, if you are lucky – to leave your cabin early, only to wait in crowded public rooms, sometimes for hours. To add insult to injury, your cabin steward – after he has received his tip, of course – will knock on the door to take the sheets off the bed so the cabin can

Disembarking from large resort ships can be tedious.

be made up for the incoming passengers. This will not happen aboard the smaller "upscale" ships.

Some companies, such as Princess Cruises, now offer a more relaxed system that allows you to stay in your cabin as long as you wish, or until your tag color is called, instead of waiting in public areas, where it's difficult to avoid the mass of wheeled luggage waiting to trip you up.

Before leaving the ship, remember to claim any items placed in your in-cabin safe. Passengers cannot go ashore until all baggage has been offloaded, and customs and/or immigration inspections or pre-inspections have been carried out. In most ports, this takes two to three hours after arrival. It is wise to leave at least three hours from the time of arrival to catch a connecting flight or other transportation. Once off the ship, you identify your baggage on the pier before going through customs inspection. Porters may be there to assist you.

Unseen by passengers: the engine room of *Oasis of the Seas*.

Duty-free liquor purchases

If you buy a box of "duty-free" liquor in the Caribbean, it will be taken from you at the gangway as you reboard and given back to you the day before you disembark. (Cruise lines want you to buy your alcohol on board.) Also, if you fly home after your cruise, you are not permitted to take any liquid items larger than 100ml in your hand luggage. Place liquor in your checked baggage, or it will be confiscated.

Engine room

For insurance and security reasons, visits to the engine room are seldom allowed. Some ships may have a technical information leaflet. Aboard others, a Behind the Scenes video may be shown on the cabin TV system.

Gift shops

The gift shop/boutique/drugstore offers souvenirs, gifts, toiletries, logo and duty-free items, as well as a basic stock of essential items. Opening hours are posted at the store and in the Daily Program.

Internet access typically costs 50–75 cents a minute.

Internet access, email, and cell phones

The trend toward cell (mobile) phone use aboard ships is certainly growing, and most cruise ships built after 2000 are wired and ready for internet and cell phone use, albeit at a price. You can use your own device, but it must be set for roaming – and extra charges will apply. The calls are handled by a marine satellite provider, which will pass on the international roaming charges to your phone operator. Before you cruise, check with your phone operator for the international roaming rates applicable to your tariff.

As for internet use, most new ships have a room – often part of the library – with computers. The best-wired ships also have strong signals to cabins and public areas, so you could use your own laptop in the privacy of your room or on deck (extra charges apply).

When a ship is close to antennae on land, or under the track of a passing telecommunications satellite, signals can be strong. But they can also fade in and out – typically just as you are finishing a long email. Waiting for web pages to appear on your computer screen can be frustrating.

The cost of internet time ranges from about 50 cents to 75 cents a minute. If you think you will use the

Tenders transport passengers when a ship can't dock.

internet a lot, perhaps for emails, it makes sense to buy a package of minutes. Typical charges are around $50 for 100 online minutes and $100 for 250 minutes.

Shipboard computers will ask you to establish a user name and password before you can access websites or your email. Each ship-received email arrives separately (unlike on your home computer) and will take longer to load. This is because ships use different software from home-based systems, and you will be sharing the space with marine requirements.

The signal strength can vary substantially from hour to hour, minute to minute. The farther north you get, the closer the telecommunications satellite is to the horizon, so signals tend to fade in and out. Mountain ranges can get in the way, too.

Keep in mind a few important tips:
● Remember to log off the computer when you are finished or your online charges will continue to accumulate.
● Peak demand for online time is on sea days, and just before and after the evening meal, slowing your connection. Avoid those times.
● Remember to take your user name and password for your favourite websites.
● Some browsers have small print that says "click here if you have a slow connection." Clicking on that may help speed the connection.
● If you can wait, an internet café ashore will be faster and cheaper.

Launch (shore tender) services

Enclosed or open motor launches ("tenders") are used when your cruise ship is unable to berth at a port or island. In such cases, a regular launch service is operated between ship and shore for the duration of the port call. Aboard the large resort ships, you'll need to obtain a tender ticket, usually given out in one of the lounges, unless you are on an organized excursion (these take priority). The procedure can take a long time.

When stepping on or off a tender, extend "forearm to forearm" to the person who is assisting you. Do not grip their hands because this has the unintentional effect of immobilizing the helper.

Laundry and drycleaning

Most ships offer a full laundry and pressing service. Some ships may in addition offer drycleaning facilities. A detailed list of services, and prices, can be found in your cabin. Your steward will collect and deliver your clothes. Some ships have self-service launderettes, well equipped with washers, dryers, and ironing facilities. There may be a charge for washing powder and for the use of the machines.

Library

Some cruise ships have a library offering a good selection of books, reference material, and periodicals. A small, refundable deposit may be required when you borrow a book. Aboard small luxury ships, the library is open 24 hours a day, and no deposit is required. Aboard the large resort ships, the library may be open only a couple of hours a day. *Aurora, Oriana, QM2, Queen Elizabeth*, and

A traditional paneled library aboard *Marina*.

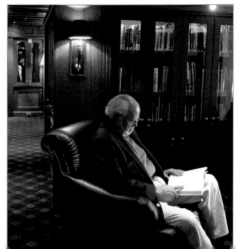

Queen Victoria have full-time, qualified librarians provided by the dedicated specialist company Ocean Books, which also sells a superb range of specialist maritime books and memorabilia aboard the three Queens.

Sadly, libraries aboard some ships are like forgotten children, with books badly organized. Aboard most other ships a member of the cruise staff or entertainment staff – with little knowledge of books or authors – staffs the library. The library may also have board games such as Scrabble, backgammon, and chess.

Lido

This is a deck devoted to swimming pools, hot tubs, showers, and general recreation, often with intrusive "background" music. Aboard most cruise ships, it has a self-serve buffet.

Lost property

Contact the reception desk immediately if you lose or find something aboard the ship.

Mail

You can buy stamps and mail letters aboard most ships, at the reception desk. Some ships use the postal privileges and stamps of their flag of registration, while others buy local stamps at ports of call. Mail is usually taken ashore by the ship's port agent just before the ship sails.

News/sports bulletins

Most ships have satellite TV for world news and sports coverage. Others print world news and sports results in the ship's newspaper or place details on a bulletin board near the reception desk or in the library. For sports results not listed, ask at the reception desk. A few ships can even print a version of your favorite newspaper.

Photographs

Professional photographers on board take digital pictures of passengers during embarkation and throughout the cruise. They cover all the main events and social functions, such as the captain's cocktail party. The pictures can be viewed without any obligation to buy, but the prices may surprise. The cost is likely to exceed $10 for a postcard-sized photograph, and a 10 x 8-inch embarkation photo aboard *Queen Mary 2* will set you back a whopping $27.50.

The reception desk is the information hub.

Postcards/stationery

These are typically available from the writing room, the library, or the reception desk. Some cruise lines now charge for them, although if you are in suite-grade accommodation, you may get stationery personalized with your name and suite number when you embark.

Pre-paid drinks

Most large resort ships offer drinks packages in an effort to "add value." However, although these booze-cruise packages mean you don't need to sign each time you order a drink, they really are a temptation to drink more (example: $29–$49 per person, per day aboard the ships of Royal Caribbean International, depending on what you want included). Some packages include wine, although the choice is the cruise line's – not yours. If you choose to travel on a low-budget ship that includes a drinks package, you could be in for a rowdy vacation.

Reception desk

This is also known as the purser's office, guest relations, or information desk. Centrally located, it is the nerve center of the ship for general passenger information and problems. Opening hours – in some ships, 24 hours a day – are posted outside the office and given in the Daily Program.

Religious services

Interdenominational services are conducted on board many ships, usually by the captain or staff captain. Costa Cruises' ships have a small private chapel. Denominational services may be taken by clergy traveling as passengers.

Room service

Beverages and snacks are available at most times. Liquor is normally limited to the opening hours of the ship's bars. Some ships charge for room service.

Sailing time

In each port of call, sailing and all-aboard times are posted at the gangway. The all-aboard time is usually half an hour before sailing. If you miss the ship, it's entirely your responsibility to get to the next port of call to rejoin the vessel.

Shipboard etiquette

Two points that are sometimes overlooked:
● If you take a video camera with you, be aware that international copyright laws prohibit you from recording the professional entertainment shows.
● It is all right to be casual but not to enter a ship's dining room in just a bathing suit, or with bare feet.

Shopping

A large resort ship with its captive audience afloat is something of a "padded sell" for retailers – hence the bargain basement stalls that spring up almost as soon as the ship sets sail. Even on formal nights, you'll see bazaar tables selling tee-shirts. It's all a bit tacky.

Many cruise lines operating in Alaska, the Bahamas, the Caribbean, and the Mexican Riviera engage an outside company that provides the services of a "shopping lecturer." This person promotes "selected" shops, goods, and services heavily, fully authorized by the cruise line (which receives a commission). This relieves the cruise director of responsibility, together with any questions concerning his involvement, credibility, and financial remuneration. Shopping maps, with "selected" stores highlighted, are placed in your cabin, and sometimes include a guarantee of satisfaction valid for 30 days.

During shore excursions, be wary of stores recommended by tour guides – they may be receiving commissions from the merchants. Shop around before you purchase. When buying local handicrafts, make sure they have indeed been made locally. Be wary of "bargain-priced" name brands, as they may be counterfeit. For watches, check the guarantee.

Some of the world's shopping havens put serious temptation in the way of cruise passengers. Top of the list are Hong Kong, Singapore, and Dubai (especially in the Mall of the Emirates – a shopping *resort* rather

Shopping in Puerto Rico during a shore excursion.

than a mall – and the Dubai Mall, with over 1,200 shops, including the only Bloomingdale's outside the USA).

A few shopping tips:
● Know in advance just what you are looking for, especially if your time is limited. If time is no problem, browsing can be fun.
● When shopping time is included in shore excursions, be careful of stores repeatedly recommended by tour guides; the guides are likely to be receiving commissions from the merchants.
● Shop around and compare prices before you buy. Good shopping hints and recommendations are often given in the cruise director's port lecture at the start of your cruise. If you notice cruise directors "pushing" certain stores, it is likely that they, too, are on commission.
● When shopping for local handicrafts, make sure they have indeed been made locally. It can happen that a so-called local product has in fact been made in Taiwan, Hong Kong, or another Far Eastern country. It pays to check.
● Be wary of "bargain priced" name brands such as Gucci bags and Rolex or Omega watches, as they may well be counterfeit. For watches, check the guarantee. If you have specific questions, ask the cruise director or shore excursion manager.
● Remember that the ship's shops are also duty-free, and, for the most part, competitive in price. The shops on board are closed while in port, however, due to international customs regulations. Worthwhile discounts are often offered on the last day of the cruise.

Swimming pools

Most ships have outdoor or indoor swimming pools, or both. They may be closed in port owing to local health regulations or cleaning requirements. Diving is not allowed – pools are shallow.

The main pool is usually on the open-air lido deck.

Parents should note that most pools are unsupervised. Some ships use excessive chlorine or bleaching agents; these could cause bathing suit colors to run.

Telephone calls

Most ships have a direct-dial satellite link, so you can call from your cabin to anywhere in the world. All ships have an internationally recognized call sign, a combination of letters and digits (example: C6SE7). Satellite calls can also be made when the ship is in port. Satellite telephone calls cost between US$5 and $12 a minute, depending on the type of equipment the ship carries.

To reach any ship, dial the International Direct Dial (IDD) code for the country you are calling from, followed by the ship's telephone number.

Anyone without a direct-dial telephone should call the High Seas Operator (in the United States, dial 1-800-SEA-CALL). The operator will need the name of the ship, together with the ocean code (Atlantic East is 871; Pacific is 872; Indian Ocean is 873; Atlantic West/Caribbean/US is 874).

● *For cell phone usage, see Internet entry (page 49).*

Television

Programming is obtained from a mixture of satellite feeds and onboard videos. Some ships lock on to live international news programs such as CNN or BBC World, or to text-only news services. Satellite TV reception can be poor because ships constantly move out of the narrow beam transmitted from the satellite.

Tipping

Aboard many ships, particularly the large resort ships, tipping appears to be mandatory rather than voluntary. Gratuities, typically at $10–$12 per person, per day, are added automatically to onboard accounts by almost all the major cruise lines, and may need to be converted to your local credit card currency at the prevailing rate, whether you have received extra service or not. However, many people, especially Europeans, don't like to be told when and how much to tip, and tipping is foreign to Asian cultures.

Gratuities are included in the cruise fare aboard a small number of ships, mainly those at the luxury end of the market, where no extra tipping is permitted – at least in theory. Even when cruise brochures state "tipping is not required," it will be expected by the staff. Aboard some ships, subtle suggestions are made regarding tips; in others, cruise directors get carried away and dictate rules.

Here are the accepted industry guidelines: dining room waiter, $3–$4 per person, per day; busboy (assistant waiter), $1.50–$2 per day; cabin steward or steward, $3–$3.50 per person, per day; Butler: $5–$6 per person, per day. Tips are normally given on the last evening of a cruise of up to 14 days' duration. For longer cruises, hand over half the tip halfway through and the rest on your last evening.

Aboard many ships, a gratuity of 10 or 15 percent is automatically added to your bar check, whether you get good service or not, and for spa treatments.

Valuables

Most ships have a small personal safe in each cabin, but items of special value should be kept in a safety deposit box in the purser's office. This is accessible during the cruise.

Water sports

Some small ships have a watersports platform that lowers from the ship's stern or side. These ships usually carry windsurfers, waterski boats, jet skis, water skis, and scuba and snorkel equipment, usually at no extra charge (except for scuba equipment).

Such facilities look good in brochures, but ships are often reluctant to use them. This is because many itineraries have too few useful anchor ports. Also, the sea must be in an almost flat calm condition – seldom the case. Insurance regulations can be restrictive too.

Wine and liquor

The cost of drinks on board is generally lower than on land, since ships have access to duty-free liquor. Drinks may be ordered in the dining room, at any of the ship's bars, or from room service. Dining rooms have extensive and reasonably priced wine lists.

Some ships sell duty-free wine and liquor to drink in your cabin. You can't normally bring these into the dining room or public rooms, nor any duty-free wine or liquor bought in port. These rules protect bar sales, a substantial source of onboard revenue. ❑

A wine appreciation session run by Regent Seven Seas Cruises.

CUISINE

Anyone determined to eat around the clock could do so aboard many ships, but the weight-conscious should exercise restraint, especially at self-service buffets

Conceited menus, rubberized duck, bitter gravy, rock-hard lobster, brittle pizza, elasticized croissants, grenade-quality fruit, coffee that tastes like army surplus paint... you can find all this and more in the cruise industry's global cafeteria. On the other hand, you can enjoy prime cuts of meat, really fresh fish and seafood, fine caviar, foie gras and vintage champagne – aboard the right ship.

The message to remember is this: generally speaking, as in most restaurants on land, you get what you pay for. High-quality food ingredients cost money, so it's pointless expecting low-cost cruises to offer anything other than low-cost food. It's not that the cruise lines don't try. They know that you will spend more time eating on board than doing anything else, so their intention is to cater as well as they can to your palate while keeping the cruise price competitive. They even boast about their food, but the reality is that meals aboard most ships are not gourmet affairs. How could they be when a kitchen has to turn out hundreds of meals at the same time? Most cruise-ship cuisine compares favorably with "banquet" food in a family restaurant – in other words, often tasteless and pedestrian. So what you can expect, therefore, is a good selection of palatable, pleasing, and complete meals served in comfortable surroundings. Maybe you will even dine by candlelight (well, electric candlelight), which at least creates some atmosphere.

Menus are typically displayed outside the dining room each day so that you can preview each meal. Menus are delivered to suites.

Fresh versus frozen

Aboard low-priced cruises, you will typically be served portion-controlled frozen food that has been reheated. Fresh fish and the best cuts of meats cost the cruise lines more, and that cost is reflected in the cruise price. Aboard some ships, the "fresh" fish – often described as "Catch of the Day" (but *which* day?) – has clearly had no contact with the sea for quite some time.

Sushi bars are a recent fad but, in 90% of cases, fish used in sushi (with rice) is steamed, and raw (sashimi-style, without rice) fish is not available, as storage and preparation facilities are inadequate. The only ships with authentic sushi bars and authentic sushi/sashimi are *Asuka II, Crystal Serenity, MSC Musica,* and *MSC Poesia.*

Note also that many items of "fresh" fruit may have been treated with 1-MCP (methylcyclopropene) to make them last longer – apples, for example, may be up to a year old.

Bread and pastry

Most bread baked aboard cruise ships is unappealing because, with little time for fermentation of natural yeast, it is made instead with instant dough that contains dried yeast from packets. Many baked goods and pastry items will be made mostly from refined flours and sugars.

A typical day

From morning till night, food is offered to the point of overkill, even aboard the most modest cruise ship. Aboard the large resort ships, pizzas, hamburgers, hot dogs, ice cream, and frozen yoghurt are almost always available. If you're still hungry, there's 24-hour room service – which, aboard some large resort ships, may cost extra. Some ships also have extra-charge bistros, cafés, and patisseries.

A Crystal Cruises head waiter prepares crêpes.

Carnival Destiny's two-level Universe Dining Room.

If you prefer to eat at set times rather than graze, these are the options:

● **6am:** hot coffee and tea on deck for early risers (or late-to-bed types).

● **Full breakfast:** typically with as many as 60 different items, in the main dining room. For a more casual meal, you can serve yourself buffet-style at an indoor/outdoor deck café, though the choice may be restricted.

● **Lunchtime:** with service in the dining room, buffet-style at a casual café, or at a separate grill for hot dogs and hamburgers, and a pizzeria, where you can watch the cooking.

● **4pm:** afternoon tea, in the British tradition, complete with finger sandwiches and scones. This may be served in a main lounge to the accompaniment of live music (it may even be a "tea-dance") or recorded classical music.

● **Dinner:** the main event of the evening, and apart from the casualness of the first and last nights, it is generally formal in style.

● **Light bites:** typically served in public rooms late at night. These have mostly replaced the traditional midnight buffet.

● **Gala midnight buffet:** It's almost extinct, but if there is one, it is usually held on the penultimate evening of a cruise when the chefs pull out all the stops. It features a grand, colorful spread, with much intricate decoration that can take up to 48 hours to prepare.

Seating arrangements

● **Open seating:** You can sit at any available table, with whomever you wish, at any time within dining room opening hours – just like going out to a restaurant ashore. You'll probably have a different waiter each time, because you'll be seated in different locations, so the attraction of your waiter learning your likes and dislikes is missing.

Unless you are with your own family or group of friends, you will be seated next to strangers. It is the responsibility of the restaurant manager – also known as the maître d'hôtel – to seat you with compatible people. If a reservation has been arranged prior to boarding, you will find a table seating card in your cabin when you embark. If not, make your reservation with the restaurant manager or an assistant as soon as you embark.

Tables for two are a rarity; most tables seat

THE RISE OF CELEBRITY CHEFS

Several cruise lines have signed up well-known chefs to devise menus for their alternative dining venues. Celebrity Cruises, for example, worked with three-star Michelin chef Michel Roux from 1989 until 2007.

Europa chef Dieter Müller.

The celebrity chef's ideal is to create food that can be mass produced, and not cooked à la minute, as on land. But because ingredients cannot be delivered daily, as on land, the choice of dishes can be a challenge.

If he is fond of cooking over charcoal-flaming grills, he's out of luck. No open flames are allowed, though ships often use induction cooking instead to achieve a similar result.

Celebrated chefs have included Georges Blanc (Carnival Cruise Lines), Elizabeth Blau (Celebrity Cruises), Jacques Pépin (Oceania Cruises), Nobu Matsuhisa (Crystal Cruises), Todd English (Cunard Line), Mauro Uliassi (MSC Cruises), Gary Rhodes and Marco Pierre White (P&O Cruises), Charlie Palmer (Seabourn), and Aldo Zilli (Thomson Cruises).

Most celebrity chefs sail only one or two cruises a year, but Germany's three-star Michelin chef Dieter Müller has set a new benchmark by sailing for up to half a year in order to run his eponymous restaurant aboard Hapag-Lloyd Cruises' *Europa*.

four, six, or eight. It is a good idea to ask in advance to be seated at a larger table, because if you are a couple seated at a table for four and you don't get along with your table partners, there is no one else to talk to. And remember, if the ship is full, it may be difficult to change tables once the cruise has started.

Depending on the size of the ship, it may have one, two or open seatings:

● **Single seating** doesn't mean seating for single passengers. It means you can choose when you wish to eat (within dining room hours) but have the same table assigned for the cruise.

● **Two seatings:** you are assigned (or choose) one of two seatings, early or late. Typical meal times for two-seating ships are: breakfast: 6.30am–8.30am; lunch: 12 noon–1.30pm; dinner: 6.30pm–8.30pm.

Some ships operate two seatings for all meals and some just for dinner. Dinner hours may vary when the ship is in port to allow for the timing of shore excursions. Ships that operate in Europe and the Mediterranean or in South America may have later meal times to suit their clientele.

● Some ships operate a mix of open seating (dine when you want) or fixed dining times, for greater flexibility.

The captain's table

The captain usually occupies a large table in or near the center of the dining room on "formal" nights, although this tradition is disappearing as ships get bigger and more fun-oriented. The table seats eight or more people picked from the passenger or "commend" list by the hotel manager. If you are invited to the captain's table, it is gracious to accept, and you will have the chance to ask questions about shipboard life.

Bolero's bar aboard RCI's *Oasis of the Seas*.

Alternative dining

Extra-cost "alternative" restaurants were pioneered by RMS *Queen Mary* in 1936 and introduced in modern times by NCL in 1988 and Crystal Cruises in 1990. Now the large resort ships, never reluctant to embrace an additional source of revenue, have joined the trend, offering their customers an escape from the huge, noisy main dining rooms with their singing, table-dancing waiters who know little about food.

These specialist restaurants are typically smaller, à la carte venues where you must make a reservation, and pay an extra charge of between $6 and $75 a person. In return, you get better food, wines, service, and ambi-

Multi-level dining aboard *Voyager of the Seas*.

ence. But the costs can soon add up, just as can happen when you dine out ashore.

As an example, take David's Supper Club aboard *Carnival Pride*. The food is good, and the ambience is modestly refined. But a couple having two glasses of decent wine each can, with the cover charge, easily end up paying over $100 for dinner.

Molecular gastronomy

The term, invented in 1992 by the physicist Nicholas Kurti, signals food's collision with science to create molecularly synthesized food. The cuisine was first introduced to the cruising industry by Italy's Emilio Bocchia in the extra-cost restaurants aboard some Costa Cruises ships.

To provide it, you'll need blast chillers, a Pacojet (a machine that can turn everyday ingredients into ice cream), liquid nitrogen, thickening gums (such as algin and xantham), malic acid, and flame retardants (such as gellan). You'll also need a serious qualification in molecular engineering.

The end result is rather like a plate of colorful toy portions of "foam food." It can look pretty, and is reassuringly expensive, but it still tastes like foam food. In the world of molecular gastronomy, bacon can be made to taste like melon. Britain's Heston Blumenthal became famous for his snail ice cream. This type of cooking is, in the most literal sense, a matter of taste.

Special needs

Cruise lines tend to cater to general tastes. If you are allergic to ingredients such as nuts or shellfish, let the cruise line know in writing well ahead of time and, once on board, check with the restaurant manager.

---

12 TOP ALTERNATIVE DINING VENUES

Dieter Muller *Europa*
Kaito *MSC Musica, MSC Poesia*
Le Champagne *Silver Spirit*
Le Cordon Bleu *Seven Seas Voyager*
Olympic Restaurant *Celebrity Millennium*
Prime 7 *Regent Seven Seas Cruises*
Red Ginger *Marina*
Remy *Disney Dream*
The Sushi Bar *Crystal Serenity*
Teppanyaki Grill *Norwegian Epic*
Umihiko *Asuka II*
Veranda Grill *Queen Elizabeth*

Vegetarians should make sure that soups are not made with a chicken stock, as I have in the past found many so-called "vegetarian" soups are aboard ships. I once came across a "vegetarian burger" with mozzarella cheese topping – but the cheese had been made with buffalo milk and animal rennet!

If you are vegetarian, vegan, macrobiotic, counting calories, want a salt-free, sugar-restricted, low-fat, low-cholesterol, or any other diet, advise your travel agent when you book, and get the cruise line to confirm that the ship can meet your needs. Cruise ship food tends to be liberally sprinkled with salt, and vegetables are often cooked with sauces containing dairy products, salt, and sugar.

Most cruise ships don't cope well with those on vegan or macrobiotic diets who regularly need fresh-squeezed juices; most large resort ships use commercial canned or bottled juices containing preservatives and aren't able to provide really fresh juices in their bars.

A Silversea Cruises chef prepares a dainty dish.

MULTI-DECK DINING

Dining rooms with balcony levels include: *Amsterdam, Carnival Legend, Carnival Pride, Carnival Spirit, Celebrity Century, Celebrity Infinity, Celebrity Mercury, Celebrity Millennium, Celebrity Summit, Costa Atlantica, Costa Mediterranea, Dawn Princess, Empress, Eurodam, Legend of the Seas, Liberty of the Seas, Maasdam, Mein Schiff, Nieuw Amsterdam, Noordam, Oosterdam, Queen Elizabeth, Queen Victoria, Rotterdam, Ryndam, Sea Princess, Splendour of the Seas, Statendam, Sun Princess, Veendam, Volendam, Zaandam,* and *Zuiderdam.*

Not to be outdone, *Adventurer of the Seas, Allure of the Seas, Explorer of the Seas, Freedom of the Seas, Independence of the Seas, Liberty of the Seas, Mariner of the Seas, Navigator of the Seas, Oasis of the Seas,* and *Voyager of the Seas* have dining halls that span three decks.

Hebridean Princess provides the antithesis to mass catering.

Plate service versus silver service

PLATE SERVICE: When the food is presented as a complete dish, as the chef wants it to look. In most cruise ships, "plate service" is now the norm. It works well and means that most people seated at a table will be served at the same time and can eat together, rather than letting their food become cold.

SILVER SERVICE: When the component parts are brought to the table separately, so that the diner, not the chef, can choose what goes on the plate and in what proportion. Silver service is best when there is plenty of time, and is rare aboard today's ships. What some cruise lines class as silver service is actually silver service of vegetables only, with the main item, whether it is fish, fowl, or meat, already on the plate.

Self-serve buffets

Most ships have self-serve buffets for breakfast and luncheon (some also for dinner), one of the effects of discounted fares and dumbing down – and fewer staff are needed. Strangely, passengers don't seem to mind lining up for self-service food (reminiscent of school lunches and army canteens) in scandalously overcrowded venues. But while buffets look fine when they are fresh, they don't after a few minutes of passengers helping themselves. And, one soon learns, otherwise sweet little old ladies can become ruthlessly competitive at opening time.

Passengers should not have to play guessing games when it comes to food, but many cruise lines forget to put proper labels on food items; this slows down any buffet line. Labels on salad dressings, sauces, cold cuts of meat, and cheeses would be particularly useful.

What's not good is that if you ask anyone behind the self-serve buffet counters what kind of apples are in the fruit bowl they haven't a clue, "red" or "green" being the

WHAT YOU'RE MOST LIKELY TO FIND ON A TRADITIONAL CRUISE SHIP MENU

APPETIZERS
Prawn Cocktail
Smoked Salmon or
  Graved Lax
Deep-Fried Camembert
Cheese Croquets
Bacon-wrapped
  Asparagus Spears
Honeydew Melon with
  Prosciutto (or Parma)
  Ham
Emmental Cheese Soufflé
Escargots Bourguignonne
Garlic-Sautéed Frog Legs
Forest Mushroom Terrine

SOUPS
French Onion Soup
Scotch Barley Broth
Cream of Spinach
Lobster Bisque
Fagioli Red Bean
Vegetable Minestrone
  Soup

Chicken Consommé
Louisiana Gumbo
Chilled Fruit Soup
Cock a Leekie Soup

MAIN COURSES
Prime Rib of Beef/Roast
  Sirloin of Beef
Roasted Pork Loin
Beef Wellington

Veal Cordon Bleu
Broiled Lobster Tail
Surf & Turf
Coq au Vin
Pan-Seared Darne of
  Salmon
Salmon Kulebiak
Duckling à L'Orange
Magret de Canard
Sautéed King Prawns

Herb-Crusted Rack
  of Lamb
London Mixed Grill
Osso Bucco
Beef (or Mushroom)
  Stroganoff
Fish, Chips, and Mushy
  Peas
Roast Turkey with
  trimmings

Boneless Chicken Kiev
Grilled Sirloin Steak/
  Filet Mignon

SALADS
Caesar Salad
Cobb Salad
Tossed Spinach Salad
  with Bacon Bits
Tossed Garden Greens
Salade Niçoise

DESSERTS
Baked Alaska
Crème Brûlée
Apple Pie à la Mode
Black Forest Cake
Sticky Toffee
  Pudding
Amaretto Soufflé
Tiramisu
Pecan Pie
Lemon Cheesecake
Chocolate Chiffon Pie

usual answer (red apples, for example, could be Brae-burn, Calville, Egremont Russet, Gala, Pink Lady, Starking Delicious, or Worcester Pearmain). Staff should know the most basic details about food on display.

Healthy eating

It's easy to gain weight when cruising – but not inevitable. In fact, taking a cruise could well be a good reason to get serious about your wellbeing. Weight-conscious passengers should exercise self-restraint, particularly at self-service buffets. The same rule applies as on dry land: eat slowly and chew well.

Many ships' menus include "heart-healthy" or "lean and light" options, with calorie-filled sauces replaced by so-called "spa" cuisine. It may also be wise to choose grilled or poached fish (salmon, or sea bass, for example), rather than heavy meat dishes or chicken – which is typically loaded with hormones and antibiotics – or fried food items.

If you have a sensitive stomach, avoid the self-serve buffets. If you must use them (some cruise lines close their main dining rooms for lunch, leaving you with little choice), salads are a wise choice.

● **Fruit and vegetables:** Quality and variety are directly linked to the per-passenger budget set by each cruise line and are dictated by suppliers, regions, and seasons. Companies operating large resort ships buy fruit at the lowest price, which can translate to unripe bananas, tasteless grapes, and hard-as-nails plums.

The smaller, more upscale ships usually carry better-quality ripe fruits as well as the more expensive varieties such as dragon fruit, carambola (star fruit), cherimoya, cactus pear, guava, kumquat, loquat, pas-

Carnival's self-serve buffets are always open.

___

sion fruit, persimmon, physalis (Cape gooseberry), rambutan, and sharon fruit.

Some cruise lines are also putting a greater emphasis on fresh vegetables, whole grains, and organic food. As well as being healthier, eating fruit regularly checks hunger pangs and so delays the need for heavier fare. If you take fruit from the buffet to your cabin, it would be wise to wash it because it may have been sprayed with pesticides and fungicides.

● **Exercise:** There are plenty of opportunities for exercise, either in the spa or gym, on the jogging track often found above the main swimming pool deck, or by signing up for active shore excursions involving biking, hiking, or river-rafting. Also, to encourage good digestion, forget about the elevator and take the stairs – you'll skip those tedious lines for the elevator on large resort ships at peak times, and you'll feel fitter, too.

___

Better-quality food is served at extra-cost restaurants.

National differences

Most cruise lines feature mainly American-style cuisine, or cuisine that is often described as international, while more European-style cuisine is typically provided aboard the ships of European cruise lines (examples: Cunard Line, Fred Olsen Cruise Lines, Hebridean Island Cruises, MSC Cruises, P&O Cruises, Phoenix Reisen, and TUI Cruises).

Beef, lamb, and pork cuts are different on both sides of the Atlantic, so what you ordered may not be the cut, shape, or size you expected. For example, there are 15 British cuts of beef, 17 American cuts, and 24 French cuts. There are six American cuts of lamb, eight British cuts, and nine French cuts. There are eight American cuts of pork, 10 British cuts, and 17 French cuts.

While American passengers typically like iced water, or a jug of iced tea at lunch, most European passengers don't like ice in their water, and few drink iced tea.

If you care about cutlery, note that only a few cruise lines with large resort ships provide the correct, specially shaped fish knives, or the correct soup spoons (oval for thin bouillon-style soups and round for creamy soups).

Dining room and kitchen staff

Celebrity chefs *(see box on page 55)* make the headlines, but it's the executive chef who plans the menus, orders the food, organizes his staff, and arranges all the meals. Although he himself rarely cooks, he oversees everything about the galley operation. He makes sure that menus are not repeated, even on long cruises. On some cruises, he works with guest chefs from restaurants ashore to offer tastes of regional cuisine. He may also purchase fish, seafood, fruit, and various other local produce in "wayside" ports and incorporate them into the menu with a "special of the day" announcement.

The restaurant manager – also known as the maître d'hôtel and not to be confused with the ship's hotel manager – is an experienced host, with shrewd perceptions about compatibility. It is his responsibility to seat you with suitable fellow passengers. If a reservation has been arranged prior to boarding, you'll find a table assignment or seating card in your cabin when you embark. If not, make your reservation with the restaurant manager or an assistant as soon as you embark.

If you are unhappy with any aspect of the dining room operation, the sooner you tell someone the better. Don't wait until the cruise is over to send a scathing letter to the cruise line – it's too late then to do anything positive.

The best waiters are those trained in European hotels or catering schools. They provide fine service and quickly learn your likes and dislikes. They normally work aboard the best ships, where dignified professionalism is expected and living conditions are good.

Many lines contract the running and staffing of dining rooms to a specialist maritime catering organization.

Ships that cruise far from their home country find that professional caterers such as Hamburg-based Sea Chefs do a good job. However, ships that control their own catering staff and food often try very hard for good quality.

Hygiene standards

Galley equipment is in almost constant use, and regular inspections and maintenance help detect potential problems. There is continual cleaning of equipment, utensils, bulkheads, floors, and hands.

Cruise ships sailing from or visiting US ports are subject to in-port sanitation inspections. These are voluntary, not mandatory inspections, based on 42 inspection items, undertaken by the United States Public Health (USPH) Department of Health and Human Services, under the auspices of the Centers for Disease Control. The cruise line pays for each inspection. A similar process takes place in Britain under the Port Health Authority, which has even more stringent requirements.

A tour of the galley proves to be a highlight for some passengers, when a ship's insurance company permits. A video of Behind the Scenes, for use on in-cabin television, may be provided instead.

In accordance with international standards, all potable water brought on board, or produced by distillation aboard cruise ships, should contain a free chlorine or bromine residual equal to or greater than 0.2 ppm (parts

How to ascertain waiting times aboard *Oasis of the Seas*.

per million). This is why drinking water served in dining rooms often tastes of chlorine.

Smoking and no-smoking areas

Most ships now have totally no-smoking dining rooms, while some still provide smoking (cigarettes only, not cigars or pipes) and no-smoking sections. Those wishing to sit in a no-smoking area should tell the restaurant manager when reserving a table.

At open seating breakfasts and luncheons in the dining room or at a casual self-serve buffet venue, smokers and non-smokers may be seated close together. ❏

HOW THE MAJOR CRUISE LINES SCORE ON CUISINE AND SERVICE

Scores out of maximum 10. Note that these ratings do not reflect extra-cost "alternative" restaurants.	Carnival Cruise Lines	Celebrity Cruises	Costa Cruises	Cunard Line	Holland America Line	MSC Cruises	Norwegian Cruise Line	P&O Cruises	Princess Cruises	Royal Caribbean Int.	Star Cruises
Food											
Dining Room/Cuisine	5.7	7.3	5.9	7.7	7.1	7.0	6.0	6.5	7.4	4.8	6.0
Buffets/Informal Dining	5.8	7.0	5.6	7.1	6.3	6.4	6.2	6.0	6.8	6.1	5.9
Quality of Ingredients	6.0	7.1	6.0	7.5	6.7	7.5	6.1	6.6	6.8	5.8	6.4
Afternoon Tea/Snacks	4.0	6.6	4.6	7.4	5.6	6.6	4.5	6.5	6.3	4.0	5.2
Wine List	5.7	7.5	5.6	8.0	6.1	7.3	6.2	6.7	6.6	5.4	5.5
Overall Food Score	**5.44**	**7.10**	**5.54**	**7.54**	**6.36**	**6.96**	**5.80**	**6.46**	**6.78**	**5.22**	**5.80**
Service											
Dining Rooms	6.0	7.6	6.0	7.6	7.4	7.3	6.6	6.8	7.5	5.7	6.3
Bars	5.8	7.4	6.2	7.6	7.1	7.5	6.4	7.1	7.5	5.6	6.0
Cabins	6.0	7.6	6.8	7.7	7.5	7.5	6.2	7.6	7.3	6.2	6.1
Open Decks	5.5	7.2	5.6	7.4	6.6	7.2	6.0	6.2	6.8	5.6	6.0
Wines	5.0	7.5	5.2	8.0	6.1	7.4	6.0	6.0	6.2	5.2	5.2
Overall Service Score	**5.66**	**7.46**	**5.96**	**7.66**	**6.94**	**7.38**	**6.24**	**6.74**	**7.06**	**5.66**	**5.92**
Combined food/service	**5.55**	**7.28**	**5.75**	**7.60**	**6.65**	**7.17**	**6.02**	**6.60**	**6.85**	**5.44**	**5.86**

THE SHOW MUST GO ON

**The bigger the ship, the bigger the production show.
But the tired old song-and-dance routines are now
being replaced by well-known Broadway musicals**

Cruise lines with large resort ships have been upping the ante lately, competing to attract attention by staging lavish, high-tech-reliant productions that are licensed versions of Broadway shows. Examples include *Chicago* and *Hair* aboard Royal Caribbean International's Oasis-class ships, with impressively large casts. These big theater shows are abridged versions specially adapted to the cruise ships' showroom stage, typically by trimming and fine-tuning them so that the performance fits in with the ship's operational schedule – not to mention dinner.

Also, on an Aqua (outdoor) combination water and stage aboard Royal Caribbean International's *Allure of the Seas* and *Oasis of the Seas*, aquabatics and comedy provide a night-time entertainment spectacular on the outside deck at the aft of the ships.

Aboard Norwegian Cruise Line's *Norwegian Epic*, the *Blue Man Group*, a mime and multi-sensory effects show which involves passengers, is a hit with families, as is a Cirque Dreams and Dinner; each show is in a dedicated venue as there's no main showlounge as such.

Then there's family favorite Disney Cruise Line with

RCI's *How to Train Your Dragon* ice spectacular.

its own superb stage shows taken from the vast choices available in the Disney stable, plus *Believe*, developed specifically for *Disney Dream*. There's also a proven family favorite, *Toy Story – The Musical*. Disney has separate entertainment shows for adults, too. And children are invited to meet and greet Disney characters in designated places and during special surprise appearances aboard its four ships.

The good news is you don't pay extra to see the show; there are few bad seats in the house; you don't have to find a parking place; you don't even have to carry tickets, or find a restaurant to eat in before or after the show. And there's always a handy bar nearby.

Onboard productions

Colorful Las-Vegas-style production shows have evolved enormously aboard the large resort ships, as have the stages, technical equipment, and facilities. Although they still can't match the budgets of Las Vegas, they can certainly beat many shore-side venues. Most shipboard production shows have two things in common: no audience contact (well, almost none), and intense volume. With few exceptions, the equation "volume = ambience" is thoroughly entrenched in the minds of the young, hearing-impaired and musically-challenged audiovisual technicians.

With few exceptions, there's little elegance in most production shows, and all are too long. The after-dinner attention span of most cruise passengers – who are generally not unlike a television studio audience – is about 35 minutes. Most production shows run for about 45 to 50 minutes, and follow the "more is better" theory. The classic show business dictum, of course, is that it's better to "leave 'em wanting more."

Most production show "dancing" today consists of stepping in place, while pre-recorded backing tracks are often synthetic and grossly imbalanced. Synthetic string sections, for example, are acceptable only to the aurally impaired.

Some cruise lines have a live showband that backs the large-scale production shows. This band plays along with a pre-recorded backing track to create an "enhanced" or larger sound. Some companies, such as Disney Cruise Line, use only a click track. This has little "feel" to it, unlike a live showband that can generate empathy and variation – as well as create work for musicians. Although live music may contain minor imperfections (which some might regard as "charac-

An Aquatheatre show aboard *Allure of the Seas*.

ter"), most passengers would prefer it to canned music – a term invented by John Philip Sousa, composer of many military marches and author, in 1906, of *The Menace of Mechanical Music*.

Great expectations

Many passengers, despite having paid comparatively little for their cruise, expect to see top-notch entertainment, headline cabaret artists, the world's most popular singers, and the most dazzling shows with slick special effects, just as one would find in the best venues in Las Vegas, London, or Paris. There are many reasons why the reality is different. Cruise line brochures tend to over-hype entertainment – just like food – to the hilt. International star acts invariably have an entourage that accompanies them to any venue: their personal manager, their musical director (often a pianist or conductor), a rhythm section with bass player and drummer, even their hairdresser.

On land, one-night shows are possible, but with a ship, an artist cannot always disembark after just one night, especially when it involves moving equipment, costumes, stage props, and baggage. This makes the deal logistically and financially unattractive for all but the very largest ships on fixed itineraries, where a marquee-name act might be a marketing plus.

For their part, most entertainers don't like to be away from their "home base" for long periods, as they rely on reliable telephone contact for managing their careers. Nor do they like the long contracts that most ships must offer in order to amortize the high costs.

A certain sameness

So many acts working aboard cruise ships are interchangeable with so many other acts also working aboard cruise ships. Ever wonder why? It relates to the limited appeal of a cruise ship gig. Entertainers aboard ships have to *live* with their audiences for several days and perhaps weeks – something unheard of on land – as well as work on stages aboard older ships that weren't designed for live performances. Nevertheless, there is no question that cruise ships have become the new location for vaudeville acts, where a guaranteed audience is a bonus for many former club-date acts, as well as fresh acts trying to break into the big time on land.

As for the "sameness" of so many shows, entertainment aboard large resort ships is market-driven. In other words, it is directed toward that segment of the industry that marketing departments are specifically targeting. This is predominantly a family audience, so the fare must appeal to a broad age range. That partly accounts for the frequency of formulaic Cirque du Soleil-style acrobatic routines and rope climbing.

A cruise line with several ships will normally employ an entertainment director and several assistants, and most cruise lines use entertainment agencies that specialize in entertainment for cruise ships. As a result, regular passengers are likely to see the same acts time after time on various ships.

Mistakes do happen. It is no use, for example, booking a juggler who needs a floor-to-ceiling height of 12ft but finds

THE COST OF STAGING A SHOW

Staging a lavish 50-minute production show can easily cost between $500,000 and $1 million, plus performers' pay, costume cleaning and repair, royalties, and so on. To justify that cost, shows must remain aboard for 18 to 24 months.

Some smaller operators see entertainment as an area for cost-cutting, so you could find yourself entertained by cheaper singers and bands that can't read musical arrangements.

Illuminations, a starry show aboard *Queen Mary 2*.

that the ship has a showlounge with a height of just 7ft (although I did overhear one cruise director ask if the act "couldn't juggle sideways"); or an acrobatic knife-throwing act (in a moving ship?); or a concert pianist when the ship only has an upright honky-tonk piano; or a singer who sings only in English when the passengers are German-speaking.

Trying to please everyone

The toughest audience is one of mixed nationalities (each of whom will expect entertainers to cater exclusively to their particular linguistic group). Given that cruise lines are now marketing to more international audiences in order to fill ever-larger ships, the problem of finding the right entertainment is far more acute.

The "luxury" cruise lines (typically those operating small ships) offer more classical music, even some light opera, more guest lecturers and top authors than the seven-day package cruises heading for the sun.

These performers, and ship entertainers generally, need to enjoy socializing. Successful shipboard acts tend to be good mixers, are presentable when in public, do not do drugs or take excess alcohol, are not late for rehearsals, and must cooperate with the cruise director.

Part of the entertainment experience aboard large resort ships is the glamorous "production show," the kind of show you would expect to see in any good Las Vegas show palace – think flesh and feathers – with male and female lead singers and Madonna or Marilyn Monroe look-alike dancers, a production

manager, lavish backdrops, extravagant sets, grand lighting, special effects, and stunning custom-designed costumes. Unfortunately, most cruise line executives, who know little or nothing about entertainment, still favor plumes and huge feather boas paraded by show-girls who *step*, but don't *dance*. Some cruise ships have coarse shows, and topless performances can be found aboard the ships of Star Cruises/Genting Hong Kong.

Book back-to-back seven-day cruises (on alternating eastern and western Caribbean itineraries, for example), and you will probably find the same two or three production shows and the same acts on the second week of your cruise. The way to avoid seeing everything twice is to pace yourself. Go to some shows during the first week and save the rest for the second week – or go sing your heart out at the karaoke sessions.

The smaller cruise lines find it economically challenging to provide high-class entertainment. Therefore they hire lower-cost singers who often turn out to be vocally challenged and bands that cannot read musical arrangements.

Other entertainment

Most ships organize acts that, while not nationally known "names," can provide two or three different shows during a seven-day cruise. These will be singers, illusionists, puppeteers, reality TV show wannabes, hypnotists, and even circus acts, with wide age-range appeal. Also, comedians who perform "clean" material can find

THE SHOWS YOU SHOULDN'T MISS

Blue Man Group *Norwegian Epic*
Chicago *Allure of the Seas* (above)
Hairspray *Oasis of the Seas*
Believe *Disney Dream*
Illuminations Planetarium *Queen Mary 2*

employment year-round on the cruise ship circuit. These popular comics enjoy good accommodation, are ministars while on board, and may go from ship to ship on a standard rotation every few days. There are raunchy, late-night "adults only" comedy acts in some of the ships with younger, clued-in audiences, but few have enough material for several shows. In general, the larger a ship, the broader the entertainment program will be.

Movies on deck

Showing movies on the open deck has been part of the cruise scene since the 1970s, when they were often classic black and white films shown at midnight. In those days, the screens were small, roll-down affairs, and the projectors were set up on makeshift pedestals. The result was often images that vibrated and sound that quivered.

Speed forward into the 21st century. Many large resort ships now have huge outdoor poolside LED (light emitting diode) movie screens 300 sq. ft (approximately 27.8 sq. meters) that cost around $1 million each. The screens are complemented by 50,000–80,000-watt sound systems for a complete "surround the deck" experience.

Princess Cruises started the trend in 2004 aboard aboard *Grand Princess* under its "Movies Under the Stars" program – not that you could always see the stars – but now all companies with large resort ships have them. The experience is reminiscent of the old drive-in movies, the difference being that cruise lines often supply blankets and even popcorn free of charge.

Movies are shown throughout the day and evening. Aboard the family-friendly ships, they may include special films for junior cruisers. Big sports events such as

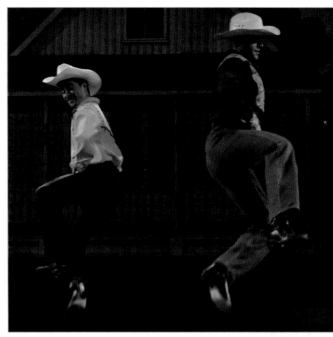

The Western-themed *X-Treme Country* aboard *Carnival Ecstasy*.

the Super Bowl or World Cup soccer are also presented.

Smaller cruise ships, expedition cruise ships and sail-cruise ships may have little or no entertainment. Aboard those ships, after-dinner conversation, reading, and relaxation becomes the entertainment of choice.

What's on

You can keep up with entertainment on offer by reading the daily program – a mini-newspaper that appears in your suite/cabin each night when your bed is turned down. It describes the next evening's shows and lists performance times. Any changes – due to bad weather, for example – are announced over the PA system. ❏

DID YOU KNOW...

● that Silvio Berlusconi, Italy's controversial premier, was once a cruise ship entertainer? He sang, and accompanying him on piano was his oldest buddy, Fedele Confalonieri, who became president of Berlusconi's Mediaset empire.

● that the cruise ship used in the 1974 movie *Juggernaut*, in which seven bombs in oil drums were placed aboard, was *Maxim Gorkiy*? The film starred Richard Harris, Omar Sharif, David Hemmings, and Anthony Hopkins.

● that the first cruise line to provide tickets for shows was Celebrity Cruises in 1991?

● that the Cunard White Star Line's *Queen Mary* was the first ship to have a system of colored lights that varied according to music (chromosonics)?

● that the 212-passenger *Seabourn Legend* was the star of the

1997 film *Speed 2: Cruise Control*? The film was shot on location in Marigot, the capital of the French side of the tiny two-nation Caribbean island of St Martin/St Maarten. The filming called for the building of almost a complete "town" at Marigot, into which the ship crashes.

● that Verdi wrote an opera to commemorate the opening of the Suez Canal? Its name is *Aida*.

● that *Titanic*, the stage musical, cost $10 million to mount in New York in 1997? That's $2.5 million more than it cost to build the original ship that made its one and only voyage in 1912.

● that the Hollywood film that made headlines by having the largest budget to date – but also made the most money – was based aboard a passenger liner? The film, of course, was *Titanic*, released in 1997.

SPAS AND WELLNESS FACILITIES

The "feelgood factor" is alive and well aboard the latest cruise ships, which offer a growing array of beauty salons and body-pampering treatments – but costs can quickly mount up

Land-based health spas have long provided a range of body treatments and services for those who wanted to hide away at a health farm in the countryside. With the increase in awareness of the body beautiful and the importance of wellbeing has come a whole new array of shipboard spas to rival those on land, particularly in the range of body-pampering treatments available. Today's cruise ships have elaborate spas where, for an extra fee, whole days of almost continuous treatments are on offer. Once the domain of adult women, spas now cater almost as equally to men.

A visit to the ship's spa will help you to relax and feel pampered. Many people not used to spas may find some of the terminology daunting: aromatherapy, hydrotherapy, ionithermie, rasul, thalassotherapy. Spa staff are used to first-time users, however, and will help you choose the massage or other treatment that best suits you and your needs. It's a good idea to visit the spa on embarkation day, when staff will be on hand to show you round, and answer your questions. Some cruise lines let you pre-book spa treatments online before your cruise. But take note of prices, which can soon add up.

Too relaxed aboard *MSC Musica* to notice the view.

Facilities

Large resort ships will have a large gymnasium with ocean views, saunas, steam rooms, rasul chamber, several body treatment rooms, thalassotherapy pool, relaxation area, changing/locker rooms, and a beauty salon. Some ships even have acupuncture treatment clinics, and some have a built-in juice bar. Some onboard spas offer a "couples" experience, and some have "spa suites" for rent by the day or half-day.

Thermal suites

Thermal suites (no, they're not specially insulated cabins) are private areas that provide a combination of various warm scented rain showers, saunas, steam rooms, thalassotherapy (saltwater) pools, and relaxation zones offer the promise of ultimate relaxation. While most ships do not charge for use of the sauna or steam room, some make a per-day charge, typically about $30–$35. Some ships even add a gratuity to a spa Day Pass, although it is supposed to be included.

Spa suites

Some ships have "spa suites," which include spa access and special amenities, and even a treatment or two, whereas regular cabin occupants pay extra to use the sauna/steam room and relaxation rooms; examples include *Costa Concordia, Costa Deliziosa, Costa Fascinosa, Costa Favolosa, Costa Luminosa, Costa Pacifica, Costa Serena, Europa*. Some even have a special spa-food-menu-only restaurant; examples include *Celebrity Eclipse, Celebrity Equinox, Celebrity Reflection, Celebrity Silhouette, Celebrity Solstice, Costa Concordia, Costa Deliziosa, Costa Fascinosa, Costa Favolosa, Costa Serena*.

Spa design

Many ship spas have Asian-themed decor, with warm woods and gently flowing water to provide a soothing atmosphere, with therapy staff dressed in the appropriate attire. But interior designers often forget to include dimmers and mood lighting, particularly in reception areas, where lighting is often too bright.

Pampering treatments

Stress-reducing and relaxation treatments are offered, combined with the use of seawater, which contains minerals, micronutrients, and vitamins. Massages might include Swedish remedial massage, shiatsu, and aroma -

therapy oils. You can even get a massage on your private balcony aboard some ships.

Having body-pampering treatments aboard a cruise ship can be wonderful, as the ship can provide a serene environment in itself; so, when enhanced by something like a massage or facial, the benefits can be more therapeutic. Ship interior designers do, however, need to pay more attention to soundproofing so that facilities can be used at all hours (lighting dimmers are also essential – it's surprising how often this simple, but essential, item is overlooked). Examples of poor soundproofing include the treatment rooms aboard *Golden Princess* and *Grand Princess*, where they are located directly underneath a sports court. So, before you actually book your relaxing massage, find out if the treatment rooms are quiet enough.

Unfortunately, treatments are usually available only until about 8pm, whereas some passengers would welcome being able to have a massage late at night before retiring to bed (the problem is that most shipboard spas are run by concessions, with wellbeing treated as a daytime-only event).

Also, be aware that the latest rip-off in the revenue game is to charge more for treatments on days at sea, and lower on port days. Check the daily program for "port day specials" and packages that make prices more palatable.

Some of the smaller, more upscale ships now offer "Spa Days" with a whole day of body-pampering treatments (often termed "wellness pack-

Working out in the gym aboard *Carnival Destiny*.

ages"). Expect to pay up to $500 a day *in addition to* the basic cruise fare.

Fitness centers

A typical large resort ship spa will include a gymnasium, probably with ocean-view windows. Virtual-reality exercise machines are found in the techno-gyms aboard most large resort ships, with state-of-the-art muscle-pumping and body-strengthening equipment, universal stations, treadmills, bicycles, rowing machines, and free weights.

Most fitness centers are open only until early evening (one exception: NCL ships, whose gyms are open 24 hours a day). And if you've forgotten your workout clothes, you can probably purchase new items on board.

Typical exercise classes include aerobics (for beginners, intermediate, and advanced), high intensity/low impact aerobics, step aerobics, interval training, stretch and relax, super body sculpting, fab abdominals, sit and be fit, and walk-a-mile.

Group exercycling, kickboxing, pilates and yoga classes, body composition analysis, and sessions with a personal trainer will cost extra.

Massage

Having a massage aboard ship is a treat that more people are discovering. Today, many ships have suites and cabins with a "private" balcony, although you'll need a balcony with

EXCELLENT SHIPBOARD SPAS

AIDAbella
AIDAluna
AIDAsol
Asuka II
Crystal Serenity
Europa
Mein Schiff
Mein Schiff 2
MSC Fantasia
MSC Splendida
Pacific Pearl
Queen Mary 2
Seabourn Odyssey
Seabourn Quest
Seabourn Sojourn
Silver Spirit

plenty of space in order to set up a proper portable massage table and allow the masseur/masseuse room to walk around it and work from all sides. It can be a real stress-busting experience, but if it's not right it can prove frustrating, and expensive.

Here are some of my favourite massages (always taken in the late afternoon or early evening, preferably just before sundown):

● Aboard *Celebrity Constellation, Celebrity Infinity, Celebrity Millennium, Celebrity Summit* (on the balcony of a Sky Suite).

● Aboard *Royal Clipper* (in a private massage hut on an outside deck).

● Aboard *SuperStar Virgo* (on the floor of a junior suite bedroom).

● Inside a beach cabana ashore on Castaway Cay or Half Moon Cay in the Bahamas, or as part of the beach, caviar, and champagne experience of ships such as *SeaDream I* and *II* in the British Virgin Islands.

Make appointments for a massage as soon after embarkation as possible, so you can obtain the time and day of your choice. Large resort ships have more staff and offer more flexibility in appointment times, although cruises tend to be shorter than those aboard smaller, more upscale ships. The cost averages $2 a minute. In some ships, a massage service may be available in your cabin (or on your private balcony), if it is large enough to accommodate a portable massage table.

While it's easy to telephone and make an appointment for a massage or facial or two (some cruise lines let you do this online), do watch the cost. When you

Best foot forward aboard *Costa Concordia*.

charge treatments to your onboard account, remember that gratuities are often added automatically (typically 10–15%). Elixirs of youth, lotions and potions, creams and scrubs – all are sold by therapists, typically at the end of your treatment, for you to use when you get home. But be warned, these are expensive items; beware of falling for subtle and flattering sales talk.

A whole range of treatments and styles has evolved from the standard Swedish Remedial Massage. The most popular are:

Swedish Massage: There are two main effects of massage – a reflex effect and a mechanical effect. There are four basic movements in this general massage: effleurage (the stroking movements that benefit the circulation of lymphatic fluids and drainage), petrissage (the picking, kneading, rolling, and wringing movements), friction (the application of circular pressure), and tapotement (percussive tapping, flicking, and hacking movements that stimulate circulation).

Wellbeing Massage: This puts more emphasis on effleurage movements, the use of complementary, warmed aromatic (aromatherapy) oils and four-hand massage (two therapists working rhythmically in unison).

Shiatsu Massage: This means "finger pressure," and in Japan for thousands of years has been applied to the pressure points of the body as a preventative measure. It typically promotes a peaceful awareness of both body and mind, and is administered in a calm environment, without oil.

Hot Stones Massage: The therapist places 24 to 36 smooth basalt volcanic stones of varying sizes in a special oven. These are then applied to various key energy points of the body, using the stones to gen-

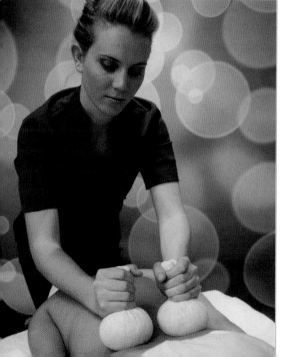

Thai Herbal Poultice Massage on *Allure of the Seas*.

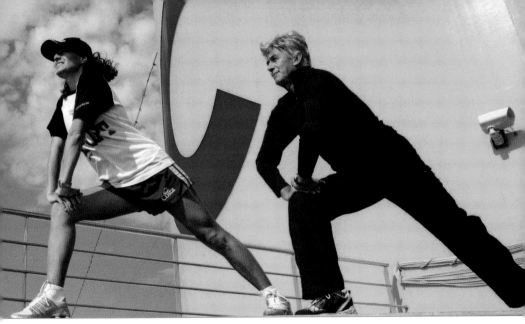

tly massage specific areas and muscles. The heated volcanic stones are then left in place while the therapist works on other parts of the body. The heat from the stones promotes a sense of deep relaxation.

Ayurvedic Head Massage: Using warmed herbal oils, the therapist will apply the oil to the scalp, neck, and shoulders to stimulate circulation and nourish the hair (you'll need to wash your hair afterwards, as it will be extremely oily). Shirodhara is the form of Ayurvedic medicine that involves gently pouring warm oil (made from tulsi, or holy basil) over the forehead. Ayurveda is a compound word meaning life and knowledge. A shirodosha experience includes bathing and polishing the feet with Himalayan salts prior to an Ayurvedic head massage, followed by a full body massage using warm oils drizzled over the body.

Underwater Massage: You soak in a large tub of warm water, possibly with rose petals floating around you, while the therapist massages joints and muscles.

Sports Massage: Typically provided by a male therapist, sports massage is a deep-tissue massage designed to unlock the kinks and knots.

Lomi-Lomi Massage: This is a more rhythmic massage inspired by Hawaiian healing traditions that restore the free flow of "mana" or life force; it is typically given using warm aromatherapy oils, and may be a two-hand or four-hand massage.

Lymphatic Massage: This detox massage is designed to improve circulation by releasing body toxins and nodes that build up in key lymphatic points. It is usually recommended for those who have poor circulation.

Thai Massage: Uses pressure points and stretching techniques employed by the therapist, using both hands and feet, to stretch and relax muscles, improve circulation, and reduce stress. It is usually carried out on a mat or thin mattress which is laid out on the floor.

Chinese Tuina: This is a therapeutic massage based on a diagnostic evaluation, manipulation of the joints and muscle fibers, and identification and prevention of wrong body postures, habits, and degenerative conditions.

Couples Massage: Sometimes known as a "duet massage," this is typically a 90-minute session for a couple that includes a hands-on lesson from a massage specialist on the art of massaging each other.

Ultimate Massage: Two therapists provide a synchronized full body massage, using Swedish massage movements to provide the ultimate in stress-busting relief. But it can be less than good if the two therapists are even slightly out of sync.

THE 10 RULES OF SPA ETIQUETTE

❶ Wear proper attire, including shoes, in the gym.

❷ Wipe the equipment off with a clean towel (or sanitized cloth) after you have used it.

❸ Limit your time on the equipment or in the hot tub to a maximum of 30 minutes when others are waiting.

❹ Most ships allow jogging on a designated deck or area at selected times which will be posted. Adhere to the times posted because cabins are usually located directly below the designated deck and you may disturb fellow passengers who are sleeping.

❺ If there's a mixed sauna, men should not shave in it – it's unclean, and uncool.

❻ Arrive at least 10 minutes before your appointment.

❼ Take a shower or wash off all suntan lotions or oils.

❽ It's better not to talk during a massage – simply close your eyes, relax and enjoy.

❾ Shipboard spas are no-smoking zones – so no quick drag in the sauna.

❿ You can cancel an appointment up to 24 hours before your treatment time without charge. If you cancel within the 24 hours before your appointment time, you will be charged for the treatment you booked.

Recent variations of massage include a warm candle massage and a bamboo tamping treatment. Aboard some ships (MSC Cruises, for example), combinations of Balinese massage and reflexology are popular.

OTHER TREATMENTS

While massage is the most popular shipboard spa treatment, some ships offer a whole range of body-pampering treatments, such as facials, manicures, pedicures, teeth whitening – even acupuncture. Most treatments are based on holistic Asian therapies. Some examples: Bali or Java, Indonesia (*ural* and *pijat* massage; mandi lulur, a scrub made from herbs, essential oils and rice to soften the skin); Balinese *boreh* (a warm herb, rice, spice, galangal water and oil body wrap for detoxification); China (acupuncture); Japan (shiatsu massage; enzyme baths made from warmed finely shaved cedar chips, rice bran, and vegetable enzymes to improve the metabolic system); Malaysia (Malay massage, which focuses on the body's 600,666 nerves); Philippines (*Hilot* massage, using virgin coconut oil and banana leaves); Thailand (Thai massage, or *nuad boran*).

Typically, the spa will provide items such as towels, robes, and slippers, but it's best to store valuables safely in your cabin prior to your appointment.

Stretching mind and body in the spa aboard *MSC Fantasia*.

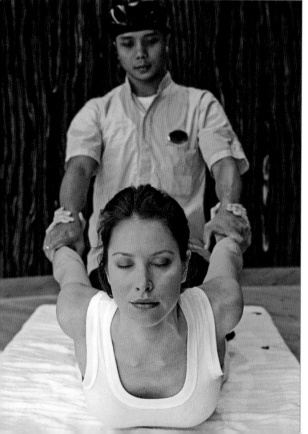

You'll typically don a robe and slippers in the changing rooms. You then go to the treatment room, and the therapist will leave while you disrobe and lie down, placing a towel over your body, ready for massage. Some spas offer disposable panties for body treatments such as a Body Salt Glow or Seaweed Wrap.

Acupuncture

This can be used to prevent and remedy many maladies. Moxibustion is the treatment which involves hair-thin needles and heat transfer based on a special plant, the *Artemisa capillaris*, placed into one of the body's 1,100-plus acupuncture points.

Body scrub

The aim of this treatment is to cleanse and soften the skin, and to draw out impurities from within, using aromatic oils, creams, lotions, and perhaps sea salt, together with exfoliation (removal of dead skin cells) using skin brushing techniques.

Body wrap

Often called a body mask, this treatment typically includes the use of algae and seaweeds applied to the whole body. The body is then covered in aluminium foil and blankets. There are many variations on this theme, using mud from the Dead Sea or Mediterranean Sea, or sea salt and ginger, or cooling cucumber and aloe, or combinations of herbs and oils that leave you with a warm glow. The aim is to detoxify, firm and tone the skin, and reduce cellulite.

Dry flotation

This hydrobath gives you the sensation of floating without getting wet; you lie on a plush warm blanket between your body and the water. A therapist then gently massages your head and neck.

Facials

Aromatherapy facial: This treatment typically uses aromatic oils such as lavender, sandalwood and geranium, plus a rejuvenating mask and accompanying creams and essences to "lift" the skin and facial muscles. **Rejuvenation facial:** This is typically a classic French facial which utilizes the latest skin care products that may include essential plant and vitamin-rich oils. This facial aims to reduce lines and wrinkles.

Other popular treatments include eye lifting, volcanic mud mask, manicure with back and neck massage, and teeth whitening.

Rasul chamber

This is a steam chamber (Hammam) that is typically fully tiled, with a domed roof and

Some RCI cruise ships have a full-size boxing ring.

Moorish decor. You paste yourself or your partner – it's a much better experience with a partner – with three types of mud, and sit down while gentle steam surrounds you. The various types of mud become heated and then you're in a mud bath, after which you rub yourself (and each other) with large crystals of rock salt.

Reflexology

The body's energy meridians exist as reflex points on the soles of the feet. The therapist uses thumb pressure to stimulate these points to improve circulation and restore energy flow throughout the body.

Thalassotherapy

The use of seawater to promote wellbeing and healing dates back to ancient Greece. Today, shipboard spas have whole bath rituals involving water and flower petals, herbs or mineral salts.

Sample prices

Prices of body-pampering treatments have escalated recently, and are now equal to the prices you would find at land-based spas in the United States. You can expect to pay up to:
$200 for a 75-minute Hot Stones Massage
$125 for a 50 minute Wellbeing Massage
$200 for a 75-minute Seaweed Wrap
$125 for a 50-minute Reflexology Session

Spa cuisine

Originally designed as low-fat, low-calorie (almost tasteless) meals for weight loss using grains, greens, and sprouts, spa cuisine now includes whole grains, seasonal fruits and vegetables, and lean proteins – ingredients low in saturated fats and cholesterol, low-fat dairy products, and reduced salt. They provide the basis for balanced nutrition and portion sizes

while maintaining some flavor, texture and taste. To eat healthier meals, choose steamed or grilled items rather than baked or fried items.

Sports facilities

Sports facilities might include basketball and paddle tennis (a sort of downsized tennis court), and electronic golf simulators. Some boutique/small "luxury" ships offer kayaking, water-skiing, jet skiing, and wake boarding for no extra charge. In reality, however, the watersports equipment is typically only used on one or two days (or part days) during a seven-day cruise. ❑

WHO RUNS THE SPAS

Aboard most ships, the spa and fitness areas are operated by a specialist concession, although each cruise line may have a separate name for the spa, such as AquaSpa (Celebrity Cruises), The Greenhouse Spa (Holland America Line), Lotus Spas (Princess Cruises), etc.

Aboard the large resort ships, spa staff tend to be young and enthusiastic "therapists" who will try hard to sell you own-brand beauty products, for a commission. Steiner Leisure is by far the largest concession, operating spas aboard more than 100 ships.

This company, founded in London in 1901 by Henry Steiner, began its ambitious growth in 1926 when Herman Steiner got involved in the family beauty salon on his father's death. He opened salons throughout England, became official cosmetician to Queen Elizabeth the Queen Mother, and won his first cruise ship contract in 1956.

The company closed its land-based salons in the 1990s as its cruise ship business burgeoned. It bought Elemis, a lifestyle range of plant-based beauty products, and acquired Mandara Spas, which it has developed in the US alongside its Elemis Spas. In 2010 it bought The Onboard Spa Company. It runs 14 training schools. Steiner's corporate headquarters is now in the Bahamas.

Other shipboard concessions include Blue Ocean (MSC Cruises), Canyon Ranch At Sea (Cunard, Oceania Cruises), Clarita, Espace Elegance, Flair (Louis), and Ocean Spa (Hapag-Lloyd).

CRUISING FOR FAMILIES

The family market is a lucrative one, but cruise lines
know that much of the appeal depends on their
ability to keep children fully occupied

It used to be that children, when they were allowed to travel on the old ocean liners, were hidden away, attended by maids and minders, and never to be seen by "real" passengers. Things have changed. Today's large resort ships actively cater to an ever-increasing number of families with children.

More than 2 million children and teens a year take a cruise; Carnival Cruise Lines alone carries over 650,000. There are few better vacations for families than a ship cruise. Active parents can have the best of all worlds: family togetherness, social contact, and privacy. Cruise ships provide a virtually crime-free, encapsulated environment, and give young passengers a lot of freedom without parents having to be concerned about where their children are at all times. Because the days aboard are long, youngsters will be able to spend time with their parents or grandparents, as well as with their peers. They can also meet senior officers and learn about the navigation, radar, and communications equipment. They will be exposed to different environments, experience many types of cuisine and, since the food is "free," they can eat as much as they want. During shore excursions, they'll discover different cultures.

Although children may not like organized school-like clubs, they will probably make new friends quickly in the surroundings of a cruise ship. Whether you share a cabin with them or book an adjoining cabin, there'll be plenty to keep them occupied.

Some cruise lines have token family programs, with limited activities and only a couple of general staff allocated to look after children, even though their brochures might claim otherwise. Other lines dedicate teams of counselors who run special programs off-limits to adults. They also provide practical facilities such as high chairs in the dining room, cots, and real playrooms.

Note that some ships provide children's programs and youth counselors only during the summer holidays, Christmas, New Year, and Easter. Check whether the cruise line offers the right product for your needs at other times.

Most of the cruise lines with large resort ships give out colored bracelets to children which must be worn at all times. These identify which muster station they belong to in the event of an emergency, as well as showing which children are enrolled in which activity programs.

If you have older children – say, between 12 and 16 – you could get them involved by putting them in charge of taking family photos. They'll probably get to experience more, and think more about location, colors and angles. And, you could put them in charge of making a family scrapbook. If you have younger children and own an expensive digital camera, it may be prudent to buy a disposable camera for each of them.

Cruise lines serious about children typically divide them into distinct age groups: Toddlers (ages 2–4), Juniors (ages 5–7), Intermediate (ages 8–10), Tweens (ages 11–13), and Teens (ages 14–17). It often seems to be children under 12 who get the most from a cruise.

Choosing a cabin

Families cruising together often find the hassle of shared cabins causes most distress. Teens need a place they can call their own, where they can put their stuff and retreat to when the world gets to be too much – in

LEFT: the good life on Holland America Line's private island, Half Moon Cay, in the Bahamas.
RIGHT: Disney Cruise Line keeps kids diverted.

Carnival ships cater well for younger children.

short, privacy. So, before booking, check the size of the cabin and pace it out at home, remembering that the size quoted on ship deck plans *includes* the bathroom. If you are a large family, some ships (such as NCL's) have three-bedroom suites that can accommodate as many as 14. Several cruise lines have special family cabins that can accommodate two adults and several junior cruisers – 14 family cabins, 39 junior suites and 12 suites aboard *Mein Schiff 2* even have an Xbox games console.

It's best to choose the largest cabin you can afford, because, if there's not enough storage space, expect to use your suitcase a lot for young children's dolls, games

THE GOOD PARENTING GUIDE

Parenting responsibilities don't end just because you're on vacation, and cruise lines will charge parents for any damage caused by their children and teens. Princess Cruises, for example, posts a short statement warning parents or guardians to supervise children and teens who are not taking part in the youth programs, to restrain children in public areas from running or engaging in loud or disruptive behavior, and to accompany children in elevators at all times. Here are a few rules worth laying down at the outset:

● Parents should establish a curfew, and stick to it.
● Children are not permitted to use the elevators unless accompanied by a parent or guardian.
● No shouting in passenger hallways.
● Tantrums should be confined to cabins, not restaurants or public areas.
● No urinating in the pool.
● No diaper-changing on deck – many ships have diaper-changing stations in both men's and women's toilets.

or toys, and for toddlers' diapers and baby food. If you have a large or extended family, cabins with interconnecting doors may be more practical.

If possible, opt for a cabin with a balcony. An interior (no view) cabin may be adequate for a short cruise, but could be claustrophobic on a 10-day Mediterranean vacation. To get access to fresh air without a balcony, you'd have to keep trudging up to the open deck, carrying the towels many large resort ships provide for use with deckchairs. If you have a baby, having a balcony gives you somewhere to escape to in the evening while keeping an eye on a (hopefully) sleeping infant.

Many ships have family-friendly cabins with two lower beds and one or two upper berths. But in some cabins, the two lower beds can't be pushed together to form a queen-sized bed for parents. This means mom and dad and one or two children all have separate beds, – so families that cruise together can't always be sure they'll sleep together as they would wish.

If you have older children, consider two adjoining cabins. Larger cabins or suites have much more space, and may include sofa beds. Some ships, such as *Disney Dream, Disney Fantasy, Disney Magic, Disney Wonder,* and *Norwegian Epic,* have cabins with two bathrooms.

Caring for babies under three

Many new or recent parents want to take their babies with them when they cruise. Perhaps the most attractive consideration is that they need to pack and unpack the baby things only once, they'll get to see new destinations, and experience life on the ocean wave. They will, however, need to adjust their normal routines a little, given the way ships operate at sea.

However, this can mean lots of baby strollers (buggies) cluttering up the open decks – and nowhere to store them. Some companies, such as Carnival Cruise

Lines, don't accept babies under six months old. This is because of concerns over specialist medical attention for problems, and the fact that there have been many instances of "naughties" in paddling pools (even if toddlers are wearing swim diapers, or even if parents are with them), making them unusable for others.

Note that Disney Cruise Line is the only line that does allow toddlers in paddling pools – that's because of a special filtration system that is cleverly disguised in Mickey's face and ears painted into the bottom of its paddling pools.

It may be difficult to bathe small children in cabins with no bathtub but only a shower enclosure with a fixed-head shower. So check with your travel agent to make sure that your little one is not too little for the cruise line you choose.

It's important to check the ship's itinerary. Why? Because it's easier if a ship docks alongside in each port, rather than being at anchor, when shore tenders must be used (these may require you to go down a rigged ladder to a small boat waiting to take you ashore – not easy with an infant in tow).

Some ships have well-equipped children's play areas.

Most cruise lines' children's programs start at age three, so if you have a toddler, you're generally on your own. And that can mean around the clock. However, some cruise lines do have nurseries, wading pools, babysitting services, and diaper-changing facilities. Children under three years old need to be potty-trained to take part in group activities.

Some cruise ships will lend you key baby equipment, such as bouncy seats, cribs, strollers, books, and toys. Check with the cruise line or your travel agent *before* you book. Disposable nappies, wipes, and sterilising fluid can be purchased aboard most child-friendly ships, but if you have very small children, you will be expected to bring your own supplies. Cots and bed guards are usually available on request and can be pre-booked when you make your reservations.

A PACKING LIST FOR PARENTS CRUISING WITH BABIES

● An inexpensive umbrella stroller is invaluable in airports, aboard ship, and ashore. Small is better because it takes up less space in cabins, elevators, and self-serve buffet areas. It will also be easier to maneuver at the cruise terminal and up the ship's gangway.

● Inflatable toys such as beach balls and zoo animals are easy to pack and inexpensive, so even if you leave one or two behind after your vacation it won't really matter. You won't be able to borrow toys from the playrooms on board.

● A sling-style baby carrier is useful for hands-free baby carrying on shore outings, or to the self-serve buffet, or pool deck.

● Disposable diapers and wipes: If you are flying, pack some in a carry-on duffel bag which on your way home may be used to carry souvenirs. In your check-in luggage, pack twice as many as you would typically go through in a week. Also pack deodorized diaper disposal bags.

Some cruise lines have nurseries.

● Swim diapers: For health reasons, regular diapers are not allowed in the pools (exception: Disney Cruise Line ships).

● Swim vest – but make sure it's of an approved type.

● Bottles and sip cups: Cruise lines don't provide these. They can be washed out in your cabin, so, a little dish detergent and bottle brush could be useful.

● Baby food. Take a few small jars in case baby's appetite turns finicky. If your baby is on formula, take small bottles of the ready-to-feed variety, although larger bottles should be fine if you know your cabin has a refrigerator.

● Spot remover and gentle soap for attending to spills on baby's clothing.

● Baby soap and shampoo: These items are not provided by the cruise lines so take your preferred branded items.

● Sunscreen and insect repellent are useful in warm weather areas – your child's paediatrician may recommend certain brands.

● A hat, for sun protection.

● A car seat for use on aircraft, and in buses and taxis.

● Picture books to keep baby amused.

● Medication, such as pain relievers and fever reducers for babies, and the name and contact details of your child's paediatrician – just in case.

If you do take baby (or babies) along, and you want some time to yourself, you'll need the services of a babysitter, so choose well. Some, but not all, ships have babysitting services; some have restricted hours (meaning you'll need to be back by midnight – or you'll change into a pumpkin); and some have only group babysitting and not in-cabin care.

From the viewpoint of a cruise line, babies do not bring much revenue (no alcohol, they don't play in the casino, or patronize the shop – except, perhaps, for diapers), and so many cruise lines would rather not bother with them. While some babies do travel well, others can also upset a lot of passengers who are older and don't want to be around them. Another reason that many cruise lines do not cater to passengers with babies is that the medical department simply isn't set up for pediatric services – nor is there a pediatrician on board, should a medical situation arise, because cruise ship doctors are generalists.

If you have a swim vest for your toddler (the ones with "floaties" built into them are *not* life vests – they are made to help children learn to swim, not to keep their head above water, and are not recommended), it's a good idea to take it

Learning the art of baking cookies on a Crystal cruise.

AN ESSENTIAL CHECKLIST FOR PARENTS CRUISING WITH CHILDREN

The basics
● What are the age restrictions for the cruise line?
● Do your children's ages qualify them for a discount?
● Are discounts available for a third and/or fourth person in your cabin?
● Are the special activities and child care/ teen centers open and available at the time you want to cruise?
● How big are the cabins?
● Will your children find the ports of call interesting? If not, is there enough to keep them happy aboard the ship?
● Is there a special place or playroom dedicated for children? For teens?

Accommodation
● Are cribs and/or day beds or cots available to put in the cabin?
● Are adjoining cabins available (for those with a large or extended family)?
● Do they have interconnecting doors? How large are the cabins?
● If there is no child's or infant's life vest in your cabin, see your steward right away and ask for one.
● Are bedrails (guardrails) available for the upper berths?

Computers for kids aboard an RCI ship.

Dining
● Does the menu offer the kind of food your children will eat? If not, are pizza and burgers and hot dogs available?
● Is a children's menu available for each meal?
● Is early seating available or does the ship feature "open" seating so that you can eat at a time close to when the children normally dine?
● Kids in the dining room can be even messier and more demanding than adults, so remember to tip accordingly.

Activities
● What activities are planned for children?
● Is there a children-only pool available on the ship?
● Will there be special movies or live entertainment that children will enjoy?
● Are any scheduled shore excursions geared toward children?
● Is a babysitting service available? If so, what are its hours and costs?
● Does the cruise lines provide after-midnight babysitting services?

Activity/Play centers
● What are the requirements for placing a child in the center such as age, vaccinations, or toilet training?
● How are the children's areas supervised? Is the teen center supervised?
● What are the hours, costs, and restrictions on the centers?
● What security methods are used when a child is picked up from the center?
● What is the ratio of children to adult staff in the children's center?
● How are staff members trained for work in the children's center? Are they insured? Do they know how to perform CPR on children and infants?

The classic carousel aboard RCI's *Allure of the Seas*.

with you. That's because the life vest provided aboard a cruise ship is for emergency use only – you can't take it off the ship when you go to the beach, or on a boating excursion ashore.

Coping with infants

You can take your infant with you, but check with the cruise line whether your new baby is old enough. Remember that you'll be responsible the whole time, unless you choose one of the few ships that has a proper nursery and qualified staff to look after toddlers. Ships with a nursery for ages 6–36 months: *Allure of the Seas, Disney Dream, Disney Fantasy, Disney Magic, Disney Wonder*, and *Oasis of the Seas*.

It's important to calculate how much ready-feed formula, baby food, diapers, and wipes you'll need for the duration of the cruise. Most lines don't sell these products on board, and those that do sell diapers – such as Disney Cruise Line – charge exorbitant prices. For diapers, take twice as many as you would normally use. If you normally give your baby ready-to-feed formula, consider using powder for the cruise, and buy bottled mineral water from the ship's bar (an expensive option) or in ports of call.

Fruit is now available in unbreakable plastic containers. If you fly to join your cruise, decide whether to carry glass vegetable jars by hand, or risk possible breakage by bubble-wrapping and packing them.

In luggage for airline check-in, remember to pack items such as baby bottles and extra nipples, baby spoon and bib, swim diapers, medicines, pacifiers, insulated bag for keeping bottles cool, picture books and toys. And a thermometer might come in handy.

Berlitz Tip: Carnival Cruise Lines is one of the few

operators to offer baby strollers for rent. If you take your own, it's best to consider one with an integral umbrella – particularly useful for strong sunlight areas. These are collapsible and can be stored easily under the bed or in a corner.

The right food

Selected baby foods, cribs, and high chairs are stocked by ships catering to children, but ask your travel agent to get confirmation in writing that they'll be provided.

Vegetables such as steamed or boiled broccoli, carrots, cauliflower, pumpkin, and potatoes are usually available on request aboard, as are steamed chicken or fish, and white rice (brown rice can be more difficult to obtain unless requested in advance). Remember that

SAFETY TIPS AT SEA

● In case children get lost or separated from their parents, most cruise lines provide them with colored wristbands, which must be worn at all times. Disney Cruise Line has "Mickey Bands" – magic bracelets that use radio tracking to locate the exact whereabouts of children at any time.

● Young children love to climb, so don't ever leave them on a balcony alone. On the open decks, ships have railings – these are either horizontal bars through which children cannot get their heads, or they are covered in glass/plexiglass under a thick wooden top rail.

● While children find their way around easily, walk with them between the playroom/activity and your cabin, so that all of you get to know the way.

● Discuss safety issues with them, and warn them not to walk into "Crew Only" areas at any time.

● Children's lifejackets are available aboard most cruise ships that carry children. However, check with your cabin steward as soon as you embark.

children can eat later aboard ships – at the self-serve buffet – than they would at home.

If you need a special brand of baby food, or a high chair in the restaurant, let your travel agent know well in advance. Parents using organic baby foods, such as those obtained from health food stores, should be aware that cruise lines buy their supplies from major general food suppliers and not from the smaller specialized food houses.

Children's entertainment

Most entertainment for children is designed to run simultaneously with adult programs; few ships have dedicated children's entertainers. An exception is Disney Cruise Line, which invites kids to meet and greet Disney characters in both designated places and during special surprise appearances.

For those cruising with very young children, baby-sitting services may be available. For example, *Queen Mary 2* has children's nurses and English nannies. *Aurora, Azura, Oceana, Oriana,* and *Ventura* have a "night nursery" for two- to five-year-olds. Some ships have children's pools and play areas, as well as junior discos, video rooms, and teen "chill-out" centers.

In some ships, stewards, stewardesses, and other staff may be available as private babysitters for an hourly charge; otherwise, group babysitting may be offered. Make arrangements at the reception desk. Aboard some ships, evening babysitting services may not start until late – check details before booking.

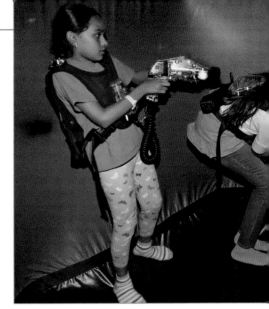
Carnival's laser tag is played in an inflatable arena.

Activities for children

Although many ships have full programs for children during days at sea, these may be limited when the ship is in port. Ships expect you to take your children with you on organized excursions, which sometimes have lower prices for children. If the ship has a playroom, find out if it is open and supervised on all days of the cruise.

When going ashore, remember that if you want to take your children swimming or to the beach, it is wise to telephone ahead to a local hotel with a beach or pool. Many hotels will be happy to show off their property to you, hoping to gain your future business.

Some cruise ships in the Caribbean have the use of a "private" island for a day, including waterpark areas for children and adults. A lifeguard will be on duty, and there will be water-sports and snorkeling equipment you can rent. But remember that the beaches on some "private" islands are fine for 200 passengers, but with 2,000 they quickly become crowded, forcing you to stand in line for beach barbecues and toilet facilities. Also, since operators take advantage of the captive market, rental of beach and water-sports items can be very expensive.

Although the sun and warm sea might attract juniors to the Caribbean, many older children will find a Baltic, Black Sea, or Mediterranean cruise fascinating as they are exposed to different cultures.

Activities for pre-teens

Supervised group activities and activity/play centers mean that you won't have to be con-

A child-size rock wall may appeal to aspiring mountaineers.

talent shows. Some Royal Caribbean International ships provide musical instruments for jam sessions. Sports include rockclimbing, basketball, and riding the wave surfer. There's usually almost unlimited food, too, although some of it may not be very nutritious.

Cruising with teens provides a chance to meet other families who cruise with teens, and the moms enjoy sharing thoughts and experiences while their teens and other kids are having fun together. But some ships simply are not big-kid-friendly, so choose wisely. Teens also tend to eat a lot, so cruising aboard one of the large resort ships makes sense, and provides excellent value for money. Just think, your teenagers can eat themselves silly if they really want to.

Balancing adult needs with teenage desires can be challenging. Teens do really well for themselves on cruises and, once they find others of a like age, you'll probably never see them again for the whole cruise. Teens can go almost anywhere aboard ship, although they can't play in the casino, or use reserved, "adult-only" sanctuary areas, and perhaps certain lounges. But they do get to go to nightclubs free.

They will, however, probably end up spending most of their free time hanging out in "chill-out" rooms – just the job for truculent teens – maybe even trying out their communication skills!

It's best if you set limits and curfews *before* you leave home. Girls end up in gaggles, while boys end up in "cool" groups (or groups *trying* to be "cool"). And teens who go cruising almost always say afterwards how surprised they were at just how many other teens were also

cerned, and will be able to go out and enjoy yourself, knowing that your children are in good hands. Some cruise lines issue beepers in case of problems. Activities would typically include scavenger hunts, make-up and cookery classes, and interactive computer programs.

Activities for teens

Many large resort ships have dedicated "no adults allowed" zones. Teen-only activities include deck parties, pool parties, sports tournaments, poolside games, karaoke, discos, dances, computer gaming consoles and

---

THE SHIPS THAT CATER WELL FOR CHILDREN

These ships have been selected for the quality of their children's programs:
Aida Cruises: *AIDAaura, AIDAbella, AIDAblu, AIDAcara, AIDAdiva, AIDAluna, AIDAsol, AIDAvita*
Carnival Cruise Lines: *Carnival Conquest, Carnival Destiny, Carnival Dream, Carnival Freedom, Carnival Glory, Carnival Legend, Carnival Liberty, Carnival Pride, Carnival Spirit, Carnival Splendor, Carnival Triumph, Carnival Valor, Carnival Victory*
Celebrity Cruises: *Celebrity Constellation, Celebrity Eclipse, Celebrity Equinox, Celebrity Infinity, Celebrity Millennium, Celebrity Reflection, Celebrity Solstice, Celebrity Summit*
Costa Cruises: *Costa Atlantica, Costa Concordia, Costa Deliziosa, Costa Fortuna, Costa Luminosa, Costa Magica,*

Some cruise lines are more child-friendly than others.

Costa Mediterranea, Costa Pacifica, Costa Serena
Cunard Line: *Queen Elizabeth, Queen Mary 2, Queen Victoria*
MSC Cruises: *MSC Fantasia, MSC Magnifica, MSC Musica, MSC Opera, MSC Orchestra, MSC Poesia, MSC Splendida*
Disney Cruise Line: *Disney Dream, Disney Fantasy, Disney Magic, Disney Wonder*

Norwegian Cruise Line: *Norwegian Dawn, Norwegian Epic, Norwegian Gem, Norwegian Jade, Norwegian Jewel, Norwegian Pearl, Norwegian Spirit, Norwegian Star, Norwegian Sun*
P&O Cruises: *Aurora, Azura, Oceana, Ventura*
Princess Cruises: *Crown Princess, Diamond Princess, Emerald Princess, Golden Princess, Grand Princess, Ruby Princess, Sapphire Princess, Star Princess*
Royal Caribbean International: *Adventure of the Seas, Allure of the Seas, Explorer of the Seas, Freedom of the Seas, Independence of the Seas, Liberty of the Seas, Mariner of the Seas, Navigator of the Seas, Oasis of the Seas, Voyager of the Seas*
Star Cruises: *SuperStar Virgo*
Thomson Cruises: *Thomson Celebration, Thomson Destiny, Thomson Dream, Thomson Spirit.*
TUI Cruises: *Mein Schiff, Mein Schiff 2*

Disney characters dominate the line's entertainment.

on board – and express their amazement at just how fast a seven-day cruise goes by.

Teens can get together in their own disco, games rooms, video arcades and activity clubs, and on deck for sports tournaments and basketball games, rockclimbing and rollerblading. With some cruise lines, the fun extends ashore, with beach barbecues and even some shore excursions aimed at younger passengers.

If your teens are inclined to be messy at home, perhaps getting an adjoining cabin for them is a good idea – and will also give them a feeling of independence. Just be sure to set some limits to what they can and cannot do in their "home away from home."

A Major Teen Gripe: Understandably, teens often want to take a dip in the swimming pool late at night, but, aboard most large resort ships, this is simply not possible. Most pools are closed and netted over by 6pm. Why? Because it's the end of the crew working shift, and no one is assigned to take over in the evening. Keeping them open would mean paying for adequate supervision, or risking negligence claims. So pools get closed, and teens get frustrated. It's about time the cruise lines started catering to their customers – after all, today's teens could be tomorrow's suite occupants.

Disney goes cruising

In 1998, Disney Cruise Line introduced the first of two large resort ships to cater to families with children, with cruises of three, four and seven days. *Disney Magic* and *Disney Wonder* were joined by *Disney Dream* in 2011, and *Disney Fantasy* will debut in 2012. The casino-free ships have ambitious entertainment programs, with everything centered around Disney and its superb stable

of famous characters *(see feature on pages 14–15)*. Disney has its own Art Deco passenger terminal at Port Canaveral, Florida, plus a fleet of motorcoaches.

Each ship carries over 40 children's and youth counselors, and families preparing to sail with children under three years of age have access to an online service that allows them to order baby supplies in advance of their cruise and have them delivered to their cabin. The service, exclusive to Disney Cruise Line passengers, is provided by Babies Travel Lite, an online retailer offering more than 1,000 brand-name baby products including diapers, baby food, infant formula and specialty travel items. On disneycruise.com, you can access a section of the Babies Travel Lite website where you can create orders for familiar brands in quantities customized to the length of your cruise.

One ship sails in the Mediterranean in summer from Barcelona, and another ship sails in Alaska in summer. Disney calls at its own 1,000-acre (400-hectare) private island on three-, four- and seven-day Bahamas and Caribbean cruises. About 50 miles (80km) north of Nassau in the Bahamas, it's called Castaway Cay – Disney's own private country, with its own ship docking pier. (Locals say it had a military landing strip that was once used by drug runners.) Beaches are divided into family-friendly and adults-only "quiet" sections.

Single parents

Only a few cruise lines have introduced their versions of the "Single Parent Plan" (e.g. Disney Cruise Line, P&O Cruises). This offers an economical way for single parents to take their children on a cruise, with parent and child sharing a two-berth cabin, or parent and children sharing a three-berth cabin. Reduced rates may apply to children of single parents in the same cabin.

Confirming a guardian's identity

A Parent and Guardian Consent Form (PGCSA) will be needed at or before embarkation if you are a grandparent, parent, or guardian with a passport surname different from that of any child traveling with you. Without this form, which includes passport information of the child's legal parent, you will be denied boarding.

Family reunions

A cruise can provide the ideal place for a family get-together, with or without children. Let your travel agent make the arrangements and ask for a group discount if there are more than 15 of you.

Take care to choose a cruise line with a suitable ambience. If possible, book 12 months or more in advance so that you can arrange cabins close to each other. If the ship operates two dinner seatings, you may also wish to arrange for everyone to be at the same one.

With pricing that includes accommodations, meals, entertainment, use of most of the ship's recreational facilities, and travel from destination to destination, any cruise represents excellent value for money spent. Cruise lines also make special offers to groups. Depending on the company, these include reduced fares for groups as small as eight guests and free berths for one in every 10 to 15 paying passengers.

Family groups may have the option to ensure even greater value by purchasing everything in advance, from cruise fares to shore excursions, drinks packages, spa packages, and even pre-paid gratuities. Additional savings can be realized through reduced fares for third and

As a single parent, you should expect to pay about one-third the normal single-person rate for your children. However, as a single parent with just one child, you may have to pay for two adults (double occupancy), so it's important to check the pricing policy of each cruise line you are interested in. It may also be better to take an adult friend and share the cost (in some cases, your child could travel free).

THE PROS AND CONS OF CRUISING WHEN PREGNANT

In 2010, a 30-year-old passenger on a four-night Baja cruise aboard *Carnival Paradise* gave birth on board to a premature baby. Both mother and baby were transported from the ship to a local hospital near San Diego, and the ship continued to its home port of Long Beach, California.

It can happen. Nevertheless, if your pregnancy is routine and healthy, there's no reason not to go on a cruise. Indeed, a cruise could be a great getaway before you deal with the things associated with an upcoming childbirth. However, if you are in your third trimester, cancel your cruise quickly, and recover any money you have already spent. Although some cruise lines may let you sail even in your 27th week of pregnancy, most will not accept you if you have entered your 24th week.

Ask about any restrictions by your chosen cruise line. Do purchase travel insurance. Although most travel insurance won't cover cancellation penalties resulting from normal pregnancy, any claims arising from

Shore excursions in hot climates can be tiring.

complications may be paid. And since you stand to lose much of your cruise fare for last-minute cancellations, insurance is a must – whether you paid for your cruise with money or with award points. Also, make sure that your medical insurance covers you in case of complications, either on board or in ports of call.

Berlitz's Pregnancy Tips:

● If you are heavily pregnant, standing in line at embarkation with heavy carry-on bags could be stressful. Ask a member of staff for an expedited embarkation (but first make sure all your documentation is correct). Most cruise line personnel will whisk you through quickly.

● Ask for extra pillows, in case your mattress is a bit worn and saggy – you'll need more support when pregnant. Your cabin steward will be happy to oblige.

● Shore excursions can be challenging for someone who is heavily pregnant – too much walking, not enough rest or comfort stops, etc.

● Don't even think of going scuba diving, parasailing, or water-skiing. Wine-tasting should be off-limits, too.

● Carry a reusable water bottle when off the ship to keep your hydration levels high.

● Carry some healthy snack items when you are off the ship, either on your own or on a shore excursion.

CHILDREN'S FARES

Children under two travel free on most cruise lines and airlines (aboard MSC Cruises, kids under 12 sail free, paying only port taxes). If they're older, however, you have to pay. Most cruise lines offer special rates for children sharing their parents' cabin. The cost is often lower than third and fourth person share rates. For best rates, book early. If you don't anticipate spending much time in your cabin, consider a cheaper interior (no-view) cabin.

Although many adult cruise rates include airfare, most children's rates don't. Also, although some lines say children sail "free," they must pay port taxes as well as airfare. The cruise line should be able to get the airfare at the best rate.

fourth passengers in each cabin, and some cruise lines offer "kids sail free" programs.

Family reunions can provide opportunities for accommodation upgrades, private events, and special shipboard credits and perks ranging from free family photos to "Fountain Soda Cards" to special family meals. Some cruise lines offer personalized shore excursions and customized programs to suit family reunions.

The diversity of itineraries and cruise experiences means there is a family-friendly cruise vacation for all interests and budgets. Some cruise lines offer vacations as short as a weekend, with an itinerary that meets your family reunion's needs. A professional travel agent – and this book – will guide you through the maze.

Birthday specials

If anyone in the group has a birthday or anniversary, tell your travel agent to arrange a special cake – most cruise lines don't charge extra for this. Private parties can also be arranged, at a price. Shore excursions, too, can be booked in advance for a group.

Finally, get everything confirmed in writing, particularly cabin assignments and locations.

Formal nights

Some ships have nights when traditional "formal attire" is the required dress code. If you don't want your children to dress formally (although some children really enjoy getting dressed up – it's a bit like going to a prom night), you can opt out of the festivities, and simply head for one of the casual dining options. Or your kids may prefer to opt out and go to the children's clubs or teen rooms and hang out while *you* go to the captain's cocktail party.

Maybe your teenage dropouts don't want anything to do with formal dress. However, once they see many other teens dressed nicely, they may want to emulate them on their next cruise. Most like it – because, today, it's actually *different* – particularly when almost everyone has gone into "dress down" mode ashore. Again, that makes cruising different. But anyone with an image-conscious teenage daughter will anticipate that it will probably take them a *long* time to get ready.

Unfamiliar languages

If you book a cruise aboard one of the ships catering to more international passengers, such as Costa Cruises, MSC Cruises, or Star Cruises, your youngsters may find themselves surrounded by children who speak other languages. This could cause a degree of confusion, but in most cases it will prove to be an adventure in learning and communication. ❏

MSC Splendida's 4D screens add a new dimension.

How Grandparents Can Bridge the Generation Gap

Many children love to go cruising with grandparents, perhaps because they anticipate fewer restrictions than they have at home. And busy parents like the idea, too, particularly if the grandparents make a contribution to the cost.

Having enrolled their grandchildren in age-related groups for daytime activities aboard ship, grandparents will be able to enjoy the adults-only facilities, such as the wellness and spa treatments. Not surprisingly, it's the large resort ships that provide the widest choice of facilities for both age groups. For those not averse to ubiquitous cartoon characters, Disney Cruise Line provides some facilities for adults and children in separate areas, but also allows them to mix in others.

Before you leave home

Grandparents should remember that their grandchildren will need their own passports. They should also bring along a letter signed by the parent authorizing any necessary medical attention. In some cases they may also need a notarized letter by a custodial parent granting permission for a child to travel with them.

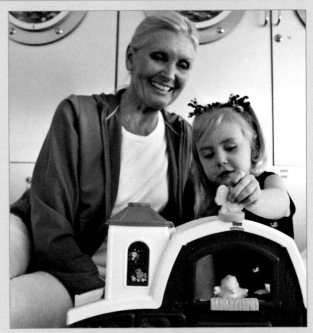

Incipient architectural ambitions aboard *Enchantment of the Seas*.

Ground rules should be established with a child's parent(s) present to avoid potential problems. An important issue is whether a child will be allowed to roam the ship unsupervised, given that some cruise lines allow children as young as eight to sign themselves out of supervised programs. Walkie-talkies are a good solution to this issue. They work well aboard ships, and allow adults and children to stay in constant touch.

You should remember to pack a grandchild's favorite toys and any medications for your journey to the ship. If flying to an embarkation port, pack games, books, a bathing suit, and a change of clothes for your grandchild in your carry-on, plus any important medication – just in case any checked-in luggage gets lost.

On embarkation day, it's wise to take essentials in a carry-on or tote bag, because your luggage may not be delivered to your cabin until several hours after you embark. This is especially so aboard the large resort ships.

On board

Most cruise lines offer scheduled activities from 9am to noon, 2–5pm, and 7–10pm. This means you can drop your grandchild off after breakfast, relax by the pool, go to a lecture, or take part in other activities, and pick them up for lunch. After a couple of hours together, they can rejoin their friends while you enjoy an afternoon movie or siesta.

Dining: Flexibility is the key. Coaxing children out of a pool, getting them dressed and ready to sit quietly through a four-course dinner every night can be tough. Work out a compromise by eating dinner together occasionally at the buffet. Most ships offer a tempting menu of children's favorites, and some ships have special mealtimes for children.

Children with special needs

If a grandchild has special needs, you'll need to advise the cruise line when you book. Children needing one-to-one care or assistance must be accompanied by a grandparent when in the children's play center.

Shore excursions

Consider your grandchild's interests before booking expensive shore excursions (example: flightseeing in Alaska). It's also best to avoid long bus rides, shopping trips and scenic tours, and better to choose excursions that feature water and/or animals. Examples include snorkeling, aquariums, or nature walks. Remember to pack snacks. In some ports, it may be better to explore on your own. If your grandchildren are really young, full-day shore excursions are a bad idea.

Disembarkation

When it's time to go home, some grandparents like to minimize post-cruise blues for the children by adding on an extra couple of days' vacation ashore. If everybody genuinely enjoyed the cruise, that's a good time to get out the brochures and start planning next year's. ❑

CRUISING FOR SENIORS

People everywhere are living longer and healthier lives, and cruise lines are keen to cater for their particular needs

Although cruise lines have been striving, with some success, to embrace all age groups, the over-60s remain an important segment of the market. Group cruising for seniors, in fact, is growing in popularity and is a good way for like-minded people to vacation together. Nowhere is this more evident than in Japan's "Golden Week," a collection of four national holidays within seven days in late April/early May, when seniors clamor for available cabins.

One trend for seniors is toward longer cruises – even round-the-world cruises if they can afford them. Some opt for an adults-only ship such as *Adonia*, *Arcadia*, or *Oriana* (all P&O Cruises); *Saga Pearl II*, *Saga Ruby*, or *Spirit of Adventure* (all Saga Cruises).

There are bargains to be had, too. Organizations for seniors such as AARP in the United States and Saga in the UK often offer discount fares and upgrades.

Some seniors who may have had major surgery or have mobility problems cannot fly, or don't wish to.

They are aided by the trend toward "Homeland Cruising," which enables them to embark at and disembark from a nearby port in their home country. In the United States, the number of homeland ports increased dramatically following the terrorist attacks of September 2001. In the UK, some cruise ships sail from ports in both the north and south of the country. The same is true elsewhere, as language-specific cruise lines and ships proliferate.

But all is far from perfect. Some cruise lines have yet to recognize that, with seniors as with other groups, one size does *not* fit all. Only a few, for example, take the trouble to provide the kind of items that millions of seniors need, such as large-print editions of daily programs, menus, and other printed matter.

Special diets

While the wide range of cuisine aboard many ships is a big attraction, cruise lines understand that many

---

WHY SENIORS LIKE CRUISING – BUT CAN OFTEN FIND IT FRUSTRATING

THUMBS UP

● A cruise is an excellent choice for those who like to be independent while having the chance to meet other like-minded people.

● Cruising is stress-free and relaxing. You don't have to keep packing and unpacking as you do on a land-based tour.

● It's safe. You travel and dine in comfort and safety, while your floating hotel takes you to a choice of around 2,000 destinations all over the world.

● Lecturers and lessons in everything from golf to computing provide a chance to learn something new.

● There's plenty of entertainment – shows, cinema, casinos, games, dances.

● All main and self-serve buffet meals are included in the fare, and those on special diets can be easily accommodated.

● Senior singles, in particular, find it easy to meet others in a non-threatening environment. Some ships provide male dance hosts, screened and subject to a strict code of ethics, who can also act as escorts on shore excursions.

● Most ships have 24-hour room service and a 24-hour reception desk.

A senior moment aboard *Oasis of the Seas*.

● The disabled can find ships that cater for their needs.

● Ships carry a medical doctor and one or more trained nurses. In an emergency, treatment can be arranged.

THUMBS DOWN

● Online check-in procedures, and unreadable Passenger Ticket Conditions and Contracts that are provided only online.

● Credit-card-sized electronic key cards to cabins that often don't make it clear which end to insert and penalize those passengers with poor eyesight.

● Booking events and meals via the in-cabin "interactive" television/keypad system; it is user-unfriendly for many seniors (all services should be readily accessible via telephone).

● Poor, difficult-to-read signage such as "You are here" deck plans unreadable from further away than an inch.

● Menus with small, hard-to-read typefaces and daily programs that require a magnifying glass.

● Buffets with plates only, requiring several visits, and cutlery too heavy to hold comfortably.

● Anything that requires a signature – for example: bar, shore excursions, spa bills with small print.

● Libraries with few books, if any, in large-print format – notably recent novels.

● The absence of a "concierge" for seniors.

● Public toilets not clearly marked.

● The lack of music-free lounges and bars for conversation and drinks.

Background reading aboard an expedition ship.

passengers are on special diets. Lighter menu options *are* available aboard most ships, as well as vegetarian and vegan choices. Options include low sodium, low fat, low cholesterol, and sugar-free entrées, and desserts. A booking agent will ensure that special dietary needs are recorded.

Healthier eating

You don't have to put on weight during a cruise. Many health-conscious seniors prefer smaller portions of food with taste and nutritional value rather than the overflowing plates that emerge from the kitchens of large floating resorts.

Heart-healthy diets are in demand, as are low-fat, low-carbohydrate, salt-free, or low-salt foods and salad dressings. Denture wearers often request food that includes softer items.

Those seeking lighter fare should be aware that most cruise lines have an "always available" section of heart-healthy items that can be cooked plainly, such as grilled or steamed salmon, skinless chicken breast, lean sirloin steak, or baked potatoes.

Gentlemen hosts

Because more female than male seniors cruise, cruise lines have developed "gentlemen host" programs. Unescorted female seniors can select cruise lines that have such hosts to enhance their cruise experience. These are gentlemen, typically over 55 years of age, selected for their social skills and competence as dance partners, for dining table conversation, and for accompanying passengers on shore excursions.

Cruise lines with gentlemen hosts include: Celebrity Cruises, Crystal Cruises, Cunard Line, Holland America Line, P&O Cruises, Princess Cruises, Regent Seven Seas Cruises, Silversea Cruises, Swan Hellenic Cruises, Seabourn, and Voyages of Discovery Cruises.

Enrichment programs

Many seniors want to learn about a destination's history and culture rather than be told which shops to visit ashore. Lecturers of academic quality are found aboard some smaller ships such as *Aegean Odyssey* (Voyages to Antiquity), *Minerva* (Swan Hellenic Cruises), *Spirit of Adventure, Saga Pearl II* and *Saga Ruby* (Saga Cruises). Some lines, such as Crystal Cruises, have special interest cruises and lecturers on topics such as archaeology, food and wine, ornithology, and military history.

Tips for seniors

● If you are traveling solo, it's important to check the price of any single supplements.
● If you take medication, make sure you have enough with you to cover all eventualities.
● Some ships are dressy, some are casual. Choose a ship according to your own lifestyle and tastes.
● If you have mobility difficulties, choose one of the newer ships that have public rooms with an "open-flow" style of interior design. Examples include *Arcadia, Balmoral, Nieuw Amsterdam, Oosterdam, Queen Elizabeth, Queen Mary 2, Queen Victoria, Westerdam, Zuiderdam*. Older ships such as *Marco Polo* have "lips" or doors between public rooms.

Best facilities

Among the cruise lines that provide the facilities and onboard environment that seniors enjoy most are: American Cruise Lines, Azamara Club Cruises, Blount Small Ship Adventures, Classic International Cruises, Crystal Cruises, Delphin Cruises, Fred Olsen Cruise Lines, Hebridean Island Cruises, Holland America Line, Noble Caledonia, Oceania Cruises, P&O Cruises, Pearl Seas Cruises, Regent Seven Seas Cruises, Saga Cruises, Sea Cloud Cruises, Seabourn, Silversea Cruises, Swan Hellenic Cruises, Voyages of Discovery, and Voyages to Antiquity. ❏
● *For contact addresses, see page 687.*

CRUISING FOR ROMANTICS

**No need to worry about getting to the church
on time – you can be married at sea, or
get engaged, or have a second honeymoon**

Two famous TV shows, *The Love Boat* (US) and *Traumschiff* (Germany), boosted the concept of cruising as a romantic vacation, though the plots didn't always match reality. The real captain of one ship, when asked the difference between his job and that of the captain of *The Love Boat*, remarked: "On TV they can do a retake if things aren't right the first time around, whereas I have to get it right the first time."

Getting engaged aboard ship

Princess Cruises has a special "Engagement Under the Stars" package that allows you to propose to your loved one in a personal video that is then screened just before an evening movie at a large outdoor screen aboard some of the company's ships. Current cost: $695.

Getting married at sea

Instead of the hassle of arranging flights, hotels, transportation and packages, you can let a specialist wedding planner do it all for you. As in all those old romantic

Cruise lines offer a variety of honeymoon packages.

black-and-white movies, a ship's captain can indeed marry you when at sea if properly certified – unless the ship's country of registry prohibits or does not recognize such marriages. You first need to inquire in your country of domicile whether such a marriage is legal, and ascertain what paperwork and blood tests are required. The onus is on you to prove the validity of such a marriage. The captain could be held legally responsible if he married a couple not entitled to be wed.

It's relatively easy to get married aboard almost any cruise ship when it is alongside in port. Carnival Cruise Lines, Celebrity Cruises, Holland America Line, and Princess Cruises, among others, offer special wedding packages. These include the services of a minister to marry you, wedding cake, champagne, bridal bouquet and matching boutonnière for the bridal party, a band to perform at the ceremony, and an album of wedding pictures. Note that US citizens and "green card" residents may need to pay sales tax on wedding packages.

Several cruise lines can arrange a marriage ceremony on a Caribbean beach. For example, Princess Cruises offers weddings on a beach in St Thomas (prices range from $525 to $1,175 per package). Or how about a romantic wedding Disney-style on its private island, Castaway Cay?

Azamara Club Cruises, Celebrity Cruises, and Princess Cruises offer weddings aboard many of their ship. The ceremonies can be performed by the captain, who is certified as a notary, when the ships' registry – Bermuda or Malta, for example – recognizes such unions.

Expect to pay about $2,500, plus about $500 for licensing fees. Harborside or shore-side packages vary according to the port. A wedding coordinator at the line handles all the details, enabling you to be married aboard ship and honeymoon aboard, too.

Even if you don't get married aboard ship, you could have your wedding reception aboard one. Contact the director of hotel services at the cruise line of your choice. The cruise line should go out of its way to help, especially if you follow the reception with a honeymoon cruise – and a cruise, of course, also makes a fine, no-worry honeymoon *(see facing page)*.

UK-based passengers should know that P&O Cruises hosts a series of cruises called the "Red-Letter Anniversary Collection" for those celebrating 10, 15, 20, 25, 30, 35, 40, 45, 50, 55, or

Two's company in an MSC Cruises spa.

60 years of marriage; the cruise comes with a complimentary gift, such as a brass carriage clock, leather photograph album, or free car parking at Southampton.

Getting married ashore

An alternative is to have a marriage ceremony in an exotic destination with your reception (and honeymoon) aboard ship afterwards. For example, you could get married on the beach in Barbados or Hawaii; on a glacier in Juneau, Alaska; in a villa in Rome or Venice; in an authentic Tahitian village; or in Central Park, New York.

Renewal of vows

Many cruise lines now perform "renewal of vows" ceremonies. A cruise is a wonderful setting for reaffirming to one's partner the strength of commitment. A handful of ships have a small chapel where this ceremony can take place; otherwise it can be anywhere aboard ship – a most romantic time is at sunrise or sunset on the open deck. The renewal of vows ceremony is conducted by the ship's captain, using a non-denominational text.

Although some companies, such as Carnival Cruise Lines, Celebrity Cruises, Holland America Line, P&O Cruises, and Princess Cruises, have complete packages for purchase, which include music, champagne, hors d'oeuvres, certificate, corsages for the women, and so on, most other companies do not charge – yet.

Cruising for honeymooners

There are many advantages in honeymooning at sea: you pack and unpack only once; it is a hassle-free and safe environment; and you get special attention, if you want it. It is easy to budget in advance, as one price often includes airfare, cruise, food, entertainment, several destinations, shore excursions, and pre- and post-cruise hotel stays. Also, some cruise lines offer discounts if you book a future cruise to celebrate an anniversary.

Although no ship as yet provides bridal suites, many ships have suites with king- or queen-sized beds. Some also provide tables for two in the dining room, should you wish to dine together without having to make friends with others. A variety of honeymoon packages is available; these might include champagne and caviar for breakfast, flowers in the suite or cabin, a complimentary cake, and a private captain's cocktail party.

Some cruise ships have Sunday departures, so couples can plan a Saturday wedding and reception before traveling to their ship. Pre- and post-cruise hotel accommodation can also be arranged.

Most large resort ships accommodate honeymoon couples well. However, couples averse to crowds might try one of the smaller, yacht-like cruise vessels such as those of Regent Seven Seas Cruises, Seabourn, Silversea Cruises, or Windstar Cruises.

And for quiet moments? The deck to the forward part of a ship, near the bridge, is the most dimly lit part and the quietest – except perhaps for some wind noise. ❏

PRACTICAL TIPS FOR HONEYMOONERS

Remember to take a copy of your marriage license or certificate, for immigration (or marriage) purposes, as your passports will not yet have been amended. Also, allow extra in your budget for things like drinks, shipboard gratuities, shore excursions, and spending money while ashore.

Since you will probably wish to share a large bed with your partner, check with your travel agent and cruise line to make sure the cabin you have booked has such a bed. Better still, book a suite if you can afford to. It's important to check and double-check to avoid disappointment.

If you plan to combine your honeymoon with getting married along the way – in Hawaii or Bermuda, for example – and need to take your wedding gown aboard, there is usually space to hang it in the dressing room next to the stage in the main showlounge, especially aboard the large resort ships.

CRUISING FOR SOLO PASSENGERS

Cruise prices are geared towards couples. Yet more than one in four cruise passengers travels alone or as a single parent. How do they fare?

Many solo passengers are prejudiced against cruising because most lines charge them a single-occupancy supplement. The reason is that the most precious commodity aboard any ship is space. Since a solo-occupancy cabin is often as large as a double and is just as expensive to build, cruise lines feel the premium price is justified, What's more, because solo-occupancy cabins are at a premium, they are unlikely to be discounted.

Single supplements

If you are not sharing a cabin, you'll be asked to pay either a flat rate or a single "supplement" if you occupy a double-occupancy cabin by yourself. Some lines charge a fixed amount – $250, for instance – as a supplement, no matter what the cabin category, ship, itinerary, or length of cruise. Such rates vary between lines, and sometimes between a particular line's ships. Because there are so few single-occupancy cabins, it's best to book as far ahead as you can.

Lines that charge low single supplements include Crystal Cruises, Peter Deilmann Ocean Cruises, Orion Expedition Cruises, and Voyages of Discovery. Saga

Cruises has no additional supplements for singles. A sneaky cruise line may try to charge you twice for port charges and government taxes (by including that non-existent second person in the cabin you occupy as a single), so check your cruise fare invoice carefully.

Guaranteed singles rates

Some lines offer singles a set price for a double cabin but reserve the right to choose the cabin. So you could end up with a rotten cabin in a poor location or a wonderful cabin that happened to be unallocated.

Guaranteed share programs

These allow you to pay what it would cost each half of a couple for a double-occupancy cabin, but the cruise line will find another passenger of the same sex (and preferences such as smoking or non-smoking) to share it with you. If the line does not find a cabin-mate, the single passenger may get the cabin to himself or herself at no extra charge. Some cruise lines do not advertise a guaranteed-share program in their brochures but will often try to accommodate such bookings at times when demand for space is comparatively light.

Solo dining

A common complaint concerns dining arrangements. Before you take your cruise, make sure that you request a table assignment based on your personal preferences; table sizes are typically for two, four, six, or eight people. Do you want to sit with other singles? Or do you like to sit with couples? Or perhaps with a mixture of both? Or with passengers who may not speak your language?

When you are on board, make sure that you are comfortable with the dining arrangements, particularly in ships with fixed table assignments, or ask the maître d' to move you to a different table. Aboard ships with open seating or with several different dining venues, you can choose which venue you want to eat in, and when; Norwegian Cruise Line (NCL) is an example of this arrangement, with its Freestyle Dining.

Cruising for single women

A cruise ship is at least as safe for single women as any major vacation destination, but of course that doesn't mean it is entirely hassle-free. It's easy to strike up conversations with other passengers, and cruising is not a "meat market" that keeps you

It's easy for single travelers to strike up conversations.

under constant observation. The easiest way to meet other singles is to participate in scheduled activities. Single black women may find there is often a dearth of single black men for dancing or socializing with.

Beware of embarking on an easy affair with a ship's officer or crew member. They meet new people on every cruise and could transmit sexual diseases. Crew members have few romantic illusions – indeed, they have been known to award an imaginary Golden Mattress to whoever can bed the most passengers.

Gentlemen cruise hosts

The female-to-male passenger ratio is typically high, especially among older people, so some cruise lines provide male social hosts. They may host a table in the dining room, appear as dance partners at cocktail parties and dance classes, join bridge games, and accompany women on shore excursions.

These men, usually over 55 and retired, are outgoing, mingle easily, and are well groomed. First introduced aboard Cunard Line's *QE2* in the mid-1970s, gentlemen hosts are now employed by a number of cruise lines, including Crystal Cruises, Cunard Line, Holland America Line, Regent Seven Seas Cruises, and Silversea Cruises.

If you think you'd like such a job, do remember that you'll have to dance for several hours most nights, and be proficient in just about every kind of dance. ❑

Cunard Line provides male hosts as dance partners.

THE BEST OPTIONS FOR GAYS AND LESBIANS

Several US companies specialize in ship charters or large group bookings for gay and lesbian passengers. These include the California-based Atlantis (tel: 310-859 8800; www.atlantis events.com), San Francisco's lesbian specialist Olivia (www. olivia.com), or New York's Pied Piper Travel (tel: 212-239 2412; http://home.att.net/~gay groupcruises).

One drawback of gay charters is that they're as much as 20% more expensive than the equivalent general cruise. Another is that they have been greeted with hostility by church groups on some Caribbean islands such as Grand Cayman, Jamaica, and Bermuda. One Atlantis cruise was even denied the right to dock. But their great advantage is that they provide an accepting environment and gay-geared entertainment, with some big-name comedians and singers.

Another idea is to join a gay affinity group on a regular cruise at normal prices; these groups may be offered amenities such as private dining

Rosie O'Donnell promotes a gay family cruise.

rooms and separate shore excursions.

Many gays, of course, have no wish to travel exclusively with other gays but may worry that, on a mainstream cruise, they might be seated for dinner with unsympathetic companions. They would prefer to sit where they want, when they want, and such open seating is offered by Norwegian Cruise Line

and Princess Cruises, and by upscale lines such as Crystal, Oceania, Regent, Seabourn and Silversea. Open seating is not offered by Carnival, Celebrity or Royal Caribbean International.

That doesn't mean that any of the major cruise companies are not gay-friendly – many hold regular "Friends of Dorothy" gatherings, sometimes scheduled and sometimes on request – though it would be prudent to realize that Disney Cruise Line, for example, will not really offer the ideal entertainment and ambience. Among the smaller companies, Windstar's sail-powered cruise yachts have a reputation for being gay-friendly.

Gay families are catered for by R Family Vacations (tel: 866-732 6822; www.rfamilyvacations.com), although it's not essential to bring children. Events may include seminars on adoption and discussion groups for teenagers in gay families. One of the company's founders was the former TV talk show host Rosie O'Donnell, herself a lesbian mother.

CRUISING TO SUIT SPECIAL NEEDS

Cruising for the physically challenged offers one of the most hassle-free vacations possible. But it's important to choose the right ship and to prepare in advance

Cruise ships have become much more accessible for people with most types of disabilities. Ships built in the past five to 10 years will have the most up-to-date suites/cabins and accessible shipboard facilities for those with special needs. Many new ships also have text telephones and listening device kits for the hearing-impaired (including showlounges aboard some ships). Special dietary needs can often be met, and many cabins have refrigerators – useful for those with diabetes who need to keep supplies of insulin cool.

Special cruises cater for dialysis patients (check out www.dialysisatsea.com and www.dialysis-cruises.com) and for those who need oxygen regularly. Some cruise lines publish a special needs brochure.

If you use a wheelchair, take it with you, as ships carry only a limited number for emergency hospital use only. An alternative is to rent an electric wheelchair, which can be delivered to the ship on your sailing date.

Arguably the weakest point of cruising for the mobility-limited is any shore tender operation. Ship tenders simply aren't designed properly for the wheelchair-bound. This is why it is important to make sure that the itinerary you have chosen will work for you if there are ports where the ship is at anchor and a tender operation takes place. Also, check that shore excursions on offer are appropriate for your physical limitations.

Six basic problems to consider

It is as well to begin with the disadvantages of a cruise for the physically challenged:

❶ Unless cabins and bathrooms are specifically designed, problem areas include the entrance, furniture configuration, closet hanging rails, beds, grab bars, height of toiletries cabinet, and wheel-in shower stall.

❷ Elevators: the width of the door is important; in older ships, controls often can't be reached from a wheelchair.

❸ Few ships have access-help hoists installed at swimming pools (exception: P&O Cruises) or angled steps with handrail, or thalassotherapy pools or shore tenders (exception: Holland America Line).

❹ It can be hard to access areas like self-serve buffets, and many large resort ships provide only oval plates (no trays) in their casual eateries. So you may need to ask for help. Also, because the plates are plastic, they're cold. Tip: Ask a supervisor to get you a "proper" china heated plate for hot food items.

❺ Some insurance companies may prohibit smaller ships from accepting passengers with severe disabilities.

❻ Only five cruise ships have direct access ramps to lifeboats: *Amadea, Asuka II, Crystal Serenity, Crystal Symphony,* and *Europa.*

12 tips to avoid pitfalls

❶ Start by planning an itinerary and date, and find a travel agent who knows your needs. But follow up on all aspects of the booking yourself to avoid slip-ups; many cruise lines have a department or person to handle requests from disabled passengers.

❷ Choose a cruise line that lets you select a specific cabin, not just a price category. If the ship does not have any specially equipped cabins, book the best outside cabin in your price range, or choose another ship.

❸ Check whether your wheelchair will fit through your cabin's bathroom door, or into the shower area whether there is a "lip" at the door. Don't accept "I think so" as an answer. Get specific measurements.

❹ Choose a cabin close to an elevator. Not all elevators go to all decks, so check the deck

Wheelchair users should check in advance what help is available.

WHAT TO ASK BEFORE YOU BOOK

● Are any public rooms or public decks inaccessible to wheelchairs – for instance, it is sometimes difficult to obtain access to outdoor decks?

● Will you be guaranteed a good viewing place in the main showlounge if seated in a wheelchair?

● Some cruise lines, such as P&O Cruises, can supply a raised toilet seat, though not aboard all ships.

● Will crew be on hand to help, or must the passengers rely on their own traveling companions?

● Will special transportation be provided to transfer you from airport to ship?

● If you need a collapsible wheelchair, can this be provided by the cruise line?

● Do passengers have to sign a medical release?

● Are the ship's tenders accessible to wheelchairs?

● How do you get from your cabin to lifeboats in an emergency if the elevators are out of action?

● Do passengers need a doctor's note to qualify for a cabin for the physically challenged?

● Does the cruise line's travel insurance (with a cancellation or trip interruption) cover you for any injuries while you are aboard ship?

● Most disabled cabins have twin beds or one queen-sized bed. Anyone with a disabled child should ask whether a suitable portable bed can be moved in.

plan. Smaller and older vessels may not even have elevators, making access to even the dining room difficult.

❺ Avoid, at all costs, a cabin down a little alleyway shared by several other cabins, even if the price is attractive. It's hard to access a cabin in a wheelchair from such an alleyway.

❻ Cabins located amidships are less affected by vessel motion, so choose something in the middle of the ship if you are concerned about possible rough seas. The larger – and therefore more expensive – the cabin, the

more room you will have to maneuver in. And a tub provides more space than a shower.

❼ Hanging rails in the closets on most ships are positioned too high for someone in a wheelchair to reach – even the latest ships seem to repeat this basic error. Many cruise ships, however, have cabins specially fitted out to suit the mobility-limited. They are typically fitted with roll-in closets and have a pull-down facility to bring your clothes down to any height you want.

❽ Meals in some ships may be served in your cabin, on special request – an advantage should you wish to avoid dressing for every meal. But few ships have enough space in the cabin for dining tables. If you opt for a dining room with two fixed-time seatings for meals, choose the second – it's more leisurely. Alert the restaurant manager in advance that you would like a table that leaves plenty of room for your wheelchair.

❾ Hand-carry medical records. Once on board, tell the reception desk help may be needed in an emergency.

❿ Make sure that the contract specifically states that if, for any reason, the cabin is not available, that you will get a full refund and transportation back home as well as a refund on any hotel bills incurred.

⓫ Advise the cruise line of the need for proper transfer facilities such as buses or vans with wheelchair ramps or hydraulic lifts.

⓬ If you live near the port of embarkation, arrange to visit the ship to check its suitability (most cruise lines will be accommodating).

Coping with embarkation

The boarding process can pose problems. If you embark at ground level, the gangway may be level or inclined. It will depend on the embarkation deck of the ship and/or the tide in the port.

Alternatively, you may be required to embark from

WHY DOORS CAN PRESENT A PROBLEM FOR WHEELCHAIR USERS

The design of cruise ships has traditionally worked against the mobility-limited. To keep water out or to prevent water escaping from a flooded area, raised edges ("lips") – unfriendly to wheelchairs – are often placed in doorways and across exit pathways. Also, cabin doorways, at a standard 24 inches (60cm) wide, are often not wide enough for wheelchairs – about 30 inches (76 cm) is needed.

Bathroom doors, whether they open outward or inward, similarly hinder maneuverability. An electrically operated sliding door would be better.

Bathrooms in many older ships are small and full of plumbing fixtures, often at odd angles, awkward when moving about in a wheelchair. Those aboard

The author tests accessibility around a ship.

new ships are more accessible, but the plumbing may be located beneath the complete prefabricated module, making the floor higher than that in the cabin, which means a ramp is needed.

Some cruise lines will, if given

advance notice, remove a bathroom door and hang a fabric curtain in its place. Many lines will provide ramps for the bathroom doorway if needed.

Access to outside decks is usually through doors that must be opened manually rather than via automatic electric-eye doors.

It's not cheap to provide facilities for wheelchair-bound passengers. Trained crew members are needed to assist them, which translates to two crew members per eight-hour shift. Thus, six crew members would be required according to the latest safety and evacuation regulations solely to provide the necessary support for one wheelchair-bound passenger – a big drain on the cruise ship's labor resources.

Elevators on newer ships have Braille text on buttons.

an upper level of a terminal, in which case the gangway could well be of the floating loading-bridge type, like those used at major airports. Some have flat floors; others may have raised lips at regular intervals. The lips can be awkward to negotiate in a wheelchair, especially if the gangway is made steeper by a rising tide.

Ship-to-shore launches

Cruise lines should – but don't always – provide an anchor emblem in brochures for those ports of call where a ship will be at anchor instead of alongside. If the ship is at anchor, the crew will lower you and your wheelchair into a waiting tender and then, after a short boatride, lift you out again onto a rigged gangway or integral platform. If the sea is calm, this maneuver proceeds uneventfully; if the sea is choppy, it could vary from exciting to somewhat harrowing.

This type of embarkation is rare except in a busy port with several ships sailing the same day. Holland America Line is one of the few companies to make shore tenders accessible to the disabled, with a special boarding ramp and scissor lift so that wheelchair passengers can see out of the shore tender's windows.

Help for the hearing-impaired

Difficulties for such passengers include hearing announcements on the public address system, using the telephone, and poor acoustics in key areas such as boarding shore tenders.

Take a spare hearing aid battery. Some cruise lines have special "alert kits." These include "visual-tactile" devices for those unable to hear a knock on the door, a telephone ringing, or the sound of an alarm clock. Crystal Cruises' *Crystal Serenity* and *Crystal Symphony*, and Celebrity Cruises' *Celebrity Century* and *Celebrity Mercury* have movie theaters fitted with special headsets for those with hearing difficulties.

Finally, when going ashore, particularly on organized excursions, be aware that most destinations, particularly in Europe and Southeast Asia, are simply not equipped to handle people with hearing impairment.

Cruising blind

Any totally or almost blind persons must be accompanied by a fully able-bodied person, occupying the same cabin. A few lines will allow seeing-eye dogs. Taking an around-the-world cruise or long voyage aboard a cruise ship is one way for them to enjoy the sea, the aromas of the world, and to feel things that they are unable to at home.

Recent improvements

Many new ships now provide mobility-limited cabin bathrooms with collapsible shower stools mounted on shower walls, and bathroom toilets have collapsible arm guards and lower washbasin. Other cabin equipment may include a vibrating alarm clock, door beacon (light flashes when someone knock on the door), television with closed caption decoders, and a flashing light as fire alarm. Look out, too, for:
● Hearing-impaired kits on request.
● Dedicated wheelchair positions in the showlounge (including induction systems).
● Electrical hoist to access pool and hot tubs.
● All elevators and cabins have Braille text. The large resort ships *MSC Fantasia* and *MSC Splendida* even have Braille pads subtly hidden under each lower section of handrail in the main foyers – very user-friendly. ❑

WHEELCHAIR ACCESSIBILITY
Each cruise ship reviewed in this book is rated in its data listing for wheelchair accessibility. The ratings are defined on page 191.

EXPEDITIONS AND NATURE CRUISES

**Like sport utility vehicles, some ships have become
crossovers, operating as expedition cruise ships
but offering a quite plush and comfortable lifestyle**

Passengers joining expeditions tend to be more self-reliant and more interested in doing or learning than in being entertained. They become "participants" and take an active role in almost every aspect of the voyage, which is destination-, exploration- and nature-intensive.

Naturalists, historians, and lecturers (rather than entertainers) are aboard each ship to provide background information and observations about wildlife. Each participant receives a personal logbook, illustrated and written by the wildlife artists and writers who accompany each cruise – a fine souvenir.

You can walk on pack ice in the islands and land masses in the Arctic Ocean and Arctic Circle, explore a huge penguin rookery on an island in the Antarctic Peninsula, the Falkland Islands or South Georgia, or search for "lost" peoples in Melanesia. Or you can cruise close to the source of the Amazon, gaze at species of flora and fauna in the Galápagos Islands (Darwin's laboratory), or watch a genuine dragon on the island of Komodo – from a comfortable distance, of course.

Briefings and lectures bring cultural and intellectual elements to expedition cruise vessels. There is no formal entertainment as such; participants enjoy this type of cruise more for the camaraderie and learning experience, and being close to nature. The ships are designed and equipped to sail in ice-laden waters, yet they

Kapitan Khlebnikov slices through the Antarctic ice.

have a shallow enough draft to glide over coral reefs.

Despite being rugged, expedition cruise vessels can provide comfortable and even elegant surroundings for up to 200 passengers, and offer good food and service. Without traditional cruise ports at which to stop, a ship must be self-sufficient, be capable of long-range cruising, and be totally environmentally friendly.

Wildlife migrations

Lars-Eric Lindblad pioneered expedition cruising in 1966. A Swedish-American, he turned travel into adventure by going to parts of the world tourists had not visited. After chartering several vessels for voyages to Antarctica, he organized the design and construction of a small ship capable of going almost anywhere in comfort and safety. In 1969, *Lindblad Explorer* was launched; it soon earned an enviable reputation in adventure travel. Others followed.

To put together cruise expeditions, companies turn to knowledgeable sources and advisers. Scientific institutions are consulted; experienced world explorers and naturalists provide up-to-date reports on wildlife sightings, migrations, and other natural phenomena. Although some days are scheduled for relaxation, participants are kept physically and mentally active. Avoid such an adventure cruise if you are not completely ambulatory.

Adventure cruise companies provide expedition parkas and waterproof boots, but you will need to take waterproof trousers for Antarctica and the Arctic.

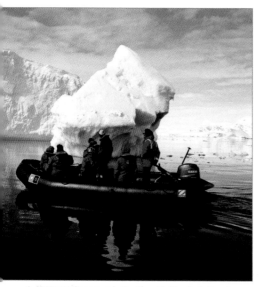

A *National Geographic Explorer* Zodiac in Antarctica.

Antarctica

While Arctic ice is only a few feet thick, the ice of Antarctica is thousands of feet thick. The continent was first sighted in 1820 by the American sealer Nathaniel Palmer, British naval officer Edward Bransfield, and Russian captain Fabian Bellingshausen.

For most, it is just a windswept frozen wasteland – it has been calculated that the ice mass contains almost 90 percent of the world's snow and ice, while its treeless land mass is twice the size of Australia. For others, it represents the last pristine place on earth, offering an abundance of marine and bird life.

As many as 36,000 people a year visit Antarctica, which has 24-hour sunshine during the austral summer but not a single native inhabitant. Its ice is as much as 2 miles (3km) thick, and its total land mass equals more than all the rivers and lakes on earth and exceeds that of China and India combined. Icebergs can easily be the size of Belgium. The region has a raw beauty.

Although visited by "soft" expedition cruise ships and even "normal"-sized cruise ships with ice-hardened hulls, the more remote "far side" – the Oates and Scott Coasts, McMurdo Sound, and the famous Ross Ice Shelf

THE LEADING EXPEDITION CRUISE VESSELS: HOW THEY RATE

Research Vessels/ True Expedition Vessels	Rating of facilities (max: 100)	Company/ Operator [1]	Built	Pass. Cabins	Max No. Passengers	Tonnage	Registry	Length (meters)
Akademik Ioffe	46	Quark Expeditions	1988	55	110	6,460	Russia	117.10
Akademik Sergey Vavilov	50	Quark Expeditions	1988	40	110	6,231	Russia	117.80
Akademik Sholaskiy	44	Quark Expeditions	1982	22	44	2,140	Russia	71.56
Antarctic Dream	35	Antarctic Shipping	1959	39	78	2,180	Panama	83.00
50 Years of Victory [2]	90	Quark Expeditions	2007	66	128	23,439	Russia	159.00
Grigoriy Mikheev	46	Oceanwide Expeditions	1990	22	44	2,000	Russia	70.00
Kapitan Dranitsyn	50	Poseidon Arctic Voyages	1980	53	113	10,471	Russia	131.00
Kapitan Khlebnikov	51	Quark Expeditions	1981	54	112	12,288	Russia	132.49
Marina Svetaeva	45	Aurora Expeditions	1989	45	100	4,575	Russia	89.98
Ocean Nova	48	Quark Expeditions	1992	45	96	2,118	Greenland	73.00
Polar Pioneer	47	Aurora Expeditions	1985	26	54	2,140	Russia	71.60
Professor Molchanov	44	Oceanwide Expeditions	1983	29	52	1,753	Russia	71.60
Professor Multanovskiy	44	Oceanwide Expeditions	1983	29	49	1,753	Russia	71.60
Spirit of Enderby	44	Heritage Expeditions	1983	22	48	6,231	Russia	72.00
Other Expedition Cruise Ships								
Bremen	77	Hapag-Lloyd Cruises	1990	82	184	6,752	Bahamas	111.51
Clipper Adventurer	57	Quark Expeditions	1976	61	122	5,750	Bahamas	100.01
Expedition	55	GAP Adventures	1972	58	120	6,336	Liberia	105.00
Hanseatic	86	Hapag-Lloyd Cruises	1993	92	194	8,378	Bahamas	122.80
Marco Polo	55	Cruise & Maritime Voyages	1965	425	915	22,080	Bahamas	176.28
Minerva	66	Swan Hellenic Cruises	1996	178	474	12,500	Bahamas	133.00
National Geographic Endeavour	51	Lindblad Expeditions	1966	62	110	3,132	Bahamas	89.20
National Geographic Explorer	45	Lindblad Expeditions	1982	81	148	6,200	Bahamas	112.00
Orion	82	Orion Expedition Cruises	2003	53	139	4,050	Bahamas	102.70
Plancius	41	Oceanwide Expeditions	1976	53	110	3,175	Holland	89.00
Quest	47	Noble Caledonia	1992	26	52	1,268	Bahamas	49.65
Sea Spirit	62	Quark Expeditions	1991	60	127	4,200	Bahamas	89.70
Silver Explorer	84	Silversea Cruises	1989	66	158	6,072	Bahamas	108.20
Ushuaia	40	Ushuaia Adventure Corp/ Antarpply Expeditions	1970	41	84	2,963	Argentina	84.73

NOTES: (1) = most expedition ships are sold by multiple expedition companies, or under full charter to one operator.
(2) = nuclear-powered.

Gentoo penguins at Brown Bluff in Antarctica.

– can be visited only by genuine icebreakers, as the katabatic winds can easily reach more than 100mph (160 km/h). The first ship carrying passengers on a circumnavigation of Antarctica was the 114-passenger *Kapitan Khlebnikov*, operated by Quark Expeditions, in 1996–7.

Only 100 passengers *per ship* are now allowed ashore at any given time, so if you sail aboard one of the larger ships that claim to include Antarctica on their itineraries, it will probably be to view it – but only from the ship. Indeed, cruise ships with more than 500 passengers have not been allowed to sail in Antarctic waters since August 2011, as the chances of rescue in the event of pack ice crushing a normal cruise ship hull are virtually nil. For real expedition cruising, choose a ship that includes a flotilla of Zodiac rubber inflatable landing craft, proper boot washing stations, expedition equipment, experienced expedition leaders, and ice captains. Two companies that stand out from the crowd are: Hapag-Lloyd Expedition Cruises and Quark Expeditions.

There are no docks in Antarctica, so venturing "ashore" is done by Zodiacs – an integral part of the experience.

Be aware that you can get stuck even aboard these specialized expedition ships, as did *Nordkapp*, which ran aground near Deception Island in 2007. In the same year, Canadian company GAP Expeditions' *Explorer* hit an iceberg in Bransfield Strait off King George Island and sank; all 91 passengers, nine expedition staff, and 54 crew members were rescued thanks to the coordination efforts of the British Coast Guard and the Hurtigruten cruise ship *Nordnorge*. In December 2008

Antarpply Expeditions' *Ushuaia* was grounded; all 89 passengers were rescued by the Chilean navy vessel *Achiles*. In 2009, Quark Expeditions' *Ocean Nova* was grounded, and in 2011 *Polar Star* grounded on an uncharted rock, with no injuries to passengers or crew.

Tip: Wear an identification bracelet or belt at all times while on an Antarctic expedition cruise. Any-

PROTECTING SENSITIVE ENVIRONMENTS

Polar bears are under threat.

In the future, only ships capable of meeting new "zero discharge" standards will be allowed to cross environmentally sensitive areas. Expedition cruise companies are concerned about the environment, and they spend much time and money in educating their crews and passengers about safe procedures.

They observe the "Antarctic Traveler's Code," based on 1978's Antarctic Conservation Act, designed to protect the region's ecosystem, flora, and fauna.

The Antarctic Treaty Meeting in Kyoto in 1994 made it unlawful, unless authorized by permit, to take native animals, birds, and certain native plants, introduce species, enter certain special pro-

tected areas (SPAs), or discharge or dispose of pollutants.

To "take" means to remove, harass, molest, harm, pursue, hunt, shoot, kill, trap, capture, restrain, or tag any native mammal or bird, or to attempt to do so. Violators face civil penalties, including a fine of up to $10,000 and one-year imprisonment for each violation. A copy of the Act can be found in the library of each adventure or expedition ship that visits the continent.

Ships carrying over 500 passengers are not allowed to land and are restricted to "scenic" cruising, so the likelihood of a single-hulled mega-ship zooming in on the penguins with 3,000-plus passengers is unlikely. Nor would it be possible to rescue so many passengers and crew in the event of an emergency. Also, the large resort ships burn heavy oil rather than the lighter oil used by the specialist expedition ships, which also have ice-strengthened hulls – so the danger of pollution arising from an "incident" is far greater.

one on a special diet should advise the cruise operator as early as possible so that any needed items can be obtained.

Wildlife you may see or come into contact with include orcas, dolphins, the six species of Antarctic seals, penguins, birds, and various species of lichen and flora, depending on the area visited.

Take plastic bags to cover your camera, so that condensation forms inside the bag and not on your camera when changing from the cold of the outside Antarctic air to the warmth of your expedition cruise vessel. Make sure you know how to operate your camera with gloves on – frostbite is a real danger.

The Arctic

Want some Northern Exposure? Try the Arctic. This is an ocean surrounded by continents, whereas Antarctica is an ice-covered continent surrounded by ocean. The Arctic Circle is located at 66 degrees, 33 minutes, and 3 seconds north, although this really designates where 24-hour days and nights begin.

The Arctic is best defined as that region north of which no trees grow, and where water is the primary feature of the landscape. It is technically a desert, receiving less than 10 inches (25cm) of rainfall a year, but actually teems with wildlife, including polar bears, walruses, seals, and Arctic birds. It has short, cool summers, long, cold winters, and frequent high winds. Canada's Northwest Territories, which cover 1.3 million sq. miles, are part of the Arctic region, as are some of Russia's northernmost islands such as Franz Josef Land.

Passenger ships that have navigated the Northwest

10 TOP EXPEDITIONS

Aleutian-Pribiloff Islands
Amazon (Manaus-Iquitos)
Antarctic Peninsula
Arctic
Galápagos Islands
Islands of Micronesia
Northwest Passage
Northeast Passage
Papua New Guinea
Ross Ice Shelf (Antarctica)

Passage linking the Atlantic and Pacific Oceans include *Lindblad Explorer* (1984), *World Discoverer* (1985), *Society Explorer* (1988), *Frontier Spirit* (1992), *Kapitan Khlebnikov* (1994, 1995, 1998, 2006, 2007, 2008), *Hanseatic* (1995, 1996, 1997, 1999, 2007), *Bremen* (2009), and both *Bremen* and *Hanseatic* (2010).

Greenland

The world's largest island, the inappropriately named Greenland, in the Arctic Circle, is 82% covered with ice – actually compressed snow – up to 11,000ft thick (3,350 meters). Its rocks are among the world's oldest, and its ecosystem is one of the newest.

The glacier at Jacobshavn, also known as Ilulissat, is the world's fastest moving and creates a new iceberg every five minutes. Greenland, which was granted home rule by Denmark in 1978, makes its living from fishing. It is said to have more dogs than people – its population is 68,400 – and dogs are an important means of transport.

The Galápagos Islands

These islands, 600 miles (960km) off the coast of Ecuador in the Pacific Ocean, are a microcosm of our planet. More than 100 islands, plus mineral-rich and lava outcroppings, make up the Galápagos, which are fed by the nutrient-rich Cromwell and Humboldt currents. The fertile waters can be cold, even on the equator.

The Ecuadorians jealously guard their islands and prohibit the movement of almost all non-Ecuadorian-registered cruise vessels within its boundaries. The best way to follow in the footsteps of Charles Darwin, who visited the islands in 1835 aboard the *Beagle*, is to fly to Quito and cruise aboard an Ecuadorian-registered vessel. Ecological fact: cruising leaves a smaller carbon footprint because it does not contribute to the building of hotels, restaurants, roads, and cars.

The government of Ecuador set aside most of the islands as a wildlife sanctuary in 1934, while uninhabited areas were declared national parks in 1959. The national park includes approximately 97 per cent of the islands' landmass, together with 20,000 sq. miles (50,000 sq. km) of ocean. The Charles Darwin Research Station was established in 1964, and the government created the Galápagos Marine Resources Reserve in 1986.

The Galápagos National Park tax doubled to $200 per person in 2009. Smoking is prohibited on the islands, and no more than 50,000 visitors a year are admitted. Some cruise lines require vaccinations for cruises that include Ecuador, although the World Health Organization does not. ❏

A booby and sea lion under observation in the Galápagos.

COASTAL CRUISES

Being all at sea doesn't appeal? You can stay close to dry land by journeying round the coasts of Australia, Europe, and North and South America

AUSTRALIA

The marine wonderland of the Great Barrier Reef, a World Heritage Site off the northeast coast of Australia, is the earth's largest living coral reef – it actually consists of more than 2,800 individual coral reefs. It is visited by around 70 local Australian boutique ship operators, who mostly offer one- to four-night cruises to the reefs and Whitsunday Islands. The area is excellent for scuba diving and snorkeling.

June through September is humpback whale-watching season; the Reef shelters the young whales while the adults nurture them in the shallow waters. Note that the Australian government levies an environmental charge of A$5 on everyone over four years of age visiting the Great Barrier Reef and its environs.

NORWAY

There is year-round coastal cruising along the shores of Norway to the Land of the Midnight Sun aboard the ships of the Hurtigruten Group, formerly known as Norwegian Coastal Voyages. The fleet consists of small, comfortable, working express coastal packet steamers and contemporary cruise vessels that deliver mail, small packaged goods, and foodstuffs, and take passengers, to the communities spread on the shoreline.

Invariably dubbed "the world's most beautiful voy-

ABOVE: glass-bottomed boat on the Great Barrier Reef.

age," this is a 1,250-mile (2,000-km) journey from Bergen in Norway to Kirkenes, close to the Russian border (half of which is north of the Arctic Circle) and takes 12 days. The service started in 1893, and the name Hurtigruten – meaning "fast route" – reflects the fact that this coastal express was once the most reliable communication link between southern Norway and its remote north. Today the company carries more than 300,000 passengers a year. It's a good way to meet Norwegians, who treat the service like a bus.

You can join it at any of the 34 ports of call and stay as long as you wish because the vessels, being working ships, sail every day of the year. At the height of sum-

HURTIGRUTEN SHIPS			
Ship	Tonnage	Built	Berths
Finnmarken	15,000	2002	638
Fram	12,700	2007	328
Kong Harald	11,200	1993	490
Lofoten	2,621	1964	147
Midnatsol	16,053	2003	652
Nordkapp	11,386	1996	464
Nordlys	11,200	1994	482
Nordnorge	11,386	1997	455
Nordstjernen *	2,621	1956	114
Polar Star *	4,998	1969	100
Polarlys	12,000	1996	479
Richard With	11,205	1993	483
Trollfjord	15,000	2002	648
Vesteralen	6,261	1983	316
* for "soft" expedition voyages only			

SMALL COASTAL CRUISE VESSELS (more than 10 cabins)

Ship	Cruise Line	Cabins	Region	Built
Admiralty Dream	Alaskan Dream Cruises	39	Alaska	1980
Alaska Dream	Alaskan Dream Cruises	21	Alaska	1986
American Glory	American Cruise Lines	27	USA Coastal Cruises	2002
American Spirit	American Cruise Lines	50	USA Coastal Cruises	2005
American Star	American Cruise Lines	52	USA Coastal Cruises	2007
Aranui 3	Campagnie Polynésienne de Transport Maritime	63	Tahiti/Marquesas	2003
Baranof Dream	Alaskan Dream Cruises	39	Alaska	1980
Belle de l'Adriatique	CroisiEurope	100	European Coast	2006
Callisto	Travel Dynamics International	17	Greek Isles	1963
Celebrity Xpedition	Celebrity Cruises	47	Galápagos Islands	2001
CoCo Explorer	CoCo Explorer Cruises	56	Philippines	1967
Coral Princess	Coral Princess Cruises	27	Australia (Great Barrier Reef)	1988
Corinthian	Ecoventura/Galápagos Network	45	Galápagos Islands	1967
Discovery	Panama Marine Adventures	12	Panama	2004
Emeraude	Emeraude Classic Cruises	38	Halong Bay (Vietnam)	2003
Fiji Princess	Blue Lagoon Cruises	34	Yasawa Islands (Fiji)	2005
Galápagos Legend	Galápagos Island Cruises	57	Galápagos Islands	1963
Grande Caribe	American Canadian Caribbean Line	48	USA Coastal Cruises	1997
Grande Mariner	American Canadian Caribbean Line	50	USA Coastal Cruises	1999
Independence	American Cruise Lines	52	USA Coastal Cruises	2009
Isabela II	Metropolitan Touring	21	Galápagos Islands	1989
La Pinta	South American Experience	24	Galápagos Islands	2008
Lord of the Glens	Magna Carta Cruises	27	Scotland	1985
Mare Australis	Cruceros Australis	64	Chilean Fjords (Patagonia)	2002
Megastar Aries	Star Cruises	33	Southeast Asia	1992
Mystique Princess	Blue Lagoon Cruises	36	Yasawa Islands (Fiji)	1996
National Geographic Endeavour	Lindblad Expeditions/National Geographic	62	Various regions	1966
National Geographic Explorer	Lindblad Expeditions/National Geographic	81	Various regions	1982
National Geographic Islander	Lindblad Expeditions/National Geographic	24	Galápagos Islands	1995
National Geographic Polaris	Lindblad Expeditions/National Geographic	41	Galápagos Islands	1960
National Geographic Sea Bird	Lindblad Expeditions/National Geographic	35	Alaska, Baja	1981
National Geographic Sea Lion	Lindblad Expeditions/National Geographic	35	Alaska, Baja	1982
Oceanic Discoverer	Coral Princess Cruises	38	Australia (Great Barrier Reef)	2005
Reef Escape (pictured below)	Captain Cook Cruises	60	Australia	1987
Safari Explorer	American Safari Cruises	18	Alaska/Mexico Coast	1998
Safari Quest	American Safari Cruises	11	Alaska/Mexico Coast	1992
Santa Cruz	Metropolitan Touring	43	Galápagos Islands	1979
Sarfaq Ittuk	Arctic Umiaq Line	26	Greenland	1992
Sea Voyager	Various tour operators	33	Central America	1982
Skorpios II	Skorpios Cruises	64	Chilean Fjords	1988
Skorpios III	Skorpios Cruises	56	Chilean Fjords	1995
Stella Australis	Cruceros Australis	100	Chilean Fjords	2010
True North	North Star Cruises	18	Australia (west coast)	2005
Tu Moana	Bora Bora Cruises	20	Tahitian Islands	2003
Via Australis	Cruceros Australis	64	Chilean Fjords (Patagonia)	2005
Via Australis	InnerSea Discoveries	30	Alaska	1983
Via Australis	InnerSea Discoveries	34	Alaska	1992

Gierangerfjord, one of Norway's stunning vistas.

mer, north of the Arctic Circle, there are 24 hours of daylight, and between November and February the northern lights create spectacular arcs across the sky. Some specialist voyages are aimed at birdwatchers and others include onboard concerts and lectures celebrating the work of Norwegian composer Edvard Grieg.

The ships can accommodate between 144 and 652 passengers. The newest ships have an elevator that can accommodate a wheelchair passenger, but otherwise, they are fairly plain and basic, practical vessels, with food that is more bistro than restaurant. Note that alcohol prices are extremely high, as they are throughout Norway, and that the currency is the Norwegian krone.

Archipelago hopping can be done along Sweden's eastern coast, too, by sailing in the daytime and staying overnight in one of the many small hotels. One vessel sails from Norrtalje, north of Stockholm, to Oskarshamn, near the Baltic island of Öland, right through the spectacular Swedish archipelago.

The Hurtigruten Group also operates utilitarian ships for expeditions to the Arctic, Antarctic, and Greenland.

SCOTLAND

The fishing town of Oban, two hours west of Glasgow by road, is the base for one of the world's finest cruise experiences. *Hebridean Princess* is a little gem, with Laura Ashley-style interiors – homely enough to have been chartered by Queen Elizabeth II for a family-only celebration of her 80th birthday in 2006. The food is excellent, and includes Scottish beef, local seafood, and seasonal vegetables. There's fine personal service.

This ship, owned by Hebridean Island Cruises, carries up to 49 passengers around some of Scotland's most magnificent coastline and islands. If you cruise from Oban, you can be met at Glasgow airport or rail station and taken to the ship by motor coach. Take lots of warm clothing, however (layers are best), as the weather can be flexible and often unkind.

As an alternative, there's the 54-passenger *Lord of the Glens*, operated by Magna Carta Steamship Company, which cruises in style through Scotland's lakes and canals. Some seven- and 10-night high-season sailings are accompanied by historians and guest lecturers.

NORTH AMERICA

Coastal cruise ships flying the American flag offer a complete change of style from the large resort cruise ships. They are American-owned and American-crewed, and very informal. Being US-registered, they can start from and return to a US port without being required to call at a foreign port along the way – which a foreign-flagged cruise ship must do.

Accommodating up to 150 passengers, the ships are more like private family affairs, and are rarely out of sight of land. These cruises are low-key, low-pace, and not for active, adventurous types. Their operators seek out lesser-known areas, offering in-depth visits to destinations inaccessible to larger ships, along both the eastern and western seaboards of the USA, including Alaska.

Most passengers are over 60, and many over 70. They may prefer not to fly, and wherever possible drive or take a train to join their ship. During the summer, you might see a couple of children on board, but in general small kids are not allowed. There are no facilities for them, and no staff to look after them.

Destinations: Eastern US and Canadian seaboard cruises include the St Lawrence River, Atlantic Coastal Waterways, New England (good for fall cruises), Cape Cod and the Islands (and Cape Cod Canal), the Great Lakes (and Welland Canal), the Colonial Deep South, and Florida waterways.

Western seaboard cruises cover Alaska, the Pacific Northwest, California Wine Country, and Baja California/Sea of Cortés. Cruises focus on historically relevant destinations, nature and wildlife spotting, and coastal

Blount Small Ship Adventures vessels have a casual style.

American Safari Cruises finds humpback whales in Mexico's Sea of Cortés and goes kayaking in Alaska.

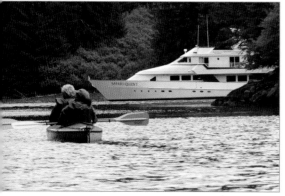

to the engines and generators than aboard the large resort ships, so generator humming noises can be disturbing at night. The quietest cabins are at the bows – although there could be noise if the ship is equipped with a bow thruster – and most cruising is done in the early morning so that passengers can sleep better at night.

Tall passengers should note that the overall length of beds rarely exceeds 6 ft (1.8 meters). While soap is provided, it's best to bring your own shampoo, conditioner, and other toiletries. The ships of Blount Small Ship Adventures do not have cabin keys.

Although some of the older ships are really basic, the latest, particularly those of American Cruise Lines, are very comfortable. Because they are not classified for open-water cruising, though, they don't have to conform to the same rigorous shipbuilding standards that larger ocean-going cruise ships do. You may find that hot and cold water lines run close to each other in your bathroom, thus delivering neither really hot nor really cold water. Sound insulation could be almost non-existent.

Activities: The main evening event is dinner in the dining room, with one seating. This can be a family-style affair, with passengers at long tables, and the food passed around.

The cuisine is decidedly American, with fresh local specialties. Menus aboard the ships of Alaskan Dream Cruises and Blount Small Ship Adventures are very limited, while those aboard the ships of American Cruise Lines offer slightly more variety, including seasonal items. You'll probably be asked in the morning to choose which of the two main courses you'd like for dinner.

Evening entertainment consists mainly of after-dinner conversation. Most vessels are in port during the time, so you can easily go ashore for the local nightlife, although most passengers simply go to bed early.

The cost: These cruises are expensive, with an average daily rate of $400–$800 a person. Suggested gratuities are high – typically about $125 per person, per seven-day cruise – but they are shared by all personnel. ❏

viewing. On some cruises, these boutique ships can dock adjacent to a town, allowing easy access on foot.

The ships: These "D-class" vessels are less than 2,500 gross tonnage, and are subject neither to bureaucratic regulations nor to union rules. They are restricted to cruising no more than 20 miles (32km) offshore, at a comfortable 12 knots (13.8mph). Public room facilities are limited. Because the vessels are American-registered, there is no casino. They really are ultra-casual, no-frills ships with the most basic of facilities, no swimming pools, little artwork, and no glitz in interior decor. They usually have three or four decks and, except for the ships of American Cruise Lines, no elevator. Stairs can be steep and are not recommended for people with walking difficulties. Because of this, some ships have an electric chair-lift on indoor or outdoor stairways.

Cabins: Accommodation is in outside-view cabins, some of which open directly onto a walking deck – inconvenient when it rains. Each has a picture window and small bathroom. They are small and basic, with very limited closet space – perhaps just a curtain across a space with a hanging rod for clothes. Many do not have a TV set or telephone. There's no room service, and you may have to turn your own bed down. Cabins are closer

---

COASTAL CRUISE LINES IN NORTH AMERICA

There are several small ship cruise companies: Alaskan Dream Cruises, American Cruise Lines, American Safari Cruises, Blount Small Ship Adventures, and Lindblad Expeditions.

What differentiates them? American Cruise Lines and American Safari Cruises provide better food and service than the others. American Cruise Lines' ships have larger cabins, and more public rooms. Drinks are included aboard the ships of American Cruise Lines only.

American Cruise Lines and Blount Small Ship Adventures operate on the USA's east coast; American Safari Cruises and Lindblad Expeditions operate on the USA's west coast and Alaska.

NORTH ATLANTIC CROSSINGS

You may be facing some unpredictable weather, but there's something romantic and adventurous about this classic ocean voyage

Crossing the 3,000 miles (4,800km) of the North Atlantic by passenger vessel can be considered an art. I have done it 157 times and always enjoy it immensely. I consider crossings as rests in musical parlance, for both are described as "passages." Indeed, musicians do often "hear" rests in between notes. So if ports of call are the musical notes of a voyage, then the rests are the days at sea – temporary interludes, when physical and mental indulgence become ends in themselves.

Experienced mariners say a ship behaves like a ship only when it is doing a crossing, for that's what a real ship is built for. Yet the days when ships were built specifically for crossings are almost gone. The only one offering a regularly scheduled transatlantic service is Cunard Line's *Queen Mary 2*, a 148,151-tonnage ship, built with a thick hull designed to survive the worst weather the North Atlantic has to offer. Some unpredictable weather, together with fog off the Grand Banks of Newfoundland, can confine the captain to torturous hours on the bridge, with little time for socializing.

When it is foggy, the crew of *Queen Mary 2* is often pestered by passengers wanting to know if the ship has yet approached latitude 41°46' north, longitude 50°14' west – where White Star Line's 43,328-ton *Titanic* struck an Arctic iceberg on that fateful April night in 1912.

Boat trains are back

In 2011, specially chartered "boat trains" were reintroduced in the UK between Glasgow and Southampton. The 324-passenger trains take passengers within yards of the Queen Elizabeth II and Mayflower terminals, with porters transferring luggage straight from the baggage car to the ship. On some trains staff members help with check-in formalities en route.

Excitement and anticipation usually precede a crossing. First there is the hubbub and bustle of check-in, then the crossing of the threshold on the gangway before being welcomed into the calmness aboard, and finally escorted to one's accommodation.

Once the umbilical cord of the gangway is severed, bow and stern mooring lines are cast off, and with three long blasts on the ship's deep whistle, the *QM2* is pried gently from its berth. Passengers on deck often observe motorboats trying to keep up with the ocean liner as it edges away from Brooklyn's excellent Red Hook Pier 12 terminal toward the Statue of Liberty, Ellis Island, then under the Verrazano-Narrows Bridge, and out to the open sea. Coming westbound, arriving in New York by ship is one of the world's thrilling travel experiences.

The *QM2* has almost year-round scheduled crossings, whereas other cruise ships crossing the Atlantic are little more than repositioning cruises – a way of moving ships that cruise the Mediterranean in summer to the Caribbean in winter, and vice versa – they offer more chances to experience the romance and adventure of a crossing, usually in spring and fall. These satisfy those wanting uninterrupted days at sea and lots of leisure time.

Most cruise ships operating repositioning crossings cross the Atlantic using the "sunny southern route" – departing from southern ports such as Fort Lauderdale, San Juan, or Barbados, and ending the journey in Lisbon, Genoa, or Copenhagen via the Azores or the Canary Islands off the coast of northern Africa. In this way, they avoid the more difficult weather often encountered in the North Atlantic. Such crossings take longer, however: between eight and 12 days. ❑

ABOVE: *Queen Mary 2* at dusk, heading for New York.

SAILING SHIPS

Want to be free as the wind? Think about cruising under sail, with towering masts, the creak of taut ropes and gleaming white sails to power you along

There is simply nothing that beats the thrill of being aboard a multi-mast tall ship, sailing under thousands of square feet of canvas through waters that mariners have sailed for centuries. This is cruising in the traditional manner of seafaring, aboard authentic sailing ships, contemporary copies of clipper ships, or aboard high-tech cruise-sail ships. But it gives you a genuine sailing experience while keeping creature comforts.

There are no rigid schedules, and life aboard equates to an unstructured lifestyle, apart from meal times. Weather conditions may often dictate whether a scheduled port visit will be made or not, but passengers sailing on these vessels are usually unconcerned. They would rather savor the feeling of being at one with nature, albeit in a comfortable, civilized setting, and without having to do the work themselves. The more luxurious sailing ships are the closest most people will get to owning their own mega-yacht.

Wind Surf offers extensive water-sports facilities.

Real tall ships

While we have all been dreaming of adventure, a pocketful of designers and yachtsmen committed pen to paper, hand in pocket and rigging to mast, and came up with a potpourri of stunning vessels to delight the eye and refresh the spirit. Examples are *Royal Clipper*, *Sea Cloud*, *Sea Cloud II*, *Star Clipper*, and *Star Flyer*.

Of these, *Sea Cloud*, built in 1931, restored in 1979, and adapted to satisfy the latest regulations in 2011, is the most romantic sailing ship afloat. It operates under charter for much of the year, and sails in both the Caribbean and the Mediterranean. A kind of stately home afloat, *Sea Cloud* remains one of the finest and most exhilarating travel experiences in the world.

The activities are few, so relaxation is the key, in a stylish but unpretentious setting. The food and service are good, as is the interaction between the 69 passengers and 60 crew, many of whom have worked aboard the ship for many years. One bonus is the fact that a doctor is available on board at no charge for emergencies or seasickness medication.

Although passengers may be able to participate occasionally in the furling and unfurling of the sails, they are not permitted to climb the rigging, as may be possible aboard some of the other, more modern tall ships.

Sea Cloud Cruises introduced a new, real tall ship in 2010, and Star Clippers is said to be thinking of building one.

Contemporary sail-cruise ships

To combine sailing with push-button automation, try *Club Med 2* (Club Mediterranée) or *Wind Surf* (Windstar Cruises) – with five tall aluminum masts, they are the world's largest sail-cruise ships – and *Wind Spirit* and *Wind Star* (Windstar Cruises), with four masts. Not a hand touches the sails; they are computer-controlled from the navigation bridge.

The traditional sense of sailing is almost absent in these ocean-going robots, because the computer keeps the ship on an even keel. Also, some people find it hard to get used to the whine of the vessels' generators, which run the lighting and air-conditioning systems 24 hours a day.

From a yachtsman's viewpoint, the sail-to-power ratio is poor. That's why these cruise ships with sails have engine power to get them into and out of port. The *Sea Cloud* and *Star Clipper* ships do it by sail alone, except when there is no wind, which doesn't happen all that often.

On some itineraries, when there is little wind, you could be motor-powered for most of the cruise, with only a few hours under sail. The three Windstar Cruises vessels and one Club Med ship are typically under sail for about 40 percent of the time.

The Windstar ships carry mainly North Americans and the Club Med vessel mainly French-speakers.

Another slightly smaller but chic vessel is *Le Ponant*. This three-mast ship caters to just 64 French-speaking passengers in elegant, yet casual, high-tech surroundings, advancing the technology of the original Windstar concept. The ship made news in 2008 when its crew was held to ransom by pirates off the Somali coast; no passengers were on board at the time.

When the engine cuts in

So, do you get to cruise under sail most of the time? Not really. Aboard the ships of Sea Cloud Cruises and Star Clippers, because they are real tall ships, you could be under sail for most of the night when the ships are under way, as long as there is wind, of course, and on the days or part days at sea.

The ship's small engine is used for maneuvering in and out of port. In the Caribbean, for example, the trade winds are good for most of the year, while in the Mediterranean and Southeast Asia the winds are not so potent. But many passengers enjoy helping to furl and unfurl the sails, and being able to climb the rigging. Lying in the netting under the ship's bows is a memorable experience.

Aboard the ships of Windstar Cruises, however, the itineraries are so port-intensive that the computer-controlled sails are hardly ever used today – so the experience can be disappointing.   ❏

Star Clipper crew members get away from it all.

HOW TO MEASURE WIND SPEEDS

Understanding wind patterns is important to sailing ships, but the numbering system for wind velocity can confuse. There are 12 velocities, known as "force" on the Beaufort scale, devised in 1805 by Sir Francis Beaufort *(left)*, an Irish-born hydrographer and officer in Britain's Royal Navy. It was adopted internationally in 1874 as the official means of recording wind velocity. They are as follows, with descriptions of the ocean surface:

Force 0 (0–1mph): Calm; glassy (like a mirror).
Force 1 (1–3mph): Light wind; rippled surface.
Force 2 (4–7mph): Light breeze; small wavelets.
Force 3 (8–12mph): Gentle breeze; large wavelets, scattered whitecaps.
Force 4 (13–18mph): Moderate breeze; small waves, frequent whitecaps.
Force 5 (19–24mph): Fresh breeze; moderate waves, numerous whitecaps.
Force 6 (25–31mph): Strong breeze; large waves, white foam crests.
Force 7 (32–38mph): Moderate gale; streaky white foam.
Force 8 (39–46mph): Fresh gale; moderate waves.
Force 9 (47–54mph): Strong gale; high waves.
Force 10 (55–63mph): Whole gale; very high waves, curling crests.
Force 11 (64–73mph): Violent storm; extremely high waves, froth and foam, poor visibility.
Force 12 (73+mph): Hurricane; huge waves, thundering white spray, visibility nil.

CARGO SHIP CRUISING

These slow voyages appeal to independent
types who don't require constant entertainment,
and the accommodation can be surprisingly comfortable

More than 3,000 passengers a year
travel by cargo ship, and the number
is growing as passengers become further disenchanted with the large resort ships
that dominate the cruise industry. Traveling
by freighter is also the ultimate way to travel
for those seeking a totally unstructured voyage
without entertainment or other diversions.

The experience has particular appeal for
retirees, relocating executives, those with far-
flung family connections, graduates returning home from an overseas college, or
professors on sabbatical leave. Freighters
travel the busiest trade routes, and you can
even take one around the world aboard the
vessels of Bank Line; the round-trip takes
about four months.

About 300 cargo ships (freighters and container ves-

Cabins on most cargo ships are surprisingly comfortable.

PASSENGER-CARRYING CARGO SHIPS

These lines, among others, offer regular passenger
voyages year-round: Andrew Weir Shipping, Christian F.
Ahrenkiel, Alpha Ship, Bank Line, H Buss, CMA CGM The
French Line, Compagnie Polynésienne de Transport
Maritime (CPTM), Coopérative de Transport Maritime &
Aérien (CTMA), Peter Doehle, French Asia Line, French
West Indies Line, Grimaldi Lines, Hamburg-Süd, Hansa
Shipmanagement, Horn Line, Independent Container Line,
Interorient Navigation, Reederei F Laeisz, Leonhardt &
Blumberg, Mare Schifffahrtsgesellschaft, Martime
Gesellschaft, Maruba Lines, MCC Passage, Mediterranean
Club Express, Melfi Lines, MSC Mediterranean Shipping
Company, NSB Freighter Cruises, Niederelbe Schif-
fahrtssgesellschaft Buxtehude, Reederei Nord, OPDR,
Oltmann Shipping, PZM Polish Steamship Company, Pearl
String Service, Rickmers Reederei, St Helena Line,
Reederei Heinrich Schepers, Reederei Karl Schlüter, H
Schuldt, Swire Shipping, Transeste Shipping, Tom Wörden,
Reederei Hermann Wulff, Zim Integrated Shipping, Kapitän
Peter Zylmann Freighter Cruises. Remember that, due to
the changing economic climate, ships may be cancelled
or laid up at short notice.

Booking and Information
www.travltips.com
www.freighterworld.com
www.cruisepeople.co.uk/freighters.htm
www.seejapan.co.uk/transport/sea/cargo.html
www.sydneytravel.com
www.freightertravel.co.nz

sels) offer berths, with German operators accounting for
more than half of them. True freighters – the general
breakbulk carrier ships and feeder container vessels –
carry up to 12 passengers; the only exception is the
Royal Mail Ship *RMS St Helena*, which carries up to
128 passengers, animals such as goats and sheep, and
goods from the UK to the island of Ascension. While
RMS St Helena carries a doctor, freighters do not, and
remember that they are working vessels, not cruise ships.

Cargo ship schedules change constantly, depending
on the whim of the owner and the cargo to be carried,
whereas container ships travel on regular schedules. For
the sake of simplicity, they are all termed freighters.
But cargo ships have changed dramatically as cost management and efficiency have become vital. Container
ships are operated as passenger liners used to be: running line voyages on set schedules. You can also make
a one-way voyage.

Most cargo ship companies don't allow children or
pregnant women to travel, and won't accept accept anyone younger than five or older than 80. You'll need to be
fully mobile – there are no elevators to connect the various decks. Because there are no medical facilities, anyone over 65 is usually required to produce a medical
certificate of good health. Also, if your ship visits a US
port at any point, non-Americans will need a full US visa
(cargo ships are not part of the visa-waiver program).

Cargo ship facilities

What do you get when you book a cargo ship voyage?
You get a cabin with double or twin beds, a small writing table, and a private bathroom. You also get good
company, cocktails with conversation, hearty food

(you'll eat in one seating with the ship's officers), an interesting voyage, a lot of water, and the allure of days at sea. What don't you get? Organized entertainment. You will certainly have time to relax and read books (some freighters have a small library), as well as observe the small crew as they help with loading, unloading, and constant upkeep, rust control and maintenance.

The accommodation will consist of a spacious, well-equipped outside-view cabin high above the water line, with a large window rather than a porthole, comfortable lounge/sitting area, and private facilities – far larger than most standard cruise ship cabins are.

How much does it cost?

On a per day basis, cargo ship travel costs between $125 and $200. The fares are mostly estimated, with final fares provided prior to sailing. If you book with a US specialist, and the cargo ship line is based in euros, there may be an additional cost depending on the rate of conversion when final payment is due.

A 28-day round-trip sailing aboard one of four CMA-CGM container vessels (Le Havre, France, to Guadeloupe and Martinique), for example, costs just over $120 (€83) per person, per day in a twin-bedded cabin, and slightly more in a single-occupancy cabin, plus any expenses incurred in getting to/from the embarkation and disembarkation ports.

Remember that voyages last much longer – typically 30 days or more – so the cost can be considerable. Most are sold out more than a year ahead – two years for some routes – and the cargo-carrying fleet has been reduced as a result of the credit crunch, so plan wisely, and remember to purchase trip cancellation insurance.

What to bring

What to take with you? Casual clothing (check with the shipping line, as some require a jacket and tie for din-

ner), all medications, cosmetics, and toiletry items, hairdryer, multi-voltage converter plug, washing powder, and other sundry items such as soap, sun protection, insect repellent, and small flashlight. There may be a small "shop" on board (for the crew) carrying bare essentials like toothpaste.

Bring along your medical certificate, travel insurance details, money in cash, and some extra photos of yourself in case the ship makes unannounced port stops and visas are required. The only gratuities needed are for the waiter and cabin steward, which are generally set at about $1–$2 per day, per person.

New international security regulations mean that if you book a one-way voyage, you must have all onward travel documents with you. Check with embassies and consulates of the countries you will visit. Note that freighters visit cargo ports, so private transportation such as taxis will need to be arranged in advance.

Cargo ships sometimes have to cancel port calls for commercial reasons at short notice. Bear this in mind if you're attracted by a particular itinerary or port. ❏

ABOVE: the *Hatsu Crystal* carries five passengers.
BELOW: *Aranui 3* off Fatu Hiva in French Polynesia.

RIVER CRUISING

More than 1 million people a year take a river or inland waterway cruise, making this one of the industry's fastest-growing sectors

Whether you want to cruise down the Nile, along the mighty Amazon or the lesser Orinoco, the stately Volga or the magnificent Rhine or the "blue" Danube, along the mystical Ayeyarwady (formerly the Irrawaddy) or the "yellow" Yangtze – to say nothing of the Don and the Dnieper, the Elbe, or Australia's Murray – there are more than 1,000 river cruise vessels to choose from.

What sort of person enjoys cruising aboard these vessels? Well, anyone who survives well without formal dinners, bingo, casinos, discos, or lavish entertainment, and those who want a totally unstructured lifestyle.

The plus points
● You need to pack and unpack only once.
● Rivercruise vessels to enable you to enjoy the ever-changing scenery (the "riverscape"), all at eye level.
● You'll wake up in a different place each day, often in the very heart of a city or town.
● You never have to take a tender ashore – you simply step off the vessel when it ties up.
● The atmosphere on board is friendly and informal, never stuffy or pretentious.

Cologne-based 1AVista Reisen permits dogs on certain cruises.

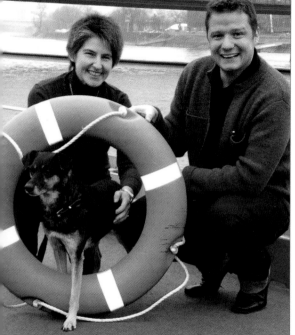

● Cruising along one of the world's rivers is a delightful way to unwind at a slow pace.
● The ride is typically silky smooth – there's no rolling like aboard many of the ocean-going cruise ships, so you won't suffer from seasickness.
● Good food and service are essential elements of a successful river cruise operation.
● All meals are provided, typically in a self-serve buffet arrangement for breakfast and lunch, with sit-down service for dinner. Additionally, basic table wines may also be included for lunch and dinner – included wines are typical of the German river cruise operators or cruise/tour packagers.
● Almost all cabins have outside views; there are virtually no interior (no view) cabins, as aboard most of the ocean-going cruise ships.
● A whole range of optional, extra-cost excursions is available, while some excursions may be included.
● You will typically sail by day, and dock at night (exceptions: Danube and Russian river cruises, where most vessels sail at night), so you can get a restful sleep without engine noise. However, bear in mind that, if your cabin is toward the aft, there may well be the soft humming of a generator, which supplies power for air-conditioning, heating, water supply, lighting, and cooking.
● You can, if you wish, leave the vessel in the evening to go out to dinner, or to the cinema, theater or a concert (exceptions: Danube and Russian river cruises).
● Rivers provide a sense of continuity – difficult to achieve from a coach tour, where you may change lodgings each night, and encounter border crossings. Also, while on board, you deal in a single currency.
● The dress code is completely casual.

The minus points
● The flow of water in almost all rivers cannot always be controlled, so there will be times when the water level is so low that even a specially constructed rivercruise vessel, with its shallow draft, cannot travel.
● If you are tall, note that the beds aboard most rivercruise vessels are less than 6ft (1.8 meters) long.
● Don't wear white. Rivercruise vessels are long and low, which means that their funnels are also low. Soot, created by the emissions

Michelangelo, on a lagoon cruise, visits Venice.

from diesel engines and generators, can be a problem, particularly at the stern of a vessel, and on the upper (open) deck.

● Aboard some of the vessels that have an aft, open but sheltered deck area, or an open upper deck – almost all rivercruise vessels have one – smokers may be seated next to you. Few vessels distinguish between smoking and non-smoking areas outdoors, though almost none allow smoking in the public rooms.

● Depending on the vessel, river, the operating company, and tour operators that send passengers to the vessels, there could be passengers of several nationalities. Communication could be a problem if you don't speak the same language.

European river cruising

Cruising down one of Europe's great waterways is a soothing experience – different from sailing on an open sea, where wave motion is a factor. These cruises provide a constant change of scenery, often passing through several countries, each with its own history and architecture, in a week-long journey.

River vessels are always close to land and provide a chance to visit cities and areas inaccessible to the large resort ships. A cruise along the Danube, for example, will take you through nine countries: Germany, Austria, Slovakia, Hungary, Croatia, Serbia, Romania, Bulgaria, and Ukraine.

The Rhine–Main–Danube waterway, at 2,175 miles (3,500km), is the longest waterway in Europe. It connects 14 countries, from Rotterdam on the North Sea to Sulina and Izmail on the Black Sea, and offers travelers varied and fascinating sights.

River vessels are long and low in the water, and

their masts fold down in order to negotiate low bridges. Although small when compared to ocean-going cruise ships, they have a unique and friendly international atmosphere. The most modern are air-conditioned and offer the discreet luxury of a small floating hotel, with several public rooms including a dining room, observation lounge, bar, heated swimming "dip" pool (some even have a small heated indoor pool), sauna, solarium, whirlpool, gymnasium, massage, hairdresser, and shop kiosk.

Although the cabins may be small, with limited closet space (take casual clothing, as informality is the order of the day), they are functional. Almost all have an outside view (facing the river), with a private bathroom, and will prove very comfortable for a one-week journey. Romantics may lament the fact that twin beds are the norm on the older vessels, but many cabins in the latest

WHAT GENDER IS A RIVER?

Whether a river is known as a he or a she depends on its behaviour. Take the River Rhône, for example – almost always referred to in the masculine because the waters can be turbulent, bothersome and rough at times. The Saône, on the other hand, is a gentler kind of river – more beautiful, more tranquil – and is thus referred to as "she," as is the "beautiful" Blue Danube (although Napoleon described the Danube as the "king of the rivers of Europe"). The Rhine is male, always referred to as "Father Rhine." The Nile is also deemed a masculine river. The River Volga is always referred to as the "dear little mother" (even though it is the mightiest river in Europe).

Rhine and Danube cruises take in the Christmas markets.

vessels have twin beds that can be converted to a queen-sized bed. They also have a safe, a mini-bar, flat-screen TV, and an alarm clock/radio.

River cruising in Europe has reached quite a sophisticated level, and you can be assured of good service and meals of a consistently good local standard. Dining is a pleasant if not a gourmet experience, although some companies (such as AMA Waterways and Avalon Waterways) are making strenuous efforts to provide fine cuisine. The best food is typically catered by Austrian, German, or Swiss companies. Breakfast and lunch are generally a buffet affair; dinners feature a set menu.

Typical fares for river cruises are from $800 to over $3,000 per person for a one-week cruise, including meals, cabin with private facilities, side trips, and airport/railway transfers. If you are already in Europe, many cruises can be purchased "cruise-only."

Theme cruises are gaining in popularity. For example, greenery lovers might enjoy the "Gardens of the Rhine," with visits to famous botanical gardens, arboretums and herbariums. There are cruises for classical and jazz music fans, gourmets (including a meal at top restaurants in France, for example), and wine lovers. Christmas Markets cruises in Germany are popular.

Although just a few years ago rivercruise vessels were little more than floating buses, today they have become like sophisticated, floating boutique hotels. While most are of the single-hull type (propulsion machinery, accommodation areas, and public rooms are all in one hull), new "twin-cruisers" have been introduced. These vessels have their power unit and navigation bridge located aft in a separate unit attached to the longer body that contains the accommodation areas and public rooms. Although this guarantees that every cabin will be ultra-quiet for sleeping, captains find that the vessels are not so easy to manoeuvre.

● **Tip:** To ensure a degree of peace and quiet, it is best to go for a cabin on a deck that doesn't have a promenade deck walkway outside it. Normally, cabins on the lowest deck have a four-berth configuration. It doesn't matter which side of the vessel you are on, as you will see a riverbank and scenery on either side.

Russia's rivers

The "Waterways of the Tsars" are a well-developed network of rivers, lakes, and canals. Geographically, river routes for tourists are divided into three main areas: Central European Russia, Northwestern European Russia, and Asian Russia. There are more than 80 river cruise vessels carrying international tourists.

In the Central Basin, Moscow is the hub of river tourism, and the newly opened waterways between Moscow and St Petersburg allow a seven-day cruise link between the present and former capitals, including the transit of the Volga-Baltic Canal System and its many locks. The best-known Russian rivers are the Don, Moskva, Neva, and Volga, but the lesser-known Belaya, Dvina (and North Dvina), Irtysh, Kama, Ob (longest river in Siberia), Oka, Svir, Tura, and Vyatka connect Russia's vast system of rivers and lakes.

Many Russian vessels are chartered to foreign cruise

THE BEST TIME TO CRUISE IN EUROPE AND ON THE NILE

There are advantages and disadvantages to every season in Europe. Early spring and late summer will be less crowded and can have beautiful weather. In July and August the weather is often more reliable, though it can be too hot for some and there are more crowds.

It's possible to time a river cruise to coincide with, say, the Rhine in Flames festival in high summer, or the paprika harvest in Hungary, or the beautiful autumn colors along the Danube's Wachau Valley. Special winter cruises operate on the Rhine and Danube to take in the Christmas markets – if you're lucky you'll get crisp, cool

It's cooler in Egypt between January and March.

weather and snow on the ground, but rain and slush are just as likely.

Russia tends to be hot and humid

in summer. Take insect repellent for travel in August and September, when midges can be a problem, and something warm to wear in the evening in spring and fall.

Nile cruises operate year-round, the peak months being January to March when it's cooler. August is really too hot for anybody except the most dedicated sun-worshipper. September is tolerable if you take things slowly, and there'll be hardly any crowds at the temples. Wearing shorts and a tank top might keep you cool, but they'll indicate a lack of respect if you wear them when visiting tombs and you may be hassled.

wholesalers and tour packagers, and dedicated to a specific onboard language. The vessels vary in quality and facilities. Some are air-conditioned and most are clean. Cruises include the services of a cruise manager and lecturers. Recommended vessels: *Volga Dream, Viking Kirov, Viking Pakhomov,* and *Viking Surkov*.

The Nile

The scenery has changed remarkably little in more than 2,000 years, and the best way to see it, of course, is from a river vessel. In all, there are over 7,000 departures every year aboard 300 or so Nile cruise vessels, which offer standards of comfort, food, and service that vary between very good and extremely poor. Most have a small, shallow "plunge" pool, lounge, piano bar, and disco.

A lecturer in ancient Egyptian history accompanies almost all sailings, which cruise the 140 miles (220km) downstream between Aswan and Luxor in three or four days. Extended cruises, of seven or eight days, cover about 295 miles (475km) and visit Dendera and Abydos. The longest cruises, of 10 to 12 days, cover 590 miles (950km) and may include visits to Sohag, El Amarna, Tuna El Gabal, and Ashmuneim, ending in Cairo.

Most Nile cruises include sightseeing excursions, accompanied by experienced guides who may reside on board, or who may meet the vessel at each call. Security in Egypt has been improved, but the terrorist threat remains, and it's wise to be vigilant. It's also prudent to subtract two stars from any rating provided in brochures or on cruise company and tour operator websites.

The best peak time to take a River Nile cruise is between December and February when the weather is hot but not quite so humid. However, if you go in March/April or October/early November, you'll find that the major hotels are not so crowded and it will be easier to get around. However, the water level can be low between October and May to conserve water at the Aswan Dam,

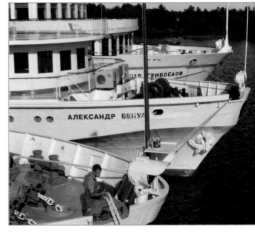

Riverships triple-parked on the Volga in Russia.

so getting through the locks at Esna can take a long time as rivercruise vessels compete with cargo vessels and feluccas to get through.

Gratuities are usually not included in the cruise fare, but any tips you give will be divided among all crew members. Some vessels accept credit cards for payment of your onboard account, but others accept only cash.

A few useful tips:

● When you visit the major historic sites and temples, note that there are few public toilet facilities. Toilet paper is not normally provided, so take tissues with you.

● Most Nile rivercruise vessels provide 220-volt outlets in cabins. If you have 110-volt appliances, take adapters (plugs have European-style two round pins).

● If you take a camera with you to any of the 62 tombs in the Valley of the Kings (only a few are open at any one time), you will need to buy a ticket for your camera, too. Museums and other major tourist sites also charge for the use of video and still cameras.

More triple-parking, on the Nile at Aswan.

THE BEST VIEWS

With a bit of cunning, you can secure a better view on a Nile cruise. As vessels head north from Aswan to Luxor, they almost always tie up on the river's left bank – except in Aswan, where they tie up on the right bank. Also, they tend to moor two or three deep. But if you ask for a starboard cabin and your vessel gets the outside position, your view across the Nile while you are in port – particularly in Luxor, where you will spend a couple of nights – will be uninterrupted. In a port cabin, all you would see would be the river bank or the vessel tied up next to you. Reverse this logic for southbound cruises.

There are several operators, but do check on the facilities, meet-and-greet service, and the newness of the vessels before booking. The best time of the year to go is May–June, and late August–October (July and early August are extremely hot and humid). However, in the Yangtze Valley, temperatures between April and September can reach 97°F (36°C), and summer rains can be torrential. Monsoons – seasonally changing winds – dominate the region's weather conditions.

River Murray, Australia

The fifth-largest river in the world, the Murray was the lifeblood of the pioneers who lived on the driest continent on earth. Today, the river flows for more than 1,250 miles (2,760km) across a third of Australia, its banks forming protected lagoons for an astonishing variety of bird and animal life. A paddlewheel boat such as *Murray Princess* even has six cabins for the physically disabled.

Barge cruising in Europe

Smaller and more intimate than river vessels and more accurately called boats, "cruise barges" ply the inland waterways and canals of Europe from spring to fall, when the weather is best. Barge cruises (usually lasting three to 13 days) offer a completely informal atmosphere, and a slow pace of life, for up to a dozen passengers. They chug along slowly in the daytime, and moor early each evening, giving you time to pay a visit to a local village and get a restful night's sleep.

Most cruise barges are comfortable and beautifully fitted out with rich wood paneling, full carpeting, custom-built furniture and tastefully chosen fabrics. Each has a dining room or lounge-bar. Captains take pride in their vessel, often displaying rare memorabilia.

Locally grown fresh foods are usually purchased and prepared each day, allowing you to live well and feel like a houseguest. Dining ranges from home-style cook-

A Yangtze cruise boards on a typically misty morning.

China's rivers

More than 50 vessels offer cruises along the Yangtze, the world's third-longest river. The most popular include the area known as the Three River Gorges, a 100-mile (160-km) stretch between Nanjin Pass in the east and White King City in the west.

The Yangtze stretches 3,900 miles (6,300km) from Shanghai through the very heartland of China. The Three Gorges include the 47-mile-long (76-km) Xiling Gorge, the 25-mile-long (40-km) Wu Gorge, and the 28-mile-long (45-km) Qutang Gorge, known locally as "Wind Box Gorge." The Lesser Three Gorges (or Three Small Gorges) are also an impressive sight, often part of the main cruise but also reached by small vessels from Wushan. If possible, take a cabin with a balcony. It is worth the extra money, and the view is better.

Standards of hygiene are generally far lower than you may be used to at home. In China, rats and rivers often go together, and rat poison may well be found under your bed. Some vessels, such as those of Viking River Cruises, have Chinese- and Western-style restaurants, a beauty salon, a small health club with sauna, and private mahjong and karaoke rooms. Fine Asian hospitality and service prevail, and cabins are kept supplied with fresh towels and hot tea.

Murray Princess paddles along Australia's Murray River.

Tranquility on the Burgundy Canal in France.

ing to some outstanding nouvelle cuisine, with all the trimmings. Often, the barge's owner, or spouse, cooks. Most cruise barges can be chartered exclusively so you can just take your family and friends. The waterways of France especially offer beauty, tranquility, and a diversity of interests, and barge cruising is an excellent way of exploring an unfamiliar area. Most cruises include a visit to a famous vineyard and wine cellar, as well as side trips to places of historic, architectural, or scenic interest. Shopping opportunities are limited; evening entertainment is impromptu.

Barging on the canals often means going through a constant succession of locks. Nowhere is this more enjoyable and entertaining than in the Burgundy region of France where, between Dijon and Mâcon, for example, a barge can negotiate as many as 54 locks during a six-day cruise. Interestingly, all lock-keepers in France are women.

Rates range from $600 to more than $3,000 per person for a six-day cruise. I don't recommend taking children. Rates include a cabin with private facilities, all meals, good wine with lunch and dinner, all other beverages, use of bicycles, side trips, and airport or railway transfers. Some operators provide a hotel the night before or after the cruise. Clothing is totally casual – but, at the beginning and end of the season, it's a good idea to take sweaters and rain gear.

United States

Although the former Delta Queen Steamboat Company no longer exists and the steamboats stopped operating in 2008, a small American company, American Cruise Lines, bought the *Columbia Queen, Empress of the North,* and *Queen of the West* steamboats in 2009, and started operations in 2010 on the Columbia and Snake rivers in the Pacific Northwest. So, the (faux) steamboat era lives on – just not on the Mississippi. The company is also building a brand new riverboat, to be introduced in 2012. ❑

RIVER CRUISING: WHO TO CONTACT

This is a complicated sector, with product details changing frequently and river cruise operators chartering their vessels to many different tour operators. The websites below will help you find what's available in your preferred destination.

EUROPE	RUSSIA AND UKRAINE
AMA Waterways	**Noble Caledonia**
www.amawaterways.com	www.noblecaledonia.com
APT Waterways	**Uniworld**
www.aptwaterways.com	www.uniworld.com
A'Rosa Cruises	**Viking River Cruises**
www.arosa.de	www.vikingrivercruises.com
Avalon Waterways	
www.avalonwaterways.com	**CHINA (YANGTZE)**
CroisiEurope	
www.croisieurope.com	**Noble Caledonia**
Feenstra Rhine Line	www.noblecaledonia.com
www.feenstrarijnlijn.nl	**Uniworld**
Grand Circle Travel	www.uniworld.com
www.gct.com	**Victoria Cruises**
Leuftner Cruises	www.victoriacruises.com
www.leuftner-cruises.com	**Viking River Cruises**
Phoenix Reisen	www.vikingrivercruises.com
www.poenixreisen.com	
Scenic Tours	**EGYPT (THE NILE)**
www.scenictours.com	
Scylla Tours	**Hilton Hotels**
www.scylla-tours.com	www.hiltonhotels.com
Sea Cloud Cruises	**Movenpick**
www.seacloud.com	www.movenpick-nilecruises.com
Tauck Tours	**Nabila Tours**
www.tauck.com	www.nabila.com/en
Uniworld	**Noble Caledonia**
www.uniworld.com	www.noblecaledonia.com
Victoria Cruises	**Oberoi Hotels**
www.victoriacruises.com	www.oberoihotels.com/cruises.asp
Viking River Cruises	**Sonesta Hotels**
www.vikingrivercruises.com	www.sonesta.com/nilecruises

AROUND-THE-WORLD CRUISES

**They sound like a great way to see the world without
having to pack and unpack constantly. But choose
carefully: some cruises spend very little time in ports**

Since Cunard operated its first world cruise aboard the *Laconia* in 1922, this has become the ultimate classic voyage. It is defined as the complete circumnavigation of the earth in a continuous one-way voyage, typically including both the Panama and the Suez Canals. Ports of call are carefully planned for their interest and diversity, and the entire voyage can last six months or longer.

Galas, themed balls, special social events, top entertainers, and, typically, well-known lecturers are all part of the package. It's a great way of exchanging the northern winter for the southern sun in a grand voyage that is

Ports of call: Barcelona, Spain; Lima, Peru.

over 32,000 nautical miles long, following in the wake of Ferdinand Magellan, who led his round-the-world voyage in 1519–22 (he himself was killed en route).

Around-the-world cruises – they are considered voyages more than cruises – pursue the sun in a westbound direction. This gives an added bonus: that of gaining an hour each time a ship goes into the next time zone. Travel in an eastbound direction – between, for example, Europe and Australia – and you lose an hour each time.

A world cruise aboard a modern ship means enjoying stabilized, air-conditioned comfort in luxury cabins, combined with extraordinary sightseeing and excursions on

shore and overland. Aboard some ships, every passenger gets to dine with the captain at least once. Such a cruise is all about experiencing a special annual event – cruise lines typically operate only one world cruise a year – exchanging familiar environments with new ones, glamorous evening soirées, special social parties, black-and-white-themed balls, and entertainment that ranges from intimate recitals to large-scale shows and headline cabaret specialty acts.

It's also about socializing, meeting new friends – and perhaps old ones, if you have previously taken a long cruise. There'll be lots of sea days, during which your suite or cabin can be a private refuge, so it's worth choosing the best you can afford.

There are four aspects to a good world cruise: itinerary, price, ship, and the cruise line's experience.

Some of the most ambitious itineraries are those operated by the German cruise lines such as Hapag-Lloyd Cruises, Phoenix Reisen, and Transocean Tours. But check brochures and itineraries carefully, because some ships spend surprisingly little time in port. On *Arcadia*'s 83-day grand voyage in 2011 (Southampton to Southampton), for example, only two port calls include an overnight stay.

World cruise segments

If you want to experience all the extra things that around-the-world cruises provide but don't have the three months needed, you should know that most lines offer the cruise in several "segments." This also allows you to "test" the ship and service levels before investing the time and money needed for a full circumnavigation. *Queen Mary 2*, for example, offers 16 segments on its 2012 around-the-world cruise, from 16 nights to 73 nights. The most popular length for a segment is around 30 days.

"Segmenters," as they are often called, typically add on a stay pre- or post-cruise in a destination combining a cruise 'n' stay vacation. In this way they can visit exotic destinations such as China, the South Pacific, the Indian Ocean, or South America while enjoying elegance, comfort, splendid food, and good company.

Bear in mind that you tend to get what you pay for. Ships rated at four stars or more will probably include shuttle buses from your ship to town centers; ships rated three stars or less will not.

Ships that roam worldwide during the year offer the most experienced world cruises or segments. Most operate at about 75% capacity, providing much more space per person than they could normally expect.

Calculating the cost

Prices for a full world cruise vary depending on the cruise line, ship, and accommodation chosen. The following examples are taken from 2012 world cruise brochures (per person rates are quoted, based on double occupancy, but single occupancy rates are typically available on request):

● *Queen Mary 2* (108 nights: from £11,699).
● *Saga Ruby* (114 nights: from £16,201).
● *Seabourn Quest* (109 days: from $107,700).

Sydney, Singapore, St Petersburg, Vietnam.

Naturally, substantial discounts (up to 50%) and special incentives are offered by many cruise lines, particularly if you book early – the earlier the better. In today's difficult economic times, it's the lowest-grade cabins

that tend to sell out fastest. Some cruise lines quote only a "from" price as a lead-in rate, and provide the price for the large suites only on application.

Passengers who book a full world cruise will probably enjoy a pre-cruise five-star hotel stay and extravagant dinner with the cruise line's top executives, onboard credit, plus other special events during the cruise (not available to "segmenters"). Note that some cruise lines reserve the right to add a surcharge if the NYNEX oil price exceeds $70 a barrel – read the fine print in the brochure. Also, the lowest prices may not include the airfare, if any is required.

Some ships include alcoholic drinks and wine in their cruise fares (examples include *Seabourn Quest, Seven Seas Voyager, Silver Spirit*), but most do not. There will inevitably be the question of gratuities to staff, which are included for the 2012 world cruises aboard *Albatros, Amadea, Asuka II, Seabourn Quest, Seven Seas Voyager* and *Silver Spirit*. You'll need to factor in about $10 per person, per day to your budget for these. On a 90-day world cruise, that's $1,800. If you are in one of the largest suites, it would be considerably more – allow about $3,000 per couple. ❏

AROUND THE WORLD CRUISES 2012

Ship	Company	Days	Date	From (Start)	Date (Finish)	To	Direction	No. of Ports
Albatros	Phoenix Reisen	119	Dec 18, 2011	Hamburg	Apr 15, 2012	Monte Carlo	Westbound	58
Amadea	Phoenix Reisen	139	Dec 18, 2011	Hamburg	May 5, 2012	Venice	Westbound	69
Amsterdam	Holland America Line	117	Jan 6, 2012	Fort Lauderdale	Apr 28, 2012	Fort Lauderdale	Westbound	38
Asuka II	NYK Cruises	97	Apr 2, 2012	Yokohama	July 8, 2012	Yokohama	Westbound	25
Aurora	P&O Cruises	99	Jan 4, 2012	Southampton	Apr 12, 2012	Southampton	Westbound	37
Black Watch	Fred Olsen Cruise Lines	106	Jan 11, 2012	Southampton	Apr 26, 2012	Southampton	Eastbound	32
Columbus	Hapag-Lloyd Cruises	175	Nov 13, 2011	Rio de Janeiro	May 7, 2012	Nice	Westbound	84
Costa Deliziosa	Costa Cruises	100	Jan 6, 2012	Savona	Jan 1, 2012	Savona	Westbound	36
Crystal Serenity *	Crystal Cruises	94	Jan 18, 2012	Los Angeles	Apr 21, 2012	Los Angeles	Westbound	35
Dawn Princess	Princess Cruises	104	May 25, 2012	Sydney	Sept 7, 2012	Sydney	Westbound	44
Europa	Hapag-Lloyd Cruises	138	Nov 19, 2011	Lisbon	Apr 6, 2012	Dubai	Westbound	70
Oriana	P&O Cruises	98	Jan 5, 2012	Southampton	Apr 10, 2012	Southampton	Eastbound	32
Pacific Princess	Princess Cruises	107	Jan 13, 2012	Fort Lauderdale	Apr 30, 2012	Venice	Westbound	44
Queen Elizabeth	Cunard Line	107	Jan 10, 2012	Southampton	Apr 27, 2012	Southampton	Eastbound	41
Queen Mary 2 **	Cunard Line	108	Jan 10, 2012	Southampton	Apr 27, 2012	Southampton	Eastbound	35
Saga Ruby	Saga Cruises	114	Jan 6, 2012	Southampton	Apr 30, 2012	Southampton	Westbound	38
Seabourn Quest	Seabourn	109	Jan 5, 2012	Fort Lauderdale	Apr 23, 2012	Venice	Westbound	38
Silver Spirit	Silversea Cruises	116	Jan 7, 2012	Fort Lauderdale	Apr 16, 2012	Monte Carlo	Westbound	43
Silver Whisper	Silversea Cruises	116	Jan 6, 2012	Fort Lauderdale	May 1, 2012	Monte Carlo	Westbound	43
Sun Princess	Princess Cruises	104	May 16, 2012	Sydney	Aug 29, 2012	Sydney	Westbound	41

* Grand Circle Pacific cruise   ** Not including North or South America

Choosing the Right Cruise

CHOOSING THE RIGHT SHIP

What's the difference between large and small ships? Are new ships
better than older ones? Should you consider a maiden voyage?
Is corporate cruising good value? Are theme cruises fun?

Which ship? There's something to suit virtually all tastes, so take into account your own personality and tastes. Ships are measured (not weighed) in gross tonnage (gt) and come in four principal size categories:

● **Large Resort Ships:** for 1,600–6,400 passengers (typically measure 50,000–220,000 gross tonnage). *Think:* double-decker bus (with some seats that are better than others).
● **Mid-Size Ships**: for 600–1,600 passengers (typically 25,000–50,000 gross tonnage). *Think:* long-distance coach (comfortable seats).
● **Small Ships**: for 200–600 passengers (typically 5,000–25,000 gross tonnage). *Think:* mini-van (some are executive types; some are more mainstream).
● **Boutique Ships**: for up to 200 passengers (typically 1,000–5,000 gross tonnage). *Think:* private car (luxury, mid-range, or compact).

Space

For an idea of the amount of the space around you, check the Passenger Space Ratio given for each ship in the listings section (gross tonnage divided by number of passengers). A Passenger Space Ratio of **50 and above** is the ultimate; **30 to 50** is very spacious; **20 to 30** is reasonably spacious; **10 to 20** is high density; and **10 or below** is extremely cramped.

LARGE RESORT SHIPS
(1,600–6,400 passengers)

Choose a large resort ship if you like being with lots of other people, in a bustling big-city environment, you enjoy being sociable, and want to have plenty of entertainment and dining (no, make that eating) options. These balcony-rich ships provide a well-packaged standard or premium vacation, usually in a seven-day cruise. It is the interaction between passengers and crew that determines the quality of the onboard experience.

Large resort ships have extensive facilities and programs for families with children of all ages. But if you meet someone on the first day

and want to see them again, make sure you appoint a very specific place and time (apart from the size of the ship, they may be at a different meal seating). These ships have a highly structured array of activities and passenger participation events each day, together with large entertainment venues, and the most lavish production shows at sea.

It is in the standard of service, entertainment, lecture programs, level of communication, and finesse in dining services that really can move these ships into high rating categories, but they must be exceptional to do so. Choose higher-priced suite accommodation and the service improves. In other words: pay more, get more.

Large resort ships are highly programmed. It is difficult, for example, to go swimming in the late evening, or after dinner – decks are cleaned and pools are often netted over by 6pm. Having champagne delivered to outdoor hot tubs late at night is virtually impossible. They have lost the flexibility for which cruise ships were once known, becoming victims of company "policy" legislation and insurance regulations. There can be a feeling of "conveyor-belt" cruising, with cultural offerings scarcely extending beyond rap, rock, alcohol, and gambling.

LEFT: *Costa Victoria* in Mykonos, Greece.
RIGHT: the large resort ships stage the most lavish Vegas-style shows.

LARGE RESORT SHIPS: Advantages

● Have the widest range of public rooms and facilities, often a walk-around promenade deck outdoors, and more space (but more passengers).
● Generally have more dining options.
● The newest ships have state-of-the-art electronic interactive entertainment facilities – good if you like computers and high-tech gadgetry.
● Generally sail well in open seas in bad weather.
● There are more facilities and activities for people of all ages, particularly for families with children.

LARGE RESORT SHIPS: Disadvantages

● Finding your way around the ship can be frustrating, and signage is often confusing.
● Lines to wait in: for embarkation, the information desk, elevators, informal buffet meals, fast food grills, shore tenders, shore excursions, security checkpoint (when returning to the ship), immigration, and disembarkation.
● They resemble floating hotels (but with constant announcements), and so many items cost extra. They are like retail parks surrounded by cabins.
● No matter how big your suite is, or how many public rooms the ship has, you can't help feeling like just one of the crowd, and the individual attention or recognition is missing. You have to mingle with all the other passengers, who may be paying less, in the public rooms.
● The itineraries may be limited by ship size, and there are typically too many tender ports where you need to take a number, sit in a lounge and wait, and wait.
● There will be a lack of elevators at peak times.
● The larger the ship, the more impersonal the service – except for "butler" service in penthouse suites.
● You may have to use a sign-up sheet to use gym equipment such as treadmills or exercise bikes.

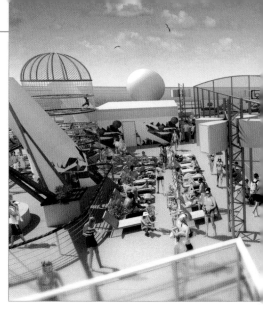

The sports deck on the new *Norwegian Epic*.

● There are too many announcements – and they could be in several languages.
● Dining room staff are so trained to provide fast service that it's almost impossible to dine in leisurely fashion.
● Food may well be bland – cooking for 5,000 is not quite the same as cooking for a dinner party of eight.
● Telephoning room service can be frustrating, particularly in ships with automatic telephone answering systems that state "your call will be answered by room service personnel in the order it was received."
● Room service breakfast is not generally available on the day of disembarkation.
● In early evening, the deckchairs are taken away, or strapped up so they can't be used.
● The in-cabin music aboard the latest ships is supplied through the television set, and it may be impossible to turn off the picture while listening.
● Some large resort ships have only two main passenger staircases. In an emergency, the evacuation of more than 4,000 passengers could be difficult.
● Waiting for a tender to take you ashore in "anchor" ports can be tiresome.
● Immigration line-up in ports of call such as St Thomas is tedious.

MID-SIZE SHIPS (600–1,600 passengers)

These suit the smaller ports of the Aegean and Mediterranean, and are more maneuverable than larger ships. Several operate around-the-world cruises and other long-distance itineraries to exotic destinations not really feasible aboard many small ships or large resort ships.

There is a big difference in the amount of space available. Accommodation varies from large "penthouse suites" complete with butler service to tiny interior (no-view) cabins. These ships will generally

MSC Sinfonia, though large, still offers solitude on balconies.

be more stable at sea than "small ships," due to their increased size and draft. They provide more facilities, more entertainment, and more dining options. There is some entertainment and more structured activities than aboard small ships, but less than aboard large resort ships.

MID-SIZE SHIPS: Advantages

● They are neither too large, nor too small; their size and facilities often strike a happy balance.
● It is easy to find one's way around.
● They generally sail well in areas of bad weather, being neither high-sided like the large resort ships, nor of too shallow draft like some of the small ships.
● Lines seldom form, except for ships approaching 1,600 passengers; if they do, they're likely to be relatively short.
● They appear more like traditional ships than most of the larger vessels, which tend to be more "boxy" in shape and profile.

MID-SIZE SHIPS: Disadvantages

● They don't offer as wide a range of public rooms and facilities as the large resort ships.
● Few have large showlounges for large-scale production shows, so entertainment tends to be more of the cabaret variety.

BOUTIQUE SHIPS (50–200 passengers) and SMALL SHIPS (200–600 passengers)

Choose a boutique or small ship for an intimate cruise experience and a small number of passengers. Some of the world's most exclusive cruise ships belong in this group – but so do most of the coastal vessels with basic, unpretentious amenities, sail-cruise ships, and the expedition-style cruise vessels that take passengers to see nature.

Select this size of ship if you don't need much entertainment, large resort ship facilities, gambling casinos, several restaurants, and if you don't like

to wait in lines for anything. If you want to swim in the late evening, or have champagne in the hot tub at midnight, it's easier aboard boutique or small ships than aboard larger ships, where more rigid programs lead to inflexible, passenger-unfriendly thinking.

BOUTIQUE/SMALL SHIPS: Advantages

● They're more like small inns than mega-resorts.
● It's easy to find your way around, and signage is usually clear and concise.
● At their best in warm weather areas.
● Capable of true culinary excellence, with fresh foods cooked individually to order.
● Most provide an "open seating" in the dining room; this means that you can sit with whomever you wish, whenever you wish, for all meals.
● Provide a totally unstructured lifestyle, offering a level of service not found aboard most of the larger ships, and no – or almost no – announcements.
● Provide an "open bridge" policy, allowing passengers to go to the navigation bridge when safe to do so.
● Some small ships have a hydraulic marina water-sports platform at the stern and carry equipment such as jet skis, windsurfers, a water-ski powerboat, and scuba and snorkeling gear.
● They can visit the more off-beat ports of call that larger ships can't get into.
● When the ship is at anchor, going ashore is easy and speedy, with a continuous tender service and no lines.
● Less crowded ports mean more exclusivity.

BOUTIQUE/SMALL SHIPS: Disadvantages

● They don't have the bulk, length, or beam to sail well in open seas in inclement weather conditions.
● They don't have the range of public rooms or open

A yoga class aboard the mid-size *Crystal Serenity*.

Corporate cruising with attitude: *Majesty of the Seas* hosts a 70,000 Tons of Metal festival cruise in 2011.

spaces that the large resort ships can provide. Options for entertainment, therefore, are limited.

What about age?

A ship built before 1990 is considered old. However, its quality depends on the level of maintenance it has received, and whether it has operated on short or longer cruises – short cruises get more passenger throughput, and so more wear and tear. Many passengers like older ships, as they tend to have fewer synthetic materials in their interior decor. It's inevitable that some older tonnage can't match the latest in high-tech, but today's ships aren't built with the same loving care as in the past.

Most cruise advertising you'll see revolves around the newer, larger ships, but some older ships have much to offer if you don't want the latest trendy facilities and city high street feel. Indeed, some of the older, smaller ships have adequate facilities, tend to have more character, and provide a more relaxing vacation experience than the go-go-go contemporary ships, where you're just one of a large crowd.

Newer ships (post-1990): Advantages

● Incorporate the latest in high-tech electronic equipment and in advanced ship design and construction.
● Meet the latest safety and operating standards.
● Typically have "pod" propulsion system, which replaces conventional propeller shafts, propellers and rudders, with the result that there is little or no vibration *(details: page 191)*.
● Have more interior public rooms, and maybe no exterior promenade deck.
● More standardized cabin layouts, fewer categories.
● Are more fuel-efficient.
● Have a shallower draft, which makes it easier for them to enter and leave ports.

● Have bow and stern thrusters, so they seldom require tug assistance in many ports, reducing operating costs.
● Have good plumbing and air-conditioning systems.
● Have the latest submersible lifeboats.

New ships: Disadvantages

● Do not "take the weather" as well as older ships – sailing across the North Atlantic in November on one of the new large resort ships can be unforgettable. Because of their shallow draft, these ships roll, even when there's the slightest puff of wind.
● Tend to have smaller standard cabins, which can mean narrow, short beds.
● Have decor made mostly from synthetic materials, due to stringent regulations, and could cause problems for passengers sensitive to such materials.
● Have thin hulls and do not withstand the bangs and dents as well as older, more heavily plated vessels.
● Have toilets of the powerful vacuum suction "barking dog" type.
● Are powered mainly by diesel or diesel-electric engines, which can cause some vibration; although on the latest vessels, the engines are mounted on pliable, floating rubber cushions and are, therefore, virtually vibration-free.
● Have cabin windows that are completely sealed instead of portholes that can be opened.

Pre-1990 ships: Advantages

● Have strong, plated hulls that can withstand tremendously hard wear and tear; they "take the weather" well.
● Have large cabins with long, wide beds/berths, because passengers needed more space in the days when voyages were much longer.
● Have toilets that are of the "gentle flush" variety instead of today's "barking dog" vacuum toilets.
● Have interiors built from traditional materials such as wood and brass, with less use of synthetic fibers, so are less likely to affect anyone allergic to synthetics.

● Have deep drafts that help them to achieve a smooth ride in the open seas.

Pre-1990 ships: Disadvantages

● They are not so fuel-efficient and therefore are more expensive to operate than new ships.
● Need a larger crew, because of the more awkward, labor-intensive layouts of the ships.
● Have a deep draft (necessary for a smooth ride) but need tugs to negotiate ports and tight berths.
● Have a tough job complying with current international fire, safety, and environmental regulations.
● Are fitted with older-type open lifeboats.

The crew

You can estimate the standard of service by looking at the crew-to-passenger ratio (provided in the ship profiles in this book). The best service levels are aboard ships that have a ratio of one crew member to every two passengers, or higher. The best ships in the world, from the point of view of crew living and working conditions, also tend to be the most expensive ones – the adage "you get what you pay for" tends to be all too true.

Most ships, with one or two exceptions, have multinational crews. Indeed, the crew mixture can resemble a miniature United Nations. However, if the crew is happy, the ship will be happy, too, and that will communicate itself to passengers.

Corporate cruising

Corporate, incentive organizations and seagoing conferences need to have such things as accommodation, food, or entertainment for their delegates organized as one contract, and cruise companies have specialized departments to deal with all the details. Helpfully, many larger ships have almost identical cabin sizes and configurations.

Once a corporate contract is signed, no refund is possible, so insurance is essential. Although you may need to charter only 70 percent of a ship's capacity for your purposes, you will have to pay for the whole ship if you want an *exclusive* charter.

Although you can contact cruise lines directly, I strongly recommend contacting the professionals at www.seasite.com, which contains all cruise brands designed for event planners by the Miami-based ship charter specialists Landry & Kling. You can download a Meeting Planner Guide for ships from the website.

Maiden and inaugural voyages

It can be fun to take part in the maiden voyage of a new cruise ship, or in joining the inaugural voyage of a refurbished, reconstructed, or stretched vessel – if you have a degree of tolerance and don't mind some

inconvenience, slow or nonexistent service in the dining room. Otherwise, wait until the ship has been in service for at least three months. Then again, if you book a cruise on the third or fourth voyage and the ship's introduction is delayed, you could find yourself on the maiden voyage.

One thing is certain: any maiden voyage is a collector's item, but Murphy's Law – "If anything can go wrong, it will" – can prevail. For example:

● Service aboard new or recently refurbished ships (or a new cruise line) is likely to be uncertain and could be a disaster. An existing cruise line may use experienced crew from its other vessels to help "bring out" a new ship, but they may be unfamiliar with the ship's layout and may have problems training other staff.
● Plumbing and electrical items tend to cause the most problems, particularly aboard reconstructed and refurbished vessels. Examples: toilets that don't flush or don't stop flushing; faucets incorrectly marked, where "hot" really means "cold"; and "automatic" telephones that refuse to function.
● In the entertainment department, items such as spare spotlight bulbs may not be in stock. Or what if the pianos arrive damaged, or "flip" charts for the lecturers didn't show up? Manuals for high-tech sound and lighting equipment may be in a foreign language.
● Items such as menus, postcards, writing paper, or TV remote control units, door keys, towels, pillowcases, glassware, and even toilet paper may be lost in the bowels of the ship, or simply not ordered.
● The galley (kitchen) of a new ship is in trouble if the right supplies don't turn up on time. ❏

RIGHT: most crews today are thoroughly multinational.

CHOOSING THE RIGHT CABIN

Does cabin size count? Are suites sweeter than cabins?
How desirable is a balcony? What about location?

Ideally, you should feel at home when at sea, so it is important to choose the right accommodation, even if most of your time in it is spent with your eyes shut. Accommodation sizes range from a whopping 4,390 sq. ft (407 sq. meters) to a minuscule 60 sq. ft (5.5 sq. meters). Like houses ashore, all cabins have good and bad points. Choose wisely, for if you find your cabin (incorrectly called a "stateroom" by some companies) is too small when you get to the ship, it may be impossible to change it or to upgrade, as the ship could be full. As for the best location, the upper decks are more expensive.

Cruise lines designate cabins only when deposits have been received – they may, however, guarantee the grade and rate requested. If this isn't done, or if you find a disclaimer such as "All cabin assignments are confirmed upon embarkation of the vessel," get a guarantee in writing that your cabin will *not* be changed on embarkation.

There are three main types of accommodation, but many variations on each theme:
● **Suites**: the largest living spaces, typically with a private balcony; and "junior" suites, with or without a private balcony.

ABOVE: a balcony suite aboard *Black Watch*.

● **Outside-view cabins**: a large picture window or one or more portholes (with or without private balcony).
● **Interior (no-view) cabins**: so called because there is no window or porthole.

Are balconies worth it?

Romeo and Juliet thought so – and they're certainly addictive. A private balcony (or "veranda," "terrace," or "lanai"), for which you pay a premium, is just that. It is a mini-terrace adjoining your cabin where you can sit, enjoy the view, dine, or even have a massage.

Some private balconies aren't so private, however. Balconies not separated by full floor-to-ceiling partitions don't quite cut it (examples: *Carnival Destiny, Carnival Triumph, Carnival Victory, Maasdam, Oriana, Queen Mary 2, Ryndam, Seven Seas Mariner, Seven Seas Voyager, Statendam,* and *Veendam*). You could get noise or smoke from your neighbor. Some ships have balconies with full floor-to-ceiling privacy partitions and an outside light (example: *Celebrity Century*, some of whose partitions are full and others partial).

Many large resort ships have balconies too small to accommodate even two reclining chairs, and may have plastic or plain painted steel decking instead of traditional, more expensive teakwood decking. The average size of a cabin balcony aboard the large resort ships is about 9ft x 6ft (2.7 by 1.8 meters). But they can measure as much as 10 times that.

Some suites with forward-facing private balconies may not be so good, as the wind speed can make them all but unusable (examples: *Seabourn Legend, Seabourn Pride, Seabourn Spirit, Silver Cloud, Silver Shadow, Sil-*

ver Spirit, Silver Whisper, Silver Wind). And when the ship drops anchor in ports of call, the noise pollution can be deafening (examples: Silver Cloud, Silver Wind).

All private balconies (except "French," or "Juliet" balconies) have railings to lean on, but some have solid steel plates between railing and deck, so you can't look out to sea when seated (Costa Classica, Costa Romantica, Dawn Princess, Oceana, Sea Princess, and Sun Princess). Better are ships whose balconies have clear glass (Aurora, Brilliance of the Seas, Celebrity Century, Empress, Mein Schiff, Mein Schiff 2, Radiance of the Seas, and Serenade of the Seas) or horizontal bars.

A "French balcony" is one where the doors open to fresh air, but there's no balcony for you to step onto unless your feet are less than six inches long.

Balcony doors can be quite heavy and difficult to open. Many ships have doors that slide open (Celebrity Century, Crystal Serenity, Grand Princess, Norwegian Gem); a few have doors that open inwards (Seabourn Legend, Seabourn Spirit, Silver Cloud, Silver Wind); some have doors that open outwards (Eurodam, Legend of the Seas, Queen Elizabeth, Queen Victoria).

Upstairs and downstairs

With the introduction of Oasis of the Seas and sister ship Allure of the Seas, "loft" accommodation – living room downstairs and sleeping quarters upstairs – will become a "must have" among regulars. Although ships such as the retired QE2, Sagafjord, and Vistafjord (now Saga Ruby) had split suites, they never shouted the fact.

How much?

The cost of accommodation is directly related to the size of the cabin, its location, and the facilities and services.
● Each line implements its own system according to ship size, age, construction, and profit potential.
● Many cruise lines still do not give accurate cabin sizes in their brochures, but you will find the size range in the ship profiles in this book.
● It may be better to book a low-grade cabin on a good ship than a high-grade cabin on a poor ship.
● If you are in a party of three or more and don't mind sharing a cabin, you'll save a lot per person, so you may be able to afford a higher-grade cabin.

Cabin sizes

Cabins provide more or less the same facilities as hotel rooms, except space. Most owners favor large public rooms over cabins. In some smaller interior (no-view) and outside cabins, changing clothes is a challenge.

The latest ships have more standardized cabin sizes, because they are made in modular form. I consider 180 sq. ft (16.7sq. meters) to be the minimum acceptable size for a "standard" cabin today.

Cabin location

● An "outside-view" cabin is recommended for first-time passengers: an "interior" cabin has no portholes or windows, making it more difficult to orient you or to gauge the weather or time.
● Cabins in the center of a ship are more stable and tend to be noise- and vibration-free. Ships powered by diesel engines (i.e. most modern vessels) create and transmit some vibration, especially at the stern.
● Take into account personal habits when choosing the cabin location. If you like to go to bed early, avoid a cabin close to the disco. If you have trouble walking, choose a cabin close to the elevator.
● Generally, the higher the deck, the higher the cabin price, and the better the service. This is an inheritance from transoceanic times, when upper-deck cabins and suites were sunnier and warmer.
● Cabins at the front of a ship are slightly crescent-shaped, given that the outer wall follows the curvature of the ship's hull. But they can be exposed to early-morning noises, such as the anchor being dropped at ports where the ship is too big to dock.
● Cabins with interconnecting doors are fine for families or close friends, but the dividing wall is usually so thin you can hear the conversation next door.
● Many brochures indicate cabins with "obstructed views." Cabins on lower decks are closer to engine noise and heat, especially at the stern of the vessel and around the engine casing. In many older ships, elevators may not operate to the lowermost decks.

Facilities

Cabins provide some, or all, of the following:
● Private bathroom (generally small) with shower, wash-basin, and toilet. Higher-grade cabins and suites may have full-size bathtubs. Some have a whirlpool bath and/or bidet, a hairdryer, and more space.
● Multi-channel radio, TV (regular satellite channels or closed circuit), and DVD player.
● Two beds or a lower and upper berth (possibly,

Typical Cabin Layouts

The following rates are typical of those you can expect to pay for ⓐ a seven-day and ⓑ a 10-day Caribbean cruise aboard a modern cruise ship. The rates are per person and include free round-trip airfare or low-cost air add-ons from principal North American gateways

Luxury outside-view suite with private veranda, separate lounge area, vanity area, extra-large double or queen-size bed, bathroom with tub, shower, and extensive closet and storage space.

ⓐ **$1,750** ⓑ **$3,000**

Luxury outside-view suite with private veranda, separate lounge, vanity area, king- or queen-size bed, bathroom with full-sized tub and separate shower, and extensive walk-in closet and storage space (plus a guest bathroom). Typical size: 550 sq. ft (50 sq. meters).

ⓐ **$2,000** ⓑ **$3,000**

■ Note that in some ships, third- and fourth-person upper berths are available for families or friends wishing to share. The upper Pullman berths, not shown on these cabin layouts, are recessed into the wall or ceiling above the lower beds.

Large outside-view double with bed and convertible daytime sofabed, bathroom with shower, and good closet and drawer space. Typical size: 270 sq.ft (23 sq. meters).

ⓐ **$1,000** ⓑ **$2,000**

Junior suite with lounge, double or queen-size beds, bathroom with tub, shower, and ample closet and storage space. Typical size: 375 sq.ft (35 sq.meters).

ⓐ **$1,500** ⓑ **$2,000**

Interior no-view cabin with two lower beds convertible to queen-size bed (plus a possible upper third/fourth berth), bathroom with shower, and some closet space. Typical size: 160 sq.ft (15 sq.meters).

ⓐ **$600** ⓑ **$800**

another one or two upper berths) or a double, queen- or king-size bed. Some twin beds can be pushed together to form a double.

● Depending on cabin size, a chair, or chair and table, or sofa and table, or, in higher grades, even a separate lounge/sitting area.

● Phone, for inter-cabin or ship-to-shore calls.

● Refrigerator/wet bar (higher grades).

● Electrical outlets for personal appliances, usually 110 and/or 220 volts.

● Vanity/desk unit with chair or stool.

● Personal safe.

● Closet space, some drawer space, plus storage room under beds for suitcases.

● Bedside night stand/table unit.

● Towels, soap, shampoo, and conditioner. (Upscale ships provide a greater selection.)

Some ships have upper and lower berths. A "berth" is a nautical term for a bed held in a wooden or metal frame. A "Pullman berth" tucks away out of sight during the day, usually into the bulkhead or ceiling. You climb up a short ladder at night to get into an upper berth.

The suite life

Suites are the most luxurious and spacious of all shipboard accommodation, and typically come with butler service. A suite (in the sense of a "suite of rooms") should measure a *minimum* 400 sq. ft (37 sq. meters), and comprise a lounge or sitting room separated from a bedroom by a solid door (not just a curtain), a bedroom with a large bed, one or more bathrooms, and an

Penthouse suite aboard the 2,852-passenger *Celebrity Solstice*.

abundance of closet, drawer, and other storage space. The best suites have the most desirable position, privacy, and good views. Many cruise lines inaccurately describe some accommodation as suites, when they are nothing more than a large cabin with a curtain that divides sitting and sleeping areas.

Suites are best on long voyages with several days at sea. Be aware that, although the large resort ships may devote a whole deck or two to penthouses and suites, you will have to share the rest of the ship with those in lower-priced accommodation.

That means there is no preferential seating in the showroom, dining rooms, or on sunbathing decks. You may get separate check-in facilities and preferential treatment upon disembarkation, but your luggage will be lumped with everyone else's. ❑

THE LARGEST SUITES AT SEA			
Ship	**Cruise Line**	**Total (sq. ft)**	**Total (sq. m)**
Norwegian Dawn	Norwegian Cruise Line	4,390.0	407.8
Norwegian Gem	Norwegian Cruise Line	4,390.0	407.8
Norwegian Jade	Norwegian Cruise Line	4,390.0	407.8
Norwegian Jewel	Norwegian Cruise Line	4,390.0	407.8
Norwegian Pearl	Norwegian Cruise Line	4,390.0	407.8
Norwegian Star	Norwegian Cruise Line	4,390.0	407.8
Celebrity Constellation	Celebrity Cruises	2,530.0	235.0
Celebrity Infinity	Celebrity Cruises	2,530.0	235.0
Celebrity Millennium	Celebrity Cruises	2,530.0	235.0
Celebrity Summit	Celebrity Cruises	2,530.0	235.0
Queen Mary 2	Cunard Line	2,249.7	209.0
Freedom of the Seas	Royal Caribbean International	2,025.0	188.0
Independence of the Seas	Royal Caribbean International	2,025.0	188.0
Liberty of the Seas	Royal Caribbean International	2,025.0	188.0
Seven Seas Mariner	Regent Seven Seas Cruises	2,002.0	186.0
Marina	Oceania Cruises	2,000.0	185.8
Disney Dream	Disney Cruise Line	1,781.0	165.5
Disney Fantasy	Disney Cruise Line	1,781.0	165.5
Silver Spirit	Silversea Cruises	1,614.0	150.0
Celebrity Century	Celebrity Cruises	1,514.5	140.7
Celebrity Mercury	Celebrity Cruises	1,514.5	140.7

NOTES: 1. Sizes shown include balconies. 2. This list does not include the suites aboard ships such as The World, which are for residents and not normal cruise passengers.

Suites aboard *Silver Shadow* (top), *Norwegian Dawn* (above), and *Freedom of the Seas* (below).

COMPARE THE MAJOR CRUISE LINES

Is big necessarily better? We compare what the world's largest cruise companies, reviewed in alphabetical order, have to offer when it comes to facilities, cuisine, service, and ambience

The mainstream cruise industry may appear diverse, but it is dominated by just a few conglomerates, principally Carnival Corporation and Royal Caribbean Cruises *(see chart on page 126)*. Dig deeper and you'll find, for example, that two Carnival subsidiaries, Holland America Line and Princess Cruises, virtually control large resort ship cruising in Alaska, where they own hotels, lodges, tour companies, and much land-based transportation (other operators have to buy their services). This came about in 2002–3 when Princess Cruises' parent company, P&O Group, sold its cruising division to the Carnival Corporation. It sounds monopolistic, although it is not really more so than some tour operators in Europe that own travel agency chains, hotels, an airline, and cruise ships.

Fortissimo: Carnival's large resort ships like their music loud.

What makes them different

Apart from Louis Cruises, today's major cruise lines are global in scale. Ships belonging to the big companies may look the same, but they differ not only in their lay-out, decor, and passenger flow but also in such facilities as tea- and coffee-making machines in passenger cabins (P&O Cruises provides them, as does RCI – but only aboard its UK-based ships). Even the size of towels varies widely – a trivial point for some, perhaps, though not for larger passengers. The panel below sums up each line's individual character.

THE MAJORS UNDER THE MICROSCOPE: WHICH CRUISE LINE DOES WHAT BEST

● **Carnival Cruise Lines** is known for all-round fun, activities, and casinos for the lively, no-sleep-needed youth market – although many passengers are over 45. Carnival doesn't sell itself as a "luxury" or "premium" cruise line, which it certainly isn't. It consistently delivers exactly the well-packaged cruise vacation its brochures promise, for which there is a huge and growing first-time cruise market. Its smart ships have the latest high-tech entertainment facilities and features, and some include extra-cost alternative dining spots for the more discerning.

● **Celebrity Cruises** has the best food, the most elegant ships and spas, and its cruises are really under-priced. Although it advertises itself as a "premium" line, some aspects are no longer premium – for example, recorded "music" blaring over pool decks 24 hours a day is not relaxing. But the term still sums up Celebrity reasonably well.

● **Costa Cruises** has the edge on European style and lively ambience, with a mix of passengers of many nationalities, but the swimming pools are full of noisy children in peak holiday periods. Costa provides first-time cruise passengers with a packaged holiday that is a mix of sophistication and basic fare, accompanied by loud music. Most passengers are Italian.

● **Cunard Line** has one real ocean liner *(Queen Mary 2)* that provides a regular transatlantic service, while its other two ships are more about regular cruising. All three are best suited to a wide range of seasoned and well-traveled couples and single passengers who enjoy the cosmopolitan setting of an ocean liner. Dressing formally for dinner is encouraged, though except in the grill rooms the cuisine is largely of mass-market quality, with many traditional British favorites and extensive French dishes.

● **Holland America Line** has all the right touches for seniors and retirees: smiling service staff, lots of flowers, traditions of the past, good cooking demonstrations, and alternative grill rooms. The ships are best suited to older couples and singles who like to mingle in a large ship, in an unhurried setting with fine-quality surroundings. There's plenty of eclectic antique artwork, decent – though not gourmet – food, and service from a smiling Indonesian/Filipino crew who don't have the finesse many passengers expect from a "premium" product.

● **Louis Cruises'** ships, some chartered to other companies, focus mainly on destinations in Europe (particularly the Greek islands) and the Middle East, and have surprisingly good food and friendly service. Although it doesn't have the newest ships around, Louis Cruises has some good attributes. One is its excellent spa concession (Flair), which is small but is

Pianissimo: a Cunard string quartet stimulates digestive juices.

What they have in common

All offer one thing: a well-packaged cruise vacation, generally of seven days, typically with a mix of days at sea and days in port, plenty of food, reasonable service, large-scale production shows and trendy cabaret acts, plus large casinos, shopping malls, and extensive, busy spa and fitness facilities. Nine offer a variety of "drive to" embarkation ports within the US ("homeland cruising").

Their ships have a lot in common, too. Except for Louis Cruises and MSC Cruises, all have art auctions, bingo, horse racing, shopping talks for ports of call (pushing "recommended" stores), programs for children and teens, wedding vows renewal programs, and wi-fi or internet connect centers. All except MSC Cruises still persevere with the "Peppermill Routine" (the waiter brings a huge peppermill to your table before you've even tasted the food), but only a few extra-charge dining venues offer tableside carving or flambé items.

Extra costs include port taxes, insurance, gratuities to staff, and use of the washer/dryers in self-serve launderettes. Some lines offer their own credit cards, with points usable for upgrades, discounts, and "free" cruises (examples: Carnival Cruise Lines, Norwegian Cruise Line, Royal Caribbean International).

Standing in line for embarkation, disembarkation, shore tenders, and for self-serve buffet meals is inevitable aboard all large resort ships. But the ships differ in their characters, facilities, maintenance, space, crew-to-passenger ratio, food and service, and crew training. You'll be escorted to your cabin aboard the ships of Cunard Line (suite-grade accommodation only), Holland America Line, and MSC Cruises. Aboard other lines, staff at the entrance simply point you in the right direction – even if you have heavy carry-on luggage – and gangway staff may even try to give you a daily program, or spa details.

a refreshing change, with really skilled staff. Another is its food operation. Yet another is its friendly crew.

● **MSC Cruises** tailors its onboard product to pan-European passengers of all ages, and displays fine Italian flair, with a high level of service and hospitality from a friendly, multilingual crew. It has evolved quickly as the "new kid on the block." Of all the major cruise lines, it's also the cleanest. It changes bed linen and towels the most; typically, bed linen is changed every second day, towels daily, and bathrobes in suites daily, unlike most other large cruise lines.

● **Norwegian Cruise Line** is good for a first cruise for families with children, with a great choice of eateries, good entertainment, and friendly service staff. NCL ships are best suited to first-time young and young-at-heart couples, single passengers, children, and teenagers who

want upbeat, color-rich surroundings, plenty of entertainment lounges and bars, and high-tech sophistication – all in one programmed but well-packaged vacation.

● **P&O Cruises** operates mainly ex-UK cruises for its predominantly UK-based passengers, with good facilities for families with children, as well as adults-only ships, and a liking for Indian curries and cuisine. it has been reinventing itself, and the result is a contemporary onboard cruise product well aimed at the high-street traveler. It specializes in providing all the little things that British passengers have come to expect, including tea/coffee-making sets in all cabins, and a choice of Indian food.

● **Princess Cruises** has consistent product delivery, although the ships have decor that is rather bland, and passengers tend to be somewhat older. Choose Princess Cruises if you

enjoy being with families and fellow passengers of mid-50s and upwards, who want a well-organized cruise experience with unpretentious middle-of-the-road cuisine, a good range of entertainment, and an excellent shore excursion program – arguably the best run of any of the major cruise lines.

● **Royal Caribbean International** is a good bet for the Caribbean (naturally), for first-time cruisers and families. It has a good variety of entertainment, and interesting programs, including many for children. RCI ships are liked by active, young-minded couples and solo cruisers of all ages, families with toddlers, children, and teenagers who enjoy mingling in a large ship setting with plenty of life, high-energy entertainment, and bright lighting everywhere. The food is more notable for quantity than quality – unless you pay extra for dining in an "alternative" restaurant (not all RCI ships have them). There's background music everywhere.

CARNIVAL CRUISE LINES

Ships

Fantasy-class ships: *Carnival Ecstasy* (1991), *Carnival Elation* (1998), *Carnival Fantasy* (1990), *Carnival Fascination* (1994), *Carnival Imagination* (1995), *Carnival Inspiration* (1996), *Carnival Paradise* (1998), *Carnival Sensation* (1993)
Destiny-class ships: *Carnival Conquest* (2002), *Carnival Destiny* (1996), *Carnival Freedom* (2007), *Carnival Glory* (2003), *Carnival Liberty* (2005), *Carnival Splendor* (2008), *Carnival Triumph* (1999), *Carnival Valor* (2004), *Carnival Victory* (2000)
Dream-class ships: *Carnival Dream* (2009), *Carnival Magic* (2011)
Spirit-class ships: *Carnival Legend* (2002), *Carnival Miracle* (2004), *Carnival Pride* (2002), *Carnival Spirit* (2001)

About the company

Israel-born Ted Arison, whose ambition was to be a concert pianist, founded Carnival Cruise Lines, now the world's largest and most successful single cruise line, in 1972 with one ship, *Mardi Gras* (formerly *Empress of Canada*). Carnival wanted to be different, youthful, and fun, and developed the "fun ship" concept. It worked, appealing to people of all ages and backgrounds.

The company's first new ship, *Tropicale*, debuted in 1982. In 1984 Carnival started advertising on television, introducing a wider public to the idea of cruising. It introduced the first cruise ship measuring over 100,000 gross tonnage, *Carnival Destiny*, in 1996.

Today, the Carnival Corporation, parent company of Carnival Cruise Lines, is run by Ted Arison's son, Micky Arison, who is chairman of the board – as well as owning the NBA's Miami Heat basketball team. More than 20 new ships have been introduced since the line was founded in 1972.

Self-dubbed the "fun ship" cruise line, the well-organized company attracts passengers of all ages, although the majority are between 30 and 55.

Micky Arison, the man behind the Carnival empire.

The line has upgraded some aspects of its operation and product. It needed to. The Fantasy-class ships are receiving an overdue multi-million-dollar makeover, including an adults-only sunbathing area, pool decks (a thatched roof over one of two hot tubs and the addition of palm trees and new mid-deck stairways), a new lobby bar, expanded children's and teens' areas, and more interconnecting cabins. Balconies have been retrofitted to 98 cabins; the Fantasy-class ship have few balcony cabins and no walk-around open promenade deck. Meanwhile, giant poolside movie screens have been fitted to most non-Fantasy-class ships.

In 2008 Carnival re-categorized cabin price grades based on the European model of charging more for those in prime position.
○ **Frequent passengers' club:** Carnival Concierge Club.

So what's it really like?

It's an all-American experience: cruising for those with a low boredom threshold – exciting, noisy, challenging, but blood pressure-raising, organized fun, slickly packaged with about 60 itineraries.

Carnival's "fun" cruising is good for families with children and teens (anyone under 21 must be accompanied by a parent, relative, or guardian) and youthful

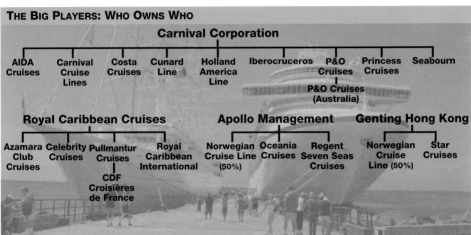

THE BIG PLAYERS: WHO OWNS WHO

Carnival Corporation

AIDA Cruises	Carnival Cruise Lines	Costa Cruises	Cunard Line	Holland America Line	Iberocruceros	P&O Cruises	Princess Cruises	Seabourn

P&O Cruises (Australia)

Royal Caribbean Cruises

Azamara Club Cruises	Celebrity Cruises	Pullmantur Cruises	Royal Caribbean International

CDF Croisières de France

Apollo Management

Norwegian Cruise Line (50%)	Oceania Cruises	Regent Seven Seas Cruises

Genting Hong Kong

Norwegian Cruise Line (50%)	Star Cruises

adults. Carnival ships are also good for whole-ship charters and incentive groups, for multi-generational passengers, and for family reunions. Typically, about half of Carnival's passengers are taking their first cruise. About 30 percent are under the age of 35, 30 percent are over 55, the other 40 percent are between 35 and 55.

The dress code is ultra-casual – indeed, the waiters are better dressed than most passengers – particularly during youth-heavy holiday seasons and spring breaks, when clothes appear almost optional. Carnival is all about "happy" and "fun" – cruise directors actually tell passengers to "make some noise," so Camp Carnival is for adults as well as children. But it's a very impersonal cruise experience, overseen by young cruise directors who are fluent in "tongue-fu" and deliver the same jokes and banter on every trip. Solo cruisegoers can get lost in the crowds of doubles. It's all about towels shaped like animals, programmed participation activities, yelling and screaming and having fun.

Perhaps the tone doesn't matter so much because this will be a first cruise for most passengers. Repeat customers, however, have a distinct sense of déjà vu, but carry a Gold Card for better recognition from hotel staff (Platinum for those who have cruised with Carnival more than 10 times).

The ships are clean and well maintained – if you don't peer too closely. Open deck space may look adequate when you board, but on days at sea you can expect your plastic deck chair, if you can find one that's free, to be kissing its neighbor – it's probably tied to it. There are no cushioned pads for the deck lounge chairs, which are hard to sit on, if you use just a towel, for any length of time.

You may well encounter lots of smokers, and masses of fellow passengers walking around in urban warfare clothing – passengers dress better on longer cruises such as Panama Canal sailings – clutching plastic sport drinks bottles at any time of the day or night. The decibel level is high: it is difficult to escape from noise and loud music, and "background" music is played even in cabin hallways and elevators 24 hours a day. Huge poolside movie screens are being fitted aboard Carnival's ships.

Expect to be subjected to a stream of flyers advertising daily art auctions, "designer" watches, gold and silver chains, and other promotions, while "artworks" for auction are strewn throughout the ships. Also, expect intrusive announcements (particularly for activities that bring revenue), and waiters hustling you to have drinks.

Carnival Capers, the ship's

ABOVE: when the pool gets boring, there's the water chute.
BELOW: Carnival's mascot, Fun Ship Freddy, struts his stuff.

daily program, is among the industry's poorest information sheets, in terms of layout and print quality, and most of it is devoted to persuading you to spend money.

There are libraries but few books, and bookshelves are always locked by 6pm, because you are expected to be out in the (revenue-earning) public areas each evening. If you enjoy casino gaming at sea, you could join Carnival's Ocean Players Club, which brings benefits to frequent players, depending on your level of skill.

Between 2008 and 2010, a multimillion-dollar renovation added 98 small balconies to existing cabins aboard the Fantasy-class ships. Also included: a new Circle "C" facility for 12- to 14-year-olds, a waterpark with water-spray area, and oversized umbrellas. An adults-only Serenity retreat was added to the aft area of the Promenade Deck. The main pool now has more of a resort-style ambience.

● **Accommodation:** In 2008 Carnival reorganized some cabin categories, and, following the European way of doing things, cabins in the best locations now cost more. Note that balconies in many of the cabins with "private" balconies aren't so private – most can be overlooked from other cabins located on the deck above and from various public locations. You may have to carry a credit card to operate the personal safes – inconvenient. High-quality mattresses and bed linen, also available for sale, have been fitted to all beds.

Changing tastes: Carnival has introduced sushi bars.

● **Passenger niggles:** The most consistent complaints are that most activities are geared around trying to sell you something. Free-to-enter onboard games have pint-sized "prizes," while the cost of playing bingo keeps rising. Many people object to the heavy sales pitches for beauty-enhancement products. The intrusive photographers are almost impossible to escape. There's no listing of the free in-cabin TV movies – only those that are pay-per-view. The non-stop recorded poolside music is intrusive. Then there's disembarkation…

There is little finesse and not enough attention to individuals. Carnival operates from many "drive to" embarkation ports in the US, and promotes a "vacation guarantee program" that is almost useless (check the Carnival brochure for details).

Decor

The decor is very creative, although you probably wouldn't want to let the ships' interior designer loose in your home. But there's no denying that Joe Farcus, the "neon-lithic" genius behind the decor, creates a dramatic impact, from the carpets to the ceiling, mixing more colors than a rainbow could aspire to. Strangely, the sensory overload works. It's pure magic, whimsical, and very entertaining.

So, if you love color, you'll be fine. If you prefer monochrome, take sunglasses. Excepted from the

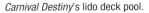

Carnival Destiny's lido deck pool.

dazzle are the clinical public toilets, which could do with a lot of cheering up – the designer clearly hasn't been in one lately.

Gratuities

These are added to your onboard account at $9.75 per person per day (the sum charged when this book went to press). You can have this amount adjusted if you visit the information desk. Additionally, 15% is added to your account for all bar, wine, and spa charges (yes, even after high treatment prices). The onboard currency is the US dollar – and this applies even when a ship is operating in European waters.

Cuisine/Dining

All Carnival ships have one or two main dining rooms, and its "Your Choice Dining" program offers three dinner seating options, including "Your Time" open seating. Dining assignments are confirmed at time of booking. Menus are standardized across the fleet, and all the dining venues are non-smoking.

Don't even think about a quiet table for two, or a candlelight dinner on deck – it's not Carnival's style – unless you pay extra at an "alternative" restaurant. Dining aboard a Carnival ship is all about table mates, social chat, lively meals, fast eating.

Tables are, however, nicely set with white tablecloths, plenty of silverware, and iced water/iced tea whenever you want it. Oh, and the tired old peppermill routine (where the waiter brings a huge peppermill to your table before you've even tasted the food) is all part of the show – delivered with friendly service that lacks polish but invites extra gratuities.

The main dining rooms marry food and show business. Waiters sing and dance, and there are constant waiter parades with flashing lights in an attempt to create some excitement.

Taste-filled food is not the company's strong point, but quantity, not quality, is – although consultant chef Georges Blanc has created daily "Georges Blanc Signature" menu items. The company has been striving to improve its cuisine and the menu choices often look good, but the actual food delivered is simply banquet-style catering, with its attendant standardization and production cooking.

While meats are of a decent quality, poultry, fish, seafood, and desserts are disappointing. Sauces and gravies are used well as disguises, and there are few garnishes. The selection of fresh green vegetables, breads, rolls, cheese, and ripe fruit is poor, and there is much use of canned fruit and jellied desserts, not to mention packets of jam, marmalade, butter, sugar – the same stuff you'd find in the average family eatery in the USA. It is virtually impossible to obtain anything remotely unusual or off-menu, and the "always available" items appear to have disappeared from the menus.

Vegetarian and children's menus are available at all meals, but they wouldn't get a generous score for their nutritional content. Spa Carnival Fare has been introduced to provide healthy dining options.

The wine list is adequate, but there are no wine waiters or decent-sized wine glasses. Carnival also has a "wines by the glass" program, with good storage and presentation facilities that enable wines to be served properly in several locations and not just in the restaurants aboard each ship.

● **Alternative Dining Spots**
Carnival Conquest, Carnival Destiny, Carnival Dream, Carnival Freedom, Carnival Glory, Carnival Liberty, Carnival Miracle, Carnival Splendor, Carnival Triumph, Carnival Valor
These extra-cost restaurants feature fine table settings, china and silverware, and leather-bound menus. Menu favorites include prime American steaks such as filet mignon (9 ounces), porterhouse steak (24 ounces) and New York strip loin (be prepared for huge cuts of meat – shown to you at your table before you order), and broiled lobster tail, as well as stone crab claws from Joe's Stone Crabs of South Miami Beach.

Reservations are necessary, and a cover charge of $30 per person for service and gratuity is payable.

The food is good, and the ambience is reasonably quiet. But if you are a couple and you have just two glasses of wine each (Grgich Hills Chardonnay or Merlot, for example, at $12.50 a glass), and pay the cover charge, that's over $100 for dinner.

Caviar (American) would cost around $30 for a 1-ounce serving.

Are alternative dining spots worth the extra money? Yes, I believe they are – the food's better, the service is slower, and it's less noisy.

● **Casual Eateries**
All ships also have large food court-style spaces for casual food, fast-food items, grilled meats, pizzas (each ship serves over 800 pizzas in a typical day), stir-fry, deli and salad items. There are self-help beverage stands, coffee that looks like rusty water, and tea provided in paper cups with a teabag (tea dust, as far as I'm concerned), plastic or wooden stirrers (no teaspoons and no saucers), and packets of chemical "milk" or "creamer."

But some people are happy to have it that way, and it's actually better than what's offered aboard the ships of its competitor, Royal Caribbean International. Late-night "snacks" consist of greasy fast-food items instead of healthy alternatives such as light fruit bites, and are usually the same every night. Breakfast buffets are as repetitive as canned laughter on television.

● **The Coffee/Tea Factor**
Regular coffee is weak and poor, scoring 1 out of 10 (paper/foam cups in buffet areas). The espresso and cappuccino coffees score 2 out of 10 (served in paper or foam cups, in buffet areas).

For Children:

Carnival is a fine family-friendly cruise line, carrying more than 575,000 children a year, and "Camp Carnival," the line's extensive child/youth program, is well organized and extensive. There are five age groups:

Loud discos celebrate Carnival's "fun ship" image.

Toddlers (ages 2–5), Juniors (6–8), Intermediate (9–11), Tweens (12–14, Circle C), and late Teens (15–17, with Club 02). Even the under-2s are now being catered to, with special programs aboard each ship. Meanwhile, Family Fun Nights are all about reconnecting parents to their children – something many can do only while on vacation.

Soft-drinks packages can be bought for children (adults, too). Note that a babysitting service is not generally available after 10pm.

Best ships for children: *Carnival Conquest, Carnival Destiny, Carnival Dream, Carnival Freedom, Carnival Glory, Carnival Legend, Carnival Liberty, Carnival Miracle, Carnival Pride, Carnival Spirit, Carnival Splendor, Carnival Triumph, Carnival Valor,* and *Carnival Victory.*

Ships with fewer facilities: *Carnival Ecstasy, Carnival Elation, Carnival Fantasy, Carnival Fascination, Carnival Imagination, Carnival Inspiration, Carnival Paradise,* and *Carnival Sensation.*

Entertainment

The ships have big showlounges, all non-smoking, and large-scale flesh-and-feather production shows. On a typical cruise, there will be one or two large-scale shows,

with male and female lead singers and a clutch of dancers backed by a 10-piece live orchestra and supported by pre-recorded backing tracks.

These are loud, ritzy-glitzy, razzle-dazzle, Las Vegas-style revues with little or no story-line or flow – lots of running around on stage and stepping in place, but little real dancing. The skimpy costumes are very colorful, as is the lighting, with extensive use of "color mover" lights. Stage "smoke" is much overused – to the irritation of anyone unfortunate enough to be seated in the front few rows.

Carnival often rotates entertainers aboard its ships, so that passengers see different acts each night, and specialty acts take center stage on nights when there's no production show. There's also live music in just about every bar and lounge – although there appears to be a trend to replace live music with more DJs – and there's also a strong trend toward late-night adults-only comedy.

Cabaret acts include vocalists, magic acts, ventriloquists, and comedy jugglers. Each cruise has karaoke nights, a passenger talent show, and a discotheque with ear-splitting volumes and megaphones to enable you to converse with your partner.

Spa/Fitness Facilities

Spa/fitness facilities are operated by Steiner Leisure, a specialist concession, whose young, revenue-conscious staff will try to sell you the company's own-brand beauty products *(more details about Steiner: page 71)*. Some fitness classes are free; others, such as yoga and kick-boxing, cost extra, and you'll need to sign up to join.

Examples of treatments: Swedish Massage ($119 for 50 minutes); Aroma Stone Massage ($195 for 75 minutes); Couples Massage ($269 for 50 minutes); Facial ($119 for 50 minutes); Seaweed Body Wrap, with half-body massage ($195 for 90 minutes). It's prudent to book appointments early, and you can book more than 30 treatments online before your cruise.

The SpaCarnival layout spaces and facilities are identical to other ships in the same "class":

● *Carnival Legend, Carnival Miracle, Carnival Pride, Carnival Spirit*

SpaCarnival spans two decks and is located directly above the navigation bridge in the forward part of the ship. Facilities on the lower level include a solarium, eight treatment rooms, lecture rooms, sauna and steam rooms for men and women, and a beauty parlor; the upper level consists of a large gymnasium with floor-to-ceiling windows on three sides, including forward-facing ocean views (with a large array of the latest in muscle-pumping electronic machines), and an aerobics room with instructor-led classes.

● *Carnival Conquest, Carnival Destiny, Carnival*

ABOVE: a jog on *Carnival Elation*'s 660-ft (200-meter) track.
BELOW: *Carnival Imagination*'s mini-golf course.

Echoes of Las Vegas glitz aboard *Carnival Ecstasy*.

Freedom, Carnival Glory, Carnival Miracle, Carnival Splendor, Carnival Triumph, Carnival Valor
SpaCarnival spans two decks and is located directly above the navigation bridge in the forward part of the ship (accessible from the forward stairway). Facilities on the lower level include a solarium, eight treatment rooms, lecture rooms, sauna and steam rooms for men and women, and a beauty parlor; the upper level consists of a large gymnasium with floor-to-ceiling windows on three sides, including forward-facing ocean views. It has the latest in muscle-pumping electronic machines, and an aerobics room with instructor-led classes, some costing extra.

● *Carnival Dream, Carnival Magic*
The expansive Serenity Spa, Carnival's largest and most elaborate health and wellness center, is positioned over three decks in the ship's front section. The uppermost deck is intended for indoor/outdoor private spa relaxation (at extra cost). A spiral staircase connects each deck, and the Steiner-operated spa offers a wide range of treatments.

● *Carnival Ecstasy, Carnival Elation, Carnival Fantasy, Carnival Fascination, Carnival Imagination, Carnival Inspiration, Carnival Paradise, Carnival Sensation*
SpaCarnival is located on Sports Deck, forward of the ship's mast, and accessed from the forward stairway. It consists of a gymnasium with ocean-view windows that look out over the ship's bow, and there's a good array of the latest in muscle-pumping electronic machines, an aerobics exercise room, men's and women's changing rooms (towels are provided), sauna and steam rooms, and beauty salon.

CELEBRITY CRUISES

Ships
Century-class ships: *Celebrity Century* (1995)
Millennium-class ships: *Celebrity Constellation* (2002), *Celebrity Infinity* (2001), *Celebrity Millennium* (2000), *Celebrity Summit* (2001)
Solstice-class ships: *Celebrity Eclipse (2010), Celebrity Equinox* (2009), *Celebrity Reflection* (2012), *Celebrity Silhouette* (2011), *Celebrity Solstice* (2008)
Other ships: *Celebrity Xpedition* (2001)

About the company
Celebrity Cruises was the brainchild of Harry H. Haralambopoulos and brothers John and Michael Chandris, the London-based Greek cargo ship owners and operators of the former Chandris Lines and Chandris Cruises. In 1989, as the cruise industry was gaining momentum, they determined to create a newer, better cruise line, with new ships, larger, more standard cabins, and focusing more on food and service in the European tradition.

In its formative years, Celebrity Cruises forged an alliance, since dissolved, with three-star Michelin chef Michel Roux. The company established an outstanding reputation for its cuisine, particularly in the main dining rooms, with a formal presentation and service.

Its image as a "premium" line is justified because the product delivery on board is superior to that of its parent company, Royal Caribbean International, which bought it in 1997 for $1.3 billion. The ships are recognizable, thanks to the "X" on the funnel denoting the third letter from the end of the Greek alphabet, the Greek "chi" or "Ch" in English, for Chandris, the founding family.

In 2007 Celebrity Cruises created a new company, Azamara Cruises (now **Azamara Club Cruises**, *see page 160*), with mid-size ships, including *Azamara Journey* (2000) and *Azamara Quest* (2000). The idea is to focus on lesser-visited destinations, and offer a more personal cruise experience. All hotel services and cruise operations are, however, operated by Celebrity Cruises.
○ **Frequent passengers' club:** Captain's Club.

So what's it really like?

The ships are usually very clean and extremely well maintained. There are always lots of flowers and flower displays – some ships have flower shops, where you can buy fresh blooms for special occasions.

There's a lot of fine artwork aboard Celebrity's ships; it may not be to everybody's taste, but it is probably the cruise industry's most remarkable collection of contemporary art. The company provides a lot of the niceties that other lines have long forgotten, although some are now playing "catch up": waiters who carry your trays when you obtain food from buffets or casual eateries; water spritzes on the pool deck. Sadly, stewards no longer escort you to your cabin on embarkation day. On days at sea in warm-weather areas, if you are sunbathing on deck, someone will bring you a cold towel, and a sorbet, iced water, or iced tea.

Regardless of the accommodation grade, Celebrity Cruises delivers a well-defined North American cruise experience at a modest price. Book a suite-category cabin for the extra benefits it brings – it's worth it. Strong points include the many European staff and the high level of service, fine spas with a good range of facilities and treatments, taste-filled food served in fine European dining tradition, a "zero announcement policy," cloth towels in public restrooms instead of paper towels. Such touches differentiate Celebrity Cruises from its competitors.

Its ships have significantly more staff than other ships of comparable size and capacity, especially in the housekeeping and food and beverage departments. This helps create a superior product.

Celebrity's ships are best suited to well-educated, more sophisticated adult couples, families with older children and teenagers, and singles who like to mingle in a large ship with stylish surroundings, reasonable entertainment, and extremely good food and service, for a fare that's excellent value.

Even so, such things as topless sunbathing spaces are now available aboard all ships (except *Azamara Journey, Azamara Quest, Celebrity Xpedition*). Some cruises aboard some ships are designated adults-only.

Unfortunately, background music is now played almost everywhere, and any lounge designated as "music-free" is typically full of activities and participation events, so it's hard to find a quiet corner to sit and read.

So, what are the differences between Celebrity Cruises and its parent, Royal Caribbean International? Here are a few examples relating to food items:
● **RCI** *(Brilliance of the Seas)*
Café: Seattle Coffee Company coffee, in paper cups.
Dining Room: no tables for two.
In the Windjammer Café, waiters don't help passengers to tables with trays; plastic plates are used, cutlery is wrapped in paper napkins, melamine mugs for coffee/tea, tea selection very poor – impossible to get hot water.
Public restrooms have paper towels.
● **Celebrity Cruises** *(Celebrity Century)*:
Café el Bacio: Coffees/teas served in china cups and saucers, with doily and chocolate.
Dining Room Food: Good quality and presentation.
Dining Room: Tables for two are available.
Lido Café: Waiters line up to help passengers with trays to tables. Real china, white cloth napkins, polished cutlery, and a decent selection of teas are provided.
Public restrooms have cloth towels.

The waterfall pool aboard *Celebrity Millennium*.

Decor

All ships: there are no glitzy atrium lobbies, rock-climbing walls, ice-skating rinks or other puffery – just good European style in the elegant interiors. The exception is in the casinos, which are simply coin boxes wrapped in garish, unfriendly lighting – like pachinko parlors. You can book spa, salon, and personal fitness appointments, make main (Celebrity Select) and specialty dining reservations, and shore excursions online before you cruise – so planning ahead will pay off (exception: *Celebrity Xpedition*).

Solstice-class ships: The layout is sensible, and the decor and colors are pleasing and elegant. There's also an abundance of designer chairs and sunloungers, including two-person clam-shell deck loungers.

Other ships: The decor is elegant – Greek, classical, minimalist, although some might find it a little antiseptic and cool in places. *Celebrity Constellation, Celebrity Infinity, Celebrity Millennium,* and *Celebrity Summit* were "Solsticized" in 2011, to make them more consistent with the latest design and culinary trends in the newer ships.

Celebrity Cruises has some of the most eclectic sculptures and original artwork, from Picasso to Warhol, found at sea. The colors don't jar the senses, and cannot be said to be glitzy – except for the casinos, which are mostly vulgar.

The ships absorb people well, and the flow is, for the most part, good, except for entrances to showlounges and in photo galleries. Each public room subtly invites you to move on to the next.

Gratuities

$11.95 per person per day is added to your onboard account. You can have this amount adjusted at the guest relations desk during the cruise. Additionally, 15% is added for all bar and wine

A balcony stateroom aboard *Celebrity Constellation*.

purchases – so, buy a bottle of mineral water at the bar and you'll pay an extra 15% "for your convenience"; 10% for spa treatments (and receipts invite you to make an additional gratuity).

For Children

Junior passengers are divided into Shipmates (3–6 years), Cadets (7–9), Ensigns (10–12), Teens (13–17).
● **Best ships for children:** *Celebrity Constellation, Celebrity Infinity, Celebrity Millennium, Celebrity Solstice, Celebrity Summit.* Almost as good: *Celebrity Century, Celebrity Mercury.*

Cuisine/Dining

The dining rooms aboard all ships are non-smoking areas. There are two seatings for dinner, and open seating for breakfast and lunch. Table settings are excellent, with fine-quality linen, china, and glassware. Tables for two are available – far more than by most other major lines. What sets Celebrity apart is the superior training and supervision of dining room waiters, and the service.

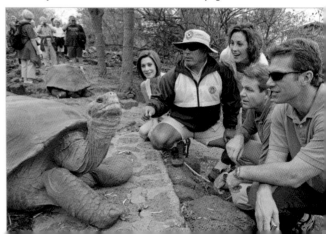

A Celebrity Cruises shore excursion on the Galápagos Islands.

The main restaurant aboard *Celebrity Solstice*.

The food represents a range of culinary influences; it is based loosely on classic French cuisine, modified to appeal to North Americans and Europeans alike, and menus are standardized across the fleet and have been dumbed down since a new regime took over from Michel Roux – meatloaf, spaghetti, and striploin for dinner are pathetic for what is supposed to be a "premium" product. Items that can be made at home cannot be considered as acceptable. For better quality, Celebrity Cruises wants you to pay extra to eat in the alternative venues. Full service in-cabin dining is also available for all meals, including dinner.

The food is generally made from good-quality ingredients. Take croissants, for example. Those found aboard Celebrity ships are made fresh each morning, while aboard most competitors' ships they are purchased ashore; there's a big difference in taste and consistency, depending on what kind of dough and butter are used.

Celebrity Cruises also has well-trained sommeliers and wine waiters who know their subject. *Celebrity Eclipse, Celebrity Equinox, Celebrity Reflection, Celebrity Silhouette,* and *Celebrity Solstice* have a special wine room for tastings. *Celebrity Constellation, Celebrity Infinity, Celebrity Millennium* and *Celebrity Summit* have special wine rooms in their "alternative" restaurants that you can dine in, and fine wines that can cost thousands of dollars a bottle. But there are also wines that start at about $20.

● **Casual Eateries**

There are casual self-serve buffets aboard all Celebrity Cruises' ships. Except for *Celebrity Eclipse, Celebrity Equinox, Celebrity Reflection, Celebrity Silhouette* and *Celebrity Solstice,* most are laid out in continuous straight lines, which can cause congestion at peak times. Celebrity is trying to be more creative with these buffets, and, like other cruise lines, has stations for pasta, faux sushi, salads, grilled and rotisserie items, and hot food items. A waiter will – or should – take your tray to a table. A bar trolley service for drinks and wines is provided at lunchtime, and wine waiters are always on hand to discuss and take wine orders for dinner. All the ships make great martinis.

● **The Coffee/Tea Factor**

Regular coffee: weak and poor. Score: 2 out of 10. Espresso/cappuccino coffees: Score: 3 out of 10. If you order espresso/cappuccino coffees in the dining room, there is a charge; they are treated like a bar item.

Café el Bacio: The cafés are in prominent locations, and provide an agreeable setting for those who like decent Italian coffees, pastries, and cakes.

Entertainment

The company has little cohesive policy regarding big production shows, although *Celebrity Eclipse, Celebrity Equinox, Celebrity Reflection, Celebrity Silhouette,* and

---

CELEBRITY'S CLASSY APPROACH

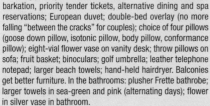

There really are four different "classes" aboard Celebrity ships: those in accommodation designated as suites; those in standard exterior-view and interior (no view) cabins; a third that comes between the two, known as Concierge Class; and Aqua Class.

Concierge Class brings added value to passengers with enhanced facilities including priority embarkation, disembarkation, priority tender tickets, alternative dining and spa reservations; European duvet; double-bed overlay (no more falling "between the cracks" for couples); choice of four pillows (goose down pillow, isotonic pillow, body pillow, conformance pillow); eight-vial flower vase on vanity desk; throw pillows on sofa; fruit basket; binoculars; golf umbrella; leather telephone notepad; larger beach towels; hand-held hairdryer. Balconies get better furniture. In the bathrooms: plusher Frette bathrobe; larger towels in sea-green and pink (alternating days); flower in silver vase in bathroom.

Aqua Class accommodation occupants get priority access to spa treatments, and special "up-rated" spa amenities.

Celebrity Solstice have better Cirque-style acrobatic shows. Shows aboard some ships are quite decent, with good costuming and lighting, but others look dated and lack storyline, flow, or connectivity. Each ship carries its own resident troupe of singers/dancers and audiovisual support staff. Bar service, available throughout shows, disrupts concentration. While some cabaret acts are good, they are the same ones seen aboard many ships. All showlounges are non-smoking.

Celebrity vessels have a variety of bands and small musical units, although there is very little music for social dancing, other than disco and pop music. Then there are the summer camp-style audience participation events, games and talent shows that don't sit well with Celebrity's quality of food and service. There are also the inevitable country line dances and playschool routines.

On days at sea the program is crammed with things to do, though the emphasis is on revenue-enhancing activities such as art auctions, bingo, and horse racing.

Spa/Fitness Facilities

Celebrity Cruises, acknowledging the popularity of spas and fitness facilities, has been improving its offerings. Spa/fitness programs are staffed and operated by Steiner Leisure, a specialist concession, whose enthusiastic staff will try to sell you Steiner's own-brand beauty products. Some fitness classes are free; others, such as yoga, and kick-boxing, cost extra.

Massage (including exotic massages such as Aroma Stone massage, Chakra Balancing massage, and other wellbeing massages), facials, pedicures, and beauty salon treatments cost extra. Examples: massage at $120 (50 minutes), facial at $120, seaweed wrap (75 minutes) at $190 – to which you need to add a gratuity of 10%. Personal training sessions in the gymnasium cost $83 for one hour.

COSTA CRUISES

Ships

Atlantica-class ships: *Costa Atlantica* (2000), *Costa Deliziosa* (2010), *Costa Luminosa* (2009), *Costa Mediterranea* (2003)
Fortuna-class ships: *Costa Concordia* (2006), *Costa Fascinosa* (2011), *Costa Favolosa* (2010), *Costa Fortuna* (2003), *Costa Magica* (2004), *Costa Pacifica* (2009), *Costa Serena* (2007)
Classica-class ships: *Costa Classica* (1992), *Costa Romantica* (1993)
Other ships: *Costa Allegra* (1992), *Costa Marina* (1990), *Costa Victoria* (1996)

About the company

Costa Cruises traces its history back to 1860, when Giacomo Costa started an olive oil business. The first

COSTA CRUISES: BEST SUITED TO...

Costa ships are best suited to young couples, singles, and families with children who enjoy big-city life, multicultural fellow passengers, outdoor cafés, constant activity, eating late, loud entertainment, and food more notable for quantity than quality. All printed materials (room service folio, menus, etc) are in six languages: Italian, English, French, German, Portuguese, and Spanish. Announcements are made in at least two languages in the Caribbean and at least four in Europe and the Mediterranean.

ship, in 1924, transported that oil. After he died in 1924, his sons, Federico, Eugenio and Enrico, inherited the business. First they bought *Ravenna*, a cargo ship, to cut transport costs for their olive oil empire. In 1948 Costa's first passenger ship, the *Anna "C"*, carried passengers in style from Genoa to South America. In 1997, Costa Cruises was bought by the USA's Carnival Corporation and UK's Airtours plc. Three years later Carnival took full control.

Costa specializes in cruises for Europeans or passengers with European tastes, and particularly Italians, during the summer. Costa has initiated an aggressive newbuild policy in recent years, in order to modernize the company's aging fleet of different-sized ships. The ships operate in three main markets: the Mediterranean, the Caribbean, and South America.

Most ships are well maintained, although there are inconsistencies throughout the fleet. The same is true of cleanliness – some ships are very clean, while others are a little dusty around the edges, as are its shore tenders. The ships have a laid-back European "feel" to their decor and manner of product delivery.
✪ **Frequent passengers' club:** Costa Club.

A yogic moment aboard *Costa Concordia*.

Costa ships incorporate eye-catching sculptures.

So what's it really like?

Costa is noted for its lively "Italian" ambience. There are few Italian crew members, however, although many officers are Italian. Nevertheless, Costa's lifestyle is perceived to be Italian – lively, very noisy, yet easygoing. The dress code is casual, even on formal nights.

Most passengers are Italian, with a generous sprinkling of other Europeans. One night at the end of each cruise is reserved for a "Roman Bacchanal," when passengers dress up toga-style for dinner and beyond. This is a cruise line for those who like to party. If you want quiet, take earplugs – good ones.

On European and Mediterranean cruises, English will be the language least spoken, as most passengers will be Italian, Spanish, French, or German. On Caribbean itineraries, a high percentage of passengers will speak Spanish, as the ships carry passengers from Latin American countries in addition to passengers from North America.

Expect to cruise with a lot of children of all ages if you book for peak holiday cruises – and remember that in Europe schoolchildren at certain times such as Easter have longer vacations. On some European itineraries, passengers embark and disembark in almost every port along the way, which makes for a disjointed cruise experience since there's almost no start or end to the cruise.

There is almost no information for passengers who want to be independent in ports of call, and not take the ship's organized general excursions.

There is extensive smoking on board. No-smoking zones and signs are often ignored to the frustration of non-smoking passengers, and ashtrays are moved at whim; many of the officers and crew also smoke, even when moving through public rooms, so they don't bother to enforce the no-smoking zones.

The cabins tend to be on the mean side in size, but the decor is fresh and upbeat, and the bathrooms are very practical units. Some ships have cabin bathrooms with sliding doors – an excellent alternative to inward-openers that use up space.

Decor

Older ships: *Costa Allegra, Costa Classica, Costa Marina, Costa Romantica, Costa Victoria* have a distinctively European feel. They are lively without being brash, or pastel-toned without being boring, depending on the ship you choose.
Newer, larger ships: *Costa Atlantica, Costa Concordia, Costa Deliziosa, Costa Fascinosa, Costa Favolosa, Costa Fortuna, Costa Luminosa, Costa Magica, Costa Mediterranea, Costa Pacifica, Costa Serena* have an "in-your-face" brashness similar to Carnival's ships, with grainy and unflattering digital artwork on walls and panels, and even inside elevators.

The "entertainment architecture," as designer Joe Farcus calls it, can't be ignored. There is an abundance of jazzy colors, fine or grotesque sculptures (depending on your taste), and huge murals that are both impressive and mind-numbing.

Gratuities

On Europe and Mediterranean cruises €7 per person per day is charged to your onboard account, plus 10% to all bar and wine orders. On Caribbean cruises, the figures are $9 per person per day and 15% for bar and wine orders. Many non-Italians would prefer to choose when to tip and how much. To have these amounts adjusted, you need to visit the information desk.

Cuisine/Dining

If you expect to be served by jovial Italian waiters, you'll be disappointed – although the restaurant managers might be Italian. All ships have two seatings for dinner; dining times on Europe/Mediterranean and South America cruises are usually later than those in the Caribbean because Europeans and Latin passengers eat much later than North Americans. Few tables for two are available, most being for four, six, or eight. All dining rooms are smoke-free – in theory.

The cuisine is best described as continental adequate, with many regional Italian dishes and much emphasis on pasta: 50 pasta dishes per cruise. Except for pasta

Big on balconies: *Costa Mediterranea.*

dishes (made fresh on board) and cream sauces, presentation and food quality are not memorable, and are the subject of many negative comments from passengers. While the quality of meat is adequate, it is often disguised with gravies and rich sauces. Fish and seafood tend to lack taste, and are often overcooked. Green vegetables are hard to come by. Breads and bread rolls are usually good, but the desserts are of supermarket quality and lack taste.

There is a wine list but no wine waiters; table waiters are expected to serve both food and wine, which does not work well. Almost all wines are young – very young.

● **Alternative Dining**
If you opt for one of the "alternative" restaurants aboard the larger ships, note that a cover charge applies: €20 per person plus 10% service charge (Europe/Mediterranean cruises), or $20 per person plus 15% service charge (Caribbean cruises).

● **Casual Eateries**
All ships have self-serve lido buffets. In most, you have to move along with your tray, but the latest ships have more active stations and individual islands. The items available are quite basic. All ships except *Costa Europa* also have a pizzeria.

● **The Coffee/Tea Factor**
Regular coffee: decent and quite strong. Score: 5 out of 10.
Espresso/cappuccino coffees (Lavazza) are among the best served by the major cruise lines: the main competition is from Celebrity Cruises' Café el Bacio; Star Cruises also serves Lavazza. Costa ships have coffee machines in most lounges/bars. Score: 8 out of 10.

For children
Junior passengers are in four groups: Kids Club is for 3–6; Junior Club is for 7–12; Teen Club is for 13–17. The program varies by ship, itinerary, and season. Group babysitting is available 6.30–11pm. During port days, babysitting is available generally 8.30am–12.30pm and 2.30–6.30pm.
● **Best ships for children:** *Costa Atlantica, Costa Concordia, Costa Fortuna, Costa Luminosa, Costa*

Magica, Costa Mediterranea, Costa Pacifica, Costa Serena. But not: *Costa Allegra, Costa Classica, Costa Marina, Costa Romantica, Costa Victoria.*

Entertainment
Each ship carries its own resident troupe of singers/dancers and audiovisual support staff, but Costa Cruises is not known for the quality of its entertainment. What it does present tends to be of the "no finesse" variety, with revue-style shows that have little storyline, poor choreography and execution, but plenty of fast-moving action – more stepping in place than dancing – and lots of volume. It's entertainment to pass the time rather than remember.

Cabaret acts – typically singers, magicians, comedy jugglers, ventriloquists, and so on – are entertaining but rather ho-hum. Most passenger participation activities include poolside games such as a "Belly Flop" competition, election of the "Ideal Couple," and other juvenile games – but some families love them. There are also dance classes, and the inevitable "Fine Art Auction."

Spa/Fitness Facilities
These vary according to ship and size. The newest and largest ships (*Costa Atlantica, Costa Concordia, Costa Fortuna, Costa Magica, Costa Mediterranea,* and *Costa Serena*) have more space and better facilities, while the others (*Costa Allegra, Costa Marina*) have only basic facilities. Spa/fitness facilities are staffed and operated by Steiner Leisure, a specialist concession,

Costa ships are packed with kids at peak holiday times.

whose young staff will try to sell you its own-brand beauty products. Some fitness classes are free, while some, such as yoga and kick-boxing, cost $10 per class.

However, being aboard will give you an opportunity to try some of the more exotic treatments, particularly some of the massages available. Massage (including exotic massages such as Aroma Stone massage, Chakra Balancing massage and other well-being massages), facials, pedicures, and beauty salon treatments cost extra – massage, for example, costs about $2 per minute, plus gratuity.

Aboard *Costa Concordia* and *Costa Serena*, Samsara Spa accommodation grades benefit from Oriental-themed decor and Samsara bathroom amenities, and 12 Samsara Suites have direct access to the Samsara Spa facilities and special packages and concessions. To use the sauna/steam and relaxation areas aboard some of the ships, you'll need to buy a day pass, for €35 per person.

CUNARD LINE

Ships:
Queen Elizabeth (2010), *Queen Mary 2* (2004), *Queen Victoria* (2007).

About the company
Cunard Line was established in 1839, as the British and North American Steam Packet Company, to carry the Royal Mail and passengers from the Old World to the New. Its first ship, *Britannia*, sailed on its maiden voyage on American Independence Day in 1840. The author

Charles Dickens crossed the Atlantic aboard the ship in 1842 together with 62 other passengers, 93 crew members, one cow, and, most important, Her Majesty's mails and despatches.

Since 1840, Cunard Line has always had ships built to sail across the North Atlantic. From 1850 until the arrival of *QE2* in 1969, all of the line's ships and those of White Star Line (with which Cunard merged in 1934) had several classes. Your luggage label, therefore, declared not only your name but also what you could afford. Today, there's no class distinction, other than by the grade of accommodation you choose. In other words, you get what you pay for, as on any cruise ship.

But one is still reminded of the company's illustrious history. For example, Cunard Line:
● was the first company to take passengers on regularly scheduled transatlantic crossings.
● introduced the first passenger ship to be lit by electricity (*Servia*, 1881).
● introduced the first steam turbine engines in an ocean liner (*Carmania*, 1905).
● introduced the first indoor swimming pool aboard a ship (*Aquitania*, 1914).
● pioneered an around-the-world cruise (*Laconia*, 1922).
● held the record for the largest passenger ship ever built (*Queen Elizabeth*, between 1940 and 1996).
● is presently the only company to sail regularly scheduled year-round transatlantic crossings (*Queen Mary 2*).
○ **Frequent passengers' club:** Cunard World Club.

So what's it really like?
Sailing with Cunard Line is quite different to being aboard a standard cruise ship. The ships incorporate a lot of maritime history and the grand traditions of ocean liners – as opposed to the other ships, with their tendency to tacky high-street trappings.

Assuming your sea legs can cope with sometimes less than calm waters, a transatlantic crossing is supremely civilized, particularly if you can enjoy being cosseted in accommodation that allows you to dine in the "grill"-class restaurants with their fine cuisine and presentation. There's less pressure from staff to get you to buy drinks than with other lines, and the itineraries are well spaced and not so hectic.

Cunard Line's three vessels – the mother ship is *Queen Mary 2*, with younger sisters *Queen Elizabeth* and *Queen Victoria* – are best suited to a wide range of seasoned and well-traveled couples and single passengers who enjoy the cosmopolitan setting of an ocean liner, with their extensive array of facilities, public rooms, dining rooms, and lecture programs. All three ships have Art-Deco decor, fine wood mosaics, and many attributes of the old ocean liners, albeit in a

Making memories aboard Cunard Line's new *Queen Elizabeth*.

Above: the three Queens meet in New York, 2011.
Below: the monarch's bust in *QE*'s Queens Room.

more modern, contemporary setting. Male social hosts – typically 10 on an around-the-world cruise – serve as dancing partners for women traveling alone.

Cunard Line is the only cruise line that lets you take your dog or cat with you (*Queen Mary 2* transatlantic crossings only). Also, one of its most successful formulas is its adherence to formal dress codes – in contrast to the downward sartorial spiral of most cruise lines.

Accommodation

Cunard has four distinct accommodation classes, with the class linked to a specific restaurant: Queens Grill, Princess Grill, Britannia Club, and Britannia.

Cuisine/Dining

Cunard Line uses good-quality ingredients, sourced in Europe and the USA. The cuisine is still of a mass-market standard – some venues have butter in packets. However, in self-serve buffets, salt and pepper are usually provided on each table. Espressos and cappuccinos are available in the dining rooms, and at extra cost in many bars. Cunard uses Italian coffee.

All ships have "grill rooms" as well as traditional large restaurants, and casual self-service dining venues. Grill rooms are more exclusive and some have à la carte menus, while the main restaurants have fixed menus. The grill rooms have seating dining at assigned tables, when you wish, while the main Britannia restaurants in all ships have two seatings.

The cuisine includes many traditional

British favorites, together with extensive French dishes as well as regional specialties from around the world, nicely presented on Wedgwood china.

For Children

Children's facilities are quite good, although not as extensive as aboard the former *Queen Elizabeth 2*. Youngsters are supervised by real English nannies.

Gratuities

The onboard currencies are the British pound and the US dollar, depending on the operating area. Gratuities are automatically charged to your onboard account – you will need to visit the information desk to change them. The amount is $13 per person per day (Grill Class accommodation, including children) or $11 per person per day (other accommodation).

In addition, 15% is added to all bar and wine, and health spa/salon bills.

Entertainment

Production shows are colourful and visual, with pre-recorded backing tracks supplementing the showband. Other shows consist of cabaret acts – typically singers, magicians, mime artistes, comedy jugglers, and, occasionally, comedians – doing the cruise ship circuit.

A number of bands and small musical units provide live music for dancing and listening.

Spa/Fitness Facilities

The spa/fitness centers are operated by Canyon Ranch *(QM2)* and The Onboard Spa Company (*Queen Elizabeth, Queen Victoria*), with prices that generally match those of land-based health resorts.

HOLLAND AMERICA LINE

Ships

Statendam-class: *Maasdam* (1993), *Ryndam* (1994), *Statendam* (1993), *Veendam* (1996)
Rotterdam-class: *Amsterdam* (2000), *Rotterdam* (1997), *Volendam* (1999), *Zaandam* (2000)
Zuiderdam-class: *Eurodam* (2008), *Nieuw Amsterdam* (2010), *Noordam* (2006), *Oosterdam* (2003), *Westerdam* (2004), *Zuiderdam* (2002)
Others: *Prinsendam* (1988)

About the company

Holland America Line was founded in 1873 as the Netherlands-America Steamship Company, shipping immigrants to the New World from Rotterdam. It moved its headquarters to New York in 1971. It bought into Alaskan hotels and transportation when it acquired Westours in 1983, and is one of the state's biggest employers. In 1989, it was acquired by Carnival Cruise Lines, but retained its Seattle-based headquarters.

HAL carries both traditional cruise passengers (senior citizens, alumni groups) and multi-generational families. It tries hard to keep its Dutch connections, with antique artifacts and traditional decor, as well as Indonesian stewards. It has a private island, Half Moon Cay, in the Bahamas.

○ **Frequent passengers' club:** Mariner Society.

So what's it really like?

Fresh management with updated ideas, the line's "Signature of Excellence" program, the food variety, and creativity have improved the HAL experience. The ships benefit from lots of fresh flowers, museum-quality art pieces, and more attention to detail than all the other major lines, with the exception of Celebrity Cruises.

The brand encompasses basically two types of ship. Younger families with children and grandchildren are best suited to the newer, larger vessels such as *Eurodam, Nieuw Amsterdam, Noordam, Oosterdam, Westerdam,* and *Zuiderdam*, whereas those of senior years – HAL's traditional audience of repeat passengers from alumni groups – are best suited to ships that are smaller and less glitzy (*Amsterdam, Maasdam, Prinsendam, Rotterdam, Ryndam, Statendam, Veendam,* and *Zaandam*). All the ships are well maintained, and cleaning takes place constantly. All ships have teakwood outdoor promenade decks, whereas most rivals have artificial grass or some other form of indoor-outdoor carpeting. Explorations Cafés have been built into its ships recently.

Holland America Line has its own training school in Jakarta, Indonesia, and so is able to "pre-train" crew members who have never been to sea before. Many crew members have been promoted to supervisory positions due to a host of new ships introduced, but few of those promoted have the formal training, professional or management skills, or experience to do the job well. Internal promotion is fine, but decreased professionalism is not the price that passengers should pay. However, HAL's mainly Indonesian crew members are willing, polite, and smile a lot – particularly if extra tips are forthcoming – which is more than can be said for service staff on land today, particularly in western countries. That said, many struggle to communicate with passengers.

HAL is one of only three major cruise lines with cinemas built into all its ships. It also operates many theme-related cruises, and has an extensive "University at Sea" program of life-enrichment lecturers. The cinemas also have superb full demonstration kitchens built in for a "Culinary Arts" program that includes celebrity chefs, and interactive cooking demos.

HAL has established smoking and no-smoking areas throughout its ships, but there are many more smokers than you might expect, depending on ship and itinerary.

Decor

Aboard *Amsterdam, Maasdam, Nieuw Amsterdam, Prinsendam, Rotterdam, Ryndam, Statendam, Veendam, Volendam, Zaandam*, the decor is rather bland (restful), with eclectic artwork that is focused on Dutch artifacts, mainly from the 16th and 17th centuries.

As part of its "Signature of Excellence" program, which involves refreshing the ships, its vessels have received a new and trendy "Mix" lifestyle facility – an open area with three themed specialty bars: Champagne (serving champagne and sparkling wines from around the world), Martinis (in individual shakers), and Spirits & Ales (a sports bar with beer, baseball, and basketball). You can play checkers and chess, air hockey, and other sports games using Microsoft Surface touch-screen technology.

Master chef Rudi Sodamin, culinary consultant to Holland America.

Holland America Line is not known for lavish shows.

Aboard the newest ships (*Eurodam, Nieuw Amsterdam, Noordam, Oosterdam, Westerdam, Zuiderdam*) the decor is more lively – acceptable for families with children who like bright things such as large wall panels with digital "in-your-face" artwork that present an *Alice in Wonderland* look. You wouldn't go for it in your living room, but aboard these large resort ships it works. It is important, therefore, to choose the right ship for your personality type, and for the facilities that appeal.

Gratuities

$10 per person per day (the amount charged when this book went to press) is added to your onboard account. You can have this amount adjusted at the information desk to do so. Additionally, 15% is added to bar and wine accounts. The onboard currency is the US dollar.

Cuisine/Dining

For dinner, Holland America Line features both open seating (on one level) or assigned tables (at fixed times, on the other level) in its two-deck dining rooms; it's called "As You Wish" dining. For breakfast and lunch in the main dining room, an open-seating policy applies. All dining venues are non-smoking.

Some tables for two are available, but most are for four, six, eight, or 10. The larger tables are ideal for multi-generational families. Fine Rosenthal china and cutlery are used. Live music is provided for dinner. "Lighter option" meals are always available for the nutrition-conscious and the weight-conscious.

Holland America Line food was much upgraded when master chef Rudi Sodamin arrived in 2005 as a consultant; he introduced his "Wild about Salmon" and other creative ideas, and the "Culinary Arts Center" (with its own dedicated live interactive demonstration kitchen and guest chef program) has been a success story. In 2008 menus were revamped to include more regional cuisine and more local ingredients.

However, while the USDA beef is very good, poultry and most fish tend to be overcooked (except when the ships are in Alaska, where halibut and salmon are excellent). What are not "premium" are the packets of sugar, and packets (instead of glass jars) of supermarket-brand breakfast jams, marmalade and honey, sugar, and butter. Also, coffee and teas are poor-quality, except in the extra-charge Explorations Café. While packets may be suitable for a family diner, they don't belong aboard ships that claim "award-winning cuisine."

Dessert and pastry items are good, suited to American tastes, but canned fruit and jellied desserts are much in evidence. Most of the "international" cheeses are highly colored, processed cheese (cruises in Europe have better access to European cheeses).

HAL also offers complimentary ice cream during certain hours of the day, as well as hot hors d'oeuvres in all bars – something other major lines seem to have dropped, or charge extra for. Cabin service breakfasts are very basic, with only Continental breakfast available and few hot food items.

HAL can provide kosher meals. As the ships do not

HAL'S SIGNATURE OF EXCELLENCE

Between 2004 and 2006, "Signature of Excellence" improvements were introduced, at a cost of $225 million. These cover dining, service, accommodation, and activities, and include "Premium-Plus" Euro-Top mattresses, 100% cotton bed linens or duvets (top suites only), massage showerheads, fruit baskets, and DVD players. Elemis personal bathroom amenities are pro-

vided for all passengers (these are better than Celebrity's present bathroom amenities, for example). Suite occupants also have access to the Neptune Lounge (with concierge services), thus in effect creating a two-class system that suite occupants like. Bathrobes and a range of personal toiletries are provided for all passengers, and hot hors d'oeuvres and canapés are always part of the pre-dinner cocktail scene.

have kosher kitchens, these are prepared ashore, frozen, and brought to your table sealed in containers.

The wine list relies heavily on wines from California and Washington State, with few decent French or German wines, other than those found in a typical supermarket ashore. A Connoisseur List is available in the Pinnacle Grill.

● Alternative Dining

All HAL ships have "alternative dining" spots called "Pinnacle Grill" (or "Pinnacle Grill at the Odyssey Restaurant"), specializing in "Pacific Northwest Cuisine." Items include sesame-crusted halibut with ginger-miso, and an array of premium-quality steaks, presented tableside prior to cooking. These are more intimate restaurants, with tablecloths, linen napkins, and decently sized wine glasses. The food is better than in the main dining rooms. There is a cover charge, and reservations are required. Bulgari china, Frette linens, and Reidel glasses are part of this enhanced dining experience.

● Casual Eateries

All ships have a Lido Deck self-serve buffet. Most are lines you move along with your tray, although the latest ships have more "active" stations (examples: omelets and pasta cooked to order) and individual islands. There are decent salad bars, dessert bars, regional specialties, and grilled fast-food items such as hamburgers, salmon

Perfecting a high-tech swing aboard *Prisendam*.

burgers, hot dogs, and French fries. These venues become overcrowded during breakfast and lunch.

● The Coffee/Tea Factor

Regular coffee: Half decent, but weak. Score: 3 out of 10. Espresso/cappuccino coffees (Dutch) are adequate, served in proper china, but not quite up to the standard of Celebrity or Costa. Score: 6 out of 10.

For Children

Club HAL: Junior passengers are divided into three age-appropriate groups: 3–8, 9–12, and teens. Programming is based on the number of children booked on any given sailing, and children's counselors are provided accordingly. HAL's children's programs are not as extensive as those of Carnival Cruise Lines, for example, although they are improving with the latest ships.

● Best ships for children: *Eurodam, Nieuw Amsterdam, Noordam, Oosterdam, Westerdam, Zaandam, Zuiderdam*, but not: *Amsterdam, Maasdam, Prinsendam, Rotterdam, Ryndam, Statendam, Veendam*.

Entertainment

Holland America Line is not known for lavish entertainment (the budgets aren't high enough). The production shows, while a good attempt, fall short on storyline, choreography, and performance, while colorful costuming and lighting hide the weak spots. Each ship carries its own resident troupe of singers and dancers and audio-visual support staff. HAL also offers a consistently good, tried and tested array of cabaret acts that constantly pop up on the cruise ship circuit. All showlounges are non-smoking venues.

A number of bands, a string ensemble, and solo musicians present live music for dancing and listening in many of the lounges and bars. Each ship has a Crow's Nest Lounge (by day an observation lounge) for social dancing, and there is always serenading string music in the Explorer's Lounge and dining room.

Each cruise includes a Crew Show; these vary from poor to very entertaining, depending on your taste. Passengers always seem enthusiastic, because they like connecting staff that they know and have seen during their cruise.

Holland America Line gets up-close to Alaska.

Spa/Fitness Facilities

The Greenhouse Spa, beauty and fitness amenities named after the Texas-based facility, aboard all HAL ships are staffed and operated by Steiner Leisure, a specialist concession, whose young staff will try to sell you Steiner's own-brand Elemis beauty products. Some fitness classes are free; others, such as yoga, kick-boxing or Pilates essentials, cost extra (a special price is offered for unlimited classes).

Massages (including exotic massages such as Aroma Stone massage, Chakra Balancing massage and other wellbeing massages), facials, pedicures, and beauty treatments cost extra. Examples: wellbeing massage $109 for 50 minutes; hot stone therapy massage $175 for 75 minutes; reflexology $109 for 50 minutes; personal fitness instruction $75 for 60 minutes.

LOUIS CRUISES

Ships

Coral (1971/2005), *Louis Cristal* (1980/2007), *Louis Majesty* (1992/2009), *Orient Queen* (1968/2006), *Sapphire* (1967/1996), *The Calypso* (1968/2000), *The Emerald* (1958/1997), *Thomson Destiny* (1982/2005), *Thomson Spirit* (1983/2002)

About the company

In the 1930s and '40s, Louis Loizou became the undisputed father of tourism in Cyprus. His venture into sea tourism started with the charter of ships transferring immigrants from Cyprus to other continents. His son, Costakis Loizou, who took over the running of the company after his death in 1971, started organizing short cruises from Cyprus, and in 1986 Louis Cruises was officially founded with the acquisition of the company's first fully owned ship, *Princesa Marissa* (now scrapped).

Today, the Louis Group owns about 20 four- and five-star hotels in the Greek islands and Cyprus. Louis Cruises has a 10-ship fleet, comprising medium-sized vessels – ideal for small island-hopping itineraries – and operates principally from Greece and ports in the Mediterranean. The company is listed on the Cyprus stock exchange.

Louis Cruises charters two of its ships to TUI Travels' UK-based Thomson Cruises and has, over the years, chartered other ships to well-known UK and European tour operators. Its ships are featured by some of the large package tour operators in the US.

The company's newest ship, *Louis Majesty*, cruises year-round in the Mediterranean, and, with a growing fleet based in Greece and Cyprus, the line has quietly become a solid performer in the industry.

So what's it really like?

It's a traditional cruise ship experience, based on the tour operator perspective of visiting as many port calls as possible. Hence, everything is centered round group shore excursions, and little help is provided to individual travelers.

Decor

Louis Cristal and *Louis Majesty* have contemporary European decor and style. The other ships, being much older, have a mix of design elements that are less than cohesive, although they become better with each refurbishment.

Gratuities

These are not included in the cruise fare, and are left to your discretion.

Cuisine/Dining

The company makes all its own breads, beefburgers, and pizzas aboard its ships from scratch – they are not supplied from ashore, as aboard several other major cruise lines – and each ship makes its own homemade jams, pâtés, and soups.

● **The Coffee/Tea Factor**

Regular coffee: fairly strong, but of standard quality. Score: 3 out of 10. Extra cost espresso/cappuccino coffees (illy brand): 8 out of 10. A selection of high-quality, extra-cost single-estate teas is also available.

For Children

Although the ships are all family-friendly, the children's facilities are minimal. Youth staff are supplied during peak holiday periods, according to demand.

Louis Cristal's beauty salon has a good reputation.

Entertainment

Louis has never invested much in entertainment, and its ships have only the most basic facilities. However, entertainment staff members are very enthusiastic, interact well with passengers, and are good at multi-tasking.

Spa/Fitness Facilities

While the facilities are really quite minimal, the staff is caring and very professional.

MSC CRUISES

Ships

Fantasia-class ships: *MSC Davina* (2012), *MSC Fantasia* (2008), *MSC Splendida* (2009)
Lirica-class ships: *MSC Armonia* (2001), *MSC Lirica* (2003), *MSC Opera* (2004), *MSC Sinfonia* (2005)
Musica-class ships: *MSC Magnifica* (2010), *MSC Musica* (2006), *MSC Orchestra* (2007), *MSC Poesia* (2008)
Other ships: *MSC Melody* (1982)

About the company

The HQ of the world's largest privately owned cruise line is in Geneva, Switzerland, home of parent company Mediterranean Shipping Company, the world's second-biggest container shipping company. Operations are based in Naples, Italy. It started in the passenger shipping business by acquiring the Italian company Star Lauro in 1995, together with two older ships, *Monterey* and *Rhapsody*. It expanded with the purchase of *Melody*, followed by almost new ships bought from the bankrupt Festival Cruises.

MSC Cruises has grown extremely fast, and has a number of large resort ships on order. It had the world's youngest fleet in 2011. Also, it is owned by a shipping-based family, not a faceless corporation.
✪ **Frequent passengers' club:** MSC Club.

So what's it really like?

MSC Cruises' ships are really suited to adult couples and singles, and families with children. They are good for those who enjoy big-city life, multicultural and multinational fellow passengers, outdoor cafés, constant activity accompanied by plenty of live music, late nights, and food ranging from adequate to very good.

MSC Cruises uses the most environmentally friendly detergents and cleaning materials in its housekeeping department and laundries. It has drastically reduced its onboard use of plastic items, and is aiming to eliminate them entirely.

The ships typically operate in five languages, with embarkation-day announcements in English, French, German, Italian, and Spanish. Thankfully, during the cruise, there are almost no announcements. Given this multilingual emphasis, production shows and other major entertainment displays are more visual than verbal. For the same reason, the ships don't generally carry lecturers. By culling news from 600 major newspapers around the world, in up to 36 languages, Newspapers Direct can supply you with a daily paper on board to your liking.

The roving band of photographers, taking your picture at every opportunity, can irritate, however. Particularly intrusive are the tacky photographs taken during dinner, when "pirates" and other costumed staff appear behind smartly dressed diners.

Cigar lovers will find a selection of Cuban (including Cohiba, Monte Cristo, Romeo e Juliet, Partagas), Dominican (Davidoff), and Italian (Toscana) smokes in the cigar lounges.

Decor

Except for the oldest ship, *MSC Melody*, the decor is decidedly European, with much understated elegance and really high-quality soft furnishings and other materials such as Italian marble. The latest ships are much brighter and more contemporary, albeit with restraint.

Gratuities

These are charged to your onboard cabin at €6 per person, per day. Note that 15% is added to all drinks and beverage orders; the basic price of drinks, however, is very reasonable.

Cuisine/Dining

MSC Cruises provides better-quality ingredients, almost all sourced in Europe, than some other major cruise lines. The cuisine is still mainstream – you'll find butter in packets. But, at the self-serve buffets, salt and pepper are typically provided on each table, not in packets as on most cruise lines. Espresso and cappuccino (Sega-

MSC offers a wide choice of newspapers with breakfast.

MSC Musica lives up to its name.

always available, with a tomato sauce freshly made each day. Many varieties of Italian breads such as bruschetta, focaccia, and panettone, are provided.

● **Alternative dining:** The newest ships have an alternative specialty restaurant. Aboard *MSC Musica* and *MSC Poesia*, it is Kaito, an authentic Japanese restaurant and sushi bar with an extensive menu. Aboard *MSC Magnifica* and *MSC Orchestra* it is Shanghai, a Chinese restaurant with real wok cooking, dim sum, and other Chinese and Asian specialties. The quality is high, and it really is worth having at least one meal in these venues; the à la carte prices are reasonable.

● **Room service:** Continental breakfast is complimentary from 7.30 to 10am, while room service snacks can be bought at any other time. A basket of fruit is provided to all cabins at embarkation, and replenished daily for suite-grade accommodation.

For Children

Up to three children over two and under 17 can cruise free when sharing a cabin with two adults (they pay only port dues). Children are divided into three age groups, with facilities to match: Mini Club for 3–9-year-olds; Junior Club for 10–13s; Teenagers Club for those over 14 (a pre-paid Teen Card is available). While the facilities and play areas are not as extensive as those aboard some other major lines, a "baby parking" service is useful when parents want to go ashore on excursions. MSC Cruises' mascot is Do-Re-Mi – the von Trapp family of *Sound of Music* fame would no doubt be delighted.

● **Best ships for children:** *MSC Fantasia, MSC Magnifica, MSC Musica, MSC Opera, MSC Orchestra, MSC Poesia, MSC Splendida.*

Entertainment

Because of the multilingual passenger mix, production shows are colorful and visual, particularly aboard the newest ships. Other shows consist of unknown cabaret acts (typically singers, magicians, mime artistes, comedy jugglers, and others) doing the cruise ship circuit. The ship carries a number of bands and small musical units that provide live music for dancing or listening, but there is no show band, and production shows use pre-recorded backing tracks.

Spa/Fitness Facilities

The spas are operated as a concession by Blue Ocean – except *MSC Musica*, which is operated by Steiner Leisure. Treatments include acupuncture, massages, facials, and other beauty enhancement services.

fredo brand Italian coffee) are available in the dining rooms, at extra cost, and in almost all bars – which also have coffees from Brazil, Costa Rica, and Peru.

Aboard the newest ships, MSC Cruises has introduced the Italian "slow food" concept. Always available items include spaghetti, chicken breast, salmon fillet, and vegetables of the day. Refreshingly, the company spotlights regional Italian cuisine and wine, so daily dining room menus feature food from regions such as Calabria, Piedmont, Lazio, Puglia, and Sicily.

All pizza dough is made on board, and risotto (featured daily) is a signature item for MSC Cruises and something the ships make really well. Spaghetti is

NCL's über-chic, 5,400-passenger *Norwegian Epic*.

NORWEGIAN CRUISE LINE

Ships

Dawn-class: *Norwegian Dawn* (2002), *Norwegian Star* (2002)
Epic-class: *Norwegian Epic* (2010)
Jewel-class: *Norwegian Gem (2007), Norwegian Jade* (2006), *Norwegian Jewel* (2005), *Norwegian Pearl* (2006)
Others: *Norwegian Sky* (1999), *Norwegian Spirit* (1998), *Norwegian Sun* (2001), *Pride of America* (2005)

About the company

Norwegian Cruise Line, the originator of contemporary cruising, was founded in 1966 by three Norwegian shipping companies as Klosters Sunward Ferries and was renamed Norwegian Caribbean Line in 1967. It was bought by Star Cruises in 2000, and has been replacing its older, smaller ships with brand new, larger vessels. NCL also operates one ship with mostly American crews and a base in Hawaii.

Freestyle Cruising is how NCL describes its operation – although it's hard to detect style in the onboard product. Its fleet is diverse, so the cruise experience can vary, although this makes for interesting character variation between the various ship categories. There is more standardization aboard the larger, newer ships. The senior officers are the only thing that's Norwegian.

Scaling an NCL rock wall.

Choose this line for a good all-round family cruise with a sporty, contemporary feel, interesting itineraries (many from "Homeland USA" ports), and lots of dining choices, particularly aboard the newest ships.

Most standard cabins are extremely small, though they have reasonably attractive decor and are functional. Closet and drawer space is limited aboard newer ships.
✪ **Frequent passengers' club:** Latitudes.

So what's it really like?

If this is your first cruise, you should enjoy a good overall vacation in a lively, upbeat setting. The lifestyle is contemporary, fresh, creative, and sporty, with a casualness typical of youthful city dwellers, and with its "eat when you want" philosophy, the shipboard ambience is ultra-casual – best described as US east coast "edgy." So is the dress code – indeed, the waiters are probably better dressed than many passengers. The staff is generally congenial, and you'll find a high percentage of females in cabin and restaurant service departments – more than most major cruise lines.

However, revenue centers are everywhere, including "inch of gold," tee-shirts, and sunscreen lotion, all sold at tables on the open decks adjacent to swimming pools. You won't find many fresh flowers, but you will find lots of tacky plastic flowers.

All ships can provide an almost full-size newspaper from a wide choice of US and European titles on the Multicast satellite delivery system (the cost: $3.95 per paper, per day). You can also request your favorite newspaper that's not in the list, although it may cost a bit more.

There's plenty of lively music, constant activity, entertainment, and food that's mainstream and acceptable but nothing more – unless you pay extra to eat in the "alternative" dining spots. All this is delivered by a smiling, very friendly service staff who lack polish but are willing. In the latest wheeze to extract revenue, NCL has started "Backstage Tours," costing $55 or $150 (depending on what's included).

● **NCL's Private Island (Great Stirrup Cay):** Only coffee and iced water are free (there's no iced tea), and all other drinks are charged.

Decor

The newest ships have colorful, eye-catching designs on their hulls, differentiating them from the competition.

Gratuities

A fixed $12 per person per day service charge can be pre-paid, or it will be added to your onboard account. Children over 13 pay the full adult rate; those aged 3–12 pay $6 per day, and under-3s pay nothing. A 15% gratuity is added to bar and wine charges. Spa gratuities are a whopping 18%. Onboard currency: the US dollar.

Cuisine/Dining

NCL has recognized the increasing trend away from formal restaurants (purpose: dining) toward bistros (purpose: eating faster). For cruising, NCL has championed more choices in dining than any other cruise line, except parent company Star Cruises, which started "Freestyle Dining."

This allows you to try different types of cuisine, in different settings, when you want. In practice, however, it means that you have to make reservations, which can prove frustrating at times, and getting it just right takes a little planning and, often, waiting. Food in the main dining rooms is poor to average and marginally better in the extra-charge venues. (NCL is not known for good for good food – choose it because the itinerary appeals to you).

Freestyle Dining works best aboard the ships that have been specially designed to accommodate it: *Norwegian Dawn, Norwegian Epic, Norwegian Gem, Norwegian Jade, Norwegian Jewel, Norwegian Pearl, Norwegian Spirit, Norwegian Star, Norwegian Sun,* and *Pride of America.*

On production show presentation nights, most people want to eat at the same time in order to see the shows, which causes massive prime-time congestion, slow service, and utter frustration; pagers are given out for anyone waiting for a table. The ships have plasma screens in various locations so you can make reservations when you want, and see at a glance the waiting times for a table; an updated version of its "Silverware" reservation program was introduced in 2009. The self-serve buffets are mostly chaotic, mob-scene affairs (and very repetitive), and should be avoided.

After-dinner espresso/cappuccino coffees are available in the dining rooms without extra charge – a nice feature. Once each cruise, there's a Chocoholics Buffet with paper plates and plastic cutlery. The wine list is quite good, with many excellent wines in the $20–$30 range. But the wine is typically served by table waiters, whose knowledge of wines is poor.

Cabin service breakfasts are very basic, with only Continental breakfast available and no hot food items – for those, you'll need to go to a restaurant or self-serve buffet. The non-breakfast Room Service menu has only two hot items available throughout the day: Oriental soup and pizza – the rest is cold (salads and sandwiches).

● **The Coffee/Tea Factor:** Regular coffee: weak and poor. Score: 2 out of 10. Iced tea: pitiful. Espresso/cappuccino coffees score 4 out of 10. Some bars have espresso/cappuccino machines, which are extra-charge items.

For Children

NCL's Junior Cruisers (Kids Crew) program divides children into three groups, according to age: Junior sailors (ages 2–5), First Mates and Navigators (6–12), Teens (13–17). Babysitting services are available (group only, not individual) at an extra change. Special packages are available for soft drinks.

● **Best ships for children:** *Norwegian Dawn, Norwegian Epic, Norwegian Gem, Norwegian Jade, Norwegian Jewel, Norwegian Pearl, Norwegian Spirit, Norwegian Star, Norwegian Sun.*

Entertainment

NCL has good production shows that provide color and spectacle in a predictable – though now dated – format. Each ship has a resident troupe of singers/dancers. There are two or three production shows in a typical seven-day cruise. They are all very colorful, high-energy, razzle-dazzle shows, with much use of laser and color-mover lights. They're not memorable – but, it

The SpiegelTent aboard *Norwegian Epic.*

must be said, they're very entertaining. Most activities and passenger participation events range from poor to extremely poor. Nintendo Wii interactive games are available on large screens.

Spa/Fitness Facilities

The spas are staffed and operated by the Hawaii-based Mandara Spa, owned by Steiner Leisure. Many of the staff are young, and will try to sell you Steiner's own-brand Elemis beauty products. Some fitness classes are free, while others, such as yoga and kick-boxing, cost extra. However, being aboard will give you an opportunity to try some of the more exotic treatments, particularly the various massages. Massage (including Aroma Stone massage, Chakra Balancing massage, and other wellbeing massages), facials, pedicures, and beauty salon treatments cost extra, and an 18% gratuity is added. Examples: Lomi Lomi Massage ($99 for 50 minutes/$140 for 80 minutes), Mandara Four Hands Massage ($180 for 50 minutes; $280 for 80 minutes).

Aboard some ships, a "Thermal Suite" (sauna, steam room, aroma-showers and relaxation area) costs $20 per day, or $75 for a seven-day pass.

P&O CRUISES

Ships
Adults-only ships: *Adonia* (2001), *Arcadia* (2005), and, after November 2011, *Oriana* (1995)
Family-friendly ships: *Aurora* (2000), *Azura* (2010), *Oceana* (2000), *Ventura* (2008)

About the company

Its full name is the Peninsular and Oriental Steam Navigation Company, though none of its ships is still operated by steam turbines. Based in Southampton,

The atrium aboard P&O Cruises' *Oceana*.

England, it was founded in 1837, just before Samuel Cunard established his company, and was awarded a UK government contract in 1840 to carry the mails from Gibraltar to Alexandria.

P&O Cruises acquired Princess Cruises in 1974, Swan Hellenic in 1982, and Sitmar Cruises in 1988. In 2000 it demerged from its parent to establish itself as P&O Princess plc. It was bought by Carnival Corporation in 2003.

○ **Frequent passengers' club:** Portunus Club (to be renamed the Peninsular Club from April 2012).

So what's it really like?

P&O Cruises has always been a traditional British cruise company, never quite matching the quality aboard the Cunard Line ships, which have more international passengers. It was known for British families who wanted to sail from a UK port – except for winter Caribbean cruises from Barbados. But now it's also known for having adults-only ships, and so the two products differ widely in their communal spaces. It also makes an effort to provide theme cruises – antiques, art appreciation, classical music, comedy, cricket, gardening and horticulture, jazz, Scottish dance, etc. The ships typically carry ballroom dance instructors. Bed linen is not changed as often (twice a week) as on some lines, such as MSC Cruises (every two days).

Decor

A mix of British "traditional" (think: comfy, dated armchairs, wood paneling, bistro-style food, non-glitzy). British artists are featured aboard all ships – *Ventura*, for example, displays works by more than 40 of them.

Gratuities

For gratuities, you should typically allow £3.50 ($5.20) per person, per day. However, if you opt for "Freedom Dining" (dine when you want), the ship will add £1.60 per person, per day to your account for waiter service, because you will get different waiters during the cruise; you should then tip your cabin steward separately.

Cuisine/Dining

The cuisine is straightforward, no-nonsense British food, reasonably well presented on nice Wedgwood china. But it tends to be rather bland and uninspiring. It is typical of mass-banquet catering with standard fare comparable to that found in a family hotel in an English seaside town like Scarborough.

The ingredients of many meals are disguised by gravies and sauces, as in Indian curries – well liked, of course, by most British passengers. Bread, desserts, and cakes are made well, and there is a wide variety. P&O Cruises always carries a decent selection of British, and some French, cheeses.

Ventura cruises past Ajaccio, Corsica.

Most of the dining room staff are from India, and provide service with a warmth that many other nationals find hard to equal. Wine service is amateurish and the lack of knowledge is lamentable.

● **Alternative Dining**
Extra-cost restaurants with menus designed by some of Britain's well-known television celebrity chefs, such as Gary Rhodes and Marco Pierre White, have been introduced aboard the ships. They are a mix of trendy bistro-style venues, and restaurants with an Asia-Pacific theme.

● **Casual Eateries**
The self-serve buffets suffer from small, cramped facilities, and passengers complain of having to share them with the countless concession staff who take over tables and congregate in groups. In other words, the buffets are too small to accommodate the needs of most passengers today.

● **The Coffee/Tea Factor:** Regular coffee: weak, and poor. Score: 3 out of 10. Good-quality tea and coffee-making set-up is provided in all cabins. Self-serve beverage stations are provided at the buffets, but it's often difficult to find proper teaspoons – often only wooden stirrers are available. Espresso/cappuccino coffees in the extra-charge venues are slightly better, but not as good as aboard the ships of Costa Cruises or MSC Cruises, for example.

For Children

P&O Cruises really excels in looking after children. The ships – apart from the adults-only ones, of course – have very good facilities and children's counselors, with lots of activities and participation events that make it a pleasure to take to take your kids with you.

Entertainment

P&O Cruises has always been known for its traditional, "end of pier" entertainment, with lots of pub-like sing-along sessions for the masses. These have been augmented with in-house production shows that provide lots of color, costume changes, and high-tech lighting. Each ship carries its own resident troupe of singers and dancers, called Headliners.

P&O Cruises does a good job in providing guest lecturers with varying themes, as well as occasional after-dinner speakers such as well-known television personalities and book authors.

Spa/Fitness Facilities

The spa/fitness facilities are operated by the UK concession Harding Brothers, which also provides a wide range of beauty products. Examples of prices: a full body massage is £60 for 50 minutes; an Indian head massage is £42 for 45 minutes; a holistic facial is £45 for 75 minutes. A manicure is £24 for 45 minutes, while a pedicure is £35 for 45 minutes.

PRINCESS CRUISES

Ships

Grand-class ships (over 100,000 gross tonnage): *Caribbean Princess* (2004), *Crown Princess* (2006), *Diamond Princess* (2004), *Emerald Princess* (2007), *Golden Princess* (2001), *Grand Princess* (1998), *Ruby Princess* (2008), *Sapphire Princess* (2005), *Star Princess* (2002)
Pacific-class ships: *Ocean Princess* (1999), *Pacific Princess* (1999)
Coral-class ships: *Coral Princess* (2002), *Island Princess* (2003)
Other ships: *Dawn Princess* (1997), *Sea Princess* (1998), *Sun Princess* (1995)

About the company

Princess Cruises was founded by Stanley McDonald in 1965 with one ship, the former passenger ferry *Princess Patricia*, for cruises along the Mexican Riviera. In 1974, the company was bought by the UK's Peninsular and Oriental Steam Navigation Company (P&O), and in 1988 P&O/Princess Cruises merged with the Italian line Sitmar Cruises. In 2000, Carnival Corporation and Royal Caribbean Cruises fought a protracted battle to buy Princess Cruises. Carnival won.

Princess Cruises benefited hugely from its involvement in the American television series *The Love Boat*, and its brand became known as "The Love Boat Cruise Line." Today it provides comfortable mainstream

Stretching to keep fit aboard a Princess cruise.

cruising aboard a fleet of mainly large resort ships (plus two mid-size ships), and covers the world. The ships have a higher-than-average Passenger Space Ratio than competitors Carnival or RCI, and the service is friendly without being showy. In 2010 the company converted to fully digital travel documents, so there are no more ticket document wallets and everything is online.

○ **Frequent passengers' club:** Captain's Circle.

So what's it really like?

Ships in both the mid-size and large resort categories are clean and always well maintained, and the open promenade decks of some ships have teak deck lounge chairs – others are plastic. Only *Coral Princess* and *Island Princess* have full walk-around open promenade decks; aboard all other Princess ships you cannot walk completely around the open promenade decks. The line also has a nice balance of officers, staff and crew members, and its British connections help it to achieve the feeling of calmness aboard its ships that some other lines lack.

There are proper cinemas aboard most ships, as well as outdoor poolside mega-screens for showing evening "movies under the skies."

Lines form at peak times for elevators, the information office, and for open-seating breakfast and lunch in the main dining rooms. Lines for shore excursions and shore tenders are a fact of life aboard large resort ships.

All passengers receive turndown service and chocolates on pillows each night, as well as bathrobes (on request) and toi-

Basketball aboard *Ruby Princess*.

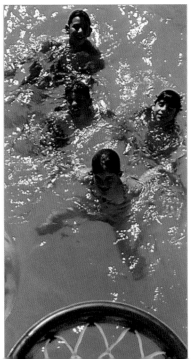

letry kits – larger, naturally, for suite/mini-suite occupants – that typically include soap, shampoo, conditioner, and hand/body lotion. A hairdryer is provided in all cabins, sensibly located at a vanity desk unit in the lounge area.

You come across countless pieces of questionable "art" everywhere – an annoying reminder that cruising aboard large resort ships is like living in a bazaar of paintings surrounded by a ship.

The dress code is either formal – usually one formal night per seven-day cruise – or smart casual. The latter is interpreted by many as jeans or tracksuits and trainers.

The newest ships – *Crown Princess, Emerald Princess, Ruby Princess* – include an adults-only area called The Sanctuary, an extra-cost retreat at the top of the ship, forward of the mast. This provides a "private" place to relax and unwind and includes attendants to provide chilled face towels and deliver light bites. It has thick-padded sunloungers both in the sun and in the shade, a swim-against-the-current pool, and there are also two outdoor cabanas for massages. I particularly recommend The Sanctuary in hot weather during Caribbean cruises. It's worth the extra $15 a head per half-day.

Princess's onboard product, especially the food and entertainment, is well established, and is totally geared to the North American market's west coast types. But British and other European nationalities should feel at home, as long as they realize that this is all about highly organized, packaged cruising, food, and service, with an increasing emphasis on onboard revenue. So you can expect to be subjected to a stream of flyers advertising daily art auctions, "designer" watches, specialized classes such as the cruise line's "ScholarShip@Sea" programs, and the like.

You'll also encounter many extra-charge items such as ice cream, non-standard coffees and pastry items taken in venues other than the restaurants, and $4 an hour for group babysitting services. There's also a charge for using washers and dryers in self-service launderettes.

Princess Cruises' ships are best suited to couples, families with children and teenagers, and older singles who like to mingle in a large ship setting with sophisticated surroundings and lifestyle, reasonably good entertainment, and fairly decent food and service, packaged affordably.

Sadly, the few staff members

on duty at the gangway when you first arrive will do no more than point you in the direction of your deck, or to the ship's elevators, instead of escorting you to your cabin – a practice now confined to MSC Cruises among the major lines.

Shipboard hospitals have live SeaMed tele-medicine link-ups with specialists at the Cedars-Sinai Medical Center in Los Angeles for emergency help – useful mainly for passengers who reside in the USA.

Princess Cays is the company's own "private island" in the Caribbean. It's all "yours" (along with a couple of thousand other passengers) for a day. However, it's a tender ride away from the ship, so getting to it can take some time.

Decor

If Carnival's ships have the brightest decor imaginable, the decor aboard Princess Cruises'

Panning for gold on a shore excursion.

ships is almost the opposite – perhaps a little bland in places, with much use of neutral tones, calm colors and pastels. This really does suit the passengers who cruise with Princess.

Gratuities

Gratuities to staff are automatically added to your account, at $10.50 ($11 for suite occupants) per person, per day; gratuities for children are charged at the same rate. If you want to pay less, go to the reception desk to have these charges adjusted – that could mean lining up with many other passengers wanting to do the same. Additionally, 15% is added to bar and wine bills. The onboard currency is the US dollar.

Cuisine/Dining

Although portions are generous, the food and its presentation are disappointing. Fish is often disguised by crumb or batter coating, the selection of fresh green vegetables is limited, and few garnishes are used. However, do remember that this is big-ship banquet catering, with all its attendant standardization and production cooking. Meats are of a decent quality, although often disguised by gravy-based sauces, and pasta dishes are acceptable (though voluminous), and are typically served by section head waiters who may also make "something special just for you" – in search of favorable comments and gratuities.

If you like desserts, order a sundae at dinner, as most other desserts are just so-so. Ice cream, when ordered in the dining room, is included, but costs extra elsewhere (Häagen Dazs can be found at poolside).

Specially designed dinnerware and good-quality linens and silverware are used, such as Dudson of England dinnerware, Frette Egyptian cotton table linens, and silverware by Hepp of Germany. All dining rooms and eateries are smoke-free.

Themed dinners are a feature. On a seven-day cruise, a typical menu cycle will include a Sail-away Dinner, Captain's Welcome Dinner, Captain's Gala Dinner, and Landfall Dinner. An extra-cost "Chef's Table Dinner" is an indulgent, three-hour "foodertain-ment" event (at $75 per person, maximum 10 persons), in which the executive chef interacts with diners; appetizers and cocktails in the galley are followed by a multi-course tasting dinner with wines paired to the meal. The wine list is reasonable, but not good. There are no dedicated wine waiters.

Passengers in balcony-grade accommodation can enjoy a full-service "Balcony Dinner" for two at $50 per person extra, plus wine, and a truly indulgent Balcony Champagne Breakfast – superb value at $32 per couple.

● **Casual Eateries**: For casual eating, each ship has a Horizon Buffet (open almost round the clock), and, at night, provides an informal dinner setting with sit-down

HOW TO GET HITCHED AT SEA

Princess Cruises has possibly the most extensive wedding program of any of the major lines, with its "Tie the Knot" wedding packages. The ship's captain can legally marry American couples at sea aboard its ships registered in Bermuda. This is by special dispensation, and should be verified when in the planning stage, and may vary according to where you reside.

The basic wedding at sea package costs $1,800, plus $450 for licensing fees, and includes a personal wedding coordinator. Live music, a candlelit celebration officiated by the captain, champagne, fresh floral arrangements, a bridal bouquet, boutonnière, a photographer, and a wedding cake can all be

laid on, with the wedding do in an exclusive wedding chapel (or other location).

You'll also get keepsake champagne flutes, and keepsake wedding certificate. Tuxedo rental is available. Harborside or shore-side packages vary according to the port. For latest rates, see Princess Cruises' website or your travel agent.

waiter service. A small, limited bistro menu is also available. The buffet displays are mostly repetitious, but far better than in past years. There is no finesse in presentation, however, as plastic plates are provided, instead of trays. The cabin service menu is quite limited, and the presentation of food items is poor.

● **The Coffee/Tea Factor:** Regular coffee: weak and poor. Score: 2 out of 10. Espresso/cappuccino coffees: Score: 3 out of 10. Except for beverage station at the serve-yourself buffets, coffees/teas in bars cost extra.

For Children

Children are divided into three age groups: Princess Pelicans (ages 2–5), Shockwaves (ages 8–12), and Off-Limits or Remix (13–17). The groups are split into age-related activities, and Princess Cruises has good children's counselors and supervised activities.

● **Best ships for children:** *Caribbean Princess, Coral Princess, Crown Princess, Dawn Princess, Diamond Princess, Emerald Princess, Golden Princess, Grand Princess, Island Princess, Ruby Princess, Sapphire Princess, Sea Princess, Star Princess, Sun Princess.* But not: *Ocean Princess, Pacific Princess.*

Entertainment

Princess Cruises' production shows have always been aimed at its slightly older, more elegant passengers. The company prides itself on its glamorous all-American shows, and they should not disappoint. For variety, there are typically two or three shows during each seven-day cruise. Each ship has a resident troupe of singers and dancers.

Passenger participation events are put on by members of the cruise staff, who would be well advised to hang on to their day jobs. Most lounges and bars have live music. Musical units range from solo pianists to string quartets, from a cappella singers to bands that can provide music for ballroom dancing. Princess Cruises also provides a number of male hosts as dance partners for women traveling alone.

Spa/Fitness Facilities

All Lotus Spa/beauty treatments and fitness facilities are operated and staffed by the Steiner Leisure

ABOVE: *Allure of the Seas*, an apartment block afloat.
BELOW: *Oasis of the Seas* employs a horticulturalist.

concession, whose offerings are similar to those already described for Celebrity Cruises and Costa Cruises. You can now make online reservations for spa treatments before your cruise, but be careful not to clash with shore excursions and other diversions. Days at sea are easiest to book online, and usually hardest to obtain on board.

ROYAL CARIBBEAN INTERNATIONAL

Ships

Oasis-class ships: *Allure of the Seas* (2010), *Oasis of the Seas* (2009)

  Freedom-class ships: *Freedom of the Seas* (2006), *Independence of the Seas* (2008), *Liberty of the Seas* (2007)

    Voyager-class ships: *Adventure of the Seas* (2001), *Explorer of the Seas* (2000), *Mariner of the Seas* (2004), *Navigator of the Seas* (2003), *Voyager of the Seas* (1999)

      Radiance-class ships: *Brilliance of the Seas* (2002), *Jewel of the Seas* (2004), *Radiance of the Seas* (2001), *Serenade of the Seas* (2003)

      Vision-class ships: *Enchantment of the Seas* (1997), *Grandeur of the Seas* (1996), *Legend of the Seas* (1995), *Rhapsody of the Seas* (1997), *Splendour of the Seas* (1996), *Vision of the Seas* (1998)

      Sovereign-class ships: *Majesty of the Seas* (1992), *Monarch of the Seas* (1991)

and comfortable cruise experience, but there's nothing royal about it except the name. The product is consistent but homogeneous. This is cruising for mainstream America. The ships are all quite pleasing, and some have really comfortable public rooms, lounges, bars, and innovative gimmicks such as ice-skating rinks.

The company competes directly with Carnival Cruise Lines, Norwegian Cruise Lines, and Princess Cruises in terms of what's offered on board, as well as the hard sell for onboard revenue (the result of highly discounted pricing in the marketplace). But RCI ships have more glass area and connection with the outdoors and the sea than Carnival's ships, and are a better bet for families with children.

RCI's largest ships are termed Oasis-class, Freedom-class, and Voyager-class *(see facing page)*. They differ from other ships in the fleet – mainly in the internal lay-out – by having a large mall-like high street – the focal point for most passengers. Many public rooms, lounges, and bars are located as adjuncts to the mall. It's rather like a mall with a ship built around it. Also, in placing so much emphasis on "active" outdoors areas, space has been taken away from the pool areas, leaving little room left just to sit and relax or sunbathe.

The next group of ships (*Brilliance of the Seas, Jewel of the Seas, Radiance of the Seas, Serenade of the Seas*) have lots of balcony cabins, and large expanses of glass. *Enchantment of the Seas, Grandeur of the Seas, Legend of the Seas, Rhapsody of the Seas, Splendour of the Seas,* and *Vision of the Seas* also have lots of glass in the public areas, but not so many balcony cabins. *Freedom of the Seas* pioneered a concierge lounge available only to suite occupants.

The oldest ships (*Majesty of the Seas, Monarch of the*

About the company

Royal Caribbean Cruise Line was set up by three Norwegian shipping company dynasties in 1969: Arne Wilhelmsen, I.M. Skaugen, and Gotaas-Larsen (who was more of a sleeping partner). Its first ship, *Song of Norway*, debuted in 1970, followed by *Nordic Prince* and *Sun Viking*. Royal Caribbean was different to Carnival and NCL in that it launched its cruise operations with brand new ships, whereas the others had only older, pre-owned tonnage. In 1978 the cruise industry's first "chop-and-stretch" operation enlarged *Song of Norway*, and 1988 saw the debut of the first really large cruise ship, *Sovereign of the Seas*.

In 1997, RCI bought Celebrity Cruises for $1.3 billion and in 2006 acquired Pullmantur Cruises for $889.9 million. In 2007 its Celebrity Cruises division created a new cruise line, Azamara Cruises, with two ships. In 2007 Royal Caribbean established CDF Croisières de France with one ship, diverted from the Pullmantur Cruises fleet.

At first the operation was excellent. But, with shareholders to please, the onboard product has slipped to equal that of Carnival Cruise Lines (whose ships, in general, have larger standard cabins). RCI's ships are shapely, with well-rounded sterns, and interesting design profiles that make them instantly recognizable. They have large, brightly lit casinos, and revenue-raising shopping galleries that passengers have to walk through to get almost anywhere else.

✪ **Frequent passengers club:** Crown and Anchor Society.

So what's it really like?

RCI provides a well-integrated, fine-tuned,

Playing the game aboard *Voyager of the Seas*.

Seas), innovative in the late 1980s, now look extremely dated. They have extremely small, barely adequate cabins, and tiny tub chairs in public rooms, for example, although the average passenger has become larger.

The onboard product is aimed at those with an active lifestyle. All ships have a rock-climbing wall with several separate climbing tracks. You'll need to plan what you want to take part in wisely, as almost everything requires you to sign up in advance.

There are few quiet places to sit and read – almost everywhere has intrusive background music, played even in elevators and all passenger hallways. Bars also have very loud music. There are many, many unwelcome announcements for activities that bring revenue, such as art auctions and bingo.

Standing in line for embarkation, the reception desk, disembarkation, for port visits, shore tenders, and for the self-serve buffet stations in the Windjammer Café is an inevitable aspect of cruising aboard large resort ships. It's often hard to escape the ship's photographers – they're everywhere. Take lots of extra pennies – you'll need them to pay for all the additional-cost items. Expect to be subjected to a stream of flyers advertising promotions, while "artworks" for auction are strewn throughout the ship, and frosted drinks in "souvenir" glasses are pushed to the hilt. There are no cushioned pads for the deck lounge chairs.

Service personnel are friendly, but not many greet you when passing in the corridors, so the hospitality factor could be improved. The elevators talk to you, though "going up/going down" is informative but monotonous. However, the signage and illuminated picture displays of decks are good, particularly aboard the Oasis-class ships.

RCI's pool tables are gyroscopically controlled.

Occupants of the Presidential Family Suite, Royal Suite, Royal Family Suite, Owner's Suite, and Grand Suite get a dedicated security line, where available. Royal and Presidential Family Suite occupants are welcomed by a senior officer and escorted aboard. Those in Grand Suites and higher categories get gold SeaPass cards for better staff recognition. On embarkation: free bottled water and a fruit plate, slippers, spa bathrobes, Vitality bathroom amenities, and Ghirardelli chocolates or petits fours at turndown. Free 24-hour room service, coffee, and tea are available throughout the cruise, along with the option of ordering from the main dining room's full breakfast, lunch and dinner menus. There's also free garment pressing on formal evenings.

Other perks include a cocktail reception with the captain, reserved showlounge seating, and priority bookings for spa/salon appointments, tender tickets and excursions. On Voyager- and Freedom-class ships, suite guests get reserved seating poolside and at Studio B ice shows. During breakfast and lunch in the casual Windjammer buffet venue, there's reserved private seating in the adjacent specialty restaurants. Aboard Radiance-, Voyager- and Freedom-class ships, suite occupants receive a Concierge Club key. Junior Suite occupants get silver SeaPass cards for extra benefits.

Decor

Interior decor is bright and contemporary, but not as neon-intensive and glitzy as Carnival's ships. There is much Scandinavian design influence, with some eclectic sculpture and artwork. The "you are here" signage and deck plans are excellent. The furniture in public lounges tends to include small "tub" chairs, often broken by large passengers.

Gratuities

Gratuities can be paid in cash or added to your onboard account daily at the suggested rate of $11.65 per person ($13.90 for suite occupants). In addition, 15% is automatically added to all bar, wine, and spa charges.

Johnny Rockets is a popular RCI fast-food venue.

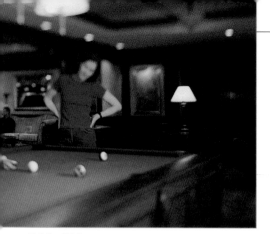

Cuisine/Dining

Most ships have large dining halls that are two or three decks high, giving a sense of space and grandeur. Few tables for two are available, most being for four, six, or eight people. All dining rooms and eateries are non-smoking. The efficient dining operation emphasizes highly programmed, extremely hurried service that many find insensitive. There are no fish knives.

"My Time Dining," rolled out fleetwide in 2009, means you can choose either a fixed dining time or any time you want. For this option, you'll need to pre-pay gratuities and enrol either on board or in advance through www.royalcaribbean.com or by asking your travel agent to arrange it via the reservations system.

The cuisine in the main dining rooms is typical of mass banquet catering, with mediocre standard fare. The food costs per passenger are below those for sister companies Azamara Club Cruises and Celebrity Cruises, so don't expect the same food quality. Dinner menus typically include a Welcome Aboard Dinner, French Dinner, Italian Dinner, International Dinner, and Captain's Gala Dinner, and all offer plenty of choice. Menu descriptions sound tempting, but the food, although well enough prepared, is unmemorable. A decent selection of light meals is provided, and there is a vegetarian menu.

The quality of meat, particularly beef, is poor – unless you pay $14.95 extra for a "better" quality sirloin steak "cooked to order." Other meats are often disguised with gravies or heavy sauces. Most fish (except salmon) and seafood items tend to be overcooked and lack taste. Green vegetables are scarce – they're provided basically for decoration – but salad items are plentiful. Rice is often used as a source of carbohydrates, potatoes being more expensive.

Breads and pastry items are generally good, although some items, such as croissants, may not be made on board. The selection of breads, rolls, and fruit could be better. Dessert items are standardized and lack flavor, and the cheese selection and crackers are poor. Caviar, once a standard menu item, is now lumpfish caviar – poor, incredibly salty, and nothing to do with real caviar.

Although prices are moderate, the wine list is not extensive, and almost all wines are very young. Only small glasses are provided. The waiters are overly friendly for some tastes – particularly on the last night of the cruise, when tips are expected.

● **Alternative Dining Venues:** All Freedom, Radiance and Voyager-class ships have two additional dining venues: Chops Grille Steakhouse (for premium veal chops and steaks, cover charge $30 per person), and Portofino (for Italian-American cuisine; cover charge $25 per person). Both venues serve food of a much higher quality than that in the main dining room. Reservations are required in both venues. Vision-class ships have one extra-charge alternative dining venue, Portofino. Be prepared to eat Texas-sized portions, presented on large plates. Note that menus do not change throughout the cruise. Oasis-class ships have more extra-cost dining venues. The dress code is smart casual.

● **Casual Eateries:** All ships have casual venues called Windjammer Café or Windjammer Marketplace for fast-food items, salads, and other informal meals. Some are of the single-line (move along with your plate) type, while the newer ships have individual islands for more variety and fewer lines. However, the actual quality of cooked food items is nutritionally poor, as are the tacky salad dressings.

Breakfast buffet items are virtually the same each day, monotonous and mostly below the standards of diner food. The same is true of lunchtime salad items. The beverage stations have only the most basic items. Hamburgers and hot dogs in self-serve buffet locations are generally left in steam tables. They are steamed rather than grilled, although you can ask for one to be grilled in front of you. Note that trays are not provided

Shrek on parade, courtesy of RCI's link-up with DreamWorks.

Water-sports off RCI's Labadee resort in Haiti.

3–5), Explorer Center (6–8), Voyager Center (9–12), and Optix Teen Center (13–17).

An unlimited soda and juice package for under-17s is available. There are lots of activities, and a host of children's counselors.

● **Best ships for children:** *Adventure of the Seas, Allure of the Seas, Explorer of the Seas, Freedom of the Seas, Independence of the Seas, Liberty of the Seas, Mariner of the Seas, Navigator of the Seas, Oasis of the Seas, Voyager of the Seas.* **Ships with fewer facilities:** *Brilliance of the Seas, Enchantment of the Seas, Grandeur of the Seas, Jewel of the Seas, Legend of the Seas, Radiance of the Seas, Rhapsody of the Seas, Serenade of the Seas, Splendour of the Seas, Vision of the Seas.* **Ships with poor facilities for children:** *Majesty of the Seas, Monarch of the Seas.*

– only oval plates – so if you are disabled or have mobility difficulties you may need to ask for help. Also, because the plates are plastic, it's impossible to get your food on a heated plate.

Almost all ships also have Johnny Rockets '50s-style diners (extra charge, per person, whether you eat in or take out, and, while the food is included, shakes and drinks cost extra). These serve hamburgers, hot dogs, desserts, and sodas, although the typical waiting time is about 30 minutes – pagers are provided, allowing you to wander off in the meantime.

Drinks packages are available in bars, in the form of cards or stickers so that you can pre-pay for a selection of soft drinks and alcoholic drinks. However, the rules for using the pre-paid packages are a bit cumbersome. There is a $3.95 charge for cabin service deliveries midnight–5am.

● **The Coffee/Tea Factor:** Regular coffee: weak, poor quality. Score: 1 out of 10. Espresso/cappuccino coffees (Seattle's Best brand) score 4 out of 10 – but they come in paper cups.

For Children

Early 2009 saw the start of RCI's new youth programs, including My Family Time dining, and extra-cost packages such as a supervised "Lunch and Play" option. An extra-cost in-cabin babysitting service was added.

Adventure Ocean is RCI's "edutainment" area. Kids are divided into four age-appropriate groups: Aquanaut Center (ages

Ziplining aboard *Oasis of the Seas*.

Entertainment

The entertainment is upbeat, similar to what you would find in a resort hotel in Las Vegas. Production shows are colorful, fast-paced, high-volume razzle-dazzle spectaculars, but with little or no storyline, poor linkage between themes and scenes, and basic choreography. The live band is augmented by pre-recorded backing tracks to make it sound like a big, professional orchestra. Each ship has its resident troupe of singers and dancers.

Then there are silly audience participation events (summer camp-style, but often funny) and activities – something RCI has always done well.

Spa/Fitness Facilities

The spa facilities are operated by the Steiner Leisure concession, with offerings similar to those already described for Celebrity Cruises and Costa Cruises.

For the more sporting, all RCI ships have a rock-climbing wall, with several separate climbing tracks. There is a 30-minute instruction period before anyone is allowed to climb, and this is done in pairs. It's free, and all safety gear is included, but you'll need to sign up. It's worth remembering that it's quieter on port days, but the hours of operation are limited – typically two hours in the morning and two in the afternoon.

Playing a round of golf in the golf simulator costs $25 per hour (for up to four persons). ❑

THE BIGGEST OF THE BIG: CRUISE SHIPS OVER 100,000 GROSS TONNAGE

Ship Name	Cruise Line	Gross Tonnage	No. of Passengers	Passenger Space Ratio	Year Built
Allure of the Seas	Royal Caribbean Int.	225,282	5,400	41.2	2010
Oasis of the Seas	Royal Caribbean Int.	225,282	5,400	41.2	2009
Freedom of the Seas	Royal Caribbean Int.	154,407	3,634	42.0	2006
Independence of the Seas	Royal Caribbean Int.	154,407	3,634	42.0	2008
Liberty of the Seas	Royal Caribbean Int.	154,407	3,634	42.0	2007
Norwegian Epic	Norwegian Cruise Line	153,000	4,200	36.4	2010
Queen Mary 2	Cunard Line	148,528	2,620	56.6	2004
Phoenicia	GNMTC (Libya)	139,400	3,502	39.6	2012
MSC Divina	MSC Cruises	139,000	3,502	39.6	2012
Explorer of the Seas	Royal Caribbean Int.	137,308	3,634	42.0	2000
Voyager of the Seas	Royal Caribbean Int.	137,280	3,634	42.0	1999
Adventure of the Seas	Royal Caribbean Int.	137,276	3,634	42.0	2001
Mariner of the Seas	Royal Caribbean Int.	137,276	3,634	42.0	2004
Navigator of the Seas	Royal Caribbean Int.	137,276	3,634	42.0	2003
MSC Fantasia	MSC Cruises	133,500	3,274	41.2	2008
MSC Splendida	MSC Cruises	133,500	3,274	41.2	2008
Carnival Breeze	Carnival Cruise Lines	130,000	3,646	35.6	2012
Carnival Dream	Carnival Cruise Lines	130,000	3,646	35.6	2009
Carnival Magic	Carnival Cruise Lines	130,000	3,646	35.6	2011
Disney Dream	Disney Cruise Lines	129,690	2,500	51.2	2011
Disney Fantasy	Disney Cruise Lines	129,690	2,500	51.2	2012
Celebrity Eclipse	Celebrity Cruises	122,000	2,852	42.7	2010
Celebrity Equinox	Celebrity Cruises	122,000	2,852	42.7	2009
Celebrity Reflection	Celebrity Cruises	122,000	2,852	42.7	2012
Celebrity Silhouette	Celebrity Cruises	122,000	2,852	42.7	2011
Celebrity Solstice	Celebrity Cruises	122,000	2,852	42.7	2008
Ventura	P&O Cruises	116,017	3,092	37.5	2008
Diamond Princess	Princess Cruises	115,875	2,674	43.3	2004
Sapphire Princess	Princess Cruises	115,875	2,674	43.3	2004
Azura	P&O Cruises	115,055	3,092	37.5	2010
Costa Fascinosa	Costa Cruises	114,500	3,012	38.0	2012
Costa Favolosa	Costa Cruises	114,500	3,012	38.0	2011
Costa Serena	Costa Cruises	114,147	3,000	38.0	2007
Crown Princess	Princess Cruises	113,561	3,114	36.4	2006
Emerald Princess	Princess Cruises	113,561	3,114	36.4	2007
Ruby Princess	Princess Cruises	113,561	3,114	36.4	2008
Caribbean Princess	Princess Cruises	112,894	3,114	36.2	2004
Costa Concordia	Costa Cruises	112,000	3,000	37.3	2006
Carnival Conquest	Carnival Cruise Lines	110,239	2,974	37.0	2004
Carnival Splendor	Carnival Cruise Lines	110,239	2,974	37.0	2008
Carnival Freedom	Carnival Cruise Lines	110,239	2,974	37.0	2007
Carnival Glory	Carnival Cruise Lines	110,239	2,974	37.0	2003
Carnival Liberty	Carnival Cruise Lines	110,239	2,974	37.0	2005
Carnival Valor	Carnival Cruise Lines	110,239	2,974	37.0	2004
Star Princess	Princess Cruises	108,977	2,602	41.8	2002
Golden Princess	Princess Cruises	108,865	2,600	41.8	2001
Grand Princess	Princess Cruises	108,806	2,600	41.8	1998
Costa Fortuna	Costa Cruises	102,587	2,716	37.7	2003
Costa Magica	Costa Cruises	102,587	2,718	37.7	2004
Carnival Triumph	Carnival Cruise Lines	101,509	2,758	36.8	1999
Carnival Victory	Carnival Cruise Lines	101,509	2,758	36.8	2000
Carnival Destiny	Carnival Cruise Lines	101,353	2,642	38.3	1996

Allure of the Seas

Queen Mary 2

MSC Fantasia

Ventura

Costa Serena

Golden Princess

Carnival Destiny

THE APPEAL OF SMALLER OPERATORS

While the major cruise lines dominate the mass market, dozens of other companies cater for more specialist tastes and can offer some exotic destinations

The international cruise industry is comprised of around 75 companies with ocean-going cruise ships providing vacations to more than 21 million passengers each year. Most major cruise lines are owned and operated by large corporations. Other operators are family-owned cruise lines. Still others are small, with just a couple of compact-sized ships. Some cruise companies don't own their own ships, but charter them from ship owning and ship management companies for year-round or seasonal operation – for example, specialized ships outfitted for Arctic and Antarctic expedition cruises only.

Some cruise lines are actually tour operators – vacation packagers, mostly in Europe, that put together airlines, hotels, car rentals, and cruises. Some own their own charter airlines. Tour operators have transferred some of their land-based tourists to the sea, aboard ships that move the destinations for them. These are the equivalent of the package vacation that first became popular in Europe in the 1970s – for example, Thomson Cruises.

These mini-profiles, in alphabetical order, include cruise lines with small or mid-size ships and small fleets, those with a small number of large resort ships, those with tall ships (with either real working sail propulsion or computer-controlled assistance), those that specialize in hardy or "soft" expedition cruises, and those which cruise along coastal and inland waterways.

The major cruise companies are profiled on pages 124–57 and so are not included in this section.

Germany-oriented AIDA Cruises is yet another Carnival brand.

Abercrombie & Kent (A&K)

Geoffrey Kent started A&K as a safari company in 1962 – there was no Mr Abercrombie, it just sounded good – and then specialized in upscale train journeys around the globe for small groups. The company got started in the cruise business when it went into a marketing agreement with the long-defunct Society Expeditions in 1990.

Two years later it bought the little expedition ship *Society Explorer* (formerly *Lindblad Explorer*) when Society Expeditions ceased operations. The ship, renamed *National Geographic Explorer*, now belongs to Lindblad Expeditions. Today, A&K specializes in escorted educational and nature cruises, and charters various ships, such as those of Swan Hellenic Cruises, for its cruise programs, taking passengers to the more remote destinations such as the Antarctic, in relative comfort. The company is also involved in river cruises and hotel barges, for which it acts as sales agents. Gratuities are not included in the cruise fare.

AIDA Cruises

The former East German shipping company Deutsche Seereederei (DSR) and its marketing arm Seetours (Deutsche Seetouristik) were assigned the traditional cruise ship *Arkona* as part of the east–west integration in 1985, which included a contractual agreement with the Treuhandanstalt to build a new ship. It did this in 1996 with the newly built *Aida*, designed to appeal to young, active German-speaking families. The concept was to create a seagoing version of the popular Robinson Clubs – a sort of German Club Med concept. When *Aida* first debuted, there were almost no passengers and the company struggled.

In 1998 the company was sold to Norwegian Cruise Line, which sold it back to its original Rostock-based owners. P&O acquired it in 1999 and it is now a very successful multi-ship brand belonging to the Carnival Corporation, under the direct control of its Costa Cruises division. AIDA Cruises, Germany's largest cruise line, is known for its über-casual cruising, with two main self-serve buffet restaurants instead of the traditional waiter service. It's a tablecloth-less method of eating, a bit like camping at sea, with little contact with the small staff numbers.

The entertainment is extremely good, however, and is provided in conjunction with the Schmidt Theatre in Hamburg. Gratuities are not included in the cruise fare.

Alaska Dream Cruises

Allen Marine Tours, an operator of local day vessels in Alaska, formed a new micro-cruise company, Alaska Dream Cruises, in 2010 after purchasing two Cruise West 78-passenger vessels when Cruise West declared insolvency and ceased operations. *Spirit of Columbia* and *Spirit of Alaska* were converted into *Admiralty Dream* and *Baranhof Dream* in 2011. Gratuities are not included in the cruise fare.

American Cruise Lines

ACL was originally formed in 1974, at the beginning of American coastal passenger shipping, but it went bankrupt in 1989, the ships were sold off, and the company lay dormant. The original owner, Charles Robertson, a renowned yachtsman who used to race 12-meter America's Cup yachts, resurrected it in 2000, and built its own ships in its own wholly owned small shipyard in Salisbury, Maryland, on the Chesapeake Bay.

ACL's ships *(American Glory, American Spirit, American Star, Independence)* ply the inter-coastal waterways and rivers of the USA's east coast between Maine and Florida, and provide an up-close, intimate experience for passengers who don't need luxury or much pampering but do like American history and culture, as well as service from an all-American college-age staff. The "D-class" vessels are less than 2,500 gross tonnage, and are subject neither to bureaucratic regulations nor to union rules. In 2011, the company also started operating *Queen of the West*, a 120-passenger paddlewheel (replica steamboat) on rivers in the USA's Pacific Northwest, and it is building another replica steamboat for service on the Mississippi. Gratuities are not included in the company's cruise fares.

American Safari Cruises

This micro-cruise line, founded in 1996, was bought in 2008 by InnerSea Discoveries, owned by the former chief executive officer of American Safari Cruises, Dan Blanchard. ASC has a fleet of very small motor yacht-type vessels for 6–36 passengers

American Safari Cruises goes whale watching.

taking expensive up-close-and-personal cruises in Alaska and the Pacific Northwest. While the vessels are decent, the onboard facilities are few and the one-seat dining experience is very casual, with little choice. The advantage of these intimate vessels is that they really can take you up close to fascinating parts of Alaska that large resort ships can't reach. Gratuities are not included.

Aurora Expeditions

This Australian company was founded in 1993 by Australian Mount Everest veteran and geologist Greg Mortimer and adventure travel specialist Margaret Werner. The company, which specializes in small-group expeditions, uses the chartered expedition ship *Polar Pioneer* for its Antarctic expedition cruise programs. Other destinations include Papua New Guinea, Australia's Kimberley region, and the Russian Far East, for which the ship is the chartered Russian expedition vessel *Marina Svaetana*. Gratuities are not included in the fare.

American Cruise Lines' *Queen of the West* paddlewheel.

The mid-size *Azamara Journey* carries 866 cruisers.

Azamara Club Cruises

This company, formerly Azamara Cruises, is an off-shoot of Celebrity Cruises, and was created in 2007. Having started with little direction, the company was revitalized in 2009–10 by a new president, Larry Pimentel, formerly with SeaDream Yacht Cruises. It operates two 700-passenger ships, taking people to smaller ports that some of the large resort ships can't get into. The company specializes in providing high-quality dining, and the ships try to provide a floating "country club" experience. They are in direct competition with the ships of Oceania Cruises – except that Oceania doesn't charge extra to dine in its specialty restaurants. But Azamara has longer port stays and more overnight port stays than Oceania – a bonus during longer itineraries.

The onboard experience is similar to that aboard the ships of parent company Celebrity Cruises (including tacky art auctions), but modified to suit those who want a more personal cruise experience aboard smaller ships. Its strengths are the food and European-style service, and each ship has two extra-charge restaurants in addition to the main dining venues. Gratuities to dining and housekeeping staff, wine with lunch and dinner, coffee and tea 24 hours a day, and shuttle buses in ports of call, where needed, are all included in the fare.

Blount Small Ship Adventures

Founded in 1966 by the late Luther H. Blount, an engineer and inventor of the American steam trawler, who built his cruise vessels in his own shipyard in Warren, Rhode Island, the company started as as a family-run venture. Today, as the oldest US-flag cruise line still operating, it is run by his daughter, Nancy Blount.

Cruises are operated like private family outings, using two unpretentious ships that were specially constructed to operate in close-in coastal areas and inland waterways of the eastern US seaboard, with forays to the Bahamas and Caribbean during the winter. The onboard experience is strictly no-frills cruising in very, very basic, down-to-earth surroundings that have a 1950s feel.

Its early-to-bed passengers – average age 72 years – are typical of those who don't like glitz or trendy, and don't need much other than basic American food. If you want a drink, bring your own – the line supplies only tonic and soft drinks – so forget wine with dinner unless you supply your own bottle. Gratuities are not included in the cruise fare.

CDF Croisières de France

Founded and wholly owned by Royal Caribbean Cruise Line (RCCL), CDF Croisières de France was created in

Chile-based Cruceros Australis runs expedition cruises.

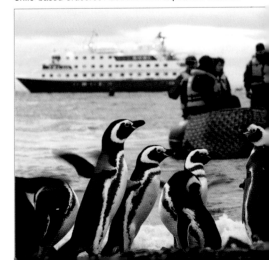

2007, with headquarters in Paris. The brand is now under the overall control of Pullmantur Cruises, also owned by RCCL. The company devotes all its resources to cruising for French-speaking passengers, with one ship, the former *Horizon*. The emphasis is on fine French cuisine and all-inclusive pricing. Gratuities are included in the cruise fare.

Celebration Cruise Line

This company, a one-ship operation, is owned by Celebration Cruise Holdings, which also owned the now defunct Imperial Majesty Cruise Line, whose reputation suffered from high-pressure telemarketing campaigns. Its *Bahamas Celebration* operates two-night cruises from the Port of Palm Beach to the Bahamas.

Despite the company's claims to "international gourmet dining," the ship provides a highly programmed but absolutely basic party getaway cruise with very standard food, and with much pressure for onboard revenue from its dining, casino, and shore excursion operations.

Classic International Cruises

This small, family-owned company is based in Lisbon, Portugal. It buys or charters older (pre-owned) deep-draft ships that have "traditional" decor and lovingly refurbishes them. George Potamianos, an engineer whose passion is restoring ships' engine rooms and machinery, and his two sons run the company, which either operates the ships itself, or charters them to various cruise and tour operators.

Nautical officers and most service staff are Portuguese, known for their warm-hearted, gracious service. The ships may be old, but they are "traditional" ships that have been extremely well maintained and provide the kind of seagoing experiences not found aboard the world's large resort ships. Gratuities are not included in the cruise fare.

A shallow draft makes disembarking easy from a Blount ship.

Club Med Cruises

Club Med became renowned for providing hassle-free vacations for the whole family. The first Club Med village was started in 1950 on the island of Mallorca, but the concept became so popular that it grew to more than 100 vacation villages throughout the world.

Club Med Cruises, an offshoot of the French all-inclusive vacation clubs, introduced its first ocean-going cruise vessel in 1990, the computer-controlled sail-cruise ship *Club Med II* (extensively refurbished in 2008). Aboard the all-inclusive ship, the *gentils ordinaires* serve as both super-cruise staff and "rah-rah" cheerleaders for the mainly French-speaking passengers. *Club Med II* has a sister ship, Windstar Cruises' *Wind Surf*, which also provides a relaxed onboard experience. Gratuities are included in the cruise fare.

Cruceros Australis

Cruceros Australis, based in Santiago, Chile, operates cruise ships on soft expedition cruises to the Chilean fjords, Patagonia and Tierra del Fuego – some of the world's most fascinating but hostile environments. Catering increasingly to an international clientele, with Spanish as the official onboard language, cruising with this company is all about Chile and its truly dramatic coastline. Don't expect high standards aboard its two ships, but service is very friendly, and its organization and operations are extremely good. The onboard languages are English and Spanish. The company introduced a brand new ship in 2010, the 210-passenger *Stella Australis*, and now operates a three-ship fleet. The other two ships are *Mare Australis* and *Via Australis (see the Coastal Cruises chart on page 98)*. Its cruises are "all-inclusive," with an open bar for all beverages, including wine, and gratuities included.

Cruise and Maritime Voyages

This UK-based company, which has existed for many years as a sales and marketing organization representing several small cruise lines, now charters two older ships owned by other companies. The company, whose owners originally worked for the now-defunct CTC Cruises, specializes in adults-only (16 and over) cruises from UK ports, and provides traditional cruise features such as mid-morning bouillon, and captain's welcome and farewell dinners. The onboard product, particularly the food, is at the lower end of the market. *Marco Polo* and *Ocean Countess* are the featured ships for ex-UK cruises. Gratuities are not included in the cruise fare.

Crystal Cruises

Crystal Cruises was founded in 1988 by Nippon Yusen Kaisha (NYK), the world's largest cargo ship and transportation logistics company, with a fleet of more than 700 ships. The American-managed company is based in Century City, Los Angeles. *Crystal Harmony*, the company's first ship, was built in Japan, and debuted in New York in May 1990 to great acclaim. Meanwhile, Crystal Cruises introduced two new ships, *Crystal Symphony* in 1995, and *Crystal Serenity* in 2000, one built in Finland, the other in France.

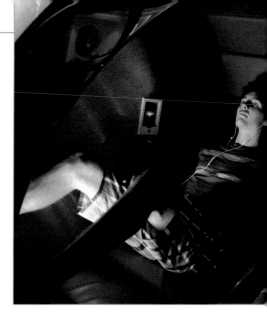

The media room in Vibe, *Disney Dream*'s teen club.

In 2006 *Crystal Harmony* was transferred to parent company NYK as *Asuka II* for its Asuka Cruise division, for Japanese speakers. Crystal Cruises continues to provide excellent food and service aboard its two spacious ships (*Crystal Serenity* and *Crystal Symphony*), including a Nobu sushi/sashimi bar aboard *Crystal Serenity*.

The ships operate worldwide itineraries with flair. Both ships are superbly maintained, and passengers who seek fine food in a sophisticated setting should be delighted with their choice of ship and company. Open-seating dining was introduced in January 2011 for the first time, or passengers can opt for a choice of fixed-time dining. Gratuities are currently not included, but in spring 2012 Crystal Cruises joins the "all-inclusive" club with drinks, wines, and gratuities included in the fare.

Disney Cruise Line

In 1932, a Disney cartoon, *Steamboat Willy*, depicted Mickey Mouse at the wheel of a ship, but it took 60 years until Disney decided to get into the cruise business, as an extension of its resort stay business, offering a "seamless vacation package."

It was Lawrence (Larry) P. Murphy, executive vice-president of the Walt Disney Company, who was the guiding light in the early 1990s behind the expansion of the company into the cruise business. Previously, the company had flirted with cruising by participating in a licensing agreement with a Florida-based cruise line, the now-defunct Premier Cruise Lines, with three vintage ships based in Port Canaveral. Murphy and other Disney executives explored the possibility of creating their own ships when the licensing agreement ran

Crystal Serenity's sushi stars Nobu Matsuhisa and Chef Tamba.

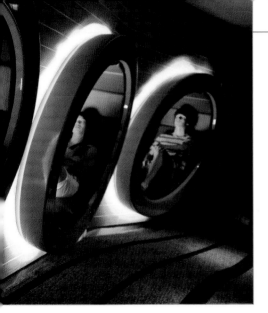

are usually retired and of senior years – typically over 65. Aboard the ships, interior design reflects traditional design features, and dressing for dinner is expected on four nights during a two-week cruise. Many theme cruises, such as gardening and horticulture, and Scottish country dancing, hosted by recognised television celebrities, are regular features. The company welcomes solo passengers as well as couples and delivers a quintessentially "British" cruise experience, albeit by a mainly Filipino hotel service staff.

The first ship dedicated exclusively to cruising debuted in 1987, and now ships cruise year-round out of UK ports such as Dover, Southampton, Liverpool, Newcastle, Greenock, Leith, Belfast, and Dublin (ideal for anyone based in the UK to join one of the ships without having to fly), with some ships operating out of Caribbean ports such as Barbados in winter.

Coffee- and tea-making facilities – much appreciated, particularly by its older passengers – are provided in each cabin. Smoking is allowed only on the open decks, and nowhere inside the ships. Gratuities are not included in the cruise fare, but are automatically charged to your onboard account. Drink prices are extremely reasonable aboard all the company's ships, where the social scene is friendly and warm.

Galápagos Cruises

Metropolitan Touring, Ecuador's foremost tour and travel company, is based in Quito, and sells its cruises through general sales agents such as the USA's Dallas-based Adventure Associates. Its boutique ships, the well-run *Isabella* and *Santa Cruz*, visit the Galápagos Islands with all-Ecuadorean crew and food. Go because of the nature-filled destination, not for the ships, which are old and have few facilities. Gratuities are not included in the cruise fare.

The atrium aboard Fred Olsen Cruise Line's *Braemar.*

out. They concluded that pairing with an established cruise line wouldn't work because of Disney's policy of generous spending on the guest experience.

The solution: create a new cruise line, wholly owned and controlled by Disney and to be known as Disney Cruise Line. The company committed an astonishing $1 billion to the project.

Its two large resort ships, *Disney Magic* (1998) and *Disney Wonder* (1999), the first cruise ships since the 1950s to be built with two funnels, cater to loyal Disney followers, and everything aboard the ships is Disney – every song, every piece of artwork, every movie and production show, and Mickey's ears adorn the ships' funnels. But there's no casino (hooray!), and no library (boo!). However, its "rotation dining" concept proved to be completely Disneylogical; you move, together with your waiter, to each of three identically sized restaurants – each with different decor – in turn.

One new, larger ship, *Disney Dream*, joined the fleet in 2011, and sister ship *Disney Fantasy* arrives in 2012.

Disney is all about families with children, and the ships cater to both. You can buy a package combining a short stay at a Disney resort and a cruise. Disney has its own cruise terminal at Port Canaveral, Florida, its design being an imaginative but close copy of the Ocean Terminal in Southampton, UK, used by yesteryear's ocean liners. The terminal and pier were extended in 2010 and connected to a new parking garage. Gratuities are not included in the cruise fare.

Fred Olsen Cruise Line

This is a Norwegian family-owned and family-run company which was founded in Hvitstein, a town on Oslofjord, Norway, in 1848. Today, a fifth-generation Olsen, Fred Jr, runs the company from its headquarters in Suffolk, England. The group also has interests in the hotels, aviation, shipbuilding, ferries, and offshore industries. The company specializes in cruises for adults who

GAP Adventures

This Canadian company, based in Toronto, was founded by Bruce Poon Tip in 1990. It has a grassroots approach to travel, creating meaningful, memorable adventures on the path less traveled. With only his own personal credit cards, GAP Adventures was born. The company has grown into one of the world's largest adventure travel companies, with over 850 employees. It charters small ships suitable for expedition-style cruises.

Hapag-Lloyd Cruises

Germany's two most famous ocean liner companies, the Bremen-based Norddeutscher Lloyd and the Hamburg-based Hamburg America Line, merged in 1970 to become Hapag-Lloyd. The company no longer operates regularly scheduled transatlantic crossings. Instead, it markets four ships in three different market segments.

Two small ships are in the specialized expedition cruise market (the 164-passenger *Bremen* and the 184-passenger *Hanseatic*); one is in the mid-priced market (the 408-passenger *Columbus*), and one ship (the 400-passenger *Europa*) is in the luxury market. All provide destination-intensive cruises aimed at the German market, with occasional dual-language cruises for the English-speaking market. Hapag-Lloyd Cruises is a member of IAATO (Association of Antarctica Tour Operators), a body committed to the highest standards of responsible tourism to Antarctica and to operating its ships in the most environmentally friendly manner.

Except for *Europa*, gratuities are not included in the cruise fare. *Columbus* operates certain cruises as "all-inclusive." Both ships operate an annual around-the-world cruise, which typically starts in November–December and lasts for three or four months. The company makes all its own breads and soups, pâtés, jams, and preserves aboard its ships from scratch.

Following the Midnight Sun with Hurtigruten.

Happy Cruises

Formerly known as Quail Cruises, this is part of Spain's Quail Travel Group. The company, a well-known tour operator, started its cruise division in 2008 by chartering one of the original Love Boats (Pacific). After several changes of ships, Happy Cruises operates several ships under charter. It offers "all-inclusive" pricing and is marketed to families with children, with cruises from Barcelona and Valencia, Spain. Gratuities are included in the cruise fare.

Hebridean Island Cruises

Hebridean Island Cruises (formerly Hebridean International Cruises) was set up in 1989 under the Thatcher government's British Enterprise Scheme. Its headquarters is in Skipton, Yorkshire. The company operates one all-inclusive boutique ship, *Hebridean Princess*, which conveys the atmosphere of English country-house life – think Laura Ashley fabrics and soft furnishings – and specializes in cruises for mature adults. Gratuities and all port taxes are included, as are most excursions. The ship runs cruises around the Scottish islands, including Fingal's Cave in the Inner Hebrides, the inspiration for Felix Mendelssohn's Hebrides Overture, Opus 26. There are occasional sailings to English ports, the Channel Islands and Norway. Each cabin has coffee- and tea-making facilities. Gratuities are not included in the cruise fare.

Hurtigruten

The company is an amalgamation of two shipping companies (OVDS and TVDS) and provides year-round service along the Norwegian coast, calling at 33 ports in 11 days. Hurtigruten, formerly known as the Norwegian Coastal Voyage, has also recently developed expedition-style cruises, albeit aboard ships that have been converted for the purpose, rather than specifically built for expedition cruises. So, as long as you think utilitarian and modest decor, you'll get the idea of life aboard one of the Hurtigruten ships, which are practical rather than beautiful. Even aboard the newest ships, the food and service are fairly basic – there's a lack of green vegetables – but the ships provide a great way to see many, many ports along the coast of Norway in a comfortable manner.

Norway's Crown Princess Mette-Marit was the godmother of the newest ship, *Fram*, a 318-berth expedition-style vessel built for polar and Greenland cruising.

Iberocruceros

Founded originally as one of the Iberojet (tour operator) companies, 75% of the venture company is owned by the Carnival Corporation, and 25% by the Orizonia Corporation. The company's ships operate well-organized, all-inclusive cruises for the Spanish-speaking market, in direct competition to Pullmantur Cruises. The onboard product has developed well and now provides a well-established style

Hebridean Princess arrives at Tobermory, Isle of Mull.

of cruise and service for the family cruise segment of Spain's growing cruise market, with three ships: *Grand Celebration, Grand Holiday,* and *Grand Voyager.* Gratuities are included in the cruise fare.

Inner Sea Discoveries

This Seattle-based company was formed by its parent, American Safari Cruises, in 2010. It bought the website and database files of now defunct Cruise West in order to expand its reach to small-ship enthusiasts. It operates two small vessels, *Wilderness Adventurer* and *Wilderness Discoverer.* Gratuities are not included in the fare.

Island Cruises

Island Cruises was founded as a joint venture between Royal Caribbean Cruises and the British low-cost tour operator First Choice Holidays. Its first ship started operations in 2002. However, in 2007, First Choice merged with Germany's largest travel company TUI, to become TUI Travel. Its two-ship fleet was reduced to one ship *(Island Escape)* in 2009, and the company is now operated as a sub-brand of Thomson Cruises. It provides its mainly British passengers with an active cruise experience in ultra-casual, lager-lout-style surroundings. Its self-serve, self-carry buffet meals from an always-busy, congested café are the mainstay of the "culinary" offerings, although slightly better food can be had in a smaller extra-cost dining venue. Gratuities are not included in the cruise fare.

Kristina Cruises

This Finnish Partanan family-owned company was founded in 1985 as Rannikkolinjat to operate short cruises on Lake Saimaa. In 1987 the company purchased its first ship and started to open Baltic and Russian-owned ports on the Gulf of Finland to international cruise passengers.

Today, Kristina Cruises owns and operates one vintage-style ship (*Kristina Brahe*), and one modern cruise vessel (*Kristina Katarina*), principally on cruises in the Baltic and Mediterranean, and continues to preserve nautical traditions on board. Gratuities are not included in the cruise fare.

Lindblad Expeditions

Lars-Eric Lindblad started the whole concept of expedition cruising with a single ship, *Lindblad Explorer*, in 1969, taking adventurous travelers to remote regions of the world. Today, his son, Sven-Olof Lindblad, runs the company, but with an array of small ships. It's all about wilderness, wildlife, off-the-beaten-path adventures, and learning. Zodiac inflatable craft are used to ferry participants ashore in remote areas such as the Arctic and Antarctica.

The ships carry excellent lecturers, who are more academic than entertaining. In partnership with the National Geographic Society, the company operates the wholly owned *National Geographic Endeavour, National Geographic Explorer, National Geographic Islander,* and *National Geographic Polaris*, together with other small ships for coastal or soft expedition-style cruising. Gratuities are not included in the cruise fare.

Mano Cruise

The company, founded by Moshe Mano, caters mainly to Israeli and Russian passengers, and the onboard product is tailored to their requirements. The company has small and mid-size ships and specializes in Mediterranean cruises. While most of passengers are Israeli, the ships also carry an increasing number of Russian tourists. The onboard ambience is quite sound, but basic. Gratuities are not included in the cruise fare.

Mitsui OSK Passenger Line

Osaka Shosen Kaisha was founded in 1884 in Osaka, Japan. In 1964 it merged with Mitsui Steamship, to become Mitsui OSK. It is now one of the oldest and largest shipping companies in the world.

It entered cruise shipping in 1989 with *Fuji Maru*, the first cruise ship in the Japanese-speaking domestic market. The company specialized in incentive, meetings and groups at sea rather than cruising for individuals. But the company (now known as MOPAS) steadily changed to more cruises for individuals. The company operates two ships, *Fuji Maru* and *Nippon Maru* (extensively refurbished in 2010), both based in Japan for Japanese-speaking passengers, with *Fuju Maru* dedicated exclusively to the corporate and charter market.

Gratuities are included in the cruise fare.

Noble Caledonia

London-based Noble Caledonia, established in 1991, operates two boutique-sized sister ships, *Corinthian II* (under charter) and *Island Sky*, each carrying around 100 passengers. It also sells cruises aboard a wide range of small ship and expedition cruise companies as well as river cruises. It markets to British passengers of mature years, and operates cruises, generally in sheltered water areas, with cultural interest themes, and so is not recommended for children.

The company, whose financial partners include Norway's Salen family, has an excellent reputation for well-organized cruises and tours, accompanied by good lecturers. It specializes in itineraries impossible to operate aboard larger ships. A Commodore Club gives repeat passengers an early warning about new voyages and special offers. Gratuities are not generally included in the

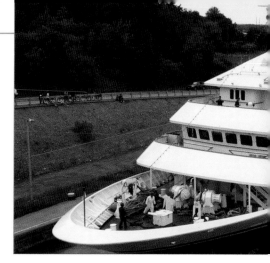

Orion's *Clelia II* traverses the St Lawrence Seaway.

cruise fare, unless otherwise stated in the brochures (whether printed or on the Noble Caledonia website).

NYK Cruises

Nippon Yusen Kaisha is the largest shipping company in the world, and owns the well-known US-based upscale brand Crystal Cruises. It created its own NYK Cruise division – today branded as Asuka Cruise – in 1989 with one Mitsubishi-built ship, *Asuka*, for Japanese-speaking passengers. In 2006, the company sold the original *Asuka* to Germany's Phoenix Reisen, and the former *Crystal Harmony* was transferred from Crystal Cruises to become *Asuka II*. The ship, known for its excellent Japanese and western food, operates an annual around-the-world cruise, plus a wide array of both short and long cruises in the Asia-Pacific region. Coffee- and tea-making facilities are provided in each cabin. Gratuities are included in the cruise fare.

Oceania Cruises

The company's ships provide faux English charm in a country-club atmosphere ideal for middle-aged and older couples seeking relaxation. Cruises are usually 10–14 days. Its trademarks are comfortable cabins, warm and attentive service, and fine dining combining French culinary expertise and top-quality ingredients. Breads and baked goods, such as Poilane-quality croissants, are outstanding.

In 2006, Oceania Cruises was bought by Apollo Management, a private equity company that owns Regent Seven Seas Cruises, and 50% of NCL. The brand was placed under the umbrella of Apollo's cruise brand, Prestige Cruise Holdings. With *Insignia, Nautica*, and *Regatta* well established, and with two new, much larger and faster ships (the first, the 1,250-passenger *Marina,* was delivered in 2010, while the second, *Riviera*, followed in 2011), the company is set to grow.

Mitsui OSK specializes in the Japanese market.

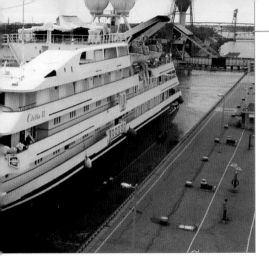

With multiple-choice dining at no extra cost, the 700- and 1,250-passenger ships suit those who prefer mid-size ships to large resort vessels. Bottled mineral water, soft drinks, and beer are included in the price. Gratuities are added at $10.50 per person, per day, and butler-service suites have an additional charge of $3 per person. Bar drinks and spa treatments have 15% added.

Orion Expedition Cruises

This Australia-based expedition cruise company was created in 2004 by Sarina Bratton, specifically for soft expedition-style cruises to Antarctica, Australia's Kimberley region, Tasmania, and Papua New Guinea and its islands, including Melanesia and the Solomon Islands. The ship, *Orion*, built in Germany, is a little gem, with handcrafted cabinetry in every cabin, together with marble bathrooms and a health spa and gymnasium. Shore excursions range from camel safaris to snorkeling over pristine coral formations. In 2008, the company was sold to the US-based KSL Capital Partners. It has acquired a second ship, the 100-passenger *Clelia II* (chartered from Travel Dynamics International), for cruises in Southeast Asia. Gratuities are not included in the fare.

P&O Cruises (Australia)

This Australian division of P&O Cruises was founded in 1932. Today it provides fun in the sand and sun cruises for the beer and bikini brigade and their families, although the line is growing up to become more of a mainstream operator – particularly with the latest ships in the fleet. With a maturing market, the company has larger, more contemporary hand-me-down ships from Carnival Corporation companies (mainly from the P&O Cruises stable), and continues to thrive, specializing in cruises in the Pacific and to New Zealand, with "Your Choice" dining. Coffee/tea-making facilities are provided in each cabin, and passengers will be pleased to learn that, in October 2010, the company scrapped automatic tipping on all ships.

Paquet Cruises (Croisières Paquet)

The company name disappeared in 1999 when it was owned by Costa Cruises, which owned the brand since 1996 (even though ACCOR, Paquet's parent company at the time, owned Costa Cruises and Ocean Cruise Lines). Its single ship, *Mermoz*, now scrapped, was sold to Louis Cruises. The company was resurrected in 2010 under new ownership in a joint venture with the French travel company TMR, based in Marseille, that operated Costa Cruises' *Costa Allegra* under a charter arrangement. Paquet Cruises acquired *Grand Mistral* from Iberocruceros in 2010 to operate as its only ship, for the French-speaking market.

Paul Gauguin Cruises

Created by Boston-based tour operator Grand Circle Travel, Paul Gauguin Cruises took over the marketing and operation of *Paul Gauguin* in 2009 from Regent Seven Seas Cruises, who had operated the ship since its inception. Also in 2009, the ship was purchased by the Tahiti-based investor Richard Bailey and his company Pacific Beachcomber, which owns Polynesian resort hotels (including four InterContinental Hotels). Gratuities are not included in the cruise fare.

Phoenix Reisen

Based in Bonn, Germany, the company for many years operated low-budget, tour-operator-style destination-intensive cruises for German speakers. It now has a loyal, widespread audience and more contemporary ships, with better food and service, particularly aboard *Amadea* and *Artania*.

To keep costs down, Phoenix charters its ships for long periods. It is consistently praised for its extremely good itineraries, particularly on world cruises, its pre- and post-cruise programs, and its excellent value for money. The utterly comprehensive Phoenix brochure provides photographs of its captains and cruise director, as well as bar lists and drink prices – a refreshing change to the brochures provided by most cruise

Oceania's *Marina* has a *Titanic*-like main staircase.

Le Ponant is a sleek sail-cruise ship with three masts.

vacations with a cultural bias toward French-speaking participants. Its cruise division chartered *Adriana* for many years, but in 2010 instead chartered a small ship, *Vistamar*. The company also sells river cruises.

Ponant Cruises

The company was founded in 1988 by Videau and Jean-Emmanuel Sauve. It started life as La Compagnie des Iles du Ponant, and is a subsidiary of the state-owned CMA CGM (Compagnie Maritime Atlantique/Compagnie Générale Transatlantique), both of which began in 1855 but merged in 1977 to become the world's third largest container shipping firm.

The cruise company, whose head office is in Marseille, France, was created in 1988, and operates three boutique-sized ships – *Le Diamant, Le Levant,* and *Le Ponant* – for French-speakers. In 2004, the company bought the Paris-based tour operator Tapis Rouge International, which specializes in upscale travel. Two new small ships – *Le Boreal*, introduced in 2010, and *L'Austral*, introduced in 2011 – provide more space and more options for passengers. The company increasingly markets cruises in both English and French cruises to international passengers, and onboard announcements are made in both languages. Gratuities are not included in the cruise fare.

Pullmantur Cruises

The company was set up as part of Pullmantur, the Spain-based holiday tour operator founded in 1971. Its cruising division was established in 2000 when it bought *Oceanic* (then known as the Big Red Boat) from the defunct Florida operator Premier Cruise Lines. In 2006, Pullmantur Cruises was bought by Royal Caribbean Cruises. The company, mainly serving the Spanish-speaking market, operates all-inclusive cruises for families with children to the Caribbean, Europe and, during the South American summer, serves the Brazilian market. While most passengers are Spanish, the company now also markets heavily to US and other cruisegoers. Gratuities are included in the fare.

Quark Expeditions

The company was founded in 1991 by Lars Wikander and silent partner Christer Salen (formerly of Salen-Lindblad Cruises). Based in Darien, Connecticut, it specializes in providing up-close-and-personal expedition cruises to some of the world's most remote regions and inaccessible areas.

In its formative years, Quark Expeditions chartered Russian icebreakers to take adventurous, hardy outdoor types to the polar regions, and has years of experience in taking participants to Antarctica. Quark Expeditions has always been committed to minimizing the environmen-

companies. Single-seating dining is standard, as are low drink prices, and there is no constant pushing for onboard revenue – again different to most rivals. In 2011 Phoenix acquired another ship, *Artania* (formerly P&O Cruises' *Artemis* and originally *Royal Princess*, named by Princess Diana). Gratuities are included in the fare.

Plantours & Partner

This company, based in Bremen, Germany, provides low-budget cruises aboard its single small, chartered cruise ship, *Vistamar*, for German speakers. The Spanish-built ship suffers from poor build quality. The onboard food and service are well-meaning, but of only the most basic standard. *Vistamar* will be replaced by *Hamburg* after that ship ceases to operate as *Columbus* for Hapag-Lloyd Cruises in May 2012. The company also sells cruises on the rivers of Europe and Russia. Gratuities are not included in the cruise fare.

Plein Cap Cruises

The company (Plein Cap Croisières in French) was created in 1985 as part of the French TVL Voyages group, founded in 1981. It specializes in cruises and land

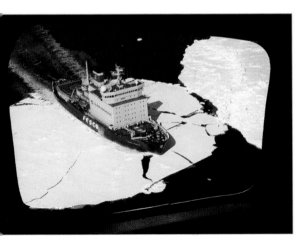

Quark's *Kapitan Khlebnikov* breaks the ice in Antarctica.

Regent Seven Seas Cruises. It strives to pay close attention to detail and provide high-quality service aboard its small fleet of three small- and mid-size cruise ships (*Seven Seas Mariner, Seven Seas Navigator,* and *Seven Seas Voyager*) operating worldwide itineraries.

In 2007 the company was bought by US-based investment group Apollo Management, and, together with Oceania Cruises, was placed under the umbrella of its Prestige Cruise Holdings. The company spent $40 million to refurbish its three ships in 2009–10.

It provides drinks-inclusive cruising, which means that drinks *and* gratuities are included in the fare, as are shore excursions. Passengers have to pay extra only for laundry services, beauty services, casino, and other personal items.

Saga Cruises

Saga, based in Folkestone, England, was created by Sydney de Haan as a company offering financial services and holidays to the over-60s (reduced to the over-50s in 1995 as the company's success grew). Its popular travel flourished because it was good at providing personal attention and competent staff. Instead of sending passengers to ships operated by other companies, it decided to purchase its own ships and market its own product under the Saga Holidays brand.

Saga Shipping (Saga Cruises), the cruising division of Saga Holidays, was set up in 1997 when it purchased *Saga Rose* (ex-*Sagafjord*), followed not long after by *Saga Ruby* (ex-*Vistafjord*) and, in 2010, *Saga Pearl II* (formerly *Astoria*). *Saga Sapphire* arrives in 2012.

Another brand, Spirit of Adventure, was added in 2006, the year that parent company Saga and Britain's

tal impact of operating in ecologically sensitive areas.

In 2007, it was sold to the UK's First Choice Holidays (founded in 1973), merged with Peregrine Shipping, and then in 2007 was bought, along with First Choice, by the large German travel company TUI.

Cruising with Quark Expeditions is all about being close to nature, wilderness, wildlife, off-the-beaten-path adventures, and learning. The company, an associate member of IAATO (Association of Antarctica Tour Operators), an association committed to the highest standards of responsible tourism to Antarctica, Quark Expeditions still specializes in chartering nuclear- and diesel-powered Russian icebreakers, the most powerful in the world, to provide participants with a truly memorable expedition experience. This is adventure cruising for toughies. Gratuities are not included in the cruise fare.

Regent Seven Seas Cruises

The company has a complicated history. It was born out of Seven Seas Cruises, which was originally based in San Francisco to market the cruise ship *Song of Flower* (belonging to "K"-Line, a cargo operator based in New Jersey) as well as expedition cruises aboard the chartered *Hanseatic* (then belonging to Hanseatic Tours). The lyre, logo of that ship, became RSSC's logo.

For many years, the company was part of the Carlson group, and operated as Radisson Seven Seas Cruises. Carlson Hospitality Worldwide ventured into cruising via its Radisson Hotels International division – hence, Radisson Diamond Cruises (when Radisson Diamond joined in 1992). In 1994 Radisson Diamond Cruises and Seven Seas Cruise Line merged to become Radisson Seven Seas Cruises, and in 2007 it became

A yoga session aboard Regent's *Seven Seas Voyager.*

Automobile Association merged. The cruise company emphasizes British seamanship and training, and its fleet manages to retain the feel of traditional, elegant, adults-only cruising aboard *Quest for Adventure, Saga Ruby,* and, from March 2012, *Saga Sapphire.* Saga Cruises offers single-seating dining, friendly, attentive service from a mainly Filipino hotel service crew, and its ships have many single-occupancy cabins. It takes care of all the many little details other lines have long forgotten.

Coffee- and tea-making facilities are provided in each cabin. All gratuities are included in the cruise fare.

Sea Cloud Cruises

The company was founded in 1979 by a consortium of shipowners and investors known as the Hansa Treuhand (active in commercial vessel management, engineering, and construction), and has its HQ in Hamburg, Germany. It owns and operates two tall ships (sailing vessels), the legendary *Sea Cloud* and *Sea Cloud II*, and two European rivercruise boats, *River Cloud I* and *River Cloud II.*

The company has many corporate clients who charter the two tall ships, while a number of upscale cruise and travel companies sell cruises to individuals. The onboard style and product delivery are quite upscale, with elegant retro decor and fine food and service. Gratuities are not included in the cruise fare.

Seabourn

Originally founded in 1986 as Signet Cruise Line, the company, then owned by Norwegian industrialist Atle Brynestad, had to change its name in 1988 as a result of a lawsuit brought by a Texas ferry company that had already registered the name Signet Cruise Lines (no ships were ever built for cruising, however). Indeed, the company's first brochure was released under the Signet Cruise Lines name.

In 1998, a consortium, which included the Carnival Corporation and Norwegian investors, bought Seabourn Cruise Line and merged its operations into Cunard Line, which was acquired from Kvaerner. The fleet then included its three present ships plus *Seabourn Goddess I* and *Seabourn Goddess II* (bought by SeaDream Yacht Cruises in 2002 and named *SeaDream I* and *SeaDream II*) and *Seabourn Sun* (which became Holland America Line's *Prinsendam*). The Carnival Corporation acquired 100% of Seabourn Cruise Line in 1999.

The company aims its product at affluent, sophisticated, well-traveled North Americans, with small ships providing a high level of European-style service, open-seating dining, all-inclusive drinks, great attention to detail, and personal pampering.

Three new, larger ships joined the company between 2009 and 2011. All three have an aft water-sports platform, as well as more dining and spa options, more space, and more passengers. Seabourn Cruise Line was briefly rebranded as The Yachts of Seabourn in 2009–10, but is now simply Seabourn. Gratuities are included in the cruise fare.

Top: *Seabourn Legend* makes a point of pampering.
Above: a *Star Clipper* tender links sea and shore.

SeaDream Yacht Cruises

Larry Pimentel, an American, and his Norwegian business partner Atle Brynestad, founder of Seabourn Cruise Line, jointly created the company by buying the former Sea Goddess Cruises' ships. They introducing them in 2002 to an audience anxious for exclusivity, personal pampering, and cuisine prepared à la minute.

The two ships, *SeaDream I* and *SeaDream II*, have been refreshed several times, and are often chartered by companies or private individuals who appreciate the refined, elegant, but casual atmosphere on board. The 100-passenger ships operate year-round in the Caribbean and Mediterranean, and provide all-inclusive beverages and open-seating dining at all times, and a high degree of personalized service, all in a cozy, club-like atmosphere, with great attention to detail and personal idiosyncrasies. Atle Brynestad is the company's chairman and sole owner, while Larry Pimentel now belongs to Azamara Cruises. Gratuities are included in the cruise fare.

Silversea Cruises

Silversea Cruises is a mostly privately owned cruise line. It was founded in 1992 by the Lefebvre D'Ovidio family from Rome (previously co-owners of Sitmar Cruises; 90% partners are the Lefebvre D'Ovidios, 10% by V-Ships), and is based in Monaco.

Antonio Lefebvre D'Ovidio was a maritime lawyer and professor of maritime law before acquiring and operating cargo ships and ferries in the Adriatic. He took the family into partnership with Boris Vlasov's Vlasov Group (V-Ships) to co-own Sitmar Cruises until that company merged with Princess Cruises in 1988.

Silversea Cruises has generated tremendous loyalty from its frequent passengers, who view the ships as their own. All six Silversea ships have teak verandas and all-inclusive beverages. Open-seating dining prevails at all times, and the company is known for its partnership with the hospitality organization Relais et Châteaux. A new, larger, 540-passenger all-suite luxury ship, *Silver Spirit*, debuted at the end of 2009, while *Silver Whisper* and *Silver Shadow* were refurbished in 2010 and 2011. Gratuities are included in the cruise fare.

Star Clippers

Swedish-born yachtsman Mikhail Krafft founded Star Clippers in 1991 with *Star Flyer* and then *Star Clipper*, both true tall ships. The company went on to build the largest tall ship presently sailing, the five-mast *Royal Clipper*. It is now building an even bigger tall ship. Good food and friendly service in a casual, laid-back setting, under the romance of sail (when there is enough wind), is what Star Clippers is all about – but the food variety and quality is extremely good.

The tall ships sail in the Caribbean, Mediterranean and Southeast Asia. Gratuities are not included in the cruise fare.

Star Cruises

Presently part of the world's third-largest cruise operator, the company was incorporated in 1993 as a subsidiary of Genting Hong Kong, which itself comes under the umbrella of Genting Berhad, founded in 1965 by the late Tan Sri (Dr) Lim Goh Tong in Malaysia as an Asian multinational corporation. The group's various business include palm oil production, power generation, property development, biotechnology, oil and gas production, together with leisure activities including resort hotels and casino/entertainment complexes in Malaysia, Manila, and Singapore, and cruise ships.

Genting Hong Kong operates ships dedicated to specific markets. Its brands include Star Cruises and Norwegian Cruise Line (jointly owned with Apollo Management).

Star Cruises is one of only two cruise lines to have its own ship simulator (the other is MSC Cruises) – useful training tools when a captain these days may be in charge of a speeding vessel measuring more than 100,000 gross tonnage. It also owns the cruise terminal at its operations base in Port Klang, Malaysia, and the jetty and pier facility in Langkawi. Its marketing base is now in Hong Kong, and the company is formally known as Star Cruises/Genting Hong Kong. Its ships are *MegaStar Aries* (1991), *SuperStar Aquarius* (1993), *SuperStar Libra* (1988), and *SuperStar Virgo* (1999). Gratuities are included in all cruise fares.

Swan Hellenic Cruises

Founded in 1954 By R.K. Swan, the company chartered small cruise ships for years. The company was purchased by P&O Cruises in 1982, and then it changed hands when Carnival Corporation merged with P&O in April 2004. In 2007, the Carnival Corporation disbanded Swan Hellenic, and its single ship *(Minerva II)* was transferred to the Princess Cruises fleet to become *Royal Princess* (now P&O Cruises' *Adonia*). Some months later, a semi-retired Lord Sterling purchased the brand from the Carnival Corporation and joined forces with the UK's Voyages of Discovery to operate as a separate brand. So, the "swanners," as its clever passengers are called, now have their very own ship *(Minerva)*.

The company's strengths are its program of highly

Thomson Destiny aims at the middle-of-the-road UK market.

academic lecturers and speakers, in a small-ship setting that is unpretentious but comfortable, and includes gratuities, drinks (on Antarctic voyages), tailor-made shore excursions, and entrance fees to museums and places of interest. The company operates special-interest themes such as archaeology, history, nature, and wildlife. Coffee- and tea-making facilities are provided in each cabin. Gratuities are included in the cruise fare.

Thomson Cruises

Thomson Cruises' first foray into cruising was in 1973 when it chartered two ships, *Calypso* and *Ithaca,* from the Greek-owned Ulysses Line. It was not a success, and the company withdrew from cruising two years later. Ulysses Line became known as Useless Line.

The company started again in 2002 after seeing rival tour operator Airtours operate ships successfully. Unlike Airtours' Sun Cruises, which no longer exists, Thomson Cruises charters its ships instead of owning them outright, preferring instead to leave ship operations, management, and catering to specialist maritime companies. The company operates cruises for the whole family aboard its small fleet of ships – *Thomson Celebration, Thomson Destiny, Thomson Dream,* and *Thomson Spirit* – catering principally to the British market, but also to the Scandinavian market.

Thomson Cruises operates subbrand Island Cruises, with just one ship, *Island Escape,* for the ultra-casual market. Basic gratuities are included in the price. The company owns its own airline, Thomsonfly, part of the TUI Travel group.

Transocean Cruises

Founded in 1954, Transocean Cruises (formerly Transocean Tours) has headquarters in Bremen, Germany. The company specializes in providing low-cost but high-value cruises aboard a ship under long-term charter *(Astor)*, with traditional decor and excellent itineraries. Gratuities and port charges are included. The company also sells river cruises, operated by chartered vessels under the banner of Transocean River Cruises. Gratuities are included in the cruise fare.

Travel Dynamics International

Founded by brothers George and Vasos Papagapitos, the company specializes in providing small and boutique cruise ships to culturally minded passengers. Long a provider of vacations and cruises to university alumni, cultural associations, and museum groups, the company seeks out unusual itineraries and destinations according to a group's interest or travel theme. The company is also known for its US Great Lakes cruises, and cruises to remote regions, as well as for its academically trained lecturers. Gratuities are not included in the cruise fare.

TUI Cruises

The German-owned TUI Group has several divisions, but started its own cruise line in 2009 with *Mein Schiff*, a large resort ship (ex-*Celebrity Galaxy*) which underwent a massive reconstruction program. *Mein Schiff 2* (formerly *Celebrity Mercury*) was added in 2011. Targeted at families with children, the onboard product – particularly the food and service – is markedly superior to that of competitor AIDA Cruises. All cabins, for example, have their own espresso machine, and there is a wide choice of dining venues and food styles, with an emphasis on healthy eating. Much emphasis has also been placed on the wellness facilities. Gratuities are included in the cruise fare.

Entertaining the customers aboard Venus Cruise's *Pacific Venus.*

Wind Surf's sails are computer-controlled.

Venus Cruise

Founded in 1988, the company's headquarters are in Osaka, Japan. Venus Cruise was first known as Japan Cruise Line, which is owned by four ferry companies: Shin Nipponkai Ferry, Kyowa Shoji, Hankyu Ferry, and Kanko Kisen. As Japan Cruise Line, the company at first operated company and incentive charter cruises before branching out into cruises for individuals. The company, catering exclusively to Japanese speakers, has one ship, *Pacific Venus*, which operates an annual around-the-world cruise as well as shorter Asia-Pacific cruises. Gratuities are included in the cruise fare.

Voyages of Discovery

UK-based Roger Allard and Dudley Smith jointly founded the company to offer low-cost cruises aboard comfortable and roomy but older mid-size ships, to UK passengers, but with good food and service. The company's *Discovery* is one of the former "Love Boats" of US television fame. The company went public in 2006 and, with the help of Lord Sterling of Plaistow, purchased Swan Hellenic Cruises. It now operates both brands from its HQ in the south of England, and also owns the premium brand Hebridean Island Cruises.

Voyages to Antiquity

Founded in 2007 by Gerry Herrod, who formerly created the now defunct Ocean Cruise Lines, the company has just one ship, painstakingly converted into a comfortable cruise ship with a fairly handsome profile. It operates seven- and 14-day cruises to ancient lands, specializing in the Aegean and Mediterranean regions. The cruises are aimed at British and American passengers who seek educational experiences. Gratuities to dining and housekeeping staff are included, as are most shore excursions, and wines with lunch and dinner.

Windstar Cruises

Founded by New York-based Karl Andren in 1984 as Windstar Sail Cruises, the company built high-class sail-cruise ships with computer-controlled sails, outfitting them in a contemporary decor designed by Marc Held. The first ship, *Wind Star*, debuted in 1986 to much acclaim, and was followed by *Wind Spirit* (1988) and *Wind Surf* (1990).

Windstar Cruises was sold to Holland America Line in 1988. The company, with headquarters in Seattle, USA, was sold again in 2007 to the Ambassadors Cruise Group, wholly owned by Ambassadors International.

The onboard style is casual and unregimented, but smart, with service by Indonesian and Filipino crew. The ships carry a variety of water-sports equipment, accessed from a retractable stern platform. Itineraries include off-the-beaten-track ports not frequented by large resort ships. The onboard product is decidedly American casual, with unfussy bistro-style cuisine, and service that lacks finesse and the small details that could make it much better. Gratuities are not included in the cruise fare.

Zegrahm Expeditions

This small expedition cruise company, which takes inquisitive travelers to remote or unusual destinations, including the Arctic and Antarctica, was founded in 1990 and bought in 2009 by TUI Travel. Although it doesn't own any ships, it charters high-quality specialized vessels. It also sells cruises operated by other expedition companies and operates safaris and small-group adventure vacations. Two- or three-week expedition cruises are headed by experienced leaders and expert naturalists. Gratuities are not included in the cruise fare. ❏

LIVING IN LUXURY

Of the 70-plus cruise lines operating internationally, only a handful provide the kind of stylish ships aboard which the word "no" is virtually unheard

L uxury cruises versus standard (large resort ship) cruises are like the difference between a Bentley and a Hyundai. "Luxury cruising" should be a flawless combination of ship, facilities, food, and service. Unfortunately, the word has been degraded by marketing people – you can even buy a "luxury" burger today – but the panel on the facing page tells you what the term ought to mean in a cruise ship.

Little and large

Size is important. Boutique and small ships can get into ports that larger ships can't. They can also get closer to the center of large cities. For example, in St Petersburg, Russia, large and mid-size ships (such as those of Crystal Cruises and Regent Seven Seas Cruises) dock about one hour from the city center, while boutique ships such as those of Hapag-Lloyd Cruises, Silversea Cruises, or Seabourn can dock right next to the Hermitage Museum in the heart of the city.

One area where "luxury" ships differ least from large resort ships is in shore excursions, particularly in the Caribbean and Alaska, where almost all cruise operators are obliged to use the same specialist tour operators ashore – simply because "luxury" is virtually unknown in these regions and local tour operators consider all cruise passengers to be the same.

Large resort ships (those carrying more than 1,600 passengers) simply cannot provide the kind of personal service and attention to detail that the boutique/small ships can. Although you can book one of the largest suites afloat aboard a large ship and have a

SeaDream's yachts provide a setting for personal indulgence.

THE CRÈME DE LA CRÈME

These 18 ships (listed alphabetically, by company) belong to six cruise lines, and are the "cream" of the cruise industry in terms of style, finesse, staff training, cuisine, service, hospitality, and finesse. Their individual facilities are fully reviewed in the ratings section of this book, and the Berlitz ratings awarded for accommodation, food, service, entertainment, and so on indicate their particular strengths.

- **CRYSTAL CRUISES**
  Crystal Serenity, Crystal Symphony
- **HAPAG-LLOYD CRUISES**
  Europa
- **REGENT SEVEN SEAS CRUISES**
  Seven Seas Mariner, Seven Seas Navigator, Seven Seas Voyager
- **SEABOURN**
  Seabourn Legend, Seabourn Odyssey, Seabourn Pride, Seabourn Sojourn, Seabourn Spirit
- **SEADREAM YACHT CRUISES**
  SeaDream I, SeaDream II
- **SILVERSEA CRUISES**
  Silver Cloud, Silver Shadow, Silver Spirit, Silver Whisper, Silver Wind

really good cruise, once you leave your "private living space" you'll have to mix with all other passengers, particularly if you want to go to a show, have an informal alfresco meal or coffee in the café, disembark at ports of call (think of the lines at the gangway security checkpoint), or go on organized shore excursions. That's when you appreciate the fact that smaller may suit you better.

These are ships suited to those not seeking the active, family- and entertainment-driven cruise experiences that large resort ships offer. The ships, companies, and comparisons in this section provide ships, facilities, and service levels hard to find elsewhere. While most of them boast about being the best, or boast the awards they receive annually from various magazines (whose respondents are almost never global in scope), not all provide the same degree of luxury, and there *are* differences in the cruise product delivered.

So, what are the differences?

Once you know the main differences, you'll be better equipped to choose the right cruise line

Caribbean idyll: *Crystal Symphony* in St Thomas.

and ship to provide the level of onboard food and service you are looking for. While most of the differences are immediately noticeable when you sail aboard (and compare) them all, some of the variations in style and service are more subtle. One thing is certain: the word "no" will be virtually unheard.

Some have more crew per passenger. Some have more expensive European crew than others. Some have better food and service. Some have entertainment, some don't. Some have more public space per passenger. It's important to weigh up the differences, so that you choose the right ship for the right reasons.

For example, the following facilities and services are found aboard the ships of Hapag-Lloyd Cruises, SeaDream Yacht Cruises, and Seabourn, but not aboard the ships of Crystal Cruises, Regent Seven Seas Cruises, or Silversea Cruises.

● Anticipation is more widely practiced aboard the smaller ships, where staff training is better in terms of passenger recognition (remembering your name).
● Waiters escort female guests (waitresses escort male guests) to the dining table and to the dining room exit after meals.
● Relaxed embarkation/disembarkation at your leisure.
● Cabin stewardesses leave handwritten notes.
● There are no announcements, and no mindless background music in public rooms, accommodation hallways, or elevators.
● The chef invites passengers to accompany him on visits to local food markets.

More space, better service

All 18 ships have an excellent amount of open deck and lounging space, and a high Passenger Space Ratio (almost all are above 40) when compared to large resort ships (which are typically under 35), the two SeaDreams being the exception.

Almost all have a better Crew to Passenger Ratio than the large resort ships. In warm-weather areas, the ships of SeaDream Yacht Cruises and Seabourn,

all of which have fold-down platforms at the stern, provide jet skis, kayaks, snorkeling gear, windsurfers and the like at no extra cost, typically for one day each cruise (the others do not).

Hapag-Lloyd's *Europa* also has a fleet of Zodiac rigid inflatable craft for in-depth exploration and shore adventures, plus an ice-hardened hull and a

WHAT YOU SHOULD EXPECT

● Flawless personal service and attention to detail.
● Champagne at embarkation.
● European hotel service crew.
● Personalized stationery.
● A crew that anticipates your needs, responds quickly to your requests, and doesn't say "no" or "impossible".
● Zero announcements (except for emergencies).
● No background music in public rooms, hallways, and elevators.
● A high Passenger Space Ratio (35 to 70 gross tonnage per passenger).
● A high Crew to Passenger Ratio (1.5 to 1 or better).
● Creative cuisine that excels in presentation, taste, variety, and ingredients.
● Highly qualified sommeliers to discuss and serve wines.
● Connoisseur wines and premium spirits.
● The finest-quality bed linens, duvets, towels, bathrobes.
● High-quality personal toiletries (e.g. Aveda, Bulgari).
● Gratuities that are included in the fare.
● No extra charge for on-demand movies or music.
● No machinery vibration (engines/propulsion equipment).
● No lines anywhere.
● More overnight port stays.
● Separate gangway for passengers and crew.
● Shoe-shine service.
● No signing for drinks or other items.
● Your fellow passengers are unlikely to flaunt ostentatious tattoos and body piercings.

crew who understands the culture of the passengers. And mattresses that are 7ft (2.1 meters) long.

Dining

Fine dining is the highlight of ships in this category, and is more of an entertainment feature than the entertainment itself – if there is any. Good company and conversation are crucial. You can expect to find plenty of tables for two, a calm refined dining atmosphere, open or one-seating dining, by candlelight (when permitted), high-quality china and silverware, large wine glasses, fresh flowers, a connoisseur wine list, and sommeliers who can discuss fine wines.

It's really about non-repetitive, highly creative menus, high-quality ingredients, moderate portions, and attractive presentation, with fresh local fish and other items provided (when available) and cooked à la minute (not in batches), and meat of the highest grade. Caviar, foie gras, black/white truffles and other exotic foods, and fresh green vegetables (instead of frozen or canned vegetables) are provided. Caviar aboard *Europa* is usually from French farmed sturgeon, and is excellent, while caviar aboard most other ships in this category is from the American farmed hackleback variety of sturgeon (not as good).

There should also be a choice of sea salt from different regions of the world, and olive oil from countries such as Greece, Italy, and Spain.

Almost all the ships provide silver covers for main courses, creating extra "wow" effect. Additionally, passengers are often invited to visit local markets with the chef aboard the ships of Hapag-Lloyd Cruises, Seabourn, and SeaDream Yacht Cruises.

Seabourn ships provide personal pampering.

Some luxury ships provide even more special touches. *Europa,* for example, makes its own breakfast preserves. Strangely, Regent Seven Seas Cruises does not have fish knives – needed if you like to de-bone the Dover sole yourself, though it can be done for you. *Europa* uses only loose tea (over 30 types) – all the others use teabags of varying quality.

Typically, lunch and dinner menus are provided in your suite/cabin in advance, and special orders (ordering off-menu) are often possible. Room service menus

HOW THE LUXURY SHIPS COMPARE

Ship	Company	Tonnage	Size	Pod Propulsion	Passenger Space Ratio
Crystal Serenity	Crystal Cruises	68,870	Mid-Size	Yes	62.6
Crystal Symphony	Crystal Cruises	51,044	Mid-Size	No	53.1
Europa	Hapag-Lloyd Cruises	28,437	Small	Yes	69.6
Seabourn Legend *	Seabourn	9,961	Boutique	No	46.9
Seabourn Odyssey	Seabourn	32,009	Small	No	71.1
Seabourn Pride *	Seabourn	9,975	Boutique	No	46.9
Seabourn Sojourn	Seabourn	32,000	Small	No	71.1
Seabourn Spirit *	Seabourn	9,975	Boutique	No	46.9
SeaDream I	SeaDream Yacht Cruises	4,253	Boutique	No	39.4
SeaDream II	SeaDream Yacht Cruises	4,253	Boutique	No	39.4
Seven Seas Mariner	Regent Seven Seas Cruises	48,015	Mid-Size	Yes	67.8
Seven Seas Navigator	Regent Seven Seas Cruises	28,550	Mid-Size	No	58.2
Seven Seas Voyager	Regent Seven Seas Cruises	41,827	Mid-Size	Yes	59.0
Silver Cloud	Silversea Cruises	16,927	Small	No	57.1
Silver Shadow	Silversea Cruises	28,258	Small	No	72.8
Silver Spirit	Silversea Cruises	36,009	Small	No	66.6
Silver Whisper	Silversea Cruises	28,258	Small	No	72.8
Silver Wind	Silversea Cruises	16,927	Small	No	57.1

* These ships also have a number of "French" balcony cabins with floor-to-ceiling doors that open for fresh air (the actual "balcony" is only about 12 inches/30cm deep).

lunch), although the wines are typically young, and not from first-class houses. However, real premium brands and classic vintage wines cost extra.

Crystal Cruises and Hapag-Lloyd Cruises charge for all alcoholic beverages. Crystal Cruises includes soft drinks and, from spring 2012, will provide an all-inclusive product, including gratuities. Regent, Sea-Dream, Seabourn, and Silversea include all drinks (but only standard brands). Hapag-Lloyd Cruises does not include alcoholic drinks, because its passengers know and want their favorite brands, many of which are well above the level of standard brands carried by those cruise lines that do include alcoholic beverages, which are normally tailored to suit North American tastes.

Other differences

Aboard the ships of Regent Seven Seas Cruises and Seabourn, white plastic deck lounge chairs are provided. Aboard the ships of SeaDream Yacht Cruises they are made of teak (or other hardwood). Aboard Hapag-Lloyd Cruises' *Europa* they are made of aluminum and wood, and aboard the ships of Silversea Cruises they are made of aluminum.

Crystal Serenity, Crystal Symphony, Seven Seas Mariner, Seven Seas Navigator, and *Seven Seas Voyager* are mid-size ships (600–1,600 passengers) that include entertainment with production shows and cabaret acts. To a lesser extent, so do the Seabourn ships and Hapag-Lloyd's *Europa,* but the other ships do not have entertainment as such, but instead rely on their intimacy and friendliness, and promote after-dinner conversation or, aboard the ships of Silversea Cruises, individual specialist cabaret acts. ❑

are extensive, and meals can be served, course by course, in your suite/cabin, either on the balcony or inside on special portable tables – some ships do this better than others. It is also possible to have a special dinner set up on deck (wonderful in the right location), with all the finery and individual service you would expect of private dining.

Drinks: included or not?

Regent Seven Seas Cruises, Seabourn, SeaDream Yacht Cruises, and Silversea Cruises provide wine with dinner (Seabourn and Silversea also include wine with

Crew to Passenger Ratio	Cabins (double)	Cabins w/balcony	Largest Suite (sq. m)	Smallest Cabin (sq. m)	Tips incl.	Water-sports toys	Hand-held showers	Toiletries
1.7	550	466	125.0	21.0	No	No	Yes	Aveda
1.7	480	276	91.2	18.7	No	No	Yes	Aveda
1.5	204	168	85.0	33.0	Yes	No	Yes	Own brand
1.3	106	6	53.5	25.7	Yes	Yes	Yes	Therapies (Molton Brown)
1.3	225	199	133.6	27.5	Yes	Yes	Yes	Therapies (Molton Brown)
1.3	106	6	53.4	25.7	Yes	Yes	Yes	Therapies (Molton Brown)
1.3	225	199	133.6	27.5	Yes	Yes	Yes	Therapies (Molton Brown)
1.3	106	6	53.4	25.7	Yes	Yes	Yes	Therapies (Molton Brown)
1.2	54	0	45.5	18.1	Yes	Yes	Yes	Bulgari
1.2	54	0	45.5	18.1	Yes	Yes	Yes	Bulgari
1.6	354	354	142.0	28.0	Yes	No	Yes	Canyon Ranch
1.5	245	196	109.0	28.0	Yes	No	Yes	Canyon Ranch
1.6	354	354	130.0	33.0	Yes	No	Yes	Canyon Ranch
1.4	148	110	122.0	22.2	Yes	No	No	Bulgari
1.3	194	157	133.3	26.6	Yes	No	No	Bulgari
1.4	270	258	150.0	29.0	Yes	No	No	Bulgari
1.3	194	157	133.3	26.6	Yes	No	No	Bulgari
1.4	148	110	122.0	22.2	Yes	No	No	Bulgari

NOTE: Only *Europa* gives the true net (interior) measurement.
All the others provide gross measurements for their suites.

THE BEST SHORE EXCURSIONS

Escorted tours in ports of call cost extra, but they are often
the best way to get a nutshell view of a destination and
make the most efficient use of your limited time ashore

Shore excursions used to be limited to city tours and venues that offered folkloric dances by local troupes. Today's excursions are almost limitless, and are very active, encompassing crocodile hunting in the Amazon, kayaking in Alaska, elephant riding in Thailand, or flying over Moscow in a MiG jet (fare $28,000). It's easily possible to spend far more on shore excursions on than on buying the cruise.

Most excursions are escorted by ship's staff, who will usually carry first-aid kits. If you explore independently and need medical help, you could risk missing the ship when it sails. Unless the destination is a familiar one, first-time cruisegoers are probably safer booking excursions organized by the ship and vetted by the cruise line. Also, if you have a problem during a tour, the cruise line should be able to sort it out on the spot.

If you do go it alone, always take the ship's port agent and telephone numbers with you, in case of emergencies (they are normally printed in the Daily Program). Allow plenty of time to get back to your ship before sailing time – the ship won't wait. Make sure your travel insurance covers you fully.

Note that if you book tours on your own, and it's a tender port where the ship has to remain at anchor offshore, you will need to wait until the ship's organized tours have been offloaded – which can take two or more hours aboard some of the large resort ships.

Venice, though crowded, is a perennially popular port of call.

A TICKET TO RIDE

Many companies with large resort ships typically charge extra for shuttle buses to take you from the port or other docking area to a local city or town center. The port with the highest charge is Venice, Italy, where the transport is by motorboat, between the cruise terminals and St Mark's Square.

How tiring are excursions?

Most tours will involve some degree of walking, and some require extensive walking. Most cruise lines grade their excursions with visual symbols to indicate the degree of fitness required.

Are there private excursions?

Yes, aboard some of the more upscale ships such as those of Hebridean Island Cruises, Hapag-Lloyd Cruises, Regent Seven Seas Cruises, SeaDream Yacht Cruises, Silversea Cruises, and Seabourn, you can have shore excursions tailored to your specific needs. But even large resort ship lines like Norwegian Cruise Line (NCL) can book something special under its Freestyle Private Touring program.

What if my first choice is sold out?

Some excursions do sell out, owing to limited space or transport, but there can be last-minute cancellations. Check with the shore excursion manager on board.

What should I take with me?

Only what's necessary; leave any valuables aboard ship, together with any money and credit cards you do not plan to use. Groups of people are often targets for pickpockets in popular sightseeing destinations. Also, beware of excursion guides who give you a colored disk to wear for "identification" – they may be marking you as a "rich" tourist for local shopkeepers. It's always prudent to wear comfortable rubber-soled shoes, particularly in older ports when there may be cobblestones or other uneven surfaces.

How can I make a booking?

Several cruise lines allow you to book shore excursions online *before* you cruise. But this means some popular excursions may sell out before you even get to your ship. So book early. Payment aboard ship is normally made via a ship's central billing system.

A street market in Ho Chi Minh City, Vietnam.

If you need to cancel a shore excursion, you usually need to do so at least 24 hours before its advertised departure time. Otherwise, refunds are at the discretion of the cruise line, and refunds of pre-paid tickets booked over the internet can take a long time to make and incur currency losses. You may be able to sell your ticket to another passenger – tickets don't normally have names or cabin numbers on them, except those that involve flights or overland arrangements. Check with the shore excursion manager to make sure it's okay to resell.

How can I know which are good?

If it's your first cruise, try to attend the shore excursion briefing. Read the excursion literature and circle tours that appeal to you. Then go to the shore excursion office and ask any other questions you may have before you book.

A few helpful tips:

● Shore excursions are put together for general interest. If you want to see something that is not described in the excursion literature, do not take it. Go on your own or with friends.

● Brochure descriptions of shore excursions, often written by personnel who haven't visited the ports of call, can be imprecise. All cruise lines should adopt the following definitions in their descriptive literature and for their lectures and presentations: The term "visit" should mean actually entering the place or building concerned. The term "see" should mean viewing from the outside – as from a bus, for example.

● City excursions are basically superficial. To get to know a city intimately, go alone or with a small group. Go by taxi or bus, or explore on foot.

● If you do not want to miss the major sightseeing attractions in each port, organized shore excursions provide a good solution. They also allow you to meet fellow passengers with similar interests.

● In the Caribbean, many sightseeing tours cover the same ground, regardless of the cruise line you sail with. Choose one and then do something different in the next port. The same is true of the history and archaeology excursions in the Greek islands, where the same ancient gods will put in frequent appearances.

What if I lose my ticket?

Report lost or misplaced tickets to the shore excursion manager. Aboard most ships, excursion tickets, once sold, become the sole responsibility of the buyer, and the cruise line is not generally able to issue replacements. ❑

GOING ASHORE INDEPENDENTLY – AND SAFELY

If you hire a taxi for sightseeing, negotiate the price in advance, and don't pay until you get back to the ship or to your destination. If you are with friends, hiring a taxi for a full- or half-day sightseeing trip can often work out far cheaper than renting a car – and it's probably safer. Try to find a driver who speaks your language.

Exploring independently is ideal in the major cruise ports of Alaska, the Bahamas, Bermuda, the Caribbean, the Mexican Riviera, the Canary Islands, the Mediterranean, Aegean ports, and the South Pacific's islands. If you don't speak the local language, carry some identification (but not your passport, unless required), the name of your ship, and the area in which it is docked. If the ship is anchored and you take a launch tender ashore, observe landmarks near the landing place, and write down the location. This will help if you get lost and need to take a taxi back to the launch.

Some small ships provide an identification tag or boarding pass at the reception desk or gangway, to be handed in each time you return to the ship. Remember that ships have schedules – and sometimes tides – to meet, and they won't wait for you if you return late. If you are in a launch port in a tropical area and the weather changes for the worse, the ship's captain could well make a decision to depart early to avoid being hemmed in by an approaching storm; it has happened, especially in the Caribbean. If it does, locate the ship's agent in the port – he's likely to be carrying a walkie-talkie – who will try to get you back.

Planning on going to a quiet, secluded beach to swim? First check with the cruise director or shore excursion manager, as certain beaches may be considered off-limits because of a dangerous undertow, drug pushers, or persistent hawkers. And don't even think of going diving alone – even if you know the area well.

100 POPULAR SHORE EXCURSIONS AROUND THE WORLD

THE CARIBBEAN

Antigua
❶ Tour of Shirley Heights and Nelson's Dockyard
Aruba, Netherlands Antilles
❷ Full-day Jeep eco-adventure trip
Barbados
Party cruise aboard the *Jolly Roger* pirate boat
Grand Cayman
❸ Go snorkeling with the stingrays at Sting Ray City
Grenada
❹ Eco-hiking tour of the Seven Sisters waterfall
Hamilton, Bermuda
❺ Guided walking tour of the former capital, St George's
Jamaica
❻ Excursion to Dunn's River Falls and Prospect Plantation (Ocho Rios)
❼ Horseback riding on the beach (Montego Bay, Ocho Rios)
❽ Zipline forest canopy tour
Nassau, Bahamas
❾ Go swimming with the dolphins
St Lucia
❿ Jungle eco-tour by Jeep
St Maarten, Netherlands Antilles
⓫ Join the America's Cup Regatta Adventure tour and compete in an actual yacht race
St Thomas, US Virgin Islands
⓬ The Coral World Underwater Aquarium and Island Drive Tour
⓭ "Screemin' Eagle" jet boat thrill ride
San Juan, Puerto Rico
⓮ El Yunque Rain Forest Tour & Hike
Tortola, British Virgin Islands
⓯ Hiking tour of the peak of Sage Mountain (National Park)
Virgin Gorda, British Virgin Islands
⓰ Trip to "The Baths," exotic pools and grottoes formed by giant boulders

MEXICO / CENTRAL AMERICA

Acapulco, Mexico
⓱ Excursion to see the rock divers
⓲ Tour of the Silver City of Taxco
Belize, Central America
⓳ Horseback riding and more in the jungles of Belize
Cabo San Lucas, Mexico
⓴ Personal dolphin encounter (for children) at the Cabo Dolphin Center

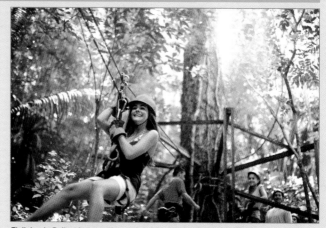

Ziplining in Belize during a Norwegian Cruise Line shore excursion.

Cozumel, Mexico
㉑ Tour of 12th-century Mayan ruins of Tulum and Xel-Ha national park

EUROPE AND THE BALTIC

Amsterdam, Holland
㉒ Go to the Anne Frank Museum
Athens (Piraeus, the port for Athens), Greece
㉓ Tour of the Acroplis and museums of ancient Athens
Barcelona, Spain
㉔ City tour to see Gaudí's architecture, the Sagrada Familia cathedral, and the Ramblas
Casablanca, Morocco
㉕ Casablanca, including the Hassan II Grand Mosque, and Rabat
Catania/Messina, Sicily
㉖ Visit to Mt Etna and Taormina
㉗ Sicilian Cooking Class tour
Copenhagen, Denmark
㉘ Guided walking tour of the famed Tivoli Gardens
Dublin, Ireland
㉙ Visit the original Guinness brewery
Dubrovnik, Croatia
㉚ Walking tour of the old walled city
Edinburgh, Scotland
㉛ Visit Edinburgh Castle and the city
㉜ The Whisky Distillery Tour
Flam/Gudvangen
㉝ Take the mountain railway excursion from Flam to Gudvangen
Helsinki, Finland
㉞ Art, city highlights, and Sibelius concert tour

Istanbul, Turkey
㉟ Tour of Topkapi Palace and the Grand Bazaar
Kusadasi
㊱ Tour of historic Ephesus, and the house of the Virgin Mary
La Coruña, Spain
㊲ Tour of Santiago de Compostela, home to the mystery of St James
Lisbon, Portugal
㊳ Tour of the Alfama (old) quarter of Lisbon and the Maritime Museum
Livorno, Italy
㊴ Full-day tour of Florence and the Leaning Tower of Pisa
London, England
㊵ River cruise along the historic River Thames for a different view of London
㊶ London by Night, including a West End musical or play
Madeira, Portugal
㊷ The toboggan ride excursion
Monte Carlo, Monaco
㊸ Tour of the Royal Palace and Grand Casino (jacket and tie required)
Naples, Italy
㊹ Boat tour to the island of Capri to visit the famous Blue Grotto caves
Nice, France
㊺ Tour of the medieval hilltop village of Eze and the Corniche
Palma de Mallorca
㊻ Tour of former Carthusian monastery of Valldemosa (Frederick Chopin and George Sand lived here in 1838)
Rhodes, Greece
㊼ Follow in the footsteps of St Paul

Rome (Civitavecchia, the port for Rome), Italy
48 Guided "Roman Holiday" walking tour, including the Colosseum
49 Visit the Vatican's Sistine Chapel

St Petersburg, Russia
50 Guided walking tour through the Hermitage Museum
51 Excursion to St Catherine's Summer Palace
52 Night tour to a ballet or classical music concert at the Mariinsky Theater

Santorini, Greece
53 Donkey-ride tour up the hillside

Sorrento, Italy
54 Visit to the ruins of Pompeii, the Amalfi Coast, and Sorrento

Stockholm, Sweden
55 Tour of the Nobel Prize Museum
56 Tour of the Viking Museum and the warship *Wasa*

Venice, Italy
57 Romantic gondola ride excursion
58 Guided walking tour of the Guggenheim Museum

Warnemunde, Germany
59 Excursion to Berlin and the Brandenburg Gate

ICELAND

Reykyavik, Iceland
60 "Ring of Fire" tour of the warm geothermal waters of the Blue Lagoon and an active volcano

INDIAN OCEAN AND THE MIDDLE EAST

Alexandria or Port Said, Egypt
61 Tour of the Temple of Karnak in Luxor

Aqaba, Jordan
62 Tour to the "Rose Red City" of Petra

Dubai, United Arab Emirates
63 4x4 Dune Drive Safari Tour

Male, Seychelles
64 Flightseeing of the atolls and inlets

Mumbai, India
65 Mumbai City Sights
66 Buddhist Trail tour to Kanheri Caves

Sharm el Sheik, Egypt
67 Go diving and snorkeling

Tripoli, Libya
68 Tour of Leptis Magna and Tripoli's Medina (when security permits!)

THE UNITED STATES

Hilo, Hawaii
69 Kilauea Volcano tour in Volcanoes National Park

Juneau, Alaska
70 Flightseeing trip to Mendenhall Glacier, and Alaska salmon bake

Ketchikan, Alaska
71 Misty Fjords flightseeing trip

Key West, Florida
72 The Conch Train Tour in Ernest Hemingway's favorite town

Los Angeles, California
73 Tour past the Hollywood homes of top movie stars

New York City
74 Take a Circle Line boat cruise around Manhattan

Sitka, Alaska
75 Sea Otter and Wildlife Quest

Skagway, Alaska
76 The historic White Pass & Yukon Route Railway train tour

AUSTRALIA, NEW ZEALAND AND THE SOUTH PACIFIC

Auckland, New Zealand
77 Tour of one of West Auckland's wineries and micro-breweries

Hamilton Island, Australia
78 Cruise/tour of Great Barrier Reef

Melbourne, Australia
79 Guided walking and tram tour, including the Gold Treasury
80 Shark diving in the aquarium tour on

Floatplane rides are popular in Alaska.

the banks of the Yarra River

Sydney, Australia
81 Full-day catamaran tour taking in the Blue Mountains and Featherdale Wildlife Park

SOUTHEAST ASIA

Bali, Indonesia
82 Balinese music and dance show

Bangkok (Laem Chabang, the port for Bangkok), Thailand
83 Tour of the Royal Palace and the sacred halls of Wat Phra Kaew

Ha Long Bay, Vietnam
84 Junk tour through the misty waters and limestone monuments

Ho Chi Minh City, Vietnam
85 Tour of the (Vietnam) War Museum

Hong Kong, China
86 The Harbour Bay cruise tour

Kuala Lumpur, Malaysia
87 Visit the Petronas Twin Tower building and night market

Osaka, Japan
88 Tour of Kyoto, Japan's former capital, and the monuments of the ancient city, now a Unesco World Heritage Site

Singapore
89 The Night Safari Tour

Yokohama, Japan
90 Tour of the famous Ginza shopping area in Tokyo
91 Kabuki Theater Performance tour

SOUTH AMERICA

92 **Buenos Aires, Argentina**
Steak and tango night tour

Puerto Madryn, Chile
93 The Penguin Safari tour (encounter 250,000 penguins, and the landscape of Patagonia)

Rio de Janeiro, Brazil
94 Tour of Sugar Loaf Mountain
95 Corcovado Tour and Christ the Redeemer Monument

Ushuaia, Argentina
96 Ride world's southernmost train

SOUTH AFRICA

Cape Town, South Africa
97 Cape Town/Table Top Mountain
98 Vintage car tour to Mount Nelson Hotel for afternoon tea

Mombasa, Kenya
99 Tour of Tsavo National Park (Kenya's oldest game preserve)

Walvis Bay, Namibia
100 Moon landscape and Welwitschia

THIS YEAR'S STAR PERFORMERS

Having reviewed 285 cruise ships, Berlitz names
the top-rating ships for 2012 and explains
why they scored as highly as they did

THE WORLD'S HIGHEST-RATED CRUISE SHIP

Despite constant cruise company claims that theirs has been named the "Best Cruise Line" or "Best Cruise Ship," *there really is no such thing* – only what's right for you. Most shipowners want to be a "luxury" cruise operator, and most passengers want to sail aboard one of the top-rated "luxury" ships. But few operators can really deliver a ship, product, and crew worthy of five Berlitz stars. For this 2012 edition, only one ship has achieved the score required for it to be awarded membership in this most exclusive club.

| *Europa* | Hapag-Lloyd Cruises | 1,852 points | ★★★★★+ |

Why? Because there is outstanding cuisine and attentive, friendly, very attentive, yet unobtrusive personal service from a staff dedicated to working aboard the world's finest cruise ship. But it's not just the ship itself and its facilities and appointments that contribute to the ship's high rating – it's also in the extensive array of details and personal attention from a fine, dedicated crew. Read the full review on pages 365–8. It all adds up to the very best cruise experience available today – unless you own a private motor yacht. Also, thanks to the pod propulsion system, there is absolutely no vibration anywhere.

Naturally, *Europa* is not a cheap ship, but one of the reasons for its continuing success is that the food is creatively produced using high-quality ingredients. The ship also offers excellent itineraries, taking passengers to many ports of call off the beaten track and inaccessible to larger cruise ships. Although *Europa* is now 12 years old, it looks almost new, thanks to the dedication of its crew and owners.

THE TOP 10 LARGE RESORT SHIPS

(more than 1,600 passengers)

Queen Mary 2 (Grill Class)	1,702	★★★★★
Queen Elizabeth (Grill Class)	1,690	★★★★★
Queen Victoria (Grill Class)	1,671	★★★★★
Celebrity Eclipse	1,612	★★★★★
Celebrity Silhouette	1,612	★★★★★
Celebrity Equinox	1,611	★★★★★
Celebrity Solstice	1,611	★★★★★
MSC Fantasia (Yacht Club)	1,570	★★★★★
MSC Splendida (Yacht Club)	1,570	★★★★★
Celebrity Constellation	1,568	★★★★★

THE TOP 10 MID-SIZE SHIPS

(600–1,600 passengers)

Crystal Serenity	1,717	★★★★★
Crystal Symphony	1,701	★★★★★
Marina	1,701	★★★★★
Asuka II	1,685	★★★★★
Seven Seas Voyager	1,654	★★★★★
Seven Seas Mariner	1,651	★★★★★
Prinsendam	1,642	★★★★★
Amadea	1,600	★★★★★
Nautica	1,575	★★★★★
Insignia	1,574	★★★★★

ABOVE: *Queen Mary 2*'s captain.
LEFT: *Europa* is given a noisy welcome in the Middle East.

THE TOP 10 SMALL SHIPS

(200–600 passengers)

Europa	1,852	★★★★★★
Seabourn Quest	1,787	★★★★★
Seabourn Odyssey	1,786	★★★★★
Seabourn Sojourn	1,783	★★★★★
Seabourn Legend	1,774	★★★★★
Silver Spirit	1,772	★★★★★
Seabourn Spirit	1,770	★★★★★
Seabourn Pride	1,769	★★★★★
Silver Whisper	1,753	★★★★★
Silver Shadow	1,750	★★★★★

THE TOP 10 BOUTIQUE SHIPS

(50–200 passengers)

SeaDream II	1,788	★★★★★
SeaDream I	1,786	★★★★★
Hanseatic	1,746	★★★★★
Sea Cloud	1,704	★★★★★
Sea Cloud II	1,702	★★★★★
Silver Explorer	1,684	★★★★★
Hebridean Princess	1,680	★★★★★
Orion	1,612	★★★★★
Island Sky	1,562	★★★★★
Bremen	1,553	★★★★★

HOW WE EVALUATE THE SHIPS

**Their facilities count, of course, but just as important
are the standards of food, service, staff, and hospitality.
This section explains how our points system works**

I have been evaluating and rating cruise ships and the onboard product professionally since 1980. In addition, I receive regular reports from my team of five trained assessors. The ratings are conducted with *total objectivity*, from a set of predetermined criteria and a modus operandi designed to work *globally*, not just regionally, across the entire spectrum of ocean-going cruise ships today, in all segments of the marketplace.

There really is no "best cruise line in the world" or "best cruise ship" – only the ship and cruise that is right for you. After all, it's the overall enjoyment of a cruise as a vacation that's really important. Therefore, different criteria are applied to ships of different sizes, styles, and market segments throughout the world (vacationers of different nationalities are looking for different things).

The evaluation and rating of cruise ships is about as contrary to soccer as you can get. In soccer, the goalposts are always in the same place. But with cruise ships, they keep changing as the industry evolves and matures. To fill ships and make a profit, ship owners, cruise operators, wholesalers, and tour packagers keep redefining their product, pricing, and marketing strategies.

This section includes 280 ocean-going cruise ships in service (or due to enter service) and chosen by the author for inclusion when this book was completed. Almost all except the newest ships have been carefully evaluated, taking into account around 400 separate items based on personal cruises, visits, and revisits to ships, as well as observations and comments from my team. These are channeled into 20 major areas, each with a possible 100 points. The maximum possible score for any ship is therefore 2,000 points.

A veranda suite aboard the award-winning *Europa*.

For the sake of clarity and user-friendliness, scores are further channeled into five main sections: Ship, Accommodation, Food, Service, and Cruise Operation.

Cruise lines, shipowners, and operators should note that the ratings may be adjusted annually as a result of increased competition, the introduction of newer ships with better facilities, and other market- or passenger-driven factors.

The ratings more reflect the *standards* of the cruise product delivered to passengers (the software: dining experience, and the service and hospitality aspects of the cruise), and less the physical plant (the hardware). Thus, although a ship may be the latest, most stunning vessel in the world in terms of design and decor, if the food, service, staff, and hospitality are not so good, the scores and ratings will reflect these aspects more clearly.

The stars beside the name of the ship at the top of each page relate directly to the Overall Rating. The highest number of stars awarded is **five stars** (★★★★★), and the lowest is one star. This system is universally recognized throughout the hospitality industry. A plus (+) indicates that a ship deserves just that little bit more than the number of stars attained. However, I must emphasize that it is the number of points achieved rather than the number of stars attained that perhaps is more meaningful to anyone comparing ships.

The star system

★★★★★+	1,851–2,000 points
★★★★★	1,701–1,850 points
★★★★+	1,551–1,700 points
★★★★	1,401–1,550 points
★★★+	1,251–1,400 points
★★★	1,101–1,250 points
★★+	951–1,100 points
★★	801–950 points
★+	650–800 points
★	501–650 points

What the ratings mean

1,851–2,000 points   ★★★★★ +
You can expect an outstanding, top-class cruise experience – it doesn't get any better than this. It should be truly memorable, and with the highest attention to detail, finesse, and personal service – how important you are made to feel is critical. The decor

Sales of "art" are often an important revenue source.

must be elegant and tasteful, measured by restraint and not flashiness, with fresh flowers and other decorative touches in abundance, and the layout of the public rooms might well follow *feng shui* principles.

Any ship with this rating must be just about unsurpassable in the cruise industry, and it has to be very, very special, with service and hospitality levels to match. There must be the very highest-quality surroundings, comfort, and service levels, the finest and freshest quality foods, including all breads and rolls baked on board. Highly creative menus, regional cuisine, and dining alternatives should provide maximum choice and variety, and special orders will be part of the dining ritual.

Dining room meals (particularly dinners) are expected to be grand, memorable affairs, correctly served on the finest china, with a choice of wines of suitable character and vintage available, and served in the correct-sized sommelier glasses of the highest quality (Reidel or Schott).

The service staff will take pleasure in providing you with the ultimate personal, yet unobtrusive, attention with the utmost of finesse, and the word "no" should not be in their vocabulary. This is the very best of the best in terms of refined, unstructured living at sea, but it is seriously expensive.

1,701–1,850 points ★★★★★
You can expect a truly excellent, memorable cruise experience, with the finesse and attention to detail commensurate with the amount of money paid. The service and hospitality levels will be extremely high from all levels of officers and staff, with strong emphasis on fine hospitality training – all service personnel members *must* make you feel important.

The food will be commensurate with the high level expected from what is virtually the best possible at sea, with service that should be very attentive yet unobtrusive. The cuisine should be memorable, with ample taste. Special orders should never be a problem, with a creative cuisine of a very high standard. There must be a varied selection of wines, which should be served in glasses of the correct size, not simply a standard-size glass for white and one for red wines.

Entertainment is expected to be of prime quality and

variety. Again, the word "no" should not be in the vocabulary of any member of staff aboard a ship with this rating. Few things will cost extra once you are on board, and brochures should be more "truthful" than those for ships with a lower rating.

1,551–1,700 points ★★★★ +
You should expect to have a high-quality cruise experience that will be quite memorable, and just a little short of being excellent in all aspects. Perhaps the personal service and attention to detail could be slightly better, but, nonetheless, this should prove to be a fine all-round cruise experience, in a setting that is extremely clean and comfortable, with few lines anywhere, a caring attitude from service personnel, and a good standard of entertainment that appeals to a mainstream market.

The cuisine and service will be well rounded, with mostly fresh ingredients and varied menus that should appeal to almost anyone, served on high-quality china.

This should prove to be an extremely well rounded cruise experience, probably in a ship that is new or almost new. There will probably be fewer "extra cost" items than ships with a slightly lower rating.

1,401–1,550 points ★★★★
You should expect to have a very good quality all-round cruise experience, most probably aboard a modern, highly comfortable ship that will provide a good range of facilities and services. The food and service will be quite decent overall, although decidedly not as "gourmet" and fanciful as the brochures with the always-smiling faces might have you believe.

The service on board will be well organized, if a little robotic and impersonal at times, and only as good as the cruise line's training program allows. You may notice a lot of things cost extra once you are on board, although the typically vague brochure tells you that the things are "available" or are an "option." However, you should have a good time, and your bank account will be only moderately damaged.

1,251–1,400 points ★★★ +
You should expect to have a decent-quality cruise experience, aboard a ship where the service levels should be good, but perhaps without the finesse that could be expected from a more upscale environment. The crew aboard any ship achieving this score should reflect a

positive attitude with regard to hospitality, and a willingness to accommodate your needs, up to a point. Staff training will probably be in need of more attention to detail and flexibility.

Food and service levels in the dining room(s) should be reasonably good, although special or unusual orders might prove more difficult. There will probably be a number of extra-cost items you thought were included in the price of your cruise – although the brochure typically is vague and tells you that the things are "available" or are an "option."

1,101–1,250 points ★★★

You can expect a reasonably decent, middle-of-the-road cruise experience, with a moderate amount of space and quality in furnishings, fixtures, and fittings. The cabins are likely to be a little on the small side (dimensionally challenged). The food and service levels will be quite acceptable, although not at all memorable, and somewhat inflexible with regard to special orders, as almost everything is standardized.

Crew attitude could be improved, the level of hospitality and cleanliness will be moderate but little more, and the entertainment will probably be weak. This is a good option, however, for those looking for the reasonable comforts of home without pretentious attitudes, and little damage to their bank statement.

951–1,100 points ★★ +

You should expect an average cruise experience in terms of accommodation (typically with cabins that are dimensionally challenged), quality of the ship's facilities, food, wine list, service, and hospitality levels, in surroundings that are unpretentious. In particular, the food and its service will probably be disappointing.

There will be little flexibility in the levels of service,

Having a decently sized balcony enhances the cruise.

hospitality, staff training and supervision, which will be no better than poor. Thus, the overall experience will be commensurate with the small amount of money you paid for the cruise.

801–950 points ★★

You should expect to have a cruise experience of modest quality aboard a ship that is probably in need of more attention to maintenance and service levels, not to mention hospitality. The food may be quite tasteless and homogenized, and of low quality, and service will leave much to be desired in terms of attitude, which will tend to be mediocre at best. Staff training is likely to be minimal, and turnover may be high. The "end-of-pier" entertainment could well leave you wanting to read a good book.

651–800 points ★ +

You can expect to have only the most basic cruise experience, with little or no attention to detail, from a poorly trained staff that is probably paid low wages and to whom you are just another body. The ship will, in many cases, probably be in need of much maintenance and upgrading, and will probably have few facilities.

Cleanliness and hygiene may well be questionable, and there will be absolutely no finesse in personal service levels, with poor attitude from the crew, and dismal entertainment as significant factors in the low score and rating. On the other hand, the price of a cruise is probably alluringly low.

501–650 points ★

You can expect to have a cruise experience that is the absolute bottom of the barrel, with almost nothing in terms of hospitality or finesse. You can forget about attention to detail – there won't be any. This will be the kind of experience that would equal a stay in the most basic motel on land, with few facilities, a poorly trained, uncaring staff, and a ship that needs better maintenance.

The low cost of a cruise aboard a ship with this rating should provide a strong clue to the complete absence of any quality. This will be particularly evident in the areas of food, service, and entertainment. In other words, this could well be a totally forgettable cruise experience.

Distribution of points

These are the percentage of the total points available which are allocated to each of the main areas evaluated:

- ● **The Ship** 25%
- ● **Accommodation** 10%
- ● **Cuisine** 20%
- ● **Service** 20%
- ● **Entertainment** 5%
- ● **The Cruise Experience** 20%

These last two categories may be combined for boutique ships, tall ships, and expedition ships.

RCI's Flowrider is a neat feature aboard some ships.

The Ship

Hardware/Maintenance/Safety

This score reflects the general profile and condition of the ship (hardware), its age and maintenance, hull condition, exterior paint, decking and caulking, swimming pool and surrounds, deck furniture, shore tenders, lifeboats, life rafts, and other safety items. It also reflects interior cleanliness (public restrooms, elevators, floor coverings, wall coverings, stairways, passageways, and doorways), food preparation areas, refrigerators, garbage handling, compacting, incineration, and waste disposal facilities.

Outdoor Facilities/Space

This score reflects the overall space per passenger on open decks, crowding, swimming pools/whirlpools and their surrounds, lido deck areas, number and type of deck lounge chairs (with or without cushioned pads) and other deck furniture, outdoor sports facilities, shower enclosures and changing facilities, towels, and quiet areas (those without music).

Interior Facilities/Space/Flow

This score reflects the use of common interior public spaces, including enclosed promenades; passenger flow and points of congestion; ceiling height; lobby areas, stairways, and all passenger hallways; elevators; public restrooms and facilities; signage, lighting, air conditioning and ventilation; and degree of comfort and density.

Decor/Furnishings/Artwork

This score reflects the overall interior decor (decoration and colors); hard and soft furnishings, wood (real, imitation, or veneer) paneling, carpeting (tuft density, color, and practicality), fit and finish, chairs (comfort, height, and support), ceilings and decor treatments, reflective surfaces, artwork (paintings, sculptures, and atrium centerpieces), and lighting.

Spa/Fitness Facilities

This score reflects any health spa, wellness center, and fitness facilities: location, accessibility, and noise levels; lighting and flooring materials; fitness and muscle-training machines and other equipment; fitness programs; sports and games facilities; indoor swimming pools; hot tubs; grand baths; hydrotherapy pools; saunas and steam rooms; treatment rooms and range of personal body treatments; changing facilities; jogging and walking tracks; and promenades.

Accommodation

Cabins: Suites and Deluxe Grades

This score reflects the design and layout of all suites and deluxe-grade cabins, private balconies (whether full floor-to-ceiling partition or part partitions, balcony lighting, balcony furniture). Also beds/berths, furniture (its placement and practicality), cabinetry, and other fittings; closets and other hanging space, drawer space, and bedside tables; vanity unit, bathroom facilities, washbasin, cabinets, and toiletries storage; lighting, air conditioning, and ventilation; audiovisual facilities; quality and degree of luxury; artwork; bulkhead insulation, noise, and vibration levels. Suites should not be so designated unless the sleeping room is completely separate from the living area.

Some large resort ships now have whole decks devoted to superior-grade accommodation, with a significant difference between this accommodation and that of "standard" cabins.

Also the soft furnishings and details like the cabin service directory, interactive TV; paper, postcards and personalized stationery (if any); telephone directory; laundry lists; tea- and coffee-making equipment; flowers (if any); fruit (if any); bathroom personal amenities kits, bathrobes, slippers, and the size, thickness and quality of towels.

Cabins: Standard Sizes

This score reflects the design and layout, beds, furniture (functionality), and other fittings. Also taken into account: closets and other hanging space, drawer space,

Cabin aboard *Carnival Freedom*, which scores ★★★+.

bedside tables, and vanity unit; bathroom facilities, washbasin, cabinets, and toiletries storage; lighting, air conditioning and ventilation; audiovisual facilities; quality and degree of fittings and furnishings; artwork; insulation, noise, and vibration levels.

In addition, we have taken into account the usefulness of the information manual (cabin directory); stationery; laundry lists; tea- and coffee-making equipment; flowers (if any); fruit (if any); and bathroom amenities, bathrobes, slippers, and the size, thickness, quality, and material content of towels.

Cuisine

Food is one of the main features of most vacations. Cruise lines put maximum emphasis on promising passengers how good their food will be, often to the point of being unable to deliver what is promised. Generally, the standard of food is good. The rule of thumb is: if you were to eat out in a good restaurant, what would you expect? Does the ship meet your expectations? Would you come back again for the food?

There are perhaps as many different tastes as there are passengers. The "standard" market cruise lines cater to a wide range of tastes, while the more exclusive cruise lines can offer better-quality food, cooked individually to your taste. As in any good restaurant, you get what you pay for.

Dining Room/Cuisine

This score reflects the physical structure of dining rooms, layout and seating (alcoves and individual chairs, with or without armrests); lighting and ambience; table set-ups; linen, china, and cutlery quality and condition; and table centerpieces (flowers). It also reflects menus, food quality, presentation, food combinations, culinary creativity, appeal, taste, texture, freshness, color, balance; garnishes and deco-

rations; appetizers, soups, pastas, tableside cooking (if any); fresh fruit and cakes; the wine list (and connoisseur wine list), price range, and wine service. Alternative dining venues are also checked for menu variety, food and service quality, decor, seating, and noise levels.

Informal Eateries/Buffets

This score reflects the hardware (hot and cold display units, sneeze guards, "active" stations, tongs, ice containers and ladles, and serving utensils); buffet displays (most are disappointing and institutionalized); trays, plates, and set-ups; correct food temperatures; food labeling; breakfast, luncheon, deck buffets, midnight buffets, and late-night snacks; decorative elements; staff attitude, service, and communication skills.

Quality of Ingredients

This score reflects the quality of ingredients used, including consistency and portion size; grades of meat, fish, and fowl; and the price paid by the cruise line for food per passenger per day. It is the quality of ingredients that most dictates the eventual presentation and quality of the finished product, as well as its taste.

Tea/Coffee/Bar Snacks

This score reflects the quality and variety of teas and coffees available, including afternoon teas/coffees and their presentation; whether mugs or cups and saucers are presented; whether milk is served in the correct open containers or in sealed packets; whether self-service or graciously served. The quality of such items as cakes, scones, and pastries, as well as bar/lounge snacks, hot and cold canapés, and hors d'oeuvres also forms part of this section.

Douglas Ward checks the quality of spa towels.

Service

Dining Room

This score reflects the professionalism of the restaurant staff: the maître d'hôtel, dining room managers, head section waiters, waiters and assistant waiters (busboys), and somme-liers and wine waiters; place settings, cut-lery, and glasses; and proper service (serving, taking from the correct side), communica-tion skills, attitude, flair, dress sense (uni-form), and finesse. Waiters should note whether passengers are right- or left-handed and, when tables are assigned, make sure that cutlery and glasses are placed on the side of preference. Cutlery and wine glasses are also included as part of this score.

Bars

This score reflects the lighting and ambience; service in bars and lounges; seating, noise levels; communication skills (between bar staff and passengers); staff attitude, personality, flair, and finesse; correct use of glasses (and correct size of glasses); and attitude when presenting the bill (aboard those ships where a charge is made).

Seabourn ships offer tempting hors d'oeuvres.

Cabins

This score reflects the cleaning and housekeeping staff, butlers (for penthouse and suite passengers), cabin stew-ards/stewardesses and their supervisory staff, attention to detail and cleanliness, food service, linen and bath-robe changes, and language and communication skills.

Open Decks

This score reflects steward/stewardess service for bev-erages and food items around the open decks; placement and replacement of towels on deck lounge chairs, towel supply, emptying of used towel bins; and general tidiness of all associated deck equipment.

Entertainment

Aboard specialist ships, such as those offering expedi-tion cruises, or tall ships, where entertainment is not a feature, it is the lecture program that forms this portion of the evaluations.

The score reflects the overall entertainment program and content as designed and targeted to specific passen-ger demographics. The entertainment has to appeal to passengers of many ages and types. Included is the phys-ical plant (stage/bandstand) of the main showlounge; technical support, lighting, set/backdrop design; all sound and light systems; pre-recorded click-tracks and special effects; large-scale production shows (including story, plot, content, cohesion, costumes, quality, chore-ography, and vocal content); cabaret; variety shows; cabaret acts; bands and solo musicians.

The cruise experience

Activities Program

This score reflects the daytime activities and events. It includes the cruise director and staff (their visibility,

availability, and professionalism), sports and water-sports programs, participation games, special interest programs, port and shopping lecturers, and mind-enrichment lecturers. Also the extent and quality of any water-sports equipment carried, instruction, staff super-vision, marina or side-retractable water-sports plat-forms, and any enclosed swimming area.

Movies/Television Programming

This score reflects movies screened in theaters and on poolside screens, picture and sound quality; videos on the in-cabin system; other programming, including a ship's own TV station programs; and content. Cabin audio channels are included.

Hospitality Standard

This score reflects the level of hospitality and profes-sionalism of senior officers, middle management, super-visors, cruise staff, and all other crew; social contact, personal appearance, and dress codes or uniforms; moti-vation; communication skills (very important).

Overall Product Delivery

This score reflects the quality of the overall cruise as a vacation – what the brochure states and promises (real or implied), and the onboard hospitality and services.

Notes on the rating results

Cruise ship evaluations and ratings have become ever more complex. Although a ship may be the newest, with all the latest facilities possible, it is the onboard food and service that often disappoint, as well as standing in lines and signing up for activities. It's about deliver-ing a cohesive, consistent onboard product.

Cruise companies say that food quality is a trade-off against lower prices. However, this implies a downward spiral that affects food quality as well as service, quality of personnel, crew training, safety, and maintenance.

In the final analysis, it is the little things that add to points lost on the great scorecard. ❑

WHAT THE DESCRIPTIONS MEAN

Each of the ship reviews that follow is preceded by a panel
providing basic data on the ship's size and facilities.
Below we explain how to interpret some of the headings

Ship Size
● Large Resort Ship (1,600–6,000+ passengers)
● Mid-Size Ship (600–1,600 passengers)
● Small Ship (200–600 passengers)
● Boutique Ship (50–200 passengers)

Lifestyle
Designated as Standard, Premium, or Luxury, according
to a general classification into which segment of the
market the ship falls. This should help you choose the
right size ship and cruise experience to fit your lifestyle.
● **Standard:** the least expensive, offering the basic
amenities, food, and service.
● **Premium:** more expensive than Standard, has generally better food, service, facilities, amenities, more
attention to detail, and differentiation of suites (with
butler service) than standard accommodation.
● **Luxury:** more expensive than Premium or Standard,
and provides more personal comfort, space, open or
one-seating dining, much better food (no processed
items, more menu creativity, and everything made as
fresh as possible), and highly trained staff.

Measuring Luxury by the Oatmeal Factor
The Oatmeal Factor shows how various cruise ships
will provide a passenger with a basic item such as a
bowl of oatmeal. The difference can be found in its
presentation. There are ships that provide one
of four levels of oatmeal presentation:
Standard: Hot oatmeal (supermarket brand oats)
mixed with water, with little or no chance of
obtaining tahini to add taste to the oatmeal. You
get it from a soup tureen at the buffet, and put it
into a plastic or inexpensive china bowl yourself
(or it may be served in the dining room by a
waiter/waitress); it is eaten with plastic or basic
canteen cutlery. It's basic, basic, basic.
Premium: Hot oatmeal, water, salt, and a little
olive oil; served in a higher-quality bowl, by a
waiter or waitress, with hotel-quality (or better)
cutlery. It's possible that the ship will have tahini,
to add taste and creaminess. It's also possible that
the waiter/waitress will ask if you'd like hot or cold
milk with your oatmeal. There may even be a doily
between the oatmeal bowl and base plate.
Luxury: Hot oatmeal (medium or large flakes),
water, salt, tahini, a little (extra virgin) olive oil
and nutmeg, with a dash of blended Scotch
(whisky); served in a high-quality brand-name

bowl (Versace), with base plate and doily, and Hepp- or
Robbe & Berking-quality silverware. Naturally, the
waiter/waitress will ask if you'd like hot or cold milk
with your oatmeal.
Incomparable: Hot Scottish (large flakes, hand-ground)
oatmeal, water, sea salt, tahini, and nutmeg (grated at the
table), high-quality cold-pressed olive oil and a layer of
rare single malt Scotch; served in small-production hand-
made china, with base plate and doily, and sterling silver
cutlery. The waiter/waitress will ask if you'd like hot or
cold milk (or anything else) with your oatmeal.
   Naturally, there are variations and some crossover
depending on the ship, supplies available, staff training,
etc. The setting and presentation play a large part. Noise
level, decor, chairs, table height, table settings, and overall comfort are all part of the evaluation process.

Cruise Line
The cruise line and the operator may be different if
the company that owns the vessel does not routinely
market and operate it. Tour operators often charter
ships for their exclusive use (e.g. Thomson Cruises).

First Entered Service
Where two dates are given, the first is for the ship's
maiden passenger voyage, and the second is the date it
began service for the current operator.

A luxury lifestyle should include a superior breakfast.

Pod propulsion: a single pod can weigh 250 tons.

Propulsion

The type of propulsion is given (i.e. gas turbine, diesel, diesel-electric, nuclear, or steam turbine), together with the output (at 100%), expressed as MW (megawatts) or KW (kilowatts) generated.

Propellers

This heading refers to the number of propellers or fixed or azimuthing pods.

The favored drivers are now eco-friendly diesel-electric or diesel-mechanical propulsion systems that propel ships at speeds of up to 28 knots (32mph). Only Cunard Line's *QM2*, with a top speed of more than 30 knots (34.8mph), is faster.

More than 70 cruise ships are now fitted with the "pod" propulsion system, first introduced to the industry in 1990. It resembles a huge outboard motor fitted below the waterline (pictured above). It replaces the long-used conventional rudder, shaft, and propeller mechanisms, saves valuable machinery space, and makes stern thrusters redundant.

The pods are compact, self-contained units powered by internal electric propulsion motors. They are turned by the hydraulic motors of the steering gear, and can turn through 360 degrees (azimuthing). This allows even the largest ships to maneuver into smaller spaces without help from tugs.

There are typically two "pods" for most ships, although some have three or even four units. Each pod typically weighs about 170 tons. But the four pods attached to *Queen Mary 2* weigh 250 tons each – more than an empty Boeing 747 jumbo jet; two are fixed, two are of the azimuthing variety. Although they are at the stern, pod units pull, rather than push, a ship through the water, thanks to their forward-facing propellers, and provide greater maneuvrability.

Ships with pod propulsion systems should have no noticeable vibration or engine noise at the stern, unlike ships with conventional propulsion systems. Competing manufacturers have different names for their pod

systems – examples: Azipod, Dolphin, Mermaid. The design of the pods has been improved, resulting in slimmer, more efficient units, including safe access for routine maintenance.

Passenger Capacity

This is based on:
● Two lower beds/berths per cabin, plus all cabins for single occupancy.
● All available beds/berths filled. (Note: This figure may not always be accurate, as cruise lines often make changes by adding or taking away third/fourth berths according to demand.)

Passenger Space Ratio (Gross Tonnage per Passenger)

Achieved by dividing the gross tonnage by the number of passengers.

Crew to Passenger Ratio

Achieved by dividing the number of passengers by the number of crew (lower beds/all possible beds and berths filled).

Cabin Size Range

From the smallest cabin to the largest suite (including "private" balconies/verandas), these are provided in square feet and square meters, rounded up to the nearest number.

Wheelchair-Accessible Cabins and Ratings

Cabins designed to accommodate passengers with limited mobility.
There are four wheelchair accessibility ratings:
Best: the ship is recommended as being most suitable for wheelchair passengers.
Good: reasonably accessible.
Fair: moderately accessible.
None: the ship is not suitable.

Dedicated Cinema/Seats

A "yes" means that there is a separate cinema dedicatedly solely to showing large-screen movies throughout the day and during the evening. This is distinct from a showlounge that may be used to screen movies during the day (afternoon) and live shows in the evening, or poolside screens. The number of seats is provided where known.

A Note about Prices

Some price examples are given throughout the ship reviews (for massage, the cover price for "alternative" restaurants, for internet access, or gratuities added to your onboard account, for example), but please note that these are provided *only* as a guideline, and may have changed since this book was completed. Always check with the cruise line, onboard concession, or your travel provider for the latest prices. ❏

HOW A NEW CRUISE SHIP IS CREATED

Ships used to be constructed from the keel up. Today they are built in as many as 100 huge sections that are joined together in a shipyard

One of 55 prefabricated ship blocks is moved into position in Meyer Werft's shipyard in Papenburg, Germany.

It is the job of the shipyard, its marine architects, consultants, interior designers, and a mass of specialist suppliers to turn those dreams and concepts into a ship without unduly straining the laws of naval architecture, safety regulations, or – crucially – budgets. Computers have simplified this complex process, although shipboard management and operations personnel often become frustrated with designers who are more idealistic than they are practical.

Today's ships begin life as huge sections – as many as 100 sections, each weighing up to 450 tons, for a large resort ship such as *Carnival Freedom* or *Celebrity Solstice*. Most are extensively pre-outfitted and may not even be constructed in the shipyard – simply assembled there.

Formerly, passenger spaces were slotted in wherever there was space within a given hull. Today, computers provide targeted ship design, enabling a new ship to be built in two years instead of the four or five it used to take in the 1950s.

Maximum noise and vibration levels allowable in the accommodation spaces and recreation areas are stipulated in any owner's contract. Vibration tests, focusing on propellers and main engines, are carried out once a ship is built and launched.

Prefabricated cabin modules, including in situ bathrooms complete with toilets and plumbing, are used today. When the steel structure of the relevant deck is ready, with main lines and insulation installed, cabin modules are then affixed to the deck, and power lines and sanitary plumbing are swiftly connected. All waste and power connections, together with hot/cold water mixing valves, are arranged in the service area of the bathroom and can be conveniently reached from the passageway outside the cabin for maintenance.

Cloning a design

With the costs of developing new designs prohibitively expensive, some companies go into "clone" mode, using the same basic platform, space, and machinery configuration for the hull, but varying the upper structure and layout of public spaces.

The best example of this is in the "Vista"-class ships, with the same basic platform shared by cruise lines belonging to the Carnival Corporation. Examples include *Carnival Legend, Carnival Miracle, Carnival Pride, Carnival Spirit* (Carnival Cruise Lines); *Costa Atlantica, Costa Luminosa, Costa Mediterranea* (Costa Cruises); *Eurodam, Nieuw Amsterdam, Oosterdam, Westerdam, Zuiderdam* (Holland America Line). More modified versions can be found in Cunard Line's *Queen Elizabeth* and *Queen Victoria*. ❏

The prefabricated bridge section is moved into position. The yard's massive cranes can carry 600 tons.

An engine unit is added. The ship looks like a stack of containers bolted together – which is pretty close to reality.

Gradually the 122,000-ton *Celebrity Solstice*, with its 14 passenger decks, assumes its final shape.

Today's ships are a compromise between a designer's ideal, maximizing use of interior space, and financial constraints.

Admiralty Dream
★★

Size:	Boutique Ship	Passenger Decks:	3	Cabins (wheelchair accessible):	0
Tonnage:	730	Total Crew:	20	Wheelchair accessibility:	None
Lifestyle:	Standard	Passengers		Cabin Current:	110 volts
Cruise Line:	Alaska Dream Cruises	(lower beds/all berths):	84/84	Elevators:	0
Former Names:	Spirit of Columbia,	Passenger Space Ratio		Casino (gaming tables):	No
	Independence, Columbia	(lower beds/all berths):	10.8/10.8	Slot Machines:	No
Builder:	Eastern Shipping (USA)	Crew/Passenger Ratio		Swimming Pools (outdoors):	0
Original Cost:	n/a	(lower beds/all berths):	4.2/4.2	Swimming Pools (indoors):	0
Entered Service:	1982/May 2011	Cabins (total):	43	Whirlpools:	0
Registry:	USA	Size Range (sq ft/m):	64–126.0/5.9–11.7	Self-Service Launderette:	No
Length (ft/m):	166.0/50.5	Cabins (outside view):	43	Dedicated Cinema/Seats:	No
Beam (ft/m):	37.0/11.2	Cabins (interior/no view):	0	Library:	Some bookshelves
Draft (ft/m):	7.5/2.2	Cabins (for one person):	2	Onboard currency:	US$
Propulsion/Propellers:	diesel/2	Cabins (with private balcony):	0		

A small Alaska coastal cruising ship with limited facilities.

OVERVIEW. This little ship, which used to be part of the Cruise West fleet, is all about eco-tourism, and can take you close to nature and wildlife for an up-close experience. It suits couples and single travelers, mostly over 60, who enjoy nature and wildlife at close quarters, with an all-American crew.

THE SHIP. Public rooms consist of a lounge that is a multi-functional space for meetings (plus a couple of bookcases with books about nature and wildlife), and a dining room. Naturalists and other specialists give talks and act as leaders on shore excursions.

The young, cheerful staff is multi-flexible, doing a little of this and a little of that. Service comes with a smile, but rarely with finesse – homely but not perfect. The captain has the flexibility to deviate to take in particular areas of interest. The dress code is utterly casual – not even a jacket for men, and no ties, please. However, do take comfortable walking shoes, as well as photographic materials for wildlife spotting. Smoking is permitted only on the outside decks. All tips are pooled by all staff, using the amounts recommended in the cruise line's brochure. Alaska cruises start and end in Sitka. A sister ship, *Baranof Dream*, also with 39 cabins, is available for groups and charters.

Note that, because the ship is small, there is an almost constant throbbing from the diesel engines/generator.

ACCOMMODATION. There are seven price categories – a

BERLITZ'S RATINGS

	Possible	Achieved
Ship	500	183
Accommodation	200	82
Food	400	199
Service	400	206
Entertainment	n/a	n/a
Cruise	500	250

OVERALL SCORE
920 points out of 2,000

lot for such a small ship. All cabins are small when compared to most cruise ships, but they are basically comfortable, and each has a large picture window – a few cabins have portholes – and a very small clothes closet. A few cabins have double beds, but most have singles that can't be moved together. Some cabins may also have upper/lower berths instead of beds). Each has its own little bathroom, with a wall-mounted shower, and there's a small washbasin. There is no room service for food or snack items.

Cool-weather clothing for the outdoors is necessary in Alaska, but there's almost no storage space for it in the tiny, utilitarian cabins aboard these small ships.

DINING. All meals are taken in the dining room at a set time, except for Continental breakfast, which is typically provided in the lounge. This tends to be early, so it's regimented and not at all flexible. Don't expect outstanding cuisine – the galley is small, and the range of food items limited, except for fresh local fish and seafood, which can be very good. It's really simple American fare.

ENTERTAINMENT. Dinner and after-dinner conversation with fellow passengers in the ship's lounge/bar constitutes the entertainment each evening.

SPA/FITNESS. There are no spa or fitness facilities.

Adonia
★★★★

Size:	Mid-Size Ship	Passenger Decks:	.9	Cabins (with private balcony):	.258
Tonnage:	.30,277	Total Crew:	.300	Cabins (wheelchair accessible):	.4
Lifestyle:	Standard	Passengers		Wheelchair accessibility:	Good
Cruise Line:	.P & O Cruises	(lower beds/all berths):	.710/838	Cabin Current:	.110 and 220 volts
Former Names:	.Royal Princess,	Passenger Space Ratio		Elevators:	.4
	Minerva II, R8	(lower beds/all berths):	.42.6/36.1	Casino (gaming tables):	Yes
Builder: .Chantiers de l'Atlantique (France)		Crew/Passenger Ratio		Slot Machines:	Yes
Original Cost:	.$150 million	(lower beds/all berths):	.1.8/2.2	Swimming Pools (outdoors):	.1
Entered Service:	.Feb 2001/May 2011	Cabins (total):	.355	Swimming Pools (indoors):	.0
Registry:	Bermuda	Size Range (sq ft/m):	.145.3–968.7/	Whirlpools:	.2 (+ 1 thalassotherapy)
Length (ft/m):	.592.0/180.45		13.5–90.0	Self-Service Launderette:	Yes
Beam (ft/m):	.83.5/25.46	Cabins (outside view):	.332	Dedicated Cinema/Seats:	No
Draft (ft/m):	.19.5/6.0	Cabins (interior/no view):	.23	Library:	Yes
Propulsion/Propellers: diesel (18,600 kW)/2		Cabins (for one person):	.0	Onboard currency:	UK£

An adults-only, homey ship, ideal for British tastes.

OVERVIEW. There may not be marble bathroom fittings, or other expensive niceties, but this adults-only ship provides value-for-money cruise and tour programs, geared specifically to more mature British passengers, in a hassle-free environment with expert lecturers. The price of drinks is quite reasonable.

THE SHIP. *Adonia*, the last of eight almost identical ships originally built for the defunct Renaissance Cruises, has the feel of an informal old-world British country hotel – warm, comfortable, cosseting, and homely. P & O's trademark buff-colored funnel balances the ship's all-white hull and superstructure. An outside lido deck has a swimming pool and good sunbathing space.

Although there is no walk-around promenade deck outdoors, there is a small jogging track above the perimeter of the swimming pool, and you can stroll on open decks on the port and starboard sides. There are no wooden decks outdoors; they are covered by Bolidt, a sand-colored rubberized material.

The interior decor, designed by a Scotsman, John McNeece, is quite elegant, a throwback to the dark woods-style of the ocean liners of the 1920s and '30s. It includes detailed ceiling cornices, both real and faux wrought-iron staircase railings, wood- and leather-paneled walls, trompe l'oeil ceilings, rich carpeting in hallways, and many other interesting and expensive-looking decorative touches.

Public rooms. These are basically spread over three decks. The reception hall has a staircase with intricate, real wrought-iron railings, but these are cleverly painted on plasti-glass panels on the stairways on other decks – a copy of the staircase aboard SS *Titanic*.

BERLITZ'S RATINGS

	Possible	Achieved
Ship	500	416
Accommodation	200	157
Food	400	287
Service	400	296
Entertainment	100	76
Cruise	400	308

OVERALL SCORE
1,540 points out of 2,000

The Library is a beautiful, grand, restful room – perhaps the nicest public room – designed in the Regency style. It has a fireplace, a high, indented, trompe l'oeil ceiling, and a collection of about 2,000 books, plus comfortable wingback chairs with footstools, and sofas to fall asleep on.

A Crow's Nest Lounge is high atop the ship, with great views from its floor-to-ceiling windows. The room has a long bar which faces forward – the barmen actually have the best view – and very comfortable seating. There is a small central bandstand and wooden dance floor forward of the bar.

Anderson's Lounge, a P&O Cruises favorite also found aboard *Aurora* and *Oriana*, is a delightful wood-paneled lounge with a fireplace, a long bar, and the feel of a proper gentleman's club.

The Cabaret Lounge is used mainly for evening theatrical shows and musical performances. There are several bars, including one in each of the restaurant entrances.

Adonia is already a much sought-after and successful ship for P&O Cruises and for passengers who simply don't like the large resort-style ships – or cruising with children. And it allows P&O regulars to sail into some of the smaller ports the larger ships in the fleet can't get into.

ACCOMMODATION. There are six basic cabin size categories, in 20 price categories (14 for double occupancy and six for single occupancy). Some cabins have interconnecting doors, and 18 cabins on Deck 6 have lifeboat-obstructed views. All grades have tea/coffee-making facilities. There are two interior accommodation passageways.

The **Standard Outside-View and Interior (no view) Cab-**

ins are compact units, and tight for two persons, particularly for cruises longer than five days. They have twin beds or a queen-size bed, with good under-bed storage, personal safe, vanity desk with large mirror, reasonable closet and drawer space in rich, dark woods, TV, and cotton bathrobe. TV sets carry major news channels, where obtainable, plus sport and several movie channels.

Cabins with Private Balcony: Cabins with private balconies – about 66 percent of all cabins – have partial, and not full, balcony partitions, sliding glass doors and, thanks to good design and layout, only 14 cabins on Deck 6 have lifeboat-obstructed views. The tiled-floor, plain wall bathrooms are compact units, and include a shower stall with a removable hand-held shower unit, wall-mounted hairdryer, 100% cotton towels, toiletries storage shelves, and retractable clothesline.

Owner's Suites/Master Suites: The six Owner's Suites and four Master Suites provide abundant space and are worth the extra cost. They are large living spaces located in the forward-most and aft-most sections of the ship. Particularly nice are those that overlook the stern, on Deck 6, 7 and 8. They have more extensive private balconies that really are private and cannot be overlooked by anyone on the decks above. There is an entrance foyer, living room, bedroom (the bed faces the sea), audio unit, bathroom with Jacuzzi tub, and small guest bathroom.

CUISINE. There are three proper restaurants, plus a casual self-serve buffet-style venue:

The *Pacific Restaurant*, in the aft section, is the most formal, with 338 seats and a raised central section. It has large ocean-view windows on three sides, and several prime tables overlook the stern. The menu changes daily for lunch and dinner. The noise level can be high, the result of its single-deck-height ceiling and noisy waiter stations. Adja-

cent to the restaurant entrance is the *Club Bar* – a cosy, open lounge and bar, with an attractive fireplace.

Ocean Grill, by Marco Pierre White, has ocean-view windows along two sides, serves steak and seafood dishes. There is a cover charge, and reservations are needed. A second reservations-only venue, *Sorrento*, offers fine Italian cuisine and has a cover charge.

Both of these L-shaped venues are the same size, and have ocean-view windows along two sides and at the stern. Tables are mostly for four or six.

The *Conservatory*, with both indoor and outdoor seating, is the ship's casual dining spot, in a self-serve style. It is open for breakfast, lunch and casual dinners – the dinner menu is the same as that in the formal dining room.

Additionally, there is a *Poolside Grill*, providing casual fast food.

ENTERTAINMENT. The Curzon Lounge, forward on Deck 5, is the venue for all main entertainment events, and occasional social functions. The entertainment consists mainly of small production shows, and cabaret shows. A Crow's Nest Lounge, which sits atop the ship at the front, has good forward views; it includes a dance floor and live music.

SPA/FITNESS. The Oasis Spa has a gymnasium with some muscle-toning equipment, a large hot tub, steam rooms for men and women (there are no saunas), several treatment rooms, and a beauty salon. A spa concession provides beauty and wellness treatments, as well as exercise classes – some of which may cost extra. Out on deck, there is a small swimming pool, two hot tubs, a jogging track, a golf practice net and shuffleboard courts.

● **For more extensive general information on what the P & O Cruises experience is like, see pages 148–9.**

Adventure of the Seas
★★★★

Size: . . . . .Large Resort Ship	Passenger Decks: 14	Cabins (with private balcony): 765
Tonnage: 137,276	Total Crew: 1,185	Cabins (wheelchair accessible): 26
Lifestyle: . . . . .Standard	Passengers	Wheelchair accessibility: . . . . .Best
Cruise Line: Royal Caribbean International	(lower beds/all berths): 3,114/3,838	Cabin Current: . . . . .110 volts
Former Names: . . . . .none	Passenger Space Ratio	Elevators: . . . . .14 (6 glass-enclosed)
Builder: . . .Kvaerner Masa-Yards (Finland)	(lower beds/all berths): 44.0/35.7	Casino (gaming tables): . . . . .Yes
Original Cost: . . . .$500 million	Crew/Passenger Ratio	Slot Machines: . . . . .Yes
Entered Service: . . . . .Nov 2001	(lower beds/all berths): 2.6/3.2	Swimming Pools (outdoors): 3
Registry: . . . . .The Bahamas	Cabins (total): 1,557	Swimming Pools (indoors): 0
Length (ft/m): 1,020.6/311.1	Size Range (sq ft/m): 151.0–1,358.0/	Whirlpools: 6
Beam (ft/m): 155.5/47.4	14.0–126.1	Self-Service Launderette: . . . . .No
Draft (ft/m): 28.8/8.8	Cabins (outside view): 939	Dedicated Cinema/Seats: . . . . .No
Propulsion: . . .diesel-electric(75,600kW)/	Cabins (interior/no view): 618	Library: . . . . .Yes
3 pods (2 azimuthing, 1 fixed/14 MW each)	Cabins (for one person): 0	Onboard currency: . . . . .US$

Big on things to do for the whole family.

OVERVIEW. *Adventure of the Seas* is a large, floating leisure resort. It provides a host of facilities, rather like a small town, yet offers a healthy amount of space per passenger. Too big for the Panama Canal, it limits its itineraries almost exclusively to the Caribbean, where only a few islands can accept it.

THE SHIP. Embarkation and disembarkation typically take place through two access points, designed to minimize lines – that's over 1,500 people for each access point. Once inside the ship, you'll need good walking shoes – it really is quite a long way from one end to the other. Spend the first few hours exploring all the facilities and public spaces and it will be time well spent.

A four-decks-high Royal Promenade is the main interior focal point; it's a good place to hang out, or to arrange to meet someone. The length of two football fields (American football, that is), it has two internal lobbies rising through 11 decks. Cafés, shops, and entertainment locations front this winding street and interior "with-view" cabins look into it from above. It is an imaginative piece of design work, and fans of shopping malls enjoy it immensely.

The long super-atrium houses a "traditional" pub. There is also a Champagne Bar, a Sidewalk Café (for continental breakfast, all-day pizzas, speciality coffees, and desserts), Sprinkles (for round-the-clock ice cream and yoghurt), and a sports bar. There are also several shops – jewelry shop, gift shop, liquor shop, perfume shop, and a logo souvenir shop. Comedy art has its place here, too, for example in the trompe l'oeil painter climbing up the walls.

The cabin hallways are warm and attractive, with artwork cabinets and wavy lines to lead you along and break up the

BERLITZ'S RATINGS		
	Possible	Achieved
Ship	500	419
Accommodation	200	149
Food	400	222
Service	400	281
Entertainment	100	82
Cruise	400	301
OVERALL SCORE		
1,454 points out of 2,000		

monotony. In fact, there are plenty of colorful, even whimsical, decorative touches to avoid what could be a very clinical environment.

The Guest Reception and Shore Excursion counters are located at the aft end of the promenade, as is an ATM machine. Things to watch for: look up to see the large moving, asteroid-like sculpture (constantly growing and contracting). At times, street entertainers appear, and parades are staged, while at other (carefully orchestrated) times it's difficult to walk through the area as it is filled to the brim with tacky shopping items – like a cheap bazaar.

Arched across the promenade is a captain's balcony, and in the center of the promenade a stairway connects you to the deck below, where you'll find the Schooner Bar (a piano lounge common to all RCI ships) and the flashy Casino Royale. Gaming includes blackjack, Caribbean stud poker, roulette, and craps, plus 300 slot machines.

Aft of the casino is the neat Aquarium Bar, with 50 tons of glass and water in four large aquariums, while close by are some neat displays of oceanographic interest. RCI has teamed up with the University of Miami's Rosenstiel School of Marine and Atmospheric Science to study the ocean and the atmosphere. A small onboard laboratory is part of the project.

There's a regulation-size ice-skating rink (Studio B), with real ice, with "bleacher" seating for up to 900, and the latest in broadcast facilities. Superb Ice Follies shows are presented here. A stunning two-deck library, open 24 hours a day, includes $12 million worth of artwork.

Other drinking places include the small and intimate Champagne Bar, Crown & Anchor Pub, and Connoisseur

Club – for cigars and cognacs. Lovers of jazz might appreciate Blue Moon, an intimate room for cool music atop the ship in the Viking Crown Lounge. Golfers might enjoy the 19th Hole, a golf bar, as they play the Adventure Links. There is a TV studio with high-tech broadcast facilities, located adjacent to rooms that can be used for trade show exhibit space, with a conference center seating 400 and a multi-media screening room that seats 60.

High atop the ship, you can tie the knot in a wedding chapel in the sky, the Skylight Chapel; located on the upper level of the Viking Crown Lounge, it has wheelchair access via an electric stairlift. Outdoors, the pool and open deck areas provide a resort-like environment.

If possible, visit the Helicopter deck at the front of the ship for great starry-sky views at night.

Passenger niggles include having to negotiate the "sale" bazaar tables along the Royal Promenade; the lunchtime chaos in the Windjammer Café on embarkation day (before you have access to your cabin); and the problem of getting a table in the extra-cost dining venues.

The ship has four sisters: *Explorer of the Seas, Mariner of the Seas, Navigator of the Seas* and *Voyager of the Seas.*

FAMILIES. Facilities for children and teenagers are quite extensive. Aquanauts is for 3–5-year-olds; Explorers is for 6–8-year-olds; Voyagers is for 9–12-year-olds. Optix is a dedicated area for teenagers, including a daytime club (with several computers), soda bar, and dance floor. Challenger's Arcade has an array of video games. Paint and Clay is an arts and crafts center for younger children. Adjacent is Adventure Beach, an area for all the family; it includes swimming pools, a water slide and game areas outdoors.

ACCOMMODATION. There is an extensive range of 22 cabin categories in four major groupings: Premium ocean-view suites and cabins, Promenade-view (interior-view) cabins, Ocean-view cabins, and Interior (no view) cabins. Many cabins are of a similar size – good for incentives groups and other large groups, and 300 have interconnecting doors – useful for families. For a more detailed explanation, see the entry for *Voyager of the Seas* on page 650.

CUISINE. The main dining room (total capacity 1,919) is massive, and is set on three levels, each named after a composer *(Mozart, Strauss, Vivaldi)* and all with the same menu. A dramatic staircase connects all three levels, and huge, fat support pillars obstruct the sight lines.

Two small private wings serve private groups: *La Cetra* and *La Notte*, each seating 58 persons. When you book, choose one of two seatings, or "My Time Dining" (eat when you want during dining room hours). Tables are for four, six, eight, 10, or 12. The place settings, china and cutlery are of good quality.

Alternative Dining Options: These are for casual and informal meals, and include:
● *Café Promenade:* for continental breakfast, all-day piz-

zas, pastries, desserts and specialty coffees (sadly provided in paper cups).
● *Windjammer Café:* for casual buffet-style breakfast, lunch and light dinner (except on the last night of the cruise).
● *Island Grill:* (actually a section inside the Windjammer Café), for casual dinner (no reservations necessary) featuring a grill and open kitchen.
● *Portofino:* the ship's "upscale" Euro-Italian restaurant, open for dinner only. Reservations are required, and there is a cover charge. The food and its presentation are better than in the main dining room, although the venue is too small for all passengers to try even once during a cruise. Choices include: antipasti, soup, salad, pasta, main dish, dessert, cheese and coffee.
● *Johnny Rockets,* a retro 1950s all-day, all-night diner-style eatery that features hamburgers, malt shakes (at extra cost), and jukebox hits, with both indoor and outdoor seating (all indoor tables feature a mini-jukebox; dimes are provided for you to make your selection of vintage records), and all-singing, all-dancing waitresses that'll knock your socks off, if you can stand the high volume.
● *Sprinkles:* for 24-hour ice cream and yoghurt.

ENTERTAINMENT. The 1,350-seat Lyric Showlounge is a stunning room located at the forward end of the ship. It spans the height of five decks, with only a few slim pillars and almost no disruption of sight lines. There's also an array of up-and-coming cabaret acts and late-night adults-only comedy.

Entertainment is always upbeat. There is even background music in all corridors and elevators, and constant music outdoors on the pool deck. If you want a quiet relaxing holiday, this is not the right ship for you.

SPA/FITNESS. The ShipShape health spa is reasonably large, and measures 15,000 sq. ft (1,400 sq. meters). It includes an aerobics room, fitness center (with the usual stairmasters, treadmills, stationary bikes, weight machines and free weights), treatment rooms, and men's and women's sauna/steam rooms. Another 10,000 sq. ft (930 sq. meters) is devoted to a Solarium (with sliding glass-dome roof) to relax in after you've exercised.

There's a 32.8-ft (10-meter) rock-climbing wall at the aft end of the funnel, with five climbing tracks. You'll get a great "buzz" being 200 ft (60 meters) above the ocean while the ship is moving. Other sports facilities include a roller-blading track, a dive-and-snorkel shop, a full-size basketball court and nine-hole, par 26 golf "course." A dive-and-snorkel shop provides equipment for rental, and diving classes.

● **For more extensive general information about a Royal Caribbean cruise experience, see pages 152–6, and for more detailed information about the Voyager-class ships, see *Voyager of the Seas* (page 650).**

Aegean Odyssey
★★★ +

Size: ....Small Ship	Propulsion/Propellers: ....diesel	Cabins (for one person):......................18
Tonnage: 11,563	(10,296kW)/2	Cabins (with private balcony):............42
Lifestyle: ....Standard	Passenger Decks: 8	Cabins (wheelchair accessible): 2
Cruise Line:.............Voyages to Antiquity	Total Crew: 200	Wheelchair accessibility: ....Fair
Golden Star Cruises	Passengers	Cabin Current: ....220 volts
Former Names:*Aegean I, Aegean Dolphin,*	(lower beds/all berths):..............378/388	Elevators: 2
Dolphin, Alkyon, Narcis	Passenger Space Ratio	Casino (gaming tables): ....Yes
Builder:......Santierul N. Galatz (Romania)	(lower beds/all berths):............30.5/ 29.8	Slot Machines:..................................Yes
Original Cost: ....n/a	Crew/Passenger Ratio	Swimming Pools (outdoors): 1
Entered Service:.............1974/May 2010	(lower beds/all berths):................1.8/1.9	Swimming Pools (indoors): 0
Registry:...Greece	Cabins (total):....................................198	Whirlpools: 0
Length (ft/m):.........................460.9/140.5	Size Range (sq ft/m): 130.0–550.0/	Self-Service Launderette:......................No
Beam (ft/m):................................67.2/20.5	12.0–51.0	Dedicated Cinema/Seats: ....No
Draft (ft/m):.................................20.3/6.2	Cabins (outside view):........................153	Library: ....Yes
	Cabins (interior/no view):....................45	Onboard currency: ....Euros

Cultural exploration and learning are the big draw.

OVERVIEW. *Aegean Odyssey* appeals to couples and single travelers looking for a life enrichment cruise experience in a smart, yet somewhat traditional classic ship environment. The credo is based on history, ancient civilizations and learning, and the main appeal is the quality of the excursions and lecturers.

THE SHIP. This is not a new ship, but it has been skillfully converted to provide an extremely comfortable environment. Its profile is quite smart, with a nicely-shaped funnel that balances the rather angular stern – the result of a $26 million "chop and stretch" operation some years ago. The present operator, Voyages to Antiquity, bought the ship in December 2007, then set about a painstaking, extensive refit and refurbishment program that ended up more like a complete rebuild, because the ship looks so much nicer.

Originally built to carry ammunition, the ship's hull is really strong. The passenger capacity has been significantly reduced – from 650 to 378, with a subsequent increase in the passenger space ratio – in what can only be described as a well thought-out conversion, refit and refurbishment. As a result, the open deck space, covered in teak, is extremely good, and measures 37,674 sq. ft (3,500 sq. meters) – a lot for a small ship.

The Promenade Deck houses most of the public rooms. There is a forward observation lounge, with many windows providing plenty of natural light. The Rendez-Vous Square – actually a large lounge with a large dance floor – is quite stunning, with its classy black and red decor.

Some materials in public rooms are held together by the

BERLITZ'S RATINGS		
	Possible	Achieved
Ship	500	315
Accommodation	200	143
Food	400	265
Service	400	276
Entertainment	100	68
Cruise	400	274

OVERALL SCORE
1,341 points out of 2,000

"patch and fix" method, but subtle, pleasing, homely color combinations – most with earth tones – help to create a spacious, light, and open feel.

Outstanding lecturers are an intrinsic part of the cruises, which are typically 14 days long, and a good-size library is an important facility. Itineraries include several port overnights. Cellphone use inside the ship is, wisely, not permitted.

Although the onboard currency is the euro, you can also pay your final bill in either US$ or UK£. Gratuities to dining and cabin staff are included in the fare, and so are most shore excursions, together with selected wines with dinner (or beer/soft drinks); otherwise, 12½% is added to bar accounts.

ACCOMMODATION. There are 14 cabin price grades, half designated as Concierge Class, and 42 cabins have a private balcony. The accommodation numbering system is nautically incorrect, however, with even numbered cabins on the starboard side instead of on the port, or left, side of the ship. Most cabins do have an outside view, with similar sizes and configuration. All have a small refrigerator.

They are reasonably spacious, considering the ship's size, and pleasantly decorated, although closet, drawer and luggage storage space for two is limited in the lower grade cabins, particularly for longer cruises. Most bathrooms are partly tiled, with decent storage space for toiletries.

Single travellers have a choice of 18 single-occupancy cabins, most of which are quite spacious.

Two owner's suites are located forward on Sun Deck. These are rather nice and have forward ocean views over the bow, and include a narrow balcony on either port or starboard side. They have a separate bedroom, a walk-in closet, and a bathroom with a tub-shower combination.

CUISINE. The *Marco Polo Restaurant*, the main dining room, is located on the lowest passenger deck. It has restful colors, and seating is mostly at large tables – there are no tables for two – in an open-seating arrangement that allows you to dine when you want and with whom you want. The amount of space around each table is good. Portholes on both sides, rather than windows, are set high up, and allow some natural light during the day. A smaller, more intimate alternative dining venue is found in the Yacht Club, for which there is no extra charge.

The cuisine is a mixture of Continental and Greek, but the selection of breads, cheeses and fruit is limited. Meats, fish and poultry items are not high-quality. For casual meals, self-serve breakfast and lunch buffets are available at the *Terrace Café*, aft on Promenade Deck, with indoor-outdoor seating that includes a Tapas Bar each evening ("Tapas on the Terrace").

ENTERTAINMENT. The Ambassador Lounge, a single-level showlounge, has a bar at one end, and seating that is mainly in tub-style chairs. The sightlines to the "stage" from many seats are obstructed, however, because of several support pillars. While the occasional cabaret act is presented for entertainment, this room serves as a presentation room for the specialist lecturers.

SPA/FITNESS. The wellness facilities are very attractive, and include a separate sauna and changing area for males and females, plus a fitness area with aft-facing views. A beauty salon is located on a lower deck.

WHO'S WHO IN SHIPBOARD ENTERTAINMENT

Although production companies differ in their approach, the following gives some idea of the various people involved behind the scenes.

Executive Producer
Transfers the show's concept from design to reality. First, the brief from the cruise line's director of entertainment might be for a new production show (the average being two major shows per seven-day cruise). After deciding on an initial concept, they then call in the choreographer, vocal coach, and musical arranger.

Choreographer
Responsible for auditioning the dancers and for creating, selecting, and teaching the routines.

Musical Director
Coordinates all musical scores and arrangements; trains the singers in voice and microphone techniques, projection, accenting, phrasing, memory, and general presentation; and oversees session singers and musicians for the recording sessions.

Musical Arranger
After the music has been selected, the musical arrangements must be made. Just one song can cost more than $2,000 for a single arrangement for a 12-piece orchestra.

Costume Designer
Provides creative original designs for a minimum of seven costume changes in one show lasting 45 minutes. The costumes must also be practical, as they will be used repeatedly.

Costume Maker
Buys all materials, and must be able to produce all required costumes in time for a show.

Graphic Designer
Provides all the set designs, whether they are physical one- two- or three-dimensional sets for the stage, or photographic images created on slide film, video, laser disk, or other electronic media.

Lighting Designer
Creates lighting patterns and effects for a production show. Sequences and action on stage must be carefully lit to the best advantage. The completed lighting plot is computerized.

Bands/Musicians
Before the big production shows and artists can be booked, bands and musicians must be hired, often for long contracts. Naturally, live musicians are favored for a ship's show band, as they are excellent music readers (necessary for all visiting cabaret artists and for big production shows). Big bands are often placed in some of the larger ships for special sailings, or for world cruises, on which ballroom dancing plays a large part. Most musicians work to contracts of about six months.

AIDAaura
★★★ +

Size:.................	Mid-size Ship
Tonnage:..................	42,289
Lifestyle:...............	Standard
Cruise Line:..........	AIDA Cruises
Former Names:.............	none
Builder:........ Aker MTW (Germany)	
Original Cost:..........	$350 million
Entered Service:........	April 2003
Registry:....................	Italy
Length (ft/m):..........	665.5/202.8
Beam (ft/m):.............	92.2/28.1
Draft (ft/m):..............	20.3/6.2
Propulsion/Propellers:.. diesel-electric	
	(27,150kW)/2
Passenger Decks:..............	10
Total Crew:..................	389

Passengers
(lower beds/all berths):.. 1,266/1,582
Passenger Space Ratio
(lower beds/all berths):..... 33.4/26.7
Crew/Passenger Ratio
(lower beds/all berths):....... 3.0/3.7

Cabins (total):	633
Size Range (sq ft/m): ... 145.3–344.4/	
	13.5–32.0
Cabins (outside view):.........	422
Cabins (interior/no view):.......	211
Cabins (for one person):..........	0
Cabins (with private balcony):.....	60
Cabins (wheelchair accessible):.....	4
Wheelchair accessibility:.......	Good
Cabin Current:............	220 volts
Elevators:....................	6
Casino (gaming tables):.........	No
Slot Machines:.................	No
Swimming Pools (outdoors):	2
Swimming Pools (indoors):	0
Whirlpools:	5
Self-Service Launderette:.......	Yes
Dedicated Cinema/Seats:	No
Library:....................	Yes
Onboard currency:	Euros

BERLITZ'S RATINGS

	Possible	Achieved
Ship	500	368
Accommodation	200	131
Food	400	259
Service	400	269
Entertainment	100	72
Cruise	400	281

OVERALL SCORE
1,380 points out of 2,000

Upbeat, family-friendly ships for no-frills cruising.

Because the facilities and cruise experience offered aboard the AIDA Cruises fleet are reasonably similar, we have combined our assessment for all nine ships.

OVERVIEW.
The ships of AIDA Cruises are for youthful German-speaking couples, singles, and particularly families seeking good value for money in a fun, upbeat party-like environment, with excellent entertainment. AIDA Cruises is part of Costa Cruises, which is itself part of the giant Carnival Corporation. Germany's largest cruise line, it is known for its über-casual cruising, with two main self-serve buffet restaurants instead of the traditional waiter service. It's a tablecloth-less method of eating, a bit like camping at sea, with little contact with the small staff numbers.

THE SHIPS.
A growing fleet of ships means that AIDA Cruises can offer a wide choice of itineraries that include the Middle East and Asia. The vessels have smart, contemporary profiles that are quite well proportioned, and each has a swept-back funnel and wedge-shaped stern. The bows display the red lips, as well as the blue eyes, of Aïda (from Verdi's opera, written to commemorate the opening of the Suez Canal in 1871).

There are differences between the various ships, due to their size and configuration, but all share the same basic concept, with self-service eateries being the mainstay. The company has developed recent ships after analyzing the popularity of certain areas in its older ships, the flow of passengers through the public rooms, and the needs of those new to cruising.

Overall, this really is cruising for urban dwellers, and for those that don't mind busy places and lines. An AIDA cruise isn't cheap, but you get a lot of high-tech entertainment, and there's always plenty of food. Some frustration occurs when shore excursions sell out, when lines form after shore excursion buses return to the ship and you have to go through the slow security check – and at peak times in the self-serve restaurants, and for shore tenders.

The AIDA-class ships (known as AIDA Clubships) evolved from the first and smallest ship, *AIDA* (over 14 years old and now named *AIDAcara*), in which the central idea was to get passengers to participate in public-area activities together, as in the Robinson Club concept on land. This led to "open plan" interiors and the feeling that the ship is one large space, but cleverly split into intimate rooms – although, in reality, rooms "flow" into each other at each fire zone section (a length of 157ft/48 meters).

One thing that's really noticeable is the fact that most of the chairs, counter stools and bar seats are really quite small, designed for thin young passengers, typically under 40. There is constant high-street music everywhere, so these ships are not for those wanting a "quiet escape" vacation, even though volume levels are well controlled.

AIDA Cruises has really grown up over the past few years, and no longer focuses on summer-camp style participation events. The ships have become more sophisticated, entertaining venues, and the old *animateurs* – somewhat like the *gentils ordinaires* of Club Med, but better – have grown up and morphed into what is now known as Club Teams. They, along with other staff, interact with passengers throughout the ship.

AIDAbella
★★★★

About 20 nationalities are represented among the crew, who are upbeat and cheerful. Staff hospitality training is now at a high level in all departments, and AIDA Cruises has its own training schools in several countries, plus a recognized training academy in Rostock.

The company's brochure accurately describes the casual, active urban lifestyle. Sport biking is part of its youthful image, with three different levels of cycling to suit differing fitness levels. AIDA Cruises has also successfully appealed to golfers, with golf-theme packages, cruises, and excursions ashore in many ports of call.

The open deck space is very tight, but sunbathing space includes some rather pleasant, reasonably quiet space above the navigation bridge. Dip pools and hot tubs, plus seating areas, are provided in a cascading, tiered setting atop the ship on the pool deck, providing a decent amount of sunbathing space. It's all designed to be in a "beach-like" environment, with splash and play areas.

There are three pricing levels – Aida Premium, Aida Vario, and Just Aida – depending on what you want to be included, plus differences in price according to accommodation size and grade, and the itinerary. Opt for the basic, price-driven Just Aida package and the cruise line chooses the ship, itinerary and accommodation for you – sort of a pot-luck cruise, based on or close to the dates you choose.

The dress code is simple: casual (no ties) at all times – there are no formal nights on board. All port taxes and gratuities are included in all packages, and, with very attractive rates, a cruise provides much better value than almost any land-based vacation.

In all the ships, several decks of public rooms and facilities are positioned above the accommodation decks. Public rooms that have become common aboard all the ships are: Aida Bar, the main social gathering place, whose principal feature is a star-shaped bar (whose combined length per ship makes them the longest at sea).

The ships have good sport and wellness facilities. Each has a bike excursion counter, dive or golf excursion counter, golf simulator (not *AIDAbella, AIDAblu, AIDAluna, AIDAmar, AIDAsol*), shore excursion counter, library, seminar rooms, duty-free shop, Nordic Walking machines, several bars and lounges, and eateries.

● *AIDAcara* (1996). The open deck space on the original ship is tight and there's not enough restaurant seating capacity at peak times, making a cruise a comfortable, but slightly cramped, experience.

● *AIDAaura* (2003), *AIDAvita* (2002). These ships' layout is much the same as for *AIDAcara*, but in a slightly rearranged manner that provides more space and seating in the Markt Restaurant, and adds more seating to the balcony level of Das Theater (the show lounge).

● *AIDAbella* (2008), *AIDAblu* (2010), *AIDAdiva* (2007), *AIDAluna* (2009), *AIDAsol* (2011). Each has a small casino with blackjack, roulette and poker gaming tables and slot machines. There are many more balcony cabins, a separate aft sports deck, a "no music" observation lounge, and an art gallery. The embarkation entryway is really innovative, and has a bar, lookout balcony, and is cheerfully painted to look like a street scene in a city such as Copenhagen (example: *AIDAbella*). It is totally different to the utilitarian gangway entry areas found aboard most cruise ships – a welcoming environment, it helps to calm tempers after waiting in a line to go through the security process for embarkation or in ports of call. *AIDAsol* is a sister to *AIDAblu* and close sister to *AIDAbella, AIDAluna* (but in a slightly modified form). *AIDAblu, AIDAmar* and *AIDAsol* have microbreweries.

Size:	Large Resort Ship
Tonnage:	69,203
Lifestyle:	Standard
Cruise Line:	AIDA Cruises
Former Names:	none
Builder:	Meyer Werft (Germany)
Original Cost:	$390 million
Entered Service:	Apr 2008
Registry:	Italy
Length (ft/m):	826.7/252.0
Beam (ft/m):	105.6/32.2
Draft (ft/m):	24.6/7.5
Propulsion/Propellers:	diesel-electric (36,000 kW)/2
Passenger Decks:	13
Total Crew:	646
Passengers (lower beds/all berths):	2,050/2,500
Passenger Space Ratio (lower beds/all berths):	33.7/27.6
Crew/Passenger Ratio (lower beds/all berths):	3.1/3.8
Cabins (total):	1,025
Size Range (sq ft/m):	145.3–473.2/ 13.5–44
Cabins (outside view):	666
Cabins (interior/no view):	359
Cabins (for one person):	0
Cabins (with private balcony):	480
Cabins (wheelchair accessible):	11
Wheelchair accessibility:	Good
Cabin Current:	110 volts
Lifts:	10
Casino (gaming tables):	Yes
Slot Machines:	No
Swimming Pools (outdoors):	3
Swimming Pools (indoors):	0
Whirlpools:	0
Self-Service Launderette:	Yes
Dedicated Cinema/Seats:	No
Library:	Yes
Onboard currency:	Euros

BERLITZ'S RATINGS

	Possible	Achieved
Ship	500	406
Accommodation	200	144
Food	400	280
Service	400	284
Entertainment	100	73
Cruise	400	298

OVERALL SCORE
1,485 points out of 2,000

AIDAblu
★★★★

Size:	Large Resort Ship
Tonnage:	71,300
Lifestyle:	Standard
Cruise Line:	AIDA Cruises
Former Names:	none
Builder:	Meyer Werft (Germany)
Original Cost:	€350 million
Entered Service:	Apr 2010
Registry:	Italy
Length (ft/m):	826.7/252.0
Beam (ft/m):	105.6/32.2
Draft (ft/m):	24.6/7.5
Propulsion/Propellers:	diesel-electric (36,000 kW)/2
Passenger Decks:	14
Total Crew:	646
Passengers (lower beds/all berths):	2,194/2,500
Passenger Space Ratio (lower beds/all berths):	34.6/28.4
Crew/Passenger Ratio (lower beds/all berths):	3.1/3.8
Cabins (total):	1,096
Size Range (sq ft/m):	145.3–473.2/13.5–44
Cabins (outside view):	715
Cabins (interior/no view):	381
Cabins (for one person):	0
Cabins (with private balcony):	491
Cabins (wheelchair accessible):	11
Wheelchair accessibility:	Good
Cabin Current:	110 volts
Elevators:	10
Casino (gaming tables):	Yes
Slot Machines:	No
Swimming Pools (outdoors):	3
Swimming Pools (indoors):	0
Whirlpools:	0
Self-Service Launderette:	Yes
Dedicated Cinema/Seats:	No
Library:	Yes
Onboard currency:	Euros

BERLITZ'S RATINGS

	Possible	Achieved
Ship	500	407
Accommodation	200	144
Food	400	281
Service	400	284
Entertainment	100	73
Cruise	400	298

OVERALL SCORE
1,487 points out of 2,000

/continued from previous page

FAMILIES.

Children are split into four age groups: Seepferdchen (4–6 years), Delfin (7–9), Orcas (10–12), and Teens (14–17). Each has its own play area. There is a diverse selection of children's and youth programs in a holiday camp atmosphere, and special Club Team members dedicated to making at all happen. Supervised by a chef, children can make their own menus for the week, and visit the galley to make cookies and other items – a novel idea more cruise lines could adopt. These really are family-friendly ships.

ACCOMMODATION.

There are eight or nine grades, from deluxe suites to interior (no view) cabins, depending on the ship, which keeps your cabin choice simple. Accommodation ranges in size, as follows:

> AIDAaura (145.3–344.4 sq.ft/13.5–32 sq. meters)
> AIDAbella (145.3–473.6/13.5–44 sq. meters)
> AIDAblu (145.3–473.6/13.5–44 sq. meters)
> AIDAcara (145.3–376.7/13.5–35 sq. meters)
> AIDAdiva (145.3–473.6/13.5–44 sq. meters)
> AIDAluna (145.3–473.6/13.5–44 sq. meters)
> AIDAmar (145.3–473.6/13.5–44 sq. meters)
> AIDAsol (145.3–473.6/13.5–44 sq. meters)
> AIDAvita (145.3–344.4 sq.ft/13.5–32 sq. meters)

Contrary to maritime traditions (even-numbered cabins on the port side, odd-numbered cabins on the starboard side), cabin numbers progress numerically (example: 8201–8276 on the port side; 8101–8176 on the starboard side). All suites and cabins have two beds (convertible to queen-size bed). Some cabins also have two extra beds/berths for children, and some cabins have interconnecting doors – useful for families.

The decor in all accommodation grades is bright, youthful, rather minimalist, and slightly whimsical. All are accented with multi-patterned fabrics, wood-trimmed cabinetry (with nicely rounded edges) and rattan or wood-look furniture. Beds have duvets and a colorful fabric canopy that goes from the headboard to the ceiling. The windows have full pull-down blackout blinds (useful in destinations with long daylight hours). Lifeboats may obstruct views in some cabins in the ship's center (AIDAaura, AIDAcara, AIDAvita).

The bathrooms are compact, practical units; they have a shower enclosure, small washbasin, and small toilet. As in the most basic hotels and motels, only a wall-mounted body wash/shampoo dispenser is provided, so take your own conditioner, hand lotion, and other toiletries you may need.

Thick 100% cotton bathrobes are provided for all grades of accommodation (AIDAbella, AIDAblu, AIDAdiva, AIDAluna, AIDAmar, AIDAsol) and for suite-grade accommodation only (AIDAaura, AIDAcara, AIDAvita, although non-suite grade passengers can obtain one from the spa). Two towels are provided – a face towel and a "bath" towel, in two different colors. The "bath" towels are not very large, at 54 by 27 inches – compared to 72 by 36 inches aboard the P&O Cruises' Ventura, for example. Although the bathrooms do not have a hairdryer, one is located in the vanity unit in the cabin. Night-time turn-down service is not provided, and there is no cabin service after 3pm.

Cabins with balconies have a sliding door that's easy to open and doesn't impinge on balcony space; a small drinks table and two small, light chairs are provided. Note that balconies on the lowest deck can be overlooked by anyone on a balcony on the decks above. Balcony cabins aboard AIDAbella,

AIDAcara
★★★ +

AIDAblu, AIDAdiva, AIDAluna, AIDAmar and *AIDAsol*) have a hammock as standard, although it only accommodates one (thin) person. Some cabins (forward on Deck 5 – Nos 5103, 5104, 5105, 5106, 5203, 5204, 5206) aboard these ships have cabins with an outside view (well, outside light), but they are totally obstructed by steel bulkheads that form the front section of the ship.

Naturally, suite-grade accommodation offers more space, including more drawer and storage space, better quality furniture and furnishings, a larger lounge area and a slightly larger bathroom with a tub – and, of course, a larger balcony (those at the front and stern of the ship have the best).

CUISINE.

Principal restaurants:
Aboard *AIDAaura, AIDAcara* and *AIDAvita* two eateries included in the cruise fare are the self-serve *Markt* and *Karibik* restaurants. There's also *Rossini*, a decent enough à la carte (extra-charge) tablecloth dining spot that serves high-quality meals cooked à la minute, and has friendly waiter service.

Aboard the larger *AIDAbella, AIDAblu, AIDAdiva, AIDAluna, AIDAmar* and *AIDAsol* there are three self-serve eateries: *Markt* (Market), *Bella Vista*, and *Weite Welt* (Wide World) restaurants plus a *Buffalo Steakhouse* (which serves excellent steaks), *Rossini*, a *Sushi Bar*, and a *Pizzeria*. The restaurants are open at set times only (there are no 24-hours-a-day outlets, because there is little demand for them), although the Pizzeria typically stays open until midnight.

Beverage stations open only during restaurant opening hours, unless you go to the extra-cost coffee bar. Vending machines dispense out-of-hours snacks.

The meal concept is simple: main meals are taken when you want them in one of the large self-serve buffet-style restaurants, with open seating at tables of four, six or eight. Cutlery can be found hanging in a rack, but there are no soup spoons, only dessert spoons.

Beer is available at the push of a button or a pull of the tap, and table wine – of the sort that would make a good drain cleaner – is usually provided in carafes on each table for lunch and dinner. It's very casual and easy-going mass catering, so think food court eating – it certainly can't be called dining, and is more like camping at sea.

The standard of food at the self-serve buffet islands ranges from adequate to quite good, with creative displays and presentation, and table-clearing service that is sometimes efficient, mostly not.

The many food islands and active stations cut down on the waiting time for food. There is always a big selection of breads, cheeses, cold cuts, fruits and make-your-own coffee and teas – with a choice of more than 30 types of loose-leaf regular and herbal teas. More than 1,200 items of food are offered. The fish section of *AIDAbella, AIDAdiva, AIDAluna, AIDAmar* and *AIDAsol* has its own fish smoking unit (which resembles a wine cabinet).

In addition, one à la carte option is available in all the ship: the "Rossini Restaurant", with waiter and sommelier service.

You can sit where you want, when you want, and with whom you want, so eating is a socially interactive occasion. In fact, it's hard to be an unsociable couple and have a table for only two. At peak times, the venues may remind you of noisy roadside cafés. Because of the large buffet rooms and self-serve dining concept, the crew to passenger ratio looks poor; but this is because there are no waiters as such (except in à la carte venues), only staff for clearing tables.

Size:	Mid-size Ship
Tonnage:	38,557
Lifestyle:	Standard
Cruise Line:	AIDA Cruises
Former Names:	*Aida, Das Clubschiff*
Builder:	Kvaerner Masa-Yards (Finland)
Original Cost:	DM300 million
Entered Service:	June 1996
Registry:	Italy
Length (ft/m):	634.1/193.3
Beam (ft/m):	90.5/27.6
Draft (ft/m):	19.6/6.0
Propulsion/Propellers:	diesel(21,720kw)/2
Passenger Decks:	9
Total Crew:	370
Passengers (lower beds/all berths):	1,180/1,339
Passenger Space Ratio (lower beds/all berths):	32.6/27.5
Crew/Passenger Ratio (lower beds/all berths):	3.1/3.7
Cabins (total):	590
Size Range (sq ft/m):	145.3–376.7/13.5–35.0
Cabins (outside view):	390
Cabins (interior/no view):	200
Cabins (for one person):	0
Cabins (with private balcony):	48
Cabins (wheelchair accessible):	6
Wheelchair accessibility:	Good
Cabin Current:	110 and 220 volts
Elevators:	5
Casino (gaming tables):	No
Slot Machines:	No
Swimming Pools (outdoors):	1
Swimming Pools (indoors):	0
Whirlpools:	2
Self-Service Launderette:	Yes
Dedicated Cinema/Seats:	No
Library:	Yes
Onboard currency:	Euros

BERLITZ'S RATINGS

	Possible	Achieved
Ship	500	355
Accommodation	200	131
Food	400	259
Service	400	269
Entertainment	100	72
Cruise	400	281

OVERALL SCORE
1,367 points out of 2,000

AIDAdiva
★★★★

Size:	Large Resort Ship
Tonnage:	69,203
Lifestyle:	Standard
Cruise Line:	AIDA Cruises
Former Names:	none
Builder:	Meyer Werft (Germany)
Original Cost:	$390 million
Entered Service:	Apr 2007
Registry:	Italy
Length (ft/m):	826.7/252.0
Beam (ft/m):	105.6/32.2
Draft (ft/m):	24.6/7.5
Propulsion/Propellers:	diesel-electric (36,000 kW)/2
Passenger Decks:	13
Total Crew:	646
Passengers	
(lower beds/all berths):	2,050/2,500
Passenger Space Ratio	
(lower beds/all berths):	33.7/27.6
Crew/Passenger Ratio	
(lower beds/all berths):	3.1/3.8
Cabins (total):	1,025
Size Range (sq ft/m):	145.3–473.2/ 13.5–44
Cabins (outside view):	666
Cabins (interior/no view):	359
Cabins (for one person):	0
Cabins (with private balcony):	480
Cabins (wheelchair accessible):	11
Wheelchair accessibility:	Good
Cabin Current:	110 volts
Lifts:	10
Casino (gaming tables):	Yes
Slot Machines:	No
Swimming Pools (outdoors):	3
Swimming Pools (indoors):	0
Whirlpools:	0
Self-Service Launderette:	Yes
Dedicated Cinema/Seats:	No
Library:	Yes
Onboard currency:	Euros

BERLITZ'S RATINGS

	Possible	Achieved
Ship	500	405
Accommodation	200	144
Food	400	280
Service	400	284
Entertainment	100	73
Cruise	400	298

OVERALL SCORE
1,484 points out of 2,000

/continued from previous page

Alternative (Extra Cost) Dining:

The *Rossini Restaurant* (à la carte), with mostly high-back seats, has an intimate atmosphere. It is open for dinner only, and has a set five- or six-course menu (plus daily specials). There is no cover charge, but an extra charge applies to everything on the à la carte menu (such as caviar, chateaubriand, rib-eye steak), and for wines. Reservations are needed. Tablecloths are provided, the food is very good, and service is sound.

Buffalo Steakhouse (AIDAbella, AIDAblu, AIDAdiva, AIDAluna, AIDAmar AIDAsol) has an open "display" kitchen, and offers various steak cuts and sizes (Delmonico, New York Strip Loin, Porterhouse and Filet, plus bison steaks), and roast lamb rack. There's a daily special – a prix-fixe meal (example: a 180 kg filet steak, house salad, and dessert). It's like going out to eat in a decent restaurant ashore – but there are no tablecloths. Wine is extra.

Sushi Bar (AIDAbella, AIDAblu, AIDAdiva, AIDAluna, AIDAmar and AIDAsol). The 12-seater sushi counter is for Japanese-style sushi and sashimi dishes. While the counter provides stool seating, two low-slung tables with well-type seating are difficult to sit at and get up from (notice to females: avoid wearing a short skirt). The sushi is "commercial" and uninspiring, but typical of what you'd expect in a sushi bar not run by Japanese sushi masters. While the presentation is appetizing, the actual fare is mediocre and light on taste – and you can be subjected to intense noise level from the adjacent "open-plan" showlounge.

Vinotheque. The wine bar, located in front of the Weide Welt (Wide World) Restaurant, has a surprisingly good list of premium wines, and Davidoff cigars (although you can't smoke them at the bar – or anywhere inside the ship). *Pizzeria* provides ever popular – and overcooked – pizzas.

ENTERTAINMENT.

The Theater, the main venue for all shows and most cabaret, is two decks high aboard *AIDAaura, AIDAcara, AIDAvita*. It has a raised stage, and amphitheater-style bench seating on all levels. The benches have back rests, and are quite comfortable, and sight lines are good from most seats, with the exception of port and starboard balcony sections, where sight lines are interrupted by thick safety railings.

Aboard *AIDAbella, AIDAblu, AIDAdiva, AIDAluna, AIDAmar* and *AIDAsol*, the Theater (called a Theatrium) is in the center of the ship, is open to the main foyer and other public areas, on three levels (Decks 9, 10, 11), and topped by a glass dome. It has amphitheater-style seating on three decks (the bench seating on the two upper levels has back supports, but not on the lower level), plus standing tables, although sight lines to the raised thrust stage area are less than good from many seats.

Also, the layout means that people constantly walk through the area, distracting you from what's on the stage. For the performers, it's a bit like being in a TV studio, and trying to perform in front of the cameras, but with the audience in a different location. It doesn't really work well (passengers can watch the rehearsals) but, hey, this is really all about an active/interactive lifestyle, and it's a fresh way of presenting professional entertainment.

The shows are produced by AIDA Cruises' in-house department in a joint venture with SeeLive (Hamburg's Schmidt's Tivoli Theater), and typically

AIDAluna
★★★★

consist of 12 performers. All vocals in the shows are performed live, to pre-recorded backing tracks that provide a mix of recorded live music and synthesized sound. The shows are trendy, upbeat, fun, and very entertaining. The whole entertainment experience is lively and fun – in fact, it's a little like going to the circus.

In addition, there is a live band in the Aida Bar, the only room with a large dance floor (except for the disco).

SPA/FITNESS.

The Wellness spas, fitness and sports programming are among the most extensive in the cruise industry. Several types of massage and body pampering treatments are offered.

"Sport Bikes" (mountain bikes with tough front and rear suspension units) are provided for conducted biking excursions in each port of call, a concession run by of Austrian downhill champion skier Erwin Resch. You can book biking, diving, and golfing excursions.

● *AIDAaura, AIDAcara, AIDAvita:*
The Wellness spa, is located forward on Deck 11. It measures 11,840 sq. ft (1,100 sq. meters), and contains two saunas (one dry, one wet, both with seats for more than 20 persons, and glass walls that look onto the deck), massage and other treatment rooms, and a large lounging area. There are also showers, and two whole "ice walls" to use when you come out of the saunas (simply lean into the ice wall for maximum effect). Forward and outside the wellness center, is an FKK (FreiKoerperKultur) nude sunbathing deck, on two levels. A beauty and hair salon is located just behind the balcony level of the showlounge (*AIDAcara*).

● *AIDAbella, AIDAblu, AIDAdiva, AIDAluna, AIDAsol:*
The Body and Soul wellness/oasis area is located on two decks (connected by a stairway), and encompasses some 2,300 sq. meters (24,757 sq. ft). There is also an open air wellness deck for (FKK) relaxation/nude sunbathing in an area atop the ship forward of the ship's mast. In keeping with the times, all the trendy treatments are featured in an appealing contemporary setting.

There are saunas and steam rooms, and 14 rooms for massage and other treatments (most named after places associated with the design theme), neat showers, funky changing rooms and a tropical garden with real (waxed) palm trees and relaxation loungers. Sporting types can play golf in the electronic simulator, or billiards, or volleyball, or squash, or go jogging.

Size:	Large Resort Ship
Tonnage:	69,203
Lifestyle:	Standard
Cruise Line:	AIDA Cruises
Former Names:	none
Builder:	Meyer Werft (Germany)
Original Cost:	$390 million
Entered Service:	Apr 2009
Registry:	Italy
Length (ft/m):	826.7/252.0
Beam (ft/m):	105.6/32.2
Draft (ft/m):	24.6/7.5
Propulsion/Propellers:	diesel-electric (36,000 kW)/2
Passenger Decks:	13
Total Crew:	646
Passengers (lower beds/all berths):	2,050/2,500
Passenger Space Ratio (lower beds/all berths):	33.7/27.6
Crew/Passenger Ratio (lower beds/all berths):	3.1/3.8
Cabins (total):	1,025
Size Range (sq ft/m):	145.3 –473.2/ 13.5–44
Cabins (outside view):	666
Cabins (interior/no view):	359
Cabins (for one person):	0
Cabins (with private balcony):	480
Cabins (wheelchair accessible):	11
Wheelchair accessibility:	Good
Cabin Current:	110 volts
Lifts:	10
Casino (gaming tables):	Yes
Slot Machines:	No
Swimming Pools (outdoors):	3
Swimming Pools (indoors):	0
Whirlpools:	0
Self-Service Launderette:	Yes
Dedicated Cinema/Seats:	No
Library:	Yes
Onboard currency:	Euros

BERLITZ'S RATINGS

	Possible	Achieved
Ship	500	406
Accommodation	200	144
Food	400	280
Service	400	284
Entertainment	100	73
Cruise	400	298

OVERALL SCORE
1,485 points out of 2,000

AIDAmar
NOT YET RATED

Size: . . . . .Large Resort Ship
Tonnage: .71,300
Lifestyle: . . . . .Standard
Cruise Line: . . . . .AIDA Cruises
Former Names: . . . . .none
Builder: . . . . Meyer Werft (Germany)
Original Cost: . . . .€350 million
Entered Service: . . . . .May 2012
Registry: . . . . .Italy
Length (ft/m): 826.7/252.0
Beam (ft/m): 105.6/32.2
Draft (ft/m): 24.6/7.5
Propulsion/Propellers: . . . . .diesel-electric
(36,000 kW)/2
Passenger Decks: 14
Total Crew: .646
Passengers
(lower beds/all berths): 2,194/2,500
Passenger Space Ratio
(lower beds/all berths): 34.6/28.4
Crew/Passenger Ratio
(lower beds/all berths): 3.1/3.8
Cabins (total): 1,096
Size Range (sq ft/m): 145.3–473.2/13.5–44
Cabins (outside view): 715
Cabins (interior/no view): 381
Cabins (for one person): 0
Cabins (with private balcony): 491
Cabins (wheelchair accessible): 11
Wheelchair accessibility: . . . . .Good
Cabin Current: . . . . .110 volts
Elevators: 10
Casino (gaming tables): . . . . .Yes
Slot Machines: . . . . .No
Swimming Pools (outdoors): 3
Swimming Pools (indoors): 0
Whirlpools: 0
Self-Service Launderette: . . . . .Yes
Dedicated Cinema/Seats: . . . . .No
Library: . . . . .Yes
Onboard currency: . . . . .Euros

BERLITZ'S RATINGS

	Possible	Achieved
Ship	500	NYR
Accommodation	200	NYR
Food	400	NYR
Service	400	NYR
Entertainment	100	NYR
Cruise	400	NYR

OVERALL SCORE
Not Yet Rated

AIDAsol
★★★★

Size: . . . . .Large Resort Ship
Tonnage: .71,300
Lifestyle: . . . . .Standard
Cruise Line: . . . . .AIDA Cruises
Former Names: . . . . .none
Builder: . . . . Meyer Werft (Germany)
Original Cost: . . . .€350 million
Entered Service: . . . . .Apr 2011
Registry: . . . . .Italy
Length (ft/m): 826.7/252.0
Beam (ft/m): 105.6/32.2
Draft (ft/m): 24.6/7.5
Propulsion/Propellers: . . . . .diesel-electric
(36,000 kW)/2
Passenger Decks: 14
Total Crew: .646
Passengers
(lower beds/all berths): 2,194/2,500
Passenger Space Ratio
(lower beds/all berths): 34.6/28.4
Crew/Passenger Ratio
(lower beds/all berths): 3.1/3.8
Cabins (total): 1,096
Size Range (sq ft/m): 145.3–473.2/13.5–44
Cabins (outside view): 715
Cabins (interior/no view): 381
Cabins (for one person): 0
Cabins (with private balcony): 491
Cabins (wheelchair accessible): 11
Wheelchair accessibility: . . . . .Good
Cabin Current: . . . . .110 volts
Elevators: 10
Casino (gaming tables): . . . . .Yes
Slot Machines: . . . . .No
Swimming Pools (outdoors): 3
Swimming Pools (indoors): 0
Whirlpools: 0
Self-Service Launderette: . . . . .Yes
Dedicated Cinema/Seats: . . . . .No
Library: . . . . .Yes
Onboard currency: . . . . .Euros

BERLITZ'S RATINGS

	Possible	Achieved
Ship	500	406
Accommodation	200	144
Food	400	286
Service	400	284
Entertainment	100	73
Cruise	400	297

OVERALL SCORE
1,490 points out of 2,000

AIDAvita
★★★ +

Size: . . . . .Mid-size Ship
Tonnage: .42,289
Lifestyle: . . . . .Standard
Cruise Line: . . . . .AIDA Cruises
Former Names: . . . . .none
Builder: . . . . .Aker MTW (Germany)
Original Cost: . . . .$350 million
Entered Service: . . . . .Apr 2002
Registry: . . . . .Italy
Length (ft/m): 666.5/202.85
Beam (ft/m): 92.2/28.1
Draft (ft/m): 20.7/6.3
Propulsion/Propellers: . . .diesel-electric/2
Passenger Decks: 10
Total Crew: .389
Passengers
(lower beds/all berths): 1,266/1,582
Passenger Space Ratio
(lower beds/all berths): 33.4/26.7
Crew/Passenger Ratio
(lower beds/all berths): 3.0/3.7
Cabins (total): 633
Size Range (sq ft/m): 145.3–344.4/
13.5–32.0
Cabins (outside view): 422
Cabins (interior/no view): 211
Cabins (for one person): 0
Cabins (with private balcony): 60
Cabins (wheelchair accessible): 4
Wheelchair accessibility: . . . . . .Good
Cabin Current: . . . . .220 volts
Elevators: 6
Casino (gaming tables): . . . . .No
Slot Machines: . . . . .No
Swimming Pools (outdoors): 2
Swimming Pools (indoors): 0
Whirlpools: 5
Self-Service Launderette: . . . . .Yes
Dedicated Cinema/Seats: . . . . .No
Library: . . . . .Yes
Onboard currency: . . . . Euros

BERLITZ'S RATINGS

	Possible	Achieved
Ship	500	368
Accommodation	200	131
Food	400	259
Service	400	269
Entertainment	100	72
Cruise	400	282

OVERALL SCORE
1,381 points out of 2,000

Albatros
★★★

Size ....Mid-Size Ship	Passenger Decks:..................8	Cabins (with private balcony): 9
Tonnage: 28,078	Total Crew: 340	Cabins (wheelchair accessible): 0
Lifestyle: ....Standard	Passengers	Wheelchair accessibility: ....Fair
Cruise Line: ....Phoenix Reisen	(lower beds/all berths): 884/1,100	Cabin Current: ....110 and 220 volts
Former Names: .Crown, Norwegian Star I,	Passenger Space Ratio	Elevators: 5
Royal Odyssey, Royal Viking Sea	(lower beds/all berths):.......31.7/25.5	Casino (gaming tables): ....Yes
Builder: ....Wartsila (Finland)	Crew/Passenger Ratio	Slot Machines: ....Yes
Original Cost: ....$22.5 million	(lower beds/all berths): 2.6/3.2	Swimming Pools (outdoors): 1
Entered Service: .....Nov 1973/Apr 2004	Cabins (total): 442	Swimming Pools (indoors): 0
Registry: ....The Bahamas	Size Range (sq ft/m): 123.7– 679.2/	Whirlpools: 3
Length (ft/m): 674.2/205.50	11.8–63.1	Self-Service Launderette: ....No
Beam (ft/m): 82.0/25.00	Cabins (outside view): 380	Dedicated Cinema/Seats: Yes/156
Draft (ft/m): 23.9/7.30	Cabins (interior/no view): 57	Library: ....Ye
Propulsion/Propellers:diesel (13,400 kW)/2	Cabins (for one person): 0	Onboard currency: ....Euros

Contemporary setting for low-price, no-frills cruising.

OVERVIEW. *Albatros* appeals to mature German-speaking adults and families seeking a low-budget, good-value vacation in a comfortable but not new ship.

THE SHIP. *Albatros*, built for long-distance cruising for the long-defunct Royal Viking Line, was refurbished in 2004 prior to replacing Phoenix Reisen's much loved but outdated *Albatros*. There is plenty of open deck and sunbathing space, although the popular aft pool area can become crowded.

The ship has a decent array of public rooms, including several lounges and bars, most of which are quite elegant and have high, indented ceilings. The Observation Lounge is particularly pleasant. Wide stairways and foyers give a sense of space, even when the ship is full. The atmosphere is very informal, and the dress code is relaxed and casual.

Albatros performs well in most sea conditions, and the onboard product is very good value for money. A 7% gratuity is added to bar accounts.

ACCOMMODATION. There are more than 20 price grades, from expansive suites with private balcony to standard outside-view cabins and small interior cabins. A Captain's Suite is located at the front, directly under the navigation bridge, with fine forward-facing views. Nine other Penthouse Suites include a private balcony (with separate bedroom and living area). Most other cabins have an outside view and are quite well appointed, and there is a good amount of storage

BERLITZ'S RATINGS		
	Possible	Achieved
Ship	500	310
Accommodation	200	128
Food	400	208
Service	400	237
Entertainment	100	60
Cruise	400	251

OVERALL SCORE
1,194 points out of 2,000

space; however, some bathrooms in the lower categories have awkward access. All cabins have a TV, bathrobe, and personal safe. Suites and "comfort cabins" also have a minibar. Occupants of eight (mostly suite) accommodation grades receive Phoenix VIP service.

CUISINE. Two dining rooms (*Mowe* and *Pelikan*) have high ceilings, and are quite spacious. Dining is in one seating, at assigned tables for two, four, six or eight. Breakfast and lunch can be taken in the dining room or outdoors in a self-service buffet by the swimming pool. Mid-morning bouillon is a Phoenix seagoing tradition, as is a Captain's Dinner (formal night), and Buffet Magnifique.

The service, by mainly Filipino waiters, is friendly and attentive, although there is little finesse. Table wines are included for lunch and dinner, although the quality is not good. Slightly better quality wines can be purchased.

The food itself is best described as "down home" simple. Casual eateries include a pizzeria at the (aft) pool bar.

ENTERTAINMENT. The large Pacific Lounge seats about 500, but thick pillars obstruct some sightlines. Small-scale production shows are presented by a small team of resident singers/dancers, and cabaret acts.

SPA/FITNESS. There's a gymnasium and sauna, two steam rooms, body treatment rooms, and a beauty salon.

Alexander von Humboldt
NOT YET RATED

Size: ....Small Ship	Passenger Decks: 7	Cabins (wheelchair accessible): 0
Tonnage: 15,343	Total Crew: 240	Wheelchair accessibility: . . . . .None
Lifestyle: ....Standard	Passengers	Cabin Voltage:...........................110 volts
Cruise Line:....All Leisure/Phoenix Reisen	(lower beds/all berths):..............508/560	Lifts: 4
Former Names: ....*Jules Verne, Walrus,*	Passenger Space Ratio	Casino (gaming tables):.....................Yes
Crown Monarch	(lower beds/all berths):............30.2/27.3	Slot Machines:.....................................Yes
Builder:............Union de Levante (Spain)	Crew/Passenger Ratio	Swimming Pools (outdoors): 1
Original Cost:........................$95 million	(lower beds/all berths):................2.3/2.6	Swimming Pools (indoors): 0
Entered Service:.......Dec 1990/May 2010	Cabins (total):....................................254	Whirlpools:...2
Registry:............................The Bahamas	Size Range (sq ft/m):139.9–398.2/13.0–37	Self-Service Launderette:.....................No
Length (ft/m):.....................494.4/150.72	Cabins (outside view):........................225	Dedicated Cinema/Seats: ....No
Beam (ft/m):...........................67.6/20.62	Cabins (interior/no view):....................30	Library: ....Yes
Draft:..18.7/5.7	Cabins (for one person):........................0	Onboard currency: ....Euros
Propulsion/Propellers: ....diesel	Cabins (with private balcony):..............10	

For discovery and learning aboard a homely ship.

OVERVIEW. The ship is best suited to adult couples and singles seeking soft-adventure and enrichment-style cruising in a small ship. The Passenger Space Ratio is reasonable for the ship's size, and it carries several Zodiac inflatable craft for shore landings and explorations. In typical Phoenix Reisen style, it's an almost all-inclusive product and excellent value-for-money.

BERLITZ'S RATINGS		
	Possible	Achieved
Ship	500	NYR
Accommodation	200	NYR
Food	400	NYR
Service	400	NYR
Entertainment	n/a	NYR
Cruise	500	NYR

THE SHIP. *Alexander von Humboldt,* formerly owned by the now-defunct Dutch company Club Cruise but bought at auction by the UK's All Leisure company in 2009, serves the UK and German-speaking markets. Named after a German explorer and naturalist, it is under charter to Phoenix Reisen from May to October. Its profile is decent and balanced, though angular, and it has a squat, swept-back funnel. The "swimming pool" is really a dip pool, but it is flanked by two hot tubs, although there is little open deck space. There's more sunbathing space on the deck above.

Most public rooms are located on one deck. The focal point of the social life is the elegant Harry's Bar – a high-ceilinged lifestyle lounge/bar, off to one side of which is the Jules Verne library/card playing area, but the library is poor.

The space per passenger remains good because Phoenix keeps the capacity to 470. Most of the hotel service crew is Filipino. All gratuities are included. Those who want a little extra can buy silver and gold packages.

ACCOMMODATION. There are 18 cabin price grades – a lot for this small ship. Aft of the bridge are 10 fairly spacious suites, each with a private balcony. The sleeping area, which includes a small sofa and drinks table, and ample drawer space, can be curtained off from the lounge area, which includes a mini-fridge. There are two balcony doors (one each from the bedroom and the lounge). The small bathrooms have a Jacuzzi tub/shower combination.

The standard cabins have all the basics, including twin beds that convert to a double, a small vanity desk and small chair, and flat-screen TV set. Bathrooms have a shower enclosure, toilet, and washbasin. There is not much drawer space, and the soundproofing between cabins could be better. Many cabins close to the engine casing are noisy. Cabins on the lowest decks have portholes, while those on upper decks have windows.

CUISINE. The 280-seat *Fier Jahreszeiten* (Four Seasons Restaurant) is quite attractive, with a slightly raised center section. Seating is at tables for two, four, six, or eight. It's an open, one-seating arrangement. Table wines are included for lunch and dinner. Alternatively, casual, serve-yourself buffet-style meals (including dinner) can be taken in the *Veranda* indoor-outdoor eatery, although in the indoor section, windows have views obstructed by lifeboats. In warm weather, the seating at outdoor tables is very popular.

ENTERTAINMENT. The Music Lounge accommodates around 300 in banquette-style seating, and has decent sight-lines to the wooden dance floor/stage, except for seats located behind the substantial support columns. A discotheque/late-night spot is adjacent to the fitness centre.

SPA/FITNESS. A wellness center is located aft of the discotheque on the uppermost deck overlooking the stern, while a beauty salon is located several decks below, as is a small unisex sauna and relaxation area.

Allure of the Seas
★★★★

Size:..............................Large Resort Ship	Passenger Decks: 16	Cabins (with private balcony):........1,956
Tonnage: 225,062	Total Crew: 2,164	Cabins (wheelchair accessible): 46
Lifestyle: ....Standard	Passengers	Wheelchair accessibility: ....Good
Cruise Line:.Royal Caribbean International	(lower beds/all berths):........5,408 /6,360	Cabin Current: ....110 volts
Former Names: ....none	Passenger Space Ratio	Elevators: 24
Builder:....................Aker Yards (Finland)	(lower beds/all berths):............41.6 /35.4	Casino (gaming tables):.....................Yes
Original Cost: ....$1. 5 billion	Crew/Passenger Ratio	Slot Machines:....................................Yes
Entered Service: ....Dec 2010	(lower beds/all berths):................2.4/2.9	Swimming Pools (outdoors):.................6
Registry:...........................The Bahamas	Cabins (total):.................................2,704	Swimming Pools (indoors): 0
Length (ft/m):.....................1181.1/360.0	Size Range (sq ft/m): 150.6–1,523.1/	Whirlpools: 10
Beam (ft/m):..........................216.5 /66.0	14.0–141.5	Self-Service Launderette:...................No
Draft (ft/m):................................30.0/9.15	Cabins (outside view):....................2,210	Dedicated Cinema/Seats: ....No
Propulsion/Propellers:.......diesel-electric	Cabins (interior/no view):..................496	Library:...Yes
(97.2 MW)/3 pods (2 azimuthing, 1 fixed)	Cabins (for one person):........................0	Onboard currency: ....US$

The world's largest, family-friendly, multi-choice ship.

OVERVIEW. The ship commands a premium over other RCI ships, but provides a fine cruise experience and wide range of choices for young adults and families with children, though the service is notably better in suites. It's packed with innovative design elements – none more so than the dramatic Central Park, taking urban greenery to sea. The ship is a benchmark for self-contained resorts with propellers.

THE SHIP. *Allure of the Seas* qualifies
as the world's largest cruise ship by less than 2 inches (5 cm) – that's how much longer it is than its twin sister, *Oasis of the Seas*. Built as "Moveable Resort Vacations" for families with children, they are stunning ships, and a massive credit to Royal Caribbean International's design team. There is a lot of outdoor and indoor/outdoor space for aqua-bathing and sports, although there's not much space for sunbathing. There are several swimming pools, three of which – "main," "beach" and "sports" – are positioned high on Deck 15 (Pool and Sports Zone) of the 16 passenger decks, as is an H₂O Zone. Two large hot tubs are cantilevered over the ship's side. The water for the swimming pools alone weighs 2,300 tons.

While *Allure*'s design from the front aspect is quite handsome, if bulky, the aft end looks as if it's been chopped off and unfinished when viewed from the side. Perhaps a more rounded stern would have improved the profile – although, when you're on board, it looks fine. The open stern makes it look like a ship with a huge aft aircraft hangar. Overall, though, it's an amazing ship.

There are minor differences between the two vessels. Where the Donut Hut is on the Boardwalk of *Oasis*, aboard

BERLITZ'S RATINGS		
	Possible	Achieved
Ship	500	433
Accommodation	200	158
Food	400	234
Service	400	295
Entertainment	100	87
Cruise	400	321
OVERALL SCORE		
1,528 points out of 2,000		

Allure it's the Boardwalk Dog House, serving hot dogs, wieners, bratwurst and sausages, and the Donut Shop is positioned adjacent to the Ice Cream Shoppe. *Allure* also has a Starbucks coffee shop on the Royal Promenade – the first Starbucks at sea. Both ships now have a 3-D movie screen.

Public spaces are arranged as seven "neighborhoods": Central Park, the Boardwalk, the Royal Promenade, the Pool and Sports Zone, Vitality at Sea Spa/Fitness Center, Entertainment Place and Youth Zone. The most popular are the Boardwalk and Central Park, both open to the air, and the indoor Royal Promenade.

The Boardwalk. An echo of Coney Island, the Boardwalk, which is open to the skies, contains shops (naturally) and an art gallery for those peculiar people who go on a cruise to peruse or buy "artwork." Art displayed in Central Park's Art Actually, where artists who contributed to the ship's multi-million dollar collection can sell items to passengers.

Eateries include the Boardwalk Donut Shop; Johnny Rockets, a burger/milk shake diner; and the covered Seafood Shack for fish and seafood. If you are in a Central Park cabin, you need to take the elevator to get to the closest pool – it's like going to the top of your building to take a dip. Let's hope the pool volleyball game doesn't end up with the ball being tossed into the park – or onto someone's balcony while they're having coffee.

Central Park. This space is 328 ft (100 meters) long. The vegetation is real, with 27 trees and almost 12,000 plants, including a vertical "living" plant wall. But, unlike its New York inspiration, it includes, at its lower level, a "town center." At night, it's just about the only quiet and serene area,

ALLURE OF THE SEAS: WHAT'S GOOD AND WHAT'S NOT

THE POSITIVES

The Passenger Space Ratio is good for such a large vessel. The design concept is a continuum of the Freedom-class ships, themselves an extension of the Voyager-class ships – and then some. However, the increase in size has meant that RCI has been able to incorporate more of the facilities that young families seek for action-packed cruise vacations, including 37 bars and more than 20 places to eat or snack. And the latest technology means that *Oasis* is 30% more energy-efficient than even the Freedom-class ships.

The ship has been designed remarkably well, with large public spaces made possible by the split superstructure design – the idea of Harri Kulovaara, who first achieved this with Silja Serenade in 1986. This gives the ship the interior space needed to provide The Boardwalk, Central Park, and the Royal Promenade (all parts of the "seven neighbourhoods" concept). Excellent, large touch-screen ship information screens provide electronic maps at each stairway, and elevators are color-coordinated in either pink or blue for the fore and aft sections of the ship. There are no elevators in the center of the ship; all are in forward and aft locations, but there are enough of them, and they are speedy.

It's all rather novel, and should appeal to families with children. The only reminder that you're aboard a ship is the presence of the other 5,400 or so passengers – in a ship that could swallow 6,295. Because Central Park and the Boardwalk are open to the elements – so you could hide under a tree – but better take an umbrella just in case it rains in the sunny Caribbean.

Although not as stunning as the Aquaventure experience at Dubai's Atlantis Resort Hotel, where you can slide 27 meters down a ziggurat through shark infested waters or sleep underwater, the Pool and Sports Zone forward of the twin funnels is a real adventurous fun place for families. An adults-only open-air solarium and rentable cabanas are part of the outdoor scene today, and Oasis provides several. Two Flow-Riders are part of the sports line-up; these are located atop the ship around the aft exhaust mast, together with basketball courts and golf. The ship also has the largest jogging track at sea.

The Solarium is the most welcoming large, light-filled and restful (despite the background music) space. High atop ship, it is frequented by few children – so adults can "escape" the Las Vegas-like atmosphere of most other parts of the ship. On the subject of casinos, the roulette tables are stunning – all electronic and touch-buttony (no need to place chips on the table – simply touch a screen with your finger). There's also blackjack, craps, Caribbean Stud Poker, and 450 slot machines, plus a player's club and poker room – but this really can be a smoke-filled place, even in the "no-smoking" area. The casino entrance is dedicated to the history of gaming.

The Caribbean itinerary for this ship includes a "private" beach day at Labadee, the company's leased island, whose facilities were upgraded in 2009. RCI has built its own 800-ft pier, making it a logistically simple matter for anyone to access the ship and beach several times during the day-long stay. Do try the zipline – it's one of the world's longest, and a real blast. Other new additions: an alpine coaster, a beach club with 20 private cabanas, new dining facilities, a larger artisans' market and a Haitian Cultural Center.

A cruise aboard *Allure of the Seas* commands a premium over other ships in the RCI fleet, but it should provide a fine family cruise experience, with a wide range of choices (many at extra cost). This means you'll need to plan how you will spend your time, and where you would like to eat, well in advance of your cruise. Overall, if you are in suite-grade accommodation, you'll be treated well, while those in anything else receive second-class service, and will hear the word "no" a lot. But that's part and parcel of a large resort ship with its "metropolitan"-style cruise experience.

THE NEGATIVES

If all 5,400 passengers want a sunlounger at the same time, forget it – and those who secure one will find them so tightly packed together that there's little space to put their belongings. It's sad to see that exterior wooden railings have mostly been replaced by fibreglass railings – this is particularly noticeable on balconies.

Live or recorded music is everywhere, 24 hours a day, whether inside or outside the ship, including elevators and accommodation hallways. Ordering room service is complicated – you can't do it by phone, only by using the interactive touch-screen television in your suite/cabin. Standing in line to make reservations for the main shows can be time-consuming and frustrating (the reservation booth is in the middle of the Royal Promenade). You could make them online before your cruise – good for families that like to plan their vacations together – but who knows in advance what you may want to do when?

Getting reservations in one of the specialty restaurants takes a bit of effort, unless you are occupying suite-grade accommodation. Smoking is permitted in several bars and lounges aboard this ship and the smell of stale smoke permeates several areas. Cigar smokers will probably be underwhelmed by the cigar lounge.

The sense of being aboard a cruise ship is somewhat lost in all the large spaces to play in, but what this ship offers is a moveable resort full of facilities. There are few quiet nooks and crannies – except for a small, cramped library, with oversized leather chairs, and perhaps the Solarium.

Passengers complain constantly about the retail shop staff and their uncaring attitude. Other niggles include waiting for elevators; that the ship is simply too large to meet friends unless you are very specific about place and time); that the Windjammer Café is always busy; about the wine packages for purchase, which can be served only in certain venues; and the fact that bars do not have any snacks such as nuts. While RCI has programming and passenger flow down to a fine art, a few bottlenecks occur – but then, they do also at baseball stadiums and airports, both of which are as impersonal as this ship.

Allure of the Seas operates from the purpose-built $75 million Terminal 18 in Port Everglades (Fort Lauderdale), whose restroom facilities are minimal. Getting to the terminal is where people experience delays and frustration.

Disembarkation notes: If the two "fly-bridge" gangways are working, disembarkation is relatively speedy. However, when only one is working, a line forms in the Royal Promenade, in which case it's better to sit somewhere until the line gets shorter. Disembarkation for non-US citizens can be appallingly slow.

and is best for couples. Vintages wine bar is a great place to chill out, and there are several reservations-required, extra-charge dining venues; the poshest is 150 Central Park, while Chops Grille and Giovanni's Table are favourites for South Beach types. There's also Vintages wine and tapas bar, a nice place to relax in the late afternoon.

The Royal Promenade really is the equivalent of a floating shopping mall, with casual food eateries, shops with all kinds of merchandise, video screens, and changing color lights at every step. It's all a bit surreal. – like being in a circus at sea, with something going on every minute. But one thing not to be missed is the "Move On! Move On!" parade, a 15-minute circus-like extravaganza that includes characters from DreamWorks Animation's *Madagascar*. Interior-view promenade cabins have balconies that look down onto the action in Central Park. An hydraulic, oval-shaped Rising Tide Bar moves slowly through three floors and links the double-width Royal Promenade with Central Park.

While 11 of the ship's 22 dining venues and food outlets charge extra, you don't have to eat in them if you don't want to. Getting reservations to some of the better ones can be a challenge (try to do it online before your cruise if possible – even though it's a bit like programming your vacation before you go).

The ship is so large that it doesn't feel so crowded in most areas, except for the pool deck and in the Windjammer Café. As far as facilities go, this ship really has it all for trendy waterside (or parkside) living. Don't be concerned about long lines at check-in – there aren't any, because RCI has a custom-built terminal in Fort Lauderdale (Port Everglades) designed to get you on board in about 15 minutes.

ACCOMMODATION. Remarkably, there are 37 price grades, reflecting the choice of location and size. Suite occupants get access to a concierge lounge and associated services. There are many family-friendly cabins, good for family reunions, but there are no single-occupancy cabins. The cabin numbering system is a bit awkward to get used to. In a first for RCI, cabin doors open outwards (towards you), as in most European and Scandinavian hotels. In many of the lower grade accommodation, access to the closet is awkward – often with small sofas in the way. Most cabins feel extremely small, given the size of the ship. All cabins have an iPod dock.

There are 475 cabins with views into either Central Park or Royal Promenade, the two horizontal atriums, from their curved interior balconies, four of which are wheelchair-accessible. This includes 80 Central Park-view cabins with windows (not balconies) and fine views. But you'll need to keep your curtains closed for privacy, which rather defeats the object. Noise could be generated along the inner promenades, particularly late at night with street parades and non-stop music. So, your balcony experience could be like a continuous street party.

Loft suites: Although a few ships such as *Saga Ruby* have upstairs/downstairs suites, RCI has introduced "loft" suites to the Oasis-class ships. These offer spectacular ocean views, with floor-to-ceiling, double-height windows. Each

has a lower living area plus a private balcony with sun chairs, and a stairway that connects to the sleeping area which overlooks the living area and has extended ocean views. Modern designs are dotted with abstract, modern art pieces.

There are 28 Loft Suites, with 25 Crown Loft suites measuring 545 sq ft (51 sq meters). Three more spacious Loft Suites (called Royal Loft Suites) measure 1,524-sq. ft (141-sq meter). Each sleeps up to six, and each a baby grand piano, and indoor and outdoor dining areas, private wet bar, a library and extended 843-sq ft (78.3-sq meter) balcony with flat-screen TV set, entertainment area and Jacuzzi. Two large Sky Loft Suites measure 722 sq. ft (67 sq meters) and 770 sq ft (71 sq meters), and a 737-sq-ft (68-sq-meter) Crown Accessible Loft Suite includes an elevator to aid disabled passengers.

Standard Cabins (balcony and non-balcony class): Electrical sockets are located below the vanity desk unit in a user-unfriendly position. This is particularly poor for anyone trying to use the hairdryer in the 50% of cabins where the sockets are positioned on the right side. Also, it's difficult to watch television from the bed.

The washbasins in non-suite grade cabins are very small and low, at just 30½ inches (77.5cm) above the floor level. Be careful – it's easy to hit your head on the mirror above. Small soap bars are provided, while shampoo is provided in a dispenser in the shower enclosure. Unfortunately, the shower head is fixed, making it difficult to wash yourself thoroughly. Although there is no soap dish, or indentation in the washbasin surround for soap, useful touches include a blue ceiling bathroom nightlight.

Cabins are exposed to noise and whatever is happening on the Boardwalk itself, including rehearsals and sports activities in the Aqua Theater aft, bells from the carousel, rowdy revelers on the Boardwalk late at night, plus screaming ziplining participants high above during the day, not to mention loud music from bands playing at one of the pools, and exceedingly loud announcements by the cruise director repeating what's already printed in the daily program.

Boardwalk-view balcony cabin occupants need to close their curtains for privacy at times. However, the curved balconies – good for storing luggage to free up space inside the cabin – connect you with the open air and provide a community feeling, as you look across at balconies on the opposite side. All have a sea view aft (just); those close to the aft Aqua Theater can use their balconies for a great view of any shows or events. The lowest deck of Boardwalk-view cabins have windows but no balcony – and actually the view is mainly of the top of things such as the carousel or beach hut-like structures. The best Boardwalk balcony cabins are, in my view, located on decks 8–12. For more privacy, however, it might be best to book a sea-facing balcony cabin, not one that overlooks the Boardwalk.

Many suite-grade cabins have bathrooms with granite-look washbasin counter tops, and two washbasins. Some have bidets, Jacuzzi tubs and a separate shower enclosure. Some Family Suite grades have a separate, small room with bunk beds; some, not all, have curtains to separate them.

CUISINE. Because *Allure of the Seas* is an extra-large resort ship, the main meals in the main dining room, which is spread over three decks, are all about well-timed production cooking and fast delivery – essentially a banquet catering operation. Almost inevitably, the food is tasteless (except for salt) and mostly underwhelming. When you book, choose one of two seatings, or "My Time Dining" (eat when you want, during dining room hours). There are tables of all sizes, including large ones for family reunions.

Alternative Dining Venues in Central Park include:

● *150 Central Park:* The most exclusive restaurant aboard the ship, combines cutting-edge cuisine with interesting design. An observation window into the kitchen allows passers-by to watch the chefs in action. KeriAnn Van Raesfeld offers a multi-course tasting menu. It's open for dinner only, reservations are required and there's an extra charge.

● *Chops Grille:* Royal Caribbean's popular "signature" steakhouse, open for dinner only, offers premium-cut meats. There's a cover charge.

● *Chef's Table,* on the upper level of the Concierge lounge, is available to all passengers, at $70 per person for dinner, and offers a six-course meal with wine. It is hosted by the executive chef, but, with just 14 seats, trying to get a reservation could be difficult.

● *Giovanni's Table* ($10 for lunch; $15 for dinner): This casual Italian dining spot has a rustic feel, yet modern flair. It offers toasted herb breads, pizzas, salads, pastas, sandwiches, braised meat dishes and stews.

● *Central Park Café* is a casual dining spot with a high level of variety and flexibility, is an indoor/outdoor food market with line-up counters, and limited waiter service. Items include freshly prepared salads, made-to-order sandwiche, paninis, crêpes and hearty soups. You order directly from the chefs behind the food stations.

● *Rita's Cantina,* on the Boardwalk, is a noisy canteen offering quasi-Mexican fare. The cover charge ($8.95) is high and you'll need to a wait to get a tablecloth-less table. But then it is a bit of a cantina – so it lives up to its name.

● *Vintages* is a wine bar with a robust selection of decent wines, accompanied by cheese and tapas (with an à la carte item charge). Price examples: a glass of Caymus is $23, Stags Leap $19, Francis Coppola Reserve $12–$25, Beringer Private Reserve $15, and Silverado $8.75.

Other snacking spots on the Boardwalk include: *Boardwalk Dog House* (for hot dogs, wieners, bratwurst and sausages); the *Donut Shop* and *Ice Cream Shoppe.*

Elsewhere, dining venues/eateries include *Izumi,* offering Japanese-style cuisine, at an à la carte price; *Sorrento's Pizzeria*; *Park Café* (for salads and light bites); and *Wipe Out Café*. For those with a sweet tooth, there's a 1940s-style *Cupcake Shop*. Naturally, if you're thinking of getting married, you could have a cupcake wedding cake. For lighter, more health-conscious fare, there's a self-serve section in the *Solarium Bistro* for breakfast and lunch – it's usually the quietest place, too.

The *Windjammer Café* is the (free) casual, self-serve eatery common to all RCI ships. However, note that no trays are provided, only oval plates, so if you are disabled or have mobility difficulties you may need to ask for help. Also, because they're plastic, it's impossible to get a hot plate. The venue is simply too small to handle the number of people that can invade it at peak times – my advice is to try some of the other venues to avoid the overcrowding. The food varies from acceptable to less than acceptable – fresh fruit tends to be hard and unripe – and it's best to arrive early, when things have just been cooked and displayed. Although there's a decent enough variety, the quality of some of the meat is poor and overcooked.

Regular coffee is available free in many venues, but espresso and cappuccinos (in paper cups) cost extra – in the first Starbucks at sea.

The longest waiting lines are for *Johnny Rockets* and *Rita's Cantina*. Note that the cover charges quoted above are subject to change – check with RCI's website or your travel provider for the latest prices.

ENTERTAINMENT. The 750-seat AquaTheater, located outside at the ship's stern with a 6,000 sq. ft stage, is a stunning combination show theatre, sound stage and events space (some great viewing places can be found high in the aft wings of the ship on both sides). The stern has some "overhang," to accommodate the venue. A (DreamWorks Animation) *Madagascar*-themed aquatic acrobatic and dive show is also presented.

DreamWorks Animation Studios provides interactive shows featuring popular animation characters such as Shrek, King Fu Panda, Madagascar, and How To Train Your Dragon. The 1,380-seat main showlounge, spread over three decks, stages the popular musical *Chicago* – an excellent, 90-minute-long production, just like a Broadway show, and is performed four times during each cruise. The Aqua Theater show is called *Ocean Aria. Frozen in Time* is a stunning, must-see ice show.

There's no charge for any of the shows, and bookings can be made at www.royalcaribbean.com up to three months before your cruise, although reservations are not required. It's extremely hard to change any reservations.

SPA/FITNESS. The The Vitality at Sea Spa includes a *Vitality Café* for extra-cost health drinks and snacks. The fitness center includes 158 cardio and resistance machines. An extra-cost thermal suite includes saunas, steam rooms, and heated tiled loungers. You can't just take a sauna for 10 minutes without paying for a one-day pass, at $30 per person. Steiner Leisure provides the staff and treatments, and gratuities are at your discretion.

The facility really is not that large, given the number of passengers carried. It's best not to book a massage when the ship is due to arrive or leave an anchor port because some treatment rooms experience immense vibration when the anchor chain is in use. Sports facilities include two surfboard pools, golf putting course, ziplining (screaming is mandatory), and an ice-skating rink.

● **For more extensive general information on what an RCI cruise is like, see pages 152–6.**

Amadea
★★★★ +

Size: . . . . .Mid-Size Ship	Passenger Decks: 8	Cabins (with private balcony): 108
Tonnage: .28,856	Total Crew: 292	Cabins (wheelchair accessible): 2
Lifestyle: . . . . .Standard	Passengers	Wheelchair accessibility: . . . . .Fair
Cruise Line: . . . . .Phoenix Reisen	(lower beds/all berths): 606/624	Cabin Current: . . . . .110 volts
Former Names: . . . . .Asuka	Passenger Space Ratio	Elevators: 5
Builder: . .Mitsubishi Heavy Industries (Japan)	(lower beds/all berths): 48.0/46.6	Casino (gaming tables): . . . . .No
Original Cost: . . . .$150 million	Crew/Passenger Ratio	Slot Machines: .No
Entered Service: . . . . . .Dec 1991/Mar 2006	(lower beds/all berths): 2.3/2.3	Swimming Pools (outdoors): 1
Registry: . . . . .The Bahamas	Cabins (total): 303	Swimming Pools (indoors): 0
Length (ft/m): 632.5/192.81	Size Range (sq ft/m): 182.9–649.0/	Whirlpools: 3
Beam (ft/m): 81.0/24.70	17.0–60.3	Self-Service Launderette: . . . . .Yes
Draft (ft/m): 21.6/6.6	Cabins (outside view): 300	Dedicated Cinema/Seats: Yes/97
Propulsion/Propellers: . . . . .diesel	Cabins (interior/no view): 3	Library: . . . . .Yes
(17,300kW)/2	Cabins (for one person): 0	Onboard currency . . . . .Euros

---

A stylish, spacious ship with excellent food and service.

OVERVIEW. *Amadea* is best suited to German-speaking couples, single travelers and families with children, who enjoy cruising in very comfortable surroundings aboard a contemporary ship. Because it absorbs people well, there is never any feeling of crowding.

THE SHIP. When introduced in 1991 as *Asuka*, this was the first all-new large ship specially designed and built in Japan for the domestic market. It was sold to Phoenix Reisen and, as *Amadea*, started cruising for German-speaking passengers in 2006.

The ship, a more upscale vessel than other ships in the Phoenix Reisen fleet, has pleasing exterior styling and a contemporary profile, with a large, rounded, but squat funnel. There is a generous amount of open deck and sunbathing space, plus a wide walk-around teakwood promenade deck outdoors, good for strolling.

The "cake-layer" stacking of the public rooms hampers passenger flow and makes it somewhat disjointed, although passengers will like the separation of public rooms from accommodation areas. There are many intimate public rooms, plenty of space and lots of light.

The interior decor is understated but elegant, with pleasing color combinations, quality fabrics and fine soft furnishings. There's some fascinating Japanese artwork, including Noriko Tamura's *Song of the Seasons*, a four-deck-high mural on the wall of the main foyer staircase.

Harry's Bar is a bar and lounge decorated in the style of a contemporary gentleman's club with wood-paneled walls and burgundy leather chairs. This popular drinking spot has a light, airy feel.

As for the dress code, there is a mix of formal and infor-

BERLITZ'S RATINGS		
	Possible	Achieved
Ship	500	398
Accommodation	200	160
Food	400	336
Service	400	327
Entertainment	100	77
Cruise	400	302
OVERALL SCORE		
1,600 points out of 2,000		

mal nights, while during the day attire is very casual. There is a self-service launderette with eight washing machines – useful for long voyages. The ship provides an extremely comfortable and serene cruising environment. All gratuities are included.

ACCOMMODATION. There are several price categories, although in reality there are just five types of suites and cabins. Three decks (8, 9, and 10) have suites and cabins with a private balcony. (The balcony floors are laid with green simulated turf, and there is no outside light.)

Suites and cabins in all grades have ocean views, although some are slightly obstructed by the ship's gangway when it is in the raised (stowed) position.

In all grades, cherry wood cabinetry, which is in beautiful condition, has nicely rounded edges. Cabin soundproofing is excellent, and there is a good amount of closet and drawer space (including lockable drawers), refrigerator, and personal safe.

All grades have bathrooms with full, deep tubs, and all have a tiled floor and bath/shower area. While the suite bathrooms are generously proportioned, the "standard" bathrooms are practical but small.

Two suites provide the largest accommodation (one is decorated in blue, the other in salmon); these are larger versions of the "A" grade cabins. Each has a separate bedroom, with walk-in closet that includes a luggage deck, and twin beds that convert to a queen-size bed, sofa, two chairs and coffee table, large vanity desk, plenty of drawer space, and large color TV set. The marble-clad bathroom is large and has a whirlpool tub set alongside large ocean-view windows overlooking the private balcony, and twin washbasins set in a marble surround; a living room, and separate guest bathroom. The private balcony is quite large and has a tall tropical plant set in a glass display enclosure.

The top grade cabins are excellent living spaces, and have twice the size and space of the standard cabins. They are very nicely decorated and outfitted, and have twin beds (convertible to a queen-size bed), sofa, two chairs and coffee table, large vanity desk, plenty of drawer space, and large color TV set. However, when in its twin-bed configuration, the room's *feng shui* is poor, as one of the beds is facing a large mirror at the writing/vanity desk – a negative for some people.

Many cabins have a private balcony with full floor-to-ceiling partition and a green synthetic turf floor (but no outside light) with floor-to-ceiling sliding door – the door handles are awkward.

There's also an illuminated walk-in closet with long hanging rail and plenty of drawer space. The bathrooms, partly tiled and generously proportioned, include a plastic, glass-fronted toiletries cabinet, and two washbasins set in a thick marble surround.

CUISINE. There are two main restaurants, both with open-seating for all meals. *The Four Seasons* has two sections; there are ocean-view windows along one side of the aft section, and along two sides of the forward section. *The Amadea Restaurant* is located on a higher deck, with ocean view windows on two sides. The cuisine is the same in both venues. For casual breakfasts and lunches, there's an informal self-serve *Lido Café* with plenty of outdoor seating, adjacent to a small pool and hot tub.

With this ship, Phoenix Reisen has taken its cuisine and service to a much higher level than that aboard its other ships (except *Artania*), by spending more money per passenger per day (this is also reflected in the cruise fare).

ENTERTAINMENT. The Atlantic Lounge is the venue for most entertainment events, including shows, social functions, and lectures. The room spans two decks, with seating on both main and balcony levels, and an extra-large wooden dance floor is provided for social dancing.

SPA/FITNESS. There is a spacious wellness center. It has large ocean-view windows, two baths, one hot tub, a sauna, steam room with wooden floor; there are several shower enclosures, plus a changing area with vanity counter. Two massage rooms are in a different location, although they are on the same deck.

WHERE NAUTICAL EXPRESSIONS COME FROM

If you've ever wondered where some terms or phrases came from, you have only to look to the sea, ships, and seamen.

Bamboozle

Today, when you intentionally deceive someone, usually as a joke, you are said to have bamboozled them. The word also was used in the days of sail, but then it meant to deceive a passing vessel as to your ship's origin or nationality by flying an ensign other than your own – a common practice by pirates. From the 17th century, it described the Spanish custom of hoisting false flags to deceive (bamboozle) enemies.

Batten down the hatches

The real hatches are the things that cover the hatchways: gratings and close-hatches. A great deal of water can come aboard either from the sea of the sky or both, so they used to cover those hatches with tarpaulins. The crew typically took battens – stout laths of wood that fit against the coaming (the raised rim of the hatchway) – and pinned the tarpaulin down to cleats on the deck, drum tight.

Barge in

The word barge has two nautical meanings. First as a term applied to a flag officer's boat or highly decorated vessel used for ceremonial occasions. The second usage refers to the more common, flat-bottomed work boat which is hard to maneuver and difficult to control. Hence the term "barge in."

Bigwigs

The senior officers in the English Navy, who once wore huge wigs, were referred to a "bigwigs."

Bitter End

If a sailor were to lay out all of the anchor warp (chain or rope) until he reached the bitter end, then he would have no more to give out. The bitter end also refers to the end of the "starter" (a short rope knotted at on end) used for punishment. Today we talk of having reached the "bitter end" when we mean that we can go no further in a task. The landlubber's phrase "stick it to the bitter end" and "faithful to the bitter end" are derivations of the nautical term and refer to anyone who insists in adhering to a course of action without regard to consequences.

American Glory
★★

Size: ....Boutique Ship	Total Crew: 22	Cabins (wheelchair accessible): 3
Tonnage: 1,287	Passengers	Wheelchair accessibility: ....None
Lifestyle: ....Standard	(lower beds/all berths): 49/49	Cabin Current: ....110 volts
Cruise Line: .....American Cruise Lines	Passenger Space Ratio	Elevators: 1
Former Names: ....none	(lower beds/all berths): 26.2/26.2	Casino (gaming tables): ....No
Builder: . .Chesapeake Shipbuilding (USA)	Crew/Passenger Ratio	Slot Machines: ....No
Original Cost: ....n/a	(lower beds/all berths): 2.2/2.2	Swimming Pools (outdoors): 0
Entered Service: ....July 2002	Cabins (total): 27	Swimming Pools (indoors): 0
Registry: ....USA	Size Range (sq ft/m): 176.0–382.0/	Whirlpools: 0
Length (ft/m): 174.0/53.00	16.3–35.4	Self-Service Launderette: ....No
Beam (ft/m): 40.5/12.30	Cabins (outside view): 27	Dedicated Cinema/Seats: ....No
Draft (ft/m): 6.5/1.98	Cabins (interior/no view): 0	Library: ....No
Propulsion/Propellers: diesel/2	Cabins (for one person): 5	Onboard currency ....US$
Passenger Decks: 4	Cabins (with private balcony): 14	

A US coastal cruise ship with limited facilities, aimed at retirees.

OVERVIEW: *American Glory* is best suited to mature couples and single travelers sharing a cabin who want to cruise in an all-American environment aboard a small ship where the itineraries and destinations are more important than food, service or entertainment.

THE SHIP. American Cruise Lines is the resurrection of a company with the same name that existed between 1974 and 1989. It now features intra-coastal waterway cruising, as well as sailings in New England and the Hudson River Valley. *American Glory* was built specifically for coastal cruising and cannot venture far from the coastline. The ship's uppermost deck is open (good for views), and there are tables and chairs, a few sunloungers, and a small putting green.

There are two public lounges. The main one, the observation lounge, is located forward, with windows on three sides, and an open bar is set up each afternoon. A second, smaller lounge is sandwiched between cabins on the same deck.

The point is to get close to the inland areas, cities and towns of America's intra-coastal waterways and coastline. There's no waiting in line – you can board whenever you want. The ship docks in town centers, or within walking distance of most towns on the itineraries. The dress code is "no ties casual". But it really is *extremely* expensive for what you get, compared even to ships of a similar size and purpose, although this is a new ship and the cabins are of a better size and are slightly better equipped. There is an elevator, which goes to all decks.

ACCOMMODATION. There are cabins for couples and

BERLITZ'S RATINGS

	Possible	Achieved
Ship	500	257
Accommodation	200	110
Food	400	208
Service	400	170
Entertainment	n/a	n/a
Cruise	500	123

OVERALL SCORE
868 points out of 2,000

singles, seven suites, and five wheelchair-accessible cabins. All cabins have twin beds that convert to a king-size bed, color TV, a small desk with chair, and clothes hanging space. The seven most expensive cabins also have a VCR and compact disc (audio) player. All cabins have a private bathroom with separate shower enclosure, washbasin and toilet (none of the cabins has a bathtub), as well as windows that open. Accommodation designated as suites also have a private balcony; although narrow, it does have two chairs and a small drinks table.

CUISINE. The dining salon, located in the latter third of the vessel, has large, panoramic picture windows on three of its sides. There's open seating (no assigned tables). There are no tables for two, and the chairs do not have armrests. The food is very much American fare – good and wholesome, featuring regional cuisines.

There is little choice of entrées, appetizers, or soups, soups, although there have been recent improvements. There is no wine list, although basic low-quality white and red American table wines are included. On the last morning of each cruise, only continental breakfast is available.

ENTERTAINMENT. There is no formal entertainment, although dinner and after-dinner conversation with fellow passengers in the ship's lounge/bar really becomes the entertainment each evening. Otherwise, take a good book.

SPA/FITNESS. There are no health spa facilities or medical facilities – but then the vessel is always close to land.

American Spirit
★★

Size:	Boutique Ship	Total Crew:	27	Cabins (wheelchair accessible):	1
Tonnage:	2,000	Passengers		Wheelchair accessibility:	None
Lifestyle:	Standard	(lower beds/all berths):	92/92	Cabin Current:	110 volts
Cruise Line:	American Cruise Lines	Passenger Space Ratio		Elevators:	1
Former Names:	none	(lower beds/all berths):	21.7/21.7	Casino (gaming tables):	No
Builder:	Chesapeake Shipbuilding (USA)	Crew/Passenger Ratio		Slot Machines:	No
Original Cost:	n/a	(lower beds/all berths):	3.4/3.4	Swimming Pools (outdoors):	0
Entered Service:	June 2005	Cabins (total):	51	Swimming Pools (indoors):	0
Registry:	USA	Size Range (sq ft/m):	204.0-240.0/	Whirlpools:	0
Length (ft/m):	220.0/67.0		18.9-22.2	Self-Service Launderette:	No
Beam (ft/m):	46.0/14.0	Cabins (outside view):	51	Dedicated Cinema/Seats:	No
Draft (ft/m):	8.2/2.5	Cabins (interior/no view):	0	Library:	Yes
Propulsion/Propellers:	diesel/2	Cabins (for one person):	5	Onboard currency	US$
Passenger Decks:	4	Cabins (with private balcony):	23		

A small, expensive coastal cruising ship for US retirees.

OVERVIEW. *American Spirit* is best suited to mature couples and single travelers sharing a cabin who want to cruise in an all-American environment aboard a small ship where the itineraries and destinations are more important than food, service or entertainment.

THE SHIP. American Cruise Lines builds its vessels in its own shipyard in Chesapeake, Maryland. The company operates intra-coastal waterway cruises, as well as sailings in New England and the Hudson River Valley. *American Spirit* is built specifically for coastal cruising and cannot venture far from the coastline. Its uppermost deck is open (good for views) behind the forward windbreaker, and the expansive open deck has many sunloungers, and a small putting green.

Inside, the public rooms include an observation lounge, with views forward and to port and starboard side (complimentary cocktails and hors d'oeuvres are offered before dinner); a library/lounge; a small midships lounge; and an elevator that goes to all decks.

Cruises are typically of seven days' duration. Given the small number of passengers, there's no waiting in line – you can board whenever you want. The ship docks in town centers, or within walking distance of most towns on the itineraries. The dress code is "no ties casual".

It really is extremely expensive for what you get, and the cabins are of a better size and are slightly better equipped than those of smaller half-sister *American Glory*.

ACCOMMODATION. There are five cabin price grades (four are doubles, one is for singles). All cabins have twin beds

BERLITZ'S RATINGS		
	Possible	Achieved
Ship	500	287
Accommodation	200	125
Food	400	210
Service	400	175
Entertainment	n/a	n/a
Cruise	500	125
OVERALL SCORE		
922 points out of 2,000		

that convert to king-size, a small desk with chair, color TV, and clothes hanging space. The seven most expensive cabins also have a DVD and CD player. All cabins have a modular bathroom with separate shower enclosure, washbasin and toilet (none has a tub), plus windows that open, and satellite-feed TV sets. Accommodation designated as suites also have a private balcony; although narrow, it has two chairs and a small drinks table. Some 23 cabins have a French balcony – you can open the door for fresh air, but it's too narrow to place chairs on.

CUISINE. The dining salon, in the latter third of the vessel, has large, panoramic picture windows on three sides. There's open seating (no assigned tables) and everyone dines at a single seating, at large tables, allowing you to get to know your fellow passengers.

The food is very much American fare – good and wholesome, with regional cuisines. There is a limited choice of entrées, appetizers, and soups. There is no wine list, although basic low-quality white and red US table wines are included. On the last morning of each cruise, only continental breakfast is available.

ENTERTAINMENT. There is no formal entertainment, although dinner and after-dinner conversation with fellow passengers in the ship's lounge/bar really becomes the entertainment each evening. Otherwise, take a good book.

SPA/FITNESS. There is a small fitness room with a few bicycles and other exercise machines.

American Star
★★

Size: ....Boutique Ship	Total Crew: 27	Cabins (wheelchair accessible): 1
Tonnage: 2,000	Passengers	Wheelchair accessibility: ....None
Lifestyle: ....Standard	(lower beds/all berths): 94/100	Cabin Current: ....110 volts
Cruise Line: ......American Cruise Lines	Passenger Space Ratio	Elevators: 1
Former Names: ....none	(lower beds/all berths): 21.2/20.0	Casino (gaming tables): ....No
Builder: ..Chesapeake Shipbuilding (USA)	Crew/Passenger Ratio	Slot Machines: ....No
Original Cost: ....n/a	(lower beds/all berths): 3.4/3.4	Swimming Pools (outdoors): 0
Entered Service: ....June 2007	Cabins (total): 52	Swimming Pools (indoors): 0
Registry:.......................USA	Size Range (sq ft/m): 204.0-240.0/	Whirlpools: 0
Length (ft/m): 220.0/67.0	18.9-22.2	Self-Service Launderette: ....No
Beam (ft/m): 46.0/14.0	Cabins (outside view): 51	Dedicated Cinema/Seats: ....No
Draft (ft/m): 8.2/2.5	Cabins (interior/no view): 0	Library: ....Yes
Propulsion/Propellers: diesel/2	Cabins (for one person): 5	Onboard currency ....US$
Passenger Decks:...................4	Cabins (with private balcony): 23	

A small coastal ship with limited facilities, for US retirees.

OVERVIEW. *American Star* suits mature couples and single travelers sharing a cabin and wishing to cruise in an all-American environment aboard a small ship where the destinations are more important than food, service or entertainment.

THE SHIP. This is one of four vessels in the fleet of American Cruise Lines, which has its own shipyard in Chesapeake, Maryland, and the company's best ship by far. The company features intra-coastal waterway cruising, as well as sailings in New England and the Hudson River Valley. *American Star* is built specifically for coastal and inland cruising to destinations unreachable by large cruise ships, in a relaxed, unregimented environment. The uppermost deck is open (good for views) behind a forward windbreaker; many sun-loungers are provided, as is a small golf putting green.

The public rooms include an observation lounge, with views forward and to port and starboard side (complimentary cocktails and hors d'oeuvres are offered before dinner); a library/lounge; a small midships lounge, and an elevator that goes to all decks, including the outdoor sun deck.

Cruises are typically of seven to 14 days' duration. The ship docks in town centers, or within walking distance of most towns and ports. The dress code is "no ties casual." It is extremely expensive for what you get. There are no additional costs, except for gratuities and port charges, because it's all included – quite different to big-ship cruising.

ACCOMMODATION. There are five cabin price grades

BERLITZ'S RATINGS

	Possible	Achieved
Ship	500	287
Accommodation	200	125
Food	400	210
Service	400	178
Entertainment	n/a	n/a
Cruise	500	125

OVERALL SCORE
925 points out of 2,000

(four are doubles, one is for singles). All cabins have twin beds, convertible to a king-size bed, a small desk with chair, flat-screen TV set, DVD player and internet access, and clothes hanging space. All cabins have internet access, a modular bathroom with separate shower enclosure, washbasin and toilet (no cabin has a bathtub), windows that open, and satellite-feed TV sets. Accommodation incorrectly designated as suites (23) also have a private balcony; although narrow, it does have two chairs and a small drinks table.

CUISINE. The dining salon, in the latter third of the vessel, has large, panoramic picture windows on three sides. Everyone dines at a single (open) seating – there are no assigned tables – at large tables, so you can get to know your fellow passengers. The cuisine is American: simple, honest food featuring regional specialties. The choice of entrées, appetizers, and soups is limited. There is no wine list, although basic white and red American table wines are included.

On the last morning of each cruise, only continental breakfast is available.

ENTERTAINMENT. There is no formal entertainment, although dinner and after-dinner conversation with fellow passengers in the ship's lounge/bar really becomes the entertainment each evening. Otherwise, take a good book.

SPA/FITNESS. There is a tiny fitness room with a few bicycles and other exercise machines.

Amsterdam
★★★★

Size: . . . . .Mid-size Ship	Total Crew: 600	Wheelchair accessibility: . . . . .Good
Tonnage: .61,000	Passengers	Cabin Current: . . . . .110 and 220 volts
Lifestyle: . . . . .Premium	(lower beds/all berths): . . .1,380/1,653	Elevators: 12
Cruise Line: . . . . . . .Holland America Line	Passenger Space Ratio	Casino (gaming tables): . . . . .Yes
Former Names: . . . . .none	(lower beds/all berths): 44.2/36.9	Slot Machines: . . . . .Yes
Builder: . . . . .Fincantieri (Italy)	Crew/Passenger	Swimming Pools (outdoors): 1
Original Cost: . . . .$400 million	Ratio (lower beds/all berths): 2.3/2.7	Swimming Pools (indoors): 1
Entered Service: . . . . .Oct 2000	Cabins (total): 690	(magrodome cover)
Registry: . . . . .The Netherlands	Size Range (sq ft/m): 184.0–1,124.8/	Whirlpools: 2
Length (ft/m): 780.8/238.00	17.1–104.5	Self-Service Launderette: . . . . .Yes
Beam (ft/m): 105.8/32.25	Cabins (outside view): 557	Dedicated Cinema/Seats: Yes/235
Draft (ft/m): 25.5/7.80	Cabins (interior/no view): 133	Library: . . . . .Yes
Propulsion/Propellers: . . . . .diesel-electric	Cabins (for one person): 0	Onboard currency . . . . .US$
(37,500 kW)/2 x 15.5 MW azimuthing pods	Cabins (with private balcony): 172	
Passenger Decks: 12	Cabins (wheelchair accessible): 20	

Dutch-style decor and friendly service for cruisers of mature years.

OVERVIEW. *Amsterdam* is extremely comfortable, with fine, elegant and luxurious decorative features. On the negative side, the quality of food and service is poor and there's a lack of understanding of what it really takes to make a "luxury" cruise experience, despite what is touted in Holland America Line's brochures.

THE SHIP. *Amsterdam*, a close sister ship to *Rotterdam*, has a nicely raked bow, as well as the familiar interior flow and design style. It was the first ship in the HAL fleet to feature an azimuthing pod propulsion system *(see page 191)*. The pods are powered by a diesel-electric system.

The decor retains much of the traditional ocean liner detailing so loved by frequent Holland America Line passengers, with some use of medium and dark wood panelling. However, some color combinations – particularly for the chairs and soft furnishings – are rather wacky. Much of the artwork reflects HAL's glorious past, as well as items depicting the city of Amsterdam's history.

The interior focal point is a three-deck high atrium, in an oval, instead of circular, shape. A whimsical "Astrolobe" is the featured centerpiece in this atrium. Also clustered in the atrium lobby are the reception desk, shore excursion desk, photo shop and photo gallery.

The ship has three principal passenger stairways – so much better than two from the viewpoint of safety, flow and accessibility. There is a glass-covered pool on the Lido Deck between the mast and the twin funnels, watched over by a sculpture of a brown bear catching salmon.

The casino, in the middle of a major passenger flow on

BERLITZ'S RATINGS		
	Possible	Achieved
Ship	500	430
Accommodation	200	165
Food	400	281
Service	400	273
Entertainment	100	78
Cruise	400	310
OVERALL SCORE		
1,537 points out of 2,000		

one of the entertainment decks, has blackjack, roulette, poker and dice tables alongside the requisite rows of slot machines.

HAL provides cappuccino and espresso coffees and free ice cream at certain times, as well as hot hors d'oeuvres in all bars – something other major lines have dropped, or charge extra for.

With one whole deck of suites (and a dedicated, private concierge lounge, with preferential passenger treatment), the company has in effect created a two-class ship. The charge to use the washing machines and dryers in the self-service launderette is petty and irritating, particularly for the occupants of high-priced cabins.

Perhaps the ship's best asset is its friendly and personable Filipino and Indonesian crew, although communication (in English) can prove frustrating at times, particularly in the dining room and informal buffet areas. The room service menu is limited, and room service is very basic.

FAMILIES. There are children's and teens' play areas – token gestures by a company that traditionally does not cater well to children. Popcorn is available at the Wajang Theater for moviegoers, while adjacent is the popular Java Café.

ACCOMMODATION. This is spread over five decks (some cabins have full or partially obstructed views), and is in 16 grades: 11 with outside views, and five interior grades (no view). There are four penthouse suites, and 50 suites – 14 more than aboard sister ship *Rotterdam*. No cabin is more than 130 ft (40 meters) from a stairway, which makes it very easy to find your way from your cabin to the public rooms. Although 81% of cabins have outside views, only 25% of those have balconies.

All of the "standard" interior and outside-view cabins are tastefully furnished, and have twin beds that convert to a queen-size bed – but the space is a little tight for walking between beds and the vanity unit. There is a decent amount of closet and drawer space, although this will be tight for longer voyages. The fully tiled bathrooms are disappointingly small, particularly on long cruises, the shower tubs are very small, and the storage for toiletries is quite basic. There is little detailing to distinguish the bathrooms from those aboard the *Statendam*-class ships. All cabin TV sets carry CNN and TNT, as well as movies, and ship information and shopping channels.

There are 50 Verandah Suites and four Penthouse Suites on Navigation Deck. The suites all share a private Concierge Lounge, with a concierge to handle such things as special dining arrangements, shore excursions and special requests. Strangely there are no butlers for these suites, as aboard ships with similar facilities. The lounge, with its wood detailing and private library, is accessible only by private key-card.

Four Penthouse Suites are extremely civilized. Each has a separate steward's entrance, as well as a separate bedroom with king-size bed, vanity desk, large walk-in closet with excellent drawer and hanging space, living room, dining room (seating up to eight), wet bar, and pantry. The bathroom is large, and has a big oval Jacuzzi tub, separate shower enclosure, two washbasins, separate toilet and bidet. A guest bathroom has a toilet and washbasin. There is a good-sized private balcony. Suite occupants get personal stationery, complimentary laundry and ironing, cocktail-hour hors d'oeuvres and other goodies, as well as priority embarkation and disembarkation.

CUISINE. The *La Fontaine Dining Room* seats 747, spans two decks, and has a huge stained-glass ceiling measuring almost 1,500 sq. ft (140 sq. meters), with a floral motif and fiber-optic lighting. There are tables for two, four, six or eight, but few tables for two. Both open seating and fixed (assigned tables and times) seating are available, while breakfast and lunch are open-seating (you'll be seated by restaurant staff when you enter). Rosenthal china and fine cutlery are provided.

Alternative (Reservations Required) Dining Spot

The 88-seat *Pinnacle Grill* is available to all passengers on a reservation-only basis, with priority reservations given to those in suite grades. There is an extra charge for dining here ($10 for lunch, $20 for dinner), but there's better food and presentation than in the main dining room (it's open for lunch and dinner). The whimsically surreal artwork features scenic landscapes. The cuisine is California-Italian in style, with small portions and few vegetables. The wine list is good, and wines are served in the correct stemware.

Another alternative, the *Lido Buffet Restaurant*, is open for casual dinners on all except the last night of each cruise, in an open-seating arrangement. Tables are set with crisp linens, flatware and standard stemware. A set menu includes a choice of four entrées.

For casual breakfasts and lunches, the Lido Buffet Restaurant provides old-style, stand-in-line serve-yourself canteen food – adequate for anyone used to TV dinner food, but most definitely not as lavish as the brochures claim. Although the salad items appear adequate when displayed, they are too cold and quite devoid of taste. The constant supply of iceberg lettuce doesn't seem to go away, but there is little choice of other, more suitable, lettuces and greens.

ENTERTAINMENT. The 577-seat Queen's Lounge is the venue for all production shows, strong cabaret, and other entertainment. It is two decks high, with main and balcony level seating. The stage has hydraulic lifts and three video screens, and closed-loop system for the hearing-impaired.

While Holland America Line is not known for its fine entertainment (the budgets aren't high enough), what the line does offer is a consistently good, tried and tested array of cabaret acts. The production shows, while a good attempt, fall short on storyline, choreography and performance, with colorful costuming and lighting hiding the weak spots.

A number of bands, a string ensemble and solo musicians present live music for dancing and listening in many of the lounges and bars. There's dancing in the Crows Nest (atop the navigation bridge), and serenading string music in the Explorer's Lounge, among other venues.

SPA/FITNESS. The Ocean Spa is located one deck above the navigation bridge at the very forward part of the ship. It includes a gymnasium with all the latest muscle-pumping exercise machines, including an abundance of treadmills. It has forward views over the ship's bows. There's an aerobics exercise area, large beauty salon with ocean-view windows to the port side, several treatment rooms, and men's and women's saunas, steam rooms and changing areas.

The spa is operated by Steiner, a specialist concession, whose young staff will try to sell you Steiner's own-brand Elemis beauty products. Some fitness classes are free, while some, such as yoga, and kick-boxing, cost $10 per class. Massage facials, pedicures, and beauty salon treatments cost extra (massage, for example, costs about $2 per minute, plus gratuity).

For the sports-minded, two paddle-tennis courts are located at the aft of the Sports Deck.

● **For more extensive general information about a Holland America Line cruise, see pages 140–3.**

Arcadia
★★★★

Size: ....Large Resort Ship	Passenger Decks: 10	Cabins (wheelchair accessible): 30
Tonnage: 82,972	Total Crew: 886	Wheelchair accessibility: ....Good
Lifestyle: ....Standard	Passengers	Cabin Current: ....110/220 volts
Cruise Line: ....P&O Cruises	(lower beds/all berths): 2,064/2,628	Elevators: 14
Former Names: ....none	Passenger Space Ratio	Casino (gaming tables): ....Yes
Builder: ....Fincantieri (Italy)	(lower beds/all berths): 41.5/32.4	Slot Machines: ....Yes
Original Cost: ....$400 million	Crew/Passenger Ratio	Swimming Pools (outdoors): 2
Entered Service: ....April 2005	(lower berds/all berths): 2.3/2.9	Swimming Pools (indoors): 0
Registry: ....Bermuda	Cabins (total): 1,032	Whirlpools: 5
Length (ft/m): 936.0/285.3	Size Range (sq ft/m): ..170–516.6/15.7–48	Self-Service Launderette: ....Yes
Beam (ft/m): 105.0/32.0	Cabins (outside view): 690	Dedicated Cinema/Seats: ....Yes
Draft (ft/m): 25.5/7.8	Cabins (interior/no view): 342	Library: ....Yes
Propulsion/Propellers: .....diesel-electric	Cabins (for one person): 0	Onboard currency ....UK£
(34,000 kW)/ 2 azimuthing pods	Cabins (with private balcony): 677	

A contemporary, adults-only ship for trendy Brits.

OVERVIEW. *Arcadia* is a trendy, modern cruise ship based in Southampton, England – so UK passengers can avoid airports. It is best suited to couples and singles looking for a large, adults-only ship, with entertainment geared to British tastes, an informal setting and plenty of public rooms.

THE SHIP. P&O's *Arcadia*, intended to be Cunard Line's *Queen Victoria* for the British cruise market, was transferred to the P&O Cruises brand (both companies are owned by the giant Carnival Corporation).

Outdoors facilities include a walk-around promenade deck (covered in the ship's forward section), with plenty of sun-loungers (and cushioned pads). A large Lido Deck pool has a moveable glass domed cover – useful in poor weather. Panoramic exterior glass-wall elevators grace the central foyer to port and starboard and travel between all 10 passenger decks. Pod propulsion is provided *(see page 191).*

The layout provides a horizontal flow, with most public rooms, shops, bars and lounges set open-plan style on two principal decks, so finding your way around is relatively easy. However, the layout of upper public room decks is not so good. The interior decor is geared towards those with youthful, contemporary – even trendy British – tastes, and can best be described as "traditionally modern." It is, however, restrained and welcoming (if a bit bland), and has many warm, earthy pastel colors, assisted by 3,000 works of art (some outstanding) by contemporary British artists, at a cost of $4 million. Although *Arcadia* is one of the Carnival Corporation's Vista-class ships, the decor is perhaps the most refined of them all, and both passenger flow and signage are generally good.

Facilities include a forward-facing Crow's Nest observa-

BERLITZ'S RATINGS		
	Possible	Achieved
Ship	500	420
Accommodation	200	150
Food	400	258
Service	400	292
Entertainment	100	81
Cruise	400	289
OVERALL SCORE		
1,490 points out of 2,000		

tion lounge high atop the ship (in a contemporary setting); a florist; a gift shop arcade; and a Monte Carlo casino, a library (with leather armchairs and a Waterstone's section for paperback sales), a 30-seat boutique screening room which replaced the cyberstudy in a 2008 refit, and The Retreat (a good place to meet and chill out). The 14 bars include the Spinnaker Bar (good for ship buffs, with its fine display of ship models), a "traditional" English pub (The Rising Sun, with Boddington's draught beer), plus a bar overlooking a very modest three decks-high atrium lobby. The lobby (there isn't one, really) is small and disappointing, particularly when compared to *Oceana.*

Arcadia blends time-honored British cruising with contemporary facilities, but it is completely different to the more traditional *Aurora, Oceana* or *Oriana.* It is registered in Bermuda, so UK and US passport holders can be legally married by the ship's captain (check with P&O Cruises for the latest requirements). You can also renew your vows in a special ceremony (£250 per couple).

The New Horizons lecture program provides an array of lectures on a range of subjects (introductory sessions at no charge; more in-depth subject matter study in smaller groups, at an additional cost, typically £5 or £10 per class).

Many extra onboard revenue centers have now appeared aboard P&O Cruises' ships, including *Arcadia* – such as paying for lectures and thalassotherapy pool use. Also, smoking is permitted only on cabin balconies and in designated spots on the open decks.

Passenger niggles: There is no room for card games such as bridge; the ship's dance floor space is pitiful; and the embarkation system keeps people waiting in a lounge after lines at the check-in desks and security until boarding card letters are called. The small public toilets lack touches such as flowers and hand towels; there are no towels at poolside (you must take them from your cabin); poolside gala receptions lack atmosphere (and "nibbles"); and pre-dinner announcements are robotic. The often noisy air conditioning cannot be turned off in cabins or bathrooms.

ACCOMMODATION. There are 26 price grades of accommodation in seven types of suites/cabins; the choice includes 23 suites, 24 mini-suites, and 685 outside-view cabins with a private balcony. While there are plenty of price grades, there are really only five types of accommodation: suites, mini-suites, cabins with private balcony, and twin-bedded cabins with or without a window. All cabin doors and elevators have numbers in Braille.

There are 67 suites and mini-suites. All accommodation has duvets as standard (blankets and pillows if you prefer), flat-screen TV sets, tea/coffee making sets (with Tetley teabags and long-life milk) , small refrigerator, vanity/writing desk, personal safe, hairdryer; bathrooms have half-size tubs/shower/washbasin, and toilet. High-quality toiletries are by Temple Spa, with larger bottles and more selection choice provided for suite occupants.

Also standard are stylish bed runners, Slumberland 8-inch sprung mattresses, 10.5 tog duvets (blankets and pillows if you prefer), Egyptian cotton towels and robes, improved tea/coffee making facilities with speciality teas (long-life is provided) and a Nick Munro-designed bespoke tray, as well as in-cabin toning and fitness facilities for passengers who would prefer to exercise in private.

In twin-bedded cabin grades (approximately 170 sq.ft.), when the beds are pushed together, there's little room to maneuver, but they are otherwise quite practical units.

Accommodation designated as suites (approximately 516 sq.ft. including balcony) and mini-suites (approximately 384 sq.ft. including balcony) benefit from more space (some are really just the size of two cabins), king-size bed, trouser press, ironing board and iron, three-seat sofa (suites) or two-seat sofa (mini-suites), wall clock, and binoculars. The bathrooms are larger, and include an aqua-jet tub, two washbasins, toilet, and separate shower enclosure (suites only).

So-called "butler" service is provided, but, unlike most lines with these kinds of grades, bottled water costs extra, as do soft drinks.

Passengers complain about the space-hogging coffee/tea-making set on the small vanity desk in standard cabin grades, although the set is comprehensive. Other gripes about standard cabins include: closets with hanging space too narrow for the width of a man's jacket; little drawer space; poor-quality plastic hangers and the hanging system, and no hooks for belts.

The room-service breakfast choice is limited, but is available between 7am and 11am.

CUISINE. The *Meridian Restaurant*, located aft, is two decks high (the two decks are connected by a spiral staircase); it has 11 superb glass-fiber optic ceiling chandeliers created by Neil Wilkin, and a podium with grand piano graces the upper level. There are two seatings in both restaurants, and tables are for two, four, six, or eight. **Alternative (extra charge) restaurants.** Two smaller, more intimate dining settings provide an escape from the main dining rooms. *Ocean Grill*, by Marco Pierre White, specializes in prime steaks and seafood. The *Orchid Restaurant* (on Deck 11) has fine panoramic views, Asian-fusion (heavy on the spices) cuisine, and its own bar for pre-meal drinks. Reservations are required in both venues.

For casual meals and snacks, there's a self-serve 24-hour food-court-style eatery *(Belvedere)*, a section of which becomes another dining venue at night, serving Indian cuisine. There's also an open-deck *Neptune Grill* (for burgers and other fast food items), and *Caffe Vivo* (for coffees and pastries, at extra cost).

ENTERTAINMENT. The Palladium show lounge is an entertainment palace with three seating tiers and the latest in high-tech staging, lighting, and sound systems. Seating is in both banquette-style and individual tub chairs, and the sightlines to the stage are generally good. There are several major production shows –some with a Cirque du Soleil feel to them – complete with major bungee-diving acrobatics and fine adagio dancers. In addition, the ship has an array of cabaret acts. Classical concerts are scheduled for many cruises (typically in the Crows Nest).

P&O Cruises typically carry professional dance hosts and teachers. But ballroom dance aficionados should note that there are few wooden dance floors aboard this ship.

SPA/FITNESS. The Ocean Spa includes a gymnasium with great forward ocean views, 10 body-pampering treatment rooms, a thermal suite that incorporates a hydrotherapy pool, sauna and steam room (£10 for two hours, in five timed sessions per day), and two very small unisex saunas at no charge, but in a location that discourages their use (the thermal suite is better), well away from the changing rooms. Additionally, The Retreat is a cool space for relation, and for calming classes like tai chi, and yoga (£5 per class). The spa is operated by the UK-based Harding Brothers. Sports facilities include a sports court for racquet or football games, a golf driving range, and the traditional shuffleboard and ring toss.

● **For more extensive general information about a P&O cruise, see pages 148–9.**

Arion
★★

Size:	.Small Ship	Passenger Decks:	.5	Cabins (wheelchair accessible):	.0
Tonnage:	.5,885	Total Crew:	120	Wheelchair accessibility:	.None
Lifestyle:	.Standard	Passengers		Cabin Current:	.220 volts
Cruise Line:	.Classic International Cruises	(lower beds/all berths):	.334/340	Elevators:	.1
Former Names:	Astra I, Istra	Passenger Space Ratio		Casino (gaming tables):	.Yes
Builder:	.Brodgradiliste (Yugoslavia)	(lower beds/all berths):	.17.6/17.3	Slot Machines:	.Yes
Original Cost:	.n/a	Crew/Passenger Ratio		Swimming Pools (outdoors):	.1
Entered Service:	.1965/1999	(lower beds/all berths):	.2.7/2.8	Swimming Pools (indoors):	.0
Registry:	.Madeira	Cabins (total):	169	Whirlpools:	.0
Length (ft/m):	.387.1/118.0	Size Range (sq ft/m): 80.7–161.4/7.5–15.0		Self-Service Launderette:	.No
Beam (ft/m):	.54.1/16.5	Cabins (outside view):	142	Dedicated Cinema/Seats:	.No
Draft (ft/m):	.18.3/5.6	Cabins (interior/no view):	.27	Library:	.Yes
Propulsion/Propellers:	diesel	Cabins (for one person):	.4	Onboard currency:	.Euros
	(11,030kW)/2	Cabins (with private balcony):	.0		

A classic little ship with friendly European service.

OVERVIEW. Arion, a charming little ship originally built for weekly service between Venice and Egypt, is best suited to adult couples, typically over 50, looking for a basic cruise holiday in a traditional ship. This could be good for your first cruise experience, in a setting that provides basic comforts, and at a price that provides fair value for money.

THE SHIP. Classic International Cruises commissioned a $15 million reconstruction – even the navigation bridge was relocated forward – after it bought the ship at auction in Haifa in 1999. It emerged in its present form in May 2000 and is operated under charter to various tour operators, attracting an international mix of passengers who like smaller ships with some character.

Arion is now a charming ship offering interesting itineraries at low prices. It is particularly suited to the "nooks and crannies" style of cruising along the Dalmatian coast. The dress code is extremely casual, there is a relaxed ambience, and the service staff is warm and friendly.

There are few public rooms and facilities, and little open deck space – although the sunloungers do have cushioned pads. Interior passageways are narrow, the public rooms are always busy and it is difficult to avoid smokers. The ship is not suitable for disabled passengers.

ACCOMMODATION. There are 12 cabin price grades, though this may depend on tour operators that charter the vessel. Except for the top two grades, the cabins are modest in size and features, and one wouldn't want to spend much time in them. Cabins 1–8, which have windows, have

BERLITZ'S RATINGS		
	Possible	Achieved
Ship	500	186
Accommodation	200	90
Food	400	182
Service	400	225
Entertainment	100	40
Cruise	400	179
OVERALL SCORE		
902 points out of 2,000		

lifeboat-obstructed views. Cabins on the higher decks have windows, while others have portholes.

Each cabin has a small TV set, personal safe, and hairdryer. There is little closet and storage space (so take the minimal amount of clothing), although each cabin has bedside drawers. Some cabins have twin beds, side by side, while others are "L"-shaped (only 13 cabins have a double bed). Some cabins have a third, or third and fourth berth. Bathrooms are tiny and basic, yet adequate.

CUISINE. The 352-seat restaurant is warm and cosy; there are ocean-view windows on two sides, and standard place settings. There are tables (quite close together) for four, six or eight. The chairs do not have armrests. All passengers dine together in one seating.

The menus are limited, although there is a good choice of breads and bread rolls. Dinner menus typically consist of one or two appetizers, two soups, and three entrées. The wine list is quite basic, and the wine glasses are small. The all-Portuguese waiters are friendly and attentive. Casual breakfasts and luncheons can be taken in the Lido Lounge, just forward of the swimming pool and the open deck aft.

ENTERTAINMENT. There is little entertainment, and what is provided is of the cabaret variety. There is a band for dancing and a pianist in the piano bar, located just aft of the main lounge, and Lido Bar.

SPA/FITNESS. None, although there is a small beauty salon. The small swimming pool is really only a "dip" pool.

Artania
★★★★ +

Size:	.Mid-Size Ship	Passengers		Cabin Current:	.110 & 220 volts
Tonnage:	.44,348	(lower beds/all berths):	.1,200/1,260	Elevators:	.6
Lifestyle:	Standard	Passenger Space Ratio		Casino (gaming tables):	.Yes
Cruise Line:	.Phoenix Reisen	(lower beds/all berths):	.36.9/35.1	Slot Machines:	.Yes
Former Names:	*Royal Princess*	Crew/Passenger Ratio		Swimming Pools (outdoors):	.2
Builder:	.Wartsila (Finland)	(lower beds/all berths):	.2.3/2.4	(+2 splash pools)	
Original Cost:	.$165 million	Cabins (total):	.600	Swimming Pools (indoors):	.0
Entered Service:	Nov 1984/Apr 2011	Size Range (sq ft/m):	.186.0–1,126.0/	Whirlpools:	.2
Registry:	The Bahamas		17.2–104.5	Fitness Center:	.Yes
Length (ft/m):	.754.5/230.0	Cabins (outside view):	.600	Self-Service Launderette:	.Yes
Beam (ft/m):	.95.8/29.2	Cabins (interior/no view):	.0	Dedicated Cinema/Seats:	.Yes/150
Draft (ft/m):	.25.5/7.8	Cabins (for one person):	.0	Library:	.Yes
Propulsion/Propellers: diesel (29,160kW)/2		Cabins (with private balcony):	.152	Onboard currency:	.Euros
Passenger Decks:	.9	Cabins (wheelchair accessible):	.4		
Total Crew:	.520	Wheelchair accessibility:	.Good		

A comfortable, spacious ship for mature-age German-speaking cruisers.

OVERVIEW. *Artania* should provide a fine cruise experience in reasonably spacious, quietly contemporary surroundings, at a very decent price. It is best suited to couples and singles seeking to cruise in a modern mid-size ship, with entertainment geared specifically for German-speaking tastes, an informal setting, really good, creative food, and a decent number of bars and lounges.

THE SHIP. *Artania*, originally Princess Cruises' *Royal Princess*, the first ship to have all-outside cabins, was transferred to Phoenix Reisen as a running mate to *Amadea*, and a second restaurant was added in order to accommodate all passengers in a single seating. There's a traditional walk-around teak deck, and the outdoor deck and sunbathing space is moderate.

The ungarish interior decor reflects the feeling of space, openness and light; the passenger flow is good. There are several nicely appointed public rooms, bars and lounges, plus wide passageways and imposing stairways.

A Panorama Lounge, set around the funnel base, has fine views and a peaceful environment during the day, while in the evening becomes a nightclub. A nice feature is a dedicated cinema. Phoenix Reisen's onboard team take good care of passengers. A 7% gratuity is added to bar accounts.

ACCOMMODATION. The all-outside view cabins (152 with private balcony) represent just four accommodation types (including suites), although there are 21 price categories. All cabins, most of which have twin beds, are comfortable and well appointed, although a trifle bland. All have a combination bathtub and shower, three-sided mirrors, color TV

BERLITZ'S RATINGS

	Possible	Achieved
Ship	500	392
Accommodation	200	154
Food	400	329
Service	400	323
Entertainment	100	76
Cruise	400	294

OVERALL SCORE
1,568 points out of 2,000

set, and European two-pin sockets. Also standard are stylish bed runners, high-quality sprung mattresses, European duvets (blankets and pillows if you prefer), cotton towels and robes. Toiletries are provided, as are bathrobes and chocolates on your pillow each night. Prompt, attentive room service is available 24 hours a day. Some cabins on both Apollo Deck and Orion Deck have full or partial lifeboat and safety equipment-obstructed views. Some cabins have extra berths fitted.

The 12 largest suites, named after famous composers, are quite attractive, but not large by today's standards, and the balconies are small. All suite occupants get an expanded range of toiletries and complimentary mineral water.

CUISINE. The *Vier Jahreszeiten* (Four Seasons) restaurant is set low down in the ship, conveniently adjacent to the lobby. It is an elegant room, and there are tables for two, four, six, or eight. One deck above is the *Artania Restaurant*, with adjacent bar. Casual meals can be taken in the 24-hour indoor-outdoor *Lido Restaurant* self-serve eatery.

ENTERTAINMENT. The Atlantik Showlounge hosts shows, drama presentations and main cabaret acts. Phoenix always provides plenty of live music for the various bars and lounges, and volume is normally kept to an acceptable level.

SPA/FITNESS. The Artania Spa contains a gymnasium with muscle-toning equipment, saunas and changing rooms for men and women, and a beauty salon. There's a wide range of beauty and wellness treatments.

Astor
★★★ +

Size: . . . . .Mid-Size Ship	Passenger Decks: 7	Cabins (wheelchair accessible): 0
Tonnage: 20,606	Total Crew: 300	Wheelchair accessibility: . . . . .Fair
Lifestyle: . . . . .Standard	Passengers	Cabin Current: . . . . .220 volts
Cruise Line: . . . . .Transocean Cruises	(lower beds/all berths): 590/650	Elevators: 3
Former Names: . . . . .Fedor Dostoyevskiy,	Passenger Space Ratio	Casino (gaming tables): . . . . .Yes
Astor (II)	(lower beds/all berths): 34.9/31.7	Slot Machines: . . . . .Yes
Builder: . . . . . . .Howaldtswerke Deutsche	Crew/Passenger Ratio	Swimming Pools (outdoors): 1
Werft (Germany)	(lower beds/all berths): 1.9/2.1	Swimming Pools (indoors): 1
Original Cost: . . . .$65 million	Cabins (total): 295	Whirlpools: 1
Entered Service: . . . . . Feb 1987/Apr 1997	Size Range (sq ft/m): 140.0–280.0/	Self-Service Launderette: . . . . .No
Registry: . . . . .The Bahamas	13.0–26.0	(ironing room)
Length (ft/m): 579.0/176.50	Cabins (outside view): 199	Dedicated Cinema/Seats: . . . . .No
Beam (ft/m): 74.1/22.61	Cabins (interior/no view): 96	Library: . . . . .Yes
Draft (ft/m): 20.0/6.10	Cabins (for one person): 0	Onboard currency: . . . . .Euros
Propulsion/Propellers: diesel (15,400kW)/2	Cabins (with private balcony): 0	

Traditional style and restful decor for German speakers.

OVERVIEW. *Astor* caters exclusively to German-speaking couples and single travelers of mature years and provides a degree of style, comfort and elegance in a relaxed, spacious setting that is less formal than a ship such as *Europa*. It offers a good-value-for-money vacation in a traditional cruise ship setting, with appealing itineraries and destinations, good food and friendly service.

THE SHIP. This is an attractive modern ship with a raked bow, a large square funnel and a nicely balanced almost contemporary profile. It is slightly larger than the first *Astor* (which is now *Saga Pearl II*), and has been well maintained and refurbished over the years. Introduced by Transocean Tours (as it then was called) in 1997, this ship was placed under a long-term charter agreement from its present owner, Premicon (which also owns a number of fine riverships).

Astor was the original name for this ship, the larger of two vessels bearing the same name in the 1980s (the other being the former Transocean Cruises ship *Astoria*), originally built for the now-defunct Astor Cruises. Its previous owners, the also defunct AquaMarin Cruises, brought back the ship's name to *Astor* from its previous identity as *Fedor Dostoyevskiy*.

This ship represents a good mix of traditional and modern styling, with restful decor that doesn't jar the senses in any way – though some say it's a little too dark. Its high standard of German construction can be seen in the fine teakwood decking, polished wood railings and interior fittings, much of it refurbished in 2010.

There is an excellent amount of open deck and sun-

BERLITZ'S RATINGS

	Possible	Achieved
Ship	500	357
Accommodation	200	141
Food	400	258
Service	400	286
Entertainment	100	62
Cruise	400	275

OVERALL SCORE
1,379 points out of 2,000

bathing space, plus cushioned pads for the sunloungers. There is a basketball court for active passengers, as well as a large deck chess game on an aft deck, and shuffleboard courts.

The public rooms and conference facilities are supremely comfortable and varied, most with high ceilings. Apart from a showlounge, there's a Captain's Club lounge, a library and card room, and two large boutiques. The wood-paneled Hanse Bar, with good German lager on draft, is a fine retreat; it has an outdoor area too, and is popular as a late-night hangout. There is no crowding anywhere and no annoying background music in hallways or elevators.

Transocean Cruises has interesting and well-designed destination-intensive worldwide itineraries, and cruises are provided at a very attractive price. The mainly European hotel staff are friendly without being obtrusive.

Transocean Cruises staff can be found aboard every cruise, some of which are designated as special-theme cruises. Port taxes, insurance and gratuities to staff are all included in the fare. The drinks prices are inexpensive, particularly when compared to land-based prices.

A service provided by ABX Logistics will collect your luggage from your house, and transport it to the ship for you; when you return, the service will collect it from the ship and bring it to your house – all for a nominal fee.

ACCOMMODATION. The accommodation, spanning 20 price categories, is spread over three decks, and comprises 32 suites and 263 outside-view and interior cabins. No matter what grade of accommodation is chosen, rosewood cabinetry and plain beige walls is the norm – a restful environment. All suites and cabins with outside-view windows have blackout blinds – good for cruises to the land of the midnight sun.

Astor Suite: This new suite measures approximately 635 sq.ft. (59 sq. meters) and includes a private balcony, with a separate bedroom and living room. The large bathroom has a tub, separate shower enclosure, dual washbasins, and a separate toilet with washbasin.

Senator Suites: These two suites (516.6 sq.ft (48 sq. meters), also added in the 2010 refit, are tastefully decorated in pastel colors, and have wood cabinetry and accents. Each has a separate bedroom, lounge/living room, private balcony, and a French balcony. The bathroom has decent-sized storage cabinets for toiletries, as well as a tub, separate shower enclosure, toilet, and dual washbasins. A wide variety of bathroom amenities is provided.

Outside-view and Interior Cabins: These cabins (139.9 sq. ft/13 sq. meters) are well appointed and tastefully decorated in fresh pastel colors, and have dark wood accents and cabinetry, making them very restful. There is plenty of closet and drawer space, as well as some under-bed storage space for luggage. The bathrooms are very practical, and each has a decent-sized cabinet for toiletries, as well as all the necessary fittings, including a white enamel washbasin.

Outside-view Family (4-Berth) Cabins: These large cabins (258.3 sq.ft/24 sq. meters) have two lower beds, one upper berth and one sofa bed – good for families with children. The tiled bathroom has a shower enclosure, white enamel washbasin and toilet.

All grades have a mini-bar and personal safe, European duvets, 100% cotton towels and bathrobe, soap, shampoo, shower cap, sewing kit and a basket of fruit. The bathroom towels, however, are small.

The cabin service menu is limited, although German-speaking passengers in general seldom use room service for food items. There is an extra charge for sandwiches, and little else is available. However, there is plenty of food elsewhere around the ship. Note that there is an extra charge for freshly-squeezed orange juice, as aboard all ships in the German-speaking market.

CUISINE. The *Waldorf Dining Room* is reasonably elegant, well laid-out, and operates two seatings. It also has one small wing – good for groups of up to 30. The service throughout is friendly and unpretentious, and the food quality and presentation has received some attention from the food caterer, although remember that you get what you pay for, and food is not a particularly high priority for Transocean Cruises.

The menus are reasonably attractive, and both quality and presentation are acceptable standard fare, but nothing special – there's certainly no "wow" factor. In addition to the regular entrées (typically three entrées for dinner), there may also be a pasta dish, and a vegetarian specialty dish. The wine list contains a decent selection of wines from many regions, and all at inexpensive to moderate price levels, but wine glasses are small.

A small alternative dining venue serving Italian cuisine is a reservations-only, extra-cost dining spot for those wanting something a little more special and as an alternative to the main dining room. Larger wine glasses are provided.

Casual breakfast and lunch buffets (both in the restaurant and another lounge) are reasonably well presented, and constantly refreshed, although they tend to be somewhat repetitive; the choice of foods is limited and there is room for improvement. In typical German style, a Frühschoppen with the appropriate music, Bavarian sausages and complimentary beer, is presented on the open lido deck once each cruise and is not to be missed.

ENTERTAINMENT. The Showlounge is a single-level room with 14 pillars obstructing the sightlines. It is better suited to cabaret and mini-concerts than large-scale staged production shows. The stage itself is also the dance floor, and cannot be raised for shows. The entertainment possibilities, therefore, are limited, with singers, magicians, and other visual acts providing the bulk of the shows.

SPA/FITNESS. The Wellness Oasis, located on the lowest passenger deck, contains a sauna (there is no steam room), solarium, indoor swimming pool, beauty salon, treatment rooms and changing areas. Massage, facials, manicures and pedicures are some of the services offered. A separate fitness center, equipped with techno-machinery and exercycles, is located on an upper deck (Bridge Deck), complete with ocean views.

Asuka II
★★★★ +

Size: ....Mid-Size Ship	Passenger Decks: 8	Cabins (with private balcony): 260
Tonnage: 50,142	Total Crew: 470	Cabins (wheelchair accessible): 4
Lifestyle: ....Luxury/Premium	Passengers	Wheelchair accessibility: ....Best
Cruise Line: ....NYK Cruises	(lower beds/all berths): 800/1,010	Cabin Current: ....115 and 220 volts
Former Names: ....*Crystal Harmony*	Passenger Space Ratio	Elevators: 8
Builder:Mitsubishi Heavy Industries, Japan	(lower beds/all berths): 52.0/45.2	Casino (gaming tables): ....Yes
Original Cost: ....$240 million	Crew/Passenger Ratio	Slot Machines: ....Yes
Entered Service: ... July1990/May 2006	(lower beds/all berths): 1.7/1.8	Swimming Pools (outdoors): 1
Registry: ....Japan	Cabins (total): 462	Swimming Pools (indoors): 0
Length (ft/m): 790.5/240.96	Size Range (sq ft/m): 198.1–949.4/	Whirlpools: 1
Beam (ft/m): 97.1/29.60	18.4–88.2	Self-Service Launderette: ....Yes
Draft (ft/m): 24.6/7.50	Cabins (outside view): 462	Dedicated Cinema/Seats: Yes/263
Propulsion/Propellers: ....diesel-electric	Cabins (interior/no view): 0	Library: ....Yes
(32,800kW)/2	Cabins (for one person): 0	Onboard currency: ....Japanese yen

An elegant, spacious ship with fine food, for Japanese cruisers.

OVERVIEW. *Asuka II* is best suited to Japanese-speaking travelers, typically over 60, seeking a sophisticated ship with fine-quality fittings and furnishings, a wide range of public rooms and facilities, and excellent food and service from a well-trained staff that enjoys providing hospitality. It is the attention to detail that makes this ship so pleasant, such as almost no announcements, and little background music.

THE SHIP. Although now 20 years old, *Asuka II,* formerly *Crystal Harmony,* underwent a four-month long drydocking and refit in 2005–06, and further refurbishment in 2009. It is a handsome, well-balanced contemporary ship with raked clipper bow, sleek lines, and NYK's double red band on the funnel. There is almost no sense of crowding anywhere, and the fact that form follows function means that comfort is built-in. There is a wraparound teakwood deck for walking, and an abundance of open deck and sunbathing space.

Inside, the layout is completely different to the previous *Asuka* in that there is a horizontal flow through the public rooms, as opposed to the previous vertical arrangement, and this better suits the age range of NYK's typical passengers. The design combines some large ship facilities with the intimacy of rooms found aboard many smaller ships. There is a wide assortment of public entertainment lounges and small intimate rooms, and passenger flow is excellent. Fine-quality fabrics and soft furnishings, china, flatware and silver are used throughout.

Outstanding are the Vista (observation) Lounge and the tranquil, elegant Palm Court, one of the nicest rooms afloat, while adjacent are an internet room and a Washitsu (Japan-

BERLITZ'S RATINGS		
	Possible	Achieved
Ship	500	427
Accommodation	200	160
Food	400	341
Service	400	337
Entertainment	100	83
Cruise	400	337
OVERALL SCORE		
1,685 points out of 2,000		

ese 12-tatami mat room). Other public spaces and facilities include the Mariner's Club Lounge (piano bar/ lounge), Cigar Bar, Bistro Café, Casino Corner, Mahjong Room with eight tables, Compass Room (meeting and activities room), a book/video library, and the Stars karaoke bar. The theater is a dedicated room with high-definition video projection. There is a self-service launderette on each deck – practical for long voyages.

Asuka II is a hotel afloat – approximately the equivalent of Tokyo's Imperial Hotel – and provides abundant choices and flexibility. It has just about everything for the discerning traveler prepared to pay for high style, space, and the comfort and the facilities of a mid-size vessel capable of long voyages. The company pays attention to its repeat passengers, particularly those in Deck 10 penthouses and suites.

Unfortunately, dining is in two seatings, which makes its timing highly structured – there are two shows, because the showlounge can't seat everyone at once. This works well in the Japanese market, and you can always choose to eat in an alternative dining venue, but the arrangement detracts from the otherwise fine setting of the ship and the professionalism of its staff. All gratuities are included.

ACCOMMODATION. There are five categories of suites and cabins (including four Royal Suites with private balcony; 26 Asuka Suites with balcony; 32 Suites with balcony; 202 Cabins with balcony; 172 Cabins without balcony). Regardless of the category, duvets and down pillows are provided, as are lots of other niceties. All cabins have a color TV set, DVD player, mini-refrigerator, personal safe, small couch and coffee table, excellent soundproofing, a refrigerator and mini-bar, full tea-making set, satellite-linked telephone, hairdryer, and slippers. A full range of toiletries (including Shiseido shampoo, hair rinse, shower cap, soap, cotton pads, razor set, hairbrush, and more) is provided, and plenty of cotton towels.

Deck 10 Penthouses: Four Royal Suites, whose entrance doorway has a door phone and camera, measure 949.4 sq. ft (88.2 sq. meters) and have a large private balcony and lounge with elegant walnut furniture, new soft furnishings, and audio-visual entertainment center (Bose audio system, Blu-Ray player); separate master bedroom with twin beds (flat-screen TV), and large walk-in closets. The excellent ocean-view Japanese-style bathrooms, with German quality fittings that include a large overhead shower, come with jet bathtub, two washbasins, and plenty of storage space for toiletries (a range of L'Occitane toiletries is provided). These fine, private, pampered living spaces at sea were totally refurbished in 2010, and include perks such as priority service, free laundry service, a wide variety of alcoholic beverages and many other goodies.

Other Deck 10 Suites: These are worth the asking price. All have a private balcony, with outside light, and plenty of space including a lounge with large couch, coffee table and chairs, large TV set, and a separate sleeping area that can be curtained off with thick drapes that allow you to sleep totally in the dark. The bathrooms are quite large, and extremely well appointed. All deck 10 suites/cabins are attended by social officers, and complimentary in-room dining service is offered.

Deck 9/8/7/5 Cabins: Many of the cabins have a private balcony (in fact, 50% of all cabins have private balconies, with outside lights), and are extremely comfortable. But they are a little tight for space, with one-way traffic past the bed. There is a reasonable amount of drawer and storage space, although the drawers are small and the closet hanging space and the storage space for shoes are very limited for long voyages. Some cabins have lifeboat-obstructed views, so it's best to check the deck plan carefully.

Although well appointed, the bathrooms (except for those in Deck 10 accommodation), are of the "you first, me next" variety – and size. But they do come with generously sized toiletries and amenities, and all bathrooms are fitted with electric "washlet" high-cleanse toilets.

CUISINE. There are several choices. The non-smoking *Four Seasons Dining Room* is quite elegant, and has a raised central section. There is plenty of space around each table, well-placed waiter service stations and a number of tables for two, as well as tables for four, six or eight.

Dinner in the main dining room is in two seatings, with no set table assignments. Afternoon tea and coffee can be taken in the Vista Lounge, a restful venue.

Alternative (extra charge) Dining: *Umihiko* is a Japanese specialty restaurant, complete with a wholly authentic sushi bar and live fish tanks for absolutely fresh sashimi. It specializes in sushi and authentic sashimi dishes, and provides a refined, intimate dining experience with fine ocean views. Reservations are required.

Prego, which has 40 seats with ocean views to starboard and aft, is for occupants of the Royal Suites and Asuka Suites. The menu is the same as the main dining room, but with more intensive waiter service.

For casual meals, beverages and ice cream, the *Lido Café*, which was completely reconstructed in the refit, has an extensive self-serve buffet area; it is located high up in the ship, and with ocean views from large picture windows. For casual meals, there is also a *Lido Garden Grill*, a large area with wooden tables and chairs, and bar.

Additionally, *The Bistro*, located on the upper level of the two-deck-high lobby, is a casual spot for coffees and pastries, served in the style and atmosphere of a European street café.

ENTERTAINMENT. The Grand Hall, the ship's showlounge, is a large room on one level, with a tiered floor. The sightlines are good from most seats, although a few pillars obstruct the view from some seats. Both banquette and individual seating is available.

In addition, there are often good-caliber cabaret acts that change constantly. The bands and musical units are also, for the most part, of a high standard, and there is plenty of music for social dancing.

SPA/FITNESS. The Grand Spa includes a large Grand Bath/ cleansing center (one for men, one for women), with integral sauna and steam room. Other facilities include the first Shiseido Salon and Spa at sea, with five treatment rooms (longevity, water, wind, prosperity, harmony) including one for couples. There's a separate sauna, steam rooms, changing rooms for men and women, a beauty salon, and a relaxation area. Another part of the spa houses the gymnasium, with ocean-view windows on one side.

Shiseido operates the spa and the staff offers a wide range of body pampering treatments using the brand products of Qi Estherapy, Carita and Decleor.

The spa also offers a kimono dressing service, which costs ¥12,600 (about $110).

There is an excellent amount of open deck space, including a swimming pool that's one of the longest aboard any cruise ship. Sports facilities include a full-size paddle tennis court, putting green, and golf driving range.

Athena
★★ +

Size: ....Small Ship	
Tonnage: 16,144	
Lifestyle: ....Standard	
Cruise Line: .Classic International Cruises	
Former Names:*Vision Athena, Athena,*	
Caribe, Valtur Prima, Italia Prima, Italia I,	
Positano, Surriento, Fridtjof Nansen,	
Volker, Volkerfreundschaft, Stockholm	
Builder: ....Varco Chiapella (Italy)	
Original Cost: $150 million (reconstruction)	
Entered Service: ....Feb 1948/May 2008	
Registry: ....Madeira	
Length (ft/m): 525.2/160.10	
Beam (ft/m): 68.8/21.04	
Draft (ft/m): 24.9/7.6	

Propulsion/Propellers: diesel (14,500kW)/2
Passenger Decks: 7
Total Crew: 280
Passengers
(lower beds/all berths): 556/640
Passenger Space Ratio
(lower beds/all berths): 29.0/25.2
Crew/Passenger Ratio
(lower beds/all berths): 1.7/2.0
Cabins (total): 277
Size Range (sq ft/m): 129.2–376.7/
12.0–35.0
Cabins (outside view): 230
Cabins (interior/no view): 47
Cabins (for one person): 2

Cabins (with private balcony): 8
Cabins (wheelchair accessible): 0
Wheelchair accessibility: ....None
Cabin Current: ....220 volts
Elevators: 2
Casino (gaming tables): ....Yes
Slot Machines: ....Yes
Swimming Pools (outdoors): 1
Swimming Pools (indoors): 0
Whirlpools: 1
Self-Service Launderette: ....No
Dedicated Cinema/Seats: ....No
Library: ....Yes
Onboard currency: ....Euros

An older, traditional ship with good service and comfort.

OVERVIEW. *Athena*, which has had many incarnations, names and operators, is best for adults and families with children, who seek an inexpensive first cruise in traditional non-glitzy surroundings with limited facilities, food and simple entertainment.

THE SHIP. *Athena* was a transatlantic "liner" before being converted into a cruise ship in 1994. It has a large "sponson" stern apron, added to aid stability. Classic International Cruises' owner, George Potamianos, has an engineering background and loves older ships. The ship is often chartered to various tour operators when not operating under the CIC brand.

The sturdily built ship, a lovingly maintained classic, holds a special charm for those not seeking the newest large resort ships. Outdoors facilities include a walk-around teakwood promenade deck and many real wooden sunloungers are provided, although open deck sunbathing space is extremely limited. The cheerful, bright colors make the interiors feel quite contemporary.

There is a good selection of public rooms, including a 400-seat auditorium for meetings, and some smart boutiques, and most public rooms are conveniently located on one deck. However, *Athena* is a high-density ship, leaving little space to move around in, and its fixed gangway may be steep, depending on the port and tidal conditions.

The small swimming pool is really just a "dip" or "plunge" pool. Book "Diplomat Suite" service and get VIP priority service and other niceties (welcome bottle of cava, flowers, bathrobe, chocolates, and room service). Gratuities are not included.

BERLITZ'S RATINGS

	Possible	Achieved
Ship	500	258
Accommodation	200	121
Food	400	208
Service	400	238
Entertainment	100	50
Cruise	400	217

OVERALL SCORE
1,092 points out of 2,000

ACCOMMODATION. There are 12 cabin price grades. All cabins have a mini-bar, TV set, and safe. Bathrooms have a combination tub/shower, as well as a good amount of indented space for toiletries. Eight suites each have a small private balcony. Each has a separate lounge/living area, with table and chairs; the bedroom's twin beds convert to a queen-size bed. The bathrooms in the suites and junior suites have whirlpool bathtubs with showers, toilet, washbasin and bidet.

Some cabins (on Promenade Deck) have lifeboat-obstructed views, and some on Mediterranean Deck may pick up noise from the public rooms on the deck above. The accommodation passageways are very narrow.

CUISINE. The 520-seat *Grand Restaurant Olissipo* is quite attractive, and has tables for two, four, six, and eight, and 520 seats. There are normally two seatings for dinner. Continental cuisine is featured, with some regional specialties. The food quality is in line with the low cruise cost. One port-side section of the restaurant has been enclosed to create a separate environment for VIP/Diplomat Suite passengers, in a more exclusive setting. There is also a self-serve buffet for breakfast and lunch in the *Lotus Buffet Restaurant*, although the selection is really basic.

ENTERTAINMENT. Many sightlines in the Main Lounge, which presents basic shows and cabaret acts, are obstructed, and there's a large bar in the aft of the room.

SPA/FITNESS. There's a workout room, sauna, steam room, body therapy rooms, and beauty salon.

Aurora
★★★★

Size: . . . . .Large Resort Ship	Total Crew: .816	Cabins (wheelchair accessible): 22
Tonnage: .76,152	Passengers	(8 with private balcony)
Lifestyle: . . . . .Standard	(lower beds/all berths): 1,868/1,975	Wheelchair accessibility: . . . . .Good
Cruise Line: . . . . .P&O Cruises	Passenger Space Ratio	Cabin Current: . . . . .110 and 220 volts
Former Names: . . . . .none	(lower beds/all berths): 40.7/38.5	Elevators: 10
Builder: . . . . .Meyer Werft (Germany)	Crew/Passenger Ratio	Casino (gaming tables): . . . . .Yes
Original Cost: . . . .$375 million	(lower beds/all berths): 2.2/2.4	Slot Machines: . . . . .Yes
Entered Service: . . . . .May 2000	Cabins (total): 934	Swimming Pools (outdoors): 3
Registry: . . . . .Great Britain	Size Range (sq ft/m): 150.6–953.0/	(1 with sliding glass dome)
Length (ft/m): 885.8/270.0	14.0–88.5	Swimming Pools (indoors): 0
Beam (ft/m): 105.6/32.2	Cabins (outside view): 655	Whirlpools: 5
Draft (ft/m): 25.9/7.9	Cabins (interior/no view): 279	Self-Service Launderette: . . . . .Yes
Propulsion/Propellers: . . . . .diesel-electric	Cabins (for one person): 0	Dedicated Cinema/Seats: Yes/200
(40,000kW)/2	Cabins (with private balcony): 406	Library: . . . . .Yes
Passenger Decks: 10		Onboard currency: . . . . .UK£

A traditional British-style ship for the whole family.

OVERVIEW: *Aurora* is best for adults of all ages (although most cruises attract the over-50s), and families with children who want a cruise that starts and ends in the UK, aboard a large ship with all the facilities of a small resort, with food and service that are very acceptable, though not as good as aboard some other cruise ships. But P&O Cruises has improved on the facilities of its older sister ship *Oriana*, with larger cabins and suites and with more dining options and choice of public areas.

THE SHIP. *Aurora* is named after the goddess of the dawn in Greek, Melanesian and Slavonic mythologies, or perhaps the carnation Dianthus Aurora. Or it could be the famous Northern and Southern Lights, aurora borealis and aurora australis. At any rate, it was built specifically for Britain's growing traditional cruise market.

As ships evolve, slight differences in layout occur, as is the case with *Aurora* compared to earlier close sister *Oriana*. One big difference can be found in the addition of a large, glass-domed indoor/outdoor swimming pool – good in all weathers. The stern superstructure is nicely rounded and has several tiers that overlook the aft decks, pool and children's outdoor facilities. There is a good amount of open deck and sunbathing space, an important plus for the outdoors-loving mainly British passengers. There is an extra-wide walk-around promenade deck outdoors, with plenty of white plastic sunloungers (cushioned pads are available).

The interiors are gentle, welcoming and restrained, with warm colors and combinations that don't clash. The public rooms and areas have been designed in such a way that

BERLITZ'S RATINGS		
	Possible	Achieved
Ship	500	406
Accommodation	200	160
Food	400	256
Service	400	307
Entertainment	100	76
Cruise	400	298
OVERALL SCORE		
1,503 points out of 2,000		

each room is individual, yet there appears to be an open, yet cohesive flow throughout all of the public areas – something difficult to achieve when a number of designers are involved. There is good horizontal passenger flow, and wide passageways help to avoid congestion. Very noticeable are the fine, detailed ceiling treatments.

As it is a ship for all types of people, specific areas have been designed to attract different age groups and lifestyles. The focal point is a four-decks-high atrium lobby and a dramatic, calming, 35-ft (10.6-meter) high, Lalique-style fiberglass sculpture of two mythical figures behind a veil of water. At the top of the atrium is the ship's library.

The carpeting throughout is excellent, much custom designed and made of long-lasting 100% wool. Original artworks by British artists include several tapestries and sculptures. For a weird experience, try standing on the midships staircase and look at the oil on the curved canvas paintings by Nicholas Hely Hutchinson – this has a dramatic effect on one's ability not to be seasick while cruising through the Bay of Biscay.

Other features include a virtual reality games room, 12 lounges/bars (among the nicest are Anderson's – similar to Anderson's aboard *Oriana*, with a fireplace and mahogany paneling), and the Crow's Nest – complete with a lovely one-sided model of a former P&O liner: *Strathnaver* of 1931, scrapped in Hong Kong in 1962. There is also a cinema that doubles as a concert and lecture hall.

The library has several writing desks, large leather audio listening chairs, a good range of hardbacks (and a librarian), and skillfully crafted inlaid wood tables. On the second day of almost any cruise, however, it will have been almost stripped of books by word-hungry passengers. The library also sells some nautical books. An internet-connect center is located on the port side, aft of the popular Crow's Nest observation lounge, but sending emails can be expensive.

The ship's layout is a little disjointed in certain places, and there are several dead-ends and some poor signage. The reception desk's opening hours (7am–8pm) are too short. Standing in line for embarkation, disembarkation, shore tenders, and for self-serve buffet meals is inevitable. Other passenger niggles include noisy air-conditioning in cabins, and the proliferation of extra-charge activities.

In the quest for more onboard revenue and shareholder value, even birthday cakes now cost extra, as do espressos and cappuccinos (fake ones, made from instant coffee, are available in the dining rooms). Also at extra cost are ice creams, and bottled water, which can add up to a considerable amount on an around-the-world cruise.

"Cashless Cruising" doesn't include tips – you should allow about £3.50 ($5.25) per person, per day. For the annual around-the-world cruise, this means carrying more than $750 in cash – though otherwise the circumnavigation is excellent value for money.

A British brass band send-off accompanies all sailings. Other touches include church bells that sound throughout the ship for the interdenominational Sunday church service. A coach service for passengers embarking or disembarking in Southampton covers much of the UK. Car parking, both under cover and in an open compound, is available.

FAMILIES. Toybox is the playroom for 2–5-year-olds, Jumpin' Jack's for 6–9 year olds, Quarterdeck for 10–13-year-olds, and Decibels for 14–17-year-olds. An entire deck includes swimming pools and whirlpools just for youngsters. Children and teens have "Club Aurora" programs with their own rooms and their own outdoor pool. Children can be entertained until 10pm, which gives parents time to have dinner and go dancing. All cabins also have a baby-listening device. A night nursery for small children (ages 2–5) is available (6pm–midnight, no charge; from midnight to 2am there's a fee), as well as slumber parties for 6–9-year-olds, Sixteen passenger cabins have interconnecting doors – good for families. At peak holiday times (summer, Christmas, Easter) there could be 400 or more children on board. However, the ship absorbs them well, and there's lots to keep them occupied.

ACCOMMODATION. There are five main grades of cabins, in 26 price categories. Included are two two-level penthouses, 10 suites with balconies, 18 mini-suites with balconies, 368 cabins with balconies, 225 standard outside-view cabins, 16 interconnecting family cabins, and 279 interior cabins.

All grades, from the largest to the smallest, provide the following common features: polished cherry wood laminate cabinetry, full-length mirror, personal safe, refrigerator, television, individually controlled air conditioning; twin

beds that convert to a queen-size double bed, sofa and coffee table. Also standard are stylish bed runners, Slumberland eight-inch sprung mattresses, 10.5 tog duvets (blankets and pillows if you prefer), Egyptian cotton towels and robes, improved tea/coffee-making facilities with speciality teas (long-life is provided) and a Nick Munro-designed bespoke tray, as well as in-cabin toning and fitness facilities for passengers who prefer to exercise in private.

There are four whole decks of cabins with private balconies (about 40% of all cabins), and these have easy-to-open sliding glass floor-to-ceiling doors; the partitions are of the almost full floor-to-ceiling type – so they really are quite private and cannot be overlooked from above.

Cabin insulation could better, and the magnetic catches in drawers and on the closet doors are noisy. Also, the TV sets provide only monaural sound. Although most doorways are 26 inches (66 cm) wide, the actual access is 2 inches (5 cm) less because of the doorframe; however, some doorways are only 21.5 inches (55 cm) wide.

A range of Molton Brown products is provided in penthouse suites, suites or mini-suites. For all other cabins, only soap is provided, plus a "sport wash" combination soap and shampoo in a dispenser in the shower (so take your favorite shampoo and conditioner), and a small pouch of assorted personal-care items. All grades get 100% cotton bathrobes, and 100% cotton towels. Except for the suites, no cabins have illuminated closets, and cabin ceilings are very plain.

Penthouse Suites: The largest cabins consist of two penthouse suites (Library Suite and Piano Suite), each 953 sq. ft (88.5 sq. meters). They have forward-facing views, being located directly underneath the navigation bridge (the blinds must be drawn at night so as not to affect navigation). Each is spread over two decks in height, and connected by a beautifully curved wooden staircase. One suite has a baby grand piano which can be played manually or electronically, while the other has a private library. The living area is on the lower deck (Deck 10), and incorporates a dining suite (a first in a P&O ship) and a small private balcony. In the bedroom, upstairs, there is a walk-in closet, while the bathroom is decked out in porcelain and polished granite, with twin basins, tub and separate shower enclosure. There is also a small private balcony.

Suites: The 10 suites measure about 445 sq. ft (41.3 sq. meters). They have a separate bedroom with two lower beds that convert to a queen-size bed. There is a walk-in dressing area and closet, with plenty of drawer space, a trouser press and ironing board. The lounge has a sofa, armchairs, dining table and chairs, writing desk, TV set, radio and stereo system. The marble-clad bathroom has a whirlpool bath, shower and toilet. The private balcony has space for two sunloungers, plus two chairs and two tables. Butler service is provided.

Mini-Suites: These measure 325 sq. ft (30.1 sq. meters), and have a separate bedroom area with two lower beds that convert to a queen-size bed. There's one double and two single closets, a good amount of drawer space, binoculars, a trouser press and ironing board. Each private balcony has a blue plastic deck covering, one deck lounge chair, one chair and table, and exterior light.

Standard Outside-view/Interior Cabins: Any cabin designated as a double with private balcony measure about 175 sq. ft (16.2 sq. meters). They have two lower beds that convert to a queen-size bed. The sitting area has a sofa and table. There's also a vanity table/writing desk, and a private balcony with blue plastic deck covering, two chairs (with only a small recline) and a small table. Note that a 110-volt (American) socket is located underneath the vanity desk drawer – in a difficult-to-access position.

Outside-view or Interior Cabins have two lower beds that convert to a queen-size bed, closet (but few drawers), and are 150 sq. ft (14 sq. meters). The bathroom has a mini-bath/shower and toilet, or shower and toilet.

All bathrooms in all grades (except those designated as suites) are compact, modular units, and have mirror-fronted cabinets, although the lighting is quite soft, and, in cabins with bathtubs, the retractable clothesline is located too high for most people to reach.

There are 22 wheelchair-accessible cabins, well outfitted for the physically challenged passenger and almost all within easy access to lifts. However, one cabin (D165 on Deck 8) is located between forward and mid-ships stairways, and it is difficult to access the public rooms on Deck 8 without first going to the deck below, due to several steps and tight corners. All other wheelchair-accessible cabins are well positioned, and eight have a private balcony.

CUISINE. The two main dining rooms (each seats about 525) have tables for 2, 4, 6, 8 and 10, in two seatings. The midships *Medina* has a vaguely Moorish theme, while *Alexandria*, with windows on three sides, has Egyptian decor. Both have more tables for two than in the equivalent restaurants aboard close sister ship *Oriana*. The china is Wedgwood, and the silverware is by Elkington.

The typical menu cycle is 14 days; anyone on a long voyage may find it quite repetitive. The cuisine is very British – a little adventurous at times, but always with plenty of curry dishes and other standard British items.

You should not expect exquisite dining, though – this is British hotel catering that doesn't pretend to offer foie gras and other gourmet foods. But what it does present is attractive and tasty, with some excellent gravies and sauces to accompany all dining room meals. In keeping with the Britishness of P&O Cruises, the desserts and cakes are good. The service is provided by a team of friendly stewards from India, with which the company has had a long relationship.

There are other dining options. You can, for example, also have dinner in the 24-hour, 120-seat French bistro-style restaurant, *Café Bordeaux*, for which there is a cover charge (for dinner only), with menus designed by Marco Pierre-White, the TV chef who starred in *Hell's Kitchen*. Breakfasts and lunches are also served here, as are several coffees: espresso, cappuccino, latte, ristretto, as well as flavored coffees. So, if you want a croque-monsieur (a toasted ham and Gruyère cheese sandwich) at 5am, you can have it. For £9.50 you can try the "Tasting Menu" – a selection of small cosmopolitan dishes, with three different menus per cruise.

Casual, self-serve breakfasts and lunches can be taken from the buffet in a colorful eatery named *The Orangery*, which has fine ocean views. Other casual dining spots include the *Sidewalk Café* (for fast-food items poolside), champagne bar and, in a first for a P&O cruise ship, *Raffles* coffee and chocolate bar (but without the ceiling fans).

ENTERTAINMENT. There is a wide variety of mainly British entertainment, from production shows to top British "name" and lesser name cabaret artists. The Headliners Theater Company is a group of resident actors, singers and dancers. They provide theater-style presentations such as mini versions of well-known musicals, "book" shows, revues, and drama presentations. There is also a program of theme cruises – antiques, art appreciation, classical music, comedy, cricket, gardening, jazz, Scottish dance, etc.

Ballroom dance fans will make use of the four good-sized wooden dance floors. The ship always carries a professional dance couple as hosts and teachers, and plenty of dancing time is included in the programming.

SPA/FITNESS. The *Oasis Spa* is midships on Lido Deck – almost at the top of the ship, just forward of the Crystal swimming pool. It is moderately large, and facilities include a gymnasium with the latest high-tech muscle-pumping and body toning equipment. There is also a sauna and steam room (both unisex, so you'll need a bathing suit). There's a beauty salon, a spiral staircase, and a relaxation area overlooking the forward Riviera swimming pool.

The spa is operated by a UK concession that provides the staff and a wide range of beauty and wellness treatments. Examples of treatments include: Body Toning (detox for the body); Seaweed Wrap; Collagen Velvet Facial Mask; and a range of aromatherapy treatments. Book spa treatments as soon after you embark as possible, as time slots fill up quickly aboard large ships such as this.

A sports court incorporates a golf practice cage and a golf simulator, for which there is an extra charge.

● **For more extensive general information about a P&O cruise experience, see pages 148–9.**

Azamara Journey
★★★★ +

Size: . . . . .Mid-Size Ship	Total Crew: 390	Cabins (wheelchair accessible): 6
Tonnage: .30,277	Passengers	Wheelchair accessibility: . . . . .Fair
Lifestyle: . . . . .Premium	(lower beds/all berths): 676/777	Cabin Current: . . . . . . .110 and 220 volts
Cruise Line: . . . . . .Azamara Club Cruises	Passenger Space Ratio	Elevators: 4
Former Names: .Blue Star, Blue Dream, R6	(lower beds/all berths): 42.7/38.9	Casino (gaming tables): . . . . .Yes
Builder: .Chantiers de l'Atlantique (France)	Crew/Passenger Ratio	Slot Machines: . . . . .Yes
Original Cost: . . . .$150 million	(lower beds/all berths): 1.8/2.5	Swimming Pools (outdoors): 1
Entered Service: . . . .Feb 2000/May 2007	Cabins (total): 338	Swimming Pools (indoors): 0
Registry: . . . . .Malta	Size Range (sq ft/m): 151.0–818.0/	Whirlpools: 2 (+ 1 thalassotherapy hot tub)
Length (ft/m): 593.7/181.0	14.0–76.0	Self-Service Launderette: . . . . .Yes
Beam (ft/m): 95.1/29.0	Cabins (outside view): 312	Dedicated Cinema/Seats: . . . . .No
Draft (ft/m): 19.85/6.0	Cabins (interior/no view): 26	Library: . . . . .Yes
Propulsion/Propellers: diesel 18,600kW)/2	Cabins (for one person): 0	Onboard currency: . . . . .US$
Passenger Decks: 9	Cabins (with private balcony): 249	

An informal ship with country-house decor and fine food.

OVERVIEW. The all-white *Azamara Journey*, virtually identical to *Azamara Quest* in features and fittings, suits mature couples seeking to get away from the crowds aboard a contemporary, mid-size ship with a wide range of bars and lounges, at a slightly lower cost than the luxury lines but with many of the same features. The overall feel is of a members-only country club.

THE SHIP. The exterior design balances the ship's high sides by combining a deep blue hull with the white superstructure and large, square blue funnel. A lido deck has a tiny – and I mean tiny – swimming pool, and good sunbathing space. There is no outdoor walk-around promenade deck, although a short jogging track encircles the pool deck (but one deck above it). The uppermost outdoors deck includes a golf driving net and shuffleboard court. There are no wooden decks outdoors; they are covered by a sand-colored rubberized material.

The interior decor is in good taste, and is a throwback to ship decor of the ocean liners of the 1920s and '30s. The public rooms are spread over three decks. The reception hall has a staircase with intricate wrought-iron railings. A large observation lounge (The Looking Glass) is high atop the ship. This has a long bar with forward views – for the barmen, that is, as passengers sitting at the bar face aft. There's a bar in each of the restaurant entrances, as well as a Martini Bar. There's also a Michael's Club – a jazz/piano lounge, and, of course, a Luxe Casino, and a shop (Boutique C). Internet connectivity is provided at Online@Celebrity. Unfortunately, tacky art auctions spoil the experience.

The Library is a beautiful, grand, restful room, designed

BERLITZ'S RATINGS		
	Possible	Achieved
Ship	500	417
Accommodation	200	157
Food	400	292
Service	400	320
Entertainment	100	78
Cruise	400	297
OVERALL SCORE		
1,561 points out of 2,000		

in the Regency style. It has a fireplace, a high, indented, *trompe l'oeil* ceiling, and a good selection of books, comfortable wingback chairs with footstools, and sofas you could sleep on. Smoking is permitted only on cabin balconies and in designated spots on the open decks – the interior space is non-smoking.

Gratuities to housekeeping and dining staff are included in the fare. Shuttle buses are provided free when needed in ports of call.

ACCOMMODATION. There are eight cabin price grades; three suite-grades and five other grades. All have so-called butler service (merely better-dressed cabin stewards). All of the standard interior and outside-view cabins (the lowest four grades) are extremely compact units. Azamara calls them staterooms (a real misnomer), but they are simply cabins – and rather tight for two persons, particularly during cruises longer than seven days. The bathrooms are postage-stamp-sized and you'll be fighting with the shower curtain, as well as storage space for toiletries. The standard cabins cannot, in any sense, be considered luxury, and even premium is stretching it a bit. But all suites and cabins receive "butler" service.

For the extra cost, it's wise to choose a suite or cabin with a balcony. Some cabins have interconnecting doors (good for families with children) while 18 cabins on Deck 6 have lifeboat-obstructed views. No matter what grade of accommodation you choose, all have TV sets that carry European news, sports channel (where obtainable), and several movie channels.

Standard Interior/Standard Outside-view Cabins: These have twin beds (convertible to a queen-size bed), with good under-bed storage areas, safe, vanity desk with large mirror, good closet and drawer space.

Ocean-view Cabins: Features: two lower beds convertible to queen size (some have an extra sofa bed); flat-screen TV; refrigerator with mini-bar; thermostat-controlled air conditioning; direct-dial telephone and voicemail; desk; in-room safe; hand-held hairdryer. Approximate size: 161 sq.ft.

Some cabins have a panorama window with an obstructed view. Those on the lowest deck have just a porthole.

Deluxe Ocean-view Cabins with Balcony: Features: two lower beds convertible to queen-size; floor-to-ceiling sliding glass doors; sitting area with sofa bed; private veranda; flat-screen TV; refrigerator with mini-bar; thermostat-controlled air conditioning; direct-dial telephone and voicemail; desk; in-room safe; hand-held hairdryer. Approximate size: 215 sq.ft.; balcony 38 sq.ft.

Sunset Verandah Cabins: Features: two lower beds convertible to queen size; floor-to-ceiling sliding glass doors; sitting area with sofa bed; private veranda; flat-screen television; refrigerator with mini-bar; thermostat-controlled air conditioning; direct-dial telephone and voicemail; desk; in-room safe; hand-held hairdryer. Approximate size: 215 sq.ft.; balcony 154 sq.ft.

Sky Suites: Superior Exterior View Cabins with Balcony: The cabins with private balconies, have partial balcony partitions, and sliding glass doors. The bathrooms, with tiled floors and plain walls, are compact units, and include either a tub/shower or a shower stall with a strong, removable hand-held shower unit, hairdryer, 100% cotton towels, toiletries storage shelves and retractable clothesline. Approximate size: 323 sq.ft.; balcony 57 sq.ft.

Royal Suites (Decks 6, 7): In reality these are large cabins, as the sleeping and lounge areas are not divided. The bathrooms have a good-sized tub and ample space for toiletries. The living area has a refrigerated mini-bar, lounge area with breakfast table, and a balcony with two plastic chairs and a table. Approximate size: 538 sq.ft.; balcony 173 sq.ft.

Penthouse De-Luxe Suite with Balcony: Providing the most spacious accommodation, these are fine, large living spaces located in the forward-most and aft-most sections of the accommodation decks (particularly nice are those that overlook the stern, on Deck 6, Deck 7 and Deck 8). An entrance foyer leads to a living room, bedroom (the bed faces the sea, which can be seen through the floor-to-ceiling windows and sliding glass door), CD player with selection of audio discs, bathroom with Jacuzzi tub, and a small guest bathroom. They have more extensive private balconies that really are private. Approximate size: 603 sq.ft.; balcony 215 sq.ft.

Suite occupants get priority boarding, tender service, alternative dining venue reservations, and light bites at 4pm, in-suite spa treatments, in-suite portrait sitting, free espressos/cappuccinos, bottled water, and silk-wrapped hangers. All suites/cabins located at the stern can suffer from vibration and noise, particularly when the ship is proceeding at or close to full speed, or maneuvering in port.

CUISINE. *Discoveries,* the main dining room, has around 340 seats, a raised central section (conversation at these tables may be difficult, due to its low ceiling height), and open-seating dining. There are large ocean-view windows on three sides, several prime tables overlooking the stern, and a small bandstand for live dinner music. Some tables for two are so close to adjacent tables for four that privacy is non-existent. The menu changes daily for lunch and dinner, and wine is included. Adjacent to the restaurant is a *Martini Bar,* with a cozy fireplace.

Alternative Dining Spots (make reservations early):

● The *Restaurant* (service charge $5) is at the aft of the ship on the port side of Deck 10; it has 96 seats, windows along two sides, and serves Mediterranean cuisine. A $50 per person Tasting Menu includes wine.

● *Prime C* (service charge $5), at the aft of the ship on the starboard side of Deck 10, has steaks and seafood. It has 98 seats, windows along two sides and a set menu.

● The *Windows Café* has indoor seating for just over 150 (not really enough when cruising in cold areas or in the winter months), and 186 seats outdoors. Many tables do, however, have ocean views. It is open for breakfast, lunch and casual dinners, and incorporates a small Sushi Café.

All dining venues have open-seating dining, although reservations are needed in the Aqualina Restaurant and Prime C, where there are mostly tables for four or six (there are few tables for two). Suite-grade occupants get two nights free, while other accommodation categories get one night free in one of the two alternative venues. All cappuccino and espresso coffees cost extra, even in the restaurants.

A *Cova Café* serves fine Italian coffees, as well as teas and pastries. And a *Wine Bar* with an extensive cellar has wine-and-food pairings, wine tasting sessions, and wines by the glass or bottle. Additionally, a *Poolside Grill* provides fast-food items. Some items are grilled to order. A self-serve soft ice cream machine is located adjacent to a beverage station. Coffee and tea are free 24 hours a day

ENTERTAINMENT. Celebrity Cabaret, located forward, is the venue for all main entertainment events. In the evenings, the entertainment consists of a mix of classical concerts, revues, as well as comedy and drama. The entertainment has a cultural tone to it. Additionally, local entertainers are brought on board in various destinations.

SPA/FITNESS. The AquaSpa has a gymnasium with some high-tech muscle toning equipment, an extra-cost thalassotherapy pool (outside, forward on deck), and several treatment rooms. Outside on deck, there is a small swimming pool, two hot tubs, and a jogging track. The spa is staffed and operated by Steiner Leisure. An "Acupuncture at Sea" clinic provides treatments that are operated independently of the spa (but also as a concession). Spa treatments are possible in your suite, too. Outside on the Lido Deck, there is a small swimming pool, two hot tubs, and a jogging track (one deck above the pool).

Azamara Quest
★★★★ +

Size: . . . . .Mid-Size Ship	Passenger Decks: 9	Cabins (with private balcony): 232
Tonnage: 30,277	Total Crew: 306	Cabins (wheelchair accessible): 4
Lifestyle: . . . . .Premium	Passengers	Wheelchair accessibility: . . . . .Fair
Cruise Line: . . . . . . .Azamara Club Cruises	(lower beds/all berths): 716/777	Cabin Current: . . . . .110 and 220 volts
Former Names: . . . . . .Blue Moon, Delphin	Passenger Space Ratio	Elevators: 4
Renaissance, R7	(lower beds/all berths): 42.2/38.9	Casino (gaming tables): . . . . .No
Builder: .Chantiers de l'Atlantique (France)	Crew/Passenger Ratio	Slot Machines: .No
Original Cost: . . . .$150 million	(lower beds/all berths): 2.3/2.5	Swimming Pools (outdoors): 1
Entered Service: . . . . .Oct 2000/Oct 2007	Cabins (total): 358	Swimming Pools (indoors): 0
Registry: . . . . .Malta	Size Range (sq ft/m): 156.0–484.3/	Whirlpools: 2 (+ 1 thalassotherapy hot tub)
Length (ft/m): 591.8/180.4	14.5–45.0	Self-Service Launderette: . . . . .Yes
Beam (ft/m): 83.3/25.4	Cabins (outside view): 332	Dedicated Cinema/Seats: . . . . .No
Draft (ft/m): 19.0/5.8	Cabins (interior/no view): 26	Library: . . . . .Yes
Propulsion/Propellers: diesel 18,600kW)/2	Cabins (for one person): 0	Onboard currency: . . . . .US$

It reminds you of an elegant country club.

OVERVIEW. Like its sister, *Azamara Journey,* this ship has the ambience of an old-world country club. For a full review, see *Azamara Journey.*

THE SHIP. *Azamara Quest* was originally *R7,* one of a series of eight almost identical ships in the now defunct Renaissance Cruises fleet (when it was in operation, between 1998 and 2001, it was the cruise industry's only totally no-smoking cruise line). It was purchased by Pullmantur in 2006, but transferred in 2007 to Celebrity Cruises' new mid-size ship brand, Azamara Cruises (renamed Azamara Club Cruises in 2009). Before entering service, the ship underwent an almost $20 million make-over. The ship has a sister in *Azamura Journey* (formerly *R6*).

An outdoors lido deck has a swimming pool, and good sunbathing space, while one of the aft decks has a thalassaotherapy pool. The exterior decks are covered with a rubber and sand-like surface (teak, although very expensive, would be much better, and more in keeping with the decor of the ship). The uppermost outdoors deck includes a golf driving net and shuffleboard court.

The interior decor is quite elegant, in the style of the ocean liner decor of the 1920s and '30s. This includes detailed ceiling cornices, both real and faux wrought-iron staircase railings, leather paneled walls, *trompe l'oeil* ceilings, rich carpeting in hallways with an Oriental rug-look center section, and other interesting (and expensive-looking, but faux) decorative touches.

The staircase in the main, two-deck-high foyer will remind you of something similar in a blockbuster hit about a certain iconic ship in which movie stars Kate Winslet and Leonardo di Caprio made their melodramatic voyage.

Passengers should be pleased with the ship's tasteful, traditional-style interiors, and with the variety of public rooms, basically spread over three decks.

Some public rooms have different names to those of *Azamara Journey* (Breeze instead of Windows Café, for example, which changes, for some unknown reason, to Breeza in the evening). Note the 15% gratuity on drinks.

BERLITZ'S RATINGS

	Possible	Achieved
Ship	500	418
Accommodation	200	157
Food	400	292
Service	400	320
Entertainment	100	78
Cruise	400	197

OVERALL SCORE
1,562 points out of 2,000

Azura
★★★★

Size: . . . . .Large Resort Ship	Passenger Decks: 14	Cabins (with private balcony): 910
Tonnage: 115,055	Total Crew: .1,239	Cabins (wheelchair accessible): 25
Lifestyle: . . . . .Standard	Passengers	Wheelchair accessibility: . . . . .Good
Cruise Line: . . . . .P&O Cruises	(lower beds/all berths): 3,096/3,574	Cabin Voltage: . . . . .220/110 volts
Former Names: . . . . .none	Passenger Space Ratio	Elevators: 12
Builder: . . . . .Fincantieri (Italy)	(lower beds/all berths): 37.2/32.1	Casino (gaming tables): . . . . .Yes
Original Cost: . . . .€535 million	Crew/Passenger Ratio	Slot Machines: . . . . .Yes
Entered Service: . . . . .Apr 2010	(lower beds/all berths): 2.4/2.8	Swimming Pools (outdoors): 3
Registry: . . . . .Bermuda	Cabins (total): 1,557	Swimming Pools (indoors): 0
Length (ft/m): 951.4/290.0	Size Range (sq ft/m): 134.5–534.0/	Whirlpools: 6
Beam (ft/m): 118.1/36.0	12.5–49.6	Self-Service Launderette: . . . . .Yes
Draft (ft/m): 27.8/8.5	Cabins (outside view): 1,117	Dedicated Cinema/Seats: . . . . .No
Propulsion/Propellers: . . . . .diesel-electric	Cabins (interior/no view): 440	Library: . . . . .Yes
(42,000kW)/2	Cabins (for one person): 18	Onboard currency: . . . . .UK£

A large ship with sedate decor to suit British tastes.

OVERVIEW. *Azura* is P&O Cruises' most advanced cruise ship. It is best suited to families with children and adult couples who want to spend time together, and are seeking a big-ship environment with comfortable, unstuffy surroundings, lots of options, and a British flavor.

THE SHIP. *Azura* and sister ship *Ventura*, which debuted in 2008, are the largest cruise ships yet built specifically for British passengers and are P&O's version of Princess Cruises' Grand-class ships. With its flat stern, *Azura* looks a bit like a giant hatchback, but its side profile is softer and more balanced. Promenade walking decks are to port and starboard sides, underneath the lifeboats. You can't walk completely around; it's narrow in some places, with deck lounge chairs in your way.

There are three main pools: two on the pool deck, one at the stern. If your cabin is towards the front of the ship, it's a long walk to get to the pool at the back. Considering the number of passengers carried, there's not a lot of outdoor deck space – unless you pay extra to go into a covered, adults-only zone called The Retreat, with its faux-grass floor, private cabanas and personal waiter service. What's new is a huge open-air movie screen, the aptly-named SeaScreen, forward of the funnel by the Aqua Pool.

Inside, a three-deck atrium, with integral dance floor, is the focal point. It's a bit like a town center at sea. Four large, three-decks-high black granite archways, sourced from India, provide "gateways" to the center. It's the place to see and be seen – as are the "alternative" dining venues – and a good location to arrange to meet friends. Also in the atrium are a smallish open-plan library that isn't at all intimate or

BERLITZ'S RATINGS

	Possible	Achieved
Ship	500	426
Accommodation	200	166
Food	400	252
Service	400	287
Entertainment	100	77
Cruise	400	306

OVERALL SCORE
1,514 points out of 2,000

good for reading in, particularly when noisy events are staged in the atrium; the library includes computers for internet access; and Java Café for extra-cost coffees, teas, cakes, pastries and snacks.

Other rooms, bars and lounges include the casino, The Exchange, an urban "warehouse" bar; the Blue Bar, the ship's social hub; Brodies, a "traditional" British pub (named after Brodie McGhie Wilcox, P&O's co-founder); and the Planet Bar, set high in the ship, featuring a video wall. There are 7,000 pieces of art on board, sourced from 55 British artists; naturally, there's an art gallery so you can also buy "artwork."

The upper-deck public room layout means you can't easily go from one end of the ship to the other without first going down, along and up. Those with mobility problems will need to plan their journey and use the most appropriate of three elevator banks. Overall, the ship attracts more traditional P&O repeaters and fewer families than sister ship *Ventura*, depending on the itinerary and cruise date.

Gratuities are optional, unless you choose Freedom Dining, when they are automatically applied to your onboard account. Smoking is permitted only on cabin balconies and in designated spots on the open decks.

FAMILIES. *Azura* is really child-friendly. There are clubs for the under-2s up to 17 years, plus a rock 'n' roll school. Children between 2 and 4 will find Noddy, the popular Enid Blyton character, on board. There's a useful Night Nursery for under-5s. Youngsters can also enjoy a dedicated Wii room; Scalextric at sea with Grand Prix-style track; 3D cinema; and interactive classes. Family shore programs include aqua and "theme parks."

ACCOMMODATION. There are 27 price grades, but really just five types of accommodation: suite with balcony; family suite with balcony; outside-view twin/queen with balcony; outside-view twin/queen; interior cabin. Although there are more balconies than aboard *Ventura*, more than a third of all cabins are of the no-view variety. Some have extra third/fourth berths that fold down from the ceiling.

Most welcome are 18 single-occupancy cabins, a first for P&O Cruises. They are located in a small section on the port side, adjacent to Brodies casino and the atrium. Also new are spa cabins, with added amenities and direct access to the ship's spa, and two large suites for extended families or groups of friends.

While the suites are reasonably spacious, they really are small when compared to those of lines such as Celebrity Cruises or Norwegian Cruise Line, whose top suites are four or five times the size. Most cabins are intelligently laid out, and manage to provide a feeling of space – well, sort of.

Standard in all cabins: bed runners, 10.5 tog duvets, Slumberland 8-inch sprung mattresses, and Egyptian cotton towels (bathrobes are polyester, except in the suites). Tea/coffee making facilities (plastic and basic), and packets of UHT milk, not fresh milk, are provided. There are UK three-pin sockets plus US-style 110-volt sockets for electrical devices.

Open closets (no doors – a money saver), provide easy access, but many passengers dislike the "no trust" attached hangars that bang against the wall when the ship is "moving". Balcony cabins have wooden railings atop glass dividers, green plastic floors, a couple of small chairs and drinks table, and an outside light. Most cabin bathrooms are small, beige modular units lacking in personality, with a shower enclosure that would challenge anyone who wears clothes of size "X" or larger. The shower head is fixed, making it difficult to wash all parts of the body – there is no hand-held shower hose unless you occupy suite-grade accommodation.

Wheelchair-accessible cabins, which have a large, user-friendly shower enclosure, are mostly located in the front section of the ship, but one of the main restaurants is aft. So be prepared for lots of wheeling time, and waiting time at the elevators. Wheelchair users should note that breakfast in the fixed dining restaurants typically ends at 9.30am on sea days and 9am on port days. To take breakfast in the self-serve casual eatery, you may need to wheel across the decks containing the forward and midship pools and lots of deck chairs – not easy. Alternatively, you can order room service breakfast – typically cold items only.

There is no room service breakfast on disembarkation day, when the company want you out of your cabin by 8am.

CUISINE. P&O's marketing blurb claims that there are 10 restaurants. There aren't. There are five genuine restaurants (Peninsular, Oriental, Meridian, Sindhu, and Seventeen), the rest are bistro-style eateries or fast food joints.

The three main dining rooms, *Peninsular, Oriental* and *Meridian*, all have the same menus. Peninsular and Oriental offer fixed seating dining, with assigned tables (typical seating times: 6:30pm or 8:45pm). In the Meridian restaurant, you can dine when you want, with whomever you

want, between 6pm and 10pm – P&O calls it "Freedom Dining," although at peak times there can be a bit of a wait and it's not open for breakfast or lunch. Occasionally, special dinners are served in the main dining rooms, one of which is a Chaîne des Rôtisseurs event.

Alternative dining venues: *Sindhu* is an Indian restaurant (reservation-only, extra-charge). This is a first aboard a P&O Cruises ship and is a natural, given the line's UK passenger profile and its links with India. It is overseen by Michelin-star chef Atul Kochhar, whose specialty is British and Indian fusion cuisine. The food is cooked to order, unlike in the three main dining rooms. But the venue's design is poor, with some cold stone flooring. Table seating includes several alcove-style areas that make it impossible for waiters to serve food correctly without reaching across others at the same table. When I was aboard, it was difficult to read the menu outside the venue because colored inks are used, but can't be read in the bright lights of the passageway.

For the *Glass House*, TV wine expert Olly Smith has helped create a "Select Dining" restaurant and wine bar. The venue offers seafood and grilled items, paired with wines chosen by Smith. You can, of course, simply have just a glass of wine, without food.

The cuisine is very good in *Seventeen*, a reservations-only, extra charge, à la carte restaurant in a quiet, refined setting. It has an outdoor terrace for warm-weather areas.

Venezia is the ship's large, casual, self-serve buffet eatery/food court, open almost around the clock, with indoor-outdoor seating for thousands – well, hundreds – but the table tops are too high for most people. On the same deck, adjacent to the forward pool, are a poolside grill and pizzeria. Verona is a family-friendly self-service eatery.

In addition, 24-hour room service is available in cabins.

ENTERTAINMENT. The 800-seat Playhouse Theatre, which spans two decks and is located at the front of the ship, is an excellent venue for shows and, with two large video screens on either side of the stage; the sightlines are very good from all seats. The Manhattan Lounge, a multi-function social/entertainment venue, hosts family shows and cabaret acts, and is a late-night disco. Malabar, another night venue, has decor based on the hotels on Marine Drive, Mumbai. Cabaret, live bands and dancing are featured here. Meanwhile, the Planet Bar, a nightclub and entertainment venue, is an activities room by day and a club by night.

SPA/FITNESS. The Oasis Spa – located forward, almost atop the ship – has a gymnasium, aerobics room, beauty salon, separate male and female sauna and steam rooms (no charge), and 11 treatment rooms. An internal stairway connects to the deck below, which contains an extra-charge Thermal Suite (£15 per person, per day, or a composite price per cruise). Harding Brothers provide the spa staff and services. Treatments include special packages for couples, and the SilverSpa Generation.

● **For more extensive general information about a P&O cruise experience, see pages 149–9.**

Bahamas Celebration
★★ +

Size: ....Mid-Size Ship	Passenger Decks: 7	Cabins (wheelchair accessible): 0
Tonnage: 35,855	Total Crew: 360	Wheelchair accessibility:...................None
Lifestyle:.....................................Standard	Passengers	Cabin Current: ....220 volts
Cruise Line: ....Celebration Cruise Line	(lower beds/all berths):......... 1,030/1875	Elevators: 4
Former Names:.........*Princesse Ragnhild*	Passenger Space Ratio	Casino (gaming tables):......................Yes
Builder: ....HDW (Germany)	(lower beds/all berths):............ 34.8/19.1	Slot Machines:...................................Yes
Original Cost: ....n/a	Crew/Passenger Ratio	Swimming Pools (outdoors): 1
Entered Service: 1981/Mar 2009	(lower beds/all berths):................ 4.1/5.2	(+1 child pool)
Registry:.....................................Bahamas	Cabins (total):....................................515	Swimming Pools (indoors): 0
Length (ft/m):......................673.2/202.25	Size Range (sq ft/m): 86–239/7.9–22.2	Whirlpools: 2
Beam (ft/m):..............................87.4/26.6	Cabins (outside view):.........................331	Self-Service Launderette:...................No
Draft (ft/m): 20.0/6.1	Cabins (interior/no view):...................184	Dedicated Cinema/Seats: ....No
Propulsion/Propellers:................. diesel/	Cabins (for one person):.........................0	Library: ....No
(36,356kW/2	Cabins (with private balcony):.............. 0	Onboard currency ....US$

Good for a short getaway, but lacks finesse.

OVERVIEW. This ship operates cheap and cheerful two- and three-night getaway "party" cruises from Florida's Port of Palm Beach that masquerade as real cruises. It appeals to adult couples and singles who enjoy gambling, and fellow passengers will typically walk around with a bottle or a glass in their hands.

THE SHIP. This ship, now with a bright blue hull and sponson ducktail stern, was originally constructed as a ferry and operated in Scandinavia by Jahre Line until 1990, and then Color Line until 2008 (some Color Line signage can still be found). In 1992, it was extensively reconstructed and lengthened by the addition of a 116-ft (35.3-meter) section. Celebration Cruise Line – which isn't really a cruise "line" but a one-ship company – is owned by Celebration Cruise Holdings, once the parent company of the now defunct Imperial Majesty Cruise Line.

The ship underwent a further extensive refit and refurbishment before starting its new life as a short-cruise ship, based in the Port of Palm Beach. The ship also provides a cargo service to the Bahamas (passengers upstairs/cargo downstairs) via two stern ro-ro ramps.

Bahamas Celebration retains its bow and stern loading doors, and has an extremely unsightly exterior ducktail (sponson) skirt – the aft part is large enough to hold a small party on. Because it was built as a ferry, it has a rather boxy, slab-sided look, and the open deck space is *extremely* limited, with plastic chairs everywhere. Consequently, the Passenger Ratio is a very poor 23.6 (and that's with two per cabin), while crew to passenger ratio is the worst in the cruise industry, at 4.1.

The pool deck, with port and starboard hot tubs and twin

BERLITZ'S RATINGS

	Possible	Achieved
Ship	500	276
Accommodation	200	111
Food	400	185
Service	400	207
Entertainment	100	54
Cruise	400	202

OVERALL SCORE
1,035 points out of 2,000

Tiki bars, is pleasant, but there is simply not enough outdoor seating for the aft-positioned self-serve buffet. However, it's good to find shuffleboard courts on deck.

Inside, a glass-walled atrium spans six decks. Public rooms include a rather large casino, cutely named Wynmore, with a double-height ceiling, but most other public rooms have low ceilings. A small library and card room exist, but there's almost no time to use them on such short cruises. Many of the chairs in the lounges and bars are of the small, Scandinavian tub chair type – too cramped for many people today and with little back support. There are many support pillars in odd locations throughout the public rooms – a throwback to the ship's days as a ferry.

One neat feature is a cut-away model of the ship, adjacent to elevators on the main deck (Deck 4). Overall, the interiors have the same kind of Scandinavian feel as the Royal Caribbean Cruise Line ships from the early 1970s. You can even see the transport decks of the original design in the model, so you can compare the old with the new. Indeed, throughout the ship, there is evidence of its original life, with signs to the trailer deck, Color Line emblems and other items remaining as a tribute to the ship's days as *Princess Ragnhild*.

Perhaps the most popular room is the warm, inviting Pub 437, with its rather comfortable leather chairs and Victorian English decor and feel.

FAMILIES. As for cruising with kids, the ship has reasonably decent facilities for its size. It features Island Club Coconuts, a club for ages 4–10, while Club Wave is for 11–14-year-olds. A number of counselors keep the children busy, and a waterpark-style aft deck outside has a 180-ft waterslide in an area called "Kids of the Caribbean."

ACCOMMODATION. There are nine cabin price grades, the price depending on location and size. When the ship was built as a cold-water Baltic ferry, it contained tiny cabins built for truckers doing an overnight sailing. These still exist, and are called Oceanview Couch cabins. Upper berths have a posted weight limit of 200lbs (90kg). Note that all cabins have European-style round-pin electrical sockets, so you may need a convertor plug for anything electrical such as phone chargers, adaptors, etc.

Most cabins are small, with plain, minimalist decor that is practical. There's room under beds to store luggage, however. Bedside reading lights in most cabins are poor. The bathrooms are of the extremely compact "you first, me next" variety, with a shower, washbasin and toilet.

Six "suites" face forward and have views over the bow (there's no balcony), while four others face aft. These have more space, although there's no separation of sleeping and lounge areas, so they are not real suites – though they have larger bathrooms (with tiny bath), and more storage space.

CUISINE. There are several dining venues. The *Crystal Dining Room* is the main dining room, with reserved tables; the restaurant entrance has beautifully polished parquet wood flooring. It's a nice room, although the chairs have "sit-up-and-beg" backs without armrests. Wine is served by the waiters. The cuisine is strictly American.

For better cuisine and slightly better service, *The Cove*, located between the Crystal Dining Room and the Wynmore Casino, is an intimate, extra-charge, reservations-only venue open for dinner only, with a $25 per person cover charge. Make your reservations as soon as possible – there are so few tables.

Rio's is a self-serve, all-you-can-east Brazilian-style buffet venue, open for breakfast, lunch and dinner, and serves meat carved by Brazilian staff moving from table to table. Other items are provided in a self-serve buffet.

The *Trattoria Di Gerry* is a casual Italian-style eatery, with plain, uninspiring, bland decor, with wooden, school classroom-style chairs that don't have armrests. However, it is lively, extremely popular, and is included in the basic cruise fare, although some items cost extra.

ENTERTAINMENT. The "View" is the ship's 630-seat showlounge/nightclub and disco. Entertainment is of the ear-splitting, in-your-face variety.

SPA/FITNESS. The Fountain of Youth "spa" – it's not much of a spa – includes a "Mussel Beach" fitness room with muscle-pumping equipment.

WHERE NAUTICAL EXPRESSIONS COME FROM

If you've ever wondered where some terms or phrases came from, you have only to look to the sea, ships, and seamen.

Above board

This term for honesty originated in the days when pirates would hide most of their crews below decks, to trick an unsuspecting victim. A ship that sh6wed its crew openly on the deck, aboveboard, was obviously an honest merchantman.

All Above Board

"All above board referred to the fact that boards or planking which made up the decks are in plain view;

hence, anything that was stored above board was in plain view of everyone. Today we tend to use "going overboard" in the sense of going to far in our reaction or in some venture. "All above board" has come to be synonymous with honest dealings.

All hands on deck

Everyone should gather together to their positions and prepare for action. It is used nowadays to mean "to gather together for some task or other."

As the crow flies

British coastal vessels customarily

carried a cage of crows. These birds hate wide expanses of water and head, "as straight as the crow flies," to the nearest land when released at sea. This was useful to vessels lost in foggy coastal weather before the days of radar. The lookout perch on sailing vessels became known as the crow's nest.

Bale out

The term is typically used in the sense of getting out of some situation - particularly a financial one. However, the verb to bale out, means to remove water, and comes from the old name 'boyle' for a bucket.

Balmoral
★★★★

Size:	Mid-Size Ship	Passenger Decks:	10	Cabins (with private balcony):	121
Tonnage:	43,537	Total Crew:	471	Cabins (wheelchair accessible):	9
Lifestyle:	Standard	Passengers		Wheelchair accessibility:	Good
Cruise Line:	Fred Olsen Cruise Lines	(lower beds/all berths):	1,340/1,930	Cabin Current:	110/220 AC
Former Names:	Norwegian Crown,	Passenger Space Ratio		Elevators:	4
	Crown Odyssey	(lower beds/all berths):	31.1/31.1	Casino (gaming tables):	Yes
Builder:	Meyer Werft (Germany)	Crew/Passenger Ratio		Slot Machines:	Yes
Original Cost:	$178 million	(lower beds/all berths):	3.03/3.03	Swimming Pools (outdoors):	2
Entered Service:	Jun 1988/Jan 2008	Cabins (total):	744	Swimming Pools (indoors):	0
Registry:	The Bahamas	Size Range (sq ft/m):	153.9–613.5/	Whirlpools:	4
Length (ft/m):	715.2/218.18		14.3–57.0	Self-Service Launderette:	Yes
Beam (ft/m):	92.5/28.2	Cabins (outside view):	562	Dedicated Cinema/Seats:	No
Draft (ft/m):	23.8/7.26	Cabins (interior/no view):	182	Library:	Yes
Propulsion/Propellers: diesel (21,330kW)/2		Cabins (for one person):	91	Onboard currency	UK£

A well-designed ship with a homely ambience.

OVERVIEW. *Balmoral* is best suited to British couples and single travelers wanting destination-intensive cruising in a ship that has European quality, style and character, a sense of space, comfortable surroundings, decent facilities, realistic pricing and provides good value for money.

THE SHIP. *Balmoral,* formerly *Norwegian Crown,* is a well-designed and built ship, originally constructed for the long defunct Royal Cruise Line. Norwegian

BERLITZ'S RATINGS		
	Possible	Achieved
Ship	500	387
Accommodation	200	150
Food	400	261
Service	400	266
Entertainment	100	65
Cruise	400	273

OVERALL SCORE
1,402 points out of 2,000

Cruise Line then operated the ship for many years, before it was transferred to Orient Lines in 2000, and then back to Norwegian Cruise Line in September 2003.

Fred Olsen Cruise Lines bought the ship in 2007 and gave it a major refurbishment, including a "chop and stretch" operation involving the addition of a 99-ft (30.2-meter) mid-section. Although the company's logo includes the Norwegian flag, the ship is registered in the Bahamas.

The all-white ship has a relatively handsome, nicely balanced exterior profile, and one of its plus features is its full, walk-around teak promenade deck outdoors, although it becomes a little narrow in the forward section of the vessel. There are many nicely polished wood railings on balconies and open decks, and there is a jogging track on the upper-most deck outdoors. Atop the ship is the Observatory Lounge, with fine ocean views, central dance floor, and bar. Out on deck, there is a heated saltwater pool, but little shade (no glass dome for inclement weather).

The main public room spaces are on Lounge Deck. At the front of the ship is the Neptune Lounge, the main showlounge, with an integral bar at the back of the room; the raised stage and wood dance floor are surrounded by amphitheater-style seating in banquettes with small drinks tables. To its aft are the shops – a curved staircase connects this deck with the reception lobby on the deck below.

Next is the Braemar Lounge, alongside a lifestyle area that includes an internet center with good separation for privacy; there's also a library, and separate card room. Aft of the Braemar Lounge is the Morning Light Pub (named after the very first Fred Olsen ship, *Morning Light*). This venue is more like a lounge than a real pub, although it does have draft beers. Aft is the Palms Café, the ship's casual self-service buffet-style café.

The high lobby has a large gold sculpture in the shape of a globe of the world by the famous sculpture artist Arnaldo Pomodoro (called Microcosm, Macrocosm); it used to revolve.

Balmoral offers a wide range of itineraries, which keeps people coming back to this very comfortable ship; passengers also receive a log of each cruise to take home. Niggles include an inflexible bed layout in some cabins, and the dated decor in some older cabins.

Port taxes are included for UK passengers. Gratuities of £4 ($6) per passenger, per day, are suggested. The drinks prices are very reasonable, but laundry/dry-cleaning prices are quite high. The mostly Filipino crew are warm and friendly, and should help make your cruise enjoyable.

ACCOMMODATION. There are 21 price categories; typically, the higher the deck, the higher the price. Most cabins are of the same size and layout, have blond wood cabinetry and accents, an abundance of mirrors, and closet and drawer space, and are very well equipped. All accommodation grades have a color TV set, a hairdryer, music console (plus a button that can be used to turn announcements on or off), personal safe, and private bathroom with shower (many upper-grade cabins have a good-sized tub).

All towels are 100% cotton, although they could be larger; soap, shampoo, conditioner, body lotion, shower cap and sewing kit are provided. Duvets (single) are standard, blankets and bed linen are available on request, as are double-bed size duvets. On-demand movies are £2.95 from the in-cabin Infotainment System.

The cabin soundproofing is generally good. Some cabins have interconnecting doors, so that they can make a two-room suite – good for families with children.

The largest accommodations are the suites on Highland Deck 10. They are quite spacious units, and provide a sleeping area and separate living room, including some nicely finished wood cabinetry and a large amount of closet and drawer space, together with a large, white marble-clad bathroom with a full-size tub and integral shower. There is a large private balcony, although some balconies can be overlooked from the deck above.

There are nine wheelchair-accessible cabins; these provide plenty of space to maneuver, and all include a bathroom with roll-in shower. But wheelchair accessibility in some ports on the many itineraries operated by this ship – particularly in Europe – may prove quite frustrating and wheelchair-accessible transportation may be limited.

Cabins in the new mid-section have attractive, contemporary decor that is light and airy. Some of those on the upper decks (Deck 8, 9) have bathrooms with a vertical window with a direct view from the large shower enclosure through the sleeping space to the outside, providing an enhanced feeling of spaciousness. Bathrooms have shower enclosures rather than tub/shower combinations (some have two washbasins), and enough storage space for toiletries.

CUISINE. The *Ballindalloch Restaurant*, in the aft third section of the ship, is the main dining room. It has ocean-view windows on port and starboard sides, and operates two seatings. It has comfortable seating at tables for two, four, six or eight. However, the waiter stations are exposed and can be extremely noisy; indeed, the noise level in this main restaurant is high, and trying to hold a conversation can be frustrating.

Two more intimate dining spots: *Avon Restaurant* and *Spey Restaurant*, both named after rivers, are located aft on Highland Deck 10 – the deck that contains the higher-priced suites. The floor-to-ceiling windows provide lots of light. The decor is contemporary and minimalist, and the noise level is low, which makes for comfortable conversation. However, these venues also operate two seatings.

The 70-seat *Palms Café* is an alternative, more intimate venue for informal self-serve meals.

All venues have open seating for breakfast and lunch.

ENTERTAINMENT. The Neptune Lounge is the setting for all entertainment shows, cabaret acts, lectures, and some social functions. It is a single level room with tiered seating levels. Sightlines are generally good, but could be better.

Revue-style production shows are staged by a resident troupe of singers and dancers, and there are cabaret acts. The quality of the shows, however, is average. Cabaret acts – typically singers, magicians, ventriloquists, comedy jugglers, and comedians – perform individually or as part of the revues.

A piece of trivia for ship buffs: a bar at the back of the showlounge was originally named Theo's bar after one of the former Royal Cruise Line's most popular bartenders.

SPA/FITNESS. There is a reasonably decent – but not large enough – indoor wellness center, which includes a fitness room with ocean views, plenty of muscle-pumping equipment, and several beauty treatment rooms. The wellness facilities and treatment staff are provided by The Onboard Spa Company.

LATITUDE AND LONGITUDE

Latitude signifies the distance north or south of the equator, while **longitude** signifies distance east or west of the 0 degree at Greenwich Observatory in London ("where time begins"). Both are recorded in degrees, minutes, and seconds. At the equator, one minute of longitude is equal to one nautical mile, but as the meridians converge after leaving the equator and meeting at the poles, the size of a degree becomes smaller. It was in 1714 that an Act of Parliament established a Board of Commissioners for the Discovery of Longitude at Sea. A prize of £20,000, then a huge sum, was set. The English clockmaker John Harrison (1693–1776) won it for his highly accurate chronometer. Indeed, none other than Captain Cook used a Harrison-designed chronometer on one of his voyages to the Pacific in 1775.

Black Watch
★★★ +

Size: Mid-Size Ship	Passenger Decks: .8	Cabins (with private balcony): .43
Tonnage: .28,613	Total Crew: .350	Cabins (wheelchair accessible): .4
Lifestyle: Standard	Passengers	Wheelchair accessibility: Fair
Cruise Line: .Fred Olsen Cruise Lines	(lower beds/all berths): .804/868	Cabin Current: .110 and 220 volts
Former Names: *Star Odyssey,*	Passenger Space Ratio	Elevators: .4
Westward, Royal Viking Star	(lower beds/all berths): .35.5/32.9	Casino (gaming tables): Yes
Builder: .Wartsila (Finland)	Crew/Passenger Ratio	Slot Machines: Yes
Original Cost: .$22.5 million	(lower beds/all berths): .2.2/2.4	Swimming Pools (outdoors): .2
Entered Service: .June 1972/Nov 1996	Cabins (total): .421	Swimming Pools (indoors): .0
Registry: .The Bahamas	Size Range (sq ft/m): .135.6–819.1/	Whirlpools: .3
Length (ft/m): .674.1/205.47	12.6–76.1	Self-Service Launderette: Yes
Beam (ft/m): .82.6/25.20	Cabins (outside view): .383	Dedicated Cinema/Seats: Yes/156
Draft (ft/m): .24.7/7.55	Cabins (interior/no view): .48	Library: Yes
Propulsion/Propellers: diesel (13,400kW)/2	Cabins (for one person): .38	Onboard currency .UK£

This older ship provides good-value cruises.

OVERVIEW. *Black Watch* is a comfortable but not luxurious ship best suited to the older UK traveler who enjoys seeking out the world's duty-free shops and wants a British cruise environment, wearing relatively formal attire. Cruises are well organized, with interesting itineraries and free shuttle buses in many ports of call.

THE SHIP. The name is taken from the famous Scottish Black Watch regiment, although the ship itself is all-white. There is a good amount of open deck and sunbathing space, and a good health and fitness area high atop the ship, as well as a wide wrap-around teakwood promenade deck with wind-breaker on the aft part of the deck.

The interior decor is quiet and restful, with wide stairways and foyers, soft lighting and no glitz anywhere, though many passengers find the artwork a little drab – it is, in reality, rather more Scandinavian eclectic than anything. In general, good materials, fabrics (including the use of the Black Watch tartan) and soft furnishings give a pleasant ambience and comfortable feeling to the public rooms. Most of these are quite spacious, with high, indented ceilings, and most (including the main dining room) are located on one deck in a user-friendly horizontal layout.

An observation lounge, The Observatory, high atop the ship, displays nautical memorabilia and has commanding views. Draft beers are available in all bars. The whole ship indoors is a smoke-free zone.

There is a good cinema (few ships today have a dedicated cinema) with a steeply tiered floor, and a pleasant library with an adjacent room containing two computer terminals for internet access.

BERLITZ'S RATINGS	Possible	Achieved
Ship	500	346
Accommodation	200	141
Food	400	248
Service	400	273
Entertainment	100	63
Cruise	400	268
OVERALL SCORE		
1,339 points out of 2,000		

A popular meeting place is the Braemar Room, a large lounge close to the restaurant; it has a self-help beverage corner for coffees and teas (open 24 hours a day, although it becomes overly busy during afternoon tea time), comfortable chairs, and large ocean-view windows along one side. The Library and Card Room is a very pleasant facility. A self-serve launderette, useful on the longer cruises, has four washing machines, five dryers, and a couple of irons in a large user-friendly room.

Although it is being well maintained, do remember that this ship is now 40 years old, which means that little problems such as gurgling plumbing, creaking joints, and other idiosyncrasies can occur, and air conditioning is not be all that it should be in some cabins. But the ship still looks good, and is very comfortable. The company suggests gratuities of £4 per passenger per day.

Black Watch offers a moderate standard of food and service from a friendly, mostly Filipino staff that provides decent, though not faultless, service. There is ample space per passenger, even when the ship is full. Port taxes are included for UK passengers.

The National Express bus operator works in conjunction with Fred Olsen Cruise Lines to provide a dedicated Cruiselink service via London's Victoria Coach Station to the UK departure ports of Dover or Southampton.

Passenger niggles include: noticeable cutbacks in food variety and quality; an increase in the use of paper napkins, packets of butter, margarine and preserves; the lack of choice of sugar; very poor coffee; long lines at the cramped buffet; poor wine service; and too few staff for the increased passenger numbers following the addition of more cabins.

ACCOMMODATION. There are 18 price categories of cabins (plus one for the owner's suite, whose price is not listed in the brochure). These include four grades of cabin, spread around most of the decks, for solo travelers. The wide range of cabins provides something for everyone, from spacious suites with separate bedrooms, to small, no-view cabins. While most cabins are for two people, some can accommodate a third, fourth, or even a fifth person.

In all grades, duvets are provided, and the decently sized bathroom towels are 100% cotton. A hairdryer and a package of Gilchrist & Soames toiletries is supplied to all passengers. Occupants of suite grades also get a cotton bathrobe and cold canapés each evening, plus priority seating in the dining rooms).

The suites and cabins on Decks 7, 8, and 9 are quiet units. A number of cabins in the aft section of Decks 3, 4, and 5 can prove to be uncomfortable, with noise from throbbing engines and generator units a major distraction, particularly in the cabins adjacent to the engine casing. The room service menu is quite limited and could be improved. **Outside-view and Interior Cabins:** Spread across Decks 3, 4, 5, 7, and 8, all cabins are quite well equipped, and there is plenty of good (illuminated) closet, drawer and storage space. Some bathrooms have awkward access, and insulation between some of the lower grade cabins could be better. The bathrooms are of a decent size. Some cabins have a small bathtub, although many have only a shower enclosure.

Deluxe/Bridge/Junior Suites: These suites, on Decks 7 and 8, have a large sleeping area and lounge area with ocean-view picture windows and refrigerator, plenty of hooks for hanging bathrobes, outerwear and luggage; and a bathroom with tub and shower (cabin 8019 is the exception, with a shower instead of a bathtub).

Marquee Suites: These suites have a large sleeping area and lounge area with bigger ocean-view picture windows and a refrigerator, more hooks for hanging bathrobes, outerwear and luggage; and a bathroom with tub and shower.

Premier Suites: Each of these nine suites is named after a place: Amalfi (9006), Lindos (9002), Nice (9004), each measuring 547.7 sq. ft/50.8 sq. meters; Seville (9001), Singapore (9003), Carmel (9005), Bergen (9007), Waterford (9009), each measuring 341.7 sq ft/31.7 sq. meters; and Windsor (9008), measuring 574.8 sq. ft/53.4 sq. meters. They have a separate bedroom with ample closet and other storage space, a lounge with large windows (with large television and VCR, refrigerator and mini-bar), and bathroom with full-size tub and shower, and separate toilet.

Owner's Suite: This measures 819.1 sq. ft/76.1 sq. meters, including a large balcony. It consists of a foyer leading into a lounge, with sofa, table and chairs, audio center (TV set, DVD player), refrigerator and mini-bar. A separate bedroom has a double bed, and ample closet and drawer space. A second bedroom has two bunk beds – good for families with children. The bathroom is large and has a full-size tub, separate shower enclosure, toilet, and two washbasins. The balcony has space enough for a table and six chairs, plus a couple of sunloungers. It is located just aft of the navigation bridge on the starboard side of the ship.

CUISINE. The *Glentanar Dining Room* has a high ceiling, a white sail-like focal point at its center, and ample space at each table. The chairs have armrests, and are quite comfortable. The Orchid Room is a smaller offshoot of the dining room, which can be reserved for more intimate, quieter dining. While breakfast and lunch are typically in an open-seating arrangement, there are two seatings for dinner. Passengers help themselves from two cold food display counters during breakfast and lunch.

The *Garden Café* is a small, more casual dining spot with a light, breezy decor reminiscent of a garden conservatory. It sometimes has themed dinners, such as French, Indian, or Thai. There is a self-help salad bar and hot food display. The venue is also the place for late-night snacks.

Fred Olsen Cruise Lines has above-average cuisine that is attractively presented, with a good range of fish, seafood, meat and chicken dishes, and has a good selection of cheeses as well as vegetarian options. The food is generally of good quality, with a decent selection of main-course items to suit most British tastes. Breakfast buffets tend to be quite repetitive, although they appear to satisfy most.

There is a reasonably decent range of wines, at really moderate prices, but few of the wine stewards have much knowledge of wines.

Coffee and tea are always available in the Braemar Room, adjacent to, and aft of, the Glentanar Restaurant.

ENTERTAINMENT. The Neptune Lounge, the ship's showlounge, seats about 400, although some sightlines are obstructed by pillars. The entertainment mainly consists of small-scale production shows presented by a small team of resident singers/dancers, and cabaret acts. Standards are quite poor, and the cast self-congratulatory.

There are also cabaret acts. To be fair, passengers who cruise aboard this ship are not especially looking for first-rate entertainment, but rather something to fill the time after dinner.

There is plenty of live music for dancing and listening in several lounges, and there are good British sing-alongs.

SPA/FITNESS. The spa/fitness facilities are located at the top and front of the ship – inaccessible for wheelchair users. There is a combined gymnasium/aerobics room, while a door provides access to steam rooms, saunas, and changing rooms. Sample treatment prices: Elemis Aromapure facial: £29; Well-being massage (50 minutes): £35; Personal Training Session (60 minutes): £20. Steiner's staff will try to sell their own-brand Elemis beauty products. Some fitness classes are free, while some, such as yoga and kick-boxing, cost extra. It's prudent to make appointments as early as possible. Sports facilities include a large paddle tennis court, golf practice nets, shuffleboard, and ring toss.

Bleu de France
★★★ +

Size: . . . . .Mid-Size Ship	Total Crew: .406	Wheelchair accessibility: . . . . .Good
Tonnage: 37,301	Passengers	Cabin Current: . . . . . . .110 and 220 volts
Lifestyle: . . . . .Standard	(lower beds/all berths): 752/1,158	Elevators: 4
Cruise Line: . . .CDF Croisières de France	Passenger Space Ratio	Casino (gaming tables): . . . . .Yes
Former Names: *Holiday Dream, SuperStar*	(lower beds/all berths): 49.6/32.2	Slot Machines: . . . . .Yes
Aries, SuperStar Europe, Europa	Crew/Passenger Ratio	Swimming Pools (outdoors): 2
Builder: . . . . . .Bremer Vulkan (Germany)	(lower beds/all berths): 1.8/2.8	(1 glass dome)
Original Cost: . . . .$120 million	Cabins (total): 374	Swimming Pools (indoors): 1 (fresh water)
Entered Service: . . . . Jan 1982/Nov 2009	Size Range (sq ft/m): 161.4–678.1/	Whirlpools: 3
Registry: . . . . .The Bahamas	15.0–63.0	Self-Service Launderette: . . . . .Yes
Length (ft/m): 654.9/199.63	Cabins (outside view): 309	Dedicated Cinema/Seats: . . . . .No
Beam (ft/m): 93.8/28.60	Cabins (interior/no view): 65	Library: . . . . .Yes
Draft (ft/m): 27.6/8.42	Cabins (for one person): 0	Onboard currency: . . . . .Euros
Propulsion/Propellers: diesel(21,270 kW)/2	Cabins (with private balcony): 6	
Passenger Decks: 10	Cabins (wheelchair accessible): 2	

A French ship that's soon to change nationality.

OVERVIEW. The ship suits French-speaking couples, singles, and families with children who want a first cruise experience in a traditional – but not new – ship, with plenty of public rooms and a lively atmosphere, and food that is quantity rather than quality. From spring 2012, the ship will have a new owner, the UK-based Saga Cruises.

THE SHIP. *Bleu de France* sounds more like a cheese than a ship. As predecessor to Hapag-Lloyd's current *Europa*, it was once the flagship of Germany's cruise industry. Originally, the ship was to have twin side-by-side funnels, but the idea was dropped in favour of a single funnel. There is a very decent amount of outdoor deck and sunbathing space, including a solarium.

Facilities include a small casino, library/internet center, karaoke room, and children's play room. The ship, which has an all drinks-inclusive policy, provides an informal, relaxed, yet quite elegant setting, with a casual dress code. Drinks and table wines are included in the price. Children are split into different age groups.

ACCOMMODATION. There is a wide range of suites and cabins, in 15 price grades. All of the original cabins are quite spacious, and all have illuminated closets, dark wood cabinetry with rounded edges, full-length mirrors, color TV/DVD player, mini-bar/refrigerator, personal safe, hairdryer, and good cabin insulation. Most cabins can accommodate one or two additional persons.

Most bathrooms have deep tubs (cabins without bathtub have a large shower enclosure), a three-head shower

BERLITZ'S RATINGS		
	Possible	Achieved
Ship	500	382
Accommodation	200	143
Food	400	256
Service	400	284
Entertainment	100	64
Cruise	400	267

OVERALL SCORE
1,396 points out of 2,000

unit, two deep washbasins (not all cabins), large toiletries cabinet and handsome toiletries. The largest living spaces are suites added during a 1999 refit, but they have lifeboat-obstructed views. Six other suites have private balconies. There is a separate bedroom with either queen-size or twin beds, illuminated closets, and vanity desk.

CUISINE. *Le Flamboyant*, the main restaurant, has ocean-view windows on two sides and two seatings for meals. *Le Panorama* self-serve buffet, with excellent ocean views, is for casual meals. The *Olive Bistro* serves light Mediterranean fare. There's also *Millesime* (for cigars and quality spirits), and the *Le Café Crème Bar*.

ENTERTAINMENT. The sightlines in the elegant main lounge (Le Grand Salon) are quite poor from many seats. The shows consist of a troupe of showgirl dancers, together with a host of cabaret acts, including singers, magicians, and comedians, among others, and are very much geared to the family audience that this ship carries. There is also plenty of live music for listening or dancing to in various bars and lounges, and there is the inevitable discotheque.

SPA/FITNESS. The 800-sq. meter (8,611 sq. ft) Aqua-Marine Spa is an extremely good indoor wellness center, and is located together with a large indoor swimming pool.

Adjacent facilities include three saunas (Finnish, hammam, herbal), fitness/exercise centre, hydrotherapy bath, 12 treatment rooms, and beauty salon. A solarium is located outdoors atop the ship.

Boudicca
★★★ +

Size:	Mid-Size Ship
Tonnage:	28,388
Lifestyle:	Standard
Cruise Line:	Fred Olsen Cruise Lines
Former Names:	Grand Latino, SuperStar Capricorn, Hyundai Keumgang, SuperStar Capricorn, Golden Princess, Sunward, Birka Queen, Sunward, Royal Viking Sky
Builder:	Wartsila (Finland)
Original Cost:	$22.5 million
Entered Service:	June 1973/Feb 2006
Registry:	The Bahamas
Length (ft/m):	674.1/205.47
Beam (ft/m):	82.6/25.20
Draft (ft/m):	24.7/7.55

Propulsion/Propellers:	diesel 13,400kW)/2 (CP)
Passenger Decks:	8
Total Crew:	320
Passengers (lower beds/all berths):	839/900
Passenger Space Ratio (lower beds/all berths):	33.8/31.5
Crew/Passenger Ratio (lower beds/all berths):	2.3/2.5
Cabins (total):	437
Size Range (sq ft/m):	135.6–579.1/12.6–53.8
Cabins (outside view):	363
Cabins (interior/no view):	39
Cabins (for one person):	35
Cabins (with private balcony):	59

Cabins (wheelchair accessible):	4
Wheelchair accessibility:	Fair
Cabin Current:	110 and 220 volts
Elevators:	5
Casino (gaming tables):	Yes
Slot Machines:	Yes
Swimming Pools (outdoors):	2
Swimming Pools (indoors):	0
Whirlpools:	2
Self-Service Launderette:	Yes
Dedicated Cinema/Seats:	No
Library:	Yes
Onboard currency	UK£

An older-style ship with a traditional British ambience.

OVERVIEW. The ship appeals to British couples and single travelers seeking a sense of space, comfortable surroundings, decent facilities, realistic pricing and good value for money, with British food and entertainment. Passengers with tattoos would not be welcomed.

THE SHIP. Acquired by Fred Olsen Cruise Lines in 2005, this well-proportioned ship, originally built for long-distance cruising for the now-defunct Royal Viking Line (it was built for one of the three original shipping partners who formed the line – Bergenske Dampskibsselskab), has a sharply raked bow and a sleek appearance. The ship was "stretched" in 1982 with the addition of a 27.7-meter (91-ft) mid section.

The outer styling is quite handsome for an early 1970s-built vessel. The single funnel bears the company's starfish logo, and balances the profile of this attractive (now contemporary-classic) ship. The name *Boudicca* (pronounced Boodicker) comes from the Queen of the Iceni tribe that occupied England's East Anglia; she led a dramatic revolt against the Romans in AD61, and her body is supposedly buried under Platform 10 of London's King's Cross Station.

The ship has a good amount of open deck and sunbathing space; in fact, there is plenty of space everywhere and little sense of crowding because the ship absorbs passengers well. There are port and starboard walking teak promenade decks outdoors, although they no longer wrap around the front of the ship. Before the ship began cruising as *Boudicca*, it was given an extensive refit, which included creating a number of cabins for solo travelers, and re-engining.

The interior decor is restful, with a mix of English and

BERLITZ'S RATINGS		
	Possible	Achieved
Ship	500	342
Accommodation	200	154
Food	400	258
Service	400	274
Entertainment	100	65
Cruise	400	264

OVERALL SCORE
1,357 points out of 2,000

Norwegian styles (particularly the artwork) with wide stairways and foyers, good passenger flow, soft lighting and no glitz. In general, good materials, fabrics and soft furnishings add to a pleasant ambience and comfortable feeling experienced throughout the public rooms, most of which are quite spacious and have high, indented ceilings.

There are lots of (small) public rooms, bars and lounges, unlike the newer (larger) ships built today, including a delightful observation lounge, a small casino, card room, large library, and the Secret Garden Lounge (with its integral café).

Boudicca is an extremely comfortable ship in which to cruise, with a moderate standard of food and service from a friendly, mostly Filipino staff, featuring extremely good value for money cruises in a relaxed environment that provides passengers with many of the comforts of home.

Although the ship has benefited from an extensive refit and refurbishment, do remember that it'll soon be 40 years old, which means that little problems such as gurgling plumbing, creaking joints, and other idiosyncrasies can occur, and air conditioning may not be all that it should be. Port taxes are included for UK passengers. Gratuities of £4 ($6) per passenger, per day, are suggested.

Passenger niggles include: noticeable cutbacks in food variety and quality, an increased use of paper napkins, packets of butter, margarine and preserves, the lack of choice of sugar, very poor coffee, long lines at the cramped buffet, and too few wine waiters. Other gripes: not enough staff for the increased passenger numbers after more cabin additions, and declining service standards.

For the ship's mainly British passengers, the National Express bus operator works in conjunction with Fred Olsen Cruise Lines to provide a dedicated Cruiselink service via London's Victoria Coach Station to the UK departure ports of Dover or Southampton.

ACCOMMODATION. There is something for every taste and wallet, from spacious family suites to small interior (no view) cabins. While most cabins are for two persons, some can accommodate a third, fourth, or even a fifth person. There are 20 price categories of cabins (plus one for the owner's suite, whose price is not listed in the brochure), including four grades of cabin for those traveling solo (these are spread across most of the cabin decks, and not just the lower decks, as is the case with some cruise lines), and three of these have a private balcony. While most cabins have bathtubs, some lower grades have only a shower enclosure.

Some of the quietest cabins are those located just under the navigation bridge, on Lido Deck, as well as those suites and cabins on Bridge Deck. In the refit, a vacuum toilet system was fitted.

In all grades, duvets are provided, the bathroom towels are 100% cotton and are quite large, and a hairdryer is provided. A package of Gilchrist & Soames personal toiletry items (bath gel, shampoo/conditioner, sewing kit, shower cap) is supplied to all passengers. Occupants of suite grades also get a cotton bathrobe and cold canapés each evening, as well as priority seating in the dining rooms.

The room service menu is quite limited and could be improved, although there is an abundance of food available at most times of the day. All cabins have had a facelift. Only a few suites have private balconies.

Outside-view/Inside (No View) Cabins: These are quite well equipped, and there is plenty of good (illuminated) closet, drawer and storage space, but insulation between some of the lower grade cabins could be better. While most cabin bathrooms are of a decent size, some have awkward access. Some have a small tub, although many have only a shower enclosure.

Deluxe/Bridge/Junior Suites: These suites, on Decks 7 and 8, have a large sleeping area and lounge area with ocean-view picture windows and refrigerator, plenty of hooks for hanging bathrobes, outerwear and luggage; and a bathroom with bathtub and shower.

Marquee Suites: These suites have a large sleeping area and lounge area with bigger ocean view picture windows and a refrigerator, more hooks for hanging bathrobes, outerwear and luggage; and a bathroom with tub and shower.

Premier Suites: Anyone wanting the most space should consider one of these suites (each is named after a place). These have a separate bedroom with ample closet and other storage space, a lounge with large windows (with large television/video player, refrigerator/mini-bar), and bathroom with full-size tub and shower, and a separate toilet.

CUISINE. The main dining room is divided into three venues: *Heligan, Tintagel,* and *Four Seasons*; each has a high ceiling, and ample space at each table. Although the decor is reserved, the chairs, which have armrests, are comfortable. Window-side tables for two are the most sought after, naturally.

Breakfast is typically in an open-seating arrangement, while there are two seatings for lunch and dinner. Cold food display counters are provided for passengers to help themselves to breakfast and lunch items.

Fred Olsen Cruise Lines has above-average cuisine that is attractively presented and includes a good range of fish, seafood, meat and chicken dishes, as well as vegetarian options, and a wide selection of cheeses, to suit most British tastes. You'll also find a number of popular British pub standards such as bangers and mash, toad in the hole, and spotted dick. Breakfast buffets tend to be a little repetitive, although they appear to satisfy most passengers. There is a reasonably decent range of wines, at unpretentious prices.

Coffee and tea are available in the *Secret Garden Café* (part of the Secret Garden Lounge), just aft of the main dining venues – but, sadly, not around-the-clock.

Casual self-serve deck buffets are provided outdoors at the *Poolside Café*, while fast-food items can be obtained from the *Marquee Bar* (also outdoors).

ENTERTAINMENT. The Neptune Lounge is the venue for shows, cabaret acts, and lectures. It is a large room that seats about 400, although some pillars obstruct sightlines from some seats. The entertainment consists of small-scale production shows presented by a small team of resident singers/dancers, and cabaret acts (these typically rotate around many cruise ships of the same standard).

There is plenty of live music for social dancing (many of the musicians are Filipino) and listening in several lounges, and good British sing-alongs are a feature on each cruise.

SPA/FITNESS. A decent amount of (windowless) space is given to providing health and fitness facilities on Atlantic Deck. However, they are split in three separate areas. Forward are the sauna/steam rooms; the center section contains a gymnasium/aerobics room, changing rooms; while the aft section houses a beauty salon.

Some fitness classes are free, while some, such as yoga and kick-boxing, cost extra.

It's best to make appointments as early as possible as treatment time slots go quickly. Sports facilities include a large paddle tennis court, golf practice nets, shuffleboard, and ring toss.

Braemar
★★★ +

Size:	Mid-Size Ship	Passenger Decks:	7	Cabins (wheelchair accessible):	4
Tonnage:	24,344	Total Crew:	371	Wheelchair accessibility:	Fair
Lifestyle:	Standard	Passengers		Cabin Current:	110 and 220 volts
Cruise Line:	Fred Olsen Cruise Lines	(lower beds/all berths):	930/930	Elevators:	5
Former Names:	*Crown Dynasty,*	Passenger Space Ratio		Casino (gaming tables):	Yes
	Norwegian Dynasty, Crown Majesty,	(lower beds/all berths):	25.9/25.9	Slot Machines:	Yes
	Cunard Dynasty, Crown Dynasty	Crew/Passenger Ratio		Swimming Pools (outdoors):	2
Builder:	Union Navale de Levante (Spain)	(lower beds/all berths):	2.3/2.3	Swimming Pools (indoors):	0
Original Cost:	$100 million	Cabins (total):	484	Whirlpools:	2
Entered Service:	July 1993/Aug 2001	Size Range (sq ft/m):	139.9–349.8/	Self-Service Launderette:	Yes
Registry:	The Bahamas		13.0–32.5	Dedicated Cinema/Seats:	No
Length (ft/m):	639.7/195.01	Cabins (outside view):	373	Library:	Yes
Beam (ft/m):	73.8/22.50	Cabins (interior/no view):	110	Onboard currency	UK£
Draft (ft/m):	17.7/5.40	Cabins (for one person):	38		
Propulsion/Propellers: diesel (13,200kW)/2		Cabins (with private balcony):	70		

A sporty ship and decor suited to casual leisure cruising.

OVERVIEW. This handsome-looking mid-size ship suits middle-aged and older UK and Scandinavian passengers who want to cruise in a casual, unstuffy environment, in a ship with British food and entertainment. It's a refreshing change for those who don't enjoy larger, warehouse-size ships. But it does roll somewhat, probably because of its shallow draft design, meant for warm-weather cruise areas.

THE SHIP. *Braemar* has attractive exterior styling, and a lot of glass space. There is a good amount of open deck and sunbathing space for its size, and this includes two outdoors bars – one aft and one midships adjacent to the two swimming pools and paddling pool – that have Boddington's and Stella Artois keg beers. Four open decks, located aft of the funnel, provide good, quiet places to sit and read.

The teak promenade deck is a complete walk-around deck, wrapping around Lounge Deck. Passengers can go right to the ship's bow – good for photographs. Faux teak floor covering is used on the pool deck, which has two pools; it looks tacky, but works well in the heat of the Caribbean, where the ship was meant to spend much of its time.

Inside, there is a pleasant five-deck-high, glass-walled atrium on the starboard side. Off-center stairways add a sense of spaciousness to a clever interior design that surrounds passengers with light. The interior decor in public spaces is warm and inviting, with contemporary, but not brash, art-deco color combinations. The artwork is quite colorful and pleasant, in the Nordic manner.

The Morning Light Club is an open-plan lounge, with its own bar, split by a walkway that leads to the showlounge (forward), the library/card room/internet center and the boutique (midships). Despite being open, it has cozy seating areas and is very comfortable, with a tartan carpet. A model of the first Fred Olsen ship named *Braemar* (4,775 gross tonnage) is displayed in the center of the room, as is a large carved wood plaque bearing the name Braemar Castle in Scotland.

The mostly Filipino staff are friendly and attentive, and the hospitality factor is good. This is noticeable in the restaurant and other food service areas. The company has come a long way from its humble beginnings, and now offers extremely good value for money cruises in a relaxed, welcoming environment that provides passengers with many of the comforts of home. The dress code is casual.

In 2008, a 102-ft (31-meter) mid-section extension was added, providing additional cabins and balcony "suites." Facilities added or changed include a second swimming pool and more sunbathing space, an observatory lounge, a new restaurant and a pub-style bar.

There can be a bit of a wait for shore tenders, and for the few elevators aboard this ship. British passengers should note that no suites or cabins have bathtubs.

Passenger niggles include: lines at the cramped self-service buffet; poor wine service (not enough wine waiters); an increase in the use of paper napkins, packets of butter, margarine and preserves; the lack of choice of sugar; weak coffee; and badly worn bathroom fittings. There is a self-service launderette (£2 for wash and dry) – and the company may charge for shuttle buses in some ports of call.

BERLITZ'S RATINGS

	Possible	Achieved
Ship	500	356
Accommodation	200	133
Food	400	235
Service	400	254
Entertainment	100	62
Cruise	400	275

OVERALL SCORE
1,315 points out of 2,000

ACCOMMODATION. There are 16 cabin price categories; the higher the deck, the higher the price. All grades have a small television and hairdryer (some are awkward to retract from their wall-mount holders), plus European-style duvets. The large bathroom towels are 100% cotton (bathrobes are available upon request in suite-grade cabins). Gilchrist & Soames toiletry items are provided. There is no separate audio system in the cabin, but music can be obtained from one of the TV channels, although you'll have to leave the picture on. Suites, however, do have a CD music system.

Standard (Outside-view)/Inside Cabins: Almost all are the same size – which is really quite small – although they are nicely furnished. Most have broad picture windows, but some deluxe cabins on Deck 6 and Deck 7 have lifeboat-obstructed views. They are practical and comfortable, with blond wood-trimmed accents and multi-colored soft furnishings, but there is very little drawer space, and hanging space is extremely limited (the ship was purpose-built originally for seven-day cruises). So take only the clothing you think necessary. Each outside-view cabin on Deck 4 has a large picture window, while those on the lower Decks 2 and 3 have a porthole. They are quite well-equipped, with a small vanity desk unit, minimal drawer space, curtained windows, and personal safe (hard to reach).

Each cabin has a private bathroom (of the "me first, you next" variety) with a tiled floor, small shower enclosure, toiletries cupboard, washbasin, and low-height toilet of the barking dog vacuum variety. There is some under-basin storage space, and an electrical socket for shavers.

When Fred Olsen Cruise Lines bought the ship, it converted a number of cabins from double-occupancy units to cabins for the single traveler.

Some cabins do suffer from inadequate soundproofing; passengers in cabins on Deck 4 in particular are disturbed by anyone running or jogging on the promenade deck above. Cabins on the lowest deck (Deck 2) in the ship's center are subject to noise from the adjacent engine room. **Suites:** On Deck 7, suites have city names such as Rio de Janeiro and Toronto. While they are not large, the suites do have a sleeping area that can be curtained off from the living area. All suites are decorated in individual styles befitting their name, and each has its own small CD player/music system.

CUISINE. The *Thistle Restaurant* is a pleasing and attractive venue, with large ocean-view windows on three sides. The focal point is a large oil painting on a wall behind the buffet food display counter. However, space is tight, and tables are extremely close together, making proper service difficult. There are tables for two, four, six or eight; the Porsgrund china has the familiar Venus pattern. The ambience, however, is warm, and service is attentive.

There are two seatings for dinner, and an open seating for breakfast and lunch. The menu is varied. Salad items are quite poor and very basic, with little variety, although there is a decent choice of dessert items. For breakfast and lunch the dual food counters are functional, but the layout is not ideal and at peak times they create much congestion. The *Grampian Restaurant* is an additional dining venue, located aft at the top of the ship, with some fine aft views.

Casual breakfasts and luncheons can also be taken in the self-service buffet located in the *Palms Café*, although these tend to be repetitive and poorly supervised, with dishes not replaced or refreshed properly. There is indoor and outdoor seating. Although it is the casual dining spot, tablecloths are provided. The indoor flooring is wood, which makes it rather a noisy room, and some tables adjacent to the galley entrance are to be avoided at all costs.

Out on the pool deck, there is a barbecue grill for casual eating – welcome when the ship is in warm-weather areas.

ENTERTAINMENT. The Neptune Showlounge sits longitudinally along one side of the ship, with amphitheater-style seating in several tiers, but its layout is less than ideal for either shows or cocktail parties. There is often congestion between first- and second-seating passengers at the entrance.

Unfortunately, 15 pillars obstruct sightlines to the stage, and the banquet and individual tub chair seating arrangement is quite poor.

The entertainment mainly consists of small-scale production shows and mini-musicals presented by a small troupe of resident singers/dancers, and cabaret acts. They are rather amateurish, but enjoyable. Apart from the production shows, there are the typical cabaret acts often found on the cruise ship circuit.

SPA/FITNESS. The health spa facilities are limited. It includes a combined gymnasium/aerobics room, and a separate room for women and men, with sauna, steam room and small changing area. Spa Rituals treatments are provided by Steiner. Some fitness classes are free; others, such as yoga and kick-boxing, cost extra.

Bremen
★★★★ +

Size: ....Boutique Ship	Total Crew: 94	Wheelchair accessibility: ....None
Tonnage: 6,752	Passengers	Cabin Current: ....110 and 220 volts
Lifestyle: ....Premium	(lower beds/all berths): 164/184	Elevators: 2
Cruise Line:Hapag-Lloyd Expedition Cruises	Passenger Space Ratio	Casino (gaming tables): ....No
Former Names: ....*Frontier Spirit*	(lower beds/all berths): 41.1/36.6	Slot Machines: ....No
Builder: Mitsubishi Heavy Industries (Japan)	Crew/Passenger Ratio	Swimming Pools (outdoors): 1
Original Cost: ....$42 million	(lower beds/all berths): 1.7/1.9	Swimming Pools (indoors): 0
Entered Service: .....Nov 1990/Nov 1993	Cabins (total): 82	Whirlpools: 0
Registry: ....The Bahamas	Size Range (sq ft/m): 174.3–322.9/16.2–30.0	Self-Service Launderette: ....No
Length (ft/m): 365.8/111.51	Cabins (outside view): 82	Lecture/Film Room: ......Yes (seats 164)
Beam (ft/m): 55.7/17.00	Cabins (interior/no view): 0	Library: ....Yes (open 24 hours)
Draft (ft/m): 15.7/4.80	Cabins (for one person): 0	Zodiacs: 12
Propulsion/Propellers: .diesel (4,855kW)/2	Cabins (with private balcony): 18	Helicopter Pad: ....Yes
Passenger Decks: 6	Cabins (wheelchair accessible): 2	Onboard currency ....Euros

A strong expedition ship for in-depth discovery.

OVERVIEW. This ship will suit anyone who enjoys nature and the natural world, and traveling off the beaten path in remote and unspoiled areas. Venturing on the wild side of cruising, *Bremen* has some superb, well-planned destination-intensive itineraries, with a good degree of comfort and useful documentation, including port information and maps. It's a charming, very friendly ship with a homely, welcoming ambience that's hard to beat.

BERLITZ'S RATINGS

	Possible	Achieved
Ship	500	363
Accommodation	200	155
Food	400	313
Service	400	319
Entertainment	n/a	n/a
Cruise	500	403

OVERALL SCORE
1,553 points out of 2,000

Bremen is a practical expedition cruise vessel, nicely refurbished in 2009 when flat-screen TV sets were placed in all cabins, and the number of internet-connect computers was increased to four. Arguably, it is a better expedition vessel than *Hanseatic*, and, although not quite as luxurious in its interiors and appointments, the ship has a loyal following. Its cruises will provide you with a fine learning and expedition experience, particularly its Antarctic cruises. All shore landings and tours are included, as is seasickness medication. There's a fine array of expert lecturers, and a friendly crew. The ship has two microscopes, and a plankton-collection net for in-depth studies.

THE SHIP. This purpose-built all-white expedition cruise vessel has a handsome, wide, though squat, contemporary profile and decent equipment. Its wide beam provides good stability and the vessel's long cruising range and ice-hardened hull allows it access to remote destinations. The ship carries the highest ice classification for passenger vessels.

Zero-discharge of waste matter is fiercely practiced; this means that absolutely nothing is discharged into the ocean that does not meet with the international conventions on ocean pollution (MARPOL). Equipment for in-depth marine and shore excursions is provided, including a boot-washing station with three water hoses and boot cleaning brushes.

There is almost a walk-around deck – you have to go up and down steps at the front of the deck to complete the "walk." A large open deck aft of the mast provides a good viewing platform that's also useful for sunbathing on warm-weather cruises).

The ship has a good number of public rooms for its size, including a forward-facing observation lounge/lecture room, and a main lounge (the Club) with a high ceiling, bandstand, dance floor and large bar, and an adjacent library with 12 bookcases (most books are in German).

The onboard ambience is completely casual, comfortable, unstuffy (no dressy clothes needed), and very accommodating. Passengers appreciate the fact that there is no music in hallways or on open decks. The reception desk is open 24 hours a day, and an "invitation to the bridge" policy applies.

Arctic/Antarctic Cruises: Parkas (waterproof outdoor jackets) and tough "snow-grip" boots are supplied, but you should take strong waterproof trousers and thick socks, plus "thermal" underwear. Each of the fleet of 12 Zodiacs (rubber-inflatable landing craft) is named after a place or region: Amazon, Antarctic, Asmat, Bora Bora, Cape Horn, Deception, Jan Mayen, Luzon, Pitcairn, San Blas, Spitzbergen, and Ushuaia. On Arctic and Antarctic cruises, it is particularly pleasing to go to the bridge wings late at night to stargaze under pollution-free skies – the watch officers will be pleased to explain star formations.

Special sailings may be under the auspices of various tour operators, although the ship is operated by Hapag-Lloyd

Expedition Cruises. Thus, your fellow expedition voyagers may well be from many different countries. Insurance, port taxes and all staff gratuities are typically included in the cruise fare, and a logbook is provided at the end of each expedition cruise for all participants – a reminder of what's been seen and done during the course of the adventure.

There's no "bulbous bow" and so the ship can pitch in some sea conditions; but it does have stabilizers. The swimming pool is small, as is the open deck space around it, although there are both shaded and open areas. In-cabin announcements cannot be turned off (on cruises in the Arctic and Antarctic regions, announcements are often made at or before 7am on days when shore landings are permitted). Sadly, the ship was not built with good cabin soundproofing.

Hapag-Lloyd publishes its own excellent handbooks, in both English and German, on expedition regions such as the Arctic, Antarctica, Amazonia and the South Sea Islands, as well as exclusive maps.

ACCOMMODATION. There are just four different configurations. All cabins have an outside view – those on the lowest deck have portholes, and the others have good-sized picture windows. All are well-equipped for the size of the vessel. Each has wood accenting, a color TV and DVD player, telephone, refrigerator (soft drinks are provided free and replenished daily), vanity desk with 220-volt European-style electrical sockets, sitting area with small drinks table, and W-LAN access.

Cabins have either twin beds (convertible to a queen-size bed, but with individual European cotton duvets) or double bed, according to location, plus bedside reading lights and alarm clock. There is a small indented area for outerwear and rubber boots, while a small drawer above the refrigerator unit provides warmth when needed for such things as wet socks and gloves.

Each cabin has a private bathroom (totally replaced in 2010) with a tiled floor, shower enclosure with curtain, toiletries shelf, washbasin and low-height toilet (vacuum type), a decent amount of under-basin storage space, and an electrical socket for shavers. Large towels and 100% cotton bathrobes are provided, as is a range of Crabtree & Evelyn toiletries (shampoo, body lotion, shower gel, soap, and shower cap).

Each cabin has a moderate amount of illuminated closet space (large enough for two weeks for two persons, but tight for longer cruises), although the drawer space is limited – suitcases can be stored under the beds. Some Sun Deck and Bridge Deck cabins also have a small balcony (*Bremen* was the first expedition cruise vessel to have these)

with blue plastic, easily cleanable decking and wooden handrail, but no exterior light. The balconies have two teak chairs and a small drinks table, but are small and narrow, with partial partitions and doors that open outwards onto the balcony, taking up space.

Two Sun Deck suites have a separate lounge area with sofa and coffee table, bedroom with wall clock, large walk-in closet, and marble bathroom with tub and basin.

CUISINE. The dining room has open seating when operating for mixed German and international passenger cruises, and open seating for breakfast and lunch, with one seating for dinner (assigned seats) when operated solely as a German-speaking cruise. It is fairly attractive, with pleasing decor and pastel colors; it has big picture windows and 12 pillars placed in inconvenient positions – the result of old shipbuilding techniques.

The food, made with high-quality ingredients, is extremely good. Although the portions are small, the presentation is appealing to the eye – and you can always ask for more. There is an excellent choice of freshly made breads and pastries, and a good selection of cheeses and fruits.

Dinner typically includes a choice of two appetizers, two soups, an in-between course, two entrées and two or three desserts, plus a cheese board (note that Europeans typically have cheese before dessert). There is always a vegetarian specialty, as well as a healthy eating option. The service is good, with smartly dressed bi-lingual (German- and English-speaking) waiters and waitresses.

As an alternative to the dining room, breakfast and luncheon buffets are available in "The Club", or outside on the Lido Deck (weather permitting), where "The Starboard Bar/Grill" provides grilled food items.

ENTERTAINMENT. The Club is the main lounge, used as a gathering place after meals and before expedition landings ashore. There is no formal entertainment as such, lectures in a dedicated lecture room being the principal feature of any expedition cruise aboard this ship (unless under charter). Occasionally, the crew may put on a little amateur dramatics event, or a seaman's choir. At the end of each cruise, the ship's chart is auctioned off one evening to the highest bidder, with profits donated to charity.

SPA/FITNESS. There is a small fitness room, a large sauna, and beauty salon with integral massage table. Out on the open deck is a small swimming pool, which is heated when the ship is sailing in cold-weather regions such as the Arctic or Antarctica.

Brilliance of the Seas
★★★★

Size: ....Large Resort Ship	Passenger Decks: 12	Cabins (with private balcony): 577
Tonnage: 90,090	Total Crew: 869	Cabins (wheelchair accessible): 24
Lifestyle: ....Standard	Passengers	Wheelchair accessibility: ....Good
Cruise Line: Royal Caribbean International	(lower beds/all berths): 2,112/2,500	Cabin Current: ....110/220 volts
Former Names: ....none	Passenger Space Ratio	Elevators: 9
Builder: ....Meyer Werft (Germany)	(lower beds/all berths): 42.6/36.0	Casino (gaming tables): ....Yes
Original Cost: ....$350 million	Crew/Passenger Ratio	Slot Machines: ....Yes
Entered Service: ....Jul 2002	(lower beds/all berths): 2.5/2.8	Swimming Pools (outdoors): 2
Registry: ....The Bahamas	Cabins (total): 1,056	Swimming Pools (indoors): 0
Length (ft/m): 961.9/293.2	Size Range (sq ft/m): 165.8–1,216.3/	Whirlpools: 3
Beam (ft/m): 105.6/32.2	15.4–113.0	Self-Service Launderette: ....No
Draft (ft/m): 27.8/8.5	Cabins (outside view): 818	Dedicated Cinema/Seats: Yes/40
Propulsion/Propellers: .....Gas turbine/	Cabins (interior/no view): 238	Library: ....Yes
2 pods (19.5 MW each)	Cabins (for one person): 0	Onboard currency ....US$

Fairly elegant decor and style for the young, active and trendy set.

OVERVIEW. This ship was constructed for longer itineraries, with more space and comfortable public areas, larger cabins and more dining options. For the more sporting, youthful passengers, there is activity galore – including a 30-ft (9-meter) rock-climbing wall with five separate climbing tracks.

THE SHIP. This is a streamlined contemporary ship, built in 66 blocks, and has a two-deck-high wrap-around structure in the forward section of the funnel. Along the port side, a central glass wall protrudes, giving great views (cabins with balconies occupy the space directly opposite on the starboard side). The gently rounded stern has nicely tiered decks, which gives the ship an extremely well-balanced look. As is common aboard all Royal Caribbean International vessels, the navigation bridge is of the fully enclosed type – good for cold-weather areas. One of two swimming pools can be covered by a large glass dome for use as an all-weather indoor/outdoor pool.

The interior decor is contemporary, yet elegant and cheerful, designed for active, young and trendy types. The artwork is abundant and truly eclectic. A nine-deck high atrium lobby has glass-walled elevators (on the port side) that travel through 12 decks, face the sea and provide a link with nature and the ocean. The Centrum (as the atrium is called) has several public rooms connected to it: the guest relations and shore excursions desks, a Lobby Bar, Champagne Bar, the Library, Royal Caribbean Online, the Concierge Club, and a Crown & Anchor Lounge. A great view can be had of the atrium by looking down through the flat glass dome high above it.

There's also a Champagne Bar, and a large Schooner

BERLITZ'S RATINGS		
	Possible	Achieved
Ship	500	415
Accommodation	200	154
Food	400	238
Service	400	262
Entertainment	100	78
Cruise	400	299
OVERALL SCORE		
1,446 points out of 2,000		

Bar that houses maritime art in an integral art gallery, not to mention the Casino Royale. There's a small, deeply tiered, movie screening room (with space for two wheelchairs), as well as a 194-seat conference center, a business center, and several conference rooms.

A Viking Crown Lounge is set around the ship's funnel. This functions as an observation lounge during the day; in the evening, the space hosts Starquest, a futuristic, high-energy dance club, and Hollywood Odyssey, a more intimate and relaxed entertainment venue for softer mood music and "black-box" theater. A computer business center has 12 PCs with high-speed internet access for sending and receiving emails. Gratuities are automatically charged to your onboard account.

FAMILIES. Youth facilities include Adventure Ocean, an "edutainment" area with four separate age-appropriate sections for junior passengers: Aquanaut Center (for ages 3–5); Explorer Center (6–8); Voyager Center (9–12); and the Optix Teen Center (13–17). Adventure Beach includes a splash pool with waterslide. Surfside has computer lab stations with entertaining software. Ocean Arcade is a video games hangout.

The largest cabins consist of a family suite with two bedrooms. One bedroom has twin beds (convertible to queen-size bed), while a second has two lower beds and two upper Pullman berths, a combination that can sleep up to eight persons – good for large families.

ACCOMMODATION. A wide range of suites and standard outside-view and interior cabins comes in 10 categories and 19 price groups. Apart from the six largest suites (called owner's suites), which have king-size beds, almost all other cabins have twin beds that convert to a queen-size bed; all sheets are 100% Egyptian cotton, although the blankets are of nylon.

All cabins have rich (faux) wood cabinetry, including a vanity desk (with hairdryer), faux wood drawers that close silently (hooray), TV set, personal safe, and three-sided mirrors. Some cabins have ceiling recessed, pull-down berths for third and fourth persons, although closet and drawer space would be extremely tight for four persons (even if two are children), and some have interconnecting doors. Audio channels are available through the TV set, so if you want to go to sleep with soft music playing you'll need to put a towel over the television screen.

Most bathrooms have tiled accenting and a terrazzo-style tiled floor, and a rather small half-moon shower enclosure, 100% Egyptian cotton towels, a small cabinet for toiletries and a small shelf. There is little space to stow toiletries for two (or more).

Occupants of cabins designated as suites get the use of a private Concierge Lounge where priority dining room reservations, shore excursion bookings and beauty salon/spa appointments can be made.

Many "private" balcony cabins are not very private, as they can be overlooked from the port and starboard wings of the Solarium, and from other locations.

CUISINE. *Minstrel*, the main dining room, spans two decks (the upper deck level has floor-to-ceiling windows, while the lower deck level has windows). It seats 1,104, and has Middle Ages music as its themed decor. There are tables for two, four, six, eight or 10 in two seatings for dinner. Two small private dining rooms (*Zephyr*, with 94 seats and *Lute*, with 30 seats) are located off the main dining room.

Choose one of two seatings, or "My Time Dining" (eat when you want during dining room hours) when you book. Minstrel is closed for lunch on most days, which leaves passengers scrambling for food and seating in the *Windjammer Café* – an awful prospect after passengers return from morning excursions.

The cuisine in the main dining room is typical of mass banquet catering that offers standard fare comparable to that found in American family-style restaurants ashore – mostly disappointing and without much taste. However, a decent selection of light meals is provided, and a vegetarian menu is available. Caviar, once a standard menu item, incurs a hefty extra charge. Special orders, tableside carving and flambéed items are not offered.

Menus typically include a "Welcome Aboard" Dinner, French Dinner, Italian Dinner, International Dinner, Captain's Gala Dinner.

There are two alternative dining spots: *Portofino*, with 112 seats, has Italian-American cuisine (choices include antipasti, soup, salad, pasta, main dish, dessert, cheese and coffee); and *Chops Grille Steakhouse*, with 95 seats and an open (show) kitchen, has premium veal chops and steaks (New York Striploin Steak, Filet Mignon, Prime Rib of Beef). Both these spots have food that is of a much higher quality than in the main dining room. There is an additional per-person cover charge for *Portofino Chops Grille*. Both venues, which are typically open between 6pm and 11pm, require reservations.

Be prepared to eat a lot of food (perhaps this justifies the cover charge), as these are Texas-sized portions presented on large plates. Menus don't change throughout the cruise. The dress code is smart casual.

Also, casual meals can be taken (for breakfast, lunch and dinner) in the self-serve, buffet-style *Windjammer Café*, which can be accessed directly from the pool deck. It has a peculiar layout, and has several islands – so you may have to hunt for the items you like. It is impossible to get a hot plate for hot food because the plates are plastic, so things go cold quickly. The selection of cold cuts of meat is poor, cheeses have absolutely no taste, and salad items almost always look unappetizing.

Additionally, the *Seaview Café* is open for lunch and dinner. Choose from the self-serve buffet, or from the menu for fast-food seafood items, hamburgers and hot dogs. The decor, naturally, is marine- and ocean-related.

ENTERTAINMENT. The Pacifica Theatre, the main showlounge, is three decks high, has 874 seats, including 24 stations for wheelchairs, and good sightlines from most seats.

SPA/FITNESS. The ShipShape Spa's health, fitness and spa facilities have themed decor, and include a 10,176 sq.-ft (945 sq.-meter) solarium with whirlpool and counter current swimming under a retractable glass roof, a gymnasium with 44 cardiovascular machines, a 50-person aerobics room, sauna and steam rooms, and therapy treatment rooms. All are on two of the uppermost decks.

Sports facilities include a 30-ft (9-meter) rock-climbing wall, golf course, jogging track, basketball court, 9-hole miniature golf course with novel decorative ornaments, and an indoor/outdoor country club with golf simulator. There is an exterior jogging track.

● **For more extensive general information about a Royal Caribbean cruise experience, see pages 152–6.**

Caribbean Princess
★★★★

Size: . . . . .Large Resort Ship	Passenger Decks: 15	Cabins (with private balcony): 881
Tonnage: 112,894	Total Crew: 1,163	Cabins (wheelchair accessible): 25
Lifestyle: . . . . .Standard	Passengers	Wheelchair accessibility: . . . . .Good
Cruise Line: . . . . .Princess Cruises	(lower beds/all berths): 3,114/3,622	Cabin Voltage: . . . . .110 volts
Former Names: . . . . .None	Passenger Space Ratio	Elevators: 14
Builder: . . . . .Fincantieri (Italy)	(lower beds/all berths): 36.2/31.1	Casino (gaming tables): . . . . .Yes
Original Cost: . . . .$500 million	Crew/Passenger Ratio	Slot Machines: . . . . .Yes
Entered Service: . . . . .Apr 2004	(lower beds/all berths): 2.6/3.1	Swimming Pools (outdoors): 4
Registry: . . . . .Bermuda	Cabins (total): 1,557	Swimming Pools (indoors): 0
Length (ft/m): 951.4/290.0	Size Range (sq ft/m): 163-1,279/	Whirlpools: 9
Beam (ft/m): 118.1/36.0	15.1-118.8	Self-Service Launderette: . . . . .Yes
Draft (ft/m): 28.3/8.6	Cabins (outside view): 1,105	Dedicated Cinema/Seats: . . . . .No
Propulsion/Propellers: . . . . .diesel-electric	Cabins (interior/no view): 452	Library: . . . . .Yes
(42,000kW)/2	Cabins (for one person): 0	Onboard currency . . . . .US$

A multi-choice large ship for informal family cruising.

OVERVIEW. The ship is a grand resort, a playground in which to roam when not ashore. Princess Cruises delivers a consistent, well-packaged vacation at an attractive price. If you're not used to large ships, it will take you some time to find your way around this one, despite the company's claim that it offers a "small ship feel, big ship choice."

THE SHIP. Caribbean Princess has the same profile as its half-sisters Golden Princess, Grand Princess, and Star Princess. However, it takes 500 more passengers, thanks to an extra accommodation deck (Riviera Deck), and the fact that two of the 17 upper decks are made of aluminum; although lighter than steel, it tends to "harden" over time.

Despite its greater capacity, the outdoor deck space remains the same, as do the number of elevators – so there's a longer wait during peak usage.

There is a good sheltered faux-teak promenade deck – it's actually painted steel – which almost wraps around the ship (three times around equals one mile). The outdoor pools have various beach-like surroundings. "Movies Under the Skies" and major sporting events are shown on a 300-sq-ft (28-sq-meter) poolside movie screen.

Unlike the outside decks, there is plenty of space inside (but also plenty of passengers), and a wide array of public rooms, with many "intimate" (a relative word) spaces. The passenger flow is well thought-out, and there is little congestion, except the wait for elevators at peak times.

High atop the stern is a ship-wide glass-walled disco pod with spectacular views from the extreme port and starboard side windows – it would make a great suite.

The interior decor is attractive, with mainly earth tones

BERLITZ'S RATINGS		
	Possible	Achieved
Ship	500	431
Accommodation	200	165
Food	400	254
Service	400	293
Entertainment	100	82
Cruise	400	314
OVERALL SCORE		
1,539 points out of 2,000		

– well suited to both American and European tastes. An extensive collection of artworks complements the interior design and colors well. Caribbean Princess also has a Wedding Chapel, and a live web-cam can relay ceremonies via the internet. The captain can legally marry American couples, thanks to the ship's Bermuda registry. The "Hearts & Minds" chapel is also useful for "renewal of vows" ceremonies.

The ship has one of the largest casinos at sea (Grand Casino), with more than 260 slot machines, and blackjack, craps and roulette tables, plus newer games such as Let It Ride Bonus, Spanish 21 and Caribbean Draw Progressive. But the highlight could well be the specially linked slot machines that provide a combined payout.

Other facilities include a small library and internet-connect room. The wood-paneled Wheelhouse Bar is finely decorated with memorabilia and ship models tracing part of parent company P&O's history. Churchill's cigar/sports bar has several TV screens. A high-tech hospital has SeaMed tele-medicine link-ups to specialists at the Cedars-Sinai Medical Center in Los Angeles.

FAMILIES. Children's facilities include a large playroom, a teens-only room, and a host of youth counselors. Children have their own pools, hot tubs, and open deck area at the stern of the ship, thankfully away from adult areas. There are good netted-in areas; one section has a dip pool, while another has a mini-basketball court. Two family suites consist of two suites with an interconnecting door, plus a large balcony. These can sleep up to 10 if at least four are children, or up to eight adults.

ACCOMMODATION. There are six principal types of cabins and configurations: (a) grand suite, (b) suite, (c) mini-suite, (d) outside-view double cabins with balcony, (e) outside-view double cabins, and (f) interior double cabins. These come in 35 different brochure price categories. The choice is quite bewildering for both travel agents and passengers; pricing depends on two things, size and location.

Cabin bath towels are small, and drawer space is limited. Even the top-grade suites are not really large in comparison to similar suites aboard some other ships. Cabin attendants have too many cabins to look after (typically 20), which does not translate to fine personal service.

(a) The largest, most lavish suite is the Grand Suite, at the stern). It has a large bedroom with queen-size bed, huge walk-in (illuminated) closets, two bathrooms, a lounge (with fireplace and sofa bed) with wet bar and refrigerator, and a large private balcony on the port side (with hot tub that can be accessed from both balcony and bedroom).

(b/c) Suites (with a semi-private balcony) have a separate living room (with sofa bed) and bedroom (with a TV set in each). The bathroom is quite large and has both a tub and shower stall. The mini-suites also have a private balcony, and a separate living and sleeping area (with a TV set in each). The differences between the suites and mini-suites are basically in the size and appointments. Suite and mini-suite passengers receive more attention, including priority embarkation and disembarkation privileges.

(d/e/f) Both interior and outside-view cabins (80% of the latter have a private balcony) are of functional, although almost no drawers are provided. They are quite attractive, with warm, pleasing decor and fine soft furnishing fabrics. Interior cabins measure 163 sq. ft (15.1 sq. meters).

The 28 wheelchair-accessible cabins, surprisingly, have no mirror for dressing, and no full-length hanging space for long dresses (yes, some passengers in wheelchairs do use mirrors and wear long dresses).

All cabins receive turndown service and chocolates on pillows each night, bathrobes (on request) and toiletry kits. A hairdryer is provided in all cabins. All bathrooms have tiled floors, and there is a decent amount of open shelf storage space for toiletries, although the plain beige decor is very basic and unappealing.

Most outside-view cabins on Emerald Deck have views obstructed by lifeboats. There are no cabins for singles.

Some cabins can accommodate a third and fourth person in upper berths. However, in such cabins, the lower beds cannot then be pushed together to make queen-size bed.

Almost all balcony suites and cabins can be overlooked both from the navigation bridge wing and from sections of the discotheque. Passengers in some the most expensive suites with balconies at the stern may experience some vibration during certain ship maneuvers.

CUISINE. The three principal dining rooms for formal dining are *Coral*, *Island*, and *Palm*. The Palm Dining Room has traditional two seating dining, while Coral and Island have "anytime dining" (you choose when and with whom

you want to eat). All are split into multi-tier sections in a non-symmetrical design that breaks what are quite large spaces into smaller sections for better ambience. Each dining room has its own galley. While four elevators go to Fiesta Deck, where the Coral and Island restaurants are located, only two go to Plaza Deck 5, where the Palm Restaurant is located (this can cause waiting problems at peak times, particularly for anyone in a wheelchair). Note that 15% is added to all beverage bills, including wines.

Alternative (Extra Charge) Dining Options: *Sabatini's Trattoria* serves Italian-style pizzas and pastas, with a variety of sauces, as well as Italian entrées including tiger prawns and lobster tail (reservation only; cover charge).

Sterling Steakhouse is located in a somewhat open area, to tempt you as you pass by, with people walking through as you eat – not a particularly comfortable arrangement. There is a cover charge.

The cuisine in the alternative dining spots is decidedly better than in the three main dining rooms, with better quality ingredients and more attention to presentation and taste.

Casual eateries include a poolside hamburger grill and pizza bar (no additional charge), while extra charges do apply if you order items to eat at the coffee bar/ patisserie, or the caviar/champagne bar. Other casual meals can be taken in the Horizon Court, open 24 hours a day.

Ultimate Balcony Dinner or Breakfast: For something different, you could try a private dinner on your balcony, an all-inclusive evening featuring cocktails, fresh flowers, champagne and a deluxe four-course meal including Caribbean lobster tail. Of course, it costs extra.

There's 24-hour room service – but some room service menu items are unavailable during early morning hours.

ENTERTAINMENT. The *Princess Theater*, the main entertainment venue, spans two decks and has comfortable seating on both main and balcony levels. It has $3 million worth of sound and light equipment, plus a nine-piece orchestra, and a scenery loading bay that connects directly from stage to a hull door for direct transfer to the dockside. The ship carries a resident troupe of singers and dancers.

Club Fusion, located aft, has cabaret spots at night, and lectures, bingo and horse racing during the day. *Explorers* can also host cabaret acts and dance bands. Other lounges and bars have live music, and Princess Cruises employs male dance hosts as partners for women traveling alone.

SPA/FITNESS/RECREATION. The Lotus Spa is located forward on Sun Deck – one of the uppermost decks. Separate facilities for men and women include a sauna, steam room, and changing rooms; common facilities include a relaxation/waiting zone, body-pampering treatment rooms, and a gymnasium with packed with high-tech muscle-pumping, cardio-vascular equipment, and great ocean views. Some fitness classes are free, while some cost extra.

● **For more extensive general information on what a Princess Cruises cruise is like, see pages 149–52.**

Carnival Conquest
★★★ +

Size: . . . . .Large Resort Ship	Total Crew: .1,160	Wheelchair accessibility: . . . . .Good
Tonnage: 110,239	Passengers	Cabin Current: . . . . .110 volts
Lifestyle: . . . . .Standard	(lower beds/all berths): 2,974/3,700	Elevators: 18
Cruise Line: . . . . . . .Carnival Cruise Lines	Passenger Space Ratio	Casino (gaming tables): . . . . .Yes
Former Names: . . . . .none	(lower beds/all berths): 37.0/29.7	Slot Machines: . . . . .Yes
Builder: . . . . .Fincantieri (Italy)	Crew/Passenger Ratio	Swimming Pools (outdoors): 2
Original Cost: . . . .$500 million	(lower beds/all berths): 2.5/3.1	(+1 with glass dome)
Entered Service: . . . . .Dec 2002	Cabins (total): 1,487	Swimming Pools (indoors): 0
Registry: . . . . .Panama	Size Range (sq ft/m):	Whirlpools: 7
Length (ft/m): 951.4/290.0	179.7–482.2/16.7–44.8	Self-Service Launderette: . . . . .Yes
Beam (ft/m): 116.4/35.5	Cabins (outside view): 917	Dedicated Cinema/Seats: . . . . .No
Draft (ft/m): 27.0/8.2	Cabins (interior/no view): 570	Library: . . . . .Yes
Propulsion/Propellers: . . . . .diesel-electric	Cabins (for one person): 0	Onboard currency . . . . .US$
(63,400kW)/2	Cabins (with private balcony): 574	
Passenger Decks: 13	Cabins (wheelchair accessible): 25	

A vivid, fun-filled ship for ultra-casual cruising.

OVERVIEW. This is quite a stunning ship, built to impress at every turn. The layout is quite logical, so finding your way around is easy. The decor features great Impressionist painters, such as Degas, Monet and Van Gogh. Murano glass flowers on antiqued brass stems are displayed in several public areas.

THE SHIP. *Carnival Conquest* has the same well-balanced profile as its sisters: *Carnival Destiny, Carnival Freedom, Carnival Glory, Carnival Liberty, Carnival Triumph* and *Carnival Victory*. Because of its size, it can't transit the Panama Canal, and is dedicated to the Caribbean area.

Amidships on the open deck is a long water slide (200 ft/60 meters long), as well as tiered sunbathing decks positioned between two swimming pools, several hot tubs and a giant poolside (Seaside Theater) movie screen. It's all about imagination, and sensorial fantasy and is more reserved than Carnival's Fantasy-class ships.

There are three decks full of lounges, 10 bars and lots of rooms to play in. There are two atriums: the largest, the forward, glass-domed Atelier Atrium spans nine decks, while the aft atrium goes through three decks. The ship has a doublewide indoor promenade.

The Tahiti casino is large and action-packed, with more than 320 slot machines. There are several other nightspots for just about every musical taste (except for opera, ballet and classical music lovers).

It is impossible to escape from noise and loud music (it's even played in cabin hallways and lifts), not to mention smokers, and people walking around in unsuitable clothing,

BERLITZ'S RATINGS		
	Possible	Achieved
Ship	500	412
Accommodation	200	157
Food	400	218
Service	400	259
Entertainment	100	82
Cruise	400	257
OVERALL SCORE		
1,385 points out of 2,000		

clutching plastic sport drinks bottles, at any time of the day or night. You have to carry a credit card to operate the personal safes, which is inconvenient.

The many pillars in the dining room make it difficult for proper food service by the waiters. The public toilets are somewhat spartan and could do with some cheering up.

FAMILIES. Children are provided with good facilities, including a two-level Children's Club with an outdoor pool, and are well cared for with "Camp Carnival", the line's extensive children's program.

ACCOMMODATION. There are 21 cabin price categories, in seven different grades: suites with private balcony; deluxe outside-view cabins with private balcony; outside-view cabins with private balcony; outside-view cabins with window; cabins with a porthole instead of a window; interior (no-view) cabins; interior cabins with upper and lower berths. The price reflects the grade, location and size.

Five decks of cabins have a private balcony – over 150 more than *Carnival Destiny, Carnival Triumph* or *Carnival Victory*, for example. But many are not so private, and can be overlooked from various public locations.

There are 18 "fitness" cabins, located directly around and behind the SpaCarnival. This allows fitness devotees to get out of bed and go straight to the treadmill without having to go through any of the public rooms first.

The standard cabins are of good size and are equipped with all the basics, although the furniture is rather angular, with no rounded edges. Three decks of cabins (eight on each deck, each with private balcony) overlook the stern. Most cabins with twin beds can be converted to a queen-size bed format. A gift basket is provided in all grades of cabin; it includes aloe soap, shampoo, conditioner, deodorant, breath mints, candy, and pain relief tablets (all in sample sizes).

Note: If you book one of the suites (Category 11 or 12 in the Carnival Cruise Lines brochure) you get "Skipper's Club" priority check-in at any US homeland port – useful for getting ahead of the crowd.

CUISINE. There are two principal dining rooms: the *Renoir Restaurant*, with 744 seats, and the larger *Monet Restaurant*, with 1,044 seats. Both are two decks high, and both have a balcony level for diners (the balcony level in the Monet Restaurant is larger). Cassat and Pissaro, two additional wings in the Renoir Restaurant, can accommodate large groups in a private dining arrangement. There's a choice of either fixed time dining (6pm or 8:15pm), or flexible dining (any time between 5:45pm and 9:30pm). Although the menu choice looks good, the cuisine delivered is typically adequate, but quite unmemorable.

The *Cézanne Restaurant* is the ship's casual self-serve international food court-style lido deck eatery, with a capacity of over 1,200. Its decor reflects the style of a 19th-century French café. It has two main serving lines, is adjacent to the aft pool and can be covered by a glass cover in poor weather. Included are Paul's Deli, PC's Wok (Chinese cuisine, with wok preparation), a 24-hour pizzeria, and a patisserie (there's an extra charge for pastries, however), as well as a grill for fast foods such as hamburgers and hot dogs. Each night, the Cézanne Restaurant is turned into the *Sea-view Bistro*, and provides a casual alternative to eating in the main dining rooms; it serves pasta, steaks, salads and desserts, typically between 6pm and 9pm. If you're still hungry, there's always a midnight buffet around the corner.

Alternative (Reservations-Only, Extra Cost) Dining: *The Point* is the reservations-only, extra cost, alternative dining spot. The decor includes wall murals in the style of Seurat's famous *Le Cirque* (The Circus). There are fine table settings, china and silverware, as well as leather-bound menus.

ENTERTAINMENT. The Toulouse-Lautrec Showlounge is a multi-deck showroom seating 1,400. It has a revolving stage, hydraulic orchestra pit, superb sound, and seating on three levels (the upper levels being tiered through two decks). A proscenium over the stage acts as a scenery loft.

SPA/FITNESS. SpaCarnival is a large health, fitness and spa complex that spans two decks (the walls display hand-painted reproductions of the artist's poster work). It is directly above the navigation bridge in the forward part of the ship and is accessed from the forward stairway.

Facilities on the lower level include a solarium, eight treatment rooms, lecture rooms, sauna and steam rooms for men and women, and a beauty parlor. The upper level consists of a large gymnasium with floor-to-ceiling windows on three sides, including forward-facing ocean views, and an aerobics room with instructor-led classes, some at extra cost.

● **For more extensive general information on what a Carnival cruise is like, see pages 126–31.**

PLIMSOLL MARK

The safety of ships at sea and all those aboard owes much to the 19th-century social reformer Samuel Plimsoll, a member of the British Parliament concerned about the frequent loss of ships due to overloading. In those days, some shipowners would load their vessels down to the gunwales to squeeze every ounce of revenue out of them. They gambled on good weather, good fortune, and good seamanship to bring them safely into port. Consequently, many ships went to the bottom of the sea – the result of their buoyancy being seriously impaired by overloading.

Plimsoll helped to enact legislation that came to be known as the Merchant Shipping Act of 1875. This required shipowners to mark their vessels with a circular disc 12 inches (30 cm) long bisected by a line 18 inches (46 cm) long, as a measure of their maximum draft; that is, the depth to which a ship's hull could be safely immersed at sea.

The Merchant Shipping Act of 1890 went even further, and required the Plimsoll mark (or line) to be positioned on the sides of vessels in accordance with tables drawn up by competent authorities.

The Plimsoll mark is now found on the ships of every nation. The Plimsoll mark indicates three different depths: the depth to which a vessel can be loaded in fresh water, which is less buoyant than salt water; the depth in summer, when seas are generally calmer; and the depth in winter, when seas are much rougher.

Carnival Destiny
★★★ +

Size:	Large Resort Ship	Total Crew:	1,000	Wheelchair accessibility:	Good
Tonnage:	101,353	Passengers		Cabin Current:	110 volts
Lifestyle:	Standard	(lower beds/all berths):	2,642/3,400	Elevators:	18
Cruise Line:	Carnival Cruise Lines	Passenger Space Ratio		Casino (gaming tables):	Yes
Former Names:	none	(lower beds/all berths):	38.3/29.8	Slot Machines:	Yes
Builder:	Fincantieri (Italy)	Crew/Passenger Ratio		Swimming Pools (outdoors):	2
Original Cost:	$400 million	(lower beds/all berths):	2.6/3.4	(+1 with glass dome)	
Entered Service:	Nov 1996	Cabins (total):	1,321	Swimming Pools (indoors):	0
Registry:	The Bahamas	Size Range (sq ft/m):	179.7–482.2/	Whirlpools:	7
Length (ft/m):	892.3/272.0		16.7–44.8	Self-Service Launderette:	Yes
Beam (ft/m):	116.0/35.3	Cabins (outside view):	806	Dedicated Cinema/Seats:	No
Draft (ft/m):	27.0/8.2	Cabins (interior/no view):	515	Library:	Yes
Propulsion/Propellers:	diesel-electric	Cabins (for one person):	0	Onboard currency	US$
	(63,400kW)/2	Cabins (with private balcony):	418		
Passenger Decks:	12	Cabins (wheelchair accessible):	25		

An vibrant ship suited to first-time casual cruising.

OVERVIEW. *Carnival Destiny* was the world's first cruise ship whose gross tonnage exceeded 100,000, which is why it can't transit the Panama Canal and is dedicated to itineraries in the Caribbean. It's a stunning vessel, but getting away from people and noise is difficult and there's no escape from repetitious announcements for activities that bring revenue, such as art auctions, bingo, and horse racing.

THE SHIP. The ship has short bows and the distinctive, large, swept-back wing-tipped funnel in red, white and blue. Amidships on the open deck is a very long water slide (200 ft/60 meters long), and tiered sunbathing decks positioned between two swimming pools, several hot tubs, and a large poolside movie screen.

The interior decor is a fantasyland for the senses. There are three decks full of lounges, 10 bars, lots of rooms to play in, and a double-wide indoor promenade. A glass-domed rotunda atrium lobby (with bar) is nine decks high. an action-packed Millionaire's Club Casino has lots of gaming tables, plus more than 320 slot machines. Tables in the All Star Bar include sporting memorabilia.

The terraced pool deck is cluttered, and there are no cushioned pads for the deck chairs. The Photo Gallery, adjacent to the atrium/purser's office, is extremely congested when photos are on display. There is constant hustling for drinks, although accompanied with a knowing smile.

From the viewpoint of safety, passengers can embark directly into the lifeboats from their secured position without having to wait for them to be lowered, thus saving time in the event of a real emergency.

BERLITZ'S RATINGS

	Possible	Achieved
Ship	500	399
Accommodation	200	157
Food	400	218
Service	400	253
Entertainment	100	81
Cruise	400	253

OVERALL SCORE
1,361 points out of 2,000

FAMILIES. Youngsters are provided with good facilities, including their own two-level Children's Club (including an outdoor pool), and are well cared for with "Camp Carnival", the line's extensive children's program.

ACCOMMODATION. There are 19 price grades, ranked by grade, size and location. Over half of all cabins have an ocean view, and at 225 sq. ft./21 sq. meters they are quite large. The cabins, spread over four decks, have private balconies with glass rather than steel balustrades for better, unobstructed ocean views. The balconies have bright fluorescent lighting.

The standard cabins are of good size and come equipped with all the basics, although the furniture is angular, with no rounded edges. Three decks of cabins (eight on each deck, each with private balcony) overlook the stern.

There are eight penthouse suites, each with a large private balcony. Although they are quite lavish in their appointments, at only 483 sq. ft (44.8 sq. meters), they are really modest when compared to the best suites even in many smaller ships. There are also 40 other suites, each with a decent sized bathroom, and lounge space

In cabins with balconies, the partition between each balcony is open at top and bottom, so you can hear noise from neighbors – or smell their cigarettes. It is disappointing to see three categories of cabins, both outside and interior, with upper and lower bunk beds – lower beds are far more preferable, but this is how the ship accommodates an extra 600 people over and above the lower bed capacity.

The cabins have soft color schemes and soft furnishings

in more attractive fabrics than some other ships in the fleet. Interactive "Fun Vision" technology lets you choose movies on demand, for a fee. The bathrooms, which have good-sized showers, have adequate storage space in the toiletries cabinet. A gift basket is provided in all grades; it includes aloe soap, shampoo, conditioner, deodorant, breath mints, candy, and pain relief tablets – albeit all in sample sizes.

Book one of the suites (Category 11 or 12 in the Carnival Cruise Lines brochure) and you get "Skipper's Club" priority check-in at any US homeland port – useful for getting ahead of the crowd.

CUISINE. The ship has two dining rooms: the *Galaxy*, forward, with windows on two sides, has 706 seats; and the *Universe*, aft, with windows on three sides, has 1,090 seats). Each spans two decks and incorporates a dozen pyramid-shaped domes and chandeliers, and a soft, mellow peachy color scheme.

The Universe dining room has a two-deck-high wall of glass overlooking the stern. There are tables for four, six and eight, and even a few tables for two that the line tries to keep for honeymooners. Choose either fixed-time dining (6pm or 8:15pm), or flexible dining (any time between 5:45 and 9:30pm). Although the menu choices look good, the actual cuisine delivered is adequate, but unmemorable.

Casual eaters will find a serve-yourself *Lido Buffet* – open for breakfast and lunch, while for dinner this turns into the *Seaview Bistro* for use as an alternative eatery for anyone not wishing to dress for the formal dining rooms (between 6pm and 9pm). These include specialty stations where you can order omelets, eggs, fajitas, Chicken Caesar salad, pasta and stir-fry items. The dining room entrances have comfortable drinking areas for pre-dinner cocktails.

There are many options for casual dining, particularly during the daytime. The *Sun and Sea Restaurant*, two decks high, is the ship's informal international food court-style eatery, which is adjacent to the aft pool and can be covered by a glass dome-shaped cover in poor weather. Included in this eating mall are a *Trattoria* (for Italian cuisine, with made-to-order pasta dishes), *Happy Valley* (Chinese cuisine, with wok preparation), a 24-hour pizzeria, a patisserie (extra charge for pastries), and a grill for fast foods such as hamburgers and hot dogs.

At night, the area becomes the *Seaview Bistro* (it typically operates 6pm–9pm), providing a dress-down alternative to the main dining rooms. It serves pasta, steaks, salads, and desserts. If you want to eat 24 hours a day, you can.

ENTERTAINMENT. The three-level Palladium showlounge, the setting for all production shows and large-scale cabaret acts, is quite stunning, and has a revolving stage, hydraulic orchestra pit, superb sound, and seating on three levels (the upper levels being tiered through two decks). A proscenium over the stage acts as a scenery loft.

SPA/FITNESS. SpaCarnival spans two decks, with a total area of 13,700 sq. ft/1,272 sq. meters, and is located directly above the navigation bridge in the forward part of the ship (it is accessed from the forward stairway). Facilities on the lower level include a solarium, eight treatment rooms, lecture rooms, sauna and steam rooms for men and women, and a beauty parlor; the upper level consists of a large gymnasium with floor-to-ceiling windows on three sides, including forward-facing ocean views, and an aerobics room with instructor-led classes (some at extra cost).

● **For more extensive general information on what a Carnival cruise is like, see pages 126–31.**

WIND SPEEDS

A navigational announcement to passengers is normally made once or twice a day, giving the ship's position, temperature, and weather information.

Various winds affect the world's weather patterns. Such well-known winds as the Bora, Mistral, Northwind, and Sirocco, among others, play an important part in the makeup of weather at and above sea level. Wind velocity is measured on the Beaufort scale, a method that was devised in 1805 by Commodore Francis Beaufort, later Admiral and Knight Commander of the Bath, for measuring the force of wind at sea. Originally, it measured the effect of the wind on a fully rigged man-of-war (which was usually laden with cannon and heavy ammunition). It became the official way of recording wind velocity in 1874, when the International Meteorological Committee adopted it.

Carnival Dream
★★★ +

Size: ....Large Resort Ship	Passenger Decks: 13	Cabins (with private balcony): 887
Tonnage: 128,251	Total Crew: 1,367	Cabins (wheelchair accessible): 35
Lifestyle: ....Standard	Passengers	Wheelchair accessibility: ....Good
Cruise Line: ....Carnival Cruise Lines	(lower beds/all berths): 3,646/4,631	Cabin Voltage: ....110 volts
Former Names: ....none	Passenger Space Ratio	Elevators: 20
Builder: ....Fincantieri (Italy)	(lower beds/all berths): 35.1/27.6	Casino (gaming tables): ....Yes
Original Cost: ....$740 million	Crew/Passenger Ratio	Slot Machines: ....Yes
Entered Service: ....Sept 2009	(lower beds/all berths): 2.6/3.3	Swimming Pools (outdoors): 2
Registry: ....Panama	Cabins (total): 1,823	Swimming Pools (indoors): 0
Length (ft/m): 1,004.0/306.0	Size Range (sq ft/m): 185.0–430.5/	Whirlpools: 7
Beam (ft/m): 158.0/48.0	17.1–40.0	Self-Service Launderette: ....Yes
Draft (ft/m): 26.2/8.0	Cabins (outside view): 1,145	Dedicated Cinema/Seats: ....No
Propulsion/Propellers: .... diesel-electric	Cabins (interior/no view): 678	Library: ....Yes
(75.6 mW)/2	Cabins (for one person): 0	Onboard currency ....US$

Fun for a first cruise, with a great water-slide.

OVERVIEW. *Carnival Dream* operates year-round Caribbean cruises from Port Canaveral. It has lots of facilities for children and there's also a Serenity adults-only, extra-charge retreat as well as a sports activity area on deck. The Ocean Plaza, with around 190 seats, is designed to be a comfortable place by day and a trendy entertainment venue by night. Its indoor/outdoor café and live music venue has a bandstand showcasing a variety of musical genres, and a large circular dance floor.

THE SHIP. This vessel and its sister, *Carnival Magic*, are the largest "fun ships" yet for this expansive cruise line. Although its bows are short, the ship's profile is nicely balanced, with a rakish front and more rounded stern than previous Carnival ships. The propulsion system consists of conventional twin rudders, with twin (six-blade) propellers.

Among the numerous pools and open-deck nooks and crannies, one thing that stands out is the ship's really long Twister Water Slide – part of The Waterworks on pool deck. However, the general open deck space is really not enough for the number of passengers carried, so your sunbed loungers will be packed in tightly.

Carnival Dream is the only Carnival ship to have a full walk-around open promenade deck, lined with deck chairs, though it can be difficult to navigate your way through them. Along the outdoor promenade, four "scenic whirlpools" are cantilevered over the water, and provide fine sea views. Higher up, Lido Deck 10 offers the best open-deck area of any Carnival ship with a tropical, resort-style main pool complete with a giant Seaside Theatre LED screen for outdoor movies. *Carnival Dream* is the first

BERLITZ'S RATINGS		
	Possible	Achieved
Ship	500	415
Accommodation	200	157
Food	400	218
Service	400	260
Entertainment	100	82
Cruise	400	263
OVERALL SCORE		
1,395 points out of 2,000		

Carnival ship to have a laser light show outdoors – which the ships of AIDA Cruises have featured since 1996.

The interior decor is bright, but well executed. Most public rooms, lounges and bars are on Dream Street or Upper Dream Street. The stunning Dream Lobby is the connection point for ship functions and people. Take the glass-walled elevators for a neat view – but you may need sunglasses. It's good to note that there are three main elevator towers: forward, midships, and aft. This is in contrast to larger ships such as *Oasis of the Seas*, which, although it carries many more passengers, has only two main elevator banks. Well done, Carnival, good for safety.

Many lounges, bars and nightspots – including a dance club with a twist, offering indoor/outdoor access – are accessible via an 11-deck-high atrium whose ground level has a neatly cantilevered bandstand atop a massive dance floor. The Page Turner (great name) is the library, while Jackpot is – you guessed it – the colourful, large, lively and noisy casino. Other rooms include The Song (Jazz Bar), and Ocean Plaza, a sort of quiet area during the day, but lively at night with live entertainment. Three dozen internet terminals are scattered around the ship, although most have no privacy. There's a 232-capacity conference room, The Chambers.

Naturally, to get to the showlounge, you need to walk through the shops and casino. This is a ship that encourages you to spend money on all the extras you'll need.

Although passenger flow is generally sound, the ship's layout is rather disjointed. There is much congestion just before the second seating, on both Upper and Lower Dream Streets, both of which are located on the starboard side. Further congestion appears around the photo gallery in the atrium lobby. Passenger niggles center around barely warm food in the two main dining rooms, poorly trained and rude staff, lines forming, particularly for self-serve food items, and congestion in the public areas just before the second seating for dinner. Gratuities are automatically charged to your onboard account.

FAMILIES: Children's facilities are purpose-built for the line's three age-related programs: "Camp Carnival" for kids aged 2–11, "Circle C" for 12- to 14-year-olds, and "Club O2" for teens ages 15 to 17, together with a full schedule of morning-to-night activities catering to each age group. About 5,000 sq.ft. of space has been devoted to junior cruisers. Carnival WaterWorks, an expansive aqua park offering exhilarating water slides and various water spray apparatus, should be a hit with active children.

ACCOMMODATION. There are 19 cabin price categories, but just six cabin types. The price depends on the accommodation grade and location. Whether you go for high end or low end, all accommodation includes the Carnival Comfort Bed with plush mattresses, good-quality duvets and linens and pillows. However, the straight accommodation deck hallways create rather a cell-block look – and they are bright, very bright, even at night. There are also lot of interior cabins. All in all, the cabins to go for are those at the stern of the ship, with great rearward ocean views on Decks 6, 7, 8, and 9.

"Deluxe" ocean-view cabins, with two bathrooms, provide comfort and convenience for families. In addition to twin beds that convert to a king, decent closet space and elegant decor, the two-bathroom configuration includes one full bathroom and a second bathroom containing a small tub with shower and sink.

Some cabins can accommodate five persons – a rarity in new ships but useful for families. There is a wide selection of balcony cabins and suites, including "Cove Balcony" cabins that are the closest to the waterline.

Additionally, adjacent to the Serenity Spa are 65 "Cloud 9" spa cabins, designated as no-smoking. They provide a number of "exclusive" amenities and privileges. Twenty of these are positioned directly aft of the lower level of the spa, with direct access to it. Some cabins located directly over loud late-night venues (such as Encore), with poor soundproofing, have resulted in many restless nights. Also, cabins on Deck 12 are subject to lots of noise from kids having fun on the deck above – so afternoon naps are out.

CUISINE. There are two main restaurants: the 1,180-seat *Crimson* (mid-ships) and the smaller 828-seat *Scarlet* (aft). Each has two levels: main and balcony (stairways connect both levels), with the galley set on the lower level. Forward of Crimson are two small restaurant annexes, which can be reserved by small groups as a private dining room.

The Gathering is the ship's self-serve buffet facility, with indoor/outdoor seating areas on the lower (main) level, and indoor-only seating on the upper level. A number of designated areas serve different types of ethnic cuisine, including a Mongolian Wok and Pasta Bar on the upper level, open 6pm–9pm for tablecloth-free, candle-less (bare table top) buffet dinners. The layout invites congestion around the beverage stands. Go off-peak and it's much better.

Alternative (Reservations-Only, Extra-Cost) Dining:
The Chef's Art Supper Club (and bar) seats 139, has great views to port and starboard from its aft location high on Spa Deck 12, and an à la carte menu. It has fine table settings, china and silverware, as well as leather-bound menus. The specialties are steaks and seafood items. It's worth paying the cover charge to get a taste of what Carnival can really deliver in terms of food. It's also the place to go for celebrating something special, or just to get away from the noise of the large dining rooms.

Wasabi is the ship's tribute-to-sushi venue; note the large fish behind the sushi bar.

ENTERTAINMENT. The 1,964-seat Encore Showlounge spans three decks at the front of the ship, with seating set in a horseshoe shape around a large proscenium arched stage; the sightlines are generally good, except from some of the seats at the back of the lowest level. Large-scale production shows, with lots of feathers and skimpy costumes, are staged, together with snappy cabaret acts, all accompanied by a live showband.

The 425-seat Burgundy Lounge, at the aft end of the ship (opposite to the showlounge, at the front), has a stage, dance floor, large bar, and is a comedy venue, including late-night in-your-face, raunchy "adult comedy."

Caliente, the ship's hot club, provides Latin music for vibrant dancing and hot-foot style and is very loud.

SPA/FITNESS. The expansive 23,750-sq-ft (2,206 sq-meter) Cloud 9 Spa is Carnival's largest and most elaborate health and wellness center to date. It is positioned over three decks in the front section of the ship. The uppermost deck includes indoor/outdoor private spa relaxation areas, at extra cost. A spiral staircase connects the two decks, and the Steiner-operated spa offers a wide range of treatments.

There are 10 treatment rooms, including a VIP room, a large massage room for couples, and a Rasul mud treatment room, plus two dry flotation rooms. An extra-charge "Thermal Suite" comes with the typical sensory-enhanced soothing heated chambers: Laconium, Tepidarium, Aroma and Oriental steam baths.

There are two steam rooms, one each for men and women, and a small unisex sauna with a floor-to-ceiling window on its starboard side. *Carnival Dream* is the first "Fun Ship" to include a two-level miniature golf course.

● **For more extensive general information on what a Carnival cruise is like, see pages 126–31.**

Carnival Ecstasy
Carnival Elation
Carnival Fantasy
Carnival Fascination
★★★

Size: . . . . .Large Resort Ships	(42,240kW)/2 *(Ecstasy, Fantasy,*	Cabins (with private balcony): 52 *(Ecstasy)*,
Tonnage: 70,367	*Fascination)*, diesel-electric 42,842 kW)/	152 *(Elation, Fantasy)*, 250 *(Fascination)*
Lifestyle: . . . . .Standard	2 azimuthing pods (14 MW each) *(Elation)*	Cabins (wheelchair accessible): 22
Cruise Line: . . . . . . .Carnival Cruise Lines	Passenger Decks: 10	Wheelchair accessibility: . . . . .Fair
Former Names: . . . .*Ecstasy, Elation,*	Total Crew: 920	Cabin Current: . . . . .110 volts
Fantasy, Fascination	Passengers	Elevators: 14
Builder: . . .Kvaerner Masa-Yards (Finland)	(lower beds/all berths): 2,056/2,634	Casino (gaming tables): . . . . .Yes
Original Cost: . . . .$225 million	Passenger Space Ratio	Slot Machines: . . . . .Yes
Entered Service: . . . .Jun 1991 *(Ecstasy)*,	(lower beds/all berths): 34.4/26.7	Swimming Pools (outdoors): 3
Mar 1998 *(Elation)*, Mar 1990 *(Fantasy)*,	Crew/Passenger Ratio	Swimming Pools (indoors): 0
Jul 1994 *(Fascination)*	(lower beds/all berths): 2.2/2.8	Whirlpools: 6
Registry: . . . . . .Panama *(Ecstasy, Elation,*	Cabins (total): . . . . .1,026 or 1,028	Self-Service Launderette: . . . . .Yes
Fantasy), The Bahamas *(Fascination)*	Size Range (sq ft/m):	Dedicated Cinema/Seats: . . . . .No
Length (ft/m): 855.8/263.6	173.2–409.7/16.0–38.0	Library: . . . . .Yes
Beam (ft/m): 103.0/31.4	Cabins (outside view): . . . . . . .618 or 620	Onboard currency . . . . .US$
Draft (ft/m): 25.9/7.9	Cabins (interior/no view): 408	
Propulsion/Propellers: . . . . .diesel-electric	Cabins (for one person): 0	

Floating fun palaces for ultra-casual first-time cruisers.

OVERVIEW. Externally angular and not at all handsome, these ships belong to Carnival's Fantasy-class series of almost identical, very successful ships, along with *Carnival Imagination, Carnival Inspiration, Carnival Paradise* and *Carnival Sensation*. They are aimed at the mainstream first-time cruiser. There are fewer balcony cabins than in the company's newer ships.

THE SHIPS. All have extremely short bows and reasonable open deck areas which quickly become inadequate when the ships are full and everyone wants to be out on deck. The aft decks tend to be less noisy, whereas all the activities are focused around the main swimming pool and hot tubs (one with a thatched shade). There's also a topless sunbathing area for those who prefer European-style sunning. There is no walk-around open promenade deck, although there is a short jogging track. The lifeboats, six of which double as twin screw shore tenders, are positioned high atop the ships.

The interior spaces are well utilized. The general passenger flow is good, and the interior design – the work of Miami-based creative genius Joe Farcus – is clever, functional, and extremely colourful. He calls it "entertainment architecture," and considers every part of a ship as a piece of a giant jigsaw puzzle. Each ship has an interior design

BERLITZ'S RATINGS

	Possible	Achieved
Ship	500	318
Accommodation	200	138
Food	400	213
Service	400	262
Entertainment	100	73
Cruise	400	243

OVERALL SCORE
1,247 points out of 2,000

theme. For example, *Carnival Fantasy*'s is mythical muses, and composers and their compositions. The interior focal point is an "open" atrium lobby, whose balconied shape recalls some of the world's great opera houses; it spans six decks, and is topped by a large glass dome.

The lowest level is where you'll find the Purser's Desk and Shore Excursion Desk. The original sculpture has gone, replaced by a lobby bar and live music; it's the most central place to meet.

There are public entertainment lounges, bars and clubs galore, with something for everyone (except quiet space). The public rooms, connected by a double-width indoor boulevard, combine a colorful mix of classic and contemporary design elements. Most public rooms and attractions lead off from this boulevard – a sort of shipboard "Main Street" which runs between the showlounge (forward) and lounge/nightclub (aft). A large casino has almost non-stop action. Conversely, there is also a fine looking library and reading room, but few books.

While the cuisine is just so-so, the real fun begins at sundown when Carnival really excels in sound, lights, razzle-dazzle shows and late-night high volume sounds. From venues such as Electricity Disco to Cleopatra's Bar, these ships' interior decor will entertain you. However, the ships are not for those who seeking a quiet, relaxing cruise experience. There are simply too many annoying announcements, and the never-ending hustling to get you to buy drinks and many other things.

Shore excursions can be booked via the in-cabin "Fun Vision" television system, but obtaining advice and suggestions isn't easy. In fact, getting anyone to answer your questions can be frustrating.

Onboard enhancements for all eight of the "Carnival Fantasy"-class ships in their 2007–9 refurbishments included: an expansive children's water park; updated design style and features for pool areas, and the creation of the Serenity adults-only deck area; a nine-hole miniature golf course on Sun Deck as well as a new Café (a patisserie serving specialty coffees and sweets, located along the Promenade Deck); a teen club (for the line's popular "Club 02" teen program), plus a new 1,600-sq-ft (149-sq-meter) Children's World play area, located on Verandah Deck, to enhance the Camp Carnival children's program.

Other additions included an art gallery, a photo gallery, an Atrium Bar, a New York-style deli in the Lido restaurant, a better internet café, and a 1,200-sq-ft (111-sq-meter) conference room. Suites/cabins include flat-screen TVs, new decor and remodeled bathrooms; 98 cabins received a small balcony. Spa Carnival got new private treatment rooms, and updated exercise equipment.

FAMILIES. Kids will, I am sure, enjoy "Children's World", a 2,500 sq. ft (230 sq. meter) play-area with games and fun stuff for youngsters of all ages, including Apple computers loaded with educational software, and an arts and crafts area with spin and sand art machines. A group babysitting service is available ($6 per hour for the first child; $4 per hour for each additional child of the same immediate family).

ACCOMMODATION. There are 13 grades of accommodation. The price you pay will depend on grade, size and location. The standard outside-view and interior cabins have decor that is rather plain and unmemorable. They are marginally comfortable, yet spacious enough and practical (most are of the same size and appointments), with good storage space and practical, well-designed no-nonsense bathrooms. However, if you have a queen-bed configuration instead of the standard twin-bed layout, note that one person has to clamber over the bed – an ungainly exercise for those of a heavier build.

Anyone booking an outside suite will find more space, whirlpool bathtubs, and some rather eclectic decor and furniture. These are mildly attractive, but so-so, and they are much smaller than those aboard ships of a similar size of competing companies. A small gift basket of toiletry samples is provided in all grades of accommodation.

Book a Category 11 or 12 suite, and you get "Skipper's Club" priority check-in at any US homeland port – useful for getting ahead of the crowd.

Room service items are available 24 hours a day, although in standard cabins, only cold food is available, while those in suite-grade accommodation get a greater range of items (both hot and cold) to choose from.

CUISINE. The two large main dining rooms, located midships and aft, are called *Wind Star* and *Wind Song* in *Carnival Ecstasy*, *Imagination* and *Inspiration* in *Carnival Elation*, *Celebration* and *Jubilee* in *Carnival Fantasy*, and *Sensation* and *Imagination* in *Carnival Fascination*. All have ocean-view windows, and are noisy, but the decor is attractive, although extremely bright. Choose either fixed-time dining (6pm or 8:15pm), or flexible dining (any time between 5:45 and 9:30pm).

The food is so-so. Presentation is simple, and few garnishes are used. Many meat and fowl dishes are disguised with gravies and sauces. The selection of fresh green vegetables, breads, rolls, cheeses and fruits is limited, and there is much use of canned fruit and jellied desserts. There's a decent wine list, but no wine waiters. The waiters sing and dance, and there are constant waiter parades.

At night, the *Seaview Bistro*, as the Windows on the Sea lido self-serve buffet restaurant is known in the evenings, provides a casual alternative to the main dining rooms, for pasta, steaks, salads and desserts – it typically operates only between 6pm and 9pm. The food selection, though limited, makes a change from the large, crowded main dining rooms.

A patisserie offers specialty coffees and sweets (extra charge), and a so-called sushi bar on Promenade Deck is open prior to dinner; if you know anything about sushi, don't expect authenticity.

Carnival Fantasy-class ships do not have "alternative" (extra-charge) dining spots.

ENTERTAINMENT. A main showlounge is the venue for large-scale production shows and major cabaret acts – although 20 pillars obstruct some views. In a typical three- or four-day cruise, there will be one or two trend-setting production shows, with a cast of two lead singers and a clutch of dancers, backed by a 10-piece live orchestra.

SPA/FITNESS. A large, glass-wrapped health, fitness and spa complex is located on the uppermost interior deck, forward of the ship's mast; it is typically open from 6am to 8pm daily. It consists of a gymnasium with oceanview windows that look out over the bow and the latest in muscle-pumping electronic machines, an aerobics exercise room, men's and women's changing rooms, sauna and steam rooms, and beauty salon. A common complaint is that there aren't enough staff to keep the area clean and tidy, and used towels are often strewn around the changing rooms.

Sporting types can play basketball or volleyball, or ping-pong. There is also a "banked" jogging track outdoors on the deck above the spa.

● **For more extensive general information on what a Carnival cruise is like, see pages 126–31.**

Carnival Freedom
★★★ +

Size: . . . . .Large Resort Ship	Total Crew: 1,150	Wheelchair accessibility: . . . . .Good
Tonnage: 110,239	Passengers	Cabin Current: . . . . .110 volts
Lifestyle: . . . . .Standard	(lower beds/all berths): 2,974/3,700	Elevators: 20
Cruise Line: . . . . . . .Carnival Cruise Lines	Passenger Space Ratio	Casino (gaming tables): . . . . .Yes
Former Names: . . . . .none	(lower beds/all berths): 37.0/29.7	Slot Machines: . . . . .Yes
Builder: . . . . .Fincantieri (Italy)	Crew/Passenger Ratio	Swimming Pools (outdoors): 2
Original Cost: . . . .$500 million	(lower beds/all berths): 2.5/3.1	(+1 with glass dome)
Entered Service: . . . . .Feb 2007	Cabins (total): 1,487	Swimming Pools (indoors): 0
Registry: . . . . .Panama	Size Range (sq ft/m):	Whirlpools: 7
Length (ft/m): 951.4/290.0	179.7–484.2/16.7–44.8	Self-Service Launderette: . . . . .Yes
Beam (ft/m): 105.6/32.2	Cabins (outside view): 917	Dedicated Cinema/Seats: . . . . .No
Draft (ft/m): 27.2/8.3	Cabins (interior/no view): 570	Library: . . . . .Yes
Propulsion/Propellers: . . . . .diesel-electric	Cabins (for one person): 0	Onboard currency . . . . .US$
(63,400kW)/2	Cabins (with private balcony): 574	
Passenger Decks: 13	Cabins (wheelchair accessible): 25	

A fun-filled, alive-at-night ship with exciting decor.

OVERVIEW. *Carnival Freedom* shares the same generally balanced profile as sisters *Carnival Conquest, Carnival Destiny, Carnival Glory, Carnival Liberty, Carnival Triumph, Carnival Valor,* and *Carnival Victory.* Being a non-Panamax ship, it is unable to transit the Panama Canal, due to its size. Immediately recognizable is the swept-back wingtip funne, Carnival's trademark.

THE SHIP. The interior decor is a kaleidoscopic blend of colors that stimulate and excite the senses, and is dedicated to time, and the decades. The deck and public room layout is logical, and finding your way around is quite easy. Most of the public rooms are located on one deck off a main interior boulevard, above a deck which contains the two main dining rooms. The public rooms include a large casino with gaming tables and over 300 slot machines.

If you remember drive-in movie theaters, Carnival's Seaside Theatre for movies on deck recalls classic drive-in movie theaters, with seating in tiered rows and the screen facing forward. The ship has bow-to-stern wi-fi internet access, including all passenger cabins.

Minor niggles include the fact that many pillars obstruct passenger flow, particularly in the dining room, where they make it difficult for the waiters to serve food properly.

FAMILIES. Youngsters are provided with their own Camp Carnival children's club with its own small outdoor pool, and are well cared for with the line's extensive children's program. Camp Carnival is located on Sun Deck, out of the way of older passengers.

BERLITZ'S RATINGS

	Possible	Achieved
Ship	500	414
Accommodation	200	157
Food	400	218
Service	400	260
Entertainment	100	82
Cruise	400	259

OVERALL SCORE
1,390 points out of 2,000

ACCOMMODATION. There are 20 cabin price categories, in seven different suite/cabin types, sizes and grades. These include suites with private balcony; deluxe outside-view cabins with private balcony; outside-view cabins with private balcony; outside-view cabins with window; cabins with a porthole instead of a window; interior cabins; and interior with upper and lower berths.

There are five decks of cabins with private balconies. Standard cabins are of good size and come equipped with all the basics, although the furniture is rather square and angular, with no rounded edges. Three decks of cabins (eight on each deck, each with private balcony) overlook the stern. Most cabins with twin beds convert to a queen-size bed format.

Book a suite (Category 11 or 12 in the Carnival Cruise Lines brochure) and you'll get "Skipper's Club" priority check-in at any US homeland port – useful for getting ahead of the crowd.

There are even "spa" cabins aboard this ship – a grouping of 18 cabins located directly around and behind Spa-Carnival; so fitness devotees can get out of bed and go straight to the treadmill without having to go through any of the public rooms first.

A gift basket of toiletries is provided in all grades of cabins; it includes aloe soap, shampoo, conditioner, deodorant, breath mints, candy, and pain relief tablets (all in sample sizes – and most in paper packets that are difficult, sometimes frustrating, to open).

CUISINE. There are two principal dining rooms (*Chic 744,* located midships; and *Posh*, aft, seating 1,122). Both are two decks high and have a balcony level (the balcony level in Posh is larger than the one in Chic). There's a choice of either fixed time dining (6pm or 8:15pm), or flexible dining (any time between 5:45pm and 9:30pm).

There are few table for two, but my favourites are the two tables for two right at the very back of the restaurant, with ocean views astern.

Alternative (Reservations-Only, Extra Cost) Dining: The *Sun King Supper Club* has fine table settings, china and silverware, as well as leather-bound menus. The featured specialties are steaks and seafood items. It's worth paying the cover charge to get a taste of what Carnival can really deliver in terms of food that is of better quality than what's served in the main dining rooms.

Casual Eateries: The *Freedom Restaurant*, a casual self-serve international food court-style lido deck eatery, has two main serving lines. Included in this eating mall are a deli, an Asian eatery with wok preparation, a 24-hour pizzeria, and a grill for fast foods such as hamburgers and hot dogs. Each night, the Freedom Restaurant morphs into the "Seaview Bistro," and provides a dress-down alternative to eating in the main dining rooms, serving pasta, steaks, salads and desserts (typically 6–9pm).

Other "nooks and crannies" (extra cost) food and drink-related places include the *Nouveau Wine Bar*, the *Viennese Café*, and the cute little *Meiji Sushi Bar*. All are located on Promenade Deck.

ENTERTAINMENT. The Victoriana Theater (named after England's Queen Victoria) is the ship's multi-deck showlounge, and seats up to 1,400. colorful Las-Vegas-style production shows and major cabaret acts. It has a revolving stage, hydraulic orchestra pit, superb sound, and seating on three levels (the upper levels being tiered through two decks). A proscenium arch acts as a scenery loft. The decor is medieval (drinks tables look like shields, and towers with stained-glass windows, shields, and coats of armor flank the stage).

An alternative entertainment venue is the aft lounge, which seats 425 and typically features live music and late-night cabaret acts including smutty adult comedy.

Body-throbbing loud music sensations can be found in the ship's discotheque; it includes a video wall with live projections from the dance floor. Meanwhile piano bar lovers should enjoy the 100-seat Lindy Hop piano bar.

SPA/FITNESS. SpaCarnival, spanning two decks with a total area of approximately 13,300 sq. ft/1,235 sq. meters, is located above the navigation bridge, and accessed from the forward stairway. Lower-level facilities include a solarium, eight treatment rooms, lecture rooms, sauna and steam rooms for men and women, and a beauty parlor; the upper level consists of a large gymnasium with floor-to-ceiling windows including forward-facing ocean views, and an aerobics room with instructor-led classes (some at extra cost) for which you'll need to sign up.

● **For more extensive general information on what a Carnival cruise is like, see pages 126–31.**

WHERE NAUTICAL EXPRESSIONS COME FROM

If you've ever wondered where some terms or phrases came from, you have only to look to the sea, ships, and seamen.

In the doldrums

Doldrums is the name of a place in the ocean that is located either side of, and near, the equator. It is characterized by unstable trade winds or even lack of winds for days, if not weeks, at a time. A sailing ship caught in the Doldrums can be stranded due to lack of wind. If the situation was bad enough, or if danger threatened, the boats might be launched in order to tow the ship until the wind picked up. Today, if we are in the doldrums, we feel stagnated or even morose.

Mind your P's and Q's

Sailors would get credit at the waterfront taverns until they were paid. The innkeeper kept a record of their drinks, and he had to mind that no pints or quarts were left off of their accounts. Today, the term usually refers to manners.

Passed with flying colors

This comes from sailing ships that, when passing other ships at sea, would fly their colors (pennants, flags) if they wanted to be identified. Today we tend to mean by this phrase that a person has passed an exam or test or trial with great marks.

Pipe down

A boatswain's call denoting the completion of an all hands evolution, and that you can go below. This expression is now used to mean "keep quiet" or "quiet down."

Port and Starboard

Originally, the old sailing ships (like the Vikings), didn't have a rudder, and were steered by a board on the right side. This came to be the "steerboard" side or starboard. The other side was called "larboard" at first, but since the side with the board could not be against the dock, the left when facing forward, it became known as the "port" side.

Round robin

The term originated in the British nautical tradition. Sailors wishing to mutiny would sign their names in a circle so the leader could not be identified. Today the term is often used in sports and competitions to denote a series of games in which all members of a league play each other one time.

Carnival Glory
★★★ +

Size:	Large Resort Ship	Total Crew:	1,160	Wheelchair accessibility:	Good
Tonnage:	110,239	Passengers		Cabin Current:	110 volts
Lifestyle:	Standard	(lower beds/all berths):	2,974/3,700	Elevators:	14
Cruise Line:	Carnival Cruise Lines	Passenger Space Ratio		Casino (gaming tables):	Yes
Former Names:	none	(lower beds/all berths):	37.0/29.7	Slot Machines:	Yes
Builder:	Fincantieri (Italy)	Crew/Passenger Ratio		Swimming Pools (outdoors):	2
Original Cost:	$500 million	(lower beds/all berths):	2.5/3.1		(+1 with glass dome)
Entered Service:	Jul 2003	Cabins (total):	1,487	Swimming Pools (indoors):	0
Registry:	Panama	Size Range (sq ft/m):		Whirlpools:	7
Length (ft/m):	951.4/290.0	179.7–482.2/16.7–44.8		Self-Service Launderette:	Yes
Beam (ft/m):	116.4/35.5	Cabins (outside view):	917	Dedicated Cinema/Seats:	No
Draft (ft/m):	27.0/8.2	Cabins (interior/no view):	570	Library:	Yes
Propulsion/Propellers:	diesel-electric	Cabins (for one person):	0	Onboard currency	US$
	(63,400kW)/2	Cabins (with private balcony):	590		
Passenger Decks:	13	Cabins (wheelchair accessible):	25		

An ultra-casual fun-filled ship for first-time cruisers.

OVERVIEW. Like its sisters – *Carnival Conquest, Carnival Destiny, Carnival Freedom, Carnival Liberty, Carnival Triumph* and *Carnival Victory* – this ship has three decks full of lounges, 10 bars and lots of rooms to play in. Its interior decor is a fantasyland of colors, with every hue of the rainbow represented. The layout is logical, so finding your way around is easy. It has extremely short bows and cannot transit the Panama Canal.

THE SHIP. Most of *Carnival Glory*'s public rooms are located off the Kaleidoscope Boulevard, the main interior promenade – great for strolling and people-watching. The larger of two atriums, The Colors Lobby, spans nine decks in the forward third of the ship. Check out the interpretative paintings of US flags at the Color Bar – the colors really are kaleidoscopic. The aft atrium goes through three decks.

Other facilities are similar to those already described for *Carnival Conquest (see page 254)*.

FAMILIES. Youngsters have good facilities, such as their own two-level Children's Club (including an outdoor pool), and are well cared for with "Camp Carnival," the line's extensive children's program. Teens have their own "Circle C" club. Note that soft-drinks packages can be purchased for children (and adults).

ACCOMMODATION. There are 20 price categories, in seven grades: suites with private balcony; deluxe outside-view cabins with private balcony; outside-view cabins with private balcony; outside-view cabins with window; cabins

BERLITZ'S RATINGS		
	Possible	Achieved
Ship	500	408
Accommodation	200	157
Food	400	218
Service	400	259
Entertainment	100	82
Cruise	400	256
OVERALL SCORE		
1,380 points out of 2,000		

with a porthole instead of a window; interior cabins; and interior cabins with upper and lower berths. There are five decks of cabins with private balcony. Facilities are similar to those aboard *Carnival Conquest (see page 254)*.

CUISINE. The two principal dining rooms, *Golden* and *Platinum*, are two decks high, and both have a balcony level for diners. The decor includes wall coverings featuring a pattern of Japanese bonsai trees. There is also a casual self-serve food court-style lido deck eatery, the two-level *Red Sail Restaurant*, which includes Paul's Deli, Mongolian Wok, a 24-hour pizzeria, and a patisserie. Alternative dining (reservations-only, extra cost) is provided in the *Emerald Room*, whose lighting fixtures resemble giant emeralds.

Dining times and food quality are similar to those for *Carnival Conquest*.

ENTERTAINMENT. The Amber Palace Showlounge is similar to the venue aboard *Carnival Conquest*. The White Heat Dance Club, the ship's discotheque, has a "Liberace-like" tall candelabra and a video wall with projections live from the dance floor.

Jazz lovers should head for the Bar Blue. The Cinn-A-Bar is a piano bar with curved aluminum walls.

SPA/FITNESS. SpaCarnival has facilities similar to those aboard *Carnival Conquest*.

● **For more extensive general information on what a Carnival cruise is like, see pages 126–31.**

Carnival Imagination
★★★

Size: . . . . .Large Resort Ship	Passenger Decks: 10	Cabins (wheelchair accessible): 22
Tonnage: 70,367	Total Crew: 920	Wheelchair accessibility: . . . . .Fair
Lifestyle: . . . . .Standard	Passengers	Cabin Current: . . . . .110 volts
Cruise Line: . . . . . . .Carnival Cruise Lines	(lower beds/all berths): 2,056/2,634	Elevators: 14
Former Names: . . . .*Imagination*	Passenger Space Ratio	Casino (gaming tables): . . . . .Yes
Builder: . . .Kvaerner Masa-Yards (Finland)	(lower beds/all berths): 34.4/26.7	Slot Machines: .Yes
Original Cost: . . . .$330 million	Crew/Passenger Ratio	Swimming Pools (outdoors): 3
Entered Service: . . . . .Jul 1995	(lower beds/all berths): 2.2/2.8	Swimming Pools (indoors): 0
Registry: . . . . .The Bahamas	Cabins (total): 1,028	Whirlpools: 6
Length (ft/m): 855.0/260.6	Size Range (sq ft/m): .173.2–409.7/16–38	Self-Service Launderette: . . . . .Yes
Beam (ft/m): 103.0/31.4	Cabins (outside view): 620	Dedicated Cinema/Seats: . . . . .No
Draft (ft/m): 25.9/7.9	Cabins (interior/no view): 408	Library: . . . . .Yes
Propulsion/Propellers: . . . . .diesel-electric	Cabins (for one person): 0	Onboard currency . . . . .US$
(42,240 kW)/2	Cabins (with private balcony): 152	

It's a fun ship filled with high-energy cruisers.

OVERVIEW. *Carnival Imagination*'s passenger flow is good, and the interior design is clever, functional, and extremely colorful. The theme of the interior decor is musical muses and classical mythology. There are public entertainment lounges, bars and clubs galore, with something for everyone – except quiet space.

THE SHIP. This *Fantasy*-class Carnival ship has an angular appearance typical of today's space-creative designs. It has expansive open deck areas, but they are inadequate when it is full and everyone wants to be out on deck. Sadly, there is no walk-around open promenade deck. The aft decks tend to be less noisy, whereas all the activities focus on the main swimming pool and hot tubs (one with a thatched roof for shade). There is a "banked" jogging track outdoors on the deck above a large, glass-enclosed health spa.

The public rooms, connected by a wide indoor boulevard, are a colorful mix of classic and contemporary design elements. There is a dramatic six-deck-high atrium, topped by a large glass dome. The large casino has almost non-stop action; an ATM machine is located outside it.

The Victorian-style library is a curious room, with intentionally mismatched furnishings (it reminds one of *Alice in Wonderland*), fine oriental rugs, and even a few books.

ACCOMMODATION. There are 13 price grades, linked to grade, size and location. See *Carnival Fantasy* for details.

CUISINE. There are two large, colorful, noisy dining rooms

BERLITZ'S RATINGS

	Possible	Achieved
Ship	500	297
Accommodation	200	138
Food	400	213
Service	400	262
Entertainment	100	73
Cruise	400	243

OVERALL SCORE
1,226 points out of 2,000

(*Pride*, located midships, and *Spirit*, located aft, with the galley between the two). Both are non-smoking. Shorts are permitted in the dining room for one dinner each cruise. There's a choice of either fixed time dining (6pm or 8:15pm), or flexible dining (any time between 5:45pm and 9:30pm).

The Lido Cafe self-serve buffets are very basic, as is the selection of breads, rolls, fruit and cheeses. At night, it changes its name to "Seaview Bistro" and provides more of a dress-down alternative to the main dining room, serving pasta, steaks, salads and desserts (usually 6–9pm). A 24-hour Pizzeria typically serves over 500 pizzas every single day.

ENTERTAINMENT. The Dynasty Showlounge is the principal venue for large-scale production shows and major cabaret acts, but 20 pillars obstruct the views from several seats.

SPA/FITNESS. The Nautica Spa is a large glass-wrapped health, fitness and spa complex consisting of a gymnasium with oceanview windows, an aerobics exercise room, men's and women's changing rooms, sauna and steam rooms, and beauty salon. A common complaint from passengers is lack of staff to keep the area clean and tidy. Used towels are often strewn around the changing rooms, particularly on the men's side.

● For more extensive information on what a Carnival cruise is like, see pages 126–31, and for more information on the Fantasy-class ships, see *Carnival Fantasy*.

Carnival Inspiration
★★★

Size:	.Large Resort Ship	Passenger Decks:	.10	Cabins (wheelchair accessible):	.22
Tonnage:	.70,367	Total Crew:	.920	Wheelchair accessibility:	.Fair
Lifestyle:	.Standard	Passengers		Cabin Current:	.110 volts
Cruise Line:	.Carnival Cruise Lines	(lower beds/all berths):	.2,056/2,634	Elevators:	.14
Former Names:	.Inspiration	Passenger Space Ratio		Casino (gaming tables):	.Yes
Builder:	.Kvaerner Masa-Yards (Finland)	(lower beds/all berths):	.34.4/26.7	Slot Machines:	.Yes
Original Cost:	.$270 million	Crew/Passenger Ratio		Swimming Pools (outdoors):	.3
Entered Service:	.Apr 1996	(lower beds/all berths):	.2.2/2.8	Swimming Pools (indoors):	.0
Registry:	.The Bahamas	Cabins (total):	.1,028	Whirlpools:	.6
Length (ft/m):	.855.0/260.6	Size Range (sq ft/m):	.173.2–409.7/16–38	Self-Service Launderette:	.Yes
Beam (ft/m):	.103.0/31.4	Cabins (outside view):	.620	Dedicated Cinema/Seats:	. No
Draft (ft/m):	.25.9/7.9	Cabins (interior/no view):	.408	Library:	.Yes
Propulsion/Propellers:	.diesel-electric	Cabins (for one person):	.0	Onboard currency	.US$
	(42,240 kW)/2	Cabins (with private balcony):	.152		

An ultra-colorful ship for first-time casual cruising.

OVERVIEW. As in its sister *Fantasy*-class ships, there is a six-deck-high atrium, topped by a large glass dome. The atrium has scrolled shapes resembling the necks and heads of violins, and a marble staircase. There is a $1 million art collection. Particularly interesting is an avant-garde rendition of Leonardo da Vinci's *Mona Lisa*, in Pablo's Lounge.

THE SHIP. *Carnival Inspiration* has expansive open deck areas that quickly become inadequate when it is full and everyone wants to be out on deck. The aft decks are less noisy, because all the activities are focused on the main swimming pool and hot tubs. Sadly, there is no walk-around open promenade deck. The diesel electric propulsion system is almost vibration-free.

The general passenger flow is good, and the interior design is functional, and extremely colorful. There is lots of neon lighting, and the color combinations are quite vivid. The decor itself is themed after the arts (in an art nouveau style) and literature. There are public entertainment lounges, bars and clubs galore. Most lead off from a wide indoor boulevard.

The Shakespeare Library is a stately room (25 of his quotations adorn the oak veneer), but there are few books. Another dazzling room is the Rock and Roll Discotheque, with its guitar-shaped dance floor and video dance club and dozens of video monitors.

ACCOMMODATION. There are 13 grades. The price you pay will depend on the grade, size and location you choose. For a detailed explanation, see the entry for *Carnival Fantasy (page 260).*

BERLITZ'S RATINGS		
	Possible	Achieved
Ship	500	295
Accommodation	200	138
Food	400	213
Service	400	262
Entertainment	100	73
Cruise	400	242
OVERALL SCORE		
1,223 points out of 2,000		

CUISINE. There are two large, rather noisy – or perhaps one should say "lively" – dining rooms: *Mardi Gras*, located midships, and *Carnival*, located aft, with the galley between them. The service is attentive, but far too fast and assertive, and lacks finesse. Choose either fixed-time dining (6pm or 8:15pm), or flexible dining (between 5:45 and 9:30pm).

Carnival meals stress quantity, not quality. Although the company works hard to improve the cuisine, food and its taste are still not the company's strongest points.

Casual meals can be taken at informal food outlets such as the *Brasserie Bar and Grill*, which also includes an always-open Pizzeria (it serves over 500 every single day). At night, the *Seaview Bistro*, as the Lido Café becomes known, provides a dress-down alternative to the main dining rooms, serving pasta, steaks, salads and desserts; it typically operates from 6pm to 9pm.

ENTERTAINMENT. The Paris Showlounge is the principal venue for large-scale production shows and major cabaret acts, although 20 pillars obstruct views from some seats.

SPA/FITNESS. The Nautica Spa is a large glass-enclosed complex consisting of a gymnasium with a large array of the latest in muscle-pumping electronic machines, an aerobics exercise room, men's and women's changing rooms, sauna and steam rooms, and beauty salon.

● **For more extensive information on what a Carnival cruise is like, see pages 126–31, and for more information on the Fantasy-class ships, see *Carnival Fantasy.***

Carnival Legend
★★★ +

Size:	.Large Resort Ship	Passenger Decks:	12
Tonnage:	.85,920	Total Crew:	.1,030
Lifestyle:	.Standard	Passengers	
Cruise Line:	.Carnival Cruise Lines	(lower beds/all berths):	.2,124/2,680
Former Names:	.none	Passenger Space Ratio	
Builder:	.Kvaerner Masa-Yards	(lower beds/all berths):	.40.4/32.0
Original Cost:	.$375 million	Crew/Passenger Ratio	
Entered Service:	.Aug 2002	(lower beds/all berths):	.2.2/2.6
Registry:	.Panama	Cabins (total):	.1,062
Length (ft/m):	.959.6/292.5	Size Range (sq ft/m):	.185–490/17.1–45.5
Beam (ft/m):	.105.6/32.2	Cabins (outside view):	.849
Draft (ft/m):	.25.5/7.8	Cabins (interior/no view):	.213
Propulsion/Propellers:	.diesel-electric	Cabins (for one person):	.0
	(62,370 kW)/2 azimuthing pods	Cabins (with private balcony):	.750
	(17.6 MW each)	Cabins (wheelchair accessible):	.16

Wheelchair accessibility:	.Good
Cabin Current:	.110 volts
Elevators:	.15
Casino (gaming tables):	.Yes
Slot Machines:	.Yes
Swimming Pools (outdoors):	.2
	+ 1 children's pool
Swimming Pools (indoor/outdoor):	.1
Whirlpools:	.5
Self-Service Launderette:	.Yes
Dedicated Cinema/Seats:	.No
Library:	.Yes
Onboard currency	.US$

For a fun-filled cruise in a contemporary setting.

OVERVIEW. *Carnival Legend* is sister to *Carnival Miracle, Carnival Pride* and *Carnival Spirit*. It is longer than the company's larger quintet (*Carnival Conquest, Carnival Destiny, Carnival Glory, Carnival Triumph,* and *Carnival Victory*). Its launch made headlines in 2002 when actress Dame Judi Dench, the celebrity chosen to break the traditional bottle of champagne on its hull, had difficulty doing so; a final hefty heave smashed the bottle, drenching Dame Judi with champagne.

THE SHIP. The colourful atrium lobby, spanning eight decks, has wall decorations best seen from any of the multiple viewing balconies on any deck above the main lobby level. Take a drink from the lobby bar and look upwards – the surroundings are stunning, with a mural of the Colossus of Rhodes the focal point.

The interior decor is dedicated to the world's great legends, from wonders of the ancient world and heroes of antiquity to 20th-century jazz masters and great athletes – an eclectic mix that somehow works well. There are two entertainment/public room decks, the upper with an exterior promenade deck – something new for this fun cruise line.

Without doubt, the most dramatic room is the Follies Showlounge. Spanning three decks in the forward section, it recalls a 1920s movie palace. Spiral stairways at the back of the lounge connect all three levels. Stage shows are best seen from the upper three levels, from where the sight lines are reasonably good. Directly underneath is the Firebird Lounge, which has a bar in its starboard aft section.

A small wedding chapel is forward of the uppermost level

BERLITZ'S RATINGS

	Possible	Achieved
Ship	500	401
Accommodation	200	148
Food	400	229
Service	400	252
Entertainment	100	81
Cruise	400	277

OVERALL SCORE
1,388 points out of 2,000

of the two main entertainment decks, adjacent to the library and internet center. Other facilities include a winding shopping street with several boutique stores, photo gallery, video games room, and an observation balcony in the center of the vessel, at the top of the multi-deck atrium. The large Club Merlin Casino has a castle-like atmosphere, with damsels, knights and wizards as murals.

The medical department offers Tele-Radiology, enabling shipboard physicians to digitally transmit X-rays and other patient information to shore-side facilities – useful for peace of mind for passengers and crew.

The lobby's small information desk gets congested. It is hard to escape from noise and loud music (it's even played in cabin hallways and lifts), not to mention smokers, and masses of people walking around in unsuitable clothing, clutching plastic sport drinks bottles, at any time of the day or night. Many private balconies are not so private, and can be overlooked from public locations.

Many pillars obstruct passenger flow (those in the dining room, for example, make it difficult for proper food service by the waiters). Books and computers are cohabitants in the ship's library/internet center, but anyone wanting a book has to lean over others who may be using a computer – an awkward arrangement. An extra-charge, adults-only Sanctuary, with bar, was added in a 2011 refit.

ACCOMMODATION. There are 20 cabin categories, priced by grade, location and size. The range of cabins includes suites (with private balcony), outside-view cabins with private balcony, 68 ocean view cabins with French doors (pseudo balconies that have doors which open, but no balcony to step out onto), and a healthy proportion of standard outside-view to interior cabins.

All cabins have spy-hole doors, and have twin beds that can be converted into a queen-size bed, individually controlled air-conditioning, TV set, and telephone. A number of cabins on the lowest deck have views that are obstructed by lifeboats. Some cabins can accommodate a third and fourth person, but have little closet space, and there's only one personal safe. There is no separate radio in each cabin – instead, audio channels are provided on the in-cabin TV system, but you can't turn the picture off. Nor can you turn off the air conditioning in cabins or bathrooms.

A gift basket of sample-size personal amenities is provided in all grades.

Book one of the suites (Category 11 or 12 in the Carnival Cruise Lines brochure) and you automatically qualify for "Skipper's Club" priority check-in at any US homeland port – useful for getting ahead of the crowd.

Among the most desirable suites and cabins are those on five of the aft-facing decks; these have private balconies overlooking the stern and ship's wash. You might think that these units would suffer from vibration, but they don't – a bonus provided by the pod propulsion system *(see page 191)*.

For extra space, it's worthwhile booking one of the larger deluxe balcony suites on Deck 6, with private teakwood balcony. These tend to be quiet suites, with a lounge and sleeping area, a good-sized bathroom with twin washbasins, toilet and bidet, and whirlpool tub. They have twin beds convertible to a queen-size bed, three (illuminated) closets, and a huge amount of drawer space. The balcony has an outside light, and a wide teakwood deck with smoked glass and wood railing (you could easily seat 10 people).

Even the largest suites, however, are quite small compared with suites aboard other ships of a similar size – for example, Celebrity Cruises' *Constellation, Infinity, Millennium,* and *Summit,* where penthouse suites measure up to 2,530 sq. ft (235 sq. meters).

CUISINE. This ship has a single, large, two-decks-high, 1,300-seat main dining room, *Truffles Restaurant,* with seating on both upper and main levels. Its huge ceiling has large murals of a china pattern made famous by Royal Copenhagen, and wall-mounted glass display cases contain fine china. The galley is located underneath the restaurant, with escalator access. Tables are for two, four, six or eight, and small rooms on both upper and lower levels can be closed off for groups of up to 60. Choose either fixed time dining (6pm or 8:15pm), or flexible dining (between 5:45pm and 9:30pm).

For casual eaters, the *Unicorn Café* is an extensive eatery that forms the aft third of Deck 9 (part of it wraps around the upper section of the huge atrium). Murals of unicorns are everywhere. The café includes a central buffet area with a deli sandwich corner, Asian corner, rotisserie, and International counter. There are salad counters, a dessert counter, and a 24-hour Pizzeria counter, all of which offer both indoor and outdoor seating. Movement around the buffet area is slow, and you have to stand in line for everything. Each night, the Unicorn Café becomes *Seaview Bistro,* for casual, serve-yourself dinners (typically 6pm–9.30pm). **Alternative (Reservations-Only, Extra Cost) Dining:** The *Golden Fleece Supper Club* is a more upscale dining spot atop the ship, with just 156 seats and a show kitchen. It is located on two of the uppermost decks of the ship, above the Unicorn Café, in the lower, forward section of the funnel housing, with great atrium views. The decor is set around the Greek legend of Jason and the Argonauts. The bar includes a large sculpture of the Golden Fleece. Fine table settings, china and silverware are provided, along with leather-bound menus.

ENTERTAINMENT. The Follies Showlounge is the ship's principal venue for large-scale production shows and cabaret shows. Shows are best seen from the upper three levels. Directly underneath the showlounge is the Firebird Lounge, which has a bar in its starboard aft section.

Almost every lounge/bar, including Billie's Bar (a piano lounge), and Satchmo's Club (a nightclub with bar and dance floor) has live music in the evening. Finally, for the very lively, there's the disco; and there's always karaoke as well as a Passenger Talent Show during each cruise.

SPA/FITNESS. SpaCarnival, spanning two decks, is located directly above the navigation bridge in the forward part of the ship and has 13,700 sq. ft (1,272 sq. meters) of space. Facilities on the lower level include a solarium, eight treatment rooms, lecture rooms, sauna and steam rooms for men and women, and a beauty parlor. The upper level consists of a large gymnasium with floor-to-ceiling windows on three sides, including forward-facing ocean views, and an aerobics room with instructor-led classes.

There are two centrally located swimming pools outdoors, and one can be used in inclement weather due to its retractable glass dome. Adjacent are two whirlpool tubs. A winding water slide two decks high is located aft. Another smaller pool is available for children. An outdoor jogging track is located around the ship's mast and the forward third of the ship; it doesn't go around the whole ship, but it's long enough for some serious walking.

● **For more extensive general information on what a Carnival cruise is like, see pages 126–31.**

Carnival Liberty
★★★ +

Size:	.Large Resort Ship	Total Crew:	1,160	Wheelchair accessibility: .Good
Tonnage:	110,239	Passengers		Cabin Current: 110 volts
Lifestyle:	.Standard	(lower beds/all berths): 2,974/3,700		Elevators: .18
Cruise Line:	Carnival Cruise Lines	Passenger Space Ratio		Casino (gaming tables): .Yes
Former Names:	none	(lower beds/all berths): 37.0/29.7		Slot Machines: .Yes
Builder:	Fincantieri (Italy)	Crew/Passenger Ratio		Swimming Pools (outdoors): .2
Original Cost:	$500 million	(lower beds/all berths): 2.5/3.1		(+1 with glass dome)
Entered Service:	Jul 2005	Cabins (total): 1,487		Swimming Pools (indoors): .0
Registry:	Panama	Size Range (sq ft/m):		Whirlpools: .7
Length (ft/m):	951.4/290.0	179.7–482.2/16.7–44.8		Self-Service Launderette: .Yes
Beam (ft/m):	116.4/35.5	Cabins (outside view): .917		Dedicated Cinema/Seats: .No
Draft (ft/m):	27.0/8.2	Cabins (interior/no view): .570		Library: .Yes
Propulsion/Propellers:	.diesel-electric	Cabins (for one person): .0		Onboard currency .US$
	(63,400kW)/2	Cabins (with private balcony): .574		
Passenger Decks:	13	Cabins (wheelchair accessible): .25		

An ultra-colorful ship for first-time casual cruising.

OVERVIEW. *Carnival Liberty* shares the same generally well-balanced profile as sisters *Carnival Conquest, Carnival Destiny, Carnival Freedom, Carnival Glory, Carnival Triumph, Carnival Valor* and *Carnival Victory*. The ship, though registered in Panama, is unable to transit the Panama Canal. A giant Seaside Theater LED movie screen adorns the open pool deck.

THE SHIP. The decor, in the public rooms, hallways and atrium, adopts a design theme saluting master trades such as ironwork, masonry, pottery and painting. The layout is logical, so finding your way around is easy. Most public rooms are located off a main boulevard (an interior promenade that is great for strolling and people watching – particularly from the Jardin Café or Promenade Bar). Other hangouts and drinking places include The Stage (live music/karaoke lounge), the Flower Bar (main lobby), Gloves Bar (sports Bar), Paparazzi (wine bar), and The Cabinet.

There are three decks full of lounges, 10 bars and lots of rooms to play in. There are two atriums: the largest, in the forward third of the ship spans nine decks (the Grand Villa Garden Atrium combines all four of the design themes), while a small aft atrium spans three decks. The large Czar's Palace Casino, with its Russian motifs and theme, is action-packed, with more than 320 slot machines.

FAMILIES. Youngsters are provided with good facilities, including their own two-level Children's Club (including an outdoor pool), and are well cared for with "Camp Carnival", the line's extensive children's program. Soft-drinks packages can be purchased for children (and adults).

BERLITZ'S RATINGS

	Possible	Achieved
Ship	500	411
Accommodation	200	157
Food	400	218
Service	400	257
Entertainment	100	82
Cruise	400	258

OVERALL SCORE
1,383 points out of 2,000

ACCOMMODATION. There are 20 cabin price categories, in seven different grades. For full details, see the entry for *Carnival Conquest* on page 254.

CUISINE. There are two principal dining rooms, *Golden Olympian Restaurant*, forward, seating 744, and *Silver Olympian Restaurant*, aft, seating 1,122. Two additional wings (the *Persian Room* and *Satin Room*) can accommodate large groups in a private dining arrangement. There is a casual self-serve international food court-style lido deck eatery, the two-level *Emile's*, which morphs into the *Seaview Bistro* in the evening to provides a casual alternative to the main dining rooms. The alternative dining venue is *Harry's*.

For details of dining times and food quality, see the entry for *Carnival Conquest*.

ENTERTAINMENT. The Venetian Palace Showlounge is a 1,400-seat multi-deck showroom for large-scale Las Vegas-style production shows and major cabaret acts. The Victoria Lounge, located aft, seats 425 and typically features live music and late-night cabaret acts, including adult comedy. The Tattooed Lady Dance Club is the ship's discotheque; it includes a video wall with projections live from the dance floor. Piano bar lovers should enjoy the 100-seat Piano Man piano bar.

SPA/FITNESS. For details of SpaCarnival's facilities, see the entry for *Carnival Conquest*.

● **For more extensive general information on what a Carnival cruise is like, see pages 126–31.**

Carnival Magic
★★★ +

Size: ....Large Resort Ship	Passenger Decks: 13	Cabins (with private balcony):...........887
Tonnage: 128,251	Total Crew: 1,367	Cabins (wheelchair accessible): 35
Lifestyle:....................................Standard	Passengers	Wheelchair accessibility: . . . . .Good
Cruise Line: ....Carnival Cruise Lines	(lower beds/all berths):........3,646/4,631	Cabin Current: ....110 volts
Former Names: ....none	Passenger Space Ratio	Elevators: 20
Builder:........................Fincantieri (Italy)	(lower beds/all berths):............35.1/27.6	Casino (gaming tables):.....................Yes
Original Cost:........................$740 million	Crew/Passenger Ratio	Slot Machines:...................................Yes
Entered Service:.....................Jun 2011	(lower beds/all berths):...............2.6/3.3	Swimming Pools (outdoors): 2
Registry:.....................................Panama	Cabins (total):................................1,823	Swimming Pools (indoors): 0
Length (ft/m):.....................1,004.0/306.0	Size Range (sq ft/m): 185.0–430.5/	Whirlpools:..7
Beam (ft/m):............................158.0/48.0	17.1–40.0	Self-Service Launderette:...................Yes
Draft (ft/m):...............................26.2/8.0	Cabins (outside view):.....................1,145	Dedicated Cinema/Seats: ....No
Propulsion/Propellers: ......Diesel-electric	Cabins (interior/no view):...................678	Library:...Yes
(75.6 MW)/2	Cabins (for one person):..........................0	Onboard currency ....US$

A family-friendly, high-energy ship for fun-filled cruising.

OVERVIEW. *Carnival Magic* is a sister ship to *Carnival Dream,* introduced in 2010, and both are 13% larger than their close sister *Carnival Splendour.* One thing that stands out, however, is the long Twister Water Slide, part of The Waterworks on pool deck, which is really for kids. There's an adults-only, extra-charge retreat called Serenity, and this is the first Carnival ship to have a pub, the Red Frog, with its own-label beer, ThirstyRedFrog.

THE SHIP. Although the ship's bows are short, its profile is nicely balanced, with a rakish front and a more rounded stern. The propulsion system consists of the conventional twin rudder, with twin propellers. However, the ship is based on the original design for *Carnival Destiny,* and includes some of the design flaws of the *Destiny*-class, with a passenger capacity that has been increased by just over 1,000. Strangely, the cabin numbering system – even numbers, starboard side; odd numbers, port side – goes against the maritime tradition that places even-numbered cabins on the port, or left, side; and odd-numbered cabins on the starboard, or right, side.

There are numerous pools (pretty small, actually), hot tubs and open deck nooks and crannies – but one less pool than the original *Carnival Destiny.* However, there's really not enough open deck space for the number of passengers, so sunbed loungers are tightly packed together, with no room for drinks tables.

The ship does have a full walk-around open promenade deck, lined with deck chairs. Four "scenic hot tubs" are cantilevered over the sea, and provide fine views, but they do get crowded, and rowdy. Higher up, Lido Deck 10 offers

BERLITZ'S RATINGS		
	Possible	Achieved
Ship	500	415
Accommodation	200	157
Food	400	218
Service	400	261
Entertainment	100	82
Cruise	400	263
OVERALL SCORE		
1,396 points out of 2,000		

a very good open-deck area, with a tropical, resort-style main pool (still small) and a large Seaside Theatre LED movie screen. *Carnival Magic* is the second Carnival ship to stage a laser light show outdoors – which AIDA Cruises' ships have had since 1996.

The interior decor is vivid – *really* vivid. The main lobby is the stunning connection point for ship functions and people. Take the glass-walled elevators for a neat view, though you may need sunglasses. It's good to see three main elevator towers: forward, midships, and aft, unlike larger ships such as *Oasis of the Seas,* which, although it carries many more passengers, has only two such towers. So, well done, Carnival, better for safety.

The Ocean Plaza, a new Carnival feature, is a comfortable area by day and a trendy entertainment venue by night. The indoor/outdoor café and live music venue has a bandstand where a variety of musical genres are showcased, a large circular dance floor, and around 190 seats. A floor-to-ceiling curved glass wall separates the room, dividing indoor and outdoor seating areas. An adjacent bar also offers espresso and cappuccino coffees, gelato ice creams, and pastries.

A wide variety of lounges, bars and nightspots, including a dance club with a twist, offering indoor/outdoor access, are accessible via an 11-deck-high atrium whose ground level has a neatly cantilevered bandstand atop a massive dance floor. The Page Turner (great name) is the ship's library, while Jackpot is – you guessed it – the colourful, large, lively and noisy casino.

Other rooms include The Song (Jazz Bar); Ocean Plaza (a sort of quiet area during the day, but lively at night with live entertainment); internet-connect computer terminals are scattered throughout the ship, but few have much privacy. There's also a 232-capacity conference room called The Chambers.

There is much congestion just before the second seating, on both Upper- and Lower Dream Streets, both located on the starboard side. Further congestion appears around the photo gallery, which surrounds the atrium lobby. All in all, this is a ship designed to encourage you to spend money on lots of extras – especially if have children with you – and it really is a good ship for junior cruisers who just want to have fun. Gratuities are charged to your onboard account.

FAMILIES: About 5,000 sq.ft. of space is devoted to the line's three age-related children's programs: "Camp Carnival" for ages 2–11, "Circle C" for 12- to 14-year-olds, and "Club O2" for teens 15–17. A full schedule of morning-to-night activities caters to each age group. Carnival Water-Works, an expansive aqua park with exhilarating water slides and water spray apparatus, appeals to active kids.

"Deluxe" ocean-view cabins, with two bathrooms, provide comfort and convenience for families. In addition to twin beds that convert to a king, decent closet space and elegant decor, the two-bathroom configuration includes one full bathroom and a second bathroom containing a small tub with shower and sink. Some cabins can accommodate five people – good for family togetherness.

ACCOMMODATION. There are 19 cabin price categories, but just six cabin types. But, whether you go for high end or low end, all accommodation includes the Carnival Comfort Bed with plush mattresses, good-quality duvets and linens and pillows. However, the straight accommodation deck hallways create rather a cell block look – and they are bright, very bright, even at night. There are also lot of interior cabins. The cabins to go for are those at the stern, with great rearward ocean views on Decks 6, 7, 8 and 9.

Apart from the Deluxe cabins described above, there is a wide selection of balcony cabins and suites, including "Cove Balcony" cabins that are the closest to the waterline.

Adjacent to the Cloud 9 Spa are 65 "Cloud 9" spa cabins, designated as no-smoking. They provide a number of "exclusive" amenities and privileges. You should be aware that some cabins are located directly over loud late-night venues, with poor soundproofing. Also, cabins on Deck 12 are subject to lots of noise from kids having fun on the deck above – so afternoon naps are out.

CUISINE. There are two main restaurants: a 1,180-seat midships dining room, and a smaller 828-seat aft dining room. Each has two levels: main and balcony, with the galley set on the lower level. Two small restaurant annexes can be reserved by small groups as a private dining room. Expect all-singing, all-dancing waiters to entertain while you search for the elusive green vegetables.

The *Lido Restaurant*, the ship's self-serve buffet facility, has indoor/outdoor seating areas on the lower (main) level, and indoor-only seating on the upper level. A number of designated areas serve different types of ethnic cuisine, including a Mongolian Wok and Pasta Bar on the upper level, open 6–9pm for tablecloth-free buffet dinners. It gets congested and the food is pretty basic, but it works, just.

Alternative (Reservations-Only, Extra-Cost) Dining: The extra-charge *Supper Club* and bar seats 139, has great views to port and starboard from its aft location high up on Spa Deck 12, and an à la carte menu. It has fine table settings, china and silverware, and leather-bound menus. The specialties are steaks and seafood items. It's worth paying the cover charge to get a taste of what Carnival can really deliver in terms of food that is of better quality than what is served in the main dining rooms. It's also the place to go for celebrating something special, or just to get away from the noise of the large dining rooms.

There's a sushi venue, too; note the large fish behind the sushi bar.

ENTERTAINMENT. The 1,964-seat showlounge spans three decks at the front of the ship, with seating set in a horseshoe shape around a large proscenium arched stage; the sightlines are generally good, except from some of the seats at the back of the lowest level. Large-scale production shows, with lots of feathers and skimpy costumes are staged, together with snappy cabaret acts, all with a live showband as accompaniment.

The 425-seat Burgundy Lounge, at the aft end of the ship – opposite to the showlounge, at the front – has a stage, dance floor, large bar, and is a comedy venue, including late-night raunchy "adult comedy." Caliente is the ship's hot club; it provides Latin music for vibrant dancing and hot-foot style, but at ear-splitting volume.

SPA/FITNESS. The expansive 23,750-sq-ft (2,206 sq-meter) Cloud 9 Spa is a large and elaborate health and wellness center; it is positioned over three decks in the front section of the ship and well appointed. The uppermost deck includes indoor/outdoor private spa relaxation areas, at extra cost. A spiral staircase connects the two decks, and the Steiner-operated spa offers a wide range of treatments.

There are 10 treatment rooms, including a VIP room, a large massage room for couples, and a Rasul mud treatment room, plus two dry flotation rooms. A "Thermal Suite" (extra charge) comes with the typical sensory-enhanced soothing heated chambers: Laconium, Tepidarium, Aroma and Oriental steam baths. There are two steam rooms, one each for men and women, and a small unisex sauna with a floor-to-ceiling window on its starboard side.

A large outdoor SportsSquare for adults is a fenced area for basketball, football and volleyball. Then there's an outdoor weight-training circuit (SkyFitness), and the cutely named Turf on Surf miniature golf course. Perhaps the highlight is SkyCourse, a 230-ft (70-meter) long outdoor ropes course, suspended above the uppermost deck. After all those activities, you'll need a cruise to relax.

● **For more extensive general information on what a Carnival cruise is like, see pages 126–31.**

Carnival Miracle
★★★ +

Size:	Large Resort Ship	Passenger Decks:	13	Cabins (wheelchair accessible):	16
Tonnage:	85,920	Total Crew:	961	Wheelchair accessibility:	Good
Lifestyle:	Standard	Passengers		Cabin Current:	110 volts
Cruise Line:	Carnival Cruise Lines	(lower beds/all berths):	2,124/2,680	Elevators:	15
Former Names:	none	Passenger Space Ratio		Casino (gaming tables):	Yes
Builder:	Kvaerner Masa-Yards	(lower beds/all berths):	40.4/32.0	Slot Machines:	Yes
Original Cost:	$375 million	Crew/Passenger Ratio		Swimming Pools (outdoors):	2+1
Entered Service:	Apr 2004	(lower beds/all berths):	2.2/2.7		children's pool
Registry:	Panama	Cabins (total):	1,062	Swimming Pools (indoors):	1
Length (ft/m):	959.6/292.5	Size Range (sq ft/m):	185.0–490.0/		(indoor/outdoor)
Beam (ft/m):	105.6/32.2		17.1–45.5	Whirlpools:	5
Draft (ft/m):	25.5/7.8	Cabins (outside view):	849	Self-Service Launderette:	Yes
Propulsion/Propellers:	diesel-electric	Cabins (interior/no view):	213	Dedicated Cinema/Seats:	No
	(62,370 kW)/2 azimuthing pods	Cabins (for one person):	0	Library:	Yes
	(17.6 MW each)	Cabins (with private balcony):	750	Onboard currency	US$

A fun-filled, family-friendly ship for high-energy cruising.

OVERVIEW. *Carnival Miracle* – sister to *Carnival Legend, Carnival Pride* and *Carnival Spirit* – is built from more than 100 blocks, each weighing up to 450 tons. It is longer than the company's larger quintet (*Carnival Conquest, Carnival Destiny, Carnival Glory, Carnival Triumph,* and *Carnival Victory*). The interior decor is very artistic and overwhelmingly colorful – there are no restful colors – with "fictional icons" as the design theme, including such luminaries as the Phantom of the Opera, Sherlock Holmes, Philip Marlowe, and Captain Ahab. Bronze statues of Orpheus and Ulysses adorn the swimming pools.

THE SHIP. For a full description of the wide range of facilities, see the entry for *Carnival Legend (page 267).*

ACCOMMODATION. There are 20 cabin categories, priced according to grade, location and size. For a complete review of this range, see the entry for *Carnival Legend.*

CUISINE. This ship has a single, large, two-decks-high, 1,300-seat main dining room called the Bacchus Restaurant, with seating on both upper and main levels. For casual eaters, Horatio's Cafe is an extensive eatery that forms the aft third of Deck 9 (part of it also wraps around the upper section of the huge atrium). The café includes a central area with small buffet counters (deli sandwich corner, Asian corner, rotisserie, and International counter); there are salad

BERLITZ'S RATINGS		
	Possible	Achieved
Ship	500	401
Accommodation	200	148
Food	400	229
Service	400	251
Entertainment	100	81
Cruise	400	277
OVERALL SCORE		
1,387 points out of 2,000		

counters, a dessert counter, and a 24-hour Pizzeria counter, all of which form a large eatery with both indoor and outdoor seating. Movement around the buffet area is slow, and you have to stand in line for everything. At night, the cafe becomes Seaview Bistro, for casual, serve-yourself dinners (typically open 6pm–9.30pm).

The ship's alternative restaurant (reservations-only, extra-cost) is called *Nick and Nora's Supper Club,* recalling Dashiell Hammett's characters in *The Thin Man.* It is more upscale, with just 156 seats.

For more details of dining times and food quality, see the entry for *Carnival Legend.*

ENTERTAINMENT. The Mad Hatter's Ball Showlounge is the venue for large-scale production shows and cabaret acts. Stage shows are best seen from the upper three levels, from where the sight lines are reasonable. Directly underneath the showlounge is the Phantom Lounge, which has a bar in its starboard aft section. Stage smoke appears to be in constant use during the production shows, and volumes are of the ear-splitting type.

SPA/FITNESS. SpaCarnival spans two decks. For a desciption of its facilities, see the entry for *Carnival Legend.*

● **For more extensive general information on what a Carnival cruise is like, see pages 126–31.**

Carnival Paradise
★★★

Size: . . . . .Large Resort Ship	Passenger Decks: 10	Cabins (wheelchair accessible): 22
Tonnage: .70,367	Total Crew: 920	Wheelchair accessibility: . . . . .Fair
Lifestyle: . . . . .Standard	Passengers	Cabin Current: . . . . .110 volts
Cruise Line: . . . . . . .Carnival Cruise Lines	(lower beds/all berths): 2,052/2,594	Elevators: 14
Former Names: . . . .*Paradise*	Passenger Space Ratio	Casino (gaming tables): . . . . .Yes
Builder: . . .Kvaerner Masa-Yards (Finland)	(lower beds/all berths): 34.2/26.7	Slot Machines: . . . . .Yes
Original Cost: . . . .$300 million	Crew/Passenger Ratio	Swimming Pools (outdoors): 3
Entered Service: . . . . .Nov 1998	(lower beds/all berths): 2.2/2.8	Swimming Pools (indoors): 0
Registry: . . . . .Panama	Cabins (total): 1,026	Whirlpools: 6
Length (ft/m): 855.0/260.6	Size Range (sq ft/m): .173.2–409.7/16–38	Self-Service Launderette: . . . . .Yes
Beam (ft/m): 103.3/31.5	Cabins (outside view): 618	Dedicated Cinema/Seats: . . . . .No
Draft (ft/m): 25.9/7.9	Cabins (interior/no view): 408	Library: . . . . .Yes
Propulsion/Propellers: . . . . .diesel-electric	Cabins (for one person): 0	Onboard currency . . . . .US$
(42,842 kW)/2 azimuthing pods	Cabins (with private balcony): 152	

A family-friendly, high-energy ship for ultra-casual cruising.

OVERVIEW. *Carnival Paradise* is the eighth (and final) in Carnival's series of Fantasy-class ships, with the same internal configuration and layout. The interior decor includes splashy, showy, public rooms and interior colors – pure Las Vegas, ideal for some tastes. Public entertainment lounges, bars and clubs galore offer something for everyone, including a large children's playroom.

THE SHIP. *Carnival Paradise* has a forthright, angular appearance typical of today's space-creative designs. It is one of only two of the Fantasy-class ships – the other is *Carnival Elation* – to have been provided with a "pod" propulsion system *(technical details: page 191).*

The ship has expansive open deck areas (there is no walk-around open promenade deck), but they quickly become inadequate when it is full and everyone wants a place in the sun. The aft decks tend to be less noisy, whereas all the activities are focused around the main swimming pool and hot tubs.

Some busy colors and design themes abound in the handsome public rooms. Much of the eclectic art collection is bright and eye-catching. The Blue Riband library is a nice room, with few books but models of ocean liners. A good hangout place is the atrium lobby bar, with live music. Facilities include a shop stuffed with low-quality merchandise, and a large casino with gaming tables for blackjack, craps, roulette, Caribbean stud poker, plus slot machines.

ACCOMMODATION. There are 13 grades, priced according to grade, size and location. See *Carnival Fantasy (page 260)* for a more detailed description.

BERLITZ'S RATINGS

	Possible	Achieved
Ship	500	296
Accommodation	200	138
Food	400	213
Service	400	260
Entertainment	100	73
Cruise	400	242

OVERALL SCORE
1,222 points out of 2,000

CUISINE. There are two dining rooms (*Destiny*, aft; and *Elation*, midships). They have splashy decor, and are large, crowded and very noisy. While menu descriptions sound inviting, the food may prove disappointing. You get what you pay for, and this company pays very little for food. There's a choice of either fixed-time dining (6pm or 8:15pm), or flexible dining (between 5:45pm and 9:30pm).

For casual meals, there's the *Lido Café*, which, aboard this ship, has some improvements worthy of note, such as an orange juice machine, where you put in oranges and out comes fresh juice – better than the concentrate stuff supplied in the dining room. The *Pizzeria* is open 24 hours a day. There's a small sushi bar. At night, the *Seaview Bistro*, as the Lido Café becomes known, provides a dress-down venue.

ENTERTAINMENT. The 1,010-seat Normandie Show-lounge is the main venue for large-scale production shows and cabaret acts, but 20 pillars obstruct some sightlines.

SPA/FITNESS. SpaCarnival is a large health, fitness and spa complex on the uppermost interior deck, forward of the ship's mast. It consists of an aerobics exercise room, men's and women's changing rooms, sauna and steam rooms, beauty salon and a gymnasium with ocean-view windows looking over the ship's bow and the latest in muscle-pumping electronic machines.

● **For more extensive information on what a Carnival cruise is like, see pages 126–31, and for more information on the Fantasy-class ships, see *Carnival Fantasy.***

Carnival Pride
★★★ +

Size: . . . . .Large Resort Ship	Passenger Decks: 12	Cabins (wheelchair accessible): 16
Tonnage: .85,920	Total Crew: .1,029	Wheelchair accessibility: . . . . .Good
Lifestyle: . . . . .Standard	Passengers	Cabin Current: . . . . .110 volts
Cruise Line: . . . . . . .Carnival Cruise Lines	(lower beds/all berths): 2,124/2,680	Elevators: 15
Former Names: . . . . .none	Passenger Space Ratio	Casino (gaming tables): . . . . .Yes
Builder: . . . . .Kvaerner Masa-Yards	(lower beds/all berths): 40.4/32.0	Slot Machines: . . . . .Yes
Original Cost: . . . .$375 million	Crew/Passenger Ratio	Swimming Pools (outdoors): . . . . .2+1
Entered Service: . . . . .Jan 2002	(lower beds/all berths): 2.2/2.6	children's pool
Registry: . . . . .Panama	Cabins (total): 1,062	Swimming Pools (indoors): 1
Length (ft/m): 959.6/292.5	Size Range (sq ft/m): 185.0–490.0/	(indoor/outdoor)
Beam (ft/m): 105.6/32.2	17.1–45.5	Whirlpools: 5
Draft (ft/m): 25.5/7.8	Cabins (outside view): 849	Self-Service Launderette: . . . . .Yes
Propulsion/Propellers: . . . . .diesel-electric	Cabins (interior/no view): 213	Dedicated Cinema/Seats: . . . . .No
(62,370 kW)/2 azimuthing pods	Cabins (for one person): 0	Library: . . . . .Yes
(17.6 MW each)	Cabins (with private balcony): 750	Onboard currency . . . . .US$

For a fun-filled cruise in a contemporary setting.

OVERVIEW. This ship is sister to *Carnival Legend, Carnival Miracle* and *Carnival Spirit,* all of which can transit the Panama Canal. Its decor is extremely eclectic, with art being the theme – even elevator doors and interiors display reproductions (blown-up, over-grainy photographic copies) of some of the great Renaissance masters such as Gauguin, Matisse and Jacopo Vignali.

THE SHIP. *Carnival Pride,* whose bows are extremely short, is longer than the company's larger quintet (*Carnival Conquest, Carnival Destiny, Carnival Glory, Carnival Triumph,* and *Carnival Victory),* all of which measure over 100,000 tons.

The lobby is immense, spanning eight decks, and the decor includes lots of larger-than-life women's breasts, bottoms, and nude men – all reproductions from the Renaissance period. The atrium lobby has a stunning 37-ft high (11-meter) reproduction of Raphael's *Nymph Galatea* that is best seen from any of the multiple viewing balconies on each deck above the main lobby floor level. There's no question about it – the surroundings are quite stunning.

One of the two centrally located outdoor swimming pools has a retractable glass dome. There are two whirlpool tubs, located adjacent to the swimming pools. A winding water slide that spans two decks in height is located at an aft, upper deck. Another smaller pool is available for children. There is also an additional whirlpool tub outdoors, plus a jogging track.

For a fuller description facilities such as the wedding chapel, library/internet center, and casino, see the entry for *Carnival Legend (page 267).*

BERLITZ'S RATINGS

	Possible	Achieved
Ship	500	401
Accommodation	200	148
Food	400	229
Service	400	251
Entertainment	100	81
Cruise	400	276

OVERALL SCORE
1,386 points out of 2,000

ACCOMMODATION. There are 20 cabin price categories, in six different grades. While the smallest cabin measures a very decent 185 sq. ft (17.1 sq. meters), the largest suite measures only 490 sq. ft (45.5 sq. meters) – small when compared with other ships of a similar size. For a complete review of the range, see the entry for *Carnival Legend.*

CUISINE. The *Normandie Restaurant,* a single, large, two-decks-high, 1,300-seat main dining room, has seating on both upper and main levels. For casual meals, the extensive *Mermaid's Grille* includes a central area with small buffet counters in an eclectic mix. Each night, Mermaid's Grille changes its name to *Seaview Bistro,* for casual, serve-yourself dinners in a dress-down setting.
Alternative (Reservations-Only, Extra Cost) Dining: *David's Supper Club* seats around 150 and includes a 12-ft (3.7-meter) replica of Michelangelo's *David.*

For details of dining times and food quality, see the entry for *Carnival Legend.*

ENTERTAINMENT. The 1,170-seat Taj Mahal Showlounge spans three decks in the forward section. Shows are best seen from the upper three levels. Directly underneath the showlounge is Butterflies, a large lounge with its own bar.

SPA/FITNESS. SpaCarnival spans two decks. For details of its facilities, see the entry for *Carnival Legend.*

● **For more extensive general information on what a Carnival cruise is like, see pages 126–31.**

Carnival Sensation
★ ★ ★

Size: ....Large Resort Ship	Passenger Decks: 10	Cabins (with private balcony): 152
Tonnage: 70,367	Total Crew: 920	Cabins (wheelchair accessible): 20
Lifestyle: ....Standard	Passengers	Wheelchair accessibility: ....Fair
Cruise Line: ......Carnival Cruise Lines	(lower beds/all berths): 2,040/2,594	Cabin Current: ....110 volts
Former Names: ....*Sensation*	Passenger Space Ratio	Elevators: 14
Builder: ...Kvaerner Masa-Yards (Finland)	(lower beds/all berths): 34.4/26.7	Casino (gaming tables): ....Yes
Original Cost: ....$300 million	Crew/Passenger Ratio	Slot Machines: ....Yes
Entered Service: ....Nov 1993	(lower beds/all berths): 2.2/2.8	Swimming Pools (outdoors): 3
Registry: ....The Bahamas	Cabins (total): 1,020	Swimming Pools (indoors): 0
Length (ft/m): 855.0/260.6	Size Range (sq ft/m): 173.2–409.7/	Whirlpools: 6
Beam (ft/m): 104.0/31.4	16.0–38.0	Self-Service Launderette: ....Yes
Draft (ft/m): 25.9/7.9	Cabins (outside view): 618	Dedicated Cinema/Seats: ....No
Propulsion/Propellers: .....diesel-electric	Cabins (interior/no view): 402	Library: ....Yes
(42,240kW)/2	Cabins (for one person): 0	Onboard currency ....US$

An ultra-colorful ship for first-time casual cruising.

OVERVIEW. *Carnival Sensation*, which is almost vibration-free, has expansive open deck areas (but, sadly, no walkaround open promenade deck), but they quickly become inadequate when the ship is full and everyone wants to be on deck. Inside, the general passenger flow is good, and the interior design is clever, functional, and extremely colorful. A dramatic six-deck-high atrium, with cool marble and hot neon, is topped by a large colored glass dome.

BERLITZ'S RATINGS		
	Possible	Achieved
Ship	500	317
Accommodation	200	138
Food	400	213
Service	400	261
Entertainment	100	73
Cruise	400	242
OVERALL SCORE		
1,244 points out of 2,000		

THE SHIP. Added during a 2007 refurbishment were a new nine-hole miniature golf course, a 1,600-sq-ft (148-sq-meter) Children's World play area, a Circle C tweens area (for 12–14 year-olds); a new "art" gallery, photo gallery, and a 1,200-sq-ft (111-sq-meter) conference room. All cabins were completely refurbished and given flat-screen TVs. The bathrooms were also updated. A new New York-style deli counter and a patisserie were added to the Lido Café, and the internet café was redesigned.

The library is a lovely room, but there are few books. The Michelangelo Lounge is a creative thinker's delight, while Fingers Lounge is sheer sensory stimulation. The casino has plenty of gaming tables and slot machines.

ACCOMMODATION. There are 13 price grades. For more detailed information, see the entry for *Carnival Fantasy (page 260)*. In 2009, another 98 cabins were given balconies and some suite balconies were enlarged.

CUISINE. There are two huge, noisy dining rooms (*Ecstasy* and *Fantasy*, each with assertive service. There's a choice of either fixed time dining (6pm or 8:15pm), or flexible dining (any time between 5:45pm and 9:30pm).

The *Lido Café* self-serve buffets are very basic, as is the selection of breads, rolls, fruit and cheeses. At night, the café becomes *Seaview Bistro*, providing a dress-down alternative to the main dining rooms and serving pasta, steaks, salads and desserts, typically between 6pm and 9pm. The Pizzeria is open 24 hours a day.

ENTERTAINMENT. The Fantasia Showlounge is the main venue for large-scale production shows and cabaret acts, although 20 pillars obstruct the views from several seats.

SPA/FITNESS. The Nautica Spa is a large health, fitness and spa complex located on the uppermost interior deck, forward of the ship's mast, and accessed from the forward stairway. It consists of a gymnasium with oceanview windows that look out over the ship's bow, an aerobics exercise room, men's and women's changing rooms, sauna and steam rooms, and beauty salon. There is a "banked" jogging track outdoors on the deck above the spa.

● **For more extensive information on what a Carnival cruise is like, see pages 126–31, and for more information on the Fantasy-class ships, see *Carnival Fantasy*.**

Carnival Spirit
★★★ +

Size: . . . . .Large Resort Ship	Passenger Decks: 12	Cabins (wheelchair accessible): 16
Tonnage: 85,920	Total Crew: 930	Wheelchair accessibility: . . . . .Good
Lifestyle: . . . . .Standard	Passengers	Cabin Current: . . . . .110 volts
Cruise Line: . . . . . . .Carnival Cruise Lines	(lower beds/all berths): 2,124/2,680	Elevators: 15
Former Names: . . . . .none	Passenger Space Ratio	Casino (gaming tables): . . . . .Yes
Builder: . . . . .Kvaerner Masa-Yards	(lower beds/all berths): 40.4/32.0	Slot Machines: . . . . .Yes
Original Cost: . . . .$375 million	Crew/Passenger Ratio	Swimming Pools (outdoors): 2
Entered Service: . . . . .Apr 2001	(lower beds/all berths): 2.2/2.6	+1 children's pool
Registry: . . . . .Panama	Cabins (total): 1,062	Swimming Pools (indoors): 1
Length (ft/m): 959.6/292.5	Size Range (sq ft/m): 185.0–490.0/	(indoor/outdoor)
Beam (ft/m): 105.6/32.2	17.1–45.5	Whirlpools: 5
Draft (ft/m): 25.5/7.8	Cabins (outside view): 849	Self-Service Launderette: . . . . .Yes
Propulsion/Propellers: . . . . .diesel-electric	Cabins (interior/no view): 213	Dedicated Cinema/Seats: . . . . .No
(62,370 kW)/2 azimuthing pods	Cabins (for one person): 0	Library: . . . . .Yes
(17.6 MW each)	Cabins (with private balcony): 750	Onboard currency . . . . .US$

For a fun-filled cruise in a contemporary setting.

OVERVIEW. Sister ships in the same class and internal layout and design are *Carnival Legend, Carnival Miracle* and *Carnival Pride*, and all can transit the Panama Canal. From October 2012, *Carnival Spirit* will be based in Sydney, Australia, and the onboard currency will be the Australian dollar.

THE SHIP. The interior design theme is a nod to the world's great architecture, from art nouveau to postmodern. The immense lobby space spans eight decks. The atrium lobby, with its two grand stairways, presents a stunning wall decoration best seen from any of the multiple viewing balconies on each deck above the main lobby floor level.

There are two entertainment/public room decks, the upper of which has an exterior promenade deck. There is also an outdoor jogging track.

A winding shopping street contains several boutique stores selling Carnival logo items. A small wedding chapel is adjacent to the combined library and internet center. Other facilities include a photo gallery, video games room, an observation balcony in the center of the vessel, and a piano lounge/bar. The casino is large (one has to walk through it to get from the restaurant to the showlounge on one of the entertainments decks), and it has all the gaming paraphernalia and array of slot machines you can imagine.

For a fuller description of these facilities, see the entry for *Carnival Legend (page 267).*

ACCOMMODATION. There are 20 cabin categories, priced according to grade, location and size. For a complete review

BERLITZ'S RATINGS

	Possible	Achieved
Ship	500	402
Accommodation	200	148
Food	400	229
Service	400	252
Entertainment	100	81
Cruise	400	278

OVERALL SCORE
1,390 points out of 2,000

of this range, see the entry for *Carnival Legend*.

CUISINE. The *Empire Restaurant*, the single, large, two-decks-high, 1,300-seat main dining room, has seating on two levels. The decor is heavily Napoleonic (early 19th-century French) style. For casual eaters, *La Playa Grille* forms the aft third of Deck 9, and at night becomes *Seaview Bistro*, for casual dinners (typically open 6pm–9.30pm). The *Nouveau Supper Club* is the reservations-only, extra-cost dining spot, located on two of the uppermost decks under a large glass dome.

For details of dining times and food quality, see the entry for *Carnival Legend.*

ENTERTAINMENT. The 1,170-seat Pharaoh's Palace Showlounge is a dramatic room which spans three decks in the forward section of the ship. Spiral stairways at the back of the lounge connect all levels. Stage shows are best seen from the upper three levels, from where the sight lines are reasonably good. Directly underneath the showlounge is the Versailles Lounge (in the highy decorative manner of 18th-century France), a large lounge with its own bar.

SPA/FITNESS. The Nautica health spa, spanning two decks. is located directly above the navigation bridge in the forward part of the ship. For details of its facilities, see the entry for *Carnival Legend.*

● **For more extensive general information on what a Carnival cruise is like, see pages 126–31.**

Carnival Splendor
★★★ +

Size: . . . . .Large Resort Ship	Total Crew: 1,150	Wheelchair accessibility: . . . . .Good
Tonnage: 110,239	Passengers	Cabin Current: . . . . .110 volts
Lifestyle: . . . . .Standard	(lower beds/all berths): 2,974/3,700	Elevators: 18
Cruise Line: . . . . . . .Carnival Cruise Lines	Passenger Space Ratio	Casino (gaming tables): . . . . .Yes
Former Names: . . . . .none	(lower beds/all berths): 37.0/29.7	Slot Machines: . . . . .Yes
Builder: . . . . .Fincantieri (Italy)	Crew/Passenger Ratio	Swimming Pools (outdoors): 3
Original Cost: . . . .$500 million	(lower beds/all berths): 2.5/3.1	(+1 with glass dome)
Entered Service: . . . . .Jul 2008	Cabins (total): 1,487	Swimming Pools (indoors): 0
Registry: . . . . .Panama	Size Range (sq ft/m):	Whirlpools: 7
Length (ft/m): 951.4/290.0	179.7–484.2/16.7–44.8	Self-Service Launderette: . . . . .Yes
Beam (ft/m): 105.6/32.2	Cabins (outside view): 917	Dedicated Cinema/Seats: . . . . .No
Draft (ft/m): 27.2/8.3	Cabins (interior/no view): 570	Library: . . . . .Yes
Propulsion/Propellers: . . . . .diesel-electric	Cabins (for one person): 0	Onboard currency . . . . .US$
(63,400kW)/2	Cabins (with private balcony): 574	
Passenger Decks: 13	Cabins (wheelchair accessible): 25	

A family-friendly, fun-filled ship with a great water-slide.

OVERVIEW. *Carnival Splendor* shares the same generally balanced profile as sisters *Carnival Conquest, Carnival Destiny, Carnival Freedom, Carnival Glory, Carnival Liberty, Carnival Triumph, Carnival Valor,* and *Carnival Victory.* It is unable to transit the Panama Canal, due to its size. The interior decor displays a vivid palette of colors that excite the senses.

THE SHIP. The deck and public room layout is logical, and finding your way around is relatively easy. Most of the public rooms are located on one deck off a main interior boulevard, above a deck which contains the two main dining rooms.

The public rooms include the large Royal Flush Casino (gaming includes blackjack, craps, roulette, three-card poker, Caribbean Stud poker, Face Up, Let it Ride, Bonus, and Wheel of Madness, and an array of more than 300 slot machines).

Recalling drive-in movie theaters, the Seaside Theater shows movies on deck, with seating in tiered rows and the screen facing forward. The ship has bow-to-stern wi-fi internet access, including all passenger cabins.

Minor niggles include the fact that many pillars obstruct passenger flow, particularly in the dining room, where they make it difficult for the waiters to serve food properly.

FAMILIES. Youngsters are provided with their own Camp Carnival children's club (with its own small outdoor pool), and are well cared for with the line's extensive children's program. Camp Carnival is located on Sun Deck, out of the way of older passengers.

BERLITZ'S RATINGS

	Possible	Achieved
Ship	500	414
Accommodation	200	157
Food	400	218
Service	400	260
Entertainment	100	82
Cruise	400	262

OVERALL SCORE
1,393 points out of 2,000

ACCOMMODATION. There are 20 cabin price categories, in seven different suite/cabin types, sizes and grades. These include suites with private balcony; deluxe outside-view cabins with private balcony; outside-view cabins with private balcony; outside-view cabins with window; cabins with a porthole instead of a window; interior (no-view) cabins; and interior (no-view) cabins with upper and lower berths. There are five decks of cabins with private balconies.

The standard cabins are of good size and come equipped with all the basics, although the furniture is angular, with no rounded edges. Three decks of cabins (eight per deck, each with private balcony) overlook the stern. Most cabins with twin beds convert to a queen-size bed format. Book one of the suites (Category 11 or 12 in the Carnival Cruise Lines brochure) and you'll get "Skipper's Club" priority check-in at any US homeland port – useful for getting ahead of the crowd.

There are even "spa" cabins – a grouping of 18 cabins located directly around and behind SpaCarnival; so fitness devotees can get out of bed and go straight to the treadmill without having to go through any of the public rooms first.

A basket of sample toiletries is provided in all cabins.

CUISINE. There are two principal dining rooms, *Black Pearl*, seating 744, located midships, and *Gold Pearl*, located aft, seating 1,122. Both are two decks high and have a balcony level (the balcony level in Gold Pearl is the larger of the two). There's a choice of either fixed-time dining (6pm or 8:15pm), or flexible dining (any time between 5:45pm and 9:30pm).

There are few tables for two, but my favorites are the two tables for two right at the very back of the Gold Pearl restaurant, with ocean views astern.

Alternative (Reservations-Only, Extra Cost) Dining: *The Pinnacle* has fine table settings, china and silverware, and leather-bound menus. The specialties are USDA dry-aged prime steaks and seafood items. It's worth paying the cover charge to get a taste of what Carnival can really deliver in terms of food that is of better quality than what is served in the main dining rooms.

Casual Eateries: The *Lido Restaurant* is a casual self-serve international food court-style eatery. It has two main serving lines and several stand-alone sections. Included in this eating mall are a New York-style deli, a 24-hour pizzeria, and a grill for fast foods such as hamburgers and hot dogs; one section has a Tandoori oven for Indian-themes items. Each night, the venue morphs into the *Seaview Bistro* to provide a dress-down alternative the main dining rooms, serving pasta, steaks, salads and desserts (typically between 6pm and 9pm). An upstairs *Rotisserie* offers chicken.

ENTERTAINMENT. The large, multi-deck Spectacular Showlounge seats 1,400, and hosts colourful large-scale entertainment including Las-Vegas-style production shows and major cabaret acts. It has a revolving stage, hydraulic orchestra pit, superb sound, and seating on three levels, the upper levels being tiered through two decks.

An alternative entertainment venue is the El Morocco, a 425-seat lounge located aft; this typically features live music and late-night cabaret acts including smutty adult comedy. Adjacent is the Grand Piano Lounge/Bar.

SPA/FITNESS. The Cloud 9 Spa spans two decks (with a total area of around 40,000 sq. ft/3,715 sq. meters including the 16 spa suites – or 13,000 sq.ft./1,235 sq. meters excluding them). Located directly above the navigation bridge in the forward part of the ship, it is accessed from the forward stairway.

Facilities on the lower level include a gymnasium, solarium, a thermal suite (a number of saunas and steam rooms – some infused with herbal aromas), thalassotherapy pool (check out the huge Chinese dogs), and a beauty salon. The upper level houses 17 treatment rooms, including two VIP suites (one for couples, one specially configured for wheelchair access), rasul (Mediterranean mud treatment – best for couples) chamber, floatation therapy room, treatment rooms and outdoor relaxation areas on both port and starboard sides with integrated massage cabana. This is Carnival's most extensive spa, and using it will cost you lots if you have several treatments – or even if you simply want to use the thermal suite. There's a charge for everything.

● **For more extensive general information on what a Carnival cruise is like, see pages 126–31.**

Carnival Triumph
Carnival Valor
Carnival Victory
★★★ +

Size: . . . . .Large Resort Ships	Propulsion/Propellers: . . . . .diesel-electric	Cabins (with private balcony): 508
Tonnage: . . . . .101,509 *(Triumph, Victory)*	(34,000 kW)/2 azimuthing pods	Cabins (wheelchair accessible): 25
110,239 *(Valor)*	(17.6 MW each)	Wheelchair accessibility: . . . . .Good
Lifestyle: . . . . .Standard	Passenger Decks: 13	Cabin Current: . . . . .110 volts
Cruise Line: . . . . . . .Carnival Cruise Lines	Total Crew: .1,100	Elevators: 14
Former Names: . . . . .none	Passengers	Casino (gaming tables): . . . . .Yes
Builder: . . . . .Fincantieri (Italy)	(lower beds/all berths): 2,758/3,473	Slot Machines: . . . . .Yes
Original Cost: . . . .$420 *(Triumph)*,	Passenger Space Ratio	Swimming Pools (outdoors): 2
$500 million *(Valor)*, $410 million *(Victory)*	(lower beds/all berths): 36.8/29.2	(+1 with glass dome)
Entered Service: . . . . .Oct 1999 *(Triumph)*,	Crew/Passenger Ratio	Swimming Pools (indoors): 0
Dec 2004 *(Valor)*, Aug 2000 *(Victory)*	(lower beds/all berths): 2.3/3.0	Whirlpools: 7
Registry: . . . . . . .The Bahamas *(Triumph)*,	Cabins (total): 1,379	Self-Service Launderette: . . . . .Yes
Panama *(Valor, Victory)*	Size Range (sq ft/m): 179.7–482.2/	Dedicated Cinema/Seats: . . . . .No
Length (ft/m): . . . . .893.0/272.2 *(Triumph,*	16.7–44.8	Library: . . . . .Yes
Victory), 951.4/290.0 *(Valor)*	Cabins (outside view): 853	Onboard currency . . . . .US$
Beam (ft/m): 116.0/35.3	Cabins (interior/no view): 526	
Draft (ft/m): 27.0/8.2	Cabins (for one person): 0	

Floating fun palaces for ultra-casual first-time cruisers.

OVERVIEW. These three ships belong to Carnival Cruise Lines' *Destiny* class, along with *Carnival Conquest, Carnival Destiny, Carnival Freedom, Carnival Glory* and *Carnival Liberty*. They are quite stunning, built to impress at every turn, and have extremely short bows. They are too big transit the Panama Canal.

THE SHIPS. The decor is quite tasteful, not like the glitzy the Fantasy-class ships, and public rooms are given a visual theme. On *Carnival Triumph* this is great cities such as Rome and Paris, on *Carnival Valor* it's famous names such as Josephine Baker and Charles Lindbergh, and on *Carnival Victory* it's oceans of the world, with seahorses, corals and shells prominent throughout the design. The layout is logical and easy to navigate.

There are three decks full of lounges, 10 bars and lots of rooms to play in. Like their smaller (though still large) predecessors, these ships have a doublewide indoor promenade, nine decks high, with statues of Neptune at both ends, and a glass-domed rotunda atrium lobby. Amidships on the open deck is the longest water slide at sea – 200ft (60 meters) long, it travels from just aft of the ship's mast. Tiered sunbathing decks are positioned between two small swimming pools and several hot tubs.

BERLITZ'S RATINGS

	Possible	Triumph	Valor	Victory
Ship	500	409	410	407
Accommodation	200	157	157	157
Food	400	218	218	218
Service	400	259	260	249
Entertainment	100	82	82	81
Cruise	400	255	253	257

OVERALL SCORES
1,379 *(Triumph)*, 1,380 *(Valor)*,
1,369 *(Victory)*

The terraced pool deck is cluttered, and there are no cushioned pads for the deck chairs. Although the outdoor deck space has been improved, there is still much crowding when the ship is full and at sea. Getting away from people and noise is extremely difficult. The photo gallery becomes extremely congested when photographs are on display.

A feature the *Fantasy*-class ships don't have is a square-shaped bar, located in the atrium, facing forward to the glass-walled lifts and sits under the 10-deck-high dome. A sports bar has tables displaying sports memorabilia.

From a safety viewpoint, passengers can embark directly into the lifeboats from their secured position without having to wait for them to be lowered, thus saving time in the event of a real emergency. Well done, Carnival.

HOW THE SHIPS DIFFER

Carnival Valor differs from *Carnival Triumph* and *Carnival Victory* in a few ways not covered in the initial data (above). Its propulsion is diesel-electric (63,400kW/2). It carries up to 3,700 passengers (2,974 in lower beds) to give a crew/passenger ratio for lower beds/all berths of 2.5/3.1. It has 917 cabins with an outside view, and 574 cabins with a private balcony.

FAMILIES. Children have good facilities, including their own two-level Children's Club, including an outdoor pool, and are well cared for with "Camp Carnival," the cruise line's extensive children's program.

ACCOMMODATION. There are 20 price categories, depending on grade, location and size. Over half of all cabins are outside, and at 225 sq. ft./21 sq. meters they are among the largest in the standard market. They are spread over four decks and have private balconies extending from the ship's side; these have glass rather than steel balustrades for unobstructed ocean views, as well as bright fluorescent lighting. The standard cabins are of good size and have all the basics, although the furniture is angular, with no rounded edges. Three decks of cabins – eight per deck, each with private balcony – overlook the stern.

There are eight penthouse suites, each with a large private balcony. Although quite lavish in their appointments, at only 483 sq. ft (44.8 sq. meters), they are really quite small when compared to the best suites even in many smaller ships. There are also 40 other suites that are nothing special, although each has a decently sized bathroom and a good amount of lounge space.

In cabins with balconies, the partition between each balcony is open at top and bottom, so you may well hear noise from neighbors or smell their cigarettes. It is disappointing to see three categories of cabins (both outside and interior) with upper and lower bunk beds – lower beds are far more preferable, but this is how the ships absorb hundreds of extra passengers over and above the lower bed capacity.

The cabins have soft color schemes and more soft furnishings in more attractive fabrics than other ships in the fleet. Interactive "Fun Vision" technology lets you choose movies on demand, for a fee. The bathrooms, which have good-sized showers, have good storage space for toiletries. All grades get a gift basket of toiletry samples.

Book one of the suites (Category 11 or 12 in the Carnival Cruise Lines brochure), and you get "Skipper's Club" priority check-in at any US homeland port.

CUISINE. The ships have two main dining rooms, one forward with windows on two sides and 706 seats, and the other aft with windows on three sides and 1,090 seats. Each dining room spans two decks, and incorporates a dozen domes and chandeliers. The aft dining room has a two-deck-high wall of glass overlooking the stern. Tables are for four, six and eight. There are even a few tables for two that the line tries to keep for honeymooners.

There's a choice of either fixed-time dining (6pm or 8:15pm), or flexible dining (any time between 5:45pm and 9:30pm). This gives you very little time to "dine" – although it should give you some idea of what to expect from your dining experience. Although the menu choice looks good, the actual cuisine delivered is adequate, but quite unmemorable.

The dining room entrances have comfortable drinking areas for pre-dinner cocktails. There are also many options for casual dining, particularly during the day.

An informal international self-serve buffet-style eatery, has seating on two levels. Included in this eatery are a New York-style deli (open 11am–11pm), a Chinese restaurant, with wok preparation, and a 24-hour pizzeria which typically serves an average of more than 800 pizzas every day.

At night, the *Seaview Bistro* provides a casual alternative to the main dining rooms, serving pasta, steaks, salads and desserts. There is also a barbecue for fast grilled foods such as chicken, hamburgers and hot dogs, and a salad bar. In addition, there is a self-serve ice cream and frozen yogurt station, at no extra charge. If you want to eat 24 hours a day, you can.

Alternative (Reservations-Only, Extra Cost) Dining: There is one reservations-only, extra-cost dining spot, *Scarlett's*, aboard *Carnival Valor*. It has fine table settings, china and silverware, as well as leather-bound menus, and a design theme set around Scarlett O'Hara, the heroine of Margaret Mitchell's classic novel *Gone With the Wind*.

ENTERTAINMENT. The three-level showlounges are stunning, with a revolving stage, hydraulic orchestra pit, superb sound, and seating on three levels, the upper levels being tiered through two decks. A proscenium over the stage acts as a scenery loft.

SPA/FITNESS. SpaCarnival spans two decks, with a total area of 13,700 sq. ft/1,272 sq. meters, and is located directly above the navigation bridge in the forward part of the ship; it is accessed from the forward stairway. Facilities on the lower level include a solarium, eight treatment rooms, lecture rooms, sauna and steam rooms for men and women, and a beauty parlor; the upper level consists of a large gymnasium with floor-to-ceiling windows on three sides, including forward-facing ocean views, and an aerobics room with instructor-led classes, some at extra cost.

● **For more extensive general information on what a Carnival cruise is like, see pages 126–31.**

Celebrity Century
★★★★

Size: ....Large Resort Ship	Passenger Decks: 10	Cabins (with private balcony): 386
Tonnage: 71,545	Total Crew: 858	Cabins (wheelchair accessible): 8
Lifestyle: ....Premium	Passengers	Wheelchair accessibility: ....Good
Cruise Line: ....Celebrity Cruises	(lower beds/all berths): 1,814/2,150	Cabin Current: ....110 and 220 volts
Former Names: ....Century	Passenger Space Ratio	Elevators: 9
Builder: ....Meyer Werft (Germany)	(lower beds/all berths): 39.4/33.2	Casino (gaming tables): ....Yes
Original Cost: ....$320 million	Crew/Passenger Ratio	Slot Machines: ....Yes
Entered Service: ....Dec 1995	(lower beds/all berths): 2.0/2.5	Swimming Pools (outdoors): 2
Registry: ....Malta	Cabins (total): 907	Swimming Pools (indoors): ...1 hydropool
Length (ft/m): 807.1/246.0	Size Range (sq ft/m): 168.9–1,514.5/	Whirlpools: 4
Beam (ft/m): 105.6/32.2	15.7–140.7	Self-Service Launderette: ....No
Draft (ft/m): 24.6/7.5	Cabins (outside view): 590	Dedicated Cinema/Seats: Yes/190
Propulsion/Propellers: ....diesel	Cabins (interior/no view): 317	Library: ....Yes
(29,250kW)/2	Cabins (for one person): 0	Onboard currency ....US$

A stylish modern ship with understated decor and good food.

OVERVIEW. The ship suits well-travelled baby-boomer couples, solo travellers, and families with children seeking a ship with reasonable quality, style, and character. It is a decent, but dated vessel for a big-ship cruise vacation. Sloppy maintenance can be found in some areas, although general cleanliness is excellent. Gratifyingly, there are few annoying announcements.

THE SHIP. The exterior profile is well balanced despite a squared-off stern. It carries the distinctive brand "X" funnel ("X" being the Greek letter "C" – for Chandris, the former owning company, before Royal Caribbean purchased it). With a high passenger space ratio for this large ship, there is no real sense of crowding, passenger flow is efficient, and the high crew/passenger ratio provides a sound basis for good passenger service.

There is a good amount of open deck space, a three-quarter, two-level teak wood promenade deck, and a walking/jogging track atop the ship. The interior decor is elegant, but contemporary and understated. A small, dedicated cinema doubles as a conference and meeting center with the latest audio-visual technology. The atrium is calm and refreshing, not glitzy.

The former cigar club (Michael's Club) is now a piano lounge; this triangular-shaped room, a favorite watering hole, has large comfortable chairs and the feel of a real gentlemen's club. Those who like gambling will find a large casino tightly packed with slot machines and gaming tables.

Outstanding are the 500 pieces of art that adorn the ship – a $3.8 million art collection and some fascinating contemporary sculptures (look for the colored violins on Deck Seven). The collection includes a comprehensive survey of the most important artists and trends since the 1960s, and embraces Abstract Expressionism, Pop, Conceptualism, Minimalism and Neo-Expressionism.

BERLITZ'S RATINGS		
	Possible	Achieved
Ship	500	411
Accommodation	200	175
Food	400	290
Service	400	298
Entertainment	100	72
Cruise	400	299

OVERALL SCORE
1,545 points out of 2,000

Gratuities are charged to your account daily, and a 15% gratuity is added to all bar and wine accounts.

Embarkation and disembarkation remain weak links in the Celebrity Cruises operation, and the cruise staff is unpolished and has little finesse. Standing in line for embarkation, disembarkation, shore tenders and for self-serve buffet meals is an inevitable aspect of cruising aboard large ships. The interactive TV system is frustrating to use, and the larger suites have three remotes for TV/audio equipment (one would be better).

In 2006, *Celebrity Century* had a $55 million make-over that added 314 balconies, 14 new "Sky Suites" and 10 other cabins. The self-serve buffet area was expanded; an "Acupuncture at Sea" facility was added, as was Murano – a specialty extra-charge restaurant, more shop space, an art gallery for art auctions, more internet-connect computers plus ship-wide wi-fi, and a neat ice-walled bar that is part of the Martini Bar. In short, the refit makes the ship more like the larger Millennium-class ships.

FAMILIES. Children and teens are well catered for. X-Treme, within the Kid's Fun Factory area, is a hangout for teens. Children's counselors are aboard for every cruise.

ACCOMMODATION. There are 12 different grades. The price depends on the grade, size, and location. The wide variety of cabin types includes 18 family cabins, each with two lower beds, two foldaway beds and one upper berth. In the 2006 refit, new minimalist washbasins were installed in cabin bathrooms; however, they are not user-friendly as water splashes everywhere.

All cabins have wood cabinetry and accenting, personal safe, mini-bar/refrigerator, and interactive flat-screen TVs and entertainment systems that enable you to shop, book shore excursions or play casino games interactively in English, German, French, Italian or Spanish. Bathrooms have hairdryers, 100% cotton towels and large shower enclosures. However, the standard 24-hour cabin menu is disappointing and limited.

The cabins are nicely equipped and decorated, with warm wood-finish furniture, and none of the boxy feel of cabins in many ships, due to the angled placement of vanity and audio-video consoles. In addition, all suites on Deck 10 (and the Sky Deck suites on Deck 12) have butler service and in-cabin dining facilities. Suites with private balconies have floor-to-ceiling windows and sliding doors; a few have outward opening doors.

For the largest space, choose one of two beautifully decorated Presidential Suites, each 1,173 sq. ft (109 sq. meters). These are amidships in the most desirable position, and each can be combined with an adjacent mini-suite via an inter-connecting door to provide a living space of 1,515 sq. ft (140.7 sq. meters). Each suite has a marble-floored foyer, a living room with mahogany wood floor and hand-woven rug. A separate dining area has a six-seat dining table, and there's a butler's pantry with wet bar, a wine bar, refrigerator and microwave.

A large private balcony has a dining table for two, chaise lounge chairs with cushioned pads, hot tub and dimmer-controlled lighting; master bedroom with king-size bed, dressed with fine fabrics and draperies, and walk-in closet with abundant storage space. The all-marble bathroom has a jet-spray shower and whirlpool bath.

All suites and cabins have European duvets instead of sheets/blankets, fresh flowers, DVD, and butler service. Electrically operated blinds and other goodies are also standard in some suites.

CUISINE. A grand staircase connects the upper and lower levels of the two-level *Grand Dining Room*. Huge windows overlook the stern. Each of the two levels has a separate finishing galley. There are two seatings for dinner (open-seating for breakfast and lunch), at tables for two, four, six, eight, or 10. The design of the two galleys is good, so food that's meant to be hot arrives hot at the table.

All meals, including full dinners, can be served, course-by-course, in all suites and cabins, no matter what grade you choose. Freshly baked boxed pizzas, for those who can't live without them, can be delivered to your cabin.

Celebrity Cruises had better food in its earlier days, but it's still decent. However, the food served as room-service items is below the standard of food featured in the dining room.

There is also a large indoor/outdoor lido café, *Islands*, with four self-service buffet lines (included is a 76-seat sushi café), as well as two-grill serving stations located adjacent to the swimming pools outdoors.

Alternative Dining. *Murano*, a reservations-only specialty restaurant off the main lobby, is a fine dining experience that takes about three hours, in a small, intimate setting – ideal for celebrating a birthday or anniversary, with refined service and an extensive wine list.

Cova Café di Milano is a seagoing version of the original Café di Milano opened in 1817 next to La Scala Opera House in Milan. The café is located on the second level of the atrium lobby, and a display case shows off the extensive range of Cova coffee, chocolates and alcoholic digestives. It is a fine meeting place for those who appreciate fine Italian coffees, pastries and superb cakes in a refined setting.

ENTERTAINMENT. The Celebrity Theater is a two-level, 1,000-seat showlounge/theater with side balconies. It has a large stage, and a split orchestra pit (hydraulic). The continuous bar service during shows can be irritating. The ship has a number of bands, although there is very little music for social dancing, other than disco and latin music.

SPA/FITNESS. The AquaSpa has 9,040 sq. ft (840 sq. meters) of space dedicated to well-being and body treatments, all set in a calming environment. It includes a large fitness/exercise area, complete with all the latest high-tech muscle machines, thalassotherapy pool, and 10 treatment rooms. The spa includes an Acupuncture at Sea clinic, and a Rasul – a mud and gentle steam bathing room.

The spa is operated by Steiner, a specialist concession whose staff provide a range of treatments. Some fitness classes are free, while others, such as yoga and kick-boxing, cost extra.

● **For more extensive general information on what a Celebrity cruise is like, see pages 131–5.**

Celebrity Constellation
★★★★ +

Size: . . . . .Large Resort Ship	Passenger Decks: 11	Cabins (wheelchair accessible): 26
Tonnage: 90,228	Total Crew: 999	(17 with private balcony)
Lifestyle: . . . . .Premium	Passengers	Wheelchair accessibility: . . . . .Best
Cruise Line: . . . . .Celebrity Cruises	(lower beds/all berths): 1,950/2,450	Cabin Current: . . . . . . .110 and 220 volts
Former Names: . . . . .Constellation	Passenger Space Ratio	Elevators: 12
Builder: . . . . .Chantiers de l'Atlantique	(lower beds/all berths): 46.2/36.8	Casino (gaming tables): . . . . .Yes
(France)	Crew/Passenger Ratio	Slot Machines: . . . . .Yes
Original Cost: . . . .$350 million	(lower beds/all berths): 1.9/2.4	Swimming Pools (outdoors): 2
Entered Service: . . . . .May 2002	Cabins (total): 975	Swimming Pools (indoors): 1
Registry: . . . . .Malta	Size Range (sq ft/m): 165.1–2,530.0/	(with glass dome)
Length (ft/m): 964.5/294.0	15.34–235.0	Whirlpools: 4
Beam (ft/m): 105.6/32.2	Cabins (outside view): 780	Self-Service Launderette: . . . . .No
Draft (ft/m): 26.2/8.0	Cabins (interior/no view): 195	Dedicated Cinema/Seats: Yes/368
Propulsion/Propellers: . . . . .gas turbine/2	Cabins (for one person): 0	Library: . . . . .Yes
azimuthing pods (19.5 MW each)	Cabins (with private balcony): 590	Onboard currency . . . . .US$

Understated decor, providing a stylish setting for families.

OVERVIEW. A cruise aboard such a large ship provides a wide range of choices and possibilities. If you travel in one of the suites, the benefits include the highest level of personal service, while cruising in non-suite accommodation is almost like in any large ship. One thing really is certain: cruising in a hassle-free environment such as this is hard to beat no matter how much or how little you pay.

THE SHIP. *Celebrity Constellation* is a sister ship to *Celebrity Infinity, Celebrity Millennium*, and *Celebrity Summit*, the line's Millennium-class ships. Jon Bannenberg, the mega-yacht designer, dreamed up the exterior featuring a royal blue and white hull – although it has turned out to look quite ungainly. It has a "pod" propulsion system *(see page 191)* coupled with a quiet, smokeless, energy-efficient gas turbine powerplant.

New AquaClass veranda staterooms and Blu, a new Mediterranean-themed specialty restaurant exclusively for AquaClass passengers, were added in a "Solsticizing" of the ship in 2010. Also added were a Celebrity iLounge (for the latest Apple products, computer classes and internet connection); a Martini Bar with a frosted countertop, a Cellar-Masters wine bar, QSine (an extra-cost fine dining venue with iPad menus), and a Bistro on Five (a crêperie).

On one side of Sky Deck, a huge bronze sculpture of a gorilla is holding a fish under its arm. Created by Angus Fairhurst, it is titled *A couple of differences between thinking and feeling*.

Inside, the ship has a similar standard of decor and materials, and public rooms that make ships in the fleet so user-friendly. The atrium, with separately enclosed room for

BERLITZ'S RATINGS

	Possible	Achieved
Ship	500	427
Accommodation	200	178
Food	400	291
Service	400	298
Entertainment	100	74
Cruise	400	300

OVERALL SCORE
1,568 points out of 2,000

shore excursions, is three decks high and houses the reception desk, tour operator's desk, and bank. Four dramatic glass-walled elevators travel through the ship's exterior (port) side, connecting the atrium with another seven decks, thus traveling through 10 passenger decks, including the tender stations – a nice ride.

Facilities include a combination Cinema/Conference Center, an expansive shopping arcade with 14,447 sq. ft (1,300 sq. meters) of retail store space (with trendy brand name labels such as Fendi, Fossil, Hugo Boss, and Versace), a lavish four-decks-high show-lounge with high-tech sound and lighting equipment, a two-level library (one level for English-language books; a second for books in other languages and reference material), card room, music listening room, and an observation lounge/ discotheque with outstanding views.

Michael's Club (originally a cigar smoker's haven), is now a piano lounge/ bar. An internet cafe has almost 20 computers with custom-made wood-surround flat-screen monitors and internet access.

The artwork throughout the ship (particularly the sculptures) is eclectic, provocative, thoughtful, and intelligent, and at almost every turn another piece appears to break the monotony associated with large spaces.

Gaming sports include the ship's overly large Fortunes Casino, with blackjack, roulette, and slot machines, and lots of bright lights and action. Families with children will appreciate the Fun Factory (for children) and The Tower (for teenagers). Children's counselors and youth activities staff provide a wide range of supervized activities.

Note that there is, sadly, no walk-around wooden promenade deck outdoors. Standing in line for embarkation, disembarkation, shore tenders and for self-serve buffet meals is an inevitable aspect of cruising aboard all large ships (however, more flexible embarkation hours do help to spread the flow), but the worst time is when large numbers of passengers return from shore excursions and have to wait to go through a security check; the result being long lines outside the ship. The ship's two seating dining and two shows detract from an otherwise excellent product, and this ship (together with sister ships *Celebrity Infinity*, *Celebrity Millennium* and *Celebrity Summit*) can be said to provide the very best of the ships in the Premium segment of the marketplace, providing a taste of luxury for those who book in the largest suites.

A 15% gratuity is added to all bar and wine accounts.

ACCOMMODATION. There are 21 grades from which to choose, depending on your preference for the grade, size and location of your living space. Almost half of the ship's cabins feature a "private" balcony; approximately 80 percent are outside-view suites and cabins, and 20 percent are interior cabins. The cabins are extremely comfortable throughout this ship, regardless of which cabin grade you choose. Suites, naturally, have more space, butler service (whether you want it or not), more and better amenities and more personal service than if you choose any of the standard cabin grades. There are several categories of suites, but those at the stern of the ship are in a prime location and have huge balconies that are really private and not overlooked from above.

Regardless of the grade you choose, all suites and cabins have wood cabinetry and accenting, interactive television and entertainment systems (you can go shopping, book shore excursions, play casino games interactively, and even watch soft porn movies). The bathrooms have hairdryers and 100% cotton towels.

Penthouse Suites (2): These, on Penthouse Deck, are the ship's largest cabins. Each occupies one half of the beam (width) of the ship, overlooking the stern. Each measures a huge 2,530 sq. ft (235 sq. meters), consisting of 1,431.6 sq. ft (133 sq. meters) of living space, plus a huge wrap-around terrace measuring 1,098 sq. ft (102 sq. meters) with 180-degree views. This terrace includes a wet bar, hot tub and whirlpool tub – but much of it can be overlooked by passengers on other decks above. Features include a marble foyer, a separate living room (complete with ebony baby grand piano – bring your own pianist if you don't play yourself – and a formal dining room. The master bedroom has a large walk-in closet, personal exercise equipment, dressing room with vanity desk, exercise equipment, marble-clad master bathroom with twin washbasins, deep whirlpool bathtub, separate shower, toilet and bidet areas, flat-screen televisions (one in the bedroom and one in the lounge), and electronically controlled drapes. Butler service is standard, and a butler's pantry, with separate entry door, has a full-size refrigerator, temperature-controlled wine cabinet, microwave oven and good-sized food preparation and storage areas. For even more space, an interconnecting door can be opened into the adjacent suite (ideal for multi-generation families).

Royal Suites (8): These measure 733 sq ft (68 sq. meters), and are located towards the aft of the ship (four each on the port and starboard sides). Each has a separate living room with dining and lounge areas (with refrigerator, mini-bar and Bang & Olufson CD sound system), and a separate bedroom. There are two entertainment centers with DVD players, and two flat-screen televisions (one in the living area, one in the bedroom), and a large walk-in closet with vanity desk. The marble-clad bathroom has a whirlpool bathtub with integral shower, and there is also a separate shower enclosure, two washbasins and toilet. The teakwood decked balcony is extensive (large enough for on-deck massage) and also has a whirlpool hot tub.

Celebrity Suites (8): Each measures 467 sq. ft (44 sq. meters) and has floor-to-ceiling windows, a separate living room with dining and lounge areas, two entertainment centers with flat-screen televisions (one in the living room, one in the bedroom), and a walk-in closet with vanity desk. The marble-clad bathroom has a whirlpool tub with integral shower (a window with movable blind lets you look out of the bathroom through the lounge to the large ocean-view windows). Interconnecting doors allow two suites to be used as a family unit; as there is no balcony, these suites are ideal for families with small children. These suites overhang the starboard side of the ship (they are located opposite a group of glass-walled lifts), and provide stunning ocean views from the glass-walled sitting/dining area, which extends out from the ship's side. A personal computer with wood-surround screen allows direct internet connectivity. Butler service is standard.

Sky Suites (30): Each measures 308 sq. ft (28.6 sq. meters), including the private balcony (note that some balconies may be larger than others, depending on the location). Although these are designated as suites, they are really just larger cabins that feature a marble-clad bathroom with bathtub/shower combination. The suites also have a VCR player in addition to a TV set, and have a larger lounge area (than standard cabins) and sleeping area. Butler service is standard.

Butler Service: Butler service in all cabins designated as suites includes full breakfast, in-suite lunch and dinner service (as required), afternoon tea service, evening hors d'oeuvres, complimentary espresso and cappuccino, daily news delivery, shoeshine service, and other personal touches.

Suite occupants in Penthouse, Royal, Celebrity and Sky suites also get welcome champagne; a full personal computer in each suite, including a printer and internet access (on request in the Sky Suites); choice of films from a video library; personalized stationery; tote bag; priority dining room seating preferences; private portrait sitting, bathrobe; and in-suite massage service.

Standard Outside-View/Interior Cabins: All other outside-view and interior cabins have a lounge area with sofa or convertible sofa bed, sleeping area with twin beds that can convert to a double bed, a good amount of closet and drawer space, personal safe, mini-bar/refrigerator (extra cost), interactive television, and private bathroom. The cabins are nicely decorated with warm wood-finish furniture, and there is none of the boxy feel of cabins in so many ships, due to the angled placement of vanity and audio-video consoles. Even the smallest cabin has a good-sized bathroom and shower enclosure.

Wheelchair-Accessible Suites/Cabins: Wheelchair accessibility is provided in six Sky Suites, three premium outside-view, eight deluxe ocean-view, four standard ocean-view and five interior cabins measuring 347–362 sq. ft (32.2–33.6 sq. meters). They are located close to lifts for good accessibility – all have doorways and bathroom doorways, and showers are wheelchair-accessible. Some cabins have extra berths for third or third and fourth occupants. Note, however, that there is only one safe for personal belongings, which must be shared.

CUISINE. The 1,198-seat *San Marco Restaurant* is the ship's formal dining room. It is two decks high, has a grand staircase connecting the two levels (on the upper level of which is a musicians' gallery), and a huge glass wall overlooking the sea at the stern of the ship (electrically operated blinds provide several different backdrops). There are two seatings for dinner (with open seating for breakfast and lunch), at tables for two, four, six, eight or 10. The dining room, like all large dining halls, can be extremely noisy.

The menu variety is good, the food is tasty, and it is very attractively presented and served in a well orchestrated operation with European traditions and training. Full service in-cabin dining is also available for all meals, including dinner.

The *Seaside Café & Grill* is a casual self-serve buffet area, with six principal serving lines, and around 750 seats, grill and pizza bar. Each evening, casual meals take place here, with tablecloths and a modicum of service. Reservations are needed, although there's no additional charge

Alternative (Reservations-Only, Extra Cost) Dining: *Ocean Liners Restaurant* is the ship's alternative dining salon; it is adjacent to the main lobby. The decor includes some lacquered paneling from the famed 1920s French ocean liner *Ile de France*. Fine tableside preparation is the feature of this alternative dining room, whose classic French cuisine and service is very good. This is haute cuisine at the height of professionalism, for this is, indeed, a room for a full savoring, and not merely for dinner, featuring the French culinary arts of découpage and flambé. However, with just 115 seats, not all passengers are able to experience it even once during a one-week cruise (reservations are necessary, and a cover charge applies). There's a dine-in wine cellar with more than 200 labels from around the world.

Café al Bacio and Gelateria: Located on the third level of the atrium lobby, this is the place to see and be seen, for coffees (espresso, cappuccino, latte), pastries, cakes, and gelato, in a trendy setting.

ENTERTAINMENT. The 900-seat Celebrity Theatre is the three-deck-high venue for the ship's production shows and major cabaret acts. It is located in the forward part of the ship, with seating on the main level and two balcony levels. The large stage is equipped with a full fly loft behind its traditional proscenium.

SPA/FITNESS. A large AquaSpa measures 24,219 sq. ft (2,250 sq. meters). It has a large thalassotherapy pool under a solarium dome, complete with health bar for light breakfast and lunch items and fresh squeezed fruit and vegetable juices. There are 16 treatment rooms, plus eight treatment rooms with showers and one treatment room specifically designed for wheelchair passengers, an aerobics room, gymnasium with over 40 exercise machines, large male and female saunas (with a large ocean-view porthole window), an extra-cost unisex thermal suite containing several steam and shower mist rooms with different fragrances, and a beauty salon.

Sports facilities include a full-size basketball court, compact football, paddle tennis and volleyball, golf simulator, shuffleboard (on two different decks) and a jogging track.

● **For more extensive general information on what a Celebrity cruise is like, see pages 131–5.**

Celebrity Eclipse
★★★★ +

Size: . . . . .Large Resort Ship	Passenger Decks: 14	Cabins (with private balcony): 1,216
Tonnage: 121,878	Total Crew: 1,253	Cabins (wheelchair accessible): 30
Lifestyle: . . . . .Premium	Passengers	Wheelchair accessibility: . . . . .Best
Cruise Line: . . . . .Celebrity Cruises	(lower beds/all berths): 2,852/3,145	Cabin Current: . . . . .110/220 volts
Former Names: . . . . .none	Passenger Space Ratio	Lifts: 12
Builder: . . . . .Meyer Werft (Germany)	(lower beds/all berths): 42.7/38.7	Casino (gaming tables): . . . . .Yes
Original Cost: . . . .$641 million	Crew/Passenger Ratio	Slot Machines: . . . . .Yes
Entered Service: . . . . .Jun 2010	(lower beds/all berths): 2.2/2.5	Swimming Pools (outdoors): 2
Registry: .Malta	Cabins (total): 1,426	Swimming Pools (indoors): 1
Length (ft/m): 1,033.4/315.0	Size Range (sq ft/m): 182.9–668.4/	Whirlpools: 6
Beam (ft/m): 120.7/36.8	17.0–155.0	Self-Service Launderette: . . . . .No
Draft (ft/m): 27.2/8.3	Cabins (outside view): 1,286	Dedicated Cinema/Seats: . . . . .No
Propulsion/Propellers: . . . . .diesel	Cabins (interior/no view): 140	Library: . . . . .Yes
(67.2 MW)/2 azimuthing pods	Cabins (for one person): 0	Onboard currency . . . . .US$

A large, stylish, premium ship for the whole family.

OVERVIEW. This is a sister ship to *Celebrity Equinox* (2009), *Celebrity Reflection* (2012), *Celebrity Silhouette* (2011) and *Celebrity Solstice* (2008). For detailed information about its facilities, see the entries for those ships on pages 287, 295, 297 and 299.

THE SHIP. *Celebrity Eclipse* has a steeply sloping stern – which includes a mega-yacht-style ducktail platform above the propulsion pods, is attractive, and nicely balances the ship's contemporary profile. One thing that's cool is an Apple "iLounge" equipped with 26 Apple MacBook Pro work stations. You can also buy Apple products.

Good points include elevator call buttons located in a floor-stand "pod" so that, when the elevator arrives, a glass panel above it turns from blue to pink. Also, the ship has a good collection of designer chairs and sunloungers.

Passenger niggles include poor drawer space in cabins; inadequate children's facilities and staff during the school holiday periods; utter congestion caused by a bottleneck when you exit the showlounge; and noise in all areas of the lobby when the martini bar is busy.

During the summer, the ship is based in the UK, when all beverage prices include a service charge, and include the following British beers: Fuller's London Pride, Old Speckled Hen, Boddingtons, Guinness, Murphy's Stout and Newcastle Brown Ale. A "Champagne High Royal Experience" (afternoon tea with white glove service, Wedgwood china, and Forte loose teas) is available for $25 per person.

ACCOMMODATION. About 90% of the accommodation is in outside-view cabins. Of these, 85% have a balcony;

BERLITZ'S RATINGS		
	Possible	Achieved
Ship	500	433
Accommodation	200	178
Food	400	303
Service	400	309
Entertainment	100	78
Cruise	400	311
OVERALL SCORE		
1,612 points out of 2,000		

indeed, this ship has more balcony cabins than any other cruise ship to date and, due to its slender width, there are very few interior cabins. There are four suite-grade categories: Royal Suite, Celebrity Suite, Sky Suite, and Penthouse Suite. If you can afford it, book a suite-category cabin for the extra benefits it brings.

All grades include: twin beds that convert to a queen-size bed, sitting area, and vanity desk with hairdryer. But there's very little drawer space. Also standard in all cabins: 32-inch flat-screen TVs (larger screens in suites), wireless internet access (for a fee), premium bedding. Although the closets have good hanging space, there's no shelving for folded items, and drawers in the vanity desk can't accommodate such items. The bathroom has a shower enclosure, toilet, and tiny washbasin but no soap dish. Accommodation designated as suites have more space and larger balconies with good-quality sunloungers.

Some 130 AquaSpa-class cabins share the relaxation room of the AquaSpa itself, incorporate select spa elements into the cabins, and allow for access to the AquaSpa's Thermal Relaxation Room and Persian Garden. Occupants also get assigned seating at the exclusive 130-seat Restaurant Blu.

CUISINE. Although this ship has almost the same dining venues as sister ships *Celebrity Equinox* and *Celebrity Solstice*, one venue is different. Called *Qsine*, it tries hard to present traditional and contemporary unordinary food from around the world, in a trendy setting. It's open for dinner only, reservations are required, and there's a cover charge.

● **For more extensive general information on what a Celebrity cruise is like, see pages 131–5.**

Celebrity Equinox
★★★★ +

Size: . . . . Large Resort Ship	Passenger Decks: 14	Cabins (with private balcony): 1,216
Tonnage: 122,000	Total Crew: 1,253	Cabins (wheelchair accessible): 30
Lifestyle: . . . . .Premium	Passengers	Wheelchair accessibility: . . . . .Best
Cruise Line: . . . . .Celebrity Cruises	(lower beds/all berths): 2,852/3,145	Cabin Current: . . . . .110/220 volts
Former Names: . . . . .none	Passenger Space Ratio	Lifts: 12
Builder: . . . . .Meyer Werft (Germany)	(lower beds/all berths): 42.7/38.7	Casino (gaming tables): . . . . .Yes
Original Cost: . . . .$641 million	Crew/Passenger Ratio	Slot Machines: . . . . .Yes
Entered Service: . . . . Aug 2009	(lower beds/all berths): 2.2/2.5	Swimming Pools (outdoors): 2
Registry: .Malta	Cabins (total): 1,426	Swimming Pools (indoors): 1
Length (ft/m): 1,033.4/315.0	Size Range (sq ft/m): . . . .182.9 –1,668.4/	Whirlpools: 6
Beam (ft/m): 120.7/36.8	17.0–155.0	Self-Service Launderette: . . . . .No
Draft (ft/m): 27.2/8.3	Cabins (outside view): 1,286	Dedicated Cinema/Seats: . . . . .No
Propulsion/Propellers: . . . . .diesel	Cabins (interior/no view): 140	Library: . . . . .Yes
(67.2 MW)/2 azimuthing pods	Cabins (for one person): 0	Onboard currency . . . . .US$

A large ship with contemporary style, for family cruising.

OVERVIEW. This is a sister ship to *Celebrity Eclipse, Celebrity Reflection* (2012), *Celebrity Silhouette*, and *Celebrity Solstice*. The steeply sloping stern, which includes a mega-yacht-style ducktail platform above the propulsion pods, is very attractive, and nicely balances the ship's contemporary profile. The bows have been rounded to accommodate a helicopter platform.

THE SHIP. Two rather slim funnels, set one behind the other distinguish the new ship from previous (single-funnel) Celebrity ships. Between the two funnels is a grass outdoor area, the Lawn Club. This grass is the real stuff, and it seems to like the salty air. The Lawn Club is open to all, so you can go putting, play croquet or bocce ball (like bowling or French boules), have a picnic on the grass, or perhaps even sleep on it.

There are several pool and water-play areas on Resort Deck: one in a solarium (with glass roof), a sports pool, a family pool, and a wet zone. However, the deck space around the two pools is not large enough for the number of passengers carried.

Inside, the decor is elegant, yet contemporary. Michael's Club is an intimate, quiet lounge with classic English leather chairs, a dramatic black glass chandelier, a grand fireplace and some contemporary artwork. Rich furnishings help create a warm atmosphere, amidst a backdrop of piano and jazz music, as well as single malt scotch and cognacs for tastings.

Other attractions include a wine bar with a sommelier, a pre-dinner cocktail lounge that reflects the jazz music of the 1930s and '40s; a bar with the look of an ocean-going yacht; Quasar, a bar with designs from the 1960s and '70s

BERLITZ'S RATINGS

	Possible	Achieved
Ship	500	433
Accommodation	200	178
Food	400	302
Service	400	310
Entertainment	100	78
Cruise	400	310

OVERALL SCORE
1,611 points out of 2,000

and large screens that create a nightly light show synchronized to music; and an observation lounge with dance floor.

Celebrity's signature Martini Bar, which has a frosted bar – and more than 100 varieties of vodka as well as martinis – has a small alcove called Crush with an ice-filled table for caviar and vodka tastings. This is a trendy, extremely noisy bar, which also makes the whole area congested.

Fortunes Casino (non-smoking) has 16 gaming tables and 200 slot machines. There's a delightful two-deck library, but books on the upper shelves – it is 12 shelves high – are impossible to reach. An innovative Hot Glass Show, created in collaboration with Corning Museum of Glass, includes demonstrations and a narrated performance of glass-blowing, housed in an outdoor studio on the open deck as part of the Lawn Club. Three resident glass-blowing artists host workshops – but after you've seen it once, it's enough.

Passenger niggles include poor drawer space in cabins; inadequate children's facilities and staff during the school holiday periods; utter congestion caused by a bottleneck when you exit the showlounge; and noise in all areas of the lobby when the martini bar is busy.

Good points include elevator call buttons located in a floor-stand "pod" so that, when an elevator arrives, a glass panel above it turns from blue to pink. Also, the ship has a good collection of designer chairs and sunloungers in various locations.

Gratuities are charged to your onboard account.

ACCOMMODATION. About 90% of the accommodation is in outside-view cabins. Of these, 85% have a balcony;

indeed, this ship has more balcony cabins than any other cruise ship to date and, due to its slender width, there are very few interior cabins. There are four suite-grade categories: Royal Suite, Celebrity Suite, Sky Suite, and Penthouse Suite. If you can afford it, book a suite-category cabin for the extra benefits it brings.

All grades of accommodation include: twin beds convertible to a queen-size bed, sitting area, vanity desk with hairdryer, but there's very little drawer space. Also standard in all cabins: 32-inch flat-screen TVs (larger screens in suites), wireless internet access (for a fee), premium bedding. However, although the closets have good hanging space, there is no shelving on which to place folded items, and drawers in the vanity desk can't accommodate such items. The bathroom has a shower enclosure, toilet, and tiny washbasin but no soap dish. Accommodation designated as suites have more space, larger balconies with good-quality sunloungers, and more personal amenities.

Some 130 AquaSpa-class cabins share the relaxation room of the AquaSpa itself, incorporate select spa elements into the cabins, and allow for specialized access to the AquaSpa's Thermal Relaxation Room and Persian Garden (with aromatherapy/steam rooms) on the same deck. Features include: a choice of four pillows (conformance, body, goose, Isotonic); express luggage delivery; shoeshine; Frette bathrobes; dining and seating preferences in other alternative dining venues; and early embarkation and disembarkation. Bathrooms include a tub plus a separate shower enclosure. Occupants also get assigned seating at the exclusive 130-seat Restaurant Blu.

Other accommodation grades are named Veranda-class; Sunset-Veranda-class; Concierge-class; Family oceanview with veranda; Deluxe Oceanview with veranda; Standard Oceanview; and Standard Interior cabins.

Cabins 1551–1597 on the port side, and 1556–1602 on the starboard side on Penthouse Deck (Deck 11) suffer from "aircraft carrier" syndrome because they are directly under the huge overhanging Resort Deck. they have little exposure to sun or light, so private balcony sunbathing is out of the question. Many thick supporting struts ruin the view from these cabins, which are otherwise pleasantly fitted out.

CUISINE. *Silhouette*, the ship's balconied main dining room (included in the cruise price), has ocean views on the port and starboard sides. The design is stunning and contemporary. At the forward end, a two-deck-high wine tower provides an eye-catching focal point. As for the food, it's a bit of a let-down – the decreased quality is all too obvious to repeat Celebrity passengers. Shame!

The following four dining venues are all located one deck above the main restaurant and galley (on Deck 5), and occupy the aft section of the ship:

● *Murano* is an extra-cost, reservations-required venue offering high-quality traditional dining with a French flair and exquisite table settings, including large Reidel wine glasses. Food and service are very good.

● *Blu* is a 130-seat specialty restaurant designated just for the occupants of AquaClass cabins. The room has pleasing, but rather cold, blue decor.

● The *Tuscan Grille*, an extra-cost venue, serves Kobe beef and premium quality steaks, and has beautifully curved archways – it's like walking into a high-tech winery. There are great views from huge aft-view windows.

● *QSine* is an extra-cost, reservations-required fine-dining venue, with iPad menus.

For snacks and less ambitious meals, the options are:

● *Bistro* on Five (Deck 5, that is) is for coffee, cakes, crêpes, pastries, and more. It gets busy at times and the serving counter is small, so it's a congested area.

● *Café al Bacio & Gelateria* is a coffeehouse serving Lavazza Italian coffee. It is on one side of the main lobby, but it's small and lines quickly form at peak times. The seating is mostly in large, very comfortable armchairs.

● *Oceanview Café and Grill* is the expansive, tray-less, casual self-serve buffet venue. There are a number of food "islands" rather than those awful straight buffet counters, but the signage is reasonably good. However, it's impossible to get a warm plate for so-called hot food items, and condiments are hard to find.

● The *AquaSpa Café* is for light, healthier options (solarium fare), but the selections are bland and boring.

● The *Mast Bar Grill and Bar* is an outside venue offering fast-food items.

ENTERTAINMENT. The 1,115-seat Equinox Theater, the ship's principal showlounge, has a main level and two balconied sections positioned amphitheatre-style around a stage with music lofts set on either side. Three circus-themed production shows highlight in-your-face, formulaic acrobatics.

Colorful theme nights are held in the Sky Observation Lounge, whose daytime bland and minimalist decor comes alive at night thanks to mood lighting effects. The 200-seat Celebrity Central hosts stand-up comedy, cooking demonstrations, enrichment lectures and feature films.

An Entertainment Court showcases street performers, psychics and caricaturists, and is in the center of the ship, linked to the adjacent Quasar nightclub, with its decor harking back to the 1960s and '70s. The Ensemble Lounge is a big-band era cocktail lounge with live jazz-styled music, set adjacent to the specialty restaurant, Murano.

SPA/FITNESS. The large AquaSpa is operated by concessionaire Steiner Leisure. The fitness center includes kinesis (pulleys against gravity) workout equipment, plus the familiar favorite muscle-pumping cardio-vascular machinery. There's also a relaxation area, AquaSpa station, and acupuncture center. Massages include fashionable things such as a Herbal Poultice massage and a Bamboo Massage using bamboo shoots and essential oils.

● **For more extensive general information on what a Celebrity cruise is like, see pages 131–5.**

Celebrity Infinity
★★★★ +

Size:	.Large Resort Ship	Passenger Decks:	.11	Cabins (wheelchair accessible):	.26
Tonnage:	.90,228	Total Crew:	.999	(17 with private balcony)
Lifestyle:	.Premium	Passengers		Wheelchair accessibility:	.Best
Cruise Line:	.Celebrity Cruises	(lower beds/all berths):	.2,154/2,570	Cabin Current:	.110 and 220 volts
Former Names:	.Infinity	Passenger Space Ratio		Elevators:	.12
Builder:	.Chantiers de l'Atlantique	(lower beds/all berths):	.46.2/36.8	Casino (gaming tables):	.Yes
	(France)	Crew/Passenger Ratio		Slot Machines:	.Yes
Original Cost:	.$350 million	(lower beds/all berths):	.1.9/2.4	Swimming Pools (outdoors):	.2
Entered Service:	.Mar 2001	Cabins (total):	.1,035	Swimming Pools (indoors):	.1
Registry:	.Malta	Size Range (sq ft/m):	.165.1–2,530.0/	(with glass dome)
Length (ft/m):	.964.5/294.0		15.34–235.0	Whirlpools:	.4
Beam (ft/m):	.105.6/32.2	Cabins (outside view):	.840	Self-Service Launderette:	.No
Draft (ft/m):	.26.2/8.0	Cabins (interior/no view):	.195	Dedicated Cinema/Seats:	.Yes/368
Propulsion/Propellers:	.gas turbine/2	Cabins (for one person):	.0	Library:	.Yes
azimuthing pods (19.5 MW each)	Cabins (with private balcony):	.590	Onboard currency	.US$

A family-friendly, high-energy ship for fun-filled cruising.

OVERVIEW. The ship provides a wide range of choices and possibilities. If you travel in one of the suites, you receive the highest level of personal service, while cruising in non-suite accommodation is almost like in any large ship – you'll be one of a number, with little access to the niceties and benefits of "upper class" cruising. It all depends how much you are willing to pay. The two-seating dining and two shows nightly detract from an otherwise excellent product.

THE SHIP. *Celebrity Infinity* is a sister ship to *Celebrity Constellation, Celebrity Millennium* and *Celebrity Summit.* Jon Bannenberg, famous for his mega-yacht designs, designed the exterior. It is fitted with a "pod" propulsion system *(see page 191)* coupled with a quiet, smokeless, energy-efficient gas turbine powerplant.

New AquaClass veranda staterooms and a new Mediterranean-themed specialty restaurant, Blu, exclusively for AquaClass passengers, were added in a "Solsticizing" of the ship in 2011. Also added were a Celebrity iLounge (for Apple products, computer classes and internet-connection), a Martini Bar with a frosted countertop, a Tuscan Grill serving steaks, a CellarMasters wine bar, Café al Bacio and Gelateria, and Bistro on Five (a crêperie). Replacing the former conservatory is QSine, a reservations-only, extra-cost "interactive" dining venue with iPad menus.

There is no walk-around wooden promenade deck outdoors. There are cushioned pads for poolside sunloungers only, but not for chairs on other outside decks. Trying to reach Cabin Service or the Guest Relations Desk to answer the phone (to order breakfast, for example, if you don't

BERLITZ'S RATINGS

	Possible	Achieved
Ship	500	425
Accommodation	200	178
Food	400	291
Service	400	298
Entertainment	100	74
Cruise	400	300

OVERALL SCORE
1,566 points out of 2,000

want to do so via the "interactive" television) is a matter of luck, timing and patience.

The atrium is the focal point inside the ship; it is three decks high and houses the reception desk, tour operator's desk, and bank. Four glass-walled elevators travel through the ship's exterior (port) side, connecting the atrium with another seven decks, thus traveling through 10 passenger decks, including the tender stations – a nice ride.

Facilities include a Cinema and Conference Center, an expansive shopping arcade with a 14,447 sq.-ft (1,300 sq.-meter) retail store space with all the favorites, a four-deck-high showlounge, a two-level library (one level for English-language books; a second level for other languages); card room; compact disc listening room; art auction center (with seating that looks more like a small chapel); Cosmos, a combination observation lounge/discotheque; a Celebrity iLounge (an Apple store/ reseller and computer center). Michael's Club, originally a cigar smoker's haven, is now a piano lounge/tasting bar. A 15% gratuity is added to bar and wine accounts.

Gaming sports include the ship's overly large Fortunes Casino, with blackjack, roulette, and slot machines, and lots of bright lights and action.

FAMILIES. The Fun Factory is designed for young children and The Tower caters to teenagers. Children's counselors and youth activities staff provide a wide range of supervised activities.

ACCOMMODATION. There are 20 different price grades.

Almost half of the ship's accommodation features a "private" balcony; approximately 80% are outside-view suites and cabins, and 20% are interior (no view) cabins. All the accommodation is extremely comfortable. Suites, naturally, have more space, butler service (whether you want it or not), more and better amenities and more personal service than standard cabin grades.

There are several categories of suites, but those at the stern are in a prime location and have huge balconies that are very private and not overlooked from above.

All suites and cabins have wood cabinetry and accenting, interactive television and entertainment systems – you can go shopping, book shore excursions, play casino games, interactively, and even watch soft-porn movies. Bathrooms have hairdryers, and 100% cotton towels.

Penthouse Suites: Two Penthouse Suites (on Penthouse Deck) are like apartments. Each occupies one half of the beam (width) of the ship, overlooking the ship's stern. Each is a huge 2,530 sq. ft (235 sq. meters): 1,431.6 sq. ft (133 sq. meters) of living space, plus a huge wrap-around balcony of 1,098 sq. ft (102 sq, meters). It includes a wet bar, hot tub and whirlpool tub, but much of this terrace can be overlooked from other decks above.

Features include a marble foyer, a separate living room complete with ebony baby grand piano, and a formal dining room. The master bedroom has a large walk-in closet; personal exercise equipment; dressing room with vanity desk; exercise equipment; marble-clad master bathroom with twin washbasins; deep whirlpool tub; separate shower; toilet and bidet areas; flat-screen televisions (one in the bedroom and one in the lounge); and electronically controlled drapes. Butler service is standard, and a butler's pantry, with separate entry door, houses a full-size refrigerator, temperature-controlled wine cabinet, microwave oven and food preparation and storage areas. For even more space, an interconnecting door can be opened into the adjacent suite.

Royal Suites: Eight Royal Suites, each measuring 733 sq. ft (68 sq. meters), are located towards the aft of the ship (four each on the port and starboard sides). Each has a separate living room with dining and lounge areas (with refrigerator, mini-bar and a Bang & Olufsen audio system), and a separate bedroom. There are two entertainment centers with DVD players, and two flat-screen TV sets (one in the living area, one in the bedroom), and a large walk-in closet with vanity desk. The marble-clad bathroom has a whirlpool tub with integral shower, and there is also a separate shower enclosure, two washbasins and toilet. The teakwood decked balcony is extensive (large enough for on-deck massage) and has a whirlpool hot tub.

Celebrity Suites (8): These measure 467 sq. ft (44 sq. meters), have floor-to-ceiling windows, a separate living room with dining and lounge areas, two entertainment centers with flat-screen TV sets (one in the living room, one in the bedroom), and a walk-in closet with vanity desk. The marble-clad bathroom has a whirlpool tub with integral shower; a window with movable shade lets you look out of the bathroom through the lounge to the large ocean-view windows. Balconies were added in the 2011 refit.

Interconnecting doors allow two suites to be used as a family unit. These suites, located opposite a group of glass-walled elevators, overhang the ship's starboard side, and provide stunning ocean views from the lounge/dining area. A personal computer with wood-surround screen connects to the internet.

Sky Suites (30): Each measures 308 sq. ft (28.6 sq. meters) including the private balcony (some balconies may be larger than others, depending on the location). Although these are designated as suites, they are really just larger cabins that have a marble-clad bathroom with tub/shower combination. The suites also have a video player in addition to a TV set, and have a larger lounge area and sleeping area than standard cabins.

Butler Service: Provided in all accommodation designated as suites, this includes full breakfast, in-suite lunch and dinner service (as required), afternoon tea service, evening hors d'oeuvres, complimentary espresso and cappuccino, daily news delivery, and shoeshine service.

Suite occupants in Penthouse, Royal, Celebrity and Sky suites also get welcome champagne; a full personal computer in each suite, including a printer and internet access (on request in the Sky Suites); choice of films; personalized stationery; tote bag; priority dining room seating preferences; private portrait sitting; bathrobe; and in-suite massage service.

Concierge Class: Positioned between the top grade suite grades and standard cabin grades, Concierge Class adds value to these "middle-class" cabins. Enhanced facilities include priority embarkation, disembarkation, tender tickets, alternative dining and spa reservations.

Here's what you get in the Concierge Class cabins that others don't (except for the suites): European duvet; double bed overlay (no more falling "between the cracks" for couples); choice of four pillows (goose down pillow, isotonic pillow, body pillow, conformance pillow); eight-vial flower vase on vanity desk; throw pillows on sofa; fruit basket; binoculars; golf umbrella; leather telephone notepad; larger beach towels; hand-held hairdryer. The balcony has better furniture. Bathrooms have plusher Frette bathrobes, larger towels in sea green and pink (alternating days), and a flower in a silver vase. It all adds up to excellent value for money.

Standard Outside-View/Interior Cabins: All other outside-view and interior cabins have a lounge area with sofa or convertible sofa bed, sleeping area with twin beds that can convert to a double bed, a good amount of closet and drawer space, personal safe, mini-bar/refrigerator (extra cost), interactive television, and private bathroom. The cabins are nicely decorated with warm wood-finish furniture, and there is none of the boxy feel of cabins in so many ships, due to the angled placement of vanity and audio-video consoles. Even the smallest cabin has a good-sized bathroom and shower enclosure.

Wheelchair-Accessible Accommodation: This is available in various grades and practical locations, close to elevators. All doorways and bathroom doorways and showers are wheelchair-accessible. Some cabins have extra berths for third or third and fourth occupants. There is only one safe for personal belongings, which must be shared.

CUISINE. The *Thellis Restaurant* is the ship's 1,170-seat formal dining room. It is two decks high, has a grand staircase connecting the two levels, a huge glass wall overlooking the sea at the stern of the ship (electrically operated shades provide several different backdrops), and a musician's gallery on the upper level, typically for a string quartet or quintet. There are two seatings for dinner (open seating for breakfast and lunch), at tables for two, four, six, eight, or 10. The dining room, like all large dining halls, can be extremely noisy. The menu variety is good, the food has taste, and it is attractively presented and served in a well orchestrated operation that displays European traditions and training. Full service in-cabin dining is also available for all meals, including dinner.

There are several other options, particularly for those seeking more casual dining, or for an extra-special (and extra cost) meal in a more intimate (and quiet) setting.

Las Olas Café and Grill is a casual self-serve buffet area, with six principal serving lines, and seating for 754; there is also a grill and pizza bar. For champagne and caviar lovers, not to mention martinis, *Carlisle's* is the place to see and be seen.

Alternative (Reservations-Only, Extra Cost) Dining Option: The *United States Restaurant* is adjacent to the main lobby. Actual glass panelling from the former United States Lines liner *United States* is featured (in 1952, the ship made the fastest transatlantic crossing by a passenger ship, taking the famed "Blue Riband" from the Cunard's *Queen Mary*). This restaurant is not as luxurious as the alternative dining salons aboard sister ships *Celebrity Constellation*, *Celebrity Millennium* or *Celebrity Summit*.

A team of chefs prepares the cuisine exclusively for this restaurant. Fine tableside preparation is the attraction, and both the classic French cuisine (but including some menu items from the *United States*) and service are very good. This is haute cuisine at the height of professionalism, for this is a room for a full dégustation, and not just a dinner. However, with only 134 seats, not all passengers will be able to experience it even once during a one-week cruise (reservations are necessary, and a per-person cover charge applies. There's a dine-in wine cellar and a demonstration galley.

QSine, with its iPad menu and wine list, was added in the 2011 refit.

Café al Bacio and Gelateria, on the third level of the atrium lobby, is the place to see and be seen, for coffees (espresso, cappuccino, latte), pastries, cakes, and gelato, in a trendy setting. *Bistro on Five* is a new crêperie.

ENTERTAINMENT. The 900-seat Celebrity Theater is the three-deck-high venue for production shows and major cabaret acts. It is located in the forward part of the ship, with seating on main, and two balcony levels. The large stage has a full fly loft behind its traditional proscenium.

SPA/FITNESS. The AquaSpa measures 24,219 sq. ft (2,250 sq. meters). It includes a large thalassotherapy pool under a solarium glass dome, complete with health bar for light breakfast and lunch items and fresh squeezed fruit and vegetable juices.

Spa facilities include 16 treatment rooms, plus eight treatment rooms with showers and one treatment room specifically designed for wheelchair passengers, aerobics room, gymnasium with over 40 exercise machines, large men's and women's saunas (with large ocean-view porthole window), an extra-cost unisex thermal suite (containing several steam and shower mist rooms with different fragrances such as chamomile, eucalyptus and mint, and a glacial ice fountain), and a beauty salon.

The spa is operated by Steiner, a specialist concession. Sports facilities include a full-size basketball court, compact football, paddle tennis and volleyball, golf simulator, shuffleboard (on two different decks), and a jogging track.

● **For more extensive general information on what a Celebrity cruise is like, see pages 131–5.**

Celebrity Millennium
★★★★ +

Size: . . . . .Large Resort Ship	Passenger Decks: 11	Cabins (wheelchair accessible): 26
Tonnage: .90,228	Total Crew: 999	(17 with private balcony)
Lifestyle: . . . . .Premium	Passengers	Wheelchair accessibility: . . . . .Best
Cruise Line: . . . . .Celebrity Cruises	(lower beds/all berths): 1,950/2,450	Cabin Current: . . . . .110 and 220 volts
Former Names: . . . .*Millennium*	Passenger Space Ratio	Elevators: 12
Builder: . . . . .Chantiers de l'Atlantique	(lower beds/all berths): 46.2/36.8	Casino (gaming tables): . . . . .Yes
(France)	Crew/Passenger Ratio	Slot Machines: . . . . .Yes
Original Cost: . . . .$350 million	(lower beds/all berths): 1.9/2.4	Swimming Pools (outdoors): 2
Entered Service: . . . . .Jun 2000	Cabins (total): 975	Swimming Pools (indoors): 1
Registry: . . . . .Malta	Size Range (sq ft/m): 170.0–2,350.0/	(with glass dome)
Length (ft/m): 964.5/294.0	15.7–235.0	Whirlpools: 4
Beam (ft/m): 105.6/32.2	Cabins (outside view): 780	Self-Service Launderette: . . . . .No
Draft (ft/m): 26.2/8.0	Cabins (interior/no view): 195	Dedicated Cinema/Seats: Yes/368
Propulsion/Propellers: . . . . .gas turbine/2	Cabins (for one person): 0	Library: . . . . .Yes
azimuthing pods (19.5 MW each)	Cabins (with private balcony): 590	Onboard currency . . . . .US$

A premium large ship with understated decor.

OVERVIEW. *Celebrity Millennium* delivers a well-defined North American cruise vacation at a very modest price. The "zero announcement policy" means there is little intrusion. My advice is to book a suite-category cabin for its many extra benefits. Although two-seating dining and two nightly shows detract from an otherwise good product, this ship (like its sisters *Celebrity Constellation*, *Celebrity Infinity* and *Celebrity Summit*) provides a premium cruise experience that's hard to beat.

THE SHIP. This was the first Celebrity Cruises ship to be fitted with a "pod" propulsion system coupled with a gas turbine powerplant. Indeed, this was the first cruise ship in the world to be powered by quiet, smokeless, energy-efficient gas turbines (two GE gas turbines provide engine power while a single GE steam turbine drives the electricity generators). The ship was dogged by technical problems in its early days.

One notable feature is a large conservatory located in a glasshouse environment and spreading across a whole foyer. It includes a botanical environment with flowers and plants. It is directly in front of the main funnel and a section of it has glass walls overlooking the ship's side. Facilities outdoors include two outdoor pools, one indoor/ outdoor pool, and six whirlpools.

There is no walk-around wooden promenade deck outdoors. There are cushioned pads for poolside deck lounge chairs only, but not for chairs on other outside decks. Passenger participation activities are amateurish and should be upgraded.

BERLITZ'S RATINGS

	Possible	Achieved
Ship	500	427
Accommodation	200	178
Food	400	291
Service	400	298
Entertainment	100	74
Cruise	400	300

OVERALL SCORE
1,568 points out of 2,000

Inside, the ship has an understated elegance, with the same high-class decor and materials (including lots of wood, glass and marble) and public rooms that have made other ships in the fleet so popular. The atrium (with separately enclosed room for shore excursions) is four decks high and houses the reception desk, tour operator's desk, and bank. Four glass-walled elevators travel through the ship's exterior (port) side, connecting the atrium with another seven decks, thus traveling through 10 passenger decks, including the tender stations – a nice ride.

A 70-person capacity sports bar, Extreme, just doesn't, somehow, belong; it is located directly in front of the main funnel and has glass walls overlooking the ship's side.

Other facilities include a cinema/conference center, an expansive shopping arcade, with more than 14,450 sq. ft (1,300 sq. meters) of retailing space, a lavish four-decks-high showlounge with the latest in high-tech staging and lighting equipment, two-level library (one level for English-language books, a second for books in other languages); card room; CD listening room; art auction center with seating that makes it look like a small chapel; Cosmos, a combination observation lounge/discotheque; and an Internet Center containing 19 computers with wood-surround flat screens.

Gaming sports include the ship's overly large Fortunes Casino, with blackjack, roulette, and slot machines, bright lights and action. Michael's Club, originally a cigar smoker's haven, is now a piano lounge/bar.

FAMILIES. The Fun Factory is designed for young children and The Tower caters to teenagers. Children's counselors and youth activities staff provide a wide range of supervised activities. Interconnecting doors on two Celebrity Suites allow them to be used as one unit; as there is no balcony, they are ideal for those with small children.

ACCOMMODATION. There are 20 different grades. Almost half of the ship's accommodation has a "private" balcony. The accommodation is extremely comfortable. Suites, naturally, have more space, butler service, more and better amenities and service. There are several categories of suites, but those at the stern are in a prime location and have huge balconies that really are private and not overlooked from above.

All suites and cabins have wood cabinetry and accenting, interactive television and entertainment systems – you can go shopping, book shore excursions, play casino games, interactively, and even watch soft porn movies. Bathrooms have hairdryers, and 100% cotton towels.

Penthouse Suites: Two Penthouse Suites (on Penthouse Deck) are the largest accommodation aboard. Each occupies one half of the ship's width, overlooking the ship's stern. Each measures a huge 2,530 sq. ft. (235 sq. meters): 1,432 sq. ft. (133 sq. meters) of living space, plus a huge wrap-around balcony measuring 1,098 sq. ft. (102 sq. meters) with 180° views plus a wet bar, hot tub and whirlpool tub. Much of this terrace, however, can be overlooked by passengers on decks above.

Features include a marble foyer, a separate living room complete with ebony baby grand piano, and a formal dining room. The master bedroom has a large walk-in closet; personal exercise equipment; dressing room with vanity desk, exercise equipment; marble-clad master bathroom with twin washbasins; deep whirlpool tub; separate shower; toilet and bidet areas; flat-screen televisions (one in the bedroom, one in the lounge) and electronically controlled drapes. Butler service is standard, and a butler's pantry, with separate entry door, has a full-size refrigerator, temperature-controlled wine cabinet, microwave oven and good-sized food preparation and storage areas. For even more space, an interconnecting door can be opened into the adjacent suite.

Royal Suites: Eight Royal Suites, each 733 sq. ft (68 sq. meters), are located towards the ship's aft (four each on the port and starboard sides). The decor in each is different, and is geographically themed: Africa, China, Mexico, France, India, Italy, Morocco and Portugal. Each has a separate living room with dining and lounge areas (with refrigerator, mini-bar and Bang & Olufsen CD audio system), and a separate bedroom. There are two entertainment centers with DVD players, and two flat-screen televisions (one in the living area, one in the bedroom), and a large walk-in closet with vanity desk. The marble-clad bathroom has a whirlpool tub with integral shower, and there is also a separate shower enclosure, two washbasins and toilet. The teakwood decked balcony is extensive (large enough for on-deck massage) and also has a whirlpool hot tub.

Celebrity Suites: Eight Celebrity Suites, each 467 sq ft (44 sq. meters), have floor-to-ceiling windows, a separate living room with dining and lounge areas, two entertainment centers with flat-screen televisions (one in the living room, one in the bedroom), and a walk-in closet with vanity desk. The marble-clad bathroom has a whirlpool tub with integral shower (a window with movable shade lets you look out of the bathroom through the lounge to the large ocean-view windows).

These suites, located opposite a group of glass-walled elevators, overhang the starboard side of the ship and provide stunning ocean views from the glass-walled sitting/dining area, which extends out from the ship's side. A computer with wood-surround screen allows direct internet connectivity. Butler service is standard.

Sky Suites: There are 30 Sky Suites, each 308 sq ft (28.6 sq. meters), including the private balcony (some balconies may be larger than others, depending on location). Although these are designated as suites, they are really just larger cabins with a marble-clad bathroom with tub/shower combination. The suites also have a VCR player in addition to a television, and have a larger lounge area (than standard cabins) and sleeping area. Butler service is standard.

Butler Service: Butler service (in all accommodation designated as suites) includes full breakfast, in-suite lunch and dinner service (as required), afternoon tea service, evening hors d'oeuvres, free espresso and cappuccino, daily news delivery, shoeshine service, and other personal touches. Suite occupants in Penthouse, Royal, Celebrity and Sky suites also get welcome champagne; a full personal computer in each suite, including a printer and internet access (on request in the Sky Suites); choice of films from a video library; personalized stationery; tote bag; priority dining room seating preferences; private portrait sitting, and bathrobe; and in-suite massage service.

Concierge Class: In 2003, Celebrity Cruises added a third service "class" to some of the accommodation grades aboard this ship. Positioned between the top grade suite grades and standard cabin grades, Concierge Class offers added value to purchasers of these "middle-class" cabins.

Enhanced facilities include priority embarkation, disembarkation, tender tickets, alternative dining and spa reservations. Concierge Class cabin occupants get double bed overlay (no more falling "between the cracks" for couples); choice of four pillows (goose down pillow, isotonic pillow, body pillow, conformance pillow); eight-vial flower vase on vanity desk; throw pillows on sofa; fruit basket; binoculars; golf umbrella; leather telephone notepad; larger beach towels; hand-held hairdryer. The balcony gets better furniture. In the bathrooms: plusher Frette bathrobes; larger towels in sea green and pink (alternating days); flower in silver vase. It all adds up to excellent value for money.

Standard Outside-View/Interior Cabins: All other outside-view and interior cabins not designated as suites have a lounge area with sofa or convertible sofa bed, sleeping area with twin beds that convert to a double, good closet and drawer space, personal safe, mini-bar/refrigerator (all items cost extra), interactive television, and bathroom. The cabins are nicely decorated with warm wood-finish furniture, and there is none of the boxy feel of cabins in so many ships, due to the angled placement of vanity and audio-video consoles. Even the smallest interior cabin has a good-sized bathroom and shower enclosure.

Wheelchair-Accessible Accommodation: This is available in six Sky Suites, three premium outside-view cabins, eight deluxe ocean-view cabins, four standard ocean-view and five interior (no view) cabins measure 347 sq. ft to 362 sq. ft (32.2 to 33.6 sq. meters) and are located in the most practical parts of the ship, close to elevators for good accessibility. All have doorways and bathroom doorways and showers that are wheelchair-accessible.

CUISINE. The *Metropolitan Dining Room*, seating 1,224, is the principal dining hall. Two decks high, it has a grand staircase connecting the two levels, a huge glass wall overlooking the sea, and a musician's gallery on the upper level, typically for a string quartet or quintet. There are two seatings for dinner (open seating for breakfast and lunch), at tables for two, four, six, eight or 10. The menu variety is good, the food has taste, and it is attractively presented. Full service in-cabin dining is also available for all meals, including dinner.

For casual meals, the self-serve buffet-style *Ocean Café* is an extensive area that can seat 754. At the aft end of the Ocean Buffet, a separate pasta bar, sushi counter, grill/rotisserie and pizza servery provide freshly created items. Pizzas are made on board from pizza dough and do not come ready made for reheating, as with many cruise lines. On selected evenings, alternative dinners can be taken here (reservations needed). There is also an outdoors grill, adjacent to the swimming pool, for fast food.

For champagne and caviar lovers, the *Platinum Club* has a platinum and silver *belle-époque* decor reminiscent of a 1930s gentleman's club.

Café al Bacio and Gelateria, located on the third level of the atrium lobby, this is the place to see and be seen, for coffees (espresso, cappuccino, latte), pastries, cakes, and gelato, in a trendy setting.

Alternative (Reservations-Only, Extra Cost) Dining: Celebrity Cruises created its first true alternative restaurant aboard this ship. The *Olympic Restaurant* is named after White Star Line's transatlantic ocean liner (sister ship to *Titanic*). It is adjacent to the atrium lobby, and has a dining lounge that is rather like an ante-room that contains figured French walnut wood paneling from the à la carte dining room of the 1911 ship, which was decorated in Louis XVI splendor. When the panelling, sold by the scrapyard, was found in a house in Southport, northern England, Celebrity Cruises bought the house in order to obtain it.

A team of chefs prepares the cuisine exclusively for this restaurant. Fine tableside preparation is the attraction of this alternative dining room, whose classic French cuisine and service are very good; this is, indeed, a room for a full dégustation, and not just a dinner.

The wine list is extremely extensive, with more than 400 labels. But the real treat for connoisseurs is an additional list of rare vintage wines, including (when I was last aboard) a magnum of 1949 Château Pétrus (at $12,400), a 1907 Heidsieck Monopole Champagne (a mere $7,000 and brought to the surface from a sunken German ship), and a Château Lafite-Rothschild Pouillac from 1890 (a snip at $2,160).

To enjoy classic French cuisine, with tableside preparation, in this fine setting is rather like dining in a living museum, and takes a minimum of three hours. However, with just 134 seats, not all passengers will be able to experience it even once during a one-week cruise; reservations are needed, and there's a cover charge. There's also a dine-in wine cellar and a demonstration galley.

ENTERTAINMENT. The 900-seat Celebrity Theater is the three-deck-high venue for the ship's production shows and major cabaret acts. It is located in the forward part of the ship, with seating on main, and two balcony levels. The large stage is equipped with a full fly loft behind its traditional proscenium.

SPA/FITNESS. Wellness facilities include a large AquaSpa measuring 24,219 sq. ft (2,250 sq. meters). It has a large thalassotherapy pool under a huge solarium dome, complete with health bar for light breakfast and lunch items and fresh squeezed fruit and vegetable juices. There are 16 treatment rooms, plus eight more with showers and one designed for wheelchair passengers, an aerobics room, gymnasium (with over 40 exercise machines), large men's and women's saunas, an extra-cost unisex thermal suite (containing several steam and shower mist rooms with fragrances such as chamomile, eucalyptus and mint, and a glacial ice fountain), and a beauty salon.

Sports facilities include a full-size basketball court, compact football, paddle tennis and volleyball, golf simulator, shuffleboard (on two different decks) and a jogging track.

● **For more extensive general information on what a Celebrity cruise is like, see pages 131–5.**

Celebrity Reflection
NOT YET RATED

Size: ....Large Resort Ship	Passenger Decks: 14	Cabins (with private balcony): 1,216
Tonnage: 126,000	Total Crew: 1,253	Cabins (wheelchair accessible): 30
Lifestyle: ....Premium	Passengers	Wheelchair accessibility: ....Best
Cruise Line: ....Celebrity Cruises	(lower beds/all berths): 3,030/3,323	Cabin Current: ....110/220 volts
Former Names: ....none	Passenger Space Ratio	Lifts: 12
Builder: ....Meyer Werft (Germany)	(lower beds/all berths): 41.5/37.9	Casino (gaming tables): ....Yes
Original Cost: ....$641 million	Crew/Passenger Ratio	Slot Machines: ....Yes
Entered Service: .... Jun 2012	(lower beds/all berths): 2.2/2.5	Swimming Pools (outdoors): 2
Registry: ....Malta	Cabins (total): 1,515	Swimming Pools (indoors): 1
Length (ft/m): 1,033.4/315.0	Size Range (sq ft/m): 182.9–668.4/	Whirlpools: 6
Beam (ft/m): 120.7/36.8	17.0–155.0	Self-Service Launderette: ....No
Draft (ft/m): 27.2/8.3	Cabins (outside view): 1,353	Dedicated Cinema/Seats: ....No
Propulsion/Propellers: ..diesel (67.2 MW)/	Cabins (interior/no view): 151/162	Library: ....Yes
2 azimuthing pods	Cabins (for one person): 0	Onboard currency: ....US$

A premium ship for family-friendly cruising.

OVERVIEW. *Celebrity Reflection* is a close sister ship to *Celebrity Eclipse* (2010), *Celebrity Equinox* (2009), *Celebrity Silhouette* (2011), and *Celebrity Solstice* (2008). For fuller details of its facilities, see the reviews for those ships. It is expected that *Celebrity Reflection* will achieve a rating similar to that for *Celebrity Silhouette*.

THE SHIP. *Celebrity Reflection* has a steeply sloping stern that includes a mega-yacht-style ducktail platform above the propulsion pods. The ship is attractive, and nicely balanced, with two slim funnels set one behind the other. The ship's name is positioned directly under the navigation bridge and not forward on the bows (for space reasons), and the rounded bows accommodate a helicopter landing pad. One thing that's cool is an Apple "iLounge" with Apple MacBook Pro work stations – and Apple products for sale.

Although *Celebrity Reflection* is sister to *Celebrity Silhouette*, it has an additional deck housing more suites and cabins, with additional seating provided in the Celebrity Theater, the main dining room, Oceanview Café, Blu and Tuscan Grille, and QSine. With more passengers, the Passenger Space Ratio is reduced.

Another new feature (also aboard *Celebrity Silhouette*) is a Lawn Club Grill, an option lets you grill your own steak. The Lawn Porch is an intimate 48-seat casual eatery, there's an Art Studio, and The Alcoves are extra-cost "private" cabanas on deck.

ACCOMMODATION. A wide range of accommodation includes the addition of a new deck of 34 Aqua-class suites.

BERLITZ'S RATINGS

	Possible	Achieved
Ship	500	NYR
Accommodation	200	NYR
Food	400	NYR
Service	400	NYR
Entertainment	100	NYR
Cruise	400	NYR

CUISINE. *Reflections*, the ship's balconied main dining room is included in the cruise price and has ocean views on the port and starboard sides. The design is stunning and contemporary. At the forward end, a two-deck-high wine tower provides a great focal point.

The following dining venues are all located one deck above the main restaurant and galley on Deck 5, and occupy the aft section of the ship:

● *Murano* is an extra-cost, reservations-required dinner venue, offering high-quality traditional dining with a French flair and gorgeous table settings, including large Reidel wine glasses. Food and service are very good.

● *Blu* is a 130-seat specialty restaurant designated exclusively for the occupants of AquaClass cabins. The room has pleasing but rather cold blue decor.

● The *Tuscan Grille*, an extra-cost venue, serves Kobe beef and premium quality steaks, and has beautifully curved archways – it's like walking into a high-tech winery. Large aft-facing windows offer a great view over the ship's wake.

● *QSine* is an extra-cost, reservations-only dining venue (it replaced *Silk Road* on other ships in the same class). It's an "interactive" venue, with iPad menus and wine list, and you can even prepare your own food items like guacamole – but your cover charge won't be reduced to reflect your own efforts. Note the waiters' jackets with their square buttons. It is open only for dinner.

For snacks and less ambitious meals, the options are:

● *Bistro on Five* (Deck 5, that is) is for coffee, cakes, crêpes, pastries, and more – it's sort of a French-style crêperie. It gets busy at times and the serving counter is small, so it's a congested area.

● *Café al Bacio & Gelateria* is a coffeehouse serving (extra cost) Lavazza Italian coffee. It is on one side of the main lobby, but it's small and lines quickly form at peak times. The seating is mostly in large, very comfortable armchairs.
● *Oceanview Café and Grill* is the expansive, tray-less, casual self-serve buffet venue. There are a number of food "islands" rather than those awful straight buffet counters, but the signage is reasonably good. However, it's impossible to get a warm plate for so-called hot food items, and condiments are hard to find.
● The *AquaSpa Café* is for light, healthier options (solarium fare), but the selections are bland and boring.
● The *Mast Bar Grill and Bar* is an outside venue that serves fast food.

ENTERTAINMENT. The 1,160-seat Reflection Theater, the ship's principal showlounge, has a main level and two balconied sections positioned amphitheater-style around a stage with music lofts set on either side. Three circus-themed production shows highlight in-your-face, formulaic acrobatics.

Colorful theme nights are held in the Sky Observation Lounge, whose daytime bland and minimalist decor comes alive at night thanks to mood lighting effects. The 200-seat Celebrity Central hosts stand-up comedy, cooking demonstrations, enrichment lectures and feature films.

An Entertainment Court showcases street performers, psychics and caricaturists, and is in the center of the ship, linked to the adjacent Quasar nightclub, with its decor harking back to the 1960s and '70s. The Ensemble Lounge is a big-band era cocktail lounge with live jazz-styled music, set adjacent to the specialty restaurant, Murano.

SPA/FITNESS. The AquaSpa is operated by concessionaire Steiner Leisure. The fitness center includes kinesis (pulleys against gravity) workout equipment, plus the familiar favorite muscle-pumping cardio-vascular machinery. There's also a relaxation area, AquaSpa station, and an acupuncture center.

● **For more extensive general information on what a Celebrity cruise is like, see pages 131–5.**

Celebrity Silhouette
★★★★ +

Size: . . . . .Large Resort Ship	Passenger Decks: 14	Cabins (with private balcony): 1,216
Tonnage: 121,878	Total Crew: 1,253	Cabins (wheelchair accessible): 30
Lifestyle: . . . . .Premium	Passengers	Wheelchair accessibility: . . . . .Best
Cruise Line: . . . . .Celebrity Cruises	(lower beds/all berths): 2,852/3,145	Cabin Current: . . . . .110 and 220 volts
Former Names: . . . . .none	Passenger Space Ratio	Elevators: 12
Builder: . . . . .Meyer Werft (Germany)	(lower beds/all berths): 42.7/38.7	Casino (gaming tables): . . . . .Yes
Original Cost: . . . .$641 million	Crew/Passenger Ratio	Slot Machines: . . . . .Yes
Entered Service: . . . . .Jun 2010	(lower beds/all berths): 2.2/2.5	Swimming Pools (outdoors): 2
Registry: . . . . .Malta	Cabins (total): 1,426	Swimming Pools (indoors): 1
Length (ft/m): 1,033.4/315.0	Size Range (sq ft/m): 182.9–668.4/	Whirlpools: 6
Beam (ft/m): 120.7/36.8	17.0–155.0	Self-Service Launderette: . . . . .No
Draft (ft/m): 27.2/8.3	Cabins (outside view): 1,286	Dedicated Cinema/Seats: . . . . .No
Propulsion/Propellers: . . . . .diesel	Cabins (interior/no view): 140	Library: . . . . .Yes
(67.2 MW)/2 azimuthing pods	Cabins (for one person): 0	Onboard currency . . . . .US$

A premium large ship with elegant decor and style.

OVERVIEW. Behind the two slim funnels, *Celebrity Silhouette* recreates the great outdoors with the Lawn Club, an area with real Bermudan (not fake) grass. You can go putting, play croquet or bocce ball, or picnic on the grass – even sleep on it. And it's a nice place to walk barefoot. If you can afford it, book a suite-category cabin for the extra benefits it brings – it really is worth it.

THE SHIP. This sleek-looking ship is sister to *Celebrity Eclipse, Celebrity Equinox, Celebrity Solstice* and, in 2012, *Celebrity Reflection.* Down on Resort Deck, several water-play areas are located: one in a glass-roofed solarium, a sports pool, a family pool, and a wet zone. But the deck space around the two pools isn't large enough for the number of passengers carried.

Inside, the decor is a contemporary interpretation of cool and chic. A favorite spot is Michael's Club, an intimate lounge with classic English leather club chairs and a handsome fireplace, plus more than 50 types of beer, whiskeys and cognacs. Also popular is the Martini Bar, which has a frosted bar and many varieties of vodka and martinis; it includes a small alcove called Crush with an ice-filled table where you can try caviar and vodka tasting, or host a private party.

Part of the Lawn Club is an interactive Lawn Club Grill, while The Porch is a 48-seat eatery overlooking the lawn, for complimentary breakfast and lunches, plus specialty coffees, wine and beer (at extra cost), in a laid-back setting. Eight cabana-style alcoves can accommodate up to four, and are available for a full- or part-day rental. The alcoves are wi-fi enabled, and you can order picnic baskets

BERLITZ'S RATINGS

	Possible	Achieved
Ship	500	433
Accommodation	200	178
Food	400	303
Service	400	309
Entertainment	100	78
Cruise	400	311

OVERALL SCORE
1,612 points out of 2,000

and beverages. Eight hammocks and two oversized Adirondack chairs are also being added.

Near the Lawn Club entrance is The Art Studio, for art demonstrations and classes on topics such as painting, drawing and mixology. While some are free, others cost extra.

ACCOMMODATION. From Penthouse Suites to small interior cabins, the accommodation is practical and comfortable. There are 24 price grades, depending on size and location. In the standard Interior and Ocean View cabins, there is little space between the bed and the wall, and usable drawer space is poor.

There are four suite-grade categories: Royal Suite, Celebrity Suite, Sky Suite, and Penthouse Suite. Most of the balcony cabins on Penthouse Deck and Sky Deck suffer from permanent shade because they are just under the wide deck overhang – the large suites surrounding the aft elevator foyers get much more sunlight.

Facilities in all grades include: twin beds that convert to queen-size, sitting area, vanity desk with hairdryer, and 32-inch flat-screen TV (larger screens in suites). But there's little drawer space. The bathroom has a shower enclosure (with foot-rail for leg-shaving), toilet, and tiny washbasin – but no soap dish, and the faucet gets in the way when washing your face or brushing your teeth. There's no retractable clothesline for washed small items; and the two hooks on the back of the bathroom door are tiny.

Also standard in all cabins: wireless internet access (for a fee), and premium bedding. Although the closets have good hanging space, there is no shelving on which to place folded items, and drawers in the vanity desk cannot accommodate them. Accommodation designated as suites have more space, larger balconies (with good quality sun-loungers), and more toiletries.

Some 130 "AquaSpa"-class cabins share the relaxation room of the AquaSpa itself, incorporate select spa elements into the cabins, and allow for specialized access to the AquaSpa's Thermal Relaxation Room and a Persian Garden (with aromatherapy/steam rooms) on the same deck, and other spa amenities. Occupants get assigned seating in the 130-seat Restaurant Blu. Facilities include: a choice of four pillows (conformance, body, goose, Isotonic); express luggage delivery; shoeshine; Frette bathrobes; dining and seating preferences in other alternative dining venues; and early embarkation and disembarkation. Bathrooms include a tub plus a separate shower enclosure.

Other accommodation grades are named Veranda-class; Sunset-Veranda-class; Concierge-class; Family Oceanview with veranda; Deluxe Oceanview with veranda; Standard Oceanview; and Standard Interior cabins.

CUISINE. The ship has a good choice of dining venues, from the main dining room included in the cruise fare to specialty venues that need reservations and cost extra. The balconied main dining room is in the ship's aft, close to the main lobby, and has ocean views on the port and starboard sides. The design is contemporary, and visually stunning.

For snacks and less ambitious meals, the options are:
● *Bistro on Five* (Deck 5, that is) is for coffee, cakes, crepes, pastries, and more. It gets busy at times and the serving counter is small, so it's a congested area.
● *Café al Bacio & Gelateria* is a coffeehouse featuring Lavazza Italian coffee and situated on one side of the main

lobby, but it's small and lines quickly form at peak times.
● *Oceanview Café and Grill* is the expansive, tray-less, casual self-serve buffet venue. There are a number of food "islands" and the signage is reasonable.
● The *AquaSpa Café* is for light, healthier options (solarium fare), but the selections are uninspiring.
● The *Mast Bar Grill and Bar* is an outside fast-food venue.

ENTERTAINMENT. The 900-seat Celebrity Theater is the three-deck-high venue for production shows and major cabaret acts. It is located in the forward part of the ship, with seating on main and two balcony levels. The large stage has a full fly loft behind its traditional proscenium.

SPA/FITNESS. The AquaSpa measures 24,219 sq. ft (2,250 sq. meters). It includes a large thalassotherapy pool under a solarium glass dome, complete with health bar for light breakfast and lunch items and fresh squeezed fruit and vegetable juices.

Spa facilities include 16 treatment rooms, plus eight treatment rooms with showers and one treatment room specifically designed for wheelchair passengers. There's also an aerobics room, a gymnasium with over 40 exercise machines, large men's and women's saunas with a sizable ocean-view porthole window, and a beauty salon. An extra-cost unisex thermal suite contains several steam and shower mist rooms with fragrances such as chamomile, eucalyptus and mint, and a glacial ice fountain.

● **For more extensive general information about the Celebrity Cruises experience, see pages 131–5.**

Celebrity Solstice
★★★★ +

Size: . . . . .Large Resort Ship	Passenger Decks: 14	Cabins (with private balcony): 1,216
Tonnage: .121,878	Total Crew: .1,253	Cabins (wheelchair accessible): 30
Lifestyle: . . . . .Premium	Passengers	Wheelchair accessibility: . . . . .Best
Cruise Line: . . . . .Celebrity Cruises	(lower beds/all berths): 2,852/3,145	Cabin Voltage: . . . . .110/220 volts
Former Names: . . . . .none	Passenger Space Ratio	Elevators: 12
Builder: . . . . .Meyer Werft (Germany)	(lower beds/all berths): 42.7/38.7	Casino (gaming tables): . . . . .Yes
Original Cost: . . . .$641 million	Crew/Passenger Ratio	Slot Machines: . . . . .Yes
Entered Service: . . . . Nov 2008	(lower beds/all berths): 2.2/2.5	Swimming Pools (outdoors): 2
Registry: . . . . .Malta	Cabins (total): 1,426	Swimming Pools (indoors): 1
Length (ft/m): 1,033.4/315.0	Size Range (sq ft/m): 182.9–1,668.4/	Whirlpools: 6
Beam (ft/m): 120.7/36.8	17.0–155.0	Self-Service Launderette: . . . . .Yes
Draft (ft/m): 27.2/8.3	Cabins (outside view): 1,286	Dedicated Cinema/Seats: . . . . .No
Propulsion/Propellers: . . . . .diesel	Cabins (interior/no view): 140	Library: . . . . .Yes
(67,200kW)/2 azimuthing pods	Cabins (for one person): 0	Onboard currency . . . . .US$

Elegant, understated decor in a premium setting.

OVERVIEW. *Celebrity Solstice,* whose decor is elegant yet contemporary, sails year-round from Fort Lauderdale (Port Everglades). There are several firmly established Celebrity "signature" rooms such as Michael's Club, an intimate, quiet lounge with classic English leather club chairs, a dramatic black glass chandelier, a grand Michelangelo marble fireplace, and some fashionable artwork.

THE SHIP. The steeply sloping stern, which includes a mega-yacht-style ducktail platform above the propulsion pods, is very attractive. Behind the two smallish funnels is a real grass outdoor area, the Lawn Club. This is the authentic stuff – not green Astroturf – and it seems to like the salty air. The club is open to all, so you can go putting, play croquet or bocce ball (like bowling or French boules), or picnic on the grass, or perhaps sleep on it. Several pool and water-play areas are positioned on Resort Deck: one in a glass-roofed solarium, a sports pool, a family pool, and a wet zone. The deck space around the two pools, however, isn't large enough for the number of passengers carried.

For the thirsty, there's a wine bar with a sommelier; a pre-dinner cocktail lounge that reflects the jazz age of the 1930s and '40s; a bar with the look of an ocean-going yacht; Quasar, a bar with designs from the 1960s and '70s and large screens that create a nightly light show synchronized to music; and an observation lounge with a dance floor.

Celebrity's signature Martini Bar, which has a frosted bar and more than 100 varieties of vodka as well as martinis, has a small alcove called Crush with an ice-filled table where you can participate in caviar and vodka tasting, or host a private party. It's very noisy and congested.

BERLITZ'S RATINGS

	Possible	Achieved
Ship	500	433
Accommodation	200	178
Food	400	302
Service	400	310
Entertainment	100	78
Cruise	400	310

OVERALL SCORE
1,611 points out of 2,000

The ship also has a delightful two-deck library, though books on the higher of the 12 shelves are impossible to reach. The card room – located, unusually, in the center of the ship, with no ocean view windows to distract players – is open, and attracts noise from adjacent areas, so it's almost useless as a serious card playing room. Fortunes Casino (non-smoking) has 16 gaming tables and 200 slot machines.

An innovative Hot Glass Show, housed in an outdoor studio on the open deck as part of the Lawn Club and created in collaboration with Corning Museum of Glass, includes demonstrations and a narrated performance of glass-blowing. However, it's a novelty, and once you've seen it, you've seen it – which may be why *Celebrity Reflection* and *Celebrity Silhouette* have replaced the glass show with an interactive Lawn Club Grill. Three resident glass-blowing artists host workshops.

Elevator call buttons are located in a floor-stand "pod" and, when the elevator arrives, a glass panel above it turns from blue to pink. Also notable is the collection of designer chairs and sunloungers in various locations.

Passenger niggles include lack of usable drawer space in cabins; inadequate children's facilities and staff during school holiday periods; congestion caused by a bottleneck when you exit the showlounge; and noise in all areas of the lobby when the martini bar is busy.

Gratuities are charged to your onboard account.

FAMILIES. Play areas include the Fun Factory (for 3–12 year-olds, featuring Leapfrog Schoolhouse's educational programs); and "X Club" – a high-tech teens-only chill-out room with coffee bar and a night-time dance club.

ACCOMMODATION. About 90% of cabins have an outside view. Of these, 85% have a balcony; indeed, this ship has more balcony cabins than any other cruise ship to date and its slender width means there are very few interior cabins. There are four suite-grade categories: Royal Suite, Celebrity Suite, Sky Suite, and Penthouse Suite. If you can afford it, book a suite-category cabin for the extra benefits – it really is worth it. Most balcony cabins on Penthouse Deck and Sky Deck suffer from permanent shade because they are just under the wide deck overhang – the large suites surrounding the aft elevator foyers get much more sunlight.

Facilities in all grades include: twin beds that convert to a queen-size bed, sitting area, vanity desk with hairdryer, and 32-inch flat-screen TV (larger screens in suites). But there's very little drawer space. The bathroom has a shower enclosure (with a useful foot-rail for leg-shaving, toilet, and tiny washbasin, but there's no soap dish, and the faucet gets in the way when washing your face or brushing your teeth. There's no retractable clothesline for hanging your washed small items; and the two hooks on the back of the bathroom door are tiny.

Also standard in all cabins: wireless internet access (for a fee), premium bedding. However, although the closets have good hanging space, there is no shelving on which to place folded items, and drawers in the vanity desk cannot accommodate them. Accommodations designated as suites have more space, larger balconies (with good quality sunloungers), and more personal amenities.

Like other cruise lines, Celebrity has added "Spa-Class" accommodation. Some 130 AquaSpa-class cabins share the relaxation room of the AquaSpa itself, incorporate select spa elements into the cabins, and allow for specialized access to the AquaSpa's Thermal Relaxation Room and Persian Garden (with aromatherapy/steam rooms) on the same deck, and other spa amenities. Occupants also get assigned seating at the exclusive 130-seat Restaurant Blu. Other bonuses include: a choice of four pillows (conformance, body, goose, Isotonic); express luggage delivery; shoeshine; Frette bathrobes; dining and seating preferences in other alternative dining venues; and early embarkation and disembarkation. Bathrooms include a tub plus a separate shower enclosure.

Other accommodation grades are named Veranda-class; Sunset-Veranda-class; Concierge-class; Family oceanview with veranda; Deluxe Oceanview with veranda; Standard Oceanview; and Standard Interior cabins.

CUISINE. *Grand Epernay*, the balconied principal dining room that's included in the cruise price, is located towards the aft section of the ship close to the main lobby, and has ocean views on the port and starboard sides. The design is stunning and contemporary; the decor is brown and beige. However, the almost-backless tub-style chairs are not comfortable and lack a separate armrest. At the forward end, a two-deck high wine tower glistens and provides a stunning focal point. As for the food, it is a bit of a let-down; the decreased quality is all too obvious to repeat Celebrity passengers.

The following four dining venues are all located one deck above the main restaurant and galley (on Deck 5), and occupy the aft section of the ship:
● *Murano* is an extra-cost, reservations-required venue offering high-quality traditional dining with a French flair and fine table settings.
● *Blu* is a 130-seat specialty restaurant designated for occupants of AquaClass cabins. The room has pleasing (but rather cold) blue decor. The ambience is cool.
● The *Tuscan Grille*, an extra-cost, reservations-required venue, serves Kobe beef and premium quality steaks, and has beautifully curved archways and great views.
● *Silk Harvest* is a Southeast Asian extra-cost dining venue serving unmemorable pan-Asian fusion cuisine. It has wood-topped tables (no tablecloths).

For snacks and less ambitious meals, the options are:
● *Bistro on Five* (Deck 5, that is) is for coffee, cakes, crêpes, pastries, and more. It gets busy at times and the serving counter is small, so it's a congested area.
● *Café al Bacio & Gelateria* is a coffeehouse serving Lavazza Italian coffee and situated on one side of the main lobby, but it's small and lines quickly form at peak times.
● *Oceanview Café and Grill* is the expansive, tray-less, casual self-serve buffet venue. There are a number of food "islands" rather than those awful straight buffet counters, but the signage is reasonable. Condiments are hard to find.
● The *AquaSpa Café* is for light, healthier options (solarium fare), but the selections need improvement.
● The *Mast Bar Grill and Bar* is a fast-food outside venue.

ENTERTAINMENT. The 1,115-seat Solstice Theater, the main showlounge, stages three circus-themed production shows featuring in-your-face, formulaic acrobatics.

Colorful theme nights are held in the Observation Lounge (whose daytime bland and minimalist decor comes alive at night thanks to mood lighting effects). The 200-seat Celebrity Central hosts stand-up comedy, cooking demonstrations, enrichment lectures and feature films. Quasar is a high-pulse, high-volume nightclub.

An Entertainment Court showcases street performers, psychics and caricaturists, and is in the center of the ship, linked to the adjacent Quasar nightclub, with its decor harking back to the 1960s and '70s. The Ensemble Lounge is a big-band era cocktail lounge with live jazz-styled music, set adjacent to the Murano, the specialty restaurant.

SPA/FITNESS. The AquaSpa is operated by Steiner Leisure. The fitness center includes kinesis (pulleys against gravity) workout equipment, plus familiar favorite muscle-pumping cardio-vascular machinery. There's also a relaxation area, AquaSpa station, and acupuncture center. Massages include fashionable things such as a Herbal Poultice massage and a Bamboo Massage using bamboo shoots and essential oils.

● **For more extensive general information on what a Celebrity cruise is like, see pages 131–5.**

Celebrity Summit
★★★★ +

Size:	Large Resort Ship	Passenger Decks:	11	Cabins (wheelchair accessible):	26
Tonnage:	91,000	Total Crew:	999		(17 with private balcony)
Lifestyle:	Premium	Passengers		Wheelchair accessibility:	Best
Cruise Line:	Celebrity Cruises	(lower beds/all berths):	1,950/2,450	Cabin Current:	110 and 220 volts
Former Names:	Summit	Passenger Space Ratio		Elevators:	12
Builder:	Chantiers de l'Atlantique	(lower beds/all berths):	46.6/37.1	Casino (gaming tables):	Yes
	(France)	Crew/Passenger Ratio		Slot Machines:	Yes
Original Cost:	$350 million	(lower beds/all berths):	1.9/2.4	Swimming Pools (outdoors):	2
Entered Service:	Nov 2001	Cabins (total):	975	Swimming Pools (indoors):	1
Registry:	Malta	Size Range (sq ft/m):	165.1–2,530.0/		(with glass dome)
Length (ft/m):	964.5/294.0		15.34–235.0	Whirlpools:	4
Beam (ft/m):	105.6/32.2	Cabins (outside view):	780	Self-Service Launderette:	No
Draft (ft/m):	26.2/8.0	Cabins (interior/no view):	195	Dedicated Cinema/Seats:	Yes/368
Propulsion/Propellers:	gas turbine/2	Cabins (for one person):	0	Library:	Yes
	azimuthing pods (19.5 MW each)	Cabins (with private balcony):	590	Onboard currency	US$

A premium ship for family-friendly cruising.

OVERVIEW. This is a sister ship to *Celebrity Constellation, Celebrity Infinity* and *Celebrity Millennium*. The accommodation is extremely comfortable in all grades, and only two-seating dining and two nightly shows detract from an otherwise excellent product.

THE SHIP. Jon Bannenberg, designer of mega-yachts, was responsible for the exterior that has a royal blue and white hull, although it has actually turned out to look extremely ungainly. In early 2012, the ship will under a "Solsticizing" program which will add more cabins, more facilities and more dining options such as QSine, an extra-cost fine dining venue with iPad menus. For details of these additions and a full description of the ship's decor and facilities, see the entry for *Celebrity Infinity* on page 289.

ACCOMMODATION. There are 20 different grades, giving you a wide choice of size and location. Almost half the accommodation has a "private" balcony; approximately 80 percent are outside-view suites and cabins, and 20 percent are interior (no view) cabins.

For comprehensive details of Penthouse Suites, Royal Suites, Celebrity Suites, Sky Suites, Butler Service, Concierge Class, Standard Outside-View and Interior Cabins, and Wheelchair-accessible accommodation, see the entry for *Celebrity Infinity*.

CUISINE. The 1,170-seat, two-deck-high *Cosmopolitan Restaurant* is the ship's formal dining room. As a tribute to

BERLITZ'S RATINGS

	Possible	Achieved
Ship	500	427
Accommodation	200	178
Food	400	291
Service	400	298
Entertainment	100	74
Cruise	400	300

OVERALL SCORE
1,568 points out of 2,000

the French Line ship *Normandie*, a statue created by Leon-Georges Baudry, called "La Normandie", that once overlooked the ship's grand staircase and for the past 47 years graced the Fontainebleu Hotel in Miami, was purchased for $250,000 and can now be seen here. The extra-cost, reservations-only alternative dining optiion is the 134-seat *Normandie Restaurant*, with gold-lacquered paneling from the smoking room of the original French Line ship. There is a dine-in wine cellar.

The *Champagne Bar* is reminiscent of a 1930s gentleman's club. There's also a *Martini Bar*. For casual eating, the *Waterfall Café* is a self-serve buffet area, with six principal serving lines and 754 seats. There is also a grill and pizza bar. *Café al Bacio and Gelateria* is the place to see and be seen for coffees, pastries, cakes, and gelato, in a trendy setting.

For more details of dining times and food quality, see the entry for *Celebrity Infinity*.

ENTERTAINMENT. The 900-seat Celebrity Theater is the three-deck-high venue for the ship's production shows and major cabaret acts.

SPA/FITNESS. For details of the AquaSpa and the many other treatment and sports facilities, see the entry for *Celebrity Infinity*.

● **For more extensive general information on what a Celebrity cruise is like, see pages 131–5.**

Celebrity Xpedition
★★★★

Size: ....Boutique Ship	Total Crew: 64	Wheelchair accessibility: ....None
Tonnage: 2,842	Passengers	Cabin Voltage: 220
Lifestyle: ....Premium	(lower beds/all berths): 90/95	Elevators: 0
Cruise Line: ....Celebrity Cruises	Passenger Space Ratio	Casino (gaming tables): ....No
Former Names: ....Sun Bay	(lower beds/all berths): 31.5/29.9	Slot Machines: ....No
Builder: ....Cassens-Werft (Germany)	Crew/Passenger Ratio	Swimming Pools (outdoors): ....No
Original Cost: ....DM 35 million	(lower beds/all berths): 1.4/1.4	Swimming Pools (indoors): ....No
Entered Service: .....Jun 2001/Jun 2004	Cabins (total): 45	Whirlpools: 1
Registry: ....The Bahamas	Size Range (sq ft/m): 156.0–460.0/	Fitness Center: ....Yes
Length (ft/m): 290.3/88.5	14.5–42.7	Sauna/Steam Room: ....Yes/No
Beam (ft/m): 45.9/14.0	Cabins (outside view): 45	Massage: ....Yes
Draft (ft/m): 11.4/3.5	Cabins (interior/no view): 0	Self-Service Launderette: ....No
Propulsion/Propellers: ....diesel	Cabins (for one person): 0	Dedicated Cinema/Seats: ....No
(3,000kW)/2	Cabins (with private balcony): 8	Library: ....Yes
Passenger Decks: 4	Cabins (wheelchair accessible): 0	Onboard currency ....US$

A comfortable small ship for exploring the Galápagos Islands.

OVERVIEW. This is the first specialist boutique ship for Celebrity Cruises and is like a small private club, providing ecotourism of the best kind. It will suit mature adults who want an intimate and casual cruise experience without the crowds, to see the nature and wildlife of the Galápagos Islands.

THE SHIP. There is a surprisingly good amount of open deck space – better, in proportion, than many larger ships, and much of it with teakwood decking, as well as teak sunloungers and patio furniture. Although there is no swimming pool – the ship's too small for one – there is a whirlpool tub on the uppermost open deck. Stabilizers were installed in 2004.

All accommodation is located forward half, with public rooms aft. The ambience is unhurried, yet subtly elegant. Except for the dining room, which can double as a conference room, there is only one public room: the main lounge, complete with bar, dance floor and bandstand.

Shore excursions by Zodiac inflatable boats are in small groups led by Ecuadorian guides. On your return, waiters greet you with refreshing drinks and towels. Included in the fare: excursions, gratuities to shipboard staff, beverages including house wine, champagne, liquor, beer and soda.

ACCOMMODATION. There are four price categories in two cabin types: nine Suites, measuring 247 sq. ft (23 sq. meters); 34 Comfort Cabins, 172 sq. ft (16 sq. meters); and three Comfort cabins, 156 sq. ft (14.5 sq. meters). All suites and cabins have twin beds (four comfort cabins have a dou-

BERLITZ'S RATINGS

	Possible	Achieved
Ship	500	336
Accommodation	200	139
Food	400	281
Service	400	302
Entertainment	n/a	n/a
Cruise	500	346

OVERALL SCORE
1,404 points out of 2,000

ble bed), TV, sofa, drinks table, vanity desk with hairdryer, mini-bar/refrigerator, and personal safe. Bathrooms all have a good-sized shower enclosure (there are no tubs) with soap/shampoo dispenser, black granite washbasin, and white marble-clad walls.

The largest accommodation is in nine suites, each with a private balcony. One suite is located forward, with forward-facing views, and has a sloping ceiling with character. Balcony partitions are almost private; the balcony deck is teak covered. Two of the suites can be joined together. One bedroom has two pull-down Murphy beds.

CUISINE. The Darwin Dining Room is an intimate room that operates on an open-seating basis. Nicely decorated, it has ocean-view windows along one side. A self-serve buffet offers salads, cold cuts and cheeses. House wines and beer are included in the fare; a few better wines can be bought. The cuisine depends on local suppliers; meat quality is disappointing, fish seafood and fruits are good, but vegetables are inconsistent.

The casual, self-serve Seagull Buffet is just behind the main lounge on the open deck, with teak tables and chairs.

ENTERTAINMENT. Dinner and after-dinner conversation with fellow passengers is the main entertainment.

SPA/FITNESS. There is a small fitness room, and adjacent unisex sauna located inside on the uppermost deck, while a small beauty salon is located on the lowest deck.

Clipper Odyssey
★★★

Boutique Ship: . . . . .5,218 tons	Total Crew: 52	Wheelchair accessibility: . . . . .Fair
Lifestyle: . . . . .Standard	Passengers	Cabin Current: . . . . .115 volts
Cruise Line: . . . . . . .Zegrahm Expeditions	(lower beds/all berths): 128/128	Elevators: 1
Former Names: . . . . . . .Oceanic Odyssey,	Passenger Space Ratio	Casino (gaming tables): . . . . .No
Oceanic Grace	(lower beds/all berths): 43.4/43.4	Slot Machines: .No
Builder: . . . . . . .NKK Tsu Shipyard (Japan)	Crew/Passenger Ratio	Swimming Pools (outdoors): 1
Original Cost: . . . .$40 million	(lower beds/all berths): 2.4/2.4	Swimming Pools (indoors): 0
Entered Service: . . . . . Apr 1989/Jun 2008	Cabins (total): .64	Whirlpools: 1
Registry: . . . . .The Bahamas	Size Range (sq ft/m): . .182.9–258.3/17–24	Self-Service Launderette: . . . . .No
Length (ft/m): 337.5/102.9	Cabins (outside view): 64	Dedicated Cinema/Seats: . . . . .No
Beam (ft/m): 50.5/15.4	Cabins (interior/no view): 0	Library: . . . . .Yes
Draft (ft/m): 14.1/4.3	Cabins (for one person): 0	Onboard currency . . . . .US$
Propulsion/Propellers: diesel (5,192kW)/2	Cabins (with private balcony): 8	
Passenger Decks: 5	Cabins (wheelchair accessible): 1	

A small expedition-style ship for discovery cruises.

OVERVIEW. *Clipper Odyssey* is liked by couples and single travelers who enjoy nature and wildlife up close and personal, and who wouldn't dream of cruising in the mainstream sense aboard ships with large numbers of people. This is for hardy, adventurous types who don't need entertainment or games, and provides a pleasing antidote to cruising aboard large ships.

THE SHIP. It has a somewhat angular, but contemporary profile. Designed in Holland and built in Japan, it tried to copy the *SeaDream* small ship/ultra-yacht concept for the Japanese market. Operated by Japan's Showa Line, it wasn't suited to Japan's often choppy seas. After 10 years, the company sold it to Clipper Cruise Line (owned by Denmark's Clipper Group, but managed by International International Shipping Partners), and in 2008 it began a five-year charter to Seattle-based Zegrahm Expeditions.

Considering its size, there are expansive areas outdoors, excellent for sunbathing or for viewing wildlife. The small swimming pool is just a "dip" pool. There is a wide teak-wood outdoor jogging track. A decompression chamber for divers is no longer used due to insurance requirements. But free snorkeling equipment is available, as is a small fleet of Zodiacs (inflatable landing craft for "soft" expedition use).

Inside, nothing jars the senses, as the interior design concept balances East–West color combinations with some Indonesian accents. The ambience is warm and intimate.

There are many pillars in almost all public areas, which spoil the decor and sightlines.

BERLITZ'S RATINGS		
	Possible	Achieved
Ship	500	358
Accommodation	200	147
Food	400	219
Service	400	237
Entertainment	n/a	n/a
Cruise	500	284

OVERALL SCORE
1,245 points out of 2,000

ACCOMMODATION. There are six cabin categories. The ship has all-outside cabins quite tastefully furnished with blond wood cabinetry, twin- or queen-size beds, living area with sofa, personal safe, mini-bar/refrigerator, TV set and VCR, and three-sided mirror. All bathrooms have a deep, half-sized tub. Some cabins have private balconies; but these are very small, with awkward door handles. The bathroom toilet seats are extremely high.

There is one suite, which is the size of two cabins. It provides more room, of course, with a lounge area, and more storage space.

CUISINE. The dining room has large ocean view picture windows. It is quite warm and inviting, and all passengers eat in a single seating. The unmemorable cuisine includes fresh foods from local ports, in a mix of regional and some Western cuisine, with open seating. There is much use of canned fruits and other cheap ingredients. A young, friendly American staff provides the service.

ENTERTAINMENT. There is no formal entertainment, although dinner and after-dinner conversation with fellow passengers in the ship's lounge/bar really becomes the entertainment each evening. Otherwise, it might be a good idea to bring a good book or two.

SPA/FITNESS. There is a tiny beauty salon, and an adjacent massage/body treatment room, while a small fitness room is located on a different deck.

Club Med 2
★★★★

Size: . . . . .Small Ship	Sail Area (sq ft/m2): 26,910/2,500	Cabins (interior/no view): 0
Tonnage: .14,983	Main Propulsion: . . . . .(a) engines (b) sails	Cabins (for one person): 0
Lifestyle: . . . . .Premium	Propulsion/Propellers: . . . . .diesel	Cabins (with private balcony): 0
Cruise Line: . . . . .Club Med Cruises	(9,120kW)/2	Cabins (wheelchair accessible): 0
Former Names: . . . . .none	Passenger Decks: 8	Wheelchair accessibility: . . . . .None
Builder: . . . .Ateliers et Chantiers du Havre	Total Crew: .200	Cabin Current: . . . . . . .110 and 220 volts
Original Cost: . . . .$125 million	Passengers	Elevators: 2
Entered Service: . . . . Dec 1992	(lower beds/all berths): 394/409	Casino (gaming tables): . . . . .No
Registry: . . . . .Wallis & Fortuna	Passenger Space Ratio	Slot Machines: . . . . .No
Length (ft/m): 613.8/187.10	(lower beds/all berths): 38.0/36.6	Swimming Pools (outdoors): 2
Beam (ft/m): 65.6/20.00	Crew/Passenger Ratio	Whirlpools: 0
Draft (ft/m): 16.4/5.00	(lower beds/all berths): 1.9/2.0	Self-Service Launderette: . . . . .No
Type of Vessel: . . . . .high-tech sail-cruiser	Cabins (total): 197	Library: . . . . .Yes
Number of Masts: . . . . . . .5 (164 ft high)/	Size Range (sq ft/m): . . .193.8–322/18–30	Onboard currency . . . . .Euros
7 computer-controlled sails	Cabins (outside view): 197	

French ambience and style that'll put wind in your sails.

OVERVIEW. This ship appeals to youthful French-speaking couples and singles who want contemporary facilities and watersports in a casual but chic setting that's different to "normal" cruise ships, with good food and service, and little or no entertainment.

THE SHIP. *Club Med 2* is one of a pair of the world's largest high-tech sail-cruisers (the other is *Wind Surf*), part-cruise ship, part-yacht. Five huge masts rise 221 ft (67.5 meters) above sea level; they carry seven triangular, self-furling Dacron sails with a total surface area of 26,881 sq. ft (2,497 sq. meters). No human hands touch the sails, as everything is controlled by computer from the bridge. This also keeps the ship on an even keel via the movement of a hydraulic ballast system, so there is no rolling over 6°. When the ship is not using the sails, four diesel-electric motors propel it at up to 12 knots. The ship was extensively refurbished in 2008, when 10 new cabins were added.

An extensive array of water sports facilities is provided (all except scuba gear are included in the cruise fare), and equipment on the aft marina platform includes 12 windsurfers, three sailboats, two water ski boats, several kayaks, 20 single scuba tanks, snorkels, and four motorized water sport boats. There are two small saltwater swimming pools (really dip pools). There is an open bridge policy.

Inside, facilities include a main lounge, meeting room and an extra-charge golf simulator, plus a fitness and beauty center, and piano bar. No gratuities are expected.

BERLITZ'S RATINGS		
	Possible	Achieved
Ship	500	385
Accommodation	200	162
Food	400	282
Service	400	278
Entertainment	100	70
Cruise	400	282
OVERALL SCORE		
1,459 points out of 2,000		

ACCOMMODATION. There are five suites and 192 standard cabins, all of equal size. All cabins are nicely equipped and very comfortable, and have an inviting decor that includes much blond wood cabinetry. They have a mini-bar/refrigerator, 24-hour room service (but you pay for food), a personal safe, color television, plenty of storage space, bathrobes, and a hairdryer. There are six, four-person cabins, and some 35 doubles are fitted with an extra Pullman berth – good for young families but cramped.

CUISINE. The two main dining rooms are *Le Mediterranée* and *Le Magellen*. Both have tables for two, for, six or eight. There is open seating, so you can sit with whom you wish. The *Grand Bleu Restaurant* has a delightful open terrace for informal meals. Complimentary wines and beers are available with lunch and dinner; there is also an à la carte wine list, at a price. Afternoon tea is a delight. The cuisine provides French, continental and Japanese specialties, and the creativity and presentation are good.

ENTERTAINMENT. Apart from occasional cabaret acts, there is live music for dancing and listening each evening.

SPA/FITNESS. The Health Spa has a unisex sauna, beauty salon, and treatment rooms for massage, facials and body wraps. There is also a decent fitness room, and a beauty salon. The spa facilities are split on three separate decks.

Columbus
★★★ +

Size:	Small Ship	Passenger Decks:	6	Cabins (with private balcony):	2
Tonnage:	14,903	Total Crew:	170	Cabins (wheelchair accessible):	2
Lifestyle:	Standard	Passengers		Wheelchair accessibility:	Fair
Cruise Line:	Hapag-Lloyd Cruises	(lower beds/all berths):	408/421	Cabin Current:	220 volts
Former Names:	none	Passenger Space Ratio		Elevators:	2
Builder:	MTW Schiffswerft (Germany)	(lower beds/all berths):	36.5/35.3	Casino (gaming tables):	No
Original Cost:	$69 million	Crew/Passenger Ratio		Slot Machines:	No
Entered Service:	Jul 1997	(lower beds/all berths):	2.4/2.4	Swimming Pools (outdoors):	1
Registry:	The Bahamas	Cabins (total):	205	Swimming Pools (indoors):	0
Length (ft/m):	472.8/144.13	Size Range (sq ft/m):	139.9–339.0/	Whirlpools:	0
Beam (ft/m):	70.5/21.50		13.0–31.5	Self-Service Launderette:	No
Draft (ft/m):	16.8/5.15	Cabins (outside view):	158	Dedicated Cinema/Seats:	No
Propulsion/Propellers:	diesel	Cabins (interior/no view):	47	Library:	Yes
	(10,560kW)/2	Cabins (for one person):	2	Onboard currency	Euros

A small ship for worldwide port-intensive cruising.

OVERVIEW: *Columbus* appeals to youthful-minded German-speaking couples and single travelers seeking good value for money on a first cruise, aboard a ship with contemporary, comfortable (but not pretentious or luxurious) surroundings, and good itineraries, at a very modest price. The level of "luxury" is below that of Hapag-Lloyd's *Europa* and *Hanseatic*, and the experience aboard this very informal ship is different – but so, of course, is the cruise price. *Columbus* will leave the Hapag-Lloyd fleet in May 2012 to become *Hamburg* for Plantours and Partner. It will be replaced by the slightly larger *Columbus 2 (see page 307).*

THE SHIP. *Columbus* has a smart contemporary profile, with a single, large funnel painted in Hapag-Lloyd's orange/blue colors. Hamburg-based Hapag-Lloyd Cruises charters the ship from its German owner, Conti Reederei.

The ship also has an ice-hardened hull, which is useful for cold-weather cruise areas. In addition, the bridge "wings" can be folded inwards (as can the overhang lights) flush with the ship's side so that the vessel can enter the locks in North America's Great Lakes region, including the St. Lawrence Seaway and Welland Canal, for which the ship was specifically built. There's a choice of well-planned itineraries and destination-intensive cruises.

First-time cruise passengers in particular will find this a fresh, comfortable, casual and unpretentious ship. You don't need to buy a new wardrobe, and you can leave your tuxedo at home; you need only informal and casual clothes.

The ship has a good passenger space ratio. Each deck has a distinctly different color scheme and carpeting, making it easy to find one's way around. There is a reasonable range of public rooms to choose from, most of which are located in a "cake-layer" vertical stacking aft of the accommodation. Although the ceilings in the public rooms are plain and unimaginative (except for the Palm Garden), the decor is really bright and upbeat, and very different to all other ships in Hapag-Lloyd's fleet.

The most popular room is arguably the delightful multi-function Palm Garden, which is also the ship's forward-facing observation lounge. There are four internet-connect computers here.

The fit and finish of the interiors can best be described as a little utilitarian – the mottled gray walls are somewhat cold, but a contrast to the splashes of color found in carpeting and other decorative touches. The artwork is, for the most part, minimal and uncoordinated, yet it all works together to create cheerful surroundings. Ship buffs will notice some superb original photographs from Hapag-Lloyd's archives adorning the stairways.

A big attraction is the excellent dining experience in a relaxed, one-seating environment. The food is extremely good, and the service and housekeeping staff are well trained, so the overall vacation experience is excellent value for money. Indeed, the ship really delivers a four-star experience based on a three-and-a-half star price. Gratuities are extra and are recommended at €5–€6 per person per day.

While it's a comfortable, trendy ship, the swimming pool is small – more like a "dip" pool – as is the open deck space, and there is no walk-around promenade deck outdoors. The ship carries 12 bicycles that passengers can use in ports, free of charge.

BERLITZ'S RATINGS

	Possible	Achieved
Ship	500	342
Accommodation	200	145
Food	400	283
Service	400	297
Entertainment	100	61
Cruise	400	270

OVERALL SCORE
1,398 points out of 2,000

ACCOMMODATION. The standard cabins are really small, and many are interior cabins. All but 10 cabins have lower berths, but the 16 price grades established really are a lot for this size of ship. Except for two forward-facing suites, there are no balcony cabins, and no room service (except for accommodation designated as suites). There are two single-occupancy cabins.

The cabin decor is bright and upbeat, and a good amount of closet and shelf space is provided. The bathrooms are fully tiled and have large shower stalls (none have tubs). All cabins have a mini-bar/refrigerator (items cost extra, as in hotels ashore), flat-screen TV, personal safe, and hairdryer. Bathrobes can be requested, at a small surcharge.

There are eight suites, each at least double the size of a standard cabin and each with a curtained partition between its lounge and sleeping areas. A wall unit houses a TV set that can be turned 360 degrees for viewing from either the lounge or bedroom.

Two suites at the bow each have a narrow private veranda with two teak lounge chairs and coffee table, a bedroom with large wall clock, and a lounge area separated by a curtain, two TV sets, and an excellent amount of closet, drawer and shelf space. The cabinetry, with its walnut-finish and bird's-eye pattern, makes these suites feel warm and luxurious.

All the suites have a small room service menu. The bathrooms have a large shower – big enough for two – hairdryer, and under-sink storage space.

CUISINE. There is one large main dining room, at the stern, with large ocean-view windows on three sides, and all pas-sengers can be seated in a single seating, at assigned tables. There are just two tables for two, but other tables can accommodate up to 16 – good for family reunions. The cuisine, presented in an unstuffy way, is extremely good, though the menu choice is small – there are typically two or three entrée options for dinner.

There is an excellent daily selection of fresh-baked breads and rolls, cold cuts and cheeses. Creatively themed dinners, as well as an extensive array of late-night snacks, make dining a delight, and the quality exceeds most passengers' expectations.

Breakfast and lunch can be taken in the bright, but casual, setting of the *Palm Garden*, which doubles as the ship's very comfortable observation lounge. Light dinners can also be taken there, with the small dance floor adding another dimension.

ENTERTAINMENT. The Columbus Lounge is a single-level, H-shaped room that is quite large, with banquette and individual seating in tub chairs, and a bar is situated on the port side in the aft corner of the room. Because the apron stage is in the center of the room, the sightlines from many seats aren't that good. Entertainment consists mainly of cabaret acts typical of the cruise ship circuit. Plenty of live music, for dancing, is provided.

SPA/FITNESS. A fitness room is located forward on the uppermost deck of the ship. There's a sauna on the lowest passenger deck, next to the beauty salon, and massage/facial treatments are available.

WHERE NAUTICAL EXPRESSIONS CAME FROM

Brass monkeys

Ever wondered where the expression "Cold enough to freeze the balls off a brass monkey" came from? Well, maritime history tells us that in the days when war ships and most freighters carried cannons (and round cannon balls) made of iron. In order to keep a supply of supply of cannon balls near each cannon, a method of keeping them from rolling around had to be found.

The best storage device consisted of a square-based pyramid. One cannon ball rested on top of four others, which rested on top of nine other, which rested on a base of sixteen. Thus, a supply of 30 cannon balls could be stacked in a small area. There was, however, a small problem – how to prevent the bottom layer from rolling out from under the others on a moving ship. The solution was a metal plate called a "monkey." It had 16 round indentations – one for each of the 16 "base layer" of cannon balls.

If the "monkey" were made of iron, the cannon balls placed on it would rust to it; the solution was to make the "monkey" out of brass. However, brass contracts more than iron when it is chilled. Unfortunately, when the temperature dipped too far, the brass indentations would shrink so much that the iron cannon balls would come adrift from the "monkey." It was, thus, a case of being "cold enough to freeze the balls off a brass monkey."

He let the cat out of the bag

On board a square-rigger 150 years ago, this would have sent shudders through one's spine – for it meant that a sailor had committed an offense serious enough to have the "cat o' nine tails" extracted from its bag.

The "cat" was a whip made of nine lengths of cord, each being about 18 inches (45 cm) long with three knots at the end, all fixed to a rope handle. It could seriously injure, or even kill, the victim. It was finally outlawed by the US Congress in 1850, and then by Britain's Royal Navy in 1879.

Columbus 2
NOT YET RATED

Size: . . . . .Mid-Size Ship	Passenger Decks: 9	Cabins (with private balcony): 232
Tonnage: .30,277	Total Crew: 386	Cabins (wheelchair accessible): 3
Lifestyle: . . . . .Premium	Passengers	Wheelchair accessibility: . . . . .Good
Cruise Line: . . . . . . .Hapag-Lloyd Cruises	(lower beds/all berths): 684/824	Cabin Voltage: . . . . .110 and 220
Former Names: . . . . .Insignia, R One	Passenger Space Ratio	Elevators: 4
Builder: . . . . . . .Chantiers de l'Atlantique	(lower beds/all berths): 44.2/36.7	Casino (gaming tables): . . . . .No
Original Cost: . . . .$150 million	Crew/Passenger Ratio	Slot Machines: .No
Entered Service: . . . . . .Jul 1998/Apr 2012	(lower beds/all berths): 1.7/2.1	Swimming Pools (outdoors): 1
Registry: . . . . .Marshall Islands	Cabins (total): 342	Swimming Pools (indoors): 0
Length (ft/m): 593.7/181.0	Size Range (sq ft/m): 145.3–968.7/	Whirlpools: . . . . . .2 (+ 1 thalassotherapy)
Beam (ft/m): 83.5/25.5	13.5–90.0	Self-Service Launderette: . . . . .Yes
Draft (ft/m): 19.5/6.0	Cabins (outside view): 317	Dedicated Cinema/Seats: . . . . .No
Propulsion/Propellers: . . . . .diesel	Cabins (interior/no view): 25	Library: . . . . .Yes
(18,600 kW)/2	Cabins (for one person): 0	Onboard currency: . . . . .Euros

A mid-size ship for worldwide port-intensive cruising.

OVERVIEW. This ship is suitable for German-speaking couples who like really good food and style, but want informality, and interesting itineraries at a reasonable price below what the luxury, more formal ships charge. Hapag-Lloyd Cruises provides an extremely high level of food and service in an informal setting that is elegant, but immediately comfortable and welcoming, with almost no announcements.

BERLITZ'S RATINGS		
	Possible	Achieved
Ship	500	NYR
Accommodation	200	NYR
Food	400	NYR
Service	400	NYR
Entertainment	100	NYR
Cruise	400	NYR

THE SHIP. *Columbus 2*, a much nicer ship than the *Columbus* it replaces, was one of a series of almost identical ships built for the now-defunct Renaissance Cruises. The all-white ship has a large, square funnel in Hapag-Lloyd orange and blue. Teak overlaid decking and teak lounge chairs enhance the pool deck outdoors, giving it an elegant look.

Although there is no walk-around promenade deck outdoors, there is a jogging track around the perimeter of the swimming pool, and port and starboard side decks.

The interior decor is quite lovely, a throwback to the ship decor of the ocean liners of the 1920s and '30s, with dark woods and warm colors, all in fine taste – although it's a bit "faux" in places. It includes detailed ceiling cornices, both real, and faux wrought-iron staircase balustrades, leather-paneled walls, trompe l'oeil ceilings, rich carpeting in hallways, and many other interesting expensive-looking decorative touches. The decor is reminiscent of the Hamburg's Four Seasons Hotel, or an old-world country club.

The public rooms are spread over three decks. The reception hall has a staircase with an intricate wrought-iron balustrade. A large Observation Lounge is located high atop ship; it's a long bar with forward ocean views – at least for the barman.

There are plenty of bars – including one in each of the restaurant entrances. Perhaps the nicest is the Martini Bar/ Lounge, a lovely room reminiscent of Europe's grand hotels. It has an inviting marble fireplace, comfortable sofas and individual armchairs.

The Library is a stunning Regency-style room, with a fireplace, a high, indented, trompe l'oeil ceiling, and an excellent selection of books, plus very comfortable wingback chairs with footstools, and sofas you could sleep on.

There may not be marble bathroom fittings, but the value for money is really good. The dress code is informal.

FAMILIES. *Columbus 2* has a Children's Club and a Teens Club. Children under 15 sharing with parents in the same suite or cabin travel free; they also get discounted shore excursions, and free soft drinks during mealtimes. And Steiff, the world's oldest maker of teddy bears, will have a new bear, Captain Knopf, on board.

ACCOMMODATION. There are nine cabin categories and price grades. The standard interior and outside-view cabins (the lowest four grades) are rather compact units – tight for two persons, particularly for longer cruises. They have twin beds or queen-size bed, with good under-bed storage areas, personal safe, vanity desk with large mirror, good closet and drawer space in rich, dark woods, 100% cotton bathrobe and towels, slippers, clothes brush and shoe horn.

There are far fewer interior cabins than aboard *Columbus*. Just 18 cabins have a lifeboat-obstructed view.

Suite occupants get enhanced bathroom amenities and other goodies, complimentary shoeshine, and cashmere throw blanket, bottle of champagne on arrival, hand-held hairdryer, and priority restaurant reservations,

Owner's Suites (6): Measuring 968.7 sq.ft (90 sq.meters), these are the most spacious accommodation. They are outstanding, decadent and exclusive living spaces located aft overlooking the stern on Decks 6, 7, and 8. Each has extensive teak-floor private balconies that really are private and can't be overlooked from the decks above. Each has an entrance foyer, living room, separate bedroom (the bed faces the sea, which can be seen through the floor-to-ceiling windows and sliding glass door), CD player, fully tiled bathroom with Jacuzzi tub, and a small guest bathroom.

Vista Suites (4): Measuring 785.7 sq.ft (73 sq.meters), these are located forward on Decks 5 and 6. They have extensive teak-floor private balconies that can't be overlooked from the decks above. The layout is similar to the Owner's Suites except that there is no guest bathroom.

Penthouse Suites (52): These measure about 322.9 sq.ft (30 sq. meters). They are not really suites, but large cabins because the bedrooms aren't separate from the living areas. They have a good-sized teak-floor balcony with sliding glass door (but with partial, and not full, balcony partitions) and teak deck furniture. The lounge area has a proper dining table and there is ample clothes storage space. The bathroom has a tub, shower enclosure, washbasin and toilet.

Cabins with Balcony: Cabins with private balconies (about 216 sq.ft/20 sq. meters), comprise about 66% of all cabins. They have partial, not full, balcony partitions and sliding glass doors, and 14 cabins on Deck 6 have lifeboat-obstructed views and no balcony. The living area has a refrigerated mini-bar, lounge area with breakfast table, and a balcony with teak floor, two teak chairs and a drinks table. The bathrooms, with tiled floors and plain walls, are compact, standard units, and include a shower stall with a strong, removable hand-held shower unit, hairdryer, toiletries storage shelves and retractable clothesline.

Outside View and Interior Cabins: These measure around 160–165 sq.ft (14.8–15.3 sq.meters), and have twin beds (convertible to a queen-size bed), vanity desk, small sofa and coffee table, and bathroom with a shower enclosure with a strong, removable hand-held shower unit, hairdryer, toiletries storage shelves, retractable clothesline, washbasin, and toilet. Although they are not large, they are quite comfortable, with decent storage space.

Note that all suites/cabins located at the stern may suffer from vibration and noise, particularly when the ship is proceeding at or close to full speed, or maneuvering in port.

CUISINE. Flexibility and choice are what the dining facilities are about. There are four restaurants:

● The *Albert Ballin Restaurant* has around 340 seats, and a raised central section, with a low ceiling height. There are large ocean-view windows on three sides, with prime tables overlooking the stern. The chairs are comfortable and have armrests.

● *Toscana Italian Restaurant* has 96 seats, windows along two sides, and a set menu.

● *Polo Grill* has 98 seats, windows along two sides and a set menu including prime steaks and seafood.

● The *Lido Café,* a self-serve buffet venue, seats 154 indoors and 186 outdoors, and is open for breakfast, lunch and casual dinners. It has a small pizzeria and grill.

All restaurants have open-seating dining, so you can dine when you want, with whom you wish. Reservations are needed in Toscana Restaurant and Polo Grill (but there's no extra charge), where there are mostly tables for four or six; there are few tables for two. There is also a *Poolside Grill* outdoors.

ENTERTAINMENT. The Lounge presents entertainment, lectures and some social events. There is also live music in several bars and lounges.

SPA/FITNESS. A lido deck has a swimming pool, and good sunbathing space, plus a thalassotherapy tub. A jogging track encircles the swimming pool deck (one deck above). The uppermost outdoors deck includes a golf driving net and shuffleboard court. The spa consists of a beauty salon, three treatment rooms, men's and women's changing rooms, and steam room (but no sauna).

Coral
★★

Size: ....Mid-Size Ship	Passenger Decks: 7	Cabins (with private balcony): 0
Tonnage: 14,155	Total Crew: 265	Cabins (wheelchair accessible): 2
Lifestyle: ....Standard	Passengers	Wheelchair accessibility: ....None
Cruise Line: ....Louis Cruises	(lower beds/all berths): 756/945	Cabin Current: ....110 and 220 volts
Former Names: . . .Triton, Cunard Adventurer,	Passenger Space Ratio	Elevators: 2
Sunward II	(lower beds/all berths): 18.7/14.9	Casino (gaming tables): ....Yes
Builder: . .Rotterdamsche Dry Dock (Holland)	Crew/Passenger Ratio	Slot Machines: ....Yes
Original Cost: ....n/a	(lower beds/all berths): 2.8/3.5	Swimming Pools (outdoors): 1
Entered Service: ......Oct 1971/May 2005	Cabins (total): 378	Swimming Pools (indoors): 0
Registry: ....Greece	Size Range (sq ft/m): 118.4–131.3/	Whirlpools: 0
Length (ft/m): 491.1/149.70	11.0–12.2	Self-Service Launderette: ....No
Beam (ft/m): 70.5/21.50	Cabins (outside view): 142	Dedicated Cinema/Seats: Yes/96
Draft (ft/m): 19.22/5.86	Cabins (interior/no view): 0	Library: ....No
Propulsion/Propellers: .diesel (19,860kW)/2	Cabins (for one person): 0	Onboard currency ....Euros

For a good basic, high-value cruise experience.

OVERVIEW. *Coral* attracts first-time passengers who want to cruise the Greek Islands in a modicum of comfort and at a modest price. The all-white ship has a smart but dated profile, a deep clipper bow, and twin funnels. It has been fairly well maintained, but is showing its age.

THE SHIP. There is a walk-around painted steel outdoors promenade deck, a decent amount of open deck space for sunbathing atop the ship, and a small swimming pool on an aft deck. Some of the open space outdoors is covered by canvas awnings, providing shelter from the summer sun.

Inside, it's easy to find your way around. The few public rooms have cheerful, warm colors, although ceilings are low. Decor and artwork are eclectic, and deck names are Greek. There is no library, just some old paperbacks. Most public rooms have been refurbished and are contemporary and comfortable. Internet-access stations are provided in a small open area; connection charges are high, at €1 a minute.

Expect lines for buffets and shore excursions. Announcements are made in several languages. Gratuities are charged to your onboard account at €8 per person, per day. The dress code is casual throughout.

ACCOMMODATION. Cabins are in 15 price grades, depending on location and size. Most are very small, narrow, and basic. The closet and drawer space is minimal, and cabin soundproofing is very poor. There are 32 cabins in the two highest grades with a tub/shower; otherwise they have very small shower enclosures, and little space for toiletries.

CUISINE. While the *Dining Room* is quite attractive and

BERLITZ'S RATINGS

	Possible	Achieved
Ship	500	231
Accommodation	200	91
Food	400	194
Service	400	216
Entertainment	100	40
Cruise	400	172

OVERALL SCORE
944 points out of 2,000

benefits from contemporary colors and ambience, it can be noisy. There are two seatings for dinner on most nights (typically an open seating for the first night), and open seating for breakfast and lunch, depending on the itinerary. Dining room seating and table assignments (except for the first night) are handled by the maître d' upon embarkation.

The cuisine is predominantly Continental, with some regional Greek specialties that rely heavily on oil and salt. Vegetarian dishes are available on lunch and dinner menus. Overall, the food is quite acceptable and varied. Service is hurried and indifferent.

Casual breakfast and lunch, with limited choices, can also be taken outside on deck poolside, or in the main lounge when the weather isn't good. Additional light refreshments are available indoors at the *Café Brazil*.

ENTERTAINMENT. The Main Lounge is a single deck height, rectangular-shaped room (no sloping floor) designed mainly for small production shows and cabaret acts. Banquette and individual seating is set around a "thrust" stage, but six pillars obstruct sightlines.

SPA/FITNESS. A small gymnasium is located aft, close to the swimming pool – it's really just a "dip" pool; adjacent is a sauna and massage room. A beauty salon is located indoors on another deck – there is no natural light, which makes tinting and coloring difficult.

Massages, aromatherapy facials, manicures, pedicures, and hair beautifying treatments are available, but facilities are minimal – it's a compact ship.

Coral Princess
★★★★

Size: . . . . .Large Resort Ship	Total Crew: 900	Cabins (wheelchair accessible): 20
Tonnage: .91,627	Passengers	Wheelchair accessibility: . . . . .Good
Lifestyle: . . . . .Standard	(lower beds/all berths): 1,974/2,590	Cabin Current: . . . . .110 volts
Cruise Line: . . . . .Princess Cruises	Passenger Space Ratio	Elevators: 14
Former Names: . . . . .none	(lower beds/all berths): 46.4/35.3	Casino (gaming tables): . . . . .Yes
Builder: Chantiers de l'Atlantique (France)	Crew/Passenger Ratio	Slot Machines: . . . . .Yes
Original Cost: . . . .$360 million	(lower beds/all berths): 2.1/2.8	Swimming Pools (outdoors): 2
Entered Service: . . . . .Dec 2002	Cabins (total): 987	(+ 1 splash pool)
Registry: . . . . .Bermuda	Size Range (sq ft/m): 156–470.0/	Swimming Pools (indoors): 0
Length (ft/m): 964.5/294.0	14.4–43.6	Whirlpools: 5
Beam (ft/m): 105.6/32.2	Cabins (outside view): 879	Self-Service Launderette: . . . . .Yes
Draft (ft/m): 26/7.9	Cabins (interior/no view): 108	Dedicated Cinema/Seats: . . . . .No
Propulsion/Propellers: . . . . .gas turbine/2	Cabins (for one person): 0	Library: . . . . .Yes
Passenger Decks: 11	Cabins (with private balcony): 727	Onboard currency . . . . .US$

A comfortable, bland large ship for mature-age cruisers.

OVERVIEW. For a large ship, the layout is quite user-friendly, and less disjointed than many ships of a similar size. Because of its slim beam, the ship can transit the Panama Canal, thus providing greater flexibility in deployment than the *Grand Princess*-class ships. In a 2009 refit, an adults-only "Sanctuary" area was added to provide a quiet zone, comfortable, padded sunloungers, and "serenity" steward service. Although there's a daily fee, it's worth it.

BERLITZ'S RATINGS		
	Possible	Achieved
Ship	500	436
Accommodation	200	154
Food	400	261
Service	400	294
Entertainment	100	85
Cruise	400	314
OVERALL SCORE		
1,544 points out of 2,000		

THE SHIP. *Coral Princess* has an instantly recognizable funnel due to two jet engine-like pods that sit high up on its structure but really are mainly for decoration. Four diesel engines provide the generating power. Electrical power is provided by a combination of four diesel and one gas turbine (CODAG) unit; the diesel engines are located in the engine room, while the gas turbine unit is located in the ship's funnel housing. The ship also has three bow thrusters and three stern thrusters.

The interior layout is similar to that of the *Grand Princess*-class ships, but with two decks full of public rooms, lounges and bars instead of just one). Sensibly, it has three major stair towers for passengers – good from the safety and evacuation viewpoint – with plenty of elevators for easy access. There's a large "Movies Under the Stars" screen in the second pool area just forward of the funnel. Unlike many modern ships, *Coral Princess* has a walk-around open promenade deck.

A flower shop allows you to order flowers and Godiva chocolates for cabin delivery – good for a birthday or anniversary – a cigar lounge (Churchill Lounge), and a martini bar (Crooners). The casino has a London theme.

An AOL Internet Cafe is conveniently located on the top level of the four-deck-high lobby. The dreaded "fine arts" get their own room, so that paintings to be sold during the art auctions are not spread all over the ship.

Adjacent is the Wedding Chapel, from which a live web-cam can relay ceremonies via the internet. The ship's captain can legally marry (American) couples, thanks to the ship's registry and a special dispensation – though this may depend on where you live and should be verified when in the planning stage. Princess Cruises offers three wedding packages – Pearl, Emerald, Diamond; the fee includes registration and official marriage certificate. The Wedding Chapel can also host "renewal of vows" ceremonies, for a fee.

ACCOMMODATION. With 33 price categories, in six types, there's a good choice: 16 Suites with balcony (470 sq. ft/43.6 sq. meters); 184 Mini-Suites with balcony (285–302 sq. ft/26.4–28.0 sq. meters); eight Mini-Suites without balcony (300 sq. ft/27.8 sq. meters; 527 Outside-View Cabins with balcony (217–232 sq. ft/ 20.1–21.5 sq. meters); 144 Standard Outside-view Cabins (162 sq. ft/15 sq. meters); Interior Cabins (156 sq. ft/144.5 sq. meters). There are 20 wheelchair-accessible cabins (217–374 sq. ft/20.1–34.7 sq. meters). All measurements are approximate. Almost all outside-view cabins have a private balcony. Some cabins can accommodate a third, or third and fourth person – good for families with children. Some cabins on Emerald Deck (Deck 8) have a view obstructed by lifeboats.

Suites: There are just 16 suites and, although none are really large when compared to such ships as *Norwegian*

Dawn and *Norwegian Star*, where the largest suites measure a whopping 5,350 sq. ft/497 sq. meters, for example, each has a private balcony. All are named after islands – mostly coral-based islands in the Indian and Pacific Oceans. All suites are located on either Deck 9 or Deck 10. In a departure from many ships, *Coral Princess* does not have any suites or cabins with a view over the stern. There are also four Premium Suites, located sensibly in the ship's center, adjacent to a bank of six elevators. Six other suites, called Verandah Suites, are located further aft.

All Accommodation: All suites and cabins are equipped with a refrigerator, personal safe, TV set with audio channels, hairdryer, satellite-dial telephone, and twin beds that convert to a queen-sized bed (there are a few exceptions). All accommodation has a bathroom with shower enclosure and toilet. Accommodation designated as suites and minisuites (there are seven price categories) has a bathtub and separate shower enclosure, and two TV sets.

All passengers receive turndown service and chocolates on pillows nightly, bathrobes on request, and toiletries (larger kits, naturally, for suite/mini-suite occupants). Cabin attendants have many cabins to look after – typically 20 – which does not translate to fine personal service.

CUISINE. The two main dining rooms, *Bordeaux* and *Provence*, are in the forward part of the ship on the two lowest passenger decks The galley is all the way forward so it doesn't intersect public spaces. Both are almost identical in design and layout. The ceilings are quite low and make the rooms appear confined. They have plenty of intimate alcoves, and tables are for two, four, six, or eight. There are two seatings for dinner, while breakfast and lunch are on an open-seating basis; you may have to stand in line at peak times, just as in many large restaurants ashore.

Horizon Court, a casual 24-hour eatery, is located in the forward section of Lido Deck, with superb ocean views. Several self-serve counters provide an array of food for breakfast and lunch buffets, and offer bistro-style casual dinners in the evening.

Alternative (Extra Charge) Eateries: There are two "alternative" dining rooms *Sabatini's* and the *Bayou Café*, both enclosed – that is, not open areas which passengers can walk through, as in some Princess Cruises ships. Both cost extra, and you must make a reservation.

Sabatini's is an Italian eatery, with colorful tiled Mediterranean-style decor; it is named after Trattoria Sabatini, the 200-year old institution in Florence. It has Italian-style pizzas and pastas, with a variety of sauces, as well as Italian-style entrées – all provided with flair and entertainment by the waiters. The food is both creative and tasty, with seriously sized portions. Sabatini's is by reservation only, and there's a cover charge.

The Bayou Café is open for lunch and dinner, and has a cover charge that includes a free Hurricane cocktail. Serving Creole food, it evokes the charm of New Orleans's French Quarter, complete with wrought-iron decoration. The room has a small stage, with baby grand piano, and live jazz is part of the dining entertainment.

Other outlets include *La Pâtisserie*, in the reception lobby, for coffee, cakes and pastries. There's also a pizzeria, hamburger grill, and an extra-charge ice cream bar. Puffers and sippers should enjoy *Churchill's*, a neat cigar and cognac lounge, cleverly sited near a little hideaway called the *Rat Pack Bar*.

ENTERTAINMENT. The Princess Theatre is two decks high, and, unusually, there is much more seating in the upper level than on the main floor below. There are typically two production shows on a seven-day cruise, and three on a 10-day cruise. These are colorful, glamorous shows with well designed costumes and good lighting.

A second entertainment lounge (Universe Lounge) is designed more for cabaret-style features. It also has two levels – a first for a Princess Cruises ship – and three separate stages, enabling nonstop entertainment to be provided without constant set-ups. The room, which has a full kitchen set, is also used for cooking demonstrations and other life-enrichment participation activities. There is a good mix of music in the various bars and lounges.

For self-improvement, Princess Cruises' "Scholar Ship@Sea" program offers about 20 courses per cruise. Although introductory classes are free, there's a charge if you want to continue any chosen subject in a smaller setting. There are four core subjects: Culinary Arts, Visual/Creative Arts, Photography, and Computer Technology.

SPA/FITNESS. The Lotus Spa is located aft on one of the uppermost decks. It contains men's and women's saunas, steam rooms, changing rooms, relaxation area, beauty salon, aerobics exercise room and gymnasium with oceanviews and the latest high-tech muscle-pumping, cardiovascular equipment. There are several large rooms for individual treatments.

● **For more extensive general information about a Princess Cruises cruise experience, see pages 149–52.**

Corinthian II
★★★★

Size:.....................Boutique Ship	Passenger Decks:..................5	Cabins (with private balcony):.........4
Tonnage:.......................4,280	Total Crew:.......................66	Cabins (wheelchair accessible):.......0
Lifestyle:..................Standard	Passengers	Wheelchair accessibility..........None
Cruise Line:...Travel Dynamics International	(lower beds/all berths):.........112/122	Cabin Current:..............110 volts
Former Names:.......*Island Sun, Regina*	Passenger Space Ratio	Elevators:.........................1
Renaissance, Renaissance VIII	(lower beds/all berths):.......38.2/38.2	Casino (gaming tables):.............No
Builder:.....Nuovi Cantieri Appaunia (Italy)	Crew/Passenger Ratio	Slot Machines:....................No
Original Cost:.............$25 million	(lower beds/all berths):..........1.7/1.8	Swimming Pools (outdoors):..........0
Entered Service:......Dec 1991/May 2005	Cabins (total):....................61	Swimming Pools (indoors):..........0
Registry:..................Mauritius	Size Range (sq ft/m):......234.6–353.0/	Whirlpools:.......................1
Length (ft/m):.............297.2/90.6	21.8–32.8	Self-Service Launderette:..........No
Beam (ft/m):.................50.1/15.3	Cabins (outside view):.............61	Dedicated Cinema/Seats:...........No
Draft (ft/m):.................12.9/2.95	Cabins (interior/no view):............0	Library:..........................Yes
Propulsion/Propellers:...diesel (5000kW)/2	Cabins (for one person):.............0	Onboard currency...............US$

For life enrichment in a small-ship environment.

OVERVIEW. This intimate vessel is very comfortable and totally inviting, and operates warm-weather cruises in regions devoid of large cruise ships. It suits mature adults who like to discover small ports in a relaxed lifestyle combined with good food and service, and itineraries that enable you to "get away from it all, but in comfort."

THE SHIP. *Corinthian II* has mega-yacht looks, a smart profile and handsome styling, with twin flared funnels and a "ducktail" (sponson) stern to provide good stability and seagoing comfort. This charming ship is operated by Travel Dynamics International year-round on "soft" destination-intensive" discovery cruises. The ship, upgraded in 2004, has a teak walk-around promenade deck outdoors, and decent amount of open deck and sunbathing space.

A baby shore tender hangs off the aft deck and acts as ship-to-shore transportation. Some equipment for watersports is carried, and active types can enjoy wind surfing, scuba diving and snorkeling, deep sea fishing, mountain biking, golfing, and hiking.

The interior design is elegant, with polished wood-finish paneling throughout. There is also a very small book and video library. Although *Corinthian II* is not up to the standard of a Seabourn or Silversea ship, it will provide a good cruise experience at a moderate cost. Gratuities are appreciated but not required.

ACCOMMODATION. The spacious cabins combine highly

BERLITZ'S RATINGS		
	Possible	Achieved
Ship	500	392
Accommodation	200	159
Food	400	309
Service	400	306
Entertainment	n/a	n/a
Cruise	500	380

OVERALL SCORE
1,546 points out of 2,000

polished imitation rosewood paneling with lots of mirrors and hand-crafted Italian furniture, lighted walk-in closets, and vanity mirrors. In fact, there are a lot of mirrored surfaces in the decor, as well as just about everything you need, including a TV set and DVD player, a refrigerator, and free soft drinks and bottled water. However, the beds are fixed, so there's no underbed storage space.

The bathrooms are extremely compact; they have real teakwood floors and marble vanities, and shower enclosures. None have tubs, not even the owner's suite. Cabins with balconies have glass panels topped with a polished wood railing.

CUISINE. The dining room operates with open seating for all meals. It is small but quite smart, with tables for two, four, six, and eight. You sit where you like, with whom you like, and at what time you like. The meals are self-service, buffet-style cold foods for breakfast and lunch, with hot foods chosen from a table menu and served properly, and sit-down service for dinner. The food quality, choice, and presentation are all very good.

ENTERTAINMENT. There is no formal entertainment in the main lounge, the venue for all social activities. Anyway, six pillars obstruct the sightlines to the small stage area.

SPA/FITNESS. Water sports facilities include an aft platform, sailfish, snorkel equipment, and Zodiacs.

Costa Allegra
★★ +

Size: ....Mid-Size Ship	Passenger Decks: 8	Cabins (with private balcony): 10
Tonnage: 28,430	Total Crew: 450	Cabins (wheelchair accessible): 8 (interior)
Lifestyle: ....Standard	Passengers	Wheelchair accessibility ....None
Cruise Line: ....Costa Cruises	(lower beds/all berths): 820/1,072	Cabin Current: ....110 and 220 volts
Former Names: ....*Annie Johnson*	Passenger Space Ratio	Elevators: 4
Builder: ....Mariotti Shipyards (Italy)	(lower beds/all berths): 34.7/26.5	Casino (gaming tables): .... Yes
Original Cost: ....$175 million	Crew/Passenger Ratio	Slot Machines: ....Yes
Entered Service: ....Dec 1992	(lower beds/all berths): 2.0/2.6	Swimming Pools (outdoors): 1
Registry:.......................Italy	Cabins (total): 410	Swimming Pools (indoors): 0
Length (ft/m): 616.1/187.8	Size Range (sq ft/m): 105.4–575.8/	Whirlpools: 2
Beam (ft/m): 83.9/25.6	9.8–53.5	Self-Service Launderette: ....No
Draft (ft/m): 23.9/7.3	Cabins (outside view): 218	Dedicated Cinema/Seats: ....No
Propulsion/Propellers: ....diesel	Cabins (interior/no view): 192	Library: ....Yes
(19,200kW)/2	Cabins (for one person): 0	Onboard currency ....Euros

A modern(ish) Italian ship for low-budget cruisers.

OVERVIEW. *Costa Allegra* provides a decent first cruise experience for young adults who enjoy European-style service and a real upbeat, almost elegant atmosphere with an Italian accent and lots of noise. The decor was changed in 2006 to provide more of an Asian ambience, while still retaining a European feel. The decks are named after famous painters.

THE SHIP. *Costa Allegra* began life as a container ship in Sweden, then underwent a skilful transformation into contemporary cruise ship, which resulted in a jazzy, angular-looking vessel with a low-slung appearance that now looks dated. Slightly longer and larger than its sister ship *Costa Marina*, it has a better standard of interior fit and finish, and more outdoors space. It has an interesting glass-enclosed stern.

There is a good amount of outdoor deck and sunbathing space, but no cushioned pads are provided for the sun-loungers outdoors. There are few public restrooms. Loud and extended announcements in several languages quickly become tiresome. The small library's opening hours are poor. Gratuities are added to your onboard account.

ACCOMMODATION. The standard cabins are quite light and airy, with splashes of fabric colors, and wood accenting, and are practical. But they're small and there's little closet and drawer space. There are many small interior cabins. All cabins suffer from poor soundproofing. Many have pulldown (Pullman-style) berths for a third or fourth occupant. The bathrooms are compact, but do have good shower enclosures, with sliding circular door instead of the usual limp curtain. The cabin service menu is extremely limited.

BERLITZ'S RATINGS

	Possible	Achieved
Ship	500	275
Accommodation	200	120
Food	400	192
Service	400	226
Entertainment	100	57
Cruise	400	222

OVERALL SCORE
1,092 points out of 2,000

On Rousseau Deck there are three forward-facing suites, each with a living room, dinette and wet bar. A further 10 slightly smaller mini-suites have a small, very narrow balcony, but it is really not private, as it can be seen from the walking track on the deck above.

CUISINE. The 310-seat *Montmartre Restaurant* operates two seatings and has an international menu. It is fairly spacious but noisy, and has expansive glass windows that look out over the stern. Tables are for four, six, eight or 10 (there are no tables for two). Adjacent is the 134-seat à la carte, pay-to-eat *Montemartre Verandah Restaurant*.

Small dining venues include *Piazzetta Allegra*, a pay-to-eat sushi and sashimi bar seating 110 with a karaoke area, and *Almalfi*, an Italian pay-to-eat à la carte restaurant seating 76 indoors and 52 outside; it has a dance floor.

ENTERTAINMENT. The Folies Bergères Showroom, a single level room, has 14 pillars that obstruct sight lines. The room is quite adequate as a cabaret lounge, however. The Flamenco Ballroom has live dance music, and the Crystal Club Discotheque is predictably loud.

SPA/FITNESS. The Caracalla Spa wellness center houses a gymnasium, eight treatment rooms, two locker rooms, two saunas and a relaxation area. It is operated by Steiner, a specialist concession. Fitness classes are free, while some cost extra. There is also a jogging track outdoors.

● **For more extensive general information on what a Costa Cruises cruise is like, see pages 135–8.**

Costa Atlantica
★★★★

Size: . . . . .Large Resort Ship	Passenger Decks: 12	Cabins (wheelchair accessible): 8
Tonnage: 85,700	Total Crew: 920	Wheelchair accessibility: . . . . .Good
Lifestyle: . . . . .Standard	Passengers	Cabin Current: . . . . .110 volts
Cruise Line: . . . . .Costa Cruises	(lower beds/all berths): 2,112/2,680	Elevators: 12
Former Names: . . . . .none	Passenger Space Ratio	Casino (gaming tables): . . . . .Yes
Builder: . . . .Kverner Masa-Yards (Finland)	(lower beds/all berths): 40.5/31.9	Slot Machines: . . . . .Yes
Original Cost: . . . .$335 million	Crew/Passenger Ratio	Swimming Pools (outdoors): 2
Entered Service: . . . . .July 2000	(lower beds/all berths): 2.3/2.9	(+1 indoor/outdoor)
Registry: . . . . .Italy	Cabins (total): 1,056	Swimming Pools (indoors): . . . . .No
Length (ft/m): 959.6/292.5	Size Range (sq ft/m): 161.4–387.5/	Whirlpools: 4
Beam (ft/m): 105.6/32.2	15.0–36.0	Self-Service Launderette: . . . . .No
Draft (ft/m): 25.5/7.8	Cabins (outside view): 843	Dedicated Cinema/Seats: . . . . .No
Propulsion/Propellers: . . . . .diesel-electric	Cabins (interior/no view): 213	Library: . . . . .Yes
(34 MW)/2 azimuthing pods	Cabins (for one person): 0	Onboard currency . . . . .Euros
(17.6 MW each)	Cabins (with private balcony): 742	

A contemporary Italian ship with volume everywhere.

OVERVIEW. Costa Cruises has been updating its image, and retraining its staff, and the results can be seen in this ship, designed to wow the trendy as well as pay homage to many of Italy's great art and past masters. *Costa Atlantica* is aimed at young (and young at heart) couples and singles plus families with children who enjoy big-city life. The international clientele are offered constant activity accompanied by Italian ambience and loud entertainment.

THE SHIP. *Costa Atlantica*, sister to *Costa Mediterranea*, has basically the same exterior design and layout as that of parent company Carnival Cruise Lines' *Carnival Legend, Miracle, Pride* and *Spirit*. There are two centrally located swimming pools outdoors, one with a retractable glass dome cover that's used in bad weather. A bar abridges two adjacent whirlpool tubs. There's a smaller pool for children, and a winding water slide spanning two decks in height – it starts on a platform bridge at the aft funnel. There is an additional whirlpool tub outdoors.

Inside, the layout is somewhat of an extension of that found in previous newbuilds for Costa Cruises – particularly that of *Costa Victoria*. The deck names are inspired by Federico Fellini movies (Roma Deck, Le Notte di Cabiria, La Voce della Luna, La Strada, La Luci del Varieta). There's even a deck named after a Fellini TV movie, Ginger and Fred. The interior design is, however, bold and brash – a mix of classical Italy and contemporary features. Good points include the fact that the interior design allows efficient passenger flow from one public space to another, and

BERLITZ'S RATINGS		
	Possible	Achieved
Ship	500	427
Accommodation	200	152
Food	400	240
Service	400	273
Entertainment	100	64
Cruise	400	280
OVERALL SCORE		
1,436 points out of 2,000		

there are several floor spaces for dancing, and a range of bars and lounges for socializing.

The lobby spans eight decks. Take a drink from the lobby bar and look upwards – the surroundings are stunning. A small chapel is located forward of the uppermost level. Other facilities include a winding shopping street with boutique stores (Fendi, Gianni Versace, Paul & Shark Yachting – as well as a shop dedicated to selling Caffe Florian products), a photo gallery, a video games room, an observation balcony, a casino and a library with internet access.

All printed materials (room service folio, menus, etc.) are in six languages (Italian, English, French, German, Portuguese, and Spanish).

Some tables in the Tiziano Dining Room have a less than comfortable view of the harsh lighting of the escalators between the galley and the two decks of the dining room.

Too many pillars obstruct passenger flow and sight lines throughout the ship. The many pillars in the dining room make it difficult for waiters to provide proper food service. The fit and finish of some interior decoration is quite poor. The hospitality levels and service are inconsistent, and below the standard of several other "major" cruise lines.

ACCOMMODATION. There are 14 categories. There is a healthy (78 percent) proportion of outside-view to interior cabins. All cabins have twin beds that convert into a queen-sized bed, individually controlled air-conditioning, television, and telephone. Many cabins have views obstructed by lifeboats on Deck 4 (Roma Deck), the lowest of the accommodation decks, as well as some cabins on Deck 5. Some cabins have pull-down (Pullman-style) berths that are fully hidden in the ceiling when not in use. There is much use of fluorescent lighting in the suites and cabins, and the soundproofing could be much better. Some bathroom fixtures – bath and shower taps in particular – are frustrating to use at first.

Some of the most desirable suites and cabins are those with private balconies on five aft-facing decks (Decks 4, 5, 6, 7, and 8) with views overlooking the stern and ship's wash. Other cabins with private balconies will find the balconies not so private – the partition between one balcony and the next is not a full partition – so you might be able to hear your neighbors.

However, balcony occupants all have good views through glass and wood-topped railings, and the deck is made of teak. The cabins are well laid out, typically with twin beds that convert to a queen-sized bed, vanity desk with built-in hairdryer, large TV set, and personal safe. One closet has moveable shelves, providing more space for storing luggage. However, the lighting is fluorescent, and much too harsh. The bathroom is a simple, modular unit that has shower enclosures with soap dispenser.

The largest suites are designated Penthouse Suites, although they are really quite small when compared with suites aboard other ships of a similar size. However, they do at least offer more space to move around in, and a slightly larger, better bathroom.

CUISINE. The large *Tiziano Dining Room* is located in the aft section of the ship on two levels, with a spiral stairway between them. There are two seatings, with tables for two, four, six or eight. Dinner on European cruises is typically scheduled at 7pm and 9pm to accommodate the later eating habits of Europeans. Themed evenings are a part of the Costa Cruises tradition, and three different window blinds help create a different feel. However, the artwork is placed at table height, so the room seems more closed-in than it should.

Alternative Dining: A reservations-only alternative for dinner, *Ristorante Club Atlantica*, with menus by Gualtiero Marchesi, has a cover charge, but suite-grade occupants get a free pass for one evening. The food, though nothing special, is decidedly better than in the main dining room.

Undoubtedly the place that most people will want to see and be seen is in the informal *Caffe Florian* – a replica of the famous indoor/outdoor cafe that opened in 1720 in St. Mark's Square, Venice. There are four separate salons (Sala delle Stagioni, Sala del Senato, Sala Liberty, and Sala degli Uomini Illustri), and the same fascinating mosaic, marble and wood floors, opulent ceiling art, and special lampshades. Even the espresso/cappuccino machine is a duplicate of that found in the real thing. The only problem is that the chairs are much too small.

Casual breakfast and luncheon self-serve buffet-style meals can be taken in the *Botticelli Buffet Restaurant*, adjacent to the swimming pools, with seating both indoors and outdoors. A grill (for hamburgers and hot dogs) and a pasta bar are conveniently adjacent to the second pool, while indoors is the *Napoli Pizzeria*. Excellent cappuccino and espresso coffees are always available in various bars around the ship, served in the right-sized china cups.

ENTERTAINMENT. A three-deck-high showlounge (the Caruso Theater) is an imposing room, with just over 1,000 seats. Spiral stairways at the back of the lounge connect all levels. Stage shows are best seen from the upper three levels, from where the sight lines are reasonably good.

Directly underneath the showlounge is the large Coral Lounge, complete with its own bar. An onboard resident troupe of singers and dancers provides the cast members for colorful, high-energy production shows – though these shows are loud and poor. For nights when there are no big shows, the showlounge presents cabaret acts such as singers, comedy jugglers, magicians, and ventriloquists.

A number of bands and small musical units provide a variety of live music in many lounges and bars, and there is a discotheque.

SPA/FITNESS. The Ischia Spa spans two decks. Facilities include a solarium, eight treatment rooms, lecture rooms, sauna and steam rooms for men and women, a beauty parlor. A large gymnasium has floor-to-ceiling windows on three sides, including forward-facing ocean views, and an aerobics room with instructor-led classes. There is a jogging track outdoors.

The spa is operated by Steiner, a specialist concession, whose young staff will try to sell you Steiner's own-brand Elemis beauty products. Some fitness classes are free, while some, such as yoga, and kick-boxing, cost extra.

Massage (including exotic massages such as Aroma Stone massage, Chakra Balancing massage and other well-being massages), facials, pedicures, and beauty salon treatments are at extra cost (massage, for example, costs about $2 per minute, plus gratuity). Do make appointments as early as possible since time slots go quickly.

● **For more extensive general information on what a Costa Cruises cruise is like, see pages 135–8.**

Costa Classica
★★★

Size: . . . . .Mid-Size Ship	Passenger Decks: 10	Cabins (with private balcony): 10
Tonnage: . . . . .52,950 tons	Total Crew: 650	Cabins (wheelchair accessible): 6 (interior)
Lifestyle: . . . . .Standard	Passengers	Wheelchair accessibility: . . . . .Good
Cruise Line: . . . . .Costa Cruises	(lower beds/all berths): 1,308/1,766	Cabin Current: . . . . .110 and 220 volts
Former Names: . . . . .none	Passenger Space Ratio	Elevators: 8
Builder: . . . . .Fincantieri (Italy)	(lower beds/all berths): 40.4/29.9	Casino (gaming tables): . . . . .Yes
Original Cost: . . . .$287 million	Crew/Passenger Ratio	Slot Machines: . . . . .Yes
Entered Service: . . . . .Jan 1992	(lower beds/all berths): 2.0/2.7	Swimming Pools (outdoors): 2
Registry: . . . . .Italy	Cabins (total): .654	Swimming Pools (indoors): 0
Length (ft/m): 718.5/220.61	Size Range (sq ft/m): 185.1–430.5/	Whirlpools: 4
Beam (ft/m): 98.4/30.80	17.2–40.0	Self-Service Launderette: . . . . .No
Draft (ft/m): 25.0/7.60	Cabins (outside view): 438	Dedicated Cinema/Seats: . . . . .No
Propulsion/Propellers: . . . . .diesel	Cabins (interior/no view): 216	Library: . . . . .Yes
(22,800kW)/2	Cabins (for one person): 0	Onboard currency: . . . . .Euros

An elegant Italian-style ship for mature passengers.

OVERVIEW. This ship, which brought Costa into the mainstream of cruising, Italian-style, has a contemporary design and styling best described as befitting European tastes. It attracts a multinational group of young (and young at heart) couples and singles who enjoy big-city life with constant activity and lots of noise.

THE SHIP. *Costa Classica* is an all-white ship, now almost 20 years old, with a slab-sided unflattering profile, which is topped by Costa Cruises' unmistakable trademark trio of tall yellow funnels.

The interior design incorporates much use of circles – large portholes instead of windows can be found in cabins on lower decks, and in the dining room, self-serve buffet area, coffee bar, and discotheque, for example. There is an excellent range of public rooms, lounges and bars, plus a number of specially designed business and meeting facilities; the rooms provide multi-flexible configurations.

Some fascinating artwork includes six hermaphrodite statues in one lounge. The multi-level atrium is stark, angular, and cold. The marble-covered staircases look pleasant, but are uncarpeted and a little dangerous if water or drinks are spilled on them when the ship is moving.

Perhaps the interior is best described as an innovative design project that almost works. A forward observation lounge/nightclub sits atop ship like a lump of cheese, and, unfortunately, fails to work well as a nightclub. Internet access is available from one of several computer terminals in an internet café.

There is no walk-around promenade deck outdoors. The ship's rather slow service speed (19.5 knots) means that

BERLITZ'S RATINGS		
	Possible	Achieved
Ship	500	331
Accommodation	200	133
Food	400	214
Service	400	267
Entertainment	100	60
Cruise	400	240
OVERALL SCORE		
1,245 points out of 2,000		

itineraries have to be carefully chosen, as the ship cannot compete with the newer ships with faster speeds.

The air-conditioning system in the Tivoli Dining Room is noisy. There are too many loud, repetitious and irritating announcements. Shore excursions are very expensive.

ACCOMMODATION. There are 11 categories. These include 10 suites, while other cabins are fairly standard in size, shape and facilities, a higher price being asked for cabins on the highest decks. All suites and cabins have twin lower beds, color TV set, and telephone.
Suites: The 10 suites, located in the center of Portofino Deck, all have a private rounded balcony, marble-clad bathroom with Jacuzzi tub, and separate shower enclosure. There is plenty of space in the living and sleeping areas, and for storing luggage, as these really are very spacious suites.
Standard Outside-View/Interior Cabins: In general, the cabins are of a fairly generous size, and are laid out in a practical manner. They have cherry wood veneered cabinetry and accenting, and include a vanity desk unit with a large mirror. There are useful (unusual, for a cruise ship) sliding doors to the bathroom and closets, and the cabin soundproofing is poor. The soft furnishings are of good quality, but the room service menu is disappointing. The suites have more space – although they are not large by any means – and hand-woven bedspreads.

Some cabins have one or two extra pull-down (Pullman-style) berths – useful for families with small children.

CUISINE. The *Tivoli Dining Room* has a lovely indented clean white ceiling, although it is extremely noisy. There are two seatings, and a number of tables for two, as well as tables for four, six or eight.

Changeable wall panels help create a European Renaissance atmosphere, albeit at the expense of blocking off windows – but during dinner, it's dark outside anyway unless you're in the far North.

For casual outdoor eating, the *Alfresco Café*, with its teak deck and traditional canvas sailcloth awning, is moderately good, depending on what you expect. Breakfast and luncheon buffets are repetitious and uncreative; there is little variety, and long lines are typical. The selection of bread rolls, fruits and cheeses is disappointing.

Excellent cappuccino and espresso coffees are always available in various bars around the ship, served in the right-sized china cups.

ENTERTAINMENT. The Colosseo Theater, the main showlounge, has an interesting amphitheater-like design. However, the seats are bolt upright, and quite uncomfortable for any length of time. The Galileo discotheque, located atop the ship, for the young at heart, late of night, and hard of hearing.

SPA/FITNESS. The Caracalla Spa, on one of the uppermost decks, contains a gymnasium with good forward-facing views over the ship's bows and high-tech muscle-pump machines, an aerobics exercise area, two hot tubs, Roman bath, health bar, sauna and steam rooms, and beauty salon. The spa is operated by Steiner, a specialist concession, whose young staff will try to sell you Steiner's own-brand Elemis beauty products.

Some fitness classes are free, while some, such as yoga and kick-boxing, cost extra. Massage (including exotic massages such as Aroma Stone massage, Chakra Balancing massage and other well-being massages), facials, pedicures, and beauty salon treatments cost extra. Make appointments as early as possible as time slots can go quickly.

● **For more extensive general information on what a Costa Cruises cruise is like, see pages 135–8.**

SHIP TALK

Abeam: off the side of the ship, at a right angle to its length.

Aft: near, toward, or in the rear of the ship.

Ahead: something that is ahead of the ship's bow.

Alleyway: a passageway or corridor.

Alongside: said of a ship when it is beside a pier or another vessel.

Amidships: in or toward the middle of the ship; the longitudinal center portion of the ship.

Anchor Ball: black ball hoisted above the bow to show that the vessel is anchored.

Astern: is the opposite of Ahead (i.e., meaning something behind the ship).

Backwash: motion in the water caused by the propeller(s) moving in a reverse (astern) direction.

Bar: sandbar, usually caused by tidal or current conditions near the shore.

Beam: width of the ship between its two sides at the widest point.

Bearing: compass direction, expressed in degrees, from the ship to a particular objective or destination.

Below: anything beneath the main deck.

Berth: dock, pier, or quay. Also means bed on board ship.

Bilge: lowermost spaces of the infrastructure of a ship.

Boat Stations: allotted space for each person during lifeboat drill or any other emergency when lifeboats are lowered.

Bow: the forward most part of the vessel.

Bridge: navigational and command control center.

Bulkhead: upright partition (wall) dividing the ship into compartments.

Bunkers: the space where fuel is stored; "bunkering" means taking on fuel.

Cable Length: a measured length equaling 100 fathoms (or 600 feet/180 meters).

Chart: a nautical map used for navigating.

Colors: refers to the national flag or emblem flown by the ship.

Companionway: interior stairway.

Course: direction in which the ship is headed, in degrees.

Davit: a device for raising and lowering lifeboats.

Deadlight: a ventilated porthole cover to prevent light from entering.

Disembark (also debark): to leave a ship.

Dock: berth, pier, or quay.

Draft (or draught): measurement in feet from the ship's waterline to the lowest point of its keel.

Embark: to join a ship.

Fantail: the rear or overhang of the ship.

Fathom: distance equal to 6 ft.

Flagstaff: a pole at the stern of a ship where the flag of its country of registry is flown.

● *More Ship Talk, page 325.*

Costa Concordia
★★★★

Size: ....Large Resort Ship	Passenger Decks: 14	Cabins (with private balcony): 571
Tonnage: 112,000	Total Crew: 1,090	Cabins (wheelchair accessible): 12
Lifestyle: ....Standard	Passengers	Wheelchair accessibility: ....Good
Cruise Line: ....Costa Cruises	(lower beds/all berths): 3,000/3,800	Cabin Current: ....110 and 220 volts
Former Names: ....none	Passenger Space Ratio	Elevators: 14
Builder: ....Fincantieri (Italy)	(lower beds/all berths): 37.3/29.4	Casino (gaming tables): ....Yes
Original Cost: ....$565 million	Crew/Passenger Ratio	Slot Machines: ....Yes
Entered Service: ....Jul 2006	(lower beds/all berths): 2.7/3.4	Swimming Pools (outdoors): 3
Registry: ....Italy	Cabins (total): 1,500	Swimming Pools (indoors): 0
Length (ft/m): 951.4/290.2	Size Range (sq ft/m): 482.2–179.7	Whirlpools: 5
Beam (ft/m): 123.0/37.5	44.8–16.7	Self-Service Launderette: ....No
Draft (ft/m): 26.4/8.05	Cabins (outside view): 914	Dedicated Cinema/Seats: ....No
Propulsion/Propellers: .....diesel-electric	Cabins (interior/no view): 586	Library: ....Yes
(34,000kW)/2 azimuthing pods	Cabins (for one person): 2	Onboard currency ....Euros

---

A colourful ship that delivers a casual Italian lifestyle.

OVERVIEW. This ship is for young, trendy families with children, who want a lare resort ship with all the trappings of a lively city. Most passengers are Italian, but there will be other nationals, too. The ship operates Mediterranean cruises year-round.

THE SHIP. This is a slightly larger, extended version of *Costa Fortuna* and *Costa Magica*. One of the three pools can be covered by a sliding glass dome in case of poor weather, and one pool has a long water slide (great for kids). There's not a lot of open deck space, but *Costa Concordia* absorbs passengers well.

There are three decks full of bars and lounges plus lots of other public rooms. This ship has a nine-decks-high, glass-domed rotunda atrium lobby, with a lively bar on the lowest deck. The Barcelona Casino is large and glitzy. There's a chapel, and a small library that could be better, an internet center, card room, art gallery, and video games room.

ACCOMMODATION. There are 20 price grades, from two-bed interior cabins to 10 grand suites with private balcony, although in reality there are only three different sizes: Suites with balcony, two- or four-bed outside view cabins, and two- or four-bed interior cabins, most measuring about 160 sq.ft/15 sq.meters. There are two single cabins. The largest accommodation is in eight Grand Suites (360 sq.ft/33.5 sq.meters). They have a queen-sized bed; bathrooms have a tub and two washbasins. As suites go, they are not large.

CUISINE. *Milano* and *Roma*, the main dining rooms, allocated by accommodation grade and location, have two seatings. Costa specializes in pasta. Almost all the wines – the

BERLITZ'S RATINGS

	Possible	Achieved
Ship	500	422
Accommodation	200	152
Food	400	251
Service	400	274
Entertainment	100	64
Cruise	400	277

OVERALL SCORE
1,440 points out of 2,000

majority Italian – are young. The two 100-seat *Samsara* dining spots are for those seeking spa food; this is prepared with reduced calories, fat and salt.

Alternative (Reservations Required) Dining Option: The *Club Concordia* is an 80-seat upscale dining venue with seating under a large glass dome. There's a cover charge of €23 per person, and it's worth it. Molecular Gastronomy, interpreted by famed Italian chef Ettore Bocchia, is featured. Molecular cooking consists of using liquid nitrogen in order to make food produced with more taste.

Casual Eatery: The *Parigi Buffet Restaurant* is a self-serve eatery for breakfast, lunch, afternoon pizzas, and coffee and tea at any time. Good cappuccino and espresso coffees are always available in various bars (at extra cost).

Caffeteria Helsinki, which has Nordic decor, is the place to go for decent (extra cost) coffees.

ENTERTAINMENT. The Athena Theater, spanning three decks, is quite stunning, and has a revolving stage, hydraulic orchestra pit, superb sound, and seating on three levels.

SPA/FITNESS. The The ship's Samsara Spa has more than 22,600 sq. ft (2,100 sq. meters) of spa/wellness facilities, spread over two decks. It includes a large fitness room, separate saunas, steam rooms, UVB.

Samsara cabin and suite occupants qualify for unlimited access to the spa plus two treatments and fitness or meditation lessons.

● **For more extensive general information on what a Costa Cruises cruise is like, see pages 135–8.**

Costa Deliziosa
★★★★

Size: . . . . .Large Resort Ship	Total Crew: .1,050	Wheelchair accessibility: . . . . .Good
Tonnage: .92,700	Passengers	Cabin Voltage: . . . . .110 volts
Lifestyle: . . . . .Standard	(lower beds/all berths): 2,260/2,826	Elevators: 12
Cruise Line: . . . . .Costa Cruises	Passenger Space Ratio	Casino (gaming tables): . . . . .Yes
Former Names: . . . . .none	(lower beds/all berths): 41.0/32.7	Slot Machines: . . . . .Yes
Builder: . . . . .Fincantieri (Italy)	Crew/Passenger Ratio	Swimming Pools (outdoors): 2
Original Cost: . . . .€548 million	(lower beds/all berths): 2.1/2.6	Swimming Pools (indoors): 1
Entered Service: . . . . .Mar 2010	Cabins (total): 1,130	(with retractable roof)
Registry: . . . . .Italy	Size Range (sq ft/m):	Whirlpools: 4
Length (ft/m): 958.0/292.0	134.5–534.0/12.5–49.6	Self-Service Launderette: . . . . .No
Beam (ft/m): 111.5/34.0	Cabins (outside view): 951	Dedicated Cinema/Seats: . . . . .No
Draft (ft/m): 26.2/8.0	Cabins (interior/no view): 179	Library: . . . . .Yes
Propulsion/Propellers: . . . . .diesel-electric	Cabins (for one person): 0	Onboard currency . . . . .Euros
(4.2 MW)/2 azimuthing pods	Cabins (with private balcony): 772	
Passenger Decks: 13	Cabins (wheelchair accessible): 12	

It's Italy afloat in this casual big-ship setting.

OVERVIEW. This ship, sister to *Costa Luminosa*, was named in Dubai, the first new cruise ship to be named in an Arab city – so, instead of champagne, a bottle of fig juice was used to name it. Most passengers will be Italian, with a sprinkling of other nationalities. Printed materials are in Italian, English, French, German, Portuguese, and Spanish.

THE SHIP. *Costa Deliziosa* has a nicely balanced profile. A 4-D cinema highlights sound and lighting effects, with scent pumped in to heighten the experience. A two-deck midships Lido area swimming pool can be covered with a sliding glass roof in poor weather. There's a large 193.7-sq ft (18-sq meter) poolside movie screen.

The interior decor, which includes fine marble and gold, pays tribute to the senses. The public rooms include 11 bars, a large casino, and lots of lounges and entertainment venues. The focal point is the atrium lobby, with a large sculpture, *Sphere*, by Arnaldo Pomodoro.

Gratuities are charged to your onboard account.

ACCOMMODATION. About 68% of all accommodation suites and cabins have an ocean view, and there are 772 balcony cabins. Four suites and 52 Samsara Spa cabins are adjacent to (and considered part of) the designated wellness area. Samsara suite/cabin occupants get unlimited access to the spa plus two treatments and fitness or meditation lessons as part of their package, and dine in one of the two Samsara restaurants.

A pillow menu, with five choices, is available to suite-grade occupants, who also get bathrobes, better amenities,

BERLITZ'S RATINGS

	Possible	Achieved
Ship	500	425
Accommodation	200	152
Food	400	252
Service	400	274
Entertainment	100	64
Cruise	400	279

OVERALL SCORE
1,446 points out of 2,000

a shaving mirror, and walk-in closets. Background music is played 24 hours a day in all hallways and elevators, so you may well be aware of it if you are a light sleeper.

CUISINE. The *Restaurant Albatros* is the ship's large, main restaurant. It is located at the aft of the ship and there are two seatings for dinner. The *Samsara Restaurant* is for occupants of Samsara-grade accommodation, and is adjacent to the *Taurus Restaurant*.

The Club Restaurant is a reservations-only, intimate restaurant that features à la carte dining with a pristine show kitchen as part of the venue. The food is cooked à la minute and so it is fresher, looks better, and tastes better than food in the main dining room, and menus are under the direction of Italy's molecular cooking master, Ettore Bocchia, Costa's consulting chef. The *Buffet Muscadins* is the self-serve casual eatery. While there appears to be a decent choice of food, the layout of the venue invites congestion.

ENTERTAINMENT. The Theater Duse, with over 800 seats, spans three decks and is the ship's principal showlounge and has the latest computer-controlled lighting.

SPA/FITNESS. This area contains 37,674 sq ft (3,500 sq meters) of Samsara Spa space. Not far away, a Grand Prix Formula One simulator is housed in a glass enclosure. A golf simulator provides a choice of 37 18-hole courses.

● **For more extensive general information on what a Costa Cruises cruise is like, see pages 135–8.**

Costa Fascinosa
NOT YET RATED

Size: ....Large Resort Ship	Passenger Decks: 13	Cabins (with private balcony): 650
Tonnage: 114,500	Total Crew: 1,090	Cabins (wheelchair accessible): 12
Lifestyle: ....Standard	Passengers	Wheelchair Accessibility: ....Good
Cruise Line: ....Costa Cruises	(lower beds/all berths): 3,016/3,780	Cabin Current: ....110/220 volts
Former Names: ....none	Passenger Space Ratio	Elevators: 14
Builder: ....Fincantieri (Italy)	(lower beds/all berths): 38.0/30.2	Casino (gaming tables): ....Yes
Original Cost: ....€510 million	Crew/Passenger Ratio	Slot Machines: ....Yes
Entered Service: ....May 2012	(lower beds/all berths): 2.7/3.4	Swimming Pools (outdoors): 3
Registry: ....Italy	Cabins (total): 1,508	Swimming Pools (indoors): 2 (glass dome)
Length (ft/m): 952.0/290.0	Size Range (sq ft/m): 179.7–482.2/	Whirlpools: 5
Beam (ft/m): 116.4/35.5	16.7–44.8	Self-Service Launderette: ....No
Draft (ft/m): 27.2/8.3	Cabins (outside view): 928	Dedicated Cinema/Seats: ....No
Propulsion/Propellers: .....diesel-electric	Cabins (interior/no view): 580	Library: ....Yes
(1.4 MW)/2 azimuthing pods	Cabins (for one person): 0	Onboard currency ....Euros

Upbeat Italian decor and style, for family cruising.

OVERVIEW. Costa Cruises is for those who like to enjoy the casual life to the full. It does a good job of providing first-time cruise passengers with a packaged seagoing vacation – particularly for families with children – that is a mix of sophistication and chaos, accompanied by loud music everywhere. Most passengers are Italian, with a sprinkling of other European nationals.

THE SHIP. With an instantly recognizable single, large yellow funnel, *Costa Fascinosa* is a sister to *Costa Concordia, Costa Favolosa, Costa Fortuna, Costa Magica, Costa Pacifica* and *Costa Serena*. On the open decks, two pool areas can be covered with retractable glass domes – useful for inclement weather conditions; one pool has a long water slide, much liked by children; there is also a large poolside movie screen. However, the open deck space is pretty cramped when the ship is full, the plastic sunloungers are crammed together, and do not have cushioned pads.

With three decks packed with 13 bars and lounges and other public rooms, there's a place for all tastes. The decor throughout is on the wild side. The focal social point is a three-deck-high atrium lobby, with four glass panoramic elevators providing a neat view over the lobby bar – a good place for espresso/cappuccino and people watching. The Casino is large and very colorful, but the slot machines occupy a separate area to the gaming tables, so serious gamers can concentrate. Other public rooms include a small library, an internet-connection center, 4D cinema, card room, art gallery, and video game room, plus a chapel – a standard aboard all Costa Cruises' ships.

Families like Costa Cruises for its perceived "Italian"

BERLITZ'S RATINGS		
	Possible	Achieved
Ship	500	NYR
Accommodation	200	NYR
Food	400	NYR
Service	400	NYR
Entertainment	100	NYR
Cruise	400	NYR

style, ambience and spirit, and most passengers will be Italian, with a sprinkling of other European nationals. However, you won't find many Italian hotel service staff on board – although many of the officers are Italian, most crew members, particularly the dining room and housekeeping staff, are from the Philippines. But the lifestyle on board is decidedly Italian – lively, noisy, and full of sparkle. Naturally, during peak European school holiday periods, especially during Christmas and Easter, you can expect to be cruising with a lot of children of all ages.

Printed materials such as the cabin service folio and menus, are provided in six languages – Italian, English, French, German, Portuguese, and Spanish – and announcements are also made in several languages.

As aboard other Costa ships, few staff members are on duty at the gangway when you arrive for embarkation; they merely point you in the direction of your deck, or to the ship's elevators and do not escort you to your cabin.

ACCOMMODATION. There are 20 accommodation price grades, from two-bed interior cabins to grand suites with private balcony, although in reality there are only three different sizes: suites with "private" balcony – which are really not particularly large in comparison with some other large ships; two- or four-bed outside view cabins; and two- or four-bed interior cabins. Fortunately, no cabins have views obstructed by lifeboats or other safety equipment views, and, in most cabins, twin beds can be changed to a double/queen-bed configuration.

Eight Grand Suites, in the center of the ship on one of the uppermost decks, comprise the largest accommodation.

They have a queen-sized bed and larger living area with vanity desk; the bathrooms have a tub and two washbasins.

A total of 103 "Samsara Spa Suites" are designated as Samsara-grade. Occupants get unlimited spa access plus two treatments, and fitness or meditation lessons as part of the package. These grades have an Oriental decorative theme, special Samsara bathroom personal amenities, and can eat in one of two designated Samsara Restaurants.

Only suite grades get bathrobes and better amenities, shaving mirror, pillow menu, and walk-in closets – although the hangars are plastic. Music is played 24 hours a day in all accommodation hallways and elevators, so you may well hear it if you are a light sleeper.

CUISINE. There are two main, large dining rooms: *Il Gattopardo* and *Otto e Mezza Restaurants*, each with two seatings, allocated according to your chosen accommodation grade and location.

Two *Samsara Restaurants* have separate entrances. While the two main restaurants offer traditional cruise fare, these spa cuisine spots are for those seeking healthier food – reduced calories, fat and salt, with menu creations under the direction of dietary consultant and Michelin-star chef Ettore Boccia. They are open for lunch and dinner to those in Samsara-grade suites and cabins, and to anyone else for dinner only at an extra charge.

A reservations-required, extra-cost restaurant, *Club Fascinosa*, has fine table settings and leather-bound menus.

There's also a self-serve, buffet-style eatery, *Tulipano Nero Buffet*, for breakfast, lunch, afternoon pizzas, and coffee or tea at any time. A balcony level provides additional seating, but you'll need to carry your own food plates because there are no trays, which makes it difficult to carry both food and a beverage at the same time.

Additionally, the *Caffeteria* is the place to go for decent, extra-cost coffees and Italian sweet pastries.

ENTERTAINMENT. The Fascinosa Showlounge seats over 800. It's three decks high and is the venue for all production shows and large-scale cabaret acts, with a revolving stage, hydraulic orchestra pit, good sound, and seating on three levels, the upper levels being tiered through two decks.

High-energy revue-style shows are performed by a small troupe of resident onboard singers/dancers), with fast-moving action and busy lighting and costume changes.

SPA/FITNESS. The Samsara Spa is a large facility occupying 64,585 sq.ft/ 6,000 sq. meters of space (including relaxation areas), spread over two decks. It has a large fitness room, separate saunas, steam rooms, UVB solarium, changing rooms for men and women, and 10 body treatment rooms. Two VIP treatment rooms, available to couples for half-day rentals, are located on the upper level.

● **For more extensive general information on what a Costa Cruises cruise is like, see pages 135–8.**

Costa Favolosa
★★★★

Size: ....Large Resort Ship	Passenger Decks: 13	Cabins (with private balcony): 579
Tonnage: 114,500	Total Crew: 1,110	Cabins (wheelchair accessible): 12
Lifestyle: ....Standard	Passengers	Wheelchair accessibility: ....Good
Cruise Line: ....Costa Cruises	(lower beds/all berths): 3,012/3,780	Cabin Voltage: ....110/220 volts
Former Names: ....none	Passenger Space Ratio	Elevators: 14
Builder: ....Fincantieri (Italy)	(lower beds/all berths): 38.0/30.2	Casino (gaming tables): ....Yes
Original Cost: ....€510 million	Crew/Passenger Ratio	Slot Machines: ....Yes
Entered Service: ....Jul 2011	(lower beds/all berths): 2.7/3.4	Swimming Pools (outdoors): 2
Registry:........................Italy	Cabins (total): 1,506	Swimming Pools (indoors): 2 (glass dome)
Length (ft/m): 952.0/290.0	Size Range (sq ft/m): 179.7–482.2/	Whirlpools: 5
Beam (ft/m): 116.4/35.5	16.7–44.8	Self-Service Launderette: ....No
Draft (ft/m): 27.2/8.3	Cabins (outside view): 926	Dedicated Cinema/Seats: ....No
Propulsion/Propellers: .....diesel-electric	Cabins (interior/no view): 580	Library: ....Yes
(1.4mW)/2 azimuthing pods	Cabins (for one person): 0	Onboard currency ....Euros

---

Upbeat Italian decor and style, for family cruising.

OVERVIEW. Costa Cruises is a line for those who like to enjoy life and party. It does a good job of providing first-time cruise passengers with a packaged seagoing vacation – particularly for families with children – that is a mix of sophistication and chaos, accompanied by loud music everywhere. Most passengers are Italian, with a sprinkling of other European nationals.

THE SHIP. Displaying a single, large funnel, *Costa Favolosa* is a close sister to *Costa Serena*. Two pool areas can be covered with retractable glass domes – useful in case of bad weather. One has a long water slide – great for kids. There is a large poolside movie screen and, on one of the upper decks, a Grand Prix simulator. However, the open deck space can be pretty cramped when the ship is full, so the sunloungers, which don't have cushioned pads, will be crammed together

There are three decks full of bars and lounges plus many other public rooms. This ship has a glass-domed rotunda atrium lobby that is nine decks high, with great upward views from the lobby bar, as well as from its four glass panoramic elevators.

The Casino is large and glitzy, but always lively and entertaining – slot machines occupy a separate area to gaming tables, so serious gamers can concentrate. There's a very small library, an internet center, card room, art gallery, 4D cinema (Belphegor), and a video game room, plus a small chapel – a standard aboard all Costa Cruises' ships.

Although Costa Cruises is noted for its "Italian" style, ambience and spirit, there are few Italian crew members on board. Although many officers are Italian, most of the crew members, particularly the dining room and housekeeping

BERLITZ'S RATINGS

	Possible	Achieved
Ship	500	425
Accommodation	200	152
Food	400	251
Service	400	275
Entertainment	100	64
Cruise	400	280

OVERALL SCORE
1,447 points out of 2,000

staff, are from the Philippines. But the lifestyle on board is perceived to be Italian – lively, noisy, with lots of love for life and a love of all things casual, even on so-called "formal" nights.

All printed materials – room service folio, menus, etc. – will typically be in six languages: Italian, English, French, German, Portuguese, and Spanish. During peak European school holiday periods, particularly Christmas and Easter, you can expect to be cruising with a lot of children of all ages.

As aboard other Costa ships, note that for embarkation, few staff members are on duty at the gangway when you arrive; they merely point you in the direction of your deck, or to the ship's elevators and do not escort you to your cabin.

ACCOMMODATION. There are 20 accommodation price grades, from two-bed interior cabins to grand suites with private balcony although in reality there are only three different sizes: suites with "private" balcony – which are really not particularly large in comparison with some other large ships; two- or four-bed outside view cabins; and two- or four-bed interior cabins. Fortunately, no cabins have views obstructed by lifeboats or other safety equipment views, and, in most cabins, twin beds can be changed to a double/queen-bed configuration.

Two Grand Suites comprise the largest accommodation, and include a large balcony with hot tub. They have a queen-sized bed and larger living area with vanity desk; the bathrooms have a tub and two washbasins.

If you are into wellness treatments, there are 12 "Samsara Spa Suites" just aft of the spa itself, although 99 cabins, including the 12 suites, are designated as Samsara-grade.

Samsara suite/cabin occupants get unlimited access to the spa plus two treatments and fitness or meditation lessons as part of their package, and dine in one of the two Samsara restaurants. All Samsara-designated accommodation grades have an Oriental decorative theme, and special Samsara bathroom personal amenities.

A pillow menu, with five choices, has been introduced in all suite-grade accommodation. Only suite grades get bathrobes and better amenities, shaving mirror, and walk-in closets – although the hangers are plastic. Music is played 24 hours a day in all hallways and elevators, so you may well hear it if you are a light sleeper.

CUISINE. There are two main dining rooms, *Duke of Burgundy* and *Duke of Orleans*, one located located aft, the other in the ship's center, allocated according to your accommodation grade and location. They offer traditional cruise fare, and there are two seatings.

Two 100-seat *Samsara Restaurants* (spa cuisine spots) are provided with separate entrances. These are for those seeking healthier food with reduced calories, fat and salt content. Menu creations are under the direction of dietary consultant and Michelin-starred chef Ettore Boccia, known for his molecular Italian cuisine. These venues are open for lunch and dinner to those in Samsara-grade suites and cabins, and to anyone else for dinner only at an extra daily or weekly charge.

Alternative (Reservations Required) Dining Option: The *Favolosa Club Restaurant* sits under a huge glass dome and Murano glass decorative elements. Fine table settings, china, silverware and leather-bound menus are provided. There's a cover charge.

Casual Eatery: A self-service *Ca d'Oro* buffet restaurant offers breakfast, lunch, afternoon pizzas, and coffee and tea at any time. A balcony level provides additional seating, but you'll need to carry your own food plates since there are no trays. Decent quality cappuccino and espresso coffees are always available in various bars, at extra cost.

Additionally, the *Caffeteria* is the place to go for decent (extra cost) coffees and Italian pastries.

ENTERTAINMENT. The Favolosa showlounge. which seats more than 800, utilizes the latest in LED technology. It is three decks high and is decorated in a Baroque style, with warm colors and a Murano glass chandelier. It is the venue for all production shows and large-scale cabaret acts, is quite stunningly glitzy, and has a revolving stage, hydraulic orchestra pit, superb sound, and seating on three levels – the upper levels are tiered through two decks.

Typically, revue-style shows are performed by a small troupe of resident onboard singers and dancers. Their fast-moving action, busy lighting and costume changes add up to a high-energy performance.

SPA/FITNESS. The Samsara Spa is a large facility that occupies 23,186 sq.ft/2,154 sq. meters of space, spread over two decks. It includes a large fitness room, separate saunas, steam rooms, UVB solarium, changing rooms for men and women, and 10 body treatment rooms. Two VIP treatment rooms, available to couples for half-day rentals, are located on the upper level.

The Spa/fitness facilities are staffed and operated by Steiner Leisure, a specialist spa/beauty concession. Some fitness classes are free, while some, such as Pathway to Yoga, Pathway to Pilates, and Pathway to Meditation, cost extra. It's wise to make appointments early as time slots can go quickly.

You can buy a day pass in order to use the sauna/steam rooms, thermal suite and relaxation area, at a cost of €35 per person. However, there is an additional no-charge sauna for men and women, but to access it you must walk through an active fitness area, maybe with your bathrobe on – not comfortable for everyone, especially women.

● **For more extensive general information on what a Costa Cruises cruise is like, see pages 135–8.**

Costa Fortuna
★★★★

Size: . . . . .Large Resort Ship	Passenger Decks: 13	Cabins (with private balcony): 522
Tonnage: 102,587	Total Crew: .1,068	Cabins (wheelchair accessible): 8
Lifestyle: . . . . .Standard	Passengers	Wheelchair accessibility: . . . . .Good
Cruise Line: . . . . .Costa Cruises	(lower beds/all berths): 2,716/3,470	Cabin Current: . . . . .220 volts
Former Names: . . . . .none	Passenger Space Ratio	Elevators: 14
Builder: . . . . .Cantieri Sestri Navale (Italy)	(lower beds/all berths): 37.7/29.5	Casino (gaming tables): . . . . .Yes
Original Cost: . . . .$381 million	Crew/Passenger Ratio	Slot Machines: . . . . .Yes
Entered Service: . . . . .Nov 2003	(lower beds/all berths): 2.5/3.2	Swimming Pools (outdoors): 3
Registry: . . . . .Italy	Cabins (total): 1,358	Swimming Pools (indoors): 0
Length (ft/m): 892.3/272.0	Size Range (sq ft/m): 179.7–482.2/	Whirlpools: 6
Beam (ft/m): 124.6/38.0	16.7–44.8	Self-Service Launderette: . . . . .No
Draft (ft/m): 27.2/8.3	Cabins (outside view): 857	Dedicated Cinema/Seats: . . . . .No
Propulsion/Propellers: . . . .diesel-electric	Cabins (interior/no view): 501	Library: . . . . .Yes
34,000kW/2 azimuthing pods (17.6 MW each)	Cabins (for one person): 0	Onboard currency . . . . .Euros

A large, colourful family-friendly Italian-style ship.

OVERVIEW. *Costa Fortuna* is built to impress the trendy city-dweller at every turn, and the ship absorbs passengers quite well, with a good passenger space ratio. While a variety of nationalities are carried, most passengers are Italian, so the ship is lively but quite noisy, with lots of children running around, particularly during school holiday periods.

THE SHIP. The name is an interesting one: in Greek mythology, Fortuna is the daughter of Poseidon, god of the sea, as well as being associated with the Temple Fortuna, located along one of Pompeii's conserved streets.

The aft decks are tiered, with cut-off quarters that make the ship look less square than it otherwise would. There are three pools, one of which can be covered by a sliding glass dome in case of inclement weather, while one pool has a long water slide. There is not a lot of open deck space for the number of passengers carried, so sunloungers tend to be crammed together, and they lack cushioned pads.

The interior decor focuses on the Italian passenger ships of yesteryear, so much of the finishing detail replicates the Art Deco interiors fitted aboard ocean liners such as the *Conte de Savoia, Michelangelo, Neptunia, Rafaello, Rex*, etc., although in the kind of contemporary colors not associated with such ships, whose interiors were rather subdued. There are surprisingly few Italians among the crew, however (except in key positions), though the Philippines is well represented.

Deck names are those of major cities in Europe and South America (Barcelona, Buenos Aires, Caracas, Lisbon, Genoa, Miami). Passenger flow is generally good, with few congestion points.

BERLITZ'S RATINGS		
	Possible	Achieved
Ship	500	426
Accommodation	200	146
Food	400	251
Service	400	275
Entertainment	100	64
Cruise	400	282
OVERALL SCORE		
1,444 points out of 2,000		

There are three decks full of lounges, and 11 bars. The interior focal point is a nine-deck high, glass-domed atrium lobby: it houses a Costa Bar on the lower level, a bank of four glass-walled elevators, and, in a tribute to ship buffs, 26 models of Italian ships past and present, glued upside down on the ceiling – it's a weird feeling to look at them and then look at your feet. The lowest three decks connect the public rooms, the upper levels being mainly for accommodation. For those who like to gamble, the Neptunia 1932 Casino is the place to go. There's also a chapel – standard aboard Costa ships – and a small library that's a bit of a token gesture, an internet center, card room, art gallery, and video games room.

ACCOMMODATION. There are 15 price grades, from two-bed interior cabins to grand suites with private balcony, although in reality there are only three different sizes: Suites with balcony, two- or four-bed outside-view cabins (some 335 of which have portholes rather than windows), and two- or four-bed interior (no-view) cabins. There are also two single cabins – quite unusual for a large ship. In an example of good design, no cabins have lifeboat obstructed views – something not easy with large ships such as this.

The largest accommodation can be found in eight Grand Suites, located in the center of the ship on one of the higher decks. They have a queen-sized bed; bathrooms have a tub and two washbasins.

Wheelchair-accessible cabins: Note that 12 of the most desirable (outside-view) wheelchair-accessible cabins are rather idiotically located a long way from elevators, while eight interior cabins are located close to elevators.

CUISINE. There are two dining rooms: the *Michelangelo 1965 Restaurant* (aft), whose ceiling features frescoes by the Great Masters, and the *Rafaello 1965 Restaurant* (midships), are both two decks high and have two seatings. Dinner on European cruises is typically scheduled at 7pm and 9pm. Over 50 types of pasta are available during a typical one-week cruise. There is a wine list, although there are no wine waiters, and nearly all the wines (mostly Italian) are young.

Alternative (Reservations Required Dining Option: The *Conte Grande 1927 Club* is an upscale dining spot with seating for around 150 under a huge glass dome – if the lights were turned out, you might be able to see the stars. In its show kitchen, chefs can be seen preparing their masterpieces. Fine table settings, china, silverware and leatherbound menus are used. Reservations are required and there is a cover charge.

The *Christoforo Columbus 1954 Buffet Restaurant* is a self-serve eatery for breakfast, lunch, afternoon pizzas, and beverages at any time. Excellent cappuccino and espresso coffees are always available in the various bars.

ENTERTAINMENT. The Rex 1932 Theater spans three decks in the ship's forwardmost section. It is a stunning setting for all production shows and large-scale cabaret acts, and has a revolving stage, hydraulic orchestra pit, superb sound, and seating on three levels (the upper levels being tiered through two decks). Volume levels are high.

SPA/FITNESS. Facilities in the two-deck high Saturnia Spa (it measures about 14,424 sq. ft/1,340 sq. meters) include a large solarium, eight treatment rooms, sauna and steam rooms for men and women, and a beauty parlor. The gymnasium, full of techno-gym equipment for those into muscle-pumping and exertion, has floor-to-ceiling windows on three sides, including forward-facing ocean views, and there's an aerobics section with instructor-led classes (some, such as yoga, kick-boxing, cost extra). If you want to be near the spa, note that there are 18 two-bed cabins with ocean view windows, located adjacent to it.

● **For more extensive general information on what a Costa Cruises cruise is like, see pages 135–8.**

SHIP TALK

Free Port: port or place free of customs duty and regulations.

Funnel: chimney from which the ship's combustion gases are propelled into the atmosphere.

Galley: the ship's kitchen.

Gangway: the stairway or ramp that provides the link between ship and shore.

Helm: the apparatus for steering a ship.

House Flag: the flag denoting the company owning a ship.

Hull: the frame and body of the ship exclusive of masts or superstructure.

Leeward: the side of a ship that is sheltered from the wind.

Luff: the side of a ship facing the wind

Manifest: a list of the ship's passengers, crew, and cargo.

Nautical Mile: one-sixtieth of a

degree of the circumference of the Earth.

Pilot: a person licensed to navigate ships into or out of a harbor or through difficult waters, and to advise the captain on handling the ship during these procedures.

Pitch: the rise and fall of a ship's bow that may occur when the ship is under way.

Port: the left side of a ship when facing forward.

Quay: berth, dock, or pier.

Rudder: a finlike device astern and below the waterline, for steering the vessel.

Screw: a ship's propeller.

Stabilizer: a gyroscopically operated retractable "fin" extending from either or both sides of the ship below the waterline in order to provide a

more stable ride.

Starboard: the right side of the ship when facing forward.

Stern: the aftmost part of the ship that is opposite the bow.

Tender: a smaller vessel, often a lifeboat, used to transport passengers between ship and shore when the vessel is at anchor.

Wake: the track of agitated water left behind a ship when in motion.

Waterline: the line along the side of a ship's hull corresponding to the water surface.

Windward: the side of a ship facing the direction in which the wind blows.

Yaw: the erratic deviation from the ship's set course, usually caused by a heavy sea.

● *More Ship Talk, page 317.*

Costa Luminosa
★★★★

Size:	.Large Resort Ship	Total Crew:	1,050	Wheelchair accessibility: Good
Tonnage:	92,700	Passengers		Cabin Voltage: 110 volts
Lifestyle:	Standard	(lower beds/all berths): 2,260/2,826		Elevators: 12
Cruise Line:	Costa Cruises	Passenger Space Ratio		Casino (gaming tables): Yes
Former Names:	none	(lower beds/all berths): 41.0/32.7		Slot Machines: Yes
Builder:	Fincantieri (Italy)	Crew/Passenger Ratio		Swimming Pools (outdoors): 2
Original Cost:	€420 million	(lower beds/all berths): 2.1/2.6		Swimming Pools (indoors): 1
Entered Service:	Jun 2009	Cabins (total): 1,130		(with retractable roof)
Registry:	Italy	Size Range (sq ft/m):		Whirlpools: 4
Length (ft/m):	958.0/292.0	134.5–534.0/12.5–49.6		Self-Service Launderette: No
Beam (ft/m):	111.5/34.0	Cabins (outside view): 951		Dedicated Cinema/Seats: No
Draft (ft/m):	26.2/8.0	Cabins (interior/no view): 179		Library: Yes
Propulsion/Propellers:	diesel-electric	Cabins (for one person): 0		Onboard currency Euros
	(42,000 kW)/2 azimuthing pods	Cabins (with private balcony): 772		
Passenger Decks:	13	Cabins (wheelchair accessible): 12		

Bold decor and big-ship facilities for families.

OVERVIEW. While a variety of nationalities are carried, most passengers are Italian, so the ship is lively but quite noisy, with lots of children running around, particularly during school holiday periods. One thing not to miss is a fascinating – and rather large, at 346 cm long (11.3-ft) – *Reclining Woman 2004* bronze sculpture by Fernando Bolero, in the Atria Supernova, the atrium lobby. Weighing 910kg (2,000 lbs), the sun-tanned, rather voluminous woman is depicted staring into the atrium space, with her legs in a dynamic position of movement.

THE SHIP. *Costa Luminosa* was constructed as what is termed a *Vista*-class ship – although it is slightly larger than *Costa Atlantica* and *Costa Mediterranea*. A 4-D cinema highlights sound and lighting effects, with scent pumped in to heighten the experience.

Its two-deck midships Lido area swimming pool can be covered with a sliding glass roof. There's also a large 194-sq ft (18-sq meter) poolside movie screen. Other sporting facilities include a roller skating track.

The interior decor, which includes marble, wood and mother of pearl, pays tribute to light and lighting, as you might expect from a ship called *Costa Luminosa*, so it feels a little like cruising in a stunning special effects bubble – remember to take your sunglasses. The public rooms include 11 bars, a large Vega Casino, and lots of lounges and entertainment venues. Sony Playstation fans can enjoy "Play Station World," an area dedicated exclusively to PS3. Playstations are also available in cabins, on the pool-deck movie screen, and in the children's and teens' clubs.

BERLITZ'S RATINGS

	Possible	Achieved
Ship	500	427
Accommodation	200	153
Food	400	241
Service	400	275
Entertainment	100	66
Cruise	400	283

OVERALL SCORE
1,445 points out of 2,000

Printed materials such as room service folio and menus are in six languages (Italian, English, French, German, Portuguese, Spanish). Gratuities are not included in the fare.

ACCOMMODATION. There are 14 price grades. About 68% of all accommodation suites and cabins have an ocean view; the 772 balcony cabins give this ship the distinction of having the largest number in the fleet to date. Four suites and 52 Samsara Spa cabins are located adjacent to (and considered part of) the designated wellness area. As part of their package, Samsara suite and cabin occupants get unlimited access to the spa plus two treatments and fitness or meditation lessons, and can dine in one of the two Samsara restaurants. All Samsara-designated accommodation grades receive Samsara bathroom amenities.

A pillow menu, with five choices, is available to suite-grade accommodation occupants, who also get bathrobes, better amenities than standard-grade cabin occupants, a shaving mirror, and walk-in closets – although the hangers are plastic. Background music is played 24 hours a day in all hallways and elevators, so you may well be aware of it if you are a light sleeper.

All of the cabins have twin beds that can be converted into a queen-sized bed, individually controlled air-conditioning, television, and telephone. Some many cabins have their views obstructed by lifeboats – on Deck 4 (Roma Deck), the lowest of the accommodation decks, as well as some cabins on Deck 5. Some cabins have pull-down Pullman berths that are fully hidden in the ceiling when not in use.

Some of the most desirable suites and cabins are those

with private balconies on the five aft-facing decks (Decks 4, 5, 6, 7, and 8) with views overlooking the stern and ship's wash. Passengers in other cabins with private balconies will find the balconies not so private – the partition between one balcony and the next is not a full partition, so you will be able to hear your neighbors, or smell their smoke. However, these balcony occupants all have good views through glass and wood-topped railings, and the deck is made of teak.

The cabins are well laid out, typically with twin beds that convert to a queen-sized bed, vanity desk with built-in hairdryer, large TV set, personal safe, and one closet that has moveable shelves – thus providing useful space for storing luggage.

The largest suites are those designated as Penthouse Suites, although they are really quite small when compared with suites aboard other ships of a similar size. However, they do at least offer more space to move around in, and a slightly larger, better bathroom.

CUISINE. The *Taurus Restaurant* is the large, main restaurant. It is located at the aft of the ship and there are two seatings for dinner, which, on European cruises is typically at 7pm and 9pm. The Samsara Restaurant is for occupants of Samsara-grade accommodation, and is located adjacent to the Taurus Restaurant.

The *Club Restaurant* is a reservations-only, intimate restaurant that features à la carte dining with a pristine show kitchen as part of the venue. The food is cooked à la minute and so it is fresher, looks better, and tastes better than food in the main dining room, and menus are under the direction of Italy's molecular cooking master, Ettore Bocchia, Costa's consulting chef. It's a good idea to go for a meal in this venue, particularly to celebrate a special occasion, because it's different, and portions are small, and cooked to order rather than prepared en masse.

The *Andromeda Buffet* is the self-serve casual eatery. While there appears to be a decent choice of food, the layout of the venue invites congestion because of some narrow passageways between the indoor seating and the food dispensing areas.

ENTERTAINMENT. The Phoenix Theater, with over 800 seats, spans three decks (the actual space of the showlounge measures 1,300 sq meters/14,000 sq ft) and is the ship's main showlounge. It appears as if it is lit by a rainbow of lighting effects, using the latest computer-controlled lighting.

SPA/FITNESS. This area contains 3,500 sq meters (37,700 sq ft) of Samsara Spa space. Not far away, a Grand Prix Formula One simulator is housed in a glass enclosure. For tee-time, a golf simulator provides a choice of 37 18-hole courses.

● **For more extensive general information on what a Costa Cruises cruise is like, see pages 135–8.**

WHERE NAUTICAL EXPRESSIONS COME FROM

If you've ever wondered where some terms or phrases came from, you have only to look to the sea, ships, and seamen.

Booby Hatch

A booby hatch is a small, covered compartment under the deck, toward the bow. Sailors were punished by confinement in the booby hatch. The term has come to mean a mental institution.

Carry on

In the days of sail, the officer of the deck kept a weather eye constantly on the slightest change in the wind so sail could be reefed or added as necessary to ensure the fastest headway. Whenever a good breeze came along, the order to "carry on" would be given. It meant to hoist every bit of canvas the yards could carry. Pity the poor sailor whose weather eye failed him and the ship

was caught partially reefed when a good breeze arrived. Through the centuries the term's connotation has changed somewhat usually meaning an order to resume work.

Clean Slate

It was the custom in sailing ships to record the vessel's courses, distances and tacks on a log slate. The new watch would start with a clean slate if things had been growing fine, disregarding what had gone before and starting anew. In a similar way, today, we refer to a new beginning or a second chance in life as starting with a "clean slate."

Davy Jones's Locker

This is seamen's slang for the bottom of the sea. There are several theories as to its origin: One is that Davy Jones was the owner of a sixteenth-century London pub where unwary sailors were drugged and

put in lockers, and then awoke aboard ship to find they had been press-ganged into the Navy.

Devil to pay

Devil and the deep blue sea: In traditional wooden ships, the sailors had to caulk or pay the seams with hot tar between the planks of the deck to prevent leakage into the bilge. The devil seam was topmost on the hull next to the scuppers at the edge of the deck and the longest and most difficult seam to caulk. Hence, if there was the "devil to pay," then this was the most difficult and dangerous job since the sailor might be knocked down (scuppered) by a large wave and find himself between the "devil and the deep blue sea." The former phrase has come to mean that there will be a big price to pay for a particular action; the latter now refers to being on the horns of a dilemma.

Costa Magica
★★★★

Size:	Large Resort Ship	Passenger Decks:	13	Cabins (with private balcony):	522
Tonnage:	102,587	Total Crew:	1,068	Cabins (wheelchair accessible):	8
Lifestyle:	Standard	Passengers		Wheelchair accessibility:	Good
Cruise Line:	Costa Cruises	(lower beds/all berths):	2,718/3,788	Cabin Current:	220 volts
Former Names:	none	Passenger Space Ratio		Elevators:	14
Builder:	Fincantieri (Italy)	(lower beds/all berths):	37.7/27.0	Casino (gaming tables):	Yes
Original Cost:	$418.5 million	Crew/Passenger Ratio		Slot Machines:	Yes
Entered Service:	Nov 2004	(lower beds/all berths):	2.5/3.2	Swimming Pools (outdoors):	3
Registry:	Italy	Cabins (total):	1,359	Swimming Pools (indoors):	0
Length (ft/m):	893.3/272.3	Size Range (sq ft/m):	179.7–482.2/	Whirlpools:	6
Beam (ft/m):	124.6/38		16.7–44.8	Self-Service Launderette:	No
Draft (ft/m):	27.2/8.3	Cabins (outside view):	857	Dedicated Cinema/Seats:	No
Propulsion/Propellers:	diesel-electric	Cabins (interior/no view):	501	Library:	Yes
34,000kW/2 azimuthing pods (17.6 MW each)		Cabins (for one person):	0	Onboard currency	Euros

A family-friendly large ship with bright Italian decor.

OVERVIEW. *Costa Magica* is built to impress at every turn. It absorbs passengers quite well, with a good passenger space ratio. While a variety of nationalities are carried, most passengers are Italian, so the ship is lively but quite noisy, with lots of children, particularly during school holiday periods.

THE SHIP. Passenger flow is generally good. There is not a lot of open deck space for the number of passengers carried, so sunloungers tend to be crammed together. The interior decor is inspired by some of Italy's "magic" places such as Costa Smerelda, Isola Bella, Portofino and Spoleto. But, except in key positions, there are few Italians among the crew, which has many Filipinos.

There are three decks full of lounges and 11 bars. A nine-deck high, glass-domed atrium lobby houses the Costa Bar on the lower level. The Sicily Casino (look out for the shiny armor, helmets and shields) is big, glitzy and noisy. There's also a chapel. The Bressanone Library is a nice room, although it is rarely open.

ACCOMMODATION. There are 15 price grades, from two-bed interior cabins to grand suites with private balcony. There are two single cabins (unusual for a large ship). No cabins have lifeboat-obstructed views. The largest accommodation can be found in eight Grand Suites, in the center of the ship on one of the higher decks. They have a queen-sized bed; bathrooms have a tub and two washbasins.

Wheelchair-accessible cabins: Note that 12 of the most desirable (outside-view) wheelchair-accessible cabins are rather idiotically located a long way from elevators, while eight interior cabins are located close to elevators.

BERLITZ'S RATINGS

	Possible	Achieved
Ship	500	427
Accommodation	200	146
Food	400	251
Service	400	275
Entertainment	100	64
Cruise	400	282

OVERALL SCORE
1,445 points out of 2,000

CUISINE. The two dining rooms, *Costa Smeralda Restaurant* (aft) and the *Portofino Restaurant* (midships), are two decks high, and have two seatings. Dinner on European cruises is typically scheduled at 7pm and 9pm. Almost all the wines are young.

Alternative (Reservations Required) Dining Option: *The Vincenza Tavernetta Club* is an upscale dining spot with seating for around 150 under a huge glass dome. Fine table settings, Versace china, woven cloth napkins, fine silverware and leather-bound menus are used. The recipes, from Belloni and Belloni, are excellent. There is a cover charge of $18.75 per person.

The *Bellagio Buffet Restaurant* is a self-serve eatery for breakfast, lunch, afternoon pizzas, and beverages at any time. The bars serve excellent cappuccino and espresso coffees.

ENTERTAINMENT. The Urbino Theater spans three decks in the forwardmost section of the ship. It is the setting for all production shows and large-scale cabaret acts, is quite stunning, and has a revolving stage, hydraulic orchestra pit, superb sound, and seating on three levels.

SPA/FITNESS. Facilities in the two-deck high Saturnia Spa include a large solarium, eight treatment rooms, sauna and steam rooms for men and women, and a beauty parlor. The gymnasium is full of techno-gym equipment. There's an aerobics section with instructor-led classes, some of which, such as yoga and kick-boxing, cost extra.

● **For more extensive general information on what a Costa Cruises cruise is like, see pages 135–8.**

Costa Marina
★★ +

Size: . . . . .Mid-Size Ship	Total Crew: 400	Cabins (wheelchair accessible): 0
Tonnage: .25,441	Passengers	Wheelchair accessibility: . . . . .None
Lifestyle: . . . . .Standard	(lower beds/all berths): 772/1,005	Cabin Current: . . . . . . .110 and 220 volts
Cruise Line: . . . . .Costa Cruises	Passenger Space Ratio	Elevators: 8
Former Names: . . . .*Axel Johnson*	(lower beds/all berths): 32.9/25.3	Casino (gaming tables): . . . . .Yes
Builder: . . . . .Mariotti Shipyards (Italy)	Crew/Passenger Ratio	Slot Machines: . . . . .Yes
Original Cost: . . . .$130 million	(lower beds/all berths): 1.9/2.5	Swimming Pools (outdoors): 1
Entered Service: . . . . .Jul 1990	Cabins (total): 386	Swimming Pools (indoors): 0
Registry: . . . . .Italy	Size Range (sq ft/m): 104.4–264.8/	Whirlpools: 3
Length (ft/m): 571.8/174.25	9.7–24.6	Self-Service Launderette: . . . . .No
Beam (ft/m): 84.6/25.75	Cabins (outside view): 183	Dedicated Cinema/Seats: . . . . .No
Draft (ft/m): 26.1/8.20	Cabins (interior/no view): 205	Library: . . . . .Yes
Propulsion/Propellers: diesel (19,152kW)/2	Cabins (for one person): 0	Onboard currency . . . . .Euros
Passenger Decks: 8	Cabins (with private balcony): 8	

A basic Italian-style ship for casual, frugal cuisers.

OVERVIEW. Since a 2002 overhaul, *Costa Marina* has been an Italian ship aimed at German-speaking passengers ("La Deutsche Vita," one might say). It appeals to young and young-at-heart couples and singles who enjoy European city life, plenty of activities, and entertainment that is consistently loud.

THE SHIP. This angular-looking vessel, converted from a container ship, has a contemporary, cutaway stern that is virtually replaced by a glass wall – in fact, the dining room windows – and a stark cluster of three yellow funnels. Today the design seems dated.

Most public rooms are above the accommodation decks and include several bars and lounges. There is generally good passenger flow, although congestion occurs between first and second dinner seatings.

The fit and finish of this vessel, when it debuted as a cruise ship, were well below standard. There is a very limited amount of open deck and sunbathing space, and no observation lounge with forward-facing views. The swimming pool is very small. There are simply too many interior cabins. The library is really poor. Tipping envelopes in your cabin state the level of tip expected.

ACCOMMODATION. There are 12 categories, ranked by grade, size and location. Both the outside view and interior cabins are quite comfortable, but have plain, almost clinical, decor. Bathrooms are functional, but there is little space for toiletries. The room service menu is poor.

CUISINE. The 452-seat *Cristal Restaurant* is fairly spa-

BERLITZ'S RATINGS		
	Possible	Achieved
Ship	500	275
Accommodation	200	120
Food	400	192
Service	400	226
Entertainment	100	58
Cruise	400	219

OVERALL SCORE
1,090 points out of 2,000

cious and has expansive glass windows overlooking the stern, while port and starboard sides have large portholes. There are two seatings but few tables for two, most tables being for four, six or eight. Romantic candlelight dining is typically featured on a formal night.

The cuisine is Continental, with some German regional specialties. The quality of meats is good, although it is often disguised with gravies and rich sauces. Fish and seafood tend to be lacking in taste and are typically overcooked, and green vegetables are hard to come by. However, good pasta dishes are served each day – the pasta is made fresh on board daily – although quantity, not quality, is what appears from the galley. While the breads and rolls are typically good, the desserts are not. There is a wine list, although almost all wines are young – very young.

Excellent cappuccino and espresso coffees are always available in various bars, served in proper china cups.

ENTERTAINMENT. The Tropicana Showroom is a single-level room. However, 14 pillars obstruct many sight lines from many seats. The room is adequate as a cabaret lounge.

SPA/FITNESS. The spa/fitness facilities are not large, but they include a solarium, several treatment rooms, sauna and steam rooms for men and women, beauty salon and gymnasium with floor-to-ceiling windows on three sides. There is a jogging track outdoors.

● **For more extensive general information on what a Costa Cruises cruise is like, see pages 135–8.**

Costa Mediterranea
★★★★

Size:	Large Resort Ship	Passenger Decks:	11	Cabins (wheelchair accessible):	8
Tonnage:	85,700	Total Crew:	920	Wheelchair accessibility:	Good
Lifestyle:	Standard	Passengers		Cabin Current:	110 volts
Cruise Line:	Costa Cruises	(lower beds/all berths):	2,112/2,680	Elevators:	12
Former Names:	none	Passenger Space Ratio		Casino (gaming tables):	Yes
Builder:	Kvaerner Masa-Yards (Finland)	(lower beds/all berths):	40.5/31.9	Slot Machines:	Yes
Original Cost:	$335 million	Crew/Passenger Ratio		Swimming Pools (outdoors):	2
Entered Service:	May 2003	(lower beds/all berths):	2.2/2.9		(+1 indoor/outdoor)
Registry:	Italy	Cabins (total):	1,056	Swimming Pools (indoors):	No
Length (ft/m):	959.6/292.5	Size Range (sq ft/m):	161.4–387.5/	Whirlpools:	4
Beam (ft/m):	105.6/32.2		15.0–36.0	Self-Service Launderette:	No
Draft (ft/m):	25.5/7.8	Cabins (outside view):	843	Dedicated Cinema/Seats:	No
Propulsion/Propellers:	diesel-electric	Cabins (interior/no view):	213	Library:	Yes
	(34,000 kW)/2 azimuthing pods	Cabins (for one person):	0	Onboard currency	Euros
	(17.6 MW each)	Cabins (with private balcony):	742		

Upbeat Italian decor and style, suitable for families.

OVERVIEW. The interior design is bold and brash – a mix of classical Italy and contemporary features. There is good passenger flow, several spaces for dancing, and a range of bars and lounges for socializing. Expect constant irritating announcements – especially for revenue activities such as art auctions, bingo, horse racing – and much hustling for drinks. The appeal is to young and young-at-heart couples and singles, plus families with children, who enjoy big-city life, loud entertainment, and an international mix of passengers.

THE SHIP. The first thing regular passengers will notice is the length of this ship, which gives it an attractive sleekness. There are two centrally located swimming pools outdoors, one with a retractable glass dome that protects it in poor weather. A bar abridges two adjacent whirlpool tubs. Another smaller pool is for children. There is a winding water slide spanning two decks in height, starting on a platform bridge located at the aft funnel. There is an additional whirlpool tub outdoors.

Inside, the layout is the same as in sister ship *Costa Atlantica*. The dramatic eight-deck atrium lobby, with two grand stairways, presents a stunning wall decoration consisting of two huge paintings and *Danza,* a 25-piece wall sculpture by Gigi Rigamonte. This is best seen from any of the multiple viewing balconies on each deck above the main lobby-floor level. The squid-shaped wall lighting sconces are neat, too. But pillars throughout the ship obstruct passenger flow and pillars in the dining room provide an obstacle course for waiters.

BERLITZ'S RATINGS		
	Possible	Achieved
Ship	500	426
Accommodation	200	152
Food	400	240
Service	400	273
Entertainment	100	64
Cruise	400	282

OVERALL SCORE
1,437 points out of 2,000

The decor is said to be inspired by many Italian palaces (some known, many not) and by a profound love of art and architecture. It is extremely upbeat, bright, glitzy, and in-your-face everywhere. I was amused by one of three larger-than-life digital faces of Dionisio in the Dionisio Lounge, with a door handle sticking out of his mouth in a style recalling Monty Python.

A small chapel is located forward of the uppermost level. Other facilities include a winding shopping street with boutique stores such as Fendi, Fossil, Paul & Shark Yachting, a photo gallery, video games room, observation balcony, a large Grand Canal Casino, and a rarely-open library with internet access but few books. Printed materials such as room service folio, and menus, are in six languages (Italian, English, French, German, Portuguese, Spanish).

ACCOMMODATION. There are 14 price grades. There is a healthy (78%) proportion of outside-view to interior cabins. All cabins have twin beds that convert into a queen-sized bed, individually controlled air-conditioning, television, and telephone. Some cabins have their views obstructed by lifeboats – on Deck 4 (Roma Deck), the lowest of the accommodation decks, as well as some cabins on Deck 5. Some cabins have pull-down Pullman berths that are fully hidden in the ceiling when not in use.

There is too much use of fluorescent lighting in the suites and cabins, and the soundproofing could be much better. Some bathroom fixtures – bath and shower taps in particular – can be frustrating to use at first.

Some of the most desirable suites and cabins are those

with private balconies on the five aft-facing decks (Decks 4, 5, 6, 7, and 8) with views overlooking the stern and ship's wash. Those in other cabins with private balconies will find the balconies not so private – the partition between them is not a full partition, so you'll be able to hear your neighbors or smell their smoke.

However, these balcony occupants all have good views through glass and wood-topped railings, and the deck is teak. The cabins are well laid out, typically with twin beds that convert to a queen-sized bed, vanity desk (with built-in hairdryer), large television, personal safe, and one closet with moveable shelves – thus providing more space for storing luggage. However, the lighting is fluorescent and too harsh. The bedside control is for a master switch only – other lights cannot be controlled.

The bathroom is a simple, modular unit that has shower enclosures with soap dispenser; there is a good amount of stowage space for personal toiletries.

The largest suites are the Penthouse Suites, although they are small when compared with suites aboard other ships of a similar size. At least they do offer more space to move around in, and a slightly larger, better bathroom.

CUISINE. The *Ristorante degli Argentiere*, the main dining room, is extremely large and is located at the aft section of the ship on two levels with a spiral stairway between them. There are two seatings, with tables for two, four, six or eight. Dinner on European cruises is typically scheduled at 7pm and 9pm. Some tables have a less than comfortable view of the harsh lighting of the escalators between the galley and the two decks of the dining room.

Alternative (Reservations-Only, Extra Cost) Dining: The *Medusa Supper Club,* a more upscale dining spot on two of the uppermost decks under a huge glass dome, seats around 150 and has a menu by Zeffirino, a famous restaurant in Genoa. It has an open kitchen where chefs can be seen preparing their masterpieces. Fine table settings, china and silverware are used, and there are leather-bound menus. Reservations are needed and there's a cover charge. You may think it's worth it in order to have dinner in a setting that's quieter and more refined than the main dining room.

The *Perla del Lago Buffet* is an extensive eatery forming the aft third of Deck 9, with part of it wrapping around the upper section of the huge atrium. It includes a central area with several small buffet counters; there are salad counters, a dessert counter, and a 24-hour Posillipo Pizzeria counter, all creating a large eatery with indoor and outdoor seating. Movement around the buffet area is very slow, and requires you to stand in line for everything. Venture outdoors and you'll find a grill for hamburgers and hot dogs, and a pasta bar, both conveniently located adjacent to the second of two swimming pools on the lido deck.

Other Venues: The place most people will want to see and be seen is the casual *Oriental Café*; it has four separate salons, which provide intimate spaces for drinks, conversation, and people-watching. Excellent cappuccino and espresso coffees are always available in various bars around the ship, served in the right-sized china cups.

ENTERTAINMENT. The Osiris Theater is the principal venue for production shows and major cabaret acts. It spans three decks, with seating on all three levels. Sightlines to the stage are better from the second and third levels. Spiral stairways at the back of the lounge connect all levels.

SPA/FITNESS. The expansive Ischia Spa spans two decks, is located directly above the navigation bridge in the forward part of the ship (accessed by the forward stairway elevators), and has approximately 13,700 sq. ft (1,272 sq. meters) of space. Lower-level facilities include a solarium, eight treatment rooms, lecture rooms, sauna and steam rooms for men and women, and a beauty parlor. The upper level has a large gymnasium with floor-to-ceiling windows on three sides, and an aerobics room with instructor-led classes – the aerobics room and gymnasium together measure almost 6,000 sq. ft (557 sq. meters).

There is a jogging track outdoors, around the ship's mast and the forward third of the ship, as well as a multi-purpose court for basketball, volleyball and deck tennis.

● **For more extensive general information on what a Costa Cruises cruise is like, see pages 135–8.**

Costa Pacifica
★★★★

Size:..................... Large Resort Ship	Passenger Decks: 13	Cabins (wheelchair accessible): 12
Tonnage:........................ 114,500	Total Crew: 1,110	Wheelchair accessibility: ....Good
Lifestyle: .... Standard	Passengers	Cabin Voltage: .... 110/220 volts
Cruise Line: .... Costa Cruises	(lower beds/all berths): 3,012/3,780	Elevators:........................... 14
Former Names: .... none	Passenger Space Ratio	Casino (gaming tables): .... Yes
Builder: .... Fincantieri (Italy)	(lower beds/all berths): 38.0/30.2	Slot Machines: .... Yes
Original Cost:................ €510 million	Crew/Passenger Ratio	Swimming Pools (outdoors): 2
Entered Service: .... Apr 2009	(lower beds/all berths): 2.7/3.4	Swimming Pools (indoors): .... 2 (glass dome)
Registry: .... Italy	Cabins (total): 1,506	Whirlpools:........................... 5
Length (ft/m): 952.0/290.0	Size Range (sq ft/m):.. 179.7–482.2/16.7–44.8	Self-Service Launderette: .... No
Beam (ft/m): 116.4/35.5	Cabins (outside view): 926	Dedicated Cinema/Seats: .... No
Draft (ft/m):...................... 27.2/8.3	Cabins (interior/no view):............... 580	Library:............................ Yes
Propulsion/Propellers: .... diesel-electric	Cabins (for one person):................ 0	Onboard currency ....Euros
(34,000kW)/2 azimuthing pods	Cabins (with private balcony):.......... 579	

A large, colourful family-friendly Italian-style ship.

OVERVIEW. Costa Cruises does a good job of providing first-time cruise passengers with a well-packaged holiday, particularly for families with children. It's a mix of sophistication and chaos, accompanied by loud music. This is a cruise line for those who like to party. This ship has a musical design theme featuring "greatest hits." The lobby, for example, is covered in musical symbols and instruments. The passenger flow inside is quite good, and the ship absorbs passengers reasonably well. It also provides a decent passenger space ratio, which means that it won't feel too crowded.

THE SHIP. Sporting a single, large funnel, *Costa Pacifica* is a sister to the popular *Costa Concordia* and *Costa Serena*. Two pool areas can be covered with retractable glass domes – good in case of poor weather – and one of the pools has a water slide that's great for kids. There is also a huge screen for poolside movies. A Grand Prix simulator is positioned on one of the upper decks.

However, the open deck space is cramped when the ship is full, so sunloungers tend to be crammed together, and they don't have cushioned pads.

There are three decks full of bars and lounges plus many other public rooms. This ship has a glass-domed atrium lobby nine decks high, with great upward views from the lobby bar, as well as from its four glass panoramic elevators.

The casino is large and glitzy, but always lively and entertaining; slot machines occupy a separate area to gaming tables, so serious gamers can concentrate. There's also a very small library, an internet-connection center, card room, art gallery, and video game room, together with sev-

BERLITZ'S RATINGS		
	Possible	Achieved
Ship	500	423
Accommodation	200	152
Food	400	248
Service	400	274
Entertainment	100	66
Cruise	400	280
OVERALL SCORE		
1,443 points out of 2,000		

eral other bars and lounges. A chapel is a standard aboard all Costa ships.

Although Costa Cruises is noted for its "Italian" style, ambience and spirit, there are few Italian crew members on board its ships. While many of the officers are Italian, most of the crew members – particularly the dining room and housekeeping staff – are from the Philippines. The lifestyle on board is, however, perceived to be Italian – lively, noisy, and embracing a casual lifestyle – even on so-called "formal" nights. Most passengers will be Italian, with a sprinkling of other European nationals.

Printed materials such as room service folio and menus will typically be in six languages (Italian, English, French, German, Portuguese, and Spanish). During peak European school holiday periods, particularly Christmas and Easter, expect to be cruising with a lot of children of all ages. Sony Play Station fans can enjoy "Play Station World," an area dedicated to PS3. Play Stations are also available in cabins, in the children's and teens' clubs, and can be used with the poolside movie screen.

As aboard other Costa ships, few staff members are on duty at the gangway when you embark; they merely point you in the direction of your deck, or to the ship's elevators and do not escort you to your cabin.

ACCOMMODATION. There are 20 price grades, from two-bed interior cabins to grand suites with private balcony, although in reality there are only three different sizes: Suites with "private" balcony (which are really not particularly large in comparison with some other large ships), two- or four-bed outside view cabins, and two- or four-bed interior cabins. No cabins have views obstructed by lifeboats or other safety equipment, and, in all cabins, twin beds can be changed to a double/queen-bed configuration.

A total of eight Grand Suites comprise the largest accommodation. These are in the center of the ship on one of the uppermost decks. They have a queen-sized bed and larger living area with vanity desk; the bathrooms have a tub and two washbasins.

If you like wellness treatments, there are 12 "Samsara Spa Suites" located just aft of the spa – although 99 cabins, including the 12 suites, are designated as Samsara-grade. Samsara suite/cabin occupants get unlimited access to the spa plus two treatments and fitness or meditation lessons as part of their package, and dine in one of the two Samsara restaurants. All Samsara-designated accommodation grades have an Oriental decorative theme, and special Samsara bathroom amenities.

A pillow menu, with five choices, is available in all suite accommodation grades. Only suite grades get bathrobes and better amenities, shaving mirror, and walk-in closets – although the hangars are plastic. Music is played 24 hours a day in all hallways and elevators, so you may well hear it if you are a light sleeper.

CUISINE. There are two main dining rooms (*New York, New York*, and *My Way*), allocated according to your accommodation grade and location. There are two seatings in each for dinner.

Two 100-seat *Samsara Restaurants* have separate entrances, adjacent to the My Way restaurant. Unlike the the main restaurants that offer traditional cruise fare, these are for people seeking spa food – this means reduced calories, fat and salt, with menus created under the direction of dietary consultant and Michelin-star chef Ettore Boccia and his molecular Italian cuisine.

These dining venues are open for lunch and dinner to those in Samsara-grade suites and cabins, and to anyone else (for dinner only) for an extra charge of €20 per day, or €120 for a seven-day cruise package.

Alternative (Reservations Required) Dining Option: *Club Blue Moon* is an elegant dining venue with seating under a huge glass dome. Fine table settings, china, silverware and leather-bound menus are provided. There's a cover charge of $20 per person, for service and gratuity.

Casual Eatery: *La Paloma Buffet Restaurant* is a self-serve eatery for breakfast, lunch, afternoon pizzas, and coffee and tea at any time. A balcony level provides additional seating. You'll need to carry your own food plates – there are no trays. Decent quality cappuccino and espresso coffees are always available in various bars, at extra cost.

Additionally, the *Caffeteria* is the place to go for decent coffees and Italian pastries, at extra cost.

ENTERTAINMENT: The showlounge seats more than 800, and utilizes the latest in LED technology. It is three decks high and is decorated in a Baroque style, with warm colors and a Murano glass chandelier. It is the venue for all production shows and large-scale cabaret acts, is quite stunningly glitzy, and has a revolving stage, hydraulic orchestra pit, superb sound, and seating on three levels (the upper levels are tiered through two decks).

Typical fare consists of revue-style shows performed by a small troupe of resident onboard singers/dancers, with fast-moving action and busy lighting and costume changes that all add up to a high-energy performance.

SPA/FITNESS. The Samsara Spa is a large facility that occupies 23,186 sq.ft/2,154 sq. meters of space, spread over two decks. It includes a large fitness room, separate saunas, steam rooms, UVB solarium, changing rooms for men and women, and 10 body treatment rooms. On the upper level, two VIP treatment rooms are available to couples for half-day rentals.

The spa/fitness facilities are staffed and operated by Steiner Leisure, a specialist spa/beauty concession. Some fitness classes are free; others, such as Pathway to Yoga, Pathway to Pilates, and Pathway to Meditation, cost extra. Make appointments early as time slots can go quickly.

You can purchase a day pass in order to use the sauna/steam rooms, thermal suite and relaxation area, at a cost of €35 per person. However, there is an additional no-charge sauna for men and women, but to access it you must walk through an active fitness area, perhaps wearing your bathrobe – an arrangement with which some women may not feel comfortable.

● **For more extensive general information on what a Costa Cruises cruise is like, see pages 135–8.**

Costa Romantica
★★★

Size: . . . . .Mid-Size Ship	Total Crew: 610	Cabins (wheelchair accessible): .6 interior
Tonnage: .53,049	Passengers	Wheelchair accessibility: . . . . .Good
Lifestyle: . . . . .Standard	(lower beds/all berths): 1,356/1,779	Cabin Current: . . . . .110 volts
Cruise Line: . . . . .Costa Crociere	Passenger Space Ratio	Elevators: 8
Former Names: . . . . .none	(lower beds/all berths): 39.1/29.8	Casino (gaming tables): . . . . .Yes
Builder: . . . . .Fincantieri (Italy)	Crew/Passenger Ratio	Slot Machines: . . . . .Yes
Original Cost: . . . .$325 million	(lower beds/all berths): 2.2/2.9	Swimming Pools (outdoors): 2
Entered Service: . . . . .Nov 1993	Cabins (total): 678	Swimming Pools (indoors): 0
Registry: . . . . .Italy	Size Range (sq ft/m): 185.1–430.5/	Whirlpools: 4
Length (ft/m): 718.5/220.61	17.2–40.0	Self-Service Launderette: . . . . .No
Beam (ft/m): 98.4/30.89	Cabins (outside view): 462	Dedicated Cinema/Seats: . . . . .No
Draft (ft/m): 25.0/7.60	Cabins (interior/no view): 216	Library: . . . . .Yes
Propulsion/Propellers: diesel (22,800kW)/2	Cabins (for one person): 0	Onboard currency . . . . .Euros
Passenger Decks: 10	Cabins (with private balcony): 10	

An elegant Italian-style ship for a mature audience.

OVERVIEW. Being Italian, the ship is chic and very tasteful, and will appeal to the sophisticated. The layout and flow are somewhat disjointed, however. It has a good number of business and conference facilities, with several flexible meeting rooms. The multi-level atrium is open and spacious, and has a revolving mobile sculpture.

THE SHIP. *Costa Romantica* is a contemporary ship with an upright yellow funnel cluster of three typical of Italian styling today. There is no walk-around promenade deck outdoors, and so contact with the sea is minimal, although there is some good open space on several of the upper decks. There is a small chapel and an internet café.

ACCOMMODATION. There are 11 price categories. These include 16 suites, 10 of which have a private semi-circular balcony, while six suites command views over the ship's bows. The other cabins are fairly standard in size, shape, and facilities; the ones on the highest decks cost more.
Suites/Mini-Suites: The 16 suites (with floor-to-ceiling windows) and 18 mini-suites are quite pleasant, except for the rounded balconies of the 10 suites on Madrid Deck where a solid steel half-wall blocks the view. A sliding door separates the bedroom from the living room, and bathrooms are of a decent size. Cherry wood walls and cabinetry help make these suites warm and attractive.

The six suites at the forward section of Monte Carlo Deck are the largest, and have huge glass windows with commanding forward views, but no balconies.
Standard Outside-View/Interior (No View) Cabins: All other cabins are of a moderately generous size, and all have

BERLITZ'S RATINGS		
	Possible	Achieved
Ship	500	333
Accommodation	200	133
Food	400	214
Service	400	267
Entertainment	100	60
Cruise	400	240
OVERALL SCORE		
1,247 points out of **2,000**		

nicely finished cherry wood cabinetry and walls. However, the cabin bathrooms and shower enclosures are quite small. There are a good number of triple and quad cabins, ideal for families with children. The company's in-cabin food service menu is extremely basic.

CUISINE. The 728-seat *Botticelli Restaurant* is of a superior design. There are several tables for two, four, six or eight. There are two seatings (dinner on European cruises is typically at 7pm and 9pm), and there are both smoking and non-smoking sections. Romantic candlelight dining is typically featured on a formal night.

For casual meals and snacks, try the *Giardino Buffet*, but note that the buffet layout is extremely tight, and the buffet items are very much standard fare, with the exception of some good commercial pasta dishes. One would expect Italian waiters, but most hail from elsewhere.

ENTERTAINMENT. The L'Opéra Theater, the main showlounge, is an interesting amphitheater-like design spanning two decks, with seating on both levels. However, the seats are bolt upright and quite uncomfortable, with 10 large pillars obstructing many sightlines.

SPA/FITNESS. The Caracalla Spa contains a gymnasium with some high-tech muscle-pump machines, an aerobics exercise area, two hot tubs, Roman bath, health bar, sauna and steam rooms, and a beauty salon.

● **For more extensive general information on what a Costa Cruises cruise is like, see pages 135–8.**

Costa Serena
★★★★

Size: . . . . .Large Resort Ship	Passenger Decks: 13	Cabins (with private balcony): 575
Tonnage: .114,147	Total Crew: 1,090	Cabins (wheelchair accessible): 12
Lifestyle: . . . . .Standard	Passengers	Wheelchair accessibility: . . . . .Good
Cruise Line: Costa Crociere (Costa Cruises)	(lower beds/all berths): 3,000/3,780	Cabin Current: . . . . .110 and 220 volts
Former Names: . . . . .none	Passenger Space Ratio	Elevators: 14
Builder: . . . . .Fincantieri (Italy)	(lower beds/all berths): 38.0/30.1	Casino (gaming tables): . . . . .Yes
Original Cost: . . . .€475 million	Crew/Passenger Ratio	Slot Machines: . . . . .Yes
Entered Service: . . . . .May 2007	(lower beds/all berths): 2.7/3.4	Swimming Pools (outdoors): 4
Registry: . . . . .Italy	Cabins (total): 1,500	Swimming Pools (indoors): 0
Length (ft/m): 952.0/290.2	Size Range (sq ft/m): 482.2–179.7/	Whirlpools: 5
Beam (ft/m): 116.4/35.50	44.8–16.7	Self-Service Launderette: . . . . .No
Draft (ft/m): 27.2/8.3	Cabins (outside view): 914	Dedicated Cinema/Seats: . . . . .No
Propulsion/Propellers: . . . .diesel-electric	Cabins (interior/no view): 586	Library: . . . . .Yes
34,000kW/2 azimuthing pods	Cabins (for one person): 0	Onboard currency . . . . .Euros

Upbeat Italian decor and style, for family cruising.

OVERVIEW. Costa Cruises does a good job of providing first-time cruise passengers with a well-packaged holiday – particularly for families with children – that is a mix of sophistication and basic fare, albeit accompanied by loud music everywhere. *Costa Serena* is a sister ship to *Costa Concordia* and *Costa Pacifica*.

THE SHIP. *Costa Serena* absorbs passengers reasonably well, and provides a decent passenger space ratio that means that it won't feel too crowded – except, perhaps, on the open decks. The delightful interior design is themed around the heavens and astrology – even the ship's deck names are those of the Zodiac.

There are three decks full of bars and lounges plus lots of other public rooms. This ship has a nine-deck-high glass-domed atrium lobby with four panoramic elevators providing great views.

The Casino is large and glitzy, but always lively and entertaining; slot machines occupy a separate area to gaming tables, so serious gamers can concentrate. There's also a very small library, an internet-connection center, card room, art gallery, and video game room, together with several other bars and lounges, plus a chapel – a standard aboard all Costa Cruises' ships.

For a full description of the ship's atmosphere and facilities, see the entry for *Costa Pacifica* on page 332.

ACCOMMODATION. There are 20 price grades, from two-bed interior cabins to grand suites with private balcony, although in reality there are only three different sizes: Suites with balcony, two- or four-bed outside view cabins, and two- or four-bed interior cabins. Eight Grand suites com-

BERLITZ'S RATINGS		
	Possible	Achieved
Ship	500	423
Accommodation	200	152
Food	400	252
Service	400	272
Entertainment	100	65
Cruise	400	278
OVERALL SCORE		
1,442 points out of 2,000		

prise the largest accommodation. For anyone who likes to take wellness (spa) treatments, there are 12 "Samsara Spa Suites" located just aft of the spa itself.

For comprehensive details of cabin sizes and facilities, see the entry for *Costa Pacifica*.

CUISINE. There are two main dining rooms: *Ceres*, located aft, and *Vesta*, in the ship's center). Two 100-seat Samsara Restaurants are for those seeking spa food with reduced calories, fat and salt. *Club Bacco* is the upscale, extra-cost dining option. The *Promotea Buffet Restaurant* is a self-serve eatery for breakfast, lunch, afternoon pizzas, and coffee and tea at any time. The *Caffeteria* is the place to go for decent coffees and Italian pastries at extra cost.

For more details of dining times and food quality, see the entry for *Costa Pacifica*.

ENTERTAINMENT. The three-deck high 1,287-seat Giove Theater is the venue for all production shows and large-scale cabaret acts. Typically, revue-style shows (performed by a small troupe of resident onboard singers/dancers) are presented, with fast moving action and busy lighting and costume changes that all add up to a high-energy performance.

SPA/FITNESS. For details of the ship's Samsara Spa and the many other treatment and sports facilities, see the entry for *Costa Pacifica*.

● **For more extensive general information on what a Costa Cruises cruise is like, see pages 135–8.**

Costa Victoria
★★★+

Size: . . . . .Large Resort Ship	Total Crew: 800	Cabins (wheelchair accessible): 6
Tonnage: 75,200	Passengers	Wheelchair accessibility: . . . . .Good
Lifestyle: . . . . .Standard	(lower beds/all berths): 1,928/2,464	Cabin Current: . . . . .110 and 220 volts
Cruise Line: . . . . .Costa Cruises	Passenger Space Ratio	Elevators: 12
Former Names: . . . . .none	(lower beds/all berths): 39.0/30.5	Casino (gaming tables): . . . . .Yes
Builder: . . . . . . .Bremer Vulkan (Germany)	Crew/Passenger Ratio	Slot Machines: . . . . .Yes
Original Cost: . . . .$388 million	(lower beds/all berths): 2.4/3.0	Swimming Pools (outdoors): 2
Entered Service: . . . . .Jul 1996	Cabins (total): 964	Swimming Pools (indoors): 0
Registry: . . . . .Italy	Size Range (sq ft/m): 120.0–430.5/	Whirlpools: 4
Length (ft/m): 823.0/251.00	11.1–40.0	Self-Service Launderette: . . . . .Yes
Beam (ft/m): 105.5/32.25	Cabins (outside view): 573	Dedicated Cinema/Seats: . . . . .No
Draft (ft/m): 25.6/7.8	Cabins (interior/no view): 391	Library: . . . . .Yes
Propulsion/Propellers: diesel (30,000kW)/2	Cabins (for one person): 0	Onboard currency . . . . .Euros
Passenger Decks: 10	Cabins (with private balcony): 246	

Bland decor in an Italian setting for mature-age cruisers.

OVERVIEW. Where this ship differs from most large ships is in its distinct European interior decor, with decidedly Italian styling. When inside, there is absolutely no feeling that this is a ship. Unusual for a new ship is a pleasant (but tiny) indoor swimming pool and a sauna. Adjacent is a steam room, and gymnasium (limited assortment of equipment), as well as a covered walking/jogging track. There is also a tennis court.

THE SHIP. *Costa Victoria* has an outdoor walk-around promenade deck (full of sunloungers). Inside is a lovely four-deck-high forward-facing observation lounge with a "beam-me-up" glass elevator; in the center is a cone-shaped waterfall. It is a stunning space, and has its own bar. The seven-deck-high "planetarium" atrium has four glass lifts that travel up to a clear crystal dome. The uppermost level of the atrium is the deck where two outside swimming pools are located, together with four blocks of showers, and an ice cream bar and grill.

Internet access is available from computer terminals in the Teens Center.

ACCOMMODATION. There are 13 price categories. The six large Panorama suites (each with third/ fourth Pullman berths in tiny, train-like compartments) and 14 mini-suites have butler service; 65% of all other cabins have outside views, but they are small (for two). While the suites are not large, all other cabins are of rather mean dimensions. Only 16 of the interior cabins accommodate four people, while all other cabins are for two or three.

All cabins have wood cabinetry. There is a decent amount of storage space for two for a one-week cruise,

BERLITZ'S RATINGS

	Possible	Achieved
Ship	500	402
Accommodation	200	152
Food	400	220
Service	400	273
Entertainment	100	71
Cruise	400	264

OVERALL SCORE
1,382 points out of 2,000

excellent air-conditioning, mini-bar/refrigerator, and electric blackout window blind. The ocean-view cabins have large picture windows. The cabin bathrooms are small but well appointed. There are six cabins for the disabled.

CUISINE. This ship has two main dining rooms: the 594-seat *Minuetto Restaurant*, and the 506-seat *Fantasia Restaurant*. There are two seatings, with smoking and no-smoking sections in both restaurants. They are expansive and feature marble and pine walls. The cuisine is good basic fare, and the presentation is adequate, but nothing special. Pasta is freshly made on board daily.

Alternative (reservations-only) dining: *Ristorante Magnifico by Zeffirino* is available six nights each week, with a service charge of €20 per person. Passengers occupying suites get a free pass for one evening.

The ship also has casual breakfast and lunch buffets with indoor/outdoor seating, although the buffet displays are very disappointing. There is also a pizzeria.

ENTERTAINMENT. The Festival Showlounge, spanning two decks, is the venue for production shows, major cabaret, and social functions.

SPA/FITNESS. The congested spa/fitness area, on a lower deck, is much too small for the size of the ship. It has a beauty salon, indoor swimming pool, treatment rooms, sauna and steam room, but cramped changing areas.

● **For more extensive general information on what a Costa Cruises cruise is like, see pages 135–8.**

Crown Princess
★★★★

Ship: . . . . .Large Resort Ship	Passenger Decks: 15	Cabins (with private balcony): 881
Tonnage: .116,000	Total Crew: .1,163	Cabins (wheelchair accessible): 25
Lifestyle: . . . . .Standard	Passengers	Wheelchair accessibility: . . . . .Best
Cruise Line: . . . . .Princess Cruises	(lower beds/all berths): 3,114/3,782	Cabin Current: . . . . .110 volts
Former Names: . . . . .none	Passenger Space Ratio	Elevators: 14
Builder: . . . . .Fincantieri (Italy)	(lower beds/all berths): 37.2/30.6	Casino (gaming tables): . . . . .Yes
Original Cost: . . . .$500 million	Crew/Passenger Ratio	Slot Machines: . . . . .Yes
Entered Service: . . . . .May 2006	(lower beds/all berths): 2.6/3.2	Swimming Pools (outdoors): 4
Registry: . . . . .Bermuda	Cabins (total): 1,557	Swimming Pools (indoors): 0
Length (ft/m): 951.4/290.0	Size Range (sq ft/m): 163–1,279/	Whirlpools: 9
Beam (ft/m): 118.1/36.0	15.1–118.8	Self-Service Launderette: . . . . .Yes
Draft (ft/m): 26.2/8.0	Cabins (outside view): 1,105	Dedicated Cinema/Seats: . . . . .No
Propulsion/Propellers: gas turbine (25 MW)/2	Cabins (interior/no view): 452	Library: . . . . .Yes
azimuthing pods (21,000 kW each)	Cabins (for one person): 0	Onboard currency . . . . .US$

A large ship with sedate decor, for mature-age cruisers.

OVERVIEW. *Crown Princess* is a grand resort playground in which to roam when you are not ashore, and Princess Cruises delivers a consistently fine, well-packaged product, always with a good degree of style, at a highly competitive price. With many choices and "small" rooms (a relative term) to enjoy, the ship has been extremely well designed, and the odds are that you'll have an enjoyable vacation. If you are not used to large ships, it will take you some time to find your way around this one, despite the company's claim that it offers passengers a "small ship feel, big ship choice."

BERLITZ'S RATINGS		
	Possible	Achieved
Ship	500	433
Accommodation	200	168
Food	400	254
Service	400	291
Entertainment	100	82
Cruise	400	313

OVERALL SCORE
1,541 points out of 2,000

The interior decor is attractive, with lots of earth tones. An extensive collection of artworks complements the interior design and colors well. If you see something you like, you will probably be able to purchase it on board.

Crown Princess also includes a Wedding Chapel with a live web-cam relaying ceremonies via the internet. The ship's captain can legally marry American couples, thanks to the ship's Bermuda registry and a special dispensation (which should be verified when in the planning stage, according to where you reside). The "Hearts & Minds" chapel is also useful for "renewal of vows" ceremonies.

THE SHIP. One nice feature is The Sanctuary, an extra-cost adults-only retreat located forward on the uppermost deck. It provides a "private" place to relax and unwind and includes attendants to provide chilled face towels and deliver light bites; there are also two outdoor cabanas for massages. It's a plush, outdoor spa-inspired setting for relaxation with attentive service.

There is a good sheltered teakwood promenade deck, which almost wraps around, and a walkway that leads to the enclosed bow of the ship. The outdoor pools have various beach-like surrounding. "Movies Under the Skies" and major sporting events are shown on a 300-sq-ft (28-sq-meter) movie screen located at the pool in front of the large funnel.

Unlike the outside decks, there is plenty of space inside. There are also plenty of passengers, but the passenger flow has been well thought-out, and there is little congestion. Atop the stern is a ship-wide glass-walled disco, Skywalkers, with spectacular views from the extreme port and starboard side windows (it would make a great penthouse).

A large casino has with more than 260 slot machines, and blackjack, craps and roulette tables, plus newer games such as Let It Ride Bonus, Spanish 21 and Caribbean Draw Progressive. A highlight may be the specially linked slot machines that provide a combined payout.

Other facilities include a decent library/computer room. Ship lovers should enjoy the wood-paneled Wheelhouse Bar, finely decorated with memorabilia and ship models tracing part of parent company P&O's history.

FAMILIES. There is a two-deck-high playroom, teen room, and a host of trained counsellors. Children have their own pools, hot tubs, and open deck area at the stern, thankfully away from adult areas. There are good netted-in areas; one section has a dip pool, while another has a mini-basketball court. There's a video games arcade, too.

Two family suites consist of two suites with an interconnecting door, plus a large balcony. These sleep up to 10 (if at least four are children) or up to eight adults.

ACCOMMODATION. There are six principal types of cabins and configurations: (a) grand suite, (b) suite, (c) mini-suite, (d) outside-view double cabins with balcony, (e) outside-view double cabins, and (f) interior (no view) double cabins. These come in a bewildering choice of 35 different brochure price categories.

(a) The Grand Suite has a large bedroom with queen-sized bed, huge walk-in closets, two bathrooms, a lounge with fireplace, sofa bed, wet bar and refrigerator, and a large private balcony on the port side with hot tub that can be accessed from both balcony and bedroom.

(b/c) Suites have a separate living room (with sofa bed) and bedroom, with a TV set in each. The bathroom is quite large and has both a tub and shower stall. The mini-suites also have a private balcony, and a separate living and sleeping area (with a TV set in each). The differences between the suites and mini-suites are basically in the size and appointments. All suite occupants receive greater attention, including priority embarkation and disembarkation, but what's not good is that the most expensive accommodation has only semi-private balconies.

(d/e/f). Both interior and outside-view cabins are functional, although almost no drawers are provided. They are quite attractive, with warm, pleasing decor and fine soft furnishing fabrics; 80% of outside-view cabins have a private balcony. Interior cabins measure 163 sq. ft (15.1 sq. meters).

The 28 wheelchair-accessible cabins measure 250–385 sq. ft (23.2–35.7 sq. meters); surprisingly, there is no mirror for dressing, and no full-length hanging space for long dresses (yes, some passengers in wheelchairs do also use mirrors and full-length clothing).

Cabin bath towels are small, and drawer space is very limited. There are no butlers, even for top-grade suites. Cabin attendants have too many cabins to look after (typically 20), which does not translate to fine personal service. All cabins receive toiletry kits and have a hairdryer.

Most outside-view cabins on Emerald Deck have views obstructed by lifeboats. There are no cabins for singles. There is 24-hour room service, but some items on the room service menu are not available during early morning hours.

Some cabins can accommodate a third and fourth person in upper berths. However, in some cabins, the lower beds cannot then be pushed together to make queen-sized bed.

Almost all balcony suites and cabins can be overlooked both from the navigation bridge wing, as well as from the port and starboard sections of the ship's discotheque – high above the ship at the stern. Cabins with balconies on Dolphin, Caribe and Baja decks can also be overlooked.

Perhaps the least desirable balcony cabins are eight located forward on Emerald Deck, as the balconies do not extend to the side of the ship and can be passed by walkers and gawkers on the adjacent Upper Promenade walkway so occupants need to keep their curtains closed most of the time). Passengers occupying some the most expensive suites with balconies at the ship's stern may experience considerable vibration during certain maneuvers.

CUISINE. Of the three principal formal dining rooms, one has traditional two-seating dining, while the other two offer "anytime dining." All are no-smoking and split into multi-tier sections in a non-symmetrical design that breaks what are quite large spaces into smaller sections. While six elevators go to Fiesta Deck, where two of the restaurants are located, only four go to Plaza Deck 5, where the *Michelangelo Restaurant* is located (this can lengthen waits at peak times, particularly for those in wheelchairs).

Specially designed dinnerware, high-quality linens and silverware, Frette Egyptian cotton table linens, and silverware by Hepp of Germany are used in the main dining rooms, and 15% is added to beverage bills, including wines. **Alternative (Extra Charge) Dining Options**: There are two: *Sabatini's* and *Crown Grill*. Both are open for dinner on days at sea. Sabatini's has Italian-style pizzas and pastas, with a variety of sauces, as well as Italian-style entrées including tiger prawns and lobster tail – all provided with flair and entertainment from by the staff of waiters. Reservations are needed and there's a cover charge for lunch or dinner). The 160-seat Crown Grill, also with cover charge, is in a wide promenade area, to tempt you as you pass by.

Casual eateries include a poolside hamburger grill and pizzeria. Some items cost extra at the *International Café* coffee bar/patisserie in the atrium lobby. *Vines* offers sushi and cheese at no extra charge, and extra-cost wine. Other casual meals can be taken in the *Horizon Court*, open 24 hours a day, with ocean views.

Ultimate Balcony Dinner/Breakfast: For something different, you could try a private dinner on your balcony, an all-inclusive evening featuring cocktails, fresh flowers, champagne and a deluxe four-course meal including Caribbean lobster tail – all served by a member of the dining staff on your private balcony; of course, it costs extra.

ENTERTAINMENT. The Princess Theater spans two decks and has comfortable seating on both main and balcony levels. It has $3 million worth of sound and light equipment, plus a nine-piece orchestra. The ship carries a resident troupe of almost 20 singers and dancers.

Club Fusion, a second entertainment lounge located aft, features cabaret acts at night, and lectures, bingo and horse racing by day. Explorers, a third entertainment lounge, can also host cabaret acts and dance bands. A variety of other lounges and bars have live music, and a number of male dance hosts act as partners for women traveling alone.

SPA/FITNESS. The Lotus Spa has separate facilities for men and women include a sauna, steam room, and changing rooms; common facilities include a relaxation/waiting zone, body-pampering treatment rooms, and a gymnasium with great ocean views and the latest high-tech equipment. Some fitness classes are free, others cost extra.

Above the spa, The Sanctuary, an adults-only retreat, offers shade and solitude. MP3 players can be rented, preloaded with a variety of music.

● **For more extensive general information on what a Princess Cruises cruise is like, see pages 149–52.**

Crystal Serenity
★★★★★

Size:	Mid-Size Ship	Total Crew:	650	Cabins (wheelchair accessible):	8
Tonnage:	68,870	Passengers		Wheelchair accessibility:	Best
Lifestyle:	Luxury/Premium	(lower beds/all berths):	1,100/1,100	Cabin Current:	110/220 volts
Cruise Line:	Crystal Cruises	Passenger Space Ratio		Elevators:	8
Former Names:	none	(lower beds/all berths):	62.6/62.6	Casino (gaming tables):	Yes
Builder:	Chantiers de l'Atlantique (France)	Crew/Passenger Ratio		Slot Machines:	Yes
Original Cost:	$350 million	(lower beds/all berths):	1.7/1.7	Swimming Pools (outdoors):	1
Entered Service:	Jun 2003	Cabins (total):	550	Swimming Pools (indoors):	1
Registry:	The Bahamas	Size Range (sq ft/m):	226–1,345.5/		(indoor/outdoor)
Length (ft/m):	820.2/250.0		21–125	Whirlpools:	2
Beam (ft/m):	111.5/34.0	Cabins (outside view):	550	Self-Service Launderette:	Yes
Draft (ft/m):	24.9/7.6	Cabins (interior/no view):	0	Dedicated Cinema/Seats:	Yes/202
Propulsion/Propellers: 2 pods/diesel power		Cabins (for one person):	0	Library:	Yes
Passenger Decks:	9	Cabins (with private balcony):	466	Onboard currency	US$

An elegant, spacious ship with good food and service.

OVERVIEW. This ship is best suited to sophisticated travelers, typically over 50, who seek contemporary ship surroundings, with fine quality fittings and furnishings, a wide range of public rooms and facilities, and excellent food and service from a well trained staff. This ship has just about everything for those prepared to pay for abundant space and the comfort and the facilities of a large vessel, including an excellent program of guest lecturers.

BERLITZ'S RATINGS		
	Possible	Achieved
Ship	500	435
Accommodation	200	168
Food	400	341
Service	400	341
Entertainment	100	86
Cruise	400	346

OVERALL SCORE
1,717 points out of 2,000

The decor in most areas is warm, inviting and contemporary. There is much use of rich wood paneling and detailing. The main lobby houses the 24-hour reception desk, concierge and shore excursion desks, and a lounge/bar (Crystal Cove) with baby grand piano.

Some of the most elegant public rooms include Palm Court, evoking images of Colonial-style grand hotel lounge; the Avenue Saloon, a favorite watering hole of the late-night crowd and a throwback to traditional gentlemen's clubs; the Connoisseur Club, for cigar and cognac enthusiasts; and the Stardust Club, a lounge/nightclub. There are new shops and a private jewelry room, a computer-learning center with 24 terminals, and an internet center. One neat feature is a Vintage Room, a private dining room where 12 invited diners can enjoy exclusive vintages, paired with food, in special wine-tasting dinners. Another is a Yamaha keyboard learning center.

The centrally located casino has no outside views to distract gamers. Instead, the location is adjacent to lifeboats on both sides; in this arrangement, the lifeboats do not obstruct views from cabins or public rooms.

THE SHIP. *Crystal Serenity* is the slightly larger but still mid-size close sister ship to *Crystal Symphony*, and has a similar look and profile. While some might not like the exterior's "apartment block" look, it is in fashion today. The ship was given an extensive $25 million refit and refurbishment in 2011 and looks almost new again.

The ship achieves a high rating because of its fine facilities, service and crew, and the attention to detail. It provides announcement-free cruising in a well-tuned, very professionally run, service-oriented ship, roughly the equivalent of a Four Seasons or Ritz Carlton hotel. The passenger mix is usually 85% North American (half from California) and 15% other nationalities.

Pod propulsion is provided *(see page 191 for details)*. Electrical power is provided by the latest generation of environmentally friendly diesel engines.

There is an excellent amount of open deck, sunbathing space, and sports facilities. The aft of two outdoor swimming pools can be covered by a retractable glass dome in poor weather. There is no sense of crowding. There is also a wide wrap-around teakwood deck for walking, pleasingly uncluttered by sunloungers.

Your evenings will be necessarily rather structured due to the fact that there are two seatings for dinner (unless you eat in one of the alternative dining spots or choose "Open Dining by Reservation," whereby you can dine at different or set times each evening in the Crystal Dining Room), and two shows (the showlounge cannot seat all passengers at once). This detracts from the ship's otherwise fine setting and the professionalism of its staff. However, many older passengers do want to eat early, while the line's younger passengers prefer to dine later, so there is some balance.

All bottled water and non-alcoholic drinks are included in the price. Gratuities are at your discretion and can be pre-paid, but 15% is added to bar accounts. Note that in May 2012, *Crystal Serenity* becomes an all-inclusive ship whose fare will include all gratuities, decent wines for lunch and dinner, and bar drinks – which means no more signing or paying extra for drinks.

ACCOMMODATION. This consists of: four Crystal Penthouses with balcony; 32 Penthouse Suites with Balcony; 72 Penthouses with balcony; 78 superior outside-view cabins with balcony; 286 outside-view cabins with balcony; 84 outside-view cabins without balcony but with large picture windows. Two whole decks of accommodation are designated as suites (Deck 11, and Deck 10), while all other accommodation is located on Decks 9, 8 and 7. All suites/cabins were completely refurbished in 2011. They are now more elegant, and tasteful, and each has an electronic "Do Not Disturb" and doorbell system.

Duvets and down pillows are provided, as are lots of other niceties, including a data socket for connecting a laptop computer. All accommodation has a refrigerator and mini-bar, TV set, satellite-linked telephone, and hairdryer. There's a full range of Aveda toiletries, a plush, cotton bathrobe, and plenty of cotton towels, the largest a generous 70 by 34 inches (180 by 85cm). The in-cabin TV programming is excellent – although why it starts at Channel 53 is unclear – and close-captioned videos are provided for the hearing-impaired. The air-conditioning in bathrooms and walk-in closets is quite loud and cannot be turned off. In suites/cabins with "private" balcony, the balcony partition is of the partial, not full, type, and so noisy neighbors, particularly if using mobile phones in ports of call, can prove intrusive. The balcony decking is teak, however.

Butlers provide excellent service in all the top category suites on Decks 10 and 11, where room service food arrives on silver trays. Afternoon tea trolley service and evening hors d'oeuvres are standard fare in "butler service" suites.

Crystal Penthouses (with balcony): There are four Crystal Penthouses with private balcony (1,345 sq. ft/125 sq. meters). These are ideally located in the center of the ship on Penthouse Deck 11, each with outstanding views and large private balconies with outside lighting. There is a lounge with audio-visual entertainment center, separate master bedroom with king-sized bed and electric curtains, large walk-in closets, and large vanity desk. The marble-clad bathrooms have ocean views; they are stunning and come with a whirlpool tub with integral shower, two washbasins, separate large shower enclosure, bidet and toilet, and lots of storage space for toiletries.

Penthouse Suites (with balcony): These measure 538 sq. ft/50 sq. meters and are on Penthouse Deck 11. Each has a separate bedroom, walk-in closet and en-suite bathroom with full-size tub with integral shower, two washbasins, separate shower enclosure, bidet, toilet, and ample space for toiletries. The lounge has a large couch, coffee table and several armchairs, and there is a dining table and four chairs.

Penthouse Deck Cabin (with balcony): Located on Penthouse Decks 10 and 11, these measure 403.6 sq. ft/37.5 sq. meters. All have a private balcony, although eight located at the the aft of Deck 11 have larger balconies. They have a sleeping area that can be curtained off from the lounge area, with its large, long vanity desk. The bathroom is large, and has a full-size tub with integral shower, separate shower enclosure, and a bidet and toilet.

Superior Deluxe Outside-View Cabins (with balcony): Measuring 269 sq. ft (25 sq. meters), these really are standard outside-view cabins – but larger than standard cabins aboard most ships. Longer than cabins without a private balcony, they have a sleeping area with clothes closets, small couch, and drinks table, vanity desk with hairdryer. The bathroom has a tub with integral shower, two washbasins, and toilet. Large patio doors open onto a private balcony.

Deluxe Outside-View Cabins (with balcony): These measure 269 sq. ft (25 sq. meters). The 286 cabins, about the same size and shape as the "Deluxe" version but on a "superior" deck (Penthouse Deck 10), are longer than cabins that don't have a private balcony. They have a sleeping area with clothes closets, small couch, and drinks table, vanity desk with hairdryer. The bathroom has a tub with integral shower, two basins, and toilet. Patio doors open to a private balcony.

Deluxe Outside-View Cabins (no balcony): These are standard outside-view cabins; they are located on Deck 7, with a walk-around promenade deck outside each cabin. They measure 226 sq. ft (21 sq. meters), and have a large window, sleeping area with clothes closets, small sofa and drinks table, and vanity desk with hairdryer. The small bathroom has a tub with integral shower, two washbasins, and toilet.

Wheelchair Accessible Accommodation: This includes two penthouse grades, two cabins with balconies, and four cabins with large picture windows.

CUISINE. There is one main dining room (the *Crystal Dining Room*), two alternative, reservations-required dining rooms. The *Crystal Dining Room* is quite elegant, with a crisp, clean style that includes plenty of space around each table. It is well laid-out, and has a raised, circular central section, although it is noisy at times and not conducive to a fine dining experience. There are tables for two, many positioned adjacent to large ocean-view windows, and for four, six or eight.

The food is attractively presented on large plates, and well served, using both plate service and silver service. It is of a high standard with fine quality ingredients. European dishes are predominantly featured, but in an American style. The menus are extremely varied, and include a fine selection of meat, fish and vegetarian dishes. Off-menu orders are available, as is caviar. Kosher meals are also available (frozen when brought on board); Kosher pots, pans and utensils are sterilized in salt water, and all plates used during service are hand-washed separately.

Overall, the food is really good for the size of ship, and, with the choice of the two alternative dining spots, receives high praise. Dining is in two seatings, unless you choose "Open Dining by Reservation," whereby you can dine at different or set times each evening.

While the early seating is simply too rushed for many, with two alternative restaurants, off-menu choices, a hand-picked European staff and excellent service, dining is often memorable. Fresh pasta and dessert flambeau specialties are made at the table each day by accommodating headwaiters.

Alternative Dining Spots (reservations required, no extra charge): There are two: one Italian and one Asian. Both are aft on Deck 7, with ocean-view windows. *Prego* is for Italian food from a menu created by Piero Selvaggio, Italian wines, and service with a flair. *Silk Road* has Asian-California "fusion" food. Although there is no extra charge, a "gratuity" of $7 per person is suggested. The alternative dining spots provide an excellent standard of culinary fare with food cooked to order at no extra charge.

A separate sushi bar with counter stools is part of *Silk Road*, which serves items selected by superb Los-Angeles-based Japanese super-chef Nobuyuki "Nobu" Matsuhisa, and skillfully prepared on board by Nobu-trained chefs; the high-cost ingredients are flown regularly to the ship. To eat in a Nobu restaurants ashore costs a considerable amount; aboard the ship, this outstanding food is free.

The Bistro: Located on the upper level of the two-deck-high lobby, this is a casual spot for coffees and pastries, served in the style and atmosphere of a European street cafe. The Bistro has unusual Crystal Cruises-logo china that can be bought in one of the ship's boutiques.

Casual Eateries: For casual meals, the *Lido Café* has an extensive self-serve buffet area. It's high up in the ship, with great views from its large picture windows. For casual poolside lunches, there is also *Trident Grill*, as well as an ice cream/frozen yoghurt counter (no extra charge). A Chinese street food zone has popular favorites like steamed dumplings.

Special themed luncheon buffets, with appropriate decor and service staff dressed accordingly, are provided at the Trident indoor/outdoor pool area. These include the popular Asian Buffet and Follow the Sun (Mediterranean) buffet.

ENTERTAINMENT. The Galaxy Lounge is the ship's principal showlounge. It is quite a large room with a high ceiling, but on one level, with a nicely sloping floor, for good visibility. Indeed, the sightlines are good from almost all seats. Both banquette and individual seating is provided. The stage, lighting, and sound equipment are all excellent.

The shows are elegant, with excellent costuming (though not much in the way of scenery), but some are seriously dated, too long, and Crystal Cruises' many repeat passengers know them too well. In addition, many nights feature cabaret acts and classical artistes that are of a good caliber, and constantly changing. The bands and musical units are also, for the most part, of a high caliber, and there is plenty of music for social dancing. The ship also provides gentlemen hosts, called Ambassador Hosts, for the many single women who enjoy traveling with Crystal Cruises.

SPA/FITNESS. The Crystal Spa is located aft on Lido Deck 12, one of the ship's uppermost decks. Facilities include men's and women's changing rooms with sauna (which has a large porthole-shaped window) and steam rooms, gymnasium with high-tech muscle-pumping equipment, an aerobics exercise area, and reception/relaxation area.

Treatments are provided under the aegis of Steiner Platinum Service (Steiner being the concession). Facilities include one room dedicated to yoga and pilates classes (no extra charge), an aerobics/exercise room, plus separate sauna, steam rooms, and changing rooms for both men and women. There are seven treatment rooms (including one for couples, and one with a "dry float bed") for massage, facials, and other treatments, and a separate beauty salon.

The ship has excellent open deck and sunbathing space, and sports facilities that include two full-size paddle tennis courts, electronic golf simulator, and golf driving range. One of two outdoor swimming pools has a retractable glass dome, while the other is one of the longest aboard any ship today. Anyone trying to sunbathe quietly on the deck under and close to the paddle tennis courts will hear the noise of bat against ball when the court is in use.

THE BRIDGE

A ship's navigation bridge is manned at all times, both at sea and in port. The captain is always on call. Other senior officers take "watch" turns for four- or eight-hour periods. In addition, junior officers are continually honing their skills as experienced navigators, waiting for the day when they will be promoted to master.

The captain is always in command at times of high risk, such as when the ship is entering or leaving a port, when the density of traffic is particularly high, or when visibility is severely restricted by poor weather.

Navigation has come a long way since the days of the ancient mariners, who used only the sun and the stars to calculate their course across the oceans. The space-age development of sophisticated navigation devices (using satellites) has enabled us to eliminate the guesswork of early navigation (the first global mobile satellite system came into being in 1979).

A ship's navigator today uses a variety of sophisticated instruments to pinpoint the ship's position at any time and establish its course.

Crystal Symphony
★★★★★

Size:	.Mid-Size Ship	Total Crew:	.545	Wheelchair accessibility:	.Best
Tonnage:	.51,044	Passengers		Cabin Current:	.110 and 220 volts
Lifestyle:	.Luxury/Premium	(lower beds/all berths):	.960/1,010	Elevators:	.8
Cruise Line:	.Crystal Cruises	Passenger Space Ratio		Casino (gaming tables):	.Yes
Former Names:	.none	(lower beds/all berths):	.53.1/50.5	Slot Machines:	.Yes
Builder:	.Masa-Yards (Finland)	Crew/Passenger Ratio		Swimming Pools (outdoors):	.2
Original Cost:	.$300 million	(lower beds/all berths):	.1.7/1.8		(1 with glass dome)
Entered Service:	.Mar 1995	Cabins (total):	.480	Swimming Pools (indoors):	.0
Registry:	.The Bahamas	Size Range (sq ft/m):	.201.2–981.7/	Whirlpools:	.2
Length (ft/m):	.777.8/237.10		18.7–91.2	Self-Service Launderette:	.Yes
Beam (ft/m):	.98.0/30.20	Cabins (outside view):	.480	Dedicated Cinema/Seats:	.Yes/143
Draft (ft/m):	.24.9/7.60	Cabins (interior/no view):	.0	Library:	.Yes
Propulsion/Propellers:	.diesel-electric	Cabins (for one person):	.0	Onboard currency	.US$
	(33,880kW)/2	Cabins (with private balcony):	.276		
Passenger Decks:	.8	Cabins (wheelchair accessible):	.7		

A highly comfortable ship with elegant, refined decor.

OVERVIEW. *Crystal Symphony* is best suited to discerning adult travelers, typically over 50, who seek contemporary ship surroundings, with fine-quality fittings and furnishings, a wide range of public rooms and facilities, and excellent food and service from a well trained staff. Crystal Cruises takes care of its ships and its staff, and it is the *staff* that makes the cruise experience special. They are well-trained, stressing hospitality and service at all times.

BERLITZ'S RATINGS		
	Possible	Achieved
Ship	500	430
Accommodation	200	163
Food	400	340
Service	400	342
Entertainment	100	84
Cruise	400	342
OVERALL SCORE		
1,701 points out of 2,000		

THE SHIP. *Crystal Symphony* was given a $23 million refurbishment in 2007 that included making the main entertainment deck more contemporary. All suites/cabins received flat-screen televisions, new Murano bedside table lamps and Rubelli fabrics, and oval glass washbasins set in granite surrounds were introduced, together with a raft of other behind-the-scenes improvements that have helped bring the ship right up to date and make it more elegant.

It has just about everything for the discerning, seasoned traveler who wants and is prepared to pay good money for fine style, abundant space and the comfort and the facilities of a large vessel capable of extended voyages, including an excellent program of guest lecturers. This is announce-ment-free cruising in a well-tuned, very professionally run, service oriented, ship, the approximate equivalent of a Four Seasons hotel.

Crystal Symphony has a nicely raked clipper bow and well-balanced lines. While some might not like the "apart-ment block" look of its exterior, it is the contemporary look, balconies having become standard aboard almost all new cruise ships. This one has an excellent amount of open deck,

sunbathing space, and sports facilities. The aft of two outdoor swimming pools can be covered by a glass dome in poor weather. There is no sense of crowding anywhere – a fine example of form following function, and high-quality construction. It combines big ship facilities with the intimacy of rooms found aboard many small vessels. There is a really wide walk-around teakwood deck for walking, uncluttered by lounge chairs.

The interior decor, much of which was refreshed in 2009, is restful, with color combinations that don't jar the senses. It has a good mixture of public entertainment lounges and small inti-mate rooms. Outstanding is the Palm Court, an observation lounge with forward-facing views over the ship's bows – it is tranquil, one of the nicest rooms afloat, and larger than its equivalent aboard sister ship, *Crystal Serenity*.

There is an excellent book, video and CD-ROM library, combined with a business center. The cinema has high-definition video projection and headsets for the hearing-impaired. Useful self-service launderettes are provided on each deck. Fine-quality fabrics and soft furnishings, china, flatware and silver are used. Excellent in-cabin television programming, including CNN, is transmitted, as well as close-captioned videos for the use of the hearing-impaired.

The Connoisseurs Club, adjacent to the Avenue Saloon, serves fine premium brands of liquor and cigars for those who appreciate them. The Computer Learning Center, with more than 20 stations, is a popular venue. Private lessons are available but expensive.

The ship achieves a high rating because of its fine facil-ities, service and crew. It is the extra attention to detail that really counts. The passenger mix is approximately 85 percent North American (typically half will be from California) and 15% other nationalities.

All bottled water and (non-alcoholic) soft drinks are included in the cost of your cruise – a feature introduced with the debut of *Crystal Serenity* that has now been applied fleet-wide. Gratuities are at your discretion, but 15% is added to bar accounts. In March 2012, *Crystal Symphony* becomes an all-inclusive ship, with all gratuities to staff, decent wines for lunch and dinner, and bar drinks included – which means no more signing or paying extra for drinks.

ACCOMMODATION. There are eight categories, with the most expensive suites located on the highest accommodation deck (Deck 10). There are two Crystal Penthouses with private balcony; 18 Penthouse Suites with private balcony; 44 Penthouse Cabins with balcony; 214 Cabins with balcony; 202 Cabins without balcony. Some cabins (grades G and I) have obstructed views. Except for the suites on Deck 10, most other cabin bathrooms are very compact units.

Duvets and down pillows are provided in all cabins, as are lots of other niceties, together with a data socket for connecting a laptop computer. All accommodation has a refrigerator and mini-bar, television, satellite-linked telephone, and hairdryer. A full range of Aveda toiletries is provided, plus a plush cotton bathrobe and plenty of cotton towels, the largest of which measures a generous 70 by 34 inches (180 by 85cm). The in-cabin television programming is excellent, and close-captioned videos are provided for the hearing-impaired.

Deck 10 Penthouses: Two delightful Crystal Penthouses measure 982 sq. ft (91 sq. meters) and have a huge private balcony with outside light, a lounge with audio-visual entertainment center, separate master bedroom with king-sized bed and electric curtains, large walk-in closets, and stunning ocean-view marble bathrooms with a Philippe Stark whirlpool tub, bidet, two washbasins, and plenty of storage space for toiletries. These really are among the best in fine, private, pampered living spaces at sea, and come with all the best perks, including laundry service.

Other Deck 10 Suites: All of the other suites on this deck have plenty of space, and a private balcony with outside light. They have a lounge with large sofa, coffee table and chairs, a sleeping area and walk-in closet. Rich wood cabinetry provides much of the warmth of the decor. The bathrooms, quite large, are extremely well appointed, with full-sized tub and separate shower enclosure, two washbasins, bidet and toilet. Any of the suites on this deck have everything necessary for refined, private living at sea.

Five butlers provide the best in personal service in all the top category suites on Deck 10 (with a total of 132 beds), where room service food arrives on silver trays. Afternoon tea trolley service and evening hors d'oeuvres are standard fare in the "butler service" suites.

Decks 5/6/7/8/9: More than 50 percent of all cabins have private balconies. All are well equipped and extremely comfortable, with excellent sound insulation. The balcony partitions, however, do not go from floor to ceiling, so you can hear your neighbors. Even in the lowest category of standard cabins, there is plenty of drawer space, but the closet hanging space may prove somewhat limited for long voyages. There are generously sized personal bathroom amenities, duvets and down pillows. European stewardesses provide excellent service and attention.

CUISINE. The *Crystal Dining Room* is quite elegant, with crisp design, plenty of space around each table, and well-placed waiter service stations. Well laid out, it has a raised, circular central section, although it is somewhat noisy at times and not conducive to a fine dining experience. There are tables for two (many adjacent to large windows), four, six or eight. For a detailed review of its food and ambience, see the entry for *Crystal Serenity*. There are two seatings, or you can choose "Open Dining by Reservation" to eat at a reserved table at different or set times each evening.

While afternoon tea in the *Palm Court* is a civilized daily event, *The Lido* provides breakfast and luncheon buffets that are fairly standard fare.

Alternative Dining Spots (reservations required, no extra charge): Two alternative dining spots are the 75-seat *Prego*, serving fine Italian cuisine created by Piero Selvaggio, with good Italian wines; and the 100-seat combination *Silk Road Restaurant* and *Sushi Bar*, with Nobu Matsuhisa-trained chefs. For further details of these and casual spots such as *The Bistro* and *Trident Grill*, see the entry for *Crystal Serenity*.

ENTERTAINMENT. The Galaxy Lounge is quite large, with a high ceiling, but it's on one level with a tiered floor, for good visibility. A few pillars obstruct sight lines from some seats. Both banquette and individual seating is provided. The stage, lighting, and sound equipment are all excellent.

The shows are elegant, with excellent costuming and scenery, but they are seriously dated, too long, and too familiar to Crystal Cruises' many repeat passengers. In addition, many nights feature cabaret acts that are of a good caliber, and constantly changing. The bands and musical units are also, for the most part, good, and there is plenty of music for social dancing. The ship also provides male hosts (called Ambassador Hosts) for single women passengers.

SPA/FITNESS. Facilities include one room dedicated to yoga and pilates classes (no extra charge), an aerobics/exercise room, plus sauna, steam rooms, and changing rooms for both men and women. There are seven treatment rooms (including one for couples, and one room featuring a "dry float bed") for various types of massage, facials, and other treatments, as well as a separate beauty salon.

For full details of treatments and sports facilities, see the entry for *Crystal Serenity* on page 339.

Dawn Princess
★★★★

Size:	Large Resort Ship	Passenger Decks:	10	Cabins (with private balcony):	446
Tonnage:	77,499	Total Crew:	900	Cabins (wheelchair accessible):	19
Lifestyle:	Standard	Passengers		Wheelchair accessibility:	Good
Cruise Line:	Princess Cruises	(lower beds/all berths):	1,950/2,250	Cabin Current:	110 and 220 volts
Former Names:	none	Passenger Space Ratio		Elevators:	11
Builder:	Fincantieri (Italy)	(lower beds/all berths):	39.7/34.4	Casino (gaming tables):	Yes
Original Cost:	$300 million	Crew/Passenger Ratio		Slot Machines:	Yes
Entered Service:	May 1997	(lower beds/all berths):	2.1/2.5	Swimming Pools (outdoors):	4
Registry:	Great Britain	Cabins (total):	975	Swimming Pools (indoors):	0
Length (ft/m):	857.2/261.3	Size Range (sq ft/m):	135.0–635.0/	Whirlpools:	5
Beam (ft/m):	105.6/32.2		12.5–59.0	Self-Service Launderette:	Yes
Draft (ft/m):	26.5/8.1	Cabins (outside view):	603	Dedicated Cinema/Seats:	No
Propulsion/Propellers:	diesel-electric	Cabins (interior/no view):	372	Library:	Yes
	(46,080kW)/2	Cabins (for one person):	0	Onboard currency:	US$

A large ship with warm decor for mature-age cruisers.

OVERVIEW. *Dawn Princess*, like sister ship *Sun Princess*, is dedicated to the Australian cruise region. As aboard most large ships, if you live in the top suites, you'll be well cared for; if not, you'll just be one of a large number of passengers. The collection of artwork is good, particularly on the stairways, and helps make the ship feel smaller than it is, although in places it doesn't always seem coordinated.

THE SHIP. *Dawn Princess*, an all-white ship, has a decent contemporary profile balanced by a large funnel containing a deck tennis/basketball/volleyball court in its sheltered aft base. There is a wide, teak walk-around promenade deck outdoors, some real teak steamer-style deck chairs complete with royal blue cushioned pads, and 93,000 sq. ft (8,640 sq. meters) of space outdoors. A great amount of glass area on the upper decks provides plenty of light and connection with the outside world. There's a large poolside movie screen and an adults-only Sanctuary relaxation area.

The interiors are pretty and warm, with attractive colors and the welcoming decor includes some attractive wall murals and other artwork. The signage could be better, however. There are a number of dead ends in the interior layout, so it's not as user-friendly as a ship this size could be. The cabin numbering system is illogical, with numbers going through several hundred series on the same deck.

The wide range of public rooms includes several intimate rooms so that you don't get the feel of being overwhelmed by large spaces. The interior focal point is a four-deck-high atrium lobby with winding, double stairways, and two panoramic glass-walled elevators.

BERLITZ'S RATINGS		
	Possible	Achieved
Ship	500	422
Accommodation	200	161
Food	400	266
Service	400	291
Entertainment	100	86
Cruise	400	301

OVERALL SCORE
1,527 points out of 2,000

There are two showlounges, one at each end of the ship; one is a 550-seat, theater-style showlounge that also screens movies, and the other is a 480-seat cabaret-style lounge, with bar.

The library, a warm room with ocean-view windows, has six large butter-colored leather chairs for listening to audio discs. There is a conference center for up to 300, as well as a business center with computers and copiers. The casino, while large, is not really in the main passenger flow and so doesn't generate the "walk-through" factor found aboard so many ships.

The most traditional room is the Wheelhouse Lounge/Bar, decorated in the style of a late 19th-century gentleman's club, with wood paneling and comfortable seating. The focal point is a large ship model, *Kenya,* from the P&O collection archives.

The captain's cocktail party is typically held in the four-deck-high main atrium so that you can come and go as you please without having to stand in line to have your photograph taken with the captain. However, cruising aboard large ships such as this one has become increasingly an onboard revenue-based product. In-your-face art auctions are overbearing, and the paintings, lithographs and framed pictures strewn throughout the ship clash irritatingly with the interior decor. This is an annoying intrusion into what should be a vacation, not a cruise inside a floating "art" emporium. Also, bazaar-like tables filled with trinket junk clutter the area outside the shops.

The swimming pools are small, given the number of passengers, and the pool deck is cluttered with white, plastic sunloungers, without cushioned pads. Waiting for tenders in anchor ports can prove irritating, but is typical of large ship operations. Charging for use of the machines and washing powder in the self-service launderette is trifling.

ACCOMMODATION. The brochure shows that there are 28 different cabin grades: 20 outside-view and eight interior cabins. Although the standard cabins are a little small, they are well designed and functional in layout, and have earth tone colors accentuated by splashes of color from the bedspreads. Proportionately, there are quite a lot of interior cabins. Many outside-view cabins have private balconies, and all seem to be quite well soundproofed, although the balcony partition is not the floor-to-ceiling type, so you can hear your neighbors clearly, or smell their smoke. The balconies are very narrow, only just large enough for two small chairs, and there is no dedicated lighting.

All cabins have a reasonable amount of closet and abundant drawer and other storage space – adequate for a seven-night cruise – plus a TV set and refrigerator. The bathrooms are practical, although they really are tight spaces, best described as one person at-a-time units. But they do have a decent shower enclosure, a small amount of shelving for toiletries, real glasses, a hairdryer and a bathrobe.

The largest accommodation is in six suites, two on each of three decks located at the stern, and measure 536–754 sq.ft (49.8–21.3 sq.meters), including large private balcony). They are well laid out, and have large bathrooms with two washbasins, a Jacuzzi tub, and a separate shower enclosure. The bedroom has generous amounts of wood accenting and detailing, indented ceilings, and TV sets in both bedroom and lounge areas. The suites also have a dining room table and four chairs.

The 32 mini-suites (374–536 sq.ft/34.7–49.7 sq.meters) typically have two lower beds that convert to a queen-sized bed. There is a separate bedroom/sleeping area with vanity desk, and a lounge with sofa and coffee table, indented ceilings with generous amounts of wood accenting and detailing, walk-in closet, and larger bathroom with Jacuzzi bathtub and separate shower enclosure.

There are 19 wheelchair-accessible cabins, which measure 213–305 sq. meters (19.7–28.2 sq.ft) and are a mix of seven outside view and 12 interior cabins.

CUISINE. There are two main dining rooms of asymmetrical design, *Florentine* and *Venetian*, each with about 500 seats. They are located adjacent to the two lower levels of the atrium lobby. Each has its own galley and each is split into multi-tier sections, which help create a feeling of intimacy, although there is a lot of noise from the waiter stations adjacent to many tables. Breakfast and lunch are provided in an open-seating arrangement, while dinner is in two seatings. The wine list is reasonable, but not good, and there are no wine waiters. Note that 15% is added to all beverage bills, including wines.

The *Horizon Buffet* is open 24 hours a day, and, at night, has an informal dinner setting with sit-down waiter service; a small bistro menu is also available. The buffet displays are, for the most part, quite repetitious, but better than they have been in the past. There is no real finesse in presentation, however, as oval plastic plates are provided, instead of trays. The cabin service menu is very limited, and presentation of the food items featured is poor.

For some good meat, try the *Sterling Steakhouse*; it's for those who want to taste four different cuts of Angus beef from the popular "Sterling Silver" brand of USDA prime meats – Filet Mignon, New York Strip, Porterhouse, and Rib-Eye – all presented on a silver tray. There is also a barbecue chicken option, plus the usual baked potato or French fries as accompaniments. This is available as an alternative to the dining rooms, between 6.30pm and 9.30pm only, at extra cost. However, it is not, as you might expect, a separate, intimate dining room, but is located in a section of the Horizon Buffet, with its own portable bar and some decorative touches to set it apart from the regular buffet.

There is also a patisserie for cappuccino/espresso coffees and pastries, a wine/caviar bar, and a pizzeria with cobblestone floors, wrought-iron decorative features, and a choice of six excellent pizzas.

ENTERTAINMENT. There are two showlounges, both theatre and cabaret style. The main one, Princess Theater, has a sloping floor, with aisle-style seating (as found in shoreside movie theaters) that is well tiered, and with good sight lines to the raised stage from most of the 500 seats.

The second showlounge, Vista Lounge, located at the aft end of the ship, has cabaret entertainment, and also acts as a lecture and presentation room. Princess Cruises has a good stable of regular cabaret acts to draw from, so there should be something for most tastes.

SPA/FITNESS. A glass-walled health spa complex located high atop the ship includes a gymnasium with the latest high-tech machines. One swimming pool is "suspended" aft between two decks. There are two other pools, although they are not large for the size of the ship.

Sports facilities are located in an open-air sports deck positioned inside the funnel and adaptable for basketball, volleyball, badminton or paddle tennis. Joggers can exercise on the walk-around open Promenade Deck.

● **For more extensive general information about the Princess Cruises experience, see pages 149–52.**

Deutschland
NOT RATED

Size: ....Small Ship	Passenger Decks: 7	Cabins (with private balcony): 2
Tonnage: 22,400	Total Crew: 270	Cabins (wheelchair accessible): 1
Lifestyle: ....Premium	Passengers	Wheelchair accessibility: ....Fair
Cruise Line: ....Peter Deilmann Reederei	(lower beds/all berths): 548/560	Cabin Current: ....230 volts
Former Names: ....none	Passenger Space Ratio	Elevators: 3
Builder: ...Howaldswerke Deutsche Werft	(lower beds/all berths): 40.8/40.0	Casino (gaming tables): ....No
Original Cost: ....DM 212 million	Crew/Passenger Ratio	Slot Machines: ....No
Entered Service: ....May 1998	(lower beds/all berths): 2.0/2.0	Swimming Pools (outdoors): 1
Registry: ....Germany	Cabins (total): 294	Swimming Pools (indoors): 1
Length (ft/m): 574.1/175.0	Size Range (sq ft/m): 129.1–365.9/	Whirlpools: 0
Beam (ft/m): 75.4/23.0	12.0–34.0	Self-Service Launderette: ....No
Draft (ft/m): 19.0/5.8	Cabins (outside view): 220	Dedicated Cinema/Seats: Yes/83
Propulsion/Propellers: ....diesel	Cabins (interior/no view): 74	Library: ....Yes
(12,300 kW)/2	Cabins (for one person): 36	Onboard currency ....Euros

A crowded ship with a heavily traditional Germanic style.

OVERVIEW. *Deutschland* is best suited to German-speaking couples and single travelers of mature years looking for a very traditional cruise ship with appealing itineraries and destinations, good food and attentive service. It could also appeal to English-speaking travelers used to being in European surroundings. The entertainment is almost totally in German, and the whole ship is geared almost exclusively to German tastes.

BERLITZ'S RATINGS		
	Possible	Achieved
Ship	500	NYR
Accommodation	200	NYR
Food	400	NYR
Service	400	NYR
Entertainment	100	NYR
Cruise	400	NYR

THE SHIP. *Deutschland,* now over 13 years old but in fine condition, has an angular, low-in-the-water profile that is not particularly handsome, and a large, single, squat, traditional funnel. The ship, built in sections by four shipyards, was assembled in Kiel, Germany. It is well maintained and kept very clean.

Although there is no walk-around promenade deck outdoors as such – it's full of chairs around the central section where a swimming pool is located – you can walk along some of the open space, although there are windbreakers to negotiate. There are also port and starboard mid-ship walking decks under the inboard lifeboats. There is a decent amount of open deck and sunbathing space for a ship of this size, including three aft decks for open-air lovers, and real teakwood deck chairs with thick royal blue cushioned pads.

The Lido Deck has sides covered by canvas shading and white support pillars – like the ones you would find on seaside piers in England – as a setting for the outdoor swimming pool. This is a self-contained deck that has not only the pool but also the casual Lido Buffet restaurant and Lido Terrasse Café. One could spend all day outdoors on this deck without having to dress to go indoors to eat. There is also a small waterfall aft of the pool.

The ship is laid out in a classic symmetrical pattern, and the interior decor has been successfully designed to recreate the atmosphere of 1920s ocean liners. The ship is finely decorated throughout (some might say overly so), with rich, dark woods and intricate brass and wrought-iron staircases that remind one of what were once called "gentlemen's clubs." There is so much detail in the decoration work, and especially in the ornate ceilings, and cleaning it all is rather labor-intensive. There are quite a number of real statues, which don't seem to fit well aboard a cruise ship, but there are also many works of art on display.

There's a good range of public rooms and spaces, although these have been possible only by making the cabins smaller than one would expect of a ship of this size. The ship has an interesting, eclectic decor from different periods, as well as a wide assortment of cabin sizes, configurations and grades.

There are two favorite drinking places: Zum Alten Fritz (Old Fritz) Bar, with dark wood interiors and belle-époque ambience; and the Lili Marleen Salon, adjacent to this Berlin Restaurant, with mahogany channeled ceiling. Another nice public room is the Lido Terrace, which would have made a superb observation lounge had the designers extended it to the forward extremes of the deck. It is reminiscent of the winter gardens aboard the early transatlantic liners, and a delightful place to read or take afternoon tea.

The late Peter Deilmann's personal touch in the heavily detailed interiors is evident everywhere. *Deutschland* is registered under the German flag, but is actually placed under a second German register that allows for the employment of many non-German staff. Thus, you will find Filipinos and other nationalities in the hotel service areas. The friendliness of the staff is good. The ship operates cashless cruising – charges must be settled on the last day of the cruise, when all purchases must, inconveniently, be made in cash.

Although the ship absorbs passengers well, the space ratio could be better. The onboard product is generally sound, with attentive service, but the food and catering side of the operation could be improved. While the interiors are very attractive, the vessel does not come close to ships such as *Europa, Silver Shadow*, and *Silver Whisper*, with their much larger suites/cabins, open-seating dining (except *Europa*, which has open seating for breakfast and lunch, and assigned tables for dinner), and their abundance of cabins with private balconies. Smoking is permitted only on open decks. There is no internet center.

Just two suites have private balconies; most other cabins are very small when compared to other ships in the luxury and premium sectors of the international market.

ACCOMMODATION. There are 10 categories (the higher the deck, the higher the cost). There are 18 outside view suites, 189 outside view doubles, 17 outside view single cabins; 12 interior doubles, and 50 interior single cabins.

While many cabins are disappointingly small, all are furnished in fancy bird's-eye maple, and all ceilings are one-piece units, unlike the metal strip ceilings of most cruise ships, and come with molded coving and ornamentation. The closet and drawer space is quite generous, and the attention to detail is very good. All beds have duvets and pillows. All cabins have a TV set, direct-dial satellite telephone, mini-bar/refrigerator, and real cabin keys (not plastic cards) are provided. Many cabins have only one electrical outlet.

The bathrooms are also generously appointed, with a pink marble sink, gold anodized fittings, gilt-edged mirrors, hairdryer, and ample space for one's toiletries. There is an electrical power outlet for shavers, with both 110 and 230 volts. Bathrobes are provided for all passengers.

Accommodations designated as suites (of which there are two grades) are reasonably large, with a living area that contains a couch, coffee table and two chairs; the bathroom has a full-size tub (all other cabins have showers only). Only the Executive Suites and Owner's Suites are, sensibly, located in the center of the ship, and each has a small private balcony. There is one wheelchair-accessible cabin (8042).

CUISINE. *Berlin*, the 300-seat main restaurant, is a homely room. All the chairs have armrests, although space for serving at window-side tables is limited, and the hard chair-backs are not really very comfortable.

There are tables for two, four, six or eight, and two seatings for dinner. Two cold buffet bars for cold cuts of meat, cheese and salad items – either your waiter can obtain the food for you or you can choose it yourself – are featured for breakfast and lunch. Overall, the cuisine is quite creative, with lots of courses, small portions of nouvelle cuisine, and a wide variety of choice and good taste. It's not really memorable, though the desserts are extremely good. The place settings are extensive.

The *Restaurant Vierjahreszeiten* (Four Seasons), with 104 seats, is an intimate dining room, principally for suite occupants and for à la carte dining, for which a reservation is necessary. There is much detailing and ornamentation in the decor, and the ornate ceiling lamps and indented ceiling coving create an elegant ambience that is relatively intimate. There are tables for two, four or six.

There is also a small private dining room, the *Chancellor Room*, with a large oval table seating 10–12 – ideal for special occasions and celebrations.

The extensive wine list includes a fine selection of wines from Germany and Austria, although the choice of wines from other countries is very limited. Eating in this restaurant takes considerably longer than in the Berlin Restaurant, and is best for those seeking an evening of fine dining and conversation.

The *Lido Restaurant* is a casual dining venue. It has large ocean-view windows on two sides and a centrally located, multi-section self-serve buffet station. Additionally, there is a *Lido Terrasse*, at the stern, with windows on three sides. It is set on two slightly different levels, houses the ship's library, and has statuary and a relaxing, garden conservatory-like setting. This room also has a bar, plus elegant tea and coffee service.

ENTERTAINMENT. The Kaisersaal (Emperor's Saloon) is the main showlounge. It is a galleried period room with red velveteen chairs and is more like a ballroom than showlounge. It is reminiscent of a small opera house, and has a beautiful, huge central chandelier. However, sight lines are obstructed from some seats on both upper and lower seating levels by many large marble-effect pillars. The entertainment is geared to German tastes, and is mostly in German.

SPA/FITNESS. The main spa area is on Deck 3, and this includes a small indoor swimming pool with a statue of a female diver at one end, sauna, solarium, thalassotherapy baths, and massage/body therapy rooms; there is also a dialysis station. Deck 6 has a fitness/sport center with a few exercise machines, a sauna with a sea view, and a steam room. A beauty salon is on Deck 7.

Diamond Princess
★★★★

Size:	Large Resort Ship	Passenger Decks:	.13	Cabins (wheelchair accessible):	.28
Tonnage:	.115,875	Total Crew:	.1,238		(18 outside/10 interior)
Lifestyle:	Standard	Passengers		Wheelchair accessibility:	Good
Cruise Line:	Princess Cruises	(lower beds/all berths):	.2,674/3,100	Cabin Current:	.110 volts
Former Names:	none	Passenger Space Ratio		Elevators:	.14
Builder: Mitsubishi Heavy Industries (Japan)		(lower beds/all berths):	.43.3/37.3	Casino (gaming tables):	Yes
Original Cost:	.$400 million	Crew/Passenger Ratio		Slot Machines:	Yes
Entered Service:	Feb 2004	(lower beds/all berths):	.2.1/2.5	Swimming Pools (outdoors):	.4
Registry:	Bermuda	Cabins (total):	.1,337	Swimming Pools (indoors):	.0
Length (ft/m):	.951.4/290.00	Size Range (sq ft/m):	.168–1,329.3/	Whirlpools:	.9
Beam (ft/m):	.123.0/37.50		15.6–123.5	Self-Service Launderette:	Yes
Draft (ft/m):	.26.4/8.05	Cabins (outside view):	.1,000	Dedicated Cinema/Seats:	No
Propulsion/Propellers:	gas turbine	Cabins (interior/no view):	.337	Library:	Yes
	(25 MW)/2 azimuthing pods	Cabins (for one person):	.0	Onboard currency	.US$
	(21,000 kW each)	Cabins (with private balcony):	.750		

A large ship with bland decor, for mature-age cruisers.

OVERVIEW. If you are not used to large ships, it will take you some time to find your way around this one, despite the company's claim that this vessel offers passengers a "small ship feel, big ship choice." The passenger flow has been well thought out, and works with little congestion. The decor is attractive, with lots of earth tones. An extensive collection of art works complements the interior design and colors well.

THE SHIP. *Diamond Princess,* sister to *Sapphire Princess,* has an instantly recognizable funnel due to two jet engine-like pods that sit high up on its structure but really are mainly for decoration. It is the first of the "Grand Class" ships to have a "pod" propulsion system *(details, page 191).* Electrical power is provided by a combination of four diesel and one gas turbine (CODAG) unit; the diesel engines are located in the engine room, while the gas turbine unit is located in the ship's funnel housing.

Four areas focus on swimming pools; one of these is two decks high and is covered by a retractable glass dome, itself an extension of the funnel housing.

There is plenty of space inside the ship – but there are also plenty of passengers – and a wide array of public rooms, with many "intimate" (this being a relative word) spaces and places to enjoy. A Wedding Chapel has a webcam that can relay ceremonies via the internet. The ship's captain can legally marry American couples, due to the ship's Bermuda registry and a special dispensation (which should be verified when in the planning stage, according to where you reside). Princess Cruises offers three wedding packages – Pearl, Emerald, Diamond; the fee includes reg-

BERLITZ'S RATINGS

	Possible	Achieved
Ship	500	431
Accommodation	200	168
Food	400	256
Service	400	293
Entertainment	100	82
Cruise	400	314

OVERALL SCORE
1,544 points out of 2,000

istration and official marriage certificate. The "Hearts & Minds" chapel is useful for "renewal of vows" ceremonies.

The large Grand Casino has more than 260 slot machines; there are blackjack, craps and roulette tables, plus several newer table games. Linked slot machines provide a combined payout.

Other facilities include a library/computer room and a card room. Ship lovers should enjoy the wood-paneled Wheelhouse Bar, housing memorabilia and ship models tracing part of parent company P&O's history. Aft of the International Dining Room is the Wake View Bar, with a spiral stairway leading down to a great viewing spot for those who want to watch the ship's wake; it is reached from the back of Club Fusion, on Promenade Deck. Skywalkers Nightclub is set around the base of the funnel structure and has a view overlooking the aft-facing cascading decks and children's pool.

A high-tech hospital has live SeaMed tele-medicine linkups with specialists at the Cedars-Sinai Medical Center in Los Angeles available for emergency help.

The bath towels are small, and drawer space is limited. Even top grade suites are not really large in comparison to similar suites aboard some other ships. Cabin attendants have too many cabins to look after (typically 20), which does not translate to fine personal service.

There are many extra-charge items such as ice cream, and freshly squeezed orange juice. There's an hourly charge for group babysitting services and a charge for using the washers and dryers in the self-service launderettes.

FAMILIES. There is a two-deck-high playroom, teen room,

and a host of specially trained counselors. Children have their own pools, hot tubs, and open deck area at the stern of the ship (away from adult areas).

ACCOMMODATION. All passengers receive turndown service and chocolates on pillows each night, as well as bathrobes on request and toiletry kits (larger for suite/mini-suite occupants). A hairdryer is sensibly located at the vanity desk unit in the living area. The tiled bathrooms have a decent amount of open shelf storage space for toiletries. Princess Cruises has BBC World, CNN, CNBC, ESPN and TNT on the in-cabin TV system (when available, depending on cruise area).

Many outside cabins on Emerald Deck have views obstructed by the lifeboats. There are no cabins for singles. Your name is typically placed outside your suite or cabin – making it simple for delivery service personnel but limiting your privacy. There is 24-hour room service, but some items on the room service menu are not available during early morning hours. Most balcony suites and cabins can be overlooked both from the navigation bridge wing. Cabins with balconies on Baja, Caribe, and Dolphin decks are also overlooked by passengers on balconies on the deck above.

CUISINE. There are five principal dining rooms with themed decor and cuisine – *International* (the largest, located aft, with two seatings and "traditional" cuisine), *Sterling Steakhouse* for steak and grilled meats, *Vivaldi* for Italian fare, *Santa Fe* for southwestern USA cuisine, and *Pacific Moon* for Asian cuisine. These offer a mix of two seatings, with seating assigned according to your cabin location, and "anytime dining," where you choose when and with whom you want to eat.

All dining rooms are split into sections in a non-symmetrical design that breaks what are quite large spaces into many smaller sections, for better ambience and less noise pollution. Specially designed dinnerware and good quality linens and silverware are featured: Dudson of England (dinnerware), Frette Egyptian cotton table linens, and silverware by Hepp of Germany.

Alternative dining options: *Sabatini's* is an informal eatery (reservations needed; cover charge). It serves an eight-course meal, including Italian-style pizzas and pastas, with a variety of sauces, as well as Italian-style entrées, all provided with flair and entertainment by the waiters. The cuisine here is better than in the other dining rooms, with better quality ingredients and more attention to presentation, taste and delivery.

A poolside hamburger grill and pizza bar (no additional charge) are additional dining spots for casual bites, while extra charges will apply if you order items to eat at either the coffee bar/patisserie, or the caviar/champagne bar.

Other casual meals can be taken in the *Horizon Court*, open 24 hours a day, with large ocean-view on port and starboard sides and direct access to the two main swimming pools and lido deck. There is no finesse in presentation, however, and plastic plates, not trays, are provided.

ENTERTAINMENT. The Princess Theatre spans two decks and has comfortable seating on both main and balcony levels. It has $3 million in sound and light equipment, plus a nine-piece orchestra.

A second large entertainment lounge, Club Fusion, presents cabaret acts acts at night, and lectures, bingo and horse racing during the day. A third entertainment lounge can also host cabaret acts and dance bands. Many other lounges and bars have live music, and a number of male dance hosts act as partners for women traveling alone.

SPA/FITNESS. The Lotus Spa complex, with Japanese-style decor, surrounds one of the swimming pools – you can have a massage or other spa treatment in an ocean-view treatment room. Lotus Spa treatments include Chakra hot stone massage, Asian Lotus ritual (featuring massage with reflexology, reiki and shiatsu massage), deep-tissue sports therapy massage, lime and ginger salt glow, wild strawberry back cleanse, and seaweed mud wraps.

Activities such as yoga, group exercise bicycling and kick boxing classes cost extra.

● **For more extensive general information about the Princess Cruises experience is like, see pages 149–52.**

Discovery
★★★

Size: ....Mid-Size Ship	Passenger Decks: 8	Cabins (with private balcony): 0
Tonnage: 21,186	Total Crew: 350	Cabins (wheelchair accessible): 2
Lifestyle: ....Standard	Passengers	Wheelchair accessibility: ....Fair
Cruise Line: ....Voyages of Discovery	(lower beds/all berths): 710/796	Cabin Current: ....110 and 220 volts
Former Names: .Platinum, Hyundai Pungak,	Passenger Space Ratio	Elevators: 4
Island Princess, Island Venture	(lower beds/all berths): 29.8/26.6	Casino (gaming tables): ....Yes
Builder: Rheinstahl Nordseewerke (Germany)	Crew/Passenger Ratio	Slot Machines: ....Yes
Original Cost: ....$25 million	(lower beds/all berths): 2.4/2.6	Swimming Pools (outdoors): 2
Entered Service: ......Feb 1972/May 2003	Cabins (total): 355	Swimming Pools (indoors): 0
Registry: ....Bermuda	Size Range (sq ft/m): 125.9–441.3/	Whirlpools: 2
Length (ft/m): 553.6/168.74	11.7–41.0	Self-Service Launderette: ....No
Beam (ft/m): 80.7/24.6	Cabins (outside view): 283	Dedicated Cinema/Seats: Yes/129
Draft (ft/m): 25.2/7.7	Cabins (interior/no view): 72	Library: ....Yes
Propulsion/Propellers: diesel (13,400 kW)/2	Cabins (for one person): 0	Onboard currency ....UK£

Sedate, tired decor lets down an otherwise comfortable ship.

OVERVIEW. The ship, well maintained and quite elegant, provides comfortable surroundings for older passengers who want plenty of space but don't want to be part of larger, more impersonal ships. It has limited entertainment and a casual dress code, but offers some interesting destinations. The decor is tasteful, with pastel colors and artwork that is pleasing to the eye, if a little bland.

THE SHIP. *Discovery*, operated from 1972 to 1999 by Princess Cruises, has a very attractive traditional ship profile and well balanced, somewhat rounded exterior styling. As the former *Island Princess*, it was, with *Pacific Princess* (presently *Pacific*), one of the pair of original stars in the American TV series *The Love Boat*. Hyundai Asan Cruises acquired it in 1999, and operated cruises from South Korea to North Korea.

In 2001, the entrepreneur Gerry Herrod, founder of the long defunct Ocean Cruise Lines and Orient Lines, bought the handsome ship and provided it under a lease-purchase scheme to Voyages of Discovery, part of the UK's All-Leisure Group. He then spent $10 million refurbishing it for its present role under the brand name of Voyages of Discovery, mainly for the British market. For the winter season, the ship carries five Zodiac inflatable shore landing craft.

One of its two outdoor swimming pools has a glass dome cover, useful in inclement weather conditions. There is no walk-around promenade deck outdoors, however.

Inside, the public areas are quite spacious considering the ship's size, and there are numerous public rooms (some with high ceilings), with reasonably wide passageways. These include a lobby with mezzanine level and curved staircase (several shops and offices are on the upper level).

BERLITZ'S RATINGS

	Possible	Achieved
Ship	500	232
Accommodation	200	102
Food	400	275
Service	400	253
Entertainment	100	44
Cruise	400	205

OVERALL SCORE
1,111 points out of 2,000

The Discovery Lounge, located aft, has a two-deck high glass wall overlooking the aft deck. There's an internet center with six computers, a library with 5,000 books provided by the Marine Society, and bridge players have tables in the Palm Court. There's a very small "casino." The forward observation lounge is also an indoor dining area.

Specialist concessions run the hotel operations, dining, spa/beauty services, and shops. A self-serve launderette or ironing room (missed by many British passengers) would be a useful addition. Niggles include the tacky plastic flowers, particularly in the dining room, and the tired appearance of parts of the ship, which has probably passed its sell-by date. All gratuities are included.

ACCOMMODATION. There are 15 price categories – a lot for a mid-sized ship. There are five suites; these are of quite a decent size, and well designed, with plenty of space to move around in. Two are located forward, just under the navigation bridge, and command good views.

Most other cabins have ample room, are quite well appointed, and there is sufficient storage space. The top category cabins (on Bridge Deck and Promenade Deck) have a full bathtub, while all others have a shower enclosure. Many have obstructed views. There are no private balconies – the ship was built before these came into vogue.

All cabins and suites have a TV set, telephone, personal safe and hairdryer. Some cabins have interconnecting doors, and some can accommodate a third/fourth person. But some have an "L" bed configuration, and the beds are rather narrow, at 30 inches (76 cm). Also, the small TV sets may be positioned too high for watching movies comfortably.

CUISINE. The *Seven Continents Dining Room* is a dated, 1970s-style space with a low ceiling and a slightly sunken center section. There are two seatings for dinner, but few tables for two, most being for four, six or eight people. Many chairs have very low backs. There are separate tables as well as banquette seating, but the banquette seating is hard and uncomfortable, canteen style, and waiters need to reach over to serve and clear dishes.

The cuisine includes many classic British favorites, and the presentation and service are good. The wine list is adequate and prices are reasonable, although the selection is small and most are young wines.

Casual breakfasts and lunches can be taken in the Yacht Club, an observation lounge with fine ocean views on three sides, or outdoors on the Lido Deck, adjacent to the swimming pool.

Alternative (Reservations Only) Dining Option: Alternative dinners can also be taken in the *Yacht Club*, with its observation lounge views on three sides, adjacent to the Lido; Continental and Italian specialties are served, and there is no cover charge. A late-riser's breakfast is always popular; you can also opt for Continental Breakfast to be served in your cabin if you wish.

ENTERTAINMENT. The "theater-in-the-round" Carousel Showlounge has banquette-style seating in several tiers, set around a "thrust" stage. The entertainment is low-key, which means only the occasional cabaret act is featured. There is live music throughout the ship for dancing.

SPA/FITNESS. The Spa Atlantis is positioned aft on two of the uppermost decks (a stairway connects the two). A beauty salon is on the upper deck, while a gymnasium with aft-facing ocean-view windows, three treatment rooms, and male and female saunas are on the lower level. It is operated by a UK-based concession, Harding Brothers, and has products from Guinot and Thalgo. Staff often try to sell beauty products forcefully.

WHERE NAUTICAL EXPRESSIONS COME FROM

If you've ever wondered where some terms or phrases came from, you have only to look to the sea, ships, and seamen.

Scuttlebutt

A small drinking ladle with scuttles or holes in it to discourage sailors from idle chit chat (scuttlebutt) around the water barrel while their water ration dribbled back into the barrel. Today it usually refers to gossip or the latest news concerning a given situation or person.

Shape up

A helmsman working off a lee shore would point up and "shape up" to his course in order to avoid danger. In modern-day usage it is used similar in sense to mean "smarten up" or "pull yourself together."

Showing your true colors

Early warships often carried flags from many nations on board in order to elude or deceive the enemy. The rules of civilized warfare called for all ships to hoist their true national ensigns before firing a shot. Someone who finally "shows his true colors" is acting like a warship, which hails another ship flying one flag, but then hoisted its own flag when the vessel got within firing range.

Skyscraper

A small, triangular shaped sail that was set above the mains on the old square-riggers to try to scrape (catch) more wind in areas of calm air. The term came ashore to represent anything that was tall enough to "scrape" the sky.

Slush fund

The fat obtained by "scraping the bottom of the barrel" by the ship's cook and secreted away in his "slush fund" for selling ashore to candle makers, tanneries, etc. Today the words describe a rainy-day fund or cash reserve. Another version of the term's derivation is that the grease (slush) from frying the salt pork on a voyage was kept and sold when the ship returned to port. The money raised was put into a "fund" for the crew.

Disney Dream
★★★★+
Disney Fantasy
NOT YET RATED

Size:	Large Resort Ship	Passenger Decks:	14	Cabins (wheelchair accessible):	37
Tonnage:	129,690	Total Crew:	1,458	Wheelchair accessibility:	Good
Lifestyle:	Standard	Passengers		Cabin Current:	110 volts
Cruise Line:	Disney Cruise Line	(lower beds/all berths):	2,500/5,007	Elevators:	14
Former Names:	none	Passenger Space Ratio		Casino (gaming tables):	No
Builder:	Meyer Werft (Germany)	(lower beds/all berths):	51.8/47.8	Slot Machines:	No
Original Cost:	€600 million	Crew/Passenger Ratio		Swimming Pools (outdoors):	3
Entered Service:	Jan 2011 (Dream)	(lower beds/all berths):	1.7/3.4	Swimming Pools (indoors):	0
	Apr 2012 (Fantasy)	Cabins (total):	1,250	Whirlpools:	4
Registry:	The Bahamas	Size Range (sq ft/m):	169–1,781/	Self-Service Launderette:	No
Length (ft/m):	1,113.8/339.5		15.7–165.5	Dedicated Cinema/Seats:	No
Beam (ft/m):	120.7/36.8 6.8	Cabins (outside view):	1,100	Library:	No
Draft (ft/m):	26.0 /7.93	Cabins (interior/no view):	150	Onboard currency	US$
Propulsion/Propellers:	diesel-electric	Cabins (for one person):	0		
	(72,000kW)/2	Cabins (with private balcony):	901		

The ultimate family-friendly floating theme park.

OVERVIEW. *Disney Dream* and *Disney Fantasy* are ideal for families with children or grandchildren. Couples and singles are also welcome, though there are few activities for couples in the daytime, but enough entertainment at night. You will, however, need to be a real Disney fan, as everything revolves around Disney characters and the family theme.

THE SHIP. Mickey's dream ship has grown up. Made of pieces of steel and pixie dust, these ships' exteriors are about 40% larger than the first two Disney ships, *Disney Magic* and *Disney Wonder*. They also have two extra decks, although the design is similar – a tribute to the grand ocean liners of the 1930s. Like all Disney ships, there are two large funnels. The bows have handsome gold scrollwork more typically seen adorning yesteryear's tall ships, and the exterior colors are also those of Mickey himself: red, white, yellow and black. Even the lifeboats are yellow, not orange, by special dispensation.

A 765-ft (233-meter) "Aqua-Duck" is a shipboard "watercoaster" with wow factor, spanning four decks in height – two-and-a-half times the length of a football field. It whisks you and one other person away in a "raft" on a high-speed flume-like ride that includes twists, drops, uphill acceleration at 20ft (6 meters) a second, and river rapids while moving along the ship's upper decks between and through the ship's two funnels. It's pure Disney, really splashtastic and beyond anything aboard any other cruise

BERLITZ'S RATINGS		
	Possible	Achieved
Ship	500	434
Accommodation	200	166
Food	400	231
Service	400	296
Entertainment	100	91
Cruise	400	337

OVERALL SCORE
1,555 points out of 2,000
● These ratings are for *Disney Dream*

ship dedicated to family cruising.

Disney whimsy and Art Deco style are the hallmarks of the interior decor. In the main three-deck-high lobby stands a bronze statue of none other than Admiral Donald (Duck). The decor is enhanced by original paintings, statues, and woodwork all bearing the characteristic Disney attention to detail. Look out for the "enchanted artwork" on some walls – it incorporates movement.

Grown-ups inhabit their own area of the ship, The District, which includes five different adults-only venues. There's also a centrally-located Concierge Lounge, for occupants of accommodation designated as Concierge Class, all on Deck 12.

Other venues include: Mickey's Mainsail, Sea Treasures, Whitecaps, and Whozits and Whatsits (retail shops); District Bar, Pink Champagne Bar, Skyline Bar, Waves Bar, Bon Voyage, Meridian Bar, 687 (sports bar), Currents Bar, Cove Café; and Arr-cade. The best place for a quiet drink, however, is in the delightful Observation Bar.

During the winter, *Disney Dream* sails on three- and four-day cruises to the Bahamas as part of a seven-night vacation package that includes a three- or four-day stay at a Walt Disney World resort hotel in Orlando; the cruise then forms the second half of the vacation. It's all tied up in one well-controlled, seamless, crime-free environment that promises escape and adventure. You can also book just the cruise without the resort stay. *Disney Fantasy* operates a seven-day itinerary. The ships call at Castaway Bay, Disney's private beach island, whose facilities were enhanced in 2010. American Express cardholders get special treatment and extra goodies. Members of Disney's Vacation Club can exchange points for cruises.

At Port Canaveral, the Disney terminal was inspired by the original Ocean Terminal in Southampton, England, from which the famous ocean liners *Queen Elizabeth, Queen Mary,* and the ill-fated *Titanic* once sailed.

Gratuities are extra, and 15% is added to all bar/drinks purchases.

FAMILIES. Almost one entire deck is devoted to catering for children and teens. It's a Small World Nursery is for children aged from three months to three years. The Oceaneer Lab and Oceaneer Club both have an interactive play floor – a sort of down-to-earth Wii, where team actions translate to movement, a novel idea.

"Edge" is for 11–13 year olds, a tween pad inside the forward funnel that's a chill-out zone including karaoke with green-screen technology. "Vibe" is for the real teens, an indoor/outdoor space for 14–17 year olds that is almost 9,000 sq. ft (830 sq. meters), accessed by a "teen-only" swipe card.

ACCOMMODATION. There are nine types of suites and cabins, but many more price grades, depending on the size and location of the accommodation.

Interior cabins have a virtual porthole that gives you the feeling that you are in an outside cabin. It's done with high-definition cameras positioned on the outside decks to feed live video to each virtual porthole. You almost expect one or more Disney characters to "pop by" your porthole.

One feature that's different about *Disney Magic* and *Disney Wonder*: all bathrooms have round tubs with a pull-down seat and hand-held shower hose – perfect for washing babies and small children. The bed frames have been elevated so that luggage can easily be stored underneath.

The largest accommodation can be found in the Concierge Royal Suite (1,781 sq. ft./165.5 sq. meters, including balcony), with hot tub. It can sleep five and has one master bedroom with a large walk-in closet, a living room (with one additional pull-down wall double bed and one pull-down single bed), two bathrooms (one has two washbasins), dining room, media library, pantry, and wet bar, plus a large balcony. These suites are located in the best possible position in the ship, with great ocean views.

If you opt for one of the 21 Concierge Class suites, you'll get higher quality bed linen (Frette 300-thread count Egyptian cotton), feather and down duvets, cotton bathrobe, and H2O Plus bath and spa products.

CUISINE. There are three main dining rooms, each with a different decor. Passengers rotate through all three, together with their regular waiter (server in Disney-speak).

Expect to see the surfer-dude sea turtle from *Finding Nemo* swimming around *Animator's Palate*, making special appearances and interacting with passengers; the room transforms into a coral reef during dinner. It's all about "foodertainment," which Disney does well, but the noise level can sometimes be a little intense.

Royal Palace has decor inspired by the classic Disney films *Cinderella, Snow White and the Seven Dwarfs, Beauty and the Beast,* and *Sleeping Beauty.*

The *Enchanted Garden* is a whimsical main dining room inspired by the gardens of Versailles, and the lighting magically transforms from day to night.

Casual Dining Venue: *Cabanas* is open to all. At night, it becomes another alternative restaurant where meals from the main dining room menu are available in an even more casual setting but with waiter service.

Alternative Dining Venues: For something different, and as an escape to the big dining rooms, *Remy* is an upscale French restaurant with menus created by Michelin-starred French chef Arnaud Lallement from l'Asiette Champagne, close to Reims in France, in conjunction with Scott Hunnel from Victoria & Albert's at Walt Disney World. An extra-cost, reservations-only venue, it offers leisurely European-style dining – ideal for an evening out (without the kids, of course), but at $75 a head for dinner (plus wine) it's not cheap. The design is rather ratty, too (think Disney's *Ratatouille*); in fact, rats are everywhere in the fine dining venue.

Palo is an Italian-cuisine themed adults-only restaurant, with à la carte items cooked to order. On days at sea, high tea is also served here, and there's a cover charge.

There's also a small coffee bar for those necessary espressos and cappuccinos.

ENTERTAINMENT. Live shows are presented at the Walt Disney Theater, the ship's 1,340-seat showlounge. It has a star-studded ceiling and proscenium arch stage.

Villains Tonight, which premiered in 2010 and features the baddies in Disney's films, is one of the shows being presented, along with other Disney favorites.

The Buena Vista Theater – which is not to be confused with the Walt Disney Theater – is the ship's movie house, with 399 seats.

SPA/FITNESS. Senses Spa and Salon has 17 treatment rooms and private outdoor verandahs. Rainforest features steam heat, misty showers and hydrotherapy for relaxation. Teens can also have specially tailored spa treatments in their own chill-out zone.

● **For a more detailed description of the Disney Cruise Line experience, see the following entries for *Disney Magic* and *Disney Wonder*. *Disney Dream* and *Disney Fantasy* are sister ships, although the names of some public rooms are different.**

Disney Magic
Disney Wonder
★★★★

Size: . . . . .Large Resort Ships	Propulsion/Propellers: . . . . .diesel-electric	Family Cabins: 80
Tonnage: . . . . .83,338 *(Disney Magic)*	(38,000kW)/2	Cabins (with private balcony): 388
85,000 *(Disney Wonder)*	Passenger Decks: 11	Cabins (wheelchair accessible): 12
Lifestyle: . . . . .Standard	Total Crew: 945	Wheelchair accessibility: . . . . .Good
Cruise Line: . . . . .Disney Cruise Line	Passengers	Cabin Current: . . . . .110 volts
Former Names: . . . . .none	(lower beds/all berths): 1,750/3,325	Elevators: 12
Builder: . . . . .Fincantieri (Italy)	Passenger Space Ratio (lower beds/	Casino (gaming tables): . . . . .No
Original Cost: . . . .$350 million each	all berths): . . . . .47.6/25.0 *(Disney Magic)*	Slot Machines: .No
Entered Service: .Jul 1998 *(Disney Magic)*	48.5/25.5 *(Disney Wonder)*	Swimming Pools (outdoors): 3
Aug 1999 *(Disney Wonder)*	Crew/Passenger Ratio	Swimming Pools (indoors): 0
Registry: . . . . .The Bahamas	(lower beds/all berths): 1.8/3.5	Whirlpools: 6
Length (ft/m): 964.5/294.00	Cabins (total): 875	Self-Service Launderette: . . . . .Yes (3)
Beam (ft/m): 105.7/32.22	Size Range (sq ft/m): 180.8–968.7/16.8–90.0	Dedicated Cinema/Seats: Yes/270
Draft (ft/m): 26.2/8.0	Cabins (outside view): 720	Library: . . . . .No
	Cabins (interior/no view): 155	Onboard currency . . . . .US$

Ultra family-friendly cruising in a casual, big ship setting.

OVERVIEW. *Disney Magic* and *Disney Wonder* are like floating versions of Disney's incredibly popular theme parks – sea-going Never-Never Lands. In reality, they provide a highly programmed, well organized, strictly timed and regimented onboard experience, with tickets, lines and reservations necessary for almost everything. The onboard product has been fine-tuned since they first put to sea. Security is very good. Whether cruising with 1,000 or more children aboard will make for a relaxing holiday for those without kids will depend on how much noise they can absorb. But for children of all ages (minimum 12 weeks old), it's hard to beat these two ships.

THE SHIPS. Disney Cruise Line's first two ships were the identical 1998-built *Disney Magic* and the 1999-built *Disney Wonder*. Their profile is sleek, and combines streamlining with tradition and nostalgia, a black hull and two large red and black funnels designed to remind you of the ocean liners of the past – *Disney Magic* was the first cruise ship built with two funnels since the 1950s. One funnel is a dummy containing various public spaces, including a teen center, Aloft.

The ships were constructed in two halves, which were then joined together in the shipyard in Venice, Italy. Their whistles even play a sort of sickly version of "When You

BERLITZ'S RATINGS

DISNEY MAGIC

	Possible	Achieved
Ship	500	422
Accommodation	200	166
Food	400	205
Service	400	287
Entertainment	100	90
Cruise	400	320

OVERALL SCORE
1,490 points out of 2,000

DISNEY WONDER

	Possible	Achieved
Ship	500	423
Accommodation	200	166
Food	400	205
Service	400	287
Entertainment	100	90
Cruise	400	320

OVERALL SCORE
1,491 points out of 2,000

Wish Upon a Star." The bows have handsome gold scrollwork that more usually was seen adorning the tall sailing ships of yesteryear. There is a walk-around promenade deck outdoors for strolling – just as passengers did aboard the classic ocean liners.

Disney Cruise Line didn't add ostentatious decoration to the exterior. However, although Mickey Mouse's face and ears are painted on the funnels, there is also a special 85-ft (26-meter) paint stripe that cleverly incorporates Disney characters into the whimsical yellow paintwork along each side of the hull at the bow. Cute. The exterior colors are those of Mickey, too. Also of note is a 15-ft (4.5-meter) Goofy hanging upside down in a bosun's chair, painting the stern of *Disney Magic*; aboard *Disney Wonder*, Goofy is replaced by a similarly sized Donald Duck and Huey.

There are three outdoor pools: one pool for adults only (in theory), one for families, and one for children. One has a large poolside movie screen, and you can guess which one has Mickey's face and ears painted into the bottom.

There's music everywhere – four different types – and it's impossible to find a quiet spot. In fact, in many seats you get two types of music blaring at you at the same time. The children's pool has a long yellow water slide (available at specified times), held up by Mickey's giant hand, although the pool itself is inadequate given the number of small children usually aboard.

Inside, the ships are quite stunning. Most public rooms have high ceilings, and the Art Deco theme of the old ocean liners or New York's Radio City Music Hall has been tastefully carried out. Have a look at the stainless steel/pewter Disney detailing on the handrails and balustrades in the three-deck-high lobby. The lobby provides a real photo opportunity, with a 6-ft (1.8-meter)-high bronze statue of Mickey Mouse in the role of a ship's helmsman *(Disney Magic)* or "The Little Mermaid" *(Disney Wonder)*. Mickey is also visible in many other areas of the lobby, albeit subtly – subtly for Disney, that is. All the artwork in public areas comes from Disney films or animation features, with many original drawings dating from the early 1930s. If you can't sleep, try counting the number of times Mickey's logo appears – it's an impossible task.

One Disney exclusive is the game show "Who Wants to be a Mouseketeer?" The prizes include free cruises and onboard credits of up to $1,000 and Tea with Wendy Darling from Disney's version of *Peter Pan*. Naturally, all the Disney characters are aboard for all cruises and there are lots of photo opportunities when they come out to play – typically when children's activities are scheduled.

Added in a 2005 refit were additional spaces for spa/fitness facilities, and Ocean Quest, *Disney Magic*'s fifth dedicated space for children; it contains a scale replica of the ship's bridge and LCD screen "windows" that let youngsters look out over the bridge via live video feed from the actual navigation bridge. Kids can sit in a captain's chair and play a simulation game where they steer into and out of various ports. Teens can go to Aloft, a teens-only dorm-like chill-out zone in the base of the dummy forward funnel; it has big-screen TV, MP3 players, computers with hi-tech games, and video games, and its decor is a cross between a college dorm and a coffee shop.

Two large shops sell an abundance of Disney-theme clothing, soft toys, collectibles and specialty items. Other public rooms include a superb, 977-seat Walt Disney Theater with tiered seating over four decks, piano bar, adults-only nightclub-cum-disco, a family lounge, and a dedicated cinema where classic Disney films are shown, as well as first-run movies.

Apart from the ports of call, the highlight for most is a day spent on Disney's private island, Castaway Cay in the Bahamas. It is an outstanding private island – perhaps the benchmark for all private islands for families with children – with its own pier so that the ship can dock alongside – and is a cruise industry first. There is a post office with its own special Bahamas/Disney postage stamp, and a whole host of dedicated, well thought-out attractions and amenities for all ages. These include a large adults-only beach, complete with massage cabanas. Watersports equipment – floats, paddleboats, kayaks, hobie cats, aqua fins, aqua trikes, and snorkels – can be rented.

Take mainly casual clothing (casual with a capital "C"), although there *are* two "formal" nights on the seven-day cruises. Members of Disney's Vacation Club can exchange points for cruises, and American Express cardholders get special treatment and extra goodies. It is expensive – but so is a stay at any Disney resort. Gratuities are extra, suggested at about $10 per person, per day, and 15% is added to all bar/beverage/wine and spa accounts.

Lines at various outlets can prove irritating – some creative Disney Imagineering is needed – as can trying to get through to Guest Services by telephone. Gripes include: poky elevators; lines and signing up for activities; the food product and delivery falls short of less expensive cruise products; there is no proper library – something many adult passengers miss; and the early-morning disembarkation and customs inspection is a definite turn-off for many.

For part of the year, *Disney Magic* operates seven-day cruises to the Eastern Caribbean and Castaway Cay in the Bahamas, offering three different itineraries. During the summer, it operates cruise in Europe and the Baltic. For part of the year, *Disney Wonder* operates three- and four-day cruises to the Bahamas as part of a seven-night vacation package that includes a three- or four-day stay at a Walt Disney World resort hotel in Orlando; the cruise then forms the second half of the vacation. *Disney Wonder* also operates Alaska cruises in summer. It's all tied up in one encapsulated, well-controlled, seamless, and crime-free environment that promises escape and adventure. You can also book just the cruise without the resort stay.

FAMILIES. The ships have three main zones: one for adults only, one for families with children, and one for familes or single parents with toddlers. Each group has its own swimming pool and open deck/sunbathing areas – adults only at the front of the ship. A 24 x 14-ft (7 x 4-meter) Goofy Pool Jumbo Screen is positioned by the family pool area, just behind the forward funnel; it shows classic Disney animated and live-action movies, TV shows and sporting events.

The children's entertainment areas measure 13,000 sq. ft (1,200 sq. meters), and more than 40 children's counselors run the extensive programmes. All registered children must wear an ID bracelet showing name, cabin number and muster station number, and parents are given pagers for emergencies. There are also separate teen clubs, "tween" clubs, and a video game arcade.

A child drop-off service is available in the evenings, and private babysitting services are available at around $11 an hour, as are character "tuck-ins" for children, and character breakfasts and lunches – all at extra cost. Free strollers are available, and parents can be provided with beepers in order to enjoy their time alone, away from their offspring for much of the day.

ACCOMMODATION. There are 12 accommodation grades, but only about six different cabin layouts; the price will depend on the grade, size and location chosen, and are linked to the resort accommodation for those taking a combined resort/cruise vacation. Spread over six decks, all suites and cabins have been designed for practicality and have space-efficient layouts.

Most cabins have common features such as a neat vertical steamer trunk for clothes storage, illuminated closets, a hairdryer located at a vanity desk or in the bathroom, and bathrobes for all passengers. Many cabins have third- and fourth pull-down berths that rise and are totally hidden in the ceiling when not in use, but the standard interior and outside cabins, while acceptable for two, are extremely tight with three or four. Some cabins can also accommodate a fifth person. The cabin decor is practical, creative, and colorful, with lots of neat styling touches. Cabins with refrigerators can have them stocked, at extra cost, with one of several drinks/soft drinks packages.

Bathrooms, although compact due to the fact that the toilet is separate, are really functional units, designed with split-use facilities so that more than one person can use them at the same time – good for families. Many have bathtubs, which are really shower tubs.

Accommodation designated as suites offers much more space, and extra goodies such as CD and DVD players, large-screen TVs, and extra beds (useful for larger families). Some suites are beneath the pool deck, teen lounge, or informal café, so there could be noise as the ceiling insulation is poor – although cabin-to-cabin insulation is good.

The two largest suites, the Walter E. Disney Suite and the Roy O. Disney Suite, are located beside the central bank of elevators. These are luxurious living spaces, each with two bedrooms, and all the Disney trimmings you'd expect.

Wheelchair-bound passengers have a variety of cabin sizes and configurations, including suites with a private balcony – unfortunately you can't get a wheelchair through the balcony's sliding door – and extra-large bathrooms with excellent roll-in showers, and good closet and drawer space. Almost all the vessel is accessible. For the sight-impaired, cabin numbers and elevator buttons are braille-encoded.

A 24-hour room service is available, and suites also get "concierge service." But the room service menu and cabin breakfast menu are limited. A 15% service charge applies to beverage deliveries, including tea and coffee.

CUISINE. Each ship has three main dining rooms, all non-smoking, each with over 400 seats, two seatings, and unique themes. *Lumiere's* (in the center of the ship on Deck 3) has Beauty and the Beast; *Parrot Cay* (Deck 4) has a tacky, pseudo-Caribbean theme; also on Deck 4 aft, with great ocean views over the stern, is *Animator's Palate*, the most visual of the three with food and electronic art that makes the evening decor change from black and white to full-color.

You will eat in all three dining rooms in rotation – twice per seven-day cruise – and move with your assigned waiter and assistant waiter to each dining room in turn, thus providing the variety of different decor and different menus. It's a great concept – and totally unlike any other cruise line. As you will have the same waiter in each of the three restaurants, any gratuities go only to "your" waiter. Parrot Cay and Lumiere's have open seating for breakfast and lunch, but the lunch menu is pitiful.

The noise level in all three dining rooms is extremely high. If the formal nights happen to fall on the evening you are due to eat in Parrot Cay, formal wear and the decor of Parrot Cay Restaurant just don't mix.

Alternative Dining Venue: *Palo* is a 140-seat reservations-only alternative restaurant with a $5 cover/gratuity charge, serving Italian cuisine. It has a 270-degree view, and is for adults only (no "Munchkins" allowed); the à la carte cuisine is cooked to order, and the wine list is good, although prices are high. Make your reservations as soon as you board or you will miss out on the ship's only decent food. Afternoon High Tea is presented here, on days at sea.

Casual Dining Venue: *Topsider's* (incorporating *Beach Blanket Buffet*) is an indoor/outdoor café serving low-quality self-serve breakfast and lunch buffets with limited choice and presentation, and a buffet dinner, consisting mostly of fried foods, for children. But the venue is often overcrowded at lunchtime, so it may be better to go to the Parrot Cay dining room, which offers breakfast and lunch buffet, too. A poolside *Goofey's Galley* has grilled panini sandwiches and wraps, and soft drinks are complimentary.

Scoops, an ice cream and frozen yogurt bar, opens infrequently; other fast-food outlets include *Pluto's* for hamburgers, hot dogs, and *Pinocchio's*, which is open all day but not in the evening, for basic pizza and sandwiches.

On one night, there is also an outdoor self-serve "Tropicalifragilisticexpialidocious" buffet.

A casual *Outlook Café*, installed in 2010, has fine views from Deck 10, just forward of the first funnel housing. Vegetarians and those looking for light cuisine will be underwhelmed by the lack of green vegetables. Guest chefs from Walt Disney World Resort prepare signature dishes each cruise, and also host cooking demonstrations.

THE LINKS WITH ORLANDO

Disney Cruise Lines' home port is Port Canaveral, where the company built a terminal costing $27 million. It is a copy of the original Ocean Terminal used by the transatlantic liners *Queen Elizabeth* and *Queen Mary* in Southampton, England. Transfers between Walt Disney World resorts in Orlando and the ship are included. Special buses feature vintage 1930s and1940s-style interior decor. Five of the 45 custom-made buses are outfitted to carry wheelchair passengers. Embarkation and disembarkation is a bit of an entertainment event rather than the hassle-laden affair that it has become for many cruise lines with large ships (if all the buses don't arrive together), and it's quite slick.

The cruise terminal's second floor has a neat 13,000 sq.ft. terrazo tile map of Florida's east coast and the Bahamas. If you drive to the port, parking for the duration of your cruise is available, at rates of around $10 per night set by the port authority.

Onboard airline check-in for post-cruise flights from Orlando is offered, with luggage transfer directly from ship to flight on any one of seven airlines: AirTran, Alaska, American, Continental, Delta, Northwest and United. You'll need to supply pre-registration information at Orlando Airport or at a hospitality desk at the Disney World Resort.

ENTERTAINMENT. The entertainment and activities programs for families and children are extremely good. There are three large-scale stage shows in the stunning 977-seat showlounge, presenting original Disney musicals: *Disney Dreams, Hercules – The Muse-ical, The Golden Mickeys*, and the latest comedy production, *Villains Tonight*, bringing together a cast of Disney baddies from many Disney films. Sadly, there is no live orchestra, although the lighting, staging and technical effects are excellent. There is also a Disney-themed Trivia Game Show.

For grown-ups, "Route 66" aboard *Disney Magic* and "Beal Street" aboard *Disney Wonder* are adult entertainments that include a wacky Hollywood-style "street," complete with three entertainment rooms. "Sessions" (*Disney Magic*) and "Cadillac" (*Disney Wonder*) are jazz piano lounges, with private headphones for listening to music of all types when no live music is scheduled. "Rockin' Bar D" (*Disney Magic*) and "Wavebands" (*Disney Wonder*) provide ear-splitting rock 'n' roll and country music. "Barrel of Laughs" offers improvisational comedy with audience participation. During the day, creative enrichment programs have been added.

Once each cruise, a late-night "Pirates In the Caribbean" poolside party includes fireworks. Special equipment installed in the Walt Disney Theatre and the Buena Vista Theatre allows participants to view Disney Digital 3-D movies.

SPA/FITNESS. The Vista Spa is a fitness/wellbeing complex measuring 10,700 sq ft/994 sq metres. The fitness/workout room, with high-tech Cybex muscle-toning equipment, has ocean-view windows overlooking the navigation bridge one deck below. There are 11 rooms for spa/beauty treatments – but note that the pounding from the basketball court on the sports deck directly overhead makes spa treatments less than relaxing. Three spa "villas" have indoor treatment suites connected to private outdoor verandahs with personal hot tub, open-air shower and chaise lounge. There are a couple of private salons for Pilates instruction and one-on-one beauty and fitness consultations.

A Thermal Zone features a "tropical rain shower," sauna, mild steam room, aromatic steam room and a fog shower. Aromatic scents such as eucalyptus, lime, peppermint, rose and sage can be infused into the mild steam room, while chamomile is used in the aromatic steam room.

Exotic massages, aromatherapy facials, pedicures, and beauty salon treatments cost extra – massage, for example, costs about $2 per minute, plus gratuity. The Rasul mud and steam room is a must for couples, but make appointments early. For something extra special, consider booking a massage at Castaway Cay in a private beach hut on the beach that is open to the sea. It's magical.

A sports deck has a paddle tennis court, table tennis, basketball court, shuffleboard, and golf driving range.

DISNEY TRIVIA

● A 15-ft tall Mickey and several brooms – representing the Sorcerer's Apprentice from the 1940 animated movie *Fantasia* (the first film with multi-channel sound) – is attached to *Disney Dream*'s stern.

● A 15-ft-tall model of Goofy hangs upside down over the stern of *Disney Magic*. He's painting the ship.

● The longest water slides at sea are aboard *Disney Dream* and *Disney Fantasy*. Each goes between the ship's two funnels, and is a blast.

● The color of the ships was determined by Mickey's colors – red, white, yellow and black.

● Children can actually "steer" the Disney ships. They can do this because each one has a duplicate navigation bridge, complete with consoles and controls that let youngsters look out over the bridge via live video feed from the actual bridge. It can be found in Ocean Quest.

● Each of the propellers of *Disney Magic* and *Disney Wonder* weighs 18.8 tons.

● There are approximately 1,850 telephones aboard *Disney Magic* and *Disney Wonder*.

● *Disney Magic* was constructed in two sections (bow and stern) in two different shipyards, 100 miles (160 km) apart in Italy. The bow was built in Fincantieri's Ancona shipyard, while the stern was constructed in Fincantieri's Marghera shipyard, close to Venice. The stern, which comprised about two-thirds of the ship, was towed to Venice by two powerful tugs. The two giant sections were then welded together in the Venice shipyard. Three gondolas – each with one gondolier and one accordionist playing "Santa Lucia" – met the bow as it entered the sloop in Venice's lagoon.

● *Disney Magic* was the first cruise ship since the 1950s built with two funnels.

● The ship's whistle even plays "When You Wish Upon a Star" – or a sort of sickly version of it.

A 6 ft-tall bronze statue of the Little Mermaid adorns the lobby of *Disney Wonder*.

● All the Disney Cruise Line ships have giant movie screens outside on deck close to one of the swimming pools.

Emerald Princess
★★★★

Size: Large Resort Ship	Passenger Decks: 15	Cabins (with private balcony): 881
Tonnage: 113,561	Total Crew: 1,200	Cabins (wheelchair accessible): 25
Lifestyle: Standard	Passengers	Wheelchair accessibility: Good
Cruise Line: Princess Cruises	(lower beds/all berths): 3,114/3,782	Cabin Current: 110 volts
Former Names: none-	Passenger Space Ratio	Elevators: 14
Builder: Fincantieri (Italy)	(lower beds/all berths): 36.2/29.8	Casino (gaming tables): Yes
Original Cost: $500 million	Crew/Passenger Ratio	Slot Machines: Yes
Entered Service: May 2007	(lower beds/all berths): 2.5/3.1	Swimming Pools (outdoors): 4
Registry: Bermuda	Cabins (total): 1,557	Swimming Pools (indoors): 0
Length (ft/m): 951.4/290.0	Size Range (sq ft/m): 163–1,279/	Whirlpools: 9
Beam (ft/m): 118.1/36.0	15.1–118.8	Self-Service Launderette: Yes
Draft (ft/m): 26.2/8.0	Cabins (outside view): 1,105	Dedicated Cinema/Seats: No
Propulsion/Propellers: diesel-electric	Cabins (interior/no view): 452	Library: Yes
(42,000kW)/2	Cabins (for one person): 0	Onboard currency US$

Very comfortable, family-oriented theme-park cruising.

OVERVIEW. The ship is a fine resort playground in which to roam when you are not ashore, and Princess Cruises consistently delivers a well-packaged product, always with a good degree of style, at an attractive, highly competitive price. Whether this is a relaxing vacation is a moot point, but with many choices and "small" rooms to enjoy, the ship has been extremely well designed, and you should have an enjoyable time.

BERLITZ'S RATINGS		
	Possible	Achieved
Ship	500	435
Accommodation	200	168
Food	400	255
Service	400	292
Entertainment	100	82
Cruise	400	314
OVERALL SCORE		
1,546 points out of 2,000		

THE SHIP. *Emerald Princess* has the same profile as sister *Crown Princess* (similar to half-sisters *Diamond Princess, Golden Princess, Grand Princess, Ruby Princess, Sapphire Princess* and *Star Princess*). Although the ship takes over 500 more passengers than the half-sisters, the outdoor deck space remains the same, as do the number of elevators, so waiting time will increase at peak periods. The Passenger Space Ratio is also considerably reduced.

One nice feature worth booking on days at sea is The Sanctuary, an extra-cost adults-only retreat located forward on the uppermost deck. It provides a "private" place to relax and unwind and includes attendants to provide chilled face towels and deliver light bites; there are also two outdoor cabanas for massages. It's worth the extra charge, calculated by the half-day.

There is a good sheltered faux teak promenade deck – it's actually painted steel – which almost wraps around (three times round is equal to one mile) and a walkway which goes to the enclosed, protected bow of the ship. The outdoor pools have various beach-like surroundings, and "Movies Under the Skies" and major sporting events are shown on a 300-sq-ft (28-sq-meter) movie screen at the pool in front of the large funnel structure.

Unlike the outside decks, there is plenty of space inside – but there are also plenty of passengers – and a wide array of public rooms, with many "intimate" (this being a relative word) spaces and places to play. The passenger flow has been well thought-out, and there is little congestion.

Just aft of the funnel housing is a ship-wide glass-walled disco called Skywalkers. It's in a lower position than in the half-sister ships, but still has fine views from the port and starboard side windows – it would make a great penthouse.

The interior decor is attractive, with lots of earth tones. An extensive collection of artworks complements the interior design and colors well. If you see something you like, you will probably be able to purchase it on board.

Emerald Princess also has a wedding chapel, with a live web-cam to relay ceremonies via the internet. The captain can legally marry (American) couples, thanks to the ship's Bermuda registry and a special dispensation (which should be verified when in the planning stage, according to where you reside). But to get married and take your close family members and entourage with you on your honeymoon may prove expensive. The "Hearts & Minds" chapel is also useful for "renewal of vows" ceremonies.

Gamblers should enjoy the large Gatsby's Casino, with more than 260 slot machines, and blackjack, craps and roulette tables, plus games such as Let It Ride Bonus, Spanish 21 and Caribbean Draw Progressive. But the highlight could well be the linked slot machines that provide a combined payout.

Other features include a decent library/computer room, and a separate card room. Ship lovers should enjoy the wood-paneled Wheelhouse Bar, finely decorated with memorabilia and ship models tracing part of parent company P&O's history. A sports bar has two billiard tables, and several television screens.

If you are not used to large ships, it will take you some time to find your way around this one, despite the company's claim that it offers passengers a "small ship feel, big ship choice." There are several points of congestion, particularly outside the shops when bazaar tables are set up outside on the upper level of the atrium lobby.

FAMILIES. There is a two-deck-high playroom, teen room, and a host of trained counselors. Children have their own pools, hot tubs, open deck and sports court area at the stern of the ship, away from the adults.

ACCOMMODATION. There are six principal types of cabins and configurations: (a) grand suite, (b) suite, (c) mini-suite, (d) outside-view double cabins with balcony, (e) outside-view double cabins, and (f) interior (no view) double cabins. These come in 35 different brochure price categories (the choice is bewildering for both travel agents and passengers), and pricing depends on size and location.

For a comprehensive description of the facilities available in each type of cabin, see the entry for *Crown Princess* on page 337.

CUISINE. Of the three main dining rooms – *Botticelli, Da Vinci*, and *Michelangelo* – one has two-seating dining and the other two have "anytime dining" that allows you to choose when and with whom you want to eat. All three are split into multi-tier sections in a non-symmetrical design that breaks what are quite large spaces into smaller sections for better ambience.

While four elevators go to the deck where two of the restaurants are located, only two go to Plaza Deck 5, where the Michelangelo Dining Room is located – this can cause waiting problems at peak times, particularly for anyone in a wheelchair.

Specially designed dinnerware, high-quality linens and silverware, Frette Egyptian cotton table linens, and silverware by Hepp of Germany are used in the main dining rooms. Note that 15% is added to all beverage bills, including wines.

Alternative (Extra Charge) Dining Options: There are two: *Sabatini's*, and *Crown Grill*. Both are open for lunch and dinner on days at sea. Sabatini's is an Italian eatery located on a high deck aft of the funnel housing, with colorful tiled Mediterranean-style decor; it is named after Trattoria Sabatini, the 200-year old institution in Florence. It includes Italian-style multi-course antipasti and pastas, as well as Italian-style entrées, including tiger prawns and lobster tail. All are provided with flair and entertainment by the staff of waiters. It's by reservation only and has a cover charge.

The Crown Grill, located aft on Promenade Deck, is a reservation-only, extra-cost steakhouse, offering prime quality steaks and seafood.

The cuisine in these two dining spots is decidedly better than in the three main dining rooms, with better quality ingredients and more attention to presentation and taste.

Casual Eateries: These include a poolside hamburger grill and pizza bar (no additional charge), while extra charges apply if you order items to eat either at the *International Café* (a coffee bar/ patisserie), or in *Vines* seafood/wine bar in the atrium lobby. Other casual meals can be taken in the *Horizon Court* (open 24 hours a day). It has large ocean-view on port and starboard sides and direct access to the two principal swimming pools and lido deck. Although there is a wide variety of food, there is no finesse in presentation, however, as plastic plates are provided

Ultimate Balcony Dinner/Breakfast: For something different, you could try a private dinner on your balcony, an all-inclusive evening featuring cocktails, fresh flowers, champagne and a deluxe four-course meal including Caribbean lobster tail – all served by a member of the dining staff on your private balcony. Of course, it costs extra.

ENTERTAINMENT. The 800-seat Princess Theater is the main entertainment venue; it spans two decks and has comfortable seating on both main and balcony levels. It has $3 million worth of sound and light equipment, plus a nine-piece orchestra. The ship has its own resident troupe of almost 20 singers and dancers.

A second entertainment lounge, Club Fusion, is located aft. It features cabaret acts and karaoke contests at night, and lectures, bingo and horse racing during the day. Explorers Lounge, a third entertainment lounge, can also host cabaret acts and dance bands.

A variety of other lounges and bars have live music, including a string quartet, and street performers who appear in the main atrium lobby

SPA/FITNESS. The Lotus Spa is located forward on Sun Deck, one of the uppermost decks. Separate facilities for men and women include a sauna, steam room, and changing rooms; common facilities include a relaxation/waiting zone, body-pampering treatment rooms, and a gymnasium with packed with the latest high-tech muscle-pumping, cardio-vascular equipment, and great ocean views. Some fitness classes are free, while others cost extra.

● **For more extensive general information on what a Princess Cruises cruise is like, see pages 149–152.**

Empress
★★★

Size: . . . . .Large Resort Ship	Passenger Decks: 9	Cabins (wheelchair accessible): 4
Tonnage: . . . . .48,563 tons	Total Crew: 685	Wheelchair accessibility: . . . . .Fair
Lifestyle: . . . . .Standard	Passengers	Cabin Current: . . . . .110 volts
Cruise Line: . . . . .Pullmantur Cruises	(lower beds/all berths): 1,600/2,020	Elevators: 7
Former Names: . . . .*Empress of the Seas,*	Passenger Space Ratio	Casino (gaming tables): . . . . .Yes
Nordic Empress	(lower beds/all berths): 30.2/24.0	Slot Machines: . . . . .Yes – 220
Builder: .Chantiers de l'Atlantique (France)	Crew/Passenger Ratio	Swimming Pools (outdoors): 1
Original Cost: . . . .$170 million	(lower beds/all berths): 2.3/2.9	(+1 wading pool)
Entered Service: . . . .Jun 1990/May 2008	Cabins (total): 800	Swimming Pools (indoors): 0
Registry: . . . . .The Bahamas	Size Range (sq ft/m): .117.0–818/10.8–76	Whirlpools: 4
Length (ft/m): 692.2/211.00	Cabins (outside view): 471	Self-Service Launderette: . . . . .No
Beam (ft/m): 100.7/30.70	Cabins (interior/no view): 329	Dedicated Cinema/Seats: . . . . .No
Draft (ft/m): 24.9/7.60	Cabins (for one person): 0	Library: . . . . .No
Propulsion/Propellers: diesel (16,200 kW)/2	Cabins (with private balcony): 69	Onboard currency . . . . .Euros

A large but dated ship suited to Spanish families.

OVERVIEW. *Empress* is best suited to young Spanish-speaking couples and singles seeking an all-inclusive cruise, and those who want a good basic getaway cruise aboard a ship that offers some good drinking places, lots of noise and good cheer, in fairly comfortable surroundings.

THE SHIP. This modern ship has a polished wood walk-around promenade deck outdoors. Although the outdoor pool is decent enough (good at night for evenings under the stars), the two swimming pools are very small for the number of passengers. There's not much open deck space, and sunloungers are crammed together.

A nine-deck-high atrium is the focal point of the interior design, which has many Scandinavian influences. Passenger flow is generally good. A three-level casino has a sailcloth ceiling, but it is a noisy room. The Viking Crown Lounge, aft of the funnel, is a two-level nightclub-disco.

Empress is a fairly smart ship with a high passenger density, and you won't be bored. But you may be overwhelmed by the public spaces, and underwhelmed by the size of the cabins. However, this is basically a well-run, fine-tuned, highly structured cruise product geared to those seeking an action-packed cruise vacation at a moderately good price.

ACCOMMODATION. There are 15 price categories. The largest accommodation, the Royal Suite, has a queen-sized bed, walk-in closet, separate living area with bar, refrigerator and entertainment center; the bathroom has a whirlpool tub, and vanity dressing area. There is a private balcony.

Nine cabins have private balconies overlooking the stern; these consist of two large owner's suites and seven "supe-

BERLITZ'S RATINGS		
	Possible	Achieved
Ship	500	325
Accommodation	200	121
Food	400	218
Service	400	257
Entertainment	100	64
Cruise	400	241
OVERALL SCORE		
1,226 points out of 2,000		

rior" ocean-view cabins. The other cabins with private balconies also have a decent amount of living space, and a small sofa, coffee table and chair, and vanity desk. Almost all the other cabins are really small, and only moderately comfortable. All cabins have twin beds that convert to a queen-size configuration. The bathrooms are nicely laid-out.

CUISINE. The *Miramar Restaurant* is two decks high, but it really is a noisy room. There are two seatings, at tables for four, six, eight or 10. The cuisine is typical of mass banquet catering that offers standard fare.

Alternative Dining Option: There is one à la carte extra-charge restaurant; reservations required. Its intimacy makes it a romantic place, with a good number of tables for two.

Casual Dining Option: For casual breakfasts and lunches, the *Panorama Buffet* provides an alternative to the dining room, although there are often lines at peak times.

ENTERTAINMENT. The two-level Broadway Showroom has poor sight lines in the upper lateral balconies. It has a main floor level as well as a balcony level. However, the sightlines from the balcony are are ruined by railings. Strong cabaret acts are also featured in the main showlounge. The entertainment throughout is upbeat – in fact, it is difficult to get away from music. There is even background music in all corridors and lifts, and constant music outdoors on the pool deck.

SPA/FITNESS. A gymnasium has some good muscle-pumping equipment. Sports fans will like the climbing wall at the stern of the ship, behind the Starlight Discotheque.

Enchantment of the Seas
★★★★

Size: . . . . .Large Resort Ship	Passenger Decks: 11	Cabins (wheelchair accessible): 20
Tonnage: .81,500	Total Crew: 840	Wheelchair accessibility: . . . . .Good
Lifestyle: . . . . .Standard	Passengers	Cabin Current: . . . . .110 and 220 volts
Cruise Line: . . . . .Royal Caribbean	(lower beds/all berths): 2,252/2,730	Elevators: 9
International	Passenger Space Ratio	Casino (gaming tables): . . . . .Yes
Former Names: . . . . .none	(lower beds/all berths): 36.1/29.8	Slot Machines: . . . . .Yes
Builder: . . .Kvaerner Masa-Yards (Finland)	Crew/Passenger Ratio	Swimming Pools (outdoors): 2
Original Cost: . . . .$300 million	(lower beds/all berths): 2.6/3.2	Swimming Pools (indoors): 1
Entered Service: . . . . .Jul 1997	Cabins (total): 1,126	(indoor/outdoor with sliding glass roof)
Registry: . . . . .The Bahamas	Size Range (sq ft/m): 158.2–1,267.0/	Whirlpools: 4
Length (ft/m): 990.1/301.8	14.7–117.7	Self-Service Launderette: . . . . .No
Beam (ft/m): 105.6/32.2	Cabins (outside view): 663	Dedicated Cinema/Seats: . . . . .No
Draft (ft/m): 25.5/7.6	Cabins (interior/no view): 463	Library: . . . . .Yes
Propulsion/Propellers: . . . . .diesel-electric	Cabins (for one person): 0	Onboard currency . . . . .US$
(50,400kW)/2	Cabins (with private balcony): 248	

A large ship with elegant decor, for mature-age cruisers.

OVERVIEW. This ship has quite attractive interiors, and will provide a good cruise vacation, particularly for first-time passengers seeking comfortable surroundings similar to those in a Hyatt Hotel, with fabrics and soft furnishings that blend together to provide a contemporary resort environment. This company provides a well organized but rather homogenous cruise experience, with the same old passenger participation activities and events that have been provided for more than 25 years.

THE SHIP. *Enchantment of the Seas,* sister to *Grandeur of the Seas,* has a long profile, with a single funnel located well aft – almost a throwback to 1950s designs. The stern is nicely rounded, and a Viking Crown Lounge is set amidships. This, together with the forward mast, provides three distinct focal points in its exterior profile. There is a walk-around promenade deck outdoors, but no cushioned pads for the tacky home patio-style plastic sunloungers.

A large Viking Crown Lounge, a trademark of all Royal Caribbean International ships, sits between funnel and mast at the top of the atrium lobby, and overlooks the forward section of the swimming pool deck, as aboard *Legend of the Seas* and *Splendour of the Seas,* with access provided from stairway off the central atrium.

The principal interior focal point is a seven-deck-high Centrum (atrium lobby), which provides a good meeting point; the Purser's Desk and Shore Excursion Desk are located on one of the lower levels. Many public entertainment rooms and facilities are located off the atrium.

This ship has good passenger flow inside. There's a var-

BERLITZ'S RATINGS

	Possible	Achieved
Ship	500	411
Accommodation	200	152
Food	400	227
Service	400	260
Entertainment	100	77
Cruise	400	280

OVERALL SCORE
1,407 points out of 2,000

ied collection of artworks, including several sculptures, principally by British artists, with classical music, ballet and theater themes. The casino is large and glitzy, and has a fascinating, theatrical glass-covered, but underfloor exhibit. The children's and teens' facilities are good, much expanded from previous ships in the fleet.

A delightful champagne terrace bar sits forward of the lower level of the two-deck-high dining room. There is a good use of tropical plants throughout the public rooms, which helps to counteract the rather plain and clinical pastel wall colors, while huge murals of opera scenes adorn several stairways.

In 2005, the ship underwent a $60 million "chop-and-stretch" operation that added a 72.8-ft (22.2-meter) midsection, increasing its overall length to 990.1 ft (301.8 meters)and its gross tonnage to 81,500.

The upgrade added another 151 passenger cabins, including two "family" cabins that can sleep six, and some public rooms were given a make-over. Sports facilities were augmented; these included two "ball zones," each with three basketball hoops of different heights to accommodate youth, teen and adult shooters. The pool deck was given more space plus soaring "suspension" bridges. Special handicap lifts were provided for the two pools, as was a new Splash Deck (children will love the 64 water jets) with a decorative night-time fiber-optic light show. "Bungee" trampolines were added to Deck 10 (above the Windjammer Café). The main dining room and Windjammer Café casual eatery were enlarged to handle the extra capacity, and so was the art auction gallery.

ACCOMMODATION. There are 16 price grades, with location and grade perhaps the most important determining factor, given that so many of the cabins are of the same or very similar size. All grades of suites and cabins are provided with a hairdryer. The room service menu has only the most basic selection.

The five grades of suites are well appointed and have pleasing decor, best described as Scandinavian Moderne, with good wood and color accenting.

Royal Suite. The largest accommodation, which contains a baby grand piano, is the Royal Suite, located directly aft of the ship's navigation bridge on the starboard side. It has a separate bedroom with kind-size bed, walk-in closet and vanity dressing area, living room with queen-sized sofa bed, refrigerator and wet bar, dining table, entertainment center, and large private balcony. The bathroom has a whirlpool tub, separate shower enclosure, two washbasins, and toilet.

Owner's Suite. The five owner's suites are at the forward end of the ship, just behind the navigation bridge, close to the Royal Suite. They have a queen-sized bed, separate living area with queen-size sofa bed, vanity dressing area, refrigerator and wet bar. The bathroom has a full-size tub, separate shower enclosure, toilet and two washbasins.

Royal Family Suite. These four suites have two bedrooms with twin beds that convert to queen-size beds, living area with double sofa bed and Pullman bed, refrigerator, two bathrooms (one with tub), and private balcony. This suite can accommodate eight, and might suit families.

Grand Suite. Features of these 12 suites include twin beds that convert to a queen-size bed, vanity dressing area, lounge area with sofa bed, refrigerator, and a bathroom with tub. There's also a private balcony.

Superior Suite. Features of these 44 suites, which include two superior suites for the disabled, have twin beds that convert to a queen-size bed, vanity dressing area, lounge area with sofa bed, refrigerator, a bathroom with tub, and private balcony. Although these are called suites, they really are little more than a larger standard cabin with balcony.

Other Grades. All standard cabins have twin beds that convert to a queen-size bed, ample closet space for a one-week cruise, and a good amount of drawer space, although under-bed storage space is not good for large suitcases. The

bathrooms have nine mirrors. Plastic buckets are provided for champagne/wine and are really tacky.

CUISINE. The 1,195-seat *My Fair Lady Dining Room* spreads over two decks, connected by a grand, sweeping staircase. When you book, choose one of two seatings, or "My Time Dining" (eat when you want, during dining hours. **Alternative dining option:** The extra-cost, reservations-needed *Chops Grill Steakhouse* is an à la carte steakhouse serving steaks and veal chops. Think big steaks, better service, and more comfortable dining.

Casual, self-serve breakfasts and luncheons can be taken in the 790-seat informal *Windjammer Marketplace*. It has a great expanse of ocean-view glass windows, the decor is bright and cheerful, and buffet "islands" contain food from around the world. An intimate *Champagne/Caviar Bar* terrace is forward of the lower level of the two-deck-high dining room and just off the atrium for those who might like to taste something a little bit out of the ordinary, in a setting that is both bright and contemporary.

ENTERTAINMENT. The Orpheum Theater, the principal showlounge, is a grand room at the forward part of the ship, and has 875 seats. This is where the big production shows and major cabaret acts are staged.

A second showlounge, the 575-seat Carousel Lounge, is located aft, and is for smaller shows and adult cabarets, including late-night blue comedy. A variety of other lounges and bars have almost constant live music; in fact, there's no bar without music to have a quiet drink in. There's even background music in all corridors and elevators, and constant music outdoors on the pool deck. If you want a quiet relaxing holiday, choose another ship.

SPA/FITNESS. The ShipShape Spa is aft of the funnel and spans two decks. Facilities include an expanded gymnasium (with all the latest machines), aerobics exercise room, sauna and steam rooms, a beauty salon, and 13 treatment rooms, including a couples massage room.

● **For more extensive general information about the Royal Caribbean cruise experience, see pages 152–6.**

Eurodam
★★★★

Size:	Large Resort Ship	Total Crew:	929	Wheelchair accessibility:	Good
Tonnage:	86,700 tons	Passengers		Cabin Voltage:	110/220 volts
Lifestyle:	Standard	(lower beds/all berths):	2,104/2,671	Elevators:	14
Cruise Line:	Holland America Line	Passenger Space Ratio		Casino (gaming tables):	Yes
Former Names:	none	(lower beds/all berths):	41.2/32.4	Slot Machines:	Yes
Builder:	Fincantieri (Italy)	Crew/Passenger Ratio		Swimming Pools (outdoors):	2
Original Cost:	$450 million	(lower beds/all berths):	2.2/2.8		+ 1 children's pool
Entered Service:	Jul 2008	Cabins (total):	1,052	Swimming Pools (indoors):	1
Registry:	The Netherlands	Size Range (sq ft/m):	170.0–1,318.6/		(indoor/outdoor with retractable dome)
Length (ft/m):	935.0/285.0		15.7–122.5	Whirlpools:	5
Beam (ft/m):	105.6/32.2	Cabins (outside view):	897	Self-Service Launderette:	No
Draft (ft/m):	25.5/7.8	Cabins (interior/no view):	155	Dedicated Cinema/Seats:	Yes/170
Propulsion/Propellers:	diesel-electric	Cabins (for one person):	0	Library:	Yes
	(34,000kW/2 pods (17.6 MW each)	Cabins (with private balcony):	708	Onboard currency	US$
Passenger Decks:	12	Cabins (wheelchair accessible):	30		

A large, spacious ship with sedate Dutch-style decor.

OVERVIEW. The ship has a bright interior decor designed to appeal to younger, more vibrant, multi-generational holidaymakers. In keeping with the traditions of Holland America Line, a large collection of artwork is a standard feature, and pieces reflect the former Dutch East Indies.

THE SHIP. *Eurodam* has two funnels, positioned close together – one behind the other instead of side by side – the result of the machinery configuration. The ship has, in effect, two engine rooms – one with three diesels, and one with two diesels. A "pod" propulsion system is provided *(see page 191 for the technicalities)*.

One neat feature consists of 22 rent-by-the-day cabanas, with goodies such as champagne, chocolate strawberries, an iPod pre-stocked with music, bathrobes, fresh fruit and chilled towels. These are designed for two adults and two children, so they may not be the promised "quiet" spaces, after all. They are located in an area on observation deck and around the Lido Pool, with a daily charge for the 14 cabanas in The Retreat – $75 for sea days and $45 on port days; for the eight Lido Deck cabanas it's $50 on sea days and $30 on port days.

There is a complete walk-around exterior teak promenade deck, and real teak "steamer" style sunloungers. Additionally, there is a jogging track outdoors, located around the ship's mast and the forward third of the ship.

Exterior glass elevators, mounted midships on both port and starboard sides, provide fine ocean views from all 11 passenger decks. There are two centrally located swimming pools outdoors, one of which can be used in inclement

BERLITZ'S RATINGS		
	Possible	Achieved
Ship	500	427
Accommodation	200	168
Food	400	275
Service	400	279
Entertainment	100	77
Cruise	400	308
OVERALL SCORE		
1,534 points out of 2,000		

weather thanks to its retractable sliding glass roof.

Two whirlpool tubs, adjacent to the swimming pools, are abridged by a bar. A smaller swimming pool is available for children, and this incorporates a winding water slide that spans two decks in height. There is an additional whirlpool tub outdoors.

The intimate lobby, which has its own bar, spans three decks. Adjacent are interior elevators, and glass wall elevators with exterior views.

There are two decks of entertainment and public rooms. Perhaps the most dramatic room is the showlounge, spanning four decks in the forward section of the ship. Other facilities include a winding shopping street with several boutique stores and logo shops, card room, an art gallery, photo gallery, and several small meetings rooms.

The casino is large – you have to walk through it to get from the restaurant to the showlounge on Lower Promenade Deck – and is equipped with all the necessary gaming paraphernalia and slot machines.

"Explorations" is a combination coffee bar (coffees and other drinks are at extra cost), lounge, extensive library and internet-connect center, all in one attractive, open "lifestyle" environment, adjacent to the Crows Nest Lounge.

While this formula doesn't work so well for loyal repeat passengers used to the line's smaller ships, *Eurodam* offers a wide range of public rooms. Art, artefacts and museum pieces from the "Dutch Golden Age" of the 16th and 17th centuries are displayed.

The information desk in the lobby is small and somewhat removed from the main passenger flow on the two decks above it. Several pillars obstruct the passenger flow and lines of sight throughout the ship.

FAMILIES. For families with children, Club HAL's Kid-Zone provides a whole area dedicated to children's facilities and extensive programming for different age groups (5–17), with one counselor for every 30 children. Free ice cream is provided at certain hours. There are no self-service launderettes – something many families with children miss, even though special laundry packages are available.

ACCOMMODATION. Of the total 1,022 suites/cabins, 86% have an outside view, while 67 of these have a private balcony. Many cabins on Upper Promenade Deck have lifeboat-obstructed views. For a detailed desciption of suites/cabins, see the entry for *Noordam*. A total of 37 cabins have inter-connecting doors. All balconies have solid steel railings instead of glass.

All suites/cabins have Signature of Excellence premium amenities: plush Mariner's Dream beds, waffle/terry cloth robes, Egyptian cotton towels, flat panel TVs, DVD players, make-up mirrors with halo lighting, massage shower heads, large hair dryers, fresh flowers and fruit baskets.

Niggles include lack of drawer space and noisy air-conditioning – the flow can't be regulated or turned off in cabins or bathrooms, the only regulation being for temperature control. Avoid cabins directly under the aft pool deck because deck chair dragging noises can be really irritating.

CUISINE. The two-deck-high *Rembrandt* main dining room is at the ship's aft, with seating at tables for two, four, six or eight on both main and upper levels; the galley is under the restaurant, accessed by port and starboard escalators. It provides a traditional HAL dining experience, with friendly service from Indonesian and Filipino stewards.

Both open seating and fixed seatings (assigned tables and time) are available, plus an open-seating arrangement for breakfast and lunch; you'll be seated by restaurant staff when you enter.

Alternative themed dining spots include the reservations-only *Pinnacle Grill*, the premium *Sterling Silver* steak and seafood restaurant and adjacent *Pinnacle Bar*; *Tamarind*, a 144-seat Pan-Asian restaurant (no charge for lunch; cover charge for dinner); and the 72-seat *Canaletto*, an Italian eatery created nightly in part of the *Lido Café*.

ENTERTAINMENT. Theatre-style seating is provided in the ship's main showlounge.

SPA/FITNESS. The Greenhouse Spa, the largest yet for HAL, includes a thermal suite (wet steam rooms with various herbal mists, plus dry saunas), and a large gymnasium. Sports enthusiasts can enjoy a basketball court, volleyball court, golf simulator.

● **For more extensive general information about Holland America Line, see pages 140–3.**

DID YOU KNOW...

● that motion pictures' most famous on-screen odd couple, Jack Lemmon and Walter Matthau, played gentlemen dance hosts intent on defrauding rich widows aboard a Caribbean cruise ship (*Westerdam*)? *Out to Sea*, a 1997 Martha Coolidge film, also starred Dyan Cannon, Gloria DeHaven, and Elaine Stritch. The "cruise ship" interior was filmed at Raleigh Studios in Hollywood.
● that Epirotiki Line's *Jupiter* was used to carry the 61 finalists of the 1976 Miss Universe contest (Epirotiki Line became part of the

now defunct Royal Olympia Cruises)?
● that on Valentine's Day, 1998, some 5,000 couples renewed their vows aboard the ships of Princess Cruises?
● that a 15-ft-high model of Goofy hangs upside down over the stern of *Disney Magic*? He's painting the ship.
● that Carnival Cruise Lines and Mattel teamed up to produce a nautical-themed Barbie Doll? She can be found in the gift shops aboard all the company's ships.
● that the spa aboard the now

withdrawn *Queen Elizabeth 2* was the first afloat to have a fully functional thalassotherapy pool; it was installed in 1994?
● that Steiner Leisure spa employees at sea massage over 30,000 bodies, deep cleanse 15,000 faces, blow dry 6,000 heads of hair, and manicure approximately 6,000 pairs of hands?
● that in 2002 Steiner Leisure purchased Mandara Spas and the Greenhouse Spas? Each brand continues to maintain its own identity.

Europa
★★★★★ +

Size: .Small Ship	Passenger Decks: 7	Cabins (wheelchair accessible): 2
Tonnage: .28,890	Total Crew: 280	Wheelchair accessibility: . . . . .Good
Lifestyle: . . . . .Utterly Exclusive	Passengers	Cabin Current: . . . . .110 and 220 volts
Cruise Line: . . . . .Hapag-Lloyd Cruises	(lower beds/all berths): 408/450	Elevators: 4
Former Names: . . . . .none	Passenger Space Ratio	Casino (gaming tables): . . . . .No
Builder: . . .Kvaerner Masa-Yards (Finland)	(lower beds/all berths): 70.4/64.2	Slot Machines: .No
Original Cost: . . . . .DM260 million	Crew/Passenger Ratio	Swimming Pools (outdoors): 1
Entered Service: . . . . .Sep 1999	(lower beds/all berths): 1.4/1.6	Swimming Pools (indoors): 1
Registry: . . . . .The Bahamas	Cabins (total): .204	(indoor/outdoor with magrodome)
Length (ft/m): 651.5/198.6	Size Range (sq ft/m): 355.2–914.9/	Whirlpools: 1
Beam (ft/m): 78.7/24.0	33.0–85.0	Self-Service Launderette: . . . . .Yes
Draft (ft/m): 20.0/6.1	Cabins (outside view): 204	(ironing room)
Propulsion/Propellers: . . . . .diesel-electric	Cabins (interior/no view): 0	Dedicated Cinema/Seats: Yes/60
(21,600 kW)/2 azimuthing pods	Cabins (for one person): 0	Library: . . . . .Yes
(13.3 MW each)	Cabins (with private balcony): 168	Onboard currency . . . . .Euros

A truly sophisticated ship for formal cruising.

OVERVIEW. *Europa* is arguably the most luxurious and finest of all the smaller cruise ships. For the German-speaking market, nothing else comes close. The crew also speaks English for the few British and American passengers, and some cruises are designated as bi-lingual English/German language voyages. Combined with an enthusiastic and well-trained crew, the tradition of luxury cruising in a contemporary setting is taken to its highest expression, with superb food and a wide range of creature comforts.

THE SHIP. *Europa* has a sleek appearance, with sweeping lines, a graceful profile, and Hapag-Lloyd's orange/ blue funnel. Look down from the aft Lido Deck fantail and you will see a rounded, graceful stern – unlike the box-like rears of so many contemporary ships. This is a very stable ship in the open sea, with no vibration or noise – thanks partly to its "pod" propulsion system *(details, page 191)*. It carries 14 Zodiac landing craft for use during close-up shore excursions; and boot-washing areas are also provided. Twenty bicycles are available free for shoreside use.

There is a walking/jogging area with rubberized deck (plus a walk-around outdoors teak promenade deck outdoors), as well as a small FKK (FreiKörperKultur) deck for nude sunbathing. The sunloungers are aluminum with teak armrests, and have thick cushioned pads.

There is one swimming pool, in a long, rectangular in shape. While not the widest, it is longer than the pools aboard many other cruise ships, measuring 56.7 by 16.8 ft (17.3 by 5.15 meters). Movies are screened poolside on

BERLITZ'S RATINGS

	Possible	Achieved
Ship	500	473
Accommodation	200	183
Food	400	373
Service	400	359
Entertainment	100	91
Cruise	400	373

OVERALL SCORE
1,852 points out of 2,000

selected evenings, and themed social events are held here.

With this ship, Hapag-Lloyd has been able to reach and maintain the high standards that its passengers demand, due to the fact that most of Europa's hotel service crew are German-speaking nationals who understand the culture and can talk in depth about German, Swiss, and Austrian life, unlike an international crew that can often barely communicate.

The space per passenger is high, there is never a hint of a line, and both restaurant and show lounge seat a full complement of passengers. *Europa* is one of the world's most spacious purpose-built cruise ships – an exquisite retreat, a world of relaxed, contemporary cruising that is intensely welcoming.

The ship is finely appointed, in the contemporary style usually described as "minimalism" in hotel-speak. Only the very best quality soft furnishings have been chosen for its interiors, subtly blending traditional with modern designs and materials. Most public rooms and hallways have extremely high ceilings, providing an enhanced sense of space and grandeur. The colors used in the interior decor are light and contemporary, with no hint of glitz or neon.

Public rooms include a Club Belvedere for afternoon tea and intimate music recitals, and the Europa Lounge, which has a U-shaped seating configuration and a proper stage, although there are several pillars. There is a Clipper Lounge/Bar with high ceilings, an Atrium Piano Bar with Steinway baby grand piano. Where a little-used casino was once located is now a multi-functional space for small cocktail parties, and serves as a high-class art gallery.

There is also a fine sidewalk Havana Bar cigar lounge.

This clubby room is equipped with three large glass-fronted, fully temperature-controlled and conditioned humidor cabinets, and carries an extensive range of cigars from Cuba and other countries. Cigars stocked include a range (from 102mm to 232mm) of top brands. The bar also serves a fine range of armagnacs, calvados and cognacs, all poured tableside, as well as Cuban beer. Embedded in a wall adjacent to the bar is a digital MP3 jukebox, with a push-button selection of 15,000 songs and instrumental music.

What's really nice in this intimate spot, with its buttery soft leather chairs and sofas, is Irish Coffee, correctly made – the glass should be rotated while the sugar is blended with the alcohol and heated gently over a candle flame, the liquor set alight before coffee and cream are added.

The nicely stocked library has an illuminated globe of the world, and is open 24 hours. There's also a small cinema/meeting/function room and a business center. There's a shuffleboard court, and dedicated rooms for hobbies (arts and crafts), and for children. Although a children's playroom is provided, *Europa* really is a ship for adults seeking a quiet, refined setting.

There is a seven-deck-high central atrium, plus two glass-walled elevators (operated by "piccolos" on embarkation day), and a lobby on the lower level with a Steinway grand piano and lobby bar, reception desk, concierge desk, shore excursion desk and a future cruise sales desk.

For wheelchair passengers, a special ramp is provided from the swimming pool/outdoors deck down to where the lifeboats are located; only three other ships have such a ramp.

There is now a children's center, and parents with infants receive a Baby Welcome Package. Also, Hapag-Lloyd Cruises has teamed up with Steiff to create the exclusive Captain Knopf teddy bear.

ACCOMMODATION. This is provided in five configurations and 10 price categories. It consists of all-outside-view suites: two Penthouse Grand Suites (Hapag, and Lloyd) and 10 Penthouse Deluxe Suites (Bach, Beethoven, Brahms, Handel, Lehár, Haydn, Mozart, Schubert, Strauss, Wagner, with each suite containing a large framed picture of the composer), 156 suites with private balcony, and 36 standard suites. There are two suites (with private balcony) for the disabled and eight suites with interconnecting doors – good for families.

Almost all suites have a private balcony with wide teak deck and lighting, and a smoked glass screen topped by a teak rail. The 12 suites that overlook the stern are among the most sought-after accommodation – six on each of two decks, each suite having a balcony with canvas "ceiling" for shade and privacy.

General Information: Each suite has a wood floor entryway, and each has a sleeping area with twin beds that can convert to a queen-sized bed, and two bedside tables with lamps and two drawers. There is a separate lounge area with curtain divider and bird's-eye maple wood cabinetry and accenting with rounded edges. Facilities include a refrigerator/mini-bar (beer and soft drinks are supplied at no extra charge), a writing/vanity desk, and couch with large

WHY DOES *EUROPA* SCORE SO HIGHLY?

The reason lies in the little details most cruise lines have long left behind in the age of discounts, the extras and the meticulous attention to personal comfort and service. If you are relaxing at the swimming pool in a hot climate, deck stewards will set your sunlounger and cover the mattress pad with a towel, serve you drinks, give you a cold herbal towel, and spray you with Evian water to keep you cool.

Naturally, only real glasses are used at the swimming pool and on the open decks – plastic glasses would not be considered. When drinks are served, they are placed on linen doilies (not paper or cork – a touch of finesse not found aboard other ships). Crystal and Dom Perignon champagne are served in Robbe and Berking silver goblets. Real flowers, pot pourri and cloth towels (paper towels are not used at this rating level) are provided in all public restrooms. Indeed, fresh flowers are everywhere.

Details, details, details – that's what *Europa* cruising is all about, and what the ship's many repeat passengers expect. The prices for drinks and wines are also very reasonable (they are not included for the simple reason that ships that include

drinks typically have a much more restricted selection, including young table wines that may not be to all tastes); also, the ship provides many social functions and parties where drinks are provided free. Birthdays and anniversaries are quietly celebrated in one's suite – there are no singing waiters in the dining room to disturb other passengers.

Excellent port information is provided (both in written form and via the TV infotainment system). All port taxes and gratuities are included, although further tipping is not prohibited. The ship's voyage chart is auctioned each cruise, with the proceeds going directly to charity.

When taking all things into account – the unhurried lifestyle of single seating dining, plenty of suites with private balconies, a fine array of classical music artists and lecturers, absolutely no vibration anywhere, and the outstanding cuisine and friendly, very attentive personal service from a staff dedicated to working aboard the world's finest cruise ship – it all adds up to the best cruise experience available today (unless you have your own private motor yacht).

While most cruise lines have been

engaged in dressing down, Hapag-Lloyd has done the opposite: dining room staff have stunning uniforms for formal nights, consisting of tails and trousers.

Although there are ships with more grandiose penthouse suites, larger balconies, show lounges, health spas and other appointments – but aboard *Europa*, everything is in scale, and in relation to the requirements of its passengers. At present, while there are plenty of imitators, there are no equals.

There are few weak points, although perhaps an indoor swimming pool might be welcome. The balcony partitions are part-partitions, but would be more private if they were of the full (floor-to-ceiling) type – although this rarely presents a problem. Occupants of suites on Penthouse Deck 10 have private assisted concierge check-in aboard the ship, rather than in the cruise terminal, wherever possible.

While *Europa* is not for everyone, the ship, which provides a more formal cruise experience than some might seek, provides the setting for the highest expression of the art of unobtrusive service and hospitality.

table in a separate lounge area. An illuminated walk-in closet provides ample hanging rail space, six drawers, personal safe that can be opened with a credit card, umbrella, shoehorn, and clothes brush. European duvets are provided, as is a full-color free daily newspaper (there's a wide choice). Almost all suites have totally unobstructed views and excellent soundproofing. All passengers receive a practical blue/beige shoulder travel bag, insulated lunch bag for shore excursions, leather keycard holder, and a generous supply of toiletries.

An integrated color TV/computer monitor and "CIN" (Cruise Infotainment System) – 24 hours per day video and audio on-demand – is provided free, so you choose when you want to watch any one of up to 100 movies, or when you want to listen to any of the 1,000+ compact audio discs.

The infotainment system includes large flat screens and direct, 24 hours-a-day internet connection via a wireless keyboard located in an adjacent vanity unit. The system displays restaurant seating plans, menus, ship's position and chart, deck plan, shore excursion video clips, plus other informational video clips. You get an assigned email address, provided with your tickets and other documentation in a proper leather document holder; there is no charge for incoming or outgoing emails, only for attachments, and for internet access. A data socket is provided should you decide to bring your own laptop computer, or the ship can supply a laptop for your use.

All suites have a 100% air-circulation system, illuminated walk-in closets and a generous amount of hanging and storage space. Western European butlers and cabin stewardesses are employed (butlers for the 12 premium suites on Deck 10, cabin stewardesses for all other suites).

The white/gray/sea green marble-tiled bathrooms are very well designed, have light decor, and include two good size cabinets for toiletries. All bathrooms have a full tub plus an integral shower and a retractable clothesline, and separate glass-fronted shower enclosure. Thick, 100% cotton bathrobes are provided, as are slippers and an array of toiletries. Parents with babies get a video baby phone (camera via PDA with vibration alarm, and wireless access).

Penthouses (Deck 10): There are two Penthouse Grand suites, redesigned in 2011, and 10 Penthouse Deluxe suites, refurbished in 2009, when electronically adjustable beds and Nespresso coffee machines were added. These have a teakwood entrance hall, spacious living room with full-size dining table and four chairs, fully stocked drinks cabinet with refrigerator butler service, complimentary bar set-up (replenished with whatever you need), laundry and ironing service included, priority spa reservations, caviar or other canapés daily before dinner, hand-made chocolates, petit-fours and other niceties at no extra charge. Balconies have teakwood decking, and white canvas ceiling shades. For the ultimate in exclusivity, the two Penthouse Grand suites have even larger bathrooms (each with a private sauna), and extensive forward views from their prime, supremely quiet location one deck above the navigation bridge; a large wrap-around private balcony; larger walk-in closet (with a window), large flat-screen TVs, and Robbe and Berking

silver champagne goblets. Well-trained butlers provide the highest level of unobtrusive service.

Spa suites: Four delightful spa suites, created in 2007, are located just forward of the Futuresse Spa on Deck 7. These incorporate a large private teak-decked balcony (good for massages); twin or queen-sized bed; walk-in closet; dark wood cabinetry housing a refrigerator stocked with fruit juices and different mineral waters, and bar set-up. There's a flat-screen TV, and storage space including a jewelry drawer, with pull-around doors that can close off everything to view, a writing/ vanity desk, and floor-to-ceiling windows. The decor colors are warm reds, yellow and gold. There is a large window between the living/sleeping area and the bathroom. The bathroom itself has warm Asian decor, underwater lighted Jacuzzi bath, separate large shower enclosure (with rain shower), toilet and gold, thick-glass washbasin, hand-held hairdryer, and plenty of storage space. Special teas and other services are provided by spa personnel. For cruises longer than 10 days, a customized spa package, including treatments, is included in the price.

Suites for the Disabled (Deck 7): These spacious suites have one electronically operated bed with hydraulic elevator plus one regular bed, while a non-walk-in closet with drawers replaces the walk-in closet in all other suites. The bathroom has a roll-in shower area. All fittings are at the correct height, and there are several grab handles, plus an emergency call-for-help button. Wheelchair-accessible public toilets are provided on the main restaurant/entertainment deck.

CUISINE. With over 5,000 separate food ingredients carried at any one time, the executive chef can produce menus that don't repeat even for around-the-world and other long voyages for which this ship excels. The cuisine is outstanding, always full of surprises. Seasonal and regional ingredients are featured, with much totally fresh fish and seafood as standard. Plated presentation of food is provided for entrées with silver service for additional vegetables, as well as tableside flambeaux. The size of portions is sensible, never overwhelming. There are four restaurants.

The *Europa Restaurant* is a beautiful two-deck-high formal dining room that can accommodate all passengers in one seating, with tables assigned for dinner only (breakfast and lunch are open seating). Passengers thus keep their favorite waiter for dinner throughout each cruise. In common with most German ships, a small smoking section is provided. There are tables for two (quite a few), four, six or eight. For superb service, there is a *chef de rang* and an assistant waiter system, so that the *chef de rang* is always at the station, with the assistant waiter acting as runner.

On days at sea, in addition to the regular, extensive breakfast, a Gourmet Breakfast menu includes items such as beef tartare, carpaccio of smoked tuna with wasabi cream, goose-liver tureen with orange confit, and other specialties rarely found aboard cruise ships today. A Cuisine Legeré menu provides light, healthy, but tasty spa cuisine.

Table settings include Dibbern china, 150-gram weight Robbe & Berking silverware and Riedel wine glasses. The cuisine is very international, but includes German favorites as well as regional dishes from around the world. The quality of food is extremely high. Although top-grade Iranian Ossetre caviar is found on dinner menus at least once each week, it is always available on request, at extra cost. Otherwise, most of the caviar comes from French farmed sturgeon, and is excellent.

An extensive wine list includes a good selection of vintage French wines, as well as a well-balanced selection of Austrian, German and Swiss wines.

Alternative dining options: In a first for the cruise industry, chef Dieter Müller, who has three Michelin stars, has his first Dieter Müller at Sea Restaurant, with a personally designed five-course menu (three courses for lunch). The menu changes three times during a world cruise, and seasonally during the rest of the year. He participates in 15 cruises a year – about half of *Europa*'s program. His restaurant, which is open for dinner nightly and for lunch on sea days, can be reserved once per cruise by all passengers – and at no extra charge.

Venezia, a second alternative dining spot, is much loved for its fine Italian cuisine – and a wide variety of olive oils and grappa. It is open for lunch and dinner, and at no extra charge. Both venues are adjacent to and forward of the main restaurant, and provide the setting for a truly intimate dining experience, by reservation only.

For more casual dining, try the elegant *Lido Café* for serve-yourself breakfasts – the ship even makes its own preserves – luncheons and dinners, with both indoor and outdoor seating (under heat lamps when needed) and adjacent indoor/outdoor bar. Themed evening dining is also featured here, with full waiter service. There is a wide variety of food, and many special lunch buffets have a number of popular themes and regional specialties.

Above the Lido Café is an indoor/outdoor bar, *Sansibar*, with great aft-facing views. It's liked by the late-night set.

Europa is famous for its real German sausages, available in the *Clipper Bar*, and at a special Bavarian Fruschoppen featured once each cruise in the Lido Café. Late each night, "light bites", beautifully presented on silver trays, are taken around the various bars and lounges.

Afternoon tea is a sheer delight, with a selection of about 30 teas (loose tea, of course, never teabags). There are also several types of coffee and impeccably made liqueur coffees, heated in a hand-turned glass enclosure, and a superb selection of cakes, made fresh every day. Nautical tradition is maintained with bouillon service each morning at sea, and other daily niceties include fresh waffles and ice cream each afternoon around the pool.

ENTERTAINMENT. The Europa Lounge, whose decor is a rich red, is the main showlounge; it has a sloping floor, providing good sightlines from most seats. The ship excels in its fine, intellectual entertainment program (it is tailored more to the theme of the cruise), which includes a constant supply of high-quality classical and contemporary musical artistes, a variety of cabaret acts, as well as a programme of expert lecturers, poetry readers, and so on, together with an occasional colorful production show, and local shows brought on board in various ports.

The smaller, more intimate Clipper Lounge is the setting for late-night cabaret. The ship carries a main showband, plus small musical units to provide live music for listening or dancing. Classical concerts and recitals are provided in the Belvedere Lounge, with its dropped central circular floor and white Steinway grand piano. A summer Ocean Sun Festival has been an outstanding, successful and worthwhile addition to the classical music cruises.

SPA/FITNESS. The Ocean Spa has a wide range of beauty services and treatments, including hot stone massage, and an array of other rejuvenating treatments, including full-day spa packages. Shiseido cosmetics are the featured cosmetic/spa products for sale. The entire spa area is a well integrated and very welcoming wellness and treatment area.

Facilities include a steam room and sauna (mixed), two shower enclosures and two foot-washing stations, relaxation room with three hot tiled beds, three wicker relax beds, and male and female changing/dressing rooms. There is a separate gymnasium with new mihabodytec machine, and a beauty salon. A Japanese Room is featured, including a two-tatami mat relaxation area; treatments include a cream body massage. A nice touch is that treatment rooms have music menus, so you can choose what music you wish to hear.

On cruises with more than four sea days, *Europa*'s shore-based wellness partner provides, at no extra charge, "Vital" specialists for lectures and wellness regimes, in addition to the ship's own fitness team.

A recent feature on cruises with four or more sea days, is father and son (or daughter) fencing, with all equipment provided by *die fechtmeister*. An electronic golf simulator room complements a golf driving range, and a PGA golf pro is carried on all cruises.

Explorer of the Seas
★★★★

Size: . . . . .Large Resort Ship	Passenger Decks: 14	Cabins (wheelchair accessible): 26
Tonnage: 137,308	Total Crew: 1,181	Wheelchair accessibility: . . . . .Best
Lifestyle: . . . . .Standard	Passengers	Cabin Current: . . . . .110 volts
Cruise Line: Royal Caribbean International	(lower beds/all berths): 3,114/3,840	Elevators: . . . . .14 (6 glass-enclosed)
Former Names: . . . . .none	Passenger Space Ratio	Casino (gaming tables): . . . . .Yes
Builder: . . .Kvaerner Masa-Yards (Finland)	(lower beds/all berths): 44.0/35.7	Slot Machines: . . . . .Yes
Original Cost: . . . .$500 million	Crew/Passenger Ratio	Swimming Pools (outdoors): 3
Entered Service: . . . . .Oct 2000	(lower beds/all berths): 2.6/3.2	Swimming Pools (indoors): 0
Registry: . . . . .The Bahamas	Cabins (total): 1,557	Whirlpools: 6
Length (ft/m): 1,020.6/311.1	Size Range (sq ft/m): 151.0–1,358.0/	Self-Service Launderette: . . . . .No
Beam (ft/m): 155.5/47.4	14.0–126.1	Dedicated Cinema/Seats: . . . . .No
Draft (ft/m): 28.8/8.8	Cabins (outside view): 939	Library: . . . . .Yes
Propulsion/Propellers: . . . . .diesel-electric	Cabins (interior/no view): 618	Onboard currency . . . . .US$
(75,600kW)/3 pods	Cabins (for one person): 0	
(2 azimuthing, 1 fixed/14 MW each)	Cabins (with private balcony): 757	

A big-ship setting designed to entertain the whole family.

OVERVIEW. In terms of sheer size, this large, stunning, floating leisure resort dwarfs most other ships in the cruise industry, but in terms of personal service, the reverse is the case, unless you have one of the top suites. Although it's large, the cabin hallways are warm and attractive, with artwork cabinets and wavy lines to lead you along and break up the monotony. There are plenty of whimsical decorative touches to prevent the environment being too clinical.

THE SHIP. *Explorer of the Seas* is sister to *Adventure of the Seas, Mariner of the Seas, Navigator of the Seas* and *Voyager of the Seas*). With its large proportions, it provides more facilities and options, yet it has a healthy amount of space per passenger. It is too large to go through the Panama Canal, limiting itineraries almost exclusively to the Caribbean, where few islands can accept it, or for use as a floating resort. Take a few hours to explore the many facilities and public spaces and it will be time well spent.

The four-decks-high Royal Promenade, 394 ft (120 meters) long and the main interior focal point, is a good place to hang out or to arrange to meet someone. The length of two American football fields, it has two internal lobbies that rise as many as 11 decks high. Restaurants, shops and entertainment locations front this winding street and interior "with-view" cabins look into it from above. The Guest Reception and Shore Excursion counters are located at the aft end of the promenade, as is an ATM machine. Look up to see the large moving, asteroid-like sculpture (constantly growing and contracting), parades and street entertainers.

Arched across the promenade is a captain's balcony. Meanwhile, a stairway in the center of the promenade con-

BERLITZ'S RATINGS

	Possible	Achieved
Ship	500	418
Accommodation	200	150
Food	400	222
Service	400	281
Entertainment	100	83
Cruise	400	307

OVERALL SCORE
1,461 points out of 2,000

nects you to the deck below, where you'll find Schooner Bar (a piano lounge that's a feature of all RCI ships) and the colorful Casino Royale. Casino gaming includes blackjack, Caribbean stud poker, roulette, and craps, as well as 300 slot machines.

Aft of the casino is the Aquarium Bar; adjacent are some neat displays of oceanographic interest. Royal Caribbean International teamed up with the University of Miami's Rosenstiel School of Marine and Atmospheric Science to study the ocean and the atmosphere. A small onboard laboratory is part of the project.

There is a regulation-size ice-skating rink (Studio B), with real ice, and stadium-style seating for up to 900, plus high-tech broadcast facilities. Ice Follies shows are also presented here. Slim pillars obstruct clear-view arena stage sightlines, however. If ice-skating in the Caribbean doesn't appeal, perhaps you'd like reading in the two-deck library, open 24 hours a day. A grand $12 million was spent on permanent artwork.

Drinking places include a neat Aquarium Bar, which comes complete with 50 tons of glass and water in four large aquariums. Other drinking places include the intimate Champagne Bar, Crown & Anchor Pub, a Sidewalk Café (for continental breakfast, all-day pizzas, specialty coffees and desserts), Sprinkles (for round-the-clock ice cream and yoghurt), and Weekend Warrior (a sports bar), and a Connoisseur Club (for cigars and cognacs). Jazz fans might like Dizzy's, an intimate room for cool music within the Viking Crown Lounge, or the Schooner Bar piano lounge. Golfers might enjoy the 19th Hole, a golf bar, as they play the Explorer Links.

There are also several shops on the Royal Promenade, including a jewelry shop, gift shop, and liquor store. At times, street entertainers appear, and parades happen.

A TV studio is adjacent to rooms useable for trade show exhibit space, with a 400-seat conference center and a multi-media screening room seating 60. You can tie the knot in the Skylight Chapel, which even has wheelchair access via an electric stairlift. Outdoors, the pool and open deck areas provide a resort-like environment.

Passenger gripes: cabin bath towels and explosively noisy (vacuum) toilets; few quiet places to sit and read – almost everywhere there is intrusive background music. And if you have a cabin with a door that interconnecting door to another cabin, be aware that you'll be able to hear everything your next-door neighbours say and do.

FAMILIES. Facilities for children and teenagers are quite extensive. "Aquanauts" is for 3–5 year olds; "Explorers" (6–8); "Voyagers" (9–12). Optix is a dedicated area for teenagers, including a daytime club with computers, soda bar, disco with disc jockey and dance floor. Challenger's Arcade has the latest video games. Paint and Clay is an arts and crafts center for younger children. Adjacent to these indoor areas is Adventure Beach, an area for all the family to enjoy: it includes swimming pools, a water slide and game areas outdoors.

ACCOMMODATION. There are 22 cabin categories, in four major groupings: Premium ocean-view suites and cabins, Promenade-view (interior-view) cabins, Ocean-view cabins, and Interior (no view) cabins. Many cabins are of a similar size – good for incentives and large groups – and 300 have interconnecting doors, good for families.

Some 138 interior cabins have bay windows – pointless, really, because you see into your neighbor's cabin unless you keep the cutains closed. The windows look into a horizontal atrium, with interior cabins that look into a central shopping plaza. All cabins except for the Royal Suite and Owner's Suite have twin beds that convert to a queen-sized unit, TV set, radio and telephone, personal safe, vanity unit, mini-bar, hairdryer and private bathroom.

The largest accommodation includes luxurious penthouse suites, whose occupants have sole access to a concierge club. The grandest is the Royal Suite, on the port side of the ship, and measures 1,146 sq. ft (106.5 sq. meters). It has a king-sized bed in a separate, large bedroom, a living room with an additional queen-sized sofa bed, baby grand piano, refrigerator/wet bar, dining table, entertainment center, and large bathroom.

There are similar facilities in the slightly smaller, but still highly desirable Owner's Suites – there are 10, all in the center of the ship, on both port and starboard sides, each measuring 468 sq. ft (43 sq. meters) and four Royal Family suites (each measures 574 sq. ft (53 sq. meters). The Royal Family suites, which have two bedrooms (including one with third/ fourth upper Pullman berths) are located at the stern of the ship and have magnificent views over the ship's wake and the accompanying seagulls.

All cabins have a private bathroom with shower enclosure (towels are 100% cotton), plus interactive television and pay-per-view movies. Cabins with "private balconies" aren't so private, as the partitions are only partial.

CUISINE. The large main dining room is set on three levels, named after explorers (*Christopher Columbus, Da Gama* and *Magellan*). All three have exactly the same menus. Choose one of two seatings, or "My Time Dining" (eat when you want, during dining room hours) when you book. Tables are for four, six, eight 10 or 12.

Alternative Dining Options: Alternative dining options for casual and informal meals at all hours (according to company releases) include:
● *Café Promenade*, for continental breakfast, all-day pizzas and speciality coffees (provided in paper cups).
● *Windjammer Café*, for casual buffet-style breakfast, lunch and light dinner (except on a cruise's last night).
● *Island Grill* (actually a section inside the Windjammer Café), for casual dinner (no reservations needed), with a grill and open kitchen.
● *Portofino*: the ship's "upscale" Italian restaurant, open for dinner only. Reservations are required, and there's a gratuity per person. The food and its presentation are better than the food in the dining room. Choices include antipasti, soup, salad, pasta, main dish, dessert, cheese and coffee. The menu does not change throughout the cruise.
● *Johnny Rockets*, a retro 1950s all-day, all-night diner-style eatery, has hamburgers, malt shakes (at extra cost), and jukebox hits, with both indoor and outdoor seating.
● *Sprinkles*, for round-the-clock ice cream and yogurt, pastries and coffee.

ENTERTAINMENT. The stunning 1,350-seat Palace Show-lounge spans five decks, with only a few slim pillars and almost no disruption of sight lines. The room has a hydraulic orchestra pit and huge stage areas, together with sonic-boom loud sound, and superb lighting equipment. The strongest cabaret acts perform in the main show-lounge, while others play the Maharaja's Lounge.

SPA/FITNESS. The large ShipShape health spa includes a large aerobics room, fitness center (with the usual techno-gym equipment), several treatment rooms, men's and women's sauna/steam rooms. Another 10,000 sq. ft (930 sq. meters) is devoted to a Solarium (with sliding glass roof) for relaxation after you've overexercised. A 32.8-ft (10-meter) rock-climbing wall has five climbing tracks. Other sports facilities include a roller-blading track, a dive-and-snorkel shop, a full-size basketball court and nine-hole, par 26 golf course.

● **For more extensive general information about the Royal Caribbean cruise experience, see pages 152–6.**

50 Years of Victory
★★★★

Size: ....Boutique	Passenger Decks: 6	Cabins (wheelchair accessible): 0
Tonnage: 23,439	Total Crew: 140	Wheelchair accessibility: ....None
Lifestyle: ....Standard (Expedition)	Passengers	Cabin Voltage:..........................110 volts
Cruise Line: ....Quark Expeditions	(lower beds/all berths): 128	Elevators: 1
Former Names:.................................*Ural*	Passenger Space Ratio	Casino (gaming tables): 0
Builder: ....Baltic Works, St. Petersburg	(lower beds/all berths):.........183.1/183.1	Slot Machines: 0
(Russia)	Crew/Passenger Ratio	Swimming Pools (outdoors):.................1
Original Cost: ....n/a	(lower beds/all berths):................0.9/0.9	Swimming Pools (indoors): 0
Entered Service:............................2009	Cabins (total):.....................................50	Whirlpools: 0
Registry: ....Russia	Size Range (sq ft/m): 148.5–367.0/	Self-Service Launderette:.................Yes
Length (ft/m):.........................523.6/159.6	13.8–34.1	Dedicated Cinema/Seats: ....No
Beam (ft/m):...........................98.4/30.0	Cabins (outside view):..........................50	Library:..Yes
Draft (ft/m):..............................36.3/11.08	Cabins (interior/no view):......................0	Onboard currency ....US$
Propulsion/Propellers: 2 x nuclear reactors,	Cabins (for one person):........................0	
with 3 propulsion motors (75,000 hp)	Cabins (with private balcony):................0	

Nuclear-powered, it's the ultimate expedition ship.

OVERVIEW. An advanced vessel of the *Arktika*-class of icebreaking ships, this outstanding polar expedition cruise ship suits adventurous, hardy outdoors types of mature years who enjoy visiting some of the earth's most inhospitable places. The ship is powered by two nuclear reactors, and carries enough fuel to power it for four years before it needs refuelling. A number of thoroughly experienced lecturers are carried on each sailing.

THE SHIP. This dramatic, very impressive vessel (*Let Pobedy* in Russian, or *50 Years of Victory* or *Fiftieth Anniversary of Victory*), the world's largest icebreaker, is the first such ship with a spoon-shaped bow, the ideal shape for breaking through really stubborn ice up to 8 ft (2.5 meters) thick. The ship has a digital automated control system. Its building, originally started in October 1989, was not completed until the beginning of 2007, work having been halted in 1994 due to insufficient funds and started again in 2003.

When the ship went through its sea trials in 2007 – actually after the 60th anniversary of the end of World War II, known to Russians as the Great Patriotic War – it was found to have exceptional maneuverability in thick ice, and a speed of more than 21 knots.

There are more crew members than passengers, giving a most impressive Passenger Space Ratio. The ship is rugged but very comfortable, and carries a fleet of Zodiac inflatable landing craft. It has a small "dip" pool at the stern, underneath the helicopter deck.

Let Pobedy typically leaves from the northern Russian city of Murmansk before heading across the Barents Sea. Approaching the North Pole – 90° north and 1,000 miles (1,600 km) from the closest tree – aboard a Russian icebreaker is the ultimate prize of a true Arctic Expedition voyage, when participants leave the ship and form a circle, holding hands, at the North Pole, the holy grail of generations of explorers. The sheer noise as the ship crushes through the meters-thick archipelago ice is stunning.

Each adventure/expedition voyage planned and operated by Quark Expeditions is something special in the world of adventure travel.

Gratuities to the staff are left to your discretion.

ACCOMMODATION. There are four "suite" grades and one cabin grade. All have windows that open, so all have outside views. Only two (46 and 48) have obstructed views. Each has private bathroom facilities.

CUISINE. There is one dining room, which operates in a single, open seating, so you sit with whomever you wish. The food is best described as carbohydrate-rich hearty fare – good for those energetic days of exploration.

ENTERTAINMENT. There isn't any as such, because this is real adventure cruising, with dinner and conversation among all participants being the main event each day.

SPA/FITNESS. Sauna, athletics (fitness) center, small swimming pool, and basketball court.

BERLITZ'S RATINGS

	Possible	Achieved
Ship	500	367
Accommodation	200	140
Food	400	260
Service	400	275
Entertainment	n/a	n/a
Cruise	500	369

OVERALL SCORE
1,411 points out of 2,000

Fram
NOT YET RATED

Size:	.Small Ship	Total Crew:	.75
Tonnage:	.11,647	Passengers	
Lifestyle:	.Standard	(lower beds/all berths):	.252/328
Cruise Line:	.Hurtigruten	Passenger Space Ratio	
Former Names:	.none	(lower beds/all berths):	.46.2/35.5
Builder:	.Fincantieri (Italy)	Crew/Passenger Ratio	
Original Cost:	.€68.6 million	(lower beds/all berths):	.3.3/4.3
Entered Service:	.Apr 2007	Cabins (total):	.126
Registry:	.Norway	Size Range (sq ft/m):	.n/a
Length (ft/m):	.374.0/114.0	Cabins (outside view):	.102
Beam (ft/m):	.66.2/20.2	Cabins (interior/no view):	.24
Draft (ft/m):	.5.1	Cabins (for one person):	.0
Propulsion/Propellers:	.Diesel (4.6mW)/2	Cabins (with private balcony):	.6
Passenger Decks:	.6	Cabins (wheelchair accessible):	.2

Wheelchair Accessibility:	.Fair
Cabin Current:	.110 volts
Elevators:	.2
Casino (gaming tables):	.No
Slot Machines:	.No
Swimming Pools (outdoors):	.0
Swimming Pools (indoors):	.0
Whirlpools:	.2
Self-Service Launderette:	.No
Dedicated Cinema/Seats:	.No
Library:	.No
Onboard currency:	.Norwegian krona

Expedition-style cruising in a modern, minimalist ship.

OVERVIEW. Designed to operate in polar waters, *Fram* sails from Reykjavik, Iceland, operating Greenland and Spitzbergen cruises from May through September, and winter cruises to and within Antarctica. It suits mature-age adults who like exploring independently in a ship that is modern and comfortable, but minimalist and unpretentious.

THE SHIP. *Fram* features Norway's culture and incorporates stylish Scandinavian decor inspired by Greenlandic culture, using an extensive mix of wool, leather and oak. The interior decor is decidedly Inuit in style and flavor. The few public rooms include the Quilac observation lounge, an internet café, board room, and a small shop. There is no walk-around promenade deck.

Hurtigruten doesn't have a culture of hospitality and service, so many passengers feel they are travelling with a ferry company – there's even a car deck – rather than a cruise line. The crew to passenger ratio is low, which does not equate to a high level of service or attention to detail.

Life on board is very relaxed, so formal attire is never needed. Smoking is allowed only on the open deck – and not at all when *Fram* is in port. The ship operates in Norwegian and English. There are no safety deposit boxes. Hurtigruten operates a no-tipping-required policy.

ACCOMMODATION. There are 13 price categories (too many), according to size and location. The good thing is that no cabins have obstructed views. The largest accommodation is one Owner's Suite, which consists of a bedroom, living room and bathroom with Jacuzzi tub. Six cabins at the aft of the ship, overlooking the stern and the ship's wake, have a shared balcony.

BERLITZ'S RATINGS		
	Possible	Achieved
Ship	500	NYR
Accommodation	200	NYR
Food	400	NYR
Service	400	NYR
Entertainment	100	NYR
Cruise	400	NYR

There are several price grades for standard cabins, which typically have one bed, and a sofa that converts to a fold-down bed, or two pull-down sofa beds; there's very little room, and almost no storage space. In other words, they are extremely small and basic (think: caravan style), when compared to normal cruise ship standards.

Only suites and mini-suites have tea and coffee-making facilities, although these and other beverages can be purchased 24 hours a day by non-suite passengers.

CUISINE. *Restaurant Imaq*, the main dining room, is located at the stern, and connects with the main lobby via an arcade. Local cuisine and recipes, including such things as bison meat and fresh fish, are featured. However, several meals are of the self-help buffet variety only – not what one would expect for the cruise prices charged, and there's little finesse in terms of presentation. An extra-charge bistro and self-serve buffet are available for more casual meals. Be aware that alcoholic drinks prices are very high, in line with Norwegian prices ashore (example: a small draught beer will set you back about $8–$10).

ENTERTAINMENT. There isn't any. Guides and lecturers organize talks and informative briefings based on the cruise area. Talks are given in both Norwegian and English.

SPA/FITNESS. Saunas for men and women are located one deck above the exercise area, forward of the funnel and two hot tubs. There are no other spa facilities, other than an exercise room, which can become really hot because there's not enough air-conditioning.

Freedom of the Seas
★★★★

Size:	.Large Resort Ship	Passenger Decks:	.15	Cabins (with private balcony):	.842
Tonnage:	.154,407	Total Crew:	.1,397	Cabins (wheelchair accessible):	.32
Lifestyle:	.Standard	Passengers		Wheelchair accessibility:	.Best
Cruise Line:	Royal Caribbean International	(lower beds/all berths):	.3,634/4,375	Cabin Current:	.110 volts
Former Names:	.none	Passenger Space Ratio		Elevators:	.14
Builder:	.Kvaerner Masa-Yards (Finland)	(lower beds/all berths):	.42.0/35.32	Casino (gaming tables):	.Yes
Original Cost:	.$590 million	Crew/Passenger Ratio		Slot Machines:	.Yes
Entered Service:	.Jun 2006	(lower beds/all berths):	.2.6/3.1	Swimming Pools (outdoors):	.2
Registry:	.The Bahamas	Cabins (total):	.1,817	Swimming Pools (indoors):	.0
Length (ft/m):	.1,112.2/339.0	Size Range (sq ft/m):	.153.0–2,025.0/	Whirlpools:	.6
Beam (ft/m):	.183.7/56.0		14.2–188.1	Self-Service Launderette:	.No
Draft (ft/m):	.27.8/8.5	Cabins (outside view):	.1,084	Dedicated Cinema/Seats:	.No
Propulsion/Propellers:	.diesel-electric	Cabins (interior/no view):	.733	Library:	.Yes
	(75,600 kW)/3 pods (42,000 kW)	Cabins (for one person):	.0	Onboard currency	.US$

A large floating theme park for the whole family.

OVERVIEW. *Freedom of the Seas* is fresh, exciting and very comfortable, with tasteful decor and many bars and lounges. It is certainly a great ship for young, active families with children, as long as you don't mind lines and signing up for popular activities like the "Flowrider" surf area (about a year ahead should do it), rock-climbing wall and full-size boxing ring.

THE SHIP. *Freedom of the Seas* (with sisters *Independence of the Seas* and *Liberty of the Seas*) is an extension of the highly successful *Voyager*-class of ships, which Royal Caribbean International introduced in 1999 with *Voyager of the Seas*. The ship's length and beam were extended, enabling an increase in the number of cabins and passenger capacity, as well as a combined pool area 43% larger than the *Voyager*-class – but with 500 more passengers.

At 1,112 ft/339 meters, the ship is the length of 37 London double-decker buses; and with a beam of 185 ft/56 meters, it is wider than Washington's White House, at 165 ft/50 meters. If you meet someone and want to meet them again, it's best to make an appointment and set a location, for this really is a large, Las Vegas-style floating resort-city.

Innovative designs are possible because of this extra length. These include two 16-person hot tubs cantilevered 12 ft (3.7 meters) over the sides of the ship in an adults-only Solarium area – although the Solarium's pool itself is small. The ship's "pod" propulsion system virtually eliminates vibration *(for details, see page 191)*.

Perhaps the "wow" factor aboard this ship is its connection with water, including a 40ft x 32ft (12.2 x 9.7 meters) "Flowrider" surfing zone that is the ship's stern. This wave

BERLITZ'S RATINGS

	Possible	Achieved
Ship	500	426
Accommodation	200	161
Food	400	235
Service	400	289
Entertainment	100	82
Cruise	400	317

OVERALL SCORE
1,510 points out of 2,000

simulator creates a wall of water, flowing at 35,000 gallons per minute, for board or body surfers – but no more than two at a time. Then there's the H_2O Zone forward of the funnel, an interactive water-themed play area for families that includes a pool fed by a waterfall, and two hot tubs.

Also included are water cannons and spray fountains, water jets and ground gushers; by night the "water park" turns into a colorfully-lit "Sculpture Garden." Twin central pools consist of a main pool and a sports pool, with grandstand-style seating and competitive games including pole jousting.

Other active sports facilities include a rock-climbing wall, in-line skating area, an ice-skating rink, and golf simulators. Then there's that full-size boxing ring in the spa, with sparring partners included in the extra-cost session.

The same facilities (public rooms, bars and lounges) featured in the *Voyager*-class ships were incorporated, but with the addition of substantial conference facilities, extensive wi-fi coverage and connectivity for cell phones. The four elements – earth, air, fire, and water – provide the decorative theme for the artwork aboard this ship.

Although this is one of the world's largest cruise ships (carry your GPS unit!), the cabin hallways have an warm, attractive feel, with some neat interactive artwork cabinets and asymmetrical flow that leads you along and breaks up the monotony. There are plenty of colorful, whimsical, decorative touches typical of Scandinavian designers.

There are 16 bars and lounges. There's a whole promenade of shops, munching and drinking spots along an indoor mall-like environment called the Royal Promenade that is four decks high (some interior cabins have great views into it). The Royal Promenade is home to fashion, jewelry and perfume shops, a general store, logo shop, Promenade Café, Ben & Jerry's ice cream outlet, a Book Nook, a barber shop called A Close Shave (a razor shave "experience" costs more than $70), a pizzeria, and an English pub, The Bull and Bear. And watch out for the stilt walkers and inflatable elephants when the circus is in town. Look at the ceiling in this large atrium and you'll see Vittoria Alata ("Winged Victory") flowing down towards you – an exact replica of the sculpture in the Piazza Venetia in Rome.

The forward section of this large space leads neatly into a large nightclub called Pharaoh's Palace, typically used for late-night adult comedy. One deck down from the Royal Promenade houses a large Casino Royale, The Crypt discotheque, Schooner Bar (piano bar), Boleros (Latin hangout), and a photo gallery, while the forward section leads you into the three-decks high 1,350-seat Arcadia Theatre. A whimsical piece of artwork on the forward starboard stairway includes a musical line whose tune is: "My Bonnie Lies Over the Ocean…"

There is also a regulation-size ice-skating rink (Studio B) with real, not fake, ice, with "bleacher" seating, and the latest in broadcast facilities. Superb "Ice Follies" shows are also presented here, but a number of slim pillars obstruct clear-view arena stage sight lines. Almost at the top of the ship is RCI's trademark Viking Crown Lounge, the cutely named Olive or Twist jazz lounge, and a wedding chapel.

Other facilities include a cigar smoker's lounge, conference center, a concierge lounge (for suite occupants only), and the comfortable 3,600-book Wilhemsen Library.

Freedom of the Seas is fresh, exciting and very comfortable, with tasteful decor and many bars and lounges. However, there are only four banks of elevators (two forward and two aft) totaling 14, so if you have a cabin in the center of the ship, you'll need to walk forward or aft in order to travel vertically between decks; and there are only two major stairways – one forward, one aft – for such a large ship. On disembarkation day, you'll need to allow plenty of time to get an elevator, and, probably, for your bags to arrive – and are no seats in the luggage hall in Miami.

FAMILIES. Children are well catered to, with Adventure Ocean for kids of six months to 17 years of age. Children will love this ship and all the fun activities and sports.

ACCOMMODATION. There is a wide range of suites and cabins in 14 categories and 21 price grades, from a Presidential Family Suite that can sleep up to 14 to twin-bed two-person interior cabins, and interior cabins that look into an interior shopping/strolling atrium promenade. Price depends on grade. There are many family-friendly cabins, good for reunions, but no single occupancy cabins. All outside-view cabins have even numbers; all interior cabins have odd numbers.

Some accommodation examples (from large to small):
Presidential Family Suite: Located in the aft section, this suite comprises five rooms. These include two master bedrooms, each with twin beds that convert to a queen-size bed

and ensuite bathroom with tub/shower (the toiletries cabinets are the same as in all other cabins); two other very small bedrooms that can sleep four; private balcony sand-colored rubberized decking, not teak, with loungers, tables, chairs, a bar, and a decent view aft – although part of the balcony is overlooked by balconies on the decks above, and there is a lot of wasted space aft of the balcony because it doesn't extend to the very stern. There's also a lounge with two sofa beds, bar. The suite can accommodate eight to 14 (that's odd numbers breathing in, even numbers breathing out!), located aft, at the opposite end of the ship to the showlounge. Size: 1,215 sq. ft. (113 sq. meters), plus Balcony: 810 sq. ft (75 sq. meters). It's a pleasant enough apartment, but nothing special – it's really quite cramped and the ceilings are plain – but it could be good value for a large family, provided everyone gets on well in a confined space.

Owner's Suite: Features include a queen-size bed, private balcony, separate living area with queen-size sofa bed, wet bar, vanity area, walk-in closet; bathroom with tub and shower. Sleeps up to five. Size: 506 sq. ft. (46 sq. meters) plus Balcony: 131 sq. ft. (12.1 sq. meters).

Royal Suite: Perhaps the nicest decor of all the suites, the Royal Suite has a very spacious lounge, with black baby grand player piano, queen-size sofa and entertainment center, wet bar, and dining table. The bedroom is quite spacious and has a queen-size bed; the bathroom has a jacuzzi bath, large walk-in shower, and two (rather gaudy) gold washbasins. Sleeps up to four. Size: 1,406 sq.ft. (130.6 sq. meters) plus 377 sq.ft. (35 sq. meters).

Grand Suite: This has two twin beds convertible to queen-size, a private balcony, sitting area (some with sofa bed), vanity area; bathroom with tub and shower. Sleeps up to four. Size: 381 sq. ft. (35.3 sq. meters) plus Balcony: 89 sq. ft. (8.2 sq. meters)

Junior Suite: Two twin beds convertible to queen-size, a private balcony, sitting area (some with sofa bed), vanity area; bathroom with tub and shower. Sleeps up to four. Size: 277 sq. ft. (25.7 sq. meters) plus Balcony: 65 sq. ft. (6.0 sq. meters).

Superior Oceanview Cabin: Two twin beds convertible to queen-size, a private balcony, sitting area (some with sofa bed), vanity area; bathroom with shower. Sleeps two (some rooms sleep three or four). Size: 202 sq. ft. (18.7 sq. meters) + Balcony: 42 sq. ft. (3.9 sq. meters).

Deluxe Oceanview Cabin: Two twin beds convertible to queen-size, a private balcony, sitting area (some with sofa bed), vanity area; bathroom with shower. Sleeps two (some rooms sleep three or four). Size: 173 sq. ft. (16.0 sq. meters) + Balcony: 46 sq. ft. (4.2 sq. meters).

Interior (promenade-view) Cabin: These 172 cabins, on three decks, are interior cabins but with bay windows that allow occupants to look into the Royal Promenade. They have two twin beds convertible to queen-size; private bathroom with shower.

Interior (no view) Cabin: Two twin beds convertible to queen-size; there's a private bathroom with shower. Sleeps two (some rooms sleep three or four). Size: 160 sq. ft. (14.8 sq.meters).

Family Ocean-view Cabin: Located at the front of the ship, it contains two twin beds (convertible to queen-size), sofa and/or Pullman beds, sitting area; bathroom, with shower. Accommodates six, and has 48-inch (122-cm) round windows. Size: 265 sq. ft. (24.6 sq. meters).

All grades of accommodation have a private bathroom with tub and shower, or shower only, washbasin and toiletries cabinet. However, they are really basic, modular and akin to bathrooms found in caravans and mobile homes. There's a vanity desk with hairdryer, mini-bar, personal safe, flat-screen TV, radio, satellite-dial telephone, and nine-inch thick mattresses and duvets. A room service menu is provided. Suite occupants have access to a Concierge Lounge, for more personal service, which saves going down to the reception desk and standing in line.

CUISINE. The extremely large main dining room is set on three levels, each with a theme and different name – *Leonardo, Isaac,* and *Galileo* – but all with exactly the same menus and food. A dramatic staircase connects the three levels, but huge, fat support pillars obstruct the sight lines from many seats. When you book, choose from one of two seatings – tables are for four, six, eight, 10, or 12 – or "My Time Dining" (eat when you want, during dining hours). **Alternative (extra-charge) Dining Options:** These venues, all non-smoking, provide casual and informal meals at all hours (according to company statements):

● *Chops Grill:* for premium steaks, chops and special seafood, set in a great location. Open for dinner only, reservations required; cover charge.

● *Portofino:* this Euro-Italian restaurant is open for dinner only. Reservations required; cover charge. Choices include: antipasti, soup, salad, pasta, main dish, dessert, cheese and coffee, and the menu doesn't change during the cruise.

● *Promenade Café:* for continental breakfast, all-day pizzas, sandwiches and coffees provided in paper cups.

● *Sprinkles:* for round-the-clock ice cream and yoghurt, pastries and coffee.

● *Windjammer Café*: self-serve casual buffet breakfast, lunch and dinner, except for the cruise's last night.

● *Jade Restaurant* (a section of the Windjammer Café): self-serve casual buffet breakfasts, lunch and dinner; no reservations necessary.

● *Johnny Rockets,* a retro 1950s all-day, all-night diner-style eatery that serves hamburgers, hot dogs and other fast-food items, malt shakes and sodas (at extra cost) with indoor and outdoor seating. All indoor tables have a mini-jukebox, and dimes are provided for you to make your selection of vintage records. The waitresses are all-singing and all-dancing. There's a cover charge.

You'll need to make reservations for Chops Grill or Portofino as early as you can in the cruise, because seating is limited and sells out quickly – not surprising when there are typically over 4,000 passengers on each cruise.

ENTERTAINMENT. The stunning Arcadia Theater is located on three decks at the forward end of the ship (actually five decks including orchestra pit and scenery storage space). It has only a few pillars and little disruption of sightlines. The room has a hydraulic orchestra pit and huge stage areas, together with sonic-boom loud sound, and some superb lighting equipment. The cast performs three production shows each cruise.

Most of the cabaret acts are not what you would call headliners. The strongest acts perform in the main showlounge, while others are presented in the Nightclub, the venue for late-night adults-only comedy. The most entertaining shows are the Ice Spectaculars. There is also a TV studio, adjacent to rooms that can also be used for trade show exhibit space (good for conventions at sea).

Royal Caribbean's production shows are colorful spectaculars that will remind you of Las Vegas casino hotels, fast-moving, razzle-dazzle shows that have little or no story line, and often poor linkage between themes and scenes, and choreography that is more stepping in place rather than dancing.

One "show" not to be missed is the "Greatest Show at Sea" Parade – a superbly executed 15-minute fun extravaganza that bumbles along the Royal Promenade at turtle speed; it replicates the parade of stars and animals at a circus of yesteryear (Barnum and Bailey's meets cruise ship). This is when it's really good to have one of those interior-view atrium cabins (sadly, the windows don't open, so you can't take photographs); otherwise, get a position early along the Royal Promenade.

SPA/FITNESS. The large Steiner-operated ShipShape health spa includes a large aerobics room, fitness center (with the usual stairmasters, treadmills, stationary bikes, weight machines and free weights), treatment rooms, and men's and women's sauna/steam rooms and relaxation areas. Some basic exercise classes are free, but the good ones (examples: yoga, personal training) cost extra.

More active passengers can bodyboard, go boxing (in the full-size boxing ring in the middle of the spa; the cost is $83 for a personal session, or $10 as part of a Power-boxing class), climb (the rock-climbing wall at the back of the funnel housing), jog, putt, swim, skate, step, surf, workout and more (including play basketball and volleyball) in the sports area of the ship, located mostly aft of the funnel.

● **For more extensive general information on what a Royal Caribbean cruise is like, see pages 152–6.**

Fuji Maru
★★★

Size: ....Small Ship	Total Crew: 190	Cabins (wheelchair accessible): 2
Tonnage: 23,340	Passengers	Wheelchair accessibility: ....None
Lifestyle: ....Standard	(lower beds/all berths): 328/603	Cabin Current: ....100 volts
Cruise Line: ...Mitsui OSK Passenger Line	Passenger Space Ratio	Elevators: 5
Former Names: ....none	(lower beds/all berths): 71.1/38.7	Casino (gaming tables): ....Yes
Builder: ....Mitsubishi (Japan)	Crew/Passenger Ratio	(gifts only, no cash prizes)
Original Cost: ....$63.5 million	(lower beds/all berths): 1.7/3.1	Slot Machines: ....No
Entered Service: ....Apr 1989	Cabins (total): 164	Swimming Pools (outdoors): 1
Registry: ....Japan	Size Range (sq ft/m): 182.9–376.7/	Swimming Pools (indoors): 0
Length (ft/m): 547.9/167.00	17.0–35.0	Whirlpools: ....0 (4 Japanese Baths)
Beam (ft/m): 78.7/24.00	Cabins (outside view): 164	Self-Service Launderette: ....Yes
Draft (ft/m): 21.4/6.55	Cabins (interior/no view): 0	Dedicated Cinema/Seats: Yes/142
Propulsion/Propellers: .diesel (15,740kW)/2	Cabins (for one person): 0	Library: ....Yes
Passenger Decks: 8	Cabins (with private balcony): 0	Onboard currency ....Japanese yen

---

Caters for the Japanese-speaking charter cruise market.

OVERVIEW. This ship suits Japanese-speaking couples and single travelers looking for modestly comfortable surroundings, decent food and service, all at low cost. It has a well thought-out, flexible design for multifunctional uses, but its main use is for incentives, conventions, as a seminar and training ship, and only occasionally for individuals.

THE SHIP. When *Fuji Maru* was completed in 1989, it was Japan's largest cruise ship. The utilitarian outdoor decks are little used. The interiors are plain and a little clinical, although there is some good artwork throughout to brighten things up. There are extensive lecture and conference facilities. The largest lecture hall is two decks high, seats 600, and converts into a sports stadium or exhibition hall for industrial product introductions. The lobby is quite elegant and open and is part of a two-level atrium.

The ship has a classic, wood-paneled library. Other features include Japanese grand baths and a traditional Washitsu tatami mat room, and lecture room. A Hanaguruma owner's room is reasonably elegant for small formal functions. The Sakura Salon is soothing, with a blend of Western and traditional Japanese design. The media and TV systems include much high-tech equipment. However, there are many more modern ships in the international marketplace (some serving Japanese passengers), with better facilities, more dining choices, and a less utilitarian ambience, and so the score for this ship is lower than it used to be.

A specialist courier company will collect your luggage from your home before the cruise, and deliver it back after the cruise (this service available only in Japan). As in any ship for Japanese passengers, tipping is not allowed.

BERLITZ'S RATINGS		
	Possible	Achieved
Ship	500	274
Accommodation	200	114
Food	400	249
Service	400	266
Entertainment	100	65
Cruise	400	218
OVERALL SCORE		
1,186 points out of 2,000		

There is a waste of open deck space, and maintenance of it is poor. The deck furniture is plastic. The lighting is too bright, which increases the noise level.

ACCOMMODATION. There are seven price grades. There are two suites that are quite lovely, with separate bedroom and living room. The deluxe cabins are also of a good standard, and have a vanity/writing desk, mini-bar/refrigerator, and full-size, deep bathtub. Almost all other standard cabins are furnished very simply, but they are good for seminar and school cruises, with many accommodating three or four persons. The cabin insulation is reasonable, but could be better. The bathrooms are small and utilitarian. The folded blankets, a MOPAS (Mitsui OSK Passenger Line) tradition, are lovely.

CUISINE. The single, large dining room is quite attractive and has a high ceiling, but rather bright lighting. Both Japanese and Western cuisines are featured for all meals, in a single seating. The food itself is quite plain and simple, but with colorful presentation, and there's a good variety.

ENTERTAINMENT. The Pacific Lounge is the venue for entertainment events, social functions, and social dancing. It is a two-deck-high room, with seating on both main and balcony levels. On most cruises, entertainers are brought on board from ashore.

SPA/FITNESS. There is no spa, but there are two Japanese Grand Baths (men's and women's) with ocean-view windows. These include washing stations and two small communal baths. There is a sauna, and massage is available.

Funchal
★★ +

Size: . . . . .Small Ship	Passenger Decks: 6	Cabins (with private balcony): 0
Tonnage: .9,563	Total Crew: 155	Cabins (wheelchair accessible): 0
Lifestyle: . . . . .Standard	Passengers	Wheelchair accessibility: . . . . .None
Cruise Line: Classic International Cruises	(lower beds/all berths): 430/524	Cabin Current: . . . . .220 volts
Former Names: . . . . .none	Passenger Space Ratio	Elevators: 3
Builder: . . .Helsingor Skibsvog (Denmark)	(lower beds/all berths): 22.218.2	Casino (gaming tables): . . . . .Yes
Original Cost: .n/a	Crew/Passenger Ratio	Slot Machines: . . . . .Yes
Entered Service: . . . . .Oct 1961/May 1986	(lower beds/all berths): 2.7/3.3	Swimming Pools (outdoors): 1
Registry: . . . . .Madeira	Cabins (total): 222	Swimming Pools (indoors): 0
Length (ft/m): 503.6/153.51	Size Range (sq ft/m): 102.2–252.9/	Whirlpools: 0
Beam (ft/m): 62.5/19.05	9.5–23.5	Self-Service Launderette: . . . . .No
Draft (ft/m): 20.6/6.40	Cabins (outside view): 151	Dedicated Cinema/Seats: . . . . .No
Propulsion/Propellers: . . . . .diesel	Cabins (interior/no view): 71	Library: . . . . .Yes
(7,356kW)/2	Cabins (for one person): 14	Onboard currency . . . . .Euros

A classic older ship with great onboard character.

OVERVIEW. *Funchal* suits couples and single travelers seeking a first cruise aboard a small ship of vintage character and charm, with few facilities, but at a low price. The ship and overall product are actually quite good if you enjoy small, vintage vessels with all their accompanying eccentricities.

THE SHIP. *Funchal* has a classic 1960s small-ship profile with well balanced, rounded lines, and pleasing real wooden decks, including one outdoor deck with two sheltered promenades, although they don't completely encircle the ship. Originally, the ship was built as the Portuguese Presidential Yacht, a dual-purpose mail/passenger ship, but was rebuilt as a one-class cruise ship in 1972–73 and has since undergone regular refurbishments. Its interior has lots of fine woodwork and heavy-duty fittings. One deck houses the main public rooms, the most appealing of which is the Porto Bar, reminiscent of a classy 19th-century drinking club. The highly polished wooden spiral stairway – a beautiful, classic piece of decoration – had to be removed in a complete 2011 refit to comply with the latest SOLAS regulations.

The mostly Portuguese staff is warm, friendly and quite attentive. This ship is popular with Europeans and Scandinavians during the summer and winter. It provides destination-intensive cruises in a pleasant, old-world atmosphere.

Funchal may be old but looks quite splendid after the 2011 renovation, and has been nicely refreshed throughout, including all-new cabins. It hovers just a tad under the three-star level – a two-and-a-half star vessel with a three-star heart. While it cannot be compared to the latest brand new, larger ships, *Funchal* has a delightful character and charm. The feeling of camaraderie and friendliness from the loyal crew, some of whom have been aboard the ship for many years, offsets some of the hardware negatives.

The ship often operates under charter to various tour packagers and operators.

ACCOMMODATION. The cabins are compact but with tasteful decor, and come in both twin and double-bedded configurations.

Each has a private bathroom, and there is just enough closet and drawer space. All bathrooms are typically provided with soap, shampoo, shower cap, shoeshine, sewing kit, and bathrobe (suites only).

CUISINE. There are two tastefully decorated dining rooms, *Lisboa* and the smaller *Coimbra*, which doubles as a video screening room after dinner. Both have ocean-view picture windows on port and starboard sides. There is just one seating, and tables are for four, six or eight (there are none for two). The food is European in style – it includes plenty of fresh fish – and is surprisingly good. The wine list includes Portuguese wines at modest prices.

ENTERTAINMENT. The Main Lounge is the showlounge, an H-shaped room that extends to the sides of the ship. The room has a flat floor, and the sight lines to the stage are poor from some seats. As this is a small and older vessel, entertainment is a low priority and has a low budget.

SPA/FITNESS. There is a small beauty salon.

BERLITZ'S RATINGS

	Possible	Achieved
Ship	500	210
Accommodation	200	101
Food	400	242
Service	400	240
Entertainment	100	55
Cruise	400	207

OVERALL SCORE
1,055 points out of 2,000

Galapagos Explorer II
★★★

Size: . . . . .Boutique Ship	Passenger Decks: 5	Cabins (with private balcony): 4
Tonnage: .4,077	Total Crew: 72	Cabins (wheelchair accessible): 0
Lifestyle: . . . . .Standard	Passengers	Wheelchair accessibility: . . . . .None
Cruise Line: . . . . .Canodros	(lower beds/all berths): 106/111	Cabin Current: . . . . .110 volts
Former Names: . . . . . .*Renaissance Three*	Passenger Space Ratio	Elevators: 1
Builder: . . . . .Cantieri Navale Ferrari (Italy)	(lower beds/all berths): 38.4/36.7	Casino (gaming tables): . . . . .Yes
Original Cost: . . . .$20 million	Crew/Passenger Ratio	Slot Machines: . . . . .Yes
Entered Service: . . . . .Aug 1990/Feb 1998	(lower beds/all berths): 1.4/1.5	Swimming Pools (outdoors): 1
Registry: .Liberia	Cabins (total): 53	Swimming Pools (indoors): 0
Length (ft/m): 293.1/89.35	Size Range (sq ft/m): 231.4–282.0/	Whirlpools: 1
Beam (ft/m): 50.1/15.30	21.5–26.2	Self-Service Launderette: . . . . .No
Draft (ft/m): 11.9/3.65	Cabins (outside view): 53	Dedicated Cinema/Seats: . . . . .No
Propulsion/Propellers: . . . . .diesel	Cabins (interior/no view): 0	Library: . . . . .No
(3,514kW)/2	Cabins (for one person): 0	Onboard currency . . . . .US$

A good ship to use as a hotel base in the Galápagos.

OVERVIEW. *Galapagos Explorer II* operates three-, four-, and seven-night Galápagos cruises year-round from San Cristobal. It suits couples and single travelers who want to cruise around the primitive islands, but want to do so in comfortable, stylish surroundings. However, the ship does not sail well in inclement weather. It has not been cared for, and maintenance is poor.

THE SHIP. This is a comfortable and inviting ship, built as one of a series of eight similar small ships for the defunct Renaissance Cruises. While it is in good condition, the maintenance could be better. Its looks are quite contemporary in the style of a mega-yacht, with handsome styling. There is a wooden promenade deck outdoors. The limited number of public rooms have smart and restful, non-glitzy decor. The main lounge doubles as a lecture room, but perhaps it is the piano bar that provides the best place to relax after dinner in the evening. A doctor is carried at all times.

This ship provides a destination-intensive, refined, quiet and relaxed cruise for those who don't like crowds or dressing up. Naturalist guides trained at the Darwin Station lead the shore excursions (included in the fare), and the ship carries two glass-bottom boats. Take your passport, short and long-sleeve cotton shirts, good walking shoes, windbreaker, mosquito repellent, sunglasses with retaining strap, and personal medication. You will need to fly from Quito to San Cristobal (via Guayaquil) to join your cruise.

Liquor, beer, cocktails, bottled water and soft drinks are included in the fare, but wine and champagne are not. Also included are guided visits to the islands. The brochure rates may or may not include the Galápagos Islands visitor tax

BERLITZ'S RATINGS

	Possible	Achieved
Ship	500	325
Accommodation	200	154
Food	400	209
Service	400	245
Entertainment	n/a	n/a
Cruise	500	311

OVERALL SCORE
1,244 points out of 2,000

(about $100), which must be paid in cash at Guayaquil or Quito airports or in the islands. Shore visits take place in "pangas" (local lingo for "dinghies").

Gratuities for shipboard staff are excessive, at a recommended $80 per person, per seven-night cruise.

Sunbathing space is cramped. The tiny "dip" pool is not a swimming pool. Plastic wood is everywhere (but looks good). The service lacks finesse, but the crew is willing. The small library is attractive, but the book selection is poor.

ACCOMMODATION. This is located forward, with public rooms aft. Pleasant, all-outside suites have a large picture window and combine gorgeous, highly polished imitation rosewood paneling with lots of mirrors, hand-crafted Italian furniture, and wet bar. All cabins have a queen-size bed, a sitting area, a mini-bar/refrigerator, TV set, VCR and hairdryer. The small bathrooms have showers with a fold-down seat, real teakwood floors and marble vanities.

CUISINE. The small, elegant dining room has open seating and tables for two, four, six, and eight. The meals are self-service buffet-style cold foods for breakfast and lunch (sometimes lunch will be on deck), with local delicacies. There is limited choice.

ENTERTAINMENT. Dinner and after-dinner conversation with fellow passengers forms the entertainment each evening.

SPA/FITNESS. There is a sauna. Water sports facilities include an aft platform, sailfish, snorkel gear, and Zodiacs.

Size: ....Mid-Size Ship	Passenger Decks: 9	Cabins (wheelchair accessible): 4
Tonnage: 19,093	Total Crew: 350	Wheelchair accessibility: ....Fair
Lifestyle: ....Standard	Passengers	Cabin Current: ....220 volts
Cruise Line: ....Happy Cruises	(lower beds/all berths): 800/940	Elevators: 4
Former Names: ...... *SuperStar Gemini,*	Passenger Space Ratio	Casino (gaming tables): ....Yes
Crown Jewel	(lower beds/all berths): 23.8/21.2	Slot Machines: ....Yes
Builder: . .Union Navale de Levante (Spain)	Crew/Passenger Ratio	Swimming Pools (outdoors): 1
Original Cost: ....$100 million	(lower beds/all berths): 2.2/2.6	Swimming Pools (indoors): 0
Entered Service: ....Aug 1992/Mar 2009	Cabins (total): 400	Whirlpools: ....3 (2 outside/1 inside)
Registry: ....Bahamas	Size Range (sq ft/m): 139.9–377.8/	Self-Service Launderette: ....No
Length (ft/m): 537.4/163.81	13.0–35.1	Dedicated Cinema/Seats: ....No
Beam (ft/m): 73.8/22.50	Cabins (outside view): 241	Library: ....Yes
Draft (ft/m): 17.7/5.40	Cabins (interior/no view): 159	Onboard currency ....Euros
Propulsion/Propellers: ....diesel	Cabins (for one person): 0	
(13,200kW)/2	Cabins (with private balcony): 10	

Suitable for a first cruise in a Spanish-speaking setting.

OVERVIEW. *Gemini* is suited to Spanish-speaking couples, singles, and families with children of all ages who want to cruise aboard a contemporary ship with decent facilities, at a reasonable price for an all-inclusive vacation. The dress code is totally casual. All in all, the ship is good value for money.

THE SHIP. *Gemini,* owned by the Clipper Group and chartered to Happy Cruises, part of Spain's Quail Travel Group, is a fairly smart-looking midsize contemporary cruise ship, with a white hull (with Happy Cruises emblazoned on the sides) and superstructure topped by a single dark blue funnel. Designed for informal cruising in warm-weather waters, it has a sister in the (now stretched) *Braemar,* operated by Fred Olsen Cruise Lines.

There is a walk-around promenade deck outdoors, and passengers can also go to right to the bows of the ship for arrivals and departures – the mooring deck is underneath. There is a reasonable amount of open deck and sunbathing space for its size, and this includes a neat area high atop the ship in front of a glass windbreak area – good for those balmy evenings outdoors, away from the crowds inside. Cushioned pads are not provided for the sunloungers, and the pool is small – very small.

Although the original interior fit and finish was poor, the decor presents a warm and upbeat look that is colourful and cheery. The ship has a traditional layout that provides reasonable horizontal passenger flow, although the passageways are quite narrow, and Deck 7, where most suites are located, is like a winding street. There are picture windows in almost all of the public rooms that connect pas-

BERLITZ'S RATINGS		
	Possible	Achieved
Ship	500	332
Accommodation	200	132
Food	400	234
Service	400	243
Entertainment	100	60
Cruise	400	251
OVERALL SCORE		
1,252 points out of 2,000		

sengers with the sea and the outside light. Many of the chairs and bar stools are of the low-back variety – made for people of small proportions.

Other features include a five-deck-high glass-walled atrium, which is set on the starboard side; it has clusters of green hanging over the balcony on each deck. Off-center stairways appear to add a sense of spaciousness to an interior design that surrounds passengers with light. The artwork is fairly plain and simple, although a colourful piece – *Georama,* by Ajis Mohamad of Malaysia, in three sections – adorns the main lobby. Public rooms include a disco-lounge, small duty-free shop, casino, video arcade, children's center, card room, and a library with two internet-connect computer stations.

The all-inclusive pricing means that (standard brand) drinks and gratuities are included. But shore excursions, use of medical facility, and spa treatments are not included, nor are room service items such as snacks or sandwiches.

There are many loud announcements. Music plays constantly in public spaces, hallways, and on open decks, making a relaxing cruise impossible. Expect crowding at self-serve buffets, tenders, and the few elevators.

ACCOMMODATION. There are 11 cabin categories, the price depending on grade, location and size. These consist of suites (220.7–377.8 sq. ft/20.5–35.1 sq. meters), junior suites (225–258.3 sq. ft/20.9–24 sq. meters), ocean-view cabins with double bed (134.5–212 sq. ft/12.5–19.7 sq. meters), ocean-view cabins with twin beds (137.8 sq. ft/12.8 sq. meters), smaller ocean-view cabins with window (114.1–148.5 sq. ft/10.6–13.8 sq. meters), and very small interior (no-view) cabins (127–150.7 sq. ft/11.8–14 sq. meters). The cabin numbering system and signage is confusing, however, and contrary to nautical tradition.

Suites. The 10 Balcony Suites, each with an audio-visual system, have a private balcony with lacquered wood floor, although the balcony partitions are not of the floor-to-ceiling type – so you can hear your neighbors clearly, or smell their smoke. The Premium and Deluxe Suites are really little larger than standard cabins, but come with more closet space. All suite category accommodation is nicely furnished, and, depending on the configuration, the sleeping area can be curtained off from the living area. Four cabins are adaptable for wheelchair users, although the ship's layout makes it quite awkward to get around.

Standard Cabins. The standard outside-view and interior cabins, almost all about the same size, are really quite small, although they are nicely furnished, and trimmed with blond wood cabinetry. Most cabins have broad picture windows (some deluxe cabins on Deck 6 and Deck 7 have lifeboat-obstructed views), while cabins on the lowest deck have portholes instead of windows. They are practical and comfortable, with wood-trimmed accents and multi-colored soft furnishings, but there is little drawer space, and the closet space is tight.

Each cabin has a compact private bathroom with a tiled floor, small shower enclosure – even in accommodation designated as suites – two small toiletries cupboards, washbasin, and low-height toilet of the barking dog vacuum variety, some under-basin storage space, and an electrical socket for shavers. The cabin soundproofing is quite poor, and there is little room for luggage, so take only what is really necessary (casual clothing only). Some toiletries are provided in all cabins. The towels are of 100% cotton. None of the cabin bathrooms has a bathtub – not even the so-called "suites" – and hairdryers are not supplied for any cabin category except suites, so take your own if you need to use one. The TV sets are of the old variety.

CUISINE. The *Ocean Palace Restaurant* is located aft; it is attractive, and has large picture windows on three sides – although accenting in the center of the ceiling makes the room appear almost circular. There are typically two seatings (dinner is 8pm and 10:15 pm), except when the ship is not full, when it may go to one open seating. It is not open for dinner each night; the schedule depends on the itinerary being operated.

The ambience is friendly, but it can be noisy, depending on the passenger nationalities carried. There are few tables for two – most are for four, six or eight. Meals highlight continental European cuisine, with a Spanish flair, and there is open seating for all meals.

There is also a casual self-serve buffet-style restaurant, *Mariners Buffet*, with indoor and outdoor seating, for breakfast, lunch and dinner.

ENTERTAINMENT. The Galaxy Showlounge and Bar, which sits longitudinally along one side of the ship, with amphitheater-style seating in several tiers, is the venue for all main entertainment events. There is often congestion between first- and second-seating passengers at the single entrance to the room, which is poorly designed for passenger movement.

Fifteen pillars obstruct the sightlines to the stage, and the seating arrangement is quite poor. Don't expect much in the way of entertainment – it's loud, and rather like reality TV. The Tropicana Lounge has a decent-size dance floor, with live music, and a large bar. Several other bars and lounges feature a mix of groups and entertaining musicians.

SPA/FITNESS. There is a health spa, although it is small and has limited facilities. It includes a combined gymnasium/relaxation room, with separate rooms for men and women, a two-person sauna, steam room and small changing/locker area. There's also a beauty salon. The day you board is the best time to book your desired treatments, which are not included in the "all-inclusive" cruise fare.

WHERE NAUTICAL EXPRESSIONS COME FROM

If you've ever wondered where some terms or phrases came from, you have only to look to the sea, ships, and seamen.

Square meal

This derives from the meals served on square wooden platters used on board ship. The platters could be easily stowed in racks between meals. Any substantial meal is now described as a "square meal."

Three Sheets to the Wind

A term said of a man under the influence of drink. A ship with three sheets in the wind would "stagger to and fro like a drunken man." Conversely, a drunken man behaves like a ship with three sheets in the wind.

To Know the ropes

There were miles and miles of cordage in the rigging of a square rigged ship. The only way of keeping track of and knowing the function of all of these lines was to know their locations. It took an experienced seaman to know the ropes.

Under the weather

Refers to a sailor being in the uncomfortable position of having his station at the weather bow, subject to the pitching of the boat with spray constantly blown in his face. Used today to mean feeling unwell.

Golden Princess
★★★★

Size:	.Large Resort Ship	Total Crew:	1,100		(18 outside/10 interior)
Tonnage:	108,865	Passengers		Wheelchair accessibility:	Best
Lifestyle:	Standard	(lower beds/all berths):	2,624/3,124	Cabin Current:	110 and 220 volts
Cruise Line:	Princess Cruises	Passenger Space Ratio		Elevators:	14
Former Names:	none	(lower beds/all berths):	41.4/34.8	Casino (gaming tables):	Yes
Builder:	Fincantieri (Italy)	Crew/Passenger Ratio		Slot Machines:	Yes
Original Cost:	$450 million	(lower beds/all berths):	2.1/2.8	Swimming Pools (outdoors):	4
Entered Service:	May 2001	Cabins (total):	1,312	Swimming Pools (indoors):	0
Registry:	Bermuda	Size Range (sq ft/m):		Whirlpools:	9
Length (ft/m):	951.4/290.0	161.4–764.2/15.0–71.0		Self-Service Launderette:	Yes
Beam (ft/m):	118.1/36.0	Cabins (outside view):	940	Dedicated Cinema/Seats:	No
Draft (ft/m):	26.2/8.0	Cabins (interior/no view):	372	Library:	Yes
Propulsion/Propellers:	diesel-electric	Cabins (for one person):	0	Onboard currency	US$
	(42,000kW)/2	Cabins (with private balcony):	720		
Passenger Decks:	13	Cabins (wheelchair accessible):	28		

A comfortable large ship with an informal style, for families.

OVERVIEW. Whether this busy ship can be considered a relaxing vacation is a moot point, but with many choices and "small" rooms to enjoy, it has been extremely well designed, and the odds are that you'll have a fine time, in a controlled, well-packaged way.

THE SHIP. *Golden Princess*, sister to *Grand Princess* and *Star Princess*, presents a bold, forthright profile, with a racy "spoiler" effect at the stern that acts as an observation lounge with aft-facing views by day, and a noisy discotheque by night. The ship has a flared snub-nosed bow and a galleon-like transom stern. At 118 ft/36 meters, with many balcony cabins overhanging the hull, it is too wide to transit the Panama Canal.

There is a good sheltered faux teak promenade deck – it's actually painted steel – which almost wraps around (three times round is equal to one mile) and a walkway that goes to the enclosed bow of the ship. The outdoor pools have various beach-like surroundings. One lap pool has a pumped "current" to swim against.

High atop the stern of the ship is a ship-wide glass-walled disco pod, with spectacular views from the extreme port and starboard side windows; it's a good place to read a book in the daytime, but at night it's a discotheque. It could well be removed soon, following in the footsteps of sister *Grand Princess*. In a 2009 refit, an extra-charge retreat, The Sanctuary, was added for adult passengers only; it has plush padded lounge chairs, two private massage cabanas and dedicated Serenity Stewards.

There is plenty of space inside the ship and a wide array of public rooms. The passenger flow has been well

BERLITZ'S RATINGS		
	Possible	Achieved
Ship	500	414
Accommodation	200	163
Food	400	252
Service	400	289
Entertainment	100	80
Cruise	400	301
OVERALL SCORE		
1,499 points out of 2,000		

thought-out, with little congestion, except at the photo gallery. The decor is attractive and warm, with lots of earth tones.

The main lobby, La Piazza, has live street entertainment; an International café for coffees, fresh cookies, pastries, panini sandwiches and tapas; and Vines, a wine bar. A new 300-sq-ft (28 sq-meter) poolside movie screen has been added. An extensive collection of art works complement the elegant, non-glitzy interior design and colors, and most of the paintings are for sale.

This ship has a Wedding Chapel, with a web-cam to relay ceremonies via the internet. The ship's captain can legally marry (American) couples, thanks to the ship's Bermuda registry and a special dispensation (this should, however, be verified when in the planning stage, and may vary according to where you reside). Princess Cruises offers three wedding packages: Pearl, Emerald, Diamond. The "Hearts & Minds" chapel can also be used for "renewal of vows" ceremonies.

The large casino, on Deck 7, has more than 260 slot machines, plus blackjack, craps and roulette tables. The wood-paneled Wheelhouse Bar is finely decorated with memorabilia and ship models tracing part of parent company P&O's history. There is an internet café – which isn't a café and doesn't even have coffee, though it does have a couple of dozen AOL-linked computer terminals.

A high-tech hospital has a live SeaMed tele-medicine link-up to specialists at the Cedars-Sinai Medical Center in Los Angeles available for emergency help.

The automated telephone system is frustrating to use,

and luggage delivery is inefficient. Lines can form at the Passenger Services Desk, and for open-seating breakfast and lunch. There are lots of extra-charge items such as for ice cream, and freshly squeezed orange juice, and activities such as yoga, group exercise bicycling and kick boxing classes. There is a charge for using the washers and dryers in the self-service launderettes (coins are needed).

FAMILIES. A two-deck-high playroom and teen room is located in the forward section of the ship, and a video games room is located at the opposite end of the ship. There is a host of trained counselors. Many cabins have additional upper berths (there are 609), good for families. Group babysitting services are available for an hourly charge.

ACCOMMODATION. There are six principal types of cabins and configurations but a bewildering 35 brochure price categories. The price depends on grade, size and location.
(a) The largest, most lavish suite is the Grand Suite (B748, at the stern. It has a large bedroom with a queen-size bed, huge walk-in closets, a large bathroom with full-size tub and separate shower enclosure, toilet, and washbasin, and a hot tub (accessed from the bedroom), a lounge (with sofa bed, dining table and chairs, wet bar and refrigerator, a guest bathroom, and a large private balcony.
(b/c) Suites (with a semi-private balcony) have a separate living room (with sofa bed) and bedroom (with a TV set in each). The bathroom is quite large and has both a tub and shower stall. The mini-suites also have a semi-private balcony, and a separate living and sleeping area (with a television in each). The bathroom is also quite spacious, with both a bathtub and shower stall. Passengers occupying the best suites receive greater attention, including priority embarkation and disembarkation. What is not good is that some of the most expensive accommodation has only semi-private balconies that can be seen from above, so there is no privacy (Suites C401, 402, 409, 410, 414, 415, 420, 421, 422, 423, 424 and 425 on Caribe Deck in particular). Also, the extremely large suites D105 and D106 (Dolphin Deck) have balconies that can be seen from above.
(d/e/f) The standard interior and outside-view (the outsides come either with or without private balcony) cabins are of a functional, practical, design, although almost no drawers are provided. They are very attractive, with warm, pleasing decor and fine soft furnishing fabrics.

Two family suites consist of two suites with an interconnecting door, plus a large balcony. These can sleep up to 10 (if at least four are children), or up to eight adults.

All passengers receive turndown service and chocolates on pillows each night, bathrobes (on request) and toiletries kits. A hairdryer is provided in all cabins.

Most outside cabins on Emerald Deck have views obstructed by lifeboats. Some cabins can accommodate a third and fourth person in upper berths. However, in such cabins, the lower beds cannot then be pushed together to make queen-size bed. There are no cabins for singles.

Cabins with balconies on Dolphin, Caribe and Baja decks are overlooked by passengers on balconies on the deck above; they are, therefore, not at all private. However, perhaps the least desirable balcony cabins are the eight located forward on Emerald Deck, as the balconies do not extend to the side of the ship and can be passed by walkers and gawkers on an adjacent walkway (so occupants need to keep their curtains closed most of the time). Those in expensive suites with balconies at the stern may experience considerable vibration during certain ship maneuvers.

Cabin attendants have too many cabins to look after (typically 20), which cannot translate to fine personal service.

CUISINE. For formal meals there are three principal dining rooms (*Bernini, Canaletto,* and *Donatello*). There are two seatings in one restaurant, and the others have "anytime dining" where you choose your time and companions. All are split into multi-tier sections in a non-symmetrical design that breaks what are quite large spaces into many smaller sections, for better ambience. Each dining room has its own galley. While four elevators go to Fiesta Deck for Canaletto and Donatello, only two go to Plaza Deck 5 for Bernini, which can mean long wait problems at peak times, particularly for anyone in a wheelchair). Note that 15% is added to beverage bills, including wines.

Alternative (Extra Charge) Dining: There are two alternative informal dining areas: Sabatini's and Crown Grill. *Sabatini's* has Italian-style pizzas and pastas, with a variety of sauces, as well as Italian-style entrées, including tiger prawns and lobster tail. Sabatini's is by reservation only, with cover charge, for lunch or dinner on sea days only. *Crown Grill*, serving premium steaks and seafood, is by reservation only and has a cover charge, and the venue has an open galley. The cuisine in both of these spots is decidedly better than in the three main dining rooms.

A poolside hamburger grill and pizza bar (no extra charge) offer casual bites. Other casual meals can be taken in the 24-hour *Horizon Court*, with large ocean-view on port and starboard sides and direct access to the two main swimming pools and lido deck. Plastic plates are used.

ENTERTAINMENT. The 748-seat Princess Theatre spans two decks and has comfortable seating on both main and balcony levels. It has a nine-piece orchestra. Princess Cruises prides itself on its glamorous all-American production shows. The Vista Lounge is a second entertainment venue. It presents cabaret acts at night, and lectures, bingo and horse racing during the day. Explorers, a third entertainment lounge, can host cabaret acts and dance bands. Many other lounges and bars have live music, and there are male dance hosts as partners for women traveling alone.

SPA/FITNESS. The Lotus Spa is a large complex that surrounds one of the swimming pools at the forward end of the ship. It comprises a large gymnasium with all the usual equipment, an aerobics room, sauna and steam rooms, beauty salon, treatment rooms, and a relaxation area.

● **For more extensive general information about the Princess Cruises experience, see pages 149–52.**

Grand Celebration
★★★

Size:............................Large Resort Ship	Passenger Decks:...............................10	Cabins (wheelchair accessible):..........14
Tonnage:.......................................47,262	Total Crew:...620	Wheelchair accessibility...........Fair
Lifestyle:.....................................Standard	Passengers	Cabin Current:...................110/220 volts
Cruise Line:.........................Iberocruceros	(lower beds/all berths):.........1,494/1,896	Elevators:...8
Former Names:......................Celebration	Passenger Space Ratio	Casino (gaming tables):......................Yes
Builder:.....................Kockums (Sweden)	(lower beds/all berths):.............31.6/24.9	Slot Machines:...................................Yes
Original Cost:.......................$130 million	Crew/Passenger Ratio	Swimming Pools (outdoors):..................3
Entered Service:.......Mar 1987/Jun 2008	(lower beds/all berths):.................2.4/3.0	Swimming Pools (indoors):....................0
Registry:..............................Panama	Cabins (total):.....................................747	Whirlpools:...2
Length (ft/m):..................732.6/223.30	Size Range (sq ft/m):.............184.0/17.1	Self-Service Launderette:..................Yes
Beam (ft/m):..........................92.5/28.20	Cabins (outside view):.......................453	Dedicated Cinema/Seats:....................No
Draft (ft/m):.............................25.5/7.80	Cabins (interior/no view):...................296	Library:...Yes
Propulsion/Propellers:.....................diesel	Cabins (for one person):.........................0	Onboard currency..........................Euros
(23,520kW)/2	Cabins (with private balcony):..............10	

A child-friendly ship for Spanish-speaking families.

OVERVIEW. This former Carnival ship is a floating playground for young, Spanish-speaking active adults who enjoy constant stimulation and lots of people. There is a wide range of entertainment and passenger participation activities, and it should prove a good choice for families with children – there are several places for kids to explore.

THE SHIP. *Grand Celebration*, now more than 20 years old, has extremely short bows, and a distinctive, large, swept-back wing-tipped blue funnel just aft of the center of the ship. The swimming pools are smaller than one would expect, and the open deck space can be extremely crowded.

It has a double-width indoor promenade and a good selection of public rooms, including a large casino. Facilities include a library and internet-connect center. Children are split into two age categories, with facilities for each: Club 5 (5–10 year olds), or Club 10 (10 years and older).

There's no escape from repetitious announcements – particularly for activities that bring revenue. All gratuities to staff are included in this "mostly-inclusive" cruise.

ACCOMMODATION. There are four grades and 13 price categories: suite with balcony; junior suite with balcony; outside-view: and interior cabins. The cabins are quite standard and mostly identical in terms of layout and decor, are of fairly generous proportions, except for the interior cabins, which are quite small. They are reasonably comfortable and well equipped, but nothing special. A 24-hour room service menu is provided.

The best living spaces on board are in 10 suites, each of which has much more space, its own private balcony, a

BERLITZ'S RATINGS		
	Possible	Achieved
Ship	500	297
Accommodation	200	121
Food	400	216
Service	400	247
Entertainment	100	66
Cruise	400	235

OVERALL SCORE
1,182 points out of 2,000

larger bathroom and more closet, drawer and storage space.

CUISINE/DINING. There are two dining rooms: *Vista Hermoza*, with 550 seats, and *Riazor*, with 450 seats). They are quite cramped when full, and extremely noisy. There are tables for four, six or eight (none for two). The decor is bright and extremely colorful. Dining is in two seatings: 8:30pm and 10:30pm. Meals for vegetarians and special children's menus are available, as is a snack at midnight.

Presentation is simple, and few garnishes are used. Many meat and fowl dishes are disguised with gravies and sauces. There is much use of canned fruit and jellied desserts. This is all about banquet catering, with all its standardization and production cooking. There is a decent wine list, but no wine waiters. For casual meals, there's the 280-seat, self-serve *Buffet Triana*, although the meals are very basic, quite disappointing, and repetitive.

ENTERTAINMENT. The Astoria Showlounge is the main venue for large-scale production shows and major cabaret acts. Large-scale, high volume production shows are featured, together with a number of European cabaret acts. Almost every lounge/bar has live bands and musical units, so there's always plenty of live music in the evening.

SPA/FITNESS. The Spa is located on the ship's uppermost deck. It has a gymnasium with muscle-pumping cardiovascular machines, men's and women's changing rooms, and saunas. The beauty salon is elsewhere. Massages, facials, pedicures, and beauty treatments cost extra.

Grand Holiday
★★★

Size: . . . . .Mid-Size Ship	Passenger Decks: 9	Cabins (with private balcony): 10
Tonnage: .46,052	Total Crew: 660	Cabins (wheelchair accessible): 15
Lifestyle: . . . . .Standard	Passengers	Wheelchair accessibility: . . . . .None
Cruise Line: . . . . .Iberocruceros	(lower beds/all berths): 1,452/1,800	Cabin Current: . . . . .110 volts
Former Names: . . . . .Holiday	Passenger Space Ratio	Elevators: 8
Builder: . . . . . . .Aalborg Vaerft (Denmark)	(lower beds/all berths): 31.7/25.5	Casino (gaming tables): . . . . .Yes
Original Cost: . . . .$170 million	Crew/Passenger Ratio	Slot Machines: . . . . .Yes
Entered Service: . . . . .Jul 1985/May 2010	(lower beds/all berths): 2.2/2.7	Swimming Pools (outdoors): 3
Registry: . . . . .The Bahamas	Cabins (total): 726	Swimming Pools (indoors): 0
Length (ft/m): 726.9/221.57	Size Range (sq ft/m): 189.2–420.0/	Whirlpools: 2
Beam (ft/m): 92.4/28.17	17.0–39.0	Self-Service Launderette: . . . . .No
Draft (ft/m): 25.5/7.77	Cabins (outside view): 447	Dedicated Cinema/Seats: . . . . .No
Propulsion/Propellers: . . . . .diesel	Cabins (interior/no view): 279	Library: . . . . .Yes
(22,360kW)/2	Cabins (for one person): 0	Onboard currency: . . . . .Euros

A casual, family-friendly ship for Spanish cruisers.

OVERVIEW. This ship is best suited to young Spanish-speaking couples seeking their first cruise experience, single passengers, tots, children and teens. The passenger flow is good, although the ship does have a high density and always feels crowded.

THE SHIP. *Grand Holiday* was formerly *Holiday*, a former Carnival ship, is a bold, high-sided, all-white contemporary ship with a very short, rakish bow and stubby stern typical of so many vessels built in the 1980s. It has a distinctive swept-back wing-tipped funnel. Iberocruceros spent €55 million to refurbish the ship in 2010, when all cabins were completely refreshed.

The decks are named after cities and towns – Seville, Valencia, Lugo, Pamplona, Avila, Elche, Barcelona, Madrid, and Ronda. There are numerous public rooms on two entertainment decks to choose from, and these flow from a double-width indoor promenade. A real red-and-cream bus is located right in the middle of one of the two promenades, and this is used as a snack café.

The bright interior decor has a distinct theme. There is plenty of music and entertainment, while junior cruisers have their own activity centers.

ACCOMMODATION. There are just four cabin categories: Suite with balcony; Junior Suite with balcony; exterior cabins, and interior cabins, in 13 different price grades. The standard outside and interior (no view) cabins are plain but functional units that provide all the basics including a small vanity/writing desk. TV sets are typically placed high in one corner and are not easy to watch. The bathrooms are

BERLITZ'S RATINGS		
	Possible	Achieved
Ship	500	293
Accommodation	200	122
Food	400	214
Service	400	241
Entertainment	100	64
Cruise	400	226
OVERALL SCORE		
1,160 points out of 2,000		

practical, with decent-size shower enclosures. Wall-mounted dispensers provide body soap and shampoo.

CUISINE. There are two main restaurants: *Cantabrico* and *Alboran*. Both are large, have low ceilings and raised center sections, and a cramped feeling.

The food is presented well, but few garnishes are used. Do remember that this really is banquet-style catering, with families and children in mind, so standardization and production cooking is the norm. Although there is a decent wine list, there are no wine waiters. The service is highly programmed, although the waiters are friendly.

The *Ensenada Buffet* is a self-serve buffet that provides all the basics (except service), although its layout is old in style and makes the venue seem more like a canteen than a restaurant. Still, it's good for that quick meal when the ship is in port and the family want to be out and about.

ENTERTAINMENT. The Grand Theater Bazan is the principal venue for large-scale production shows and major cabaret acts – although pillars obstruct the views from several seats. It has a main and upper level.

Most lounges and bars have live music, so there's always plenty of life. There are two discos – one large, one small overlooking the ship's single swimming pool.

SPA/FITNESS. Some fitness classes are free, while some may cost extra. Do make early appointments for massages, facials or other beauty treatments such as manicures and pedicures), because time slots go quickly.

Grand Mistral
★★★ +

Size: ....Mid-Size Ship	Passenger Decks: 8	Cabins (with private balcony): 80
Tonnage: 48,200	Total Crew: 470	Cabins (wheelchair accessible): 2
Lifestyle: ....Standard	Passengers	Wheelchair accessibility: ....Fair
Cruise Line: ....Iberocruceros	(lower beds/all berths): 1,196/1,600	Cabin Current: ....110 and 220 volts
Former Names: ....*Mistral*	Passenger Space Ratio	Elevators: 6
Builder: ...Chantiers de l'Atlantique (France)	(lower beds/all berths): 39.5/30.1	Casino (gaming tables): ....Yes
Original Cost: ....$245 million	Crew/Passenger Ratio	Slot Machines: ....Yes
Entered Service: ......Jul 1999/May 2005	(lower beds/all berths): 2.4/3.4	Swimming Pools (outdoors): 2
Registry: ....Marshall Islands	Cabins (total): 598	Swimming Pools (indoors): 0
Length (ft/m): 709.9/216.4	Size Range (sq ft/m): 139.9–236.8/	Whirlpools: ....2 (thalassotherapy)
Beam (ft/m): 94.6/28.84	13.0–22.0	Self-Service Launderette: ....No
Draft (ft/m): 22.4/6.85	Cabins (outside view): 375	Dedicated Cinema/Seats: ....No
Propulsion/Propellers: ......diesel-electric	Cabins (interior/no view): 223	Library: ....Yes
(31,680 kW)/2	Cabins (for one person): 0	Onboard currency: ....Euros

---

Child-friendly, casual cruising for Spanish families.

OVERVIEW. *Grand Mistral* is best suited to youthful Spanish-speaking couples and singles, and families with children that enjoy big-city life and outdoor cafés, constant activity accompanied by lots of noise, late nights, entertainment that is loud, and food that focuses on quantity rather than quality.

THE SHIP. *Grand Mistral* is owned by a consortium of French investors and banks, and chartered to Iberocruceros, a vibrant tour operator that's part of the giant Carnival Corporation, for the Spanish-speaking family market. The ship's profile is similar to that of most new cruise ships, although the built-up stern makes it look bulky and less than handsome.

The lido deck surrounding the outdoor swimming pools – which are small, and regulated for use by various age groups in several time of day zones – has whirlpool tubs and a large bandstand is set in raised canvas-covered pods. Sunloungers have cushioned pads. There is no full walk-around promenade deck outdoors, although there is a partial walking deck on port and starboard sides under the lifeboats, plus an oval jogging track atop ship. The interior layout and passenger flow is good, as are the "you are here" deck signs, and the ship absorbs passengers quite well.

The interior layout and passenger flow is good, as are the "you are here" deck signs. It is light and cheerful without being glitzy in any way (with not even a hint of colored neon), and there is much use of blonde/cherry wood paneling and rich, textured soft furnishings.

Public rooms, bars and lounges have names inspired by European places or establishments such as San Remo Casino, San Marco Lounge, Cafe Guon and Richlieu

BERLITZ'S RATINGS

	Possible	Achieved
Ship	500	369
Accommodation	200	135
Food	400	240
Service	400	252
Entertainment	100	58
Cruise	400	261

OVERALL SCORE
1,315 points out of 2,000

Library. There is a smoking room (Le Diplomate), with all the hallmarks of a gentleman's club of former times, a piano bar, and a library that has real writing desks – something many ships seem to omit.

Atop the ship is an observation lounge with a twist – it faces aft, instead of forward; it doubles as a discotheque for the late-night set. There's a video games room for teens, and a children's center. A conference center provides facilities for meetings.

Smokers are difficult to avoid, towels are small, and the square chairs in the Café Navona are uncomfortable and impractical. Standing in line for embarkation, disembarkation, shore tenders and for self-serve buffet meals is inevitable aboard all ships of this size. The onboard currency is the euro except when the ship operates in Brazil during the Brazilian summer season, when the Brazilian Real is used. Gratuities are included.

An optional drinks package (standard drink brands) can be bought for €16 per person, per day or €8 for a non-alcoholic drinks package for minors.

ACCOMMODATION. There are three basic cabin types, in nine different price grades. These include 80 "suites" (each with a private balcony, although partitions are of the partial, and not the full type), ocean-view standard cabins and interior standard cabins. The price you pay will depend on grade, size and location.

The cabins on Deck 10 are subject to noise from the Lido Deck above. Good planning and layout means that no outside-view cabins have lifeboat-obstructed views. The cabin numbering system goes against maritime tradition, where even-numbered cabins are on the port side and odd-numbered cabins on the starboard; in *Grand Mistral*, the opposite is in effect.

All cabins have twin beds that convert to a queen-size unit, bold, colorful bedspreads (with blankets and sheets, not duvets), a personal safe, a TV set, a personal safe, and a good amount of closet and drawer space for a one-week cruise. The bathrooms, although not large, do have a good-size shower enclosure, and there is a decent amount of stowage space for toiletries.

Accommodation designated as suites – which are really only larger cabins and not suites, as there is no separation of lounge and sleeping space – have more space, larger (walk-in) closets, more drawers and better storage space, plus a two-person sofa, coffee table and additional armchair, vanity desk, floor-to-ceiling mirrors and hairdryer; bathrooms have a tub/shower combination.

Six Grand Suites are well-designed units that have a separate bedroom with flat-screen TV, bedside tables, vanity desk, floor-to-ceiling windows, and door to balcony; the lounge has an audio-visual center, sofa, dining table, and lots of space, plus a balcony door. A large bathroom has contemporary styling, two Villeroy & Boch washbasins, dark hardwood storage cabinets, large Jacuzzi tub, separate shower enclosure (hand-held shower), and bathrobes.

In addition, there are two interior wheelchair accessible cabins for the handicapped, which provide more spacious interiors than standard cabins.

CUISINE. There are two dining rooms (and two seatings for meals), which can be configured in any of several different ways. Both have ocean-view windows. The principal dining room – *Restaurant Mallorca*, with 610 seats – has round tables for two, four, six or eight, and a small podium with baby grand piano.

Restaurant Formentor, a second dining venue seating 380 in chairs with no armrests, is on a different deck. Smaller and more intimate, it is for passengers occupying Deck 10 accommodation; it has tables for two, four or six, and ocean-view windows.

The food is quite sound, and, with varied menus and decent presentation, should prove a highlight for most passengers. The wine list features a good variety of standard wines at reasonable prices, but almost all are young.

There's a casual *Bahia de Palma* cafeteria for al fresco self-serve buffet-style breakfasts and lunches, with ocean-view windows, but the flow is awkward and cramped. Additionally, there's an outdoor pool bar; plus a pleasant little coffee bar (*Café Navona*, serving Brazilian coffee) on the upper level of the two-deck high lobby, with lifeboat-restricted ocean views.

ENTERTAINMENT. The Grand Theatre Ibiza, the show-lounge, spans two decks, has a sloping floor, and good sight lines from most seats (there is banquette-style seating), and there is a small balcony level at the rear. Sadly, the designer forgot to include space for a live band, and the lighting facilities are less than high-tech. There's also a bar/lounge, (Salon Formentera) on the lower level at the entrance to the showlounge. Entertainment is, without doubt, the weak link in the chain for Iberocruceros.

SPA/FITNESS. The Santai Spa health/fitness facilities, located forward of the mast, are quite decent. Included is a gymnasium with high-tech muscle-pump equipment, lifecycles and life-rowing machines and a view over the bow of the ship through large floor-to-ceiling windows.

Other facilities include a thalassotherapy room, and beauty salon, six rooms for massage and other body treatments, as well as a sauna each for men and women, plus an aerobics exercise room. It's best to make appointments early, as the best time slots can go fairly quickly.

Grand Princess
★★★★

Size: . . . . .Large Resort Ship	Total Crew: 1,100	Cabins (wheelchair accessible): 28
Tonnage: 108,806	Passengers	(18 outside/10 interior)
Lifestyle: . . . . .Standard	(lower beds/all berths): 2,600/3,100	Wheelchair accessibility: . . . . .Best
Cruise Line: . . . . .Princess Cruises	Passenger Space Ratio	Cabin Current: . . . . . . .110 and 220 volts
Former Names: . . . . .none	(lower beds/all berths): 41.8/35.0	Elevators: 14
Builder: . . . . .Fincantieri (Italy)	Crew/Passenger Ratio	Casino (gaming tables): . . . . .Yes
Original Cost: . . . .$450 million	(lower beds/all berths): 2.3/2.8	Slot Machines: . . . . .Yes
Entered Service: . . . . .May 1998	Cabins (total): 1,300	Swimming Pools (outdoors): 4
Registry: . . . . .Bermuda	Size Range (sq ft/m): 161.4–764.2/	Swimming Pools (indoors): 0
Length (ft/m): 951.4/290.0	15.0–71.0	Whirlpools: 9
Beam (ft/m): 118.1/36.0	Cabins (outside view): 928	Self-Service Launderette: . . . . .Yes
Draft (ft/m): 26.2/8.0	Cabins (interior/no view): 372	Dedicated Cinema/Seats: . . . . .No
Propulsion/Propellers: . . . . .diesel-electric	Cabins (for one person): 0	Library: . . . . .Yes
(42,000kW)/2	Cabins (with private balcony): 710	Onboard currency: . . . . .US$
Passenger Decks: 13		

A multi-choice large ship for informal family cruising.

OVERVIEW. Whether *Grand Princess* provides a genuinely relaxing holiday is a moot point, but with many choices and "small" rooms to enjoy, it has been extremely well designed. The odds are that you'll have a fine time, in a controlled, well-packaged way. The ship is full of revenue centers, designed to help you part with more money.

THE SHIP. *Grand Princess*, first of the *Grand*-class ships, was given a new look following an extensive 2011 refit and now has a flared dolphin-like bow and a galleon-like transom stern. It is too wide to transit the Panama Canal, with many balcony cabins overhanging the hull. There is a good sheltered faux teak promenade deck – it's actually painted steel – which almost wraps around, and a walkway that goes right to the enclosed, protected bow. The outdoor pools have various beach-like surroundings. One lap pool has a pumped "current" to swim against.

Unlike the outside decks, there is plenty of space inside the ship – but also plenty of passengers – and a wide array of public rooms, with many "intimate" (this being a relative word) spaces. The decor is attractive and warm, with lots of earth tones, and an extensive collection of art complements the interior design and colors well.

Four areas center on swimming pools, one of which is two decks high and can be covered by a retractable glass dome. The former Skywalkers Nightclub was repositioned to a lower deck (Deck 15) in 2011. Now called One5 (cute), it has improved the ship's former shopping-cart look.

Other facilities include a new Piazza Atrium, with an integral International Café, Vines wine bar (including tapas and sushi items and wines for purchase); and Leaves Tea Lounge and Library (with "tea sommelier" to create personalized "artisan" teas). There's a Wedding Chapel with a web-cam to relay ceremonies via the internet. The ship's captain can legally marry US citizens, due to the ship's Bermuda registry and a special dispensation. Contact the line for more details.

Another neat feature is the motion-based "virtual reality" room with its enclosed motion-based rides, and a "blue screen" studio, where passengers can star in their own videos. There is an excellent library/computer room, and a separate card room. Youngsters have a two-deck-high playroom, teen room, and trained counselors.

Gamblers should enjoy the large casino, with more than 260 slot machines with dolphin-shaped handles; there are blackjack, craps and roulette tables. Look out for Neptune's Lair, a multimedia gaming extravaganza.

Ship enthusiasts will savor the wood-paneled Wheelhouse Bar, decorated with memorabilia and ship models tracing part of the history of sister company P&O.

The dress code has been simplified to formal or smart casual. Gratuities are automatically added to your account, and tips for children are charged at the same rate. If you want to pay less, you'll have to line up at the reception desk.

Niggles? The automated telephone system frustrates many passengers, and luggage delivery could be more efficient.

ACCOMMODATION. There are six types of cabins and configurations but a bewildering choice of 35 brochure price categories. Many cabins have additional upper berths (there

BERLITZ'S RATINGS

	Possible	Achieved
Ship	500	413
Accommodation	200	163
Food	400	252
Service	400	287
Entertainment	100	80
Cruise	400	301

OVERALL SCORE
1,496 points out of 2,000

are 609 of them), which is good for families with children.
(a) The plushest accommodation is the Grand Suite, with a hot tub accessible from both the private balcony and from the bedroom, two bedrooms, lounge, two bathrooms, a huge walk-in closet, and lots of drawer and storage space.

(b/c) Suites (with a semi-private balcony) have a separate living room with sofa bed, and bedroom – with a TV set in each. The bathroom is quite large and has both a tub and shower stall. The mini-suites also have a private balcony, and a separate living and sleeping area, with a TV set in each. The differences between the suites and mini-suites are basically in the size and appointments. Passengers in both receive priority attention, including speedy embarkation and disembarkation. What is unacceptable is that the most expensive accommodation has only semi-private balconies that can be seen from above and so there is no privacy (Suites C401, 402, 409, 410, 414, 415, 420, 421/422, 423, 424, and 425 on Caribe Deck). The suites D105 and D106 (Dolphin Deck) are extremely large, but their balconies can be seen from above.

(d/e/f) Both interior and outside-view cabins – the outsides come either with or without private balcony – are functional and practical, although there are almost no drawers. They are attractive, with warm, pleasing decor and fine soft furnishing fabrics. The tiled bathrooms have a good amount of open shelf storage space for toiletries.

There are also two family suites. These consist of two suites with an interconnecting door, plus a large balcony, and can sleep up to 10 (if at least four are children), or up to eight adults.

Most outside cabins on Emerald Deck have views obstructed by lifeboats. Sadly, there are no cabins for singles. Your name is placed outside your suite or cabin – making it simple for delivery service personnel but compromising privacy. Some cabins can accommodate a third and fourth person in upper berths – but in such cabins, the lower beds cannot then be pushed together to make a queen-size bed.

Perhaps the least desirable balcony cabins are the eight located forward on Emerald Deck, as the balconies do not extend to the side of the ship and can be passed by walkers and gawkers on the adjacent Upper Promenade walkway. Also, passengers occupying some the most expensive suites with balconies at the stern may experience considerable vibration during certain ship maneuvers.

The cabin bath towels are small, and drawer space is limited. There are no butlers – even for the top-grade suites. Cabin attendants have many cabins to look after (typically 20), which cannot translate to fine personal service.

CUISINE. For formal meals, there are three main dining rooms, *Botticelli*, with 504 seats, *Da Vinci* (486), and *Michelangelo* (486). There are two seatings in one restaurant, while the other two have "anytime dining" where you choose when, and with whom, you want to eat. All three split into multi-tier sections in a non-symmetrical design that breaks what are quite large spaces into many smaller sections. Each dining room has its own galley. While four elevators go to Fiesta Deck for the Botticelli and Da Vinci restaurants, only two go to Plaza Deck 5 for the Michaelangelo Restaurant – this can cause long waits at peak times, especially for wheelchair users.

Alternative (Extra Charge) Dining: There are several alternative informal dining areas, open for lunch and dinner, all requiring reservations and imposing a cover charge.

Sabatini's is an Italian eatery, with colorful tiled Mediterranean-style decor. It has Italian-style pizzas and pastas, with a variety of sauces, as well as Italian-style entrées that include tiger prawns and lobster tail.

Crown Grill is a steakhouse. *Painted Desert*, an open area, has "southwestern American food" for lunch or dinner on sea days only. The cuisine in these spots is better than in the three main dining rooms.

The poolside hamburger grill and pizza bar (no additional charge) are additional dining spots for casual bites, while extra charges apply if you order items to eat at either the coffee bar/patisserie, or the caviar/champagne bar.

Other casual meals can be taken in the *Horizon Court* buffet – open 24 hours a day, with large ocean-view on port and starboard sides and direct access to the two main swimming pools and lido deck. Plastic plates are used.

ENTERTAINMENT. The 748-seat Princess Theater spans two decks and has comfortable seating on both main and balcony levels. The Vista Lounge, a second entertainment lounge, presents cabaret acts at night, and lectures, bingo and horse racing during the day. Explorers, a third lounge, can also host cabaret acts and dance bands. Many lounges and bars have live music, and a number of gentlemen dance hosts act as partners for women traveling alone.

SPA/FITNESS. The Lotus Spa is a large complex that surrounds one of the swimming pools at the forward end. It comprises a large gymnasium with all the usual equipment, an aerobics room, sauna and steam rooms, beauty salon, ocean-view treatment rooms, and a relaxation area.

● **For more extensive general information about the Princess Cruises experience, see pages 149–52.**

Grand Voyager
★★★ +

Size:	.Mid-Size Ship	Passenger Decks:	.8	Cabins (with private balcony):	.12
Tonnage:	.24,391	Total Crew:	.360	Cabins (wheelchair accessible):	.4
Lifestyle:	.Standard	Passengers		Wheelchair accessibility:	.Good
Cruise Line:	.Iberocruceros	(lower beds/all berths):	.840/920	Cabin Current:	.110 and 230 volts
Former Names:	.Olympia Voyager,	Passenger Space Ratio		Elevators:	.4
	Olympic Voyager	(lower beds/all berths):	.29.0/26.5	Casino (gaming tables):	.Yes
Builder:	.Blohm & Voss (Germany)	Crew/Passenger Ratio		Slot Machines:	.Yes
Original Cost:	.$150.8 million	(lower beds/all berths):	.2.3/2.5	Swimming Pools (outdoors):	.1
Entered Service:	.Jul 2000/Jun 2004	Cabins (total):	.420	Swimming Pools (indoors):	.0
Registry:	.The Bahamas	Size Range (sq ft/m):	.140.0–375.0/	Whirlpools:	.0
Length (ft/m):	.590.5/180.0		13.0–34.8	Self-Service Launderette:	.No
Beam (ft/m):	.83.6/25.5	Cabins (outside view):	.294	Dedicated Cinema/Seats:	.No
Draft (ft/m):	.23.2/7.1	Cabins (interior/no view):	.126	Library:	.Yes
Propulsion/Propellers: diesel (37,800 kW)/2		Cabins (for one person):	.0	Onboard currency:	.Euros

A small but cramped ship for Spanish speakers.

OVERVIEW. *Grand Voyager* is best suited to Spanish-speaking couples and single travelers who want to see as much as possible of their destinations in contemporary, comfortable, but not luxurious surroundings, and with food and service that are acceptable but nothing special, all at a very modest cruise fare. This is a "mostly-inclusive" product that especially suits families – although facilities for children are few.

THE SHIP. The exterior hull design, called a "fast monohull," is similar to that of naval frigates, with a slender fore-body, and two engine rooms (forward and midships) that can provide a 28-knot speed – and even some additional power in reserve. The ship is well suited to destination-intensive, port-hopping itineraries, allowing passengers more time in each port – or more ports per cruise. Its funnel is of a streamlined, swept-back design.

There is a limited amount of open deck space, although there aren't many sunloungers. All exterior railings are made – unusually – of stainless steel, topped with thick, beautifully polished wood. The seawater swimming pool is located aft, and is quite small; adjacent are two shower enclosures.

The interior design combines contemporary touches with restrained decor, intended to remind one of the Mediterranean region the ship is designed for, with warm colors and an abundance of wood and opaque glass paneling. Perhaps the most striking, yet subtle, features in terms of design and decoration can be found in the artwork. Of particular note are two flowing poems, from Greece and Cyprus, etched in backlit opaque glass panels on the stairways. To read the poems, you'll need to walk down the complete set

BERLITZ'S RATINGS		
	Possible	Achieved
Ship	500	369
Accommodation	200	135
Food	400	240
Service	400	252
Entertainment	100	58
Cruise	400	260
OVERALL SCORE		
1,314 points out of 2,000		

of stairways. One poem, *Ithaca*, from 1911 by the Greek poet Constantinos Petrou Kavafis, complements the other poem, *Let's Say*, by Cypriot poet Yannis Papadopoulos.

Most public rooms are located on one principal deck in a horizontal-flow layout that makes it easy to quickly find your way around. A slightly winding open passageway links several leisure lounges in one neat "street scene." There's a smoking room, adjacent to the main show lounge, for cigar and cognac devotees, with a black fireplace from the 1890s. In the popular Piano Bar, three ship models are cleverly displayed behind large glass wall panels. There's a nightclub, a small library and a card room. A casino has its own bar as well as table games and slot machines.

There is no full walk-around promenade deck, although you can walk around parts of the vessel outdoors. There is considerable vibration when the ship is underway at high speed, and when maneuvering at slow speeds. There are no dedicated facilities or rooms for the large numbers of children or teens that are typically carried during the July/August summer holidays. None of the public toilets is accessible by wheelchair. There are not enough sunloungers considering the number of passengers carried, and not enough open deck space.

An optional drinks package (standard drink brands) can be bought for €16 per person, per day or €8 for a non-alcoholic drinks package for minors. When the ship operates in Brazil during the local summer season, the onboard currency changes to the Brazilian Real.

ACCOMMODATION. There are five categories – suite with

balcony, suite with bay window, junior suite with window but no balcony, outside cabin, and interior cabin – and nine price grades, including one for wheelchair accessible cabins with spacious bathrooms and roll-in showers. The price will depend on grade, location and size.

Standard Cabins: The standard interior and outside-view cabins are quite compact but practically laid-out, and the decor includes warm blond wood cabinetry, accents and facings, and pleasing soft furnishings. The bathrooms are small, but have a decent-size shower enclosure, and good storage facilities for toiletries. All cabins include TV set, hairdryer, mini-bar/refrigerator and personal safe. Only one personal safe is provided in each cabin, although there could be as many as four persons sharing a cabin.

Outside-View Superior Cabins: These simply have a little more room than the standard interior and outside-view cabins, and some have bay windows that extend over the side of the ship. The bathrooms are small, but have a decent-size shower enclosure, and good storage for toiletries.

Balcony Suites: The largest accommodation is in 12 Sky Suites high atop the ship in the forward-most section. They have large private balconies (some are more like large terraces), floor-to-ceiling windows, limited butler service, and 24-hour dining service.

Some suites have walk-in closets, while others have closets facing the entranceway, but all have an abundance of drawer and hanging space, and a chrome pullout shoe rack and tie rack. The bathroom has a combination tub/shower – although the tub is extremely small and is really only for sitting in – and a retractable clothesline.

All suites have wood paneled walls with vanity desk, mini-bar/refrigerator, sofa, drinks table (it's fixed, and cannot be raised), and sleeping area partly separated from the lounge area by a wood/glass divider. Four of the suites have large structures above their balconies that are the port side and starboard side gangway lowering mechanisms; they are noisy in ports of call and anchor ports, and so the balconies cannot be considered very private.

Also, when the ship is traveling at speed, considerable wind sweeps across the balconies, rendering them almost useless. The balconies have expensive stainless-steel rail-ings instead of glass, topped with a thick wood railing. Outside-view and interior cabins located aft on Deck 3 (Neptune Deck: Numbers 3120–3138, and 3121–3151) are subject to a substantial amount of throbbing noise from the diesel engines, and should be avoided – unless you like throbbing engine noise, that is.

CUISINE. The 470-seat *Main Restaurant,* located aft, is one deck below the main "street" of public rooms and thus out of the main flow. It has picture windows on three sides and a semi-circular walkway, with minimalist decor, as its entrance. Its interior decor is warm and welcoming, and quite tasteful, finished in what is best described as a "Greek Moderne" style. The chairs, however, don't have armrests. There are two seatings, and tables for two, four, six or eight. A few tables close to the entrance to the galley's escalators suffer from the service area, and, because of the single-deck ceiling height and open waiter stations, the noise level can be considerable at times, partly depending on the nationalities of your fellow passengers.

For casual breakfast and lunch self-service buffets, the *Garden Buffet* is a pleasant but basic room, with large picture windows and an open feel. It has seating for 210 indoors and about 200 outdoors (where smokers congregate), and a bar outdoors is covered with a sailcloth-style cover. The two small self-service buffet lines have a user-unfriendly layout that invites congestion.

Additional munching outlets include a pizza serving area/salad bar, and an ice cream bar.

ENTERTAINMENT. The Main Lounge is the venue for entertainment events. It is a single-level room with 420 seats, although many pillars obstruct the sight lines from many seats – about 40 per cent are almost useless. Entertainment is limited aboard this ship, whose show lounge is best for cabaret-style shows. There's a disco.

SPA/FITNESS. One of the nicest and most useful facilities can be found in the Spa. It includes a large fitness room, several massage/treatment rooms, sauna, steam room, and a rest/changing area.

Grande Caribe
★ +

Size: ....Boutique Ship	Total Crew: 17	Cabins (wheelchair accessible): 0
Tonnage: 99	Passengers	Wheelchair accessibility: ....None
Lifestyle: ....Standard	(lower beds/all berths): 100/100	Cabin Current: ....110 volts
Cruise Line: Blount Small Ship Adventures	Passenger Space Ratio	Elevators: 0
Former Names: ....none	(lower beds/all berths): 0.99/0.99	Casino (gaming tables): ....No
Builder: ....Blount Industries (USA)	Crew/Passenger Ratio	Slot Machines: ....No
Original Cost: ....$8 million	(lower beds/all berths): 5.8/5.8	Swimming Pools (outdoors): 0
Entered Service: ....Jun 1997	Cabins (total): 50	Swimming Pools (indoors): 0
Registry: ....USA	Size Range (sq ft/m): 72.0–96.0/	Whirlpools: 0
Length (ft/m): 183.0/55.7	6.6–8.9	Self-Service Launderette: ....No
Beam (ft/m): 40.0/12.1	Cabins (outside view): 41	Dedicated Cinema/Seats: ....No
Draft (ft/m): 6.5/1.9	Cabins (interior/no view): 9	Library: ....Yes
Propulsion/Propellers: diesel (1,044kW)/2	Cabins (for one person): 0	Onboard currency ....US$
Passenger Decks: 3	Cabins (with private balcony): 0	

A tiny ship for coastal cruising, with minimal facilities.

OVERVIEW. This ship is best for mature-age couples and single travelers who enjoy nature and wildlife up close, who wouldn't dream of cruising in the mainstream sense aboard warehouse-size ships and who don't demand a high standard of service. It's a basic, no-glitz vessel, providing an all-American cruise experience, albeit at a high price, and is not for children.

THE SHIP. *Grande Caribe* is the largest, most contemporary Blount-built vessel. Like sister ship *Grande Mariner*, it has stabilizers. During emergency drill, passengers are taught how to use fire extinguishers – a useful piece of training.

The ship's shallow draft enables it to cruise into off-the-beaten-path destinations well out of reach of larger ships. It also has a retractable navigation bridge – practical for those low bridges along inland waterways. An underwater video camera allows passengers, while seated in comfort in the lounge, to view on large-screen TV monitors what a scuba diver might see underneath the ship. Underwater lights, which attract fish and other marine life, are fitted. There are two 24-passenger launches, one of which is a glass-bottomed boat, and snorkeling equipment.

There is one lounge/bar, located on a different deck to the dining room. The style is casual – no jackets or ties – by day and night. An electric stairway chair-lift is provided for those whose mobility is restricted. Gratuities given by passengers (high at the suggested $10–$15 per person, per day) are pooled and shared by all the staff.

BERLITZ'S RATINGS

	Possible	Achieved
Ship	500	164
Accommodation	200	67
Food	400	155
Service	400	181
Entertainment	n/a	n/a
Cruise	500	189

OVERALL SCORE
756 points out of 2,000

ACCOMMODATION. The cabins are all extremely small, relatively utilitarian units, with very little closet space but just enough drawers. The very small bathrooms have new vacuum toilets. The twin beds convert to queen-size beds, with good storage space under them. There is no room service menu, and only soap is supplied – bring your own toiletries. Each cabin has its own air conditioner, so passengers do not have to share air with the rest of the ship. Refreshingly, there are no cabin keys. Be prepared for noise from the generators.

CUISINE. The dining room seats all passengers in one open seating, so you dine with whomever you wish, making new friends each day– it is also good for small groups. The tables convert to card tables for use between meals. Passengers are welcome to bring their own alcohol, as the company doesn't sell it aboard ship. Effervescent, young American waitresses provide the service, although there is no finesse.

A hand-held Colonial bell is rung to summon passengers to the dining room.

ENTERTAINMENT. There is no formal entertainment, so conversation with fellow passengers in the ship's lounge/bar becomes the entertainment each evening. If that isn't appealing, take a good book.

SPA/FITNESS. There are no facilities.

Grande Mariner
★ +

Size:	Boutique Ship
Tonnage:	99
Lifestyle:	Standard
Cruise Line:	Blount Small Ship Adventures
Former Names:	none
Builder:	Blount Industries (USA)
Original Cost:	$8 million
Entered Service:	Jun 1998
Registry:	USA
Length (ft/m):	183.0/55.7
Beam (ft/m):	40.0/12.1
Draft (ft/m):	6.5/1.9
Propulsion/Propellers:	diesel (1,044kW)/2
Passenger Decks:	3
Total Crew:	17
Passengers	
(lower beds/all berths):	100/100
Passenger Space Ratio	
(lower beds/all berths):	0.99/0.99
Crew/Passenger Ratio	
(lower beds/all berths):	5.8/5.8
Cabins (total):	50
Size Range (sq ft/m):	72.0–96.0/6.6–8.9
Cabins (outside view):	41
Cabins (interior/no view):	9
Cabins (for one person):	0
Cabins (with private balcony):	0
Cabins (wheelchair accessible):	0
Wheelchair accessibility:	None
Cabin Current:	110 volts
Elevators:	0
Casino (gaming tables):	No
Slot Machines:	No
Swimming Pools (outdoors):	0
Swimming Pools (indoors):	0
Whirlpools:	0
Self-Service Launderette:	No
Dedicated Cinema/Seats:	No
Library:	Yes
Onboard currency:	US$

A coastal cruise ship with basic food and minimal facilities.

OVERVIEW. This ship is best for mature-age couples and single travelers who enjoy nature and wildlife up close, and who wouldn't dream of cruising in the mainstream sense aboard warehouse-size ships and who doesn't demand a high standard of service. It's a basic, no-glitz vessel, providing an all-American cruise experience, albeit at a high price, and is not for children.

THE SHIP. *Grande Mariner* is the second of two almost identical Blount-built vessels. Like sister ship *Grande Caribe*, it has stabilizers. During emergency drill, passengers are taught how to use fire extinguishers – a useful piece of training.

The ship's shallow draft enables it to cruise into off-the-beaten-path destinations well out of reach of larger ships. It also has a retractable navigation bridge – practical for those low bridges along inland waterways. An underwater video camera allows passengers, while seated in comfort in the lounge, to view on large-screen TV monitors what a scuba diver might see underneath the ship. Underwater lights, which attract fish and other marine life, are fitted. There are two 24-passenger launches, one of which is a glass-bottomed boat, and snorkeling equipment.

There is one lounge/bar, located on a different deck to the dining room. The style is casual – no jackets or ties – by day and night. An electric stairway chair-lift is provided for those whose mobility is restricted. Gratuities given by passengers (high at the suggested $10–$15 per person, per day) are pooled and shared by all the staff.

BERLITZ'S RATINGS

	Possible	Achieved
Ship	500	159
Accommodation	200	67
Food	400	155
Service	400	181
Entertainment	n/a	n/a
Cruise	500	185

OVERALL SCORE
747 points out of 2,000

ACCOMMODATION. The cabins are all extremely small, relatively utilitarian units, with very little closet space but just enough drawers. The very small bathrooms have new vacuum toilets. The twin beds convert to queen-size beds, with good storage space under them. There is no room service menu, and only soap is supplied – bring your own toiletries. Each cabin has its own air conditioner, so passengers do not have to share air with the rest of the ship. Refreshingly, there are no cabin keys. Be prepared for noise from the generators.

CUISINE. The dining room seats all passengers in open seating, so you dine with whomever you wish, making new friends each day– it is also good for small groups. The tables convert to card tables for use between meals. Passengers are welcome to bring their own alcohol, as the company doesn't sell it aboard ship. Effervescent, young American waitresses provide the service, although there is no finesse.

A hand-held colonial bell is rung to summon passengers to the dining room.

ENTERTAINMENT. There is no formal entertainment, so conversation with fellow passengers in the ship's lounge/bar becomes the entertainment each evening. If that isn't appealing, take a good book.

SPA/FITNESS. There are no facilities.

Grandeur of the Seas
★★★★

Size:	Large Resort Ship	Total Crew:	760	Wheelchair accessibility: Good

Size: ....Large Resort Ship
Tonnage: 74,137
Lifestyle: ....Standard
Cruise Line: Royal Caribbean International
Former Names: ....none
Builder: ...Kvaerner Masa-Yards (Finland)
Original Cost: ....$300 million
Entered Service: ....Dec 1996
Registry: ....The Bahamas
Length (ft/m): 916.0/279.6
Beam (ft/m): 105.6/32.2
Draft (ft/m): 25.5/7.6
Propulsion/Propellers: .....diesel-electric
(50,400kW)/2
Passenger Decks: 11

Total Crew: 760
Passengers
(lower beds/all berths): 1,950/2,446
Passenger Space Ratio
(lower beds/all berths): 38.0/30.3
Crew/Passenger Ratio
(lower beds/all berths): 2.5/3.2
Cabins (total): 975
Size Range (sq ft/m): 158.2–1,267.0/
14.7–117.7
Cabins (outside view): 576
Cabins (interior/no view): 399
Cabins (for one person): 0
Cabins (with private balcony): 212
Cabins (wheelchair accessible): 14

Wheelchair accessibility: ....Good
Cabin Current: ....110 and 220 volts
Elevators: 9
Casino (gaming tables): ....Yes
Slot Machines: ....Yes
Swimming Pools (outdoors): 1
Swimming Pools (indoors): 1
(indoor/outdoor with sliding glass roof)
Whirlpools: 6
Self-Service Launderette: ....No
Dedicated Cinema/Seats: ....No
Library: ....Yes
Onboard currency: ....US$

Big-ship cruising with multiple choice dining.

OVERVIEW. This ship has good interior passenger flow. There is a good, varied collection of artworks including several sculptures, principally by British artists, with classical music, ballet and theater themes. Huge murals of opera scenes adorn several stairways The children's and teens' facilities are good.

THE SHIP. *Grandeur of the Seas* has an attractive contemporary profile, with a single funnel located well aft – almost a throwback to some ship designs used in the 1950s – and has a nicely rounded stern. A Viking Crown Lounge is set amidships. This, together with the forward mast, provides three distinct focal points in its exterior profile. There is a walk-around promenade deck outdoors, but no cushioned pads for the tacky home patio-style plastic sunloungers.

A large Viking Crown Lounge, a trademark of Royal Caribbean International ships, sits between funnel and mast at the top of the atrium lobby, and overlooks the forward section of the swimming pool deck, with access provided from stairway off the central atrium.

The principal interior focal point is a seven-deck-high Centrum (atrium lobby), which is a good meeting point – the Purser's Desk and Shore Excursion Desk are on one of the lower levels. Many public entertainment rooms and facilities are located off the atrium. The casino is large and glitzy, and has a fascinating, somewhat theatrical glass-covered, but under-floor exhibit.

A neat champagne terrace bar sits forward of the lower level of the two-deck-high dining room. There is a good use of tropical plants throughout the public rooms, which

BERLITZ'S RATINGS

	Possible	Achieved
Ship	500	411
Accommodation	200	152
Food	400	227
Service	400	260
Entertainment	100	77
Cruise	400	280

OVERALL SCORE
1,407 points out of 2,000

helps counteract the rather plain and clinical pastel wall colors.

ACCOMMODATION. There are 16 price grades. The price depends on grade, size and location, with location and grade perhaps more important since so many of the cabins are of the same, or a very similar size. There are five grades of suites. All are well appointed and have pleasing decor, best described as Scandinavian Moderne, with good wood and color accenting.

Royal Suite. The largest accommodation is the Royal Suite, located directly aft of the ship's navigation bridge on the starboard side. It has a separate bedroom with king-size bed, walk-in closet and vanity dressing area, living room with queen-size sofa bed, baby grand piano, refrigerator and wet bar, dining table, entertainment center, and large private balcony. The bathroom has a whirlpool tub, separate shower enclosure, two washbasins, and toilet.

Owner's Suite. The five owner's suites are at the forward end of the ship, just behind the navigation bridge. They have a queen-size bed, separate living area with queen-size sofa bed, vanity dressing area, refrigerator and wet bar. The bathroom has a full-size tub, separate shower enclosure, toilet and two washbasins.

Royal Family Suite. These four suites each include two bedrooms with twin beds that convert to queen-size beds, living area with double sofa bed and Pullman bed, refrigerator, two bathrooms (one with tub), and private balcony. They can accommodate eight, and so might suit families.

Grand Suite. These 12 suites have twin beds that convert to a queen-size bed, vanity dressing area, lounge area with sofa bed, refrigerator, and a bathroom with tub, plus a private balcony.

Superior Suite. These 44 suites, including two suites for the disabled, have twin beds that convert to a queen-size bed, vanity dressing area, lounge area with sofa bed, refrigerator, plus private balcony, and a bathroom with tub. Although they are called suites, they really are little more than larger standard cabins with a balcony.

Other Grades. All standard cabins have twin beds that convert to a queen-size bed, ample closet space for a one-week cruise, and a good amount of drawer space, although under-bed storage space is not good for large suitcases. The bathrooms have nine mirrors. Plastic buckets are provided for champagne or wine and are really tacky.

All grades of suite/cabin include a hairdryer. Room service menu is minimal, with only the most basic selection – no hot items for breakfast, for example.

CUISINE. The 1,195-seat *Great Gatsby Dining Room* is spread over two decks, with both levels connected by a grand, sweeping staircase. When you book, choose one of two seatings, or "My Time Dining" (eat when you want, during dining room hours).

The cavernous, 790-seat *Windjammer Café* is a casual eatery. It has a great expanse of ocean-view glass windows, and is where breakfast and lunch buffets are available as an alternative to the dining room. An intimate terrace *Champagne Bar* is forward of the lower level of the two-deck-high dining room and just off the atrium for those who might like to taste something a little out of the ordinary, in a setting that is bright and contemporary.

ENTERTAINMENT. The Palladium Theater is the principal showlounge. It is located at the forward part of the ship, and is used for big production shows. It has excellent sight-lines from 98 percent of the 875 seats. Another showlounge, the 575-seat South Pacific Lounge, is used for smaller shows and cabaret acts, including late-night adult comedy.

SPA/FITNESS. The ShipShape Spa is aft of the funnel and spans two decks. Facilities include a gymnasium with all the latest muscle-pumping exercise machines, aerobics exercise room, sauna and steam rooms, a beauty salon, and a clutch of treatment rooms.

For the sporting, there is activity galore – including a rock-climbing wall with several separate climbing tracks. It is located outdoors at the aft end of the funnel.

● **For more extensive general information about the Royal Caribbean experience, see pages 152–6.**

DID YOU KNOW...

● that Silvio Berlusconi, Italy's former premier, was once a cruise ship entertainer? He sang, and accompanying him, on piano, was Fedele Confalonieri, his oldest buddy, now president of Berlusconi's Mediaset empire.

● that the cruise ship used in the 1974 movie *Juggernaut*, in which seven bombs in oil drums were placed aboard, was *Maxim Gorkiy*? The film starred Richard Harris, Omar Sharif, David Hemmings, and Anthony Hopkins.

● that musical instruments of some of the stars of rock and pop can be found aboard Holland America Line's *Zaandam*? They were acquired from the "Pop and Guitars" auction at Christie's in London, and a Fender Squire Telecaster guitar signed by the Rolling Stones; A Conn Saxophone signed on the mouthpiece by former US President Bill Clinton; an Ariana acoustic guitar signed by David Bowie and Iggy Pop; a Fender Stratocaster guitar signed in silver ink by the members of the rock band Queen; a Bently "Les Paul" style guitar signed by various artists, including Carlos Santana, Eric Clapton, BB King, Robert Cray, Keith Richards and Les Paul.

● that the Cunard White Star Line's *Queen Mary* was the first ship to have a system of colored lights that varied according to music (chromosonics)?

● that Verdi wrote an opera to commemorate the opening of the Suez Canal? Its name is *Aïda*.

● that the 212-passenger *Seabourn Legend* was the star of the film *Speed 2: Cruise Control*, released in 1997 in the US? The film was shot on location in Marigot, the capital of the French side of the tiny two-nation Caribbean island of St. Martin/St. Maarten. The filming called for the building of almost a complete "town" at Marigot, into which the ship crashes.

● that *Titanic*, the stage musical, cost $10 million to mount in New York in 1997? That's $2.5 million more than it cost to build the original ship that debuted in 1912. The play debuted at the Lunt-Fontanne Theater in April 1997 (the ship sank on April 14, 1912).

● that the Hollywood film that made headlines by having the largest budget to date – but also made the most money – was based aboard a passenger liner? The film, of course, was *Titanic*, released in 1997.

Hamburg
★★★ +

Size: ....Small Ship	Total Crew: 170	Cabins (wheelchair accessible): 2
Tonnage: 14,903	Passengers	Wheelchair accessibility ....Fair
Lifestyle: ....Standard	(lower beds/all berths): 408/421	Cabin Current: ....220 volts
Cruise Line: ....Plantours & Partner	Passenger Space Ratio	Elevators: 2
Former Names: ...._Columbus_	(lower beds/all berths): 36.5/35.3	Casino (gaming tables): ....No
Builder: ....MTW Schiffswerft (Germany)	Crew/Passenger Ratio	Slot Machines: ....No
Original Cost: ....$69 million	(lower beds/all berths): 2.4/2.4	Swimming Pools (outdoors): 1
Entered Service: ....Jul 1997/May 2012	Cabins (total): 205	Swimming Pools (indoors): 0
Registry: ....The Bahamas	Size Range (sq ft/m): 139.9–339.0/	Whirlpools: 0
Length (ft/m): 472.8/144.13	.........................13.0–31.5	Self-Service Launderette: ....No
Beam (ft/m): 70.5/21.50	Cabins (outside view): 158	Dedicated Cinema/Seats: ....No
Draft (ft/m): 16.8/5.15	Cabins (interior/no view): 47	Library: ....Yes
Propulsion/Propellers: diesel (10,560kW)/2	Cabins (for one person): 2	Onboard currency ....Euros
Passenger Decks: 6	Cabins (with private balcony): 2	

A small ship for port-intensive cruising.

OVERVIEW. This ship appeals to German-speaking couples and single travelers seeking good value for money on a first cruise, aboard a ship with contemporary, comfortable (but not pretentious or luxurious) surroundings, and good itineraries, at a modest price. Only casual clothes are needed.

THE SHIP. _Hamburg_ has a smart contemporary profile, with a single, large funnel. Plantours & Partner Cruises has chartered it from its German owner, Conti Reederei, starting in May 2012, when it is transferred from Hapag-Lloyd Cruises, which operated it as _Columbus._ The ship has an ice-hardened hull, useful in cold-weather cruise areas. There's a choice of busy itineraries and destination-intensive cruises.

The ceilings in the public rooms are plain and unimaginative (except for the Palm Garden), but the decor is bright and upbeat. Interior fit and finish is utilitarian – with mottle-effect walls that are cold but a contrast to the splashes of color found in carpeting and other decorative touches. The artwork is, for the most part, minimal and uncoordinated.

While it's a comfortable, trendy ship, the swimming pool is small – more like a "dip" pool – as is the open deck space, and there is no walk-around promenade deck outdoors.

ACCOMMODATION. The standard cabins are really small, and there are many interior cabins. Except for two forward-facing suites, there are no balcony cabins, and no room service (except for accommodation designated as suites). There are two single-occupancy cabins. The cabin decor is bright and upbeat, and a good amount of closet and shelf space is provided. The fully tiled bathrooms have large

BERLITZ'S RATINGS

	Possible	Achieved
Ship	500	342
Accommodation	200	145
Food	400	283
Service	400	297
Entertainment	100	61
Cruise	400	270

OVERALL SCORE
1,398 points out of 2,000

shower stalls (none have tubs). All cabins have a mini-bar/refrigerator, flat-screen TV, personal safe, and hairdryer.

Eight suites, double the size of a standard cabin, have curtained partitions between lounge and sleeping areas. A TV set can be turned 360° for viewing in either lounge or bedroom.

Two suites at the bow have a narrow private veranda with two teak lounge chairs and coffee table, a bedroom with large wall clock, and a lounge area separated by a curtain, two TV sets, and an excellent amount of storage space. The cabinetry makes these suites feel warm and luxurious. All suites have a small room service menu. The bathrooms have a large shower – big enough for two – hairdryer, and under-sink storage space.

CUISINE. The large dining room, at the stern, has ocean-view windows on three sides. There are just two tables for two, but other tables can accommodate up to 16. The cuisine is presented (by Ligabue) in an unstuffy way. There is a decent daily selection of fresh breads, cold cuts and cheeses.

Breakfast and lunch can be taken in the bright but casual setting of the Palm Garden, which doubles as the ship's observation lounge. Light dinners can also be taken there, and there's a small dance floor.

ENTERTAINMENT. The Showlounge is a single-level, H-shaped room, with banquette and individual seating in tub chairs. Sightlines from many seats are quite poor.

SPA/FITNESS. There's a fitness room, a sauna, and a beauty salon. Massage and facial treatments are available, but the facility is rather poor.

Hanseatic
★★★★★

Size: . . . . .Boutique Ship	Total Crew: 122	Cabins (wheelchair accessible): 2
Tonnage: .8,378	Passengers	Wheelchair accessibility: . . . . .None
Lifestyle: .Luxury	(lower beds/all berths): 184/194	Cabin Current: . . . . .220 volts
Cruise Line: Hapag-Lloyd Expedition Cruises	Passenger Space Ratio	Elevators: 2
Former Names: . . . . . .Society Adventurer	(lower beds/all berths): 45.5/43.1	Swimming Pools (outdoors): 1
Builder: . . . . .Rauma Yards (Finland)	Crew/Passenger Ratio	Whirlpools: 1
Original Cost: . . . .$68 million	(lower beds/all berths): 1.5/1.5	Self-Service Launderette: . . . . .No
Entered Service: . . . . .Mar 1993	Cabins (total): 92	Lecture/Film Room: . . . . . .Yes (seats 160)
Registry: . . . . .The Bahamas	Size Range (sq ft/m): 231.4–470.3/	Library: . . . . .Yes
Length (ft/m): 402.9/122.80	21.5–43.7	Zodiacs: 14
Beam (ft/m): 59.1/18.00	Cabins (outside view): 92	Helicopter Pad: . . . . .Yes
Draft (ft/m): 16.1/4.91	Cabins (interior/no view): 0	Onboard currency: . . . . .Euros
Propulsion/Propellers: .diesel (5,880kW)/2	Cabins (for one person): 0	
Passenger Decks: 7	Cabins (with private balcony): 0	

A lovely, small "soft" expedition ship for discovery.

OVERVIEW. *Hanseatic* provides destination-intensive, nature and life-enrichment cruises and expeditions in elegant but unstuffy surroundings, to some of the world's most fascinating destinations, at a suitably handsome price that ensures really good food and high-quality service. It is at its best in the Arctic and Antarctic, but infirm passengers should be wary of the difficult conditions for shore landings in these areas.

THE SHIP. *Hanseatic,* operated by Hapag-Lloyd Cruises, was designed for worldwide expedition-style cruises in contemporary, but quite luxurious, surroundings. It is extremely environmentally friendly, and is one of the very few ships that will allow you to tour the engine room. It has a fully enclosed bridge and an ice-hardened hull with the highest passenger vessel ice classification, plus the very latest in high-tech navigation equipment.

A fleet of 14 Zodiac inflatable craft, each named after a famous explorer, is used for in-depth shore landings. These craft provide the ship with tremendous flexibility in itineraries, with excellent possibilities for up-close wildlife viewing in natural habitats. Rubber boots, parkas, boot-washing and storage rooms are provided – particularly useful for Arctic and Antarctic cruises. For warmer climes, a Bike Box, with 10 bicycles for passenger use at no charge, is offloaded in each port the ship is alongside, where possible. There's a Marine Lab, for examination of items.

Inside, the ship is equipped with fine-quality luxury fittings and soft furnishings, and exudes a microclimate of good taste. There is a choice of several public rooms – most located aft, with accommodation forward. All are well-furnished and decorated, and all have high ceilings which help

BERLITZ'S RATINGS		
	Possible	Achieved
Ship	500	436
Accommodation	200	172
Food	400	346
Service	400	343
Entertainment	n/a	n/a
Cruise	500	449
OVERALL SCORE		
1,746 points out of 2,000		

make the ship feel much larger than its actual size. The library/observation lounge provides a good selection of hardback books in English and German, including many geographical, travel, wildlife and archaeology titles; it has a sunken bar, and a warm, inviting atmosphere, and two internet-access computer stations. A large lecture hall, with excellent audio-visual facilities, on a lower deck, can accommodate almost all passengers.

The passenger count is generally kept to about 150, which means plenty of comfort, no lines, and lots of space. In passageways and suites/cabins, 400 large, framed, black and white photographs depict wildlife and expedition experiences. Bouillon is served at 11am.

Safety is paramount, particularly in the Antarctic, and here the ship excels with professionalism, pride and skilled seamanship. Most of each day is taken up with being ashore, and evenings consist mainly of dinner and daily recaps. Lectures, briefings, and the amount of information provided about the itinerary and ports of call are excellent, and, for some cruises, include useful pocket-size color port booklets. Well-qualified lecturers and naturalists accompany each cruise, and a discreet crew and service staff providing unobtrusive service are hallmarks of this ship. A full passenger list and an expedition cruise logbook is typically provided at the end of each voyage for all passengers – a fine reminder of the cruise.

Hanseatic operates in two languages, English and German, though many staff speak several languages, and caters well to both sets of passengers. All port taxes, insurance, staff gratuities, and Zodiac trips are included. A relaxed ambience and informal dress code prevail.

There are just a few negatives. The ship is marketed mainly to German- and English-speakers, so other nationalities may find it hard to integrate. Hapag-Lloyd publishes its own excellent handbooks (in both English and German) on expedition regions such as the Arctic, Antarctica, Amazonia and the South Sea Islands, as well as exclusive maps.

ACCOMMODATION. There are no bad cabins, and accommodation is priced in seven grades. The all-outside cabins, located in the forward section, are large and very well equipped, and include a separate lounge area next to a large picture window (which has a pull-down blackout blind as well as curtains), superb, high-intensity, moveable bedside reading lights, and refrigerator.

All furniture is in warm woods such as beech, and everything has rounded edges. Wood trim accents the ceiling perimeter, and acts as a divider between bed and lounge areas. Each cabin has a mini-bar, flat-screen interactive TV with internet access, when available, and wireless keyboard. A complete infotainment system includes movies and audio tracks on demand at no extra charge. There's a separate bedside three-channel radio, two locking drawers, a retro alarm clock, and plenty of closet and drawer space, as well as two separate cupboards and hooks for all-weather outerwear. One useful feature of all cabins is a blue, night/safety light, nicely hidden in each bathroom. A privacy curtain between the cabin door and the sleeping area of the cabin would be useful – you can be seen from the hallway when the cabin door is opened.

All cabin bathrooms, superbly remodelled in 2009, have a large shower enclosure with curved glass wall, toiletries cabinets, wall-mounted hairdryer, and bathrobe. There are only two types of cabins; 34 have double beds, others have twin beds. The bath-size towels are large, bed linens and pillowcases are 100% cotton, and individual cotton-filled duvet covers are provided. Laundry, dry cleaning and pressing are available.

Suites and cabins on Bridge Deck have impeccable butler service and in-cabin dining privileges, plus personalized stationery and a larger flat-screen TV. Free soft drinks in the refrigerator are replenished daily, but all liquor costs extra. Bulgari and Crabtree and Evelyn amenities are provided, as are anti-sunburn lotion and hair mist.

CUISINE. The 186-seat, no smoking *Marco Polo* restaurant is elegant, warm and welcoming, with large picture windows on two sides as well as aft. There is one seating for dinner, and open seating for breakfast and lunch, although many passengers like to be seated at their "regular" table. On embarkation day, waiters introduce themselves after the meal, so hungry passengers won't be delayed by small talk.

The cuisine and service are absolutely first-rate, but are slightly more informal than, for example, aboard the larger *Europa*, which is at or close to the same price level. Top-quality ingredients are always used, and most items are bought fresh when available. In some ports, passengers can go "shopping with the chef" to source local, regional ingredients and fresh fish.

The meals are very creative and nicely presented, each being appealing to the eye as well as to the palate. There is always an outstanding selection of breads, cheeses, desserts and pastry items. In the Arctic or Antarctic, table set-ups are often minimal, due to possible movement of the ship – stabilizers can't be used in much of the Antarctic – so cutlery is provided and changed for each course. Three types of sugar are presented when coffee or tea are ordered – it should never be placed on the table during meal service.

An alternative dining spot is the *Columbus Lounge*, with 74 seats indoors, as well as copious seating at outdoor tables. An informal, open seating, self-serve (or waiter service) buffet-style eatery by day, it changes into a second dining room night, suitably called *Ethno*, with themed dinners and barbeques featuring region-specific food. Reservations are required – you make them in the morning of the day you want to dine there – but there is no extra charge and no tipping at any time.

Also, each cruise includes a full Viennese teatime, as well as a daily teatime with a selection of cakes, pastries and finger sandwiches befitting a Viennese coffee house.

ENTERTAINMENT. There is no showlounge as such, although there is a lecture room. Entertainment is certainly not a priority aboard this ship, but the itinerary and destinations are the main show. There is no formal entertainment – except on some summer cruises, when a small classical music ensemble may be aboard – nor does the ship normally carry a band.

Lectures, by some of the foremost authorities and experts in various fields associated with expeditions and nature are a principal attraction of any cruise – unless the ship is under charter for special theme cruises during the summer – as are after-dinner recaps of the day. Occasionally, the ship's crew may put on a little amateur dramatics event, or a seamen's choral presentation.

SPA/FITNESS. The spa facilities include a decently-sized gymnasium (with up-to-date cardio-vascular and muscle-toning equipment, treadmills and exercycles), and sauna, all located forward on the Sun Deck in an area that also includes a solarium and hot tub. There's also a cosmetics/make-up room. Massage is available, at €46 for 60 minutes, and €38 for 45 minutes, in a rather clinical room within the medical facility, on a lower deck.

Happy Dolphin
★★★

Size: . . . . .Mid-Size Ship	Passenger Decks: 8	Cabins (with private balcony): 177
Tonnage: 21,884	Total Crew: 250	Cabins (wheelchair accessible): 2
Lifestyle: . . . . .Standard	Passengers	Wheelchair accessibility . . . . .Fair
Cruise Line: . . . . .Happy Cruises	(lower beds/all berths): 650/650	Cabin Current: . . . . .110 volts
Former Names: . . . . . . .Delphin Voyager,	Passenger Space Ratio	Elevators: 4
Orient Venus	(lower beds/all berths): 33.6/33.6	Casino (gaming tables): . . . . .No
Builder: . . .Ishikawajima Heavy Industries	Crew/Passenger Ratio	Slot Machines: .No
Original Cost: . . . .$150 million	(lower beds/all berths): 2.6/2.6	Swimming Pools (outdoors): 1
Entered Service: . . . . . .Jul 1990/Apr 2011	Cabins (total): 325	Swimming Pools (indoors): 0
Registry: . . . . .The Bahamas	Size Range (sq ft/m): 182.9–592.0/	Whirlpools: 0
Length (ft/m): 570.8/174.00	17.0–55.0	Self-Service Launderette: . . . . .Yes
Beam (ft/m): 78.7/24.00	Cabins (outside view): 269	Dedicated Cinema/Seats: . . . . .No
Draft (ft/m): 21.3/6.52	Cabins (interior/no view): 56	Library: . . . . .Yes
Propulsion/Propellers:diesel (13,830 kW)/2	Cabins (for one person): 0	Onboard currency: . . . . .Euros

A ship for that suits Spanish-speaking families.

OVERVIEW. This ship is best suited to youthful Spanish-speaking couples and single travelers who want to travel in comfortable surroundings at a moderate cost. Most public rooms are set on just one deck, which means it's easy to find your way around. The cruises provide good value for money, and drink prices are very reasonable.

THE SHIP. Originally built as *Orient Venus* for Japan's Venus Cruise, this is a conventionally shaped ship with a pleasant profile. There is a reasonable amount of open deck and sunbathing space, including an expansive amount of open deck space for sunbathing, aft of the funnel.

Good views can be had from the Panorama Bar, a large, high-mounted observation lounge wrapped around the funnel housing. Although there is no elevator access for disabled passengers, a chair-lift is provided. There's a good array of public rooms with tasteful, European decor, including a three-deck-high entrance lobby, the focal meeting point.

ACCOMMODATION. There are eight cabin grades, the three highest designated as "suite" grades. The standard cabins have decor best described as light but plain, with a reasonable amount of closet space; however, the drawer space is quite limited. The largest suites have an expansive lounge area with large, plush armchairs, coffee table, and window-side chairs and drinks table, large windows, and a larger private balcony. There is a separate sleeping room, curtained off from the living room, with twin- or queen-size bed, vanity/office desk, and larger bathroom.

BERLITZ'S RATINGS		
	Possible	Achieved
Ship	500	331
Accommodation	200	128
Food	400	229
Service	400	241
Entertainment	100	61
Cruise	400	253

OVERALL SCORE
1,243 points out of 2,000

All grades have a flat-screen TV, telephone, hairdryer, and refrigerator. All cabins have a shower, except for the three suites, which have a bathtub and separate shower. Some 36 cabins have life-boat obstructed views.

New cabins were installed in a 2007 refit, when the original ones didn't receive much attention. So it's best to book one of the new cabins.

CUISINE. The main dining room – single seating with assigned tables – is quite attractive. It's actually split into two sections: the *Atlantic Restaurant*, located on the port side in a "railway carriage" format, and the *Pacific Restaurant*, located aft. There's plenty of space around the dining tables. The aft section of the Pacific Restaurant is the most desirable section, with views over the stern.

The table settings are standard, and the wine glasses are small. The food is average, and it certainly wouldn't win any awards – but everything is done to a tight budget.

ENTERTAINMENT. The horseshoe-shaped Showlounge is a single-level room with good sightlines to the platform stage. On most cruises, entertainers such as singers, instrumentalists, storytellers and dance champions are brought on board from ashore.

SPA/FITNESS. There is a small spa, which consists of a gymnasium, saunas, and treatment rooms. There is also a special room with five fully-equipped dialysis stations for special cruises, when a dialysis technician is on board.

Hebridean Princess
★★★★ +

Size: ....Boutique Ship	Passenger Decks: 5	Cabins (with private balcony): 4
Tonnage: 2,112	Total Crew: 37	Cabins (wheelchair accessible): 0
Lifestyle: ....Luxury	Passengers	Wheelchair accessibility: ....None
Cruise Line: ....Hebridean Island Cruises	(lower beds/all berths): 49/49	Cabin Current: ....240 volts
Former Names: ....Columba	Passenger Space Ratio	Elevators: 0
Builder: ....Hall Russell (Scotland)	(lower beds/all berths): 43.1/43.1	Casino (gaming tables): ....No
Original Cost: ....n/a	Crew/Passenger Ratio	Slot Machines: ....No
Entered Service: 1964/May 1989	(lower beds/all berths): 1.3/1.3	Swimming Pools (outdoors): 0
Registry: ....Great Britain	Cabins (total): 30	Swimming Pools (indoors): 0
Length (ft/m): 235.0/71.6	Size Range (sq ft/m): 144.0–340.0/	Whirlpools: 0
Beam (ft/m): 46.0/14.0	13.4–31.6	Self-Service Launderette: ....No
Draft (ft/m): 10.0/3.0	Cabins (outside view): 24	Dedicated Cinema/Seats: ....No
Propulsion/Propellers: ....diesel	Cabins (interior/no view): 6	Library: ....Yes
(1,790kW)/2	Cabins (for one person): 11	Onboard currency: ....UK£

This English country house afloat is the real McCoy.

OVERVIEW. This charming little ship has a warm, totally cosseted, traditional Scottish country house ambience and stately home service that is unobtrusive but always at hand when you need it. It suits mature-age adult couples and single travelers who enjoy learning about nature and the natural sciences, geography, history, gardening, art, architecture, and like being aboard a very small ship with almost no entertainment.

THE SHIP. Small and old can be chic and comfortable. *Hebridean Princess*, originally one of three Scottish ferries built for for David MacBayne Ltd – although actually owned by the British government – was skillfully converted into a gem of a cruise ship in order to operate island-hopping itineraries in Scotland, together with the occasional jaunt to Norway and an occasional sailing around the UK coast. It was renamed in 1989 by the Duchess of York.

There is an outdoors deck for occasional sunbathing and al fresco meals, as well as a bar where occasional formal cocktail parties are held when weather conditions are right. There is no walk-around promenade deck, although there is an open deck atop ship. The ship carries a Zodiac inflatable runabout, as well as a rowing boat for passenger use and two Hardy shore tenders (*Scarba* and *Shona*).

Use of the ship's small boats, speedboat, a dozen or so bicycles, and fishing gear are included in the price, as are entrance fees to gardens, castles, other attractions, and the occasional coach tour, depending on the itinerary. The destination-intensive cruises have very creative itineraries and there is plenty to do, despite the lack of big-ship features. Specialist guides, who give daily talks about the destinations to be visited and some fascinating history and the

BERLITZ'S RATINGS		
	Possible	Achieved
Ship	500	410
Accommodation	200	174
Food	400	350
Service	400	342
Entertainment	n/a	n/a
Cruise	500	404

OVERALL SCORE
1,680 points out of 2,000

local folklore, accompany all cruises.

The principal public room inside the ship is the charming Tiree Lounge, which has a real brick-walled inglenook fireplace, plus a very cozy bar with a wide variety of whiskies – the selection of single malts is excellent – and cognacs for connoisseurs. Naturally, the ship specializes in Scottish spirits.

Agatha Christie's Inspector Hercule Poirot would be very much at home here, particularly in the Tiree Lounge – although he may be wary of the secret and intrigue evoked by "Glen Etive" (a figure that dates from 1911– you'll need to go aboard to find it). Who needs megaships when you can take a retro-cruise aboard this little gem? Direct bookings are accepted.

What passengers appreciate is the fact that the ship does not have photographers or some of the trappings found aboard larger ships. They also love the fact that there is no bingo, art auctions, or mindless parlor games.

Hebridean Princess has UK officers and an excellent Latvian service crew; all are discreet and provide unobtrusive service. This little ship remains one of the world's best-kept travel secrets, although Queen Elizabeth II chartered the ship for a family-only celebration of her 80th birthday in 2006.

A roughly polished gem, it is especially popular with single passengers. More than half the passengers are repeaters. Children under nine are not accepted. Despite the shortcomings of the ship itself, it's the food that rates highly.

If you cruise from Oban, you can be met at Glasgow station (or airport) and taken to/from the ship by private motor coach. Passengers are "piped aboard" at embarkation by a Scottish bagpiper – a neat touch. All drinks (except premium brands, which incur a small charge), soft drinks and bottled Scottish mineral water are included in the fare, as are gratuities – the company requests that no additional gratuities be given.

Although this vessel is strong, it does have structural limitations and noisy engines that cause some vibration. However, the engines do not run at night because the ship anchors before bedtime, providing soul-renewing tranquility – except for the sound of a single generator. The ship does not have an elevator, so anyone with walking disabilities may find it challenging – and there may be several tender ports on each itinerary. It is often cold and very wet in the Scottish highlands and islands, so take plenty of warm clothing for layering.

ACCOMMODATION. All cabins have different color schemes and names – there are no numbers, and, refreshingly, no door keys, although cabins can be locked from the inside. No two cabins are identical – they are individually created, with delightfully eclectic curtains, sweeping drapes over the beds, and lots of cushions. They really are quite different to almost all other cruise ships, and come in a wide range of configurations (some with single, some with double, some with twin beds), including four with a private balcony – a private and self-indulgent bonus.

All except two cabins have a private bathroom with bath or shower (two cabins share a bathroom). All have a refrigerator, ironing board with iron, trouser press, brass clock, and tea/coffee making set – there's something magical about getting up in the morning, making fresh tea in your cabin using mineral water and organic teas and sitting outside on a protected balcony watching Scotland's islands come and go. All seems right with the world.

Cabins have Victorian-style bathroom fittings, many gold-plated, and some have brass cabin portholes or windows that actually open. Three of the newest cabins are outfitted in real Scottish Baronial style. All towels and bathrobe are 100% cotton, as is the bed linen. Some cabins in the front of the ship are subject to the noise of the anchor being weighed each morning.

CUISINE. The *Columba Restaurant* has ocean-view windows, and tables laid with crisp white linen, and sometimes with lace overlays. Classic white Schonwald china is provided. There is a single seating, at assigned tables. Some chairs have armrests while some do not. While days are casual, dinner means jackets and ties, and formal attire typically twice per cruise.

The cuisine is extremely creative, and at times outstanding – and about the same quality and presentation as *SeaDream I* and *SeaDream II*, although, typically, menus offer just one meat and one fish dish (a different fish each day), plus an alternative, casual option. Fresh, taste-filled ingredients are sourced and purchased locally, supporting Scottish suppliers such as H. D. Ferguson Butchers of Lochgilphead, Argyll – a welcome change from the mass catering of most ships. Although there are no flambeau items – the galley has electric, not gas, ranges – what is created is beautifully presented and of the highest standard. The desserts are also worth saving space for.

The breakfast menu is standard each day, although you can always ask for any favorites, and each day there's a speciality item. Try the "porridge and a wee dram (Scotch whisky – single malt, of course)" – it's lovely on a cold morning, and it sets you up for the whole day.

Not to be missed is the exclusive theatrical treat "a tasting o' haggis wi' bashed neeps an champit tatties," accompanied by bagpipe music and an "address to the haggis" ceremony, traditionally given by the captain. Although there is waiter service for most things, there is also a good buffet table display during breakfast and luncheon. Wines are provided at lunch and dinner, although an additional connoisseur's list is available for those seeking fine vintage wines. Highly personal and attentive service from an attentive Latvian service staff completes the picture.

ENTERTAINMENT. The Tiree Lounge is the equivalent of a main lounge aboard this very small ship. Dinner is *the* entertainment of the evening. Occasionally, there might be after-dinner drinks, poetry readings, and an occasional storyteller, but little else (passengers neither expect nor need it).

SPA/FITNESS. There is no spa, as the ship is too small. The only concessions to fitness are an exercycle, treadmill, power stepper and slide (row) machine.

DID YOU KNOW...

Should staff name badges be on the left or right side of the body?

In the hospitality industry, name badges are worn on the *left* side of the body. There are two principal reasons for this:

● Typically 81 percent of humans are right-handed, and the human eye naturally goes towards the right (that is, the left side of the body of the person facing you).

● The right side of the body is considered reserved for the military, whose name badges are always worn on the right side of the body (medals being worn on the left, or most important, side). You may also notice that when cameras pan in a documentary film made by painstaking professionals (such as in nature films), it is normal to pan from right to left.

Independence
★★

Size: . . . . .Boutique Ship	Total Crew: 27	Cabins (wheelchair accessible): 1
Tonnage: 2,300	Passengers	Wheelchair accessibility: . . . . .None
Lifestyle: . . . . .Standard	(lower beds/all berths): 94/100	Cabin Current: . . . . .110 volts
Cruise Line: . . . . . .American Cruise Lines	Passenger Space Ratio	Elevators: 1
Former Names: . . . . .none	(lower beds/all berths): 24.4/23.0	Casino (gaming tables): . . . . .No
Builder: . .Chesapeake Shipbuilding (USA)	Crew/Passenger Ratio	Slot Machines: .No
Original Cost: .n/a	(lower beds/all berths): 3.4/3.4	Swimming Pools (outdoors): 0
Entered Service: . . . . .Jun 2010	Cabins (total): .52	Swimming Pools (indoors): 0
Registry: . . . . .USA	Size Range (sq ft/m): 204.0–240.0/	Whirlpools: 0
Length (ft/m): 223.0/67.9	18.9–22.2	Self-Service Launderette: . . . . .No
Beam (ft/m): 51.0/15.5	Cabins (outside view): 51	Dedicated Cinema/Seats: . . . . .No
Draft (ft/m): 8.2/2.5	Cabins (interior/no view): 0	Library: . . . . .Yes
Propulsion/Propellers: diesel/2	Cabins (for one person): 5	Onboard currency: . . . . .US$
Passenger Decks: 4	Cabins (with private balcony): 23	

A very small coastal cruising ship for US retirees.

OVERVIEW. This ship is for couples and single travelers of mature years sharing a cabin and wishing to cruise in an all-American environment aboard a small ship where the destinations are more important than food, service or entertainment. It is extremely expensive for what you get, compared to ships in the wider cruise industry – although this is a new ship and the cabins *are* larger and marginally better equipped than those of the slightly smaller sister ships.

THE SHIP. *Independence* is the fourth vessel in this cruise line's growing fleet (sister ships: *American Glory, American Spirit, American Star*). The company builds the ships in its own shipyard in Chesapeake, Maryland. *Independence* is built specifically for coastal and inland cruising, in a casual, unregimented setting, to destinations unreachable by large cruise ships.

The uppermost deck is open – good for views – behind a forward windbreaker; many plenty of sunloungers are provided, as is a small golf putting green.

The public rooms include an observation lounge, with views forward and to port and starboard side (complimentary cocktails and hors d'oeuvres are offered before dinner); a library/lounge; a small midships lounge, and an elevator that goes to all decks, including the outdoor sun deck.

Cruises are typically 7–14 days long. The ship docks in the center, or within walking distance of most towns and ports. The dress code is "no ties casual." There are no additional costs, except for gratuities and port charges, because it's all included – quite different to big-ship cruising.

BERLITZ'S RATINGS

	Possible	Achieved
Ship	500	292
Accommodation	200	127
Food	400	210
Service	400	180
Entertainment	n/a	n/a
Cruise	500	153

OVERALL SCORE
962 points out of 2,000

ACCOMMODATION. There are five cabin price grades – four are doubles, one is for singles. All cabins have twin beds that convert to a king-size bed, a small desk with chair, flat-screen television, DVD player, and clothes hanging space.

All cabins have internet access, a private (modular) bathroom with separate shower enclosure, washbasin and toilet (no cabin has a bathtub), windows that open, and satellite-feed TV sets.

Accommodations incorrectly designated as suites (23) also have a private balcony; although narrow, it does have two chairs and a small drinks table.

CUISINE. The dining salon, in the latter third of the vessel, has large, panoramic picture windows on three sides. Everyone eats in a single, open seating, at large tables, so you can get to know your fellow passengers; there are no assigned tables or places. The cuisine is mainstream American: simple, honest food highlighting regional specialties. The choice of entrées, appetizers, and soups is limited. There is no wine list, although basic white and red American table wines are included. On the last morning of each cruise, continental breakfast only is available.

ENTERTAINMENT. Dinner and after-dinner conversation with fellow passengers in the ship's lounge/bar *is* the entertainment each evening. Otherwise, take a good book.

SPA/FITNESS. There is a tiny fitness room with a few bicycles and other exercise machines.

Independence of the Seas
★★★★

Size: ....Large Resort Ship	Passenger Decks: 15	Cabins (wheelchair accessible): 32	
Tonnage: 154,407	Total Crew: 1,397	Wheelchair accessibility: ....Good	
Lifestyle: ....Standard	Passengers	Cabin Current: ....110 volts	
Cruise Line: Royal Caribbean International	(lower beds/all berths): 3,634/4,376	Elevators: 14	
Former Names: ....none	Passenger Space Ratio	Casino (gaming tables): ....Yes	
Builder: . . .Kvaerner Masa-Yards (Finland)	(lower beds/all berths): 42.0/35.2	Slot Machines: ....Yes	
Original Cost: ....$590 million	Crew/Passenger Ratio	Swimming Pools (outdoors): 2	
Entered Service: ....May 2008	(lower beds/all berths): 2.6/3.1	Swimming Pools (indoors): 0	
Registry: ....The Bahamas	Cabins (total): 1,817	Whirlpools: 6	
Length (ft/m): 1,112.2/339.0	Size Range (sq ft/m): 149.0–2,025.0/	Self-Service Launderette: ....No	
Beam (ft/m): 184.0/56.0	13.8–188.1	Dedicated Cinema/Seats: ....No	
Draft (ft/m): 27.8/8.5	Cabins (outside view): 1,084	Library: ....Yes	
Propulsion/Propellers: .....diesel-electric	Cabins (interior/no view): 733	Onboard currency: ....US$	
(75,600 kW)/3 pods (2 azimuthing, 1	Cabins (for one person): 0		
fixed/14 MW each)	Cabins (with private balcony): 842		

Provides abundant family facilities and entertainment.

OVERVIEW. The "wow" factor aboard the ship is its connection with water in the design of a dramatic water theme park. It is now based year-round in the UK for cruises from Southampton, although the onboard currency remains the US dollar, which makes drinks about twice the cost of those aboard the P&O Cruises vessels, also based in Southampton.

THE SHIP. *Independence of the Seas* has the same layout and facilities as *Freedom of the Seas* and *Liberty of the Seas*, and is an extension of the successful *Voyager*-class of ships, which RCI introduced in 1999 with *Voyager of the Seas*. Extending its length and beam enabled an increase in the number of cabins and passenger capacity, as well as a combined pool area 43 percent larger than the *Voyager*-class (but with 500 more passengers). More innovative design elements were incorporated, too, such as two 16-person hot tubs cantilevered 12 ft (3.7 meters) over the ship's sides in an adults-only Solarium. The pod propulsion system virtually eliminates vibration (*for details, see page 191*).

This *Freedom*-class ship is essentially split into three separate areas, rather like the Disney cruise ships: adults-only, family, or main.

By day, the H₂O Zone, aft of the funnel, has an interactive water-themed play area for families that includes water cannons and spray fountains, water jets and ground gushers; by night the "water park" turns into a colourfully-lit sculpture garden. The central pool has become a sports pool, with grandstand seating and competitive games that include pole jousting. Other active sports facilities include

BERLITZ'S RATINGS		
	Possible	Achieved
Ship	500	426
Accommodation	200	161
Food	400	235
Service	400	289
Entertainment	100	82
Cruise	400	317
OVERALL SCORE		
1,510 points out of 2,000		

a boxing ring, rock-climbing wall (10 ft/3 meters taller than in the *Voyager*-class ships), in-line skating area, an ice-skating rink, and golf simulators.

Note that, during winter cruises, it's too cold to use some of the outdoor facilities – things like the Flow Rider, for example – so the ship can become quite crowded at times, with too many bingo games and quizzes.

ACCOMMODATION. There is a wide range of suites and cabins in 14 categories and 21 price grades; the price you pay depends on the grade, from the 14-person Presidential Suite to twin-bed two person interior (no view) cabins, and interior cabins that look into an inside shopping/strolling atrium promenade. There are many family-friendly cabins, good for reunions. For a detailed description of the accommodation, see *Freedom of the Seas (page 373)*.

CUISINE. The main dining room is large and is set on three levels, each has a theme and different name: *Galileo, Isaac*, and *Leonardo*. A dramatic staircase connects all three levels, and huge, fat support pillars obstruct the sightlines from many seats. All three have the same menus and food.

When you book, choose one of two seatings, or "My Time Dining" (eat when you want, during dining room hours). Tables are for four, six, eight, 10, or 12.

Alternative Dining Options: Alternative dining options for casual and informal meals at all hours, according to company statements, include:

● *Promenade Café*: for continental breakfast, all-day pizzas (Sorrento's), sandwiches and coffee in paper cups.

● *Windjammer Café*: for casual buffet-style breakfast, lunch and light dinner, except for the cruise's last night.

● *Island Grill* (a section of the Windjammer Café): for casual dinner, with a grill and open kitchen. No reservations necessary.

● *Portofino*: this is an "upscale" Euro-Italian restaurant, open for dinner only. Reservations are required, and a there's a cover charge. Choices include: antipasti, soup, salad, pasta, main dish, dessert, cheese and coffee. The menu does not change during the cruise.

● *Chops Grill:* an intimate restaurant for steaks and seafood. There's a cover charge.

● *Johnny Rockets*, a retro 1950s all-day, all-night diner-style eatery that serves hamburgers, hot dogs and other fast-food items, malt shakes, and jukebox hits, with both indoor and outdoor seating. All indoor tables have a mini-juke-box; dimes are provided for you to make your selection of vintage records. The all-singing, all-dancing waitresses will knock your socks off, if you can stand the volume. There is a cover charge.

● *Sprinkles:* for round-the-clock ice cream and yoghurt, pastries and coffee.

ENTERTAINMENT. The Showlounge is a stunning space at the forward end of the ship. It spans five decks in height, with only a few slim pillars and almost no disruption of sightlines. The room has a hydraulic orchestra pit and huge stage area, together with sonic-boom loud sound, and superb lighting equipment.

The ship has an array of cabaret acts. The strongest perform in the main showlounge, while others are presented in the Nightclub, the venue for smutty late-night adults-only comedy. The most entertaining shows are the Spectaculars on Ice. There is also a television studio, adjacent to rooms that could be used, for example, for trade show exhibit space – good for conventions at sea.

SPA/FITNESS. The large Independence Day Spa includes an aerobics room, ShipShape fitness center (with the usual stairmasters, treadmills, stationary bikes, weight machines and free weights), treatment rooms, and men's and women's sauna/steam rooms and relaxation areas. Some basic exercise classes are free, but the good ones (examples: yoga, personal training) cost extra.

More active passengers can bodyboard, climb the rock wall at the back of the funnel housing, jog, putt, swim, skate, step, surf, or workout.

Basketball and volleyball are available in the sports area of the ship, located mostly aft of the funnel, and there's a full-size boxing ring in the middle of the spa. Personal sessions and Powerboxing classes cost extra.

● **For more extensive general information on what a Royal Caribbean cruise is like, see pages 152–6.**

DID YOU KNOW...

● that the first regular steamship service across the North Atlantic was inaugurated on March 28, 1838, when the 703-ton steamer *Sirius* left London for New York via Cork, Ireland?

● that the winter of 1970–71 was the first time since 1838 that there was no regular passenger service on the North Atlantic?

● that the first scheduled trans-atlantic advertisement appeared in the *New York Evening Post* on October 27, 1817, for the 424-ton sailing packet *James Monroe* to sail from New York to Liverpool on January 5, 1818, and for *Couvier* to sail from Liverpool to New York on January 1?

● that Cunard Line held the record from 1940 to 1996 for the largest passenger ship ever built (RMS *Queen Elizabeth*)?

● that the Dollar Steamship Line featured a round-the-world cruise that started October 15, 1910, from New York, aboard the ss *Cleveland*? The cruise was advertised as "one-class, no over-crowding" voyage. The cost was "$650 and up," according to an advertisement.

● that a round-the-world cruise was made in 1922–23 by Cunard's *Laconia* (19,680 grt), a three-class ship that sailed from New York? The itinerary included many ports of call that are still popular with world cruise passengers today. The vessel accommodated 350 persons in each of its first two classes, and 1,500 in third class, giving a total capacity of 2,200 passengers, more than many current ships.

● about the lady who went to her travel agent, who asked if she had enjoyed her cruise around the world? The lady replied, "Yes, but next year I want to go somewhere different."

Insignia
★★★★ +

Size: ....Mid-Size Ship	Passenger Decks: 9	Cabins (with private balcony): 232
Tonnage: 30,277	Total Crew: 386	Cabins (wheelchair accessible): 3
Lifestyle: ....Premium	Passengers	Wheelchair accessibility: ....Good
Cruise Line: ....Oceania Cruises	(lower beds/all berths): 684/824	Cabin Voltage: ....110 and 220
Former Names: ....R One	Passenger Space Ratio	Elevators: 4
Builder: ....Chantiers de l'Atlantique	(lower beds/all berths): 44.2/36.7	Casino (gaming tables): ....Yes
Original Cost: ....$150 million	Crew/Passenger Ratio	Slot Machines: ....Yes
Entered Service: ......Jul 1998/Apr 2004	(lower beds/all berths): 1.7/2.1	Swimming Pools (outdoors): 1
Registry: ....Marshall Islands	Cabins (total): 342	Swimming Pools (indoors): 0
Length (ft/m): 593.7/181.0	Size Range (sq ft/m): 145.3–968.7/	Whirlpools: ......2 (+ 1 thalassotherapy)
Beam (ft/m): 83.5/25.5	13.5–90.0	Self-Service Launderette: ....Yes
Draft (ft/m): 19.5/6.0	Cabins (outside view): 317	Dedicated Cinema/Seats: ....No
Propulsion/Propellers: ....diesel	Cabins (interior/no view): 25	Library: ....Yes
(18,600 kW)/2	Cabins (for one person): 0	Onboard currency: ....US$

An informal premium ship for mature-age cruisers.

OVERVIEW. *Insignia* is best suited to couples who like good food and style, but want informality with no formal nights on board, and interesting itineraries, all at a very reasonable price well below what the luxury ships charge. Note that the ship will cease operating for Oceania Cruises in April 2012, and become *Columbus 2* for Hapag-Lloyd Cruises, under a two-year charter.

THE SHIP. *Insignia*, almost identical to *Nautica* and *Regatta*, is an all-white ship with a large, square white funnel. The addition of teak overlaid decking and teak lounge chairs has greatly improved what was once a bland pool deck outdoors, but the front rows of double sunloungers ("cabanas") cost $100 a day.

The interior decor is quite stunning, a throwback to ship decor of the ocean liners of the 1920s and '30s, with dark woods and warm colors, all carried out in fine taste, although a bit faux in places. This includes detailed ceiling cornices, both real and faux wrought-iron staircase railings, leather-paneled walls, trompe l'oeil ceilings, rich carpeting in hallways with an Oriental rug-look center section, and many other interesting and expensive-looking decorative touches. It feels like an old-world country club.

The public rooms are spread over three decks. The reception hall has a staircase with intricate wrought-iron railings. A large observation lounge, the Horizon Bar, is high atop ship. This has a long bar with forward views – for the barmen, that is. There are plenty of bars, including one in each restaurant entrance. Perhaps the nicest is the casino bar/lounge, a beautiful room reminiscent of London's grand hotels. It has an inviting marble fireplace, comfortable sofas, individual chairs, and a martini bar.

BERLITZ'S RATINGS

	Possible	Achieved
Ship	500	417
Accommodation	200	160
Food	400	312
Service	400	295
Entertainment	100	77
Cruise	400	313

OVERALL SCORE
1,574 points out of 2,000

The Library, a grand Regency-style room, has a fireplace, a high, indented, trompe l'oeil ceiling, and an excellent selection of books, plus very comfortable wingback chairs with footstools, and sofas you could sleep on. Oceania @Sea is the internet center.

There may not be marble bathroom fittings, or caviar and other expensive niceties, but the value for money is good. The dress code is "smart casual." Gratuities are added at $10.50 per person, per day, and accommodation designated as suites have an extra $3 per person charge for the butler. A 15% gratuity is added to bar and spa accounts.

There is no walk-around promenade deck outdoors, but there is a small jogging track around the perimeter of the swimming pool, and port and starboard side decks. What's really nice is the lack of announcements.

Oceania Cruises is a young company with a refreshing vision and desire to provide an extremely high level of food and service in an informal setting that is at once elegant yet comfortable, and that is exactly what it has achieved in a short space of time.

ACCOMMODATION. There are six cabin categories, and 10 price grades: three suite price grades, five outside-view cabin grades, and two interior cabin grades. All of the standard interior (no view) and outside-view cabins – the lowest four grades – are extremely compact units, and extremely tight for two persons, particularly for cruises longer than five days. They have twin beds or queen-size bed, with good under-bed storage areas, personal safe, vanity desk with large mirror, good closet and drawer space in rich, dark woods, 100% cotton bathrobe and towels, slippers, clothes brush and shoe horn. TV sets carry a major news channel, where obtainable, plus a sports channel and round-the-clock movie channels.

About 100 cabins qualify as "Concierge Level" accommodation, and occupants get extra goodies such as enhanced bathroom amenities, complimentary shoeshine, tote bag, cashmere throw blanket, bottle of champagne on arrival, hairdryer, priority restaurant reservations, priority embarkation and dedicated check-in desk,

Owner's Suites. The six Owner's Suites, measuring 962 sq.ft/89.3 sq.meters, are the most spacious accommodation. They are fine, large living spaces located aft overlooking the stern on Decks 6, 7, and 8 – they are, however, subject to more movement and some vibration. They have extensive teak-floor private balconies that really are private and can't be overlooked from the decks above. Each has an entrance foyer, living room, separate bedroom (the bed faces the sea, which can be seen through the floor-to-ceiling windows and sliding glass door), CD player with selection of audio discs, fully tiled bathroom with Jacuzzi tub, and a small guest bathroom.

Vista Suites. There are four, each around 785.7 sq.ft/73 sq.meters, and located forward on Decks 5 and 6. They have extensive teak-floor private balconies that can't be overlooked from the decks above. Each has an entrance foyer, living room, separate bedroom with similar layout to that in the owner's suites, CD player plus audio discs, and a fully tiled bathroom with Jacuzzi tub.

Penthouse Suites. There are 52 of these – though they are not suites at all but large cabins because the bedrooms aren't separate from the living areas. They measure around 322.9 sq.ft (30 sq. meters), and have a good-sized teak-floor balcony with sliding glass door (but with partial, and not full, balcony partitions) and teak deck furniture. The lounge area has a proper dining table and there is ample clothes storage space. The bathroom has a tub, shower enclosure, washbasin and toilet.

Cabins with Balcony. Cabins with private balconies (around 216 sq.ft/20 sq. meters), comprise about two-thirds of all cabins. They have partial, not full, balcony partitions and sliding glass doors, and 14 cabins on Deck 6 have lifeboat-obstructed views and no balcony. The living area has a refrigerated mini-bar, lounge area with breakfast table, and a balcony with teak floor, two teak chairs and a drinks table. The bathrooms, with tiled floors and plain walls, are compact, standard units, and include a shower stall with a strong, removable hand-held shower unit, hairdryer, toiletries storage shelves and retractable clothesline.

Outside View and Interior Cabins. These measure around 160–165 sq.ft (14.8–15.3 sq.meters), and have twin beds that convert to a queen-size bed, vanity desk, small sofa and coffee table, and bathroom with a shower enclosure with a strong, removable hand-held shower unit, hairdryer, toiletries storage shelves, retractable clothesline, washbasin, and toilet. Although they are not large, they are quite comfortable, with decent storage space.

All suites/cabins located at the stern may suffer from vibration and noise, particularly when the ship is proceeding at or close to full speed, or maneuvering in port.

CUISINE. Flexibility and choice are what the dining facilities aboard the Oceania ships are all about. There are four different restaurants:

● The *Grand Dining Room* has around 340 seats, and a raised central section, but the problem is the noise level: it's atrocious when the dining room is full – the effect of the low ceiling height. Being located at the stern, there are large ocean-view windows on three sides – prime tables overlook the stern. The chairs are comfortable and have armrests. The menus change daily for lunch and dinner.

● The *Toscana Italian Restaurant* has 96 seats, windows along two sides, and a set menu plus daily chef's specials.

● The cozy *Polo Grill* has 98 seats, windows along two sides and a set menu including prime steaks and seafood.

● The *Terrace Café* has seats for 154 indoors – not enough during cruises to cold-weather areas – and 186 outdoors. It is open for breakfast, lunch and casual dinners, when it has tapas (Tapas on the Terrace) and other Mediterranean food. As the ship's self-serve buffet restaurant, it incorporates a small pizzeria and grill. There are basic salads, a meat carving station, and a reasonable selection of cheeses.

All restaurants have open-seating dining, so you can dine when you want, with whom you wish. Reservations are needed in Toscana Restaurant and Polo Grill (but there's no extra charge), where there are mostly tables for four or six; there are few tables for two. There is a Poolside Grill Bar. All cappuccino and espresso coffees cost extra.

The food and service staff is provided by Apollo, a respected maritime catering company with an interest in Oceania Cruises. The consultant chef is Jacques Pépin, well-known in the US as a TV chef. The company's brochure reference to "cuisine so extraordinary it's unrivalled at sea" is hogwash – it's good, but not that good. It is a foodie's ship, though, with really high-quality ingredients and a wide selection of dining venues. Especially delicious are the breads, rolls, croissants and brioches, all made on board from French flower and d'Isigny butter.

ENTERTAINMENT. The Regatta Lounge has entertainment, lectures and some social events. Because of the intensive nature of the itineraries, there is little entertainment. However, there is live music in several bars and lounges.

SPA/FITNESS. A lido deck has a swimming pool and good sunbathing space, plus a thalassotherapy tub. A jogging track circles the swimming pool deck – but one deck above. The uppermost outdoors deck includes a golf driving net and shuffleboard court. The Canyon Ranch SpaClub consists of a beauty salon, three treatment rooms, men's and women's changing rooms, and steam room. There is no sauna. Note that 18% is added to your spa account, whether you like it or not.

Island Escape
★★★

Size: ....Mid-Size Ship	Passenger Decks: 10	Cabins (wheelchair accessible): 3
Tonnage 40,132	Total Crew: 540	Wheelchair accessibility: . . . . .None
Lifestyle: ....Standard	Passengers	Cabin Current: ....110 volts
Cruise Line: ....Island/Thomson Cruises	(lower beds/all berths):........1,504/1,710	Elevators: 5
Former Names: ....*Viking Serenade,*	Passenger Space Ratio	Casino (gaming tables):.....................Yes
Stardancer, Scandinavia	(lower beds/all berths):............26.6/23.4	Slot Machines:....................................Yes
Builder: ....Dubigeon-Normandie (France)	Crew/Passenger Ratio	Swimming Pools (outdoors): 1
Original Cost:........................$100 million	(lower beds/all berths):.................2.7/3.1	(magrodome)
Entered Service:.........Oct 1982/Apr 2009	Cabins (total):....................................757	Swimming Pools (indoors): 0
Registry:....................................Bahamas	Size Range (sq ft/m): 143.1–398.2/	Whirlpools: 0
Length (ft/m):......................623.0/189.89	13.3–37.0	Self-Service Launderette:....................No
Beam (ft/m):..........................88.6/27.01	Cabins (outside view):......................462	Dedicated Cinema/Seats: ....No
Draft (ft/m):.............................23.6/7.20	Cabins (interior/no view):..................295	Library:...Yes
Propulsion/Propellers: ....diesel	Cabins (for one person):........................0	Onboard currency: ....UK£
(19,800 kW)/2	Cabins (with private balcony):................5	

Family-friendly, low budget, no-frills cruising.

OVERVIEW. This is cruising in utterly casual, comfortable, unpretentious surroundings that are quite upbeat, with a totally relaxed ambience that appeals to anyone looking for a first cruise in a laid-back setting with plenty of life and entertainment for everyone, with food that is quantity rather than quality, and a low price. In summer the ship operates specifically for the British family market, providing one-week cruises.

THE SHIP. *Island Escape*, built for a cruise-ferry service between New York and Freeport, Bahamas, was extensively reconstructed in 1991 to become a full-fledged cruise ship. Today it is run by Island Cruises, which is owned and operated by Thomson Cruises, part of the TUI group. This is the company's most laid-back ship.

It has only a token bow, a fairly decent amount of open deck and sunbathing space, and a pool (more a "dip" pool) with a sliding glass dome that can be used in case of inclement weather. It suffers from having an extremely boxy, angular shape with a short, stubby funnel, and has a "sponson" skirt that goes around the stern at the waterline – this is required for stability reasons.

Inside, the accommodation is mostly located forward, while the public rooms are mostly in the aft third of the ship. There is a decent amount of public rooms and facilities, including six bars and a lounge/discotheque is cantilevered around the funnel with good ocean views. The decor employs tasteful colors and furnishings of decent quality, though some have seen better days. Other facilities include an internet connection center, and a coffee/pastry shop with three internet computer stations. The ceilings in many public areas and accommodation hallways

BERLITZ'S RATINGS		
	Possible	Achieved
Ship	500	276
Accommodation	200	108
Food	400	203
Service	400	236
Entertainment	100	56
Cruise	400	230
OVERALL SCORE		
1,109 points out of 2,000		

are quite low – a legacy of the ship's original role as a cruise-ferry.

Vacations can be extended with a "cruise-and-stay" package, with special pricing to make an extended break more affordable. If you book two cruises back-to-back, some entertainment may be repeated for the second week. Children should enjoy themselves with "Palmy" a character they can eat with, and there are well-supervised activities.

Background music is played almost everywhere inside the ship and on deck around the pool, making it difficult to find quiet spots to relax, chill out and simply read a book. Passenger participation events tend to be quite amateurish.

Standing in line for embarkation, disembarkation, shore tenders and for self-serve buffet meals can be an inevitable aspect of cruising aboard all ships carrying more than 1,500 passengers. Basic gratuities are included.

ACCOMMODATION. There are just six categories, so choosing the right one shouldn't be difficult. The price will depend on grade, size and location. The cabins, however, are quite small, with little closet space, so take as few clothes as possible. They are moderately appointed with soft furnishings that are very cheerful, with upbeat colors.

Almost all cabins have twin beds that can be pushed together to form a queen-size bed; some cabins have an L-shaped arrangement, with immovable beds. All grades have a TV set, telephone, and three-channel radio, dressing table and mirror. There are many interior cabins, and drawers and other storage space is extremely limited. If you'd like more space, it's best to go for one of the suite categories. Room service is available 24 hours a day, at extra cost.

The cabin bathrooms are really small, so you can expect to dance with the shower curtain, particularly if you are bigger than average – only some of the accommodation designated as suites have a bathtub. Eleven outside-view cabins have even numbers, and all interior cabins have odd numbers. Also, if you are cruising with young children, there's almost no space for baby strollers. If, after looking at the deck plans, you want to book a specific cabin number, it currently costs £35 per cabin extra.

Some cabins have extra Pullman upper berths – good for families with young children. An in-cabin room service menu is available, but all items cost extra.

Island Suite: Towards the aft on the port side, this is the largest accommodation. Although it doesn't have a balcony, it's relatively spacious. There's a walk-in closet, and mini-bar/refrigerator. The bathroom has a tub and shower.

Club Suites: Five other cabins with balconies at the stern are designated as suites. These have great views over the wash created by the ship's propellers, although they may be subject to a little vibration now and then. A tub and shower are provided in the marble-clad bathroom, and there's a walk-in closet in the sleeping area, and mini-bar/refrigerator and entertainment center in the living room. Additionally, another two suites (without balcony or bathtub) are located in the forward third of the ship one deck lower than the aft-facing suites, but with the same facilities.

CUISINE. The *Island Restaurant*, the main dining room, has ocean-view windows on two sides, and upbeat decor. There are tables for two, four, six, or eight. It is open for breakfast, lunch and dinner; you can serve yourself from the buffets, or be served by a waiter. It's a very casual open-seating arrangement, and so waiters do not get to know your preferences. Although there is much repetition of salad items for lunch, there are plenty of main dish and dessert choices. The menus contain a fair variety of British-style food items.

Oasis is a smaller, more intimate, exclusive and quieter restaurant, one deck below the Island Restaurant. This à la carte, extra-cost dining spot, with seats for two or four, is open only for dinner (reservations required), with full waiter service for all courses. The wine list is typical of a high-street eatery, with European prices that provide decent value for money.

The ceiling is low in both venues, which provides a sense of intimacy, but the noise level is intense.

For breakfast, lunch and dinner – in fact, 24 hours a day – there is another place to go: the *Beachcomber Café*. This is really casual, and is ideal for grabbing a bite to eat while "taking the sun" on the open decks. Again, it's a self-serve buffet, with food being constantly refreshed. Tea and coffee are provided at a beverage station, with plastic cups and mugs. Additionally, there's the *Café Brazil* for pastries, extremely sinful cakes and pastries, and a range of espresso and cappuccino coffees, all at extra cost.

ENTERTAINMENT. The Ocean Theater is a single-level showlounge, with banquette and individual seating surrounding a "thrust" stage. Although it is a comfortable room, several pillars obstruct sight lines from some seats.

A resident troupe of young, enthusiastic singer/dancers provide the low-budget revue-style "shows" that are, at best, amateurish, with weak recorded tracks but lots of color. In addition, visiting cabaret acts – typically strong singers, magicians, and smutty comedians – are presented, both in their own shows and as the middle of a "pie" that includes the ship's resident troupe.

There is a ship's band, and several small musical units and pianists provide live music for dancing and listening in the bars and lounges. There's a throbbing discotheque.

SPA/FITNESS. The Ship Shape Hair and Beauty Spa is surprisingly good for the size of the ship. There are treatment rooms for massage, separate saunas and changing rooms for men and women, and a large beauty salon. The gymnasium itself is quite large and contains lots of muscle-pumping, body toning equipment. It is located just aft of the main swimming pool on the port side of the ship.

Spa staff are provided by Harding Brothers, and treatments offered include massages, aromatherapy facials, manicures, pedicures, and hair beautifying treatments. Do book appointments early, as time slots go quickly.

Island Princess
★★★★

Size: ....Large Resort Ship	Total Crew: 900	Wheelchair accessibility: ....Good
Toannage: 91,627	Passengers	Cabin Current: ....110 volts
Lifestyle: ....Standard	(lower beds/all berths): 1,974/2,590	Elevators: 14
Cruise Line: ....Princess Cruises	Passenger Space Ratio	Casino (gaming tables): ....Yes
Former Names: ....none	(lower beds/all berths): 46.4/35.3	Slot Machines: ....Yes
Builder: Chantiers de l'Atlantique (France)	Crew/Passenger Ratio	Swimming Pools (outdoors): 2
Original Cost: ....$360 million	(lower beds/all berths): 2.1/2.8	(+ 1 splash pool)
Entered Service: ....Jun 2003	Cabins (total): 987	Swimming Pools (indoors): 0
Registry: ....Bermuda	Size Range (sq ft/m): 156–470.0/14.4–43.6	Whirlpools: 5
Length (ft/m): 964.5/294.0	Cabins (outside view): 879	Self-Service Launderette: ....Yes
Beam (ft/m): 105.6/32.2	Cabins (interior/no view): 108	Dedicated Cinema/Seats: ....No
Draft (ft/m): 26/7.9	Cabins (for one person): 0	Library: ....Yes
Propulsion/Propellers: .....gas turbine/2	Cabins (with private balcony): 727	Onboard currency: ....US$
Passenger Decks: 11	Cabins (wheelchair accessible): 20	

A comfortable but bland ship for mature-age cruisers.

OVERVIEW. For a large ship, the layout is quite user-friendly, and less disjointed than many ships of a similar size. Because of its slim beam, it is able to transit the Panama Canal, thus providing greater flexibility in deployment than the *Grand Princess*-class ships. It's good to see that the dreaded "fine arts" get their own room, so that paintings to be sold during the art auctions are not spread all over the ship.

THE SHIP. *Island Princess*, sister ship to *Coral Princess*, has an interior layout similar to that of the *Grand Princess*-class ships, but with two decks full of public rooms, lounges and bars instead of just one. Sensibly, it has three major stair towers for passengers – good from the safety and evacuation viewpoint – with plenty of elevators for easy access.

What is very civilized is the fact that sunbathers who use the "quiet" deck forward of the mast have their own splash pool, so they won't have to go down two decks to get to the two main pools. Strollers will like the ship's full walk-around exterior promenade deck.

Facilities include a flower shop where you can order flowers and Godiva chocolates for cabin delivery – good for a birthday or anniversary – a neat cigar and cognac lounge (Churchill Lounge), and a martini bar (Crooners). The casino has a London theme.

An AOL Internet Café is conveniently located on the top level of the four-deck-high lobby. Adjacent is the Wedding Chapel, with a live web-cam to relay ceremonies via the internet. The captain can legally marry (American) couples, thanks to the ship's registry and a special dispensation (this should, however, be verified when in the planning

BERLITZ'S RATINGS

	Possible	Achieved
Ship	500	434
Accommodation	200	154
Food	400	261
Service	400	294
Entertainment	100	85
Cruise	400	314

OVERALL SCORE
1,542 points out of 2,000

stage, and may depend on where you live). Princess Cruises offers three wedding packages – Pearl, Emerald, Diamond; the fee includes registration and official marriage certificate. The Wedding Chapel can host "renewal of vows" ceremonies, for a fee.

ACCOMMODATION. There are 33 price categories, in six types: 16 Suites with balcony (470 sq. ft/43.6 sq. meters); 184 Mini-Suites with balcony (285–302 sq. ft/26.4–28.0 sq. meters; eight Mini-Suites without balcony (300 sq. ft/27.8 sq. meters); 527 Outside-View Cabins with balcony (217–232 sq. ft/ 20.1–21.5 sq. meters); 144 Standard Outside-view Cabins (162 sq. ft/15 sq. meters); Interior (no view) Cabins (156 sq. ft/144.5 sq. meters). There are also 20 wheelchair-accessible cabins (217–374 sq. ft/20.1–34.7 sq. meters).

Almost all outside-view cabins have a private balcony. Some cabins can accommodate a third, or third and fourth person – good for families with children. Some cabins on Emerald Deck (Deck 8) have a view obstructed by lifeboats. **Suites:** There are just 16 suites and, although none are really that large compared to such ships as *Norwegian Dawn* and *Norwegian Star*, each has a private balcony. All are named after islands – mostly coral-based islands in the Indian and Pacific Oceans. All suites are located on either Deck 9 or Deck 10. In a departure from many ships, *Island Princess* doesn't have any suites or cabins with a view of the stern. There are four Premium Suites, located sensibly in the center of the ship, adjacent to a bank of six elevators. Further aft are six other suites (Verandah Suites).
All Accommodation: Suites and cabins have a refrigerator, personal safe, TV set with audio channels, hairdryer,

satellite-dial telephone, and twin beds that convert to a queen-size bed (there are a few exceptions). All accommodation has a bathroom with shower enclosure and toilet. Accommodation designated as suites and mini-suites (there are seven price categories) have a bathtub and separate shower enclosure, and two TV sets.

All passengers receive turndown service and chocolates on pillows each night, bathrobes on request, and toiletry kits. Most "outside-view" cabins on Emerald Deck have views obstructed by lifeboats. There are no cabins for singles. Nor are there butlers – even for the top-grade suites. Cabin attendants have too many cabins to look after (typically 20), which does not translate to fine personal service.

CUISINE. The two main dining rooms, *Bordeaux* and *Provence*, are in the forward section of the ship on the two lowest passenger decks, with the galley all the way forward so it doesn't intersect public spaces – an example of good design. Both are almost identical – the ceilings are quite low, making the rooms seem more cramped than they are – and have plenty of intimate alcoves and cozy dining spots, with tables for two, four, six, or eight. There are two seatings for dinner, while breakfast and lunch are on an open-seating basis; you may have to stand in line at peak times.

Horizon Court, a casual 24-hour eatery, is in the forward section of Lido Deck, with superb ocean views. Self-serve counters provide food for breakfast and lunch buffets, and bistro-style casual dinners are available each evening.
Alternative Eateries: There are two extra-charge dining rooms, *Sabatini's* and the *Bayou Café*, both enclosed and both requiring reservations. Sabatini's, with colorful tiled Mediterranean-style decor, has Italian-style pizzas and pastas, with a variety of sauces, as well as Italian-style entrées including tiger prawns and lobster tail, all provided with flair and entertainment by the waiters. The food that is both creative and tasty, with seriously sized portions. There is a cover charge for lunch or dinner on sea days only.

The Bayou Café is open for lunch and dinner, and has a cover charge that includes a Hurricane cocktail. It evokes the charm of New Orleans' French Quarter, with wrought-iron decoration, and serves Creole food. Platters include Peel 'n' Eat Shrimp Piquante, Sausage Grillades, Oysters Sieur de Bienville and N'Awlins Crawfish "Mud Bug" Bisque, delivered to the table when you arrive. Popular entrées include Seafood Gumbo, and Chorizo Jambalaya with fresh seafood and traditional dried spice mixes, as well

as Cajun Grill items such as Smothered Alligator Ribs, Corn Meal Fried Catfish, Blackened Chicken Brochette, and Red Pepper Butter Broiled Lobster. Desserts include sweet potato pie and banana whiskey pound cake. The room has a small stage, with baby grand piano, and live jazz is part of the dining scenario.

Other outlets include *La Pâtisserie*, in the reception lobby, a coffee, cakes and pastries spot and good for informal meetings. There's also a pizzeria, hamburger grill, and an ice cream bar (extra charge for the ice cream).

ENTERTAINMENT. The Princess Theatre is two decks high, and, unusually, there is much more seating in the upper level than on the main floor below. A second entertainment venue, Universe Lounge, is designed more for cabaret-style features. It also has two levels, and three separate stages, enabling non-stop entertainment to be provided without constant set-ups. Some 50 of the room's seats are equipped with a built-in laptop computer. The room is also used for cooking demonstrations (it has a full kitchen set), and other life enrichment participation activities.

Princess Cruises always provides plenty of live music in bars and lounges, with a wide mix of light classical, jazz, and dance music, from solo entertaining pianists to showbands, and volume is normally kept to an acceptable level.

Those craving education can learn aboard ship with the "ScholarShip@Sea" program, which includes about 20 courses per cruise (six on any given day at sea). Although all introductory classes are free, fees apply if you want to continue any chosen subject in a smaller setting. There are four core subjects: Culinary Arts, Visual/ Creative Arts, Photography, and Computer Technology. A full culinary demonstration kitchen set is built into the Universe Lounge, which is also used for wine tastings, and there's a pottery studio with kiln.

SPA/FITNESS. The Lotus Spa is located aft on one of the ship's uppermost decks. It contains men's and women's saunas, steam rooms, changing rooms, relaxation area, beauty salon, aerobics exercise room and gymnasium with aft-facing ocean-views packed with the latest high-tech muscle-pumping, cardio-vascular equipment. There are several large rooms for individual treatments.

● **For more extensive general information about the Princess Cruises experience, see pages 149–52.**

Island Sky
★★★★ +

Size: . . . . .Boutique Ship	Passenger Decks: 5	Cabins (with private balcony): 4
Tonnage: 4,280	Total Crew: 66	Cabins (wheelchair accessible): 0
Lifestyle: . . . . .Standard	Passengers	Wheelchair accessibility: . . . . .None
Cruise Line: . . . . .Noble Caledonia	(lower beds/all berths): 116/116	Cabin Voltage: 110
Former Names: . . . . .*Regina Renaissance,*	Passenger Space Ratio	Elevators: 1
Renaissance VIII	(lower beds/all berths): 36.8/36.8	Casino (gaming tables): . . . . .No
Builder: . . .Nuovi Cantieri Appaunia (Italy)	Crew/Passenger Ratio	Slot Machines: . . . . .No
Original Cost: . . . .$25 million	(lower beds/all berths): 1.7/1.7	Swimming Pools (outdoors): 0
Entered Service: . . . .Dec 1991/May 2004	Cabins (total): .59	Swimming Pools (indoors): 0
Registry: . . . . .The Bahamas	Size Range (sq ft/m): 234.6–353.0/	Whirlpools: 1
Length (ft/m): 297.2/90.6	21.8–32.8	Self-Service Launderette: . . . . .No
Beam (ft/m): 50.1/15.3	Cabins (outside view): 59	Dedicated Cinema/Seats: . . . . .No
Draft (ft/m): 12.9/2.95	Cabins (interior/no view): 0	Library: . . . . .Yes
Propulsion/Propellers: .diesel (5000kW)/2	Cabins (for one person): 0	Onboard currency: . . . . .UK£

A delightful small ship for life-enrichment cruises.

OVERVIEW. This intimate ship is very comfortable and totally inviting, and operates cruises in areas devoid of large cruise ships. Although it isn't quite up to the standard of a Seabourn or Silversea vessel, it will provide a good cruise experience at a moderate cost. It suits seasoned travelers who like a relaxed lifestyle combined with good food and service, and an itinerary that promises "get away from it all, but in comfort."

THE SHIP. *Island Sky* has contemporary mega-yacht looks and handsome styling, with twin flared funnels that give it a smart profile, and a "ducktail" (sponson) stern that provides stability and seagoing comfort. This ship was originally built as one of a series of eight similar ships for the now-defunct Renaissance Cruises. It was completely refurbished in 2010.

There is a teak walk-around promenade deck outdoors, and a reasonable amount of open deck and sunbathing space. A "baby island" tender hangs off the aft deck and acts as ship-to-shore transportation. Some equipment for watersports is carried, together with a fleet of Zodiac inflatables for shore landings.

Inside, the interior design is elegant, with polished wood-finish paneling throughout. There is a very small library with two internet-connect workstations. Gratuities are included, as are house wine, beer and soft drinks during lunch and dinner.

BERLITZ'S RATINGS

	Possible	Achieved
Ship	500	396
Accommodation	200	161
Food	400	312
Service	400	307
Entertainment	n/a	n/a
Cruise	500	386

OVERALL SCORE
1,562 points out of 2,000

ACCOMMODATION. The spacious cabins combine highly polished imitation rosewood paneling with lots of mirrors and hand-crafted furniture, lighted walk-in closets, three-sided vanity mirrors – in fact, there are a lot of mirrored surfaces in the decor – and just about everything you need, including a refrigerator, a TV set and player, and wi-fi access. The bathrooms are extremely compact; they have real teakwood floors and marble vanities, and shower enclosures, but none have tubs, not even the owner's suite. All were replaced in the 2010 refit.

CUISINE. The dining room operates with open seating for all meals. It is small but quite smart, with tables for two, four, six, and eight. You simply sit where you like, with whom you like, and at what time you like. The meals are self-service, buffet-style foods for breakfast and lunch, with hot foods chosen from a table menu and served properly. The dining room operation works well. The food quality, choice, and presentation are all very decent.

ENTERTAINMENT. There is no formal entertainment in the main lounge, the venue for all social activities. Anyway, six pillars obstruct sightlines to the small stage area.

SPA/FITNESS. Water sports facilities include an aft platform, and Zodiacs.

Jewel of the Seas
★★★★

Size: . . . . .Large Resort Ship	Total Crew: 858	Cabins (wheelchair accessible): 14
Tonnage: .90,090	Passengers	(8 with private balcony)
Lifestyle: . . . . .Standard	(lower beds/all berths): 2,110/2,500	Wheelchair accessibility: . . . . .Good
Cruise Line: Royal Caribbean International	Passenger Space Ratio	Cabin Voltage: .110
Former Names: . . . . .none	(lower beds/all berths): 42.9/36.0	Elevators: 9
Builder: . . . . .Meyer Werft (Germany)	Crew/Passenger Ratio	Casino (gaming tables): . . . . .Yes
Original Cost: . . . .$350 million	(lower beds/all berths): 2.4/2.9	Slot Machines: . . . . .Yes
Entered Service: . . . . .Jun 2004	Cabins (total): 1,055	Swimming Pools (outdoors): 2
Registry: . . . . .The Bahamas	Size Range (sq ft/m): 165.8–1,216.3/	Swimming Pools (indoors): 0
Length (ft/m): 961.9/293.2	15.4–113.0	Whirlpools: 3
Beam (ft/m): 105.6/32.2	Cabins (outside view): 817	Self-Service Launderette: . . . . .No
Draft (ft/m): 27.8/8.5	Cabins (interior/no view): 238	Dedicated Cinema/Seats: Yes/40
Propulsion/Propellers: . . . . .Gas turbine/2	Cabins (for one person): 0	Library: . . . . .Yes
azimuthing pods (20 MW each)	Cabins (with private balcony): 577	Onboard currency: . . . . .US$
Passenger Decks: 12		

A large resort ship for family-friendly casual cruising.

OVERVIEW. This ship is best suited to young-minded adult couples and singles of all ages, families with toddlers, tots, children, and teenagers who like to mingle in a large ship setting with plenty of life and high-energy entertainment. The food is acceptable, stressing quantity rather than quality unless you pay extra to dine in the "alternative" restaurant. While the ship is quite delightful in many ways, the onboard operation suffers from a lack of service staff.

BERLITZ'S RATINGS		
	Possible	Achieved
Ship	500	428
Accommodation	200	158
Food	400	247
Service	400	297
Entertainment	100	81
Cruise	400	309
OVERALL SCORE		
1,520 points out of 2,000		

Royal Caribbean Online (an internet center with 12 computers), a Concierge Club, and a Crown & Anchor Lounge. A great view can be had of the atrium by looking down through the flat glass dome high above it.

Other facilities include a large Schooner Bar that houses maritime art in an integral art gallery, and a rather large, noisy and colorful Casino Royale. There's also a small dedicated screening room for movies (with space for two wheelchairs), as well as a 194-seat conference center, and a business center.

THE SHIP. *Jewel of the Seas* is a streamlined, contemporary ship, with a two-deck-high wrap-around structure in the forward section of the funnel. Along the starboard side, a central glass wall protrudes, giving great views – cabins with balconies occupy the space directly opposite on the port side. The gently rounded stern has nicely tiered decks, which gives the ship an extremely well-balanced look.

As is common aboard almost all new cruise ships today, the navigation bridge is of the fully enclosed type. In the very front of the ship is a helipad, which also acts as a viewing platform. Pod propulsion power *(see page 191 for description)* is provided.

Inside, the decor is contemporary, yet elegant, bright and cheerful, designed for young, active, hip types. The artwork is quite eclectic and provides a spectrum and a half of color works. The interior focal point is a nine-deck high atrium lobby with glass-walled elevators that travel through 12 decks, face the sea and provide a link with nature and the ocean. The Centrum, as the atrium is called, has several public rooms connected to it: the guest relations and shore excursions desks, a lobby bar, Champagne bar, a small library,

This ship also contains a Viking Crown Lounge, a large structure set around the base of the ship's funnel. It functions as an observation lounge during the daytime, with views forward over the swimming pool. In the evening, the space becomes a futuristic, high-energy dance club, as well as a more intimate and relaxed entertainment venue for softer mood music and "black box" theater.

The onboard product delivery is more casual and unstructured than RCI has previously been delivering. *Jewel of the Seas* offers more space, more comfortable public areas and several more intimate spaces, slightly larger cabins and more dining options than most of the larger ships in the RCI fleet. A 15 percent gratuity is added to all bar and spa bills.

Niggles? There are no cushioned pads for sunloungers, and the deck towels are quite thin and small. It is virtually impossible to escape background music anywhere.

FAMILIES. Youth facilities include Adventure Ocean, an "edu-tainment" area with four separate age-appropriate sections for junior passengers: Aquanaut Center (for ages 3–5); Explorer Center (6–8); Voyager Center (9–12); and the Optix Teen Center (13–17). There is also Adventure Beach, which includes a splash pool complete with waterslide; Surfside, with computer lab stations with entertaining software; and Ocean Arcade, a video games hangout.

ACCOMMODATION. There is a wide range of suites and standard outside-view and interior cabins to suit different tastes, requirements, and depth of wallet, in 10 different categories and 19 different price groups.

Apart from the largest suites (six owner's suites), which have king-size beds, almost all other cabins have twin beds that convert to a queen-size bed. All sheets are of 100% Egyptian cotton, although blankets are of nylon. All cabins have rich but faux wood cabinetry, including a vanity desk with hairdryer, faux wood drawers that close silently (hooray), a TV set, personal safe, and three-sided mirrors. Some cabins have ceiling-recessed, pull-down berths for a third and fourth person, although closet and drawer space would be extremely tight for four (even if two are children). Some have interconnecting doors, allowing families with children to cruise together in adjacent cabins. Audio channels are available through the TV set, so you can't switch off its picture while listening. Data ports are provided in all cabins.

Many "private" balcony cabins are not very private, as they can be overlooked by anyone standing in the port and starboard wings of the Solarium, and from other locations.

Most cabin bathrooms have tiled accenting and a terrazzo-style tiled floor, and a shower enclosure in a half-moon shape (it is rather small, however, considering the size of some passengers), 100% Egyptian cotton towels, a small cabinet for toiletries and a small shelf. There is little space to stow toiletries for two or more.

The largest accommodation consists of a family suite with two bedrooms. One bedroom has twin beds that convert to a queen-size bed, while a second has two lower beds and two upper Pullman berths, a combination that can sleep up to eight persons – this would be suitable for large families.

Occupants of accommodation designated as suites also get the use of a private Concierge Lounge where priority dining room reservations, shore excursion bookings and beauty salon/spa appointments can be made.

CUISINE. *Reflections*, the main dining room, spans two decks; the upper deck level has floor-to-ceiling windows, while the lower deck level has picture windows. It is a fine, but inevitably noisy dining hall, and eight huge, thick pillars obstruct the sightlines. It seats 1,104, and the decor

has a cascading water theme. There are tables for two, four, six, eight or 10 in two seatings. Two small private dining rooms (*Illusions* and *Mirage*) are located off the main dining room. There is an adequate wine list, with moderate prices.

Alternative Restaurants: *Portofino*, with 112 seats, offers Italian cuisine, and *Chops Grille Steakhouse*, with 95 seats and an open "show" kitchen, serves premium meats in the form of chops and steaks. Both have food that is of a much higher quality than in the main dining room and are typically open 6pm–11pm. There is an additional charge, and reservations are required. The dress code is smart casual.

Casual Eateries: Casual breakfasts, lunches and dinners can be taken in the self-serve, buffet-style *Windjammer Café*, which can be accessed directly from the pool deck. It has about 400 seats, and islands dedicated to specific foods, and indoors and outdoors seating. Additionally, there is the *Seaview Café*, open for lunch and dinner. You can choose from the self-serve buffet, or from the menu for casual, fast-food seafood items including fish sandwiches, popcorn shrimp, fish 'n' chips, as well as non-seafood items such as hamburgers and hot dogs.

ENTERTAINMENT. Facilities include the three-level Coral Reef Theater, with 874 seats, including 24 wheelchair stations. The sightlines are good from most seats due to steep tiers. A second entertainment venue is the Safari Club, which hosts cabaret shows, late-night adult comedy, and dancing to live music. All the ship's entertainment is upbeat – so much so that it's virtually impossible to get away from music and noise.

SPA/FITNESS. The ShipShape health, fitness and spa facilities have themed decor, and include a 10,176 sq.-ft (945 sq.-meter) solarium with whirlpool and counter current swimming under a retractable glass roof, a gymnasium with 44 cardiovascular machines, a 50-person aerobics room, sauna and steam rooms, and therapy treatment rooms.

For the more sporting, there is activity galore, including a rock-climbing wall that's 30 ft (9 meters) high, with five separate climbing tracks. It's free, and all safety gear is included, but you'll need to sign up.

Other sports facilities include a nine-hole miniature golf course, and an indoor/outdoor country club with golf simulator, a jogging track, and basketball court. Want to play pool? You can, thanks to two special tables whose technology adjusts automatically to the movement of the ship.

● **For more extensive general information about Royal Caribbean International cruises, see pages 152–6.**

Kapitan Khlebnikov
★★★

Size: . . . . .Boutique Ship	Passenger Decks: 6	Cabins (wheelchair accessible): 0
Tonnage: .12,288	Total Crew: 60	Wheelchair accessibility: . . . . .None
Lifestyle: . . . . .Standard	Passengers	Cabin Current: . . . . .220 volts
Cruise Line: . . . . . . .Murmansk Shipping/	(lower beds/all berths): 108/114	Elevators: 1
Quark Expeditions	Passenger Space Ratio	Casino (gaming tables): . . . . .No
Former Names: . . . . .none	(lower beds/all berths): 113.7/107.7	Slot Machines: .No
Builder: . . . . .Wartsila (Finland)	Crew/Passenger Ratio	Swimming Pools (outdoors): 0
Original Cost: .n/a	(lower beds/all berths): 1.8/1.9	Swimming Pools (indoors): 1
Entered Service: 1981	Cabins (total): .54	Whirlpools: 0
Registry: . . . . .Russia	Size Range (sq ft/m): 150.6–269/	Lecture/Film Room: . . . . .No
Length (ft/m): 434.6/132.49	14.0–25.0	Library: . . . . .Yes
Beam (ft/m): 87.7/26.75	Cabins (outside view): 54	Zodiacs: 4
Draft (ft/m): 27.8/8.50	Cabins (interior/no view): 0	Helicopter Pad: . . . . .Yes (1 helicopter)
Propulsion/Propellers: . . . . .diesel-electric	Cabins (for one person): 0	Onboard currency: . . . . .US$
(18,270 kW)/3	Cabins (with private balcony): 0	

An icebreaking expedition vessel for the adventurous.

OVERVIEW. This type of cruising suits adventurous, hardy outdoors types of mature years who enjoy being with nature in some of the earth's most inhospitable places. The ship offers only basic cruise amenities and very spartan, no-frills decor. Also, be prepared for some tremendous roaring noise when the ship breaks through pack ice.

After March 2012 *Kapitan Khlebnikov* will be under contract with the Russian government for icebreaking duties and will no longer operate as an expedition vessel.

THE SHIP. *Kapitan Khlebnikov* is a real, working icebreaker, one of a fleet of 10 built in Finland to exacting Russian specifications. Converted to exclusive passenger use in 1994 and since upgraded, it has an incredibly thick hull, forthright profile, a bow like an inverted whale head, and much technical equipment. In 1997, *Kapitan Khlebnikov* became the first vessel ever to circumnavigate Antarctica with passengers. "KK," as it is affectionately known, has also transited the Northwest Passage more times than any other expedition ship. An open-bridge policy allows passengers to visit the bridge at almost any time. Strong diesel-electric engines (delivering 24,000 horsepower) allow it to plow through ice several feet thick. There is plenty of open deck and observation space, and a heated but very small indoor swimming pool – really a "dip" pool.

There is always a team of excellent naturalists and lecturers aboard. A helicopter, when carried, can be used for sightseeing forays, as is a fleet of Zodiac rubber landing craft for in-your-face shore landings and wildlife spotting.

BERLITZ'S RATINGS

	Possible	Achieved
Ship	500	263
Accommodation	200	113
Food	400	233
Service	400	224
Entertainment	n/a	n/a
Cruise	500	311

OVERALL SCORE
1,144 points out of 2,000

Kapitan Khlebnikov is particularly good for tough expedition cruising, and will provide thoroughly practical surroundings, a friendly, experienced and dedicated group of crew members, and excellent value for the money. Suggested gratuities are $9–$12 per day.

ACCOMMODATION. The cabins, in four price categories, are spread over four decks in an accommodation block, and all have private facilities and plenty of storage space. Although nothing special, they are quite comfortable, with two lower beds (typically one is fixed, the other being a convertible sofa bed, either in a twin or an L-shaped format), large closets, storage for outerwear and boots, and portholes that actually open. The bathrooms are practical units, although storage space for toiletries is tight. Four units designated as "suites" have more room, including a larger bathroom.

CUISINE. The one dining room is plain, yet quite comfortable. There is a single seating, with assigned tables. The food is hearty, with generous portions and an emphasis on fish and potatoes. Fruits, vegetables and international cheeses can be in limited supply. Quark Expeditions has its own catering team. The wine list is pretty basic.

ENTERTAINMENT. Dinner is the main event of the evening, followed by discussion of what lies ahead for the next day. You might actually do a shore landing at night.

SPA/FITNESS. There is a gymnasium with some basic equipment, a small indoor pool, and a sauna.

L'Austral
★★★★

Size: .Small Ship	Passenger Decks: 6	Cabins (with private balcony): 125
Tonnage: 10,944	Total Crew: 140	Cabins (wheelchair accessible): 0
Lifestyle: . . . . .Premium	Passengers	Wheelchair accessibility: . . . . .Fair
Cruise Line: . . . . .Ponant Cruises	(lower beds/all berths): 224/264	Cabin Voltage: . . . . .110 and 220 volts
Former Names: . . . . .none	Passenger Space Ratio	Elevators: 2
Builder: . . . . .Fincantieri (Italy)	(lower beds/all berths): 48.4/41.4	Casino (gaming tables): . . . . .No
Original Cost: . . . .$100 million	Crew/Passenger Ratio	Slot Machines: . . . . .Yes
Entered Service: . . . . .May 2011	(lower beds/all berths): 1.5/1.8	Swimming Pools (outdoors): 2
Registry: . . . . .Wallis & Fortuna	Cabins (total): .132	Swimming Pools (indoors): 0
Length (ft/m): 465.8/142.0	Size Range (sq ft/m): 215.2–301.3/	Whirlpools: 0
Beam (ft/m): 9.0/18.0	20.0–28.0	Self-Service Launderette: 0
Draft (ft/m): 15.4/4.7	Cabins (outside view): 132	Dedicated Cinema/Seats: . . . . .No
Propulsion/Propellers: . . . . .diesel-electric	Cabins (interior/no view): 0	Library: . . . . .Yes
(4,600kW)/2	Cabins (for one person): 0	Onboard currency: . . . . .Euros

A contemporary ship and style to suit French speakers.

OVERVIEW. *L'Austral* is best suited to young-minded couples and singles who want sophisticated facilities in a relaxed but chic yacht-like environment quite different to most cruise ships, with very good food and decent service. The ship is often chartered or part-chartered by "premium" travel organizers who prefer smaller ships, such as Abercrombie & Kent, Gohagen, and Tauck Tours.

THE SHIP. One of two identical new ships catering to French speakers, *L'Austral* (South Wind) is a gem of contemporary design – chic and uncluttered. With a dark hull and sleek white superstructure, it looks like a large private yacht, not a traditional cruise ship. The Passenger Space Ratio, a healthy 53.5, decreases if the 40 suites that convert into 20 are all occupied by two persons.

The ship has a smart "sponson" skirt built-in at the stern for operational stability, and carries a fleet of 12 Zodiac landing craft for soft expedition voyages. For Antarctic voyages, passenger numbers are kept to a maximum of 199, although the ship does not have boot storage lockers.

There is some sunbathing space outdoors forward of the funnel, and around the small pool aft of the casual eatery one deck below, which an shower enclosure. Aft of the funnel, is an outdoor bar (Copernico) and grill, but seating is limited.

Almost all public rooms are aft, with accommodation located forward; the elevators go to all decks except the uppermost (Deck 7). The decor is minimalist and super-yacht chic – relaxing and pleasant, with lots of browns and creams and a splash of red here and there. Glitz is entirely absent, although there are many reflective surfaces and the overall feeling of the decor is cool rather than warm.

BERLITZ'S RATINGS		
	Possible	Achieved
Ship	500	415
Accommodation	200	155
Food	400	301
Service	400	304
Entertainment	n/a	n/a
Cruise	500	368

OVERALL SCORE
1,543 points out of 2,000

The focal point is the main lobby, with a central, circular seating and tiled floor surround; its small central section spans two decks. The other flooring is wood, which can be noisy. The lower decks of the main stairway are made of faux gray wood, while the upper decks are carpeted – a strange combination that somehow works.

This is all-inclusive cruising – except for spa treatments – with drinks, table wine for lunch and dinner, bottled mineral water, port charges, and Zodiac excursions on expedition-style cruises all included in the fare. The crew is English- and French-speaking, with many hotel service staff from Asia.

Passenger niggles? There's no outside walking or jogging deck. The interior stairways are a quite steep and have short steps. The restaurant is noisy. The entertainment system is not user-friendly. Overall, it's difficult for French-speaking and non-French-speaking passengers to mix.

ACCOMMODATION. Of the 132 suites/ cabins, there are three Prestige Suites (301 sq.ft. plus 54 sq.ft. balcony); while 40 of the 94 deluxe cabins (200 sq.ft. plus 43 sq.ft. balcony) can be combined into 20 larger suites, each with two bathrooms, and separate living area and bedroom. All cabinetry is made in elegant dark woods.

Each deluxe and standard cabin has a large ocean-view window, two beds that convert to a queen-size bed, and a long vanity desk, with good lighting. Features include a TV set, DVD player, refrigerator, and personal safe. The marble-appointed bathrooms have heavy hand-held shower hoses. Amenities include a minibar, personal safe, hairdryer, bathrobe, and French bathroom products. Wi-fi costs extra.

All other cabins have good-sized beds, although the bed-frame corners are square, so you need to be careful when passing between bed and a storage unit that's quite large, with two deep drawers, refrigerator, television and wall mirror. Other facilities include good-sized wardrobe-style closet (armoire) with personal safe, and a vanity desk with drawer and a small shelf.

The small cabin bathrooms (the entrance door is only 20½ inches wide) have a glass wall that is just over 20 inches wide with a sliding partition door, enabling you to see through the cabin to the ocean, and a deep, half-size tub/shower combination. The lip between floor and bathroom is just over 6 inches (16cm) high.

There are no shelves for toiletries, but there are two drawers under the washbasin – although they are not really practical in use. A separate cubicle houses the vacuum toilet. Balconies have faux-wood decking, and a fine (real) wood handrail, although solid paneling obstructs the views when seated, and makes the cabin seem dark – glass panels would have been nicer. The closet space is good, but the doors, with excellent white leather handles, are wide – at 31 inches (79cm), they are wider than the cabin door, and can't be opened without first closing the bathroom and toilet doors which are directly opposite.

Good quality bedlinen, overlays and cushions are provided, although there is no choice of pillows.

CUISINE. The main restaurant is chic but not pretentious. It accommodates all passengers in an open-seating arrangement, and has two integral wine display cabinets (not temperature-controlled). The chairs are square and have thin armrests and low backs – but they look good.

An indoor/outdoor *Grill* (though there is no grill), has casual seating for up to 130, with self-serve buffet set-up for breakfast and lunch, and a "fast grill" dinner in an al fresco setting. But the layout is disjointed, and the port and starboard sides are separated by two elevators. There are two main buffet display units (one for cold food, one for hot), and a separate table set-up for bread, and an active cooking station (eggs for breakfast, pasta dishes at lunchtime).

ENTERTAINMENT. French Line, the showlounge/lecture hall, has amphitheater-style seating for 260, and a raised stage suited to concerts and cabaret. The production shows are weak, repetitive, and loud. The venue is also used for expert specialist lecturers, and expedition-style recaps. Two large pillars obstruct the sightlines from several seats.

SPA/FITNESS. Ponant Yacht Spa facilities include a fitness room with starboard-side ocean views, adjacent kinetic wall, and a steam room, but no changing room. A wide range of massage and body treatments are provided by Carita of Paris, which staffs and oversees the facility.

RULES OF THE ROAD

Ships, the largest moving objects made by man, are subject to stringent international regulations. They must keep to the right in shipping lanes, and pass on the right (with certain exceptions). When circumstances raise some doubt, or shipping lanes are crowded, ships use their whistles in the same way an automobile driver uses directional signals to show which way he will turn. When one ship passes another and gives a single blast on its whistle, this means it is turning to starboard (right). Two blasts mean a turn to port (left).

The other ship acknowledges by repeating the same signal. Ships switch on navigational running lights at night — green for starboard, red for port, plus two white lights on the masts, the forward one lower than the aft one.

Flags and pennants form another part of a ship's communication facilities and are displayed for identification purposes. Each time a country is visited, its national flag is shown. While entering and leaving a port, the ship flies a blue-and-white vertically striped flag to request a pilot, while a half-red, half-white flag (divided vertically) indicates that a pilot is on board. Cruise lines also display their own "house" flag from the mast.

A ship's funnel (smokestack) is one other means of identification, each line having its own design and color scheme. The size, height, and number of funnels were all points worth advertising at the turn of the 20th century. Most ocean liners of the time had four funnels and were called "four-stackers."

There are numerous customs at sea, many of them older than any maritime law. Superstition has always been an important element, as in the following example quoted from the British Admiralty Manual of Seamanship: "The custom of breaking a bottle of wine over the stem of a ship when it is being launched originates from the old practice of toasting prosperity to a ship with a silver goblet of wine, which was then cast into the sea in order to prevent a toast of ill intent being drunk from the same cup. This was a practice that proved too expensive, and it was replaced in 1690 by the breaking of a bottle of wine over the stem."

Le Boreal
★★★★

Size: . . . . .Small Ship	Passenger Decks: 6	Cabins (with private balcony): 125
Tonnage: .10,700	Total Crew: 140	Cabins (wheelchair accessible): 0
Lifestyle: . . . . .Premium	Passengers	Wheelchair accessibility: . . . . .Fair
Cruise Line: . . . . .Ponant Cruises	(lower beds/all berths): 224/264	Cabin Voltage: . . . . .110 and 220 volts
Former Names: . . . . .none	Passenger Space Ratio	Elevators: 2
Builder: . . . . .Fincantieri (Italy)	(lower beds/all berths): 53.5/40.5	Casino (gaming tables): . . . . .No
Original Cost: . . . .$100 million	Crew/Passenger Ratio	Slot Machines: . . . . .Yes
Entered Service: . . . . .May 2010	(lower beds/all berths): 1.5/1.8	Swimming Pools (outdoors): 2
Registry: . . . . .Wallis & Fortuna	Cabins (total): .132	Swimming Pools (indoors): 0
Length (ft/m): 465.8/142.0	Size Range (sq ft/m): 215.2–301.3/	Whirlpools: 0
Beam (ft/m): 9.0/18.0	20.0–28.0	Self-Service Launderette: 0
Draft (ft/m): 15.4/4.7	Cabins (outside view): 132	Dedicated Cinema/Seats: . . . . .No
Propulsion/Propellers:diesel-electric	Cabins (interior/no view): 0	Library: . . . . .Yes
(4,600kW)/2	Cabins (for one person): 0	Onboard currency: . . . . .Euros

Exudes French ambience and super-yacht chic.

OVERVIEW. *Le Boreal* is best suited to young-minded couples and singles who want sophisticated facilities in a relaxed but chic yacht-like environment quite different to most cruise ships, with very good food and decent service. The ship is often chartered or part-chartered by "premium" travel organizers who prefer smaller ships, such as Abercrombie & Kent, Gohagen, and Tauck Tours.

THE SHIP. One of two identical new ships catering to French speakers, *Le Boreal* (North Wind) is a little gem of contemporary design – chic and uncluttered. For a full description of its facilities and a list of passenger niggles, see the preceding entry for *L'Austral*.

ACCOMMODATION. Of the 132 suites/ cabins, there are three Prestige Suites (301 sq.ft. plus 54 sq.ft. balcony); while 40 of the 94 deluxe cabins (200 sq.ft. plus 43 sq.ft. balcony) can be combined into 20 larger suites, each with two bathrooms, and separate living area and bedroom.

For a full description of the suites and cabins, see the preceding entry for *L'Austral*.

CUISINE. The main restaurant, *La Licorne*, is chic but not pretentious. It accommodates all passengers in an open-seating arrangement, and has two integral wine display cab-

BERLITZ'S RATINGS

	Possible	Achieved
Ship	500	415
Accommodation	200	155
Food	400	301
Service	400	304
Entertainment	n/a	n/a
Cruise	500	368

OVERALL SCORE
1,543 points out of 2,000

inets (not temperature-controlled). The chairs are rather square and have very thin armrests and low backs – but they look good.

La Boussole, an indoor/outdoor Grill (though there's no grill), has casual seating for up to 130, with self-serve buffet set-up for breakfast and lunch, and a "fast grill" dinner in an al fresco setting. But the layout is disjointed, and the port and starboard sides are separated by two elevators. There are two main buffet display units – one for cold food, one for hot – and a separate table set-up for bread, and an active cooking station (eggs for breakfast, pasta at lunchtime).

ENTERTAINMENT. French Line, the show lounge/lecture hall, has amphitheater-style seating for 260, and a raised stage suited to concerts and cabaret presentations. The production shows are weak, repetitive, and loud. The venue is also used for expert specialist lecturers, and expedition-style recaps. Two large pillars obstruct the sightlines from several seats.

SPA/FITNESS. Spa Ponant Yacht Spa facilities include a fitness room with starboard-side ocean views, adjacent kinetic wall, and a steam room, but no changing room. A wide range of massage and body treatments are provided by Carita of Paris, which staffs and oversees the facility.

Le Diamant
★★★

Size: ....Boutique Ship	Passenger Decks: 6	Cabins (wheelchair accessible): 0
Tonnage: 8,282	Total Crew: 140	Wheelchair accessibility: ....None
Lifestyle: ....Premium	Passengers	Cabin Current: ....220 volts
Cruise Line: ....Ponant Cruises	(lower beds/all berths): 198/198	Elevators: 2
Former Names: ....*Song of Flower,*	Passenger Space Ratio	Casino (gaming tables): ....Yes
Explorer Starship	(lower beds/all berths): 41.8/41.8	Slot Machines: ....Yes
Builder: ....KMV (Norway)	Crew/Passenger Ratio	Swimming Pools (outdoors): 1
Original Cost: ....n/a	(lower beds/all berths): 1.4/1.4	Swimming Pools (indoors): 0
Entered Service: 1986/May 2004	Cabins (total): 99	Whirlpools: 1
Registry: ....Wallis and Fortuna	Size Range (sq ft/m): 183.0–398.0/	Self-Service Launderette: ....No
Length (ft/m): 407.4/124.2	17.0–37.0	Dedicated Cinema/Seats: ....No
Beam (ft/m): 52.4/16.0	Cabins (outside view): 99	Library: ....Yes
Draft (ft/m): 16.0/4.9	Cabins (interior/no view): 0	Onboard currency: ....Euros
Propulsion/Propellers: diesel	Cabins (for one person): 0	
(5,500kW)/2 (CP)	Cabins (with private balcony): 10	

French casual cruising in a small, tired ship setting.

OVERVIEW. *Le Diamant* is for young-minded French-speaking couples and singles who want fairly contemporary facilities in a very relaxed but chic, yacht-like small ship setting that is different to "normal" cruise ships, with very good food and decent service. Totally understated elegance and a warm, informal lifestyle are the hallmarks of a cruise aboard this nice ship.

THE SHIP. *Le Diamant* is a boutique-size cruise ship, originally built as the ro-ro vessel *Begonia* in 1974 and fully converted for cruising in 1986. Operated for many years by Radisson Seven Seas Cruises (now Regent Seven Seas Cruises), the ship was sold to the France's Ponant Cruises/Tapis Rouges, a joint venture. The ship has tall, twin funnels (with a platform between them) that give a somewhat squat profile. If only the foredeck and bow could be a little longer, it would provide a more sleek appearance. The ship has fairly been well maintained and is clean, although its interiors now look really tired. There's a good amount of sheltered open deck and sunbathing space. Water sports facilities include snorkel equipment.

The interior decor is warm, with pastel colors, accented by splashes of color are used throughout the public rooms, passageways, and stairways. Good quality soft furnishings and fabrics are provided, and make the ship feel chic and comfortable, though not luxurious.

The ship has a warm and caring crew that really tries hard to make you feel at home and comfortable and at home during your cruise vacation. *Le Diamant* should provide you with a pleasing, destination-intensive, yet relaxing cruise

BERLITZ'S RATINGS

	Possible	Achieved
Ship	500	293
Accommodation	200	125
Food	400	248
Service	400	255
Entertainment	100	58
Cruise	400	240

OVERALL SCORE
1,219 points out of 2,000

experience, delivered with a decent amount of style and panache. The tender is in poor shape and needs replacing.

ACCOMMODATION. There are 10 elegant suites; 10 cabins are strictly non-smoking. All others are well equipped, complete with bathrobes and slippers, refrigerator, and video player. All come with excellent closet and drawer space. Many have bathtubs, but they are tiny – shower tubs would be a better description. Disabled passengers should choose a cabin with a shower instead of a bath.

There are no in-cabin dining facilities for dinner. When compared with the Seabourn and Silversea ships, the cabins are really rather plain.

CUISINE. The dining room is really most charming and has warm colors, a welcoming ambience, and one seating, with no assigned tables – tables are for two, four or six. Dining is in open seating. Free wines accompany lunch and dinner. The cuisine is, naturally, classic French, with small portions that are attractively presented. The personal service from the warm, highly personable and attentive staff is good.

ENTERTAINMENT. The well-tiered show lounge is a good, comfortable room, and there are good sight lines from almost all the banquette-style seating.

SPA/FITNESS. The health spa facility is very compact and short on space, but is reasonably adequate, and includes a beauty salon and sauna.

Le Levant
★★★★

Size: ....Boutique Ship	Total Crew: 50	Wheelchair accessibility: ....None
Tonnage: 3,504	Passengers	Cabin Current: ....110 and 220 volts
Lifestyle: ....Premium	(lower beds/all berths): 90/90	Elevators: 1
Cruise Line: ....Ponant Cruises	Passenger Space Ratio	Casino (gaming tables): ....No
Former Names: ....none	(lower beds/all berths): 38.9/38.9	Slot Machines: ....No
Builder: ....Leroux & Lotz (France)	Crew/Passenger Ratio	Swimming Pools (outdoors): 1
Original Cost: ....$35 million	(lower beds/all berths): 1.8/1.8	Swimming Pools (indoors): 0
Entered Service: ....Jan 1999	Cabins (total): 45	Whirlpools: 0
Registry: ....Wallis and Fortuna	Size Range (sq ft/m): 199.1/18.5	Self-Service Launderette: ....No
Length (ft/m): 328.0/100.00	Cabins (outside view): 45	Dedicated Cinema/Seats: ....No
Beam (ft/m): 45.9/14.00	Cabins (interior/no view): 0	Library: ....Yes
Draft (ft/m): 11.4/3.50	Cabins (for one person): 0	Onboard currency: ....Euros
Propulsion/Propellers: diesel (3,000 kW)/2	Cabins (with private balcony): 0	
Passenger Decks: 5	Cabins (wheelchair accessible): 0	

French casual-style cruising in a chic setting.

OVERVIEW. *Le Levant* appeals to young-minded couples and singles who want contemporary and sophisticated facilities in a very relaxed but chic, yacht-like small ship setting that is different to "normal" cruise ships, with very good food and decent service. Each cruise has life-enrichment lecturers aboard, as well as tour leaders.

THE SHIP. *Le Levant* is a sleek vessel with mega-yacht looks. It has two slim funnels that extend over port and starboard sides to carry any soot away from the vessel. It was built in a specialist yacht-building yard in St Malo, France. There is an "open bridge" policy, so you can visit the bridge at any time, except when the ship is maneuvering in difficult conditions.

A stern "marina" platform is used for scuba diving, snorkeling or swimming. Two landing craft are carried for shore visits, as well as six inflatable Zodiacs for landings in "soft" expedition areas such as the Amazon.

Inside, the vessel has contemporary, clean and uncluttered decor, and all the facilities of a private yacht. The public rooms are quite elegant, with much use of wood trim and accenting. Particularly pleasing is the wood-paneled library. There is one grand salon, which accommodates all passengers, and is used by day as a lecture room, and by night as the main lounge/bar. A resident scuba dive master is aboard for all Caribbean sailings.

This ship is sometimes under charter to the New York-based Travel Dynamics International, which operates it in some offbeat destinations and cruise regions. In summer it may be in the Great Lakes, sailing between Toronto and Chicago – its pencil-slim beam allows it to navigate the

BERLITZ'S RATINGS		
	Possible	Achieved
Ship	500	384
Accommodation	200	155
Food	400	272
Service	400	276
Entertainment	n/a	n/a
Cruise	500	328

OVERALL SCORE
1,415 points out of 2,000

locks. In the fall it heads to Canada and New England, and in winter to the Caribbean and South America.

This is all-inclusive cruising, with all port charges, gratuities, and shore excursions included in the fare. The crew is almost entirely French.

ACCOMMODATION. There are 45 ocean-view cabins – the brochure incorrectly calls them "suites" – and all are midships and forward, in five price categories – a lot for such a small ship. Each cabin has a large ocean-view window, inlaid wood furniture and accenting, designer fabrics, two beds that convert to a queen-size bed, a TV set and DVD player, refrigerator, safe, and toiletry kits in the marble-appointed bathrooms, all of which have a shower with a circular door – nicer than a shower curtain. There are no bathtubs.

CUISINE. The *Lafayette Restaurant* is a warm, cozy wood-panelled room with round and oval tables (but no tables for two). The informal *Panoramique Restaurant* has a great view overlooking the stern, with both indoor and outdoor seating. Dining is in open seating. Free wines accompany lunch and dinner. The cuisine is, naturally, classic French.

ENTERTAINMENT. The Grand Salon accommodates all passengers. It is the only room where smoking is allowed, and there are built-in video screens for showing movies. The only other entertainment is a singer/pianist; the room has a small dance floor in its center.

SPA/FITNESS. There is a small fitness room, and a steam room (there is no sauna) and shower.

Le Ponant
★★★ +

Boutique Ship:	1,489 tons	Main Propulsion:	(a) engine (b) sails	Cabins (interior/no view):	0
Lifestyle:	Premium	Propulsion/Propellers:	diesel/	Cabins (for one person):	0
Cruise Line:	Ponant Cruises		sail power/1	Cabins (with private balcony):	0
Former Names:	none	Passenger Decks:	3	Cabins (wheelchair accessible):	0
Builder:	SFCN (France)	Total Crew:	30	Wheelchair accessibility:	None
Original Cost:	n/a	Passengers		Cabin Current:	220 volts
Entered Service:	1991	(lower beds/all berths):	64/67	Elevators:	No
Registry:	France	Passenger Space Ratio		Casino (gaming tables):	No
Length (ft/m):	288.7/88.00	(lower beds/all berths):	23.2/22.2	Slot Machines:	No
Beam (ft/m):	39.3/12.00	Crew/Passenger Ratio		Swimming Pools (outdoors):	0
Draft (ft/m):	13.1/4.00	(lower beds/all berths):	2.1/2.2	Whirlpools:	0
Type of Vessel:	high tech sail-cruiser	Cabins (total):	32	Self-Service Launderette:	No
No. of Masts:	3	Size Range (sq ft/m):	139.9/13.0	Library:	Yes
Sail Area (sq ft/sq m):	16,150/1,500	Cabins (outside view):	32	Onboard currency:	Euros

Chic decor for trendy French casual cruising.

OVERVIEW. *Le Ponant* is best suited to young-minded couples and singles who want contemporary, sophisticated facilities in a very relaxed but chic setting that is different to "normal" cruise ships, with good food and service, no entertainment, and plenty of time for quiet relaxation.This is *très* French, and *très* chic, and venturing off the beaten path is what cruising aboard *Le Ponant* is all about.

THE SHIP. Ultra sleek, and very efficiently designed, this contemporary sail-cruise ship has three masts that rise 54.7 ft (16.7 meters) above the water line, and electronic winches assist in the furling and unfurling of the sails. The total sail area measures approximately 1,500 sq. meters/16,140 sq. ft. This captivating ship has plenty of room on its open decks for sunbathing. Although they have padded cushions, somehow the off-white plastic sunloungers are not at all elegant – teak would be so much more in keeping with the otherwise ultra-yacht look of the ship, but there is probably no space for them.

The very elegant, no-glitz interior design is clean, stylish, functional and high-tech. Three public lounges have pastel decor, soft colors and great European flair.

One price fits all. The ship is marketed mainly to young, sophisticated French-speaking passengers who love yachting and the sea. The company also has a stunning mega-yacht cruise vessel, *Le Levant*. Gratuities are not "required", but they are expected.

ACCOMMODATION. There are five cabins on Antigua Deck (the open deck) and 27 on Marie Galante Deck (the lowest deck). Crisp, clean blond woods and pristine white cabins

BERLITZ'S RATINGS

	Possible	Achieved
Ship	500	382
Accommodation	200	143
Food	400	272
Service	400	288
Entertainment	n/a	n/a
Cruise	500	300

OVERALL SCORE
1,385 points out of 2,000

have twin beds that convert to a double. There's a mini-bar, personal safe, and a private bathroom. All cabins have portholes, crisp artwork, and a refrigerator. There is limited storage space, however, and few drawers – they are also very small. The cabin bathrooms are quite small, but efficiently designed.

CUISINE. The lovely *Karukera* dining room has an open-seating policy, so you can sit where you wish and dine with anyone you want. There is fresh fish daily, when available, and dinner is always treated as a true *affaire gastonomique*. The chef goes out to buy fresh local food items, including fresh fish, produce and fruit.

Free wines are included for lunch and dinner, and the cuisine is, naturally, classic French. That Frenchness also means the selection of cheeses, breads and breakfast croissants is good. There are free cappuccinos and espressos.

For casual breakfasts and luncheons, there is a charming outdoor café under a canvas sailcloth awning.

ENTERTAINMENT. There is no professional entertainment as such, although occasionally the crew may put on a little soirée. Dinner is the main event each evening, and, being a French product, dinner can provide several hours' worth of entertainment in itself.

SPA/FITNESS. There is no spa, fitness room, sauna, or steam room. However, for recreation, there are water sports facilities, and these include an aft marina platform from which you can swim, windsurfers, water-ski boat, scuba and snorkel equipment. Scuba diving is an extra-cost item, charged per dive.

Legend of the Seas
★★★★

Size: . . . . .Large Resort Ship	Total Crew: 720	Wheelchair accessibility: . . . . .Good
Tonnage: .69,130	Passengers	Cabin Current: . . . . .110 and 220 volts
Lifestyle: . . . . .Standard	(lower beds/all berths): 1,800/2,076	Elevators: 11
Cruise Line: Royal Caribbean International	Passenger Space Ratio	Casino (gaming tables): . . . . .Yes
Former Names: . . . . .none	(lower beds/all berths): 38.3/33.2	Slot Machines: . . . . .Yes
Builder: Chantiers de l'Atlantique (France)	Crew/Passenger Ratio	Swimming Pools (outdoors): 2
Original Cost: . . . .$325 million	(lower beds/all berths): 2.5/2.8	(1 with sliding roof)
Entered Service: . . . . .May 1995	Cabins (total): .900	Swimming Pools (indoors): 0
Registry: . . . . .The Bahamas	Size Range (sq ft/m): 137.7–1,147.4/	Whirlpools: 4
Length (ft/m): 867.0/264.2	12.8–106.6	Self-Service Launderette: . . . . .No
Beam (ft/m): 105.0/32.0	Cabins (outside view): 575	Dedicated Cinema/Seats: . . . . .No
Draft (ft/m): 23.9/7.3	Cabins (interior/no view): 325	Library: . . . . .Yes
Propulsion/Propellers: . . . . .diesel	Cabins (for one person): 0	Onboard currency: . . . . .US$
(40,200 kW)/2	Cabins (with private balcony): 231	
Passenger Decks: 11	Cabins (wheelchair accessible): 17	

Refined European decor for mature-age cruisers.

OVERVIEW. Royal Caribbean International has designed a ship with much larger standard cabins than in any of the company's previous vessels except its sister, *Splendour of the Seas*. The ship is based in Britain during the summer, and operates Europe/Med cruising for both American and British passengers. It can be difficult to find relaxation areas without music, except for the Viking Crown Lounge during the day.

THE SHIP. *Legend of the Seas* has a contemporary profile and a nicely tiered stern. The pool deck amidships overhangs the hull to provide an extremely wide deck, while still allowing the ship to navigate the Panama Canal. With engines placed midships, there is little noise and no noticeable vibration, and the ship has an operating speed of up to 24 knots.

The interior decor is colorful, if slightly glitzy for European tastes. The outside light is brought inside in many places, with over 2 acres (8,000 sq. meters) of glass providing contact with sea and air. There's an innovative single-level sliding glass roof over the more formal setting of one of two swimming pools, providing a multi-activity, all-weather indoor-outdoor area called the Solarium. The glass roof provides shelter for the Roman-style pool and the health and fitness facilities (which are good) and slides aft to cover the miniature golf course when required – both cannot be covered at the same time, however.

Golfers are offered an 18-hole, 6,000-sq. ft (560 sq.-meter) miniature golf course. It has the topography of a real course, complete with trees, foliage, grass, bridges, water hazards, and lighting for play at night. The holes

BERLITZ'S RATINGS

	Possible	Achieved
Ship	500	399
Accommodation	200	153
Food	400	227
Service	400	275
Entertainment	100	76
Cruise	400	284

OVERALL SCORE
1,414 points out of 2,000

themselves are 155-230 sq. ft (14.3–21.3 sq. meters).

Inside, two full entertainment decks are sandwiched between five decks full of cabins, so there are plenty of public rooms to lounge and drink in. A multi-tiered seven-deck-high atrium lobby, complete with a huge stainless steel sculpture, connects with the impressive Viking Crown Lounge via glass-walled lifts. The casino is expansive, disorientingly glitzy but usually packed. The library, outside of which is a bust of Shakespeare, is a nice facility, with around 2,000 books. There is, sadly, no separate cinema.

ACCOMMODATION. There are 17 different grades, but no cabins for single occupancy. Some cabins on Deck 8 also have a larger door for wheelchair access in addition to the 17 cabins for the physically disabled, and the ship is very accessible, with ample ramped areas and sloping decks.

All cabins have a sitting area and beds that convert to double configuration, and there is ample closet and drawer space. There is not much space around the bed, though, and the showers could have been better designed. Those cabins with balconies have glass railings rather than steel/wood to provide less intrusive sightlines.

The largest accommodation is the Royal Suite, which is beautifully designed, finely decorated, and has a baby grand piano and whirlpool bathtub. Several quiet sitting areas are located adjacent to the best cabins amidships.

CUISINE. The *Romeo and Juliet Dining Room* has dramatic two-deck-high glass side walls, so many passengers both upstairs and downstairs can see both the ocean and each other in reflection; it is quite noisy when full, and would perhaps have been even better located at the stern). When you book, choose one of two seatings, or "My Time Dining" (eat when you want, during dining room hours).

A cavernous indoor-outdoor *Windjammer Café*, located towards the bow and above the bridge, has good views on three sides from large ocean-view windows. A good-sized snack area provides even more informal eating options.

ENTERTAINMENT. The That's Entertainment Theatre seats 802 and is a single-level showlounge with tiered seating levels: sightlines are generally good from almost all seats.

Strong cabaret acts are also presented in the main showlounge. A second entertainment lounge, the Anchors Aweigh Lounge, is where cabaret acts, including late-night adult comedy are presented. Other lounges and bars have live music for listening and dancing.

The entertainment throughout is upbeat – in fact, it is difficult to get away from music and noise – but is typical of the kind of resort hotel found ashore in Las Vegas. There is even background music in all corridors and elevators, and constant music outdoors on the pool deck. If you want a quiet relaxing holiday, choose another ship.

SPA/FITNESS. The ShipShape Fitness Center has a gymnasium, located on the port side of the ship, aft of the funnel, and has a small selection of high-tech muscle-pumping equipment. There is also an aerobics studio (classes are offered in a variety of keep-fit regimes), a beauty salon, and a sauna, as well as treatment rooms for such pampering procedures as massages and facials. While the facilities are quite small when compared with those aboard the company's newer ships, they are adequate for the short cruises that this ship operates.

For more sporting passengers, there is activity galore – including a rock-climbing wall with several separate climbing tracks. It is located outdoors at the aft end of the funnel.

● **For more extensive general information about the Royal Caribbean experience, see pages 152–6.**

FUN FACTS

● Cruise ship design is interesting. The beauty of design lies in curves, not in straight lines. Today's large resort ships, designed merely for cruising in warm weather regions and not for voyaging across the North Atlantic (heaven forbid, the delivery voyage was enough), are made of straight lines. They are boxy and cold in appearance, although they provide much more usable space inside the ship (some call it warehouse cruising). Take a look at *Saga Ruby* (the former *Vistafjord*) and you won't find a straight line anywhere. Then look at *Carnival Imagination* and compare the two.

● Beatrice Muller, in her early 80s, makes her permanent home at sea. She lives year-round aboard Cunard Line's *Queen Victoria*, paying a set amount to reside in her chosen cabin. She prefers being aboard the ship rather than sit around in a retirement home in Britain's damp climate, and proves that the world is her oyster. She loves it because she doesn't have to deal with the daily drudgery of shopping, doesn't need a car, or pay electric, gas or telephone bills. She communicates with her family by using the computer center's email service.

● Cruise lines and charity go hand in hand. Cunard donated 1,500 pieces of classic furniture from the 1994 refit of *QE2* to the Salvation Army for its adult rehabilitation program. Crew aboard the same ship donate money to buy guide dogs for the blind, or an ambulance for the St. John's Ambulance Brigade in the UK. Princess Cruises made a "sizeable" contribution to UNICEF following the death of Audrey Hepburn in 1993 (she named the company's *Star Princess*, now operating as *Sea Princess* for Princess Cruises). Passengers of Hapag-Lloyd's *Europa* have donated more than 1 million euros to children's homes in Vietnam. Both Holland America Line and Princess Cruises have contributed heavily to the Raptor Center in Juneau, Alaska.

● Someone forgot to "score" the champagne bottle when Dame Judi Dench named *Carnival Legend* in Harwich, England, on August 21, 2002. On the first two tries, the bottle didn't break. Then Dame Judi took the bottle in her own hands and smashed it against the side of the ship. It broke, and the foam and champagne went all over her. She was dubbed Dame Judi Drench.

● In the mid-1960s there were 12 "bell boys" ("piccolos" in hotelspeak) aboard the Cunard Line's RMS *Queen Elizabeth* and *Queen Mary*. They manned the elevators and opened the doors to the various restaurants. Each day, before they were allowed to work, they all lined up and their fingernails were inspected. Those were the days.

Liberty of the Seas
★★★★

Size:	Large Resort Ship	Passenger Decks:	15	Cabins (wheelchair accessible):	32
Tonnage:	154,407	Total Crew:	1,397	Wheelchair accessibility:	Best
Lifestyle:	Standard	Passengers		Cabin Current:	110 volts
Cruise Line:	Royal Caribbean International	(lower beds/all berths):	3,634/4,375	Elevators:	14
Former Names:	none	Passenger Space Ratio		Casino (gaming tables):	Yes
Builder:	Kvaerner Masa-Yards (Finland)	(lower beds/all berths):	42.0/35.3	Slot Machines:	Yes
Original Cost:	$590 million	Crew/Passenger Ratio		Swimming Pools (outdoors):	2
Entered Service:	May 2007	(lower beds/all berths):	2.6/3.1	Swimming Pools (indoors):	0
Registry:	The Bahamas	Cabins (total):	1,817	Whirlpools:	6
Length (ft/m):	1,112.2/339.0	Size Range (sq ft/m):	149.0–2,025.0/	Self-Service Launderette:	No
Beam (ft/m):	184.0/56.0		13.8–188.1	Dedicated Cinema/Seats:	No
Draft (ft/m):	27.8/8/5	Cabins (outside view):	1,084	Library:	Yes
Propulsion/Propellers:	diesel-electric	Cabins (interior/no view):	733	Onboard currency:	US$
(75,600 kW)/3 pods (2 azimuthing,		Cabins (for one person):	0		
1 fixed/14 MW each)		Cabins (with private balcony):	842		

A large resort ship for family-friendly casual cruising.

OVERVIEW. The facilities (such as public rooms, bars and lounges) of the *Voyager*-class ships have been incorporated, but with more conference and meetings facilities, extensive wi-fi capabilities and connectivity for cell phones. Other facilities include a large casino. If you want to arrange to meet someone, make an appointment and specify a location, for this really is a large, Las Vegas-style floating resort-city.

THE SHIP. *Liberty of the Seas* (like sister ships *Freedom of the Seas* and *Independence of the Seas*) is essentially split into three separate areas, rather like the Disney cruise ships – adults-only, family, and main.

The "wow" factor is its connection with water in the design of a dramatic water theme park afloat. By day, the H2O Zone (aft of the funnel) has an interactive water-themed play area for families that includes water cannons and spray fountains, water jets and ground gushers; by night the "water park" turns into a colourfully-lit sculpture garden. The ship's central pool is a sports pool, with grandstand seating and competitive games that include pole jousting. Other active sports facilities include a boxing ring, rock-climbing wall, in-line skating area, an ice-skating rink, and golf simulators.

The cabin hallways have an extremely warm, attractive feel, with artwork cabinets and asymmetrical flow to lead you along and break up the monotony. In fact, there are plenty of colorful, even whimsical, decorative touches.

ACCOMMODATION. There is a wide range of cabins in 14 categories and 21 price grades. There are many family-

BERLITZ'S RATINGS

	Possible	Achieved
Ship	500	426
Accommodation	200	161
Food	400	235
Service	400	289
Entertainment	100	82
Cruise	400	317

OVERALL SCORE
1,510 points out of 2,000

friendly cabins, good for family reunions. Some accommodation examples (from large to small):

Presidential Family Suite: Two master bedrooms, each with twin beds that convert to queen-size, private balcony, sofa bed, bar, private bathroom, bathtub, vanity, hair-dryer, closed-circuit flat screen TV and phone. Great views over the ship's stern. Occupants have access to the Concierge Club lounge and services. There is only one Presidential Family Suite, which can take up to 14, though this would be quite cramped. Size: 1,215 sq. ft. (112.8 sq. meters), plus balcony: 810 sq. ft (75.2 sq. meters), set with lounge area and dining table.

Royal Suite: There's a separate bedroom with king-size bed, private balcony, living room with queen-size sofa bed and private bathroom. Measures: 1,406 sq. ft. (130.6 sq.meters); balcony 377 sq. ft. (35.0 sq.meters)

Royal Family Suite: There are two bedrooms with twin beds that convert to queen-size beds (one room has third and fourth Pullman beds), a private balcony, two bathrooms and living area with double sofa bed. Measures 588 sq. ft. (54.6 sq.meters); balcony 234 sq. ft. (21.7 sq.meters)

Owners Suite: There's a queen-size bed, private balcony, separate living area with queen-size sofa bed, wet bar, vanity area, walk-in closet; bathroom with tub and shower, plus access to the Concierge Club lounge and attendant services. Sleeps up to five. Size: 506 sq. ft. (46 sq. meters) + Balcony: 131 sq. ft. (12.1 sq. meters).

Grand Suite: Two twin beds convert to queen-size. There's a private balcony, sitting area (some with sofa bed), vanity area; bathroom with tub and shower. Access to the Concierge

Club lounge and services. Sleeps up to four. Size: 381 sq. ft. (35.3 sq.meters) + Balcony: 89 sq. ft. (8.2 sq. meters).

Junior Suite: Two twin beds convertible to queen-size, private balcony, sitting area (some with sofa bed), vanity area; bathroom with tub and shower. Sleeps up to four. Size: 285.2 sq. ft. (26.5 sq.meters) + Balcony: 101 sq. ft. (9.3 sq.meters).

Superior Oceanview Cabin: Two twin beds convertible to queen-size, a private balcony, sitting area (some with sofa bed), vanity area; bathroom with shower. Sleeps two (some rooms sleep three or four). Size: 202 sq. ft. (18.7 sq. meters) + Balcony: 42 sq. ft. (3.9 sq. meters).

Deluxe Oceanview Cabin: Same facilities as Superior Oceanview cabins, but size is different: 173 sq. ft. (16.0 sq. meters) + Balcony: 46 sq. ft. (4.2 sq. meters).

Promenade Cabin (interior, but overlooking the Royal Promenade): A view of the Royal Promenade with bay windows, two twin beds that convert to queen-size, and private bathroom. Measures: 149 sq. ft. (13.8 sq.meters).

Promenade Family Cabin: There are two twin beds that convert to queen-size, and private bathroom. Measures: 300 sq. ft. (27.8 sq.meters).

Interior (no view) Cabin: Two twin beds convertible to queen-size; private bathroom with shower. Sleeps two (some rooms sleep three or four). Size: 152sq. ft. (14.1 sq. meters).

Family Ocean-view Cabin: Located at the front of the ship, it contains two twin beds (convertible to queen-size), sofa and/or Pullman beds, sitting area; bathroom, with shower. Accommodates six, and has 48-inch (122-cm) round windows. Size: 265 sq. ft. (24.6 sq. meters).

All cabins have a private bathroom (with tub and shower, or shower only), vanity desk with hairdryer, mini-bar, safe, flat-screen TV, iPod dock, radio, and satellite telephone. A room service menu is provided. Suite occupants have access to a Concierge Lounge, for more personal service – this saves standing in line at the reception desk.

CUISINE. The main dining room is extremely large and is set on three levels (each has a theme and name: *Galileo, Isaac,* and *Leonardo*). A dramatic staircase connects all three levels, and huge, fat support pillars obstruct the sightlines from many seats. All three have the same menus and food. When you book, choose one of two seatings, or "My Time Dining" (eat when you want, during dining room hours). Tables are for four, six, eight 10 or 12.

Alternative Dining Options: Alternative dining options for casual and informal meals at all hours, according to company statements, include:

● *Promenade Café:* for continental breakfast, all-day pizzas (*Sorrento's*), sandwiches and coffee (in paper cups).

● *Windjammer Café:* for casual buffet-style breakfast, lunch and light dinner, except for the cruise's last night.

● *Island Grill* (a section of the Windjammer Café): for casual dinner (no reservations necessary) featuring a grill and open kitchen.

● *Portofino:* this is an "upscale" Euro-Italian restaurant, open for dinner only. Reservations are required, and there's gratuity. Choices include: antipasti, soup, salad, pasta, main dish, dessert, cheese and coffee (the menu does not change during the cruise).

● *Chops Grill:* an intimate restaurant for steaks and seafood. There's a cover charge.

● *Johnny Rockets*, a retro 1950s all-day, all-night diner-style eatery that has hamburgers, hot dogs and other fast-food items, malt shakes, and jukebox hits, with both indoor and outdoor seating (indoor tables have a mini-jukebox), and all-singing, all-dancing waitresses that'll knock your socks off, if you can stand the volume. There's a cover charge.

● *Sprinkles:* for round-the-clock ice cream and yoghurt, pastries and coffee.

ENTERTAINMENT. The Showlounge is a stunning space at the forward end of the ship, spanning the height of five decks, with only a few slim pillars and almost no disruption of sightlines. The room has a hydraulic orchestra pit and huge stage areas, together with sonic-boom loud sound, and superb lighting equipment. *Saturday Night Fever: The Musical* is one of the featured production shows. The most entertaining shows are the Spectaculars on Ice.

In addition, the ship has an array of cabaret acts. The strongest are presented in the main showlounge, while others perform in the Nightclub, the venue for late-night adults-only comedy.

There is also a television studio, located adjacent to rooms that could be used, for example, for trade show exhibit space – good for conventions at sea.

A performance not to be missed is the "Greatest Show at Sea" Parade – a superbly executed 15-minute extravaganza that bumbles along the Royal Promenade at turtle speed; it replicates the parade of stars and animals at a circus of yesteryear (Barnum and Bailey's meets cruise ship). This is when it's really good to have one of those interior-view atrium cabins – although the windows don't open, so you can't take photographs. Otherwise, get a position early along the Royal Promenade.

SPA/FITNESS. The ShipShape health spa is large. It includes a large aerobics room, fitness center, treatment rooms, and men's and women's sauna/steam rooms and relaxation areas. The spa facility is operated by Steiner. Some basic exercise classes are free, but the good ones such as yoga and personal training cost extra.

More active passengers can bodyboard, go boxing in the full-size boxing ring, climb the rock-climbing wall, jog, putt, swim, skate, step, surf, and workout. There's also basketball and volleyball.

● **For more extensive general information on what a Royal Caribbean cruise is like, see pages 152–6.**

Louis Cristal
★★★

Size: ....Mid-Size Ship	Propulsion/Propellers: diesel (19,120kW/2)	Cabins (with private balcony): 10
Tonnage: 25,611	Passenger Decks: 7	Cabins (wheelchair accessible): 6
Lifestyle: ....Standard	Total Crew: 400	Wheelchair accessibility: ....None
Cruise Line: ....Louis Cruises	Passengers	Cabin Voltage: 110/220
Former Names: ... Silja Opera, SuperStar	(lower beds/all berths): 966/1,278	Elevators: 4
Taurus, Leeward, Sally Albatross,	Passenger Space Ratio	Casino (gaming tables): ....Yes
Viking Saga	(lower beds/all berths): 26.5/20.0	Slot Machines: ....Yes
Builder: ....Wartsila (Finland)	Crew/Passenger Ratio	Swimming Pools (outdoors): 1
Original Cost: ....n/a	(lower beds/all berths): 2.4/3.1	Swimming Pools (indoors): 0
Entered Service: 1980/Jul 2007	Cabins (total): 483	Whirlpools: 1
Registry: ....Malta	Size Range (sq ft/m): 107.6–462.8/10.0–43.0	Self-Service Launderette: ....No
Length (ft/m): 530.5/161.7	Cabins (outside view): 318	Dedicated Cinema/Seats: ....No
Beam (ft/m): 100.0/30.5	Cabins (interior/no view): 165	Library: ....Yes
Draft (ft/m): 20.1/6.1	Cabins (for one person): 0	Onboard currency: ....Euros

A casual ship with a friendly crew for destination-intensive cruises.

OVERVIEW. This ship appeals to first-time passengers who simply want to cruise the Greek Islands in a modicum of comfort, and at a bargain price. The dress code is casual throughout, with no formal nights. Gratuities are not included in the fare. The ship is due to be refitted/refurbished.

THE SHIP. *Louis Cristal* has undergone a number of changes, modifications and mishaps during its busy life. Originally built as a Viking Line passenger ferry, it was extensively reconstructed in 1995 to the tune of $60 million, after which it operated under charter to Norwegian Cruise Line as *Leeward*. It was bought by Louis Cruises for almost $50 million as a replacement for *Sea Diamond*, which sank off Santorini, Greece, in 2007.

The ship has a smart wedge-shaped profile with a squared-off stern and short, stubby bows, and the enclosed bridge looks like it's really one deck lower than it should be. But *Louis Cristal* does benefit from a good, walk-around teakwood promenade deck. The pool deck is very cramped, although the pool itself can be covered by a sliding glass dome. There is no forward-facing observation lounge atop the ship, but there is a reasonable array of public rooms, lounges, bars and meeting places.

ACCOMMODATION. There are three suite categories (Grand, Imperial, and Royal, plus an interior "suite"), and a mix of several outside-view cabins (some of which have balconies) and interior cabins in 19 price grades.

The top-grade suites have neatly-angled private bal-

BERLITZ'S RATINGS

	Possible	Achieved
Ship	500	321
Accommodation	200	131
Food	400	230
Service	400	246
Entertainment	100	65
Cruise	400	243

OVERALL SCORE
1,236 points out of 2,000

conies and provide a decent amount of space for short cruises; the bathrooms have a tub, separate shower, and good storage facilities for toiletries. Most of the standard cabins are really quite small, but adequate enough for the three- and four-day Greek Isles cruises this ship operates. The bathrooms really are dimensionally-challenged – dancing with the shower curtain comes to mind. Also, note that some cabins have views obstructed by safety equipment.

CUISINE. There are two principal dining rooms, plus a number of other dining spots and casual eateries. There are two seatings for dinner on most nights (typically an open seating for the first night), and open seating for breakfast and lunch. Seating and table assignments are made by the maître d' during embarkation.

The cuisine is predominantly Continental, with some Greek specialties involving much use of oil and salt. All tables are laid with crisp white linen. Spa and vegetarian dishes are available on lunch and dinner menus. Louis Cruises makes all its own breads, soups, pâtés, jams, pizzas and beefburgers on board from scratch.

ENTERTAINMENT. The show lounge has tiered seating and decent sightlines, but entertainment is a weak link in the overall cruise experience.

SPA/FITNESS. Facilities include a beauty salon, fitness room, and sauna. Massages, aromatherapy facials, mani-cures, pedicures, and hair treatments are available.

Louis Majesty
★★★ +

Size:	Mid-Size Ship	Passenger Decks:	.9	Cabins (with private balcony):	.0
Tonnage:	.40,876	Total Crew:	.620	Cabins (wheelchair accessible):	.7
Lifestyle:	Standard	Passengers		Wheelchair accessibility	None
Cruise Line:	.Louis Cruises	(lower beds/all berths):	.1,462/1,792	Cabin Current:	.110 and 220 volts
Former Names:	.Norwegian Majesty,	Passenger Space Ratio		Elevators:	.6
	Royal Majesty	(lower beds/all berths):	.27.9/22.8	Casino (gaming tables):	.Yes
Builder: Kvaerner Masa-Yards STX (Finland)		Crew/Passenger Ratio		Slot Machines:	.Yes
Original Cost:	.$229 million	(lower beds/all berths):	.2.0/2.5	Swimming Pools (outdoors):	.2
Entered Service:	.Sep 1992/Dec 2009	Navigation Officers:	.Norwegian	Swimming Pools (indoors):	.0
Registry:	.Malta	Cabins (total):	.731	Whirlpools:	.3
Length (ft/m):	.679.4/207.10	Size Range (sq ft/m): 118.4–374.5/11.0–34.8		Self-Service Launderette:	.No
Beam (ft/m):	.90.5/27.60	Cabins (outside view):	.481	Dedicated Cinema/Seats:	.No
Draft (ft/m):	.20.3/6.20	Cabins (interior/no view):	.249	Library:	.Yes
Propulsion/Propellers:diesel (21,120 kW)/2		Cabins (for one person):	.0	Onboard currency:	.Euros

A modestly stylish ship for casual, friendly cruising.

OVERVIEW. This family-owned ship is excellent value for money. It absorbs passengers well and provides a very comfortable cruise experience in warm, crisp surroundings, with good food, and decent hospitality from a really friendly crew. You can expect a multinational passenger mix, with announcements in four or five languages.

THE SHIP. Smart and modestly stylish, this is generally a well-designed vessel, ideally suited to year-round Mediterranean cruising. Inside, it is quite pretty warm, with lots of wood paneling and chrome/copper accents, reasonably discreet lighting, soothing colors, and no glitz. Wide passageways and high ceilings in some areas help provide a feeling of inner spaciousness, and the ship has a nice touch of contemporary elegance. There are several public rooms, bars and lounges, and a small library/internet room. The Monte Carlo Casino, the only room where smoking is permitted, is large and equipped with blackjack and roulette tables, and lots of slot machines. "Kids' Corner" has a full program of activities. Gratuities are at your discretion.

Passenger niggles? There are no cushioned pads for the plastic deck chairs. The self-serve buffet area is too small.

ACCOMMODATION. There are 17 different price grades. Almost all outside-view and interior cabins are on the small side, but quite comfortable. All have flat-screen TVs. The closets are really small, but luggage can be stored under the bed. The bathrooms are a little tight, although there is a generous amount of room in the shower enclosures.

Two large suites (901, 903) have a separate bedroom with walk-in closet and bathroom with combination tub

BERLITZ'S RATINGS

	Possible	Achieved
Ship	500	328
Accommodation	200	137
Food	400	246
Service	400	267
Entertainment	100	65
Cruise	400	251

OVERALL SCORE
1,294 points out of 2,000

and shower; there is a step of about nine inches (24cm). The lounge has a dining table, plus a sofa and chairs in the bay window. There are bay windows in both the lounge and bedroom, and separate TV sets/DVD players; a tea/coffee-making setup and late-afternoon snacks are provided. The Junior Suites (902–923) are smaller, but do have a curtain separating lounge and bedroom. Suite-grade bathrooms have a tub and shower combination.

CUISINE. The main dining venues are: *Seven Seas Restaurant*, with 636 seats, and the *Four Seasons Restaurant*, with 266 seats. The food, menu, creativity and service are sound, with generous portions. The restaurants have an open seating arrangement. Louis Cruises makes all its own breads, soups, sauces, pâtés, jams, pizzas and beefburgers on board. The wine list is quite decent and very reasonably priced. **Alternative Dining.** The intimate 56-seat *Le Bistro Restaurant* serves Italian- and Continental-style cuisine. No reservations are needed, but there's a cover charge of €15.
Casual Eateries. *Café Royale* is an indoor buffet venue with 112 seats. An outdoor grill serves fast food.

ENTERTAINMENT. The Palace Showlounge has banquette and individual tub chairs. There are several small musical units, but shows and entertainment events are weak links.

SPA/FITNESS. Sana contains a small gymnasium with muscle-toning equipment, an aerobics area, men's and women's saunas, a beauty salon, and four massage/body treatment rooms including one for couples. The spa concession is Flair, and the therapists are really excellent.

Maasdam
★★★★

Size: . . . . .Mid-Size Ship	Passenger Decks: 10	Cabins (with private balcony): 150
Tonnage: 55,451	Total Crew: 557	Cabins (wheelchair accessible): 6
Lifestyle: . . . . .Premium	Passengers	Wheelchair accessibility: . . . . .Good
Cruise Line: . . . . . . .Holland America Line	(lower beds/all berths): 1,266/1,627	Cabin Current: . . . . .110 and 220 volts
Former Names: . . . . .none	Passenger Space Ratio	Elevators: 8
Builder: . . . . .Fincantieri (Italy)	(lower beds/all berths): 43.8/34.0	Casino (gaming tables): . . . . .Yes
Original Cost: . . . .$215 million	Crew/Passenger Ratio	Slot Machines: . . . . .Yes
Entered Service: . . . . .Dec 1993	(lower beds/all berths): 2.2/2.9	Swimming Pools (outdoors): 1
Registry: . . . . .The Netherlands	Cabins (total): 632	Swimming Pools (indoors): 1 (glass dome)
Length (ft/m): 719.3/219.30	Size Range (sq ft/m): 186.2–1,124.8/	Whirlpools: 2
Beam (ft/m): 101.0/30.80	17.3–104.5	Self-Service Launderette: . . . . .Yes
Draft (ft/m): 24.6/7.50	Cabins (outside view): 502	Dedicated Cinema/Seats: Yes/249
Propulsion/Propellers: . . . . .diesel-electric	Cabins (interior/no view): 131	Library: . . . . .Yes
(34,560 kW)/2	Cabins (for one person): 0	Onboard currency: . . . . .US$

Dutch-style decor for mature-age cruisers.

OVERVIEW. Holland America Line is constantly fine-tuning its performance and its regular passengers, almost all of whom are North American, find the company's ships comfortable and well-run. HAL continues its strong maritime traditions and keeps its ships clean and tidy, although the food and service components still let the rest of the cruise experience down.

THE SHIP. *Maasdam* is one of a series of four almost identical ships, along with *Statendam, Ryndam* and *Veendam*. Although the exterior styling is rather angular (some would say boxy – the funnel certainly is), it is softened and balanced somewhat by the black hull. There is a full walk-around teak promenade deck outdoors – excellent for strolling – and, thankfully, no sign of synthetic turf anywhere. The sunloungers on the exterior promenade deck are wood, and have comfortable cushioned pads, while those at the swimming pool on Lido Deck are of white plastic. There is good passenger flow throughout the public areas.

In the interiors of this "S" -class ship, an asymmetrical layout helps to reduce bottlenecks and congestion. Most of the public rooms are concentrated on two decks, Promenade Deck, and Upper Promenade Deck, which creates a spacious feel to the ship's interiors. In general, the interior styling is restrained, using a mixture of contemporary materials combined with traditional woods and ceramics. There is, thankfully, little glitz anywhere.

What is noticeable is the $2 million-worth of artworks, assembled and nicely displayed to represent HAL's fine Dutch heritage and to present a balance between standard itineraries and onboard creature comforts. Several oil

BERLITZ'S RATINGS

	Possible	Achieved
Ship	500	372
Accommodation	200	150
Food	400	248
Service	400	287
Entertainment	100	72
Cruise	400	283

OVERALL SCORE
1,412 points out of 2,000

paintings of the line's former ships by Stephen Card, an ex-captain, adorn stairway landings. Also noticeable are the fine flower arrangements in the public areas and foyers – used to good effect to brighten up what to some is dull decor. Atop the ship, with forward facing views that wrap around the sides, is the Crow's Nest Lounge. By day it makes a fine observation lounge, with large ocean-view windows; by night it turns into a nightclub with extremely variable lighting.

The atrium foyer is three decks high, although its light-catching green glass sculpted centerpiece (*Totem* by Luciano Vistosi, composed of almost 2,000 pieces of glass) makes it look a little crowded, and leaves little room in front of the Front Office. A hydraulic glass roof covers the reasonably-sized swimming pool/whirlpools and central Lido area, whose focal point is a large dolphin sculpture, so that this can be used in either fine or poor weather.

This ship has a large, relaxing Leyden Library; a card-room, an Explorer's Lounge (good for afternoon tea and after-dinner coffee), an intimate Piano Bar, and a casino. Holland America Line's many repeat passengers seem to enjoy the fact that social dancing is always on the menu. In the final analysis, however, the score for this ship ends up just a disappointing tad under what it could be if the food and food service staff were more memorable – more professional training might help.

Niggles? An escalator travels between two of the lower decks, one of which was originally planned to be the embarkation point, but it is almost pointless. The charge to use the washing machines and dryers in the self-service launderette is petty, particularly for suite occupants, as they pay high prices for their cruises. The men's urinals in public restrooms are unusually high.

Perhaps the ship's best asset is its friendly and personable Filipino and Indonesian crew, although communication can prove frustrating and service is inconsistent.

ACCOMMODATION. The accommodation ranges from small interior cabins to a large penthouse suite, in 17 price categories. The interior and outside standard cabins have twin beds that convert to a queen-size bed, and there is a separate living space with sofa and coffee table. Although the drawer space is generally good, the closet space is very tight, particularly for long cruises, although more than adequate for a seven-night cruise. Bathrobes are provided for all suites and cabins, as are hairdryers, and a small range of toiletries. The bathrooms are quite well laid out, but the tubs are small units better described as shower tubs.

On Navigation Deck, 28 suites have accommodation for up to four. These have in-suite dining as an alternative to the dining room, for reclusive meals. These are spacious, tastefully decorated and well laid-out, and have a separate, good-sized living room, a bedroom with two lower beds that convert to a king-size bed, dressing room, plenty of closet and drawer space (walk-in closet), marble bathroom with Jacuzzi tub and separate toilet/washroom with bidet.

The largest accommodation is the single penthouse suite, on the starboard side of Navigation Deck at the forward staircase. It has a king-size bed and vanity desk; large walk-in closet with superb drawer space, oversize whirlpool bath (it could seat four) and separate shower enclosure, separate washroom with toilet, bidet and washbasin; living room with writing desk, large TV set and full set of audio equipment; dressing room, large private balcony (with teak lounge chairs and drinks tables, dining table and four chairs), mini-bar/refrigerator, a pantry with large refrigerator, toaster unit, and full coffee/tea making facilities and food preparation area. There's a separate entrance from the hallway, a guest toilet and floor-to-ceiling windows.

CUISINE. The *Rotterdam Dining Room* spans two decks. It is located aft, is quite dramatic, and has a grand staircase, panoramic views on three sides, and a music balcony. Both open seating and assigned seating are available, while breakfast and lunch are open-seating – you'll be seated by restaurant staff when you enter. The waiter stations are very noisy for anyone seated near them.

Alternative dining option: The 66-seat *Pinnacle Grill* is located just forward of the balcony level of the main dining room on the starboard side. It serves Pacific Northwest cuisine such as Dungeness crab, Alaska salmon, halibut and other regional specialties (reservations needed, cover charge applies). A Bulgari show plate, Rosenthal china, Reidel wine glasses, and Frette table linen are used. The Pinnacle Grill is a much better, more relaxed dining experience than the main dining room and worth it for that special celebration.

For more casual evening eating, the *Lido Buffet* is open for casual dinners on all except the last night of each cruise, in an open-seating arrangement. Tables are set with crisp linens, flatware and stemware. A set menu includes a choice of several entrees. The buffet is also open for casual breakfasts and lunches. Again there is much use of canned fruits and packeted items, although there are several commercial low-calorie salad dressings. The beverage station lets it down, for it is no better than those found in family outlets ashore in the United States. In addition, a poolside grill provides basic American hamburgers and hot dogs.

Passengers have to use the Lido Buffet on days when the dining room is closed for lunch, which is typically once or twice per cruise, depending on the itinerary.

ENTERTAINMENT. The Showroom at Sea, in the forward part of the ship, spans two decks, with banquette seating on both main and upper levels. It is basically a well-designed room, but the ceiling is low and the sight lines from the balcony level are quite poor.

SPA/FITNESS. The Ocean Spa is located one deck below the navigation bridge at the very forward part of the ship. It has ocean views and includes a gymnasium with all the latest muscle-pumping exercise machines, including an abundance of treadmills. There's also an aerobics exercise area, large beauty salon with ocean-view windows to the port side, several treatment rooms, and men's and women's sauna, steam room and changing areas.

● **For more extensive general information on what a Holland America Line cruise is like, see pages 140–3.**

Majesty of the Seas
★★★

Size: . . . . .Large Resort Ship	Passenger Decks: 11	Cabins (with private balcony): 62
Tonnage: .73,941	Total Crew: 827	Cabins (wheelchair accessible): 4
Lifestyle: . . . . .Standard	Passengers	Wheelchair accessibility: . . . . .Fair
Cruise Line: Royal Caribbean International	(lower beds/all berths): 2,380/2,774	Cabin Current: . . . . .110 volts
Former Names: . . . . .none	Passenger Space Ratio	Elevators: 11
Builder: .Chantiers de l'Atlantique (France)	(lower beds/all berths): 30.8/26.3	Casino (gaming tables): . . . . .Yes
Original Cost: . . . .$300 million	Crew/Passenger Ratio	Slot Machines: . . . . .Yes
Entered Service: . . . . .Apr 1992	(lower beds/all berths): 2.8/3.3	Swimming Pools (outdoors): 2
Registry: . . . . .The Bahamas	Cabins (total): 1,190	Swimming Pools (indoors): 0
Length (ft/m): 879.9/268.2	Size Range (sq ft/m): 118.4–670.0/	Whirlpools: 2
Beam (ft/m): 105.9/32.3	11.0–62.2	Self-Service Launderette: . . . . .No
Draft (ft/m): 24.9/7.6	Cabins (outside view): 732	Dedicated Cinema/Seats: . . . . .No
Propulsion/Propellers: . . . . diesel	Cabins (interior/no view): 458	Library: . . . . .Yes
(21,844 kW)/2	Cabins (for one person): 0	Onboard currency: . . . . .US$

A well-worn large ship for casual family cruising.

OVERVIEW. This fairly smart-looking resort ship provides a well tuned, yet impersonal, short cruise experience (three- and four-day Bahamas cruises year-round from Miami) for a lot of passengers. The dress code is very casual. You will probably be overwhelmed by the public spaces, and underwhelmed by the size of the cabins. The open deck space is very cramped when full, as aboard any large ship, although there seems to be plenty of it.

THE SHIP. When first introduced, this ship (together with sisters *Monarch of the Seas* and *Sovereign of the Seas*) was an innovative vessel. Royal Caribbean International's trademark Viking Crown lounge and bar surrounds the funnel and provides a great view, but it has no soul and looks dated. There is a basketball court.

The interior layout is a little awkward, as it is designed in a vertical stack, with most public rooms located aft, and the accommodation located forward, which ensures quiet areas. There's an impressive array of spacious and elegant public rooms, although the decor calls to mind the IKEA school of interior design, despite a revitalization in 2007 when cabins were refreshed and more casual eating options introduced. A stunning five-deck-high Centrum lobby has cascading stairways and two glass-walled elevators.

There is a decent two-level showlounge and a selection of shops, albeit with lots of tacky merchandise, and an "All items at $10" store – good for souvenirs. Casino gamers will find blackjack, craps, Caribbean stud poker and roulette tables, plus an array of slot machines in Casino Royale.

Among the public rooms, the library is a nice feature for quite relaxation, and there is a decent selection of books.

BERLITZ'S RATINGS

	Possible	Achieved
Ship	500	333
Accommodation	200	119
Food	400	221
Service	400	260
Entertainment	100	66
Cruise	400	247

OVERALL SCORE
1,246 points out of 2,000

An internet center has 10 workstations, but the cost is quite high; the ship is also wi-fi enabled – but there's a charge. The entertainment program is quite sound, and there's a decent range of children's and teens' programs (teens have their own chill-out room – adults not allowed) and cheerful youth counselors.

Because the public rooms are mostly located aft, with accommodation in the forward section, there is often a long wait for elevators, particularly at peak times after dinner, shows, and talks. But at least the restrooms are quite welcoming.

ACCOMMODATION. There are 17 categories, priced by grade, size, and location.

Suites: Thirteen suites on Bridge Deck are reasonably large and nicely furnished (the largest is the Royal Suite), with separate living and sleeping spaces. They provide more space, with better service and more perks than standard-grade accommodation.

Standard Cabins: The standard outside-view and interior cabins are incredibly small, although an arched window treatment and colorful soft furnishings give an illusion of more space. Almost all cabins have twin beds that convert to a queen-size or double-bed configuration, together with moveable bedside tables, and flat-screen TV sets. All standard cabins have very little closet and drawer space – you will need some luggage engineering to stow your cases. You should, therefore, think of packing only minimal clothing, which is all you really need for a short cruise.

All cabins have a private bathroom, with shower enclosure, toilet and washbasin. All are provided with good mattresses, and duvets.

CUISINE. There are two main dining rooms: *Moonlight*, located on the lowest level of the atrium lobby, and *Starlight*, one deck higher. When you book, choose one of two seatings, or "My Time Dining" (eat when you want, during dining room hours at tables for two to eight). The dining operation is well orchestrated, with emphasis on highly programmed, extremely hurried service that many find insensitive and intrusive.

For casual breakfasts and lunches, there's *Windjammer Marketplace*. It is split into various specialty areas including American, Asian, Latin, and Mediterranean fare. *Compass Deli* is a bar in which you can make up your own sandwich. *Johnny Rockets* is a 1950s retro diner for fast foods such as hamburgers and hot dogs, sodas and shakes, located on an upper deck section of the Windjammer Marketplace (cover charge applies). At no extra cost, there is *Sorrento's* for American-Italian pizzas.

Café Latte-tudes serves Seattle's Best Coffee brand (extra-cost) in paper cups. And for ice cream lovers, there's *Freeze Ice Cream*.

ENTERTAINMENT. A Chorus Line is the ship's principal showlounge; it has both main and balcony levels, with banquette seating, but many pillars supporting the balcony level provide less than good sightlines from the side seats on the lower level.

Royal Caribbean's large-scale production shows are extremely colorful spectaculars that will remind you of Las Vegas casino hotel shows, with their high-energy hype, presentation and glitz. They are fast-moving, razzle-dazzle shows that rely a lot on lighting and special effects, but have little or no storyline, often poor linkage between themes and scenes, and choreography that's more stepping in place than dancing. Strong cabaret acts are also presented in the main showlounge.

The entertainment throughout is upbeat but is typical of the kind of resort hotel found in Las Vegas. There is even background music in all corridors and elevators, and constant music outdoors on the pool deck.

SPA/FITNESS. The Majesty Day Spa has a gymnasium with aft-facing views and high-tech muscle-pumping equipment. There is an aerobics studio, and classes are offered in a variety of keep-fit regimes. There is also a beauty salon, and a sauna, and 10 treatment rooms for pampering massages, facials, and so on. While the facilities are not as extensive as those aboard the company's newer ships, they are adequate for the short cruises that this ship operates.

For the more sporting, there is activity galore – including a rock-climbing wall with several separate climbing tracks. It is located outdoors at the aft end of the funnel.

● **For more extensive general information about the Royal Caribbean cruise experience, see pages 152–6.**

EXPEDITIONS: DID YOU KNOW...

● that Quark Expeditions made maritime history in July/August 1991, when its chartered Russian icebreaker, *Sovetskiy Soyuz*, made a spectacular 21-day voyage to negotiate a passage from Murmansk, Russia, to Nome, Alaska, across the North Pole? Although the polar ice cap had been navigated by the US nuclear submarines *Skate* and *Nautilus*, as well as by dirigible and airplane, this was the first passenger ship to make the hazardous crossing.

● that in 1984, Salen Lindblad Cruising made maritime history by negotiating a westbound voyage through the Northwest Passage, a 41-day epic that started from St. John's, Newfoundland, in Canada, and ended at Yokohama, Japan? The search for a Northwest Passage to the Orient attracted brave explorers for more than four centuries. Despite numerous attempts and loss of life, including Henry Hudson in 1610, a "white passage" to the East remained an elusive dream. Amundsen's 47-ton ship *Gjoa* eventually navigated the route in 1906, taking three years to do so. It was not until 1943 that a Canadian ship, *St. Roch*, became the first vessel in history to make the passage in a single season. *Lindblad Explorer* became the 34th vessel, and the first cruise vessel, to complete the Northwest Passage.

● that the most expensive expedition cruise excursion was a cruise/dive to visit the resting place of RMS *Titanic* aboard the two deep-ocean submersibles *Mir I* and *Mir II* used in James Cameron's Hollywood blockbuster. Just 60 participants went as observers in 1998, and another 60 were taken in 1999.

● that a passenger once asked the operations director of a well-known expedition cruise ship where the best shops were in Antarctica? His reply: "On board, madam!"

Marco Polo
★★ +

Size: . . . . .Mid-Size Ship	Passenger Decks: 8	Cabins (with private balcony): 0
Tonnage: 22,080	Total Crew: 356	Cabins (wheelchair accessible): 2
Lifestyle: . . . . .Standard	Passengers	Wheelchair accessibility: . . . . .Fair
Cruise Line: . . .Cruise & Maritime Voyages	(lower beds/all berths): 848/915	Cabin Current: . . . . .110 and 220 volts
Former Names: . . . . .Aleksandr Pushkin	Passenger Space Ratio	Elevators: 4
Builder: . . . . . .VEB Mathias Thesen Werft	(lower beds/all berths): 26.0/24.1	Casino (gaming tables): . . . . .No
(Germany)	Crew/Passenger Ratio	Slot Machines: .No
Original Cost: .n/a	(lower beds/all berths): 2.3/2.5	Swimming Pools (outdoors): 1
Entered Service: . . . . .Apr 1966/Apr 2008	Cabins (total): 425	Swimming Pools (indoors): 0
Registry: . . . . .The Bahamas	Size Range (sq ft/m): 93.0–484.0/8.6–44.9	Whirlpools: 3
Length (ft/m): 578.4/176.28	Cabins (outside view): 292	Self-Service Launderette: . . . . .No
Beam (ft/m): 77.4/23.60	Cabins (interior/no view): 133	Dedicated Cinema/Seats: . . . . .No
Draft (ft/m): 26.8/8.17	Cabins (for one person): . . .many doubles	Library: . . . . .Yes
Propulsion/Propellers: .diesel(14,444 kW)/2	are sold for single occupancy	Onboard currency: . . . . .UK£

Modest ship, food and service, for frugal cruisers.

OVERVIEW. This is a comfortable vessel and, with its deep draft, rides well in unkind sea conditions. It appeals to couples and single travelers of mature years who enjoy visiting interesting destinations in the comfort of a ship that is traditional in style, unpretentious yet pleasing, and without much entertainment or organized parlor games. It operates adults-only cruises from the UK with Tilbury (London International Cruise Terminal) as its home port.

BERLITZ'S RATINGS		
	Possible	Achieved
Ship	500	273
Accommodation	200	120
Food	400	198
Service	400	219
Entertainment	100	56
Cruise	400	216

OVERALL SCORE
1,082 points out of 2,000

As soon as you walk aboard, you feel a warm, welcoming, homely ambience. There is a wide range of public rooms, most of which are arranged on one horizontal deck. A sense of spaciousness pervades, as most have high ceilings. The interior decor is quite tasteful, with careful use of mirrored surfaces and colors that do not clash but aren't boring. The subdued lighting helps maintain an air of calmness and relaxation.

Now more than 40 years old, the ship is still in decent shape. Indeed, it's

THE SHIP. Marco Polo was built as one of five sister ships for the Russian/Ukrainian fleet. Originally designed in 1966 to re-open the Leningrad to Montreal transatlantic route in 1966, inoperative since 1949, it has a traditional "real-ship" profile, an extremely strong ice-strengthened hull, and huge storage spaces for long voyages.

The ship passsed to Norwegian Cruise Line in 1998, and in 2007 to new Greek owners. In 2008, it began a charter operation for Germany's Transocean Tours, which had chartered it 20 years previously and now intended to operate it until 2012. Instead, Transocean Tours sub-chartered it to Cruise & Maritime Voyages, the UK's newest cruise line, and it was given a £3 million refit/refurbishment in 2009.

Marco Polo is fitted with the latest navigational aids and biological waste treatment center, and carries 10 Zodiac landing craft for in-depth shore trips in eco-sensitive areas. There are two large, forward-facing open-deck viewing areas, and a helicopter pad. The teakwood-decked aft swimming pool/lido deck area is kept in good condition. Joggers and walkers can circle around the ship – not on the promenade deck, but one deck above, although this goes past vast air intakes that are noisy, and the walkway is narrow.

in better shape than many ships only 10 years old, and its interiors are constantly being refurbished and refreshed. It operates well-planned destination-intensive cruises, and offers really good value for money in very comfortable, unpretentious but tasteful surroundings, while an accommodating crew helps to make a cruise a pleasant, no-hassle experience. Gratuities are automatically applied to your onboard account.

Passenger niggles? There is no observation lounge with forward-facing views over the bows. There are many "lips" or raised thresholds, so you need to be on your guard when walking through the ship and particularly when negotiating the exterior stairways, which could prove difficult for mobility-limited passengers.

ACCOMMODATION. The cabins, which come in 15 price grades, depending on location and size, are a profusion of different sizes and configurations. All are pleasingly decorated, practical units with good, solid, rich wood cabinetry, wood and mirror-fronted closets, adequate drawer and storage space, TV set, thin cotton bathrobe (upper grades only), and bathroom-mounted hairdryer and non-vacuum, nonnoisy toilets. Carpets, curtains and bedspreads are all nicely color-coordinated. Weak points include extremely poor sound insulation between cabins – you can probably hear you neighbors brushing their hair – and the fact that the bathrooms are small, with little storage space for toiletries, which is a particular concern during long cruises.

The largest accommodation is found in two suites: Dynasty and Mandarin, on Columbus Deck. These have a separate living room, and marble bathroom with tub/ shower, walk-in closet, refrigerator, and a TV set/DVD unit. Slightly smaller are two Junior Suites, on Pacific Deck. All suites have superior locations with forward-facing views over the ship's bow.

Also quite comfortable are the Superior Deluxe ocean-view cabins that have two lower beds (some can be converted to a queen-size bed), marble bathroom with tub/ shower, and refrigerator.

Some cabins on Upper Deck and Sky Deck have lifeboat-obstructed views. It would be advisable to avoid cabins 310/312 as these are located close to the engine room doorway and the noise level is considerable. No cabins have a balcony because the ship was built for long-distance ocean/sea crossings before they became popular.

CUISINE/DINING. The *Waldorf*, in the ship's center, is nicely decorated in soft pastel colors, practical in design, and functions well, but it has a low ceiling, is noisy, and the tables are very close together. There are two seatings, with tables for two to 10, and good place settings/china. The food itself is of a modest standard, but presentation, quality and taste could certainly be improved. The wine and prices are reasonable, although most wines are young.

Marco's Restaurant is for informal self-serve breakfasts and lunches – there is seating inside as well as outdoors around the ship's single, aft swimming pool. On some evenings during each cruise, it also becomes an alternative dining spot for about 75 people. Reservations are required, but there is no extra charge. A 15% gratuity is added to all bar and wine accounts.

ENTERTAINMENT. The Ambassador Lounge is the principal venue for shows, cabaret acts, and lectures. A single-level room, it has banquette seating and fairly decent sightlines, although several pillars obstruct the view from some seats. Entertainment is low-key and low-budget, and consists of cabaret acts such as singers, magicians, and comedians. There's live music for social dancing and listening in several bars and cocktail lounges.

SPA/FITNESS. This is an older ship that was built when spa and wellbeing facilities were not really thought about. A Health Spa was added in a later refit. It is located aft on Upper Deck, and contains a gymnasium – it's not large, but there are a few treadmills, exercycles, and some muscle-toning equipment. There's also a beauty salon, a sauna, changing facilities, and treatment rooms for massages, facials, and other body pampering treatments.

The spa is operated by Mandara Spa, and treatments have an Asian flavor – Indonesian facials, coconut body polish, aromatherapy massages.

WASTE DISPOSAL

Environmental concerns are taken very seriously by the cruise industry. Cruise ships must be capable of efficient handling of garbage and waste materials, as trash generated by passengers and crew must be managed, stored, and disposed of efficiently and economically. The larger the ship, the more waste is created, and the greater the need for reliable disposal systems.

The sheer magnitude of waste materials can be highly problematic, especially on long cruises. If solid waste is not burnable, or cannot be disposed of overboard (this must be biodegradable), it must be stored for later off-loading and disposal on land.

The latest cruise ships have "zero-discharge" facilities. These include incinerators and food waste handling systems that include vacuum transportation from feeding stations in all galleys and food preparation areas, recycling and storage systems for ash, glass, metal and paper. But many older cruise ships have outdated garbage handling equipment.

Food waste is typically sent to a pulping machine that has been partially filled with water. Cutting mechanisms reduce the waste and allow it to pass through a special sizing ring to be pumped directly overboard or into a holding tank or an incinerator when the ship is within three-mile limits.

Marina
★★★★★

Size: ....Mid-Size Ship	Total Crew: 800	Cabins (wheelchair accessible): 6
Tonnage: 66,048	Passengers	Wheelchair accessibility: ....Good
Lifestyle: ....Premium	(lower beds/all berths): 1,258/1,258	Cabin Current: ....110, 220 volts
Cruise Line: ....Oceania Cruises	Passenger Space Ratio	Elevators: 6
Former Names: ....none	(lower beds/all berths): 51.6/51.6	Casino (gaming tables): ....Yes
Builder: ....Fincantieri (Italy)	Crew/Passenger Ratio	Slot Machines: ....Yes
Original Cost: ....$530 million	(lower beds/all berths): 1.5/1.5	Swimming Pools (outdoors): 1
Entered Service: ....Jan 2011	Cabins (total): 629	Swimming Pools (indoors): 0
Registry: ....Marshall Islands	Size Range (sq ft/m): 172.2–2,000/	Whirlpools: 3
Length (ft/m): 776.5/236.7	16.0–185.0	Self-Service Launderette: ....Yes
Beam (ft/m): 105.3/32.1	Cabins (outside view): 611	Dedicated Cinema/Seats: ....No
Draft (ft/m): 24.2/7.4	Cabins (interior/no view): 18	Library: ....Yes
Propulsion/Propellers: .....diesel-electric	Cabins (for one person): 0	Onboard currency: ....US$
Passenger Decks: 11	Cabins (with private balcony): 593	

Premium country club style for mature-age cruisers.

OVERVIEW. *Marina* exudes the same intimacy as Oceania Cruises' three smaller ships, *Insignia* (due to leave the fleet in April 2012), *Nautica*, and *Regatta* – in other words, it's really homey and comfortable, although you will need to walk a little more. It will suit mature-age adults who appreciate refined quality and style, with no lines but plenty of space, plus excellent cuisine and service, in a semi-casual setting with realistic pricing.

BERLITZ'S RATINGS		
	Possible	Achieved
Ship	500	450
Accommodation	200	182
Food	400	336
Service	400	322
Entertainment	100	82
Cruise	400	329
OVERALL SCORE		
1,701 points out of 2,000		

THE SHIP. Built in 55 blocks, *Marina* is the first newbuild for this growing small cruise line. Its profile is quite handsome, with a nicely rounded front and topped by a swept-back funnel. Able to cruise at a speed 25% faster than the three other ships in the fleet, it can operate cruises over longer distances.

Oceania Cruises has been careful to try to keep the warm and tasteful "country house" decor style for which it has become known – the smaller ships were designed by the Scottish designer John McNeece – together with an uncomplicated layout that's easy to master quickly. *Marina* is an interior decorator's delight, and high-quality furnishings and soft furnishings have been provided throughout the public rooms. It's opulent, decadent, and elegant.

The interior focal point is the stunning wrought-iron and Lalique glass horseshoe-shaped staircase in the main lobby. Public rooms include nine bars and lounges. There is a 2,000-book library, set on the port side of the funnel housing, which also contains the staffed Oceania@Sea computer center, and Barista's coffee bar/lounge, with excellent Italian coffee. The Monte Carlo Casino is located between two bars – the Grand Bar and Martinis – and has its own soft lavender-colored Casino Bar. Martinis houses a beautiful Dakota Jackson special edition Steinway baby grand piano – a baby that cost well over $100,000. There are three boutiques, and a choice of several dining venues.

Something new for Oceania Cruises is the Culinary Center, a cooking demonstration kitchen and 24 workstations run in conjunction with the US-based *Bon Appétit* magazine – there's a fee for each of several cookery classes, but at least you get to eat your creations. An Artist's Loft hosts constantly changing artists – bring your own paintbrushes.

Other classes may include photography, needlepoint, scrapbooking, drawing, and quilting. If you like art, look for the genuine Picassos on board; there are 16 of them, including six in the casino.

The dress code is "elegant country club attire" – no pyjamas or track suits, but no ties either. In other words, perfect for the Aventura, Palm Springs or Scottsdale fraternity, but not the Monte Carlo set. Despite a couple of niggly items, the ship just manages to squeeze into the "Berlitz 5-Star Club." A 15% gratuity is added to bar and spa accounts.

ACCOMMODATION. There are 17 price categories, with four suite grades: Owner's suite; Oceania suite; Vista suite; Penthouse suite – and four cabin grades: Concierge-Level Verandah cabin; Verandah cabin; De-Luxe Ocean-View cabin; and Interior cabin. Price depends on size and location, but all have one thing in common – a good-sized bathroom with tub and separate but small shower enclosure.

Around 96% of all accommodation has teak-decked balconies. All suites/cabins have a bathtub and shower, and his 'n' hers toiletry cabinets. There's no tie rack in the closets because the dress code is "country club casual." The decor includes chocolate brown, cream and white – the sort of earthy colors that don't jar the senses. All suites and cabins have dark wood cabinetry with rounded edges.

Standard veranda cabins measure 282 sq. ft (26 sq. meters). Veranda and Concierge-level cabins have a sitting area and teak balcony with faux wicker furniture. Concierge-level grades get L'Occitane toiletries.

Penthouse Suites measure 420 sq. ft (39 sq. meters) with living/dining room separate from the sleeping area, walk-in closet and bathroom with a double vanity. The large veranda has a hot tub.

Oceania Suites measure about 1,030 sq.ft (96 sq. metres) and have a living room, dining room, separate bedroom, walk-in closet, teak-decked balcony with Jacuzzi tub, main bathroom, and a second bathroom for guests.

Vista Suites range from 1,200–1,500 sq. ft (111–139 sq. meters) and offer the same features as Oceania Suites but add floor-to-ceiling windows overlooking the bow.

The **Owner's Suite**, at more than 2,000 sq. ft (186 sq. meters), spans the ship's entire beam. It is decked out in furniture, fabrics, lighting and bedding from the Ralph Lauren Home collection with design by New York-based Tocar, Inc. It is outfitted with a Yamaha baby grand piano, private fitness room, laptop computers, Bose audio system, and a teak-decked balcony with Jacuzzi tub.

Suite-category occupants get niceties like Champagne on arrival, 1,000-thread-count bed linen, 42-inch plasma TV sets, Hermès and Clarins bath amenities, butler service and ensuite delivery from any of the ship's restaurants. Amenities include Tranquility beds, wi-fi laptop computer, refrigerated mini bar with unlimited free soft drinks and bottled water replenished daily, personal safe, writing desk, cotton bathrobes, slippers and marble and granite bathroom. Priority check-in and early embarkation and priority luggage delivery are extra perks.

Occupants of Owner's, Vista, Oceania and Penthouse suites can have in-suite course-by-course dining from any restaurant menu, making private dining possible as a change to being in the restaurants.

Some grades get access to an Executive Lounge or Concierge Lounge. These are great little hideaways, with sofas, internet-connect computers, Continental breakfast items, soft drinks and magazines.

Self-service launderettes are on each accommodation deck – useful for long voyages.

CUISINE. Six main open-seating dining venues provide plenty of choice, enough even for long cruises, although banquette seating in some venues does not evoke the image of premium dining as much as individual seating does. Also, it would be hard to describe some of the alternative dining venues as intimate. This is, however, a foodie's ship,

with really high-quality ingredients and effectively fancy presentation. Particularly notable are the delicious breads, rolls, croissants and brioches – all made on board from French flower and d'Isigny butter.

The *Grand Dining Room* has 566 seats, and a domed, or raised, central ceiling. Versace bone china, Christofle silver, and fine linens are used. Canyon Ranch spa dishes are available for all meals.

French celebrity chef Jacques Pépin, Oceania's executive culinary director, has his first sea-going restaurant, *Jacques*, with 124 seats. It has antique oak flooring, antique flatware and Lalique glassware, and offers fine dining in an elegant but informal setting, with roast free-range meats, nine classic French dessert items and a choice of 12 AOC cheeses.

Polo Grill, with 134 seats, serves steaks and seafood, including Oceania's signature 32-ounce bone-in King's Cut prime rib. The setting is classic traditional steakhouse, with dark wood paneling and classic white tablecloths, although the tables are a little close together.

The 124-seat *Toscana* features Italian-style cuisine, served on Versace china.

Privée, with seating for up to 10 in a private setting, invites exclusivity for its seven-course dégustation menu.

La Réserve offersa choice of two seven-course small-portion dégustation menus (discovery, and explorer), paired with wines. With just 24 seats, it's really intimate.

The *Terrace Café* is the casual self-serve buffet-style venue; outdoors, as an extension of the café is *Tapas on the Terrace* – good for light bites (although the ceiling is low, and it can be very noisy).

Red Ginger is a specialty restaurant which offers "classic and contemporary" Asian cuisine; the setting is visually refined, with ebony and dark wood finishes, but the banquette-style seating lets the venue down. Your waiter will ask you to choose your chopsticks from a lacquered presentation box.

The poolside *Waves Grill*, shaded from the sun, serves Angus beef burgers, fishburgers, veggie burgers, reuben sandwiches, seafood and other fast food, cooked to order.

Baristas coffee bar overlooks the pool deck and has excellent illy Italian coffee.

ENTERTAINMENT. The 600-seat Marina Lounge spans two decks, with tiered amphitheater-style seating. It's more cabaret-style entertainment than big production shows, in keeping with the cruise line's traditions.

SPA/FITNESS. The Canyon Ranch Spa Club provides wellness and personal spa treatments. The facility includes a fitness center, beauty salon, several treatment rooms (including a couples room), thalassotherapy pool (hot tub), and sauna and steam rooms. A jogging track is located aft of the funnel, above two of the specialty restaurants and, sensibly, away from all accommodation decks.

Mariner of the Seas
★★★★

Size: . . . . .Large Resort Ship	Passenger Decks: 14	Cabins (wheelchair accessible): 26
Tonnage: 137,276	Total Crew: 1,185	Wheelchair accessibility: . . . . .Best
Lifestyle: . . . . .Standard	Passengers	Cabin Current: . . . . .110 volts
Cruise Line: Royal Caribbean International	(lower beds/all berths): 3,114/3,840	Elevators: . . . . .14 (6 glass-enclosed)
Former Names: . . . . .none	Passenger Space Ratio	Casino (gaming tables): . . . . .Yes
Builder: . . .Kvaerner Masa-Yards (Finland)	(lower beds/all berths): 44.0/35.7	Slot Machines: . . . . .Yes
Original Cost: . . . .$500 million	Crew/Passenger Ratio	Swimming Pools (outdoors): 3
Entered Service: . . . . .Nov 2004	(lower beds/all berths): 2.6/3.2	Swimming Pools (indoors): 0
Registry: . . . . .The Bahamas	Cabins (total): 1,557	Whirlpools: 6
Length (ft/m): 1,020.6/311.1	Size Range (sq ft/m): 151.0–1,358.0/	Self-Service Launderette: . . . . .No
Beam (ft/m): 155.5/47.4	14.0–126.1	Dedicated Cinema/Seats: . . . . .No
Draft (ft/m): 28.8/8.8	Cabins (outside view): 939	Library: . . . . .Yes
Propulsion/Propellers: . . . . .diesel-electric	Cabins (interior/no view): 618	Onboard currency: . . . . .US$
(75,600kW)/3 pods (2 azimuthing,	Cabins (for one person): 0	
1 fixed/14 MW each)	Cabins (with private balcony): 765	

A large resort ship for family-friendly casual cruising.

OVERVIEW. This ship dwarfs most other cruise ships in size, but in terms of personal service, the reverse tends to be the case unless you happen to reside in a top suite. But Royal Caribbean International does try hard to provide a good standard of programmed service from its hotel service staff. Take lots of extra pennies – you'll need them to pay for all the extra-cost items.

THE SHIP. *Mariner of the Seas* is a stunning, large, floating leisure resort, sister to *Adventure of the Seas, Explorer of the Seas, Navigator of the Seas* and *Voyager of the Seas*. It has a healthy passenger space ratio (the amount of space per passenger) and extensive facilities such as a regulation-size ice-skating rink, Studio B, with real, not fake, ice.

For full details of the ship's facilities, see the entry for *Explorer of the Seas* on page 369.

FAMILIES. "Aquanauts" is for 3–5 year-olds; "Explorers" is for 6–8-year-olds; "Voyagers" is for 9–12-year-olds. Optix is a dedicated area for teenagers, including a daytime club with computers, soda bar, and dance floor. "Challenger's Arcade" has an array of video games. Paint and Clay is an arts and crafts center for younger children. Adjacent is Adventure Beach, an area for all the family; it includes swimming pools, a water slide and game areas outdoors.

ACCOMMODATION. There is an extensive range of 22 cabin categories in four major groupings: Premium ocean-view suites and cabins, Promenade-view (interior-view) cabins, Ocean-view cabins, and Interior (no-view) cab-

ins. For a detailed description of their facilities, see the entry for *Explorer of the Seas* on page 369.

CUISINE. The main dining room, with a seating capacity of 1,919, is set on three levels: *Rhapsody in Blue, Top Hat and Tails,* and *Sound of Music,* all offering exactly the same menus and food. Choose your seating options when you book. The alternative dining options for casual meals at all hours include *Café Promenade, Windjammer Café, Island Grill, Portofino, Johnny Rockets,* and *Sprinkles.*

For a detailed assessment of their food, service, and ambience, see the entry for *Explorer of the Seas.*

ENTERTAINMENT. The 1,350-seat Savoy showlounge is a stunning room that could well be the equal of many such rooms on land. In addition, the ship has a whole array of cabaret acts. The strongest of these perform in the main showlounge, while lesser acts are presented in the Lotus Lounge, also the venue for late-night adult comedy.

For a review of the shows and their quality, see the entry for *Explorer of the Seas.*

SPA/FITNESS. The large ShipShape health and fitness spa measures 15,000 sq. ft (1,400 sq. meters). For fdetails of its facilities and other sports facilities such as a rock-climbing wall, a roller-blading track and a dive-and-snorkel shop, see the entry for *Explorer of the Seas.*

● **For more extensive general information about the Royal Caribbean experience, see pages 152–6.**

BERLITZ'S RATINGS

	Possible	Achieved
Ship	500	418
Accommodation	200	150
Food	400	222
Service	400	277
Entertainment	100	83
Cruise	400	307

OVERALL SCORE
1,457 points out of 2,000

Mein Schiff 1
★★★★

Size: . . . . .Large Resort Ship	Passenger Decks: 10	Cabins (with private balcony): 430
Tonnage: 77,713	Total Crew: 780	Cabins (wheelchair accessible): 8
Lifestyle: . . . . .Standard	Passengers	Wheelchair accessibility: . . . . .Good
Cruise Line: . . . . .TUI Cruises	(lower beds/all berths): 1,948/2,725	Cabin Current: . . . . .110 and 220 volts
Former Names: . .Celebrity Galaxy, Galaxy	Passenger Space Ratio	Elevators: 10
Builder: . . . . .Meyer Werft (Germany)	(lower beds/all berths): 39.8/28.5	Casino (gaming tables): . . . . .Yes
Original Cost: . . . .$320 million	Crew/Passenger Ratio	Slot Machines: . . . . .Yes
Entered Service: . . . .Dec 1996/May 2009	(lower beds/all berths): 2.0/3.4	Swimming Pools (outdoors): 2
Registry: .Malta	Cabins (total): 974	Swimming Pools (indoors): 0
Length (ft/m): 865.8/263.9	Size Range (sq ft/m): 169.0–1,219.0/	Whirlpools: 4
Beam (ft/m): 105.6/32.20	15.7–113.2	Self-Service Launderette: . . . . .No
Draft (ft/m): 25.2/7.70	Cabins (outside view): 665	Dedicated Cinema/Seats: Yes/200
Propulsion/Propellers: . . . . .diesel	Cabins (interior/no view): 309	Library: . . . . .Yes
(31.5 MW)/2	Cabins (for one person): 0	Onboard currency: . . . . .Euros

Contemporary style for family-friendly cruising.

OVERVIEW. *Mein Schiff 1* is for German-speaking families with children who want to cruise aboard a large ship with a contemporary environment, good itineraries, decent food and good European-style service from a well-trained crew that delivers a product that's fresh and surprisingly good. In fact, the product is worth much more than the cruise fare charged when you compare it with several other large-ship cruise lines.

BERLITZ'S RATINGS		
	Possible	Achieved
Ship	500	414
Accommodation	200	165
Food	400	282
Service	400	308
Entertainment	100	71
Cruise	400	306
OVERALL SCORE		
1,546 points out of 2,000		

THE SHIP. *Mein Schiff,* originally built for Celebrity Cruises as *Galaxy,* was transferred in 2009 to newcomer TUI Cruises (part of TUI Travel – Europe's largest tour operator) specifically for German-speaking passengers, in a joint venture with Royal Caribbean Cruises, parent of Royal Caribbean International. The ship underwent a major conversion at that time. Its name ("My Ship") was suggested by several entrants to a magazine competition; the winner, whose name was drawn from a hat, was Oliver Krimmel, a Stuttgart designer.

This large, all-inclusive resort ship has just about all you need for an enjoyable and rewarding cruise experience, and provides competition for AIDA Cruises, whose ships, by comparison, do not have a traditional dining room, and have few service staff. TUI Cruises has got the onboard product just about right for German-speaking passengers, with many more dining and eating choices and more class and style than AIDA's ships, and with far better food and plenty of snappily-dressed service personnel. With 10 bars, four restaurants and six bistros, and good facilities for families, *Mein Schiff 1* has become the benchmark for a high-value, full-service cruise vacation in Germany.

The ship has good tender loading platforms. But, although there are more than 4.5 acres (1.8 hectares) of space on the open decks, it does seem a little small and crowded when the ship is full. Some 10 charming two-person cabanas can be rented on an upper, outside deck, with great ocean views, but insulated from the life that goes on around the ship.

Inside, a four-deck-high main foyer houses the reception desk and shore excursion station. There's a small, dedicated cinema, which doubles as a conference and meeting center with all the latest audio-visual technology, including simultaneous translation and headsets for the hearing-impaired.

There are still one or two pieces of the whimsical works of art originally chosen by Christina Chandris, whose family founded Celebrity Cruises. The interior decor is at once contemporary in style, but with many restful colors and combinations throughout.

Relaxation is a key element of the product, and *Mein Schiff 1* is equipped with individual hammocks in various locations, including on cabin balconies as well as in public areas. Additionally, "Meditation Islands" are installed on deck: the ship's rail is fitted with mini-balconies, equipped with special blinds. Here, passengers are able to enjoy a private space for relaxation.

Making it even more user-friendly for families is the all-inclusive pricing introduced in 2010, though this excludes the extra-cost restaurants Richard's Fines Essen, Blaue Welt Sushi Bar and the Surf 'n' Turf steakhouse and also excursions and spa treatments. The dress code throughout the ship is smart casual.

ACCOMMODATION. There are 10 price grades, depending on the size and location of your living space, but the accommodation is very comfortable throughout. Every cabin has its own Nespresso coffee machine, which takes pre-portioned packets of espresso coffee. The first two are included, but any additional packets cost €1 each. All accommodation grades are designated no-smoking.

Most suites with private balconies have floor-to-ceiling windows and sliding doors to balconies, and a few have outward opening doors. Suite-grade accommodation gets European duvets on the beds, instead of sheets and blankets. A balcony massage service is also available – it's worth it. Suite occupants get special cards to open their doors, plus priority service throughout the ship and for embarkation and disembarkation, free cappuccino/espresso coffees served by a butler, welcome champagne, flowers, video recorder, and picnic baskets as required. Suite occupants also get a private, 100-seat concierge lounge/bar and social venue (the "X" Lounge) atop the ship, with great ocean views – a good place for reading a book during the day.
Penthouse Suites: These two suites, located amidships, are the largest. Each is 1,173 sq. ft (108.9 sq. meters), and has its own butler's pantry. There is an inter-connecting door so that it can link to the suite next door to become an impressive 1,515-sq. ft (141-sq. meter) apartment.

Most of the Deck 10 suites and cabins are of generous proportions, are beautifully equipped, and have balconies with full floor-to-ceiling partitions, and large flat-screen TV sets. The Sky Deck suites are also excellent, and most of them have huge balconies; unfortunately, the partitions are not quite of the floor-to-ceiling type, so you can hear your neighbors. Also included are wall clock, large floor-to-ceiling mirrors, marble-topped vanity/writing desk, excellent closet and drawer space, and even dimmer-controlled ceiling lights.
Standard Outside-view/Interior Cabins: All of the standard interior and outside cabins are of a good size – larger than those aboard the ships of AIDA Cruises, for example – and come nicely furnished with twin beds that convert to a queen-size unit. The bathrooms are spacious and well equipped, and have generous-size showers, hairdryers, and space for personal toiletries. Baby-monitoring telephones are provided in all cabins. There are no cabins for single occupancy.

CUISINE. Restaurants and bistros range from self-serve buffet style to service, with a focus on healthy eating. There is no pre-defined seating, so you can dine when you want, and with whomever you want – good for multi-generational families. The emphasis is on healthy food, including power food, brain food, soul food, erotic food, new food (quinoa, soya and tofu dishes), including fresh fish.

The *Atlantik Restaurant* is a stunning, two-level dining hall – somewhat reminiscent of the dining halls aboard the ocean liners of the 1930s – with a grand staircase that flows between both levels and perimeter alcoves that provide more intimate dining spaces. However, there's one big difference, in that this restaurant has two-meter-wide trapeze bars built into its center (talk about swinging food – or is that food for swingers?). Tables are for two, four, six, eight, or 10.
Alternative dining venue: *Richard's Gourmet Restaurant* is an à la carte, reservations-only venue, with a calming, restful wood-laden interior where high-quality fine dining and service can be found.
Other dining venues: *Surf 'n' Turf Steakhouse* serves premium steaks and grilled seafood, with aged beef commanding different price points.

In a venue covered by a retractable glass dome, in the aft section of the ship, three eateries, combined with a communal bar provide completely different food experiences: *Bistro La Vela* for Italian cuisine, including an "active" pasta cooking station, and pizza; *Gosch Sylt*, for fresh fish and seafood; *Tapas Y Mas*, for tapas-tasting dishes. This venue is a most popular place to meet the fashionable set.

Other dining spots around the ship include: *La Vida Sana*, for wellness cuisine; *Blaue Welt* (Blue World) Sushi Bar, on the upper level of the atrium; *Vino*, a wine tasting bar; and a coffee lounge set around the atrium lobby, for specialty coffees and pastries.

For informal breakfasts and lunches, the two-level self-serve *Anckelmannsplatz Buffet* – the name comes from the road on which the TUI Cruises offices are located in Hamburg – is the place to go. There are several serving counters and "active" food islands; the venue has warm wood-accented decor, and eight bay windows provide some prime seating spots. There are also two poolside grills – one located adjacent to the midships pools, the other wedged into an area aft of the swimming pool/hot tub cluster.

ENTERTAINMENT. The Theater is a 927-seat showlounge spanning two decks, with seating on both main and cantilevered balcony levels. There are good sightlines from all seats. The large-scale production shows are excellent. It has a revolving stage, "hard" curtain and large fly tower.

SPA/FITNESS. The Spa and More, located at the front of the ship one deck above the navigation bridge, has 18,299 sq. ft (1,700 sq. meters) of space. It includes a large fitness/exercise area with all the latest muscle machines and video cycles; beauty salon; thalassotherapy pool; seven treatment rooms; a Rasul room, for Mediterranean mud and gentle steam bathing: and private "spa suites." Private "spa suites," with fine, relaxing views are located above the ship's navigation bridge and can be rented for the morning, afternoon, or the whole day. Atop the ship at the front is a healthy FKK (*freikorperkulture*) deck for the naked sunbathing set.

Mein Schiff 2
★★★★

Size: ....Large Resort Ship	Total Crew: 909	Wheelchair accessibility: ....Good
Tonnage: 77,713	Passengers	Cabin Current: ....110 and 220 volts
Lifestyle: ....Premium	(lower beds/all berths): 1,870/2,681	Elevators: 10
Cruise Line: ....TUI Cruises	Passenger Space Ratio	Casino (gaming tables): ....Yes
Former Names: *Celebrity Mercury, Mercury*	(lower beds/all berths):.......41.5/28.9	Slot Machines: ....Yes
Builder: ....Meyer Werft (Germany)	Crew/Passenger Ratio	Swimming Pools (outdoors): 2
Original Cost: ....$320 million	(lower beds/all berths):..........2.0/2.9	Swimming Pools (indoors): 1
Entered Service: ....Nov 1997/May 2011	Cabins (total): 935	indoor/outdoor (glass dome)
Registry: ....Malta	Size Range (sq ft/m): 171.0–1,219.0/	Whirlpools: 4
Length (ft/m): 865.8/263.90	15.8–113.2	Self-Service Launderette: ....No
Beam (ft/m): 105.6/32.20	Cabins (outside view): 639	Dedicated Cinema/Seats: Yes/183
Draft (ft/m): 25.2/7.70	Cabins (interior/no view): 296	Library: ....Yes
Propulsion/Propellers: ....diesel	Cabins (for one person): 0	Onboard currency: ....Euros
(31,500 kW)/2	Cabins (with private balcony): 220	
Passenger Decks: 10	Cabins (wheelchair accessible): 8	

A stylish large ship for family-friendly cruising.

OVERVIEW. *Mein Schiff II* is for German-speaking families with children who want to cruise aboard a large ship with a contemporary environment, good itineraries, great food and good European-style service from a well-trained crew that delivers a cruise that's fresh and surprisingly good. The product is worth much more than the cruise fare charged when compared to several other large-ship cruise lines.

THE SHIP. *Mein Schiff 2*, originally built as *Mercury* for Celebrity Cruises, was transferred in 2011 to newcomer TUI Cruises (part of TUI Travel, Europe's largest tour operator) specifically for German-speaking passengers, in a joint venture with Royal Caribbean Cruises, parent of Royal Caribbean International. The ship underwent a major conversion at that time.

This large, all-inclusive resort ship has just about all you need for an enjoyable and rewarding cruise experience, and provides competition for AIDA Cruises, whose ships, by comparison, do not have a traditional dining room, and have few service staff. TUI Cruises has got the onboard product absolutely spot-on for youthful German-speaking passengers, with many more dining and eating choices and more class and style than AIDA's ships, and with far better food and plenty of snappily-dressed service personnel. There are 10 bars, four restaurants and six bistros, and good facilities for families. Indeed, *Mein Schiff 2* is on track to become the benchmark for a high-value cruise vacation in Germany since the decor and finish are even smarter than they are aboard sister ship *Mein Schiff 1*.

The ship has good tender loading platforms. But,

BERLITZ'S RATINGS

	Possible	Achieved
Ship	500	406
Accommodation	200	162
Food	400	278
Service	400	306
Entertainment	100	71
Cruise	400	295

OVERALL SCORE
1,518 points out of 2,000

although there are more than 4.5 acres (1.8 hectares) of space on the open decks, it does seem a little small and crowded when the ship is full. Some 10 charming two-person cabanas can be rented on an upper, outside deck, with great ocean views, but insulated from the life that goes on around the ship.

Inside, a four-deck-high main foyer houses the reception desk and shore excursion station. There's a small cinema, which doubles as a conference and meeting center with the latest audio-visual technology, including simultaneous translation and headsets for the hearing-impaired.

There are still one or two pieces of the whimsical works of art originally chosen by Christina Chandris, whose family founded Celebrity Cruises. The interior decor is at once contemporary in style, but with many restful colors and combinations throughout.

Mein Schiff 2 has individual hammocks in various outdoor locations, including on cabin balconies. "Meditation Islands" are also installed on the open deck: the ship's rail is fitted with mini-balconies, equipped with special blinds, for private relaxation space.

Making it even more user-friendly for families is the all-inclusive pricing, though this excludes spa treatments, excursions and the extra-cost restaurants: Richard's Fines Essen, Blaue Welt Sushi Bar, and Surf 'n' Turf steakhouse. The dress code is smart casual.

ACCOMMODATION. There are 10 price grades, depending on the size and location of your living space, but the accommodation is very comfortable. Every cabin has its own Nespresso coffee machine, which takes pre-portioned packets of espresso coffee. The first two are included, but any additional packets cost €1 each. All accommodation grades are designated no-smoking.

Most suites with private balconies have floor-to-ceiling windows and sliding doors to balconies, and a few have outward opening doors. Suite-grade accommodation gets European duvets on the beds instead of sheets and blankets. A balcony massage service is also available – it's worth it. Suite occupants get special cards to open their doors, plus priority service throughout the ship and for embarkation and disembarkation, free cappuccino and espresso coffees served by a butler, welcome champagne, flowers, video recorder, and picnic baskets as required. Suite occupants also get a private, 100-seat concierge lounge/bar and social venue (the "X" Lounge) atop the ship, with great ocean views – a good place for reading a book during the day.

Penthouse Suites: These two suites, located amidships, are the largest. Each is 1,173 sq. ft (108.9 sq. meters), and has its own butler's pantry. There is an inter-connecting door so that it can link to the suite next door to become an impressive 1,515-sq. ft (141-sq. meter) apartment.

Most of the Deck 10 suites and cabins are generously proportioned, beautifully equipped, and have balconies with full floor-to-ceiling partitions, and large flat-screen TV sets. The Sky Deck suites are also excellent, and most of them have huge balconies; unfortunately, the partitions are not quite of the floor-to-ceiling type, so you can hear your neighbors. Also included are wall clock, large floor-to-ceiling mirrors, marble-topped vanity/writing desk, excellent closet and drawer space, and even dimmer-controlled ceiling lights.

Standard Outside-view/Interior Cabins: All of the standard interior and outside cabins are of a good size – larger than those aboard the ships of AIDA Cruises, for example – and come nicely furnished with twin beds that convert to a queen-size unit. The bathrooms are spacious and well equipped, and have generous-size showers, hairdryers, and space for toiletries. Baby-monitoring telephones are provided in all cabins. Mineral stones provide filtration for the ship's own bottled water. There are no cabins for single occupancy.

CUISINE. Restaurants and bistros range from self-serve buffet style to service. There is no pre-defined seating, so you can dine when you want, and with whomever you want – good for multi-generational families. The emphasis is on healthy food, including power food, brain food, soul food, erotic food, new food (quinoa, soya and tofu dishes), including fresh fish.

The *Atlantik Restaurant* is a lovely, two-level dining hall – somewhat reminiscent of the dining halls aboard the ocean liners of the 1930s – with a grand staircase that flows between both levels and perimeter alcoves that provide more intimate dining spaces. Tables are for two, four, six, eight, or 10.

Richard's Gourmet Restaurant, an alternative dining venue, is à la carte and reservations-only, with a restful wood-laden interior and high-quality fine dining and service. A dégustation menu and three specialty vegetarian menus are also available.

Surf 'n' Turf Steakhouse serves premium steaks and grilled seafood, with aged beef commanding different price points. In an area covered by a retractable glass dome in the aft section of the ship, three eateries and a communal bar provide very different food experiences: *Bistro La Vela* for Italian cuisine, including an "active" pasta cooking station, and pizza; *Gosch Sylt* for fresh fish and seafood (it's hugely popular, so make a reservation early); and *Tapas Y Mas* for tapas-tasting dishes. This venue is a most popular place to meet the fashionable set.

Other dining spots include: *La Vida Sana* for Italian cuisine; *Blaue Welt* (Blue World) Sushi Bar, on the upper level of the atrium; *Vino*, a wine tasting bar; *Cliff 24*, a 24-hour poolside grill; and a coffee lounge set around the atrium lobby for specialty coffees and pastries.

For informal breakfasts and lunches, the two-level self-serve *Anckelmannsplatz Buffet* – the name comes from the road on which the TUI Cruises offices are located in Hamburg – is the place to go. There are several serving counters and "active" food islands; the venue has warm wood-accented decor, and eight bay windows provide some prime seating spots. There are also two poolside grills – one adjacent to the midships pools, the other wedged into an area aft of the swimming pool/hot tub cluster.

ENTERTAINMENT. The Theater is a 927-seat showlounge spanning two decks, with seating on both main and canti-levered balcony levels. There are good sightlines from all seats. The large-scale production shows are excellent. It has a revolving stage, "hard" curtain and large fly tower.

SPA/FITNESS. The Spa and More, located at the front of the ship one deck above the navigation bridge, has 18,299 sq. ft (1,700 sq. meters) of space. It includes a large fitness/exercise area with the latest muscle machines and video cycles; a beauty salon; a thalassotherapy pool; seven treatment rooms; and a Rasul room for Mediterranean mud and gentle steam bathing. Private "spa suites," with fine, relaxing views, are located above the ship's navigation bridge and can be rented for the morning, afternoon, or the whole day. The balcony adjacent to the sauna is designated as a *freikorperkulture* (FKK) deck for nude sunbathing

Size: ....Small Ship	Propulsion/Propellers: diesel/2	Cabins (for one person): 4
Tonnage: 12,500	(3,480 kW)/2	Cabins (with private balcony): 12
Lifestyle: ....Standard	Passenger Decks: 6	Cabins (wheelchair accessible): 2
Cruise Line: ....Swan Hellenic	Total Crew: 157	Wheelchair accessibility: ....Fair
Discovery Cruises	Passengers	Cabin Current: ....220 Volts
Former Names: *Explorer II, Alexander von*	(lower beds/all berths): 352/474	Elevators: 2
Humboldt, Saga Pearl, Minerva, Okean	Passenger Space Ratio	Casino (gaming tables): ....No
Builder: ....Mariotti (Italy)	(lower beds/all berths): 35.5/26.3	Slot Machines: ....No
Original Cost: ....n/a	Crew/Passenger Ratio	Swimming Pools (outdoors): 1
Entered Service: ....Apr 1996/May 2008	(lower beds/all berths): 2.1/3.0	Swimming Pools (indoors): 0
Registry: ....The Bahamas	Cabins (total): 178	Whirlpools: 0
Length (ft/m): 436.3/133.0	Size Range (sq ft/m): 139.9–360.6/	Self-Service Launderette: ....Yes
Beam (ft/m): 65.6/20.0	13.0–33.5	Dedicated Cinema/Seats: Yes/96
Draft (ft/m): 19.6/6.0	Cabins (outside view): 126	Library: ....Yes
	Cabins (interior/no view): 52	Onboard currency: ....UK£

A homely ship with an emphasis on discovery and learning.

OVERVIEW. *Minerva* is mainly aimed at the so-called Swanners, as Swan Hellenic passengers are affectionately known – couples and single travelers of a mature age who seek to cruise off the beaten track in comfortable surroundings, and who don't need the highly organized entertainment found aboard larger ships. Despite small cabins and tiny bathrooms, the "soft expedition" vessel is valued for excellent food, friendly service and a fine library. It is not recommended for children.

THE SHIP. Originally intended as a spy ship (*Okean*) for the Soviet navy, the strong, 1989-built ice-strengthened hull was built at Nikolajev on the River Ingul in Ukraine; it had a stern ramp for launching submersibles for submarine tracking. The hull was bought by Monaco-based V-Ships, the present owners, who towed it to Italy for conversion into a "soft expedition" cruising vessel. The ship, under charter for six years, now operates for Swan Hellenic Discovery Cruises, part of the UK's All Leisure Group's Voyages of Discovery.

It has quite an angular profile, with a single, central funnel, and a slightly rounded stern. It doesn't handle unkind seas well, and the navigation bridge looks as if it should have been located one deck higher. There's ample open and shaded deck space, particularly in the aft section, and there is also a teak walk-around promenade deck. The uppermost passenger deck is artificial turf – awful when wet.

A fleet of rubber inflatable Zodiacs is carried for excursions ashore, ideal for inhospitable locations such as in Antarctica without landing piers or formal docking arrangements. The interior decor is homely and restrained, like a country house hotel, not in the slightest bit glitzy, for passengers with good taste, although cushions would be a welcome addition to the many sofas. Lectures and briefings take place in the Auditorium, the ship's main lounge. Fine wool carpets inhabit the passageways and public rooms.

Perhaps the most appreciated and used public room is the excellent library with its classical decor and motifs and a great range of reference books, many of university-standard. Shackleton's Lounge, exuding a country-house atmosphere, is a fine place for a relaxing drink. Cigar smokers are provided with a smoking room and humidor service, and high-back leather chairs that provide a sense of well-being and privacy. All gratuities are included, although port charges are extra.

ACCOMMODATION. There are five different grades of cabins, in 16 price categories. The price depends on grade and location rather than any great difference in size. Most standard cabins really are quite small, particularly when compared to the "standard" cabin size on the latest ships today. There are few cabins with private balcony.

Owner's Suites (2): These Bridge Deck suites measure 360 sq. ft (33.5 sq. meters). Facilities include a queen-size bed, an extra-large double closet and ample drawer space; separate lounge area with sofa, table and chair, and vanity table/writing desk, television/DVD player combo, refrigerator, hairdryer and binoculars; floor-to-ceiling patio doors leading to a private balcony; bathroom with bath/shower combination and toilet.

Suites (10): These suites on Bridge Deck measure 290 sq. ft (27 sq. meters). Facilities include twin beds or queen-size bed, two double closets and ample drawer space; separate lounge area with sofa, table and chair, and vanity table/writing desk (poor lighting), small television/DVD player combo, refrigerator, hairdryer and binoculars; floor to ceiling patio doors leading to private (Astroturf-covered) balcony; bathroom with tub/shower and toilet.

Deluxe: These measure 226 sq. ft (21 sq. meters). Facilities include twin beds or queen-size bed, two double closets and ample drawer space; separate lounge area with sofa, table and chair, and vanity table/writing desk, television and player, refrigerator, hairdryer and binoculars; large picture window; bathroom with bath/shower and toilet.

Superior: These measure 162 sq. ft (15 sq. meters). Facilities include twin beds or queen-size bed, two double closets and ample drawer space; separate lounge area with sofa, table and chair, and vanity table/writing desk, television and player, refrigerator, hairdryer and binoculars; large picture window; bathroom with bath/shower and toilet.

Standard Outside-View or Interior Cabins: These "standard" cabins are small (140 sq. ft/13 sq. meters) when compared to the 182 sq. ft (17 sq. meters) cabins aboard today's newest ships. Facilities include twin beds or queen-size bed, two double closets and ample drawer space; separate lounge area with sofa, table and chair, and vanity table/writing desk, TV and player, refrigerator, hairdryer and binoculars; large picture window (outside-view cabins only; or porthole, depending on deck and price category); bathroom with small shower enclosure and toilet.

The bathrooms have a raised "lip" to step over, are totally white, and have very small showers (except for the suites, which have bathtubs and green/black marble floors), although plumbing fixtures were poorly installed. All grades of accommodation have a hairdryer, 100% cotton bathrobe, TV with music channels, and a direct-dial telephone. However, there is little space for hanging outerwear parkas and other gear for expedition cruises, and some cabins on B Deck are subject to noise and vibration from the ship's engines/generators.

Because the insulation is quite poor, Bridge Deck suites suffer from noise that bleeds through from the Darwin lounge below. This happens on itineraries with evening entertainment rather than on itineraries to the Antarctic, when fewer passengers are carried.

CUISINE. The *Dining Room* has open-seating dining, allowing you to dine with whomever you wish, in both the main restaurant and the informal indoor/outdoor café. The menus are very good, and the food itself is of a really high quality. It's also very creative, attractively presented, and has plenty of taste. The wine list is really good, and so is the rather special champagne. The service staff provide fine service, and they are very pleasant, friendly and willing.

Coffees and teas are available 24 hours a day from a beverage station in the self-serve *Bridge Café*, in which you can have casual breakfasts, luncheons, and dinners in an open-seating arrangement; for dinner, the menu is the same as in the main dining room.

ENTERTAINMENT. Although there is a main lounge, this is used principally for lectures, and occasionally for cabaret acts and classical music ensembles. The ship has a small band and solo entertaining musicians to provide live music for dancing and listening.

SPA/FITNESS. There is a small gymnasium on Funnel Deck (with side-facing views), while a beauty salon is located near the restaurant. Massages and aromatherapy facials, manicures, pedicures and hair beautifying treatments are available, and there is also a small sauna and adjacent shower, but no changing facilities.

DID YOU KNOW...

● that on the earliest cruise ships there was little entertainment, and passengers were expected to clean their own cabins? Orders enforced on all ships sailing from Great Britain in 1849, for example, instructed all passengers to be in their beds by 10pm.

● that the first "en suite" rooms (with private bathroom) were on board Cunard Line's *Campania*, which made its debut in 1893?

● that the first single-berth cabins built as such were also aboard the *Campania*?

● that the first ships to incorporate private balconies were the *Saturnia* and *Vulcania* in the early 1900s?

● that the first ship to be fitted with interior plumbing was the 6,283-ton *Normandie*, which introduced it in 1883?

● that the first liner to offer private terraces with their first-class suites was *Normandie* in 1935 – the Trouville Suite had no fewer than four bedrooms as well as a private terrace?

● that the first ship fitted with an internal electric lighting system was the Inman liner *City of Berlin* in 1879?

● that Carnival Cruise Lines places more than 10 million chocolates on passenger pillows each year?

Monarch of the Seas
★★★

Size: . . . . .Large Resort Ship	Passenger Decks: 11	Cabins (with private balcony): 62
Tonnage: .73,937	Total Crew: 858	Cabins (wheelchair accessible): 4
Lifestyle: . . . . .Standard	Passengers	Wheelchair accessibility: . . . . .Fair
Cruise Line: Royal Caribbean International	(lower beds/all berths): 2,384/2,774	Cabin Current: . . . . .110 volts
Former Names: . . . . .none	Passenger Space Ratio	Elevators: 11
Builder: .Chantiers de l'Atlantique (France)	(lower beds/all berths): 31.0/26.6	Casino (gaming tables): . . . . .Yes
Original Cost: . . . .$300 million	Crew/Passenger Ratio	Slot Machines: . . . . .Yes
Entered Service: . . . . .Nov 1991	(lower beds/all berths): 2.8/3.3	Swimming Pools (outdoors): 2
Registry: . . . . .The Bahamas	Cabins (total): 1,192	Swimming Pools (indoors): 0
Length (ft/m): 879.9/268.2	Size Range (sq ft/m): 118.4–670.0/	Whirlpools: 2
Beam (ft/m): 105.9/32.3	11.0–62.2	Self-Service Launderette: . . . . .No
Draft (ft/m): 24.9/7.6	Cabins (outside view): 732	Dedicated Cinema/Seats: . . . . .No
Propulsion/Propellers: . . . . .diesel	Cabins (interior/no view): 460	Library: . . . . .Yes
(21,844 kW)/2	Cabins (for one person): 0	Onboard currency: . . . . .US$

A modestly large, busy ship, good for a first cruise.

OVERVIEW. This floating resort provides a well-tuned, yet very impersonal, short cruise experience for a lot of passengers. The range of facilities is decent enough, with consistently sound, with highly programmed service from a reasonably attentive young staff. You will probably be overwhelmed by the public spaces, and underwhelmed by the size of the cabins.

THE SHIP. *Monarch of the Seas* is almost identical in size and appearance to sister ship *Majesty of the Seas* but with an improved internal layout, better public room features, passenger flow and signage. Royal Caribbean International's trademark Viking Crown lounge and bar surrounds the funnel and provides a stunning view, although the original Scandinavian tub chairs are extremely small and have no back support. The open deck space is very cramped when full, as aboard any large ship, although there seems to be plenty of it. There is a basketball court for sports lovers.

The interior layout is a little awkward, as it is designed in a vertical stack, with most public rooms located aft, and the accommodation forward. But there's an impressive array of spacious and elegant public rooms, although the decor brings to mind the IKEA school of interior design. A stunning five-deck-high Centrum lobby has cascading stairways and two glass-walled elevators.

There is an adequate two-level showlounge and several shops, albeit with lots of tacky merchandise. Casino gamers will find blackjack, craps, Caribbean stud poker and roulette tables, plus an array of slot machines.

The dress code is very casual. Among the public rooms, the library offers space for relaxation and has a decent

BERLITZ'S RATINGS

	Possible	Achieved
Ship	500	334
Accommodation	200	119
Food	400	221
Service	400	260
Entertainment	100	66
Cruise	400	248

OVERALL SCORE
1,248 points out of 2,000

selection of books. The children's and teens' programs are good, overseen by enthusiastic youth counselors, and there is a busy but sound activities program for adults.

ACCOMMODATION. There are 17 categories, priced by grade, size, and location. Note that there are no cabins with private balconies.

Suites: Thirteen suites on Bridge Deck are fairly large and nicely furnished (the largest is the Royal Suite), with separate living and sleeping spaces. They provide more space, with better service and more perks than standard-grade accommodation.

Standard Cabins: The standard outside-view and interior (no view) cabins are very small, although an arched window treatment and colorful soft furnishings do give the illusion of more space.

Almost all cabins have twin beds that convert to a queen-size or double bed configuration, together with moveable bedside tables. However, when in a queen-bed configuration, the bed is typically flush against the wall, and access is from one side only. All standard cabins have very little closet and drawer space. You should, therefore, pack only minimal clothing, which is all you really need for a short cruise.

All cabins have a private bathroom, with a shower enclosure, toilet and washbasin.

CUISINE. The two large dining rooms, *Claude's* and *Vincent's*, are located off the Centrum lobby. There are tables for four, six or eight, but none for two. When you book, choose one of two seatings, or "My Time Dining" (eat when you want, during dining room hours). The dining operation is well-orchestrated, with emphasis on highly programmed service. The cuisine is typical of mass banquet catering that offers standard fare comparable to that found in American family-style restaurants ashore. While menu descriptions are tempting, the actual food may be somewhat disappointing and unmemorable. Many items are pre-prepared ashore to keep costs down.

A decent selection of light meals is provided, and a vegetarian menu is available. But the selection of breads, rolls, fruit and cheese could do with improvement. The wine list is not extensive, but the prices are moderate. The waiters, many from Caribbean countries, eastern Europe and Goa, are perhaps overly friendly for some tastes – particularly on the last night of the cruise, when tips are expected.

For casual breakfasts and lunches, the *Windjammer Café* is the place to go, although there are often long lines at peak times. Although the selection is just average, several themes, such as Mexican and Indian, are featured. On the aft of the upper level of the venue is *Sorrento's Pizzeria*.

ENTERTAINMENT. The Sound of Music is the name of the principal showlounge; it has both main and balcony levels, with banquette seating, although sightlines from many of the balcony seats are poor.

A smaller entertainment venue, the April in Paris Lounge, is where cabaret acts, including late-night adult comedy are featured, as well as music for dancing.

The entertainment throughout is upbeat – in fact, it is difficult to get away from music and noise. There is even background music in all corridors and elevators, and constant music outdoors on the pool deck. If you want a quiet relaxing holiday, choose another ship.

SPA/FITNESS. The ShipShape Fitness Center has a gymnasium with aft-facing views and a selection of high-tech muscle-pumping equipment. There is also an aerobics studio, and classes are offered in a variety of keep-fit regimes. There is a beauty salon, and a sauna, as well as treatment rooms for pampering massages and facials. While the facilities aren't as extensive as those aboard RCI's newer ships, they're adequate for the short cruises this ship operates.

For the more sporting, there is activity galore – including a rock-climbing wall with several separate climbing tracks. It is located outdoors aft of the funnel and wraparound Viking Crown Lounge.

● **For more extensive general information about the Royal Caribbean experience, see pages 152–6.**

QUOTABLE QUOTES

These are some of the questions I have been asked by newcomers to cruising:
"Does the crew sleep on board?"
"How far above sea level are we?"
"Is the island surrounded by water?"
"Are all Caribbean islands the same size?"
"How many fjords to the dollar?"

"How does the captain know which port to go to?"
"Can we get off in the Panama Canal?"
"Does the ship generate its own electricity?"
"Does this elevator go up as well as down?"
"Will this elevator take me to my cabin?"
"What time's the midnight buffet?"

"Are there two seatings at the midnight buffet?"
"Does the chef cook himself?"
"What happens to the ice sculptures after they melt?"
"What time's the 2 o'clock tour?"
"Where's the bus for the walking tour?"
"Can you see the Equator from the deck?"
"Why is the sauna so hot?"

MSC Armonia
★★★ +

Size: . . . . .Large Resort Ship	Passenger Decks: 10	Cabins (with private balcony): 132
Tonnage: .58,625	Total Crew: 710	Cabins (wheelchair accessible): 2
Lifestyle: . . . . .Standard	Passengers	Wheelchair accessibility: . . . . .Good
Cruise Line: . . . . .MSC Cruises	(lower beds/all berths): 1,566/2,223	Cabin Current: . . . . .110 and 220 volts
Former Names: . . . . . . .European Vision	Passenger Space Ratio	Elevators: 9
Builder: .Chantiers de l'Atlantique (France)	(lower beds/all berths): 37.4/26.3	Casino (gaming tables): . . . . .Yes
Original Cost: . . . .$245 million	Crew/Passenger Ratio	Slot Machines: .Yes
Entered Service: . . . .Jun 2001/May 2004	(lower beds/all berths): 2.2/3.1	Swimming Pools (outdoors): 2
Registry: . . . . .Italy	Cabins (total): 783	Swimming Pools (indoors): 0
Length (ft/m): 823.4/251.0	Size Range (sq ft/m): 139.9–236.8/	Whirlpools: . . . . .1 (thalassotherapy)
Beam (ft/m): 94.4/28.8	13.0–22.0	Self-Service Launderette: . . . . .No
Draft (ft/m): 22.4/6.85	Cabins (outside view): 511	Dedicated Cinema/Seats: . . . . .No
Propulsion/Propellers: . . . . .diesel-electric	Cabins (interior/no view): 272	Library: . . . . .Yes
(31,680kW)/2 azimuthing pods	Cabins (for one person): 0	Onboard currency: . . . . .Euros

A comfortable large ship for pan-European cruisers.

OVERVIEW. *MSC Armonia* will suit those comfortable with multilingual fellow passengers, although the staff is more focused on Italian passengers than those with a different native language. It is best for adult couples and singles, and families with children, who enjoy big-city life, constant activity accompanied by lots of noise, late nights, entertainment that is loud and of questionable quality, and food that is quantity rather than quality.

THE SHIP. As *European Vision*, the ship began its working life auspiciously, having been selected to be a floating hotel to accommodate the leaders and staff of the G8 summit in 2001. When its owner, Festival Cruises, ceased operations in 2004, it was bought by MSC Cruises for €215 million and renamed *MSC Armonia*. It is fitted with a high-tech azimuthing "pod" propulsion system *(see page 191)*.

The exterior deck space is barely adequate for the number of passengers carried. The lido deck surrounding the outdoor swimming pool also has whirlpool tubs and a large bandstand is set in raised canvas-covered pods. All sun-loungers have cushioned pads.

Inside, the layout and passenger flow is good, as are the "you are here" deck signs. The decks are named after European cities – e.g. Oxford Deck (with British public room names), Venice Deck (with Italian names), and Biarritz Deck (with French names). The decor is "European Moderne" – whatever that means – but it does include crisp, clean lines, minimalism in furniture designs – including some chairs that look interesting but are totally impractical. However, the interior colors are good; nothing jars the senses, but rather calms them, unlike the effect aboard many ships.

BERLITZ'S RATINGS		
	Possible	Achieved
Ship	500	387
Accommodation	200	152
Food	400	233
Service	400	294
Entertainment	100	55
Cruise	400	272

OVERALL SCORE
1,393 points out of 2,000

Facilities include Amadeus, a nightclub; Ambassador, a cigar smoking room with all the hallmarks of a gentleman's club; and Vivaldi, a piano lounge. The Goethe Library/Card Room has real writing desks – something many ships omit. There is an extensive internet café, and an English pub, the White Lion. The Lido Casino has blackjack, poker and roulette games, plus an array of slot machines.

Standing in line for embarkation, disembarkation, shore tenders and self-serve buffet meals is an inevitable aspect of cruising aboard large ships. Announcements are in several languages.

If you are considering two back-to-back seven-day cruises, note that some ports may be duplicated, and menus and entertainment are based on a seven-day cycle, so there is much product repetition – including the cruise director's jokes. Regular passenger complaints include poor ports of call information.

The wheelchair-bound should note that there is no access to the uppermost forward and aft decks, although access throughout most of the interior is good. The passenger hallways are a little narrow on some accommodation decks to pass when housekeeping carts are in place.

The company keeps prices low by providing air transportation that may be at inconvenient times, or that involves long journeys by bus. In other words, be prepared for a little discomfort in getting to and from your cruise in exchange for low cruise rates. Note that 15% is added to all drinks and beverage orders.

ACCOMMODATION. There are 11 categories, the price depending on grade, size and location. These include 132 suites with private balcony (the partitions are only of the partial and not the full type), outside-view cabins and interior (no view) cabins.

Suite grade accommodation – they are not true suites, as there is no separate bedroom and lounge – has more room, a larger lounge area, walk-in closet, wall-to-wall vanity counter, a bathroom with combination tub and shower, toilet, and private balcony with light. Bathrobes are provided. In general, the "suites" are practical and nicely furnished. However, except for the very highest category, the bathrooms are very plain, with white plastic washbasins and white walls, and mirrors that steam up.

Even the smallest interior cabins are acceptable , with plenty of space between two lower beds. All grades of accommodation have a TV, mini-bar/refrigerator, personal safe cleverly positioned behind a vanity desk mirror, hairdryer, and bathroom with shower and toilet. But standard grade cabins, at a modest 140 sq. ft (13 sq. meters), are quite small when compared to many other ships.

CUISINE. The principal dining room, the 610-seat *Marco Polo Restaurant*, has two seatings for dinner, and open seating for breakfast and lunch. However, for breakfast and lunch, you may well be seated with others with whom you may not be able to communicate very satisfactorily, given the mix of languages on board.

In general, the cuisine is acceptable, if unmemorable. The menus are varied and the presentation is generally sound, and should prove a highlight for most passengers. The wine list has a wide variety of wines at fairly reasonable prices, although most of the wines are very young.

La Pergola, the most formal restaurant, has stylish Italian cuisine. It is assigned to all passengers occupying accommodation designated as suites, although other passengers can dine in it too, on a reservations-only basis.

Chez Claude, on the starboard side aft, adjacent to the ship's funnel, is a grill area for fast-food. *La Brasserie* is a casual, self-serve buffet eatery, open 24 hours a day (including a sit-down, casual dinner each evening with waiter service). The selections are very standardized – i.e. minimal. *Café San Marco*, on the upper, second level of the main lobby, serves coffee and pastries.

ENTERTAINMENT. La Gondola Theater, two decks high, is the main venue for production shows, cabaret acts, plays and other theatrical presentations. It is a well designed room, except for the fact that no space was allocated for a live showband. The sightlines from most seats are good, and four entrances allow easy access and exit.

Entertainment is weak. Other shows consist of unknown cabaret acts such as singers, magicians, mime artistes, and comedy jugglers. A number of bands and small musical units provide live music for dancing or listening.

SPA/FITNESS. The Atlantica Spa has numerous body-pampering treatments, a gymnasium with ocean views, and high-tech, muscle-toning and strengthening equipment. A thermal suite has different kinds of steam rooms combined with aromatherapy infusions such as chamomile and eucalyptus, and a rasul chamber provides a combination of two or three kinds of application mud, and gentle steam shower. The spa, operated by the Italian concession OceanView, offers a wide range of well-being treatments.

There's a simulated climbing wall outdoors, a volleyball/basketball court, and mini-golf.

● **For more extensive general information about the MSC Cruises experience, see pages 144–5.**

MSC Divina
NOT YET RATED

Size:	.Large Resort Ship	Passenger Decks:	.13
Tonnage:	.139,400 tons	Total Crew:	.1,388
Lifestyle:	.Standard	Passengers	
Cruise Line:	.MSC Cruises	(lower beds/all berths):	.3,502/ 4,345
Former Names:	.none	Passenger Space Ratio	
Builder:	.STX France	(lower beds/all berths):	.39.8/ 32.0
Original Cost:	.$760 million	Crew/Passenger Ratio	
Entered Service:	.Jun 2012	(lower beds/all berths):	.2.5/ 3.1
Registry:	.Panama	Cabins (total):	.1,751
Length (ft/m):	.1,093.5/333.3	Size Range (sq ft/m): 148.5–568.3/13.8–52.8	
Beam (ft/m):	.124.6/38.0	Cabins (outside view):	.1,166
Draft (ft/m):	.27.72/8.45	Cabins (interior/no view):	.405
Propulsion/Propellers:	.diesel-electric	Cabins (for one person):	.0
	(40mW)/2	Cabins (with private balcony):	.1,125

Cabins (wheelchair accessible):	.45
Wheelchair Accessibility:	.Good
Cabin Current:	.110 volts
Elevators:	.16
Casino (gaming tables):	.Yes
Slot Machines:	.Yes
Swimming Pools (outdoors):	.3
Swimming Pools (indoors):	.0
Whirlpools:	.13
Self-Service Launderette:	.No
Dedicated Cinema/Seats:	.No
Library:	.Yes
Onboard currency:	.Euros

A super comfortable large family-friendly ship for Europeans.

OVERVIEW. This large resort ship has a trendy infinity pool, and will appeal to young adult couples, singles, and families with children and teens that enjoy an urban lifestyle, with a mix of mostly European nationalities and style. You can drive an F1 Ferrari racing car in a simulator, and experience hair-raising, seat-of-your pants rides in a 4D theatre, all in a really elegant setting.

THE SHIP. *MSC Divina*, the largest ship yet for MSC Cruises, has the latest in green-technology engines, blast chiller evaporators. It also has one more forward bow thruster than close sisters *MSC Fantasia* and *MSC Splendida*, plus two additional elevators to cope with the ship's increased size. Originally to be called *MSC Meraviglia*, the replacement, easier-to-pronounce name was chosen before the traditional coin-laying ceremony in the shipyard.

An area called the MSC Yacht Club – an exclusive community "suite-grade" accommodation, is larger than that aboard the sister ships. It includes a Top-Sail Lounge (an observation/lifestyle lounge and social meeting place), private sunbathing with integral dip pool, two hot tubs, and concierge services for making dining reservations, booking excursions and spa treatments, and arranging private parties. There's also a private Yacht Club restaurant located within this exclusive area – so you really can cruise "in private" if you so wish – even aboard a ship as large as this.

Facilities for all passengers include a large three-deck-high theater-style showlounge, a nightclub/discotheque, library, card room, an internet center, virtual reality center, shopping gallery, and large casino with gaming tables and an array of slot machines. Drinking places include many lounges and bars, most with live music. One lounge in the

BERLITZ'S RATINGS

	Possible	Achieved
Ship	500	NYR
Accommodation	200	NYR
Food	400	NYR
Service	400	NYR
Entertainment	100	NYR
Cruise	400	NYR

aft section of the ship is for adults only, as is an aft swimming pool and relaxation deck. For a general idea of the ship's features, see the entries for *MSC Fantasia* and MSC *Splendida*.

FAMILIES. The ship is designed to cater for families with children, who have their own extensive collection of play centers (a children's club and jungle adventure playground), youth counselors, and activity programs tailored to specific age groups.

ACCOMMODATION. All suite-grade (Yacht Club) accommodation grades come with full butler service, and all grades have an interactive TV, minibar, personal safe, hairdryer and satellite-link telephone.

CUISINE. *Le Muse* is the main restaurant. There are also three other restaurants, plus a casual Lido-style eatery for breakfasts and lunches, and served but casual dinners.

ENTERTAINMENT. Because passengers are multinational, the shows concentrate on visual entertainment such as mime, magic, dancing, and acrobatics, and are performed with recorded music.

SPA/FITNESS. The large Aurea Wellbeing Center houses a beauty salon, body treatment rooms, and a gymnasium with great ocean views. A thermal suite contains different kinds of steam rooms combined with herbal aromatherapy infusions, in a calming Asia-themed environment.

● **For more extensive general information about the MSC Cruises experience, see pages 144–5.**

MSC Fantasia
★★★★ to ★★★★ +

Size:	.Large Resort Ship	Passenger Decks:	.13
Tonnage:	.133,500	Total Crew:	.1,325
Lifestyle:	.Standard	Passengers	
Cruise Line:	.MSC Cruises	(lower beds/all berths):	.3,274/3,959
Former Names:	.none	Passenger Space Ratio	
Builder:	.STX Europe (France)	(lower beds/all berths):	.40.7/33.7
Original Cost:	.$550 million	Crew/Passenger Ratio	
Entered Service:	.Dec 2008	(lower beds/all berths):	.2.5/3.0
Registry:	.Panama	Cabins (total):	.1,637
Length (ft/m):	.1,093.5/333.3	Size Range (sq ft/m):	.161.4–699.6/15–65
Beam (ft/m):	.124.3/37.9	Cabins (outside view):	.1,354
Draft:	.27.72/8.45	Cabins (interior/no view):	.283
Propulsion/Propellers:	.diesel-electric	Cabins (for one person):	.0
	(40mW)/2	Cabins (with private balcony):	.1,260

Cabins (wheelchair accessible):	.43
Wheelchair accessibility	.Best
Cabin Voltage:	.110 volts
Elevators:	.14
Casino (gaming tables):	.Yes
Slot Machines:	.Yes
Swimming Pools (outdoors):	.3
Swimming Pools (indoors):	.1
(with glass dome)	
Whirlpools:	.13
Self-Service Launderette:	.No
Dedicated Cinema/Seats:	.No
Library:	.Yes
Onboard currency:	.Euros

Comfort, space and a European lifestyle for families.

OVERVIEW. This ship appeals to young adult couples, singles, and families with children and teens who enjoy big ships and a big-city lifestyle with a mix of nationalities, mostly European. You can drive an F1 Ferrari racing car in a simulator, and experience hair-raising, seat-of-your pants rides in a 4D theater.

THE SHIP. Built in 67 blocks, some more than 600 tons, *MSC Fantasia* is the largest ship ever built for a European cruise company. It is 10 meters longer than the Eiffel Tower is high, and the propulsion power is the equivalent of 120 Ferraris. There are four swimming pools, one of which can be covered by a glass dome.

The interior design is an enlargement and extension of the smaller *MSC Musica* and *MSC Orchestra*-class ships, but with some superb new additions, including an exclusive area called the MSC Yacht Club for occupants of the 99 suites. This club includes a Top-Sail Lounge, private sunbathing with integral dip pool, two hot tubs, and concierge services such as making dining reservations, and booking excursions and spa treatments.

Facilities include a large three-deck-high theater-style showlounge, a nightclub/discotheque, numerous lounges and bars, library, card room, an internet center, virtual reality center, and shopping gallery. The shops are integrated with many bars, lounges and entertainment areas so that shopping becomes a city-like environment. Note that 15% is added to all drinks/beverage orders. The Monte Carlo Casino features blackjack, poker and roulette games, plus an array of slot machines.

BERLITZ'S RATINGS

	Possible	Achieved	Yacht Club
Ship	500	425	426
Accommodation	200	162	162
Food	400	260	283
Service	400	300	313
Entertainment	100	77	76
Cruise	400	304	310

OVERALL SCORE
1,528 points/1,570 (Yacht Club)
out of 2,000

Drinking places include a pub-like venue and several comfortable lounges with live music. A neat mini-golf course is on the port side of the funnel, and a walking and jogging track encircles the two swimming pools.

FAMILIES. The ship is designed to accommodate families with children, who have their own play centers (a children's club and jungle adventure playground), youth counselors, and activity programs.

ACCOMMODATION. Eighty percent of cabins have an outside view, and 95% of these have a balcony – a standard balcony cabin will measure almost 172 sq. ft (16 sq. meters), plus bathroom and balcony. There are 99 suites in a "MSC Yacht Club" VIP section; each measures 312 sq. ft (29 sq. meters) and comes with full butler service. The private area, on two decks, consists of a pool with skydome, and sun deck with access via private elevators, an observation lounge/bar, direct access to the spa, a private galley for room service, and a private concierge lounge with an integral library.

A black marble floor leads to a magnificent Swarovski glass staircase which connects the concierge facilities between Deck 15 and 16 under a glass-domed ceiling.

CUISINE. There are four dining venues. The two-deck-high *Il Cherchio d'Oro*, the main restaurant, is in the aft section. It has a ship-wide balcony level, with a stairway to connect its two levels. As well as its Mediterranean cuisine, light "always available" choices are provided.

Red Velvet is a specialty restaurant, with a different menu each evening devoted to a different region of Italy. The Murano chandeliers are notable.

L'Etoile is a classic French restaurant, with decor reminiscent of the Belle Epoque era. Menus focus on one of three themes: the sea, the countryside, and the kitchen garden, and change seasonally. There's also an extra-charge Tex-Mex restaurant, *El Sombrero*, serving large portions of burritos, fajitas, enchiladas, tacos, tortillas and more, with a choice of several Mexican beers.

Casual breakfasts, lunches and sit-down, served, but casual dinners can be taken in the large self-serve *L'Africana Café*, a buffet-style eatery.

Another casual spot for people-watching is the *Il Cappuccino* coffee bar. Located two decks above the main reception area, it serves all types of coffees and teas, as well as fine chocolate delicacies.

La Cantina Toscana is a wine bar that pairs wines with food from several regions of Italy, in a setting which includes alcove seating, and *L'Africana*, which has a decor of dark African hardwoods.

ENTERTAINMENT. L'Avanguardia, the main showlounge, has 1,603 seats, and facilities that rival almost any to be found on land.

SPA/FITNESS. The Aurea Wellbeing Center has a beauty salon, several treatment rooms, and a gymnasium with great ocean views. A thermal suite contains different kinds of steam rooms combined with herbal aromatherapy infusions, in a calming Asia-themed environment. The spa is operated by OceanView, a specialist spa provider.

Sports facilities include deck quoits, shuffleboard courts, large tennis/basketball court, mini-golf, and a jogging track.

● **For more extensive general information about the MSC Cruises experience, see pages 144–5.**

ENVIRONMENTAL ISSUES

There are three types of waste water: bilge water, black water (or sewage) and grey water.

Bilge water is oily engine run-off and condensation that collects in the bilge, a compartment at the bottom of a vessel's hull where water is collected and later pumped out. Grey water comes from showers and sinks. Black water, perhaps the most damaging to the environment, comes from the toilets and from the drains and sinks of the medical center. When water is treated to reduce its oil content below 15 parts of oil per million parts of water, international law allows it to be discharged virtually anywhere.

Few accidents have happened, and most cruise ships' environmental standards meet or surpass all international laws; the cruise industry represents only 0.2% of all ocean-going vessels worldwide.

Cruise ship owners are working towards stricter emission limits for particulate matter and sulfur oxides, and reducing nitrogen oxide levels (compared to existing emissions levels) that will probably be imposed within the next few years. Older engines (those built before January 1, 2000) are required to achieve a 20% reduction in nitrogen oxides.

The latest generation of propulsion machinery (engines) is, however, much more fuel efficient than older ships. For example, RCI's *Freedom*-class ships are 10% more fuel efficient than the *Voyager*-class ships, and the company's *Oasis*-class ships, introduced in 2009, are 15% more fuel efficient than the *Freedom*-class ships.

In the past 10 years, cruise ships have spent huge sums of money in new technology; the result is that waste and garbage has been almost cut in half, while sustaining cruise capacity growth just approaching around eight percent annually. The latest hull coatings increase fuel efficiency; the coating, which reduces surface resistance in the water, is completely non-toxic. Many large resort ships now have environmental officers on board to oversee compliance with environmental regulations and requirements.

Cruise lines reduce the solid waste they generate by purchasing in bulk, encouraging suppliers to use more efficient packaging, reusing packaging when possible and packaging more environmentally friendly materials. Other examples:

● Advanced purification systems treat all onboard wastewater.

● Ships actively recycle glass, metals, wood, cardboard and paper.

● Excess heat from engine boilers is rerouted to power evaporators used in the process of turning sea water into potable water.

● Special high-tech compacters process garbage (the one aboard *Queen Mary 2*, for example, is four decks high).

● Dry cleaning machines now use non-hazardous detergents formulated with soy, banana and orange extracts.

● Materials printed on board can be produced using soy-based inks.

● Some ships "plug in" to clean, local hydroelectric when they dock in ports cities such as Seattle and Juneau.

● The only solid waste discharged to sea is food waste, considered safe because, either fish consume it or natural elements break it down in the water. And some use only seafood farmed from sustainable sources. NCL and NCL America ships offload their used cooking oil for recycling to bio-diesel.

What you can do to help

Specially marked garbage containers are scattered throughout each ship for you to use.

MSC Lirica
★★★★

Size:	...............Large Resort Ship	Passenger Decks:	10	Cabins (with private balcony):	132
Tonnage:	59,058	Total Crew:	701	Cabins (wheelchair accessible):	4
Lifestyle:	..................Standard	Passengers		Wheelchair accessibility:	.........Good
Cruise Line:	.............MSC Cruises	(lower beds/all berths):	.....1,560/2,065	Cabin Current:	.........110/220 volts
Former Names:	.................none	Passenger Space Ratio		Elevators:	9
Builder: .Chantiers de l'Atlantique (France)		(lower beds/all berths):	........37.5/28.3	Casino (gaming tables):	............Yes
Original Cost:	............$266 million	Crew/Passenger Ratio		Slot Machines:	...................Yes
Entered Service:	............Mar 2003	(lower beds/all berths):	.........2.2/2.9	Swimming Pools (outdoors):	2
Registry:	....................Panama	Cabins (total):	780	Swimming Pools (indoors):	0
Length (ft/m):	...........830.7/253.25	Size Range (sq ft/m):	......139.9–302.0/	Whirlpools:	2
Beam (ft/m):	............94.4/28.8		.......................13.0–28.0	Self-Service Launderette:	..........No
Draft (ft/m):	.................22.4/6.85	Cabins (outside view):	504	Dedicated Cinema/Seats:	..........No
Propulsion/Propellers:	..........diesel	Cabins (interior/no view):	276	Library:	............................Yes
	(31,680kW)/2 azimuthing pods	Cabins (for one person):	0	Onboard currency:	.............Euros

---

A large, Euro-style, informal, family-friendly ship.

OVERVIEW. *MSC Lirica* is best suited to young adult couples, singles, and families with tots, children and teens who enjoy big-ship surroundings and facilities, and passengers of different nationalities and languages (mostly European). The decor has many Italian influences, including clean lines, minimalism in furniture design, and an eclectic collection of colors and soft furnishings that somehow work well together without any hint of garishness.

THE SHIP. *MSC Lirica*, sister to *MSC Opera*, was the first of a pair of newbuilds for Mediterranean Shipping Cruises (MSC), Italy's largest privately owned cruise line. The blue funnel is quite sleek, with a swept-back design, and the ship is fitted with an azimuthing pod propulsion system *(for details, see page 191).*

Inside, the layout and passenger flow is quite good with the exception of a couple of points of congestion – typically when the first seating comes out of the dining room and passengers on second seating are waiting to go in.

Real wood and marble are used extensively in the interiors, and the high quality reflects MSC's commitment to the vessel's future. The "fit and finish" of the interior decor, and most carpeting, is very good.

Facilities include the ship's main showlounge, a nightclub/discotheque, several lounges and bars, an internet center with 10 terminals, a virtual reality center, a children's club, and a shopping gallery named Rodeo Drive with stores that have an integrated bar and entertainment area so that shopping becomes a city-like environment where you can shop, drink, and be entertained all in one convenient area. The Las Vegas Casino offers blackjack,

BERLITZ'S RATINGS		
	Possible	Achieved
Ship	500	407
Accommodation	200	156
Food	400	236
Service	400	299
Entertainment	100	55
Cruise	400	286
OVERALL SCORE		
1,439 points out of 2,000		

poker and roulette games, together with an array of slot machines. There is also a card room, but the integral library is small and disappointing and there are no hardback books.

The ship is designed to accommodate families with children, who have their own play center, youth counselors, and activity programs. Anyone wheelchair-bound should note that there is no access to the uppermost forward and aft decks, although access throughout most of the interior is very good and there are also several wheelchair-accessible public restrooms. But the passenger hallways are a little narrow on some decks for you to pass when housekeeping carts are in place.

Some things that passengers find irritating: the ship's photographers always seem to be in your face; the telephone numbering system to reach such places as the information bureau (2224) and hospital (2360) are not easy to remember – single digit numbers would be better. Gratuities are extra even though bar drinks already include the 15% service charge added to all drinks/beverage orders.

ACCOMMODATION. There are 11 different price levels for accommodation, depending on grade and location: one suite category, five outside-view cabin grades, and five interior (no view) cabin grades. Included are 132 "suites" with private balcony (though partitions between balconies are of the partial type), outside-view cabins and interior cabins.

All cabins have a mini-bar and personal safe, satellite-linked television, several audio channels, and 24-hour room service. While tea and coffee are complimentary, snacks for room service have a delivery charge of €2.50.

Accommodation designated as suites – they are not true

suites, as there is no separate bedroom and lounge – has more room, a larger lounge area, walk-in closet, wall-to-wall vanity counter, a bathroom with combination tub and shower, toilet, and semi-private balcony with a light but partitions that are partial, not full. The bathrobes are 100% cotton. However, except for the very highest category, the suite bathrooms are very plain, with white plastic washbasins and white walls, and mirrors that steam up.

Some cabins on Scarlatti Deck have views obstructed by lifeboats, while those on Deck 10 aft (10105–10159) can be subject to late-night noise from the discotheque on the deck above.

CUISINE. There are two dining rooms: *La Bussola Restaurant*, and the smaller, slightly more intimate *L'Ippocampo* Restaurant, located one deck above. Both have large oceanview picture windows at the aft end of the ship. There are two seatings for meals, in keeping with all other ships in the MSC fleet, and tables are for two, four, six, or eight.

La Pergola is the most formal restaurant, offering stylish Italian cuisine. It is assigned to passengers in accommodation designated as suites, although other passengers can dine in it too, on a reservations-only basis. The food and service are superior to that in the main dining room.

Casual, self-serve buffets for breakfast and lunch can be taken in *Le Bistrot Cafeteria,* which is also open for sit-down, served, but casual dinners each evening. For fast foods, there is also a grill and a pizzeria, both located outside, adjacent to the swimming pool and ship's funnel.

The *Coffee Corner*, located on the upper, second level of the main lobby, is the place for coffees and pastry items – as well for people-watching throughout the day. Although there are windows, the view is not of the ocean, but of the stowed gangways and associated equipment.

ENTERTAINMENT. The Broadway Theater, the main showlounge, is located in the forward section. It has tiered seating set in a sloping floor, and sightlines are good for most seats. The room can also serve as a venue for large social functions. There is no separate bandstand, and the shows work with recorded music; hence there is little consistency in orchestration and sound balance.

High-quality entertainment has not, to date, been part of MSC's mindset. Hence, production shows and variety acts tend to be adequate at best. The Lirica Lounge, one deck above the showlounge, is the place for social dancing, with live music. For the young and lively set, there is The Blue Club, the ship's throbbing, ear-melting discotheque.

SPA/FITNESS. The Lirica Health Center is located one deck above the navigation bridge at the forward end of the ship. The complex has a beauty salon, several treatment rooms offering massage and other body-pampering treatments, plus a gymnasium with ocean views and an array of high-tech equipment. There's also a thermal suite, containing different kinds of steam rooms combined with aromatherapy infusions, at extra cost.

The health center is run as a concession by the Italian company OceanView, with European hairstylists and Balinese massage and body treatment staff. Gratuities are not included, but left to your discretion.

● **For more extensive general information about the MSC Cruises experience, see pages 144–5.**

SAFETY MEASURES

Fire Control
If anyone sounds the fire alarm, an alarm is automatically set off on the bridge. A red panel light will be illuminated on a large plan, indicating the section of the ship that has to be checked so that the crew can take immediate action.

Ships are sectioned into several zones, each of which can be tightly closed off. In addition, almost all ships have a water-fed sprinkler system that can be activated at the touch of a button, or automatically activated when sprinkler vials are broken by fire-generated heat. New electronic fire detection systems are being installed aboard ships in order to increase safety further.

Emergency Ventilation Control
This automatic fire damper system also has a manual switch that is activated to stop or control the flow of air to all areas of the ship, in this way reducing the fanning effect on flame and smoke via air-conditioning and fan systems.

Watertight Doors Control
Watertight doors throughout the ship can be closed off, in order to contain the movement of water flooding the ship. A master switch activates all the doors in a matter of seconds. All watertight doors can be operated electrically and manually, which means that nobody can be trapped in a watertight compartment.

Stabilizers Control
The ship's two stabilizing fins can be extended, housed, or controlled. They normally operate automatically under the command of a gyroscope located in the engine control room.

MSC Magnifica
★★★★

Size: . . . . .Large (Resort) Ship	Total Crew: 987	Cabins (wheelchair accessible): 17
Tonnage: 92,409	Passengers	Wheelchair accessibility: . . . . .Good
Lifestyle: . . . . .Standard	(lower beds/all berths): 2,518/3,013	Cabin Voltage: . . . . .110 volts
Cruise Line: . . . . .MSC Cruises	Passenger Space Ratio	Elevators: 13
Former Names: . . . . .none	(lower beds/all berths): 37.0/30.9	Casino (gaming tables): . . . . .Yes
Builder: . . . . .Aker Yards (France)	Crew/Passenger Ratio	Slot Machines: . . . . .Yes
Original Cost: . . . . .n/a	(lower beds/all berths): 2.5/3.0	Swimming Pools (outdoors): 2
Entered Service: . . . . .Mar 2010	Cabins (total): 1,259	Swimming Pools (indoors): 0
Registry: . . . . .Panama	Size Range (sq ft/m): 150.6–301.3/	Whirlpools: 4
Length (ft/m): 963.9/293.8	14.0–28.0	Self-Service Launderette: . . . . .No
Beam (ft/m): 105.6/32.2	Cabins (outside view): 1,000	Dedicated Cinema/Seats: . . . . .No
Draft (ft/m): 25.2/7.7	Cabins (interior/no view): 275	Library: . . . . .Yes
Propulsion/Propellers: diesel/2	Cabins (for one person): 0	Onboard currency: . . . . .Euros
Passenger Decks: 13	Cabins (with private balcony): 827	

A large, family-friendly ship with bright decor.

OVERVIEW. The ship is designed to accommodate families with children, who have their own play center, video games room, youth counselors, and activity programs. The interior layout and passenger flow are quite good, and decks are named after Mediterranean destinations, such as Capri, Positano, Porto Venere, Ischia. Some of the artwork is quite whimsical, but in keeping with the ship's contemporary design.

THE SHIP. *MSC Magnifica* is one of a quartet of the same class, the others being *MSC Musica*, *MSC Poesia* and *MSC Orchestra*. It has a blue funnel with a swept-back design that balances an otherwise large-ship profile. The hull has large circular porthole-style windows instead of square or rectangular ones. The ship is powered by diesel motors driving electric generators to provide power to two conventional propellers.

The decor has plenty of Italian and Mediterranean influences, including clean lines, minimalism in furniture design, and a collection of colors, soft furnishings and fabrics that work well together. Real wood and marble have been used extensively in the Italianate interiors, and the high quality reflects the commitment that MSC Cruises has in the vessel's future.

The focal point is the main three-deck high lobby, with a water-feature backdrop and a crystal piano on a small stage that appears to float on a pond. Other facilities include a large main showlounge, a nightclub, a discotheque that houses two bowling lanes, numerous lounges and bars (including L'Olimpiade sports/wine/food bar), a library, a card room, an internet center, a 4-D virtual reality center, children's club, and a dedicated cigar lounge with special-

ized smoke extraction and stocking a selection of Cuban (including Cohiba, Monte Cristo, Romeo e Juliet, Partagas), Dominican (Davidoff), and Italian (Toscana) smokes.

One of the nicest venues is the Tiger Lounge, with its animal-themed decor and sumptuous but heavy chairs and long curvy bar. A shopping area, which includes an electronics store, has an integrated bar and entertainment area that flows through the main lobby so that shopping becomes a city-like environment where you can shop, drink, and be entertained all in one convenient area.

Drinking places include a pub-like venue as well as several comfortable lounges with live music. Note that 15% is added to all bar drink prices. A mini-golf course is on the port side of the funnel, while a walking/jogging track encircles an upper level above the two swimming pools.

Although access throughout most of the interior is very good, anyone who is wheelchair-bound should note that the passenger hallways are narrow on some decks for you to pass when housekeeping carts are in place. Sadly, there is no walk-around open promenade deck.

ACCOMMODATION. There are 12 price levels, depending on grade and location: suites, outside-view cabins, and interior (no view) cabins. Included are 18 "suites" with private balcony, mini-suites, outside-view cabins and interior cabins. Contrary to nautical convention, the cabin numbering system has even numbered cabins on the starboard side, and odd numbered cabins on the port side.

All cabins have high-quality Italian bed linen (400-count cotton for suites, 300-count cotton for all other cabins), a mini-bar, safe, satellite flat-screen TV set, several audio channels, and 24-hour room service. Continental breakfast is complimentary in cabins from 7:30am to 10am, and room service snacks are available at extra cost at any other time.

Accommodation designated as "suites" – they are not true suites, as there is no separate bedroom and lounge – also has more space, although they are small compared to suites on some other major cruise lines. They have a larger lounge area, walk-in closet, and vanity desk with drawer-mounted hairdryer; a bathroom with combination tub and shower, toilet, and semi-private balcony with light. The partitions between each balcony are of the partial, not full, type. The bathrobes and towels are 100% cotton, and a pillow menu with a choice of five pillows is available.

Many cabins on Camogli Deck have views obstructed by lifeboats. Some of the most popular cabins are those at the aft section of the ship, with views over the stern from the balcony cabins. The 17 cabins for the disabled are spacious and well-equipped.

CUISINE. There are two principal dining rooms: *L'Edera* and *Quattro Venti*. They are located aft, with large ocean-view picture windows. There are two seatings for meals, and tables are for two, four, six or eight. Seating is both banquette-style and in individual chairs – although the chairs are slim and do not have armrests. All dining venues are managed and supervised by experienced Italians.

Casual, self-serve buffets for breakfast and lunch are set out in the *Sahara Cafeteria*, which is also open for sit-down, served, but casual dinners each evening, or at a pool deck fast-food eatery. Coffee/tea and pastries are available in several bars adjacent to the midships atrium lobby.

Alternative Dining Spots: Enclosed in the ship's center, on Amalfi Deck, *Shanghai* is a Chinese à la carte extra-cost restaurant. *L'Oesi* is a reservation-required, extra-charge, à la carte dining spot that, by day, forms the aft section of the Sahara Cafeteria, with its Moroccan decor. Dinners are cooked to order from the adjacent galley.

The *Sports Bar* is a venue for lite-bite snack foods (examples: chicken breast and rocket salad; eggs stuffed with salmon roe; smoked salmon rosettes; assorted sole rolls – all at a small additional cost).

Silver trays full of late-night snacks are taken throughout the ship by waiters, and on some days, special late-night desserts, such as flambé items, are showcased in various lounges. The ship makes its own ice cream.

All sorts of coffees, available in the many bars and lounges, cost extra but are still good value.

ENTERTAINMENT. The Royal Theater is the large, principal show lounge, and its tiered seating spans three decks in the forward section of the ship, with good sightlines from most of the plush, comfortable seats. The room can also serve as a venue for large groups or social functions. All the large-scale production shows are performed to prerecorded music – there is no showband.

The L'Amethista Lounge is the place for social dancing and functions such as cooking demonstrations, with live music provided by a band. For the young and lively crowd, there's the ear-melting T32 discotheque. With its floor-to-ceiling windows, it is a quiet, pleasant place to relax and read during sea days.

Additionally, big-screen movies are shown on a megascreen above the forward pool, just behind the ship's mast.

SPA/FITNESS. The Aurea Spa is one deck above the navigation bridge at the forward end of the ship. The complex has a beauty salon, several treatment rooms offering massage and other body-pampering treatments, and a gymnasium with forward ocean views and an array of muscle-toning and strengthening equipment. There's also a Middle East-themed thermal suite, containing steam rooms and saunas with aromatherapy infusions, and a relaxation/hot tub room; there's an extra charge for using these facilities.

Sports facilities include table tennis, a tennis court minigolf course, golf practice net, two shuffleboard courts, and a jogging track.

● **For more extensive general information about the MSC Cruises experience, see pages 144–5.**

MSC Melody
★★★

Size: . . . . .Mid-Size Ship	Passenger Decks: 9	Cabins (with private balcony): 0
Tonnage: .36,500	Total Crew: 535	Cabins (wheelchair accessible): 4
Lifestyle: . . . . .Standard	Passengers	Wheelchair accessibility: . . . . .Fair
Cruise Line: . . . . .MSC Cruises	(lower beds/all berths): 1,098/1,600	Cabin Current: . . . . .110 volts
Former Names: .Star/ShipAtlantic, Atlantic	Passenger Space Ratio	Elevators: 4
Builder: . . . . .C.N.I.M. (France)	(lower beds/all berths): 33.2/22.8	Casino (gaming tables): . . . . .Yes
Original Cost: . . . .$100 million	Crew/Passenger Ratio	Slot Machines: . . . . .Yes
Entered Service: . . . . .Apr 1982/Jun 1997	(lower beds/all berths): 2.0/2.9	Swimming Pools (outdoors): 1
Registry: . . . . .Panama	Cabins (total): 549	Swimming Pools (indoors): 1
Length (ft/m): 671.9/204.8	Size Range (sq ft/m): 137.0–427.0/	Whirlpools: 3
Beam (ft/m): 89.7/27.4	12.7–39.5	Self-Service Launderette: . . . . .No
Draft (ft/m): 25.5/7.8	Cabins (outside view): 392	Dedicated Cinema/Seats: Yes/227
Propulsion/Propellers: . . . . .diesel	Cabins (interior/no view): 157	Library: . . . . .Yes (2 book racks)
(22,070 kW)/2	Cabins (for one person): 0	Onboard currency: . . . . .Euros

A well-worn older ship for budget-minded families.

OVERVIEW. The ship suits couples, singles, and families with children and teens who enjoy big-ship surroundings and a big-city life with all its attendant noise, and passengers of different nationalities. The food quality generally is adequate for the price, but doesn't live up to menu descriptions.

THE SHIP. *MSC Melody* has a short, stubby, foreshortened bow and squat funnel, and an all-white hull and superstructure. There is a good amount of outdoor deck space, but noise levels can be high when the ship is full, particularly in summer. The interior is quite spacious, with plenty of public rooms, mostly high-ceilinged. The decor is somber in places, and the lighting is quite subdued. There is a generous amount of stainless steel and teakwood trim. A large observation lounge, with good views from large picture windows, is rather wasted as an informal eating area.

A fairly good indoor-outdoor pool area can be covered in bad weather. There is a reasonable children's program at peak periods, and several children's and teens' counselors. About 60% of passengers will be Italian. Expect lots of extra charges. A 15% gratuity is added to all drinks/beverage orders. There may be a charge for shuttle buses in some ports of call.

Niggles? The almost constant loud announcements are intrusive. There is no walk-around promenade deck outdoors, and the sunloungers don't have cushioned pads. The ship has only four elevators – not nearly enough, and they aren't linked. Standing in line for embarkation, disembarkation, and buffet meals is inevitable aboard large ships. There is often extreme congestion in the foyer adjacent to

BERLITZ'S RATINGS

	Possible	Achieved
Ship	500	297
Accommodation	200	126
Food	400	220
Service	400	240
Entertainment	100	58
Cruise	400	234

OVERALL SCORE
1,175 points out of 2,000

the showlounge, particularly on gala evenings when show audiences and the captain's cocktail party crowd merge.

ACCOMMODATION. There are 12 categories and price grades. Six suites have plenty of space for families of four, and have a decent walk-in closet. The bathroom is large and has a full-size tub, oversize basin, and an uncomfortable square toilet. Other outside-view and interior cabins are of a good size, and have ample closet and drawer space. Many cabins have upper berths – good for families, although luggage space is minimal. The cabin soundproofing is extremely poor, and the room service menu is quite basic.

CUISINE. The *Galaxy Restaurant*, on a lower deck (Restaurant Deck), is large and quite attractive even though the decor is from the 1980s, but the tables are very close together and the noise level is extremely high. There are two seatings, and many Italian dishes. Each cruise usually includes two gala evenings. There is a limited wine list.

ENTERTAINMENT. The Club Universe is just forward of midships on Lounge Deck. Although the ceiling is high, it is a single-level room with banquette seating. The ship has a showband and several small musical units.

SPA/FITNESS. The SeaSport Health and Fitness Center has a gymnasium (with treadmills, exercycles, and muscle-pumping equipment), beauty salon, and massage room.

● **For more extensive general information about the MSC Cruises experience, see pages 144–5.**

MSC Musica
★★★★

Size:	.Large Resort Ship	Passenger Decks:	.13	Cabins (with private balcony):	.827
Tonnage:	.92,409	Total Crew:	.987	Cabins (wheelchair accessible):	.17
Lifestyle:	.Standard	Passengers		Wheelchair accessibility:	.Good
Cruise Line:	.MSC Cruises	(lower beds/all berths):	.2,550/3,013	Cabin Voltage:	.110/220 volts
Former Names:	.none	Passenger Space Ratio		Elevators:	.13
Builder:	.Aker Yards (France)	(lower beds/all berths):	.36.2/30.6	Casino (gaming tables):	.Yes
Original Cost:	.$360 million	Crew/Passenger Ratio		Slot Machines:	.Yes
Entered Service:	.Jul 2006	(lower beds/all berths):	.2.6/3.0	Swimming Pools (outdoors):	.2
Registry:	.Panama	Cabins (total):	.1,275	Swimming Pools (indoors):	.0
Length (ft/m):	.963.9/293.8	Size Range (sq ft/m):	.150.6–301.3/	Whirlpools:	.4
Beam (ft/m):	.105.6/32.2		14.0–28.0	Self-Service Launderette:	.No
Draft (ft/m):	.25.2/7.7	Cabins (outside view):	.1,000	Dedicated Cinema/Seats:	.No
Propulsion/Propellers:	.diesel	Cabins (interior/no view):	.275	Library:	.Yes
	(31,680kW)/2	Cabins (for one person):	.0	Onboard currency:	.Euros

Lively Italian decor and style for family cruising.

OVERVIEW. *MSC Musica* suits young adult couples, singles, and families with tots, children and teens who enjoy big-ship surroundings and a noisy, big-city lifestyle, with of different nationalities and languages, mostly European. The ship is designed to accommodate families with children, who have their own play center, video games room, youth counselors, and activity programs.

THE SHIP. *MSC Musica* is an extension and evolution of the slightly smaller *MSC Lirica* and *MSC Opera*. The blue funnel is quite sleek, with a swept-back design and carries the MSC logo in gold lettering, and forward of the mast, additional decks provide a more balanced profile. The hull has large circular porthole-style windows instead of square or rectangular windows. From a technical viewpoint, the ship is powered by diesel motors driving electric generators to provide power to two conventional propellers.

The interior layout and passenger flow is quite good with the exception of a couple of points of congestion, typically when the first seating exits the two main dining rooms and passengers on the second seating are waiting to enter. The musically-themed decor has many Italian influences, including clean lines, minimalism in furniture design, and a collection of colors, soft furnishings and fabrics that work well together, although it's a little more garish than one would expect.

Real wood and marble have been used extensively in the interiors, and the high quality reflects the commitment that MSC Cruises has in the vessel's future.

The focal point of the ship is the main three-deck high lobby, with a water-feature backdrop and a crystal piano

BERLITZ'S RATINGS		
	Possible	Achieved
Ship	500	412
Accommodation	200	156
Food	400	243
Service	400	298
Entertainment	100	62
Cruise	400	291

OVERALL SCORE
1,462 points out of 2,000

on a small stage that appears to float on a pond. Other facilities include a large main show lounge, a nightclub, discotheque, numerous lounges and bars (including a wine bar), library, card room, an internet center, virtual reality center, children's club, and cigar lounge with specialized smoke extraction and a selection of Cuban, Dominican and Italian (Toscana) smokes.

A shopping gallery, which includes an electronics store, has an integrated bar and entertainment area that flows through the main lobby so that shopping becomes a city-like environment where you can shop, drink, and be entertained all in one convenient area. The expansive San Remo Casino has blackjack, poker and roulette games, and an array of slot machines.

Drinking places include a pub-like venue as well as several comfortable lounges with live music. A 15% gratuity is added to all drinks/beverage orders. A mini-golf course is on the port side of the funnel, while a walking/jogging track encircles an upper level above the two swimming pools.

Some of the artwork is whimsical, but fishermen will appreciate the stuffed head from a blue marlin caught by Pierfrancesco Vago, president of MSC Cruises in 2004; it weighs 588 pounds (266.7 kg) and stands at the Blue Marlin Bar on the pool deck. And do check out the "restroom with a view" – the men's/ladies toilets adjacent to the Blue Marlin pool deck bar have a great ocean view and you can even watch the passing scenery while sitting on the toilet if you leave the door open.

Although access throughout most of the interior of the ship is very good, anyone who is wheelchair-bound should note that the passenger hallways are a little narrow on some decks for you to pass when housekeeping carts are in place. There is no walk-around open promenade deck.

ACCOMMODATION. There are 12 price levels, depending on grade and location: suites, outside-view cabins, and interior (no view) cabins. Included are 18 "suites" with private balcony, mini-suites, outside-view cabins and interior cabins. Contrary to nautical convention, the cabin numbering system has even-numbered cabins on the starboard side, and odd-numbered cabins on the port side.

All cabins have a mini-bar and personal safe, satellite flat-screen TV with audio channels, and 24-hour room service. Continental breakfast is complimentary from 7:30 to 10am, but room service snacks cost extra at any other time.

Accommodation designated as "suites" – they are not true suites, as there is no separate bedroom and lounge – also has more room, although they are small compared to suites on some on other cruise lines. They have a larger lounge area, walk-in closet, and vanity desk with drawer-mounted hairdryer, and a bathroom with combination tub and shower. There is a semi-private balcony with light, but the partitions between each balcony are of the partial, not full, type. The suite bathrooms are plain, with white plastic washbasins and white walls, and mirrors that steam up.

Many cabins on Forte Deck have views obstructed by lifeboats. Cabins on the uppermost accommodation deck (Cantata Deck) may be subject to the noise of sunloungers being dragged across the deck above when it is set up or cleaned early in the morning. Some of the most popular cabins are those at the aft end of the ship, with views over the ship's stern from the balcony cabins (on Virtuoso, Adagio, Intermezzo and Forte decks). The 17 cabins for the disabled are spacious and well-equipped.

CUISINE. There are two main dining rooms, *L'Oleandro* and *Le Maxim's*, both located aft, with large ocean-view picture windows. There are two seatings for meals, and tables are for two, four, six or eight. Seating is both banquette-style and in individual chairs; the chairs, however, are slim and lack armrests. All dining venues are managed by Italians.

Passengers occupying accommodation designated as suites and deluxe grades are typically assigned the best tables in the quietest sections of Le Maxim's restaurant, which is quieter than L'Oleandro, the main dining room.

The *Gli Archi Cafeteria* (one section of which forms the reservations-only Il Giardino) is for casual, self-serve buffets for breakfast and lunch and for sit-down, served, but casual dinners each evening. There's also an outside fast-food eatery on the pool deck. Several bars adjacent to the midships atrium lobby serve coffee, tea and pastries.

Alternative Dining Spots:
● *Il Giardino* is an à la carte dining spot that costs extra and requires reservations.

● *Kaito* is a Japanese sushi bar with counter and table seating and a menu that has a fine array of extra-cost à la carte sashimi pieces, nigiri and temaki sushi and maki rolls, tempura and teriyaki items, and a choice of several types of cold or hot sake, and Japanese beer. Reservations are needed.
● *Enoteca Wine Bar*, a very creative wine bar, provides a selection of famous regional cheeses, hams and wine in a relaxing and entertaining bistro-style setting.

There are more dining choices than aboard other previous MSC Cruises ships, if you are willing to pay extra.

Silver trays full of late-night snacks are taken throughout the ship by waiters, and on some days, special late-night desserts, such as flambé items, are showcased in various lounges like the Il Tucana Lounge. The ship makes its own ice cream.

ENTERTAINMENT. The Theatro La Scala, the large, principal show lounge, is in the ship's forward section. It has tiered seating on two levels, and the sightlines are good from most of the plush, comfortable seats. The room can also serve as a venue for large groups or social functions.

High-quality entertainment has not, to date, been a priority for MSC Cruises. Production shows and variety acts tend to be amateurish. There is no showband, and all shows are performed to recorded music pre-recorded tracks.

The Il Tucano (Tucan) Lounge, aft of the show lounge, is the place for social dancing and functions such as cooking demonstrations, with live music provided by a band. Another nightclub, the Crystal Lounge, provides music for social dancing. The young and lively crowd have the ear-melting G32 discotheque; with its floor-to-ceiling windows, it is a quiet, pleasant place to relax and read by day.

Big-screen movies are shown on a large screen above the forward pool, just behind the ship's mast.

SPA/FITNESS. The Aloha Beauty Farm is one deck above the navigation bridge at the forward end of the ship. The complex has a beauty salon, several treatment rooms offering massage and other body-pampering treatments, and a gymnasium with forward ocean views and an array of high-tech, muscle-toning and strengthening equipment. There's also a Middle East-themed thermal suite, containing steam rooms and saunas with aromatherapy infusions, and a relaxation/hot tub room; it costs extra to use these facilities.

The spa is run as a concession by Steiner Leisure, with European hairstylists and massage/body treatment staff.

Sports facilities include table tennis, a tennis court mini-golf course, golf practice net, two shuffleboard courts, and a jogging track.

● **For more extensive general information about the MSC Cruises experience, see pages 144–5.**

MSC Opera
★★★★

Size: ....Large Resort Ship	Passenger Decks: 10	Cabins (with private balcony): 200
Tonnage: 59,058	Total Crew: 701	Cabins (wheelchair accessible): 4
Lifestyle: ....Standard	Passengers	Wheelchair accessibility: ....Good
Cruise Line: ....MSC Cruises	(lower beds/all berths): 1,756/2,200	Cabin Voltage: ....110 and 220
Former Names: ....none	Passenger Space Ratio	Elevators: 9
Builder: .Chantiers de l'Atlantique (France)	(lower beds/all berths): 33.6/26.8	Casino (gaming tables): ....Yes
Original Cost: ....$266 million	Crew/Passenger Ratio	Slot Machines: ....Yes
Entered Service: ....Mar 2004	(lower beds/all berths): 2.5/3.1	Swimming Pools (outdoors): 2
Registry:.......................Italy	Cabins (total): 878	Swimming Pools (indoors): 0
Length (ft/m): 830.7/256.25	Size Range (sq ft/m): 139.9–302.0/	Whirlpools: 2
Beam (ft/m): 94.4/28.8	13.0–28.0	Self-Service Launderette: ....No
Draft (ft/m): 22.4/6.85	Cabins (outside view): 504	Dedicated Cinema/Seats: ....No
Propulsion/Propellers: ....diesel	Cabins (interior/no view): 276	Library: ....Yes
(31,680kW)/2 azimuthing pods	Cabins (for one person): 0	Onboard currency: ....Euros

A family-friendly ship with pan-European decor.

OVERVIEW. *MSC Opera* suits young adult couples, singles, and families with tots, children and teens who enjoy big-ship surroundings and a noisy, big-city lifestyle, with of different nationalities and languages, mostly European. The ship is designed to accommodate families with children, who have their own play center, video games room, youth counselors, and activity programs.

THE SHIP. *MSC Opera* was the second of the new ships built for MSC Cruises, Italy's largest privately owned cruise line. The first was *MSC Lirica*, which had almost 100 fewer cabins than *MSC Opera*. The blue funnel is quite sleek, with a swept-back design and carries the MSC logo in gold lettering. Although similar in size and structure to *MSC Lirica*, there are many modifications, mostly in technical spaces, and an improved layout in public rooms. More cabins have a private balcony.

All decks are named after operas. The interior layout and passenger flow are quite good, except for a couple of points of congestion, typically when the first seating exits the dining room and passengers on second seating are waiting to enter. The decor has many Italian influences, including clean lines, minimalism in furniture design, and a collection of colors, soft furnishings and fabrics that work well together, and without any hint of garishness. Real wood and marble have been used extensively in the interiors. The "fit and finish" of the interior decor, and most carpeting, is very good.

Facilities include the ship's main showlounge, a nightclub/discotheque, several lounges and bars, an internet center with 10 terminals, a virtual reality center, a children's club, a shopping gallery named Via Conditti with shops that

BERLITZ'S RATINGS		
	Possible	Achieved
Ship	500	410
Accommodation	200	156
Food	400	234
Service	400	298
Entertainment	100	62
Cruise	400	285
OVERALL SCORE		
1,445 points out of 2,000		

have an integrated bar and entertainment area so that shopping becomes a city-like environment where you can shop, drink, and be entertained all in one convenient area. The Monte Carlo Casino has blackjack, poker and roulette games, together with an array of slot machines. There is also a card room, but the integral library is small and disappointing, and there are no hardback books.

Drinking places include the Sotto Vento Pub (under the showlounge), and the La Cabala lounge. A 15% gratuity is added to all drinks/beverage orders.

Outside on deck, a neat eight-hole mini-golf course wraps around the funnel, while a walking/jogging track encircles the two swimming pools. The ship is designed to accommodate families with children, who have their own play center, youth counselors, and programming.

Anyone who is wheelchair-bound should note that there is no access to the uppermost forward and aft decks, although access throughout most of the interior of the ship is very good, and there are several wheelchair-accessible public restrooms. In passenger hallways it can be a squeeze to get past housekeeping carts at certain hours.

Minor niggles include the "in your face" photographers; constant music in every lounge; and the fact that standing in line for embarkation, disembarkation, shore tenders and for self-serve buffet meals is an inevitable aspect of cruising aboard all large ships, although lines are minimal when the ship operates from Port Everglades. Smokers are everywhere, and are virtually impossible to avoid. There is no forward observation lounge.

ACCOMMODATION. There are 11 price levels, depending

on grade and location: one suite category, five outside-view cabin grades, and five interior (no view) cabin grades. Included are 172 "suites" with private balcony, outside-view cabins and interior cabins. The cabin numbering system has even-numbered cabins on the starboard side, and odd-numbered cabins on the port side – contrary to nautical convention.

All cabins have a mini-bar and personal safe, satellite TV, several audio channels, and 24-hour room service. Tea and coffee are complimentary, but snacks delivered by room service cost extra.

Accommodation designated as suites – they are not true suites, as there is no separate bedroom and lounge – has more room, a larger lounge area, walk-in closet, wall-to-wall vanity counter, a bathroom with combination tub and shower, toilet, and semi-private balcony with a light but partitions between each balcony that are partial, not full. Cotton bathrobes are provided. Except for the very highest category, the suite bathrooms are very plain, with white plastic wash-basins and white walls, and mirrors that steam up.

Some cabins on Othello Deck and Rigoletto Deck have views obstructed by lifeboats, while those on Turandot Deck aft (10192–10241) may be subject to late-night and early morning noise from the cafeteria on the deck above. Cabins on the uppermost accommodation deck are subject to deck chairs and tables being dragged across the deck when it is set up or cleaned early in the morning.

CUISINE. There is one principal dining room, *La Caravella Restaurant*, with large ocean view picture windows in the aft section of the ship. There are two seatings for meals, in keeping with other ships in the MSC Cruises fleet, and tables are for two, four, six, or eight.

L'Approdo Restaurant is assigned to all passengers occupying accommodation designated as suites, although other passengers can dine in it too, on a reservations-only basis. As you might expect, the food and service are superior to that in the main dining room.

Casual, self-serve buffets for breakfast and lunch can be taken in *Le Vele Cafeteria,* although the serving lines on both port and starboard sides are quite cramped and the food is quite basic, or at the pool deck outside the fast food eatery, with grill and pizzeria. Le Vele is also open for sit-down, served, but casual dinners each evening. Extra-cost coffee/tea and pastries are served in the *Aroma Café*, on the upper level of the two-deck-high atrium lobby, but annoying videos constantly play on TVsets in the forward sections.

ENTERTAINMENT. The 713-seat Theatre dell Opera is the ship's main showlounge, located in the forward section of the ship. It has tiered seating set in a sloping floor, and the sightlines are good from most seats, which are plush and comfortable. The room can also serve as a venue for large social functions. There is no separate bandstand and the shows use recorded music, so there's little consistency in orchestration and sound balance.

High-quality entertainment has not, to date, been a priority for MSC Cruises. As a result, production shows and variety acts tend to be amateurish at best when compared to some other major cruise lines.

The Opera Lounge, one deck above the show lounge, is for social dancing, with a live band. Meanwhile, for the young and lively set, there is the Byblos Discotheque, the ship's throbbing, ear-melting discotheque.

SPA/FITNESS. The Opera Health Center is one deck above the navigation bridge at the forward end of the ship. The complex has a beauty salon, several treatment rooms offering massage and other body-pampering treatments, as well as a gymnasium with ocean views and an array of high-tech, muscle-toning and strengthening equipment. There's also a thermal suite, containing different kinds of steam rooms combined with aromatherapy infusions, at extra cost.

The health center is run as a concession by the excellent Italian company OceanView, with European hairstylists and Balinese massage and body treatment staff. Gratuities are not included, and are at your discretion.

● **For more extensive general information about the MSC Cruises experience, see pages 144–5.**

MSC Orchestra
★★★★

Size:	Large Resort Ship	Passenger Decks:	13	Cabins (with private balcony):	827
Tonnage:	92,409	Total Crew:	987	Cabins (wheelchair accessible):	17
Lifestyle:	Standard	Passengers		Wheelchair accessibility:	Good
Cruise Line:	MSC Cruises	(lower beds/all berths):	2,550/3,013	Cabin Voltage:	110/220 volts
Former Names:	none	Passenger Space Ratio		Elevators:	13
Builder:	Aker Yards (France)	(lower beds/all berths):	36.2/30.6	Casino (gaming tables):	Yes
Original Cost:	$360 million	Crew/Passenger Ratio		Slot Machines:	Yes
Entered Service:	May 2007	(lower beds/all berths):	2.6/3.0	Swimming Pools (outdoors):	2
Registry:	Italy	Cabins (total):	1,275	Swimming Pools (indoors):	0
Length (ft/m):	963.9/293.8	Size Range (sq ft/m):	150.6–301.3/	Whirlpools:	4
Beam (ft/m):	105.6/32.2		14.0–28.0	Self-Service Launderette:	No
Draft (ft/m):	25.2/7.7	Cabins (outside view):	1,000	Dedicated Cinema/Seats:	No
Propulsion/Propellers:	diesel electric	Cabins (interior/no view):	275	Library:	Yes
	(40.4MW)/2	Cabins (for one person):	0	Onboard currency:	Euros

A large, family-friendly ship with elegant decor.

OVERVIEW. *MSC Musica* suits young adult couples, singles, and families with tots, children and teens who enjoy big-ship surroundings and a noisy, big-city lifestyle, with of different nationalities and languages, mostly European. The ship is designed to accommodate families with children, who have their own play center, video games room, youth counselors, and activity programs.

THE SHIP. *MSC Orchestra* is a sister to *MSC Musica* and *MSC Poesia*, though its fabrics and furnishings are much nicer and softer. Among the numerous lounges and bars, the Out of Africa Savannah Lounge is stunning. A delightful four-piece classical ensemble regularly performs in the atrium lobby.

For a full description of other drinking places and facilities, see the entry for *MSC Musica* on page 453.

ACCOMMODATION. There are 12 price levels, depending on grade and location. For details of their facilities, see the entry for *MSC Musica*.

CUISINE. There are two main dining rooms, *Villa Borghese Restaurant* and *L'Ibiscus*, located in the aft section of the ship, and with large ocean-view picture windows. There are two seatings for dinner, and open seating for breakfast and lunch. Tables are for two, four, six or eight, and some alcove banquette seating. Those occupying upper-grade accommodation typically get better tables in quieter areas.

La Piazzetta Café is for casual, self-serve buffet-style breakfasts and for sit-down, served, but casual dinners.

Alternative (extra-cost) Dining Venues:

● The *Shanghai Chinese Restaurant* makes a change from

BERLITZ'S RATINGS		
	Possible	Achieved
Ship	500	413
Accommodation	200	156
Food	400	243
Service	400	298
Entertainment	100	62
Cruise	400	293

OVERALL SCORE
1,465 points out of 2,000

the main restaurants. This is the first real Chinese restaurant aboard any cruise ship – mainly because of the challenges of providing high-temperature wok and deep fryer preparation. Dim sum steamed dishes are also served, typically for lunch. The food embraces four main cuisines – Beijing, Cantonese, Shanghai and Szechzuan – and there's Tsing Tao beer.

● The *Four Seasons Restaurant* offers extra-cost à la carte Italian cuisine in a garden-like setting with fine china.

ENTERTAINMENT. Covent Garden is the ship's stunning large show lounge. The Opera Lounge, one deck above, is the place for social dancing, with live music. The G32 discotheque is for the more energetic. A large poolside movie screen provides movie-goers with more choices. Activities are provided by a team of multi-lingual animators.

SPA/FITNESS. The Orchestra Health Center, run by the Italian company OceanView, has a beauty salon, several treatment rooms offering massage and other body-pampering treatments, as well as a gymnasium with ocean views and high-tech equipment.

There's also a thermal suite, containing different kinds of steam rooms combined with aromatherapy infusions, at extra cost. There's a neat juice/smoothie bar opposite the reception desk. Gratuities are at your discretion.

There are also deck quoits, two shuffleboard courts, a tennis and basketball court, mini-golf, and a jogging track.

● **For more extensive general information about the MSC Cruises experience, see pages 144–5.**

MSC Poesia
★★★★

Size: . . . . .Large Resort Ship	Total Crew: .987	Cabins (wheelchair accessible): 17
Tonnage: .92,490	Passengers	Wheelchair accessibility: . . . . .Good
Lifestyle: . . . . .Standard	(lower beds/all berths): 2,550/3,013	Cabin Voltage: . . . . .110/220 volts
Cruise Line: . . . . .MSC Cruises	Passenger Space Ratio	Elevators: 13
Former Names: . . . . .none	(lower beds/all berths): 36.2/30.6	Casino (gaming tables): . . . . .Yes
Builder: . . . . .Fincantieri (Italy)	Crew/Passenger Ratio	Slot Machines: . . . . .Yes
Original Cost: . . . .$360 million	(lower beds/all berths): 2.6/3.0	Swimming Pools (outdoors): 2
Entered Service: . . . . .Oct 2008	Cabins (total): 1,275	Swimming Pools (indoors): 0
Registry: . . . . .Panama	Size Range (sq ft/m): 150.6–301.3/	Whirlpools: 4
Length (ft/m): 963.9/293.8	14.0–28.0	Self-Service Launderette: . . . . .No
Beam (ft/m): 105.6/32.2	Cabins (outside view): 1,000	Dedicated Cinema/Seats: . . . . .No
Draft (ft/m): 26.2/8.0	Cabins (interior/no view): 275	Library: . . . . .Yes
Propulsion/Propellers: diesel (58,000kW)/2	Cabins (for one person): 0	Onboard currency: . . . . .Euros
Passenger Decks: 13	Cabins (with private balcony): 827	

A large Euro-style informal and family-friendly ship.

OVERVIEW. *MSC Poesia* suits young adult couples, singles, and families with tots, children and teens who enjoy big-ship surroundings and a noisy, big-city lifestyle, with of different nationalities and languages, mostly European. The ship is designed to accommodate families with children, who have their own play center, video games room, youth counselors, and activity programs.

THE SHIP. *MSC Poesia* is a sister ship to *MSC Musica* and *MSC Orchestra*. The focal point of the ship is the main three-deck high lobby, with a water-feature backdrop and a crystal piano on a small stage that appears to float on a pond.

For a full description of all the ship's facilities, see the entry for *MSC Musica* on page 453.

ACCOMMODATION. There are 12 price levels, depending on grade and location. For a detailed description of their facilities, see the entry for *MSC Musica*.

CUISINE. There are two principal dining rooms, both aft with large ocean-view picture windows. There are two seatings for meals, as aboard other ships in the MSC Cruises fleet, and tables are for two, four, six, or eight; seating is both banquette-style and in individual chairs; the chairs, however, are slim and do not have armrests.

All dining venues are managed by Italian nationals.
Alternative Dining Spots:
● A *Tex-Mex Restaurant* is the ship's extra-cost à la carte dining spot; reservations are necessary.
● *Kaito* is an extra-cost Japanese restaurant, with a sushi bar and an extensive à la carte menu. Reservations needed.

BERLITZ'S RATINGS		
	Possible	Achieved
Ship	500	414
Accommodation	200	156
Food	400	243
Service	400	298
Entertainment	100	62
Cruise	400	294
OVERALL SCORE		
1,467 points out of 2,000		

● The *Wine Bar* provides a selection of famous regional cheeses, hams and wine in a bistro-style setting that is relaxing and entertaining.

The *Villa Pompeina Cafeteria* is for casual, self-serve buffets for breakfast and lunch and for sit-down, served, but casual dinners. Outside, there's a fast-food eatery on the pool deck. Coffee/tea and pastries are available in several bars adjacent to the midships atrium lobby.

Silver trays full of late-night snacks are taken throughout the ship by waiters, and on some days, special late-night desserts, such as flambé items, are showcased in various lounges.

ENTERTAINMENT. There is one large, principal show-lounge, located in the forward section of the ship. It has tiered seating on two levels – the sightlines are good from most of the plush, comfortable seats. The room can also be a venue for large groups or social functions. There is no showband, and all shows are performed to pre-recorded music tracks.

Another large lounge, aft of the showlounge, is the place for social dancing and functions such as cooking demonstrations, with live music provided by a band.

Big-screen movies are shown on a large screen above the forward pool, just behind the ship's mast.

SPA/FITNESS. The Poesia Health Center is run by the Italian company OceanView. For details of its facilities and other sporting options, see the entry for *MSC Musica*.

● **For more extensive general information about the MSC Cruises experience, see pages 144–5.**

MSC Sinfonia
★★★ +

Size: . . . . .Large Resort Ship	Passenger Decks: 10	Cabins (wheelchair accessible): 2
Tonnage: . . . . .58,600 tons	Total Crew: 710	Wheelchair accessibility: . . . . .Good
Lifestyle: . . . . .Standard	Passengers	Cabin Current: . . . . .110 and 220 volts
Cruise Line: . . . . .MSC Cruises	(lower beds/all berths): 1,566/2,223	Elevators: 9
Former Names: . . . .*European Stars*	Passenger Space Ratio	Casino (gaming tables): . . . . .Yes
Builder: Chantiers de l'Atlantique (France)	(lower beds/all berths): 37.4/27.6	Slot Machines: . . . . .Yes
Original Cost: . . . .$245 million	Crew/Passenger Ratio	Swimming Pools (outdoors): 1
Entered Service: . . . . .Apr 2002/Mar 2005	(lower beds/all berths): 2.2/3.1	Swimming Pools (indoors): 0
Registry: . . . . .Italy	Cabins (total): 783	Whirlpools: . . . . .1 (thalassotherapy)
Length (ft/m): 823.4/251.0	Size Range (sq ft/m): .139.9–236.8/13–22	Self-Service Launderette: . . . . .No
Beam (ft/m): 94.4/28.8	Cabins (outside view): 511	Dedicated Cinema/Seats: . . . . .No
Draft (ft/m): 22.4/6.85	Cabins (interior/no view): 272	Library: . . . . .Yes
Propulsion/Propellers: . . . . .diesel	Cabins (for one person): 0	Onboard currency: . . . . .Euros
(31,680 kW)/2 azimuthing pods	Cabins (with private balcony): 132	

A large Euro-style, informal and family-friendly ship.

OVERVIEW. *MSC Sinfonia* is best for adult couples and singles, and families with children, who enjoy big-city life, constant activity accompanied by lots of noise, late nights, entertainment that is loud and of questionable quality, and food that is quantity rather than quality. The constant push for onboard revenue is irritating – you have to pay extra even to visit the ship's navigation bridge.

THE SHIP. *MSC Sinfonia* is a sister of *MSC Armonia*, with a decor that's decidedly "European Moderne." The international mix of passengers adds to the overall ambience of the cruise experience. For a full description of its facilities, see the entry for *MSC Armonia* on page 443.

ACCOMMODATION. For an assessment of facilities offered by the 11 price categories, see the entry for *MSC Armonia*.

CUISINE. There are two main dining rooms, the 610-seat *Il Galeone Restaurant* and the *Il Covo Restaurant*; both have two seatings and share the same menu. The cuisine is reasonably sound, and, with varied menus and good presentation, should prove a highlight for most passengers. The wine list has a wide variety of wines at fairly reasonable prices, although almost all are very young.

La Terrazza is a casual, self-serve buffet eatery, open 24 hours a day, including sit-down, served, but casual dinners. The selections are very standardized and could be better. *Café del Mare*, adjacent to one of two swimming pools and

to the ship's funnel, is a grill area for fast food.

Extra-cost coffee/tea and pastries are available in *Le Baroque Café*, set around the upper level of the two-deck-high atrium lobby. It's a good location for people-watching, but annoying music videos are constantly played on TV monitors in the forward sections.

ENTERTAINMENT. The two-deck-high Gondola Theater is used for production shows, cabaret acts, plays and other theatrical presentations. Entertainment is a weak area for MSC Cruises, although this could improve as more ships are brought into service and more money is assigned to this important aspect of the company's cruise product. Other shows consist of unknown cabaret acts doing the cruise ship circuit – typically singers, magicians, mime artistes, and comedy jugglers. The principal difficulty aboard this ship is that the ship operates year-round in five or six languages, making entertainment other than visual acts such as mime, magic or juggling virtually impossible.

The ship carries a number of bands and small musical units that provide live music for dancing or listening in various lounges and bars throughout the ship.

SPA/FITNESS. For details of the Atlantica Spa's facilities and other sports options, see the entry for *MSC Armonia*.

● **For more extensive general information about the MSC Cruises experience, see pages 144–5.**

BERLITZ'S RATINGS

	Possible	Achieved
Ship	500	388
Accommodation	200	152
Food	400	233
Service	400	295
Entertainment	100	55
Cruise	400	273

OVERALL SCORE
1,396 points out of 2,000

MSC Splendida
★★★★ to ★★★★ +

Size:.............................Large Resort Ship	Passenger Decks:................................13	Cabins (with private balcony):.........1,260
Tonnage:.......................................133,500	Total Crew:.......................................1,313	Cabins (wheelchair accessible):...........43
Lifestyle:.....................................Standard	Passengers	Wheelchair accessibility:..........Good
Cruise Line:...........................MSC Cruises	(lower beds/all berths):.........3,274/3,900	Cabin Voltage:...........................110 volts
Former Names:................................none	Passenger Space Ratio	Elevators:..14
Builder:....................Aker Yards (France)	(lower beds/all berths):............40.7/34.2	Casino (gaming tables):......................Yes
Original Cost:........................$550 million	Crew/Passenger Ratio	Slot Machines:...................................Yes
Entered Service:........................Jul 2009	(lower beds/all berths):.................2.4/2.9	Swimming Pools (outdoors):...................3
Registry:......................................Panama	Cabins (total):..................................1,637	Swimming Pools (indoors): 1 (glass dome)
Length (ft/m):.....................1,093.5/333.3	Size Range (sq ft/m):..........161.4–699.6/	Whirlpools:...13
Beam (ft/m):............................124.6/38.0	15–65	Self-Service Launderette:....................No
Draft:...27.2/8.45	Cabins (outside view):.....................1,354	Dedicated Cinema/Seats:....................No
Propulsion/Propellers:.....................diesel	Cabins (interior/no view):..................283	Library:..Yes
(40,000 kW)/2	Cabins (for one person):..........................0	Onboard currency:..........................Euros

A large, family-friendly ship with elegant decor.

OVERVIEW. This ship appeals to young adult couples, singles, and families with children and teens who enjoy big ships with a mix of nationalities, mostly European. Children appreciate Virtual World's five white-knuckle 4D rides in a 10-seat thrill room. It all feels rather like a European city-center.

THE SHIP. This is a sister ship to *MSC Fantasia.* The public rooms include a large showlounge, a nightclub/disco, many lounges and bars (most with live music), library, card room, an internet center, and an extensive shopping gallery.

The ship is well designed to accommodate families with children, who have their own play centers (a club and jungle adventure playground), youth counselors, and programs. A 15% gratuity is added to all drinks/beverage orders.

ACCOMMODATION. Eighty percent of the cabins are outsides, of which 95% have a balcony – the standard balcony cabin is almost 172 sq ft (16 sq meters), plus bathroom and balcony. It's worth paying extra to stay in one of the 99 "suites" (each 312 sq ft (29 sq. meters) in the Yacht Club area at the top, front end of the ship. Here, you'll get silver-tray room service, a reserved section of the Villa Verde restaurant, plus access to a "members only" sundeck sanctuary area that includes its own bar and food counters, small dip pool, two hot tubs, and open lounging deck. It's a world away from the hustle and bustle of the main pool decks.

The Yacht Club has its own serene concierge lounge, small library and concierge reception desk. A Svarovski glass stairway leads to the Yacht Club accommodation

BERLITZ'S RATINGS

	Possible	Achieved	Yacht Club
Ship	500	425	426
Accommodation	200	162	162
Food	400	260	283
Service	400	300	313
Entertainment	100	77	76
Cruise	400	304	310

OVERALL SCORE
1,528 points/1,570 (Yacht Club)
out of 2,000

suites, and a private elevator accesses the Aurea Spa one deck below. The lounge has its own galley and dedicated chef. Each day, he prepares small plate dishes, artfully presented using fresh, local ingredients.

CUISINE. *Villa Verde* is the main restaurant, with two seatings for dinner, and open seating for breakfast and lunch. Tables are for two, four, six or eight, and there's some alcove banquette seating. *L'Olivo* is an Italian/Mediterranean extra-cost à la carte venue, *Santa Fe* is an extra-cost Tex-Mex restaurant, and *Bora Bora Cafeteria* is a large casual self-serve lido buffet-style eatery open for breakfast, and lunch and for sit-down, casual, served dinners in the evening.

ENTERTAINMENT. The Strand Theater has plush seating in tiers for as many as 1,700, and good sightlines. Because the passengers are multilingual, the shows concentrate on visual entertainment such as mime, magic, dancing, and acrobatics, and are performed with recorded music.

SPA/FITNESS. The Aurea Spa (16,000 sq ft/1,485 sq meters) and has a beauty salon, well-equipped treatment rooms, and a large gymnasium with ocean views. Included is a large thermal suite, and saunas. The decor is welcoming and restful. The spa is run as a concession by the Italian company OceanView. Sports facilities include deck quoits, large tennis/basketball court, minigolf, and a jogging track.

● **For more extensive general information about the MSC Cruises experience, see pages 144–5.**

National Geographic Endeavour
★★

Size:	Boutique Ship
Tonnage:	3,132
Lifestyle:	Standard
Cruise Line:	Lindblad Expeditions
Former Names:	*Caledonian Star,*
	North Star, Lindmar, Marburg
Builder:	A.G. Weser Seebeckwerft (Germany)
Original Cost:	n/a
Entered Service:	1966/1984
Registry:	The Bahamas
Length (ft/m):	292.6/89.20
Beam (ft/m):	45.9/14.00
Draft (ft/m):	20.3/6.20
Propulsion/Propellers:	diesel (3,236kW)/1

Passenger Decks:	6
Total Crew:	64
Passengers	
(lower beds/all berths):	113/124
Passenger Space Ratio	
(lower beds/all berths):	27.7/25.2
Crew/Passenger Ratio	
(lower beds/all berths):	1.7/1.9
Cabins (total):	62
Size Range (sq ft/m):	191.6–269.1/17.8–25.0
Cabins (outside view):	62
Cabins (interior/no view):	0
Cabins (for one person):	14
Cabins (with private balcony):	0

Cabins (wheelchair accessible):	0
Wheelchair accessibility:	None
Cabin Current:	110/220 volts
Elevators:	0
Casino (gaming tables):	No
Slot Machines:	No
Swimming Pools (outdoors):	1
Whirlpools:	0
Self-Service Launderette:	No
Lecture/Film Rooms:	Yes
Library:	Yes
Zodiacs:	10
Helicopter Pad:	No
Onboard currency:	US$

A very small ship, for nature and wildlife cruises.

OVERVIEW. This ship and its type of soft exploration cruising are best suited to adventurous, hardy types who enjoy being with nature and wildlife in some of the most interesting places, but cosseted aboard a small, modestly comfortable ship. Specialized lecturers accompanying each cruise make this a real life-enrichment experience for a clientele wanting to travel and learn.

THE SHIP. Renamed in 2005, the former *Endeavour* was built as a stern factory fishing trawler for North Sea service, before being morphed into a passenger ship. Today, it is tidy and well cared for as an expedition cruise vessel operating "soft" expedition cruises. There is an open bridge policy for all passengers. The vessel carries Zodiac landing craft for in-depth excursions, and there is an enclosed shore tender. A steep aft stairway leads down to the landing craft platform. The ship has a warm, intimate ambience, and a casual dress code.

This small ship has a reasonable number of public rooms and facilities, including a lecture room/lounge/bar/library, where videos are also stocked for in-cabin use. There's a good book selection.

This likeable, homey ship runs well-organized destination-intensive, soft expedition-style cruises, at a very reasonable price. It attracts loyal repeat passengers who don't want to sail aboard ships that look like apartment blocks. The itineraries include Antarctica, where this ship has been operating since 1998.

The interior stairways are a little steep, as is the exterior stairway to the Zodiac embarkation points. Noise

BERLITZ'S RATINGS		
	Possible	Achieved
Ship	500	198
Accommodation	200	86
Food	400	193
Service	400	217
Entertainment	n/a	n/a
Cruise	500	251

OVERALL SCORE
945 points out of 2,000

from the diesel engines can be irksome, particularly on the lower decks. Recommended gratuities are $10 per person, per day.

ACCOMMODATION. There are five categories of cabins: one suite category and four non-suite categories. The all-outside-view cabins (all above the waterline) are very compact, but reasonably comfortable, and they are decorated in warm, muted tones. All cabins have a mini-bar/refrigerator, video player, a decent amount of closet and drawer space – though it's tight for long voyages – and a clock. The bathrooms are tight, with little space for storing toiletries.

Four "suites" are basically double the size of a standard cabin, and have a wood partition separating the bedroom and lounge area. The bathroom is still small, however.

CUISINE. The open-seating dining room is small and charming, but the low-back chairs are not very comfortable. The cuisine is European in style with reasonably high quality, fresh ingredients, but not a lot of menu choice. Salad items, in particular, are rather scarce on variety, as are international cheeses. Service is attentive and friendly.

ENTERTAINMENT. The main lounge is the venue for lectures, slide shows and occasional film presentations. There are no shows (none are needed), and no facilities for them.

SPA/FITNESS. There is a small fitness room – about three people and it's full – and a tiny sauna.

National Geographic Explorer
★★

Size: ....Small Ship	Total Crew: 70	Wheelchair Accessibility: ....None
Tonnage: 6,471	Passengers	Cabin Current: ....110 volts
Lifestyle: ....Standard	(lower beds/all berths): 148/181	Elevators: 1
Cruise Line: ....Lindblad Expeditions	Passenger Space Ratio	Casino (gaming tables): ....No
Former Names: ...*Midnatsol II, Midnatsol*	(lower beds/all berths): 43.7/35.7	Slot Machines: ....No
Builder: ....Ulstein Hatlo (Norway)	Crew/Passenger Ratio	Swimming Pools (outdoors): 0
Original Cost: ....n/a	(lower beds/all berths): 2.1/2.5	Swimming Pools (indoors): 0
Entered Service: 1982/Jun 2008	Cabins (total): 81	Whirlpools: 0
Registry: ....The Bahamas	Size Range (sq ft/m): ....n/a	Self-Service Launderette: ....No
Length (ft/m): 367.4/112.0	Cabins (outside view): 81	Dedicated Cinema/Seats: ....No
Beam (ft/m): 54.1/16.5	Cabins (interior/no view): 0	Library: ....Yes
Draft (ft/m): 15.0/4.5	Cabins (for one person): 14	Onboard Currency: ....US$
Propulsion/Propellers: diesel/2	Cabins (with private balcony): 3	
Passenger Decks: 6	Cabins (wheelchair accessible): 1	

A small, sturdy ship for nature and wildlife cruises.

OVERVIEW. This ship suits hardy, adventurous types who enjoy being with nature and wildlife in some of the most interesting and occasionally inhospitable places on earth, cosseted aboard a small but comfortable ship.

THE SHIP. Originally built as *Midnatsol* for Hurtigruten, the ship was purchased by Lindblad Expeditions in 2007 and extensively refitted and outfitted for expedition-style cruising, with some decent facilities and expedition equipment, including kayaks, Zodiac inflatable landing craft, a semi-submersible vehicle, hydrophones, and a high-definition underwater camera.

The ship, which sits long and low in the water, has an ice-strengthened hull. Stabililizers were added in a 2008 refit so that movement is minimized in the sometimes tough Arctic and Antarctic operating conditions. The twin funnel uptakes are located almost at the stern. There is little outdoor deck space, but it's not really needed in cold-weather operating areas such as the Arctic or Antarctic.

Kayaks and Zodiac inflatable craft are carried, as well as an ROV (remotely operated vehicle – it's actually an underwater video camera in a cage that is controlled from the ship) that can dive to 1,000 ft (300 meters). It then displays images – such as those from underneath ice shelves or icebergs – on high-definition screens in the ship's lounges and in-cabin television system.

Facilities include a lecture room and bistro bar with espresso machine adjacent to the restaurant boot washing stations (which have lockers for stowing your wet gear). An expedition voyage aboard this ship is all about learning and exploration. The dress code is casual, and layered cloth-

BERLITZ'S RATINGS		
	Possible	Achieved
Ship	500	172
Accommodation	200	75
Food	400	177
Service	400	212
Entertainment	n/a	n/a
Cruise	500	220
OVERALL SCORE		
856 points out of 2,000		

ing is recommended. Gratuities to staff are not included in the price.

ACCOMMODATION. The price you pay depends on size and location. The cabins are small, as are the bathrooms, although they are nicely designed, practical units. Some have a fixed queen-size bed configuration, others have twin beds (some can be pushed together, some are fixed). There are several cabins for single occupancy. The tiled bathrooms have shower enclosures, and small shelves for toiletries. Suites have two washbasins, premium bedding, and feather-fluffy duvets.

There is a decent supply of electrical outlets and an ethernet connection for laptops, but don't expect satellite signals to be consistent – you may not be able to upload or download for long periods, depending on the ship's operating area. Closet doors are of the sliding type instead of the outward opening type, to minimize noise and banging when the ship is in tough weather conditions. Naturally, a National Geographic Atlas is provided.

CUISINE. There is one main dining room, as well as areas for self-serve buffet-style food. The food is hearty and fairly healthy, although you should not expect to find fresh greens in some of the more out-of-the-way areas.

ENTERTAINMENT. Lectures, briefings and recaps.

SPA/FITNESS. There are two treatment rooms with skylights, for wildlife-inspired wellness, facials, and massage, including a special "ice-bear massage," as well as a fitness/workout room.

National Geographic Polaris
★★

Size: ....Boutique Ship	Passenger Decks: 4	Cabins (wheelchair accessible): 0
Tonnage: 2,214	Total Crew: 44	Wheelchair accessibility: ....None
Lifestyle: ....Standard	Passengers	Cabin Current: ....220 volts
Cruise Line: ....Lindblad Expeditions	(lower beds/all berths): 82/84	Elevators: 0
Former Names: *Polaris, Lindblad Polaris,*	Passenger Space Ratio	Casino (gaming tables): ....No
Oresund	(lower beds/all berths): 27.0/26.3	Slot Machines: ....No
Builder: ....Aalborg Vaerft (Denmark)	Crew/Passenger Ratio	Swimming Pools (outdoors): 0
Original Cost: ....n/a	(lower beds/all berths): 1.8/1.8	Whirlpools: 0
Entered Service: 1960/May 1987	Cabins (total): 41	Self-Service Launderette: ....No
Registry: ....Ecuador	Size Range (sq ft/m): .99.0–229.2/9.2–21.3	Lecture/Film Room: ....No
Length (ft/m): 236.6/72.12	Cabins (outside view): 41	Library: ....Yes
Beam (ft/m): 42.7/13.03	Cabins (interior/no view): 0	Zodiacs: 8
Draft (ft/m): 13.7/4.30	Cabins (for one person): 0	Helicopter Pad: ....No
Propulsion/Propellers: diesel (2,354 kW)/2	Cabins (with private balcony): 0	Onboard currency: .Ecuadorian sucre/US$

A small ship for cruising in the Galápagos islands.

OVERVIEW. This is a decent enough small vessel, operating year-round nature-intensive "soft" expedition cruises based in and around the Galápagos Islands. This type of cruising is best suited to adventurous, hardy outdoors types who enjoy being with nature and wildlife in one of the most interesting places on earth.

THE SHIP. This cute "soft" expedition cruise vessel is of modest proportions, and has a dark blue hull and white superstructure. It has been well maintained and operated, having been skillfully converted from a Scandinavian ferry. It has a fantail and an aft lounge area outdoors, and carries several Zodiac inflatable rubber landing craft, as well as a glass-bottom boat.

Inside, there are few public rooms, although the Scandinavian-style interior furnishings and decor are very tidy and welcoming (if dated), accented by lots of wood trim. There's a friendly, very intimate atmosphere on board, with Filipino service staff, and a good team of lecturers and nature observers whose daily recaps are a vital part of the experience. A restful, well-stocked library helps passengers learn more about the region and the natural world.

If you are going on a Galápagos cruise, it is important to take with you: passport, short and long-sleeve cotton shirts, good walking shoes, windbreaker, mosquito repellent (mosquitoes are at their worst between December and July, particularly in Bartolome), sunglasses with retaining strap, and any personal medication. You will need to take a flight from Quito to San Cristobal, via Guayaquil, to join your cruise.

It's an area to which the ship is well suited because only

BERLITZ'S RATINGS		
	Possible	Achieved
Ship	500	189
Accommodation	200	85
Food	400	186
Service	400	216
Entertainment	n/a	n/a
Cruise	500	267

OVERALL SCORE
943 points out of 2,000

90 passengers from any one ship are allowed at any one time in the islands, where tourism is managed well by the local Equadorians. In fact, this ship is among the best suited to this region.

Bottled water is provided at no extra charge. All port charges are included in this product, which is marketed by Lindblad Expeditions and Noble Caledonia.

ACCOMMODATION. There are five price grades. The cabins, all above the waterline (while most have windows, a few have portholes), are fairly roomy and nicely appointed, but there is little drawer space. Some have been refurbished, and have large (lower) beds. Each cabin has either a double bed or two single beds, a small writing desk, and hairdryer. Some of the larger cabins also have a third (upper) berth. The cabin bathrooms are tiny and the towels are small, too.

CUISINE. The *Dining Room* has big picture windows and a wrap-around view. Seating is now at individual tables (it used to be family-style) in a leisurely single seating.

The cuisine is basically sound, with emphasis on local fish and seafood, and other Ecuadorian regional specialties, but meats are poor. Breakfast and lunch are self-serve buffet-style. The wine selection is very limited.

ENTERTAINMENT. Lectures, briefings and recaps are the main onboard entertainment events, together with dinner and after-dinner conversation.

SPA/FITNESS. There is a small fitness room, large enough for two. Beauty isn't a big concern on such cruises.

National Geographic Sea Bird
★ +

Size:	Boutique Ship	Propulsion/Propellers:	diesel/2	Cabins (with private balcony):	0
Tonnage:	99.7	Passenger Decks:	4	Cabins (wheelchair accessible):	0
Lifestyle:	Standard	Total Crew:	22	Wheelchair accessibility:	None
Cruise Line:	Lindblad Expeditions/	Passengers		Cabin Current:	110 volts
	National Geographic	(lower beds/all berths):	70/70	Elevators:	0
Former Names:	Sea Bird,	Passenger Space Ratio		Casino (gaming tables):	No
	Majestic Explorer	(lower beds/all berths):	1.4/1.4	Slot Machines:	No
Builder:	Whidbey Island (USA)	Crew/Passenger Ratio		Swimming Pools (outdoors):	0
Original Cost:	n/a	(lower beds/all berths):	3.1/3.1	Swimming Pools (indoors):	0
Entered Service:	1981	Cabins (total):	36	Whirlpools:	0
Registry:	The Bahamas	Size Range (sq ft/m):	.73.0–202.0/6.7–18.7	Self-Service Launderette:	No
Length (ft/m):	151.9/46.3	Cabins (outside view):	36	Dedicated Cinema/Seats:	No
Beam (ft/m):	30.8/9.4	Cabins (interior/no view):	0	Library:	No
Draft (ft/m):	8.0/2.4	Cabins (for one person):	2	Onboard currency:	US$

A basic smaller, older ship for nature-watching.

OVERVIEW. This ship is best suited to senior-age couples and single travelers who enjoy learning about nature, geography, history and other life sciences in casual, non-dressy surroundings with no pretension. They are likely to be hardy, outdoors types who don't need a lot of entertainment or parlor games. Lectures and recap sessions are held daily.

THE SHIP. *National Geographic Sea Bird* carries a fleet of motorized Zodiac landing craft for use as shore tenders and for up-close shore exploration. A number of sea kayaks are also carried. An open-bridge policy means you can go to the navigation bridge at any time. The vessel is small enough to operate in ports and narrow inlets inaccessible to larger ships.

This small craft – sister ship *National Geographic Sea Lion* – is adequate for looking at nature and wildlife close-up, in modest but comfortable surroundings that provide an alternative to big-ship cruising. Cruises visit Alaska, Baja California and the Sea of Cortes. Tipping is suggested at about $7 per person per day.

In the cabins, the mattresses are enclosed in a wood frame with sharp corners, which you bang into constantly.

ACCOMMODATION. All cabins have rudimentary furniture, but all have an outside view through picture windows, except for those on the lowest deck, which have portholes

BERLITZ'S RATINGS

	Possible	Achieved
Ship	500	141
Accommodation	200	71
Food	400	149
Service	400	185
Entertainment	n/a	n/a
Cruise	500	197

OVERALL SCORE
743 points out of 2,000

but no view. Some cabins have double beds, and some have twin beds that can be pushed together to form a queen-size bed. Some are for singles, at a surcharge of 150%. There is just enough room to stow your luggage.

All cabins have a private bathroom, although it really is tiny. There is no room service for food or beverages.

CUISINE. The dining room, which has ocean-view picture windows, is large enough to accommodate all passengers in a single seating. The tables are not assigned, and so you can sit with whoever you like. The food is unpretentious, good and wholesome, although its presentation is very plain, with no frills, and features regional specialties.

The wine list is very limited, and is comprised mostly of wines from California.

ENTERTAINMENT. There is no formal entertainment, although dinner and after-dinner conversation with fellow passengers in the ship's lounge/bar really becomes the entertainment. So, if you're not in the mood to talk to your fellow passengers, you can retire with a good book, or go outside, where you'll usually find that nature provides varied entertainment.

SPA/FITNESS. There are no spa or fitness facilities aboard this very small cruise vessel.

National Geographic Sea Lion

★ +

Size: ....Boutique Ship	Propulsion/Propellers: diesel/2	Cabins (with private balcony): 0
Tonnage: 99.7	Passenger Decks: 4	Cabins (wheelchair accessible): 0
Lifestyle: ....Standard	Total Crew: 22	Wheelchair accessibility: ....None
Cruise Line: ......Lindblad Expeditions/	Passengers	Cabin Current: ....110 volts
National Geographic	(lower beds/all berths): 72/76	Elevators: 0
Former Names: ....Sea Lion,	Passenger Space Ratio	Casino (gaming tables): ....No
Great Rivers Explorer	(lower beds/all berths): 1.3/1.3	Slot Machines: ....No
Builder: ....Whidbey Island (USA)	Crew/Passenger Ratio	Swimming Pools (outdoors): 0
Original Cost: ....n/a	(lower beds/all berths): 3.2/3.4	Swimming Pools (indoors): 0
Entered Service: 1982	Cabins (total): 37	Whirlpools: 0
Registry: ....The Bahamas	Size Range (sq ft/m): .73.0–202.0/6.7–18.7	Self-Service Launderette: ....No
Length (ft/m): 151.9/46.3	Cabins (outside view): 37	Dedicated Cinema/Seats: ....No
Beam (ft/m): 30.8/9.4	Cabins (interior/no view): 0	Library: ....No
Draft (ft/m): 8.0/2.4	Cabins (for one person): 2	Onboard currency: ....US$

A small, older ship for wildlife and nature watching.

OVERVIEW. This ship is best suited to older couples and single travelers who enjoy learning about nature, geography, history and other life sciences, in casual, non-dressy surroundings without a hint of pretension. They are likely to be hardy, outdoors types who don't need entertainment or silly parlor games. The ship is small enough to operate in ports and narrow inlets inaccessible to larger vessels.

THE SHIP. *National Geographic Sea Lion* carries a fleet of motorized Zodiac landing craft for use as shore tenders and for up-close shore exploration. A number of sea kayaks are also carried. An open-bridge policy means that you are allowed to go to the navigation bridge at any time.

This small craft is adequate for looking at nature and wildlife up close, in modest but comfortable surroundings that provide an alternative to big-ship cruising. Lectures and recap sessions are held each day.

Cruises visit Alaska, Baja California and the Sea of Cortes. Tipping is suggested at about $7 per person per day. Note that in the cabins, the mattresses are enclosed in a wood frame with sharp corners, which you can all too easily bang into constantly.

ACCOMMODATION. All the cabins aboard this little ship have an outside view through picture windows, except for

BERLITZ'S RATINGS

	Possible	Achieved
Ship	500	141
Accommodation	200	71
Food	400	149
Service	400	185
Entertainment	n/a	n/a
Cruise	500	197

OVERALL SCORE
743 points out of 2,000

those on the lowest deck, which have portholes. Some cabins have double beds, some have twin beds that can be pushed together to form a queen-size bed. Some are for singles, at a surcharge of 15%. There is plenty of room to stow your luggage.

All cabins have a private bathroom, although it really is tiny. There is no room service for food or beverages.

CUISINE. The dining room, which has ocean-view picture windows, is large enough to accommodate all passengers in a single seating. The tables are not assigned, and so you can sit with whoever you like. The food is unpretentious, good and wholesome, although its presentation is very plain, with no frills, and features regional specialties.

The wine list is very limited, and is comprised mostly of wines from California.

ENTERTAINMENT. There is no formal entertainment, although dinner and after-dinner conversation with fellow passengers in the ship's lounge/bar really becomes the entertainment each evening. So, if you don't want to talk to your fellow passengers, take a good book, or go outside, where you'll find nature provides the rest of the entertainment.

SPA/FITNESS. There are no spa or fitness facilities aboard this very small cruise vessel.

Nautica
★★★★ +

Size:	Mid-Size Ship	Total Crew:	386
Tonnage:	30,277	Passengers	
Lifestyle:	Premium	(lower beds/all berths):	684/824
Cruise Line:	Oceania Cruises	Passenger Space Ratio	
Former Names:	R Five	(lower beds/all berths):	44.2/36.7
Builder:	Chantiers de l'Atlantique	Crew/Passenger Ratio	
Original Cost:	£150 million	(lower beds/all berths):	1.7/2.1
Entered Service:	Dec1998/Nov 2005	Cabins (total):	342
Registry:	Marshall Islands	Size Range (sq ft/m): 145.3–968.7/13.5–90.0	
Length (ft/m):	593.7/181.0	Cabins (outside view):	317
Beam (ft/m):	83.5/25.5	Cabins (interior/no view):	25
Draft (ft/m):	19.5/6.0	Cabins (for one person):	0
Propulsion/Propellers:	diesel (18,600 kW)/2	Cabins (with private balcony):	232
Passenger Decks:	9	Cabins (wheelchair accessible):	3

Wheelchair accessibility:	Good
Cabin Current:	110/220 volts
Elevators:	4
Casino (gaming tables):	Yes
Slot Machines:	Yes
Swimming Pools (outdoors):	1
Swimming Pools (indoors):	0
Whirlpools:	2 (+1 thalassotherapy)
Self-Service Launderette:	Yes
Dedicated Cinema/Seats:	No
Library:	Yes
Onboard currency:	US$

A stylish premium ship for mature-age cruisers.

OVERVIEW. *Nautica* is best suited to couples who like good food and style, but want informality with no formal nights on board, and interesting itineraries, all at a very reasonable price, well below what the luxury ships charge. Oceania Cruises is a young company with a refreshing vision and desire to provide an extremely high level of food and service in an informal setting that is at once elegant yet comfortable, and that is exactly what it has achieved.

BERLITZ'S RATINGS		
	Possible	Achieved
Ship	500	418
Accommodation	200	160
Food	400	312
Service	400	295
Entertainment	100	77
Cruise	400	313
OVERALL SCORE		
1,575 points out of 2,000		

THE SHIP. *Nautica,* almost identical to *Insignia* and *Regatta*, is an all-white ship with a large, square white funnel. The addition of teak overlaid decking and teak lounge chairs has greatly improved what was once a bland pool deck outdoors, but the front rows of double sunloungers ("cabanas") cost $100 a day.

The interior decor is quite stunning, a throwback to ship decor of the ocean liners of the 1920s and '30s, with dark woods and warm colors, all carried out in fine taste, although a bit faux in places. This includes detailed ceiling cornices, both real and faux wrought-iron staircase railings, leather-paneled walls, trompe l'oeil ceilings, rich carpeting in hallways with an Oriental rug-look center section, and many other interesting and expensive-looking decorative touches. It feels like an old-world country club.

The public rooms are spread over three decks. The lobby has a staircase with intricate wrought-iron railings. A large observation lounge, the Horizon Bar, is high atop ship.

There are plenty of bars – including one in each of the restaurant entrances. Perhaps the nicest is the casino bar/ lounge, a beautiful room reminiscent of London's grand hotels and includes a martini bar. It has an inviting marble fireplace, comfortable sofas and individual chairs.

The Library is a grand Regency-style room, with a fireplace, a high, indented, trompe l'oeil ceiling, and excellent selection of books, plus very comfortable wingback chairs with footstools, and sofas you could sleep on. Oceania@Sea is the internet connect center.

Gratuities are automatically added to your onboard account. Accommodations designated as suites pay more, for the butler. A 15% gratuity is added to bar and spa accounts.

The stairways, though carpeted, are tinny. Passenger niggles include all the "inventive" and highly irritating extra charges that can be incurred. What's nice is the fact that there are almost no announcements.

ACCOMMODATION. There are six cabin categories, and 10 price grades: three suite price grades, five outside-view cabin grades, and two interior cabin grades. All of the standard interior (no view) and outside-view cabins – the lowest four grades – are extremely compact units, and extremely tight for two persons, particularly for cruises longer than five days. They have twin beds or queen-size bed, with good under-bed storage areas, personal safe, vanity desk with large mirror, good closet and drawer space in rich, dark woods, 100% cotton bathrobe and towels, slippers, clothes brush and shoe horn. TV sets carry a major news channel, where obtainable, plus a sports channel and round-the-clock movie channels.

About 100 cabins qualify as "Concierge Level" accommodation, and occupants get extra goodies such as enhanced bathroom amenities, complimentary shoeshine, tote bag, cashmere throw blanket, bottle of champagne on arrival, hairdryer, priority restaurant reservations, priority embarkation and dedicated check-in desk,

Owner's Suites. The six Owner's Suites, measuring 962 sq.ft/89.3 sq.meters, are the most spacious accommodation. They are fine, large living spaces located aft overlooking the stern on Decks 6, 7, and 8 – they are, however, subject to more movement and some vibration. They have extensive teak-floor private balconies that really are private and can't be overlooked from the decks above. Each has an entrance foyer, living room, separate bedroom (the bed faces the sea, which can be seen through the floor-to-ceiling windows and sliding glass door), CD player with selection of audio discs, fully tiled bathroom with Jacuzzi tub, and a small guest bathroom.

Vista Suites. There are four, each around 785.7 sq.ft/73 sq.meters, and located forward on Decks 5 and 6. They have extensive teak-floor private balconies that can't be overlooked from the decks above. Each has an entrance foyer, living room, separate bedroom with similar layout to that in the owner's suites, CD player plus audio discs, and a fully tiled bathroom with Jacuzzi tub.

Penthouse Suites. There are 52 of these – though they are not suites at all but large cabins because the bedrooms aren't separate from the living areas. They measure around 322.9 sq.ft (30 sq. meters), and have a good-sized teak-floor balcony with sliding glass door (but with partial, and not full, balcony partitions) and teak deck furniture. The lounge area has a proper dining table and there is ample clothes storage space. The bathroom has a tub, shower enclosure, washbasin and toilet.

Cabins with Balcony. Cabins with private balconies (around 216 sq.ft/20 sq. meters), comprise about two-thirds of all cabins. They have partial, not full, balcony partitions and sliding glass doors, and 14 cabins on Deck 6 have lifeboat-obstructed views and no balcony. The living area has a refrigerated mini-bar, lounge area with breakfast table, and a balcony with teak floor, two teak chairs and a drinks table. The bathrooms, with tiled floors and plain walls, are compact, standard units, and include a shower stall with a strong, removable hand-held shower unit, hairdryer, toiletries storage shelves and retractable clothesline.

Outside View and Interior Cabins. These measure around 160–165 sq.ft (14.8–15.3 sq.meters), and have twin beds that convert to a queen-size bed, vanity desk, small sofa and coffee table, and bathroom with a shower enclosure with a strong, removable hand-held shower unit, hairdryer, toiletries storage shelves, retractable clothesline, washbasin, and toilet. Although they are not large, they are quite comfortable, with decent storage space.

All suites/cabins located at the stern may suffer from vibration and noise, particularly when the ship is proceeding at or close to full speed, or maneuvering in port.

CUISINE. Flexibility and choice are what the dining facilities aboard the Oceania ships are all about. There are four different restaurants:

● The *Grand Dining Room* has around 340 seats, and a raised central section, but the problem is the noise level: it's atrocious when the dining room is full – the effect of the low ceiling height. Being located at the stern, there are large ocean-view windows on three sides – prime tables overlook the stern. The chairs are comfortable and have armrests. The menus change daily for lunch and dinner.

● The *Toscana Italian Restaurant* has 96 seats, windows along two sides, and a set menu plus daily chef's specials.

● The cozy *Polo Grill* has 98 seats, windows along two sides and a set menu including prime steaks and seafood.

● The *Terrace Café* has seats for 154 indoors – not enough during cruises to cold-weather areas – and 186 outdoors. It is open for breakfast, lunch and casual dinners, when it has tapas (Tapas on the Terrace) and other Mediterranean food. As the ship's self-serve buffet restaurant, it incorporates a small pizzeria and grill. There are basic salads, a meat carving station, and a reasonable selection of cheeses.

All restaurants have open-seating dining, so you can dine when you want, with whom you wish. Reservations are needed in Toscana Restaurant and Polo Grill (but there's no extra charge), where there are mostly tables for four or six; there are few tables for two. There is a Poolside Grill Bar. All cappuccino and espresso coffees cost extra.

The food and service staff is provided by Apollo, a respected maritime catering company with an interest in Oceania Cruises. The consultant chef is Jacques Pépin, well-known in the United States as a television chef. This is a foodie's ship, with really high-quality ingredients, and a wide selection of dining venues. Particularly notable are the delicious breads, rolls, croissants and brioches – all made on board from French flower and d'Isigny butter.

On sea days, an elegant teatime is presented in the *Horizon Lounge*, with formally dressed staff, cake display trolleys, and an excellent array of cake and scones. Sadly, teabags – not loose tea – prevail.

ENTERTAINMENT. The Nautica Lounge has entertainment, lectures and some social events. There is little entertainment because of the intensive nature of the itineraries. However, there is live music in several bars and lounges.

SPA/FITNESS. A lido deck has a swimming pool, and good sunbathing space, plus a thalassotherapy tub. A jogging track circles the swimming pool deck, but one deck above. The uppermost outdoors deck includes a golf driving net and shuffleboard court. The Canyon Ranch SpaClub consists of a beauty salon, three treatment rooms, men's and women's changing rooms, and steam room. There is no sauna. An 18% gratuity applies to massages and treatments.

Navigator of the Seas
★★★★

Size: ....Large Resort Ship	Passenger Decks: 14	Cabins (with private balcony): 765
Tonnage: 137,276	Total Crew: 1,185	Cabins (wheelchair accessible): 26
Lifestyle: ....Standard	Passengers	Wheelchair accessibility: ....Best
Cruise Line: Royal Caribbean International	(lower beds/all berths): 3,114/3,835	Cabin Current: ....110 volts
Former Names: ....none	Passenger Space Ratio	Elevators: ....14 (6 glass-enclosed)
Builder: ...Kvaerner Masa-Yards (Finland)	(lower beds/all berths): 44.0/35.7	Casino (gaming tables): ....Yes
Original Cost: ....$500 million	Crew/Passenger Ratio	Slot Machines: ....Yes
Entered Service: ....Dec 2002	(lower beds/all berths): 2.6/3.2	Swimming Pools (outdoors): 3
Registry: ....The Bahamas	Cabins (total): 1,557	Swimming Pools (indoors): 0
Length (ft/m): 1,020.6/311.1	Size Range (sq ft/m): 151.0–1,358.0/	Whirlpools: 6
Beam (ft/m): 155.5/47.4	14.0–126.1	Self-Service Launderette: ....No
Draft (ft/m): 28.8/8.8	Cabins (outside view): 939	Dedicated Cinema/Seats: ....No
Propulsion/Propellers: ....diesel-electric	Cabins (interior/no view): 618	Library: ....Yes
(75,600 kW)/3 pods	Cabins (for one person): 0	Onboard currency: ....US$

A colorful, fun-filled ship for family-friendly cruising.

OVERVIEW. *Navigator of the Seas* is a large, floating leisure resort. It provides a host of facilities, rather like a small town, with plenty of entertainment for all ages, yet offers a healthy amount of space per passenger. The food focuses on quantity rather than quality unless you are prepared to pay extra in the "alternative" restaurant. Too big for the Panama Canal, it limits its itineraries mostly to the Caribbean, where only a few islands can accept it.

BERLITZ'S RATINGS		
	Possible	Achieved
Ship	500	418
Accommodation	200	150
Food	400	222
Service	400	276
Entertainment	100	83
Cruise	400	307
OVERALL SCORE		
1,456 points out of 2,000		

THE SHIP. *Navigator of the Seas* is a sister to *Adventure of the Seas*, *Explorer of the Seas*, and *Voyager of the Seas*. For a full run-down of the ship's facilities, including its many bars and lounges, its full-size ice-skating rink, wedding chapel, casino, and shopping choices, see the entry for *Adventure of the Seas* on page 196.

FAMILIES. Facilities for children and teenagers are extensive – much larger than aboard sister ships *Adventure of the Seas, Explorer of the Seas and Voyager of the Seas.*

An area called Adventure Ocean is split into age-related areas: "Aquanauts" is for 3–5-year-olds; "Explorers" is for 6–8-year-olds; "Voyagers" is for 9–12-year-olds. The Living Room and Fuel are dedicated areas for teenagers, that include a daytime club with several computers, soda bar, and disco; there's also an array of the latest video games. Paint and Clay is an arts and crafts center for younger children. Adjacent to these indoor areas is Adventure Beach, an area for all the family; this includes swimming pools, a water slide, and game areas outdoors.

ACCOMMODATION. There is an extensive range of 22 cabin categories, in four major groupings: Premium ocean-view suites and cabins, Promenade-view (interior-view) cabins, Ocean-view cabins, and Interior (no view) cabins. For a full description of these categories and their facilities, see the entry for *Voyager of the Seas* on page 650.

CUISINE. Apart from the main dining room, with a capacity of almost 2,000, alternative dining options include *Café Promenade, Windjammer Café, Chops Grill, Portofino, Johnny Rockets,* and *Sprinkles*. For details of dining times and food quality, see the entry for *Adventure of the Seas*.

ENTERTAINMENT. The 1,350-seat Metropolis Showlounge is the main theater for big production shows. The Ixtapa Lounge is the venue for cabaret acts and late-night adults-only comedy. For more information about the entertainment facilities, see the entry for *Adventure of the Seas*.

SPA/FITNESS. For details of the ShipShape Spa's facilities and information about other sporting options such as the rock-climbing wall, roller-blading track, basketball court and nine-hole, par 26 golf course, see the entry for *Adventure of the Seas*.

● For more extensive general information about a Royal Caribbean cruise experience, see pages 152–6, and for more detailed information about the Voyager-class ships, see *Voyager of the Seas* (page 650).

Nieuw Amsterdam
★★★★

Size:	...............Large Resort Ship	Passenger Decks:	12
Tonnage:	86,273	Total Crew:	929
Lifestyle:	...................Premium	Passengers	
Cruise Line:	.......Holland America Line	(lower beds/all berths):	.....2,106/2,671
Former Names:	.................none	Passenger Space Ratio	
Builder:	..............Fincantieri (Italy)	(lower beds/all berths):	.......40.9 /32.2
Original Cost:	.....................n/a	Crew/Passenger Ratio	
Entered Service:	..............Jul 2010	(lower beds/all berths):	..........2.2/2.8
Registry:	..............The Netherlands	Cabins (total):	1,053
Length (ft/m):	.............935.0/285.0	Size Range (sq ft/m):	.....170.0–1,318.6/
Beam (ft/m):	...............105.6/32.2		15.7–122.5
Draft (ft/m):	..................25.5/7.8	Cabins (outside view):	897
Propulsion/Propellers:	.....diesel-electric	Cabins (interior/no view):	156
	(34,000 kW/2 azimuthing pods	Cabins (for one person):	0
	(17.6 mW each)	Cabins (with private balcony):	708

Cabins (wheelchair accessible):	30
Wheelchair accessibility:	..........Good
Cabin Current:	...........110/220 volts
Elevators:	14
Casino (gaming tables):	............Yes
Slot Machines:	....................Yes
Swimming Pools (outdoors):	2
	+ 1 children's pool
Swimming Pools (indoors):	1
	(indoor/outdoor with retractable dome)
Whirlpools:	5
Self-Service Launderette:	...........No
Dedicated Cinema/Seats:	.......Yes/170
Library:	..........................Yes
Onboard currency:	...............US$

Dutch decor, traditions and comfort for mature cruisers.

OVERVIEW. The ship is designed to appeal to younger, more vibrant, multigenerational holidaymakers. Neat little tented cabanas on the aft deck provide private shaded space in an open-air environment. They are filled with goodies such as champagne, chocolate strawberries, an iPod pre-stocked with music, bathrobes, fresh fruit and chilled towels for two adults and two children. Naturally, these canvas havens cost extra.

THE SHIP. *Nieuw Amsterdam* is a Vista-class ship, sister to *Eurodam, Noordam, Oosterdam, Westerdam* and *Zuiderdam*. It is named after the Dutch name for New York City and the interior design reflects the great city. The ship, the latest in a line of HAL ships to carry this name, has two upright "dustbin lid" funnels in a close-knit configuration – one in front of the other. There's a "pod" propulsion system *(see page 191 for details)*.

As aboard the other Vista-class Holland America Line ships, the main pool deck can be covered with a glass dome roof for use in cooler regions. There is a complete

BERLITZ'S RATINGS

	Possible	Achieved
Ship	500	428
Accommodation	200	168
Food	400	274
Service	400	278
Entertainment	100	77
Cruise	400	310

OVERALL SCORE
1,535 points out of 2,000

walk-around exterior teak promenade deck, and real teak "steamer" style sunloungers are provided.

There are two whole entertainment/public room decks. Perhaps the most dramatic room aboard this ship is the showlounge, spanning four decks in the forward section of the ship. Other facilities include a winding shopping street with boutique stores and logo shops, card room, an art gallery, large casino, photo gallery, and small meeting rooms.

Gratuities are automatically added to your onboard account.

Passenger niggles? These include noisy cabin airconditioning – the flow can't be regulated or turned off, the only regulation being for temperature control.

● **For more extensive comments about a Holland America Line cruise, see pages 140–3, and for detailed information about *Nieuw Amsterdam*'s facilities, dining venues, entertainment and spa/fitness facilities, see the entry for *Eurodam* on page 363.**

Nippon Maru
★★★★

Size:	Small Ship	Total Crew:	230	Cabins (wheelchair accessible):	2
Tonnage:	22,472	Passengers		Wheelchair accessibility:	Fair
Lifestyle:	Standard	(lower beds/all berths):	408/607	Cabin Current:	100 volts
Cruise Line:	Mitsui OSK Passenger Line	Passenger Space Ratio		Elevators:	5
Former Names:	none	(lower beds/all berths):	55.0/37.0	Casino (gaming tables):	Yes
Builder:	Mitsubishi Heavy Industries	Crew/Passenger Ratio			(gifts only, no cash prizes)
Original Cost:	$59.4 million	(lower beds/all berths):	2.5/3.7	Slot Machines:	No
Entered Service:	Sep 1990	Cabins (total):	204	Swimming Pools (outdoors):	1
Registry:	Japan	Size Range (sq ft/m):	150.6–430.5/	Swimming Pools (indoors):	0
Length (ft/m):	546.7/166.65		14.0–40.0	Whirlpools:	4 Japanese baths
Beam (ft/m):	78.7/24.00	Cabins (outside view):	184	Self-Service Launderette:	Yes
Draft (ft/m):	21.4/6.55	Cabins (interior/no view):	18	Dedicated Cinema/Seats:	Yes
Propulsion/Propellers: diesel (15,740 kW)/2		Cabins (for one person):	6	Library:	Yes
Passenger Decks:	7	Cabins (with private balcony):	27	Onboard currency:	Japanese Yen

Modern styling for Japanese mature-age cruisers.

OVERVIEW. *Nippon Maru* is best suited to Japanese-speaking couples and single travelers who want very comfortable surroundings, and who enjoy decent food and quiet Japanese "Omotenashi" service, all at a decent cost. The ship has a lot of public rooms for its size, and some have high ceilings, giving a good sense of spaciousness.

THE SHIP. *Nippon Maru* had an ambitious four-month refit in 2009–10, when a new hydraulic tender loading platform was created. Deck extensions created space for more public rooms such as a new dining room for suite-class and deluxe-grade passengers, a piano lounge, and a new health/fitness facility. New suites and balcony cabins were created, balconies were added to 26 cabins, and existing public rooms and hallways were given a facelift.

The interior's focal point is an atrium lobby that spans six decks. Public rooms include a showlounge, piano lounge, a 54-seat screening room/lecture room (Mermaid Theatre), a gaming corner with give-aways rather than cash prizes, and a washitsu tatami room within the Horizon Lounge. The Neptune Bar has probably the most extensive assortment of Scotch whiskies at sea. A Smoking Lounge has eight chairs, and special extraction. Organized children's activities are provided on certain cruises.

The service staff and crew provide really warm, friendly service with a smile. Refreshingly, tipping is not allowed.

ACCOMMODATION. The new suites, on Deck 6, are large and have a separate sleeping and living areas. A sofa, two chairs, and coffee table occupy one section of the lounge; there is also a vanity/writing desk with Nespresso machine

BERLITZ'S RATINGS

	Possible	Achieved
Ship	500	377
Accommodation	200	147
Food	400	307
Service	400	301
Entertainment	100	81
Cruise	400	290

OVERALL SCORE
1,503 points out of 2,000

and tea-making facilities. The sleeping area's two beds can be pushed together. The bathroom includes a "washlet." Slippers and bathrobes are provided, plus an excellent variety of grooming items. Nine new suites, added in the refit, include two suites with huge balconies, on the starboard side. Suites and deluxe-grade cabins are nicely decorated, and the living area has a table and two chairs, and two beds; there's also a personal computer.

All standard cabins have blond wood cabinetry and good drawer space. Many have a third (or third and fourth) pull-down upper Pullman berth.

CUISINE. The *Mizuho* dining room, which seats around 320, serves both traditional Japanese cuisine and Western dishes. There is one open seating. The ship is known for its high-quality food. A premium dining room, *Kasuga*, has been added for suite- and deluxe-grade occupants; adjacent is the excellent *Shiosai* sushi bar.

ENTERTAINMENT. The Dolphin Hall has a prosceniumarched stage, wooden dance floor, and seating on both the main and balcony levels of this two-deck-high room. There's social dancing, with gentlemen hosts available as partners, and a rich program of lecturers and classical music artistes, including traditional Japanese instruments.

SPA/FITNESS. The Terraké Spa includes beauty and nail treatment rooms, three body treatment rooms, and a small fitness room. There's a traditional Japanese Grand Bath (one for women, one for men, open until 1am), with washing stations and a sauna. Adjacent is a sports massage room.

Noordam
★★★★

Size: . . . . .Large Resort Ship	Passenger Decks: 11	Cabins (wheelchair accessible): 28
Tonnage: 82,300	Total Crew: 820	Wheelchair accessibility: . . . . .Good
Lifestyle: . . . . .Premium	Passengers	Cabin Current: . . . . .110 volts
Cruise Line: . . . . .Holland America Line	(lower beds/all berths): 1,918/2,457	Elevators: 14
Former Names: . . . . .none	Passenger Space Ratio	Casino (gaming tables): . . . . .Yes
Builder: . . . . .Fincantieri (Italy)	(lower beds/all berths): 42.9/33.4	Slot Machines: . . . . .Yes
Original Cost: . . . .$400 million	Crew/Passenger Ratio	Swimming Pools (outdoors): 2
Entered Service: . . . . .Feb 2006	(lower beds/all berths): 2.3/2.9	+ children's pool
Registry: . . . . .The Netherlands	Cabins (total): 959	Swimming Pools (indoors):1 (indoor/outdoor)
Length (ft/m): 935.0/285.0	Size Range (sq ft/m): 170.0–1,318.6/	Whirlpools: 5
Beam (ft/m): 105.6/32.25	15.7–122.5	Self-Service Launderette: . . . . .No
Draft (ft/m): 25.5/7.8	Cabins (outside view): 806	Dedicated Cinema/Seats: Yes/170
Propulsion/Propellers: . . . . . .diesel-electric	Cabins (interior/no view): 153	Library: . . . . .Yes
(34,000 kW)/2 azimuthing pods	Cabins (for one person): 0	Onboard currency: . . . . .US$
(17.6 MW each)	Cabins (with private balcony): 641	

Dutch decor, traditions and comfort for mature cruisers.

OVERVIEW. *Noordam* offers a wide range of public rooms with a reasonably intimate atmosphere and the overall feel of the ship is quite homely and comforting, with fresh flowers everywhere, as well as some nicely showcased Dutch artifacts and museum pieces from the 16th and 17th centuries. Perhaps the ship's best asset is its friendly and personable crew – most are from Indonesia and the Philippines.

THE SHIP. *Noordam*, with 35 cabins more than its close sisters *Oosterdam, Westerdam* and *Zuiderdam*, is one of the Vista-class of ships in the Holland America Line fleet, designed to appeal to multi-generational holidaymakers. The twin working funnels are the result of the slightly unusual machinery configuration; the ship has, in effect, two engine rooms – one with three diesels, and one with two diesels and a gas turbine. A pod propulsion system is provided *(see page 191 for explanation)*, powered by a diesel-electric system, with a small gas turbine located in the funnel for the reduction of emissions.

There is a complete walk-around exterior teak promenade deck, with teak "steamer" style sunloungers. A jogging track outdoors is located around the mast and the forward third of the ship. Exterior glass elevators, mounted midships on both port and starboard sides, provide fine ocean views from any one of 10 decks. One of the two centrally located swimming pools outdoors can be used in inclement weather due to its retractable sliding glass roof. Two whirlpool tubs, adjacent to the swimming pools, are abridged by a bar. A smaller swimming pool for children incorporates a winding water slide that spans two decks in

BERLITZ'S RATINGS

	Possible	Achieved
Ship	500	427
Accommodation	200	162
Food	400	269
Service	400	275
Entertainment	100	77
Cruise	400	309

OVERALL SCORE
1,519 points out of 2,000

height. There is an additional whirlpool tub outdoors.

The intimate lobby spans three decks, and is topped by a beautiful, rotating, Waterford Crystal globe of the world. Adjacent are interior and glass wall elevators with exterior views. The interior decor is bright in many areas (in order to attract a younger clientele), and the ceilings are particularly noticeable. A large collection of artwork is a standard feature, and pieces reflect the history of the former Dutch East Indies.

There are two whole entertainment/public room decks. Perhaps the most dramatic room is the showlounge, spanning four decks in the forward section. Other facilities include a winding shopping street with several boutique stores and logo shops, card room, an art gallery, photo gallery, and several small meetings rooms. The large casino is equipped with an array of gaming paraphernalia and slot machines, and you have to walk through it to get from the restaurant to the showlounge.

"Explorations" is a combination coffee bar (where coffees and other drinks cost extra), lounge, extensive library and internet-connect center, all contained in one attractive, open "lifestyle" environment – it's a popular area for relaxation and reading, although noise from the coffee machine can interrupt concentration.

The information desk in the lobby is small and somewhat removed from the main passenger flow on the two decks above it. Many pillars obstruct the passenger flow and lines of sight throughout the ship. There are no self-service launderettes – something families with children miss, although special laundry packages are available.

FAMILIES. Club HAL's KidZone provides a whole area dedicated to children's facilities and extensive programming for different age groups (5–17), with one counselor for every 30 children. Free ice cream is provided at certain hours, plus hot hors d'oeuvres in all bars. Some cabins have interconnecting doors – good for families with children.

ACCOMMODATION. There are 24 price categories: 16 outside-view/eight interior (no view). The views from some cabins on the lowest accommodation deck (Main Deck) are obstructed by lifeboats. Some cabins that can accommodate a third and fourth person have very little closet space, and only one personal safe. Occupants of suites get exclusive use of the Neptune Lounge and concierge service, priority embarkation and disembarkation, and other benefits. In many of the suites/cabins with private balconies, the balconies are not so private, and can be overlooked from various public locations.

Penthouse Verandah Suites (2): These offer the largest accommodation (1,318 sq. ft/122.5 sq. meters, including balcony). These have a separate bedroom with a king-size bed; there's also a walk-in closet, dressing room, living room, dining room, butler's pantry, mini-bar and refrigerator, and private balcony. The main bathroom has a large whirlpool tub, two washbasins, toilet, and plenty of storage space for toiletries. Personalized stationery and free dry cleaning are included, as are hot hors d'oeuvres and other goodies daily.

DeLuxe Verandah Suites (60): These suites measure 563 sq. ft (52.3 sq. meters). They have twin beds that convert to a king-size bed, vanity desk, lounge area, walk-in closet, mini-bar and refrigerator, and bathroom with full-size tub, washbasin and toilet. Personalized stationery and complimentary dry cleaning are included, as are hot hors d'oeuvres and other goodies.

Verandah Suites (100): Actually they are cabins, not suites, and measure 284 sq. ft (26.3 sq. meters). Twin beds can convert to a queen-size bed. There is also a lounge area, mini-bar and refrigerator, while the bathroom has a tub, washbasin and toilet. Floor to ceiling windows open onto a private balcony.

Outside-view Cabins: Standard outside cabins (197 sq. ft/18.3 sq. meters) have twin beds that can convert to a queen-size bed. There's a small sitting area, while the bathroom has a tub/shower combination. The interior cabins are slightly smaller (182.9 sq. ft/17 sq. meters).

Niggles include noisy cabin air-conditioning – the flow can't be regulated or turned off; the only regulation is for temperature control.

CUISINE. The 1,045-seat *Vista Dining Room* is two decks high, with seating at tables for two, four, six or eight on both main and balcony levels and is at the stern. It provides a traditional Holland America Line dining experience, with friendly service from smiling Indonesian and Filipino stewards. Both open seating and assigned seating seating are available, while breakfast and lunch are open-seating – you'll be seated by restaurant staff when you enter.

Holland America Line can provide Kosher meals, although these are prepared ashore, frozen, and brought to your table sealed in their original containers.

Alternative Dining Option: The 148-seat *Pinnacle Grill* is a more upscale dining spot, with higher quality ingredients and better presentation than in the larger main dining room. On Lower Promenade Deck, it fronts onto the second level of the atrium lobby; tables along its outer section are open to it and can suffer from noise from the Atrium Bar one deck below, though these tables are good for those who like to see and be seen. Pacific Northwest cuisine is featured, with items such as sesame-crusted halibut with ginger-miso, and an array of premium-quality steaks. The wine list includes some fine wines from around the world, including many gorgeous Bordeaux reds. Reservations are required and there is a cover charge.

Informal Eateries: For casual eating, there is an extensive *Lido Café*, an eatery that wraps around the funnel, with indoor-outdoor seating and ocean views. It includes several sections including a salad bar, Asian stir-fry and sushi section, deli sandwiches, and a separate dessert buffet, although lines can form for made-to-order items such as omelets for breakfast and pasta for lunch.

An outdoor grill bar adjacent to the Lido pool has fast food such as hamburgers, veggie burgers, hot dogs, chicken and fries. On certain days, barbecues and other culinary specialties are available poolside.

ENTERTAINMENT. The 867-seat Vista Lounge is the principal venue for Las Vegas-style revues and major cabaret shows. The main floor level has a bar in its starboard aft section. Spiral stairways at the back of the lounge connect all levels. Stage shows are best seen from the upper levels, from where the sightlines are quite good.

SPA/FITNESS. The Greenhouse Spa, a large, two-decks-high health spa, is located directly above the navigation bridge. Facilities include a solarium, hydrotherapy pool, unisex thermal suite – a unisex area incorporating a Laconium (gentle sauna), Hammam (mild steam), and Chamomile Grotto (small aromatic steam room).

There is a beauty salon, 11 massage/therapy rooms (including one for couples), and a large gymnasium with floor-to-ceiling windows on three sides and forward-facing ocean views, and the latest high-tech muscle-toning equipment. Sports enthusiasts can enjoy a basketball court, volleyball court, golf simulator.

● **For more extensive general information on what a Holland America Line cruise is like, see pages 140–3.**

Norwegian Dawn
★★★★

Size: . . . . .Large Resort Ship	Passenger Decks: 11	Cabins (with private balcony): 511
Tonnage: 91,740	Total Crew: .1,069	Cabins (wheelchair accessible): 20
Lifestyle: . . . . .Standard	Total Crew: .1,069	Wheelchair accessibility: . . . . .Best
Cruise Line: . . . . .Norwegian Cruise Lines	Passengers	Cabin Current: . . . . .110 volts
Former Names: . . . . .none	(lower beds/all berths): 2,476/3,072	Elevators: 12
Gross Tonnage: 91,000	Passenger Space Ratio	Casino (gaming tables): . . . . .Yes
Builder: . . . . .Meyer Werft (Germany)	(lower beds/all berths): 36.7/29.6	Slot Machines: . . . . .Yes
Original Cost: . . . .$400 million	Crew/Passenger Ratio	Swimming Pools (outdoors): 2
Entered Service: . . . . .Oct 2002	(lower beds/all berths): 2.3/2.8	Swimming Pools (indoors): 1
Registry: . . . . .Bahamas	Cabins (total): 1,238	Whirlpools: . . .4 (+ 1 children's whirlpool)
Length (ft/m): 964.9/294.13	Size Range (sq ft/m): 142.0–5,350.0/	Self-Service Launderette: . . . . .No
Beam (ft/m): 105.6/32.2	13.2–497.0	Dedicated Cinema/Seats: Yes/151
Draft (ft/m): 26.9/8.2	Cabins (outside view): 847	Library: . . . . .Yes
Propulsion/Propellers: . . . .diesel-electric/	Cabins (interior/no view): 393	Onboard currency: . . . . .US$
2 azimuthing pods (19.5MW each)	Cabins (for one person): 0	

A large casual ship for lively, family-friendly cruising.

OVERVIEW. More choices, including many dining options, add up to a very attractive holiday package, particularly suitable for families with children, in a very contemporary floating leisure center that really does provide ample facilities for you to have an enjoyable time. Despite the company's name, Norwegian Cruise Line, there's almost nothing Norwegian about this product, except for some senior officers.

THE SHIP. *Norwegian Dawn*, sister to *Norwegian Star*, was built in 64 sections and has a "pod" propulsion system *(see page 191 for a definition)*. The hull displays interesting logos on top of its white paint, depicting the ship's itineraries: the port side features the cruise itinerary from New York to the Bahamas and Florida, while the starboard side features the winter itinerary from Miami to the Caribbean. Dolphins, the Statue of Liberty, and representations of the four original paintings displayed on board: the Impressionists Matisse, Renoir, and Van Gogh, and the pop artist Andy Warhol. It is a colorful concept, and makes the ship easy to spot in a sea of similar-sized ships in port.

In 2011, 58 additional suites/cabins were added, which makes the ship more crowded and dining venues a little busier. In general, the ship absorbs passengers well, but the open deck space has become more congested.

Facilities include a large Dawn Club Casino gaming area, an internet café with 24 computers, an 1,150-seat showlounge, a 3,000-book library, a card room, a writing and study room, a business center, conference and meeting rooms, and a large retail shopping complex.

BERLITZ'S RATINGS

	Possible	Achieved
Ship	500	418
Accommodation	200	156
Food	400	267
Service	400	285
Entertainment	100	67
Cruise	400	294

OVERALL SCORE
1,487 points out of 2,000

While the initial cruise fare seems very reasonable, the extra costs and charges soon mount up if you want to sample more than the basics. With many dining choices, some costing extra, your overall experience will be determined by how much you are prepared to spend. You will need to plan where to eat well in advance, and make reservations. The dress code is very casual – no jacket and tie needed, although you are welcome to dress formally if you so wish.

Although service levels and finesse are sometimes inconsistent, the level of hospitality is very good – made much better and brighter by the great number of Asian female staff rather than the inconsistent Caribbean Basin staff still found aboard some NCL ships. The staff includes many Southeast Asians who have served aboard parent company Star Cruises' big ships.

The ship is full of revenue centers designed to help part you from your money. You can expect to be subjected to a stream of flyers advertising daily art auctions, "designer" watches, "inch of gold/silver" and other promotions.

Gratuities for staff – cabin attendants, dining room waiters, etc. – are automatically added to your onboard account, or you can pre-pay on-line. You can, however, reduce or otherwise amend these if necessary before you disembark. In addition, a 15% gratuity is added to all bar purchases, and 18% for spa treatments.

Music played in some areas bleeds through into others; for example, Latin music played in Salsas on the second level of the lobby is heard throughout the lobby and the internet café on the third level of the lobby and is most disconcerting. Communication, particularly between passengers and some of the Asian staff, is weak. Standing in line for embarkation, disembarkation, shore tenders and for self-serve buffet meals is an inevitable aspect of cruising aboard all large ships.

FAMILIES. A good deal of space is devoted to children's facilities such as the T-Rex Kids' Center and Teen Club. All are tucked well away from adult recreation areas, at the aft end. Children of all ages will get to play in a superb wet 'n' wild space-themed water park, complete with large pool, water slide, and paddle pool. There's a room full of cots for toddlers to use for sleepovers, and even the toilets are at a special low height. Teens, too, are well catered for, and get their own cinema (with DVD movies), discotheque with dance floor, and their own hot tub. Some cabins have interconnecting doors – good for families with children.

ACCOMMODATION. Although the suites and junior suites are quite spacious, the standard interior and outside-view cabins are very small when compared to those of other major cruise lines such as Carnival or Celebrity, particularly when occupied by three or four persons; the bathrooms, however, are of quite a decent size, and have large shower enclosures. There are 29 price grades.

All cabins have tea- and coffee-making sets – but only "coffee creamer" is provided, so tea drinkers who want fresh milk need to arrange this with their steward, or call room service. All cabins also have rich cherry wood cabinetry, bathroom with sliding door and separate toilet, shower enclosure and washbasin compartments, and European duvets. The private balconies of the top suites have teak decks, while most other cabins with balconies have a "Bolidt" (rubberized sand-like) deck, and smoked glass/wood rail panels that provide good sightlines. Audio channels are on the in-cabin TV system, but you cannot turn off the picture. Elemis personal amenities are provided.

Garden Villas (2). The largest living spaces, Vista and Horizon, sit high atop the ship in a pod located forward of the funnel, and overlooking the main swimming pool and recreation deck. These villas have huge glass walls and landscaped private roof gardens for outdoor dining – with whirlpool tubs, naturally – and huge private sunbathing areas completely shielded from anyone. Each has three bedrooms and bathrooms, and a large living room overlooking the lido/pool deck. These units have their own private elevator access and private stairway. Each measures 5,350 sq ft. (497 sq meters) and can be combined to create a huge, double-size "house" measuring 10,700 sq ft (994-sq-meters), including a private outdoor Italian garden. Butler service is provided.

Owner's Suites (4). Located in the very front of the ship, each measures 750 sq.ft. (69.6 sq. meters). Two are nestled under the enclosed navigation bridge wings on Deck 11, and the other two are in the equivalent space on the deck below. They have an entrance with wooden door front, large lounge/dining room, and separate bedroom with king-size bed beneath a mirrored ceiling, and TV set with integral DVD player. The bathroom – almost as large as a standard cabin – has a full-size tub with shower and TV; separate shower enclosure, separate toilet, and a dressing area with his-and-hers walk-in closets. There are forward-facing (open) and side-facing (enclosed) private balconies. Butler service is provided. If you don't need the entertaining space of the Garden Villas, these suites are delightful living spaces. However, they do suffer occasionally from noise generated in Spinnaker's nightclub/disco on the deck above. Each Owner's Suite can also be interconnected to a Penthouse Suite and balcony cabin – useful for large families when parents value privacy.

Penthouse Suites (30). Each measures 366 sq.ft./34 sq. meters. Facilities include a bedroom with queen-size bed, walk-in closet, living room with dining table, and bathroom with separate shower enclosure and tub. Penthouse Suites on Deck 11 can be interconnected to a children's cabin with double sofa bed and a pull-down Pullman-style bed, separate bathroom and shower enclosure. These suites also have a private balcony, and butler service.

Romance Suites (4). Each measures 288 sq.ft. (26.7 sq. meters). They include a separate bedroom with queen-size bed, a sitting area with double sofa bed, and living and dining areas. The bathroom has a full-size tub and shower. There is a private balcony.

Mini Suites (107). These measure 229 sq. ft (21.2 sq. meters), and each has two lower beds that convert to a queen-size bed, and a sitting area with double sofa bed. The bathroom has a full-size tub and shower. Floor-to-ceiling windows open onto a private balcony.

All suites are well furnished, most in rich cherry wood, although closet space in some of the smaller units is tight. Some suites have extras like a trouser press, and a full range of toiletries. Suites also get butlers, who can serve all meals en-suite from the menus of a number of restaurants.

Although nicely furnished and quite well equipped, the standard outside-view and interior cabins are quite small, particularly for three or four people. Many cabins have third- and fourth-person pull-down berths or trundle beds.

A small room service menu is available; non-food items cost extra, and a 15% service charge and a gratuity are added to your account. Bottled water is placed in each cabin, but you are charged if you open the bottle.

CUISINE. With "Freestyle Dining", you can choose which restaurant to eat in, at what time, and with whom – there are no assigned dining rooms, tables or seats. While this is fine in theory, in practice it means that you have to make reservations for a specific time, so "freestyle dining" actually turns out to be programmed dining.

Apart from three principal dining rooms, there are a number of other themed eateries, giving a wide range of choice – though some cost extra, and require advance reservations. Two entire decks are filled with 10 restaurants and eateries. NCLs dress code states that "jeans, T-shirts, tank tops and bare feet are not permitted in restaurants."

● *Venetian*: the first main dining room (seats 472) offers traditional six-course dining (open 5.30pm–midnight). It is located aft, with good views over the ship's stern – at least in the daytime – although the sightlines from some seats are obstructed by 14 pillars. The room has a baby grand piano. If you want a quieter table, choose one of two wings in the forward section near the entrance/steps.

● *Aqua:* the second main dining room seats 344 and offers traditional six-courses from 5.30pm to midnight.

● *Impressions:* the third main dining room, seating 236, offers lighter cuisine from 5.30pm to midnight. The waiter stations are too close to the tables and are very noisy.

● *Bamboo (a Taste of Asia):* a Japanese/Thai/Chinese restaurant, with 140 seats, has a sit-up conveyor-belt style sushi/sashimi bar, sake bar, show galley, and separate room with a teppanyaki grill. In the evenings, music from Gatsby's lounge/bar on the deck below completely fill the restaurant through an open lobby-like well, and a quiet meal is almost impossible. All items cost extra and there is an "all you can eat" sushi charge of $10.

● *Le Bistro:* a French restaurant with 72 seats, serving nouvelle cuisine. The decor includes four Impressionist paintings on loan from the private collection of the chairman of Star Cruises, NCL's parent company, although they don't really match the room's decor. There's a cover charge and also a line for you to add an *extra* gratuity – very cheeky. But it's the best food on board and worth the extra cost.

● *Blue Lagoon:* a food court-style eatery; 68 seats; serving hamburgers, fish & chips, pot pies and wok fast dishes.

● *Garden Café:* an indoor/outdoor self-serve buffet (seats 490). It includes "action stations" with made-to-order omelets, waffles, fruit, soups, ethnic specialities and pasta.

● *Salsa:* a Spanish tapas eatery and bar (seats 112) with a selection of hot and cold tapas dishes and authentic entertainment, located on the second level of the atrium lobby.

● *La Trattoria:* located inside the indoor/outdoor buffet (seats 162); serves pasta, pizza and other Italian fare.

● *Cagney's Steak House:* arranged atop the ship; seats 112; incorporates a show kitchen, and serves US prime steaks and seafood. Be prepared for large portions. Reservations are required and a cover charge applies.

Other eating/drinking spots include the *Pearly Kings,* an English pub for draft beer and perhaps a game of darts; *Havanas,* a cigar and cognac lounge; *Java,* an atrium lobby café and bar (hot and frozen coffees, teas and pastries); a *Beer Garden* (grilled foods); a *Gelato Bar* (ice cream); and a *Gym and Spa Bar* (health food snacks and drinks).

ENTERTAINMENT. The 1,037-seat Stardust Theatre is the venue for colorful Las-Vegas-style production shows and major cabaret acts. It is designed in the style of an opera house, spans three decks, and has a steeply tiered main floor and port and starboard balconies. There are three production shows in a typical seven-day cruise, ably performed by the Jean Ann Ryan Company. These are very colorful, high-energy, razzle-dazzle shows with much use of pyrotechnics, laser and color-mover lighting. They're not particularly memorable but they are very entertaining.

A number of bands and solo entertaining musicians provide live music for listening and dancing in several lounges and bars. Throughout the ship, loud Latin music prevails. In Spinnakers Lounge nightclub, a Pachanga Party (a Miami South Beach rave) is held each cruise.

SPA/FITNESS. Wellness devotees should enjoy the two-deck-high El Dorado health spa complex, operated by the Steiner-owned and Hawaii-based Mandara Spa. Located at the stern, it has large ocean-view windows on three sides. There are many facilities and services, almost all at extra cost, including Thai massage in the spa, outdoors on deck, in your cabin, or on your private balcony.

There is an indoor lap pool measuring 37 ft/11.2 meters, a hydrotherapy pool, two sit-in deep tubs, aromatherapy and wellness centers, and mud treatment rooms (there are 15 treatment rooms in all, including one specifically designed for couples). The fitness and exercise rooms, with the latest Cybex muscle-pumping equipment, are located not within the spa, but at the top of the glass-domed atrium lobby. Included is a room for exercycle classes. Some classes, such Pathway to Yoga, Body Cycling Class and Body Beat Class (cardio kick-boxing), cost extra.

Recreational sports facilities include a jogging track, golf driving range, basketball and volleyball courts, as well as four levels of sunbathing decks.

● **For more extensive general information on what an NCL cruise is like, see pages 146–8.**

Norwegian Epic
★★★★

Size:	Large Resort Ship	Passenger Decks:	15	Cabins (wheelchair accessible):	42
Tonnage:	155,873	Total Crew:	1,730	Wheelchair accessibility:	Good
Lifestyle:	Standard	Passengers		Cabin Current:	110 volts
Cruise Line:	Norwegian Cruise Line	(lower beds/all berths):	4,200/5,400	Elevators:	16
Former Names:	none	Passenger Space Ratio		Casino (gaming tables):	Yes
Builder:	STX Europe (France)	(lower beds/all berths):	37.1/28.8	Slot Machines:	Yes
Original Cost:	$735 million	Crew/Passenger Ratio		Swimming Pools (outdoors):	4
Entered Service:	Jun 2010	(lower beds/all berths):	2.4/3.1	Swimming Pools (indoors):	1
Registry:	Panama	Cabins (total):	2,100	Whirlpools:	9
Length (ft/m):	1,080.7/329.4	Size Range (sq ft/m):	850.3–100.1/79–9.3	Self-Service Launderette:	No
Beam (ft/m):	133.0/40.5	Cabins (outside view):	1,415	Dedicated Cinema/Seats:	No
Draft:	28.5/8.6	Cabins (interior/no view):	685	Library:	Yes
Propulsion/Propellers:	diesel-electric	Cabins (for one person):	128	Onboard currency:	US$
	(79.8 MW)/2	Cabins (with private balcony):	1,415		

An epic-sized, family-friendly, multiple-choice ship.

OVERVIEW. *Norwegian Epic* is a blast for youthful adults, and kids alike. It's all about lifestyle – bistro eateries, lots of dining choices, color and noise, the perceived über-chic South Beach life at sea, stuffed with entertainment. If you want to be part of it all, it could cost you well above the price of your cruise – and you'll need stamina. The ship sails on alternating seven-day eastern and western Caribbean itineraries during the winter season, and operates Mediterranean cruises in summer.

BERLITZ'S RATINGS		
	Possible	Achieved
Ship	500	432
Accommodation	200	158
Food	400	277
Service	400	287
Entertainment	100	85
Cruise	400	304
OVERALL SCORE		
1,543 points out of 2,000		

THE SHIP. *Norwegian Epic* is is perhaps the most extreme example of "all-exclusive" cruising, and is a throwback to the days when First Class, Cabin Class, and Tourist Class meant passengers could not access certain areas of the ship – the familiar "pay more, get more" philosophy. This is a ship for the "effortlessly casual." It's all about cruising with attitude – and volume.

The largest ship ever constructed in STX Europe's French shipyard, in St Nazaire, *Norwegian Epic* is just a tad larger than *Queen Mary 2*. Its profile isn't very handsome because several decks above the navigation bridge make it look really top heavy, like a square lump of cheese. But the two side-by-side funnels – between which is a 60-ft wide rock climbing wall – bring some semblance of balance. The ship is about 30% wider than the Norwegian Jewel-class ships, and is a prototype for NCL.

The pool deck has an Aqua Park, with three major water slides – one involves inner tubes that give you a spin before spitting you out into a big bowl, reminiscent of a washing machine – and a large rock-climbing wall and rappelling wall. Aft is a large movie screen with amphitheater-style

seating, and a nightclub within an area called Spice H₂O, which also includes a sun deck. However, despite the ship's size, the open deck space for sunbathing is extremely small and cramped – much diminished by the "exclusive" Courtyard block in the forward section, whose occupants do have enough sunbathing space.

The three lowest passenger decks contain the main entertainment venues, restaurants and other dining venues, show lounges and a large casino. Some spaces open to two or three decks in height to create an illusion of space – like mini-atriums, but the overall flow is disjointed and invites congestion, particularly around a casino walk-through area. A dramatic three-deck-high chandelier in the lobby is the largest at sea.

Two escalators do nothing to diminish congestion – they even encourage gridlock at peak times. Sandwiched between these three lower entertainment decks and the upper entertainment decks are seven decks mainly comprised of accommodation units. Something new for NCL is a bridge viewing room, just behind the navigation bridge.

NCL will extract more money from you with a number of "exclusive" experiences, including a members-only POSH Beach Club, above the more exclusive Courtyard area atop the ship. This has a Miami South Beach vibe and includes four pay-extra experiences: (1) POSH Vive, 6–9am, when you can participate in yoga classes and treatments in private cabanas. (2) POSH Rehab till noon, so you can recover from a hard night, with Bloody Marys and chill-out music. (3) POSH Sol, noon–6pm, when you can can lounge on day beds and enjoy a beach-themed atmosphere. (4) Pure POSH, echoing Caesar's Palace in Las Vegas, where you can drink and dance under the stars. It's all just a little bit decadent – shades of the Savoy without the finesse.

Other ship features include a novel Ice Bar, a chill-out, chat-up venue inspired by the original ice bars and ice hotels of Scandinavia. In this frozen chamber of iced vodka, the centerpiece is a giant ice cube that glows and changes color. The Ice Bar accommodates 25 passengers who are given fur coats, gloves and hats because the room's temperature does not rise above −8°C (around 17°F). Naturally, there's a cover charge (ice charge!), but it includes two drinks. Svedka vodka and Canada's Inniskillin ice wine are featured.

Then there's Halo, an über-bar, where garden and courtyard villa occupants, who pay a premium for much better accommodation, have exclusive access, although other passengers can use it by paying a cover charge. This bar sits at the top of the ship on Deck 16 and showcases art and jewelry, "modeled" by shop staff. Everything's available to buy, of course.

Facilities, lounges and bars include the hedonistic Bliss Ultra Lounge and Nightclub – it's a bit like Saturday night on Ocean Drive on Miami's South Beach, although boa constrictors are not permitted on board. Already popular on *Norwegian Gem* and *Norwegian Pearl*, this bowling alley by day and hot bed club by night is a popular venue for late-night owls.

Spice H$_2$O is a tiered pool, stage and movie screen complex for adults only, at the stern. It's a smaller version of the AquaTheatre aboard RCI's *Oasis*-class ships. With all-day-long music and a huge screen, different themes prevail: (1) Sunny Spice 8am–11am, including spicy drinks and breakfast; (2) Daytime Aqua Spice with sun and water and Chinese take-away food items; (3) Evening Sunset Spice, with a perfect sunset every day; (4) All Spice at night, offering a show of aqua ballet and dancing. A "Beyond the Velvet Rope" package for all clubs is available at extra cost.

Despite the marketing hype about this exceptionally trendy ship, few major public rooms, except the main show-lounge and aft restaurant, are more than one deck high.

It's a big ship, but the elevators are forward and aft – there are none in the middle of the ship, which is tough for mobility-limited passengers. Yet *Norwegian Epic* has more elevators than the much larger *Oasis of the Seas*.

A "ship within a ship" two-deck complex provides a private courtyard/pool area, male and female steam rooms, concierge lounge, and private dining rooms and lounge for those willing to pay more for exclusivity.

Because the ship spends winter in the Caribbean and summer in the Mediterranean, you might – if you have time and enjoy days at sea – try a repositioning voyage.

Niggles include the cigarette smokers in the casino, a walk-through area. Gratuities are automatically charged to your onboard account, or you can pre-pay on-line. Bar purchases incur a 15% gratuity, spa treatments a severe 18%.

FAMILIES. Family-friendly cabins are within easy access to the Kid's Crew facilities, in two zones: for Kids 2–9, and tweens of 10–12 years of age. Nickleodeon is the family

entertainment brand on all cruises, as part of NCL's children's programming. Activities include: Slime Time Live, an interactive game; Nick Live, with poolside entertainment; Character breakfast, at extra charge; and meet and greet. There's also a Nickleodeon in-cabin TV channel. So expect to see Sponge Bob, Dora the Explorer, Patrick Star, Diego as part of the family-themed entertainment. Preschoolers can be kept amused year-round.

ACCOMMODATION. There are an astonishing 38 different accommodation price levels in 13 accommodation grades, including the first Loft Suites at sea – although upstairs/downstairs suites have been available for years aboard ships such as *Saga Ruby* and the now withdrawn *QE2*. In true nautical tradition, even-numbered cabins are on the port side (red carpet), with odd-numbered cabins on the starboard side (blue carpet); if you're color-blind, forget it.

The Courtyard Suites (Decks 16, 17) are located in the "block of cheese" in the forward section, above the navigation bridge. There are six courtyard "villas" – two face forward, while six overlook the central pool section, although none has a private balcony. Occupants, however, have access to a four-deck gated-community style grouping of facilities, including a concierge lounge, private courtyard and pool, his-and-hers steam rooms, and private sunbathing areas – so no need to go to the rest of the ship underneath you, except to disembark or go out to the entertainment decks to play, or escape.

All outside-view suites/cabins have a "private" balcony. In a "New Wave" concept, the designers introduced curved walls in a wave shape for a contemporary look and feel to cabins. LED lighting, backlit domed ceiling, comfortable sofa seating (except Standard Cabins), vanity desk, and minibar. A palette of soft, warm colors in each cabin melds beautifully with walnut and rosewood colored veneers and stark white surfaces. See-through bathrooms have a separate toilet; tub or tub/shower combination, and separate vanity washbasin (few people like the see-through toilet).

Although they are about the same size as current standard industry cabins, there is an efficient use of space, achieved by separating the toilet and shower unit to either side of the entryway, and by curving the bulkheads and furniture to give the cabins a more open, wavy, and contemporary feel – a sort of Uri Geller effect.

Eight Spa Suites have private key-card entry to the adjacent Mandara Spa, and complimentary 24-hour access to the inner Thermal Spa. These have more space and larger balconies, so of course they're more expensive.

Solo travellers can take one of the 128 Studio cabins, many of which are interconnecting – reminiscent of a capsule hotel. A small window looks out into the passageway. On Decks 11 and 12, these are priced for single occupancy – although they can be occupied by two persons (and two toothbrushes only) since there is a double bed. They measure 100 sq. ft (9.3 sq. meters), and occupants have access to a common lounge with hostess, and free espressos/cappuccinos. In Interior Cabins and Studio categories, the bed faces the cabin door, so there's no privacy.

CUISINE. There are certainly plenty of dining choices. With 21 restaurants, dining venues and casual eateries, it will take some planning in order to eat where you want, when you want, despite NCL's claim to "Freestyle Dining." Actually, there is no "main" dining room as such. In other words, just like in a city or town, you choose where to eat – unless, of course, there are no tables available, which is possible at peak times when everyone wants to see a show simultaneously, and you'll have to wait for a table. There is also no Lido self-service buffet as aboard almost all other large resort ships. Instead, different food outlets have been created in numerous locations – 11 are included in the cruise fare, while the others have a cover charge of between $5 and $25 a person. Because gratuities are automatically added to your onboard account, if you change dining venues every time you eat, you don't need to think about tips.

● *Cagney's Steakhouse & Churrascaria*, with 276 seats, expands the New York-style favorite of earlier NCL ships to include Argentine churrasco offerings of skewered meats presented by tableside passadors. The spot adds a large self-help salad bar in its center.

● *Taste*, in the atrium on Deck 5, is touted as a European retro-chic restaurant with brick details and floor to ceiling velvet curtains. The menu includes traditional and contemporary cuisine for breakfast, lunch and dinner.

● *The Manhattan Room*, located aft, is two-decks-high, and reminiscent of an elegant Art Deco supper club, with dance floor, and live Celebrity Look-Alike shows. It's the closest thing to a main dining room, and has a spectacular glass window wall aft.

● *La Cucina* is for… what else but Italian-style dishes, from Tuscany, of course. It's at the front of the ship, providing great ocean views, one deck above the navigation bridge.

● The 124-seat *Le Bistro* serves French cuisine; there has been a Le Bistro aboard all NCL ships since the first one was installed aboard the now scrapped *Norway*.

● Multiple Asian-themed venues include *Shanghai's* for Chinese dishes and noodle bar specialties with an open kitchen and 133 seats; the 20-seat *Wasabi* for sushi and sakes; and a showy, food-chopping venue, the adjacent *Teppanyaki Grill*, with 115 seats.

● The *Epic Club and Courtyard Grill*, in the Courtyard Villas complex, are exclusive to suite and villa occupants and split between an elegant, private club-style restaurant with a large wine display and a casual outdoor area for breakfast and lunch. It can accommodate 127.

● *O'Sheehan's* is a neighborhood-style sports bar and grill, open 24 hours (no extra charge). It is adjacent to a bowling alley, though I'm not sure why – it disturbs the ambience.

● *Café Jardin* (Garden Café) is a large self-serve buffet venue, with 728 seats, and is modeled on an English country garden conservatory – but with a French name and excellent ocean views. The casual venue includes "action" stations where chefs prepare pasta and other items, made to order – join the line. The outdoor seating area, the *Great Outdoors*, looks over the Aqua Park. A section for children, the *Kids Café*, has low height tables and seats.

ENTERTAINMENT. The two-deck-high Epic Theater, at the front of the ship, presents major production shows and mainline cabaret acts. Another entertainment venue is the Bliss Ultra Lounge, a decadent venue which contains a bowling alley or two – there's another one in Sheehan's on the deck above. This is where late-night comedy and some cabaret acts are presented.

Celebrity look-alike shows conjuring up the likes of Elvis, Janet Jackson, Madonna, Neil Diamond and Tina Turner, is part of the entertainment offering. They are produced by Legends in Concert, the Las Vegas company that has provided shows for "The Strip" for over 25 years.

The Spiegel Tent is a two-deck-high Cirque-like space, combining a show with dinner, similar to the Teatro Zin-Zanni dinner theatre in San Francisco and Seattle. It's a mix of in-your-face street theatre, acrobatics, Berlin-style "foodertainment," with lots of clowning and satire during a poorly scripted two-hour show. There's a cover charge.

As part of NCL's creative "Check In, Rock Out" program, guitar enthusiasts can, for a daily fee, rent a real Gibson guitar and a set of headphones to play in the comfort of their cabin.

SPA/FITNESS. The Smile Spa and Pulse Fitness Center complex is possibly the largest at sea (31,000 sq.ft/2,880 sq. meters). Operated by the Steiner-owned Mandara Spa, it is in the center of the ship, and some of the 24 treatment rooms have no view. The Fitness Center has port-side ocean views; the aerobics room has no view. Numerous facilities and services are offered, almost all at extra charge.

Sports facilities include six bowling lanes in two venues (O'Sheehans Neighborhood Bar & Grill, and Bliss Ultra Lounge). There's also a full-size basketball court, volleyball, soccer, dodge ball, a batting cage, bungee trampoline, and a 24-ft (7.3-meter) tall climbing cage called the spider web, and an abseiling wall. Walkers should note that only 2.2 laps around the walking track equals 1 mile.

● **For more extensive general information on what an NCL cruise is like, see pages 146–8.**

Norwegian Gem
★★★★

Size: . . . . .Large Resort Ship	Passenger Decks: 12	Cabins (with private balcony): 540
Tonnage: .93,530	Total Crew: 1,126	Cabins (wheelchair accessible): 27
Lifestyle: . . . . .Standard	Passengers	Wheelchair accessibility: . . . . .Good
Cruise Line: . . . . . .Norwegian Cruise Line	(lower beds/all berths): 2,394/2,846	Cabin Current: . . . . .110 volts
Former Names: . . . . .none	Passenger Space Ratio	Elevators: 12
Builder: . . . . .Meyer Werft (Germany)	(lower beds/all berths): 39.0/32.8	Casino (gaming tables): . . . . .Yes
Original Cost: . . . .$390 million	Crew/Passenger Ratio	Slot Machines: . . . . .Yes
Entered Service: . . . . .Oct 2007	(lower beds/all berths): 2.1/2.5	Swimming Pools (outdoors): 2
Registry: . . . . .Panama	Cabins (total): 1,197	Swimming Pools (indoors): 0
Length (ft/m): 964.8/294.1	Size Range (sq ft/m): 142.0–4,390.0/	Whirlpools: 6
Beam (ft/m): 105.6/32.2	13.2–407.8	Self-Service Launderette: . . . . .Yes
Draft (ft/m): 26.9/8.2	Cabins (outside view): 792	Dedicated Cinema/Seats: . . . . .No
Propulsion/Propellers: . . . .diesel-electric/	Cabins (interior/no view): 405	Library: . . . . .Yes
2 pods (19.5MW each)	Cabins (for one person): 0	Onboard currency: . . . . .US$

A large, family-friendly ship with multiple eating venues.

OVERVIEW. Plenty of choices, including many dining options, add up to a very attractive vacation package, highly suitable for families with children, in a floating leisure center that provides ample facilities for enjoyment. The initial cruise fare is reasonable, but extra costs and charges soon mount up if you want to sample more than the basics.

THE SHIP. The design and layout is similar to that of *Norwegian Pearl*, and there is a "pod" propulsion system for vibration-free cruising *(details: page 191)*. The white hull has a colourful, funky string of gems along its sides as a design. There are plenty of deck lounge chairs – in fact, more than the total of passengers. Water slides are included for the adult swimming pools. Children have their own pools at the ship's stern – out of sight of adult areas.

Inside the ship is an entertaining mix of bright, funky, but warm colors and decor that you probably wouldn't have in your home, and yet somehow they all work extremely well in this large resort ship setting designed to attract the young, active, and trendy.

The dress code is ultra-casual: no jacket and tie needed, although you are welcome to dress formally – but jeans are probably essential. Although service levels and finesse may be inconsistent, the level of hospitality aboard Norwegian Cruise Line ships is good – made better by the addition of a good number of Asian staff. Despite the company's name, there's little that's Norwegian about this product, except for some senior officers. There's plenty of lively music, constant activity, entertainment, and food that is mainstream and acceptable but nothing more – even when you pay extra to eat in the "alternative" dining spots.

BERLITZ'S RATINGS		
	Possible	Achieved
Ship	500	418
Accommodation	200	156
Food	400	267
Service	400	285
Entertainment	100	67
Cruise	400	294

OVERALL SCORE
1,487 points out of 2,000

There are 11 bars and lounges, including "Bar Central," four specialty bars: martini bar, champagne and wine bar, beer and whiskey bar, and a cigar lounge; these interconnect with the lobby, yet have distinct personalities. The lobby houses a Java Bar, plus a two-deck-high movie screen, typically used to show sports events and Wii activities. One neat room is the "Bliss Ultra Lounge & Night Club," at the aft end of the ship; it houses a 24-hours a day V-shaped sports bar and lounge complex, including a bowling alley with four real bowling lanes – the cost is $5 per person, including special playing shoes, and it is limited to six persons per lane. The lounge doesn't have many seats, but does have a couple of beds.

The casino is typical of larger resort ship casinos, with plenty of gaming tables, slot machines, noise, and smoke. So, if you walk through the casino to get from the showlounge to other public rooms, you'll be subject to cigarette smoke. A new twist in the onboard casino scene has appeared, with poolside blackjack now established in its own "open-air casino" on the pool deck.

The ship is full of revenue centers designed to help you part with even more money than you paid for your cruise ticket. Expect to be subjected to a stream of flyers advertising art auctions, "designer" watches, gold and silver chain by the inch, and other promotions – and the cruise director's long programme announcements three times a day.

Per-person gratuities are automatically added to your onboard account daily; you can, however, reduce or otherwise amend these if necessary before you disembark. Alternatively, you can pre-pay online. A 15% gratuity is added to all bar purchases, and 18% for spa treatments.

FAMILIES. Because NCL is all about cruising with families of all ages, much space is devoted to children's facilities, all thoughtfully tucked well away from adult recreation areas, at the aft end of the ship. Children of all ages will get to play in a superb wet 'n' wild space-themed water park (the Aqua Kid's Club), complete with large pool, water slide, and paddle pool. There's a 30-ft by 19-ft climbing wall at the funnel. Teens are well catered for, and have their own cinema, discotheque with dance floor, and hot tub. There's a room full of cots for toddlers to use for sleepovers.

More than 250 cabins have interconnecting doors – good for families with children. That means interior cabins can connect; outside view cabins can connect; and outside view and balcony cabins can connect. Also for families, many cabins also have third- and fourth-person pull-down berths or trundle beds.

ACCOMMODATION. There are 32 different price grades, from small interior (no view) cabins to lavish suites in a private courtyard setting.

Although they are nicely furnished and quite well equipped, the standard outside-view and interior cabins are quite small, particularly when occupied by three or four people. A small room service menu is available – all non-food items cost extra cost, and a 15% service charge is automatically added to your account. Bottled water is placed in each cabin, but you will be charged if you open the bottle.

The following suites are available:

Courtyard Villas/Garden Villas: The two Garden Villa Suites, each measuring 4,390 sq.ft. (407.8 sq.meters), and 10 Courtyard Villas share a private courtyard with its own small pool, hot tub, and small fitness room, and have butler service. These units enjoy exclusivity – rather like accommodation in a gated community – where others cannot live unless they pay the asking price.

Deluxe Owner's Suites: These two suites, named Black Pearl and Golden Pearl, are set high atop all other accommodation, have stunning ocean views, and consist of a master bedroom with king-size bed, a dining/lounge area, a decent-sized balcony, and access to the private courtyard.

Penthouse Suites: Located at the front of the ship, they have a partly private balcony under the navigation bridge.

CUISINE. There are two main dining rooms: the 304-seat *Grand Palace*, with its minimalist decor; and the 558-seat *Magenta Restaurant*. There are several other themed eating spots, giving a wide range of choice; some cost extra, and require advance reservations, particularly for dinner. All are part of NCL's "Freestyle Dining" – there are no assigned dining rooms, tables or seats, so you'll need to plan your meals and times accordingly.

With 17 video screens located around the ship, you can check how busy each dining spot is and make a booking and find out if, or how long, you'll need to wait for a table; pagers are also available, so you can go bar-hopping while you wait for a table in your chosen venue. The system generally works well, with colored bars to indicate whether a restaurant is "full," "moderately busy," or "empty." This has cut down the frustration of waiting a long time for a table, although on "formal" nights, when you may want to see the production shows, congestion certainly does occur. Note that NCL's dress code states that "jeans, T-shirts, tank tops and bare feet are not permitted in restaurants."

Alternative Restaurants/Eateries include *Cagney's Steak House* (serving steaks from 5oz to 48oz); *Blue Lagoon* (for trendy fast-food street snacks); *Le Bistro* for classic French cuisine; *Orchid Garden*, an Asian eatery complete with sushi bar and Teppanyaki grill (where the chef puts on a display in front of you); *La Cucina*, serving Italian cuisine; *Latin Restaurant*; the *Garden Café*, a large self-serve buffet-style restaurant, for casual meals; *Kids' Café*; and a *Java Café*, which serves Lavazza coffee, in the lobby.

ENTERTAINMENT. The Stardust Theater, seating 1,042, is the venue for colorful Las-Vegas-style production shows and major cabaret acts. It is designed in the style of an opera house, spans three decks, and has a steeply tiered main floor and port and starboard balconies.

There are three production shows in a typical seven-day cruise, all ably performed by the Jean Ann Ryan Company. They are colorful, high-energy, razzle-dazzle shows with much use of pyrotechnics, laser and color-mover lighting.

A number of bands and solo entertaining musicians provide live music for listening and dancing in several lounges and bars. Throughout the ship, loud Latin music prevails. In the nightclub, a Pachanga Party (a Miami South Beach rave) is held each cruise.

SPA/FITNESS. Wellness devotees should enjoy the two-deck-high Yin-Yang Health Spa complex, operated by the Steiner-owned and Hawaii-based Mandara Spa. It is located in the front of the ship, with large ocean-view windows on three sides. There are many facilities and services to pamper you – almost all at extra charge – including Thai massage (in the spa, outdoors on deck, in your cabin or on your private balcony), and 18 treatment rooms. There's also a 37-ft (11.2-meter) indoor lap pool, hydrotherapy pool, two sit-in deep tubs, aromatherapy and wellness centers, and mud treatment room.

The Body Waves fitness and exercise rooms are within the spa and have the latest Cybex muscle-pumping equipment. Some classes, such as Pathway to Yoga, Body Cycling Class and Body Beat Class (cardio kick-boxing) cost extra.

Recreational sports facilities include a jogging track, golf driving range, basketball and volleyball courts, as well as several levels of sunbathing decks, plus the four bowling lanes, and a funnel-mounted rock-climbing wall.

● **For more extensive general information on what an NCL cruise is like, see pages 146–8.**

Norwegian Jade
★★★★

Size: . . . . .Large Resort Ship	Passenger Decks: 12	Cabins (with private balcony): 763
Tonnage: 93,558	Total Crew: 1,076	Cabins (wheelchair accessible): 27
Lifestyle: . . . . .Standard	Passengers	Wheelchair accessibility: . . . . .Good
Cruise Line: . . . . . .Norwegian Cruise Line	(lower beds/all berths): 2,466/2,890	Cabin Current: . . . . .110 volts
Former Names: . . . . .Pride of Hawaii	Passenger Space Ratio	Elevators: 12
Builder: . . . . .Meyer Werft (Germany)	(lower beds/all berths): 37.9/32.3	Casino (gaming tables): . . . . .Yes
Original Cost: . . . .$390 million	Crew/Passenger Ratio	Slot Machines: . . . . .Yes
Entered Service: . . . .May 2006/Mar 2008	(lower beds/all berths): 2.2/2.6	Swimming Pools (outdoors): 2
Registry: . . . . .The Bahamas	Cabins (total): 1,233	Swimming Pools (indoors): 0
Length (ft/m): 964.8/294.1	Size Range (sq ft/m): 142.0–4,390.0/	Whirlpools: 6
Beam (ft/m): 105.6/32.2	13.2–407.8	Self-Service Launderette: . . . . .No
Draft (ft/m): 26.9/8.2	Cabins (outside view): 834	Dedicated Cinema/Seats: . . . . .No
Propulsion/Propellers: . . . .diesel-electric/	Cabins (interior/no view): 425	Library: . . . . .Yes
2 azimuthing pods (20.0MW each)	Cabins (for one person): 0	Onboard currency: . . . . .US$

Entertainment and a casual lifestyle for the whole family.

OVERVIEW. *Norwegian Jade*, with an all-American crew and service, suits youthful adult couples, single passengers, and families with children and teenagers who want upbeat surroundings, good facilities, a wide range of entertainment lounges and bars, and high-tech sophistication – all in a neat, highly programmed and well packaged cruise. But, although the initial fare seems very reasonable, the extra costs and charges soon mount up if you want to sample more than the basics.

BERLITZ'S RATINGS		
	Possible	Achieved
Ship	500	416
Accommodation	200	155
Food	400	267
Service	400	283
Entertainment	100	67
Cruise	400	293
OVERALL SCORE		
1,481 points out of 2,000		

THE SHIP. Built from 67 blocks, this is a sister ship to *Norwegian Jewel*. After service as *Pride of Hawaii*, it underwent a small transformation, including the addition of a casino, to become *Norwegian Jade*, for cruising in Europe and the Caribbean – though some interior decor elements from the ship's former life in Hawaii remain. The interior decor is decidedly bright and cheerful, and it has a "pod" propulsion system *(see page 191 for an explanation)*.

Norwegian Jade's interior focal gathering place is "Bar Central" – three specialty bars (Magnum's Champagne/Wine Bar, Mixers' Martini/Cocktail Bar, and Tankard's Beer/Whiskey Bar) that are connected but have distinct personalities. They are located on the deck above the reception lobby. All told, there are a dozen bars and lounges on board. Other facilities include a casino, three meeting rooms, a chapel, card room, bridge viewing room, and the SS *United States* Library with original photography and material about America's last ocean liner.

The dress code is very casual; no jacket and tie are needed, although you are welcome to dress formally if you wish. The ship is full of revenue centers designed to help

you part with more of your money. You can expect to be subjected to a stream of flyers advertising daily art auctions, "designer" watches, and many other promotions including poolside "Inch of Gold" sales outlets.

A non-changeable service charge for staff – which is not quite the same thing as a gratuity – is automatically added to your onboard account, or you can pre-pay online.

Passenger niggles include waiting to use the interactive dining reservation screens in the public areas; lines for breakfast in the main dining spots, particularly before the shore excursions start; and poor service and hospitality in some areas.

FAMILIES. Children are well provided for, and have their own facilities, including a Kids' Club; teens have their own disco, the Wipe-Out Club. More than 250 cabins have interconnecting doors – good for families with children. That means interior cabins can connect; outside view cabins can connect; and outside view and balcony cabins can connect. Also for families, many cabins also have third- and fourth-person pull-down berths or trundle beds.

ACCOMMODATION. There are 33 price grades, determined by size and location. Although they are nicely furnished and quite well equipped, the standard outside-view and interior cabins are quite small, particularly when occupied by three or four people.

A small room service menu is available; all non-food items cost extra, and a 15% service charge is added to your account. Bottled water is placed in each cabin, but a charge is made to your account if you open the bottle.

Garden Villas: Two multi-room villas have great views over the pool deck and ocean. Each has a roof terrace and private garden, with open-air dining, hot tub, and private sunning and relaxation areas. They are among the most extravagant suites at sea today. Each has a living room with Bose audio-visual equipment (including a CD/DVD library), grand piano, wet bar, and refrigerator. Each has three bedrooms (king- or queen-size bed) with ensuite bathroom and walk-in closet. Each Garden Villa measures approximately 4,390 sq ft./407.8 sq meters – the ultimate in living space, exclusivity and privacy.

Courtyard Villas: 10 Courtyard Villas (up to 660 sq.ft./61 sq.m.) share a private courtyard with its own small pool, hot tub, massage bed, and fitness room – all in a setting that is distinctly Asian. They also share a private concierge lounge with the two largest villas, as well as butler and concierge service. These units enjoy exclusivity – rather like accommodation in a gated community. The two Garden Villas each have three bedrooms with ensuite bathroom, living room, dining room, and stunning views.

Owner's Suites: Each of these five units (approximately 1,195 sq.ft/111 sq.meters) has a large bedroom with king-size bed and audio-visual entertainment center, and a living room with dining area. The bathroom has a tub, separate shower enclosure and powder room. Some Owner's suites can interconnect with Penthouse Suites.

Penthouse Suites: There are 24 of these, measuring up to 600 sq.ft. (55.5 sq.meters). They have a bedroom with queen-size bed, and living room with dining area. The bathroom has a tub/shower or separate shower enclosure. Some can be interconnect to a kid's room with double sofa bed and a Pullman bed with separate bathroom with shower.

All villas and suites have a private balcony, walk-in closet, rich cherry wood cabinetry, tea/coffee/espresso/cappuccino makers, plus butler and concierge service.

CUISINE. "Freestyle Dining" has no assigned dining rooms, tables or seats, so you can choose which restaurant to eat in, at what time, and with whom. In practice, this means you have to make reservations for a specific time, so "freestyle dining" turns out to be programmed dining. Ten restaurants and eateries are spread over two entire decks. Some are included in the cruise fare, others cost extra.

The two main restaurants, included in the cruise fare, are *Alizar* (310 seats) and *Grand Pacific* (486 seats). Favorite NCL alternative dining venues include *Cagney's Steak House* (176 seats), *Blue Lagoon* (a casual eatery serving American food and seating 94), and *Le Bistro* (a classic French restaurant, with 129 seats – check out the beautiful, and real, Van Gogh painting).

Paniola (100 seats) offers trendy tapas and salsa fare. *Jade Garden* (including a sushi counter, sake bar, and a 32-seat Teppanyaki Grill), has Southeast Asian cuisine. The 70-seat *Papa's Italian Kitchen* has a long wooden table that creates a farmhouse ambience. Self-serve buffet-style meals can be taken in the *Garden Café,* and its outdoor section. Lavazza (Italian) coffees can be found in the *Aloha Café.*

You can make reservations through the Freestyle Dining information system; plasma screens showing waiting times for the various venues are located in high-traffic areas.

ENTERTAINMENT. The 1,042-seat Stardust Theatre is the venue for colorful Las-Vegas-style production shows and major cabaret acts. It is designed in the style of an opera house, spans three decks, and has a steeply tiered main floor and port and starboard balconies. Colorful, high-energy, razzle-dazzle production shows are ably performed by the Jean Ann Ryan Company.

Bands and solo entertaining musicians provide live music for listening and dancing in several lounges and bars. Throughout the ship, loud music prevails. In Spinnakers Lounge, a nightclub located high atop the ship with great ocean views on three sides, a Pachanga Party (a Miami South Beach rave) is held during each cruise.

SPA/FITNESS. The two-deck-high Yin and Yang health spa complex, operated by the Steiner-owned Mandara Spa, is at the stern, with large ocean-view windows on three sides. There are many facilities and services, almost all costing extra. In addition, there is a 37-ft (11.2-meter) indoor lap pool, hydrotherapy pool, two sit-in deep tubs, aromatherapy and wellness centers, and mud treatment rooms, including one for couples. Spa treatments incur an 18% gratuity.

The fitness and exercise rooms, with the latest Cybex muscle-pumping equipment, are located not within the spa, but at the top of the glass-domed atrium lobby. Included is a room for exercycle classes.

Recreational sports facilities include a jogging track, two golf driving nets (there's a golf pro shop, too), basketball and volleyball courts, paddle tennis, mini-golf, oversized chess, and several sunbathing decks.

● **For more extensive general information on what an NCL cruise is like, see pages 146–8**.

Norwegian Jewel
★★★★

Size: . . . . .Large Resort Ship	Passenger Decks: 12	Cabins (with private balcony): 540
Tonnage: 93,000	Total Crew: 1,089	Cabins (wheelchair accessible): 27
Lifestyle: . . . . .Standard	Passengers	Wheelchair accessibility: . . . . .Good
Cruise Line: . . . . . .Norwegian Cruise Line	(lower beds/all berths): 2,376/2,846	Cabin Current: . . . . .110 volts
Former Names: . . . . .none	Passenger Space Ratio	Elevators: 12
Builder: . . . . .Meyer Werft (Germany)	(lower beds/all berths): 39.1/32.6	Casino (gaming tables): . . . . .Yes
Original Cost: . . . .$390 million	Crew/Passenger Ratio	Slot Machines: . . . . .Yes
Entered Service: . . . . .Aug 2005	(lower beds/all berths): 2.1/2.6	Swimming Pools (outdoors): 2
Registry: .Panama	Cabins (total): 1,188	Swimming Pools (indoors): 0
Length (ft/m): 964.8/294.1	Size Range (sq ft/m): 142.0–4,390.0/	Whirlpools: 6
Beam (ft/m): 105.6/32.2	13.2–407.8	Self-Service Launderette: . . . . .No
Draft (ft/m): 26.9/8.2	Cabins (outside view): 783	Dedicated Cinema/Seats: . . . . .No
Propulsion/Propellers: diesel-electric/2	Cabins (interior/no view): 405	Library: . . . . .Yes
azimuthing pods (20.0MW each)	Cabins (for one person): 0	Onboard currency: . . . . .US$

A large, casual ship for lively and family-friendly cruising.

OVERVIEW. Plenty of choices, including many dining options, add up to a very attractive vacation package, highly suitable for families with children, in a floating leisure center that provides ample facilities for enjoyment. The dress code is very casual – no jacket and tie needed – although you are welcome to dress formally if you wish. The initial cruise fare is reasonable, but extra costs and charges soon mount up if you want to sample more than the basics.

THE SHIP. The ship, assembled from 67 blocks, has a basic design and layout similar to that of *Norwegian Gem* and *Norwegian Pearl*, and a "pod" propulsion system *(see page 191 for explanation)*. The white hull has a colourful, funky design on its sides featuring sparkling jewels. There are plenty of sunloungers – in fact, more than the number of passengers carried. Water slides are included for the adult swimming pools. Children have their own pools at the ship's stern, out of sight of adult areas.

Inside the ship, you'll be met by an eclectic mix of colors and decor that you probably wouldn't have in your home, and yet somehow it works extremely well in this large resort ship setting designed to attract the young, active, and trendy.

There are 13 bars and lounges, including "Bar Central," three specialty bars that are connected but have distinct personalities. Shakers Martini and Cocktail Bar is a 1960s-inspired lounge; Magnum's Champagne and Wine Bar recalls Paris of the 1920s and the liner *Normandie*; and Maltings Beer and Whiskey Pub is a contemporary bar with artwork themed around whiskey and beer production.

The level of hospitality aboard Norwegian Cruise Line ships is good – made better and brighter by the addition of

BERLITZ'S RATINGS

	Possible	Achieved
Ship	500	417
Accommodation	200	156
Food	400	267
Service	400	285
Entertainment	100	67
Cruise	400	294

OVERALL SCORE
1,486 points out of 2,000

a great number of Asian female staff. Despite the company's name, there's little that's Norwegian about this product, except for some senior officers. There's plenty of lively music, constant activity, entertainment, and food that is mainstream and acceptable but nothing more, unless you pay extra to eat in the "alternative" dining spots. All this is delivered by a smiling, friendly service staff that lacks polish but is willing.

The ship is full of revenue centers designed to part you from your cash. Expect to be subjected to a stream of flyers advertising daily art auctions, "designer" watches, and "inch of gold/silver."

Gratuities for staff are automatically added to your onboard account at $10 per person, per day; you can, however, reduce or otherwise amend these if necessary before you disembark. Alternatively, you can pre-pay online. In addition, a 15% gratuity is added to all bar purchases, and 18% for spa accounts.

FAMILIES. A good deal of space is devoted to children's facilities, which are all tucked well away from adult recreation areas, at the aft end of the ship. Children of all ages will get to play in a superb wet 'n' wild space-themed water park complete with large pool, water slide, and paddle pool. There's a room full of cots for toddlers to use for sleepovers, and even the toilets are at a special low height. Teens, too, are well catered for, and have their own cinema, discotheque with dance floor, and hot tub.

More than 250 cabins have interconnecting doors – good for families with children. That means interior cabins can connect; outside view cabins can connect; and outside view and balcony cabins can connect. Also for families, many cabins also have third- and fourth-person pull-down berths or trundle beds.

ACCOMMODATION. There are 26 price grades, so there's something for all tastes, from small interior cabins to lavish penthouse suites in a private courtyard setting. Although they are nicely furnished and quite well equipped, the standard outside-view and interior cabins are quite small, particularly when occupied by three or four people.

A small room service menu is available; all non-food items are at extra cost, and a 15% service charge is automatically added to your account. Bottled water is placed in each cabin, but you will be charged if you open the bottle. **Courtyard Penthouses/Suites:** Two Garden Villas (each measures 4,390 sq ft./407.8 sq meters), and 10 Courtyard Villas share a private courtyard with its own small pool, hot tub, massage bed, and fitness room – all in a setting that is distinctly Asian. They also share a private concierge lounge with the two largest villas, as well as butler and concierge service. These units enjoy exclusivity – rather like accommodation in a gated community – where others cannot live unless they pay the asking price. The two largest are duplex apartments, with a spiral stairway between the upper and lower quarters.

CUISINE. "Freestyle Dining" has no assigned dining rooms, tables or seats, so you can choose which restaurant to eat in, at what time, and with whom. In practice, this means you have to make reservations for a specific time, so "freestyle dining" turns out to be programmed dining. Ten restaurants and eateries are spread over two entire decks. Some are included in the cruise fare, others cost extra.

There are two main dining rooms: the 552-seat *Tsar's Palace*, designed to look like the interior of Catherine the Great's St. Petersburg palace in Russia, and the 310-seat *Azura*. There are also a number of other themed eating establishments, giving a wide range of choice – though some cost extra, and require advance reservations.

The 17 video screens around the ship enable you to check how long you'll have to wait for a table at each dining spot. Pagers are available, so you can go bar-hopping while you wait for a table. The system works well, although on "formal" nights when you may want to see the show, congestion can occur. NCL's dress code states that "jeans, T-shirts, tank tops and bare feet are not permitted in restaurants."

Alternative Restaurants/Eateries: *Cagney's House* (for fine steaks and seafood), *Blue Lagoon* (Asian street food), and *Le Bistro* (French cuisine) are NCL favorites. *Tango* is a contemporary spot with bright colors and Latin/tapas fare. *Chin Chin* is an Asian eatery with a Teppanyaki Grill and sushi counter. *Mama's Italian Kitchen* is novel in that it has a long wooden table running through the room to cre-

ate the ambience of a Tuscan farmhouse. For really casual (self-serve) buffet-style eating, there's the light, airy *Great Outdoors*. Finally, the *Garden Café* incorporates an ice cream bar, and *Kid's Café*, with its own kid-height counter, is wisely located opposite the children's play areas. For coffee, head to the *Java Café* in the lobby – it's a great place for people watching. Three of the "alternative" restaurants incur a cover charge, while others are free.

ENTERTAINMENT. The Stardust Theatre, seating 1,037, is the venue for colorful Las-Vegas-style production shows and major cabaret acts. It is designed in the style of an opera house, spans three decks, and has a steeply tiered main floor and port and starboard balconies.

There are two or three production shows in a typical seven-day cruise, all ably performed by the Jean Ann Ryan Company). These are all very colorful, high-energy, razzle-dazzle shows with much use of pyrotechnics, laser and color-mover lighting. By the end of the evening, you may well be too tired to remember much about the shows, which are nevertheless very entertaining.

A number of bands and solo entertaining musicians provide live music for listening and dancing in lounges and bars. Throughout the ship, loud Latin music prevails. In Spinnakers Lounge, a nightclub, a Pachanga Party is held each cruise (a Miami South Beach rave).

SPA/FITNESS. Wellness devotees should enjoy the two-deck-high Bora Bora health spa complex, operated by the Hawaii-based Mandara Spa, located in the front of the ship with large ocean-view windows on three sides. There are many facilities and services to pamper you, almost all at extra charge, including Thai massage in the spa, outdoors on deck, in your cabin or on your private balcony.

In addition, there is a 37-ft (11.2-meter) indoor lap pool, hydrotherapy pool, two sit-in deep tubs, aromatherapy and wellness centers, and mud treatment rooms. There are 15 treatment rooms in all, including one specifically designed for couples, and heated tile loungers in a relaxation area.

The fitness and exercise rooms, with the latest Cybex muscle-pumping equipment, are located not within the spa, but at the top of the glass-domed atrium lobby. Included is a room for exercycle classes. Some classes, such as Pathway to Yoga, Body Cycling Class and Body Beat Class (cardio kick-boxing) cost extra.

Recreational sports facilities include a jogging track, golf driving range, basketball and volleyball courts, as well as four levels of sunbathing decks.

● **For more extensive general information on what an NCL cruise is like, see pages 146–8.**

Norwegian Pearl
★★★★

Size: . . . . .Large Resort Ship	Passenger Decks: 12	Cabins (with private balcony): 540
Tonnage: .93,530	Total Crew: 1,087	Cabins (wheelchair accessible): 27
Lifestyle: . . . . .Standard	Passengers	Wheelchair accessibility: . . . . .Good
Cruise Line: . . . . . .Norwegian Cruise Line	(lower beds/all berths): 2,394/2,846	Cabin Current: . . . . .110 volts
Former Names: . . . . .none	Passenger Space Ratio	Elevators: 12
Builder: . . . . .Meyer Werft (Germany)	(lower beds/all berths): 39.0/32.8	Casino (gaming tables): . . . . .Yes
Original Cost: . . . .$390 million	Crew/Passenger Ratio	Slot Machines: . . . . .Yes
Entered Service: . . . . .Dec 2006	(lower beds/all berths): 2.2/2.6	Swimming Pools (outdoors): 2
Registry: . . . . .Panama	Cabins (total): 1,197	Swimming Pools (indoors): 0
Length (ft/m): 964.8/294.1	Size Range (sq ft/m): 142.0–4,390.0/	Whirlpools: 6
Beam (ft/m): 105.6/32.2	13.2–407.8	Self-Service Launderette: . . . . .Yes
Draft (ft/m): 26.9/8.2	Cabins (outside view): 792	Dedicated Cinema/Seats: . . . . .No
Propulsion/Propellers: . . . .diesel-electric/	Cabins (interior/no view): 405	Library: . . . . .Yes
2 pods (19.5MW each)	Cabins (for one person): 0	Onboard currency: . . . . .US$

Big-ship casual cruising in a family-friendly setting.

OVERVIEW. Plenty of choices, including many dining options, add up to a very attractive vacation package, highly suitable for families with children, in a floating leisure center that provides ample facilities for enjoyment. The dress code is very casual – no jacket and tie needed – although you are welcome to dress formally if you wish. The initial cruise fare is reasonable, but extra costs and charges soon mount up if you want to sample more than the basics.

THE SHIP. One neat room is the "Bliss Ultra Lounge & Night Club," at the aft end of the ship; rather like a South Beach club, it houses a 24-hours-a-day sports bar and lounge complex. This includes a bowling alley with four real bowling lanes – the first aboard any cruise ship. It costs $5 per person, including special playing shoes, and is limited to six persons per lane. The lounge doesn't actually have many seats, but does have a couple of beds, as well as arcade games that include a Mad Wave Motion Theater, with its wild, moving seats.

For a full description of the many bars and lounges, details of children's facilities, and an assessment of the ship's ambience and quality of service, see the preceding entry for *Norwegian Jewel*.

ACCOMMODATION. There are 32 different price grades. For a general description of their facilities, see the entry for *Norwegian Jewel*.

BERLITZ'S RATINGS

	Possible	Achieved
Ship	500	418
Accommodation	200	156
Food	400	267
Service	400	284
Entertainment	100	67
Cruise	400	293

OVERALL SCORE
1,485 points out of 2,000

The following suites are available: **Courtyard Villas/Garden Villas:** The two Garden Villa Suites, each 4,390 sq.ft. (407.8 sq.m), and 10 Courtyard Villas share a private courtyard with its own small pool, hot tub, and small fitness room, and have butler service.

Deluxe Owner's Suites: These two suites, Black Pearl and Golden Pearl, are set high atop all other accommodation, have stunning ocean views, and consist of a master bedroom with king-sized bed, a dining/lounge area, and a decent-sized balcony, and access to the private courtyard.

CUISINE. The two principal dining rooms are the 304-seat *Indigo*, with its minimalist decor; and the 558-seat *Summer Palace*, plus eight other themed eating spots. For details of these alternative restaurants and cafés, see the entry for *Norwegian Jewel*.

ENTERTAINMENT. For details of the 1,042-seater Stardust showlounge and other entertainment facilities, see the entry for *Norwegian Jewel*.

SPA/FITNESS. For details of the facilities in the two-deck-high South Pacific Health Spa complex, see the entry for *Norwegian Jewel*.

● **For more extensive general information on what an NCL cruise is like, see pages 146–8.**

Norwegian Sky
★★★ +

Size:	Large Resort Ship
Tonnage:	77,104
Lifestyle:	Standard
Cruise Line:	Norwegian Cruise Line
Former Names:	Pride of Aloha, Norwegian Sky
Builder:	Lloyd Werft (Germany)
Original Cost:	$332 million
Entered Service:	Aug 1999/Jun 2008
Registry:	The Bahamas
Length (ft/m):	853.0/260.00
Beam (ft/m):	105.8/32.25
Draft (ft/m):	26.2/8.00
Propulsion/Propellers:	diesel-electric (50,000 kW)/2
Passenger Decks:	12
Total Crew:	914
Passengers (lower beds/all berths):	2,002/2,450
Passenger Space Ratio (lower beds/all berths):	38.5/31.4
Crew/Passenger Ratio (lower beds/all berths):	2.1/2.6
Cabins (total):	1,001
Size Range (sq ft/m):	120.5–488.6/ 11.2–45.4
Cabins (outside view):	574
Cabins (interior/no view):	427
Cabins (for one person):	0
Cabins (with private balcony):	252
Cabins (wheelchair accessible):	6
Wheelchair accessibility:	Good
Cabin Current:	110 volts
Elevators:	12
Casino (gaming tables):	Yes
Slot Machines:	Yes
Swimming Pools (outdoors):	2
Swimming Pools (indoors):	0
Whirlpools:	5
Self-Service Launderette:	No
Dedicated Cinema/Seats:	No
Library:	Yes
Onboard currency:	US$

A multi-choice ship for casual family-friendly cruising.

OVERVIEW. *Norwegian Sky*, a resort at sea, caters well to a multi-generational clientele, with lots of choices for dining and entertainment. It provides a fine, comfortable base from which to explore. The outdoor space is quite generous, including an extra wide pool deck with two swimming pools and four hot tubs.

THE SHIP. In 2004 *Norwegian Sky* was "Hawaiianized" and morphed into *Pride of Aloha* for NCL's Hawaii cruise operation. It withdrew from that market in May 2008 and was transferred to NCL for short cruises in the Caribbean. The interior decor reflects its operating area, and the focal point is an eight-deck-high atrium lobby, with spiral sculptures and rainbow-colored sails.

Public rooms include a shopping arcade, children's playroom, internet center with 14 terminals and coffee available from an adjacent bar, several lounges and bars, small conference room, the Mark Twain library; and Captain Cook's for cigars and cognac. Those with a black belt in shopping may seek out the Black Pearl Gem Shop.

The hustling for passengers to attend art auctions is aggressive and annoying, as is the constant bombardment for revenue activities and the daily junk mail that arrives at one's cabin door. There are many announcements – particularly annoying are those that state what is already written in the daily program. There is little connection to the sea from many public rooms. Passenger hallways are quite plain.

ACCOMMODATION. There are 19 price categories: 13 for outside-view suites and cabins, and six for interior (no view) cabins. All the standard outside-view and interior cabins have

BERLITZ'S RATINGS

	Possible	Achieved
Ship	500	395
Accommodation	200	149
Food	400	258
Service	400	232
Entertainment	100	74
Cruise	400	280

OVERALL SCORE
1,388 points out of 2,000

two lower beds that convert to a queen-size bed, a small lounge area with sofa and table, and a decent amount of closet space, but very little drawer space, and the cabins themselves are disappointingly small. However, each is decorated in colorful Hawaiian style, with an explosion of floral themes and vibrant colors.

More than 200 outside-view cabins have their own private balcony. Each cabin has a small vanity/writing desk, color TV set, personal safe, climate control, and a laptop computer connection socket. Audio can be obtained only through the TV set. Bottled water is placed in each cabin – but your account will be charged if you open it.

The largest accommodation is four Owner's Suites. Each has a hot tub, large teak table, two chairs and two sunloungers outside on a huge, very private, forward-facing teakwood floor balcony just under the ship's navigation bridge, with large floor-to-ceiling windows. Each suite has a separate lounge and bedroom. The lounge has a large dining table and four chairs, two two-person sofas, large TV set, DVD/CD unit, coffee table, queen-size pull-down Murphy's bed, guest closet, writing desk, wet bar with two bar stools, refrigerator and sink, several cupboards for glasses, and several drawers and other cupboards for storage. The bedroom, which has sliding wood half-doors that look into the lounge, has a queen-size bed (with European duvet) under a leaf-glass chandelier, vanity desk, TV, walk-in closet with plenty of hanging rail space, five open shelves and large personal safe. The white-tiled bathroom, although not large, has a full-size tub with retractable clothesline, separate shower enclosure with glass doors, deep washbasin, and toiletries cabinets.

There are 10 Junior Suites, each with a private teak decked balcony; these suites face aft in a secluded position and overlook the ship's wash. They have almost the same facilities as those in the owner's suites, except for the outdoor hot tub, and the fact that there is less space.

CUISINE. You can choose which restaurant you would like to eat in, at what time, and with whom.

The main dining rooms – *Palace Restaurant*, with 510 seats, and *Crossings Restaurant*, with 556 seats – have tables for four, six, or eight and an open-seating arrangement. The cuisine in both includes regional specialties However, it's best to have dinner in one of the specialty restaurants, as the food in these two large dining rooms is just so-so.

A smaller eatery, the 83-seat *Plantation Club Restaurant*, is an à la carte, light-eating option serving "healthy" spa dishes and tapas. It has half-moon shaped alcoves and several tables for two. The wine list is quite decent and well arranged, with moderate prices, although you won't find many good vintage wines. The cutlery is very ordinary and there are no fish knives.

For classic and nouvelle French cuisine, the 102-seat *Bistro* has an à la carte menu. The decor is inspired by royal and aristocratic gardens. For premium steaks and lamb chops, there's *Cagneys Restaurant*, with 84 seats, intimate seating alcoves and good food, at extra cost.

Other eateries include *Pacific Heights*, a casual Pacific Rim/Asian Fusion eatery that has steaks plus local fish and seafood. Casual, self-serve buffet-style meals can be taken in the *Garden Café*.

ENTERTAINMENT. The 1,000-seat two-decks-high (main and balcony levels) Stardust Theater is the venue for production shows and major cabaret acts, although the sightlines are quite poor from some seats. A number of bands and solo entertaining musicians provide live music for listening and dancing in several lounges and bars.

SPA/FITNESS. Body Waves is a large health/fitness spa – including an aerobics room and a separate gymnasium, and several treatment rooms. Mandara Spa, headquartered in Honolulu but owned by Steiner Leisure, operates it and provides all staff and treatments as the concession. A whopping 18% gratuity is added to spa treatments.

Sports fans will appreciate the large basketball/volleyball court, baseball-batting cage, golf-driving net, platform tennis, shuffleboard, and table tennis facilities. A sports bar, with baseball and surfing themes, has live satellite television coverage of sports events and major games on several TV screens. Joggers can take advantage of a walk-around indoor/outdoor jogging track.

● **For more extensive general information on what an NCL cruise is like, see pages 146–8.**

QUOTABLE QUOTES

These are some of the questions I have been asked by newcomers to cruising:

"How many knots does the ship go to the gallon?"

"How does the captain know which port to go to?"

"Does the island float?"

"Do you send the laundry ashore?"

"Do these stairs go up as well as down?"

"Why is it that my 3-year old can wear shorts to dinner but I can't?"

"Do we have to eat dinner at both seatings?"

"I know that ships often serve smoked salmon, but I am a non-smoker"

"Can the iced tea be served hot?"

"Can you please change this spoon for a fork? I've already got five spoons"

"Why can't the late-night show be in the morning?"

"Do we have to leave the ship to go on tour?"

Overheard in Livorno: "Can we book a tour to Pizza from here?"

Overheard aboard an Alaska cruise: "Does the helicopter tour leave from the upper deck?"

Overheard on an around-the-world cruise: "Why did we stop so often?"

Norwegian Spirit
★★★★

Size:	.............Large Resort Ship	Passenger Decks:	10	Cabins (with private balcony):	374
Tonnage:	75,338	Total Crew:	948	Cabins (wheelchair accessible):	4
Lifestyle:	..................Standard	Passengers		Wheelchair accessibility:	.........Good
Cruise Line:	......Norwegian Cruise Line	(lower beds/all berths):	.....1,976/2,475	Cabin Current:	..............240 volts
Former Names:	.........SuperStar Leo	Passenger Space Ratio		Elevators:	9
Builder:	........Meyer Werft (Germany)	(lower beds/all berths):	.......38.1/30.4	Casino (gaming tables):	............Yes
Original Cost:	............$350 million	Crew/Passenger Ratio		Slot Machines:	...................Yes
Entered Service:	.....Oct 1998/May 2004	(lower beds/all berths):	.........2.0/2.6	Swimming Pools (outdoors):	2
Registry:	...................Panama	Cabins (total):	983	Swimming Pools (indoors):	0
Length (ft/m):	...........879.2/268.0	Size Range (sq ft/m):	......150.6–638.3/	Whirlpools:	4
Beam (ft/m):	..............105.6/32.2		14.0–59.3	Self-Service Launderette:	..........No
Draft (ft/m):	...............25.9/7.9	Cabins (outside view):	609	Dedicated Cinema/Seats:	..........No
Propulsion/Propellers:	........2 diesels	Cabins (interior/no view):	379	Library:	........................Yes
	(50,400kW)/2	Cabins (for one person):	0	Onboard currency:	...............US$

A casual and lively lifestyle in a large ship setting.

OVERVIEW. Because this is quite a stunning ship and offers a wide choice of dining venues, keeping consistency of product delivery will depend on the quality of the service and supervisory staff. There are many extra-cost items in addition to the à la carte/extra charge dining spots, and there is constant intrusion into your cruise experience with announcements for things such as art auctions, bingo and horse racing.

THE SHIP. As *SuperStar Leo*, this was the first brand-new ship ordered by parent company Star Cruises specifically for the Southeast Asia market. It was moved to NCL as *Norwegian Spirit* in 2004 in a fleet redeployment. A full walk-around promenade deck outdoors is good for strolling, and has lots of space, including a whole area devoted to children's outdoor activities and pool.

Inside, there are two indoor boulevards and a large, stunning, two-deck-high central atrium lobby with three glass-walled lifts and ample space to peruse the shops and cafés that line its inner sanctum. The lobby itself is modeled after the lobby of Hong Kong's Hyatt Hotel, with little clutter from the usual run of desks found aboard other cruise ships.

The interior design theme revolves around art, architecture, history and literature. The ship has a mix of both eastern and western design and decor details. Three stairways are each carpeted in a different color, which helps new cruise passengers find their way around easily.

A 450-seat room atop the ship functions as an observation lounge during the day and a nightclub at night, with live music. From it, a spiral stairway takes you down to a navigation bridge viewing area, where you can see the captain and bridge officers at work.

BERLITZ'S RATINGS		
	Possible	Achieved
Ship	500	418
Accommodation	200	156
Food	400	267
Service	400	284
Entertainment	100	67
Cruise	400	293
OVERALL SCORE		
1,485 points out of 2,000		

There is a business and conference center – good for small groups – and writing room, and a smoking room for those who enjoy cigars and cognac. A shopping concourse is set around the second level of the lobby.

The casino complex is at the forward end of the atrium boulevard on Deck 7 (not between showlounge and restaurant as in most Western ships). This includes Maharajah's, a large general-purpose, brightly lit casino, with gaming tables and slot machines.

The dress code is extremely casual – no jacket and tie needed. Watch out for the extra costs and charges to mount up if you order more than the basics. With many dining choices, some of which cost extra, to accommodate different tastes and styles, your cruise and dining experience will largely depend on how much you are prepared to spend. Gratuities for staff are added to your onboard account, or you can pre-pay online, and 15% is added to all bar purchases, while 18% is added for spa treatments.

Note that standing in line for embarkation, disembarkation, shore tenders and for self-serve buffet meals is an inevitable aspect of cruising aboard all large ships.

FAMILIES. Teens have their own huge video arcade, while younger children get to play in a wet 'n' wild aft pool (complete with pirate ship and caves) and two whirlpool tubs. Plus there's all the fun and facilities of Charlie's childcare center, which includes a painting room, computer learning center, and small cinema. Even the toilets are at a special low height, and there's a room full of cots for toddlers. Over 15,000 sq. ft (1,400 sq. meters) is devoted to children's facilities – all tucked well away from adult recreation areas.

ACCOMMODATION. Three whole decks of cabins have private balconies, while two-thirds of all cabins have an outside view. Both the standard outside-view and interior cabins really are very small – particularly given that all cabins have extra berths for a third/fourth person – although the bathrooms have a good-sized shower enclosure. So, take only the smallest amount of clothing you can get away with. All cabins have a personal safe, 100% cotton towels and 100% cotton duvets or sheets. In cabins with balconies, the balconies are extremely narrow, and the cabins themselves are very small – the ship was originally constructed for three- and four-day cruises.

Choose one of the six largest Executive Suites (named Hong Kong, Malaysia, Shanghai, Singapore, Thailand and Tokyo) and you'll have an excellent amount of private living space, with separate lounge, and bedroom. Each has a large en-suite bathroom that is part of the bedroom and opens onto it. It has a gorgeous mosaic tiled floor, kidney bean-shaped whirlpool tub, two sinks, separate shower enclosure with floor-to-ceiling ocean-view window, and separate toilet with glass door. There are TV sets in the lounge, bedroom and bathroom. The Singapore and Hong Kong suites and the Malaysia and Thai suites can be combined to form a double suite – good for families with children. Butler service and a concierge come with the territory.

Choose one of the 12 Zodiac suites, each named after a sign of the Zodiac, are the second largest accommodation, and also have a butler and concierge. Each suite has a separate lounge, bedroom, and bathroom, and an interconnecting door to an ocean-view cabin with private balcony – good for families. All cabinetry features richly lacquered woods, large (stocked) wet bar with refrigerator, dining table with a top that flips over to reveal a card table, and four chairs, plus sofa, drinks table, and trouser press. The bedrooms are small, but have a queen-size bed; there is a decent amount of drawer space, although the closet space is rather tight because it contains two personal safes. The large ensuite bathrooms are similarly designed to those in the Executive Suites.

A small room service menu is available; all non-food items cost extra, and both a 15% service charge as well as a gratuity are added to your account.

CUISINE. There is certainly plenty of choice when it comes to formal dining and casual eateries. There are eight places to eat, two at extra cost, so you need to plan where you want to eat well in advance or you may be disappointed.
Windows Restaurant: The equivalent of a main dining room, it seats 632 in two seatings, is two decks high at the aft-most section, and has huge cathedral-style windows set in three sections overlooking the ship's stern and wake. Waiter stations are tucked neatly away in side wings, which help to keep down noise levels.

The *Garden Room Restaurant:* This venue has 268 seats.
Raffles Terrace Café: a large self-serve buffet restaurant with indoor/outdoor seating for 400 and pseudo-Raffles Hotel-like decor, with rattan chairs, overhead fans, etc.
Moderno Churrascaria: Installed in a 2011 refit, this Brazilian steakhouse has passadors who serve skewered meats tableside. Reservation are required and there's a cover charge.
Taipan: a Chinese Restaurant, with traditional Hong Kong-themed decor and items such as dim sum made from fresh, not frozen, ingredients. Cover charge, reservations needed.
Shogun Asian Restaurant: a Japanese restaurant and sushi bar, for sashimi, sushi, and tempura. A section can be closed off to make the Samurai Room, with 22 seats, while a traditional Tatami Room has seats for eight. There's also a teppanyaki grill, with 10 seats, where the chef cooks in front of you.
Maxim's: a small à la carte restaurant with ocean-view windows; fine cuisine in the classic French style. Cover charge applicable, reservations necessary.
Blue Lagoon Café: a small, casual street cafe with about 24 seats, featuring noodle dishes, fried rice and other Southeast Asian cuisine. Adjacent is a street bar called *The Bund*.
The Café: a pâtisserie serving several types of coffees, teas, cakes and pastries, at extra cost, in the atrium lobby.

ENTERTAINMENT. The Moulin Rouge Showlounge, with 973 seats, is the main venue. It is two decks high, with a main and balcony levels. The room has almost no support columns to obstruct the sightlines, and a revolving stage for Broadway-style reviews and other production shows – typically to recorded music since there's little space for an orchestra. The show lounge is also used as a large-screen cinema, and has excellent surround sound.

SPA/FITNESS. The Roman Spa and Fitness Center is on one of the uppermost decks, just forward of the Tivoli Pool. It has a gymnasium full of high-tech muscle-toning equipment, and aerobics exercise room, hair and beauty salon, and saunas, steam rooms, and changing rooms for men and women, as well as several treatment rooms, and aqua-swim pools that provide counter-flow jets (swimming against the current). The spa facility is operated by the Hawaii-based Mandara Spa, owned by Steiner Leisure.

The fitness and exercise rooms, with the latest Cybex muscle-pumping equipment, are located not within the spa, but at the top of the glass-domed atrium lobby. Included is a room for exercycle classes. Sports facilities include a jogging track, golf driving range, basketball and tennis courts, and there are four levels of sunbathing decks.

● **For more extensive general information on what an NCL cruise is like, see pages 146–8.**

Norwegian Star
★★★★

Size: . . . . .Large Resort Ship	Passenger Decks: 12	Cabins (with private balcony): 509
Tonnage: 91,740	Total Crew: 1,063	Cabins (wheelchair accessible): 20
Lifestyle: . . . . .Standard	Passengers	Wheelchair accessibility: . . . . .Best
Cruise Line: . . . . . .Norwegian Cruise Line	(lower beds/all berths): 2,244/2,846	Cabin Current: . . . . .110 AC
Former Names: . . . . .none	Passenger Space Ratio	Elevators: 12
Builder: . . . . .Meyer Werft (Germany)	(lower beds/all berths): 40.8/32.0	Casino (gaming tables): . . . . .Yes
Original Cost: . . . .$400 million	Crew/Passenger Ratio	Slot Machines: . . . . .Yes
Entered Service: . . . . .Dec 2001	(lower beds/all berths): 2.1/2.6	Swimming Pools (outdoors): 2
Registry: . . . . .Panama	Cabins (total): 1,122	Swimming Pools (indoors): 1
Length (ft/m): 964.9/294.13	Size Range (sq ft/m): 142.0–5,350.0/	Whirlpools: . . .4 (+ 1 children's whirlpool)
Beam (ft/m): 105.6/32.2	13.2–497.0	Self-Service Launderette: . . . . .No
Draft (ft/m): 26.9/8.2	Cabins (outside view): 787	Dedicated Cinema/Seats: Yes/151
Propulsion/Propellers: . . .diesel-electric/2	Cabins (interior/no view): 335	Library: . . . . .Yes
azimuthing pods (19.5 MW each)	Cabins (for one person): 0	Onboard currency: . . . . .US$

A family-friendly, multi-choice ship for active people.

OVERVIEW. More choices, including more dining options, add up to a very attractive package, particularly suitable for families with children, in a very contemporary floating leisure center that really does provide ample facilities for enjoyment. While the initial cruise fare seems very reasonable, the extra costs and charges soon mount up if you want more than the basics.

THE SHIP. *Norwegian Star* is a sister ship to *Norwegian Dawn*, and has a "pod" propulsion system *(see page 191 for explanation)*. A large structure located forward of the funnel houses a children's center, and, one deck above, the two outstanding "villa" suites. The hull is adorned with a decal consisting of a burst of colorful stars and streamers.

There are plenty of sunloungers – in fact, more than the number of passengers carried. Water slides are included for the adult swimming pools. Children have their own pools at the ship's stern – out of sight of adult areas.

Facilities include an internet café with 17 computer stations, a 1,150-seat showlounge with main floor and two balcony levels, 3,000-book library, card room, writing and study room, business center, karaoke lounge, conference and meeting rooms and associated facilities, a large retail shopping complex, and a casino.

With so many dining choices, some costing extra, the amount you are prepared to spend will determine what your final cruise and dining experience will be like. The dress code is very casual – no jacket and tie needed, although you are welcome to dress formally if you wish. Although service levels and finesse are sometimes inconsistent, the level of hospitality is very good – made so much better and

BERLITZ'S RATINGS

	Possible	Achieved
Ship	500	417
Accommodation	200	155
Food	400	269
Service	400	280
Entertainment	100	67
Cruise	400	297

OVERALL SCORE
1,485 points out of 2,000

brighter by many Southeast Asians who have service experience aboard parent company Star Cruises' big ships. But the hustling for passengers to attend art auctions is aggressive and annoying. Reaching room service tends to be an exercise in frustration.

Gratuities for staff are added to your onboard account daily; you can reduce or otherwise amend these if necessary before you disembark, or you can pre-pay online. In addition, a 15% gratuity is added for all bar purchases, and 18% for spa treatments.

FAMILIES. Children of all ages will get to play in a superb wet 'n' wild space-themed water park complete with large pool, water slide, and paddle pool. They also get their own dedicated cinema in which DVD movies are featured all day long, a jungle gym, painting area, and computer center. Even the toilets are at a special low height. Teens get their own cinema with DVD movies, discotheque with dance floor, and whirlpool tub.

ACCOMMODATION. With 29 price grades, this is a mix that includes something for everyone. There are 36 suites, including two of the largest aboard any cruise ship; 372 "balcony-class" standard cabins with private balconies, 415 outside-view cabins (no balcony); 363 interior (no view) cabins; 36 suites with balconies, and 20 wheelchair-accessible cabins. Suites and cabins with private balconies have easy-to-use sliding glass doors.

All have a powerful hairdryer (located in the cabin itself, and not, thankfully, in the bathroom), and a tea and coffee making sets, rich cherry wood cabinetry, and a bathroom with a sliding door and a separate toilet, shower enclosure and washbasin compartments. There is plenty of wood accenting in all accommodation, including wood frames surrounding balcony doors – a nice touch that will be subliminally appreciated by passengers.

The largest accommodation is in two huge Garden Villas (Vista and Horizon), located high atop the ship in a pod that is located forward of the ship's funnel, and overlooks the main swimming pool. Each measures 5,350 sq ft. (497 sq meters) and can be combined to create a huge, double-size "house." These villas have huge glass walls and landscaped private roof gardens (one has a Japanese-style garden, the other a Thai-style garden) for outdoor dining (with whirlpool tubs, naturally), and huge private sunbathing areas that are completely shielded

Each suite has three bedrooms, one with a sliding glass door that leads to the garden, and bathrooms. One bathroom has a large corner tub, and two washbasins set in front of large glass walls that overlook the side of the ship as well as the swimming pool, although most of the view is of the overlarge waterslide, and a large living room with Yamaha baby grand piano, glass dining table and eight chairs. These units have their own private elevator and private stairway.

There are many suites (the smallest measures 290 sq. ft/ 27 sq. meters) in several different configurations. Some overlook the stern, while others are in the forward part of the ship. All are lavishly furnished, although closet space in some of the smaller units is tight.

Although the suites and junior suites are quite spacious, the standard interior and outside-view cabins are very small when compared to those of other major cruise lines such as Carnival or Celebrity, particularly when occupied by three or four people. The bathrooms, however, are of quite a decent size, and have large shower enclosures. Some cabins have interconnecting doors – good for families with children – and many cabins have third- and fourth-person pull-down berths or trundle beds.

A small room service menu is available; all non-food items cost extra, and a 15% service charge are automatically added to your account. Bottled water is placed in each cabin, but a charge is made if you open the bottle.

CUISINE. NCL operates "Freestyle Dining", so you can choose which restaurant to eat in, at what time, and with whom. Ten restaurants and eateries, with 11 different menus nightly, are spread over two decks.

● *Versailles*, the ornate 375-seat first main dining room, is decorated in brilliant red and gold. This offers traditional six-course dining experience and has excellent views through windows that span two decks.

● *Aqua:* a contemporary-styled 374-seat second main dining room, offering lighter cuisine, and an open galley where you can view the preparation of pastries and desserts.

● *Soho:* Pacific Rim mixes Californian and Asian cuisine. It has a live lobster tank – the first aboard a ship outside Southeast Asia. A main dining area seats 132, and private dining rooms each seat 10.

● *Ginza:* a Japanese restaurant, with 193 seats, a sit-up sushi bar, tempura bar, show galley, and separate "teppan-yaki grill" room.

● *Le Bistro:* a French restaurant, with 66 seats, serving nouvelle cuisine and six courses.

● *Blue Lagoon:* a funky food court-style eatery with 88 seats, both indoors and outdoors, with hamburgers, fish and chips, potpies and fast (wok stir-fried) dishes.

● *Market Café:* a large indoor/outdoor self-serve buffet eatery, with almost 400 ft (120 meters) of buffet counter space. "Action Stations" has made-to-order omelets, waffles, fruit, soups, ethnic specialities and pasta dishes.

● *La Trattoria,* an Italian, evening-only dining spot within the buffet area, has pasta, pizza and other Italian fare.

● *Steakhouse:* prime USDA beef steaks and lamb chops.

● *Endless Summer:* a Hawaiian themed restaurant, incorporating a performance stage and a large movie screen.

Other spots include the *Red Lion*, an English pub for draft beer and a game of darts; *Havana Club*, a cigar and cognac lounge; *Java Café*, an atrium lobby bar-café for hot and frozen coffees, teas and pastries; a *Beer Garden* for grilled foods; a *Spinkles*, an ice cream bar; a *Gym and Spa Bar* for health food snacks and drinks; and *Gatsby's* wine bar.

Overall, the food is adequate, but lacks taste and presentation quality, although the menus make the dishes sound good. There's a reasonably decent selection of breads, rolls, cheeses and fruits. The wine list is quite good and moderately priced, though the glasses are small.

A lavish "chocoholics" buffet is available once each cruise – a firm favorite among regular passengers.

ENTERTAINMENT. The Stardust Theatre, seating 1,037, is the venue for colorful Las-Vegas-style production shows and major cabaret acts. Two or three production shows are presented in a typical seven-day cruise, all ably performed by the Jean Ann Ryan Company. They're very entertaining if not particularly memorable.

A number of bands and solo entertainers provide live music for listening and dancing in several lounges and bars.

SPA/FITNESS. The two-deck-high Barong health spa complex, operated by the Steiner-owned and Hawaii-based Mandara Spa, is at the stern, with large ocean-view windows on three sides.

The many facilities and services, almost all cost extra, include Thai massage (in the spa, outdoors on deck, in your cabin or on your private balcony). There is an indoor lap pool measuring 37 ft (11.2 meters), hydrotherapy pool, aromatherapy and wellness centers, and 15 treatment rooms.

The fitness and exercise rooms, with the latest muscle-pumping equipment, are at the top of the atrium lobby. Recreational sports facilities include a jogging track, golf driving range, basketball and volleyball courts, as well as four levels of sunbathing decks.

● **For more extensive general information on what an NCL cruise is like, see pages 146–8.**

Norwegian Sun
★★★ +

Size:	Large Resort Ship	Passenger Decks:	12	Cabins (with private balcony):	252
Tonnage:	78,309	Total Crew:	916	Cabins (wheelchair accessible):	6
Lifestyle:	Standard	Passengers		Wheelchair accessibility:	Good
Cruise Line:	Norwegian Cruise Line	(lower beds/all berths):	1,936/2,400	Cabin Current:	110 volts
Former Names:	none	Passenger Space Ratio		Elevators:	12
Builder:	Lloyd Werft (Germany)	(lower beds/all berths):	40.4/32.6	Casino (gaming tables):	Yes
Original Cost:	$332 million	Crew/Passenger Ratio		Slot Machines:	Yes
Entered Service:	Nov 2001	(lower beds/all berths):	2.1/2.6	Swimming Pools (outdoors):	2
Registry:	The Bahamas	Cabins (total):	968	Swimming Pools (indoors):	0
Length (ft/m):	853.0/260.00	Size Range (sq ft/m):	120.5–488.6/	Whirlpools:	4
Beam (ft/m):	105.8/32.25		11.2–45.4	Self-Service Launderette:	No
Draft (ft/m):	26.2/8.00	Cabins (outside view):	676	Dedicated Cinema/Seats:	No
Propulsion/Propellers:	diesel-electric	Cabins (interior/no view):	292	Library:	Yes
	(50,000 kW)/2	Cabins (for one person):	0	Onboard currency:	US$

Big-ship casual cruising in a family-friendly setting.

OVERVIEW. What this offers is plenty of bars and lounges to play in, and multiple dining and snacking options. But the food in the large dining rooms is a weak point, and the ship is full of revenue centers, designed to help you part you from your money.

THE SHIP. *Norwegian Sun* is a close sister ship to *Norwegian Sky*, but with better outfitting and finishing detail, plus one extra deck of balcony cabins and additional cabins to accommodate the extra 200 crew needed for the Freestyle dining concept. The outdoor space is quite good, especially the ultra-wide pool deck, with two swimming pools and four Jacuzzi tubs, and plenty of sunloungers, albeit arranged in camp-style rows.

A separate cabaret venue, Dazzles Lounge, has an extremely long bar. A large casino operates 24 hours a day. There's a shopping arcade, children's playroom, and a video arcade. Other facilities include a small conference room, library and beauty salon, a lounge for smoking cigars and drinking cognac, and an internet café with 20 computers. You can expect to be subjected to a stream of flyers advertising daily art auctions, "designer" watches, and other promotions, while "artworks" for auction are strewn throughout the ship.

Gratuities for staff are added daily to your onboard account; you can, however, reduce or otherwise amend these before you disembark. Alternatively, you can pre-pay online. In addition, a 15% gratuity is added for bar purchases, and a hefty 18% for spa treatments.

The standard interior (no-view) and outside-view cabins are very small when compared to those of other major cruise lines. There are many plastic plates, Styrofoam and

BERLITZ'S RATINGS

	Possible	Achieved
Ship	500	400
Accommodation	200	149
Food	400	258
Service	400	232
Entertainment	100	74
Cruise	400	280

OVERALL SCORE
1,393 points out of 2,000

plastic cups and plastic stirrers in use in the casual eateries.

FAMILIES. Young passengers will find an array of facilities, which include a children's playroom called Kid's Corner (for "junior sailors" ages 3–5; First Mates (ages 6–9); Navigators (ages 10–12); and Teens (ages 13–17).

ACCOMMODATION. There are 30 different categories, including six grades of suites, 15 grades of outside-view cabins, and nine grades of interior cabins.

All of the standard outside-view and interior cabins have common facilities, such as two lower beds that can convert to a queen-size bed, a small lounge area with sofa and table, and a decent amount of closet and drawer space, although the cabins themselves are disappointingly small. Over 200 outside-view cabins have a private balcony.

There are two Honeymoon/Anniversary Suites, each with a separate lounge and bedroom.

The largest accommodation is in two Owner's Suites – each with a hot tub, large teak table, two chairs and two sunloungers outside on a huge, private, forward-facing teak floor balcony just under the navigation bridge, with large floor-to-ceiling windows. There are a number of other suites, each with a private teakwood balcony. They share some facilities with the owner's suites, except for the outdoor hot tub and the fact that there's less space.

All cabins have tea/coffee-making sets, a safe, satellite-linked telephone, and bathroom with bath or shower.

CUISINE. NCL has "Freestyle Dining", so you can choose which restaurant you would like to eat in, at what time, and with whom. Apart from two large dining rooms, there are a number of other themed eating establishments – although it would be wise to plan in advance, particularly for dinner. Some incur an extra charge. The dress code states that: "jeans, T-shirts, tank tops and bare feet are not permitted in restaurants."

The two main dining rooms – the 564-seat *Four Seasons Dining Room*, and the 604-seat *Seven Seas Dining Room*, have tables for two, four, six or eight. Sandwiched between the two (rather like a train carriage) is a third, 84-seat Italian Restaurant, *Il Adagio*, available as an à la carte (extra charge, reservations required) option, with window-side tables for two or four persons. Reservations are necessary.

Other options, most on one of the upper-most decks, with great views from large picture windows, include:

● *Le Bistro:* a 90-seat dining spot for French-style meals, including tableside cooking. Reservations required.

● *Las Ramblas:* a Spanish/Mexican style eatery serving tapas (light snack items).

● *Ginza:* a Japanese Restaurant, with a sushi bar and a teppanyaki grill (show cooking in a U-shaped setting where you sit around the chef). Reservations required.

● *East Meets West:* a Pacific Rim Fusion Restaurant, featuring à la carte California/Hawaii/Asian cuisine. Reservations are necessary for dinner.

● *Moderna Churrascaria:* Brazilian steakhouse and salad bar, with table-side meat carving. Reservations required.

● *Garden Café:* a busy 24-hour restaurant indoor/outdoor self-serve buffet-style eatery with fast foods and salads.

Although the menus make meals sound appetizing, overall the food is rather unmemorable, lacking taste and mostly overcooked. However, the presentation is generally quite good. There is a reasonable selection of breads, rolls, and pastry items, but the selection of cheeses is very poor.

The wine list is well balanced, and there is also a connoisseur list of premium wines, although the vintages tend to be young. There are many types of beer (including some on draught in the popular Sports Bar & Grill).

There is no formal afternoon tea, although you can make your own at beverage stations (but it's difficult to get fresh milk as non-dairy "creamers" are typically supplied). The service is, on the whole, adequate, nothing more.

A lavish "chocoholics" buffet is featured once each cruise – a firm favorite among NCL passengers.

ENTERTAINMENT. The Stardust Theater is a two-level show lounge with more than 1,000 seats and a large proscenium stage. However, the sightlines are obstructed in a number of seats by several slim pillars. Two or three production shows are presented in a typical seven-day cruise (all ably performed by the Jean Ann Ryan Company). These are very colorful, high-energy, high-volume razzle-dazzle shows with much use of pyrotechnics, laser and color-mover lighting. The ship carries a number of bands and solo entertaining musicians. These provide live music for listening and dancing in several of the lounges and bars, including the loud Dazzles, home to musical groups.

SPA/FITNESS. Bodywaves, at the top of the atrium, is a large health/fitness spa (including an aerobics room and separate gymnasium), several treatment rooms, and men's and women's saunas/steam rooms and changing rooms.

There is an indoor-outdoor jogging track. a large basketball/volleyball court, baseball-batting cage, golf-driving range, platform tennis, shuffleboard and table tennis facilities, and sports bar with 24-hour live satellite TV coverage of sports events and major games.

● **For more extensive general information on what an NCL cruise is like, see pages 146–8.**

Oasis of the Seas
★★★★

Size: ....Large Resort Ship	Total Crew: 2,164	Wheelchair accessibility: ....Good
Tonnage: 222,900	Passengers	Cabin Voltage: ....110 volts
Lifestyle: ....Standard	(lower beds/all berths): 5,408/6,360	Elevators: 24
Cruise Line: Royal Caribbean International	Passenger Space Ratio	Casino (gaming tables): ....Yes
Builder: ....Aker Yards (Finland)	(lower beds/all berths): 41.6/35.4	Slot Machines: ....Yes
Original Cost: ....$1.5 billion	Crew/Passenger Ratio	Swimming Pools (outdoors): 6
Entered Service: ....Dec 2009	(lower beds/all berths): 2.4/2.9	Swimming Pools (indoors): 0
Registry: ....The Bahamas	Cabins (total): 2,704	Whirlpools: 10
Length (ft/m): 1181.1/360.0	Size Range (sq ft/m): ....n/a	Self-Service Launderette: ....No
Beam (ft/m): 216.5/66.0	Cabins (outside view): 2,210	Dedicated Cinema/Seats: ....No
Draft (ft/m): 30.0/9.15	Cabins (interior/no view): 494	Library: ....Yes
Propulsion/Propellers: .....diesel-electric	Cabins (for one person): 0	Onboard currency: ....US$
(97.2MW)/3 pods	Cabins (with private balcony): 1,956	
Passenger Decks: 16	Cabins (wheelchair accessible): 46	

A huge floating resort for families with boundless energy.

OVERVIEW. *Oasis of the Seas* commands a premium over other RCI ships, but it provides a good all-round cruise and wide range of choices for young adults and families with children, though the service is notably better in suite-class accommodation. The ship is packed with innovative design elements – none more so than the dramatic Central Park, the first real park at sea. Essentially a large block of apartments sitting on a white hull, it's a benchmark for floating self-contained resorts.

THE SHIP. Technically, this is no longer the world's largest cruise ship because its sister, *Allure of the Seas*, is almost 2 inches (5cm) longer. In almost every other way, however, the ships are identical, and innovations aboard *Allure* such as a 3-D movie screen have been retrofitted to *Oasis*. Therefore, for a comprehensive account of these record-breaking vessels, turn to the 3,700-word review of *Allure of the Seas* on pages 209–12. The discussion of "What's Good and What's Not" about *Allure* on page 210 applies equally to *Oasis*.

Both ships arrange their public spaces as seven neighborhoods: Central Park, the Boardwalk, the Royal Promenade, the Pool and Sports Zone, Vitality at Sea Spa/Fitness Center, Entertainment Place and Youth Zone. The most popular are the Boardwalk and Central Park, both open to the air, and the indoor Royal Promenade.

ACCOMMODATION. Remarkably, there are 37 price grades, reflecting the choice of location and size. Suite occupants get access to a concierge lounge and associated services. There are many family-friendly cabins but no no single-

BERLITZ'S RATINGS	Possible	Achieved
Ship	500	431
Accommodation	200	158
Food	400	234
Service	400	295
Entertainment	100	87
Cruise	400	321

OVERALL SCORE
1,526 points out of 2,000

occupancy cabins. Most cabins feel extremely small, given the size of the ship. There are 475 cabins with views into either Central Park or Royal Promenade, the two horizontal atriums, from their curved interior balconies.

CUISINE. The meals in *Opus*, the main dining room, which is spread over three decks, are all about well-timed production cooking and fast delivery – essentially a banquet catering operation, so the food is tasteless (except for salt) and utterly underwhelming. There's a host of other eateries and extra-cost dining venues. The longest waiting lines are for *Johnny Rockets* and the *Seafood Shack*.

ENTERTAINMENT. The 1,380-seat Opal Theatre, spread over three decks, is the main showlounge, which stages the popular musical *Hairspray*. There's also an aerial acrobatic show, *Come Fly With Me*. The 750-seat AquaTheater presents the comedy dive show *Splish Splash*, a sort of take-off of *Le Rêve* in at the Wynn in Las Vegas. *Frozen in Time* is a stunning, must-see ice show in Studio "B."

SPA/FITNESS. The Vitality at Sea Spa (Vass) includes a Vitality Café for extra-cost health drinks and snacks. The fitness center includes 158 cardio and resistance machines. An extra-cost thermal suite includes saunas, steam rooms, and heated tiled loungers. Sports facilities include two surfboard pools, golf putting course, ziplining (screaming is mandatory), and an ice-skating rink.

● **For more extensive general information on what an RCI cruise is like, see pages 152–6.**

Ocean Countess
★★★

Size: . . . . .Mid-Size Ship	Propulsion/Propellers: diesel (15,670 kW)/2	Cabins (with private balcony): 0
Tonnage: .17,593	Passenger Decks: 8	Cabins (wheelchair accessible): 0
Lifestyle: . . . . .Standard	Total Crew: 350	Wheelchair accessibility: . . . . .None
Cruise Line: Cruise and Maritime Voyages	Passengers	Cabin Current: . . . . .110 and 220 volts
Former Names: . . . . . .Olympia Countess,	(lower beds/all berths): 780/898	Elevators: 2
Olympic Countess, Awani Dream I,	Passenger Space Ratio	Casino (gaming tables): . . . . .Yes
Cunard Countess	(lower beds/all berths): 22.5/19.5	Slot Machines: . . . . .Yes
Builder: . . . .Burmeister & Wein (Denmark)	Crew/Passenger Ratio	Swimming Pools (outdoors): 1
Original Cost: . . . .£12 million	(lower beds/all berths): 2.2/2.5	Swimming Pools (indoors): 0
Entered Service: . . . . .Aug 1976/Apr 2010	Cabins (total): 400	Whirlpools: 2
Registry: . . . . .Madeira	Size Range (sq ft/m): 87.1–322.9/8.1–30.0	Self-Service Launderette: . . . . .No
Length (ft/m): 536.6/163.56	Cabins (outside view): 265	Dedicated Cinema/Seats: Yes/126
Beam (ft/m): 74.9/22.84	Cabins (interior/no view): 135	Library: . . . . .Yes
Draft (ft/m): 19.0/5.82	Cabins (for one person): 20	Onboard currency: . . . . .UK£

A basic, casual ship for frugal seniors.

OVERVIEW. Anyone seeking a casual, child-free, destination-intensive cruise will probably like this comfortable vessel, which is a change from today's newer, larger ships. It's a very high-density ship, with small cabins, wuited to British adult couples and solo travelers seeking a traditional ship with decent facilities, quite basic food, and well-meaning, friendly service.

THE SHIP. *Ocean Countess* has had an eventful history. One of a pair, it was ordered for a US airline, Overseas National Airways, which went bankrupt, after which Cunard Line took over the contract and operated it as an informal Caribbean cruise vessel. Cunard sold it to Awani Dream Cruises, of Indonesia, and in 1997 it was bought by Royal Olympic Cruises. In 2004, when Royal Olympia Cruises ceased operating, the ship was sold to Piraeus-based Majestic International Cruises at auction in Durban (price $6.1 million), and renamed *Ocean Countess*. Look closely and, despite its many identities, you'll still find some Cunard items on board.

After a $6 million refit in 2009, the ship was placed on charter to UK operator Cruise & Maritime Voyages, which explains the intitials CM on the funnel.

Ocean Countess still displays a fairly smart, modern profile with crisp lines, blue hull and a distinctive blue swept-back funnel. Its almost identical twin presently operates as *Golden Iris* for Israel's Mano Cruise.

Inside, there is a good selection of public rooms, most with attractive, light colors and cheerful decor, and most located on one deck, making access easy. The showlounge is a single-level room with raised seating on its port and starboard sides – eight pillars obstruct the sightlines, how-

BERLITZ'S RATINGS		
	Possible	Achieved
Ship	500	307
Accommodation	200	114
Food	400	221
Service	400	239
Entertainment	100	61
Cruise	400	236
OVERALL SCORE		
1,178 points out of 2,000		

ever, and the ceiling is low. Aft of the showlounge is The Hamptons, an indoor-outdoor entertainment lounge/nightclub that incorporates a large aft open deck area and is pleasant during warm-weather cruises.

Gratuities, which are pooled among the crew, are applied to your onboard account (£5 per person, per night; £4 for cruises longer than 16 nights).

ACCOMMODATION. There are 14 price grades: three for suites, five with outside view windows or portholes, and four for interior cabins. Prices depend on grade, location and size. Note that 20 cabins in two price categories have been assigned as single occupancy units; because they were originally for two persons, this gives solo travelers a little more space. **Deluxe/Standard Outside View/Interior Cabins:** These are mostly of a standard, very compact size, and come in light colors and plain, but pleasant decor that's adequate for short cruises. They are best described as space-efficient units with metal fixtures and poor insulation – you can talk to your neighbors without having to use the telephone! All standard cabins have two lower beds; some are in a twin shape, while others are in an L shape, but they are fixed and cannot be moved together. Many cabins also have a third upper berth. The cabins on the lowest deck (Admiral Deck 3) suffer from vibration and the odor of diesel fuel, and have portholes, as do cabins on the deck above, Main Deck 4. All other cabins on the upper decks have windows. The cabin bathrooms are small modular units – good for one, but impossible for two people to use at the same time. They contain a shower enclosure, toilet and washbasin, but little storage space for toiletries.

The largest accommodation is in the "suites" on Promenade Deck 7 and Upper Deck 6. These all have a double bed, a good amount of closet space, lounge area with sofa or chairs, TV, and a larger bathroom with tub and shower, toilet and washbasin. If you are seeking more space, these are the rooms to go for. There are four price grades.

Two Owner's Suites, each able to accommodate a third person on a sofa bed, were added immediately forward and adjacent to the Kensington Restaurant. Both of these almost L-shaped suites measure 322.9 sq.ft (30 sq. meters), have a layout that allows lots of light through large picture windows (but no balconies), and provide the most space of any accommodation aboard this ship. Each has a queen-size bed, vanity/writing desk, and lounge area with minibar. The bathroom has a tub and shower.

CUISINE. The *Kensington Restaurant* is located in the middle of the ship; it is one deck high, and seats 487. It has large ocean-view picture windows on two sides, and seating is mostly at tables for four, six, or eight, in two seatings. Banquet-style catering is standard, tailored for international passengers. There is a limited selection of fresh fruits and cheeses, but cheerful service from an attentive, friendly staff.

A casual self-serve open-air area, the *Boat House*, located at the stern on Upper Deck 6, is for breakfast, lunches and sometimes, depending on the itinerary, buffet dinners. The choice of food is limited, and lacks creativity, variety and presentation – think British school canteens and overcooked food and you'll get the general idea.

ENTERTAINMENT. The 400-seat Holyrood Show Lounge is the venue for shows and entertainment events. It is a single-level, rectangular-shaped room with a black granite dance floor, designed for cabaret acts rather than production-style shows. Although the sides of the room are raised, several pillars obstruct the sightlines.

The ship has a main showband, together with small musical units and solo pianists to provide live music for dancing and listening in the various lounges and bars. These include the Tower Piano Bar, situated in what is a very nice observation lounge that includes a small library and card playing area.

SPA/FITNESS. A small gymnasium, the 20 Twelves Gym, is located on one side of the funnel housing, on the pool deck. A jogging track on the deck above is difficult to use because it is narrow and passengers tend to place their deck chairs there for sunbathing. Limited massage facilities and a small changing area are provided on the opposite side to the gymnasium. A beauty salon is located indoors on another deck (Upper Deck 6), aft of the restaurant.

DID YOU KNOW...

● that most of the major cruise lines have replaced Champagne with sparkling wine for the captain's welcome aboard cocktail party?

● that the liner *Amerika* in 1938 was the first ship to have an alternative restaurant open separately from the dining saloons? It was named the Ritz Carlton.

● that the first à la carte restaurant aboard a passenger ship was in the German ship *Amerika* of 1905?

● that TUI Cruises' *Mein Schiff* is the only ship with an espresso coffee machine in every cabin?

● that a whole county in Iowa raises all its beef cattle for sale to Carnival Cruise Lines?

● that the first "en suite" rooms (with private bathroom) were on board Cunard Line's *Campania* of 1893?

● that the first single-berth cabins built as such were also aboard the *Campania*?

● that the first liner to offer private terraces with their first-class suites was *Normandie* in 1935 (the Trouville Suite had four bedrooms as well as a private terrace)?

● that the first ships to feature private balconies were the *Saturnia* and *Vulcania* in the early 1900s?

● that the first ship to be fitted with interior plumbing was the 6,283-ton *Normandie* of 1883?

● that the first ship fitted with an internal electric lighting system was the Inman liner *City of Berlin* in 1879?

● that Carnival Cruise Lines places more than 10 million chocolates on passenger pillows each year?

● that the whole disc of the sun is visible for 24 hours a day at some points north of the Arctic Circle? North Cape (May 14–July 29); Hammerfest (May 16–July 27); Tromso (May 20–July 22); Harstad (May 26–July 19); Bodo (June 4–July 8).

Ocean Dream
★★★

Size: . . . . .Mid-Size Ship	Passenger Decks: 10	Cabins (wheelchair accessible): 11
Tonnage: .35,190	Total Crew: 550	Wheelchair accessibility: . . . . .Fair
Lifestyle: . . . . .Standard	Passengers	Cabin Current: . . . . .110/220 volts
Cruise Line: . . . . .Pullmantur Cruises	(lower beds/all berths): 1,022/1,350	Elevators: 8
Former Names: . . . .*Pacific Star,*	Passenger Space Ratio	Casino (gaming tables): . . . . .Yes
Costa Tropicale, Tropicale	(lower beds/all berths): 34.4/26.0	Slot Machines: . . . . .Yes
Builder: . . . . . .Aalborg Vaerft (Denmark)	Crew/Passenger Ratio	Swimming Pools (outdoors): 3
Original Cost: . . . .$100 million	(lower beds/all berths): 1.8/2.5	Swimming Pools (indoors): 0
Entered Service: . . . . .Jun 1982/Mar 2008	Cabins (total): 511	Whirlpools: 0
Registry: . . . . .The Bahamas	Size Range (sq ft/m): 180.0–398.2/16.7–37.0	Self-Service Launderette: . . . . .Yes
Length (ft/m): 671.7/204.76	Cabins (outside view): 324	Dedicated Cinema/Seats: . . . . .No
Beam (ft/m): 86.7/26.45	Cabins (interior/no view): 187	Library: . . . . .Yes
Draft (ft/m): 23.3/7.11	Cabins (for one person): 0	Onboard currency: . . . . .Euros
Propulsion/Propellers: diesel (19,566kW)/2	Cabins (with private balcony): 12	

A good-value cruise vacation for Spanish-speaking families.

OVERVIEW *Ocean Dream* is best suited to Spanish-speaking families, young couples, and singles seeking a standard cruise in modestly contemporary surroundings. This is a very standard product, with banquet catering. But there are plenty of opportunities for gaming and partying, and the fact that all drinks and gratuities are included makes a vacation easy to budget.

THE SHIP. This was the first new ship ordered by Carnival Cruise Lines. It was sent to Costa Cruises in 2001, and in 2008 Pullmantur Cruises – which caters to young cruisers and their parents, particularly during school vacations – acquired and refurbished it. It has a fairly distinctive, though boxy look and profile. Open deck space is very limited, and there is no walk-around promenade deck outdoors.

The interior layout and passenger flow is generally good. The public rooms are bright and cheerful, with many bold, bright color splashes. Rooms include a card room, internet center, piano bar, and several bars and lounges.

ACCOMMODATION. There are nine cabin price categories. Most of the "standard" interior and outside-view cabins are all of the usual cookie-cutter variety (but of a decent size), with an imaginative European-style decor, and just enough closet and drawer space for a week's cruise. A number of cabins have third and fourth person upper berths – useful for families with small children. The bathrooms are plain, but adequate for short cruises, although there's little storage space for toiletries.

The largest accommodation is in 12 "suites" – each with

BERLITZ'S RATINGS

	Possible	Achieved
Ship	500	271
Accommodation	200	113
Food	400	209
Service	400	246
Entertainment	100	58
Cruise	400	213

OVERALL SCORE
1,110 points out of 2,000

a narrow semi-private balcony. Naturally, there is more space, since the living and sleeping areas are divided. The bathrooms are marginally larger, too. But all these suites have their views largely blocked by the positioning of lifeboats. The cabin soundproofing could be better, and the room service menu is quite basic.

CUISINE. The *Restaurant Principal* is on the ship's lowest deck. It is colorful, very cheerful, brightly lit, but noisy and rather cramped, making proper service quite difficult. There are tables for four, six or eight (none for two), and dining is in two seatings. Dinner on European cruises is typically at 7pm and 9pm.

The *Buffet Panorama* is a self-service buffet facility, with European selections that are quite basic, as is the selection of breads, rolls, fruit and cheeses. At night, as the *Lido Café*, it becomes a bistro and provides a dress-down alternative to eating in the main dining room. There's also a pizzeria. Good cappuccino and espresso coffees are available in the various bars.

ENTERTAINMENT. The Salon de Espectaculos (show-lounge) is a single-level room that has bright, cheerful decor, although sightlines to the stage are obstructed from several seats. A mix of banquette and individual seating is provided, together with small drinks tables.

SPA/FITNESS. The spa/fitness area is located just behind the mast, and is small. It contains a gymnasium, sauna and changing rooms for men and women.

Ocean Pearl
★★ +

Size: . . . . .Mid-Size Ship	Passenger Decks: 8	Cabins (wheelchair accessible): 0
Tonnage: .22,945	Total Crew: 450	Wheelchair accessibility: . . . . .None
Lifestyle: . . . . .Standard	Passengers	Cabin Current: . . . . .110 volts
Cruise Line: . . . . .Happy Cruises/ISP	(lower beds/all berths): 1,076/1,257	Elevators: 4
Former Names: . . . . Clipper Pacific,	Passenger Space Ratio	Casino (gaming tables): . . . . .Yes
Clipper Pearl, Dream, Dream Princess,	(lower beds/all berths): 21.3/18.2	Slot Machines: . . . . .Yes
Sundream, Song of Norway	Crew/Passenger Ratio	Swimming Pools (outdoors): 1
Builder: . . . . .Wartsila (Finland)	(lower beds/all berths): 2.3/2.7	Swimming Pools (indoors): 0
Original Cost: . . . .$13.5 million	Cabins (total): 538	Whirlpools: 0
Entered Service: . . . . .Nov 1970/Mar 2010	Size Range (sq ft/m):	Self-Service Launderette: . . . . .No
Registry: . . . . .The Bahamas	118.4–265.8/11.0–24.7	Dedicated Cinema/Seats: . . . . .No
Length (ft/m): 637.5/194.32	Cabins (outside view): 346	Library: . . . . .Yes
Beam (ft/m): 78.8/24.03	Cabins (interior/no view): 192	Onboard currency: . . . . .Euros
Draft (ft/m): 21.9/6.70	Cabins (for one person): 0	
Propulsion/Propellers: diesel (13,400kW)/2	Cabins (with private balcony): 0	

A crowded, tired ship for family-friendly cruising.

OVERVIEW. This ship is best suited to young Spanish-speaking families who are used to package holidays, tight budgets, and the inclusive aspects they offer. There is a reasonable amount of open deck space, but it really feels crowded when the ship is full, particularly around the small swimming pool.

THE SHIP. This ship, originally built more than 40 years ago as one of Royal Caribbean Cruise Line's first three ships, still looks fairly smart, and has a large amount of open deck space for sports. There is a polished walk-around wooden deck outdoors – good for strolling, but make sure you wear shoes with non-slip soles.

The decor has fairly bright, crisp colors. The accommodation passageways are narrow, but do contain artwork and some wood trim. There are several lounges and bars, including a casino, piano bar, discotheque, internet center, and video games room. Children have their own Club Pelicanos.

There are many loud announcements. The space per passenger is poor. The cabin TV sets are small, except for those in the "suites". Couples without children will be surrounded by large number of youngsters in summer.

All-inclusive pricing means that standard-brand drinks and gratuities are covered by the fare. Shore excursions, use of medical facility, and spa treatments are not included, nor are room service items such as snacks or sandwiches.

ACCOMMODATION. The cabins are split into just four price grades (Standard, Superior, Promenade and Deluxe) and six types, making it easy to select the type of accommodation you want. Most cabins are of a similar size – in a word,

BERLITZ'S RATINGS

	Possible	Achieved
Ship	500	252
Accommodation	200	104
Food	400	217
Service	400	238
Entertainment	100	58
Cruise	400	211

OVERALL SCORE
1,080 points out of 2,000

small – and the insulation between them is quite poor. There's very little storage space, perhaps because the ship was built originally for Caribbean cruising, but they are adequate for a one-week cruise. The bathrooms are very small – functional rather than attractive – and the showers have a flimsy curtain.

The largest cabins are named after famous explorers. Only the owner's suite has a refrigerator. The cabin voltage is 110 volts and sockets have American-style two-flat-pins, so you may need adapters for hairdryers and the like.

CUISINE. The main dining room is reasonably attractive, but noisy, and there are two seatings. The food is unmemorable. It's basic, no-frills cuisine, but there's plenty of it. Table wines are included in the fare. There's a self-serve buffet for casual meals and a café for coffees.

ENTERTAINMENT. The Salon Espectaculo is a single-level room designed for cabaret acts rather than large-scale productions. Many seats have poor sightlines, obstructed by several pillars. Revue-style shows are performed by an energetic, well-meaning cast of young people who also double as cruise staff during the day, together with professional cabaret acts. Another, smaller lounge, with a stage and dance floor, is used mainly as a nightclub.

SPA/FITNESS. A beauty salon is located on Main Deck, and there's a small fitness room and sauna. Hairdressing services are available, as are manicures, pedicures, and massage. Sports facilities include basketball.

Ocean Princess
★★★★

Size: . . . . .Mid-Size Ship	Passenger Decks: 9	Cabins (with private balcony): 232
Tonnage: .30,277	Total Crew: 373	Cabins (wheelchair accessible): 3
Lifestyle: . . . . .Standard	Passengers	Wheelchair accessibility: . . . . .Good
Cruise Line: . . . . .Princess Cruises	(lower beds/all berths): 688/826	Cabin Current: . . . . .110 and 220 volts
Former Names: .Tahitian Princess, R Four	Passenger Space Ratio	Elevators: 4
Builder: Chantiers de l'Atlantique (France)	(lower beds/all berths): 44.1/36.6	Casino (gaming tables): . . . . .Yes
Original Cost: . . . .$150 million	Crew/Passenger Ratio	Slot Machines: . . . . .Yes
Entered Service: . . . . .Nov 1999/Dec 2002	(lower beds/all berths): 1.8/2.2	Swimming Pools (outdoors): 1
Registry: . . . . .Gibraltar	Cabins (total): 344	Swimming Pools (indoors): 0
Length (ft/m): 593.7/181.0	Size Range (sq ft/m): 145.3–968.7/	Whirlpools: . . . . . .2 (+ 1 thalassotherapy)
Beam (ft/m): 83.5/25.5	13.5–90.0	Self-Service Launderette: . . . . .Yes
Draft (ft/m): 19.5/6.0	Cabins (outside view): 317	Dedicated Cinema/Seats: . . . . .No
Propulsion/Propellers: . . . . .diesel-electric	Cabins (interior/no view): 27	Library: . . . . .Yes
(18,600kW)/2	Cabins (for one person): 0	Onboard currency: . . . . .US$

An informal ship for mature-age cruisers.

OVERVIEW. This ship is best suited to young and not-so-young couples, and older singles who like to mingle in a mid-size ship setting with pleasing, sophisticated surroundings and lifestyle, reasonably good entertainment and fairly decent food and service, all at an affordable price.

THE SHIP. *Ocean Princess* (known as *Tahitian Princess* until 2009) and its sister ship *Pacific Princess* are an ideal size for smaller ports. The value for money is extremely good, and gives you with a chance to cruise in comfort aboard a mid-size ship with some interesting dining choices. There's very little entertainment, but it is not really needed in its main cruise areas such as Europe and Australasia. *Ocean Princess* is much more about relaxation than the larger ships in the Princess Cruises fleet, and would make a good child-free vessel.

The interior decor is stunning and elegant, a throwback to ship decor of the ocean liners of the 1920s and '30s. This includes detailed ceiling cornices, both real and faux wrought-iron staircase railings, leather- and cherry wood paneled walls, *trompe l'oeil* ceilings, rich carpeting in hallways with an Oriental rug-look center section, and many other interesting and expensive-looking decorative touches. The overall feel is of an old-world country club. The staircase in the main, two-deck-high foyer may remind you of the one in the 1998 movie *Titanic*.

The public rooms are spread over three decks. The reception hall has a staircase with intricate wrought-iron railings. The Nightclub, with forward-facing views, sits high in the ship and has Polynesian-inspired decor and furniture.

There are plenty of bars – including one in the entrance

BERLITZ'S RATINGS

	Possible	Achieved
Ship	500	406
Accommodation	200	155
Food	400	265
Service	400	287
Entertainment	100	72
Cruise	400	302

OVERALL SCORE
1,487 points out of 2,000

to each restaurant. Perhaps the nicest can be found in the casino bar/lounge, a beautiful room reminiscent of London's grand hotels and understated gaming clubs. It has an inviting marble fireplace, comfortable sofas and individual chairs. There is also a large card room, which incorporates an internet center, with eight stations.

The Library, a grand room designed in the Regency style by the Scottish interior designer John McNeece, has a fireplace, a high, indented, *trompe l'oeil* ceiling, and an excellent selection of books, plus some comfortable wingback chairs with footstools, and sofas you can easily fall asleep on – it's the most relaxing room aboard.

There is no walk-around promenade deck outdoors, though there's a small jogging track around the perimeter of the swimming pool, and port and starboard side decks. There are no wooden decks outdoors; instead, they are covered by Bollidt, a sand-colored rubberized material. There is no sauna. Stairways, although carpeted, are tinny. To keep prices low, the air routing to get to and from your ship is often not the most direct. There is a charge for using machines in the self-service launderette and you have to obtain tokens from the reception desk – a change machine in the launderette itself would be better.

Drinks prices are moderate, while beer prices are high. As with all Princess Cruises ships, 15% is added to bar and spa accounts and a standard gratuity (about $10 per person, per day) is added to your onboard account. To reduce the amount, you must visit the reception desk.

ACCOMMODATION. There are about eight different cabin types. All of the standard interior and outside-view cabins (the lowest four grades) are extremely extremely tight for two persons, particularly for cruises longer than seven days. Cabins have twin beds (or queen-size bed), with good under-bed storage areas, personal safe, vanity desk with large mir-ror, good closet and drawer space in rich, dark woods, and bathrobe. Color TVs carry a major news channel, where obtainable, plus a sports channel and several round-the-clock movie channels. The bathrooms, which have tiled floors and plain walls, are compact, standard units, and include a shower enclosure with a removable, strong hand-held shower unit, hairdryer, 100% cotton towels, toiletries storage shelves and a retractable clothesline.

The suites/cabins that have private balconies (66 percent of all suites/cabins, or 73 percent of all outside-view suites/cabins) have partial, and not full, balcony partitions, sliding glass doors, and, due to good design and layout, only 14 cabins on Deck 6 have lifeboat-obstructed views. The bal-cony floor is covered in thick plastic matting – teak would be nicer – and some awful plastic furniture.

Mini-Suites: The 52 accommodation units designated as mini-suites are in reality simply larger cabins than the stan-dard varieties, as the sleeping and lounge areas aren't divided. While not overly large, the bathrooms have a good-sized tub and ample space for storing toiletries. The living area has a refrigerated mini-bar, lounge area with break-fast table, and a balcony with two plastic chairs and a table.

Owner's Suites: The 10 Owner's Suites, the most spacious accommodation, are fine, large living spaces in the for-ward-most and aft-most sections of the accommodation decks – particularly nice are those that overlook the stern, on Deck 6, 7 and 8. They have more extensive balconies that can't be overlooked by anyone from the decks abqve. There is an entrance foyer, living room, bedroom, CD player, bathroom with Jacuzzi tub, as well as a small guest bathroom. The bed faces the sea, which can be seen through the floor-to-ceiling windows and sliding glass door.

Be aware that all suites/cabins located at the stern may suffer from vibration and noise, particularly when the ship is close to full speed, or maneuvering in port.

CUISINE. Flexibility and choice are what this mid-size ship's dining facilities are all about. There is a choice of four different dining spots, including a self-serve buffet:
● *The Club Restaurant* has 338 seats, all with armrests, and a large raised central section. There are large ocean-view windows on three sides, several prime tables over-looking the stern, and a small bandstand for occasional live dinner music. The noise level can be high, due to its single deck height ceiling. This restaurant is operated in two seatings, with dinner typically at 6pm and 8.15pm – the others have an open dining hours.
● *Sabatini's Trattoria* is an extra-charge, reservations-required Italian restaurant, with 96 seats (all with armrests), windows along two sides, and a set "Bellissima" three-hour dégustation menu.
● *Sterling Steakhouse* is an extra-charge, reservations-required "American steak house" with 98 seats (all with armrests), and windows along two sides. There's a set menu, together with added daily chef's specials. The cover charge is $8 per person. There are few tables for two.
● *The Lido Café* has seating for 154 indoors and 186 out-doors with white plastic patio furniture. It is open for break-fast, lunch and casual dinners. As the ship's 24-hour-a-day self-serve buffet restaurant, it incorporates a small pizzeria and grill. Basic salads, a meat carving station, and a rea-sonable selection of cheeses are served daily.

There is a *Poolside Grill and Bar* for fast food.

ENTERTAINMENT. The 345-seat Cabaret Lounge has a stage, and circular hardwood dance floor with banquette and individual tub chair seating, and raised sections on port and starboard sides. It is not large, and not really designed for production shows, so cabaret acts form the main focus, with mini-revue style shows presented by a troupe of resi-dent singer/dancers in a potted version of what you might experience aboard the large ships of Princess Cruises.

A band, small musical units, and solo entertaining pianists provide live music for shows and dancing in the various lounges and bars before and after dinner.

SPA/FITNESS. A gymnasium has ocean-view windows, high-tech muscle-toning equipment and treadmills, steam rooms (no sauna), changing areas for men and women, and a beauty salon with ocean views. The spa is operated by Steiner, a specialist concession. A lido deck has a swim-ming pool, and good sunbathing space, while an aft deck has a thalassaotherapy pool. A jogging track circles the pool deck, but one deck above. The uppermost outdoors deck includes a golf driving net and shuffleboard court.

● **For more extensive general information about the Princess Cruises experience, see pages 149–52.**

Ocean Star Pacific
★★ +

Size: . . . . Mid-Size Ship	Total Crew: 432	Cabins (wheelchair accessible): 0
Tonnage:. 23,149	Passengers	Wheelchair accessibility . . . . : None
Lifestyle:. . . . . Standard	(lower beds/all berths):. 1,050/1,158	Cabin Current: . . . . 110/220 volts
Cruise Line:. . . . . . . Ocean Star Cruises	Passenger Space Ratio	Elevators: 4
Former Names:. . . . Aquamarine, Arielle,	(lower beds/all berths):. 22.0/19.9	Casino (gaming tables): . . . . Yes
Aquamarine, Carousel, Nordic Prince	Crew/Passenger Ratio	Slot Machines: . . . . Yes
Builder: . . . . Wartsila (Finland)	(lower beds/all berths):. 2.4/2.6	Swimming Pools (outdoors): 1
Entered Service:. . . . . . Jul 1971/Apr 2011	Cabins (total): 520	Swimming Pools (indoors): 0
Registry: . . . . n/a	Size Range (sq ft/m): 119.4–482.2/	Whirlpools: 0
Length (ft/m): 637.4/194.3	11.1–44.8	Self-Service Launderette: . . . . No
Beam (ft/m): 78.8/24.03	Cabins (outside view): 334	Dedicated Cinema/Seats: . . . . No
Draft (ft/m): 21.9/6.70	Cabins (interior/no view):. 186	Library:. . . . . No
Propulsion/Propellers:. . diesel 3,400kW)/2	Cabins (for one person): 0	Onboard currency:. . . . . . . Mexican peso
Passenger Decks:. 7	Cabins (with private balcony): 0	

For casual domestic Mexican cruises in a tired ship.

OVERVIEW. This ship is best suited to young Mexican couples, singles, and young families on tight budgets. Good for a first cruise in reasonably comfortable but basic surroundings, with a decent number of facilities, including low-budget food and entertainment.

THE SHIP. *Ocean Star Pacific,* originally built for Royal Caribbean International, underwent a "shop and stretch" operation as *Nordic Prince* in 1980 that added a mid-section, including more public rooms and cabins. It began its present life as a Mexican ship in 2011 after a stint with Louis Cruises.

There is a polished walk-around promenade deck outdoors (slippery when wet) and nicely varnished wooden railings. The main open deck space for sunbathing is limited and noisy when the ship is full, although there are quieter spots forward and aft. The interior layout and passenger flow is sound, with rather tired, eclectic 1970s decor. The accommodation deck hallways are narrow and not well lit.

The major public rooms – showlounge, à la carte restaurant, buffet restaurant, card room/library, small casino, an internet center, and an Irish pub – are conveniently located on one main deck and therefore easy to find. Taxes are included in the fare, but gratuities to staff are not.

FAMILIES. There are many children aboard during peak holiday periods, but children's facilities are really minimal.

ACCOMMODATION. Most cabins are extremely small, and

BERLITZ'S RATINGS

	Possible	Achieved
Ship	500	225
Accommodation	200	100
Food	400	196
Service	400	234
Entertainment	100	52
Cruise	400	207

OVERALL SCORE
1,014 points out of 2,000

soundproofing between them is poor, but remember that this ship is over 40 years old. The cabins also have little closet and storage space, although all have a small TV (larger in suite-grade accommodation), radio, personal safe, hairdryer, and telephone.

Many cabins have pull-down upper berths – good, but tight, for families. The bathrooms are small. Only the two top grades have bathrooms with a tub; all other cabins have showers.

There are two L-shaped suites, both on Promenade Deck; these consist of a lounge/living area, separate bedroom and bathroom. Although there's no private balcony, they are very spacious.

CUISINE. A 610-seat à la carte restaurant is quite large, and has tables for four, six or eight. The food, provided by Apollo Ship Chandlers, is reasonable and there's plenty of it. Casual meals can be taken in the self-serve bistro buffet, located aft. Alternatively, fast food and grilled items are available at a poolside "tavern."

ENTERTAINMENT. The Broadway Showroom has a "thrust" stage and hardwood dance floor, but some seats have obstructed sightlines. The single-level room best suits cabaret acts. Shows are typically of the revue or variety style, with a cadre of youthful singers and dancers.

SPA/FITNESS. A beauty salon, fitness room, and sauna are in different locations. Treatment prices are reasonable.

Oceana
★★★★

Size: ....Large Resort Ship	Passenger Decks: 10	Cabins (with private balcony): 410
Tonnage: 77,499	Total Crew: 850	Cabins (wheelchair accessible): 19
Lifestyle: ....Standard	Passengers	Wheelchair accessibility: ....Good
Cruise Line: ....P&O Cruises	(lower beds/all berths): 1,950/2,272	Cabin Current: ....110 and 220 volts
Former Names: ....Ocean Princess	Passenger Space Ratio	Elevators: 11
Builder: ....Fincantieri (Italy)	(lower beds/all berths): 39.7/34.1	Casino (gaming tables): ....Yes
Original Cost: ....$300 million	Crew/Passenger Ratio	Slot Machines: ....Yes
Entered Service: .....Feb 2000/Nov 2002	(lower beds/all berths): 2.2/2.5	Swimming Pools (outdoors): 4
Registry: ....Bermuda	Cabins (total): 975	Swimming Pools (indoors): 0
Length (ft/m): 857.2/261.30	Size Range (sq ft/m): 158.2–610.3/	Whirlpools: 5
Beam (ft/m): 105.6/32.20	14.7–56.7	Self-Service Launderette: ....Yes
Draft (ft/m): 25.9/7.9	Cabins (outside view): 603	Dedicated Cinema/Seats: ....No
Propulsion/Propellers: .....diesel-electric	Cabins (interior/no view): 372	Library: ....Yes
(28,000 kW)/2	Cabins (for one person): 0	Onboard currency: ....UK£

Family-friendly cruising in a sedate environment.

OVERVIEW. This ship is all about Britishness and will be comfortably familiar for families with children who want to go abroad but take their British traditions and food with them. It is best suited to adults of all ages and families with children of all ages, and offers excellent value for money to first-time cruisers who enjoy reading tabloids.

THE SHIP. The all-white *Oceana* has a pleasing profile for a large ship, and is well balanced by its large funnel, which contains a deck tennis/basketball/volleyball court in its sheltered aft base. There is 93,000 sq. ft (8,600 sq. meters) of space and a wide, teakwood walk-around promenade deck outdoors. A great amount of glass area on the upper decks provides plenty of light and connection with the outside world. The ship underwent a few changes to make it more user-friendly for British passengers.

The ship, while large, absorbs passengers well, although its open lounge architecture means bleed-through music and little sense of intimacy. Its interiors are pretty and warm, with attractive colors and welcoming decor that includes some attractive wall murals and other artwork.

There is a wide range of public rooms, with several intimate rooms and spaces, so that you don't feel overwhelmed by large spaces. The interior focal point is a large four-deck-high atrium lobby with winding, double stairways and two panoramic glass-walled lifts.

There is plenty of space throughout the public areas, and the traffic flow is quite good. The library is a warm room with ocean-view windows and has six large buttery leather chairs for listening to audio discs.

The collection of artwork is decent, particularly on the

BERLITZ'S RATINGS		
	Possible	Achieved
Ship	500	416
Accommodation	200	159
Food	400	254
Service	400	286
Entertainment	100	81
Cruise	400	298

OVERALL SCORE
1,494 points out of 2,000

stairways, and this helps make the ship feel smaller than it really is. The Monte Carlo Club Casino, while large, is not in the main passenger flow and so does not generate the "walk-through" factor found aboard so many ships. The most traditional room is the Yacht and Compass Bar, decorated in the style of a turn-of-the-century gentleman's club, with wood paneling and comfortable seating.

Ballroom dance fans will be pleased to note that there are several good-sized wooden dance floors. The ship usually carries a professional dance couple as hosts and teachers, and there is plenty of dancing time included in the entertainment programming.

As is the case aboard most large ships, if you live in the best accommodation – a suite – you will be well attended. Otherwise you will merely be one of a large number of passengers aboard a ship that caters to families with children – lots of them in peak vacation periods. Most cabin stewards and dining room personnel are from India, and provide service with a well-balanced smile and warmth that many other nationals find difficult to equal.

One nice feature is the Captain's cocktail party, held in the four-deck-high main atrium so you can come and go as you please, with no standing in line to have your photograph taken with the captain if you don't want to.

There are a number of dead ends in the interior layout, so it's not as user-friendly as it should be. Standing in line for disembarkation, shore tenders and for self-serve buffet meals is an inevitable aspect of cruising aboard large ships.

The swimming pools are actually rather small and will be crowded when the ship is full; also the pool deck is cluttered with white, plastic deck lounge chairs, which don't have cushioned pads. The rule about not leaving sunloungers unattended for more than half an hour is flouted by most British passengers, who are keen to keep their favored position.

While the ship's interior space is a non-smoking environment, smoking is permitted on cabin balconies and in designated spots on the open decks.

In the quest for increased onboard revenue and shareholder value, even birthday cakes are an extra-cost item, as are espressos and cappuccinos (fake ones, made from instant coffee, are available in the dining rooms). Also at extra cost are ice cream, and bottled water – items that can add up to a considerable amount. Expect to be subjected to a stream of flyers advertising daily art auctions, "designer" watches and other promotions. For gratuities, which are optional, you should typically allow £3.50 (about $5.50) per person, per day.

A British brass band send-off often accompanies sailings from Southampton. Other touches include church bells that sound throughout the ship for the interdenominational Sunday church service. A coach service for passengers embarking or disembarking in Southampton covers much of the UK. Car parking is also available – there is one rate for undercover parking, and another rate for parking in an open compound.

FAMILIES. Children have their own Treasure Chest (for ages 2–5), The Hideout (6–9-year-olds), and for older children (aged 10–13) there is The Buzz Zone. P&O Cruises provides an abundance of staff to look after the children, as well as many activities to keep them out of adult areas. A night nursery is available from 6pm to 2am, with a per-child charge after midnight. While many children don't like organized clubs, they will probably find they make new friends quickly during a cruise.

ACCOMMODATION. There are 19 different cabin grades, designated as: suites with private balcony, mini-suites with private balcony, outside-view twin-bedded cabin with balcony, outside-view twin bedded cabin, and interior twin-bedded cabins. Although the standard outside-view and interior cabins are a little small, they are well designed and functional in layout, and have earth tone colors accentuated by splashes of color from the bedspreads. Proportionately, there are quite a lot of interior cabins.

The cabin numbering system is illogical, with numbers going through several hundred series on the same deck. The walls of the passenger accommodation decks are very plain – some artwork would be an improvement.

Many of the outside-view cabins have private balconies, and all seem to be quite well soundproofed, although the balcony partition is not of the floor to ceiling type, so you can hear your neighbors clearly, or smell their smoke. The balconies are very narrow – just large enough for two small chairs – and there is no dedicated outdoor balcony lighting. Many cabins have third- and fourth-person upper bunk beds – good for families with children. All cavins have tea and coffee-making facilities – a comforting addition.

There is a reasonable amount of closet and abundant

drawer and other storage space in all cabins; although this is adequate for a seven-night cruise, it could prove to be quite tight for longer. Also provided are a color television, and refrigerator, and each night a chocolate will appear on your pillow. The cabin bathrooms are practical, and come complete with all the details one needs – although, again, they really are tight spaces, best described as one person at a time units. Fortunately, they have a shower enclosure of a decent size, a small amount of shelving for your toiletries, real glasses, and a hairdryer.

High-quality toiletries are by Temple Spa; suite occupants get larger bottles and a wider selection.

Also standard in all cabins are Slumberland eight-inch sprung mattresses, 10.5 tog duvets (blankets and pillows if you prefer), Egyptian cotton towels, improved tea/coffee making facilities with speciality teas (long-life is provided) and a Nick Munro-designed bespoke tray.

Suites: The largest accommodation is in six suites, two on each of three decks at the aft of the ship, with a private balcony giving great views over the stern. Each of these suites – Oronsay, Orcades, Orion, Orissa, Orsova, Orontes, all P&O ships of yesteryear – has a large private balcony. They are well laid out, and have large, marble-clad bathrooms with two washbasins, a Jacuzzi tub, and a separate shower enclosure. The bedroom has generous amounts of wood accenting and detailing, indented ceilings, and TV sets in both bedroom and lounge areas, which also have a dining room table and four chairs.

Mini-Suites: Mini-suites typically have two lower beds that convert to a queen-size bed. There is a separate bedroom/sleeping area with vanity desk, and a lounge with sofa and coffee table, indented ceilings with generous amounts of wood accenting and detailing, walk-in closet, and a larger, marble-clad bathroom with Jacuzzi tub and a separate shower enclosure. There is a private balcony.

Standard Outside-view/Interior Cabins: A reasonable amount of closet and abundant drawer and other storage space is provided in all cabins – adequate for seven nights but a little tight for longer cruises. There's a TV set and refrigerator. Each night a chocolate will appear on your pillow. The cabin bathrooms are practical, and come with all the details one needs, although they really are tight spaces. But they do have a decent shower enclosure, a small amount of shelving for toiletries, real glasses, and a hairdryer.

You can receive BBC World channel on the in-cabin color television system (when available, depending on cruise area), as well as movies – the ship doesn't have a dedicated theater. The cabin service menu is rather limited, and presentation of the food items could be better.

CUISINE. There are two principal asymmetrically-designed dining rooms, *Adriatic* and *Ligurian*, each seating about 500, located adjacent to the two lower levels of the four-deck-high atrium lobby. The location of your accommodation determines which dining room you are assigned to. Each has its own galley and is split into multi-tier sections, which help create a feeling of intimacy, although there is a lot of noise from the waiter stations adjacent to many tables.

Breakfast and lunch are provided in an open-seating arrangement, while dinner is in two seatings.

The cuisine is decidedly British – a little adventurous at times, but always with plenty of curry dishes and other standard British items. Don't expect exquisite dining – this is British hotel catering that doesn't pretend to gourmet standards. What it does present is attractive and tasty, with some excellent gravies and sauces to accompany meals.

In keeping with the Britishness of P&O Cruises, the desserts are always good. A statement in the onboard cruise folder states that P&O Cruises does not knowingly purchase genetically modified foods, though it makes no mention of all those commercial American cereals.

The service is provided by a team of friendly stewards – most from India, with which P&O has had a long relationship. The wine list is quite reasonable.

The Plaza, a self-serve buffet, is located above the navigation bridge, with some commanding views. At night, this large room (there are two food lines – one each on both port and starboard sides) is transformed into an informal dinner setting with sit-down waiter service. For an extra £9.50 you can experience the "Tasting Menu" – a selection of small cosmopolitan dishes, with three different menus per cruise.

Outdoors on deck, with a sheltered view over the Riviera Pool, the *Horizon Grill* has fast-food items for those who don't want to change from their sunbathing attire.

For other informal eats, there is *Café Jardin*, with a Frankie's Bar & Grill-style menu serving Italian-inspired dishes such as antipasti, glazed belly pork Marco Polo and rib-eye steak alla rosmarino. Upgraded in a March 2008 refit, it is on the uppermost level of the four-deck-high atrium lobby.

Explorer's serves for cappuccino, espressos and pastries, and *Magnums* is a Champagne/caviar bar.

ENTERTAINMENT. There are two showlounges – Footlights Theatre, and Starlights – one at each end of the ship. The Footlights, located at the forward end, is a superb 550-seat, theater-style showlounge, for production shows and the-ater events; movies can also be shown here. Starlights is a 480-seat cabaret-style lounge with bar.

P&O Cruises places a big emphasis on a decent quality of entertainment. To this end, there's a resident group of actors, singers and dancers who provide theater-style presentations such as cut-down versions of well-known musicals. In addition, the ship features a whole array of cabaret acts. Although many of these aren't what you would call headliners, they do regularly travel the cruise ship circuit. Classical concerts are scheduled for many cruises.

The ship has several good-sized wooden dance floors for ballroom dancing. P&O Cruises carries a professional dance couple as hosts and teachers, and there's plenty of dancing time included in the entertainment programming.

SPA/FITNESS. The Ocean Spa has facilities that are contained in a glass-walled complex on one of the highest decks at the aft part of the ship. It includes a gymnasium, with all the associated high-tech muscle-pumping equipment, a combination aerobics/exercise class room, sauna, steam room, and several treatment rooms.

The spa is operated by Harding Brothers, a UK concession that provides the staff and range of beauty and wellness treatments. Examples of treatments include: Body Toning (detox for the body); Body Bien Etre (body scrub and massage); Seaweed Wrap; Collagen Velvet Facial Mask.

One swimming pool is "suspended" aft between two decks, forming part of the spa complex, and two other pools are located in the ship's center. They are not large for the size of the vessel. Sports facilities are located in an open-air sports deck positioned inside the ship's funnel structure and can be adapted to basketball, volleyball, badminton or paddle tennis. Joggers can exercise on the walk-around open Promenade Deck. There's an electronic golf simulator, so no need to bring your own clubs.

● **For more extensive general information about the P&O Cruises experience, see pages 148–9.**

Oosterdam
★★★★

Size: . . . . .Large Resort Ship	Passenger Decks: 11	Cabins (wheelchair accessible): 28
Tonnage: 81,769	Total Crew: 800	Wheelchair accessibility: . . . . .Good
Lifestyle: . . . . .Premium	Passengers	Cabin Current: . . . . .110 volts
Cruise Line: . . . . . . .Holland America Line	(lower beds/all berths): 1,918/2,387	Elevators: 14
Former Names: . . . . .none	Passenger Space Ratio	Casino (gaming tables): . . . . .Yes
Builder: . . . . .Fincantieri (Italy)	(lower beds/all berths): 43.6/34.2	Slot Machines: . . . . .Yes
Original Cost: . . . .$400 million	Crew/Passenger Ratio	Swimming Pools (outdoors): 2
Entered Service: . . . . .Aug 2003	(lower beds/all berths): 2.3/2.9	+1 children's pool
Registry: . . . . .The Netherlands	Cabins (total): 924	Swimming Pools (indoors): 1
Length (ft/m): 935.0/285.0	Size Range (sq ft/m): 185.0–1,318.6/	(indoor/outdoor)
Beam (ft/m): 105.6/32.25	17.1–122.5	Whirlpools: 5
Draft (ft/m): 25.5/7.80	Cabins (outside view): 788	Self-Service Launderette: . . . . .No
Propulsion/Propellers: . . . . .diesel-electric	Cabins (interior/no view): 136	Dedicated Cinema/Seats: Yes/170
(34,000 kW)/2 azimuthing pods	Cabins (for one person): 0	Library: . . . . .Yes
(17.6 MW each)	Cabins (with private balcony): 623	Onboard currency: . . . . .US$

A contemporary ship with Dutch decor, suitable for families.

OVERVIEW. This ship offers a range of public rooms with a reasonably intimate atmosphere and the overall feel is quite homely and comforting. Perhaps the ship's best asset is its friendly and personable Filipino and Indonesian crew, although communication in English can be frustrating. In keeping with the traditions of Holland America Line, there is a large collection of artwork.

THE SHIP. *Oosterdam* (sister ships: *Eurodam, Nieuw Amsterdam, Noordam, Westerdam* and *Zuiderdam*) is one of the new generation of "Vista"-class ships for Holland America Line, designed to appeal to younger, more vibrant, multi-generational, family-oriented holidaymakers.

The twin working funnels are the result of the slightly unusual machinery configuration; the ship has, in effect, two engine rooms – one with three diesels, and one with two diesels and a gas turbine. A pod propulsion system is provided *(see page 191)*, powered by a diesel-electric system, with a small gas turbine located in the funnel for the reduction of emissions.

There is a complete walk-around exterior teak promenade deck, with teak "steamer" style sunloungers. An outdoor jogging track is located around the mast and the forward third of the ship. Exterior glass elevators, mounted midships on both port and starboard sides, provide fine ocean views from any one of 10 decks. There are two centrally located swimming pools outdoors, and one can be used in inclement weather thanks to its retractable sliding glass roof. Two whirlpool tubs, adjacent to the swimming pools, are abridged by a bar. Another smaller pool is available for children; it incorporates

BERLITZ'S RATINGS	Possible	Achieved
Ship	500	428
Accommodation	200	162
Food	400	269
Service	400	277
Entertainment	100	76
Cruise	400	308

OVERALL SCORE
1,520 points out of 2,000

a winding water slide that spans two decks in height. There is an additional whirlpool tub outdoors.

The intimate lobby spans three decks, and is topped by a beautiful, rotating, Waterford crystal globe of the world. Adjacent are interior and glass wall elevators with exterior views. The interior decor, is bright, yet comfortable – designed to attract a younger clientele. The ceilings are particularly noticeable in the public rooms. Included are some superb paintings of former Holland America Line ships on the mid-ship stairwells by maritime artist Captain Stephen Card. Also notable are many pieces reflecting the former Dutch East Indies. The cast-aluminum elevator doors are interesting – the design being inspired by the deco designs from New York's Chrysler Building.

There are two decks of entertainment/public rooms. The most dramatic room is the showlounge, spanning four decks in the forward section. A winding shopping street has several boutiques, and there's an internet center, library, card room, an art gallery, photo gallery, and several small meetings rooms. The casino, equipped with all the gaming paraphernalia and slot machines you can think of, is large, and you have to walk through it to get from the restaurant to the showlounge. There is free coffee at the Java Bar, free ice cream at certain hours, and hot hors d'oeuvres in all bars.

The information desk in the lobby is small and somewhat removed from the main passenger flow on the two decks above it. Many pillars obstruct passenger flow and lines of sight throughout the ship. There are no self-service launderettes – something families with children might miss, although special laundry packages are available.

FAMILIES. Club HAL's KidZone provides a whole area dedicated to children's facilities and extensive programming for different age groups (5–17), with a ratio of one counselor for every 30 children. Some cabins have interconnecting doors – good for families with children.

ACCOMMODATION. There are 24 price categories: 16 outside-view and eight interior. Lifeboats obstruct the view from some cabins on the lowest accommodation deck (Main Deck). Some cabins that can accommodate a third and fourth person have very little closet space, and only one personal safe. Occupants of suites get exclusive use of the Neptune Lounge and concierge service, priority embarkation and disembarkation, and other benefits. In many of the suites/cabins with private balconies the balconies are not so private and can be overlooked from various public locations.

Penthouse Verandah Suites (2): These measure 1,318 sq. ft (122.5 sq. meters), including balcony. Each has a separate bedroom with a king-size bed; there's also a walk-in closet, dressing room, living room, dining room, butler's pantry, mini-bar and refrigerator, and private balcony. The main bathroom has a large whirlpool tub, two washbasins, toilet, and plenty of storage space for toiletries. Personalized stationery and free dry cleaning are included, as are hot hors d'oeuvres and other goodies daily.

DeLuxe Verandah Suites (60): These measure 563 sq. ft (52.3 sq. meters). These have twin beds that convert to a king-size bed, vanity desk, lounge area, walk-in closet, mini-bar and refrigerator, and bathroom with full-size tub, washbasin and toilet. Personalized stationery and complimentary dry cleaning are included, as are hot hors d'oeuvres and other goodies.

Verandah Suites (100): Actually, they are cabins, not suites, and measure 284 sq. ft (26.3 sq. meters). Twin beds can convert to a queen-size bed; there is also a lounge area, mini-bar and refrigerator, while the bathroom has a tub, washbasin and toilet. Floor to ceiling windows open onto a private balcony.

Outside-view Cabins: Standard outside cabins measure 197 sq. ft (18.3 sq. meters) and have twin beds that convert to a queen-size bed. There's a small sitting area, while the bathroom has a tub/shower combination. The interior cabins are slightly smaller (182.9 sq. ft/17 sq. meters).

Niggles include noisy air-conditioning – the flow in cabins and bathrooms can't be turned off and the only regulation is for temperature control.

CUISINE. The 1,045-seat *Vista Dining Room,* at the stern, is two decks high, with seating at tables for two, four, six or eight on both main and balcony levels. The galley is underneath the restaurant, accessed by port and starboard escalators. It provides a traditional Holland America Line dining, with friendly service from smiling Indonesian and Filipino stewards. Both open seating and fixed (assigned tables and times) seating are available, while breakfast and lunch are open-seating, when you'll be seated by restaurant staff on entry.

Holland America Line can provide Kosher meals, although these are prepared ashore, frozen, and brought to your table sealed in their original containers.

Alternative Dining Option: The 130-seat *Pinnacle Grill* is slightly more upscale, with higher quality ingredients, and better presentation than in the larger main dining room. It is on Lower Promenade Deck, and fronts onto the second level of the atrium lobby. Pacific Northwest cuisine is featured, with items such as sesame-crusted halibut with ginger-miso, Peking duck breast with blackberry sauce, and an array of premium quality steaks. There are fine table settings, china and silverware, and leather-bound menus. The wine bar offers mostly American wines. Reservations are needed and there's a cover charge.

Informal Eateries: For casual eating, there is an extensive *Lido Café,* an eatery that wraps around the funnel housing and extends aft; there are also some fine views over the ship's central multi-deck atrium. It includes a pizzeria/Italian specialties counter, a salad bar, Asian stir-fry counter, deli sandwiches, and a separate dessert buffet, although movement around the buffet area can be very slow.

There is an outdoor self-serve buffet, adjacent to the fantail pool, serving fast-food such as hamburgers and hot dogs, chicken and fries, as well as two smaller buffets adjacent to the midships swimming pool area, and an extra-cost *Windsurf Café* in the atrium lobby (open 20 hours a day), for coffee, pastries, snack foods, deli sandwiches and, in the evenings, liqueur coffees.

ENTERTAINMENT. The 867-seat Vista Lounge is the principal venue for Las Vegas-style revues and major cabaret shows. The main floor level has a bar in its starboard aft section. Spiral stairways at the back of the lounge connect all levels. Stage shows are best seen from the upper levels, from where the sightlines are quite good.

SPA/FITNESS. The Greenhouse Spa is a large, two-decks-high health spa, located directly above the navigation bridge. Facilities include a solarium, hydrotherapy pool, unisex thermal suite – a unisex area incorporating a Laconium (gentle sauna), Hammam (mild steam), and Camomile Grotto (small aromatic steam room). There is also a beauty parlor, 11 massage/therapy rooms including one for couples, and a large gymnasium with floor-to-ceiling windows on three sides and forward-facing ocean views, and the latest high-tech muscle-toning equipment.

Sports enthusiasts can enjoy a basketball court, volleyball court, and golf simulator.

● **For more extensive general information on what a Holland America Line cruise is like, see pages 140–3.**

Oriana
★★★★

Size: . . . . .Large Resort Ship	Passenger Decks: 10	Cabins (with private balcony): 118
Tonnage: .69,153	Total Crew: .760	Cabins (wheelchair accessible): 8
Lifestyle: . . . . .Standard	Passengers	Wheelchair accessibility: . . . . .Good
Cruise Line: . . . . .P&O Cruises	(lower beds/all berths): 1,818/2,179	Cabin Current: . . . . . . .110 and 220 volts
Former Names: . . . . .none	Passenger Space Ratio	Elevators: 10
Builder: . . . . .Meyer Werft (Germany)	(lower beds/all berths): 38.0/31.7	Casino (gaming tables): . . . . .Yes
Original Cost: . . . .£200 million	Crew/Passenger Ratio	Slot Machines: . . . . .Yes
Entered Service: . . . . .Apr 1995	(lower beds/all berths): 2.3/2.5	Swimming Pools (outdoors): 3
Registry: . . . . .Bermuda	Cabins (total): 909	Swimming Pools (indoors): 0
Length (ft/m): 853.0/260.0	Size Range (sq ft/m): 150.6–500.5/	Whirlpools: 5
Beam (ft/m): 105.6/32.2	14.0–46.5	Self-Service Launderette: . . . . .Yes
Draft (ft/m): 25.9/7.9	Cabins (outside view): 592	Dedicated Cinema/Seats: Yes/189
Propulsion/Propellers: . . . . .diesel	Cabins (interior/no view): 317	Library: . . . . .Yes
(47,750 kW)/2	Cabins (for one person): 0	Onboard currency: . . . . .UK£

British decor, style and food for adults-only cruising.

OVERVIEW. Anyone cruising aboard *Oriana*, an adults-only ship from November 2011, will get a well organized, "traditional" cruise experience. It's all about Britishness for those wanting to go abroad but take their values and food preferences with them, and sail from a UK port. It suits mature adults seeking to cruise aboard a large ship with the facilities of a small resort.

THE SHIP. Although more than 15 years old, this ship has a feeling of timeless elegance. There is a good amount of outdoor space, with enough sunloungers for all passengers, and there is an extra-wide, traditional walk-around outdoor promenade deck. The stern superstructure is nicely rounded, with several tiers that overlook a swimming pool and hot tubs. In October 2011, a refit transformed *Oriana* from a ship for family cruising to an adults-only ship – and, as such, much better suited to long cruises. Its score will be modified once the ship has settled down in its new role.

Inside, the design provides good horizontal passenger flow, and wide passageways, with decor that is gentle, welcoming and refined. Of note are the fine, detailed ceiling treatments. The interior focal point is a four-deck-high atrium with a soft waterfall. It is elegant but not glitzy, and is topped by a dome of Tiffany glass. The many public rooms provide plenty of choice, with lots of nooks and crannies in which to sit and read.

The L-shaped Anderson's Lounge – named after Arthur Anderson, founder of the Peninsular Steam Navigation Company in the 1830s – contains an attractive series of 19th-century marine paintings, and is decorated in the manner of a fine British gentleman's club.

BERLITZ'S RATINGS

	Possible	Achieved
Ship	500	415
Accommodation	200	157
Food	400	246
Service	400	308
Entertainment	100	82
Cruise	400	289

OVERALL SCORE
1,497 points out of 2,000

Atop the ship and forward is the Crow's Nest, a U-shaped room with one small wing that can be closed off for small groups. A long bar includes a model of the former P&O ship *Ranpura* in a glass case. Two small stages are set into the forward port and starboard sections, and there is a wooden dance floor. Smoking is permitted only on cabin balconies and in designated spots on the open decks.

The library is a fine room, with a good range of hardback books and a librarian, inlaid wood tables and bookcases crafted by Lord Linley's company, and some comfortable chairs. By the second day of almost any cruise, the library will have been almost stripped of books by word-hungry passengers. Adjacent is Thackeray's, a writing room named after the novelist William Makepeace Thackeray, a P&O passenger in 1844. Lord's Tavern, decorated with cricket memorabilia, is the most sporting place to pitch a beverage or two, or take part in a singalong. There's also a small casino with table games and slot machines, and, unusually for ships today, a small cinema/lecture room.

The carpeting throughout is of a high quality, much of it custom designed and made from 100% wool. Some fine pieces of sculpture add the feeling of a floating museum, and original artworks by all-British artists include several tapestries and sculptures.

There is a wide variety of mainly British entertainment. P&O Cruises has a successful program of theme cruises covering areas such as antiques, art appreciation, classical music, comedy, cricket, gardening, jazz, motoring, popular fiction, Scottish dance.

Most cabin stewards and dining room personnel are from India, and provide service with a warm smile. However, in the quest for increased onboard revenue, even birthday cakes cost extra, as do real espressos and cappuccinos – fake ones, made from instant coffee, are available in the dining rooms. Ice cream and bottled water also cost extra.

A British brass band send-off usually accompanies sailings from Southampton. Other touches include church bells sounded for the interdenominational Sunday service. For gratuities, which are optional, allow £3.20 (around US$4.80) per person, per day.

ACCOMMODATION. With the change to an adults-only ship, the former children's playrooms were converted into additional cabins. There are 14 price categories, priced according to size and location.

Standard interior cabins and outside-view cabins are well equipped, but compact. There is much use of rich, warm limed oak or cherry wood, which makes even the least expensive interior cabin inviting. All cabins have good closet and drawer space, a small refrigerator, full-length mirror, and blackout curtains (essential for North Cape cruises). All cabins have premium Slumberland mattresses, duvets and high-quality bedlinen. Some can accommodate a third or third/fourth person, so sharing with friends can make for an economical cruise. Satellite television typically includes BBC World. Cabin soundproofing could be better.

There are a number of cabins for passengers traveling alone. Singles who share a cabin should note that only one personal safe is provided in most twin-bedded cabins.

The modestly-sized standard cabin bathrooms have mirror-fronted cabinets, although the lighting is quite soft; all have a wall-mounted hairdryer. High-quality toiletries are by Temple Spa; suite occupants get larger bottles and more of a choice.

There are eight suites, each measuring 500 sq. ft (46 sq. meters), with butler service. Facilities include a separate bedroom with two lower beds convertible to a queen-size bed, walk-in dressing area, two double closets, and plenty of drawer space. The lounge area has a sofa, armchairs and table, writing desk, binoculars, umbrella, trouser press, iron and ironing board, two TV sets, video player, personal safe, hairdryer and refrigerator. The bathroom has a whirlpool bath, shower and toilet, and there is also a guest bathroom. All in all, the suites, and particularly the bathrooms, are disappointing when compared with similarly sized suites in other ships. The private balcony has two sunloungers, tables and chairs. Suite occupants get priority embarkation, and their own lounge in the Southampton cruise terminal.

Other balcony cabins (called outside deluxe) measure 210 sq. ft (19 sq. meters). There is plenty of closet and drawer space. The bathrooms are somewhat disappointing and dated, and have a very small, plain washbasin. One would expect marble or granite units in these grades.

CUISINE. *Peninsula* (located amidships), and *Oriental* (aft) are the two restaurants, each with two seatings and with one galley between them. Both are moderately handsome, with tables for two, four, six or eight. But in the aft dining room the noise level can be high at many tables, because of the room's position above the propellers. The meals are mostly of the "Middle-England" variety, and the presentation generally lacks creativity. Curries and other Indian-style dishes are heavily featured, particularly on luncheon menus. Afternoon tea is disappointing. The typical menu cycle is 14 days; anyone on a long voyage may find it quite repetitive.

The former *Oriana Rhodes* (a Gary Rhodes at Sea) restaurant has been changed into a Marco Pierre White venue, called the *Ocean Grill* (Marco Pierre White also has restaurants aboard *Adonia* and *Arcadia*). Reservations are required and there's a per-person cover charge. An adjacent *Tiffany's Bar* serves as a pre-dinner ante-room for drinks.

Sorrento's, added in the 2011 refit, serves Italian fare, and has ocean views from its upper-level location.

The Conservatory is for casual self-serve breakfast and luncheon buffets, and 24-hour self-serve beverage stands, although the selection of teas is poor. On some evenings, it becomes a reservation-only alternative restaurant.

ENTERTAINMENT. The Theatre Royal, a well-designed room, has a sloping floor, and good sightlines from most seats. The fare is mainly British, from production shows staged by a resident company to top British "names" and lesser artists. A second, smaller Pacific Lounge is a multi-function venue for cabaret acts, including late-night comedy, and can also be used as a lecture room. However, pillars obstruct the stage view from a number of seats.

Ballroom dance fans will be pleased to make use of the four good-sized wooden dance floors. The ship always carries a professional dance couple as hosts and teachers.

SPA/FITNESS. The Oasis Spa is reasonably large, and provides the latest alternative treatment therapies. A gymnasium has high-tech muscle toning equipment. The unisex sauna is a large facility; there is also a steam room and several treatment rooms, plus a relaxation area incorporating two hot tubs.

● **For more extensive general information on the P&O Cruise experience, see pages 148–9.**

Orient Queen
★★★

Size: ....Mid-Size Ship	Passenger Decks: 7	Cabins (with private balcony): 0
Tonnage: 16,916	Total Crew: 400	Cabins (wheelchair accessible): 2
Lifestyle: ....Standard	Passengers	Wheelchair accessibility: ....None
Cruise Line: ....Louis Cruises	(lower beds/all berths): 828/910	Cabin Current: ....110/220 volts
Former Names: ....Orient Queen, Bolero,	Passenger Space Ratio	Elevators: 4
Starward	(lower beds/all berths): 26.3/18.5	Casino (gaming tables): ....Yes
Builder: .........A.G. Weser (Germany)	Crew/Passenger Ratio	Slot Machines: ....Yes
Original Cost: ....n/a	(lower beds/all berths): 2.4/2.9	Swimming Pools (outdoors): 2
Entered Service: .....Dec 1968/Aug 2006	Cabins (total): 414	Swimming Pools (indoors): 0
Registry: ....Greece	Size Range (sq ft/m): 111.9–324.0/	Whirlpools: 0
Length (ft/m): 525.9/160.30	10.4–30.1	Self-Service Launderette: ....No
Beam (ft/m): 74.9/22.84	Cabins (outside view): 192	Dedicated Cinema/Seats: Yes/210
Draft (ft/m): 22.5/6.86	Cabins (interior/no view): 200	Library: ....Yes
Propulsion/Propellers: diesel (12,950kW)/2	Cabins (for one person): 0	Onboard currency: ....Euros

---

A traditional small, casual ship for frugal cruisers.

OVERVIEW. This ship suits adult couples and single travelers who want to visit the Greek Islands in some comfort. It provides a good basic cruise experience in rather crowded, but moderately comfortable surroundings, at a modest price. The dress code is casual.

THE SHIP. The open deck and sunbathing space is very limited and some of the decks are of plain, painted steel. On the aft decks, there's a clutter of wooden sunloungers and sun shade umbrellas. Just forward of the twin funnels is an enclosed sports facility. Aft of the mast is a large solarium-style shielded housing, with multi-level lounge/bar/disco that's adjacent to one of the ship's small swimming pools.

There is a decent choice of public rooms, including six bars, all with clean, contemporary furnishings, upbeat fabric colors, and a mix of traditional and contemporary decor. The Greek staff is friendly and welcoming.

The noisy diesel engines tend to "throb" in some parts of the vessel, particularly when the ship is going full speed, including in many cabins on the lower decks.

ACCOMMODATION. There are four Royal Suites, and 54 "suites." The other cabins are very compact units that are moderately comfortable, and decorated in soft colors. But they are adequate for a short cruise, particularly as the ship is in port each day. While closet space is very limited, there are plenty of drawers, although they are metal and tinny.

The bathrooms are small and tight, and the towels are not large. Toilets are of the "gentle flush" (non-vacuum)

BERLITZ'S RATINGS

	Possible	Achieved
Ship	500	279
Accommodation	200	94
Food	400	221
Service	400	245
Entertainment	100	56
Cruise	400	208

OVERALL SCORE
1,103 points out of 2,000

variety. Soundproofing between cabins is poor, and the air-conditioning is quite noisy.

The four Royal suites have decent space for the size of the ship. There is ample floor space, a king-size bed, vanity desk, curtained-off closet, plenty of drawer and storage space for luggage, a lounge with a sofa that converts into an additional bed, drinks table and two chairs. A large pillar obstructs the room's flow. The bathroom has a small but deep Jacuzzi tub with integral handheld shower. All accommodation has flat-screen TV sets, refrigerator and telephone.

CUISINE. There are four eateries. The 444-seat *Mermaid Restaurant* is cheerful, even almost charming, and has some prime tables that overlook the stern. Seating is at tables for four, six or eight, with two seatings. The cuisine is Mediterranean, with some Greek specialties, while the wine list consists mainly of young wines.

Breakfast and lunch buffets are provided indoors at the casual self-serve *Horizon Café*, with outdoor seating at tables around the aft swimming pool, but space is tight.

ENTERTAINMENT. The 420-seat El Cabaret showlounge, a single-level room, provides "low budget, low quality" entertainment. There's also a nightclub/discotheque. A casino operates during cruises from Beirut.

SPA/FITNESS. There is a beauty salon, and a massage/body treatment room – on two different decks.

Orion
★★★★ +

Size: . . . . .Boutique Ship	Total Crew: 75	Cabins (wheelchair accessible): 0
Tonnage: 4,050	Passengers	Wheelchair accessibility: . . . . .None
Lifestyle: . . . . .Premium	(lower beds/all berths): 106/125	Elevators: 1
Cruise Line: . . . . .Orion Expedition Cruises	Passenger Space Ratio	Casino (gaming tables): . . . . .No
Former Names: . . . . .none	(lower beds/all berths): 38.2/32.4	Slot Machines: .No
Builder: . . . . . . .Cassens-Werft (Germany)	Crew/Passenger Ratio	Swimming Pools (outdoors): 0
Original Cost: .n/a	(lower beds/all berths): 1.4/1.6	Swimming Pools (indoors): 0
Entered Service: . . . . .Nov 2003/Mar 2006	Cabins (total): .53	Whirlpools: 1
Registry: . . . . .The Bahamas	Size Range (sq ft/m):	Self-Service Launderette: . . . . .No
Length (ft/m): 337.0/102.7	175.0–345.0/16.3–32.1	Lecture/Film Room/Seats: Yes/98
Beam (ft/m): 46.0/14.00	Cabins (outside view): 53	Library: . . . . .Yes (open 24 hours)
Draft (ft/m): 12.6/3.8	Cabins (interior/no view): 0	Onboard currency: . . . . .Australian $
Propulsion/Propellers: diesel/1	Cabins (for one person): 0	
Passenger Decks: 5	Cabins (with private balcony): 9	

For Australia-based "soft" expedition and adventure cruising.

OVERVIEW. This small ship is liked by mature couples and single travelers who enjoy learning about nature and wildlife up close and quietly exploring the world around them. It offers life enrichment in high-class surroundings and the company of well-traveled people. Cruising is really the wrong word for this type of eco-travel; it's more like having a magic carpet whisk to you to destinations most people have never heard of – particularly on the spectacular Papua New Guinea itineraries.

THE SHIP. *Orion* is the latest attempt in the quest to build the ideal expedition cruise ship. It has all the comforts of home, and then some – as well as specialist equipment for expedition cruising. Although small, it has stabilizers, bow and stern thrusters for maximum maneuverability, and a fleet of 10 heavy-duty Zodiac inflatable landing craft and a fishing boat, *BeeKay*. There is also an aft marina platform for swimming off.

Orion Expedition Cruises, owned by KSL Capital Partners in Denver, Colorado, has a long-term charter of this fine boutique vessel. There is no swimming pool, nor is one needed, but there is a hot tub set amid an open deck, which also houses a bar, and a small rock garden/water feature. All outdoor tables, chairs, and steamer-style sun-loungers are made of hardwood.

The interior decor is really warm and inviting, providing a cozy, cosseting atmosphere far removed from the majority of today's larger expedition-style cruise ships. Public rooms include an observation lounge (Galaxy Lounge), which opens onto a walk-around open promenade deck; it also connects with the small Vega Health Spa.

BERLITZ'S RATINGS

	Possible	Achieved
Ship	500	422
Accommodation	200	163
Food	400	309
Service	400	300
Entertainment	n/a	n/a
Cruise	400	418

OVERALL SCORE
1,612 points out of 2,000

Other public rooms include Leda Lounge (main lounge), a boutique, and a dedicated Cosmos Lecture Hall with surround sound system for lectures and movies. Typically, five expedition, culture, history and marine biology lecturers are carried on each expedition.

The reception desk is open 24 hours a day, and there's an internet-connect computer (A$50 for two hours) in the library, which has green leather seating). Some rooms are clustered around a glass-walled atrium and the single elevator. A special "mud room," complete with boot washing stations, is adjacent to a Zodiac/tender loading platform on the port side. The artwork focuses on exploration and myths associated with exploration. According to one myth, Neptune was Orion's father, for example, while Queen Eurayle of the Amazon was his mother.

This is about as far away from big cruise ships as you can get, with well-planned itineraries to some of the southern hemisphere's most remote regions, including the islands of Papua New Guinea, Australia's Kimberly region, "Wild" Tasmania, and Antarctica's McMurdo Sound and Ross Sea regions. If you want magic moments in soft adventure travel, wrapped in the comfort of fine surroundings and good food, it would be hard to beat *Orion*. But make sure you can walk well – some expeditions are quite demanding.

Note that when the ship operates in Australian waters (on Kimberly itineraries, for example), an Australian sales tax is added to all wine and beverage accounts. Drinks really should be included with this kind of product. Bottled water is provided for all passengers at no charge.

ACCOMMODATION. There are four grades of suites, and

two grades of cabins, and the facilities in all of them are top-rate. All have twin beds that convert to a queen-size bed, a TV set, a DVD/CD player, a mini-refrigerator, ample closet space, and a small personal safe.

The marble-clad bathroom has a small toiletries cabinet, single washbasin, and a large shower enclosure, with a retractable clothes line. Toiletries are by Escada. All the cabinetry was custom-made, and the bathrooms were fitted individually, which is rare in today's modular-fit world.

There are 13 suites, nine of which have a small "French" balcony (meaning you can just about step out onto it), four owner's suites, six balcony suites, two Deluxe suites, and one rather odd-shaped but delightful Junior suite. These have more space, and some share a narrow communal balcony (meaning there is no partition between them), sofa, glass drinks table, and good-sized vanity desk. Only the four owners' suites have a bathtub; all other suites/cabins have large shower enclosures.

All cabins display black and white photographs of yachts, by Beken of Cowes.

CUISINE. The *Constellation Restaurant* has ocean-view picture windows, artwork based on the astrological signs, and operates one open seating. Its low ceiling, however, makes it rather noisy. The cuisine is extremely good and varied, and, in addition to an à la carte menu, each dinner includes a four-course signature menu by one of Australia's new breed of high-profile chefs, Serge Dansereau of The Bathers' Pavilion in Sydney.

The portions are not large but they are colourful and creative. Expect to find Tasmanian oysters, crocodile, emu, and kangaroo among the offerings. Place settings include Bauscher china and Hepp silverware.

The ship carries a decent range of mostly Australian wines, including delightful reds such as Wolf Blass Black Label, and Yalumba's The Octavius Old Vine Shiraz; and whites such as Leeuwin Estate's Art Series Chardonnay, and Devil's Lair 5th Leg Chardonnay-Sauvignon. There are less-pricey alternatives whites such as the Bunnamagoo Estate Chardonnay, and the Chain of Ponds Unwooded Chardonnay; and reds such as the Penfolds Bin 389, and the perfectly acceptable Bunnamagoo Merlot. If you want champagne, several French champagnes are available, such as the top of the range Krug Grande Cuvée, or the tasty Veuve Cliquot. There is no sommelier on board, but the wines are well served by the waiters or maître d' hotel.

Delphinus Outdoor Café, an open deck aft of the Leda Lounge, serves as an al fresco dining spot for casual breakfasts, lunches, and occasional barbecue dinners.

Continental breakfast and afternoon tea are also served in the *Galaxy Lounge*, and espresso/cappuccinos are available at no extra charge in two lounges/bars and restaurant, and do try the delicious brownies on the bar counter.

The service staff is Filipino; they are warm, and communicate well with passengers.

ENTERTAINMENT. There is no formal entertainment, although the ship typically carries an entertaining duo. Each evening, lecturers provide daily recaps and fascinating, in-depth talks on marine or plant biology.

SPA/FITNESS. The Vega Health Spa consists of a fitness center, sauna, shower enclosure, and a private treatment room (for massages). A beauty salon is located two decks below. Four 90-minute top-to-toe massage experiences are called Top End, Island and Reef, Tasmania, and Antarctica, and include an aromatherapy massages. The ship carries a range of personal beauty products used on board and also for sale; creams, oils and other ingredients are mixed by the therapist and tailored to your own needs.

QUOTABLE QUOTES

Overheard in Alaska:
"Are the glaciers always here?"

Overheard in the cigar smoking room: "I'm looking for a no-smoking seat"

Overheard in the dining room in the Caribbean:
"Is all the salmon smoked? I am a non-smoker"

"Waiter, this vichyssoise is cold."
"Was the fish caught this morning by the crew?"

Overheard on an Antarctic cruise:
"Where is the good shopping in Antarctica?"

Overheard on a cruise taking in the British Isles:
"Windsor Castle is terrific. But why did they build it so close to the airport?"

Overheard on an Athens tour:
"Why did the Greeks build so many ruins?"

Overheard in the dining room:
Passenger: "Waiter: What is caviar?"
Waiter: "Fish eggs, sir."
Passenger: "In that case, I'll have two, over-easy!"

Overheard on a QE2 round-the-world cruise, in Kagoshima, with Mount Suribaya in the background:
"Can you tell me what time the volcano will erupt? I want to be sure to take a photograph."

Orion II
★★★★

Size: . . . . .Boutique Ship	Passenger Decks: 5	Cabin Current: . . . . .110 volts
Tonnage: .4,077	Total Crew: 60	Elevators: 1
Lifestyle: . . . . .Premium	Passengers	Casino (gaming tables): . . . . .No
Cruise Line: . . . .Orion Expedition Cruises	(lower beds/all berths): 100/100	Slot Machines: . . . . .No
Former Names: *Clelia II, Renaissance Four*	Passenger Space Ratio	Swimming Pools (outdoors): 0
Builder: . . . .Cantieri Navale Ferrari (Italy)	(lower beds/all berths): 40.7/40.7	Swimming Pools (indoors): 0
Original Cost: . . . .$20 million	Cabins: 50	Whirlpools: 1
Entered Service: . . . .Jan 1991/May 2011	Size Range (sq ft/m): .215.0–258.3/20–24	Self-Service Launderette: . . . . .No
Registry: . . . . .Malta	Cabins (outside view): 50	Dedicated Cinema/Seats: . . . . .No
Length (ft/m): 289.0/88.1	Cabins (interior/no view): 0	Library: . . . . .Yes
Beam (ft/m): 50.1/15.3	Cabins (for one person): 0	Onboard currency: . . . . .Australian $
Draft (ft/m): 13.4/4.1	Cabins (with private balcony): . . . . :16	
Propulsion/Propellors: . . . . .diesel	Cabins (wheelchair accessible): 0	
(3,514kW)/2 (CP)	Wheelchair accessibility: . . . . .None	

A ship for "soft" expedition and adventure cruising.

OVERVIEW. This charming, even elegant, little ship suits mature adults who want a small ship environment that offers comfort and style, combined with excellent lecturers, decent cuisine, and exploration-style itineraries. With the look and feel of a private yacht, it has handsome interior styling, although the exterior profile isn't overly attractive.

THE SHIP. *Orion II* provides an expedition-style vacation, but also a relaxing cruise for those who don't like large ships and crowds. There are two teakwood walk-around promenade decks outdoors. A water jet-propelled shore tender hangs over the stern, and the ship carries a fleet of Zodiac inflatable craft for shore landings. The open deck and sunbathing space is limited, however.

All accommodation is located forward, with public rooms aft. The interior colors are pleasing, refined, and stylish.

The few public rooms include a small library, a lounge, and a comfortable lecture room that can accommodate all passengers (good for lectures and expedition recaps), and a piano bar/lounge. There is no lounge with a forward view, and thus the ship is not good for cruising in expedition regions such as Antarctica. Smoking is allowed only on open decks. Extensive pre-cruise documentation is provided.

ACCOMMODATION. The all-outside cabins, called "suites" in the brochure, combine highly polished imitation rosewood paneling with lots of mirrors, and fine, hand-crafted Italian furniture. All suites have twin beds that can convert to a queen-size bed, a sitting area with three-person sofa, one chair, coffee table, minibar-refrigerator, a color TV/DVD

BERLITZ'S RATINGS		
	Possible	Achieved
Ship	500	378
Accommodation	200	154
Food	400	245
Service	400	278
Entertainment	n/a	n/a
Cruise	500	349

OVERALL SCORE
1,404 points out of 2,000

player, and direct-dial satellite phone. Closet space is good, but space for stowing luggage is tight, and there is little drawer space. There are no music channels in the cabins, and there is no switch to turn off announcements.

Marble-clad bathrooms are compact units that have reasonably sized showers (no bathrooms have a tub). There's a real teakwood floor, marble vanity, large mirror, recessed towel rail (good for storing toiletries), large oval washbasin, and built-in hairdryer. There is a high "lip" into the bathroom.

There are also 16 balcony suites with real teak wood balconies and polished railings, although the balcony is steel rather than glass. The suites provide a little more space that includes an office/large vanity desk.

CUISINE. *The Restaurant*, with single, open-seating dining, is bright (overly bright at night), and welcoming. It is on the lowest deck and has portholes rather than windows. There are tables for two, four, six, or eight. Dinners are normally sit-down affairs, although there could be an occasional self-serve buffet. Breakfast and lunch are usually buffets and can also be taken at an outdoor bar/café (weather permitting). Continental dishes are complemented by local regional delicacies. The food quality, choice and presentation are all good.

ENTERTAINMENT. Lecturers and recaps provide the main after-dinner entertainment. Early nights are the norm.

SPA/FITNESS. There is a small aft-facing fitness room, and a beauty salon.

Pacific Dawn
★★★

Size: . . . . .Large Resort Ship	Total Crew: 710	Cabins (wheelchair accessible): 13
Tonnage: .70,285	Passengers	Wheelchair accessibility: . . . . .Fair
Lifestyle: . . . . .Standard	(lower beds/all berths): 1,596/2,020	Cabin Current: . . . . .110 and 220 volts
Cruise Line: . . . . . .P&O Cruises (Australia)	Passenger Space Ratio	Elevators: 12
Former Names: . . . .*Regal Princess*	(lower beds/all berths): 44.0/34.7	Casino (gaming tables): . . . . .Yes
Builder: . . . . .Fincantieri Navali (Italy)	Crew/Passenger Ratio	Slot Machines: . . . . .Yes
Original Cost: . . . .$276.8 million	(lower beds/all berths): 2.2/2.8	Swimming Pools (outdoors): 2
Entered Service: . . . . .Aug 1991/Nov 2007	Cabins (total): 798	Swimming Pools (indoors): 0
Registry: . . . . .Great Britain	Size Range (sq ft/m): 189.4–586.6/	Whirlpools: 4
Length (ft/m): 811.0/247.2	17.6–54.5	Self-Service Launderette: . . . . .Yes
Beam (ft/m): 105.6/32.2	Cabins (outside view): 620	Dedicated Cinema/Seats: . . . . .No
Draft (ft/m): 25.5/7.8	Cabins (interior/no view): 178	Library: . . . . .Yes
Propulsion/Propellers: diesel (24,000kW)/2	Cabins (for one person): 0	Onboard Currency: . . . . .Australian $
Passenger Decks: 11	Cabins (with private balcony): 148	

This dated large ship provides family-friendly cruising.

OVERVIEW. This ship provides a very pleasant cruise in elegant and comfortable surroundings, and a friendly staff will make you feel welcome. The sunbathing space is really limited when the ship is full, but as many passengers are over 50 years old, perhaps this is not quite so crucial.

THE SHIP. *Pacific Dawn*'s open deck space is extremely limited for the number of passengers carried. There is no walk-around promenade deck outdoors – the only walking space being along the sides of the ship. Inside, the understated decor of soft pastel shades is highlighted by some colorful artwork. A striking, elegant three-deck-high atrium has a grand staircase with fountain sculpture; stand-up cocktail parties are held here. The Dome, an observation dome set high atop the ship, houses a multi-purpose lounge/comedy club with live music.

Regular passenger gripes include the automated telephone system and luggage delivery. Lines often form, particularly at the reception office, and for open-seating breakfast and lunch in the dining room. But some good news: P&O Australia scrapped automatic tipping in 2010.

FAMILIES. Children have their own play areas: Pacific Cove (ages 3–6); Shark Shack (ages 7–10); Children's Center (ages 11–17), and there's a dedicated team of youth counselors to keep them occupied.

ACCOMMODATION. There are many different price grades, ranked by location and size. In general, the cabins are well designed, with large bathrooms and good soundproofing. All cabins have walk-in closets, refrigerator, personal safe,

BERLITZ'S RATINGS

	Possible	Achieved
Ship	500	295
Accommodation	200	132
Food	400	213
Service	400	244
Entertainment	100	60
Cruise	400	237

OVERALL SCORE
1,181 points out of 2,000

TV set and an interactive video system. Twin beds convert to queen-size beds in standard cabins. Lifeboats obstruct the view from the outside-view cabins for disabled passengers.

The 14 most expensive suites, each with a large private balcony, are very well equipped, and storage space is generous, adequate even for long cruises.

CUISINE. The *Palm Court Dining Room* has two seatings. Portions are generous, but the bland food and its presentation are somewhat disappointing.But do remember that this is big-ship banquet catering. Meats are of a decent quality, but often disguised by gravy-based sauces. The quality of fish is poor, the selection of fresh green vegetables is limited. Pasta dishes are large.

Ice cream ordered in the dining room is included in the cruise price; anywhere else, it costs extra.

There is a good pizzeria for informal meals. Themed late-night buffets are provided, but afternoon teas are poor. There's an extra-cost patisserie in the spacious lobby.

ENTERTAINMENT. The International Showlounge spans two decks. There's plenty of live music for the various bars and lounges, with a wide mix of light classical, jazz, and dance music, from solo entertaining pianists to large show bands, and volume is normally kept to an acceptable level.

Three times during each cruise, a stunning laser light and sound show is presented in the atrium.

SPA/FITNESS. The Steiner-operated spa/fitness center has a gymnasium, aerobics exercise room, steam room, sauna and changing areas. Images is the beauty salon.

Pacific Jewel
★★★ +

Size: . . . . .Large Resort Ship	Passenger Decks: 11	Cabins (wheelchair accessible): 10
Tonnage: 70,310	Total Crew: 621	Wheelchair accessibility: . . . . .Fair
Lifestyle: . . . . .Standard	Passengers	Cabin Current: . . . . .110 and 220 volts
Cruise Line: . . . . . .P&O Cruises (Australia)	(lower beds/all berths): 1,708/2,014	Elevators: 9
Former Names: . . . . . .*Ocean Village Two,*	Passenger Space Ratio	Casino (gaming tables): . . . . .Yes
AIDAblu, A'RosaBlu, Crown Princess	(lower beds/all berths): 41.1/34.9	Slot Machines: . . . . .Yes
Builder: . . . . .Fincantieri Navali (Italy)	Crew/Passenger Ratio	Swimming Pools (outdoors): 2
Original Cost: . . . .$276.8 million	(lower beds/all berths): 2.5/2.9	Swimming Pools (indoors): 0
Entered Service: . . . . . Jul 1990/Dec 2009	Cabins (total): 832	Whirlpools: 4
Registry: . . . . .Great Britain	Size Range (sq ft/m): 188.3–538.2/	Self-Service Launderette: . . . . .Yes
Length (ft/m): 805.7/245.6	17.5–50.0	Dedicated Cinema/Seats: . . . . .No
Beam (ft/m): 105.8/32.25	Cabins (outside view): 628	Library: . . . . .No
Draft (ft/m): 26.9/8.21	Cabins (interior/no view): 197	Onboard Currency: . . . . .Aus$
Propulsion/Propellers: . . . . .diesel-electric	Cabins (for one person): 0	
(24,000kW)/2	Cabins (with private balcony): 198	

This large ship provides family-friendly Aussie cruising.

OVERVIEW. This ship is best suited to young Australian couples, single travelers, families, and single parent families with children seeking a good value for money first cruise in a large, casual ship setting, with appealing itineraries and destinations, and a range of fun-filled activities. The young, vibrant staff make passengers feel welcome.

THE SHIP. Originally ordered by Sitmar Cruises, this ship debuted in 1990 as *Crown Princess* but has since assumed many identities. It was moved to the A'Rosa brand and, as *A'Rosa Blu*, began operating cruises for the German-speaking family market in 2002. Two years later, it was refitted and renamed *AIDAblu* for AIDA Cruises, then became *Ocean Village Two* for the UK's Ocean Village brand. In 2009 it turned into *Pacific Jewel*, specifically for the Australian market.

It has a dolphin-like upper front structure made of lightweight aluminum alloy, originally designed to keep the weight down in line with stability requirements. It was designed by Renzo Piano, the renowned Italian architect behind Paris's revolutionary Centre Georges Pompidou and Japan's Kansai International Airport, Osaka. A large swept-back funnel, also made from aluminum alloy, is placed aft.

Facilities are in line with the tastes of young, active Aussie families, single parents with children, and single travelers. The interior layout is a bit disjointed, however. Some innovative and elegant styling is mixed with traditional features and a reasonably spacious interior layout. An understated decor of soft pastel shades is highlighted by splashes of colour, as well as some colorful artwork.

BERLITZ'S RATINGS		
	Possible	Achieved
Ship	500	350
Accommodation	200	140
Food	400	263
Service	400	273
Entertainment	100	72
Cruise	400	267

OVERALL SCORE
1,365 points out of 2,000

The oval-shaped atrium lobby is three decks high and has a grand staircase as its focal point; it provides a good meeting and gathering point. Shops, bars and lounges span out from the lobby on three decks. Other facilities include a cyber-zone for internet connection, and several bars. Child-free areas include the extra-cost Oasis, a sunbathing quiet zone aft on Deck 10, and the Aqua Spa and Health Center.

There is no decent outdoor or indoor forward observation viewpoint, and no walk-around promenade deck outdoors, the only walking space being along the port and starboard sides of the ship. In fact, there's little contact with the outdoors, and sunbathing space is quite limited. Other niggles include the many support pillars throughout the public rooms which obstruct sightlines and impede passenger flow, and there's no library – so bring along your own reading material.

P&O Cruises (Australia) scrapped automatic tipping from Oct 2010, so tips are at your discretion.

FAMILIES. There is a good range of facilities for children, including a paddling pool for babies, a base camp and night nursery for supervised sleepovers, a chill-out room for teens (The Attic), and a noisy video games room.

ACCOMMODATION. There are 15 price categories, including suites with private balconies, outside view cabins and interior cabins, and special cabins for the disabled. Generally, accommodation on the higher decks will cost more because, aboard ship, location is everything. Occupants of accommodation designated as suites (there are 14 of them) and junior suites (there are 36) also have access to an extra-cost private lounge in which to escape from the constant music and noise everywhere else.

Pacific Jewel has also recognized that single-parent families comprise an increasing number of today's cruise passengers, and a good number of two-bed cabins also have a third (or third/fourth) pull-down berth.

In general, the cabins are well designed and have large bathrooms as well as decent soundproofing. Walk-in closets, refrigerator, kettle, personal safe, color TV and interactive video system are provided in all of them. Twin beds convert to queen-size beds in most cabins. Bathrobes and toiletries are provided. Views from the outside-view cabins for the disabled are obstructed by lifeboats, as are some other cabins on the same deck (Deck 8).

Suites: The most expensive suites have a private balcony, and are quite well laid out to a practical design. The bedroom is separated from the living room by a heavy wooden door; there are TV sets in both rooms, and closet and drawer space are generous.

CUISINE. There are two principal restaurants, several decks apart: *Plantation* and *The Waterfront*. There are a few tables for two, but most are for four, six or eight. Plantation is open 24 hours a day, while The Waterfront is open for à la carte breakfasts, lunches and dinner at times given in the daily program. There's a neat table for six persons in the Wine Room, which is part of the Waterfront Restaurant.

Alternative Dining Options: For a treat or special celebration, extra-charge full service dining is available in the intimate bistro-style restaurant, *Salt Grill* by Luke Mangan, located forward of the main pools, on the starboard side, accessed by the forward stairway. The cover charge is worth it because the meals have more taste and neat flavor combinations, but the TV screens showing meals being prepared in the kitchen are intrusive and not at all appetizing.

La Luna, a small, casual deck restaurant adjacent to the aft pool and funnel, serves Asian-style cuisine.

For coffee, tea and sweet snacks during the day, and drinks in the evening, *Charlie's Bar* is an extra-cost patisserie/bar on the lower level of the spacious lobby.

ENTERTAINMENT. The Marquee Theatre, the venue for main entertainment events, spans two decks, with seating on both main and balcony levels. Several support pillars obstruct sightlines from a number of seats. There's plenty of colorful entertainment, including a song and dance troupe, and cabaret acts. A high-energy acrobatic-and-dance deck show is provided for warm nights under the stars, on a stage and acrobatic archway fitted during one of the ship's refits.

Connexions is an adults-only comedy venue that doubles as a karaoke and live music venue.

SPA/FITNESS. The Aqua Spa and Health Club, an extensive wellness center, spans two decks and measures almost 14,000 sq. ft (1,300 sq. meters); a staircase connects two levels. Located at the top of the ship at the forward stairway, it occupies the space in the "dolphin head" section. With its curved surfaces, walking the treadmills or exercycling and facing out to sea (albeit on the port side) makes you feel you're doing so in the upper deck of a Boeing 747.

Panoramic saunas and Hammam steam room are on the lower level; a seven-day pass for the sauna and steam rooms costs extra. The reception area has a waterfall and cypress trees, and there are 11 treatment rooms for facials, massages (including hot stones and couples massage), manicure and pedicure, dry float and hydrobath. There is also a solarium, and a four-person relaxation room. One other neat feature is a small food bar with a choice of healthy spa dishes. It's a very nice spa facility.

The spa is operated by a specialist concession. Some exercise classes and health talks are free; others may incur a charge.

Pacific Pearl
★★★ +

Size:	Large Resort Ship	Passenger Decks:	12	Cabins (wheelchair accessible):	8
Tonnage:	63,524	Total Crew:	514	Wheelchair accessibility:	Good
Lifestyle:	Standard	Passengers		Cabin Current:	220 volts
Cruise Line:	P&O Cruises (Australia)	(lower beds/all berths):	1,624/1,692	Elevators:	9
Former Names:	Ocean Village, Arcadia,	Passenger Space Ratio		Casino (gaming tables):	Yes
	Star Princess, FairMajesty	(lower beds/all berths):	39.1/37.5	Slot Machines:	Yes
Builder:	Chantiers de L'Atlantique (France)	Crew/Passenger Ratio		Swimming Pools (outdoors):	3
Original Cost:	$200 million	(lower beds/all berths):	3.1/3.2	Swimming Pools (indoors):	0
Entered Service:	Mar 1987/May 2010	Cabins (total):	812	Whirlpools:	4
Registry:	Great Britain	Size Range (sq ft/m):	148.0–538.2/	Self-Service Launderette:	Yes
Length (ft/m):	810.3/247.00		13.7–50.0	Dedicated Cinema/Seats:	Yes/205
Beam (ft/m):	105.6/32.20	Cabins (outside view):	622	Library:	No
Draft (ft/m):	26.9/8.20	Cabins (interior/no view):	190	Onboard currency:	Australian $
Propulsion/Propellers:	diesel-electric	Cabins (for one person):	0		
	(39,000kW)/2	Cabins (with private balcony):	64		

A dated family-friendly ship for casual cruising.

OVERVIEW. *Pacific Pearl* is best suited to young couples and singles of all ages and families with children and teenagers who like to mingle in a large ship with plenty of life, music and entertainment for everyone, with food that is quantity rather than quality, delivered with friendly but unpolished service, at an attractive price. In marketing terms, this is a dress-down product designed for informal cruising.

THE SHIP. *Pacific Pearl* was originally designed and built as *Arcadia* for Sitmar Cruises just as the company was absorbed into Princess Cruises. In 2003, after a refurbishment that brightened the interior passageways, public rooms and dining spots, it morphed into *Ocean Village*, a trendy ship designed for younger couples and families who wanted to cruise without the sedentary "eat when we tell you to and relax" image typical of traditional cruise ships. Several new cabins were added during that refit, but the number of crew was reduced because fewer were needed for this more casual style of cruising. The casino was also relocated, displacing the library, and the former casino became an internet center/bar. In 2010, the ship was transferred to P&O Cruises (Australia) to become *Pacific Pearl* for Australasian passengers.

Pacific Pearl is a well-proportioned ship, with a decent amount of open deck and sunbathing space. On the open leisure deck are two pools, one with sloping steps, the other with vertical steps, and one has a sit-in bar. The aft pool will probably be used by families with children. Four hot tubs sit on a raised platform, and two shower cubicles stand adjacent to a poolside Splash Bar.

BERLITZ'S RATINGS

	Possible	Achieved
Ship	500	356
Accommodation	200	138
Food	400	249
Service	400	273
Entertainment	100	74
Cruise	400	274

OVERALL SCORE
1,364 points out of 2,000

The interiors are upbeat and trendy in a high-street sort of way with decor by the designers who did a great job with the ships of AIDA Cruises – like P&O Cruises, part of Carnival Corporation. But they also include a few items that have a link with the past, such as the art deco stainless steel balustrades and the soulless stainless steel elevators. There aren't a lot of public rooms, although one nice feature is the fact that they do have ceilings higher than the average for contemporary cruise ships.

The focal point of the interior is a three-deck-high foyer, highlighted by a large blue and yellow stainless-steel kinetic sculpture resembling a Swiss Army knife; its blades move slowly, and it directs one's attention to a multi-deck horseshoe-shaped staircase. The Dome, an observation lounge, sits atop the ship, forward of the mast. It is a restful spot for cocktails; at night it turns into a night-spot/discotheque with a sunken dance floor.

For retail therapy, several shops are clustered around the second and third levels of the atrium lobby, plus a dedicated cinema. Other facilities include a casino, aft of the upper level of the two-deck-high showlounge, The Oval lounge/bar (good for sports fans), Connexions Bar (for adult-only comedy, and karaoke), and the Blue Bar, a more traditional drinking lounge.

Active sports provided include mountain biking, abseiling, jet skiing, jeep safaris, quad biking, parasailing, helicopter flight-seeing, and snorkeling, all at extra cost. The ship carries a "fleet" of mountain bikes. Both active and passive cruising, therefore, are on offer.

It's a pity there is no full walk-around promenade deck

outdoors – open port and starboard walking areas stretch only partly along the sides. There is no library. The elevators have a "London Underground" voice that intones "mind the doors." Note that duty- and tax-free shopping is not available on Australian coastal cruises, except on Queensland cruises that take in Willis Island.

FAMILIES. The children's facilities are extensive. There is an indoor play area – Turtle Cove for 3–6-year-olds, and Shark Shack for 7–10-year-olds – at the aft of the ship. The exterior aft deck has a paddling pool and games area. Teenagers have their own area, the Gaming Room.

A number of cabins have third- and-fourth person berths – good for families with children, but the drawer and storage space becomes tight, and there is only one personal safe.

ACCOMMODATION. There are four basic types, in 14 different price grades, the price depending on grade, location and size. These include two grades of suites: 36 suites with private balcony and bathtub, plus separate shower enclosure, two suites with shower, but no balcony. There are also 28 suites with private balcony, and shower. All other accommodation consists of standard outside-view and interior grade cabins, which are of a decent size. If you like to fall asleep with soft music playing, note that because music is available only through the TV set, you can't access any of the music channels without having a TV picture on.

Standard Outside-view/Interior Cabins: All are equipped with twin beds that can, in most cases, be placed together to form a queen-size bed. All have a good amount of storage space, including wooden drawer units, plus some under-bed space for luggage, and a walk-in closet. A direct-dial telephone is provided. However, the sound insulation between cabins is quite poor – TV sound late at night can be particularly irritating, as can loud children, or fellow passengers banging drawers.

The bathrooms are of a modular design, and are of quite a decent size, with good shower enclosures, and a retractable clothesline. None have tubs, except in one of the grades designated as suites, as the ship was originally built for American passengers, who prefer showers to baths. Soap is provided, and a soap/shampoo dispenser is fitted into the shower enclosure, although there is no conditioner. Coffee- and tea-making facilities are provided in all cabins.

CUISINE. The dining concept is simple: meals are taken in a self-serve buffet style setting, so you can dress as casually as you like and pick the most appropriate dining spot. There are two large self-serve buffet restaurants, *Plantation* and *Waterfront*. Plantation, high up in the ship, has great ocean views. The Waterfront also has large ocean-view windows and self-serve buffet display counters. There are plenty of tables, most of which are for four, six, or eight persons. Plantation is open 24 hours a day, while the blandly decorated Waterfront has set opening hours, detailed in the daily program. At night, Plantation serves Asian and Oriental themed buffets.

There's also a bistro and *La Luna* pizzeria on deck for lunch or dinner (with a cover charge at night, when reservations are needed).

In general, the food is typical of what you would find in a couples-only or family-style holiday village – modern British with a Mediterranean touch – with plenty of choices for families with children. It is straightforward, unfussy and unpretentious, with little use of garnishes. Vegetarian dishes are included daily. The service is warm and lighthearted. Bar snacks such as peanuts or crisps cost extra.

For better-quality, freshly prepared food, try *Salt Grill*, located in one corner on the port side of the Waterfront Restaurant. This dining spot serves fine New World cuisine created by celebrity chef Luke Mangan. There's a cover charge, and reservations are needed.

ENTERTAINMENT. The Marquee Theatre is the venue for all of the principal entertainment events. A horseshoe-shaped room, with main and balcony levels, it has adequate sightlines from most of the banquette-style seating, although sightlines from the front row seats on the upper level are obstructed by the required balcony railing.

There is a wide variety of entertainment, from production shows to cabaret-style acts that may or may not be well-known "names" – lesser artistes, and comedians. There is also live music throughout the many lounges and bars – in fact, there is no bar without music, so sitting down for a quiet drink or two is not an option.

SPA/FITNESS. Facilities include a beauty salon, gymnasium, and the Aqua Wellness/Fitness Center, with a sauna/steam room complex. It is located on the lowest passenger deck, and is not particularly attractive or inviting.

It is wise to book treatments (massages, facials, etc) as soon as possible after you embark, as time slots do fill up quickly aboard large ships such as this. Some exercise classes are free, but most incur a charge.

Pacific Princess
★★★★

Size: ....Mid-Size Ship	Passenger Decks: 9	Cabins (wheelchair accessible): 3
Tonnage: 30,277	Total Crew: 373	Wheelchair accessibility: ....Good
Lifestyle: ....Standard	Passengers	Cabin Current: ....110 and 220 volts
Cruise Line: ......P&O Cruises Australia/	(lower beds/all berths): 688/826	Elevators: 4
Princess Cruises	Passenger Space Ratio	Casino (gaming tables): ....Yes
Former Names: ....R Three	(lower beds/all berths): 44.1/36.6	Slot Machines: ....Yes
Builder: Chantiers de l'Atlantique (France)	Crew/Passenger Ratio	Swimming Pools (outdoors): 1
Original Cost: ....$150 million	(lower beds/all berths): 1.8/2.2	Swimming Pools (indoors): 0
Entered Service: .....Aug 1999/Nov 2002	Cabins (total): 344	Whirlpools: ......2 (+ 1 thalassotherapy)
Registry: ....Gibraltar	Size Range (sq ft/m): 145.3–968.7/	Self-Service Launderette: ....Yes
Length (ft/m): 593.7/181.0	13.5–90.0	Dedicated Cinema/Seats: ....No
Beam (ft/m): 83.5/25.5	Cabins (outside view): 317	Library: ....Yes
Draft (ft/m): 19.5/6.0	Cabins (interior/no view): 27	Onboard currency: ....US$
Propulsion/Propellers: .....diesel-electric	Cabins (for one person): 0	
(18,600kW)/2	Cabins (with private balcony): 232	

English country house decor for mature-age cruisers.

OVERVIEW. *Pacific Princess* appeals to mature adults seeking value for money aboard a comfortable mid-size ship with plenty of dining choices and limited entertainment. It cruises for part of the year under the Princess Cruises banner in French Polynesia, and for six months from Sydney, Australia, under the P&O Cruises brand name.

THE SHIP. *Pacific Princess* has an all-white hull instead of black, which makes the ship appear larger, and a large, square-ish funnel. A lido deck has a swimming pool and good sunbathing space, while one of the aft decks has a thalassotherapy pool. A jogging track circles the swimming pool deck, but one deck above. The uppermost outdoors deck includes a golf driving net and shuffleboard court.

There is no walk-around promenade deck outdoors, although there is a small jogging track around the perimeter of the swimming pool, and port and starboard side decks. Instead of wooden decks outdoors, they are covered by Bollidt, a sand-colored rubberized material. There is no sauna. The room service menu is extremely limited. Stairways, although carpeted, are tinny. In order to keep the prices low, often the air routing to get to/from your ship is not the most direct.

The interior decor is quite stunning and elegant, a throwback to ship decor of the ocean liners of the 1920s and '30s, executed in fine taste. This includes detailed ceiling cornices, both real and faux wrought-iron staircase railings, leather- and cherry wood-paneled walls, *trompe l'oeil* ceilings, and rich carpeting in hallways with an Oriental rug-look center section. The overall feel echoes that of an old-world country club. The staircase in the main, two-deck-

BERLITZ'S RATINGS		
	Possible	Achieved
Ship	500	406
Accommodation	200	155
Food	400	265
Service	400	287
Entertainment	100	72
Cruise	400	302

OVERALL SCORE
1,487 points out of 2,000

high foyer recalls the staircase in the 1997 movie *Titanic*.

The public rooms are spread over three decks. The reception hall has a staircase with intricate wrought-iron railings. The Nightclub, with forward-facing views, sits high in the ship and has Polynesian-inspired decor and furniture.

There are plenty of bars – including one in the entrance to each restaurant. Perhaps the nicest of all bars and lounges are in the casino bar/lounge that is a beautiful room reminiscent of London's grand hotels and understated gaming clubs. It has an inviting marble fireplace – in fact, there are three such fireplaces aboard – and comfortable sofas and individual chairs. There is also a large Card Room, which incorporates an internet center with eight stations.

The Library is a beautiful, grand Regency-style room, with a fireplace, a high, indented, *trompe l'oeil* ceiling, and an excellent selection of books, plus very comfortable wing-back chairs with footstools, and sofas you could sleep on; it's the most relaxing room aboard. There's very little entertainment, but it is not needed in the cruise areas featured. *Pacific Princess* is much more about relaxation than the larger ships in the Princess Cruises fleet.

As with all Princess Cruises ships, 15% is added to all bar and spa accounts – drink prices are moderate, but beer prices are high. A standard gratuity (about $10 per person, per day) is automatically added to onboard accounts – to reduce the amount, you'll need to go to the reception desk.

There is a charge – tokens must be obtained from the reception desk – for using the machines in the self-service launderette. A change machine in the launderette itself would be more user-friendly.

ACCOMMODATION. There is a variety of about eight different cabin types to choose from, with prices linked to grade, location and size.

All of the standard interior and outside-view cabins are extremely compact units, and extremely tight for two persons – especially for cruises longer than seven days. Cabins have twin beds or queen-size bed, with good under-bed storage areas, personal safe, vanity desk with large mirror, good closet and drawer space in rich, dark woods, and bathrobe. Color TVs carry a major news channel, where obtainable, plus a sports channel and several round-the-clock movie channels. The bathrooms, which have tiled floors and plain walls, are compact, standard units, and include a shower enclosure with a removable, strong hand-held shower unit, hairdryer, 100% cotton towels, toiletries storage shelves and a retractable clothesline.

The suites/cabins that have private balconies (66 percent of all suites/cabins, or 73 percent of all outside view suites/cabins) have partial, and not full, balcony partitions, and sliding glass doors. Thanks to good design and layout, only 14 cabins on Deck 6 have lifeboat-obstructed views. The balcony floor is covered in thick plastic matting – teak would be nicer – and some awful plastic furniture.

Mini-Suites (52): Units designated as mini-suites are in reality simply larger cabins than the standard varieties, as the sleeping and lounge areas are not divided. While not overly large, the bathrooms have a good-sized tub and ample space for storing toiletries. The living area has a refrigerated mini-bar, lounge area with breakfast table, and a balcony with two plastic chairs and a table.

Owner's Suites (10): The most spacious accommodation, these are fine, large living spaces in the forward-most and aft-most sections of the accommodation decks. Particularly nice are those that overlook the stern, on Deck 6, 7 and 8. They have more extensive balconies that really are private and cannot be overlooked by anyone from the decks above. There is an entrance foyer, living room, bedroom, CD player, bathroom with Jacuzzi tub, as well as a small guest bathroom. The bed faces the sea, which can be seen through the floor-to-ceiling windows and sliding glass door.

All suites/cabins located at the stern may suffer from vibration and noise, particularly when the ship is proceeding at or close to full speed, or maneuvering in port.

CUISINE. There are four different dining spots – three restaurants and one casual self-serve buffet:
● *The Club Restaurant* has 338 seats, all with armrests, and includes a large raised central section. There are large ocean-view windows on three sides, and some prime tables that overlook the stern, as well as a small bandstand for occasional live dinner music. However, the noise level can be high because of the single-deck-height ceiling.

● *Sabatini's Trattoria*, an extra-cost Italian restaurant, has 96 seats (all chairs have armrests), windows along two sides, and a set *bellissima* three-hour dégustation menu.
● *The Sterling Steakhouse* is an "American steak house" with a good selection of large, prime steaks and other meats. It has 98 comfortable seats, all with armrests, and windows along two sides. It has a set menu, together with added daily chef's specials. There is a cover charge.
● *The Lido Café* has seating for 154 indoors and 186 outdoors, with white plastic patio furniture. It is open for breakfast, lunch and casual dinners. The ship's self-serve buffet restaurant, it is open 24 hours a day and has a small pizzeria and grill.

All restaurants have open-seating dining, so you dine when you want, although reservations are necessary for Sabatini's Trattoria and Sterling Steakhouse, where there are mostly tables for four or six – there are few tables for two. In addition, there is a *Poolside Grill and Bar* for fast-food items.

ENTERTAINMENT. The 345-seat Cabaret Lounge, in the forward part of the ship on Deck 5, is the main venue for entertainment events and some social functions. The single-level room has a stage, and circular hardwood dance floor with adjacent banquette and individual tub chair seating, and raised sections on port and starboard sides. It is not a large room, and not really designed for production shows, so cabaret acts and local entertainment form the main focus, with mini-revue style shows with colorful costumes, presented by a troupe of resident singer/dancers in a potted version of what you might experience aboard the large ships of Princess Cruises. Inevitably, art auctions and bingo are pushed almost daily.

The ship carries a band, small musical units, and solo entertaining pianists to provide live music for shows and dancing in the lounges and bars before and after dinner.

SPA/FITNESS. Facilities, which are located in the forward part of the ship on a high deck (Deck 9) include a gymnasium with ocean-view windows and some high-tech muscle-toning equipment and treadmills. There are steam rooms but no sauna, changing areas for men and women, and a beauty salon with ocean view windows.

The spa is operated by Steiner, a specialist concession whose retail products will be pushed. Some fitness classes, such as Stepexpress, Power Walk, Total Body Conditioning, Xpress Circuit, are free. Others, such as yoga and kick-boxing, cost extra, as do massage, facials, pedicures, and beauty salon treatments.

● **For more extensive general information about the Princess Cruises experience, see pages 149–52.**

Pacific Sun
★★★

Size:	Mid-Size Ship	Passenger Decks:	.9	Cabins (with private balcony):	.10
Tonnage:	.47,262	Total Crew:	.670	Cabins (wheelchair accessible):	.14
Lifestyle:	Standard	Passengers		Wheelchair accessibility:	.Fair
Cruise Line:	.P&O Cruises (Australia)	(lower beds/all berths):	.1,486/1,896	Cabin Current:	.110 volts
Former Names:	.*Jubilee*	Passenger Space Ratio		Elevators:	.8
Builder:	.Kockums (Sweden)	(lower beds/all berths):	.31.8/24.9	Casino (gaming tables):	.Yes
Original Cost:	.$134 million	Crew/Passenger Ratio		Slot Machines:	.Yes
Entered Service:	.Jul 1986/Nov 2004	(lower beds/all berths):	.2.2/2.8	Swimming Pools (outdoors):	.3
Registry:	.The Bahamas	Cabins (total):	.743	Swimming Pools (indoors):	.0
Length (ft/m):	.733.0/223.4	Size Range (sq ft/m):	.182.9–419.8/	Whirlpools:	.2
Beam (ft/m):	.92.5/28.2		17.0–39.0	Self-Service Launderette:	.Yes
Draft (ft/m):	.24.7/7.5	Cabins (outside view):	.453	Dedicated Cinema/Seats:	.No
Propulsion/Propellers:	.diesel	Cabins (interior/no view):	.290	Library:	.Yes
	(23,520 kW)/2	Cabins (for one person):	.0	Onboard currency:	.Australian $

A family-friendly ultra-casual ship for Australians.

OVERVIEW. Freemantle-based *Pacific Sun*, although 25 years old, will provide novice Aussie and Kiwi cruisegoers with a good first-cruise experience in comfortable, but visually busy surroundings. It is best suited to those seeking a good basic getaway cruise aboard a ship that has some good drinking places, lots of noise, good cheer, and upbeat surroundings, with friendly service that lacks polish.

THE SHIP. Formerly *Jubilee*, the third new-build ordered by former owner Carnival Cruise Lines, this ship has a bold, forthright, angular all-white profile, short bows, and a slim funnel. In 2004, it was transferred to P&O Cruises (Australia), renamed and refurbished to provide passenger facilities for year-round cruises from Australia and New Zealand.

The ship has a youthful, sporty image. There is a decent amount of sunbathing space outdoors, and one of the two swimming pools has a twisting, two-deck high controlled water slide that empties you into it. The top deck is now an adults-only sanctuary area.

Most public rooms are arranged on Atlantic Deck, making for easy-access passenger flow. A double-wide indoor promenade, Park Lane, acts as a boulevard, off which a variety of bars and lounges and other public rooms are located. The decor consists of contemporary colors in all the public rooms except for the rather more elegant Churchill's Library, a decent place to sit and read or connect to the internet – watch out for the knights in suits of armor. A large Sporting Club Casino with gaming tables for blackjack, roulette, pokies, and lots of slot machines provides almost round-the-clock action.

BERLITZ'S RATINGS	Possible	Achieved
Ship	500	294
Accommodation	200	119
Food	400	233
Service	400	232
Entertainment	100	62
Cruise	400	227
OVERALL SCORE		
1,167 points out of 2,000		

The ship lays on constant entertainment and activities designed for passenger participation in a party-like setting, and is a floating playground for young, active adults who enjoy constant stimulation, close contact with lots and lots of others, as well as glitz, glamour and gambling. There's plenty for kids to do, too, and facilities including a children's club and activity center cater for up to 300 youngsters.

Standing in line for embarkation, disembarkation, shore tenders and for self-serve buffet meals is an inevitable aspect of cruising aboard large ships and this one is no exception. There is no walk-around promenade deck outdoors. The bad news: those ridiculous art auctions persist, with the same tacky, useless "art" seen aboard so many other cruise ships, particularly Carnival Corporation vessels. But it's all part of "Funship Cruising" in the down-under world. The good news: P&O Australia scrapped automatic tipping in 2010.

ACCOMMODATION. There are several different price categories for ocean-view and interior cabins – most of which are of the same approximate size – and two categories for suites. Typically, the higher the deck, the more you pay.

Especially nice are 10 large suites on Verandah Deck, each with a private balcony, although there are obstructed views from four of them. Almost all other cabins are relatively spacious units that are neatly appointed and have attractive, though rather spartan, decor.

The ocean-view cabins have large picture windows, and you should try to book one of these cabins if this is your first cruise. There are many, many interior cabins, although they are actually quite spacious, and good for anyone on a low budget. They have two lower beds, a small vanity unit, and a reasonable-sized bathroom. Some cabins have additional upper berths, and even rollaway beds – good for families with small children, although space will be extremely limited unless the kids are very, very small.

CUISINE/DINING. There are two dining rooms: *Burgundy*, located midships, and *Bordeaux*, located aft, with the galley between them. They are quite cramped when full, and extremely noisy – particularly at those tables adjacent to the large waiter stations – and they have low ceilings in their raised center sections. There are tables for four, six, or eight, but none for two, and many banquette seats (individual chairs don't have armrests). Window-side tables are for six and are typically also the quietest tables. The decor is bright, extremely colorful and jolly. At night, the elegant setting of Churchill's Library becomes a steakhouse.

The Lido Deck poolside self-serve *Outback Bar & Grill* offers casual meals. At night, it provides a dress-down alternative to eating in the main dining rooms, serving pasta, steaks, salads and desserts. For casual food there's also a sushi bar and a poolside pizzeria. New Zealand natural ice cream is served at a counter close by.

ENTERTAINMENT. The Atlantis Showlounge, the principal venue for production shows and major cabaret acts, is two decks high, decorated in high glitz, and has seating on both main and balcony levels. However, pillars obstruct the sight lines on the main level, and railings obstruct sight lines from many seats on the balcony level. In a typical cruise, there will be several production shows, typically with a cast of two lead singers and a clutch of dancers, backed by a live orchestra. The room also doubles as a cinema for big-screen movies. Almost every lounge/bar has live bands and musical units, so there is always plenty of live music happening, mostly in the evenings.

SPA/FITNESS. The Lotus Spa is on the ship's uppermost deck, just aft of the mast, and accessed by the center stairway and lifts. The facility is small by today's standards, but a former gymnasium is now a relaxation area, while a new gymnasium with some high-tech muscle-pumping cardio-vascular machines has views over the stern. There are changing rooms and saunas for men and women. The beauty salon is elsewhere, just aft of the Showlounge.

Spa/beauty treatments and fitness facilities are operated by Steiner Leisure, a concession whose young staff will try to sell you its own-brand beauty products. Some fitness classes such as Stepexpress, Power Walk, Total Body Conditioning, and Xpress Circuit are free. Others, such as yoga and kick-boxing, cost extra.

Being aboard will give you an opportunity to try some of the more exotic treatments. Massages and other treatments such as seaweed mud wraps, facials, pedicures, and beauty salon treatments cost extra.

If you want to book spa and beauty treatments, do so as soon after you embark as possible, as the limited number of time slots do fill up quickly. There are fewer treatments than aboard Caribbean ships because many Australians consider wellbeing treatments rather "namby pamby."

Pacific Venus
★★★★

Size:	Mid-Size Ship	Passenger Decks:	7	Cabins (wheelchair accessible):	1
Tonnage:	26,518	Total Crew:	220	Wheelchair accessibility:	Fair
Lifestyle:	Standard	Passengers		Cabin Current:	110 volts
Cruise Line:	Venus Cruise	(lower beds/all berths):	476/620	Elevators:	4
Former Names:	none	Passenger Space Ratio		Casino (gaming tables):	Yes
Builder:	Ishikawajima Heavy	(lower beds/all berths):	55.7/42.7	Slot Machines:	3
	Industries (Japan)	Crew/Passenger Ratio		Swimming Pools (outdoors):	1
Original Cost:	$114 million	(lower beds/all berths):	2.1/2.8		(+ 1 for children)
	(13 billion yen)	Cabins (total):	238	Swimming Pools (indoors):	0
Entered Service:	Apr 1998	Size Range (sq ft/m):	164.6–699.6/	Whirlpools:	1
Registry:	Japan		15.3–65.0	Self-Service Launderette:	Yes (5)
Length (ft/m):	601.7/183.4	Cabins (outside view):	238	Dedicated Cinema/Seats:	Yes/94
Beam (ft/m):	82.0/25.0	Cabins (interior/no view):	0	Library:	Yes
Draft (ft/m):	21.3/6.5	Cabins (for one person):	0	Onboard currency:	Japanese yen
Propulsion/Propellers: diesel (13,636 kW)/2		Cabins (with private balcony):	20		

Comfortable decor and style for Japanese cruisers.

OVERVIEW. *Pacific Venus* is best suited to Japanese-speaking couples and single travelers of mature years who enjoy traveling in very comfortable surroundings, and who enjoy good food and service, all at a moderate cost. The ship is often operated under charter to various travel organizations, so drinks may or may not be included in the cruise price; when operated by Venus Cruise, alcoholic beverages are not included.

THE SHIP. Venus Cruise is part of Japan Cruise Line, which is itself part of SHK Line Group, a joint venture between the Shin Nohonkai, Hankyu and Kanpu ferry companies, which operate more than 20 ferries. There is a decent amount of open deck space aft of the funnel – good for deck sports – while protected sunbathing space is provided around the small swimming poo. All sunloungers have cushioned pads. The open walking promenade decks are rubber-coated steel – teak would be more desirable.

The base of the funnel itself is the site of a day/night lounge, which overlooks the swimming pool – it is slightly reminiscent of Royal Caribbean International's funnel-wrapped Viking Crown lounges aboard its first ships. There is plenty of space per passenger. The decor is clean and fresh, with much use of pastel colors and blond woods, giving the interiors a feeling of warmth.

The dining rooms are located off Deck 7, which has a double-width indoor promenade, with high ceiling height. The atrium, three decks high, has a crystal chandelier as its focal point, and a white baby grand piano on its lower level, where the Reception Desk is situated.

There are special rooms for meetings and conference orga-

BERLITZ'S RATINGS		
	Possible	Achieved
Ship	500	395
Accommodation	200	147
Food	400	309
Service	400	316
Entertainment	100	76
Cruise	400	305
OVERALL SCORE		
1,548 points out of 2,000		

nizers, for times when the ship is chartered. A piano salon has colorful low-back chairs, and a large main hall has a finely sculptured high ceiling and over 700 moveable seats and hosts production shows. There's a 350-seat main lounge for cabaret shows and ballroom dancing, a small movie theater, and a library/writing room and card room. A casino gaming area is located as part of the Top Lounge set at the front of the funnel. There's also a smoking room, Chashitsu (tatami mat) room, karaoke room (for rent) and card room/mah jong room, free self-service launderettes on each accommodation deck, and two (credit card/coin) public telephone booths.

Overall, this company provides a well-packaged cruise in a ship that has a very comfortable, serene environment. The dress code is relaxed, and no tipping is allowed.

The ship has two classes: Salon Class and Standard Class. Salon Class passengers pay more, but get suite-grade accommodation, eat in the Grand Siècle private dining room (it used to be an à la carte restaurant when the ship debuted), and lots of extra goodies and services, including a welcome embarkation basket, more toiletries, and priority tickets for shows and shore tenders.

ACCOMMODATION. There are four types: royal suites, suites, deluxe cabins, state cabins (in four price grades), and standard cabins. All are located from the uppermost to lowermost decks, respectively. All suites and cabins have an outside view, but few cabins have a private balcony.

The four Royal Suites (Archaic, Elegant, Modern, and Noble) are decorated in two different styles – one contemporary, one more traditional Japanese style. Each has a private balcony, with sliding door (balcony table and two chairs), an expansive lounge area with large sofa and plush armchairs, coffee table, window-side chairs and drinks table, floor-to-ceiling windows, and a large flat-screen TV set, with separate DVD unit. There is a separate bedroom, with twin- or queen-size bed, vanity/writing desk, large walk-in closet with personal safe. Also provided are high-quality binoculars, camera tripod, humidifier, coffee/tea making set, and free minibar set-up. The large bathroom has ocean-view windows, Jacuzzi tub, a separate shower enclosure, and his/hers washbasins.

Sixteen other suites have private balconies (with teak table and two chairs), a good-sized living area with vanity/writing desk, dining table, chair and curved sofa, separate sleeping area, and bathroom with deep tub slightly larger than the Royal suites, and single large sink. There is ample lighted closet and drawer space (two locking drawers instead of a personal safe), and a DVD unit.

The 20 Deluxe cabins have large picture windows fronted by a large, curtained arch, sleeping area with twin or queen beds, plus a daytime sofa that converts into a third bed.

The "state" cabins, many of which have upper berths for third passengers, are in three price levels, have decor that is best described as basic, with reasonable closet space, but very little drawer space.

The standard cabins are really plain, but can accommodate three persons – useful for families – although the drawer and storage space is a bit tight.

All accommodation grades have a tea drinking set with electric hot water kettle, TV set, telephone, stocked minibar/refrigerator – all items included in the cruise price. Bathrooms have a hairdryer, and lots of Shiseido toiletries, particularly in the suites. All room service menu items cost extra – this is typical of all Japanese cruise ships – except for Salon-class suite-grade accommodation. All passengers receive a yukata (a Japanese-style light cotton robe). Suite occupants also get a plush bathrobe, and all accommodation grades have electric, automatic toilets (washlets) with heated seats.

CUISINE. The *Primavera Restaurant* is located aft, with ocean views on three sides, and has a high ceiling. Passengers dine in one seating, and tables are for six, 10, or 12. The food consists of both Japanese and Western items; the menu is varied and the food is attractively presented. For breakfast and lunch it includes a self-serve buffet, while dinner is typically a fully-served set meal.

A separate intimate 42-seat restaurant, *Grand Siècle*, is reserved for occupants of suite-grade (Salon Class) accommodation; it is tastefully decorated in Regency-style, with fine wood-paneling and a detailed, indented ceiling. It has mostly tables for two (with plenty of space for correct service), better quality chopsticks, nori sea-weed, and better quality and variety of fine china. Cold and hot towels are provided, and the whole dining experienced is far better than in the Primavera.

ENTERTAINMENT. Le Pacific Main Lounge is the venue for all shipboard entertainment and also functions as a lecture and activities room during the day. It is a single-level room with seating clustered around a "thrust" stage so that entertainers are in the very midst of their audience.

On most cruises, special featured entertainers such as singers, instrumentalists, storytellers, and dance champions are brought on board from ashore.

SPA/FITNESS. Spa facilities include male and female Grand Baths, which include two bathing pools and health/cleansing stations, ocean-view windows, a steam room, a gymnasium with ocean-view windows (in a different location just aft of the funnel); and a sauna.

Japanese massage is available, as are hairdressing and barber services in the small salon, located on the lowest passenger-accessible deck of the ship.

Paul Gauguin
★★★★

Size: . . . . .Small Ship	Passenger Decks: 7	Cabins (with private balcony): 89
Tonnage: 19,200	Total Crew: 215	Cabins (wheelchair accessible): 1
Lifestyle: . . . . .Premium	Passengers	Wheelchair accessibility . . . . .Fair
Cruise Line: . . . . . . .Paul Gauguin Cruises	(lower beds/all berths): 332/332	Cabin Current: . . . . .110 volts
Former Names: . . . . .none	Passenger Space Ratio	Elevators: 4
Builder: Chantiers de l'Atlantique (France)	(lower beds/all berths): 57.8/57.8	Casino (gaming tables): . . . . .Yes
Original Cost: . . . .$150 million	Crew/Passenger Ratio	Slot Machines: . . . . .Yes
Entered Service: . . . . .Jan 1998/Jan 2010	(lower beds/all berths): 1.5/1.5	Swimming Pools (outdoors): 1
Registry: . . . . The Bahamas	Cabins (total): 166	Swimming Pools (indoors): 0
Length (ft/m): 513.4/156.50	Size Range (sq ft/m): 200.0–588.0/	Whirlpools: 0
Beam (ft/m): 72.1/22.00	18.5–54.6	Self-Service Launderette: . . . . .No
Draft (ft/m): 16.8/5.15	Cabins (outside view): 166	Dedicated Cinema/Seats: . . . . .No
Propulsion/Propellers: . . . . .diesel-electric	Cabins (interior/no view): 0	Library: . . . . .Yes
(9,000 kW/2	Cabins (for one person): 0	Onboard currency: . . . . .US$

An elegant ship for casual warm-weather cruising.

OVERVIEW. This ship is best suited to couples and single travelers, typically over 50, seeking specialized itineraries, good regional cuisine and service, with almost no entertainment, all wrapped up in a contemporary ship that is elegant and understated. Where it really shines is in its variety of water-sports equipment, and its shallow draft that allows it to navigate and anchor in lovely little places that larger ships couldn't possibly reach.

THE SHIP. Built by a French company specifically to operate in shallow waters, *Paul Gauguin* is now under long-term charter to Pacific Beachcombers of Tahiti, which also own the Intercontinental Tahiti, Intercontinental Bora Bora Le Moana, Intercontinental Bora Bor and Intercontinental Moorea. The ship cruises around French Polynesia and the South Pacific and, while it could carry many more passengers, it is forbidden to do so by French law. It had a $9 million refurbishment in 2009, has a well-balanced, all-white profile, and a single funnel.

This smart ship also has a retractable aft marina platform, and carries two water skiing boats and two inflatable craft for water sports. Windsurfers, kayaks, plus scuba and snorkeling gear are available for your use; all except scuba gear, are included in the cruise fare. Islands, beaches and watersports are what *Paul Gauguin* is good at. Perhaps the best island experience is in Bora Bora. Its shallow draft means there could be some movement, as the ship is a little high-sided for its size.

Inside, there is a pleasant array of public rooms, and both the artwork and the decor have a real French Polynesia look and feel. The interior colors are quite restful, although a trifle bland.

BERLITZ'S RATINGS		
	Possible	Achieved
Ship	500	397
Accommodation	200	169
Food	400	304
Service	400	320
Entertainment	100	71
Cruise	400	286
OVERALL SCORE		
1,547 points out of 2,000		

Expert lecturers on Tahiti and Gauguin accompany each cruise, and a Fare (pronounced *foray*) Tahiti Gallery offers books, videos, and other materials on the unique art, history, and culture of the islands. Three original Gauguin sketches are displayed under protective glass.

The dress code is very relaxed – every day. The standard itinerary means the ship docks only in Papeete, and shore tenders are used in all other ports. There is little entertainment, as the ship stays overnight in several ports – so little is needed. The high crew-to-passenger ratio translates to a high level of personalized service. The ship has become a favorite of travelers to these climes, and the quiet, refined atmosphere on board makes it sort of clubby, with passengers getting to know each other easily. Wi-fi spots are provided, but internet charges are high.

Le Casino is a small casino with just two tables, and a few slot machines. The library is pleasant enough, although it could be larger. The spa is very small, and the fitness room is windowless.

All in all, it's a delightful cruise and product, and all gratuities are included. Soft drinks and mineral water are included in the cruise price.

ACCOMMODATION. There are eight suite/cabin grades, priced according to location and size. The outside-view cabins, half of which have private balconies, are nicely equipped, although they are strictly rectangular and none have more interesting shapes. Most have large windows, except those on the lowest accommodation deck, which have portholes. Each has queen- or twin-size beds convertible to queen, and wood-accented cabinetry with rounded edges. A mini-bar/refrigerator stocked with complimentary soft drinks, a DVD player, personal safe, hairdryer and umbrellas are standard.

The marble-look bathrooms are large and pleasing and have a tub as well as a separate shower enclosure. All passengers are provided with 100% cotton bathrobes, cotton slippers. The two largest suites have a private balcony at the front and side of the vessel. Although there is a decent amount of in-cabin space, with a beautiful long vanity unit and plenty of drawer space, the bathrooms are disappointingly small and plain, and too similar to all other standard cabin bathrooms.

Butler service is provided in all accommodation designated as Owners Suite, Grand Suites, Ocean-view "A" and "B" category suites.

CUISINE. *L'Etoile*, the main dining room, is open for dinner only, while *La Veranda*, an alternative dining spot, serves breakfast, lunch and dinner. Both have "open seating" which means you can choose when you want to dine and with whom. This provides a good opportunity to meet new people for dinner each evening. The chairs have armrests, making it more comfortable for a leisurely mealtime. La Veranda provides dinner by reservation, with alternating French and Italian menus; the French menus are provided by Jean-Pierre Vigato, a two-star Michelin chef with his own restaurant, Apicius, in Paris.

The dining operation is well orchestrated, with cuisine and service of a high standard. Select wines and liquor are included in the fare, while premium wines cost extra.

An outdoor (but covered) *Le Grill* provides informal café fare on deck aft of the pool, although there are no tables for two. Each evening it becomes *Pacific Grill* and serves Polynesian cuisine.

The Connoisseur Club offers a luxurious retreat for cigars, cognacs, and wine tasting.

ENTERTAINMENT. Le Grand Salon is the venue for shows and cabaret acts. It is a single-level room, and seating is in banquette and individual tub chairs. Sightlines are quite good from most seats, although there are some obstructions. Don't expect lavish production shows (there aren't any), as the main entertainment consists of local Polynesian shows brought on board from ashore, plus the odd cabaret act. A new piano lounge was added in a 2006 refit.

SPA/FITNESS. The Spa, on Deck 6 in the ship's center, is the wellbeing space. It includes a fitness centre with muscle-pumping and body toning equipment, a steam room, several treatment rooms, changing area (very small), and beauty salon. The Spa/beauty services and staff are provided by Algotherm. There is no sauna, but use of the steam room is complimentary. Body pampering treatments include various massages, aromatherapy facials, manicures, pedicures, and hairdressing services.

THE TRUTH ABOUT TONNAGE

The International Convention of Tonnage Measurement of Ships, was introduced in 1969, implemented in 1982, and actually came into force on July 18, 1994. It required ship owners to re-measure the (former) gross register tonnage of their vessels (1 grt = 100 cubic ft of enclosed space/2.8 cubic meters).

The Convention states: "The gross tonnage (GT) of a ship shall be determined by the following formula: GT-K1V where V = Total volume of all enclosed spaces of the ship in cubic meters; and K1 = 0.2+0.02 log 10 V..." Actually, measurements of gross and net tonnage are really dimensionless numbers. So the word "ton" is no longer used in maritime terminology.

Tonnage (gt) was originally a key measure of the carrying capacity of a ship was *not* how much it weighed,

but how much space it had available for cargo. A common cargo was wine, which was shipped in large casks called "tuns." A tun held 8 barrels of wine or about 242 gallons. Soon they started measuring the cargo area based on how many of these boxes or tuns could be fit in. Thus, a ship that could transport 8,000 barrels of wine was known as a 1,000 tun ship. "Tun" evolved into "ton" and then into "Gross Registered Ton." The clipper (tall) ships in the mid-1800s ranged in size from 400 grt to 4,000 grt.

The advent of steel hulled ships and steam engines allowed the building of larger vessels, with, for example, the *Titanic* measuring what was then a large 48,000 gt.

What is "displacement tonnage?"
Displacement tonnage is an estimate

of the weight of a merchant vessel's structure to the nearest 100 long tons or metric tons (they are not quite the same); or volumetric tonnage (measured by volume).

How does a giant ship stay afloat?
As the Greek scientist Archimedes (c.287–212BC) discovered, an object will float provided its weight is equal to or less than the amount of water it displaces.

Large resort ships such as *Oasis of the Seas*, which has a tonnage of 222,900, displace a lot of water, although they are essentially hollow, because most of the internal weight, such as engines and propulsion machinery, is placed at the bottom of the hull. This allows the ship to remain upright, even though many decks tower above the waterline.

Pride of America
★★★ +

Size: . . . . .Large Resort Ship	Passenger Decks: 11	Cabins (wheelchair accessible): 22
Tonnage: .81,000	Total Crew: 1,000	Wheelchair accessibility: . . . . .Good
Lifestyle: . . . . .Standard	Passengers	Cabin Current: . . . . .110 volts
Cruise Line: . . . . . .Norwegian Cruise Line	(lower beds/all berths): 2,144/2,440	Elevators: 10
Former Names: . . . . .none	Passenger Space Ratio	Casino (gaming tables): . . . . .Yes
Builder: . . . . . .Ingalls Shipbuilding (USA)/	(lower beds/all berths): 37.7/33.1	Slot Machines: . . . . .Yes
Lloyd Werft (Germany)	Crew/Passenger Ratio	Swimming Pools (outdoors): 2
Original Cost: . . . .$450 million	(lower beds/all berths): 2.1/2.4	Swimming Pools (indoors): 0
Entered Service: . . . . .Jul 2005	Cabins (total): 1,072	Whirlpools: . . . . .n/a
Registry: . . . . .USA	Size Range (sq ft/m): 129.1–1,377.8/	Self-Service Launderette: . . . . .No
Length (ft/m): 921.9/281.0	12.0–128.0	Dedicated Cinema/Seats: . . . . .No
Beam (ft/m): 106.6/32.2	Cabins (outside view): 843	Library: . . . . .Yes
Draft (ft/m): 26.25/8.0	Cabins (interior/no view): 229	Onboard currency: . . . . .US$
Propulsion/Propellers: . . . .diesel-electric/	Cabins (for one person): 0	
2 pods (17MW each)	Cabins (with private balcony): 665	

A large, family-friendly ship for Hawaiian cruises.

OVERVIEW. The ship suits first-time young couples, single passengers, children and teenagers who enjoy city nightlife and who want contemporary, upbeat surroundings, plenty of entertainment lounges and bars and high-tech sophistication – all in one neat, well-packaged cruise vacation, with plenty of music, constant activity and entertainment. But don't expect good service – the majority of the crew simply don't cut it.

THE SHIP. *Pride of America,* which sank during its dockside reconstruction at Germany's Lloyd Werft shipbuilders, sails on inter-island cruises, focusing on Hawaii's islands. The 85,850 sq.-ft. (7,975 sq.-meter) open deck space includes a sunbathing/pool deck inspired by Miami's South Beach – think Ocean Drive/Lincoln Mall – and an Art Deco area.

The stunning interior design is modeled after a "Best of America" theme, with public rooms named after famous Americans. Facilities include the Capitol Atrium (a lobby spanning eight decks and said to be inspired by the Capitol Building and White House), a large casino, a conservatory complete with tropical landscaped garden and live exotic birds, Soho Art Gallery (holding art auctions), Washington Library, and Newbury Shopping Center. The Rascal's Kids Center and Kids' Pool is a supervised facility designed around a theme of America's native animals.

Six dedicated meetings rooms range in size from boardrooms for 10 people to an auditorium for up to 250. American corporations qualify for tax-deductible meetings expenses as the ship sails under the US flag, at least until January 2012. The ship has a mainly Hawaiian crew.

BERLITZ'S RATINGS

	Possible	Achieved
Ship	500	383
Accommodation	200	149
Food	400	219
Service	400	205
Entertainment	100	74
Cruise	400	238

OVERALL SCORE
1,268 points out of 2,000

A non-changeable service charge (as distinct from a gratuity) for staff is added to your onboard account at $10 per person ($5 for children aged 3–12) per day; this is pooled for all crew and provides payment when they are on vacation. You will also be expected to provide gratuities. In addition, a 15% gratuity, plus Hawaii sales tax (because of the ship's US registry) is added to all bar and spa treatment accounts.

Although the islands are pleasant, a cruise aboard this ship is likely to test your patience. *Pride of America* is a good example of how not to run a cruise ship, and cabin cleanliness in particular is poor. Many people use their cellphones when in sight of land – an annoyance to some fellow passengers.

ACCOMMODATION. Of the 950 cabins, 77% have outside views, while 64% of these have private balconies. There are also a large number of family-friendly interconnecting cabins. Many cabins have third/fourth upper berths, and some family-special cabins can accommodate as many as six. Some suites have king-size beds, while most cabins have twin beds that can be placed together to make a queen-size bed.

A number of cabins are wheelchair-accessible, while some are equipped for the hearing-impaired.

Grand Suite: The largest accommodation is in the Grand Suite, with around 1,400 sq. ft. (130 sq. meters) of living space. It is located high atop the ship forward of the sun deck and offers sweeping views from its walk-around outdoor terrace. It has a large living room with Bang & Olufsen entertainment center (television, DVD/CD player with library), internet-access computers, and wet bar, separate dining room with dining table and six chairs. A butler is included. The master bedroom has a king-size bed, large bathroom, with whirlpool tub and separate shower enclosure; dressing area with flat-screen TV, and walk-in closet. At the entrance to the suite is a guest powder room. There is a wrap-around veranda, and facilities include open-air dining and a hot tub, plus a private sunbathing and entertainment area.

Owner's Suites (5): Measuring around 870 sq.ft. (80 sq. meters), these are named after indigenous flowers in Hawaii such as Bird of Paradise, Gardenia, Orchid, Plumeria. Each has a bedroom with king-size bed, walk-in closet, dressing area, separate living room with Bang & Olufsen entertainment center, and internet-access computer. The bathroom has a whirlpool tub and separate shower enclosure. There is also a large private balcony with hot tub, outdoor dining facilities and sun beds.

Deluxe Penthouse Suites (6): These measure around 735 sq.ft. (68 sq. meters). They have a separate bedroom with king-size bed and walk-in closet; the bathroom has a whirlpool tub, separate shower enclosure, two washbasins, dressing area; living room with Bang & Olufsen entertainment center, wet bar, and private balcony.

Penthouse Suites (28): These measure 504–585 sq.ft (47–54.5 sq. meters). These have a separate bedroom with king-size bed and walk-in closet; the bathroom has a whirlpool tub, separate shower enclosure, two washbasins, dressing area; living room with Bang & Olufsen entertainment center, wet bar, and private balcony.

Family Suites (8): These measure around 360 sq.ft. (33.5 sq. meters). Each has a main bedroom with two twin beds that convert to a queen-size bed, a living room with double sofa bed and entertainment center, separate den with single sofa bed. Another four family "suites," measuring 330–380 sq.ft. (30.5–35 sq. meters), have an interconnecting door between two cabins; there are thus two bathrooms.

Standard Outside-View and Interior Cabins: Outside-view cabins have either a window or porthole, depending on location. All cabins have twin beds that can convert into a queen-size bed, TV, satellite-dial telephone, and personal safe; the bathrooms have a built-in hairdryer.

CUISINE. NCL's ships operate "Freestyle Cruising," which means that there are several restaurants and informal dining spots. You can choose from two main dining rooms, and six other à la carte, informal and casual spots, some of which incur a cover charge.

The 628-seat *Skyline Restaurant*, the first main restaurant, has decor inspired by the skyscrapers of the 1930s. The 496-seat *Liberty Dining Room*, the second main restaurant, has two seatings.

Alternative Dining Options:

● The *Lone Star Steak House* seats 106. It is a contemporary steak house with Texan decor – the artwork includes Houston Space Center, Texas Rangers and Dallas Cowboys.

● *China Town* is a Pacific Rim/Asian Fusion restaurant that has a sushi/sashimi bar and a Teppanyaki grill room with two tables (food is prepared in front of you with a bit of showmanship) that can accommodate up to 32.

● *Jefferson's Bistro*, which seats 104, is the ship's "signature" restaurant, with an à la carte menu of classic and nouvelle French cuisine. The decor is inspired by that of Thomas Jefferson's home in Monticello – Jefferson was the US ambassador to France from 1785 to 1789 before becoming America's third president.

● *Little Italy,* a casual Italian eatery, serves pasta, pizza and other popular light Italian fare. It has 116 seats.

● *Cadillac Diner* accommodates 106 (70 indoors, 36 outdoors) and is open 24 hours a day. It has Cadillac seats and a video juke box. There's fast food galore, with hamburgers and hot dogs, fish and chips, potpies, and wok dishes.

● *Aloha Cafe/Kids Café* is an indoor/outdoor self-serve buffet-style eatery with a Hawaiian theme; there are 322 indoor and 310 outdoor seats. A special section for children has counter tops just the right height, as well as chairs and tables that have been shrunk to a child-friendly size.

Other indoor eateries and bars include the *Napa Wine Bar* (wines by the glass), *Pink's Champagne and Cigar Bar* (inspired by Hawaii's Pink Palace Hotel on Waikiki Beach), the *Gold Rush* pub (with karaoke, plus a darts board and bar billiards), and the *John Adams Coffee Bar*. Outdoor eateries and drinking places include the *Key West Bar and Grill*, and the *Waikiki Bar*.

ENTERTAINMENT. The Hollywood Theater seats 840 and stages large-scale production shows and local Hawaiian shows. A 590-seat cabaret lounge, the Mardi Gras Lounge, has cabaret entertainment including late-night comedy.

SPA/FITNESS. The Santa Fe Spa and Fitness Center, decorated with artifacts from New Mexico, is designed to be a tranquil center for mind and body. It is staffed and operated by Mandara Spa (originating in Bali, now headquartered in Hawaii, but owned by Steiner Leisure), and includes Ayurvedic-style treatments.

While some fitness classes are free, others – such as yoga, and kick-boxing – usually cost extra.

Massage (including exotic massages such as Hot Stone, Lomi Lomi, and other well-being massages), facials, pedicures, and beauty salon treatments also cost extra.

● **For more extensive general information on what an NCL cruise is like, see pages 146–8.**

Princess Danae
★★★

Size:.....................Small Ship	Passenger Decks:..................7	Cabins (wheelchair accessible):.......0
Tonnage:.....................16,531	Total Crew:.....................240	Wheelchair accessibility:.........None
Lifestyle:..................Standard	Passengers	Cabin Current:..............220 volts
Cruise Line: .Classic International Cruises	(lower beds/all berths):........568/707	Elevators:.........................2
Former Names: *Baltica, Starlight Express,*	Passenger Space Ratio	Casino (gaming tables):.............Yes
Danae, Therisos Express, Port Melbourne	(lower beds/all berths):.......29.5/23.9	Slot Machines:....................Yes
Builder:............Swan, Hunter (UK)	Crew/Passenger Ratio	Swimming Pools (outdoors):..........1
Original Cost:....................n/a	(lower beds/all berths):.........2.3/2.7	Swimming Pools (indoors):..........0
Entered Service:........Jul 1955/1996	Cabins (total):....................283	Whirlpools:........................2
Registry:...................Panama	Size Range (sq ft/m): ..183.0–270.0/17.25	Self-Service Launderette:..........No
Length (ft/m):..........532.4/162.30	Cabins (outside view):.............217	Dedicated Cinema/Seats:.......Yes/130
Beam (ft/m):..............70.0/21.34	Cabins (interior/no view):...........66	Library:........................Yes
Draft (ft/m):..............25.2/7.69	Cabins (for one person):.............6	Onboard currency:.............Euros
Propulsion/Propellers: .diesel (9,850 kW)/2	Cabins (with private balcony):........6	

A pleasant traditional ship with good space and feel.

OVERVIEW. This ship has a traditional ambience, with some contemporary features and provides a moderately comfortable cruise in unpretentious surroundings. It is often chartered to tour operators, so its character and the level of food and service can change and may not always justify the ratings given here.It typically operates Caribbean cruises in winter and European cruises in summer.

THE SHIP. *Princess Danae* began as a cargo-passenger liner, was turned into a cruise ship in 1972, and was almost destroyed by fire in Genoa in 1991. Well-built with a deep draft, it is a good sea ship, and quite stable in all sea conditions. There is a decent amount of open deck space for sunbathing. It was refurbished in 2005–6, and some public rooms were revamped.

The interior decor is pleasing, but quite traditional, in keeping with the ship's character. The thick, real wood railings are constantly maintained to perfection, as are the brass fittings in the navigation bridge. Public rooms include a cinema – unusual for a ship of this size – a shop, small casino, piano bar, and a club room/library with integral bar.

The officers and crew are very friendly, and the service is warm and heartfelt. Gratuities, not included in the fare, are at your discretion.

Passenger niggles include the fact that there is no observation lounge with forward-facing views over the bows; much of the open deck area is covered with Astroturf; the white plastic sunloungers (wood or stainless would be better) look tacky and spoil the traditional feel of the ship.

ACCOMMODATION. There are 11 price grades. Most cab-

BERLITZ'S RATINGS

	Possible	Achieved
Ship	500	295
Accommodation	200	116
Food	400	234
Service	400	230
Entertainment	100	42
Cruise	400	218

OVERALL SCORE
1,135 points out of 2,000

ins are of good size, are quite comfortable, and have rather heavy-duty furniture and fittings with a decent amount of storage space. The lower-grade cabins are plain but adequate, with bathrooms that are minimal and functional, but uninviting. While 210 cabin bathrooms have a tub and shower, 70 have only a shower. Accommodation designated as suites (six with a private balcony) and junior suites also have a writing/ vanity desk, minibar, hairdryer, and satellite-link telephone. The towels are small.

CUISINE. The 394-seat *Mimosa Restaurant* is decorated quite nicely and has a high ceiling. It has open seating, and tables are for four, six or eight. The chairs do not have armrests. The cuisine is Continental/European, with some regional specialties. Typically, a self-serve buffet table is set up in the center of the restaurant for breakfast items, salads and cheeses for lunch, dinner and late-night snacks.

Casual, self-serve buffet meals are available in the *Lido Bar*, with its indoor-outdoor bamboo seating. There's a charming little *Garden Café* with bamboo furniture.

ENTERTAINMENT. The Main Lounge is a single-level room with 380 seats, and a thrust stage best used for cabaret acts. Stage lighting is minimal, and could be better. The ship carries a main band, and several small musical units, and solo pianists to provide live music for dancing or listening.

SPA/FITNESS. There is a gymnasium and sauna, and a windowless beauty salon.

Princess Daphne
★★★

Size: ....Small Ship	Propulsion/Propellers: diesel (9,850 kW)/2	Cabins (with private balcony): 6
Tonnage: 15,833	Passenger Decks: 7	Cabins (wheelchair accessible): 0
Lifestyle: ....Standard	Total Crew: 240	Wheelchair accessibility: ....None
Cruise Line: .Classic International Cruises	Passengers	Cabin Current: 220
Former Names: ....Ocean Monarch,	(lower beds/all berths): 479/594	Elevators: 2
Switzerland, Daphne,	Passenger Space Ratio	Casino (gaming tables): ....Yes
Akrotiri Express, Port Sydney	(lower beds/all berths): 33.0/26.6	Slot Machines: ....Yes
Builder: ....Swan, Hunter (UK)	Crew/Passenger Ratio	Swimming Pools (outdoors): 1
Original Cost: ....n/a	(lower beds/all berths): 1.9/2.4	Swimming Pools (indoors): 0
Entered Service: ....Mar 1955/2008	Cabins (total): 241	Whirlpools: 2
Registry: ....Madeira	Size Range (sq ft/m): ...200–270/18.5–25	Self-Service Launderette: ....No
Length (ft/m): 532.7/162.39	Cabins (outside view): 188	Dedicated Cinema/Seats: ....No
Beam (ft/m): 70.0/21.34	Cabins (interior/no view): 53	Library: ....Yes
Draft (ft/m): 41.9/12.80	Cabins (for one person): 0	Onboard currency: ....Euros

An older ship with lots of character and comfort.

OVERVIEW. *Princess Daphne* is best suited to adult couples and solo travelers of mature years who seek to cruise aboard a traditional style of ship that is of a handy size, with moderate facilities that are unpretentious yet quite comfortable, and at a modest cruise price. Refurbished in 2008, it provides a very comfortable cruise experience.

THE SHIP. *Princess Daphne*, sister to *Princess Danae*, is a solid ship built over half a century ago as a cargo-passenger liner for voyages between the UK and Australia, and converted in 1972 to a full-time cruise ship. Now, several owners later, it is run by Lisbon-based Classic International Cruises and also operates under charter to various other companies.

It has a pleasing, traditional profile, and the interior decor and furnishings combine the classic and contemporary. There are four bars, an internet-connect center, a library and card room, photo shop, boutique, fitness center, and a really good amount of outdoors space for sunbathing. The Portuguese crew are always polite and provide warm, friendly service.

There is, unfortunately, no forward observation lounge. Gratuities, not included in the fare, are at your discretion. Drinks prices are very reasonable.

ACCOMMODATION. There are 13 cabin price grades. All suites/cabins have a bathroom either with a full-size tub/shower combination or shower only, personal safe, multi-channel audio, TV set, and satellite-linked telephone. All cabins have good solid fittings, heavy-duty doors and plain decor. There really is plenty of closet and drawer space, but the cabin insulation is poor.

BERLITZ'S RATINGS

	Possible	Achieved
Ship	500	290
Accommodation	200	110
Food	400	225
Service	400	235
Entertainment	100	51
Cruise	400	217

OVERALL SCORE
1,128 points out of 2,000

Suites: The largest accommodation is in six of the 27 suites. Each has a separate bedroom, with double bed. The living room has a sofa, large glass-topped coffee table, writing desk, TV set, radio channels, hairdryer and personal safe. The bathroom has a full-size tub/shower, washbasin and toilet. Each suite has a private balcony.

Standard Exterior View or Interior Cabins: Some grades have double beds, while others have an L-shaped two lower bed configuration.

CUISINE. *The Restaurant* has 476 seats, large picture windows, and an uncluttered seating arrangement, with several tables for two located by large picture windows; other tables are for four, six or eight. Breakfast, lunch, and dinner are served in a single seating. Casual self-serve buffet lunches can also be taken in the *Neptune Bar*, with views aft over the ship's swimming pool and hot tubs.

ENTERTAINMENT. The Main Lounge, seating 350, is designed for cabaret acts. There is a wooden dance floor, and a marginally raised "stage", but it's not a showlounge – just a lounge with a small stage. There are several slim pillars, and seating is in tub chairs. Sightlines from seats not close to the stage are quite poor. However, entertainment is a low-key affair. The room is better as a lecture hall, and for dancing.

SPA/FITNESS. There is a decent-sized health spa, built in what was formerly a cinema. It houses a gymnasium, with a reasonable array of muscle-toning equipment, changing area, sauna, and several massage/treatment rooms.

Prinsendam
★★★★ +

Size: . . . . .Mid-Size Ship	Passenger Decks: 9	Cabins (with private balcony): 166
Tonnage: 37,983	Total Crew: 443	Cabins (wheelchair accessible): 10
Lifestyle: . . . . .Premium	Passengers	Wheelchair accessibility: . . . . .Best
Cruise Line: . . . . . . .Holland America Line	(lower beds/all berths): 837/837	Cabin Current: . . . . .110 volts
Former Names: . . . .*Seabourn Sun,*	Passenger Space Ratio	Elevators: 4
Royal Viking Sun	(lower beds/all berths): 45.3/45.3	Casino (gaming tables): . . . . .Yes
Builder: . . . . .Wartsila (Finland)	Crew/Passenger Ratio	Slot Machines: .Yes
Original Cost: . . . .$125 million	(lower beds/all berths): 1.8/1.8	Swimming Pools (outdoors): 2
Entered Service: . . . .Dec 1988/May 2002	Cabins (total): 395	Swimming Pools (indoors): 0
Registry: . . . . .The Netherlands	Size Range (sq ft/m): 137.7–723.3/	Whirlpools: 4
Length (ft/m): 674.2/205.5	12.8–67.2	Self-Service Launderette: . . . . .Yes
Beam (ft/m): 91.8/28.0	Cabins (outside view): 388	Dedicated Cinema/Seats: Yes/101
Draft (ft/m): 23.6/7.2	Cabins (interior/no view): 31	Library: . . . . .Yes
Propulsion/Propellers: diesel (21,120 kW)/2	Cabins (for one person): 3	Onboard currency: . . . . .US$

A very comfortable ship that provides a premium ambience.

OVERVIEW. This ship is best suited to older adult couples and singles who like to mingle in a mid-size ship operating longer cruises, in an unhurried setting with some eclectic, antique artwork, good food and service from a smiling Indonesian and Filipino crew who like to serve but who lack finesse. It is an extremely comfortable vessel – smaller than other Holland America Line ships, and more refined.

THE SHIP. *Prinsendam* is a contemporary, well-designed ship with sleek, flowing lines, a sharply raked bow, and a well-rounded profile, with lots of floor-to-ceiling glass. Having started life as *Royal Viking Sun*, it was bought by Seabourn Cruise Line in 1998 and refitted as *Seabourn Sun*. In 2002, it was transferred to Holland America Line as *Prinsendam*, and the hull color was changed from all-white to a dark blue hull with white superstructure. A 2007 refit added an Explorations Café and expanded the shopping arcade. In 2009 an aft deck, including 21 new cabins, was added.

Wide teak wood decks provide excellent walking areas including a decent walk-around promenade deck outdoors. The swimming pool, outdoors on Lido Deck, is not large, but it is quite adequate, while the deck above has a croquet court and golf driving range. The interior layout is very spacious – it is even more ideal when no more than 600 passengers are aboard. Impressive public rooms and tasteful decor now reign. Two handrails – one of wood, one of chrome – are provided on all stairways, a thoughtful touch.

The Crow's Nest, the forward observation lounge, is an elegant, contemporary (at least in decor), lounge. Pebble Beach is the name of the electronic golf simulator room,

BERLITZ'S RATINGS		
	Possible	Achieved
Ship	500	416
Accommodation	200	174
Food	400	315
Service	400	326
Entertainment	100	82
Cruise	400	329
OVERALL SCORE		
1,642 points out of 2,000		

complete with wet bar, with play possible on 11 virtual courses.

The Erasmus Library (formerly the Ibsen Library) is well organized, although it is simply not large enough for long-distance cruising. The former Compass Rose room has now become the Explorer's Lounge.

The Oak Room is the ship's cigar/pipe smoker's lounge; it has a marble fireplace, which sadly cannot be used due to United States Coast Guard regulations. I have always thought it would make a fine library, although it is also excellent as a cigar smoking room. There is a computer-learning center, with several workstations.

Whether by intention or not, the ship has a two-class feeling, with passengers in "upstairs" penthouse suites and "A" grade staterooms gravitating to the quieter Crow's Nest lounge, particularly at night, while other passengers go to the main entertainment deck.

The wide range of facilities includes a concierge, self-service launderettes (useful on long voyages), a varied guest lecture program, 24-hour information office, and true 24-hour cabin service for the discriminating passenger who demands spacious personal surroundings and good food and service, regardless of price. This ship operates mainly long-distance cruises in great comfort, and free shuttle buses are provided in almost all ports of call.

While *Prinsendam* isn't perfect, the few design flaws (for example: poorly designed bar service counters) are minor points. The elegant decorative features include Dutch artwork and memorabilia. Added benefits include a fine health spa facility, spacious, wide teakwood decks and many teak sunloungers.

However, the good points are marred by the bland quality of the dining room food and service, and, whatever the company's brochures state, the lack of understanding of what it takes to make a "luxury" cruise experience.

There are only four elevators, so anyone with walking disabilities may have to wait for some time during periods of peak usage, such as before meals. This spacious ship shows signs of wear and tear in some areas, particularly in the accommodation passageways, despite recent refurbishments. The library is too small, especially for some of the long cruises, and is difficult to enter for anyone in a wheelchair. The shore tenders are thoughtfully air-conditioned.

ACCOMMODATION. There are 15 grades, ranging from Penthouse Verandah Suites to standard interior cabins. All suites and cabins have undergone some degree of refurbishment since the ship was taken over by Holland America Line in 2002.

Penthouse Verandah Suite: The Penthouse Verandah Suite (723 sq. ft/67 sq. meters), is a most desirable living space, although not as large as penthouse suites aboard some other ships. It is light and airy, with two bathrooms, one of which has a large whirlpool tub with ocean views, and anodized gold bathroom fittings. The living room contains a large dining table and chairs, and large sofas. There is also a substantial private balcony, and butler service.

Deluxe Verandah Suites: There are 18 of these (eight on Sports Deck, 10 on Lido Deck). Located in the forward section, they have large balconies, two sofas, and large bar/entertainment center (mini-bar/refrigerator, color television, video and CD players). Bathrooms have separate toilet, sink and toiletries cabinets, connecting sliding door into the bedroom, large mirror, two toiletries cabinets, plenty of storage space, full bathtub, and anodized gold fittings. Each evening the butler brings different goodies – hot and cold hors d'oeuvres and other niceties. If you do choose one of these suites, it might be best on the starboard side where they are located in a private hallway, while those on the port side (including the Penthouse Verandah Suite) are positioned along a public hallway. The 10 suites on Lido Deck are positioned along private port and starboard side hallways.

Passengers in Penthouse and Deluxe Verandah Suites are provided with a private concierge lounge, high tea served in the suite each afternoon, hors d'oeuvres before dinner each evening (on request), complimentary laundry pressing and dry cleaning, private cocktail parties with captain, priority disembarkation, and more.

Other Cabin Grades: Most of the other cabins, spread over six other decks, are of generous proportions and have just about everything you would need, including a video player. About 38 percent have a small, private balcony. All cabins have walk-in closets, lockable drawers, full-length mirrors, hairdryers, and ample cotton towels. A few cabins have third berths, while some have interconnecting doors – good for couples who want two bathrooms and more space or for families with children.

In all grades of accommodation, passengers receive a basket of fresh fruit, fluffy cotton bathrobes, evening turn-down service, and a Holland America Line signature tote bag. Filipino and Indonesian cabin stewards and stewardesses provide unobtrusive personal service.

Four well-equipped, L-shaped cabins for the disabled are quite well designed, fairly large, and equipped with special wheel-in bathrooms with shower facilities and closets.

CUISINE. *La Fontaine Dining Room* wraps around the aft end of Lower Promenade Deck and has extensive ocean-view windows; along the starboard side is a second, smaller and quieter section. There is plenty of space around tables. A good number of window-side tables are for two persons, although there are also tables for four, six or eight. Crystal glasses, and Rosenthal china and fine cutlery are provided.

There are two seatings for dinner, at assigned tables, and an open-seating arrangement for breakfast and lunch – you'll be seated by restaurant staff when you enter.

Alternative Dining Option: A small, quiet dining spot on the port side is the *Pinnacle Dining Room*, with 48 seats, wood-paneled decor that increases the feeling of intimacy and privacy, and great ocean views. Table settings include Bulgari china, Reidel glassware, and Frette table linens. The venue specializes in fine steaks and seafood. Seating preference is given to suite occupants. Reservations are required, and there is a cover charge. There is a well-chosen wine list, although there is a great deal of emphasis on California wines, with prices that are quite high.

There is also an enlarged *Lido Restaurant*, for decent casual dining and self-serve buffet-style meals. This eatery has both indoor and outdoor seating.

ENTERTAINMENT. The Queens showlounge is an amphitheater-style layout, with a well tiered floor, and both banquette and individual seating. While Holland America Line isn't known for fine entertainment, what it does offer is a consistently good, tried and tested array of cabaret acts. There are male "dance hosts" who act as partners for women traveling alone.

SPA/FITNESS. The extensive Greenhouse Health Spa includes six treatment rooms with integral showers, a rasul chamber (for mud and gentle steam heat treatments, combined with gentle steam), a gymnasium with views over the stern, and separate sauna, steam room, and changing rooms for men and women. The spa is operated by Steiner.

● **For more extensive general information on what a Holland America Line cruise is like, see pages 140–3.**

Professor Multanovskiy
★★

Size:	Boutique Ship	Total Crew:	25
Tonnage:	1,753	Passengers	
Lifestyle:	Standard	(lower beds/all berths):	49/49
Cruise Line:	Oceanwide Expeditions	Passenger Space Ratio	
Former Names:	none	(lower beds/all berths):	35.7/35.7
Builder:	Wartsila (Finland)	Crew/Passenger Ratio	
Original Cost:	n/a	(lower beds/all berths):	1.9/1.9
Entered Service:	1983	Cabins (total):	29
Registry:	Russia	Size Range (sq ft/m):	n/a
Length (ft/m):	213.2/65.0	Cabins (outside view):	29
Beam (ft/m):	42/12.8	Cabins (interior/no view):	0
Draft (ft/m):	15.0/4.6	Cabins (for one person):	9
Propulsion/Propellers: diesel (2,327 kW)/2		Cabins (with private balcony):	0
Passenger Decks:	3	Cabins (wheelchair accessible):	0

Wheelchair accessibility:	None
Cabin Current:	220 volts
Elevators:	0
Casino (gaming tables):	No
Slot Machines:	No
Swimming Pools (outdoors):	0
Swimming Pools (indoors):	0
Whirlpools:	0
Self-Service Launderette:	No
Dedicated Cinema/Seats:	No
Library:	Yes
Onboard currency:	US$

A small ship for nature and wildlife cruises.

OVERVIEW. This is expedition-style cruising in a very small ship with limited facilities. It appeals to hardy, adventurous couples and single travelers who enjoy viewing nature and wildlife at close quarters, and don't feel the need for onboard entertainment. Bigger ships cannot get this close to Antarctica or the Arctic, but this little vessel will take you as close to the ice as possible.

THE SHIP. *Professor Multanovskiy,* which has a dark hull and white superstructure, was originally built in Finland for the former Soviet Union's polar and oceanographic research programme run by the Russian Academy of Science. It should not be taken as a cruise ship, although it was converted in the early 1990s to carry passengers, and then fitted out specifically for expedition cruising when refurbished in 1996. Other ships in the series are *Akademik Boris Petrov, Akademik Golitsyn, Akademik M.A. Laurentiev, Akademik Nikolaj Strakhov, Akademik Shokalskiy, Livonia, Professor Khromov,* and *Professor Molchanov.*

This ship is usually operated under charter to various "expedition" cruise companies. It has an ice-hardened, steel hull, which is good for cruising in both the Arctic and Antarctic, and strong Russian diesel engines. All passengers have access to the navigation bridge. There are several inflatable Zodiac landing craft for close-in shore excursions and nature observation trips. Inside, the limited public rooms consist of a library and lounge/bar. The dining rooms are also used for lectures. Medical facilities are good.

The ship provides a somewhat primitive, but genuine

BERLITZ'S RATINGS		
	Possible	Achieved
Ship	500	227
Accommodation	200	87
Food	400	203
Service	400	188
Entertainment	n/a	n/a
Cruise	500	242
OVERALL SCORE		
947 points out of 2,000		

adventure experience, taking you up-close and personal to places others only dream about. Quark Expeditions charters it for the Antarctic (winter) season, and has its own staff and lecturers on board. It also oversees the food, to make sure that everything is up to its usual high standard.

ACCOMMODATION. There are five grades, the price depending on grade and location. Except for one "suite," almost all cabins are very small, spartan, and rather clinical. There are two-berth cabins with shower and toilet, and two-bed cabins on the lowest deck, whose occupants have to share a bathroom.

CUISINE. There are two dining rooms, with the galley between them) and a single seating. The meals are hearty international fare, with no frills. When the ship is under charter to Quark Expeditions, Western rather than Russian chefs oversee the food operation, and the quality of meals and variety of foods is much better.

ENTERTAINMENT. There is no formal entertainment, although dinner and after-dinner conversation with fellow passengers in the ship's lounge/bar really becomes the entertainment each evening. So, if you don't want to talk to your fellow passengers, take a good book, or go outside, where you'll find nature is nothing less than diverting.

SPA/FITNESS. There are no spa or fitness facilities, although there is a sauna.

Queen Elizabeth
★★★★+ to ★★★★

Size: . . . . .Large Resort Ship	Passenger Decks: 12	Cabins (with private balcony): 820
Tonnage: .90,900	Total Crew: .1,003	Cabins (wheelchair accessible): 20
Lifestyle: . . . . .Standard	Passengers	Wheelchair accessibility:: . . . . .Good
Cruise Line: . . . . .Cunard Line	(lower beds/all berths): 2,092/2,172	Cabin Current: . . . . .110/220 volts
Former Names: . . . . .none	Passenger Space Ratio	Elevators: 12
Builder: . . . . .Fincantieri (Italy)	(lower beds/all berths): 43.4/41.8	Casino (gaming tables): . . . . .Yes
Original Cost: . . . . €634 million	Crew/Passenger Ratio	Slot Machines: . . . . .Yes
Entered Service: . . . . .Oct 2010	(lower beds/all berths): 2.0/2.1	Swimming Pools (outdoors): 2
Registry: . . . . .Great Britain	Cabins (total): 1,046	Swimming Pools (indoors): 0
Length (ft/m): 964.5/294.0	Size Range (sq ft/m): . .152.0–1,493 sq.ft/	Whirlpools: 5
Beam (ft/m): 105.9/32.3	14.0–138.5	Self-Service Launderette: . . . . .Yes
Draft (ft/m): 26.2/8.0	Cabins (outside view): 892	Dedicated Cinema/Seats: . . . . .No
Propulsion/Propellers: . . . . diesel-electric	Cabins (interior/no view): 154	Library: . . . . .Yes
(64.0 MW)/2 azimuthing pods	Cabins (for one person): 0	Onboard currency: . . . . .US$

A delightful interior decor that represents British heritage.

OVERVIEW. *Queen Elizabeth*, a cruise ship that longs to be an ocean liner, suits mature adults and solo travelers, and families with children. It is pitched at traditionalists who like to dress more formally for dinner, and sail with a sense of occasion and style. Cunard purports to offer a resolutely British experience – although the marketing hype is undermined by the use of US dollars as the onboard currency, and trying to find British service staff is challenging.

THE SHIP. The red ensign continues, as does the instantly recognizable Cunard red funnel. *Queen Elizabeth*, named in the company's 170th year, is the second largest Cunarder ordered in that long history. The first section of the keel, weighing 364 tons, was laid on 2 July 2009 in Fincantieri's Monfalcone shipyard.

The ship is a pretend ocean liner, and, with its "Vista"-class hull design, is susceptible to rolling and pitching, like sister ship *Queen Victoria*. Anyone comparing this ship with the former *Queen Elizabeth 2* can't fail to notice the difference in the design of the stern – *QE2*'s was beautifully rounded, while the new ship's is totally flat and boxy. However, it does allow for more open lido deck/pool space – good on warm weather cruises. The foredeck is disappointing.

Once you are inside, the ship feels instantly comfortable, rather like a mini-*QE2*. It has less somber colors than *Queen Victoria*, commendably little glitzy brass or chrome surfaces in the public areas, and more of the look and feel of a real ocean liner, including some gorgeous carpeting. The decor is

BERLITZ'S RATINGS

Grill Class	Possible	Achieved
Ship	500	433
Accommodation	200	166
Food	400	331
Service	400	333
Entertainment	100	84
Cruise	400	343
Britannia Class		
Ship	500	404
Accommodation	200	125
Food	400	274
Service	400	292
Entertainment	100	84
Cruise	400	314

OVERALL SCORE
1,690 points (Grill Class)
1,493 (Britannia Class)
out of 2,000

classic and timeless. Unlike *Queen Mary 2*, it can transit the Panama Canal – useful for long voyages.

Nice touches like destination-themed sail-away music, the afternoon tea experience, a wide variety of entertainment – including an extremely varied Cunard Insights lecture program – and decent service, albeit lacking in finesse, help Cunard to stand out from the crowd. It provides a traditional setting for those who enjoy dressing properly for dinner. Passengers get cocktail parties, and enjoy the lecturers and speakers who sail on each voyage – Cunard cunningly calls them voyages, not cruises.

The ship has a few more cabins, and therefore more passengers, than *Queen Victoria*, but the dimensions and number of elevators remain the same. Outdoors facilities include a promenade deck; unfortunately it's not teak, but a rubberized deck covering made to look like wooden planking, which gets hot and stays hot in warm weather areas. You can almost walk around – the forward section is for marine use only – with several deck lounge chairs with comfortable Cunard-logo cushioned pads; it's a good place to read a book. In fact, there are lots of nooks and crannies to sit and read.

One open deck atop the ship has a life-size chess board, adjacent to the crocquet and bowls area.

Other features include a majestic three-deck high Grand Lobby with a sweeping staircase, sculpted balconies and elegant decorative touches, and an adjacent Cunarders' Galleria floating museum whose glass cabinets display memorabilia.

In the Yacht Club is the original Asprey silver model of *QE2*, and there's a nice model of the original *Queen Elizabeth* in a cabinet at the back of the Café Carinthia.

One "wow" factor in the main lobby is a painting of the Queen by Isobel Peachey, at 31 the youngest person to paint the monarch. Commissioned by Cunard, it shows Her Majesty in the yellow drawing room at Buckingham Palace, dressed in blue and wearing Queen Victoria's collet necklace and earrings. Another beautiful piece of art is a stunning 18½-ft (5.6-meter) David Linley marquetry panel "sculpture" that adorns the three-deck grand stairway. Crafted from nine natural woods, it depicts the port bow of the original *Queen Elizabeth* as seen from sea level.

Several public rooms are two decks high; these include the gold-beige Queen's Room, with a large, wooden ballroom dance floor measuring about 1,000 sq.ft (93 sq. meters); above are two huge ceiling-mounted chandeliers. The bandstand is fronted by a large proscenium arch, while cantilevered balconies line the room's starboard side.

Traditional British afternoon tea is served in this art deco-style grand room with Twinings tea or premium teas from the Twinings Rituals Collection. Artwork in entrance to this ballroom includes a gold bust of the Queen by Oscar Nemon; a replica of the Cunard-commissioned portrait of Princess Elizabeth and the Duke of Edinburgh displayed in *Caronia*'s main lounge before being moved to *QE2*; and *QE2* launch ceremonies painted by the Italian artist Diego Bormida.

The Royal Arcade is a cluster of several shops, selling goods connected with traditional and modern-day Britain, all set in an arcade-like environment; they include Hackett (country clothing), Penhaligon's, and Aspinal of London. There's a separate Fortnum & Mason shop.

The Library is a stunning two-deck-high wood-paneled 6,000-book facility serviced by full-time librarians, although there are few chairs in which to sit in and read. Few ships today have such a fine library. There's a good bookshop (on the same deck as the lower level of the library) selling maritime-related books, memorabilia, maps and stationery.

Gratuities – called a Hotel and Dining charge, of $11–$13 per person, depending on your accommodation grade – are added to your onboard account daily.

Passenger niggles? The layout is a little disjointed on the uppermost decks, although the general flow is reasonably good. Access between the aft deck and the pool area and Winter Garden can be gained mainly by going through the expansive buffet area. This causes congestion at the self-serve buffet as people are constantly passing through, as in a railway carriage. Some formerly free classes now incur a charge (example: the computer class costs $30). Despite the hype, afternoon tea in the Queens Room could be better (Cunard must know the British use freshly boiled water).

Despite these minor reservations, *Queen Elizabeth* provides an elegant setting for a traditional cruise experience, with a wide choice of public rooms, bars and lounges, and a mostly attentive staff that provides the kind of service that's hard to find on land today. But, in the final analysis, the finesse is missing, and the ship's Princess-style cabins are below the standard expected of a real Cunarder.

ACCOMMODATION. There are three class categories of accommodation: Queens Grill, seven price grades; Princess Grill, four price grades; Britannia Accommodation, 21 price grades. That's 32 different price grades! Still, it's all about location, location, location. Yet however much or little you pay, passengers all embark and disembark via the same gangway. In keeping with maritime tradition, even-numbered cabins are on the port side, with odd-numbered cabins on the starboard side. The six top suites are named after former Cunard commodores, all of whom have been knighted by the Queen.

The amount of drawer space in the standard cabins is less than one would expect, and there is little room for luggage storage. Note that the air conditioning cannot be turned off in cabins or bathrooms.

Grand Suites: four units, measuring 1,918–2,131 sq.ft (178–184 sq. meters). Named Bisset, Charles, Illingworth and Rostron, they are located aft, with great ocean views from their private wrap-around balconies, which contain a complete wet bar. The suites have two bedrooms with walk-in closets; bathroom with tub and separate shower enclosure; lounge; and dining room with seating for six. In-suite dining from the Queens Grill menus is also available.

Master Suites: two units, measuring 1,100 sq.ft (102 sq. meters). Named Britten and Thomson, they are located in the center of the ship.

Penthouse Suites, measuring 520–707 sq.ft (48–65 sq. meters).

Queens Suites, measuring 508–771 sq.ft (47–72 sq. meters).

Princess Suites, measuring 342–513 sq.ft (32–48 sq. meters).

Balcony Cabins, measuring 242–472 sq.ft (22–44 sq. meters).

Outside-View Cabins, measuring 180–201 sq.ft (17–9 sq. meters).

Interior (no-view) Cabins, measuring 151–243 sq.ft (14–23 sq. meters).

All accommodation grades have both British three-pin (240-volt) sockets and American and European-style two-pin (110-volt) sockets. Gilchrist & Soames toiletries are supplied to all passengers, and a hairdryer is stored in the vanity desk units. Some cabins have nicely indented ceilings with suffused lighting.

The regular cabins (Grades C/D) are small, but functional. However, the cabinetry resembles that in an Ibis hotel – a bit austere and lacking in character. There's a lack of drawer space in a cabin supposedly designed for two persons – it's noticeable on long voyages, and the additional drawers located under the bed may prove challenging for some to use. The premium mattresses are excellent – as is the bed linen. European duvets are standard.

The bathrooms, too, are rather bland, similar to those found aboard the ships of Princess Cruises, with small washbasins, and little storage space for toiletries. The fixed-head shower doesn't permit the thorough wash that handheld flexible hoses do. Overall, the standard (lower-grade) cabins are a little underwhelming – so, for more space and quality, consider booking one of the higher-grade cabins, or, better still, go for Grill-class accommodation – the perks and increased attention and service are really worth it. The walls in most accommodation passageways are rather plain, and could do with a little artwork to dress them up.

CUISINE. Cunard Line is respected for its old-world cuisine and service, with a wide variety of well-prepared and presented dishes made from good ingredients. The 878-seat *Britannia Restaurant* – the name is taken from a former Cunard ocean liner of 1914–50 – is located in the aft section. It is two decks high, with seating on both main and balcony levels, and two seatings for dinner; stairways link both levels. An adjacent Britannia Club Restaurant houses "Britannia Club" passengers, who get single-seat dining. Waterford Wedgwood china is provided.

Exclusive Dining (Queens Grill, Princess Grill): As with its sister ships, there are two special Grill-Class-only restaurants. These have a single-seating arrangement, providing a more intimate and exclusive dining experience than can be found in the two-seating main Britannia Restaurant.

The 142-seat *Queens Grill* (on the port side), with single-seating dining, is for those in suites and the top accommodation grades, and provides the best cuisine and service aboard the ship. The beloved Cunard Grill experience includes alfresco dining in *The Courtyard*, a seldom-used courtyard terrace protected from the wind, and access for Grill-class passengers only to an exclusive lounge and bar to their own upper terrace deck, with dedicated staff.

The 132-seat *Princess Grill* (on the starboard side), with single-seating dining, is for passengers in middle-class accommodation grades.

The *Verandah Restaurant* is a beautiful "alternative" à la carte dining venue, available to all passengers. It has a bar and is on the second level of the three-deck high lobby. The decor and ambience recreate the Verandah Grill restaurant aboard the original *Queen Elizabeth* and *Queen Mary*. The classic French cuisine is exceptionally good, and makes for a fine dining experience. Reservations are required, and there's a cover charge for lunch or dinner.

Casual Eatery: The *Lido Café* (on Deck 11) has panoramic views, indoor/outdoor seating for approximately 470, and operates a fairly standard multi-line self-serve buffet arrangement. It's a bit downmarket for what is supposed to be a stylish ship – the original *Queen Elizabeth* didn't have such a facility – but then, these are different times. At night, the venue is transformed into three distinct flavours: *Asado* (South American Grill); *Aztec* (Mexican cuisine); and *Jasmine* (Asian cuisine), each with a small cover charge.

For coffees, teas and light bites, there's the Parisian-style *Café Carinthia*, one deck above the Purser's Desk and adjacent to the popular *Veuve Clicquot* champagne bar.

For traditional British pub food, the *Golden Lion Pub* offers fish 'n' chips, steak and mushroom pie, a ploughman's lunch, and, of course, bangers (sausages) and mash. There's a wide range of draft beers and lagers.

ENTERTAINMENT. The 830-seat, three-deck-high Royal Court Theatre is designed in the style of a classic opera house. It has 20 private "royal boxes" that can be reserved by anyone for special nights, and a special package includes champagne, chocolates and a ticket printed with name and box number – in the tradition of a real London West End theatre. There's a lounge for pre-show drinks.

Colorful, large cast production shows and a good variety of cabaret entertainment are presented here. The Royal Court Theatre is also used to show large-screen movies. The ship has a number of bands, small combos and solo entertainers. A Big Band night is sometimes held in the Queens Room, where afternoon tea is served and live music is provided. Some bars and lounges have live jazz.

SPA/FITNESS. The Cunard Royal Health Club and Spa consists of a beauty salon, large gymnasium with high-tech muscle-pumping equipment and great ocean views; an aerobics area; separate changing rooms for men and women, each with its own ocean-view sauna; a Thermal Area with sauna and steam rooms (extra-cost day passes are available if you don't book a treatment, at $35 per day, or at less per day cost for a multi-use pass); several body treatment rooms; a rasul chamber for private Hammam-style mud/steam bathing; and a relaxation area. A 12½% gratuity is added to all spa treatment prices.

Sports include paddle tennis, croquet, British bowls, and life-size chess.

● **For more extensive general information on what a Cunard Line cruise is like, see pages 138–9.**

Queen Mary 2
★★★★★ to ★★★★

Size: . . . . .Large Ocean Liner	Passenger Decks: 12	Cabins (wheelchair accessible): 30
Tonnage: .148,528	Total Crew: 1,254	Wheelchair accessibility: . . . . .Best
Lifestyle: . . . . .Luxury/Premium/Standard	Passengers	Cabin Current: . . . . .110 and 220 volts
Cruise Line: . . . . .Cunard Line	(lower beds/all berths): 2,620/3,090	Elevators: 22
Former Names: . . . . .none	Passenger Space Ratio	Casino (gaming tables): . . . . .Yes
Builder: Chantiers de l'Atlantique (France)	(lower beds/all berths): 56.6/48.0	Slot Machines: . . . . .Yes
Original Cost: . . . .$800 million	Crew/Passenger Ratio	Swimming Pools (outdoors): 3
Entered Service: . . . . .Jan 2004	(lower beds/all berths): 2.0/2.4	Swimming Pools (indoors): 2
Registry: . . . . .Great Britain	Cabins (total): 1,310	Whirlpools: 8
Length (ft/m): 1,131.9/345.03	Size Range (sq ft/m): 194.0–2,249.7/	Self-Service Launderette: . . . . .Yes
Beam (ft/m): 134.5/41.00	18.0–209	Dedicated Cinema/Seats: . . . . .Yes
Draft (ft/m): 32.6/9.95	Cabins (outside view): 1,017	Library: . . . . .Yes
Propulsion/Propellers: . . . . . .gas turbine	Cabins (interior/no view): 293	Onboard currency: . . . . .US$
(103 MW) and diesel-electric/4 pods	Cabins (for one person): 0	
(2 azimuthing, 2 fixed/21.5 MW each)	Cabins (with private balcony): 953	

A real ocean liner built for transatlantic crossings.

OVERVIEW. *Queen Mary 2* offers the pleasures of crossing the North Atlantic comfortably on a regular schedule, with the latest high-tech facilities and conveniences. It is best suited to couples and single travelers who enjoy the cosmopolitan setting of a floating city at sea with an unequaled maritime heritage and background and an extensive array of facilities, public rooms, and dining rooms. A powerful propulsion system allows the ship to go backwards faster than many cruise ships can go forwards.

THE SHIP. RMS *Queen Mary 2*, designated a Royal Mail Ship by the British Post Office, is the largest passenger ship ever built – in terms of gross tonnage, length, and beam, though not passengers carried – and is five times the length of Cunard Line's first ship, *Britannia*, which plied the North Atlantic from 1840. Taller than the Empire State Building, it is the first new ship to be built for Cunard Line since 1969, when *QE2* first sailed from Southampton to New York. In additon to its scheduled transatlantic crossings, *QM2* operates an annual round-the-world cruise.

Its exterior design resembles that of the now retired *QE2*, and for good reason: it was designed by naval architect Stephen Payne, an ocean liner specialist. This superbly designed ship is able to weather any unkind conditions on the North Atlantic, or anywhere else – hence the long foredeck, extra-thick plating and hull, designed to maintain a high speed and battle against unkind sea conditions. It has a large, contemporary funnel and beautifully tiered stern, but it is

BERLITZ'S RATINGS		
Grill Class	Possible	Achieved
Ship	**500**	**440**
Accommodation	**200**	**175**
Food	**400**	**325**
Service	**400**	**335**
Entertainment	**100**	**84**
Cruise	**400**	**343**
Britannia Class		
Ship	**500**	**408**
Accommodation	**200**	**147**
Food	**400**	**280**
Service	**400**	**295**
Entertainment	**100**	**83**
Cruise	**400**	**328**

OVERALL SCORE
1,702 points (Grill Class)
1,541 (Britannia Class)
out of 2,000

too wide to transit the Panama Canal.

The ship is propeled by the world's first four-pod propulsion system (Rolls-Royce), which can power through the waters of the North Atlantic at up to 30 knots – the contracted top speed is 29.3 knots, but the ship can easily exceed this. Each pod weighs 270 tons – more than an empty Boeing 747 jumbo jet – and they are powered by a diesel-electric system.

One of the many delightful features is the ship's Tyfon whistle: (there are two: one is new, and the other a copy of the whistle from the original *Queen Mary*). Both whistles are tuned so that they do not disturb passengers on deck, yet they can be heard 10 miles away.

Almost everything about the liner is British in style, but with some American decor input and accents, and even the four tender stations have London names: Belgravia, Chelsea, Kensington and Knightsbridge. There is a wide walk-around promenade deck outdoors, with the forward section under cover from the weather or wind. Three times around is 6,102 ft (1,860 meters), or 1.1 miles (1.6 km). Inside are several other walking promenades – good if the weather is poor. A full line of teak "steamer" chairs are provided on the open walk-around promenade deck, but still leaves plenty of room for walkers to pass. However, plastic sunloungers are provided on some other open decks – particularly at the aft of the ship.

Robert Tillberg, the interior designer, produced a stylish, elegant interior design, with towering public spaces, sweeping staircases and grand public rooms that exude a feeling of timelessness. High ceilings – typically two decks of *QM2* are the equivalent of three decks in height of a regular cruise vessel – provide a great sense of space and grandeur. While many ships are designed inward with a central atrium, *QM2* is different. You enter the public rooms from a central location and will always be looking out, with the sea in the background. Deck signage is good, and it's quite easy to find one's way around the ship for the most part, although more fore and aft signs would be useful.

There are a few ostentatious gold pillars and tacky decorative elements, including some awful "bas-reliefs" in the accommodation passageways – perhaps the "Miami Beach" view of what a transatlantic liner looks like. But, for the most part, the ship's interiors are quite stunning, and subtly so. The use of wood laminate paneling may abhor ship buffs, as did the plastic laminates when *QE2* debuted in 1968–69, but is the result of stringent SOLAS regulations.

The atrium lobby, spanning six decks, has an elegant staircase and exclusive works of art. In the main elevator lobby attached to the central atrium, a wall mural of Samuel Cunard welcomes you aboard; it looks like an enlarged photograph, although it is made from almost 700 postage stamp-sized digital images of previous Cunard ships.

Here's a deck-by-deck look at the facilities and public rooms, starting at the lowest deck and working our way upward, forward to aft:

● Deck 2 has Illuminations (with planetarium), and the Royal Court Theatre, the lower level of the six-deck high atrium lobby, the Purser's Desk, Video Arcade, Empire Casino, Golden Lion Pub, and the lower level of the two-deck high Britannia Restaurant.

● Deck 3 has the upper level of Illuminations and the Royal Court Theatre, the second level of the six-deck high atrium lobby, Mayfair Shops, Sir Samuel's, The Chart Room, Champagne Bar (Veuve Clicquot is the "house" champagne), the upper level of the Britannia Restaurant, the Queens Room, and the G32 Nightclub.

● Decks 4/Deck 5/Deck 6 have accommodation and the third, fourth and fifth levels of the six-deck high atrium lobby; at the aft end of Deck 6 are the facilities for children, including an outdoor pool (Minnows Pool).

● Deck 7 has the Canyon Ranch Spa, the Winter Garden, the sixth and uppermost level of the six-deck high atrium lobby, expansive Kings Court Buffet, Queens Grill Lounge, Queens Grill and Princess Grill dining salons.

● Deck 8 (forward) has the upper level of the Canyon Ranch Spa, and the Library and Bookshop. The center section has accommodation. In the aft section are the alternative restaurant Todd English, Terrace Bar, and swimming pool outdoors.

● Deck 9 (forward) has the Commodore Club, Boardroom and the Cigar Club (Churchills). The rest of the deck has accommodation and a Concierge Club for suite occupants.

● Deck 10 has accommodation only.

● Deck 11 (forward) has an outdoors observation area. The rest of the deck has accommodation. The aft section outdoors has a whirlpool tub and sunbathing deck.

● Deck 12 (forward) has accommodation. The mid-section has an indoor/outdoor pool with sliding glass roof, and golf areas (Fairways), located just aft of the public restrooms. The aft section has the Boardwalk Café, dog kennels, and shuffleboard courts.

● Deck 13 has the Sports Centre, Regatta Bar, a splash pool, and extensive outdoor sunbathing space.

There are 14 lounges, clubs and bars. An observation lounge, the delightful Commodore Club, has commanding views forward over the bows; light jazz is played in this bar, which is connected to the Boardroom, and Cigar Lounge. Other drinking places include a Golden Lion Pub, a wine bar (Sir Samuel's), a nautically-themed cocktail bar (The Chart Room), and Champagne/Coffee Bar. Bars outdoors include the Regatta Bar and Terrace Bar. The G32 nightclub, which has a main and mezzanine level, is at the aft end of the ship, away from passenger cabins; it is named after the number designated to the ship by its French builder. The Empire Casino has a bar, as well as the latest high-tech slot machines, and traditional gaming tables.

The Queens Room is a grand ballroom, and, with the largest dance floor at sea, is a stunning, gloriously proportioned room, with a Hollywood-Bowl-style bandstand canopy. It has a dramatic high ceiling, two huge crystal chandeliers, highly comfortable armchairs, and is used for dancing, cocktail parties, and afternoon teas.

Illuminations, the first full-scale planetarium at sea, is a stunning multi-purpose show lounge space that also functions as a 473-seat grand cinema and broadcast studio. As a planetarium, it has tiered seating rows, with 150 very comfortable reclining seats and plush fabrics, allowing you to sit in a special area under a dome, which is 38 ft/11.5 meters in diameter and almost 20 ft/6 meters deep that forms the setting for the night sky. It's worth reserving a seat for at least one of the five outstanding 20-minute programs, when the dome is lowered and 13 computers take you out of this world as you listen to narrations by Harrison Ford, Robert Redford, and Tom Hanks. The specially equipped venue also screens 3D movies using RealD projection.

A Maritime Quest Exhibit provides a beautifully constructed Cunard history plus shipbuilding milestones throughout history, including John Brown's shipyard that built the original *Queen Mary* in the 1930s.

Just aft of the Canyon Ranch Spa is a colonial-style Winter Garden reminiscent of London's Kew Gardens, where flowers bloom year-round – this means they are artificial, and some are downright tacky. This peaceful garden setting is for relaxation; a string quartet could well be play-

COMPARING *QM2* AND *QE2*

Cunard Line's many repeat passengers who loved *QE2* inevitably make comparisons between the two ships. *QM2* has two classes and only four staircases; *QE2* had three classes and 10 staircases. *QE2* had many cabins for single occupancy; *QM2* has none, and single-occupancy premiums are extremely high. *QE2* had a Baggage Master; *QM2* does not. *QE2*'s Queens Grill and Princess Grill restaurants were far more intimate, and had nicer decor than those of *QM2*. Aboard *QM2* there is no private lounge for Princess Grill passengers; but they do share the Queens Grill Lounge.

ing for afternoon tea, which is also served in the much larger, elegant Queen's Room.

There are five swimming pools, including one that can be enclosed under a retractable glass roof – useful in bad weather. A large area of open sunning space includes a sports bar at one end. Sports facilities include an electronic golf simulator, giant chess board and a paddle tennis court.

The ship's Library and Bookshop, the world's largest floating bookshop, is located forward and staffed by full-time librarians from Ocean Books, with a superb display of 8,000 books in several languages. The area includes leather sofas and armchairs, several internet-connect computers, and a large selection of magazines. It is a delightful facility, but there are few chairs, and the adjacent bookshop is quite small.

ConneXions, an education center, includes seven sophisticated classrooms for Oxford University's "Oxford Discovery" programs. Classes in such things as computer learning, seamanship and navigation, art and wine appreciation, history, languages and photography are taught. Meanwhile, fast-access internet connectivity and a multitude of computer terminals populate the Internet Center, with a choice of connection packages. Full wi-fi service for your laptop is available round the clock in many public rooms.

Children have their own spaces, with a dedicated play area, the Play Zone. English nannies supervise toddlers, while older children use The Zone.

ACCOMMODATION. Although there are four separate categories – Queens Grill, Princess Grill, Britannia Club, and Britannia – QM2 really operates as a two-class ship (Grill Class and Britannia Class), and the restaurant to which you are assigned depends on your accommodation grade. You even get a different cabin breakfast menu depending on

whether you travel in Grill Class or Britannia Class accommodation. Twenty-five price grades cover everything from standard outside-view cabins to the most opulent suites.

Perhaps the most noticeable difference between this ship and QE2 is the addition of a large number of cabins with private balconies – 75 percent of all cabins have them, although they are of little use when crossing the North Atlantic and have steel bulkheads that obscure ocean views when you are seated. Some 12 cabins look inwards to the atrium lobby, which spans six decks.

All grades have a 20-inch (or larger) TV set, and all beds have fluffy European duvets. There's a mini-fridge, safe, and hand-held hairdryer All bathrooms have toiletries supplied by Canyon Ranch, the spa/fitness concession. Other features include digital video on demand (English-, French- and German-language movies are available), music on demand with 3,000 titles, and audio books on demand. One channel covers Cunard Line's eventful history since 1840.

A number of cabins can accommodate a third or fourth person, although they are so small as to be useful only for contortionists. They are, however, the most inexpensive way of experiencing this fine ship.

For the largest accommodation in the cruise industry, two combinations offer the equivalent of a large house at sea. At the front of the ship, you can combine the Queen Elizabeth and Queen Mary suites with the Queen Anne and Queen Victoria suites to produce one huge suite measuring 5,016 sq. ft (466 sq. meters). Even this can be eclipsed at the other end of the ship, by joining Grand Duplex apartments at the lower level to the adjacent penthouses to produce an unprecedented 8,288 sq. ft (770 sq. meters).

Balmoral/Sandringham Duplexes (Grade Q1): The

THE NEGATIVE ASPECTS OF THE *QM2* EXPERIENCE

Queen Mary 2 really is a floating city – with an elite Grill-class section – and, like any city, there are several parts of town. Some are elegant, some not so elegant, and some are slightly tacky.

The framed, animated cartoons on display, and for sale, in The Gallery don't quite go with the *QM2*'s ocean liner image; neither do art auctions or bazaar stalls selling gold chains, tee-shirts and other tacky items found aboard many cruise ships today. Gratuities are charged to your onboard account at $11–$13 per person, per day, according to the grade of accommodation chosen. A 15% gratuity is included in all beverage and wine orders. As for extra charges, drinks prices are quite reasonable, but a 10-inch by 8-inch embarkation photo can cost close to $30.

A crossing or voyage aboard *QM2* can be considered luxurious only if you travel in Queens Grill accommodation. Otherwise, the experience ranges from "standard" to

"premium" in the other accommodation grades (and little different to regular cruise ships in these market segments). While there are a few delightful wooden sunloungers with green padded cushions, the majority of sunloungers, particularly on the open decks aft, are plastic. To the disappointment of many regular transatlantic passengers, there are no single cabins.

QM2, unlike *QE2*, has no dedicated cinema – a shame since the ship is specifically built for the North Atlantic crossings, when a cinema is most appreciated by frequent passengers (films are, however, shown daily in Illuminations or the Royal Theatre). The grill rooms are too large to be intimate, and are more akin to the kind of steakhouses one finds in large North American cities.

QM2 passengers are a mixed bunch. Most are well dressed, although numerous "tracksuiters'" inhabit the ship, particularly in the Kings Court. Overall, some may feel overwhelmed by the decor's understated

look, or by the bold carpets, but, whatever you may think, the ship absorbs passengers well. While not as ornate as some would like, *QM2* is decidedly spacious and comforting, once you find your way around, although it'll take a week to discover all the out-of-the-way nooks and crannies.

Where several tender ports are included in itineraries, spending time obtaining tender tickets to go ashore detracts from the overall experience – although itineraries have been planned to include as many "alongside" ports as possible.

The passenger flow is generally sound, although there are difficulties in accessing some of the public rooms due to the rather disjointed interior design, and the ship absorbs passengers extremely well with no sense of crowding.

Sadly, there is nowhere to have breakfast outdoors if you don't have a balcony cabin, and lunch at the outdoors Boardwalk Café consists mainly of fast-food items.

largest stand-alone accommodation can be found in the Balmoral and Sandringham Duplexes (2,249 sq. ft/209 sq. meters). These are located aft in prime real estate territory, with superb views along the length of the ship. Upstairs is a bedroom with wood-framed king-size bed, and large (not so private) balcony; downstairs is a living room with sofa, coffee table, dining table, and writing desk. There are two marble-clad bathrooms with whirlpool bath and separate shower enclosure, toilet and bidet, and two washbasins.

Queen Elizabeth/Queen Mary Suites (Grade Q2): The Queen Elizabeth Suite and Queen Mary Suite (1,194 sq. ft/111 sq. meters) are both located just under the navigation bridge, with good views over the ship's long bows. There are living and dining areas, with a large private balcony (but not as large as the Balmoral/ Sandringham duplex balconies). The master, marble-clad bathroom has a whirlpool tub and shower enclosure, and a second bathroom with a shower enclosure (no tub). Each suite has the convenience of private elevator access.

Duplex Apartments (Grade Q2): There are three duplex apartments: Buckingham and Windsor (each 1,291 sq. ft/ 120 sq. meters), and Holyrood (1,566 sq. ft/145 sq. meters). Each has a gymnasium, balcony, butler and concierge service, and superb views over the stern.

Queen Anne/Queen Victoria Suites (Grade Q3): These two suites (796.5 sq. ft/74 sq. meters) have the most commanding views over the ship's long bows. They consist of a bedroom with master, marble-clad bathroom with whirlpool tub and separate shower enclosure; separate living/dining area, and a second bathroom with a shower enclosure (no tub).

Penthouse Suites (Grade Q4): The six penthouse suites (758 sq. ft/70 sq. meters) have a living and dining area, large private balcony, bedroom and dressing room with master, marble-clad bathroom with whirlpool tub and separate shower enclosure.

Suites (506 sq ft (Grade Q5/Q6): These 82 suites (506 sq. ft/47 sq. meters) have a large private balcony, living area, dressing room, marble-clad bathroom with whirlpool tub/shower. Beds can be arranged as king-size or twins.

Junior Suites (Grade P1/P2): There are 76 Junior Suites (381 sq. ft/35 sq. meters). Each has a lounge area, large private balcony, and marble-clad bathroom with whirlpool tub and separate shower enclosure. Beds can be arranged in a king-size or twin-bed configuration.

Deluxe/Premium Balcony Cabins: These 782 cabins (248 sq. ft/23 sq. meters) include a sitting area with sofa, and bathroom with shower enclosure. Beds can be arranged in a king-size or twin-bed configuration.

Standard Outside-View/Interior Cabins: There are 62 outside-view cabins and 281 interior (no view) cabins measuring 194 sq. ft/18 sq. meters). Beds can be arranged in a king-size or twin-bed configuration.

Atrium View Cabins: Each of these 12 interior cabins (194 sq. ft/18 sq. meters) has an unusual view – into the six-deck high atrium lobby. Beds can be arranged as king-

---

HOW FIDO AND FELIX CAN COME TOO

You can take your dog along on transatlantic crossings – but not on cruises – and 12 kennels are overseen by a kennel master. Dogs and cats receive a gift pack containing a QM2-logo coat, frisbee, name tag, food dish and scoop; a portrait with pet owners; a crossing certificate and personalized cruise card. Other pet perks include toys, cat posts and scratchers, plus premium pet foods. You can make kennel reservations when you book. The cost: $300–$500. Dogs must be fitted with a microchip, issued with a PETS certificate or official PET passport, and vaccinated against rabies.

---

size or twins. An en-suite bathroom has a shower enclosure, washbasin, toilet, and toiletries cabinet.

Wheelchair-Accessible Cabins: There are 30 wheelchair-friendly suites and cabins in various categories. All have pull-down closet hanging rails, above-bed emergency pull-cord, and large, well-equipped bathrooms with roll-in showers and handrails. Facilities for blind passengers include Braille signs and tactile room signs. Eight wheelchair-accessible elevators service the dining areas. Additionally, some 36 cabins have been designated to accommodate deaf or hearing-impaired passengers. There are headsets in the Royal Theatre and Planetarium, and closed-caption TV.

CUISINE. There are no fewer than 14 bars and seven galleys serving 10 dining rooms and eateries, all of which have ocean-view windows. The wines and champagnes have been selected by Michael Broadbent, one of the world's top wine experts.

Britannia Restaurant: This main dining room seats 1,347, and spans the ship's full beam. A lavish room almost three decks high, it has two grand sweeping staircases which enable you to make your entry in style. Breakfast and lunch are open-seating, while dinner is in two seatings, all with crisp linen and fine china. Vegetarian options are included on all lunch and dinner menus. One downside of open seating for breakfast or lunch is that you will probably have a different waiter each time, who won't know your preferences. Another is that if you are seated on the lower level underneath the balcony formed along the port and starboard sides of the upper level, you'll feel enclosed in an inferior space. It's better to get a table in the central well or on the upper level.

In 46 staterooms graded Category AA, occupants eat in an exclusive private dining area within the Britannia Restaurant (Britannia Club Class). This single-seating club-like venue offers the Britannia Restaurant menu, plus various à la carte options and tableside flambé service.

Queens Grill/Princess Grill: There are two Grill Rooms (the 200-seat Queens Grill and the 178-seat Princess Grill), which are small dining salons. Which you dine in depends on your accommodation grade and fare. Both are located aft and have, in theory, fine ocean-view windows – although walkers passing by on the exterior promenade deck can be disturbing in the daytime, so window blinds are kept down. Both rooms feature in their entrances an ungainly black marble contemporary statue I call the "Black Widow." Passengers in the best suites may feel less special, being mixed, as they are, among all others in Grill Class accommodation. Canyon Ranch Spaclub recommendations and vegetarian options are provided on all lunch and dinner menus.

The Queens Grill has retained waiter stations, which can be noisy at times. The chairs are comfortable, and many have armrests, and the dining table height is just right. There's an impressive à la carte menu in addition to the regular menu. The excellent dining experience includes free caviar, an extra-cost item in the Princess Grill.

Todd English Restaurant: This alternative 216-seat reservations-only restaurant is named after the American TV chef whose restaurant in Boston (Olives) has a fine reputation. With its Moorish decor, it serves his noted Mediterranean cuisine. The room has been designed with intimate detailing and overlooks the Pool Terrace, allowing for al fresco dining. Food presentation is excellent, although overly fussy at times, but the venue is disappointing.

Kings Court: This truly nondescript, informal eatery has 478 seats and obnoxious daytime lighting, and is more suited to a land-based shopping mall. It offers self-serve breakfast and lunch. Breakfast is repetitive, but includes British traditional standards: eggs, bacon, kippers and fried tomatoes. The lunch menu changes daily, and includes Indian dishes such as curried rice and chicken. Pizza, however, cannot be recommended – think card-board with toppings. The beverage station has wooden stirrers – not acceptable for an ocean liner.

At night, decorated screens transform Kings Court into four different dining venues: an Italian Trattoria (*La Piazza*), Asian cuisine (*Lotus*), a British eatery (*The Carvery*) for roast meats, and a *Chef's Galley*; all have full sit-down tablecloth service. The 36-seat Chef's Galley has a live demonstration of your meal's preparation.

Comfort foods are served in the outdoors *Boardwalk Café*, weather permitting, while pub lovers can find traditional British fare in the popular *Golden Lion Pub*. You can also order from the restaurant menus and have breakfast, lunch and dinner served in your own suite or cabin.

ENTERTAINMENT. The Royal Court Theatre, a lovely venue, has tiered seating for 1,094, though some sightlines are less than ideal. It stages lavish West End-style productions and hosts headline entertainers and cabaret acts. The Royal Academy of Dramatic Art (RADA) supplies a company of actors to perform, lead acting workshops and take part in "street theater" performances.

A number of high-class bands, small musical units, duos and solo entertainers provide live music in most of the 14 lounges and bars. Under a partnership with Oxford University, the ship's enrichment program features specialist lecturers such as authors, artists, historians, scientists and other celebrated intellectuals. Also, under a partnership with New York's Juilliard School of Music, selected jazz musicians join spring, summer and fall transatlantic crossings.

SPA/FITNESS. Health Spa and Beauty Services are provided in a 20,000 sq. ft (1,850 sq. meters) Canyon Ranch Spa Club arranged on two decks. Wellbeing treatments include many massages and skin treatments. There's a thalassotherapy pool, whirlpool, and thermal suite (with saunas and aromatic steam rooms, and a Rasul treatment chamber. There is a daily charge for using the facilities, although this is waived if you purchase a treatment. In all, there are 24 body and skincare treatment rooms.

You could also have a "Euphoria" treatment, which is a bath, facial and scalp massage followed by a body massage. Treatment prices are slightly less on port days than on sea days.

A gymnasium has the latest equipment, as well as free weights. In addition, a beauty salon offers a full menu of services for hair and skin, and Canyon Ranch's own range of natural skincare products (Living Essentials) can be purchased. As there are only six hairdressing chairs, appointments should be booked as early as possible. The spa is staffed by 51 Canyon Ranch employees and operated as a concession.

● **For more extensive information on what a Cunard Line cruise is like, see pages 138–9.**

TRANSATLANTIC CROSSINGS ON *QM2*

The ship is supremely quiet in operation, with almost no vibration, even when traveling at top speed in poor weather. The large amount of personal luggage allowed is especially useful for anyone relocating, or for extended holidays. When you arrive in New York or Southampton, after six days of not having to lift a finger, it often proves to be a bittersweet anticlimax after the calming effects of *QM2* on one's inner being. I can think of little that is more pleasing to the soul or more civilized than a transatlantic crossing, of being cosseted for seven days dining in any of the grill restaurants with their fine cuisine and presentation (Grill Class accommodation only).

As a transatlantic ocean liner, this ship has no equal; it rides extremely well, and displays superb sea-keeping characteristics, with virtually no vibration from its pod propulsion system. If you can afford to travel in Grill Class accommodation, you will be cosseted in high comfort, and experience the best service available in the grand transatlantic ocean liner traditions of today (including reserved open deck sunning space). If you travel in Britannia Class accommodation, the ship will provide you with a way to cross the North Atlantic, but with dining arrangements that are more akin to many of the large resort ships of today – although this equates to a dumbing down of food quality and presentation.

Note that, if you travel in accommodation with a balcony and you want sunshine on the crossing from Southampton to New York (westbound), book a suite/cabin on the port side. Eastbound, book on the starboard side. Going westbound, the Statue of Liberty will normally be on the port side, and, on leaving New York, on the starboard side.

QM2 berths not in Manhattan but at the Red Hook Pier 12 passenger terminal in Brooklyn. In Southampton, England, the ship docks at the Queen Elizabeth II Ocean Terminal. Four special transatlantic packages are named The Queens, The Princess, The Buckingham and The Windsor. Each provides a combination of a one-way crossing with hotels and flights of differing classes and standards, according to the fare paid. Tailor-made programs are also available.

A few niggling items dent the premium image. One example is wooden stirrers (instead of real spoons) in the Kings Court – an indication of the "Carnivalization" of Cunard Line, although, to be honest, without the Carnival Corporation, Cunard Line would not have survived in today's harsh economic climate.

Another regret is the removal of an old transatlantic favorite, mid-morning bouillon service on deck.

Queen Victoria
★★★★ + to ★★★★

Size: . . . . .Large Resort Ship	Passenger Decks: 12	Cabins (with private balcony): 718
Tonnage: .90,049	Total Crew: 1,001	Cabins (wheelchair accessible): 20
Lifestyle: . . . . .Premium	Passengers	Wheelchair accessibility: . . . . .Good
Cruise Line: . . . . .Cunard Line	(lower beds/all berths): 2,014/2,172	Cabin Current: . . . . .110/220 volts
Former Names: . . . . .none	Passenger Space Ratio	Elevators: 12
Builder: . . . . .Fincantieri (Italy)	(lower beds/all berths): 44.7/41.4	Casino (gaming tables): . . . . .Yes
Original Cost: . . . .$390 million	Crew/Passenger Ratio	Slot Machines: . . . . .Yes
Entered Service: . . . . .Dec 2007	(lower beds/all berths): 2.2/2.4	Swimming Pools (outdoors): 2
Registry: . . . . .Great Britain	Cabins (total): 1,007	Swimming Pools (indoors): 0
Length (ft/m): 964.5/294.0	Size Range (sq ft/m): 143.0–2,131.3/	Whirlpools: 5
Beam (ft/m): 105.9/32.3	13.2–198.0	Self-Service Launderette: . . . . .Yes
Draft (ft/m): 26.2/8.0	Cabins (outside view): 864	Dedicated Cinema/Seats: . . . . .No
Propulsion/Propellers: . . . . .diesel-electric	Cabins (interior/no view): 143	Library: . . . . .Yes
(63.4mW)/pod propulsion (2)	Cabins (for one person): 0	Onboard currency: . . . . .US$

A pretend ocean liner that suits British tastes.

OVERVIEW. *Queen Victoria*, a very comfortable, likeable cruise ship posing as an ocean liner, is best suited to a couples and single travelers who enjoy the cosmopolitan setting of a ship that offers traditional British ocean liner-style decor, world-wide itineraries, and dressing for dinner. But the proclaimed "Britishness" is largely marketing hype since trying to find British staff is like looking for a needle in a haystack.

THE SHIP. *Queen Victoria* flies the British Red Ensign for the ship's UK registry, and is aimed at the North American and British markets, but will appeal to any Anglophile, because Cunard is still a resolutely British experience.

Basically a stretched, modified platform and layout as the "Vista" series of ships (examples: *Arcadia, Carnival Legend, Costa Atlantica, Costa Luminosa, Costa Mediterranea, Oosterdam*), the

BERLITZ'S RATINGS

	Possible	Achieved
Grill Class		
Ship	500	428
Accommodation	200	166
Food	400	327
Service	400	329
Entertainment	100	82
Cruise	400	339
Britannia Class		
Ship	500	397
Accommodation	200	125
Food	400	274
Service	400	292
Entertainment	100	83
Cruise	400	312

OVERALL SCORE
1,671 points (Grill Class)
1,483 (Britannia Class)
out of 2,000

Cunard version has an additional passenger deck, a specially strengthened hull lengthened by 36 ft (11 meters), giving the ship more of an "ocean liner" feel. It also has a modified, more traditional interior layout reminiscent of yesteryear's ocean liners.

The promenade deck is not teak but a rubberized deck covering made to look like wooden planking, which gets hot and stays hot in warm weather areas. You can almost walk around – the forward section is for marine use only – and several deck lounge chairs with comfortable Cunard-logo cushioned pads make it a good place to read a book. One open deck atop the ship has a life-size chess board.

Queen Victoria also has a rather classy interior layout that takes the best and most favourite public rooms, bars and lounges aboard *QM2* and from the now retired *QE2* and sets them into a high-tech ship designed to offer both trans-Atlantic and trans-Pacific crossings – but with a maximum speed of 23.7 knots – as well as squeeze through the Panama Canal and offer a mix of short and long voyages.

The interior decor is "traditional" in Cunard-speak, with many public rooms finely decorated in Edwardian/Victoria styles, with wrought-iron balustrading on the staircases and in some bars. Most rooms have fine wood (veneer) paneling and decorative accents like wrought-iron horseshoe-shaped stairways, scrolled woodwork and etched glass panels. The majestic three-deck-high Grand Lobby has a sweeping staircase and sculpted balconies. The Cunardia museum's glass cabinets display models of former Cunard Line ships, old menus and daily programs.

Several public rooms are two decks high; these include the gold-beige Queen's Room, with a large, proper wooden ballroom dance floor; above are two huge ceiling-mounted chandeliers. The bandstand is fronted by a large proscenium arch, while cantilevered balconies line the room's starboard side. Traditional British afternoon tea is served in this art deco-style grand room, although the tea itself is pretty basic – it's made with tea bags, not loose tea, so it's difficult to get the strength you like.

The Royal Arcade is a cluster of seven shops, including

Harrods, Royal Doulton and Wedgwood, set in an arcade-like environment. At the forward end of the ship is a horseshoe-shaped staircase, above which is a magnificent British-made chiming pillar clock made by Dent of London – the company that created Big Ben at the Houses of Parliament and was official clockmaker to Queen Victoria herself, since 1841.

Some other venues worth noting:
● **The Library** is a really stunning two-deck-high wood-panelled 6,000-book facility with two full-time librarians. But there are few chairs on which to sit in and read. A bookshop in another location sells maritime-related books, memorabilia, maps and stationery. The Library is a great place to meet people, quietly, and the carpet is rather special, with the names of great authors scattered throughout.
● **Golden Lion Pub** – a must aboard a Cunarder. This one lies along the starboard side, and is a good gathering place for karaoke, sing-along, and quiz enthusiasts – plus, it has good pub food.
● The **Commodore Club** acts as a large observation lounge, with its ocean views on three sides, and late-night room for low-volume interactive entertainment.
● The adjacent **Churchill's Cigar Lounge**, on the starboard side, is a haven for smokers.
● **Chart Room Bar**, adjacent to the Britannia Restaurant – a place for a quiet drink before dinner.
● **Hemispheres**, positioned aft of the mast and adjacent to the Commodore Club, overlooks the wood-decked Pavilion Pool; this is the high-volume disco and themed nightclub.
● There's also a fairly large **casino** (no smoking) on the port side of the lower level of the Royal Court.

A grand conservatory (Winter Gardens), with central fountain and retractable glass roof, has a moveable glass wall to an open-air swimming pool. Rattan furniture and ceiling fans help to conjure up the area's colonial theme.

Art works worth more than $2 million, including original etchings by the liner's namesake and her husband Prince Albert, adorn various walls. An Internet Center is adjacent to the Reception Desk on Deck 1.

The layout is a little disjointed on the uppermost decks, although the general flow is reasonably good. Access between the aft deck and the pool area and Winter Gardens can be gained only by going through the expansive buffet area. This makes for congestion at the self-serve buffet as people are constantly passing through, as in a railway carriage; but it's a very popular area and provides a wide choice of food items and special themed buffet food.

The pitiful amount of drawer space in the standard cabins is disappointing, even though new under-bed drawers were added at the end of 2008, leaving almost no space for luggage storage.

Queen Victoria provides a suitable setting for passengers who enjoy dressing properly for dinner, either in formal or semi-formal attire. Passengers get cocktail party invitations, and enjoy the intellectual lecturers and specialist speakers who sail on each voyage – Cunard wisely calls them voyages, not cruises.

A per person, per day gratuity is charged to your onboard

account, and a 15% gratuity is added to all bar and wine accounts. Gratuities – called a Hotel and Dining charge – of $11–$13, depending on accommodation grade, are automatically added to your onboard account daily. The onboard currency is the US dollar – another reason to take the Britishness claims with a pinch of salt.

ACCOMMODATION. There are 31 price grades but just eight types of accommodation, which ranges from "ample" to opulent: seven Queens Grill, eight Princess Grill, and 20 Britannia grades. In the accommodation hallways, cabins on the port side (left side of the ship, facing forward) will find a red carpet, while those on the starboard (right) side will find a blue carpet. The air conditioning can't be turned off in cabins or bathrooms. In the measurements below, which are approximate, balconies are included.

Grand Suites: four, measuring 1,918–2,131 sq.ft (178–197 sq. meters). They are located aft, with great ocean views from their private wrap-around balconies, which contain a complete wet bar. The suites have two bedrooms with walk-in closets; bathroom with bathtub and separate shower enclosure; lounge; dining room (with seating for six). In-suite dining from the Queens Grill menus is also available.

Master Suites: two, measuring 1,100 sq.ft (102 sq. meters), located in the center of the ship (Deck 7).

Penthouse Suites: 25, measuring 520–707 sq.ft (48–66 sq. meters).

Queens Suites: 35, measuring 508–771 sq.ft (47–72 sq. meters).

Princess Suites: 61, measuring 342–513 sq.ft (32–48 sq. meters).

Balcony Cabins: 581, measuring 242–472 sq.ft (22–44 sq. meters).

Outside-View Cabins: 146, measuring 180–201 sq.ft (17–19 sq. meters).

Interior (no-view) Cabins: 143, measuring 151–243 sq.ft (14–19 sq. meters).

All accommodation grades have both British three-pin (240-volt) sockets and American and European-style two-pin (110-volt) sockets. Gilchrist & Soames toiletries are supplied to all passengers, and a hairdryer is stored in the vanity desk units. Some cabins have nicely indented ceilings with suffused lighting. However, the flat-screen TV sets are small – not good for bedtime movie watching.

The regular cabins (Grades C/D) are small, but functional, although completely lacking in "wow" factor. The cabinetry resembles that in an Ibis hotel – a bit austere and lacking character. There is a distinct lack of drawer space in a cabin supposedly designed for two persons – it's very noticeable on long voyages, and the additional drawers located under the bed may prove challenging for some to use. The premium mattresses are, however, excellent, as is the bed linen; European duvets are standard.

The bathrooms, also, are stunningly bland, similar to those found aboard the ships of Princess Cruises, with small washbasins and little storage space for toiletries, and cold, tiled floors. The fixed-head shower doesn't permit the thorough wash that hand-held flexible hoses do. Overall, the standard (lower grade) cabins are a little underwhelming – so, for more space and quality, consider booking one of the higher grade cabins, or, better still, go for Grill-class accommodation – the perks and increased attention and service are worth it. The walls in most accommodation passageways are rather plain, and could do with a little artwork.

CUISINE. Cunard is respected for its cuisine and service, with a wide variety of well-prepared and presented dishes made from good ingredients. The *Britannia Restaurant* – the name is taken from a former Cunard ocean liner of 1914–50 – is located in the aft section. It is two decks high, with seating on both the main level (two seatings for dinner, but open seating for breakfast and lunch) and balcony level (which houses what are known as Britannia Club passengers, with single seat dining). A horseshoe-shaped stairway links both levels. While the lower level diners have a good sea view through large picture windows, balcony diners get a promenade view. Waterford Wedgwood china is used, and there's a wide range of wines (and prices).

Queens Grill and *Princess Grill*, two Grill-Class-only restaurants, provide exclusive dining. These have a single-seating arrangement, providing a much more intimate and exclusive dining experience than can be found in the two-seating main Britannia Restaurant.

On the port side, the 142-seat Queens Grill, with its single-seating dining, is for passengers in suites and top category accommodation grades, and provides the best cuisine and service aboard the ship. The famous Cunard Grill experience also includes alfresco dining in a seldom used courtyard terrace *(The Courtyard)*, suitably protected from the wind, and exclusive access for Grill-class passengers to their own upper terrace deck, with dedicated staff as well as the Grills' lounge and bar.

On the starboard side, the 132-seat Princess Grill, with single-seating dining, is for passengers in middle-class accommodation grades.

Alternative Dining Venue: The 87-seat *Todd English Restaurant* has the look and feel of a classic English dining salon, with fussy Mediterranean cuisine based on Todd English's chain of Olive-brand restaurants in the USA and presented on creative china. The restaurant is on the second level of the three-deck high lobby. Reservations are required, and there is a cover charge for both lunch and dinner.

Casual Eatery: The *Lido Café*, on Deck 11, has good panoramic views, indoor/outdoor seating for 468, and offers a fairly standard multi-line self-serve buffet arrangement. For excellent Lavazza coffees from Maria (the coffee machine), and light bites, there's the Parisian-style *Café Carinthia*, located one deck above the Purser's Desk and adjacent to the popular *Veuve Clicquot* champagne bar.

For traditional British pub food, the *Golden Lion Pub* serves fish 'n' chips, steak and mushroom pie, ploughman's lunch, and, of course, bangers (sausages) and mash – particularly good at lunchtime – with a nice draft pint of bitter, naturally.

Cabin service is available 24 hours a day, so you can always have extra items when you are feeling peckish.

ENTERTAINMENT. The 830-seat, three-deck-high Royal Court Theatre is designed in the style of a classic opera house. In the tradition of a real London West End theatre, it provides 20 private "royal boxes" which can be reserved by any passengers for special nights. A special package includes champagne and chocolates, and ticket printed with name and box number. There's also a lounge for pre-show drinks.

A "Victoriana" show is all about good old British tradition. Other production shows include Celtic Heartbeat and Stroke of Genius, and a good variety of cabaret entertainment is presented. The Royal Court Theatre is also used to show large-screen movies. The ship has a number of bands, small combos and solo entertainers. A Big Band night is sometimes held in the Queens Room, and live jazz can be heard in several bars and lounges.

SPA/FITNESS. The Cunard Royal Health Club and Spa consists of a beauty salon, large gymnasium with high-tech muscle-pumping equipment and great ocean views; aerobics area; changing rooms for men and women (each with its own ocean-view sauna); a Thermal Area with sauna and steam rooms (extra-cost day passes are available if you don't book a treatment, at $35 per day, or at less per day cost for a multi-use pass); several body treatment rooms; a rasul chamber for private Hammam-style mud/steam bathing; and a relaxation area.

● **For more extensive general information on what a Cunard Line cruise is like, see pages 138–9.**

Radiance of the Seas
★★★★

Size: . . . . .Large Resort Ship	Total Crew: 858	Cabins (wheelchair accessible): 14
Tonnage: .90,090	Passengers	(8 with private balcony)
Lifestyle: . . . . .Standard	(lower beds/all berths): 2,146/2,542	Wheelchair accessibility: . . . . .Good
Cruise Line: Royal Caribbean International	Passenger Space Ratio	Cabin Current: . . . . .110/220 volts
Former Names: . . . . .none	(lower beds/all berths): 42.0/35.4	Elevators: 9
Builder: . . . . .Meyer Werft (Germany)	Crew/Passenger Ratio	Casino (gaming tables): . . . . .Yes
Original Cost: . . . .$350 million	(lower beds/all berths): 2.5/2.9	Slot Machines: . . . . .Yes
Entered Service: . . . . .Apr 2001	Cabins (total): 1,072	Swimming Pools (outdoors): 2
Registry: . . . . .The Bahamas	Size Range (sq ft/m): 165.8–1,216.3/	Swimming Pools (indoors): 0
Length (ft/m): 961.9/293.2	15.4–113.0	Whirlpools: 3
Beam (ft/m): 105.6/32.2	Cabins (outside view): 829	Self-Service Launderette: . . . . .No
Draft (ft/m): 27.8/8.5	Cabins (interior/no view): 237	Dedicated Cinema/Seats: Yes/40
Propulsion/Propellers: . . . . .Gas turbine/2	Cabins (for one person): 0	Library: . . . . .Yes
azimuthing pods (20 MW each)	Cabins (with private balcony): 578	Onboard currency: . . . . .US$
Passenger Decks: 12		

A large, family-friendly ship for casual-style cruising.

OVERVIEW. *Radiance of the Seas* offers more space, more comfortable public areas and slightly larger cabins for the younger, active, and trendy set than some RCI ships. The grand amount of glass provides more contact with the ocean. While the ship is quite delightful in many ways, however, the onboard operation is less so, and suffers from having too few service staff with finesse.

THE SHIP. *Radiance of the Seas* was the first Royal Caribbean International ship to use gas and steam turbine power instead of the more conventional diesel or diesel-electric combination. Pod propulsion is provided *(see page 191 for a detailed explanation)*. In the very front of the ship is a helipad, which also acts as a viewing platform for passengers.

This is a contemporary ship, with a two-deck-high walk-around structure in the forward section of the funnel. Along the ship's starboard side, a central glass wall protrudes, giving great views – cabins with balconies occupy the space directly opposite on the port side. The gently rounded stern has nicely tiered decks. One of two swimming pools can be covered by a large glass dome for use as an indoor/outdoor pool.

Inside, the decor is contemporary, yet elegant, bright and cheerful. A nine-deck-high atrium lobby has glass-walled elevators that travel through 12 decks, face the sea and provide a link with nature and the ocean. The Centrum, as the atrium is called, has several public rooms connected to it: the guest relations and shore excursions desks, a Lobby Bar, Champagne Bar, the Library, Royal Caribbean Online, the Concierge Club, and a Crown & Anchor Lounge.

BERLITZ'S RATINGS

	Possible	Achieved
Ship	500	415
Accommodation	200	154
Food	400	238
Service	400	262
Entertainment	100	78
Cruise	400	299

OVERALL SCORE
1,446 points out of 2,000

Other facilities include a delightful, but very small library. A large Schooner Bar houses maritime art in an integral art gallery. Casino Royale has a French Art Nouveau decorative theme and 11 crystal chandeliers. There's also a small dedicated screening room for movies, with space for two wheelchairs, plus a 194-seat conference center, and a business center.

The Viking Crown Lounge is a large structure set around the base of the ship's funnel. It functions as an observation lounge during the daytime, with views forward over the swimming pool. In the evening, the space hosts Starquest – a futuristic, high-energy dance club, and Hollywood Odyssey – a more intimate and relaxed entertainment venue for softer mood music and "black box" theater.

Royal Caribbean Online is a center with 12 computers, located in a semi-private setting; in addition, shipwide wi-fi is available (for a fee). More internet-access terminals are located in Books 'n' Coffee, a bookshop with coffee and pastries, located in an extensive area of shops.

The artwork aboard this ship is really eclectic, providing a spectrum and a half of color works. It ranges from Jenny M. Hansen's *A Vulnerable Moment* glass sculpture to David Buckland's *Industrial and Russian Constructionism 1920s* in photographic images on glass and painted canvas, to a huge multi-deck high contemporary bicycle-cum-paddlewheel sculpture design suspended in the atrium.

FAMILIES. Youth facilities include Adventure Ocean, an "edutainment" area with four separate age-appropriate sections for junior passengers: Aquanaut Center (for ages 3–5);

Explorer Center (6–8); Voyager Center (9–12); and the Optix Teen Center (13–17). There is also Adventure Beach, which includes a splash pool complete with waterslide; Surfside, with computer lab stations with entertaining software; and Ocean Arcade, a video games hangout.

ACCOMMODATION. There is a wide range of suites and standard outside-view and interior cabins in 10 different categories and 19 different price groups.

Apart from the largest suites (six owner's suites), which have king-size beds, almost all other cabins have twin beds that convert to a queen-size bed, All sheets are of 100% Egyptian cotton, although the blankets are synthetic. All cabins have rich (but faux) wood cabinetry, including a vanity desk with hairdryer, faux wood drawers that close silently (hooray), a TV set, personal safe, and three-sided mirrors. Some cabins have ceiling recessed, pull-down berths for third and fourth persons, although closet and drawer space would be extremely tight for four persons even if two of them were children, and some have interconnecting doors – so families with children can cruise together in separate but adjacent cabins. Audio channels are available through the TV set, whose picture cannot be turned off while listening to an audio channel.

Most bathrooms have tiled accenting a terrazzo-style tiled floor, and a small shower enclosure in a half-moon shape, 100% Egyptian cotton towels, a small cabinet for toiletries and a small shelf. In reality, there is little space to stow toiletries for two (or more).

The largest accommodation consists of a family suite with two bedrooms. One bedroom has twin beds that convert to queen-size bed, while a second has two lower beds and two upper Pullman berths, a combination that can sleep up to eight persons – this would be suitable for large families.

Many of the "private" balcony cabins are not very private, as they can be overlooked from various locations.

CUISINE. *Cascades*, the main dining room, spans two decks. The upper deck level has floor-to-ceiling windows, while the lower deck level has picture windows. It is a lovely, but noisy, dining hall – reminiscent of those aboard the transatlantic liners in their heyday, although eight huge, thick pillars obstruct the sight lines. It seats 1,104, and has cascading water themed decor. There are tables for two, four, six, eight or 10. Two small private dining rooms – the 94-seat *Breakers* and the 30-seat *Tides* – are located off the main dining room. When you book, choose one of two seatings, or "My Time Dining" that enables you to eat when you want, during dining room hours.

Giovanni's Italian Table and *Rita's Cantina* were added in a 2011 refit, as well as a *Park Café* deli-style eatery and an "exclusive" *Chef's Table* dining experience.

Alternative dining options: *Chops Grill Steakhouse*, with 95 seats and an open kitchen, serves premium meats in the form of veal chops and steaks (New York Striploin Steak, Filet Mignon, and Prime Rib of Beef). The food here is of a much higher quality than in the main dining room, though the menus don't change during the cruise. There is a per-person cover charge for Giovanni's Table and Chops Grille (including gratuities), and reservations are required. They are typically open 6pm–11pm, and the dress code is smart casual.

Casual meals can be taken for breakfast, lunch and dinner in the self-serve, buffet-style *Windjammer Café*, accessible directly from the pool deck. It has islands dedicated to specific foods, and indoors and outdoors seating.

Additionally, *Samba Grill Brazilian Steakhouse* (Churrascaria) is open for dinner, with tableside meat carving.

ENTERTAINMENT. The three-level Aurora Theater has 874 seats, including 24 stations for wheelchairs, and good sightlines from most seats. The Colony Club hosts casual cabaret shows, including late-night adult comedy, and provides live music for dancing. The entertainment throughout is upbeat. There is even background music in all corridors and elevators, and constant music outdoors on the pool deck. If you want a quiet, relaxing holiday, choose another ship.

SPA/FITNESS. The ShipShape Spa's health, fitness and spa facilities have themed decor, and include a gymnasium with 44 cardiovascular machines, a 50-person aerobics room, sauna and steam rooms, and therapy treatment rooms. All are located on two of the uppermost decks, forward of the mast, with access from the forward stairway.

A climate-controlled 10,176-sq.-ft (945-sq.-meter) indoor/outdoor Solarium has a sliding glass roof that can be closed in cool or inclement weather. It has a fascinating African themed decor, and includes a whirlpool and counter-current swimming.

More sporting passengers are offered a 30-ft (9-meter) rock-climbing wall with five separate climbing tracks. There is also an exterior jogging track. Other sports facilities include a nine-hole miniature golf course with novel 17th-century decorative ornaments, and an indoor/outdoor country club with golf simulator, a jogging track, and basketball court. There are two specially stabilized pool tables.

● **For more extensive general information about the Royal Caribbean experience, see pages 152–6.**

Regatta
★★★★ +

Size: . . . . .Mid-Size Ship	Total Crew: 386	Cabins (wheelchair accessible): 3
Tonnage: .30,277	Passengers	Wheelchair accessibility: . . . . .Good
Lifestyle: . . . . .Premium	(lower beds/all berths): 684/824	Cabin Current: . . . . .110 and 220 volts
Cruise Line: . . . . .Oceania Cruises	Passenger Space Ratio	Elevators: 4
Former Names: . . . . .R Two	(lower beds/all berths): 44.2/36.7	Casino (gaming tables): . . . . .Yes
Builder: . . . . . . .Chantiers de l'Atlantique	Crew/Passenger Ratio	Slot Machines: . . . . .Yes
Original Cost: . . . .£150 million	(lower beds/all berths): 1.7/2.1	Swimming Pools (outdoors): 1
Entered Service: Dec1998/Dec 2003	Cabins (total): .342	Swimming Pools (indoors): 0
Registry: . . . . .Marshall Islands	Size Range (sq ft/m): 145.3–968.7/	Whirlpools: . . . . . . .2 (+1 thalassotherapy)
Length (ft/m): 593.7/181.0	13.5–90.0	Self-Service Launderette: . . . . .Yes
Beam (ft/m): 83.5/25.5	Cabins (outside view): 317	Dedicated Cinema/Seats: . . . . .No
Draft (ft/m): 19.5/6.0	Cabins (interior/no view): 25	Library: . . . . .Yes
Propulsion/Propellers: . . .diesel (18,600 kW)/2	Cabins (for one person): 0	Onboard currency: . . . . .US$
Passenger Decks: 9	Cabins (with private balcony): 232	

An informal premium ship for mature-age cruisers.

OVERVIEW. Oceania Cruises is a young company with a refreshing desire to provide a high level of food and service in an informal setting that is elegant yet comfortable. *Regatta* is best suited to couples who like good food and style, but want informality with no formal nights on board, and interesting itineraries, all at a very reasonable price well below what the luxury ships charge.

THE SHIP. *Regatta* was originally one of eight almost identical ships built for the now-defunct Renaissance Cruises. The exterior design manages to balance the ship's high sides by painting the whole ship white (it previously had a dark blue hull), with a large, square white funnel. The addition of teak overlaid decking and teak lounge chairs have greatly improved what was formerly a bland pool deck outdoors – but it costs $100 a day to use the front rows of double sunloungers (cabanas).

There is no walk-around promenade deck outdoors as such – there is, however, a small jogging/walking track above the swimming pool. Stairways, though carpeted, are tinny.

The stunningly elegant interior decor is a throwback to the ocean liners of the 1920s and '30s, with dark woods and warm colors, all carried out in fine taste – if a bit *faux* in places. It feels like an old-world country club.

The public rooms are spread over three decks. The reception hall has a staircase with intricate wrought-iron railings. A large observation lounge, the Horizon Bar, is located high atop ship. There are plenty of bars, including one in each of the restaurant entrances. Perhaps the nicest is the casino bar/lounge, a beautiful room reminiscent of London's grand hotels and including a martini bar. It has an inviting marble fireplace, comfortable sofas and individual chairs.

BERLITZ'S RATINGS

	Possible	Achieved
Ship	500	416
Accommodation	200	160
Food	400	312
Service	400	295
Entertainment	100	76
Cruise	400	313

OVERALL SCORE
1,572 points out of 2,000

The Library is a grand Regency-style room, with a fireplace, a high, indented, *trompe l'oeil* ceiling, and excellent selection of books, plus very comfortable wingback chairs with footstools, and sofas you could sleep on. Oceania@Sea is the internet center.

The dress code is "smart casual." Gratuities are added at $10.50 per person, per day, and accommodation designated as suites have an extra $3 per person charge for the butler. A 15% gratuity is added to bar accounts.

Passenger niggles include all the "inventive" extra charges that can be incurred. What's really nice is the fact that there are almost no intrusive announcements.

ACCOMMODATION. There are six cabin categories, and 10 price grades (three suite price grades; five outside-view cabin grades; two interior cabin grades. All of the standard interior and outside-view cabins (the lowest four grades) are extremely tight for two persons, particularly for cruises longer than five days. They have twin beds or a queen-size bed, with good under-bed storage areas, personal safe, vanity desk with large mirror, good closet and drawer space in rich, dark woods, 100% cotton bathrobe and towels, slippers, clothes brush and shoe horn. Color TVs carry a major news channel, where obtainable, plus a sports channel and round-the-clock movie channels.

Certain cabin categories (about 100 of them) qualify as "Concierge Level" accommodation, and occupants get extra goodies such as enhanced bathroom amenities, complimentary shoeshine, tote bag, cashmere throw blanket, bottle of champagne on arrival, a hand-held hairdryer, priority restaurant reservations, and priority embarkation.

Owner's Suites (6). Measuring around 962 sq.ft (89.3 sq.meters), these fine living spaces provide the most spacious accommodation. Located aft overlooking the stern on Decks 6, 7, and 8, they are subject to more movement and some vibration. They have extensive teak-floor private balconies that really are private and cannot be overlooked by anyone. Each has an entrance foyer, living room, separate bedroom, CD player, fully tiled bathroom with Jacuzzi tub, and a small guest bathroom. The bed faces the sea, which can be seen through the floor-to-ceiling windows and sliding glass door.

Vista Suites (4). These measure around 785.7 sq.ft (73 sq.meters), and located forward on Decks 5 and 6. They have extensive teak-floor private balconies that can't be overlooked by anyone from the decks above. Each has an entrance foyer, living room, separate bedroom, CD player (with selection of audio discs), and fully tiled bathroom with Jacuzzi tub. The bed faces the sea, visible through the floor-to-ceiling windows and sliding glass door.

Penthouse Suites (52). Actually, these are large cabins rather than suites as the bedrooms aren't separate from the living areas, but they measure around 322.9 sq.ft (30 sq. meters). They have a good-sized teak-floor balcony with sliding glass door – but with partial, not full, balcony partitions – and teak deck furniture. The lounge area has a proper dining table and there is ample clothes storage space. The bathroom has a tub, shower enclosure, washbasin and toilet.

Cabins with Balcony. Measuring around 216 sq.ft (20 sq. meters), these comprise about 66% of all cabins. They have partial, not full, balcony partitions, sliding glass doors, and only 14 cabins on Deck 6 have lifeboat-obstructed views. The living area has a refrigerated mini-bar, lounge area with breakfast table, and a balcony with teak floor, two teak chairs and a drinks table. The bathrooms, with tiled floors and plain walls, are compact, standard units, and include a shower stall with a strong, removable hand-held shower unit, hairdryer, toiletries storage shelves and retractable clothesline.

Outside View and Interior Cabins. These measure around 160–165 sq.ft (14.8–15.3 sq. meters), and have twin beds that convert to a queen-size bed, vanity desk, small sofa and coffee table, and bathroom with a shower enclosure with a strong, removable hand-held shower unit, hairdryer, toiletries storage shelves, retractable clothesline, washbasin, and toilet. Although they aren't large, they are quite comfortable, with a decent amount of storage space.

All suites/cabins located at the stern of the ship may suffer from vibration and noise, particularly when the ship is maneuvering in port.

CUISINE. Flexibility and choice are what the dining facilities aboard Oceania Cruises ships are all about. There are four different restaurants:

● The *Grand Dining Room* has around 340 seats, and a raised central section, but the problem is the noise level – because of the low ceiling height, it's atrocious when the dining room is full. Being located at the stern, there are large ocean-view windows on three sides, and prime tables overlook the stern). The chairs are comfortable, with armrests. The menus change daily for lunch and dinner.

● *Toscana Italian Restaurant* has 96 seats, windows along two sides, and a set menu plus daily chef's specials.

● The cozy *Polo Grill* has 98 seats, windows along two sides and a set menu including prime steaks and seafood.

● The *Terrace Café* has seats for 154 indoors – not enough during cruises to cold-weather areas – and 186 outdoors. It is open for breakfast, lunch and casual dinners, when it has excellent tapas (Tapas on the Terrace) and other Mediterranean food. As the ship's self-serve buffet restaurant, it incorporates a small pizzeria and grill. There are basic salads, a meat carving station, and daily specials. A poolside *Waves Grill* serves fishburgers, veggie burgers, and reuben sandwiches, as well as Angus beef burgers, and hot dogs.

All restaurants have open-seating dining, so you can dine when you want, with whom you wish. Reservations are needed in Toscana Restaurant and Polo Grill (but there's no extra charge), where there are mostly tables for four or six; there are few tables for two. There is a Poolside Grill Bar. All cappuccino and espresso coffees cost extra.

The food and service staff is provided by Apollo, a respected maritime catering company that also has an interest in Oceania Cruises. The consultant chef is American TV chef Jacques Pepin. Oceania Cruises' brochure claims "Cuisine so extraordinary it's unrivaled at sea" is hogwash – it's good, but not that good. This is, however, a foodie's ship, with really high-quality ingredients and a wide selection of dining venues. Particularly notable are the delicious breads, rolls, croissants and brioches – all made on board from French flower and d'Isigny butter.

On sea days, an elegant teatime is presented in the Horizon Lounge, with formally dressed staff, cake display trolleys, and an excellent array of cake and scones. Sadly, teabags, not loose tea, prevail.

ENTERTAINMENT. The Regatta Lounge has entertainment, lectures, some social events, and a mix of production shows and cabaret acts. There is live music in several bars and lounges.

SPA/FITNESS. A lido deck has a swimming pool, and good sunbathing space, plus a thalassotherapy tub. A jogging track circles the swimming pool deck but is one deck above. The uppermost outdoors deck includes a golf driving net and shuffleboard court. The Canyon Ranch SpaClub consists of a beauty salon, three treatment rooms, men's and women's changing rooms, and steam room. There is no sauna. Note that 18% is added to your spa account, whether you like it or not.

Rhapsody of the Seas
★★★★

Size:	Large Resort Ship	Passenger Decks:	11	Cabins (with private balcony):	229
Tonnage:	78,491	Total Crew:	765	Cabins (wheelchair accessible):	14
Lifestyle:	Standard	Passengers		Wheelchair accessibility:	Good
Cruise Line:	Royal Caribbean International	(lower beds/all berths):	2,000/2,435	Cabin Current:	110 and 220 volts
Former Names:	none	Passenger Space Ratio		Elevators:	9
Builder: Chantiers de l'Atlantique (France)		(lower beds/all berths):	39.2/32.2	Casino (gaming tables):	Yes
Original Cost:	$275 million	Crew/Passenger Ratio		Slot Machines:	Yes
Entered Service:	May 1997	(lower beds/all berths):	2.6/3.1	Swimming Pools (outdoors):	1
Registry:	The Bahamas	Cabins (total):	1,000	Swimming Pools (inside/outside):	1
Length (ft/m):	915.3/279.0	Size Range (sq ft/m):	135.0–1,270.1/	Whirlpools:	6
Beam (ft/m):	105.6/32.2		12.5–118.0	Self-Service Launderette:	No
Draft (ft/m):	24.9/7.6	Cabins (outside view):	593	Dedicated Cinema/Seats:	No
Propulsion/Propellers:	diesel-electric	Cabins (interior/no view):	407	Library:	Yes
	(50,400kW)/2	Cabins (for one person):	0	Onboard currency:	US$

Pleasant decor for casual, family-friendly cruising.

OVERVIEW. What makes this ship feel warm and cozy are the use of fine, light wood surfaces throughout its public rooms, as well as the large array of potted plants everywhere. There is a large shopping area, although the merchandise is consistently tacky. Throughout the ship, the artwork is really upbeat and colorful, and has a musical theme: classical, jazz, popular and rock 'n' roll.

THE SHIP. This all-white ship, sister to *Vision of the Seas*, shares design features that make many, but not all, Royal Caribbean International ships identifiable, including a Viking Crown Lounge and a multi-level nightspot – the music can be loud and overbearing, however.

The Viking Crown Lounge (also the ship's disco) is positioned just aft of the center of the ship, above the central atrium lobby. The funnel is well aft – a departure from many other RCI ships to date – which positions the Viking Crown lounge around the funnel or at its base. The stern is beautifully rounded. There is a reasonable amount of open-air walking space, although this tends to become cluttered with sunloungers.

There's a wide range of interesting public rooms, lounges and bars, and the interiors have been cleverly designed to avoid congestion and aid passenger flow into revenue areas. Speaking of which, for those who enjoy gambling, the astrologically-themed casino is large and rather glitzy – although not as bold as aboard some of the company's other ships. Again, this is typical of most new large ships; a couple of pieces of "electrostatic" art in globe form provide fascinating relief.

The atrium lobby is the interior focal point – this is

BERLITZ'S RATINGS		
	Possible	Achieved
Ship	500	425
Accommodation	200	166
Food	400	240
Service	400	286
Entertainment	100	81
Cruise	400	292
OVERALL SCORE		
1,490 points out of 2,000		

always a good place to arrange to meet anyone, and has a large kinetic sculpture, *Diadem*. It is a multi-material construction that spans six decks, and has an astrological theme, as do many of the decorative elements throughout the ship. The interior decor throughout is imaginative, and provides a connection between sea and stars. Much improved over previous new ships in the fleet is the theater, with more entrances and fewer bottlenecks, though pillars still obstruct sightlines from many seats. Also improved are facilities for children and teens.

Ship enthusiasts will like the chair fabric in the Shall We Dance lounge, with its large aft-facing windows, and the glass case-enclosed mechanical sculptures.

ACCOMMODATION. There are 18 grades, priced by grade, size and location. The standard interior and exterior view cabins are of an adequate size, and have just enough functional facilities to make them comfortable for a one-week cruise, but longer might prove confining. The decor is bright and cheerful, although the ceilings are plain; the soft furnishings make this home away from home look like the inside of a modern Scandinavian hotel – with minimalist tones, and splashes of color. Twin lower beds convert to queen-size beds, and there is a reasonable amount of closet and drawer space, but there is little room to maneuver between the bed and the desk/television unit.

The bathrooms are small but functional. The shower units themselves are small, too, and there is no cabinet for toiletries. The towels should be larger and thicker. In the passageways, upbeat artwork depicts musical themes.

Choose a "C" grade suite if you want spacious accommodation that includes a curtained-off sleeping area, a good-sized outside balcony with part, not full, partition, a lounge with sofa, two chairs and coffee table, three closets, plenty of drawer and storage space, television and video player. The bathroom is large and has a full-size tub, integral shower, and two washbasins with two toiletries cabinets.

For the best accommodation, choose the Royal Suite. It resembles a Palm Beach apartment, and comes complete with a white baby grand piano. It has a separate bedroom with king-size bed, living room with queen-size sofa bed, refrigerator/mini-bar, dining table, entertainment center, and vanity dressing area. The decor is simple and elegant, with pastel colors, and wood-accented ceiling treatments. Located just under the starboard side navigation bridge wing, it has its own private balcony.

CUISINE. The two-level *Edelweiss Dining Room* is attractive and works well, although the noise level can be high. When you book, choose one of two seatings, or "My Time Dining" (eat when you want, during dining room hours).

The *Windjammer Café* is the casual dining spot for self-serve buffets. The area is well designed, with contemporary decor and colors, but the food is basic fare and disappointing; the self-service buffet area is small for the number of passengers using it. More money needs to be spent for better ingredients and more variety. Each evening, the room offers an alternative to the more formal dining room. The evening buffets have a different theme, something this company has been doing for more than 25 years – perhaps the time has come for more creativity.

There is a hamburger/hot dog grill counter in the Solar-ium, but typically you don't get a choice of how well done or not so well done you get your hamburgers – everything appears to be well done. The company has introduced a drinks package, available at all bars, in the form of cards or stickers. This enables you to pre-pay for a selection of standard soft drinks and alcoholic drinks, but the packages are not exactly easy to understand.

ENTERTAINMENT. The Broadway Melodies Theater is the principal showlounge. It is a large, but well-designed room with main and balcony levels, and good sight lines from most of the banquette seats.

Other cabaret acts are presented in the Shall We Dance Lounge, located aft, and include late-night adult comedy, as well as live music for dancing. A number of other bars and lounges have live music of differing types.

The entertainment throughout is upbeat. There is even background music in all passenger hallways and elevators, and constant music outdoors on the pool deck. If you want a quiet relaxing holiday, choose another ship.

SPA/FITNESS. There are good health spa facilities, set in a spacious environment on one of the uppermost decks. The decor has Egypt as its theme, with pharaohs lining the pool. The spa is operated by Steiner, a specialist concession.

For the more sporting, there is activity galore – including a rock-climbing wall with several separate climbing tracks. It is located outdoors at the aft end of the funnel.

● **For more extensive general information on what a Royal Caribbean cruise is like, see pages 152–6.**

See pages 152–6.

QUOTABLE QUOTES

These are some of the questions I have been asked over the years by newcomers to cruising:

"Will we have time to take the shore excursion?"

"Are the entertainers paid?"

"Why don't we have a Late Night Comedy Spot in the afternoon?"

"Is the mail brought in by plane?"

"Why aren't the dancers fully dressed?"

"How do we know which photos are ours?"

"Will the ship wait for the tour buses to get back?"

"Will I get wet if I go snorkeling?"

"Do the Chinese do the laundry by hand?"

"Does the ship dock in the middle of town?"

"Is the doctor qualified?"

"Who's driving the ship if the captain is at the cocktail party?"

"Does the sun always rise on the left side of the ship?"

"Is trapshooting held outside?"

"I'm married, but can I come to the Singles Party?"

"Should I put my luggage outside the cabin before or after I go to sleep?"

"Does an outside cabin mean it's outside the ship?"

Riviera
NOT YET RATED

Size: ....Mid-Size Ship	Total Crew: 800	Cabins (wheelchair accessible): 6
Tonnage: 66,048	Passengers	Wheelchair Accessibility: ....Good
Lifestyle: ....Premium	(lower beds/all berths): 1,258/1,258	Cabin Current: ....110, 220 Volts
Cruise Line: ....Oceania Cruises	Passenger Space Ratio	Elevators: 6
Former Names: ....none	(lower beds/all berths): 51.6/51.6	Casino (gaming tables): ....Yes
Builder: ....Fincantieri (Italy)	Crew/Passenger Ratio	Slot Machines: ....Yes
Original Cost: ....$530 million	(lower beds/all berths): 1.5/1.5	Swimming Pools (outdoors): 1
Entered Service: ....Jul 2012	Cabins (total): 629	Swimming Pools (indoors): 0
Registry:.............Marshall Islands	Size Range (sq ft/m): 172.2–2,000/	Whirlpools: 3
Length (ft/m): 776.5/236.7	16.0–185.0	Self-Service Launderette: ....Yes
Beam (ft/m): 105.3/32.1	Cabins (outside view): 611	Dedicated Cinema/Seats: ....No
Draft (ft/m): 24.2/7.4	Cabins (interior/no view): 18	Library: ....Yes
Propulsion/Propellers: ...diesel-electric/2	Cabins (for one person): 0	Onboard currency: ....US$
Passenger Decks: 11	Cabins (with private balcony): 593	

A homey, comfortable ship with a country-club feel.

OVERVIEW. This ship suits mature-age adults who appreciate refined quality and style, plenty of space and comfort (no lines), and excellent cuisine and service, in a semi-casual setting with realistic pricing. Oceania Cruises has succeeded in keeping the warm, tasteful "country house" decor style for which its ships are known, as well as an uncomplicated layout.

THE SHIP. *Riviera* is the second new-build (sister to *Marina*) for this popular, small premium-ship cruise line. Its profile is quite handsome, with a nicely rounded front, and is topped by a swept-back funnel. Able to cruise at a speed 25% faster than Oceania Cruises' three smaller ships – *Insignia* (which will leave the fleet in April 2012), *Nautica* and *Regatta* – the ship can therefore operate more longer-distance cruises.

The interior focal point is a stunning wrought-iron and Lalique glass horseshoe-shaped staircase in the main lobby. Public rooms include nine bars and lounges. There is a 2,000-book library, set on the port side of the funnel housing, which also contains the staffed Oceania @ Sea computer center, and Barista's coffee bar/lounge (serving the excellent illy brand Italian coffee).

A Monte Carlo Casino is located between two bars – the Grand Bar and Martinis, with its own soft lavender-colored Casino Bar. Martinis houses a beautiful Dakota Jackson special edition Steinway baby grand piano that cost well over $100,000. There are also three boutiques, and several dining venues. There aren't that many different lounges as such because most are drinking venues.

A Culinary Center comprises a cooking demonstration kitchen and 24 workstations, with various classes run in

BERLITZ'S RATINGS		
	Possible	Achieved
Ship	500	NYR
Accommodation	200	NYR
Food	400	NYR
Service	400	NYR
Entertainment	100	NYR
Cruise	400	NYR

conjunction with the US-based *Bon Appétit* magazine – there's a charge for these, but you get to eat your creations.

You can bring your paintbrushes to an Artist's Loft that has constantly changing artists. Other classes may include photography, needlepoint, scrapbooking, drawing and quilting.

The dress code is "elegant country club attire" – no pyjamas or track suits, but no ties either (so there's no tie rack in the closets). In other words, perfect for the Aventura, Palm Springs or Scottsdale fraternity, but not Monte Carlo or Tokyo.

A 15% gratuity is added to bar and spa accounts.

ACCOMMODATION. There are 17 price categories, including four suite grades and four cabin grades. Price depends on size and location, but all have one thing in common – a good-sized bathroom with tub and separate shower enclosure, plus his 'n' hers toiletry cabinets. All suites/cabins have dark wood cabinetry with rounded edges. The decor includes chocolate brown, cream and white – the sort of earthy colors that don't jar the senses. Around 96% of all accommodation has teak-decked balconies.

● **Standard veranda cabins** measure 282 sq. ft (26 sq. meters). Veranda and Concierge-level cabins have a sitting area and teak balcony with faux wicker furniture. Concierge-level grades get L'Occitane toiletries.

● **Penthouse Suites** measure 420 sq. ft (39 sq. meters) with living/dining room separate from the sleeping area, walk-in closet and bathroom with a double vanity. The large veranda has a hot tub.

● **Oceania Suites** measure about 1,030 sq.ft (96 sq. metres) and have a living room, dining room, separate bedroom, walk-in closet, teak-decked balcony with Jacuzzi tub, main bathroom, and a second bathroom for guests.

● **Vista Suites** range from 1,200 sq. ft to 1,500 sq. ft (111–139 sq. meters) and offer the same features as Oceania Suites plus floor-to-ceiling windows overlooking the bow.

● **The Owner's Suite**, at more than 2,000 sq. ft (186 sq. meters), spans the entire beam of the ship (about 105 ft/32 meters). It is decked out in furniture, fabrics, lighting and bedding from the Ralph Lauren Home collection with design by New York-based Tocar, Inc. It is outfitted with a Yamaha baby grand piano, private fitness room, laptop computers, Bose audio system, and a teak-decked balcony with Jacuzzi tub.

Suite-category occupants get niceties like champagne on arrival, 1,000-thread-count bed linen, 42-inch plasma TV sets, Hermès and Clarins bath amenities, butler service and ensuite delivery from any of the ship's restaurants. Amenities include Tranquility beds, wi-fi laptop computer, refrigerated mini-bar with unlimited free soft drinks and bottled water replenished daily, personal safe, writing desk, cotton bathrobes, slippers and marble and granite bathroom. Priority check-in and early embarkation and priority luggage delivery are extra perks.

Occupants of Owner's, Vista, Oceania and Penthouse suites can have in-suite course-by-course dining from any restaurant menu, allowing private dining as a change from restaurant dining – a nice alternative on longer voyages.

Some grades get access to an Executive or Concierge Lounge. These are great little hideaways, with sofas, internet-connect computers, Continental breakfast items, soft drinks, magazines, and more. Self-service launderettes are on each accommodation deck – useful for long voyages.

CUISINE. This really is a food lover's ship that uses high-quality ingredients and has a wide selection of dining venues, providing plenty of choice, even for long cruises. However, banquette seating in some venues does not evoke the image of premium dining as much as individual seating does. Particularly notable are the breads, rolls, croissants and brioches – all made on board from French flower and d'Isigny butter –the best!

The six main open-seating dining venues are:

● The *Grand Dining Room* has 566 seats, and a domed, or raised, central ceiling. Versace bone china, Christofle silver, fine linens are used. Canyon Ranch spa dishes are available for all meals.

● *Jacques*, with 124 seats, is the second sea-going restaurant for French celebrity chef Jacques Pépin, Oceania's executive culinary director. It has antique oak flooring, antique flatware and Lalique glassware, and provides fine dining in an elegant but informal setting, with roast free-range meats, nine classic French dessert items and a choice of 12 AOC cheeses.

● *Polo Grill*, with about 130 seats, serves steaks and seafood, including Oceania's signature 32-ounce bone-in King's Cut prime rib. The setting is classic traditional steak-house, with dark wood paneling and classic white tablecloths, although the tables are close together.

● *Toscana* is a 124-seat venue serving Italian-style cuisine (including some tasty desserts), and has Versace china.

● *Privée*, with seating for up to 10 in a private setting, invites exclusivity for its seven-course dégustation menu.

● *La Réserve* is the venue for wine and food, offering two different seven-course small-portion dégustation menus. With just 24 seats, it's also really intimate.

The *Terrace Café* is the ship's casual self-serve buffet-style venue. Outdoors, as an extension of the café, is *Tapas on the Terrace*, good for light bites – although the ceiling is low, so it can be very noisy.

Red Ginger is a specialty restaurant which offers "classic and contemporary" Asian cuisine; the setting is visually refined, with ebony and dark wood finishes, but the banquette-style seating lets the venue down. You'll be asked by the waiter to choose your chopsticks from a lacquered presentation box.

The poolside *Waves Grill*, shaded from the sun, is for burgers (including fishburgers and veggie burgers), seafood and other fast food, cooked to order. *Baristas* coffee bar overlooks the pool deck and has excellent illy Italian coffee.

ENTERTAINMENT. The 600-seat Marina Lounge, spans two decks, with tiered amphitheater-style seating. It's more cabaret-style entertainment than big production shows, in keeping with the cruise line's traditions.

SPA/FITNESS. The Canyon Ranch SpaClub provides wellness and personal spa treatments. The facility includes a fitness center, beauty salon, several treatment rooms (including a couples room), sauna and steam rooms, and a thalassotherapy pool (hot tub). A jogging track is located aft of the funnel, above two of the specialty restaurants, and, sensibly, away from all accommodation decks. All treatments incur an automatic 18% gratuity – almost one-fifth of the treatment price.

Rotterdam
★★★★

Size: . . . . .Mid-Size Ship	Passenger Decks: 12	Cabins (with private balcony): 192
Tonnage: 59,855	Total Crew: 600	Cabins (wheelchair accessible): 25
Lifestyle: . . . . .Premium	Passengers	Wheelchair accessibility: . . . . .Best
Cruise Line: . . . . . . .Holland America Line	(lower beds/all berths): 1,404/1,802	Cabin Current: . . . . .110 and 220 volts
Former Names: . . . . .none	Passenger Space Ratio	Elevators: 12
Builder: . . . . .Fincantieri (Italy)	(lower beds/all berths): 42.6/33.2	Casino (gaming tables): . . . . .Yes
Original Cost: . . . .$250 million	Crew/Passenger Ratio	Slot Machines: . . . . .Yes
Entered Service: . . . . .Dec 1997	(lower beds/all berths): 2.3/3.0	Swimming Pools (outdoors): 1
Registry: . . . . .The Netherlands	Cabins (total): 702	Swimming Pools (indoors): 1 (glass cover)
Length (ft/m): 777.5/237.00	Size Range (sq ft/m): 184.0–1,124.8/	Whirlpools: 2
Beam (ft/m): 105.8/32.25	17.1–104.5	Self-Service Launderette: . . . . .Yes
Draft (ft/m): 25.5/7.80	Cabins (outside view): 577	Dedicated Cinema/Seats: Yes/235
Propulsion/Propellers: . . . . .diesel-electric	Cabins (interior/no view): 125	Library: . . . . .Yes
(37,500kW)/2	Cabins (for one person): 0	Onboard currency: . . . . .US$

Dutch traditions and decor for senior-age cruisers.

OVERVIEW. This is a most contemporary ship for Holland America Line, with light, bright decor. It is an extremely comfortable vessel with fine, elegant and luxurious decorative features. But these are marred somewhat by the poor quality of dining room food and service and a lack of understanding of what it takes to make the "luxury" cruise experience touted in the company's brochures.

THE SHIP. This latest *Rotterdam*, the sixth Holland America Line ship to bear the name, is capable of 25 knots – useful for longer itineraries. It has been built to look like a slightly larger but much sleeker version of the *"S"-class* ships, while retaining the graceful lines of its immediate predecessor, including a nicely raked bow and a more rounded exterior. Also retained are the familiar interior flow and design style, and twin-funnel.

Two decks, Promenade Deck and Upper Promenade Deck, house most of the public rooms, and are sandwiched between several accommodation decks. The layout is quite easy to learn, and the signage is good.

The interior decor is restrained, with much use of wood accenting. As a whole, the decor is extremely refined, with much of the traditional ocean liner detailing so loved by frequent HAL passengers. A three-deck-high atrium has an oval, instead of circular, shape. Its focal point is a huge "one-of-a-kind" custom-made clock, based on an antique Flemish original, that includes an astrolabe, an astrological clock and 14 other clocks.

One room has a glass ceiling similar to that aboard a former *Statendam*. The Ambassador's Lounge has an interesting brass dance floor, similar to the dance floor that adorned

BERLITZ'S RATINGS		
	Possible	Achieved
Ship	500	428
Accommodation	200	165
Food	400	281
Service	400	279
Entertainment	100	76
Cruise	400	310
OVERALL SCORE		
1,539 points out of 2,000		

the Ritz-Carlton room aboard the previous *Rotterdam*.

Instead of just two staircases aboard the "S"-class ships, *Rotterdam* has three – better from the viewpoint of safety, passenger accessibility and evacuation. A pool, on the Lido Deck between the mast and the ship's twin funnels, is covered by a glass dome.

Popcorn is available at the Wajang Theatre for moviegoers, while adjacent is the popular Java Café. The casino, located in the middle of a major passenger flow, has blackjack, roulette, poker and dice tables alongside the requisite rows of slot machines.

Holland America Line has a long legacy in Dutch maritime history. The $2 million-worth of artwork here consists of a collection of 17th-century Dutch and Japanese artifacts together with contemporary works specially created for the ship, although there seems little linkage between some of the items.

HAL's "Signature of Excellence" program has created a "Mix," a new open area. The trendy, upbeat space combines three specialty theme bars: Champagne (serving champagne and sparkling wines from around the world), Martinis (in individual shakers), and Spirits & Ales (a sports bar with beer, baseball and basketball). Microsoft Surface touch-screen technology enhances checkers and chess, air hockey, and other sports games.

With one whole deck of suites – and a dedicated, private concierge lounge, and preferential passenger treatment – the company has in effect created a two-class ship. Passenger niggles include inadequate room service, poor staff communication, and the charge to use the washing machines and dryers in the self-service launderette – petty and irritating, particularly for the occupants of suites, as they pay high prices for their cruises.

In a 2009 refit, 23 Verandah Deck cabins were converted into "Spa Cabins," while new Lancei-style cabins were created on Lower Promenade Deck.

FAMILIES. The ship has allotted more space to children's and teens' play areas, although these really are token gestures by a company that traditionally does not cater well to children. However, grandparents do take their grandchildren with them – pleasing parents, who get a well-deserved break. Enhanced children's programming is brought into play according to the number of children carried.

ACCOMMODATION. There are 17 categories, priced by grade, size and location. Accommodation is spread over five decks, and some cabins have full or partially obstructed views. Interestingly, no cabin is more than 144 ft (44 meters) from a stairway, which makes it easier to get from cabins to public rooms. All cabin doors have a bird's-eye maple look, and hallways have framed fabric panels to make them less clinical. Cabin televisions carry CNN and TNT.

All standard inside and outside cabins are tastefully furnished, with twin beds that convert to queen-size, though space is tight for walking between beds and vanity unit. There is a decent amount of closet and drawer space, but this will prove tight for longer voyages.

The fully-tiled bathrooms are disappointingly small, particularly for long cruises, and have small shower tubs, utilitarian toiletries cupboards, and exposed under-sink plumbing. There is no detailing to distinguish them significantly from bathrooms aboard the "S"-class ships.

There are 36 full verandah suites on Navigation Deck, including four penthouse suites, which share a private Concierge Lounge with a concierge to handle such things as special dining arrangements, shore excursions and special requests – although strangely there are no butlers for these suites, as aboard many ships with similar facilities. Each suite has a separate steward's entrance and separate bedroom, dressing and living areas. Suite passengers get personal stationery, complimentary laundry and ironing, cocktail-hour hors d'oeuvres and other goodies, as well as priority embarkation and disembarkation. The concierge lounge, with its latticework teak detailing and private library is accessible only by private key-card.

Disabled passengers have a choice of 20 cabins, including two of the large "penthouse" suites that include concierge services. However, there are different cabin configurations, and it is wise to check with your booking agent.

CUISINE. The *La Fontaine Dining Room* seats 747, spans two decks, and has are tables for four, six or eight, but only nine tables for two. Both open seating and fixed (assigned tables and times) seating are available, while breakfast and lunch are open-seating where you'll be seated by restaurant staff when you enter. Fine Rosenthal china and good cutlery are provided.

Alternative Dining Option: There is also an 88-seat *Odyssey* reservations-required Italian restaurant, decorated in the manner of an opulent 17th-century baroque Italian villa, and available to all passengers. The room, whose basic color is black with gold accenting, is divided into three sections. Cuisines from Italy's Perugia, Tuscany and Umbria regions are featured.

ENTERTAINMENT. The 577-seat Showlounge at Sea is the venue for all production shows, strong cabaret, and other entertainment. It is two decks high, with main and balcony level seating. The decor includes umbrella-shaped gold ceiling lamps of Murano glass, and the stage has hydraulic lifts and three video screens, as well as a closed-loop system for the hearing-impaired.

SPA/FITNESS. The Ocean Spa is one deck above the navigation bridge at the very forward part of the ship. It includes a gymnasium with all the latest muscle-pumping exercise machines, including an abundance of treadmills, with forward views over the ship's bows. There's an aerobics exercise area, large beauty salon with ocean-view windows to the port side, several treatment rooms, and men's and women's sauna, steam room and changing areas.

● **For more extensive general information on what a Holland America Line cruise is like, see pages 140–3.**

Royal Clipper
★★★★

Size: ....Small Ship	Sail Area (sq ft/m2): 56,000/5,204.5	Cabins (interior/no view): 6
Tonnage: 5,061	Main Propulsion: ....42 sails	Cabins (for one person): 0
Lifestyle: ....Premium	Propulsion/Propellers: diesel (3,700kW)/1	Cabins (with private balcony): 14
Cruise Line: ....Star Clippers	Passenger Decks: 5	Cabins (wheelchair accessible): 0
Former Names: ....none	Total Crew: 106	Wheelchair accessibility: ....None
Builder: ....De Merwede (Holland)	Passengers	Cabin Current: ....220 volts
Original Cost: ....$75 million	(lower beds/all berths): 228/255	Elevators: 0
Entered Service: ....Oct 2000	Crew/Passenger Ratio	Casino (gaming tables): ....No
Registry: ....Luxembourg	(lower beds/all berths): 2.1/ 2.4	Slot Machines: ....No
Length (ft/m): 439.6/134.0	Crew/Passenger Ratio	Swimming Pools (outdoors): 3
Beam (ft/m): 54.1/16.5	(lower beds/all berths): 2.2/2.5	Whirlpools: 0
Draft (ft/m): 18.5/5.6	Cabins (total): 114	Self-Service Launderette: ....No
Type of Vessel: sail-cruise (square rigger)	Size Range (sq ft/m): 100.0–320.0/9.3–29.7	Library: ....Yes
Number of Masts: 5	Cabins (outside view): 108	Onboard currency: ....Euros

The ultimate tall ship, exuding character and charm.

OVERVIEW. *Royal Clipper* best suits couples and singles who would probably never even consider a "normal" cruise ship, but who enjoy sailing and the thrill of ocean and wind, but want a package that includes accommodation, food, like-minded companions and interesting destinations, and don't want the bother of owning or chartering their own yacht. What gives the ship a little extra in the scoring department is the fact that many water sports are included in the price of your cruise.

THE SHIP. The culmination of an owner's childhood dream, *Royal Clipper* is a stunning sight under sail. Being marketed as the world's largest true fully rigged sailing ship, this is a logical addition to the company's two other, smaller, 4-masted tall ships (*Star Clipper* and *Star Flyer*). *Royal Clipper*'s 5-masted design is based on the only other 5-masted sailing ship to be built, the 1902-built German tall ship *Preussen*, and has approximately the same dimensions, albeit 46 ft (14 meters) shorter (it is much larger than the famous *Cutty Sark*, for example). It is almost 40 ft (12.1 meters) longer than the largest sailing ship presently in commission – the four-mast Russian barkentine *Sedov*. To keep things in perspective, *Royal Clipper* is the same length overall as *Wind Spirit* and *Wind Star* – the computer-controlled cruise-sail vessels of Windstar Cruises.

The construction time for this ship was remarkably short, owing to the fact that its hull had been almost completed (at Gdansk shipyard, Poland) for another owner (the ship was to be named *Gwarek*) but became available to Star Clippers for completion and fitting out. The ship is instantly recognizable due to its geometric blue and white hull mark-

BERLITZ'S RATINGS		
	Possible	Achieved
Ship	500	406
Accommodation	200	157
Food	400	288
Service	400	296
Entertainment	n/a	n/a
Cruise	500	393
OVERALL SCORE		
1,540 points out of 2,000		

ings. Power winches, as well as hand winches, are employed in deck fittings, as well as a mix of horizontal furling for the square sails and hydraulic power assist to roll the square sails along the yardarm. The sail handling system, which was designed by the ship's owner, Mikael Krafft, is such that it can be converted from a full rigger to a schooner in an incredibly short time.

Its masts reach as high as 197 ft (60 meters) above the waterline, and the top 19 ft (5.8 meters) can be hinged over 90° to clear bridges, cable lines and other port-based obstacles. Watching the sailors manipulate ropes, rigging and sails is like watching a ballet – the precision and cohesion of a group of men who make it all look so simple.

As a passenger, you are allowed to climb to special lookout points aloft – maybe even for a glass of champagne. Passengers are also allowed on the bridge at any time (but not in the galley or engine room).

There is a large amount of open deck space and sunning space aboard this ship – something most tall ships lack, although, naturally, this is laid with ropes for the rigging. A marina platform can be lowered at the stern of the vessel, from where you can use the surfboards, sailing dinghies, take a ride on the ship's own banana boat, or go water-skiing or swimming. Snorkeling gear is available free, but there is a charge for scuba diving gear. You will be asked to sign a waiver if you wish to use the water-sports equipment.

Inside, a midships atrium three decks high sits under one of the ship's three swimming pools, and sunlight streams down through a piano lounge on the uppermost level inside the ship and down into the dining room, which is on the lower level. A forward observation lounge is a real plus, and this is connected to the piano lounge via a central corridor. An Edwardian library/card room is decorated with a *belle époque* fireplace. A lounge, the Captain Nemo Club, is where passengers can observe fish and sea life when the ship is at anchor, through thick glass portholes (floodlit from underneath at night to attract the fish).

This delightful, quite spectacular tall ship for tourists operates seven-night and 14-day cruises in the Grenadines and Lower Windward Islands of the Caribbean during the winter and seven-night and 14-night cruises in the Mediterranean in summer. It is good to note that the officers navigate using both traditional (sextant) and contemporary methods (advanced electronic positioning system).

Being a tall ship with true sailing traditions, there is, naturally, a parrot (sometimes kept in a large, gilded cage, but often seen around the ship on someone's shoulder), which is part of the crew, as aboard all Star Clippers' ships. The general ambience is extremely relaxed, friendly and casual – completely unpretentious. The passenger mix is international (often consisting of a good cross-section of yachting types) and the dress code is casual at all times (shorts and casual tops are the order of the day – yachting wear), with no ties needed at any time.

There is no doubt that *Royal Clipper* is a superb vessel for the actual experience of sailing – a tall ship probably without equal, as much more time is spent actually under sail than aboard almost any other tall ship, including the smaller *Sea Cloud* and *Sea Cloud II*. However, apart from the sailing experience, it is in the cuisine and service that the lack of professionalism and poor standards of delivery shows. The result is a score that could be higher if the cuisine and service were better.

The suites and cabins are larger than those aboard the tall ships of the Windjammer Barefoot Cruises fleet, while, in general, smaller than aboard *Sea Cloud* and *Sea Cloud II*. While the food and service are far superior to the Windjammers, both are well below the standard found aboard *Sea Cloud* and *Sea Cloud II*. I do not include the Windstar Cruises ships (*Wind Spirit, Wind Star, Wind Surf*), because they cannot, in any sense of the word, be considered tall ships. *Royal Clipper*, however, is exactly that – a real, working, wind-and-sails-in-your-face tall ship with a highly per-

sonable captain and crew that welcome you as if you were part of the team.

This vessel is not for the physically impaired, or for children. The steps of the internal stairs are steep, as in most sailing vessels. The tipping system, where all tips are pooled – the suggested amount is around $8 per passenger, per day – causes concern for many passengers.

ACCOMMODATION. There are eight accommodation grades (the price you pay will depend on the grade, size and location you choose): Owner's Suite (2), Deluxe Suite (14), and Categories 1–6. No matter what grade you choose (price will depend on location and size), all have polished wood-trimmed cabinetry and wall-to-wall carpeting, personal safe, full-length mirror, small television with audio channels and 24-hour text-based news, and private bathroom. All have twin beds (86 of which convert into a queen-size bed, while 28 are fixed queen-size beds that cannot be separated), hairdryer and satellite-linked telephone. The six interior cabins and a handful of other cabins have a permanently fixed double bed.

Most cabins have a privacy curtain, so that you cannot be seen from the hallway when the cabin attendant opens the door (useful if you are not wearing any clothes). In addition, 27 cabins sleep three.

The two owner's suites, located at the very aft of the ship, provide the most lavish accommodation, and have one queen-size bed and one double bed, a separate living area with semi-circular sofa, large vanity desk, wet bar/refrigerator, marble-clad bathroom with whirlpool bathtub, plus one guest bathroom, and butler service. The two suites have an interconnecting door, so that the combined super-suite can sleep eight persons. However, there is no private balcony.

The 14 "Deck Suites" have interesting names: Ariel, Cutty Sark, Doriana, Eagle Wing, Flying Cloud, France, Golden Gate, Gloria, Great Republic, Passat, Pommern, Preussen, and Thermopylae. However, they are not actually suites, as the sleeping area cannot be separated from the lounge – they are simply larger cabins with a more luxurious interior, more storage space and a larger bathroom. Each has two lower beds convertible to a queen-size, small lounge area, mini-bar/ refrigerator, writing desk, small private balcony, and marble-clad bathroom with combination whirlpool tub/shower, washbasin and toilet, and butler service. The door to the balcony can be opened so that fresh air floods the room; note that there is a 12-inch (30-cm) threshold to step over.

There are no curtains, only roll-down shades for the windows and balcony door. The balcony itself typically has two white plastic chairs and drinks table; however, teak chairs and table would be more in keeping with the nature of the ship. The 14 balconies are not particularly private, and most have ship's tenders or Zodiacs overhanging them, or some rigging obscuring the views.

A SAILS GUIDE TO ROYAL CLIPPER

Up to 42 sails can be used aboard *Royal Clipper*. 26 square sails (fore upper topgallant, fore lower topgallant, fore upper topsail, fore lower topsail, foresail, main royal, main upper topgallant, main lower topgallant, main upper topsail, main lower topsail, mainsail, middle royal, middle upper topgallant, middle lower topgallant, middle upper topsail, middle lower topsail, middle course, mizzen upper topgallant, mizzen lower topgallant, mizzen upper topsail, mizzen lower topsail, mizzen course, jigger topgallant, jigger upper topsail, jigger lower topsail, crossjack), 11 staysails (main royal staysail, main topgallant staysail, main topmast staysail, middle royal staysail, middle topgallant staysail, middle topmast staysail, mizzen royal staysail, mizzen topgallant staysail, mizzen topmast staysail, jigger topgallant staysail, jigger topmast staysail); 4 jibs (flying jib, outer jib, inner jib, fore topmast staysail) and 1 gaff-rigged spanker, it looks quite magnificent when under full sail – an area of some 54,360 sq. ft (5,050 sq. meters).

Two other name cabins (Lord Nelson and Marco Polo – designated as Category 1 cabins) are located aft, but do not have private balconies, although the facilities are similar.

The interior (no view) cabins and the lowest grades of outside-view cabins are extremely small and tight, with very little room to move around the beds. Therefore, take only the minimum amount of clothing and luggage. When in cabins where beds are linked together to form a double bed, you will have to clamber up over the front of the bed, as both sides have built-in storm barriers (this applies in inclement weather conditions only).

There is a small room service menu (all items cost extra).

CUISINE. The Dining Room is constructed on several connecting levels (getting used to the steps is not easy), and seats all passengers at one seating under a three-deck-high atrium dome. You can sit with whom you wish at tables for four, six, eight or 10. However, it is a noisy dining room, due to the positioning of the many waiter stations, and the waiting staff are poorly trained, making mealtimes less enjoyable than one would wish. Some tables are badly positioned so that correct waiter service is impossible, and much reaching over has to be done in order to serve everyone.

One corner can be closed off for private parties. Breakfasts and lunches are self-serve buffets, while dinner is a sit-down affair with table service, although the ambience is always friendly and lighthearted. The wine list consists of very young wines, and prices are quite high.

The cuisine is certainly nothing to write home about.

Although perfectly acceptable, it certainly cannot be considered in the same class as that found aboard ships such as *Sea Cloud* or *Sea Cloud II*.

ENTERTAINMENT. There are no entertainment shows, nor are any expected by passengers aboard a tall ship such as this, where sailing is the main purpose of a cruise. There is, however, live music, which is provided by a single lounge pianist/singer. Otherwise, dinner is the main evening event, as well as "Captain's Storytime", recaps of the day's interesting events, and conversation with fellow passengers in the lounge or on deck (under the stars) provides engaging entertainment.

During the daytime, when the ship is sailing, passengers can learn about the sails, and the captain or chief officer will give briefings as the sails are being furled and unfurled. The closest this tall ship comes to any kind of "show" is when, one evening towards the end of each cruise, a "sailor's choir", comprised of the ship's crew, presents a nautical performance of sea songs, sea shanties, and other light diversions.

SPA/FITNESS. The Royal Spa is located on the lowest passenger deck and, although not large, incorporates a beauty salon, Moroccan steam room (for which there is a charge), and a small gymnasium with porthole views, several muscle-pump machines body toning equipment, treadmills, rowing machines, and exercycles. Thai massage as well as traditional massage, aromatherapy facials, and other beauty treatments, are available.

Ruby Princess
★★★★

Size: . . . . Large Resort Ship	Passenger Decks: 15	Cabins (with private balcony): 881
Tonnage:. 113,561	Total Crew: 1,200	Cabins (wheelchair accessible): 25
Lifestyle: . . . . Standard	Passengers	Wheelchair accessibility: . . . . .Good
Cruise Line: . . . . Princess Cruises	(lower beds/all berths): 3,114/3,782	Cabin Current: . . . . 110 volts
Former Names: . . . . none	Passenger Space Ratio	Elevators: 14
Builder: . . . . Fincantieri (Italy)	(lower beds/all berths): 36.4/30.0	Casino (gaming tables): . . . . Yes
Original Cost: . . . . $500 million	Crew/Passenger Ratio	Slot Machines: . . . . Yes
Entered Service: . . . . Sep 2008	(lower beds/all berths): 2.5/3.1	Swimming Pools (outdoors): 4
Registry: . . . . Bermuda	Cabins (total): 1,557	Swimming Pools (indoors): 0
Length (ft/m): 951.4/290.0	Size Range (sq ft/m): 163–1,279/	Whirlpools: 9
Beam (ft/m): 118.1/36.0	15.1–118.8	Self-Service Launderette: . . . . Yes
Draft (ft/m): 26.2/8.0	Cabins (outside view): 1,105	Dedicated Cinema/Seats: . . . . No
Propulsion/Propellers: . . . . . diesel-electric	Cabins (interior/no view): 452	Library: . . . . Yes
(42,000kW)/2)	Cabins (for one person): 0	Onboard currency: . . . . US$

A large ship with sedate decor, for family-friendly cruising.

OVERVIEW. This ship, among the best ships in the standard family market, is a veritable resort playground in which to roam when not on a shore excursion. Princess Cruises delivers a consistently fine, well-packaged vacation product, always with a good degree of style, at a highly competitive price. Passenger flow is well thought-out and, despite its large capacity, there is little congestion.

THE SHIP. *Ruby Princess* has the same profile, interior layout and public rooms as sister ships *Crown Princess* (2006) and *Emerald Princess* (2007). Although it accommodates over 500 more passengers than earlier half-sisters such as *Diamond Princess*, the outdoor deck space remains the same, as do the number of elevators – so waiting time can be frustrating during peak usage. The Passenger Space Ratio is also considerably reduced.

The Sanctuary, an extra-cost adults-only retreat, is a facility worth paying extra for if you are cruising in a warm-weather area. It is located forward on the uppermost deck, it provides a "private" place to relax and unwind and includes attendants to provide chilled face towels and deliver water and light bites; there are also two outdoor cabanas for private couples massage.

While The Sanctuary steals space from what used to be a communal passenger area, it is worth the extra cost of $10 a half-day if you are seeking some quiet time, in or out of the sun. The ship's flags flap incessantly on the mast structure within the venue, though, which reduces the tranquility.

There's a good sheltered faux wood promenade strolling deck – it's actually painted steel – which almost wraps around the front and aft sections of the ship; three times

BERLITZ'S RATINGS

	Possible	Achieved
Ship	500	435
Accommodation	200	168
Food	400	256
Service	400	292
Entertainment	100	82
Cruise	400	314

OVERALL SCORE
1,547 points out of 2,000

round is equal to one mile. The outdoor pools have beach-like surroundings, and "Movies Under the Skies" and major sporting events are shown on a 300-sq-ft (28-sq-meter) movie screen located at the pool in front of the large funnel structure. Movies afloat in the open are a big hit with passengers.

With the interior layout and flow similar to that of the sister ships, the main public bars and lounges are located off one double-wide promenade deck. The main lobby is the focal meeting point. Called La Piazza, it's like a town square. It houses a 44-seat International Café with a patisserie/deli and lots of nice cakes and pastries, and Vines, a wine, cheese and corner combined with a sushi/tapas counter.

The library is in a little corner adjacent to the Wheelhouse Bar. There are pleasant bars and lounges. One intimate lounge is Crooners, a New York-style piano bar, with around 70 seats on the upper level of the lobby. Perhaps the nicest of all is Adagio's, a gem of a room.

High atop the stern is a ship-wide glass-walled disco pod. It looks like an aerodynamic "spoiler" and is positioned high above the water, with spectacular views. It would make a great penthouse, but is a good place to read a book during the day. The interior decor is attractive, with lots of earth tones well suited to both American and European tastes, with nothing too glitzy.

Ruby Princess also includes a wedding chapel, Hearts and Minds, also good for renewal of vows ceremonies; a live web-cam can relay ceremonies via the internet. The ship's captain can legally marry American couples, thanks to the ship's Bermuda registry and a special dispensation – which should be verified when in the planning stage, according to where you reside. But to get married and take close family members and friends with you on your honeymoon is going to cost a lot.

The casino, Gatsby's, has more than 260 slot machines, and blackjack, craps and roulette tables, plus newer games. A highlight might be the linked slot machines that provide a combined payout.

Ship lovers should enjoy the wood-paneled Wheelhouse Bar, finely decorated with memorabilia and ship models. A high-tech hospital has SeaMed tele-medicine link-ups to specialists at the Cedars-Sinai Medical Center in Los Angeles, who are available for emergency help.

Whether you'll have a relaxing vacation is a moot point. But, with so many choices and "small" rooms, the ship has been extremely well designed, and odds are you'll enjoy it. If you aren't used to large ships, it will take you some time to find your way around, despite the company's claim that it offers passengers a "small ship feel, big ship choice."

FAMILIES. For children, there are several playrooms, a teen room, and a host of trained counselors. Children have their own pools, hot tubs, and open deck area at the stern, away from adult areas. There are good netted-in areas; one section has a dip pool, while another has a mini-basketball court. The Wizard's Academy is an enrichment program from the California Science Center.

ACCOMMODATION. There are six main types of cabins and configurations: (a) grand suite, (b) suite, (c) mini-suite, (d) outside-view double cabins with balcony, (e) outside-view double cabins, and (f) interior double cabins. These come in 35 different brochure price categories. The choice is quite bewildering for both travel agents and passengers, but pricing will depend on two things: size and location. By comparison, the largest suite is slightly smaller, and the smallest interior cabin is slightly larger than the equivalent suites/cabins aboard *Golden, Grand* and *Star Princess*.

Cabin bath towels are small, and drawer space is very limited. There are no butlers – even for the top-grade suites, which are not large in comparison to similar suites aboard some other similarly-sized ships. Cabin attendants have too many cabins to look after – typically 20 – which does not translate to fine personal service.

(a) The largest, most lavish suite is the Grand Suite: A750, located at the stern. It has a large bedroom with queen-size bed, huge walk-in closets, two bathrooms, a lounge with fireplace, sofa bed, wet bar and refrigerator, and a large private balcony on the port side, with a hot tub accessible from both balcony and bedroom.

(b/c) Suites, with a semi-private balcony, have a separate living room with sofa bed, and bedroom, with a TV set in each. The bathroom is quite large and has both a tub and shower stall. The mini-suites also have a private balcony, and a separate living and sleeping area, with a TV set in each. The differences between the suites and mini-suites are basically in the size and appointments, the suite being more of a square shape while mini-suites are more rectangular and have few drawers. Both suites and mini-suites

have plush bathrobes, and fully tiled bathrooms with ample open shelf storage space. Passengers in both receive greater attention, including priority embarkation and disembarkation privileges. What is not good is that the most expensive accommodation has only semi-private balconies that can be seen from above, so there is little privacy – Suites C401, 402, 404, 406, 408, 410, 412, 401, 405, 411, 415 and 417 on Riviera Deck 14. Also, the suites D105 and D106 (Dolphin Deck 9), which are extremely large, have balconies that are overlooked from above.

(d/e/f). Both interior and outside-view cabins – the outsides come either with or without private balcony – are of a functional, practical, design, although almost no drawers are provided. They are quite attractive, with warm, pleasing decor and fine soft furnishing fabrics; 80 percent of the outside-view cabins have a private balcony. Interior cabins measure 163 sq. ft (15.1 sq. meters).

The 28 wheelchair-accessible cabins measure 250–385 sq. ft (23.2–35.7 sq. meters); surprisingly, there is no mirror for dressing, and no full-length hanging space for long dresses – some passengers in wheelchairs *do* use mirrors and full-length clothing. Additionally, two family suites consist of two suites with an interconnecting door, plus a large balcony. These can sleep up to 10 if at least four are children, or up to eight adults.

All cabins receive turndown service and heart-shaped chocolates on pillows each night, bathrobes (on request unless you are in suite-grade accommodation) and toiletries. A hairdryer is provided in all cabins, sensibly located at the vanity desk unit in the living area. All bathrooms have tiled floors, and there is a decent amount of open shelf storage space for toiletries, although the plain beige decor is basic and unappealing.

Most outside-view cabins on Emerald Deck have views obstructed by lifeboats. There are no cabins for singles. Your name is placed outside your suite or cabin in a documents holder, making it simple for delivery service personnel but also reducing privacy. There is 24-hour room service, but some items on the room service menu are not available during early morning hours.

Some cabins can accommodate a third and fourth person in upper berths. However, in such cabins, the lower beds can't then be pushed together to make queen-size bed.

Almost all balcony suites and cabins can be overlooked both from the navigation bridge wing, as well as from the port and starboard sections of the ship's discotheque – high above the ship at the stern. Cabins with balconies on Dolphin, Caribe and Baja decks can be overlooked by passengers on balconies on the decks above; they are, therefore, not at all private.

Passengers occupying some the most expensive suites with balconies at the stern of the vessel may experience some vibration during certain ship maneuvers. Many cabins on Emerald Deck 8 have a lifeboat-obstructed view.

CUISINE. As befits the ship's size, there's a lot of dining options. There are three main dining rooms, plus Sterling Steakhouse, and Sabatini's Trattoria.

The three rooms for formal dining are *Botticelli, Da Vinci,* and *Michelangelo.* The Botticelli Dining Room has traditional two seating dining (typically 6pm and 8:15pm for dinner), while "anytime dining" – where you choose when and with whom you want to eat – is offered in Da Vinci and Michelango. All are split into various sections in a non-symmetrical design that breaks the large spaces into smaller parts for better ambience, and each restaurant has its own galley.

Dinnerware by Dudson of England, high-quality linens and silverware, Frette Egyptian cotton table linens, and silverware by Hepp of Germany are used in the main dining rooms. Note that 15% is added to all beverage bills, including wines.

Alternative Dining Options: *Sabatini's* and *Crown Grill,* both extra-charge and reservations needed, are open for lunch and dinner on days at sea. Sabatini's is a 132-seat Italian eatery with some painted scenes of Tuscan villas and gardens and colorful tiled Mediterranean-style decor; it is named after Trattoria Sabatini, the 200-year old institution in Florence. It has Italian-style pizzas and pastas, with a variety of sauces, as well as Italian-style entrées, including tiger prawns and lobster tail, all provided with flair and entertainment by the waiters. It is also open for breakfast for suite/mini-suite occupants only – when it really is a quiet haven.

The 138-seat-seat Crown Grill serves an excellent array of steaks, chops and sizzled seafood items. It is located off the main indoor Deck 7 promenade. Seating is mainly in semi-private alcoves, and the venue incorporates a show kitchen for those who like to watch the action.

The cuisine in the alternative dining venues is deservedly better than in the three main dining rooms. It is cooked à la minute, with better quality ingredients and more attention to presentation and taste.

Casual eateries include a poolside hamburger grill and pizza bar (no additional charge), while extra charges do apply if you order items to eat at the coffee bar/patisserie, or the caviar/champagne bar.

Other casual meals can be taken in the 312-seat *Horizon Court,* with its indoor-outdoor seating, open 24 hours a day. It has large ocean-view windows on port and starboard sides and direct access to the principal swimming pools and lido deck forward, and a more secluded aft pool deck and several terraces. There is no real finesse in presentation, however, as plastic plates are provided and the central display sections are really crowded.

An aft section, *Café Caribe,* provides themed menus (Italian, French, Bavarian, for example) each evening, and

may be provide welcome change from the busy main dining venues.

A "Pub Lunch" is offered on sea days in the *Wheelhouse Bar.* It includes bangers (sausages) and mash, cottage pie, fish and chips, and ploughman's lunch – at no extra cost.

The *International Café,* on Deck 5 in The Piazza, is the place for coffees and specialty coffees, pastries, light lunches, and delightful afternoon cakes, most at no extra cost.

Ultimate Balcony Dinner/Breakfast: For something different, you could try a private dinner on your balcony, an all-inclusive evening featuring cocktails, fresh flowers, champagne and a deluxe multi-course meal – all served by a member of the dining staff. It costs extra – $50 per person for dinner, or $32 per couple for the Ultimate Balcony Breakfast – which really is superb value for money.

Chef's Dinner: For a $75 per person charge, this exclusive dining experience showcases the talents of the executive chef in a mini-dégustation that includes an array of appetizers in the galley. It really is a fine dining experience that includes good wines paired with high-quality meat and seafood dishes, and extremely creative presentation. It's worth taking the three hours needed to enjoy this special dinner; the slow-cooked roast veal shank is outstanding.

ENTERTAINMENT. The Princess Theater, the main entertainment venue, spans two decks and has comfortable seating on both main and balcony levels. It has $3 million worth of sound and light equipment, plus a nine-piece orchestra. The ship has a resident troupe of 19 singers and dancers, plus an army of audio-visual support staff.

Club Fusion, a second entertainment lounge, is located aft. It presents cabaret acts at night, and lectures, bingo and horse racing during the day. Explorers, a third entertainment lounge, can also host cabaret acts and dance bands. A variety of other lounges and bars have live music, and Princess Cruises employs a number of male dance hosts as partners for women traveling alone.

SPA/FITNESS. The Lotus Spa is located forward on Sun Deck – one of the uppermost decks. Separate facilities for men and women include a sauna, steam room, and changing rooms; common facilities include a relaxation/waiting zone, body-pampering treatment rooms, and a gymnasium with the latest high-tech muscle-pumping, cardio-vascular equipment, accompanied by great ocean views. Some fitness classes are free, while others cost extra.

● **For more extensive general information on what the Princess Cruises experience is like, see pages 149–52.**

Ryndam
★★★★

Size: . . . . .Mid-Size Ship	Passenger Decks: 10	Cabins (with private balcony): 150
Tonnage: .55,451	Total Crew: 557	Cabins (wheelchair accessible): 6
Lifestyle: . . . . .Premium	Passengers	Wheelchair accessibility: . . . . .Fair
Cruise Line: . . . . . . .Holland America Line	(lower beds/all berths): 1,266/1,627	Cabin Current: . . . . .110 and 220 volts
Former Names: . . . . .none	Passenger Space Ratio	Elevators: 8
Builder: . . . . .Fincantieri (Italy)	(lower beds/all berths): 43.8/34.0	Casino (gaming tables): . . . . .Yes
Original Cost: . . . .$215 million	Crew/Passenger Ratio	Slot Machines: . . . . .Yes
Entered Service: . . . . .Nov 1994	(lower beds/all berths): 2.2/2.9	Swimming Pools (outdoors): 1
Registry: . . . . .The Netherlands	Cabins (total): 633	Swimming Pools (indoors): .1 (glass dome)
Length (ft/m): 719.3/219.3	Size Range (sq ft/m): 186.2–1,124.8/	Whirlpools: 2
Beam (ft/m): 101.0/30.8	17.3–104.5	Self-Service Launderette: . . . . .Yes
Draft (ft/m): 24.6/7.5	Cabins (outside view): 502	Dedicated Cinema/Seats: Yes/249
Propulsion/Propellers: . . . . .diesel-electric	Cabins (interior/no view): 131	Library: . . . . .Yes
(34,560kW)/2	Cabins (for one person): 0	Onboard currency: . . . . .US$

Dutch decor and artifacts to suit senior-age cruisers.

OVERVIEW. This ship has fairly decent interior fit and finish. Holland America Line constantly fine-tunes its performance as a cruise operator and regular passengers, almost all of whom are North American, find its ships very comfortable and well-run, even though the current food and service let down the rest of the cruise experience. The ship is deployed year-round in the Caribbean, where its rather dark interior decor contrasts with the strong sunlight.

THE SHIP. *Ryndam* is one of a series of four almost identical ships, the others being *Maasdam, Statendam,* and *Veendam.* The exterior styling is rather angular – some would say boxy – although it is softened and balanced by the black hull. There is a full walk-around teakwood promenade deck outdoors – excellent for strolling, and, thankfully, there's no sign of synthetic turf. The sunloungers here are wooden, with comfortable cushioned pads, while those at the swimming pool on Lido Deck are of white plastic. Holland America Line keeps its ships clean and tidy, and there is good passenger flow throughout the public areas.

A 2010 refurbishment created "Mix," which combines library, lounge, internet center, and coffee bar; and 16 cabins near the spa were transformed into "spa" cabins.

In the interiors of this "S"-class ship, an asymmetrical layout helps to reduce bottlenecks and congestion. Most public rooms are concentrated on two decks, Promenade Deck and Upper Promenade Deck, which creates a spacious feel. In general, a restrained approach to interior styling is taken, using a mixture of contemporary materials combined with traditional woods and ceramics. There is, fortunately, little "glitz" anywhere.

BERLITZ'S RATINGS		
	Possible	Achieved
Ship	500	372
Accommodation	200	150
Food	400	254
Service	400	287
Entertainment	100	72
Cruise	400	285
OVERALL SCORE		
1,420 points out of 2,000		

What is outstanding is the array of artworks throughout the ship, costing about $2 million), assembled and nicely displayed to represent the cruise line's fine Dutch heritage. Also noticeable are the fine flower arrangements throughout the public areas and foyers – used to good effect to brighten up what some consider dull decor.

Atop the ship, with forward-facing views that wrap around the sides, is the Crow's Nest Lounge. By day it is a fine observation lounge with large ocean-view windows, while by night it turns into a nightclub with extremely variable lighting. The three-deck-high atrium foyer is attractive, although its sculptured centerpiece makes it look a little crowded and leaves little room in front of the reception office. A hydraulic glass roof covers the reasonably sized swimming pool/whirlpools and central Lido area (whose focal point is a large dolphin sculpture) so that this can be used in all weathers. There is a large and relaxing reference library. The line's many repeat passengers seem to like the fact that social dancing is on the menu.

The company provides complimentary cappuccino and espresso coffees, and free ice cream during certain hours of the day, as well as hot hors d'oeuvres in all bars – something other major lines seem to have dropped, or charge extra for. However, the score for this ship ends up a tad under what it could be if the food and waiting staff were better – more professional training might help.

An escalator travels between two of the lower decks (one of which was originally planned to be the embarkation point), but it is almost pointless. The charge to use the washing machines and dryers in the self-service launderette is petty, particularly for suite occupants, as they pay steep prices for their cruises. The men's urinals in public restrooms are unusually high. Perhaps the ship's best asset is its personable Filipino and Indonesian crew, although communication can prove frustrating.

ACCOMMODATION. This ranges from small interior cabins to a large penthouse suite, in seven types and almost 30 price categories. All cabin TV sets carry CNN.

The interior and outside-view standard cabins have twin beds that convert to a queen-size bed, and there is a separate living space with sofa and coffee table. However, although the drawer space is generally good, the closet space is very tight, particularly for long cruises – although more than adequate for a seven-night cruise). Bathrobes are provided for all suites/cabins, as are hairdryers, and a small range of personal amenities. The bathrooms are quite well laid out, but the tubs are small units better described as shower tubs. Some cabins have interconnecting doors.

On Navigation Deck, 28 suites have accommodation for up to four. These suites also have in-suite dining as an alternative to the dining room. These are very spacious, tastefully decorated and well laid-out, with a separate living room, bedroom with two lower beds (convertible to a king-size bed), a good sized living area, dressing room, plenty of storage space, and a marble bathroom with Jacuzzi tub.

The largest accommodation, a single penthouse suite, is on the starboard side of Navigation Deck at the forward staircase. It has a king-size bed, a TV set and video player, and a vanity desk, a large walk-in closet with superb drawer space, oversize whirlpool bath (it could seat four) and separate shower enclosure, and a washroom with toilet, bidet and basin. The living room has a writing desk, a large TV set and a full set of audio equipment. There's a dressing room, a large private balcony (with teak lounge chairs and drinks tables, dining table and four chairs), a pantry (with large refrigerator, toaster unit, a full coffee/tea making facilities and food preparation area, and a separate entrance from the hallway), mini-bar/refrigerator, a guest toilet and floor to ceiling windows. There is no bell push.

CUISINE. The Rotterdam Dining Room, at the stern, spans two decks. It is quite dramatic, with two grand staircases to connect the two levels, panoramic views on three sides, and a music balcony. Both open seating and fixed (assigned tables and times) seating are available, while breakfast and lunch are open-seating (you'll be seated by restaurant staff when you enter). There are tables for two, four, six or eight.

The waiter stations in the dining room are very noisy for anyone seated adjacent to them. Fine Rosenthal china and cutlery are used, although there are no fish knives. Live music is provided for dinner each evening; once each cruise, there's a Dutch Dinner (hats are provided), as is an Indonesian Lunch. "Lighter option" meals are always available for the health-conscious.

Alternative Dining Option: An intimate restaurant, the *Pinnacle Grill*, is located just forward of the balcony level of the main dining room on the starboard side. The 66-seat dining spot (reservations are necessary, and a cover/service charge applies) serves Pacific Northwest cuisine such as fresh Alaskan salmon and halibut, and other regional specialties, plus a selection of premium steaks such as filet mignon from Black Angus beef. The Pinnacle Grill is a much better dining experience than the main dining room and enhances that special celebration.

For more casual evening eating, the *Lido Buffet* is open for dinners on all except the last night of each cruise, in an open-seating arrangement; part of it is designated as Canaletto for dinner, featuring Italian fare. Tables are set with crisp linens, flatware and stemware. The set menu includes a choice of four entrées. The self-serve Lido Buffet is also the place for casual breakfasts and lunches. Again there is much use of canned fruits and packets of items, although there are several commercial low-calorie salad dressings. The choice of cheeses (and accompanying crackers) is very poor. The beverage stations are no better than those found in the average family outlet ashore in the United States. In addition, a poolside grill provides basic American hamburgers and hot dogs.

Passengers will need to eat in the Lido Buffet on days when the dining room is closed for lunch – typically once or twice per cruise, depending on the ship's itinerary.

ENTERTAINMENT. The Showroom at Sea spans two decks, with banquette seating on both main and upper levels. It is basically a well designed room, but the ceiling is low and the sightlines from the balcony level are poor.

While Holland America Line is not known for its fine entertainment, what the line does offer is a consistently good, tried and tested array of cabaret acts that constantly rove the cruise ship circuit. The production shows, however, while a good attempt, fall short on storyline, choreography and performance, with colorful costuming and lighting hiding the weak spots.

A number of bands, a string ensemble and solo musicians play live music in many lounges and bars. There's evening dancing in the Crow's Nest, and serenading string music in the Explorer's Lounge and dining room.

SPA/FITNESS. The Greenhouse Spa is one deck below the navigation bridge at the very forward part of the ship. It includes a gymnasium with ocean views, an aerobics exercise area, large beauty salon with ocean-view windows to the port side, several treatment rooms, and men's and women's sauna, steam room and changing areas. The spa is operated by Steiner, a specialist concession.

● **For more extensive general information on what a Holland America Line cruise is like, see pages 140–3.**

Saga Pearl II
★★★ +

Size:	Small Ship	Passenger Decks:	8	Cabins (with private balcony):	40
Tonnage:	18,591	Total Crew:	252	Cabins (wheelchair accessible):	0
Lifestyle:	Standard	Passengers		Wheelchair accessibility:	Fair
Cruise Line:	Saga Cruises	(lower beds/all berths):	456/456	Cabin Current:	220 volts
Former Names:	*Astoria, Arkona, Astor*	Passenger Space Ratio		Elevators:	3
Builder:	Howaldtswerke Deutsche Werft	(lower beds/all berths):	40.7/40.7	Casino (gaming tables):	No
(Germany)		Crew/Passenger Ratio		Slot Machines:	No
Original Cost:	$55 million	(lower beds/all berths):	1.8/1.8	Swimming Pools (outdoors):	1
Entered Service:	Dec 1981/Mar 2010	Cabins (total):	258	Swimming Pools (indoors):	1
Registry:	The Bahamas	Size Range (sq ft/m):	150.0–725.0/	Whirlpools:	0
Length (ft/m):	539.2/164.35		13.4–65.3	Self-Service Launderette:	Yes
Beam (ft/m):	74.1/22.60	Cabins (outside view):	178	Dedicated Cinema/Seats:	No
Draft (ft/m):	20.0/6.11	Cabins (interior/no view):	82	Library:	Yes
Propulsion/Propellers: diesel (13,200kW)/2		Cabins (for one person):	60	Onboard currency:	UK£

A comfortable small ship for adults-only cruising.

OVERVIEW. This ship is best suited to English-speaking couples, and single travelers of mature years who seek a good value for money holiday in a traditional cruise ship setting, with appealing itineraries and destinations, good food and friendly service. Saga Cruises staff, aboard every cruise, go out of their way to ensure you have an excellent time in very comfortable surroundings. In May 2012, the ship will change its name to *Quest for Adventure* and join the Spirit of Adventure cruise brand, which is owned and operated by Saga Cruises.

THE SHIP. *Saga Pearl II*, originally *Astor*, is a traditional-looking cruise ship originally built for the long-defunct Astor Cruises. A multi-million pound 2009 refit added a superb new 3,000-book library, an array of balcony cabins, and new galleys. There is a good amount of open deck and sunbathing space for its size, with some good teakwood decks, polished wood railings, and cushioned pads for sunloungers. There is no walk-around promenade deck outdoors, but a small walking area under the lifeboats exists on both sides. Unusually for this size of ship, there is an indoor swimming pool and wellness center.

The interior fittings and decor are pleasing, and include a great deal of rosewood paneling and wood accenting. The ship has been maintained extremely well. Subdued lighting and soothing ambience, highlighted by fine artwork, make for a relaxing, non-glitzy experience. The well-stocked library is a good meeting and relaxation venue. The ship has British navigation and engineering officers and traditional European-style hotel service, with a mostly Filipino hotel service staff. The reception desk is open 24 hours a day.

BERLITZ'S RATINGS		
	Possible	Achieved
Ship	500	320
Accommodation	200	134
Food	400	264
Service	400	287
Entertainment	100	72
Cruise	400	273
OVERALL SCORE		
1,350 points out of 2,000		

Saga Pearl II provides good value for money cruising in comfort, and is best recommended for passengers who appreciate quality, fine surroundings, and excellent destination-intensive itineraries, all packaged neatly in an informal setting. Many cruises have special themes. Port taxes, insurance and gratuities to staff are all included in the cruise fare.

ACCOMMODATION. The accommodation consists of 24 price categories, including 10 grades for single-occupancy cabins, and is spread over four accommodation decks. Some 40 "French" balconies were added in the 2009 refit, which means occupants can open the doors for fresh air, but there is no balcony to step out onto.

Grand Suites: Two Boat Deck suites (725 sq. ft/65.3 sq. meters) provide really large spaces, and have just about everything needed for refined, private living aboard this ship. There is a separate bedroom with double bed, living room with sofa, dining table and chairs. The tiled bathroom has a large tub, separate shower enclosure, and plenty of storage space for toiletries.

Suites: 34 Suites (269.1 sq. ft/25 sq. meters) have a separate bedroom with twin beds, living room with sofa, dining table and chairs. The tiled bathroom has a large tub, separate shower enclosure, and plenty of space for toiletries.

Outside-view Cabins/Interior Cabins: The standard cabins (139.9 sq. ft/13 sq. meters) are quite well appointed and decorated, and all have crisp, clean colors – some might find them plain. The bathrooms are quite compact units, although there is a decent-sized shower enclosure. They are fully tiled, however, and have a decent cabinet for storing toiletries. Passengers in all grades get 100% cotton towels, and bathrobe. The cabin service menu is very limited.

CUISINE. The *Dining Room*, fairly high in the ship, has big, ocean-view picture windows and is reasonably attractive, with dark wood paneling and restful decor. There is a single, open seating, at tables for four, six or eight. Two small wings, each with one 12-seat table, can be used for small groups. The wine list has a decent selection of wines from many regions, at inexpensive to moderate prices.

Self-serve buffets, for breakfast and lunch, and as a casual alternative to dinner in the Dining Room, can be taken in the *Verandah Restaurant*, which overlooks the aft pool and open deck area.

ENTERTAINMENT. The Discovery Lounge is the main showlounge. It is a single-level room, although there are 14 pillars that obstruct the sight lines from many of the seats. The stage also acts as the dance floor and cannot be raised for shows. The entertainment, therefore, consists of cabaret-style shows typically with singers, magicians and other visual acts.

SPA/FITNESS. The spa is located on the lowest passenger deck, and contains a sauna (but no steam room), solarium, indoor swimming pool, treatment rooms and changing areas. Massage, facials, manicures and pedicures are some of the services offered, although the beauty salon itself is on the deck above the spa.

KNOTS AND LOGS

A knot is a unit of speed measuring one nautical mile. (A nautical mile is equal to one-60th of a degree of the earth's circumference and measures exactly 6,080.2 ft (1,852 km). It is about 800 ft (243 meters) longer than a land mile. Thus, when a ship is traveling at a speed of 20 knots (note: this is never referred to as 20 knots per hour), it is traveling at 20 nautical miles per hour (1 knot equals 1.151 land miles).

This unit of measurement has its origin in the days prior to the advent of modern aids, when sailors used a log and a length of rope to measure the distance that their boat had covered, as

well as the speed at which it was advancing. In 1574, a tract by William Bourne, entitled A Regiment for the Sea, records the method by which this was done. The log was weighted down at one end while the other end was affixed to a rope. The weighted end, when thrown over the stern, had the effect of making the log stand upright, thus being visible. Sailors believed that the log remained stationary at the spot where it had been cast into the water, while the rope unraveled. By measuring the length of rope used, they could ascertain how far the ship had traveled, and were thus able to calculate its speed.

Sailors first tied knots at regular intervals, eventually fixed at 47 ft 3 inches (14.4 meters) along a rope, then counted how many knots had passed through their hands in a specified time (later established as 28 seconds), and measured by the amount of sand that had run out of an hourglass. They then used simple multiplication to calculate the number of knots their ship was traveling at over the period of an hour.

The data gathered in this way were put into a record, called a logbook. Today, a logbook is used to record the day-to-day details of the life of a ship and its crew as well as other pertinent information.

Conversion Chart

10 knots = 11.5 mph (18.50 km)	18 knots = 20.7 mph (33.31 km)
11 knots = 12.65 mph (20.35 km)	19 knots = 21.85 mph (35.16 km)
12 knots = 13.8 mph (22.20 km)	20 knots = 23.00 mph (37.01 km)
13 knots = 14.95 mph (24.05 km)	21 knots = 24.15 mph (38.86 km)
14 knots = 16.1 mph (25.90 km)	22 knots = 25.3 mph (40.71 km)
15 knots = 17.25 mph (27.76 km)	23 knots = 26.45 mph (42.56 km)
16 knots = 18.4 mph (29.61 km)	24 knots = 27.6 mph (44.41 km)
17 knots = 19.55 mph (31.46 km)	25 knots = 28.75 mph (46.26 km)

Saga Ruby
★★★★

Size: . . . . .Mid-Size Ship	Total Crew: 380	Cabins (wheelchair accessible): 4
Tonnage: .24,492	Passengers	Wheelchair accessibility: . . . . .Fair
Lifestyle: . . . . .Premium	(lower beds/all berths): 655/655	Cabin Current: . . . . .110 volts
Cruise Line: . . . . .Saga Cruises	Passenger Space Ratio	Elevators: 6
Former Names: . . . . . . .Caronia, Vistafjord	(lower beds/all berths): . . . . . . .37.3/37..3	Casino (gaming tables): . . . . .No
Builder: . . . . .Swan, Hunter (UK)	Crew/Passenger Ratio	Slot Machines: .No
Original Cost: . . . .$35 million	(lower beds/all berths): 1.7/1.7	Swimming Pools (outdoors): 1
Entered Service: . . . .May 1973/Mar 2005	Cabins (total): .376	Swimming Pools (indoors): 1
Registry: . . . . .Great Britain	Size Range (sq ft/m): 66.7–871.9/	Whirlpools: 2
Length (ft/m): 626.9/191.09	6.2–81.0	Self-Service Launderette: . . . . .Yes
Beam (ft/m): 82.1/25.05	Cabins (outside view): 324	Dedicated Cinema/Seats: Yes/190
Draft (ft/m): 27.0/8.23	Cabins (interior/no view): 52	Library: . . . . .Yes
Propulsion/Propellers: diesel (17,900kW)/2	Cabins (for one person): 70	Onboard currency: . . . . .UK£
Passenger Decks: 9	Cabins (with private balcony): 25	

A classic cruise ship for traditionalists over 50 years old.

OVERVIEW. This ship is best suited to couples and single travelers, almost all English, who seek a holiday afloat in a classic ship setting that is unpretentious, yet provides decent accommodation, good food and friendly service, as well as interesting itineraries and destinations. Passengers must be over 50, although spouses and partners can be as young as 45. Male dance hosts are provided for the many single women who travel with Saga Cruises.

BERLITZ'S RATINGS		
	Possible	Achieved
Ship	500	362
Accommodation	200	151
Food	400	280
Service	400	274
Entertainment	100	80
Cruise	400	274
OVERALL SCORE		
1,421 points out of 2,000		

THE SHIP. Saga Ruby, formerly Cunard Line's Caronia, has classic liner styling and profile, and really does look like a traditional ship. It was built with excellent quality materials for long-distance, low-density cruising – the original capacity was just 500 passengers – and has been well maintained. Smooth and quiet in operation, it is stable at sea due to its deep draft. Each day, the ship's bell is sounded at noon in accordance with maritime tradition. Saga Cruises gave it a £17 million refit in 2004–5.

The open decks and sunbathing space are expansive. There is a wide teak walk-around promenade deck outdoors, and sunloungers have cushioned pads – ideal for resting, relaxation, and for reading a good book. Bouillon is served on sea days.

Inside, the spacious and elegant public rooms – mostly located on Veranda Deck – have high ceilings and tasteful decor, and wide interior stairwells are subtly illuminated. The interior decor and soft furnishings are of soft, earth-toned colors that provide a calm, soothing and non-threatening environment for the longer cruises that Saga passengers enjoy. This child-free ship provides a refined, user-friendly environment with a wide range of public rooms. The Bri-

tannia Lounge is at the front of Veranda Deck; behind it are the Theater (dedicated cinema), Card Room, Ballroom (show lounge) and the Lido Café. There's an expansive and well-used library, a computer learning center, and separate internet-connect center. Few ships of this size can match the relaxing ambience and gracious service from a well-organized, friendly and happy mix of European and Filipino service staff. There are refreshingly few announcements and interruptions.

Saga Cruises includes many things other UK-based operators charge extra for: transfers to the ship, all gratuities, shuttle buses in ports of call, where possible, and newspapers in the library in each port of call, when available.

ACCOMMODATION. The brochure lists 21 cabin categories (seven of which are for single travelers wanting a cabin to themselves), from duplex penthouse suites with huge private balconies, to small interior cabins, in a wide range of different configurations. The cabins are smaller than those aboard former sister ship Saga Rose but all are well appointed, with good-sized bathrooms. Some cabins have a full-size bathtub, while others have a shower enclosure only; hand-held shower hoses are standard – better and more hygienic than fixed showers.

The grandest living spaces are the two duplex suites, Concerto and Symphony. They are superb living spaces and occupy two levels. The lower level has a large bedroom and marble-clad bathroom with Jacuzzi tub. The upper level has an expansive living room with floor-to-ceiling windows with unobstructed front and side views, a Bang & Olufsen sound system, treadmill, private bar, and a large bathroom (with Jacuzzi tub) and separate private sauna. There is a huge, private balcony outdoors on deck, complete with a two-person hot tub, a teak deck, and great views. A private internal stairway connects the upper and lower levels.

Most other cabins designated as suites (on Bridge Deck lower level, and Sun Deck) have private balconies, are nicely equipped, and have ample closet and drawer space (some also have a large walk-in closet), vanity desk, large beds, and bookshelves filled with suitable destination books or novels. The marble-clad bathrooms are large and have a full-size Jacuzzi tub, two washbasins, toilet and bidet.

All other cabins are tastefully decorated, and all have a refrigerator, mini-bar, personal safe, European duvets in two thicknesses, a range of Molton Brown toiletries (Temple Spa amenities in suites), and thick 100% cotton bathrobes. The wooden cabinetry has nicely rounded edges. Bathrooms have a whisper-quiet (non-vacuum) toilet.

This ship has an excellent range of cabins for single travelers, unlike almost all new cruise ships. Some Sun Deck and Promenade Deck suites have obstructed views. All suites and cabins have a flat-screen TV with integral DVD player.

CUISINE. Although it lacks the grandeur, high ceiling or grand stairway of former sister ship *Saga Rose*, the *Saga Dining Room* is elegant, and offers single-seating dining at assigned tables – refreshing, when so many of today's cruise ships have two seatings. There more tables for two than aboard many other cruise ships, as well as tables for two, four, six and eight. Senior officers often host tables for dinner – and always on formal nights. Single-waiter service is provided by Filipino waiters, in the European tradition. Some tables are a little close together, however, making it hard for waiters to serve properly in some areas.

The wide range of menu items include many British favorites, with a reasonably high standard of quality and variety. A cold table is set for such things as breads and cheeses at lunchtime, and passengers can help themselves or be served. Salad items, many salad dressings, juices, and a selection of international cheeses are always available. Plate service (where vegetables and entrées are set on the main course plate) is provided, and extra vegetables are available on request. This is service in the classic seagoing tradition, in unhurried style.

For afternoon tea, there is a good selection of cakes and pastries – and scones, of course. Vegetarian items and diabetic desserts are always available and other special dietary items can be provided with sufficient notice. The wine list has a good selection, and is excellent value for money.

Alternative Dining: *View* is a delightful à la carte restaurant that is elegant and very intimate, with only 12 tables. It has the feel of a small, exclusive bistro, with excellent cuisine from a varied menu. Reservations are required, but there is no extra charge.

Casual Eatery: The *Lido Café* is a well laid out casual dining area with a range of self-service buffets for breakfast, lunch and dinner. While there is some repetition of breakfast items, other meals offer a wide variety of hot and cold food items. A self-serve tea/coffee/beverage station is available 24 hours a day; a machine provides espresso and cappuccino at no extra cost, and ice cream is free, too – most ships now charge extra for these items.

Bar drinks (and wine) prices are extremely reasonable, and include gratuities. Once each cruise, there is a champagne breakfast.

ENTERTAINMENT. The Ballroom is the main venue for entertainment, revue shows, cabaret acts, lectures, and social functions such as the Captain's Cocktail Party. It is among the nicest such rooms afloat for proper cocktail parties (where you stand and mingle, rather than sit), with furniture that can be moved for almost any configuration, and a large real wood dance floor. The port and starboard side seating sections are raised, and sight lines are good from most seats. The ship has conservative, reasonably sophisticated, classically oriented entertainment. A resident troupe of singers and dancers presents mini-revue shows.

Most of the other entertainment consists of cabaret acts such as vocalists, magicians, ventriloquists and comedy jugglers, and there is a large, proper ballroom floor for social dancing, an important feature for many passengers. A number of bands and musical units provide ample live music for dancing or listening in the various lounges and bars. Each evening, the Preview Club, which overlooks the outdoor swimming pool at the aft end of the ship, becomes the late-night spot.

SPA/FITNESS. The Spa Aquarius is located low down in the ship, on "C" Deck, where there is also a rather nice indoor pool, gymnasium, men's and women's sauna and changing rooms with adjacent shower enclosures, plus a unisex steam room. A gymnasium, with elevator access, is high up on Bridge Deck; it has high-tech equipment and great port and starboard ocean views.

The spa treatments and beauty services are staffed and operated by Harding Brothers, a concession whose staff also run the fitness and aerobics classes. Spa treatments offered include several types of massage, aromatherapy facials, seaweed body wraps, and hair beautifying services.

Saga Sapphire
NOT YET RATED

Size:	.Mid-Size Ship	Passenger Decks:	.10	Cabins (wheelchair accessible):	.2
Tonnage:	.37,301	Total Crew:	.415	Wheelchair accessibility:	.Good
Lifestyle:	.Standard	Passengers		Cabin Current:	.110 and 220 volts
Cruise Line:	.Saga Cruises	(lower beds/all berths):	.706/706	Elevators:	.4
Former Names:	.Bleu de France,	Passenger Space Ratio		Casino (gaming tables):	.Yes
	Holiday Dream, SuperStar Aries,	(lower beds/all berths):	.49.6/49.6	Slot Machines:	.Yes
	SuperStar Europe, Europa	Crew/Passenger Ratio		Swimming Pools (outdoors):	.2
Builder:	.Bremer Vulkan (Germany)	(lower beds/all berths):	.1.7/1.7		(1 glass dome)
Original Cost:	.$120 million	Cabins (total):	.374	Swimming Pools (indoors): 1 (fresh water)	
Entered Service:	.Jan 1982/Mar 2012	Size Range (sq ft/m):	.161.4–678.1/	Whirlpools:	.3
Registry:	.The Bahamas		15.0–63.0	Self-Service Launderette:	.Yes
Length (ft/m):	.654.9/199.63	Cabins (outside view):	.309	Dedicated Cinema/Seats:	.No
Beam (ft/m):	.93.8/28.60	Cabins (interior/no view):	.65	Library:	.Yes
Draft (ft/m):	.27.6/8.42	Cabins (for one person):	.56	Onboard currency:	.UK£
Propulsion/Propellers: diesel (21,270 kW)/2		Cabins (with private balcony):	.19		

An elegant ship for British cruisers over 50.

OVERVIEW. This ship is best suited to couples and single travelers, almost all English, seeking a holiday afloat in a spacious, classy ship setting, and provides decent accommodation, good food and friendly service, plus interesting itineraries and destinations. Passengers must be over 50, but spouses and partners can be as young as 45. Male dance hosts are aboard each cruise for the many single women passengers.

BERLITZ'S RATINGS		
	Possible	Achieved
Ship	500	NYR
Accommodation	200	NYR
Food	400	NYR
Service	400	NYR
Entertainment	100	NYR
Cruise	400	NYR

THE SHIP. *Saga Sapphire* was originally built as the fifth incarnation of *Europa* for Hapag-Lloyd Cruises, and was for many years the pride of the German cruise industry. Although it is now 30 years old, it is in remarkably fine shape. Saga Cruises will tailor the ship to British tastes when it takes delivery in April 2012.

It has a deep blue hull and white upper structure, and a sponson stern – a kind of "skirt" added in order to comply with the latest stability regulations. But it still maintains its moderately handsome, balanced profile. There is a really decent amount of open outdoor deck space. The ship has both outdoor and outdoor/indoor pools, one of which can be covered by a retractable glass dome. While there is no walk-around outdoors promenade deck, there are half-length teak port and starboard promenades.

Saga Sapphire has a good range of good-sized public rooms, and wide interior stairways create a feeling of spaciousness on a grand scale. Contemporary yet restful colors have been applied to many public rooms and cabins, and subtle, hidden lighting is used throughout, particularly on the stairways. The public rooms are located aft in a "cake-layer" stacking, with accommodation located forward, thus separating potentially noisy areas from quieter ones. Facilities include a delightful observation lounge (The Drawing Room), with an integral library combined with an internet center (iPads are provided); light entertainment is presented here in the evenings.

The ship provides an informal, relaxed, yet elegant setting, with many public rooms that have a high ceiling. Saga Cruises includes many things other UK-based operators charge extra for – that's why its cruises may appear to cost more – such as private car transfers to the ship (check brochure for details), all gratuities, shuttle buses in ports of call where possible, and newspapers in the library in each port of call, when available.

ACCOMMODATION. There is a wide range of suites and cabins, in an astonishing 33 price grades. All of the original cabins are quite spacious, and have illuminated closets, dark wood cabinetry with rounded edges, full-length mirrors, color TV/DVD player, mini-bar/refrigerator, personal safe, hairdryer, and good cabin insulation.

Most bathrooms have deep tubs (cabins without a bathtub have a large shower enclosure), a three-head shower unit, two deep washbasins (not all cabins), large toiletries cabinet and handsome toiletries.

The largest living spaces are in the suites. However, because of their location – they were created from former bridge officers' cabins in a 1999 refit – they have lifeboat-obstructed views. Six other suites had private balconies added, and all provide generous living spaces. There is a separate bedroom with either a queen-size or twin beds, illuminated closets, and a vanity/writing desk. The lounge includes a wet bar with refrigerator and glass cabinets and large audio-visual center complete with large-screen TV set and DVD player. The marble-clad bathroom has a large shower enclosure, with retractable clothesline.

Even the standard, lower-priced cabins are very comfortable, the ship having been designed for long voyages.

CUISINE. *Pole to Pole*, the main restaurant, seats 620 diners and has ocean-view windows on two sides, yet still manages to have an intimate, "clubby" feel thanks to different areas styled to the theme of four different continents: Africa, Asia, Europe and the Americas. Both self-serve buffet and full-service meals are provided. There is open seating, so you can dine wherever you choose. For dinner, a number of tables can be reserved for fixed dining times when you book.

The Grill, an indoor/outdoor venue, provides lighter, healthier grilled meals, with food cooked to order in a show kitchen. It's open for breakfast, lunch and relaxed dinner.

Asian-fusion cuisine (Indian, Sri Lankan and Thai) is served in the intimate 64-seat *East to West* restaurant, whose decor includes traditional wood carvings, reflecting the mood of the East. Adjacent is *The Grill*, specialising in steaks and seafood, in a room with an open kitchen.

The Pier, adjacent to the indoor/outdoor pool, provides fish and chips and other light British fare, traditional desserts, and ice cream.

ENTERTAINMENT. The Britannia Lounge is the venue for major social events and shows. The sightlines are mostly good, although some thick pillars present problems from some seats – the room was originally built more for use as a single-level concert salon than a room for shows. But the setting is certainly elegant. The shows consist of a small troupe of female dancers, plus a number of cabaret acts. There is live music for listening or dancing in various bars and lounges.

SPA/FITNESS. An area of about 8,611 sq. ft. (800 sq. meters) is host to a rather nice, homely retreat – an indoor wellness center. It includes an indoor swimming pool (few ships have them today) that's larger than most outdoor pools aboard much bigger ships. Adjacent facilities include saunas and steam rooms, a fitness/exercise area, several treatment rooms, and a beauty salon.

PET PEEVES: 30 THINGS THAT EXASPERATE PASSENGERS

❶ Long lines and waiting periods for disembarkation.

❷ The number of merchandising flyers put under the cabin door.

❸ Tiny tub chairs (for size-challenged passengers).

❹ Superfluous language (example: "sleep system" instead of "bed").

❺ Cruise brochures that use models, and provide the anticipation of an onboard product that a ship cannot deliver; the result is a big disappointment for passengers.

❻ Cruise brochures that state that their ship has a "small ship feel, big ship choice" when it really caters to more than 3,000 passengers.

❼ Aboard large resort ships, getting Cabin Services, or the "Guest Relations Desk," or an Operator to answer the telephone can be an exercise in frustration, patience, and gross irritation.

❽ Constant, irritating, and repetitive announcements for bingo, horse racing, art auctions, and the latest gizmos for sale in the shops.

❾ "Elevator" music playing non-stop in passageways and on open decks (even worse: rock and rap music).

❿ Any announcement that is repeated. Any announcement that is repeated.

⓫ In-cabin announcements at any time, except for emergencies; they are completely unnecessary for programmed events and shore excursions.

⓬ Flowers in one's cabin that are not watered by the steward(ess).

⓭ Bathrobes provided but never changed during the cruise.

⓮ Mini-bar/refrigerators that lack limes and lemons for drink mixes.

⓯ Skimpy towels.

⓰ Garnishes, when "parsley with everything" seems to be the rule of the seagoing entrée experience.

⓱ Baked Alaska parades.

⓲ Paper, plastic, or polystyrene plastic cups for drinks of any kind.

⓳ Paper napkins for meals or buffets; they should be linen or cotton.

⓴ Plastic plates, often too small, for buffets.

㉑ Buffets where only cold plates are available, even for hot food items.

㉒ Artwork placed aboard ships, but with the cruise line not caring or knowing enough about it to place the name of the artist and the year of creation alongside, whether it is a painting or a sculpture.

㉓ Repetitious breakfast and luncheon buffets and uncreative displays.

㉔ Shopping lecturers, shopping videos, art auctions, carpet auctions.

㉕ Shore-side porters who take your bags when you get off the bus, or out of your car, then stand there until tipped (worst ports: Fort Lauderdale and Miami).

㉖ Cabin stewards/stewardesses who place small folded pieces of paper in cabin door frames to show when their passengers have left their cabins.

㉗ Audiovisual technicians who think that the volume level of the show should equal that for a major rock concert.

㉘ Private island days, when the tender ride to get to the island is longer than the flight to get to the ship.

㉙ Ships that ask you to settle your shipboard account before the morning of disembarkation.

㉚ The use of cellphones in ships' public rooms.

More Pet Peeves: page 569

Sapphire
★★ +

Size: . . . . .Small Ship	Propulsion/Propellers: diesel (11,050kW)/2	Cabins (with private balcony): 0
Tonnage: .12,263	Passenger Decks: 8	Cabins (wheelchair accessible): 0
Lifestyle: . . . . .Standard	Total Crew: 250	Wheelchair accessibility: . . . . .None
Cruise Line: . . . . .Louis Cruises	Passengers	Cabin Current: . . . . .110 volts
Former Names: . . . . . .*Princesa Oceanica,*	(lower beds/all berths): 576/650	Elevators: 5
Sea Prince V, Sea Prince, Ocean	Passenger Space Ratio	Casino (gaming tables): . . . . .Yes
Princess, Princess Italia, Italia	(lower beds/all berths): 21.1/18.7	Slot Machines: . . . . .Yes
Builder: . . .Cantieri Navale Felszegi (Italy)	Crew/Passenger Ratio	Swimming Pools (outdoors): 1
Original Cost: .n/a	(lower beds/all berths): 2.3/2.6	Swimming Pools (indoors): 0
Entered Service: . . . . .Aug 1967/Apr 1996	Cabins (total): .288	Whirlpools: 0
Registry: . . . . .Marshall Islands	Size Range (sq ft/m): .75.3–226.0/7.0–21.0	Self-Service Launderette: . . . . .No
Length (ft/m): 491.7/149.8	Cabins (outside view): 157	Dedicated Cinema/Seats: Yes/170
Beam (ft/m): 70.9/21.5	Cabins (interior/no view): 131	Library: . . . . .Yes
Draft (ft/m): 22.3/6.8	Cabins (for one person): 0	Onboard currency: . . . . .Euros

---

A small ship for casual cruising with minimal style.

OVERVIEW. This ship is best suited to couples and single travelers (but not recommended for children) for a first cruise in a comfortable, clubby setting that provides a decent array of public rooms and facilities, and a destination-intensive cruise that is decent value for money. For most of the year it operates seven-day Greek Island and Egypt cruises from Cyprus.

THE SHIP. *Sapphire* has had many previous names and owners, and an interesting life. In 1993, it sank in the Amazon River before being bought by its present owners and refitted. It has long, low-slung, handsome lines and a swept-back aft-placed funnel – all of which combine to provide a very attractive profile. Louis Cruises purchased the ship in 1995 and, after an extensive refurbishment, put it into service in 1996. Since then, the company has lavished much care and attention in keeping the ship in good condition. There is a good amount of open deck and sunbathing space, but the heated swimming pool is very small – really only a "dip" pool.

Inside, the contemporary decor is fairly smart. There is a mix of attractive colors, together with much use of mirrored surfaces, which help make the public rooms feel spacious and warm. Most public rooms do have a low ceiling height, however. Harry's Bar is the most popular gathering place, although there are few seats – the gaming tables are adjacent. Other public rooms include the Marco Polo Lounge for evening shows, the Monte Carlo Casino, the Starlight Theater (a cinema with comfortable seating), and a card room and token library.

The ceilings are quite low throughout the ship, exception in a couple of public rooms. Some cabins are subject to

BERLITZ'S RATINGS		
	Possible	Achieved
Ship	500	242
Accommodation	200	105
Food	400	206
Service	400	225
Entertainment	100	48
Cruise	400	204
OVERALL SCORE		
1,030 points out of 2,000		

noise from the engines and generators.

Sapphire will take you to some decent destinations in reasonably contemporary surroundings, and in a relaxed, casual yet comfortable style. The realistic, inexpensive fare is a bonus for first-time passengers seeking a cruise aboard a mid-size ship that's still considered very much a "traditional" cruise ship rather than one of the floating mega-resorts operated by the major lines. Gratuities are added to your onboard account.

ACCOMMODATION. There are five price grades: Premier Outside (the largest), Superior Outside, Standard Outside, Superior Interior, and Standard Interior. The price will depend on the grade, size and location; generally, the higher the deck, the more expensive the accommodation.

The outside-view and interior cabins are reasonably sized, and have pleasing, though plain, decor, soft furnishings, and fittings. In almost all cases, storage space is very limited. A few cabins have a double bed, while most have two beds and many have a third or third and fourth upper berth – good for families with young children.

All cabins have tiled bathrooms, with a shower enclosure, toilet and washbasin, but they are small, and there is little storage space for toiletries. There is a 24-hour cabin service menu, although there is only a limited choice of items, which cost extra.

The Premier Outside cabins are the largest, and have two beds, plus a sofa bed, and the bathroom has either a shower or tub. Nine out of the 15 Premier Outside grade cabins have a lifeboat-obstructed view, as do two of the Super Outside grade cabins.

CUISINE. The 330-seat *Four Seasons Restaurant* is quite a charming room with an art deco feel, a raised center ceiling, and glass dividers, although the noise level from the waiter stations can be high. There are two seatings. The cuisine is international, but remember that this is a low-cost cruise, so you shouldn't expect high-class cuisine. What is provided, however, is surprisingly decent fare that is tasty and well presented. The service from a willing, friendly staff is reasonably attentive. Low-cost vegetarian lunch boxes are available upon request for those taking shore excursions. The price of drinks is extremely reasonable, as are wines – but don't expect good vintages.

The indoor *Café de Paris*, looking out onto the pool deck, serves casual breakfasts and lunches, and has a bar. The self-serve breakfast buffets are a little repetitive.

ENTERTAINMENT. The Marco Polo Lounge, a single-level room designed for cabaret acts rather than "production" shows, is the venue for all entertainment events and most social functions. The sight lines are fair from most seats but best from the first few rows closest to the stage. The room also has a hardwood dance floor. A resident troupe of dancers provides "openers and closers" for the revue-style shows, where a cabaret act (such as a singer, magician, comedian, or musical specialist) is inserted into the middle "star" spot.

Because this is a small ship operating low-budget cruises, don't expect much in the way of quality entertainment. There's a band and a couple of small musical units for live dancing and listening music.

SPA/FITNESS. There are no facilities except for a small beauty salon, where basic hairdressing and hair beautifying treatments are available.

PET PEEVES: 30 MORE THINGS THAT EXASPERATE PASSENGERS

Continued from page 567

❸ Sunbed hoggers.

❸ Cabin air-conditioning that cannot be turned off.

❸ Obscenely overcrowded casual self-serve stuff-your-face buffet venues.

❸ No small "clutch purse" shelves in women's public restrooms.

❸ Hairdryers with "on" buttons that must be kept pressed.

❸ Personal safes located at floor level, or so high that you can't reach.

❸ Overuse by staff of the word "excellent" (as in "how are you today?").

❸ Aboard most ships, 15 percent is automatically added to wine bills. For doing the same job for a $125 wine as for one costing $15 he makes a lot more. You should insist on adding your own gratuity.

❸ Daily programs printed in blue ink (hard to read).

❹ Tacky trinket tables set up as tourist traps outside the onboard shops.

❹ Overly bright shopping malls (RCI's Royal Arcades aboard Oasis-, Freedom, and Voyager-class ships).

❹ User-unfriendly automated telephone answering systems that provide number options to connect you to various services – you start to wonder whether the answering service is located in a call center in India.

❹ Fluorescent lighting in bathrooms.

❹ Bathroom mirrors that steam up.

❹ Toilet tissue paper that is too thin (2-ply) so you need twice as much.

❹ Toilet paper folded to a point, then sealed with a gummed label.

❹ Soap bars that are not large enough to wash the hands of a leprechaun.

❹ Pool towels provided in passenger cabins. This is user-unfriendly for anyone on the lowest accommodation decks, who are expected to carry them up to exterior decks, and down again, when they may be wet and heavy.

❹ If you want to reduce, or otherwise change, the "automatic gratuities" charged to your cabin aboard the large resort ships, you may have to provide the reason, in writing, to present to the reception desk.

❺ Mechanically obtuse bath plugs.

❺ Cost of bottled mineral water.

❺ Cabin air conditioning that can't be turned off.

❺ Frequent and annoying onboard revenue announcements.

❺ Outrageously high Alaska excursion prices.

❺ Intrusive bazaar stalls and sales tables everywhere.

❺ Pushy spa sales people.

❺ Overcrowded buffet venues.

❺ Poorly trained food service staff.

❺ Announcements giving details of items that were already printed in the daily program.

❻ Lack of port information for independent passengers not wishing to take organized excursions.

Sapphire Princess
★★★★

Size: ....Large Resort Ship	Total Crew: 1,238	Cabins (wheelchair accessible): 28
Tonnage: ....115,875 tons	Passengers	(18 outside/10 interior)
Lifestyle: ....Standard	(lower beds/all berths): 2,674/3,100	Wheelchair accessibility: ....Good
Cruise Line: ....Princess Cruises	Passenger Space Ratio	Cabin Current: ....110 volts
Former Names: ....none	(lower beds/all berths): 43.3/37.3	Elevators: 14
Builder: Mitsubishi Heavy Industries (Japan)	Crew/Passenger Ratio	Casino (gaming tables): ....Yes
Original Cost: ....\$400 million	(lower beds/all berths): 2.1/2.5	Slot Machines: ....Yes
Entered Service: ....May 2004	Cabins (total): 1,337	Swimming Pools (outdoors): 4
Registry: ....Bermuda	Size Range (sq ft/m): 168–1,329.3/	Swimming Pools (indoors): 0
Length (ft/m): 951.4/290.00	15.6–123.5	Whirlpools: 9
Beam (ft/m): 123.0/37.50	Cabins (outside view): 1,000	Self-Service Launderette: ....Yes
Draft (ft/m): 26.4/8.05	Cabins (interior/no view): 337	Dedicated Cinema/Seats: ....No
Propulsion/Propellers: ....gas turbine	Cabins (for one person): 0	Library: ....Yes
(25 MW)/2	Cabins (with private balcony): 750	Onboard currency: ....US\$
Passenger Decks: 13		

A multi-choice large ship for informal family cruising.

OVERVIEW. This ship is a grand playground in which to roam and play when you are not ashore. Princess Cruises delivers a fine, well-packaged holiday product, with some sense of style, at an attractive, highly competitive price, and this ship will appeal to those who really enjoy big-city life with all the trimmings, and lots of fellow passengers.

THE SHIP. *Sapphire Princess* has an instantly recognizable funnel due to two jet engine-like pods that sit high up on its structure, but really are mainly for decoration. This was the second ship to be built by a Japanese shipyard for Princess Cruises, following sister ship *Diamond Princess*. The ship is similar in size and internal layout to *Golden Princess*, *Grand Princess* and *Star Princess*, although of a slightly greater beam. Unlike its half-sister ships, however, all of which had a "spoiler" containing a discotheque located aft of the funnel, this has been removed from both *Diamond Princess* and *Sapphire Princess*, being replaced by a more sensible aft-facing nightclub/discotheque, Skywalkers Nightclub, set around the base of the adjoining the funnel structure. The view from the nightclub overlooks aft-facing cascading decks and children's pool.

Four areas focus on swimming pools, one of which is two decks high and is covered by a retractable glass dome, itself an extension of the funnel housing.

The interiors are overseen and outfitted by the Okura Group, whose Okura Hotel is one of the best in Tokyo. Fit and finish quality is superior that of the Italian-built *Golden Princess*, *Grand Princess* and *Star Princess*. Unlike the outside decks, there is plenty of space inside the ship – but

BERLITZ'S RATINGS		
	Possible	Achieved
Ship	500	431
Accommodation	200	168
Food	400	256
Service	400	293
Entertainment	100	82
Cruise	400	314

OVERALL SCORE
1,544 points out of 2,000

there are also plenty of passengers – and a wide array of public rooms, with many "intimate" (this being a relative word) spaces and places to enjoy. The passenger flow has been well thought out, and there's little congestion. The decor is attractive, with lots of earth tones, well suited to both American and European tastes. An extensive collection of art works complements the interior design and colors well.

A Wedding Chapel has a live webcam to relay ceremonies via the internet. The ship's captain can legally marry American couples, due to the ship's Bermuda registry and a dispensation which should be verified in advance according to where you reside. Princess Cruises offers three wedding packages – Pearl, Emerald, Diamond. The "Hearts & Minds" chapel is also useful for "renewal of vows" ceremonies.

Grand Casino is one of the largest casinos at sea, with more than 260 slot machines; there are blackjack, craps and roulette tables, plus newer games. The highlight could well be the specially linked slot machines that provide a combined payout.

Other facilities include a library/computer room, and a card room. The wood-paneled Wheelhouse Bar is finely decorated with memorabilia and ship models tracing part of the history of sister company P&O. The Wake View Bar has a spiral stairway leading down to a great viewing spot for those who want to watch the ship's wake.

A high-tech hospital has live SeaMed tele-medicine link-ups to the Cedars-Sinai Medical Center in Los Angeles, with specialists available for emergency help.

The ship is full of revenue centers. Expect to be subjected to a stream of flyers advertising daily art auctions, "designer" watches and the like, while "artworks" for auction are strewn throughout the ship.

The dress code is formal or smart casual – interpreted by many as jeans and trainers. Gratuities to staff are automatically added to your account, with gratuities for children charged at the same rate. If you want to pay less, you can have these charges adjusted at the reception desk.

Lines form for many things aboard large ships, but particularly so for the information office, and for open-seating breakfast and lunch in the four main dining rooms. Long lines for shore excursions and shore tenders are also a fact of life aboard such large ships, as is waiting for elevators at peak times, and embarkation and disembarkation – though an "express check-in" option is available for embarkation if you fill in some forms 40 days before your cruise.

The many extra-charge items include ice cream and freshly squeezed orange juice. Yoga, group exercise bicycling and kick boxing classes cost extra. There's an hourly rate for group babysitting services, and a charge for using washers and dryers in the self-service launderettes.

FAMILIES. For youngsters and teenagers there is a two-deck-high playroom, teen room, and a host of specially trained counselors. Children have their own pools, hot tubs, and open deck area at the stern, away from adult areas.

ACCOMMODATION. All passengers receive turndown service and nightly chocolates on pillows, bathrobes (on request) and toiletries. A hairdryer is provided in all cabins, sensibly located at the vanity desk unit in the living area. All bathrooms are tiled and have a decent amount of open shelf storage space for toiletries.

The majority of outside cabins on Emerald Deck have views obstructed by the lifeboats. Sadly, there are no cabins for singles. Your name is typically placed outside your suite or cabin – handy for delivery service personnel but eroding your privacy. Most balcony suites and cabins can be overlooked from the navigation bridge wing. There is 24-hour room service, though some items on the room service menu aren't available during early morning hours.

Cabins with balconies on Baja, Caribe, and Dolphin decks are overlooked by passengers on balconies on the deck above. Cabin bath towels are small, and drawer space is limited. There are no butlers, even for the top grade suites – which are not really large in comparison to similar suites aboard some other ships. Cabin attendants have too many cabins to look after – typically 20 – which does not encourage fine personal service.

CUISINE. All dining rooms are located on one of two decks in the ship's center. There are five principal dining rooms with themed decor and cuisine: *Sterling Steakhouse* for steak and grilled meats, *Vivaldi* for Italian fare, *Santa Fe* for southwestern USA cuisine, *Pacific Moon* for Asian cuisine, and *International*, the largest, located aft, with two seat-

ings and "traditional" cuisine. These offer a mix of two seatings, with seating assigned according to your cabin's location, and "anytime dining" where you choose when and with whom you want to eat. All dining rooms are split into sections in a non-symmetrical design that breaks what are quite large spaces into many smaller sections, for better ambience and less noise pollution.

Specially designed dinnerware and good-quality linens and silverware are used. Note that 15% is added to all beverage bills, including wines.

Alternative Dining Option: *Sabatini's* is an informal eatery (reservations required; cover charge). It offers an eight-course meal, including Italian-style pizzas and pastas, with a variety of sauces, as well as Italian-style entrées including tiger prawns and lobster tail. Its cuisine is potentially better than in all the other dining rooms – better quality ingredients and more attention to presentation and taste.

A poolside hamburger grill and pizza bar (no additional charge) are additional dining spots for casual bites. You have to pay extra if you order items to eat at either the coffee bar/patisserie, or the caviar/champagne bar.

Other casual meals can be taken in the *Horizon Court*, open 24 hours a day, with large ocean-view on port and starboard sides and direct access to the two principal swimming pools and lido deck. There is no finesse in presentation, however, as the plates are plastic.

ENTERTAINMENT. The Princess Theatre, spanning two decks, has comfortable seating on both main and balcony levels. It has $3 million in sound and light equipment, plus a nine-piece orchestra.

Princess Cruises prides itself on its glamorous all-American production shows, and the two or three shows on a typical seven-day cruise should not disappoint. There is a resident troupe of singers/dancers.

A second large entertainment lounge, Club Fusion, presents cabaret acts at night, and lectures, bingo and horse racing during the day. A third entertainment lounge can also host cabaret acts and dance bands. Many lounges and bars have live music, and a number of male dance hosts act as partners for women traveling alone.

SPA/FITNESS. The Lotus Spa is forward on Sun Deck – one of the uppermost decks. Separate facilities for men and women include a sauna, steam room, and changing rooms; common facilities include a relaxation/waiting zone, body-pampering treatment rooms, and a gymnasium packed with the latest high-tech muscle-pumping, cardiovascular equipment, and providing great ocean views. Some fitness classes are free, while others cost extra.

The Lotus Spa is operated by Steiner Leisure. You can make online reservations for any spa treatments before your cruise – a great time-saver.

● **For more extensive general information on what the Princess Cruises experience is like, see pages 149–52.**

Sea Cloud
★★★★★

Size:	Boutique Ship	Number of Masts: 4 (17.7 meters)/30 sails		Cabins (outside view):	34
Tonnage:	2,532	Sail Area (sq ft/m2):	32,292/3,000	Cabins (interior/no view):	0
Lifestyle:	Luxury	Main Propulsion:	sail power	Cabins (for one person):	0
Cruise Line:	Sea Cloud Cruises	Propulsion/Propellers: diesel (4,476kW)/2		Cabins (with private balcony):	0
Former Names:	Sea Cloud of Grand	Passenger Decks:	3	Cabins (wheelchair accessible):	0
	Cayman, IX-99, Antama, Patria,	Total Crew:	60	Wheelchair accessibility:	None
	Angelita, Sea Cloud, Hussar	Passengers		Cabin Current:	220 volts
Builder:	Krupp Werft (Germany)	(lower beds/all berths):	68/69	Elevators:	0
Entered Service:	Aug 1931/1979	Passenger Space Ratio		Casino (gaming tables):	No
	(restored)	(lower beds/all berths):	37.2/36.6	Slot Machines:	No
Registry:	Malta	Crew/Passenger Ratio		Swimming Pools (outdoors):	0
Length (ft/m):	359.2/109.5	(lower beds/all berths):	1.1/1.1	Whirlpools:	0
Beam (ft/m):	48.2814.9	Cabins (total):	34	Self-Service Launderette:	No
Draft (ft/m):	16.8/5.13	Size Range (sq ft/m):	102.2–409.0/	Library:	Yes
Type of Vessel:	barque		9.5–38.0	Onboard currency:	Euros

Simply the most beautiful tall ship in the world.

OVERVIEW. *Sea Cloud* is the most romantic sailing ship afloat. It is best suited to couples and singles (not children) who would probably never consider a "normal" cruise ship, but who enjoy sailing aboard a real tall ship that is packaged to include accommodation, good food, like-minded companions and interesting destinations. It operates under charter for much of the year, and sails in both the Caribbean and European/Mediterranean waters.

BERLITZ'S RATINGS		
	Possible	Achieved
Ship	500	423
Accommodation	200	173
Food	400	348
Service	400	335
Entertainment	n/a	n/a
Cruise	500	425
OVERALL SCORE		
1,704 points out of 2,000		

this ship is its "Blue Lagoon," located at the stern. Weather permitting, you can lie down on the thick blue padding and gaze up at the stars and night sky – it's one of the great pleasures – particularly when the ship is under sail, with engines turned off.

The original engine room, with diesel engines, is still in operation for the rare occasions when sail power can't be used. An open-bridge policy is the norm, except during poor weather or navigational maneuvers.

THE SHIP. *Sea Cloud*, a completely authentic 1930s barque whose 80th birthday was celebrated in 2011, is the largest private yacht ever built – three times the size of Captain Cook's *Endeavour* – and a stunningly beautiful ship when under sail. Its three masts are almost as high as a 20-story building, the main one being 178 ft (54 meters) above the main deck. This was the largest private yacht ever built when completed in 1931 by Edward F. Hutton for his wife, Marjorie Merriweather Post, the American cereal heiress. Originally constructed for $1 million as *Hussar* in the Germany's Krupp shipyard in Kiel, the steel-hulled vessel saw action during World War II as a weather observation ship, under the code name *IX-99*. You can still see five chevrons on the bridge, one for each half-year of duty, serving as a reminder of those important years.

There is plenty of deck space, even under the vast expanse of white sail, and the promenade deck outdoors still has wonderful varnished sea chests. The decks themselves are made of mahogany and teak, and wooden "steamer"-style sunloungers are provided.

One of the most beautiful aspects of sailing aboard

In addition to its retained and refurbished original suites and cabins, some newer, smaller cabins were added in 1979 when a consortium of German yachtsmen and businessmen bought the ship and spent $7.5 million refurbishing it. The interiors exude warmth, and are finely hand-crafted. There is much antique mahogany furniture, fine original oil paintings, gorgeous carved oak paneling, parquet flooring and burnished brass everywhere, as well as some finely detailed ceilings. Marjorie Merryweather Post had been accustomed to the very finest things in life.

Passengers are not allowed to climb the rigging, as they are aboard some other tall ships. This is because the mast rigging on this vintage sailing ship is of a very different type to more modern sailing vessels such as *Royal Clipper*, *Star Clipper*, *Star Flyer*, and *Sea Cloud II*. However, passengers may be able participate occasionally in the furling and unfurling of the sails.

A cruise aboard *Sea Cloud* is really exhilarating. A kind of stately home afloat, it remains one of the world's best travel experiences. The activities are few, and so relaxation is the key, in a setting that provides fine service and style, but in an unpretentious way. The only "dress-up" night is the Captain's Welcome Aboard Dinner, but otherwise, smart casual clothing is all that is needed.

However, mini-skirts would be impractical because of the steep staircases in some places – trousers are more practical. Also bear in mind that a big sailing vessel such as this can heel to one side occasionally, so flat shoes are preferable to high heels.

Sea Cloud sails, for part of each year, under charter to Hapag-Lloyd Cruises. On those occasions, white and red wines and beer are included for lunch and dinner, and soft drinks, espresso and cappuccino coffees are included at any time. Shore excursions are an optional extra, as are gratuities. Details may differ for other charter operators such as Abercrombie & Kent.

Although now 75 years young, *Sea Cloud* is so lovingly maintained and operated that anyone who sails aboard it cannot fail to be impressed and totally absorbed by the character of this beautiful tall ship. The food and service are good, as is the interaction between passengers and crew, many of whom have worked aboard the ship for many, many years. The crew is of mixed nationality, and the sailors who climb the rigging and set the sails include women as well as men. On a cruise's last night, the sailors' choir sings seafaring songs. One bonus is the fact that the doctor on board is available at no charge for medical emergencies or seasickness medication.

Gratuities can be charged to your onboard account.

In 2001, the ship suffered a fire while in Rijeka, which put it out of commission for many months. However, all necessary repairs were painstakingly made and it is now in a beautiful original condition.

Hamburg-based Sea Cloud Cruises also operates the rivercruise vessels *River Cloud* and *River Cloud II* for cruising along the rivers of Europe, and, in 2001 introduced a brand new companion sailing ship, *Sea Cloud II*.

ACCOMMODATION. Because *Sea Cloud* was built as a private yacht, there is a wide variation in cabin sizes and configurations. Some cabins have double beds, while some have twin beds (side by side or in an L-shaped configuration) that are fixed and cannot be placed together. Many of the original cabins have a fireplace, now with an electric fire.

All the cabins are very comfortable, but those on Main Deck (Cabins 1–8) were part of the original accommodation. Of these, the two owner's suites (Cabins 1 and 2) are really opulent, and have original Chippendale furniture, fine gilt detailing, a real fireplace, French canopy bed, and large Italian Carrara marble bathrooms with gold fittings.

Owner's Cabin Number 1 is decorated in white throughout, and has a French double bed, a marble fireplace and Louis Phillippe chairs; the bathroom is appointed in Carrara marble, with cut-glass mirrors, and faucets (taps) in the shape of swans. Owner's Cabin Number 2, completely paneled in rich woods, retains the mahogany secretary used 60 years ago by Edward F. Hutton, its dark wood decor reminiscent of the 1930s.

Other cabins – both the original ones, and some newer additions – are beautifully furnished. All were refurbished in 1993 and are surprisingly large for the size of the ship. There is a good amount of closet and drawer space and all cabins have a personal safe and telephone. The cabin bathrooms, too, are quite luxurious, and equipped with everything you will need, including bathrobes and hairdryer, and an assortment of toiletries. There is a 110-volt AC shaver socket in each bathroom. The "new" cabins are rather small for two persons, so it's best to take minimal luggage.

There is no cabin food or beverage service. Also, if you occupy one of the original cabins on Main Deck you may be subjected to some noise when the motorized capstans are used to raise and lower or trim the sails. On one day each cruise, an "open-house" cocktail party is held on the Main Deck, with all cabins available for passengers to see.

CUISINE. The exquisitely elegant dining room, created from the original owner's living room/saloon, is in the center of the vessel, and also houses the ship's library. It has beautiful wood paneled walls and a wood beam ceiling. There is ample space at each table for open-seating meals. German chefs are in charge, and the high-quality cuisine is very international, with a good balance of nouvelle cuisine and regional dishes, although there is little choice, due to the size of the galley. There is always excellent seafood and fish, purchased locally, when available, as are most other ingredients.

For breakfast and lunch, there are self-serve buffets. European wines accompany lunch and dinner. Soft drinks and bottled water are included in the fare, while alcoholic drinks cost extra. On the last day of each cruise, homemade ice cream is produced.

HOW TO RECOGNIZE THE RIGGING

For the yachting types among you, the sails are, in order, from fore to aft mast, top to bottom:

Fore Mast: flying jib, outer jib, inner jib, fore topmast staysail, fore royal, fore topgallant, fore upper-top sail, fore lower-top sail, foresail.

Main Mast: main royal staysail, main topgallant staysail, main topmast staysail, skysail, main royal, main topgal-lant, main upper topsail, main lower topsail, main sail.

Mizzen Mast: mizzen royal staysail, mizzen topgallant staysail, mizzen topmast staysail, mizzen royal topsail, mizzen topgallant, mizzen upper topsail, mizzen lower topsail, mizzen course.

Spanker Mast: spanker top mast staysail, spanker staysail, spanker-gaff topsail, spanker.

ENTERTAINMENT. A keyboard player/singer is available for the occasional soirée, but after-dinner conversation constitutes the main entertainment each evening.

SPA/FITNESS. There are no spa or fitness facilities. However, for recreation (particularly at night), there is the Blue Lagoon, an area of seating with blue cushioned pads at the very aft of the ship, where you can lie down and watch the heavens.

Sea Cloud II
★★★★★

Size: . . . . .Boutique Ship	Sail Area (sq ft/m2): 32,292/3,000	Cabins (outside view): 48
Tonnage: 3,849	Main Propulsion: . . . . .sail power	Cabins (interior/no view): 0
Lifestyle: .Luxury	Propulsion/Propellers: diesel (2,500kW)/2	Cabins (for one person): 0
Cruise Line: . . . . .Sea Cloud Cruises	Passenger Decks: 4	Cabins (with private balcony): 0
Former Names: . . . . .none	Total Crew: 60	Cabins (wheelchair accessible): 0
Builder: Astilleros Gondan, Figueras (Spain)	Passengers	Wheelchair accessibility: . . . . .None
Original Cost: . . . . .DM 50 million	(lower beds/all berths): 96/96	Cabin Current: . . . . .110 and 220 volts
Entered Service: . . . . .Feb 2001	Passenger Space Ratio	Elevators: 0
Registry: . . . . .Malta	(lower beds/all berths): 40.0/40.0	Swimming Pools (outdoors): 0
Length (ft/m): 383.8/117.0	Crew/Passenger Ratio	Whirlpools: 0
Beam (ft/m): 52.9/16.15	(lower beds/all berths): 1.6/1.6	Self-Service Launderette: . . . . .No
Draft (ft/m): 17.7/5.4	Cabins (total): .48	Library: . . . . .Yes
Type of Vessel: . . . . .barque	Size Range (sq ft/m): 215.2–322.9/	Onboard currency: . . . . .Euros
Number of Masts: . . . . .3 (24 sails)	20.0–30.0	

A fine tall ship providing sail-cruises for couples.

OVERVIEW. This is as exclusive as it gets – sailing in the lap of luxury aboard one of the world's most luxurious true sailing ships – although your experience will depend on which company is operating the ship under charter when you sail, and exactly what is to be included in the package.

THE SHIP. This three-mast tall ship is slightly longer and beamier than the original *Sea Cloud*, and has the look, ambience and feel of a 1930s sailing vessel while benefiting from the latest high-tech navigational aids. It complements the company's original, 1931-built *Sea Cloud* in almost every way, including its external appearance – except for a very rounded stern in place of the counter stern of the original ship.

The interior designers have managed to replicate the same beautiful traditional look and special decorative touches, so anyone who has sailed aboard *Sea Cloud* will feel instantly at home. Whether the modern materials used will stand up to 70 years of use like those of the original ship remains to be seen, although they are of a high quality. In any event, comparisons are bound to be made, and if you have sailed aboard the original *Sea Cloud*, you will probably be disappointed with the more limited space and decoration of the equivalent cabins aboard this ship.

The main lounge is truly elegant, with sofa and large individual tub chair seating around oval drinks tables. The ceiling is ornate, with an abundance of wood detailing, and an oval centerpiece is set around skylights to the open deck above. A bar is set into the aft port side of the room, which has audio-visual aids built in for lectures and presentations.

A treasured aspect of sailing aboard this ship is its "Blue

BERLITZ'S RATINGS		
	Possible	Achieved
Ship	500	435
Accommodation	200	173
Food	400	337
Service	400	333
Entertainment	n/a	n/a
Cruise	500	424

**OVERALL SCORE
1,702 points out of 2,000**

Lagoon", at the very stern – part of the outdoor bar and casual dining area. Weather permitting, you can lie on thick blue padding and gaze up at the stars and warm night sky – it's a huge pleasure, particularly when the ship is under sail, with the engines turned off.

In terms of interior design, degree of luxury in appointments, the passenger flow, fabrics, food and service, the ceiling height of public rooms, larger cabins, great open deck space, better passenger space ratio and crew to passenger ratio, there is none better than *Sea Cloud II*. I have sailed aboard both vessels and I can promise you a memorable sail-cruise experience.

A small water sports platform is built into the aft quarter of the starboard side (with adjacent shower), and the ship carries four inflatable craft for close-in shore landings, as well as snorkeling equipment.

Rigging: This consists of up to 24 sails: flying jib, outer jib, inner jib; fore royal, fore topgallant, fore upper topsail, fore lower topsail, fore course; main royal staysail, main topgallant staysail, main topmast staysail; sky sail, main royal, main topgallant, main upper topsail, main lower topsail, main sail; mizzen topgallant staysail, mizzen topmast staysail; mizzen gaff topsail, mizzen upper gaff sail, mizzen lower gaff sail, middle gaff, upper gaff.

ACCOMMODATION. The decor in the cabins is very tasteful 1920s retro, with lots of bird's-eye maple wood paneling, brass accenting, and beautiful molded white ceilings. All cabins have a vanity desk, hairdryer, refrigerator (typically stocked with soft drinks and bottled water), and a combination TV/video player.

All cabins have a private bathroom with shower enclosure (or tub/shower combination), and plenty of storage space for toiletries. The cabin current is 220 volts, although all bathrooms also include a 110-volt socket for shavers.

There are two suites. Naturally, these have more space – but not as much space as the two owner's suites aboard *Sea Cloud* – and comprise a completely separate bedroom, with four-poster bed, and living room, while the marble-clad bathroom has a full-size tub.

There are 16 junior suites. These provide a living area and sleeping area with twin beds that convert to a queen-size bed. The marble-clad bathroom is quite opulent, and has a small tub/shower combination, with lots of cubbyholes to store toiletries.

CUISINE. The one-seating dining room operates an open-seating policy, so you can dine with whom you wish, when you wish. It is decorated in a light, modern maritime style, with wood and carpeted flooring, comfortable chairs with armrests, and circular light fixtures. The gold-rimmed plates used for the captain's dinner – typically a candlelit affair – have the ship's crest embedded in the white porcelain; they are extremely elegant and highly collectible. The place settings for dinner, also often by candlelight, are navy blue, white and gold Bauscher china.

There is always excellent seafood and fish, purchased fresh, locally, when available, as are most other ingredients. For breakfast and lunch, there are self-serve buffets. These are really good, and beautifully presented – usually indoors for breakfast and outdoors on the Promenade Deck for lunch. Meal times are announced by the ship's bell.

European wines typically accompany lunch and dinner – mostly young vintages. Soft drinks and bottled water are included in the fare, while alcoholic drinks cost extra. On a cruise's last day, homemade ice cream is produced.

ENTERTAINMENT. There is a keyboard player/singer for the occasional soirée, but nothing else – nothing else is needed since the thrill of sailing is the entertainment. Dinner and after-dinner conversation with fellow passengers really becomes the main activity each evening. So, if you are feeling anti-social and don't want to talk to your fellow passengers, take a good book or two.

SPA/FITNESS. There is a health/fitness area, with a small gymnasium, and sauna. Massage is available.

Sea Princess
★★★★

Size: . . . . .Large Resort Ship	Passenger Decks: 10	Cabins (with private balcony): 411
Tonnage: 77,690	Total Crew: 850	Cabins (wheelchair accessible): 19
Lifestyle: . . . . .Standard	Passengers	Wheelchair accessibility: . . . . .Good
Cruise Line: . . . . .Princess Cruises	(lower beds/all berths): 2,016/2,272	Cabin Current: . . . . .110 and 220 volts
Former Names: . . . . . .Adonia, Sea Princess	Passenger Space Ratio	Elevators: 11
Builder: . . . . .Fincantieri (Italy)	(lower beds/all berths): 39.3/34.1	Casino (gaming tables): . . . . .Yes
Original Cost: . . . .$300 million	Crew/Passenger Ratio	Slot Machines: . . . . .Yes
Entered Service: . . . . . . .Dec 1998/Apr 2005	(lower beds/all berths): 2.2/2.5	Swimming Pools (outdoors): 4
Registry: . . . . .Great Britain	Cabins (total): 1,008	Swimming Pools (indoors): 0
Length (ft/m): 857.2/261.3	Size Range (sq ft/m): 158.2–610.3/	Whirlpools: 5
Beam (ft/m): 105.6/32.2	14.7–56.7	Self-Service Launderette: . . . . .Yes
Draft (ft/m): 26.5/8.1	Cabins (outside view): 603	Dedicated Cinema/Seats: . . . . .No
Propulsion/Propellers: . . . . . .diesel-electric	Cabins (interior/no view): 405	Library: . . . . .Yes
(46,080kW)/2	Cabins (for one person): 0	Onboard currency: . . . . .US$

A large, family-friendly ship with relaxing decor.

OVERVIEW. *Sea Princess,* which is marketed to both British and North American passengers, operates cruises from the UK in summer and in the Caribbean in winter. As is the case aboard most large ships, you will be well attended if you live in the top-grade cabins; otherwise, you'll be one of a very large number of passengers.

THE SHIP. This all-white ship (sister ships: *Dawn Princess, Sun Princess*) has a profile balanced by a large, swept-back funnel which contains a deck tennis/basketball/volleyball court in its sheltered aft base. There is a wide, teak walk-around promenade deck outdoors, some real teak steamer-style deck chairs with cushioned pads, and 93,000 sq. ft (8,640 sq. meters) of outdoors space. A large glazed area on the upper decks provides plenty of light and connection with the outside world.

Sea Princess absorbs passengers well and has a decent passenger space ratio for a large ship. Some areas even have an intimate feel to them, which is what the interior designers intended. The interiors are attractive and welcoming with pastel colors and decor that includes countless wall murals and other artwork. There is a wide range of public rooms, including 13 bars, with several intimate rooms and spaces so that you aren't overwhelmed. A large, four-deck-high atrium lobby has winding, double stairways and two panoramic glass-walled elevators.

There is a library, a warm room with ocean-view windows and large buttery leather chairs for listening to CDs and audio books, a card room and reading room. The artwork collection is good, particularly on the stairways, and helps make the ship feel smaller than it is. The Grand

BERLITZ'S RATINGS		
	Possible	Achieved
Ship	500	413
Accommodation	200	159
Food	400	255
Service	400	283
Entertainment	100	78
Cruise	400	299
OVERALL SCORE		
1,487 points out of 2,000		

Casino is slightly out of the main passenger flow and so doesn't generate the "walk-through" factor found aboard so many ships. Cyberspace is a lounge and internet connect room close to the pools on Riviera Deck.

Perhaps the most popular drinking venue is the Wheelhouse Bar, with decor that is a pleasing mix of traditional and modern, a bandstand and dance floor; it's like a gentleman's club, with its wood paneling and comfortable seating. For families with children, plenty of space is provided in The Fun Zone children's center, on the starboard side of the Riviera Deck.

One nice feature is the fact that the captain's cocktail party is normally held in the four-deck-high main atrium, so you can come and go as you please. But, in the quest for increased onboard revenue, even birthday cakes are now an extra-cost item, as are espressos and cappuccinos – fake ones, made from instant coffee, are available in the dining rooms. Also at extra cost are ice cream, except in the restaurant, and bottled water; these can add up to a considerable amount on a long cruise.

There are a number of dead ends in the interior layout, so it could be more user-friendly. The swimming pools are quite small for the number of passengers carried, and the pool deck is cluttered with plastic sunloungers. The digital voice announcing lift deck stops is annoying for many.

ACCOMMODATION. There are 19 different cabin price grades, designated as suites with private balcony, mini-suites with private balcony, outside-view twin-bedded cabins with balcony, outside-view twin-bedded cabins, and interior twin-bedded cabins. Although the standard outside-view and interior cabins are a little small, they are functional, and have earth tone colors accentuated by splashes of color from the bedspreads. Proportionately, there are quite a lot of interior cabins.

Many outside-view cabins have private balconies, and all seem to be quite well soundproofed, although the balcony partition is not of the floor to ceiling type, so you can hear your neighbors – or smell their smoke. The balconies are very narrow – just big enough for two small chairs – and there is no outdoor balcony light. Some cabins have third- and fourth-person upper bunk beds – good for families with children.

There is a reasonable amount of closet space and abundant drawer and other storage space in the cabins; although adequate for a seven-night cruise, it can prove challenging for longer cruises. Also provided are a TV set and refrigerator, and each night a chocolate will appear on your pillow. The cabin bathrooms are practical units, and come complete with all the facilities one needs – although, again, they really are tight spaces. Fortunately, they have a shower enclosure of a decent size, real glasses, a hairdryer, and a small amount of shelving for toiletries.

Suites: The largest cabins are six suites, two on each of three decks at the stern, each with its own large private balcony. These suites are well laid out, and the large bathrooms have two washbasins, a Jacuzzi tub and separate shower enclosure. The bedroom has generous amounts of wood accenting and detailing, indented ceilings, TV sets in the bedroom and lounge areas, and a dining table and four chairs.

Mini-Suites: These typically have two lower beds that convert into a queen-size bed. There is a separate bedroom/ sleeping area with vanity desk, and a lounge with sofa and coffee table, indented ceilings, generous amounts of wood accenting and detailing, walk-in closet; the bathroom has a Jacuzzi tub and separate shower enclosure.

Standard Outside-view/Interior Cabins: The cabin bathrooms are practical, but compact. They do, however, have a decent shower enclosure, real glasses, a hairdryer, and a small amount of shelving for toiletries.

The cabin numbering system is quite illogical, with numbers going through several hundred series on the same deck. The room service menu is very limited.

CUISINE. *Rigoletto* and *Traviata* are the two main, asymmetrically designed dining rooms, each seating about 500 and adjacent to the two lower levels of the four-deck high atrium lobby. Your cabin location determines which you are assigned to. Each has its own galley and each is split into multi-tier sections that help create a feeling of intimacy, although there is a lot of noise from the waiter stations. Breakfast and lunch have open seating, and dinner

is in two seatings. The wine list is quite reasonable; 15% is added to all beverage bills, including wines.

Horizon Court is the ship's 24-hour casual, self-serve buffet. At night, this large room, which resembles a food court, can be transformed into an informal bistro dinner setting with waiter service. Reservations are necessary and there may be a cover charge.

Outdoors on deck, with a sheltered view over the Riviera Pool, the *Terrace Grill* serves fast-food items to those who don't want to change from sunbathing attire. In the evening, the grill offers steaks, seafood, and a "white sisters" mixed grill. There's a cover charge for dining under the stars.

For informal eats, *Verdi's*, on the uppermost level of the atrium lobby, serves steaks and pizza at extra cost. In addition, there's a patisserie for cappuccino/espresso coffees and pastries opposite the reception desk on the atrium's lowest deck, and a wine/caviar bar, *Rendezvous*, on Promenade Deck. Coffee or tea from any of the bars costs extra.

ENTERTAINMENT. The Princess Theater, located forward, is a 550-seat, theater-style showlounge, where the main production shows are staged and movies can be shown. The second theater, Vista Lounge, located aft, is a 480-seat lounge and bar for cabaret entertainment and lectures.

In addition, the ship has an array of cabaret acts. Although many are not what you would call headliners, they regularly travel the cruise ship circuit. Classical concerts are scheduled for many cruises throughout the year.

SPA/FITNESS. The Lotus Spa has facilities that are contained in a glass-walled complex located on Lido Deck – one of the highest decks, at the aft section of the ship.

It includes a gymnasium with ocean views aft and to port, with all the associated high-tech muscle-pumping and body toning equipment, a combination aerobics/exercise room, sauna and steam room, and several wellbeing treatment rooms. Some fitness and exercise classes may cost extra.

Forming part of the outside area of the spa complex, one swimming pool is "suspended" aft between two decks (two other pools are located in another area in the center of the ship), although they are not large for the size of the vessel. Sports facilities are located in an open-air sports deck positioned inside the funnel and adaptable for basketball, volleyball, badminton, or paddle tennis.

Joggers can exercise on the wrap-around open Promenade Deck. There's also an electronic golf simulator – no need to bring your own clubs.

● **For more extensive general information about the Princess Cruises experience, see pages 149–52.**

Sea Spirit
★★★ +

Size: . . . . .Boutique Ship	Total Crew: 64	Cabins (wheelchair accessible): 0
Tonnage: 4,200	Passengers	Cabin Current: . . . . .110 volts
Lifestyle: . . . . .Standard	(lower beds/all berths): . . . . . . .120 /127	Dining Rooms: 1
Cruise Line: . . . . .Quark Expeditions	Passenger Space Ratio	Elevators: 1
Former Names: *Spirit of Oceanus, MegaStar*	(lower beds/all berths): 35.0/33.0	Casino (gaming tables): . . . . .No
Sagittarius, Sun Viva, Renaissance Five	Crew/Passenger Ratio	Slot Machines: .No
Builder: . . . .Nuovi Cantieri Apuania (Italy)	(lower beds/all berths): 1.8/4.7	Swimming Pools (outdoors): 1
Entered Service: 1991/Oct 2011	Cabins (total): .60	Swimming Pools (indoors): 0
Registry: . . . . .The Bahamas	Size Range (sq ft/m): 215.0–353.0/	Whirlpools: 1
Length (ft/m): 294.5/89.7	20.0–32.7	Self-Service Launderette: . . . . .No
Beam (ft/m): 50.1/15.30	Cabins (outside view): 60	Dedicated Cinema/Seats: . . . . .No
Draft (ft/m): 13.2/4.05	Cabins (interior/no view): 0	Library: . . . . .Yes
Propulsion/Propellers: .diesel (5,000kW)/2	Cabins (for one person): 0	Onboard currency: . . . . .US$
Passenger Decks: 5	Cabins (with private balcony): 12	

A comfortable ship for exploring Antarctica up close.

OVERVIEW. This ship is best suited to couples and single travelers who enjoy nature and wildlife up close in a contemporary small-ship setting, and who would not dream of cruising in the mainstream sense aboard ships with large numbers of people.

THE SHIP. *Sea Spirit* (formerly *Spirit of Oceanus*) has a modern exterior with a private yacht-like look, with twin, flared funnels. There is a narrow teakwood walking deck outdoors, and a reasonable amount of open deck and sunbathing space, and Deck 5 has a hot tub. The deck furniture is also teak, as is a platform at the stern of the ship, used by passengers for passengers to decant into inflatable, rubber expedition landing craft.

The main lounge, the focal point for social activities, has six pillars that destroy sightlines to the small stage/floor area. There is a very small book and video library.

The ship is under charter to Quark Expeditions for its 2011–12 Antarctic season, including a Falklands wildlife cruise. Kayaking and camping options are available.

ACCOMMODATION. There are several price categories. Fine all-outside-view cabins (called "suites" in the brochure) combine highly polished imitation rosewood paneling with lots of mirrors, and fine, hand-crafted Italian furniture. All suites have twin beds that convert to a queen-size bed, a sitting area with three-person sofa, one individual chair, coffee table, mini-bar/refrigerator (stocked with juices

BERLITZ'S RATINGS		
	Possible	Achieved
Ship	500	339
Accommodation	200	150
Food	400	215
Service	400	237
Entertainment	n/a	n/a
Cruise	500	281
OVERALL SCORE		
1,222 points out of 2,000		

and bottled water), flat-screen TV and DVD player, direct-dial satellite telephone, and a bowl of fresh fruit on embarkation day. While closet space is good, space for stowing luggage is tight, and there is little drawer space. There are no music channels in the cabins, and there is no switch to turn off announcements in your cabin.

The marble bathrooms are compact units that have showers (no bathrooms have a tub) with fold-down (plastic) seat, real teakwood floor, marble vanity, large mirror, recessed towel rail, and built-in hairdryer. There is a high "lip" into the bathroom.

CUISINE. *The Restaurant*, which has an open-seating policy, is bright, elegant, and welcoming. It is on the lowest deck and has portholes rather than windows, due to international maritime construction and insurance regulations. There are tables for two, four, six, or eight. Dinners are normally sit-down affairs, although, depending on the itinerary and length of cruise, there could be an occasional buffet. Breakfast and lunch are typically self-serve buffets and can be taken at the poolside (weather permitting), in your cabin, or in the restaurant.

ENTERTAINMENT. There is no formal entertainment, so dinner and after-dinner conversation with fellow passengers in the ship's lounge/bar really is the entertainment.

SPA/FITNESS. Small fitness center. Massage is available.

Seabourn Legend
★★★★★

Size: ....Small Ship	Passenger Decks: 6	Cabins (wheelchair accessible): 4
Tonnage: 9,961	Total Crew: 160	Wheelchair accessibility: ....None
Lifestyle: ....Luxury	Passengers	Cabin Current: ....110 and 220 volts
Cruise Line: ....Seabourn	(lower beds/all berths): 212/212	Elevators: 3
Former Names: ....*Queen Odyssey,*	Passenger Space Ratio	Casino (gaming tables): ....Yes
Royal Viking Queen	(lower beds/all berths): 46.9/46.9	Slot Machines: ....Yes
Builder: .... Schichau Seebeckwerft	Crew/Passenger Ratio	Swimming Pools (outdoors): 1
(Germany)	(lower beds/all berths): 1.3/1.3	(plus 1 aft marina-pool)
Original Cost: ....$87 million	Cabins (total): 106	Swimming Pools (indoors): 0
Entered Service: ....Mar 1992/July 1996	Size Range (sq ft/m): 277.0–575.8/	Whirlpools: 3
Registry: ....Bahamas	25.7–53.5	Self-Service Launderette: ....Yes
Length (ft/m): 442.9/135.0	Cabins (outside view): 106	Dedicated Cinema/Seats: ....No
Beam (ft/m): 62.9/19.20	Cabins (interior/no view): 0	Library: ....Yes
Draft (ft/m): 16.4/5.0	Cabins (for one person): 0	Onboard currency: ....US$
Propulsion/Propellers: diesel (7,280kW)/2	Cabins (with private balcony): 6	

A small, cozy, elegant ship for mature-age cruisers.

OVERVIEW. *Seabourn Legend*, which can cruise to places where large cruise ships can't, thanks to its ocean-yacht size, provides an outstanding level of personal service and a very civilized cruise. For a grand, small-ship vacation in fine surroundings, with just over 100 other couples as neighbors and excellent food that approaches gourmet standards, it's hard to beat. It is best suited to sophisticated, well traveled couples, typically over 50, but possibly younger.

BERLITZ'S RATINGS		
	Possible	Achieved
Ship	500	449
Accommodation	200	186
Food	400	347
Service	400	353
Entertainment	100	86
Cruise	400	353
OVERALL SCORE		
1,774 points out of 2,000		

THE SHIP. *Seabourn Legend* is a contemporary ship with a handsome profile, almost identical in looks and size to *Seabourn Pride* and *Seabourn Spirit*, but younger and built to a much higher standard, with streamline "decorator" bars made by Mercedes Benz located along the side of the upper superstructure and a slightly different swept-over funnel design. The sunloungers have thankfully been changed to a steel-mesh design, but they are hard-surfaced and need pads to make them comfortable for more than a few minutes. There is no walk-around promenade deck outdoors.

The ship has two fine mahogany water taxis for use as shore tenders. An aft water sports platform and marina can be used in suitably calm warm-water areas. Water sports facilities include a small, enclosed "dip" pool, sea kayaks, snorkel equipment, windsurfers, water ski boat, and Zodiac inflatable boats.

Inside, a wide central passageway divides port and starboard side accommodation. The finest quality interior fixtures, fittings and fabrics have been combined in its sumptuous public areas to present an outstanding, elegant decor, with warm color combinations and some fine art-

work. There is no glitz anywhere. The dress code, relaxed by day, is more formal at night.

There have been many recent complaints about falling standards aboard the Seabourn ships, particularly in regard to maintenance – they are more than 10 years old. Food, presentation and service, passengers said, wasn't what it used to be. However, I am happy to report that the product delivered now is extremely good, and more consistent, particularly in food and service, than, say, the Silversea Cruises ships, which are larger and carry more passengers.

All drinks, except premium brands and connoisseur wines, are included in the fare. So are gratuities, fine aromatherapy Molton Brown bath products and large soaps by Bronnley, Chanel and Hermès, short massages ("massage moments") on deck, open-seating dining, use of watersports equipment, one included Exclusively Seabourn shore excursion per cruise, and movies under the stars.

The three Seabourn ships, which provide an excellent hotel service product, are superior to other upscale ships such as *Seven Seas Mariner* and *Seven Seas Voyager*, but still not up to the standard of *Europa*'s fine product delivery and hospitality.

Niggles? The range of cigars offered is limited. The Club suffers from over-amplified music. Non-American passengers should note that almost all entertainment and activities are geared towards American tastes, despite the increasingly international passenger mix.

DHL can provide luggage pick-up and delivery service. Port charges and insurance are not included.

ACCOMMODATION. This is spread over three decks, and there are nine price categories. All suites are comfortably large and comprehensively equipped. They are, for example, larger than those aboard the smaller *SeaDream I* and *SeaDream II*, but then the ship is also larger, with almost twice as many passengers.

All suites have a sleeping area with European duvets and Frette linens. A separate lounge area has a Bose wave radio/CD unit, DVD player and flat-screen TV, vanity desk with hairdryer and personalized stationery, world atlas, mini-bar and refrigerator stocked with soft drinks and two bottles of your favorite liquor at embarkation, a large walk-in closet illuminated automatically when you open the door, digital personal safe, and wall-mounted clock and barometer. A full passenger list is provided – a rarity today – as are a fresh fruit basket, replenished daily, and flowers.

Marble-clad bathrooms have one or two washbasins, depending on accommodation grade, a decent but not full-size tub (four suites have a shower enclosure only – no bathtub), plenty of storage areas, 100% thick cotton towels, plush terrycloth bathrobe, and designer soaps. A selection of five Molton Brown aromatherapy bath preparations can be ordered from your stewardess, who will prepare your bath for you.

Course-by-course in-cabin dining is available during dinner hours – the cocktail table raises to form a dining table – and there is 24-hour room service. Also provided are personalized stationery, and fancy ticket wallet, suitably boxed and nicely packaged before your cruise. Non-smoking cabins are available. Menus for each dinner are delivered to your suite during the day.

In 2001, 36 French balconies were added to suites on two out of three accommodation decks. These are not balconies in the true sense, but have two doors that open wide onto a tiny teakwood balcony that is just 27 cm (about 10.6 inches) wide. The balconies do allow you to have fresh sea air, however, together with some salt spray.

Four Owner's suites (Ibsen/Grieg, each 530 sq. ft/49 sq. meters and Eriksson/Heyerdahl, each 575 sq. ft/53 sq. meters), and two Classic Suites (Queen Maud/Queen Sonja, each 400 sq. ft/37 sq. meters) are superb, private living spaces. Each has a walk-in closet, second closet, full bathroom plus a guest toilet with washbasin. There is a fully secluded forward- or side-facing balcony, with sun lounge chairs and wooden drinks table (Ibsen/ Grieg don't have balconies). The living area has ample bookshelf space, including a complete edition of *Encyclopaedia Britannica*, large refrigerator/drinks cabinet, television and DVD player, plus a second TV set in the bedroom. All windows, as well as the door to the balcony, have manually operated blackout blinds, and a complete blackout is possible in both bedroom and living room.

CUISINE. *The Restaurant* is a part-marble, part-carpeted dining room that has portholes and elegant decor but it is not as warm and intimate as that found aboard the smaller SeaDream ships, with their wood paneling. The silverware (150 gram weight – the best available) is by Robbe & Berking. Open-seating dining means that you can dine when you want, with whom you wish. Course-by-course meals can be served in your cabin.

Dining is memorable. The menus, overseen by celebrity chef Charlie Palmer, are creative and well-balanced, with a wide selection of foods, including regional dishes. Seabourn's cuisine is artfully presented, with many items cooked to order. Special orders are available, as is caviar (sevruga). Flambeaus and flaming desserts can be cooked at your table. The selection of exotic fruits and cheeses is good.

Each day, basic table wine is included for lunch and dinner, but the decent ones cost extra. The wine list is quite extensive, with prices ranging from moderate to high; many of the wines come from the smaller, more exclusive vineyards. The European dining room staff is hand-picked and provides excellent, unhurried service.

Relaxed breakfasts until 11am, lunch buffets and casual, themed candlelight dinners (including a new "2" tasting menu) can be taken in the popular *Veranda Café*, adjacent to the swimming pool, instead of in the dining room. The *Sky Grill* provides an above-poolside setting complete with candlelit dining and specializing in steaks and seafood.

ENTERTAINMENT. The King Olaf Lounge is the venue for all entertainment events, including shows, cabaret acts, lectures, and most social functions. It has a sloping floor that provides good sightlines from just about every seat. Because this is a small, upscale ship, the typically four-person "production" shows are of limited scope, as dinner is almost always the main event. You can, however, expect to see the occasional cabaret act.

Singers also tend to do mini-cabaret performances in The Club, one deck above the showlounge, the gathering place for late-night drinkers.

SPA/FITNESS. The Spa at Seabourn, a small, well-equipped health spa/fitness center, is located just aft of the navigation bridge. It provides sauna and steam rooms with separate facilities for men and women, and integral changing room; plus a separate exercise room with video tapes for private, individual aerobics workouts; and a beauty salon.

It is staffed and operated by concession Elemis by Steiner. Treatment prices are equal to those in an expensive land-based spa. The beauty salon offers hair beautifying treatments and conditioning, while in the gymnasium, personal training sessions, yoga classes, mat Pilates, and body composition analysis are available at extra cost.

Seabourn Odyssey
★★★★★

Size:	Small Ship	Total Crew:	330	Cabins (wheelchair accessible):		7
Tonnage:	32,000	Passengers		Wheelchair accessibility:		Good
Lifestyle:	Luxury	(lower beds/all berths):	450/462	Cabin Voltage:		110 volts
Cruise Line:	Seabourn	Passenger Space Ratio		Elevators:		3
Former Names:	none	(lower beds/all berths):	71.1/69.2	Casino (gaming tables):		Yes
Builder:	Mariotti (Italy)	Crew/Passenger Ratio		Slot Machines:		Yes
Original Cost:	$250 million	(lower beds/all berths):	1.3/1.4	Swimming Pools (outdoors):		2
Entered Service:	Jun 2009	Cabins (total):	225	Swimming Pools (indoors):		0
Registry:	Bahamas	Size Range (sq ft/m):	295.0–438.1/	Whirlpools:		6
Length (ft/m):	649.6/198.0		27.5–133.6	Self-Service Launderette:		Yes
Beam (ft/m):	83.9/25.6	Cabins (outside view):	225	Dedicated Cinema/Seats:		No
Draft (ft/m):	21.3/6.5	Cabins (interior/no view):	0	Library:		Yes
Propulsion/Propellers:	diesel-electric/2	Cabins (for one person):	0	Onboard currency:		US$
Passenger Decks:	10	Cabins (with private balcony):	199			

An elegant, upscale ship for mature-age cruisers.

OVERVIEW. This is a ship with a yacht-like ambience – well, a big yacht, sort of like Roman Abramovich's *Eclipse*. Its strong points are the staff, high service levels, attention to detail, and the fitness/wellness facilities. The ship operated a 108-day around-the-world cruise in 2010 – Seabourn's first such cruise.

THE SHIP. This, the first of three new, larger ships for Seabourn, looks like an up-sized version of its three smaller vessels – *Seabourn Legend, Seabourn Pride, Seabourn Spirit*. However, this ship and sister ships *Seabourn Quest* and *Seabourn Sojourn* have the second highest passenger space ratio in the cruise industry – only the passenger space ratio of the expedition ship *50 Years of Victory* is greater – so passengers will never feel crowded. Also, unlike the smaller ships, *Seabourn Odyssey, Seabourn Quest* and *Seabourn Sojourn* are full of balcony cabins.

There are two outdoor swimming pools, midships and aft; the aft pool is in a more secluded area, although there's not a lot of sunbathing space and the sunloungers are of the steel mesh variety, not comfortable without a pad. One of the most pleasing outdoor areas is the Sky Bar – good for those balmy evenings in the right cruise areas. But for stargazing, the hot tub located by the ship's bow is a delight, and it's dimly lit and peaceful. While real teak is used in most outdoor areas, Flexteak (faux teak) is used in some locations.

All accommodation areas are in the forward section, with most public rooms aft – so accommodation is quiet, but you'll need to pass through several decks to get to some public rooms. An Observation Lounge, which has great views, is a well laid-out, very comfortable room. The Marina, at the stern, has a staging area from which watersports are organized when the weather is suitable. The interior decor uses light woods, tame colors and suitably rich soft furnishings create a contemporary, restrained and relaxing environment, which is good considering the low ceiling height in most public rooms.

Seabourn Square, a "concierge lounge," has a relaxed and club-like ambience designed to encourage sociability. The area – although considered the "town square," it's not in the center of the ship – includes a library, internet-connect computers, an outdoor terrace and a coffee bar that's particularly good for late-riser coffees and pastries. Its "concierges" can provide in-port shopping tips, set up shore excursions, get dinner reservations in ports of call, and so on. Wi-fi is available throughout. There's a "private" diamond showroom, The Collection.

Drinks, wines with meals, and all gratuities are included, though premium brands and high-quality wines cost extra.

Passenger niggles include the high charge for internet-connectivity ($39 a day). The "vertical stacking" layout is not really user-friendly. The cabin doors are rather narrow, and doors within the cabins are of varying heights and sizes, and feel utilitarian rather than luxurious. A second washbasin is pretty pointless, really, unless you wash at the same time as your spouse or partner. Most public rooms are of a single deck height, which doesn't create a good feeling of spaciousness, and support pillars are everywhere – Mariotti should look at *Europa* and learn that it's not necessary to have so many pillars – or fire doors that protrude outside bulkheads instead of being integral to them.

ACCOMMODATION. There are 13 different grades of suites

BERLITZ'S RATINGS

	Possible	Achieved
Ship	500	457
Accommodation	200	186
Food	400	347
Service	400	354
Entertainment	100	87
Cruise	400	355

OVERALL SCORE
1,786 points out of 2,000

in 18 price categories, although the smaller units are really large cabins. Fully 90 percent of cabins have a private balcony. Even the smallest cabin is a generous 269 sq.ft (25 sq. meters). All cabins have a separate tub and shower enclosure in a granite bathroom setting, twin beds convertible to a queen-size bed, flat-screen TV plus CD and DVD player, minibar, vanity desk with hairdryer, world atlas, personalized stationery, and large walk-in closet with personal safe.

The interior designers have created a very homely, contemporary living space in the suites and cabins, although the walls are rather plain and unimaginative. It's good to see that the beds are high enough off the floor to enable even the largest suitcases to be stowed underneath. All drawers are fitted with soft gel, which means they are quiet – no more "slamming" contests with your next-door neighbor.

The cabins are bathed in soft earthy tones, although a splash of color wouldn't go amiss. The cabinetry has many seams and strips covering joints which suggest that the ship's outfitters would benefit from a joinery course. One neat feature is a leather-clad vanity stool/table that converts into a backgammon table. The design of a "cube table" that can be "inserted" under a glass-topped table when not being used as a footrest is a smart idea for making more space.

Seabourn Suites and Veranda Suites are quite narrow, and feel cramped, with little space in the passageway between the bed and the opposite wall. However, the bathrooms are generously proportioned, with gray and chocolate-brown decor; there are two washbasins, a bathtub, and a separate shower enclosure.

Some size examples (excluding balcony): Grand Suites 1,135 sq.ft (105 sq. meters), including two-bedrooms; Signature Suites 819 sq. ft (76 sq. meters); Wintergarden Suites 914 sq.ft (85 sq. meters). Rather neat suites within a glass-enclosed solarium, set in front of the funnel, with a side balcony; Owners Suites 611–675 sq.ft (57–63 sq. meters); Penthouse Suite 436–611 sq.ft (41–57 sq. meters); Veranda Suite 269–298 sq.ft (25–28 sq. meters); Seabourn Suite (295 sq.ft (27 sq. meters).

DINING. There are three dining venues plus a poolside grill:
● *The Restaurant* has open-seating dining at tables for two, four, six or eight, with menus designed by American celebrity chef Charlie Palmer. It is a large venue that actually feels a bit "clinical" rather than "classical" with its white-on-white decor and double-height ceiling in its central section. The most sought-after seats are in the center rather than along the port and starboard sides, which have a window, but low ceiling height.

● *Restaurant 2*, with around 50 seats, has regional, seasonal cuisine and tasting menus, perhaps for a mini-dégustation; however, the ceiling height is rather low, which makes the feeling cramped. The cuisine is contemporary, with a flirtation with fusion, where taste and flavours are what the experience is all about. This venue shares the same galley as the adjacent The Colonnade.

● *The Colonnade*, located aft, has indoor/outdoor seating and is nicely decorated, although its "free-flow" design could be better; there's too little outdoor seating for the demand in warm-weather areas, when many passengers like to eat outdoors. During dinner, passengers who are dressed formally on designated formal nights have to share the space with those who are more casually dressed. The venue is also adjacent to one of the fine dining restaurants.

● The *Patio Grill* is in a casual poolside setting outdoors – and most enjoyable on a balmy evening, as a change to the air-conditioned interior dining venues.

In addition, a 24-hour, in-suite menu offers the à la carte items served in the main dining room during dinner hours.

ENTERTAINMENT. The Grand Salon is a nicely configured main entertainment venue for cabaret performances, social dancing, and for use as a cinema. However, the stage is small – large enough for a live band, but performers need to use the dance floor area – and the room has so many pillars that it's awkward to see anything, and a decorative steel ceiling grating in the central section is cold and unappealing. Small production shows are performed well to pre-recorded tracks. The audio equipment and sound dispersion in the room is excellent.

The Club is a cool, trendy nightclub/disco with minimalist design. Located beneath the Grand salon, it incorporates a comfortable casino.

SPA/FITNESS. The Spa at Seabourn, operated by Elemis, occupies the aft section of two decks, and is quite large, at 11,500 sq.ft (1,068 sq. meters). It offers full services in a very pleasant setting that includes a two-deck-high waterfall at the entrance and seven indoor/outdoor treatment rooms, as well as a thalassotherapy pool, thermal suite (for which a pass costs extra) and complete salon facilities, while a hot tub and relaxation area on the deck above is accessed by a spiral staircase. Separate saunas and steam rooms for men and women are provided, but they are extremely small. In the gymnasium, personal training sessions, yoga classes, mat Pilates and body composition analysis are available at extra cost, but some basic exercise programs are free.

Seabourn Pride
★★★★★

Size: ....Small Ship	Total Crew: 160	Cabins (wheelchair accessible): 4
Tonnage: 9,975	Passengers	Wheelchair accessibility: ....None
Lifestyle: ....Luxury	(lower beds/all berths): 212/212	Cabin Current: ....110 and 220 volts
Cruise Line: ....Seabourn	Passenger Space Ratio	Elevators: 3
Former Names: ....none	(lower beds/all berths): 47.09/47.09	Casino (gaming tables): ....Yes
Builder: ....Seebeckwerft (Germany)	Crew/Passenger Ratio	Slot Machines: ....Yes
Original Cost: ....$50 million	(lower beds/all berths): 1.3/1.3	Swimming Pools (outdoors): 1
Entered Service: ....Dec 1988	Cabins (total): 106	(plus 1 aft marina-pool)
Registry: ....Bahamas	Size Range (sq ft/m): 277.0–575.0/	Swimming Pools (indoors): 0
Length (ft/m): 439.9/134.10	25.7–53.4	Whirlpools: 3
Beam (ft/m): 62.9/19.20	Cabins (outside view): 106	Self-Service Launderette: ....Yes
Draft (ft/m): 16.8/5.15	Cabins (interior/no view): 0	Dedicated Cinema/Seats: ....No
Propulsion/Propellers: ..diesel (5,355kW)/2	Cabins (for one person): 0	Library: ....Yes
Passenger Decks: 6	Cabins (with private balcony): 6	Onboard currency: ....US$

A small, inclusive ship for stylish senior cruising.

OVERVIEW. *Seabourn Pride* is best for sophisticated, well-traveled couples – typically over 50, but possible younger – looking for a small ship with excellent food that approaches gourmet standards, and fine European-style service in surroundings that border on the elegant and luxurious. The ship is able to cruise where large cruise ships can't, thanks to its ocean-yacht size. You sail with only 100 other couples, and a sense of intimate camaraderie.

THE SHIP. This pleasantly appointed cruise vessel has sleek exterior styling, handsome profile with swept-back, rounded lines, and is an identical twin to *Seabourn Spirit.* It has two fine mahogany water taxis for use as shore tenders. An aft water sports platform and marina can be used in suitably calm warm-water areas. Water sports facilities include a small, enclosed "dip" pool, sea kayaks, snorkel equipment, windsurfers, water ski boat, and Zodiac inflatable boats.

The sunloungers have thankfully been changed from plastic to a steel mesh design. There is no walk-around promenade deck outdoors. There is only one dryer in the self-service launderette. Non-American passengers should note that almost all entertainment and activities are geared towards American tastes, despite the increasingly international passenger mix.

A wide central passageway divides port and starboard side accommodation. Inviting, sumptuous public areas have warm colors. Fine quality interior fixtures, fittings, artwork and fabric combine to present an outstanding, elegant decor. For a small ship, there's wide range of public rooms. These include a main lounge that stages small cabaret shows, a nightclub, an observation lounge with

BERLITZ'S RATINGS

	Possible	Achieved
Ship	500	452
Accommodation	200	186
Food	400	347
Service	400	348
Entertainment	100	86
Cruise	400	350

OVERALL SCORE
1,769 points out of 2,000

bar, large, deep armchairs, and a cigar smoking area complete with cabinet, cigar humidor and small selection of good cigars. There is a small business center, small meeting room, and a small casino with roulette and black-jack tables, plus a few slot machines.

Not for the budget-minded, this ship is for those desiring supremely elegant, stylish, small-ship surroundings, but is perhaps rather small for long voyages in open waters. During the past few years, there have been complaints about falling standards aboard the Seabourn ships, particularly with regard to maintenance – they are now over 20 years old – and that food, presentation and service had deteriorated. However, the company has now turned things around, and the product delivered is again good.

Seabourn Pride provides an outstanding level of personal service and an utterly civilized cruise. All drinks except premium brands and connoisseur wines are included. So are gratuities, fine aromatherapy bath selections from Molton Brown and soaps by Bronnley, Chanel and Hermès, short massages on deck ("massage moments"), open-seating dining, use of watersports equipment, one free Exclusively Seabourn shore excursion per cruise, and movies under the stars. Port charges and insurance are not included.

The Seabourn ships are superior to other upscale ships such as *Seven Seas Mariner* and *Seven Seas Voyager*, but still not up to the standard of *Europa*'s fine product delivery and hospitality.

DHL provides luggage pick-up and delivery service.

ACCOMMODATION. This is spread over three decks, with nine price categories. The all-outside cabins (called suites in brochure-speak) are comfortably large and beautifully equipped with everything one could reasonably need. Electric blackout blinds are provided for the large windows in addition to curtains. All cabinetry is made of blond woods, with softly rounded edges, and cabin doors are neatly angled away from the passageway.

All the suites have a sleeping area, with European duvets and Frette linens as standard. A separate lounge area has a Bose Wave audio unit, DVD player and flat-screen TV, vanity desk with hairdryer and personalized stationery, world atlas, mini-bar and refrigerator (stocked with soft drinks and two bottles of your favorite liquor when you embark). There's a large walk-in closet illuminated automatically when you open the door, wooden hangers, electronic personal safe, umbrella, and wall-mounted clock and barometer. A full passenger list is also provided – a rarity these days – as are a fresh fruit basket, replenished daily, and flowers.

Marble-clad bathrooms have one or two washbasins, depending on the accommodation grade, a decent but not full-size tub (four suites have a shower enclosure only – no tub), plenty of storage areas, 100% thick cotton towels, plush terrycloth bathrobe, designer soaps and Molton Brown personal amenities. A selection of five Molton Brown aromatherapy bath preparations can be ordered from your stewardess, who will prepare your bath.

In 2001, Seabourn added 36 French balconies to suites on two out of three accommodation decks. These are not balconies in the true sense of the word, but they do have two doors that open wide onto a tiny teakwood balcony that is just 10.6 inches (27 cm) wide. The balconies allow you to have fresh sea air, together with some salt spray.

Course-by-course in-cabin dining is available during dinner hours, and the cocktail table can be raised to form a dining table. There is 24-hour room service. Also provided are personalized stationery, and fancy ticket wallet. Non-smoking cabins are available. Menus for each dinner are delivered to your suite during the day.

Four Owner's suites (King Haakon/King Magnus, each measuring 530 sq. ft (49 sq. meters), and Amundsen/ Nansen, each 575 sq. ft (53 sq. meters), and two Classic Suites (King Harald/King Olav, each 400 sq. ft (37 sq. meters) offer superb, private living spaces. Each has a walk-in closet, second closet, full bathroom plus a guest toilet with washbasin. There is a fully secluded forward- or side-facing balcony, with sunloungers and wooden drinks table. The living area has ample bookshelf space including a complete edition of *Encyclopedia Britannica*, large refrigerator/ drinks cabinet, television and DVD player, plus a second TV

set in the bedroom. All windows, as well as the door to the balcony, have manually operated blackout blinds, and a complete blackout is possible in both bedroom and living room.

CUISINE. *The Restaurant* is a part-marble, part-carpeted dining room with portholes and elegant decor. The silverware (150 gram weight – the best available) is by Robbe & Berking. Open-seating dining means that you can dine when you want, with whom you wish.

The menus, overseen by celebrity chef Charlie Palmer, are creative and well-balanced, with a wide selection of foods and regional cuisine. Seabourn's fine, creative cuisine is artfully presented, with many items cooked to order. Special orders are available, and caviar is always available on request. Tableside flambeaus and flaming desserts can be presented at your table. There is always a good selection of exotic fruits and cheeses.

Each day, basic table wine is included for lunch and dinner, but the decent bottles cost extra. The wine list is quite extensive, with prices ranging from moderate to high; many of the wines come from the smaller, more exclusive vineyards. The hand-picked European dining room staff provide excellent, unhurried service.

In addition, relaxed breakfasts (available until 11am) and lunch buffets and casual, themed candlelight dinners, including a new "2" tasting menu, can be taken in the popular *Veranda Café* adjacent to the swimming pool.

The *Sky Grill* provides an above-poolside setting for candlelit dining. It specializes in steaks and seafood.

ENTERTAINMENT. The Magellan Lounge has a sloping floor that provides good sight lines from just about every seat. "Production" shows are of limited scope, as dinner is usually the main event. You can, however, expect to see the occasional cabaret act. Singers also tend to do mini-cabaret performances in The Club, one deck above the showlounge, the gathering place for late-night drinkers.

SPA/FITNESS. The Spa at Seabourn is a small but well-equipped health spa/fitness center. It has sauna and steam rooms (separate facilities for men and women), an equipment-packed gymnasium – but the ceiling height is low – and a beauty salon.

The spa is staffed and operated by concession Elemis by Steiner. Treatment prices equal those in an expensive land-based spa. The beauty salon has hair beautifying treatments and conditioning. In the gymnasium, personal training sessions, yoga classes, mat Pilates, and body composition analysis are available at extra cost.

Seabourn Quest
★★★★★

Size: ....Small Ship	Total Crew: 330	Cabins (wheelchair accessible): 7
Tonnage: 32,000	Passengers	Wheelchair accessibility: ....Good
Lifestyle: ....Luxury	(lower beds/all berths): 450/462	Cabin Current: ....110 volts
Cruise Line: ....Seabourn	Passenger Space Ratio	Elevators: 3
Former Names: ....none	(lower beds/all berths): 71.1/69.2	Casino (gaming tables): ....Yes
Builder: ....Mariotti (Italy)	Crew/Passenger Ratio	Slot Machines: ....Yes
Original Cost: ....$250 million	(lower beds/all berths): 1.3/1.4	Swimming Pools (outdoors): 2
Entered Service: ....Jun 2011	Cabins (total): 225	Swimming Pools (indoors): 0
Registry: ....Bahamas	Size Range (sq ft/m): 295.0–438.1/	Whirlpools: 6
Length (ft/m): 649.6/198.0	27.5–133.6	Self-Service Launderette: ....Yes
Beam (ft/m): 83.9/25.6	Cabins (outside view): 225	Dedicated Cinema/Seats: ....No
Draft (ft/m): 21.3/6.5	Cabins (interior/no view): 0	Library: ....Yes
Propulsion/Propellers: ...diesel-electric/2	Cabins (for one person): 0	Onboard currency: ....US$
Passenger Decks: 10	Cabins (with private balcony): 199	

An elegant, all-inclusive ship for mature-age cruisers.

OVERVIEW. This ship's big attractions are its staff and service levels, and the wellness facilities. Like its sister ships *Seabourn Odyssey* and *Seabourn Sojourn*, it has the highest passenger space ratio in the cruise industry, so passengers will never feel crowded. Expect it to receive a similar score and rating to that of its sisters.

THE SHIP. This, the last of Seabourn's three new, larger ships, has two outdoor swimming pools, midships and aft; the aft pool is in a delightful area, although there's not a lot of sunbathing space. One of the most pleasing outdoor areas is the Sky Bar – good for those balmy evenings in the right cruise areas. But for stargazing, the hot tub located by the ship's bow is a delight, and it's dimly lit and peaceful.

All the accommodation areas are in the forward section, with most public rooms located aft, so accommodation is quiet, but you'll need to traverse through several decks to get to some of the public rooms. The Marina, at the stern, has a staging area from which watersports are organized.

Seabourn Square, a "concierge lounge," has a relaxed, club-like ambience. The area includes a library, shops, eight internet-connect computers, an outdoor terrace and a coffee bar. Its "concierges" can provide in-port shopping tips, set up shore excursions, get dinner reservations in ports of call, etc. Wi-fi is available throughout the ship. There's a private diamond showroom, called The Collection. Drinks, wines with meals, and all gratuities are included, though premium brands and high-quality wines cost extra.

BERLITZ'S RATINGS		
	Possible	Achieved
Ship	500	457
Accommodation	200	186
Food	400	347
Service	400	355
Entertainment	100	87
Cruise	400	355
OVERALL SCORE		
1,787 points out of 2,000		

What's not so good? The "vertical stacking" layout is not really user-friendly. While real teak is used in most outdoor areas, Flexteak (faux teak) is used in other areas. The cabin doors are rather narrow, and doors within the cabins are of varying heights and sizes, and feel utilitarian rather than luxurious. A second washbasin is pretty pointless unless you and your partner usually wash at the same time.

Most public rooms are of a single deck height, so there's not such a good feeling of spaciousness, and support pillars are everywhere – Mariotti, the shipbuilder, should look at *Europa* to see it's not necessary to have so many pillars.

ACCOMMODATION. There are 13 grades of suites in 18 price categories, although the smaller units are really large cabins. For details of their sizes and facilities, see the entry for *Seabourn Odyssey* on page 581.

CUISINE. There are three venues, plus a poolside grill. For assessments of their food and service, see the entry for *Seabourn Odyssey*.

ENTERTAINMENT. For details of the Grand Salon and The Club nightclub/disco, see the entry for *Seabourn Odyssey*.

SPA/FITNESS. The Spa at Seabourn is the largest aboard any luxury ship. For details of its facilities, see the entry for *Seabourn Odyssey*.

Seabourn Sojourn
★★★★★

Size:	Small Ship	Total Crew:	330	Cabins (wheelchair accessible):	7
Tonnage:	32,000	Passengers		Wheelchair accessibility:	Good
Lifestyle:	Luxury	(lower beds/all berths):	450/462	Cabin Current:	110 volts
Cruise Line:	Seabourn	Passenger Space Ratio		Elevators:	3
Former Names:	none	(lower beds/all berths):	71.1/69.2	Casino (gaming tables):	Yes
Builder:	Mariotti (Italy)	Crew/Passenger Ratio		Slot Machines:	Yes
Original Cost:	$250 million	(lower beds/all berths):	1.3/1.4	Swimming Pools (outdoors):	2
Entered Service:	Jun 2010	Cabins (total):	225	Swimming Pools (indoors):	0
Registry:	Bahamas	Size Range (sq ft/m):	295.0–438.1/	Whirlpools:	6
Length (ft/m):	649.6/198.0		27.5–133.6	Self-Service Launderette:	Yes
Beam (ft/m):	83.9/25.6	Cabins (outside view):	225	Dedicated Cinema/Seats:	No
Draft (ft/m):	21.3/6.5	Cabins (interior/no view):	0	Library:	Yes
Propulsion/Propellers:	diesel-electric/2	Cabins (for one person):	0	Onboard currency:	US$
Passenger Decks:	10	Cabins (with private balcony):	199		

An upscale, elegant small ship for mature-age cruisers.

OVERVIEW. This ship's big attractions are its staff and service levels, and the wellness facilities. Like its sister ships *Seabourn Odyssey* and *Seabourn Quest*, it has the highest passenger space ratio in the cruise industry, so passengers will never feel crowded.

THE SHIP. This, the second of Seabourn's three new, larger ships, has two outdoor swimming pools, midships and aft; the aft pool is in a delightful area, although there's not a lot of sunbathing space. One of the most pleasing outdoor areas is the Sky Bar – good for those balmy evenings in the right cruise areas. But for stargazing, the hot tub located by the ship's bow is a delight, and it's dimly lit and peaceful.

All the accommodation areas are in the forward section, with most public rooms located aft, so accommodation is quiet, but you'll need to traverse through several decks to get to some of the public rooms. The Marina, at the stern, has a staging area from which watersports are organized.

Seabourn Square, a "concierge lounge," has a relaxed, club-like ambiance. The area includes a library, shops, eight internet-connect computers, an outdoor terrace and a coffee bar. Its "concierges" can provide in-port shopping tips, set up shore excursions, get dinner reservations in ports of call, etc. Wi-fi is available throughout the ship. There's a private diamond showroom, called The Collection. Drinks, wines with meals, and all gratuities are included, though premium brands and high-quality wines cost extra.

BERLITZ'S RATINGS		
	Possible	Achieved
Ship	500	457
Accommodation	200	186
Food	400	347
Service	400	354
Entertainment	100	87
Cruise	400	352

OVERALL SCORE
1,783 points out of 2,000

Minus points? The "vertical stacking" layout is not really user-friendly. While real teak is used in most outdoor areas, Flexteak (faux teak) is used in other areas. The cabin doors are rather narrow, and doors within the cabins vary in height and size, and feel utilitarian, not luxurious. A second washbasin is pretty pointless unless you and your partner usually wash at the same time.

Most public rooms are of a single deck height, so there's not such a good feeling of spaciousness, and support pillars are everywhere – Mariotti, the shipbuilder, should look at *Europa* to see it's not necessary to have so many pillars.

ACCOMMODATION. There are 13 grades of suites in 18 price categories, although the smaller units are really large cabins. For details of their sizes and facilities, see the entry for *Seabourn Odyssey* on page 581.

CUISINE. There are three venues, plus a poolside grill. For assessments of their food and service, see the entry for *Seabourn Odyssey*.

ENTERTAINMENT. For details of the Grand Salon and The Club nightclub/disco, see the entry for *Seabourn Odyssey*.

SPA/FITNESS. The Spa at Seabourn is the largest aboard any luxury ship. For details of its facilities, see the entry for *Seabourn Odyssey*.

Seabourn Spirit
★★★★★

Size: . . . . .Small Ship	Total Crew: 160	Cabins (wheelchair accessible): 4
Tonnage: .9,975	Passengers	Wheelchair accessibility: . . . . .None
Lifestyle: .Luxury	(lower beds/all berths): 212/212	Cabin Current: . . . . .110 and 220 volts
Cruise Line: . . . . .Seabourn	Passenger Space Ratio	Elevators: 3
Former Names: . . . . .none	(lower beds/all berths): 47.0/47.0	Casino (gaming tables): . . . . .Yes
Builder: . . . . .Seebeckwerft (Germany)	Crew/Passenger Ratio	Slot Machines: . . . . .Yes
Original Cost: . . . .$50 million	(lower beds/all berths): 1.3/1.3	Swimming Pools (outdoors): 1
Entered Service: . . . . .Nov 1989	Cabins (total): .106	(plus aft marina-pool)
Registry: . . . . .Bahamas	Size Range (sq ft/m): 277.0–575.0/	Swimming Pools (indoors): 0
Length (ft/m): 439.9/134.10	25.7–53.4	Whirlpools: 3
Beam (ft/m): 62.9/19.20	Cabins (outside view): 106	Self-Service Launderette: . . . . .Yes
Draft (ft/m): 16.8/5.15	Cabins (interior/no view): 0	Dedicated Cinema/Seats: . . . . .No
Propulsion/Propellers: . .diesel (5,355kW)/2	Cabins (for one person): 0	Library: . . . . .Yes
Passenger Decks: 6	Cabins (with private balcony): 6	Onboard currency: . . . . .US$

A contemporary small ship for mature-age cruisers.

OVERVIEW. *Seabourn Spirit* is best for sophisticated, well traveled couples – typically over 50, but possible younger – looking for a small ship with excellent food that approaches gourmet standards, and fine European-style service in surroundings that border on the elegant and luxurious. The ship is able to cruise where large cruise ships can't, thanks to its ocean-yacht size. You sail with only 100 other couples, and a sense of intimate camaraderie.

THE SHIP. This pleasantly appointed cruise vessel has sleek exterior styling, handsome profile with swept-back, rounded lines, and is an identical twin to *Seabourn Pride*. The Seabourn ships provide an excellent product, superior to other upscale ships such as *Seven Seas Mariner* and *Seven Seas Voyager*, but still not up to the standard of *Europa*'s fine product delivery and hospitality.

For full details of *Seabourn Spirit*'s facilities and ambi-

BERLITZ'S RATINGS

	Possible	Achieved
Ship	500	453
Accommodation	200	186
Food	400	347
Service	400	348
Entertainment	100	86
Cruise	400	350
OVERALL SCORE		
1,770 points out of 2,000		

ence, see the entry for *Seabourn Pride* on page 583.

ACCOMMODATION. This is spread over three decks, and there are nine price categories. For full details of sizes and facilities, see the entry for *Seabourn Pride.*

CUISINE. For assessments of their food and service in *The Restaurant*, the *Veranda Café* and the *Sky Grill*, see the entry for *Seabourn Pride.*

ENTERTAINMENT. The Amundsen Lounge is the venue for all entertainment events and there are mini-cabaret performances in The Club. For an assessment of the entertainment, see the entry for *Seabourn Pride.*

SPA/FITNESS. For details of The Spa at Seabourn's facilities, see the entry for *Seabourn Pride.*

SeaDream I
★★★★★

Size:	Boutique Ship
Tonnage:	4,253
Lifestyle:	Luxury
Cruise Line:	Seadream Yacht Club
Former Names:	Seabourn Goddess I, Sea Goddess I
Builder:	Wartsila (Finland)
Entered Service:	Apr 1984/May 2002
Registry:	The Bahamas
Length (ft/m):	343.8/104.81
Beam (ft/m):	47.9/14.60
Draft (ft/m):	13.6/4.17
Propulsion/Propellers:	diesel (3,540kW)/2
Passenger Decks:	5
Total Crew:	95
Passengers (lower beds/all berths):	112/112
Passenger Space Ratio (lower beds/all berths):	37.9/37.9
Crew/Passenger Ratio (lower beds/all berths):	1.1/1.1
Cabins (total):	54
Size Range (sq ft/m):	195.0–446.7/ 18.1–41.4
Cabins (outside view):	56
Cabins (interior/no view):	0
Cabins (for one person):	0
Cabins (with private balcony):	0
Cabins (wheelchair accessible):	0
Wheelchair accessibility:	None
Cabin Current:	110 and 220 volts
Elevators:	1
Casino (gaming tables):	Yes
Slot Machines:	Yes
Swimming Pools (outdoors):	1
Swimming Pools (indoors):	0
Whirlpools:	1
Self-Service Launderette:	No
Dedicated Cinema/Seats:	No
Library:	Yes
Onboard currency:	US$

BERLITZ'S RATINGS

	Possible	Achieved
Ship	500	439
Accommodation	200	173
Food	400	371
Service	400	370
Entertainment	n/a	n/a
Cruise	500	433

OVERALL SCORE
1,786 points out of 2,000

Nice mega-yachts for informal but stylish cruising.

OVERVIEW. *Sea Dream I* and *Sea Dream II*, reviewed here together, are best suited to sophisticated, independent and well-traveled couples who are typically over 40, but possible younger. Rejecting today's huge standard resort cruise ships, they are looking for a small ship with excellent food approaching gourmet standards, and fine European-style service in surroundings that border on the elegant and refined while remaining trendy. Note that, because these ships are popular for small company charters, you may find that the date and itinerary you want will not be available, so you may be asked to change to the sister ship and a different itinerary.

THE SHIPS. The *SeaDreams* were originally funded by about 800 investors, and operated under the Norske Cruise banner. They have an ultra-sleek profile, with deep blue hull and white superstructure, and the ambiance of a private club. After they were bought by SeaDream Yacht Club in 2001, they were completely refurbished, with many changes to public rooms and outdoor areas, and several new features added to create what are contemporary, chic, and desirable, if aging, vessels.

A "Top of the Yacht" bar, crafted in warm wood, was added to both ships. So were eight special alcoves set to the port and starboard sides of the funnel, equipped with two-person sun loungers with thick pads (and two equipped for one person); however, there is quite a bit of noise from the adjacent funnel. You are encouraged to sleep under the stars if you wish, and cotton sleep suits are provided.

At the front part of the deck there are more sun loungers and a couple of large hammocks, as well as a golf simulator with a choice of 30 courses.

Inside, there is a feeling of unabashed but discreet sophistication. Elegant public rooms have flowers and pot pourri everywhere. The main social gathering places are the lounge, a delightful library/living room with a selection of about 1,000 books, a piano bar – which can be more like a karaoke bar at times – and a small casino with two blackjack tables and five slot machines.

The two SeaDream ships really are the ultimate exclusive boutique vessels – it's like having your own private yacht in which hospitality, anticipation and personal recognition are art forms practiced to a high level. The staff is delightful and accommodating – "no" is not in their vocabulary. The dress code is resort casual. Fine-quality furnishings and fabrics are used throughout, with marble and blond wood accents.

So what type of persons will enjoy the SeaDream Yacht Club experience? This is for experienced, independent travelers who don't like regular cruise ships, large ships, glitzy lounges, a platoon of people and kids running around, or dressing up – no tuxedos or gowns are allowed, and ties are not needed. The *SeaDreams* provide the setting for personal indulgence and refined, unstructured and langorous private living at sea, in a casual, private setting akin to that on a mega-yacht. One delightful feature of each cruise in warm weather areas is a "caviar in the surf" beach barbecue.

Life could hardly be better at sea – so, as many regular SeaDream Yacht Club passengers say, why bother with ports of call at all? Embarkation never starts before 3pm, in case you are eager to get aboard.

All drinks (with the exception of premium brands and connoisseur wines), American farmed sevruga caviar, and gratuities are included, but port charges

SeaDream II
★★★★★

Size:	Boutique Ship
Tonnage:	4,333
Lifestyle:	Luxury
Cruise Line:	SeaDream Yacht Club
Former Names:	Seabourn Goddess II, Sea Goddess II
Builder:	Wartsila (Finland)
Original Cost:	$34 million
Entered Service:	May 1985/Jan 2002
Registry:	The Bahamas
Length (ft/m):	343.8/104.81
Beam (ft/m):	47.9/14.60
Draft (ft/m):	13.6/4.17
Propulsion/Propellers:	diesel (3,540kW)/2
Passenger Decks:	5
Total Crew:	95
Passengers (lower beds/all berths):	112/112
Passenger Space Ratio (lower beds/all berths):	37.9/37.9
Crew/Passenger Ratio (lower beds/all berths):	1.1/1.1
Cabins (total):	54
Size Range (sq ft/m):	195.0–446.7/ 18.1–41.5
Cabins (outside view):	56
Cabins (interior/no view):	0
Cabins (for one person):	0
Cabins (with private balcony):	0
Cabins (wheelchair accessible):	0
Wheelchair accessibility	None
Cabin Current:	110 and 220 volts
Elevators:	1
Casino (gaming tables):	Yes
Slot Machines:	Yes
Swimming Pools (outdoors):	1
Swimming Pools (indoors):	0
Whirlpools:	1
Self-Service Launderette:	No
Dedicated Cinema/Seats:	No
Library:	Yes
Onboard currency:	US$

and insurance are not. The price of a cruise is just that: the price of a cruise. Air and/or other travel arrangements can be made on your own, or through your own travel agent, or you can use the excellent services of Total Travel Marine, whose offices in London and Miami specialize in first, business or coach air arrangements as partner to SeaDream Yacht Club, with 24-hour, 365-day service.

These were the first of the mega-yacht-style ships when built, and none of the cabins has a private balcony – ships with private balconies made their debut just a couple of years later, and, anyway, yachts don't have balconies. One not so positive item is the fact that the reception desk is now called the Concierge, although it is doubtful whether the staff has the kind of in-depth knowledge that is expected of a concierge.

ACCOMMODATION. There are three types, and six price categories (depending on location, size and grade): Yacht Club (standard) Cabin, Commodore Club Suite, Admiral Suite and Owner's Suite.
Yacht Club Cabins: Incorrectly called "suites" in the brochure, the standard cabins are, more correctly, fully equipped "mini-suites" with an outside view through windows or portholes, depending on deck and price category. Each measures 195 sq. ft (18.1 sq. meters), which isn't large by today's cruise ship standards; however, it is large compared to cabins aboard many private motor yachts, and extremely large when compared to ocean-going racing yachts. The sleeping area has twin beds that can be put together to form a queen-size configuration; beds are positioned next to the window or porthole so that you can entertain in the living area without going past the sleeping area, as you must aboard the slightly larger Seabourn or Silversea ships, for example; a curtain separates the sleeping and lounge areas. All cabinetry and furniture is of thick blond wood, with nicely rounded edges.

A long vanity desk in the sleeping area has a large mirror above it; however, there is no three-sided mirror for women to check the back of their hair. There are two small drawers for cosmetic items, and a brass clock is positioned on one wall. A mirror is placed opposite the bed, which won't please those who follow feng shui principles.

In the lounge area, a long desk has six drawers, plus a vertical cupboard unit that houses a sensible safe, refrigerator and drinks cabinet stocked with your choice of drinks. There is also a 20-inch (52-mm) flat-screen television, CD and DVD player, and an MP3 audio player with a choice of more than 100 selections. The beds have the finest linens, including thick cotton duvets, and non-allergenic pillows are also available. There's little room under the beds for luggage, although this can be taken away and stored.

One drawback is the fact that the insulation between cabins is not particularly good, although rarely does this present a problem as most passengers aboard the SeaDreams are generally extremely quiet, considerate types who are allergic to noise. Incidentally, a sleep suit is supplied in case you want to sleep out on deck under the stars in one of the on-deck two-person beds – but more of those later.

When the ships became *SeaDreams I* and *II* all the bathrooms were totally refurbished. The old tiling was discarded and replaced by new cheerful decor that is more hip and trendy, with softer colors and larger (beige) marble tiles. The former tiny sit-in bathtubs have been taken out – these will be missed by many regular European passengers – and replaced by a multi-jet power

BERLITZ'S RATINGS

	Possible	Achieved
Ship	500	440
Accommodation	200	173
Food	400	371
Service	400	370
Entertainment	n/a	n/a
Cruise	500	434

OVERALL SCORE
1,788 points out of 2,000

glassed-in shower enclosure. A new washbasin set in a marble-look surround and two glass shelves make up the facilities, while an under-sink cupboard provides further space for larger toiletries. Bulgari toiletries are provided. Gorgeously thick, plush, 100% cotton SeaDream-logo bathrobes and towels are also supplied.

However, the bathrooms really are small, particularly for those who are of larger than average build, despite their having been completely rebuilt. Also, the doors still open inward, so space inside is at a premium. The toilet is located in a rather awkward position, and, unless you close the door, you can see yourself in the mirror facing of the closets, opposite the bathroom door.

Commodore Club Suites: For larger accommodation, choose one of 16 Commodore Club Suites. These consist of two standard cabins with an interconnecting door, thus providing you with a healthy 380 sq. ft (36 sq. meters) of living space. One cabin is made into a lounge and dining room, with table and up to four chairs, while the other becomes your sleeping area. The advantage is that you get two bathrooms. One disadvantage is that the soundproofing between cabins could be better.

Admiral Suite: Added in 2008–09, this suite occupies space previously devoted to the ship's boutique, and adjacent to the piano bar/library. It's a little smaller than the Owner's Suite, but is well laid out and extremely comfortable.

Owner's Suite: For the largest living space, go for the Owner's Suite. This measures a grand 490 sq. ft (45.5 sq. meters). It's the only accommodation with a bathroom that incorporates a real full-size tub; there's also a separate shower enclosure and lots of space for toiletries.

In all grades of accommodation, passengers receive personalized stationery, a personal email address, a 100% cotton sleep suit, Bulgari toiletries, 24-hour room service, and "sweet dreams" chocolates.

CUISINE. The dining salon, called *The Restaurant*, is elegant and inviting, and has bird's-eye maple wood paneled walls and alcoves showcasing beautiful hand-made glass creations. It is cozy, yet with plenty of space around each table for fine service, and the ship provides a floating culinary celebration in an open-seating arrangement, so you can dine whenever, and with whomever, you want. Course-by-course meals can also be served out on deck.

Tables can be configured for two, four, six, or eight. They are laid with a classic setting of a real glass base (show) plate, Porsgrund china, pristine white monogrammed table linen, and fresh flowers.

Candlelit dinners are part of the inviting setting. There is even a box of spare spectacles for menu reading in case you forget your own. You get leather-bound menus, and close to impeccable personalized European service.

The SeaDream Yacht Club experience really is all about dining. The ships will not disappoint, and culinary excellence prevails. Only the very freshest and finest quality ingredients are used in the best culinary artistry. Fine, unhurried European service is provided. Additionally, good-quality champagne is available whenever you want it, and so is caviar – American farmed Hacklefish malossol caviar, sadly, and not Russian caviar, whose purchase and supply today is challenging. The ice cream, made on board, is excellent.

The ships provide extremely creative cuisine, and everything is prepared individually to order. Special orders are possible, although the former popular flaming desserts have almost disappeared. You can also dine, course by course in your suite for any meal, at any time – you can also eat à la carte 24 hours a day if you wish. The dining room is not open for lunch, which disappoints those who do not want to eat outside, particularly in hot climates.

Good-quality table wines are included in the cruise fare for lunch and dinner. Real wine connoisseurs, however, will appreciate the availability of an extra wine list, full of special vintages and premier crus at extra cost. If you want to do something different with a loved one, you can also arrange to dine one evening on the open (but covered) deck, overlooking the swimming pool and stern – it can be a magical and very romantic setting.

The *Topside Restaurant* is an informal open-air dining venue created from what used to be the outdoor café. Now it has glass sides and a glass ceiling. Informal dining is its theme, whether for breakfast, lunch or the occasional dinner. Teak tables and chairs add a touch of class.

ENTERTAINMENT. There is no evening entertainment as such, other than a duo or solo musician to provide music for listening and dancing in the lounge. Dinner is the main event, and videos are available to take to your cabin.

SPA/FITNESS. The holistic approach to wellbeing plays a big part in relaxation and body pampering aboard the *Sea-Dreams*. To this end, when you enter the Asian Spa/Wellness Centre, which has a good-sized gymnasium and a small beauty salon, you enter another world. There are three massage rooms, a small sauna, and steam shower enclosure.

The spa, located in a private area forward on Deck 4, is staffed and operated as a concession by Universal Maritime Services. Massage on the beach is available when the ship stages its famous beach party.

For golfers, there's an electronic golf simulator, and choice of several golf courses to play. There is a small, retractable, water sports platform at the stern. Equipment carried includes a water-ski boat, sailboat, wave runners (jet skis), kayaks, wake boards, snorkeling equipment and two Zodiacs. The use of all this equipment is included in the price of a cruise.

The sea conditions have to be just right (minimal swell) for these items to be used, which, on average is once or twice during a typical seven-night cruise. You may be allowed to swim off the stern platform if conditions permit. Ten mountain bikes are carried, to use when ashore.

Serenade of the Seas
★★★★

Size: . . . . .Large Resort Ship	Total Crew: 858	Cabins (wheelchair accessible): 14
Tonnage: .90,090	Passengers	(8 with private balcony)
Lifestyle: . . . . .Standard	(lower beds/all berths): 2,100/2,500	Wheelchair accessibility: . . . . .Best
Cruise Line: Royal Caribbean International	Passenger Space Ratio	Cabin Current: . . . . .110/220 volts
Former Names: . . . . .none	(lower beds/all berths): 42.9/36.0	Elevators: 9
Builder: . . . . .Meyer Werft (Germany)	Crew/Passenger Ratio	Casino (gaming tables): . . . . .Yes
Original Cost: . . . .$350 million	(lower beds/all berths): 2.4/2.9	Slot Machines: .Yes
Entered Service: . . . . .Aug 2003	Cabins (total): 1,050	Swimming Pools (outdoors): 2
Registry: . . . . .The Bahamas	Size Range (sq ft/m): 165.8–1,216.3/	Swimming Pools (indoors): 0
Length (ft/m): 961.9/293.2	15.4–113.0	Whirlpools: 3
Beam (ft/m): 105.6/32.2	Cabins (outside view): 813	Self-Service Launderette: . . . . .No
Draft (ft/m): 27.8/8.5	Cabins (interior/no view): 237	Dedicated Cinema/Seats: Yes/40
Propulsion/Propellers: . . . . .gas turbine/2	Cabins (for one person): 0	Library: . . . . .Yes
azimuthing pods (20 MW each)	Cabins (with private balcony): 577	Onboard currency: . . . . .US$
Passenger Decks: 12		

A large resort ship for family-friendly casual cruising.

OVERVIEW. Life aboard is more casual and unstructured than is often the case with Royal Caribbean International. This ship offers more space, more comfortable public areas, and several more intimate spaces, slightly larger cabins and more dining options than most of the larger ships in the fleet. But, while it is delightful in many ways, the onboard operation is less than spectacular, and suffers from a lack of service staff.

THE SHIP. *Serenade of the Seas* uses gas and steam turbine power, as do sister ships *Brilliance of the Seas* and *Radiance of the Seas*, instead of the formerly conventional diesel or diesel-electric combination. Pod propulsion power is also provided *(see page 191)*.

As aboard all RCI vessels, the navigation bridge is of the fully enclosed type – good for cruising in cold-weather areas such as Alaska. In the very front of the ship is a helipad, which also acts as a viewing platform for passengers – good for up-close-and-personal cruising in Alaska. One of two swimming pools can be covered by a large glass dome for use as an indoor/outdoor pool.

Serenade of the Seas is a streamlined contemporary ship, and has a two-deck-high walk-around structure in the forward section of the funnel. Along the starboard side, a central glass wall protrudes, giving great views; cabins with balconies occupy the space directly opposite on the port side. The gently rounded stern has nicely tiered decks, which gives the ship an extremely well-balanced look.

The interior decor is contemporary yet elegant, bright and cheerful, designed for young, active, hip and trendy types. The artwork is quite eclectic, catering for most tastes,

BERLITZ'S RATINGS

	Possible	Achieved
Ship	500	424
Accommodation	200	158
Food	400	242
Service	400	291
Entertainment	100	78
Cruise	400	298

OVERALL SCORE
1,491 points out of 2,000

and provides a spectrum and a half of color works.

The interior focal point is a nine-deck high atrium lobby with glass-walled elevators (on the port side of the ship only) that travel through 12 decks, face the sea and provide a link with nature and the ocean. The Centrum, as the atrium is called, has several public rooms connected to it: the guest relations office and shore excursions desks, a Lobby Bar, Champagne Bar, the Library, an internet-connect center, the Concierge Club, and a Crown & Anchor Lounge. A great view of the atrium can be had by looking down through the flat glass dome high above it.

Other facilities include a delightful, but very small library and, in the atrium lobby, a Coffee Shop that also sells pastries and cakes – it's rather like a small Seattle coffee house. The large Schooner Bar is popular aboard RCI ships, with nautical riggings, ship replicas, maritime art and other nautically-themed ephemera. Gamblers should enjoy the rather large, noisy and very colorful Casino Royale. There's also a small dedicated screening room for movies, with space for two wheelchairs, as well as a 194-seat conference center and a business center.

This ship has a Viking Crown Lounge, a Royal Caribbean International trademark, set around the base of the funnel. It is an observation lounge by day, with views forward over the swimming pool. In the evening, the space transforms itself into a futuristic, high-energy dance club, as well as a more intimate and relaxed entertainment venue for softer mood music and "black box" theater.

Royal Caribbean Online, located in a semi-private setting, has 12 computers providing high-speed internet access for sending and receiving email. Four more internet terminals are located in Books 'n' Coffee, a bookshop with coffee and pastries, located in an extensive area of shops.

A grand amount of glass allows contact with the ocean around you; of course, more glass means more cleaning of glass. A 15% gratuity is added to all bar and spa bills.

Many "private" balcony cabins are not private, as they can be overlooked by anyone standing in the port and starboard wings of the Solarium, and from other locations. There are no cushioned pads for the sunloungers, and the deck towels provided are quite thin and small. Spa treatments are extravagantly expensive – as they are aboard most ships today, in line with land-based spa prices in the United States. It is virtually impossible to escape background music anywhere.

Standing in lines for embarkation, the reception desk, disembarkation, for port visits, shore tenders and for the self-serve buffet stations in the Windjammer Café is an inevitable aspect of cruising aboard this large ship.

FAMILIES. Youth facilities include Adventure Ocean, an "edutainment" area with four separate age-appropriate sections for junior passengers: Aquanaut Center (for ages 3–5); Explorer Center (6–8); Voyager Center (9–12); and the Optix Teen Center (13–17). There is also Adventure Beach, which includes a splash pool complete with waterslide; Surfside, with computer lab stations with entertaining software; and Ocean Arcade, a video games hangout.

Some cabins have interconnecting doors, so families with children can cruise together in adjacent cabins.

ACCOMMODATION. There is a wide range of suites and standard outside-view and interior cabins, in 10 different categories and 19 price groups.

Apart from the largest suites (six owner's suites), which have king-size beds, almost all other cabins have twin beds that convert to a queen-size bed, All sheets are of 100% Egyptian cotton, although blankets are of synthetic fabric. All cabins have rich (but faux) wood cabinetry, including a vanity desk with hairdryer, faux wood drawers that close silently (hooray), a TV set, personal safe, and three-sided mirrors. Some cabins have a recessed ceiling, pull-down berths for third and fourth persons, although closet and drawer space would be extremely tight for four people, even if two of them are children.

Audio channels are available through the TV set; however, if you want to go to sleep with soft music playing in the background you'll need to put a towel over the television screen, as it is impossible to turn off the picture. Data ports are provided in all cabins.

Most cabin bathrooms have tiled accenting and a terrazzo-style tiled floor, and a rather small shower enclosure in a half-moon shape, 100% Egyptian cotton towels, a small cabinet for toiletries and a small shelf. In reality, there is little space to stow toiletries for two or more people.

The largest accommodation consists of a family suite with two bedrooms. One bedroom has twin beds that con-

vert to a queen-size bed, while a second has two lower beds and two upper Pullman berths, a combination that can sleep up to eight people – this would suit large families.

Occupants of accommodation designated as suites also get the use of a private Concierge Lounge, where priority dining room reservations, shore excursion bookings and beauty salon/spa appointments can be made.

CUISINE. *Reflections*, the main dining room, spans two decks; the upper deck level has floor-to-ceiling windows, while the lower level has picture windows. It is a pleasant but inevitably noisy dining hall, reminiscent of those aboard the transatlantic liners in their heyday. However, eight huge, thick pillars obstruct sightlines.

Reflections seats 1,104 hungry persons, and its decor features a cascading water theme. There are tables for two, four, six, eight or 10. Two small private dining rooms – *Illusions* with 94 seats and *Mirage* with 30 seats – are located off the main dining room. When you book, choose one of two seatings, or "My Time Dining" (eat when you want, during dining room hours).

The cuisine is typical of mass banquet catering that offers standard fare comparable to that found in American family-style restaurants ashore. The menu descriptions make the food sound better than it is – the ship uses many mixes and pre-prepared items. However, a decent selection of light meals is provided, and a vegetarian menu is available. The selection of breads, rolls, fruit and cheese is quite poor, however. Caviar, once a standard menu item, now incurs a hefty extra charge. Menus typically include a "Welcome Aboard" Dinner, French Dinner, Italian Dinner, International Dinner, Captain's Gala Dinner.

One thing this company does once each cruise is to put on a "Galley Buffet" whereby passengers go through a section of the galley picking up food for a midnight buffet. There is an adequate wine list, moderately priced.

Alternative Restaurants. There are two: *Portofino*, with 112 seats, serving Italian cuisine, and *Chops Grill Steakhouse*, with 95 seats and an open "show" kitchen, serving premium meats in the form of veal chops and steaks.

Both these dining spots, typically open 6pm–11pm, have food that's of a higher quality than in the main dining room, with extremely good presentation and experienced service. The menus don't change throughout the cruise. In both restaurants, a cover charge applies, reservations are required, and the dress code is smart casual. Be prepared to eat a lot of food and so do justice to the cover charge.

Casual Eateries: Casual breakfasts, lunches and dinners can be taken in the self-serve, buffet-style *Windjammer Café*, accessed directly from the pool deck. It has islands dedicated to specific foods, and indoors and outdoors seating, but it gets seriously crowded at peak times. Additionally, the *Seaview Café* is open for lunch and dinner. Choose from the self-serve buffet, or from the menu for casual, fast-food seafood items including fish sandwiches, popcorn shrimp, fish 'n' chips, as well as non-seafood items such as hamburgers and hot dogs. The decor, naturally, is marine- and ocean-related.

ENTERTAINMENT. Facilities include the three-level Tropical Theater, with 874 seats, including 24 stations for wheelchairs. There are good sight lines from most seats. Strong cabaret acts are also presented in the main showlounge.

A second entertainment venue is the Safari Club. This is where more casual cabaret shows, including late-night adult comedy, and live music for dancing are performed.

All of the entertainment is upbeat – in fact, it is virtually impossible to get away from music and noise – and is typical of the kind of resort hotel found in Las Vegas. There is even background music in all corridors and elevators, and constant music on the pool deck. If you want a quiet holiday, choose another cruise line.

SPA/FITNESS. The ShipShape Spa's health, fitness and spa facilities have themed decor, and include a 10,176 sq.-ft (945 sq.-meter) solarium, a gymnasium with 44 cardiovascular machines, 50-person aerobics room, sauna and steam rooms, and therapy treatment rooms. All are located on two of the uppermost decks, forward of the mast, with access from the forward stairway.

The climate-controlled 10,176 sq. ft (945 sq. meters) indoor/outdoor Solarium has a sliding glass dome roof that can be closed in cool or inclement weather conditions, and provides facilities for relaxation. It has Balinese-themed decor, and includes a whirlpool and counter-current swimming. One neat feature is the Temple Gate Falls, a carved wooden gateway with water cascading down its sides.

For the more sporting passengers, there is activity galore – including a rock-climbing wall that's 30ft (9 meters) high, with five separate climbing tracks. It is located outdoors at the aft end of the funnel.

Other sports facilities include a nine-hole miniature golf course, and an indoor/outdoor country club with golf simulator, a jogging track, and basketball court.

Want to play pool? Well, you can, thanks to two special tables (called STables), whose technology adjusts to the movement of the ship automatically. You can find them in the Bombay Billiard Room, part of the Colony Club.

● **For more extensive general information about the Royal Caribbean experience, see pages 152–6.**

WORLD CRUISES: DID YOU KNOW...

● that the first regular steamship service across the North Atlantic was inaugurated on March 28, 1838, when the 703-ton steamer *Sirius* left London for New York via Cork, Ireland?

● that the winter of 1970–71 was the first time since 1838 that there was no regular passenger service on the North Atlantic?

● that the first scheduled transatlantic advertisement appeared in the *New York Evening Post* on October 27, 1817, for the 424-ton sailing packet *James Monroe* to sail from New York to Liverpool on

January 5, 1818, and for *Couvier* to sail from Liverpool to New York on January 1?

● that Cunard Line held the record from 1940 to 1996 for the largest passenger ship ever built (RMS *Queen Elizabeth*)?

● that the Dollar Steamship Line featured a round-the-world cruise that started October 15, 1910, from New York, aboard the SS *Cleveland*? The cruise was advertised as "one-class, no overcrowding" voyage. The cost was "$650 and up," according to an advertisement.

● that a round-the-world cruise was

made in 1922–23 by Cunard's *Laconia* (19,680 grt), a three-class ship that sailed from New York? The itinerary included many ports of call that are still popular with world cruise passengers today. The vessel accommodated 350 persons in each of its first two classes, and 1,500 in third class, giving a total capacity of 2,200 passengers, more than many current ships.

● about the lady who went to her travel agent, who asked if she had enjoyed her cruise around the world? The lady replied, "Yes, but next year I want to go somewhere different."

Seven Seas Mariner
★★★★ +

Size: . . . . .Mid-Size ship	Passenger Decks: 9	Cabins (with private balcony): 354
Tonnage: .48,015	Total Crew: .445	Cabins (wheelchair accessible): 6
Lifestyle: . . . . .Luxury/Premium	Passengers	Wheelchair accessibility: . . . . .Best
Cruise Line: . .Regent Seven Seas Cruises	(lower beds/all berths): 708/752	Cabin Current: . . . . .110 volts
Former Names: . . . . .none	Passenger Space Ratio	Elevators: 6
Builder: Chantiers de l'Atlantique (France)	(lower beds/all berths): 67.8/63.8	Casino (gaming tables): . . . . .Yes
Original Cost: . . . .$240 million	Crew/Passenger Ratio	Slot Machines: . . . . .Yes
Entered Service: . . . . .Mar 2001	(lower beds/all berths): 1.6/1.7	Swimming Pools (outdoors): 1
Registry: . . . . .The Bahamas	Cabins (total): 354	Swimming Pools (indoors): 0
Length (ft/m): 713/217.3	Size Range (sq ft/m): 301.3–2,002.0/	Whirlpools: 3
Beam (ft/m): 95.1/29.0	28.0–186.0	Self-Service Launderette: . . . . .Yes (3)
Draft (ft/m): 21.4/6.5	Cabins (outside view): 354	Dedicated Cinema/Seats: . . . . .No
Propulsion/Propellers: . . .diesel-electric/2	Cabins (interior/no view): 0	Library: . . . . .Yes
azimuthing pods (8.5 MW each)	Cabins (for one person): 0	Onboard currency: . . . . .US$

An all-inclusive premium ship for senior-age cruisers.

OVERVIEW. This ship is best suited to well-traveled couples and single travelers, typically over 50, who seek excellent itineraries, fine food and good service, with some entertainment, all wrapped up in a contemporary ship that is elegant and quiet in its appointments and comfort levels. Its passenger space ratio is the highest in the cruise industry, just a fraction above *Europa*'s.

THE SHIP. The largest ship in the Regent Seven Seas Cruises fleet, this was the first to receive a "pod" propulsion system *(see page 191)*, replacing the traditional shaft and rudder system. It was extensively refurbished in 2009.

There is a wide range of public rooms, almost all located under the accommodation decks. Three sets of stairways (forward, center, aft) mean it is easy to find your way around. An atrium lobby spans nine decks, with the lowest level opening directly onto the tender landing stage.

Facilities include a delightful observation lounge, a casino, a shopping concourse complete with open market area, a garden lounge/promenade arcade, a large library with internet-connect computers, business center, card room and a conference room, a, cigar-smoking lounge (the Connoisseur Club, and a photo gallery.

With *Seven Seas Mariner*, Seven Seas Cruises embraced a new breed of larger ships that are more economical to operate, and offer passengers more choices. But there is a loss of the sense of intimacy that the company's smaller ships used to have, even though some of the personal service of the smaller ships has been absorbed into the larger structure. Another downside is the fact that this ship is too large to enter the small harbors and

BERLITZ'S RATINGS

	Possible	Achieved
Ship	500	438
Accommodation	200	177
Food	400	318
Service	400	310
Entertainment	100	83
Cruise	400	325

OVERALL SCORE
1,651 points out of 2,000

berths that the company's smaller ships could access, so loses some of the benefits of small upscale ship cruising.

It's swings and roundabouts, then, when it comes to rating the ship. At present, it scores very highly in terms of hardware and software, but operationally may lose a few points if it is deemed that it can enter only mid-size ship ports. So *Seven Seas Mariner* has ended up just a tad under the score base needed for it to join the "Berlitz Five Star" Club.

Service and hospitality are mostly sound. The same carpeting is used throughout the public areas, with no relief or change of color or pattern on the stairwells. The decor is more restrained, but with a contemporary look and feel. Much of the intimacy and close-knit ambiance of smaller vessels is missing, and, because of all those cabins with balconies, the feeling of privacy and relaxation can also translate into fewer passengers in public rooms and for entertainment events, depending on the passenger mix.

Basic gratuities are included, as are all alcoholic and non-alcoholic beverages and table wines for lunch and dinner – although premium and connoisseur selections are available at extra cost. Shore excursions and pre- or post hotel stays are also included, depending on the itinerary.

ACCOMMODATION. There are 13 categories of cabins. *Seven Seas Mariner* was the cruise industry's first "all-suite, all-balcony" ship – though that's not technically correct as not all accommodation has sleeping areas completely separated from living areas.

All grades of accommodation have private, marble-clad bathrooms with tub, and all suite entrances are neatly recessed away from the passenger hallways, to provide extra quietness. In comparison with *Seven Seas Navigator*, the bathrooms aboard this ship are not as large in the lower grade of accommodation.

Master Suites: The largest accommodation (1,580 sq. ft/147 sq. meters), in two Master Suites, has two separate bedrooms, living room with TV/VCR and CD player, walk-in closet, dining area, large, two marble-clad bathrooms with tub and separate shower enclosure, and two private teakwood-decked balconies. Butler service is provided, as is a Nespresso coffee machine.

Mariner Suites: Six Mariner Suites (739 sq. ft/69 sq. meters), on the port and starboard sides of the atrium on three separate decks, have a separate bedroom, living room with large audio-visual center, walk-in closet, dining area, large, marble-clad bathroom with tub and separate shower enclosure, and a good sized private balcony. Butler service is provided, as is a Nespresso coffee machine.

Grand Suites: Two Grand Suites (707 sq. ft/66 sq. meters) are located one deck above the ship's navigation bridge. The facilities are similar to those in Mariner Suites.

Seven Seas Suites: Six spacious suites (697 sq. ft/65 sq. meters) overlook the ship's stern (two suites are located on each of four decks) and have very generous private balcony space and good wrap-around views over the ship's stern and to port or starboard. However, the balconies are only semi-private and can be partly overlooked. Another two Seven Seas Suites are located just aft of the ship's navigation bridge. They are slightly smaller, at 600 sq ft (56 sq. meters), and have balconies. They have a separate bedroom, living room with audio-visual center, walk-in closet, dining area, and marble-clad bathroom with a combination tub/shower.

Horizon Suites: The 12 Horizon Suites (522 sq. ft/48 sq. meters) overlook the stern and have a good-sized balcony and good views. These suites have a separate bedroom, living room with TV/DVD, walk-in closet, dining area, large, marble-clad bathroom with a combination tub/shower.

All Other Cabins: All other cabins (Categories A–H in the brochure, listed as Deluxe Suites and Penthouse Suites) measure 300 sq. ft (28 sq. meters) and have twin beds that convert to a queen-size bed (European duvets are standard), small walk-in closet, marble-lined bathroom with combination tub/shower, 100% cotton Anichini bathrobe and towels, vanity desk, hairdryer, TV/DVD, refrigerator (stocked with soft drinks and bar set-up on embarkation), and personal safe. In these suites, the sleeping area is separated from the living area only by partial room dividers, and therefore is a cabin – albeit a good-sized one – and not a suite.

Six wheelchair-accessible suites are located as close to an elevator as one could possibly get, and provide ample living space, together with a large roll-in shower and all bathroom fittings located at the correct height.

CUISINE. Four different dining venues all operate on an open-seating basis, so that you can choose your companions. Reservations are required in two of the four dining spots. In general, the cuisine is good to very good, with creative presentation and a wide variety of food choices.

The main dining room, the 570-seat *Compass Rose Restaurant*, has a light, fresh decor, and seating at tables for two, four, six or eight – although, as tables for six or eight predominate, it's not that intimate and, with a single-deck height, the restaurant has a rather cramped feeling.

The 80-seat *Prime Seven Steakhouse*, is the smallest of the specialty alternative dining spots. It serves a range of USDA prime, dry-aged steaks as well as chops, oven-roasted half chicken, Alaskan king crab legs and Maine lobster. It's the most intimate dining spot – though, again, the single-deck ceiling height makes it feel cramped. There is seating for two, four or six, and reservations are required.

The 120-seat *Signatures* "supper club" has ocean views along the room's port side. It is directed and staffed by chefs wearing the white toque and blue riband of Le Cordon Bleu, the prestigious culinary society, and the cuisine is classic French. Doors open onto a covered area outdoors, complete with small stage and dance floor. Seating is at tables of two, four, or six, and reservations are required. However, the single-deck ceiling height robs the room of the grandeur that suits fine classic French cuisine.

For more casual meals, *La Veranda* is a large self-serve indoor/outdoor café with seats for 450, and the decor is fresh and light. This eatery has several food islands and substantial counter display space. There is also an outdoor grill, adjacent to the swimming pool.

You can also choose to dine in your cabin – most passengers do so for breakfast, for example, and some do for dinner. There is a 24-hour room service menu, and, during regular dinner hours, the full dining room menu is available.

ENTERTAINMENT. The Constellation Theater spans two decks and is quite stunning, with very good sight lines from almost all seats. The proscenium stage includes a "thrust" stage that's good for presenting more intimate cabaret acts. Seven Seas Cruises has an eclectic entertainment program that is tailored to each individual ship.

Seven Seas Mariner presents both production shows and cabaret acts. A troupe of eight singers/dancers perform the colorful shows – the cast is, however, small for the size of the stage. Cabaret acts tend to feature vocalists, magicians and comedy jugglers, among others.

There is also Stars nightclub, with an oval-shaped dance floor, and a Horizon Lounge – both rooms could be used for late-night cabaret. A number of bands, small musical units and solo pianists provide live music in lounges and bars.

SPA/FITNESS. Health and fitness facilities include an extensive health spa with gymnasium and aerobics room, beauty parlor, and separate changing, sauna and steam rooms for men and women. The spa is located not at the top of the ship, as is common with many other ships today, but just off the atrium in the center of the ship. Canyon Ranch SpaClub operates the spa and beauty services as a concession, and provides the staff. There's a range of beauty products for the body and wellbeing books for sale.

Sports devotees can play in the paddle tennis court, golf driving and practice cages.

Seven Seas Navigator
★★★★ +

Size:	Small Ship	Passenger Decks:	8	Cabins (with private balcony):	196
Tonnage:	28,550	Total Crew:	325	Cabins (wheelchair accessible):	4
Lifestyle:	Luxury/Premium	Passengers		Wheelchair accessibility:	Good
Cruise Line:	Regent Seven Seas Cruises	(lower beds/all berths):	490/530	Cabin Current:	110 and 220 volts
Former Names:	none	Passenger Space Ratio		Elevators:	5
Builder:	T. Mariotti (Italy)	(lower beds/all berths):	58.2/53.8	Casino (gaming tables):	Yes
Original Cost:	$200 million	Crew/Passenger Ratio		Slot Machines:	Yes
Entered Service:	Aug 1999	(lower beds/all berths):	1.5/1.6	Swimming Pools (outdoors):	1
Registry:	Bermuda	Cabins (total):	245	Swimming Pools (indoors):	0
Length (ft/m):	559.7/170.6	Size Range (sq ft/m):	301.3–1,173.3/	Whirlpools:	2
Beam (ft/m):	71.5/21.8		28.0–109.0	Self-Service Launderette:	Yes
Draft (ft/m):	21.3.0/6.5	Cabins (outside view):	245	Dedicated Cinema/Seats:	No
Propulsion/Propellers:	diesel	Cabins (interior/no view):	0	Library:	Yes
	(13,000kW/2	Cabins (for one person):	0	Onboard currency:	US$

A premium, all-inclusive ship for mature-age cruisers.

OVERVIEW. This ship is best suited to well-traveled couples and single travelers, typically over 50, who seek excellent itineraries, fine food and good service, with some entertainment, all wrapped up in a contemporary ship that's elegant and quiet in its appointments and comfort levels. Designed for worldwide cruise itineraries, this is one of the upscale ships in the diverse Regent Seven Seas Cruises fleet.

THE SHIP. *Seven Seas Navigator* was built using a hull already constructed in St. Petersburg, Russia, as the research vessel *Akademik Nikolay Pilyugin*. The superstructure was incorporated into the hull in an Italian shipyard – the result being that, in effect, a new ship was delivered in record time. The result is less than handsome – particularly at the stern – but it's large enough to be stable over long stretches of water, and there is an excellent amount of space per passenger. In 2009, a "ducktail" stern was added to aid stability and buoyancy.

The interiors have a mix of classical and contemporary Italian styling and decor, with warm, soft colors and fine quality soft furnishings and fabrics. Galileo's, a large piano lounge, has good views over the stern. A Navigator's Lounge has warm mahogany and cherry wood paneling and large, comfortable, mid-back tub chairs. Next door, cigars and cognac can be taken in the delightful Connoisseur's Club – the first aboard a Regent Seven Seas Cruises vessel. The extensive library also has several computers with direct internet access, for a fee.

There is no walk-around promenade deck outdoors, although there is a jogging track high atop the aft section around the funnel housing. Two of the upper, outer decks are

BERLITZ'S RATINGS		
	Possible	Achieved
Ship	500	414
Accommodation	200	180
Food	400	307
Service	400	304
Entertainment	100	78
Cruise	400	312
OVERALL SCORE		
1,595 points out of 2,000		

laid with green Astroturf, which cheapens the look of the ship – they would be better in teak. The ceilings in several public rooms (including the main restaurant) are quite low, which makes the ship feel smaller and more closed-in than it is. It suffers from a considerable amount of vibration, which detracts from the comfort level when compared with other vessels of the same size.

Basic gratuities are included in the fare, as are alcoholic and non-alcoholic beverages, plus table wines for lunch and dinner. Shore excursions and any pre- or post-hotel stays are also included.

ACCOMMODATION. There are 11 price grades, and the company markets this as an "all-suite" ship. Even the smallest suite is quite large, and all have outside views. Almost 90 percent of all suites have a private balcony, with floor-to-ceiling sliding glass doors, while 10 suites are interconnecting, and 38 have an extra bed for a third occupant. By comparison, even the smallest suite is more than twice the size of the smallest cabin aboard the world's largest cruise ships, Royal Caribbean International's *Voyager*-class ships.

All grades of accommodation have a walk-in closet, European king-size bed or twin beds, wooden cabinetry with nicely rounded edges, plenty of drawer space, minibar/refrigerator stocked with complimentary soft drinks and bar set-up on embarkation, TV/DVD player, and personal safe. The marble-appointed bathroom has a full-size tub, as well as a separate shower enclosure, 100% cotton bathrobe and towels, and hairdryer.

The largest living spaces are in four master suites, with forward-facing views and double-length side balconies.

Each suite has a completely separate bedroom with dressing table; the living room has a full dining room table and chairs for up to six persons, wet bar, counter and bar stools, large three-person sofa and six armchairs, an audio-visual console/entertainment center, and a Nespresso coffee machine. Each suite has a large main, marble-clad, fully tiled bathroom with full-size tub and separate shower enclosure, a separate room with bidet, toilet and washbasin, with plenty of space for toiletries. There is a separate guest bathroom.

Next in size are the superb Navigator Suites, which have a completely separate bedroom, walk-in closet, large lounge with mini-bar/refrigerator stocked with complimentary soft drinks and bar set-up on embarkation, personal safe, compact disc player, large TV/DVD player, and dining area with large table and four chairs. The marble-clad, fully tiled bathroom has a full-size tub with hand-held shower, plus a separate shower enclosure (the door to which is only 18 inches/45 cm, however), large washbasin, toilet and bidet, and ample shelf space for toiletries.

It is unfortunate that the Navigator Suites are located in the center of the ship, as they are directly underneath the swimming pool deck. They are thus subject to noise attacks at 6am daily, when deck cleaning is carried out, and chairs are dragged across the deck directly over the suites. You are also aware of pool deck stewards dragging and dropping sunloungers into place. Despite these disadvantages, the Navigator Suites are delightful living spaces.

Four suites for the physically challenged have private balconies, and are ideally located adjacent to the elevators. However, while they are very practical, it is almost impossible to access the balcony because of the "lip" or "threshold" at the bottom of the sliding glass door.

CUISINE. The *Compass Rose Dining Room* has large ocean-view picture windows and open-seating dining, which means that you can choose your companions. There are a few tables for two, but most are for four, six, or eight persons. With a low ceiling height and noisy waiter stations, the overall feeling is cramped and unbecoming in terms of the lack of space and grace. Complimentary wines are served during dinner, and a connoisseur wine list is available at extra cost). The company also promotes "heart healthy" cuisine.

An alternative dining spot, *La Veranda*, for informal dining, serves dinners with an emphasis on regional cuisine, with reservations required. *Prime 7*, for steaks and seafood, is in an elegant new setting (reservations required). For fast-food, there is a small outdoor *Grill* on the deck above.

You can also dine in your cabin. There is a 24-hour room service menu and, during regular dinner hours, you can choose from the full dining room menu.

ENTERTAINMENT. The Seven Seas Lounge, a two-deck-high showlounge, has reasonable sightlines from most seats on both main and balcony levels, although pillars obstruct the views from some side balcony seats. Seven Seas Cruises has an eclectic entertainment program tailored to each ship. *Seven Seas Navigator* puts on both production shows and cabaret acts. Bands and small musical units and solo pianist entertainers provide live music in several lounges and bars.

SPA/FITNESS. The spa, fitness center and beauty salon are in the most forward part of the top deck. Canyon Ranch Spa-Club operates the spa and beauty services as a concession, provides the staff, and sells its own beauty products.

Seven Seas Voyager
★★★★+

Size: . . . . .Mid-Size Ship	Passenger Decks: 9	Cabins (with private balcony): 354
Tonnage: .41,827	Total Crew: 445	Cabins (wheelchair accessible): 4
Lifestyle: . . . . .Luxury/Premium	Passengers	Wheelchair accessibility: . . . . .Best
Cruise Line: . .Regent Seven Seas Cruises	(lower beds/all berths): 708/752	Cabin Current: . . . . .110 volts
Former Names: . . . . .none	Passenger Space Ratio	Elevators: 6
Builder: . . . . .T. Mariotti (Italy)	(lower beds/all berths): 59.0/55.6	Casino (gaming tables): . . . . .Yes
Original Cost: . . . .$240 million	Crew/Passenger Ratio	Slot Machines: . . . . .Yes
Entered Service: . . . . .Mar 2003	(lower beds/all berths): 1.65/1.6	Swimming Pools (outdoors): 1
Registry: . . . . .The Bahamas	Cabins (total): .354	Swimming Pools (indoors): 0
Length (ft/m): 669.2/204.0	Size Range (sq ft/m): 356.0/1,399.3/	Whirlpools: 3
Beam (ft/m): 94.5/28.8	33.0–130.0	Self-Service Launderette: . . . . .Yes (3)
Draft (ft/m): 23.0/7.0	Cabins (outside view): 354	Dedicated Cinema/Seats: . . . . .No
Propulsion/Propellers: . . .diesel-electric/2	Cabins (interior/no view): 0	Library: . . . . .Yes
azimuthing pods (8.5MW each)	Cabins (for one person): 0	Onboard currency: . . . . .US$

Premium all-inclusive cruising with space and style.

OVERVIEW. This ship is best suited to well-traveled couples and single travelers, typically over 50, seeking excellent itineraries, fine food and good service, with some entertainment, in a contemporary ship that's elegant and comfortable. The passenger space ratio is among the highest in the cruise industry, at about the same as the smaller, but better-built *Europa*.

THE SHIP. *Seven Seas Voyager* was built in 32 blocks, with the same basic hull design as *Seven Seas Mariner*, with a few modifications. Like its sister, it has a pod propulsion system *(see page 191)*. It has a decent range of public rooms, almost all located under the accommodation decks. Three sets of stairways (forward, center, aft) mean it is easy to find your way around. An atrium lobby spans nine decks, with the lowest level opening directly onto the tender landing stage.

Facilities include a showlounge that spans two decks, an observation lounge – the only place aboard this ship where you can see the bows – a casino, a shopping concourse complete with an open "market" area, a large library, internet-connect center and business center (Club.com, and Coffee.com), a card room and a small conference room. There is also a nightclub, Voyager, with an oval-shaped dance floor, a cigar-smoking lounge, the Connoisseur Club, for cigars and cognacs, and the usual photo gallery. The decor is a little glitzy in places, plain in others.

Regent Seven Seas Cruises has clearly moved into a new breed of larger ships that are more economical to operate, provide better economies of scale, as well as more choices for passengers. However, there are downsides such as a loss of intimacy and a limit on the size of harbors and

BERLITZ'S RATINGS

	Possible	Achieved
Ship	500	437
Accommodation	200	177
Food	400	324
Service	400	306
Entertainment	100	83
Cruise	400	327

OVERALL SCORE
1,654 points out of 2,000

berths it can access; these points are discussed on pages 594–5 in the entry for *Seven Seas Mariner*.

Basic gratuities are included, as are all drinks, including table wines for lunch and dinner (premium and connoisseur selections are available at extra cost). Shore excursions and any pre- or post-hotel stays are also included, depending on the itinerary. Service and hospitality levels have decreased since the introduction of the drinks-inclusive policy, so the overall delivery of a quality onboard experience is on the downward slope.

Passenger gripes: there is no walk-around outdoor promenade deck, and there is no forward-viewing exterior deck with views over the ship's bows.

ACCOMMODATION. There are 12 accommodation price grades. As the ship was built with a central corridor design, this has allowed for larger suites and much larger bathrooms than aboard *Seven Seas Mariner*, with which many repeat passengers will no doubt compare it. This is Regent Seven Seas Cruises' second "all-suite all-balcony" ship – although that's not strictly correct as not all sleeping areas are completely separated from living areas.

All grades of accommodation have private, marble-clad bathrooms with tub – although marble floors can be very cold on bare feet – walk-in closet with personal safe, and most suite entrances are neatly recessed away from passenger hallways (a central corridor), so as to provide extra quietness. All have a "private" balcony, although all measure only 50 sq. ft (4.6 sq. meters) except for those in the Master Suites and Grand Suites; all have pleasing teak decking. Partitions are of the partial type, except for the

Master Suites and Grand Suites, which have full floor-to-ceiling partitions, and are completely private.

Master Suites (1,162 sq. ft/108 sq. meters). These two suites, 1100 and 1001, each measure 1,403 sq. ft (130.3 sq. meters) when added with one Grand Suite via an interconnecting door, while 700 and 701 measure 1,335 sq. ft (124 sq. meters). Each has two separate bedrooms, living room with TV/DVD player, walk-in closet with personal safe, dining area, large, two marble-clad bathrooms with tub and separate shower enclosure, and private teakwood-decked balconies. These suites are on the deck under the navigation bridge. Butler service is provided, as is a Nespresso coffee machine. The bathrooms, which are open to the bedroom, have a stand-alone tub with integral shower, separate shower enclosure, toilet, bidet and washbasin. The private balcony, with floor-to-ceiling partitions, has teak decking and teak deck furniture – two chairs and drinks table.

Grand Suites (876 sq. ft/81.3 sq. meters). Two Grand Suites (1104, 1005) are one deck above the navigation bridge. They are very pleasant living spaces, and have a separate bedroom, living room with TV/DVD player, walk-in closet, dining area, and two marble-clad bathing areas. One bathing area, open to the bedroom, although a curtain can be used to close it off, has a large five-sided sit-in tub placed in a glass walled enclosure on the balcony – but with no access door to the balcony, which can be accessed only from the lounge/dining area. The second is a bathroom with separate shower enclosure, bidet, toilet and washbasin. The suites have a private balcony with port or starboard views. There is also a guest toilet. Butler service is provided, as is a Nespresso coffee machine. The private balcony is similar to that in the Master Suites.

Voyager Suites (603 sq. ft/56 sq. meters). Eight Voyager Suites, on port and starboard sides of the atrium on three decks, have a separate bedroom, living room with TV/DVD player, walk-in closet, dining area, large, marble-clad bathroom with tub and separate shower enclosure, and a good sized private balcony with either port or starboard views. Butler service is provided. The balcony has teakwood deck, part partitions, and white plastic deck furniture.

Seven Seas Suites (657 sq. ft/61 sq. meters) Aft. Six spacious suites overlook the ship's stern – two on each of four decks – and have a generous wrap-around balcony, and good views over the stern and to port or starboard. However, the balconies can be partly overlooked. They have teak decking, but white plastic deck furniture. Butler service is provided. Another four Seven Seas Suites, located amidships, measure a slightly smaller 545 sq. ft (50.6 sq. meters), and have small balconies with either port or starboard views. They have a separate bedroom, living room with audio-visual center, walk-in closet, dining area, large, and marble-clad bathroom with a combination tub/shower. Again, butler service is provided.

Penthouse Suites (370 sq. ft/34.3 sq. meters). There are 32 Category "A" Penthouse Suites and 32 Category "B" Penthouse Suites – Category "A" Suites have the better location, but the size is the same. These have a sleeping area with dressing table and adjacent lounge area, walk-in closet, and bathroom with tub, washbasin, separate shower enclosure, and toilet. The balcony is accessed from the lounge. The balcony has teakwood deck, part partitions, and white plastic deck furniture. Butler service is provided.

Horizon Suites (522 sq. ft/48.4 sq. meters). The 29 Horizon Suites overlook the stern, some being sandwiched between the larger Seven Seas Suites, and have a good-sized balcony (though not as large as those of the Seven Seas Suites) and delightful aft-facing views. They have a separate bedroom, living room with TV/DVD player, walk-in closet, dining area, large, marble-clad bathroom with a combination tub/shower. The balcony has teakwood deck, part partitions, and white plastic deck furniture.

All Other Cabins (356 sq. ft/33 sq. meters). Categories C–H in the brochure, listed as Deluxe Suites, are larger than those of the same grade aboard *Seven Seas Mariner*. They have twin beds that convert to a queen-size bed (European duvets are standard), small walk-in closet, marble-lined bathroom with combination tub/shower, 100% cotton bathrobe and towels, vanity desk, hairdryer, TV/DVD player, refrigerator stocked with soft drinks and bar set-up on embarkation, and personal safe. In these suites, the sleeping area is separated from the living area only by partial room dividers, and therefore they are cabins – albeit good-sized ones – rather than suites.

Four wheelchair-accessible suites (761, 762, 859, and 860) are all as close to an elevator as one could possibly get, and provide ample living space, together with a large roll-in shower and all bathroom fittings at the correct height.

CUISINE. For food entertainment, make a reservation in Latitudes. It has real show business flair and an open "show" kitchen, also used for Le Cordon Bleu cooking demos. Dinner is at a set time, typically 7.30pm, and consists of a set menu, the only choice being the main course, which is fish or meat. Seating is in alcoves or at open tables.

The other dining venues – *Compass Rose Restaurant, Signatures, Prime 7* and *La Veranda* – and fast-food outlets are very similar to their namesakes aboard *Seven Seas Mariner* (for details, see listing on pages 594–5). As aboard *Seven Seas Mariner*, you can also dine in your cabin from the full Compass Rose menu.

ENTERTAINMENT. The stunning Constellation Showlounge spans two decks, and sightlines are very good from almost all seats. A troupe of 10 singers/dancers provides colorful mini-Las Vegas-style revues and production shows. Cabaret acts provide stand-alone evening shows. The ship carries a main showband, several small musical units, and soloists such as a singer/harpist and singer/pianist.

SPA/FITNESS. For details of the Canyon Ranch SpaClub and other sporting facilities, see the listing for *Seven Seas Mariner*.

Silver Cloud
★★★★+

Size: . . . . .Small Ship	Passenger Decks: 6	Cabins (with private balcony): 110
Tonnage: 16,927	Total Crew: 212	Cabins (wheelchair accessible): 2
Lifestyle: .Luxury	Passengers	Wheelchair accessibility: . . . . .Fair
Cruise Line: . . . . .Silversea Cruises	(lower beds/all berths): 296/329	Cabin Current: . . . . .110 and 220 volts
Former Names: . . . . .none	Passenger Space Ratio	Elevators: 4
Builder: . . . . .Visentini/Mariotti (Italy)	(lower beds/all berths): 57.1/51.4	Casino (gaming tables): . . . . .Yes
Original Cost: . . . .$125 million	Crew/Passenger Ratio	Slot Machines: . . . . .Yes
Entered Service: . . . . .Apr 1994	(lower beds/all berths): 1.4/1.5	Swimming Pools (outdoors): 1
Registry: . . . . .The Bahamas	Cabins (total): .148	Swimming Pools (indoors): 0
Length (ft/m): 514.4/155.8	Size Range (sq ft/m): 240.0–1,314.0/	Whirlpools: 2
Beam (ft/m): 70.62/21.4	22.2–122.0	Self-Service Launderette: . . . . .Yes
Draft (ft/m): 17.3/5.3	Cabins (outside view): 148	Dedicated Cinema/Seats: Yes/306
Propulsion/Propellers: . . . . .diesel	Cabins (interior/no view): 0	Library: . . . . .Yes
(11,700kW)/2	Cabins (for one person): 0	Onboard currency: . . . . .US$

An all-inclusive small ship for mature-age cruisers.

OVERVIEW. *Silver Cloud* is best suited to discerning, well-traveled couples, typically over 50, who seek a small ship with excellent food and fine European-style service in surroundings that border on the elegant. The passenger mix includes many nationalities, although the majority of passengers are North American. Children are sometimes seen aboard, although they are not really welcomed by most passengers, who enjoy cruising without them.

BERLITZ'S RATINGS		
	Possible	Achieved
Ship	500	411
Accommodation	200	177
Food	400	333
Service	400	335
Entertainment	100	74
Cruise	400	334
OVERALL SCORE		
1,664 points out of 2,000		

THE SHIP. *Silver Cloud* has quite a handsome profile, with a sloping stern reminiscent of an "Airstream" trailer. The size is just about ideal for highly personalized cruising in an elegant environment. The vertical cake-layer stacking of public rooms aft and the location of accommodation forward ensures quiet cabins. There is a synthetic turf-covered walk-around promenade deck outdoors, and a spacious swimming pool deck with teak/aluminum deck furniture. Little "Silversea" touches such as cold towels, water sprays and fresh fruit provide poolside pampering on hot days.

The spacious interior is well planned, with elegant decor and fine quality soft furnishings throughout, accented by the gentle use of brass fittings (some of sub-standard quality and now showing blotchy patches in several places), fine woods and creative ceilings. In 2009, an extensive refit saw the addition of a proper observation lounge, with covered passageway to access it – so passengers don't have to go outside to do so. All suites were also refreshed.

There is a business center as well as an audio and hard-back book library, open 24 hours a day. An excellent amount of space per passenger means there is no hint of a line anywhere in this unhurried environment. Good documentation is provided before your cruise in a high-quality document wallet.

An elegant, announcement-free onboard ambience prevails, and there is no pressure or hype, and an enthusiastic staff to pamper you, including a high ratio of Europeans. All drinks, gratuities and port taxes are included, and no further tipping is necessary – though it is not prohibited. This ship is ideal for those who enjoy spacious surroundings, excellent food, and some entertainment. It would be hard not to have a good vacation aboard this ship, albeit at a fairly high price.

Silversea Cruises has "all-inclusive" fares, including gratuities, but now charges extra for insurance. The fares do not, however, include vintage wines, or massage, or other personal services, but they do include many things that cost extra aboard the ships of many rivals.

The onboard product delivered is very good, particularly the cuisine and its presentation. Shuttle buses are provided in most ports of call, and all the little extras passengers receive makes a cruise an extremely pleasant experience. The surroundings are very comfortable and contemporary without being extravagant, with open seating dining and drinks included, cold canapés and hot hors d'oeuvres served in the bars in the pre-dinner cocktail hour, a captain's welcome aboard and a farewell cocktail party.

"Personalized Voyages" enable you choose the port of embarkation and disembarkation and the length of cruise you want (minimum five days). While this adds flexibility, the onboard programming is already set, so you may be joining and leaving in the middle of a "normal" cruise.

Niggles? Some vibration is evident when bow thrusters or the anchors are used, particularly in the forward-most cabins. The self-service launderette is not large enough for longer cruises. Crew facilities are minimal, leading to a high crew turnover which undermines service.

ACCOMMODATION. There are seven price grades in this "all-suite" ship. The all-outside-view suites, 75% of which have fine private teakwood balconies, have convertible queen-to-twin beds and are beautifully fitted out. They have large floor-to-ceiling windows, large walk-in closets, dressing table, writing desk, stocked mini-bar/refrigerator (no charge), and fresh flowers.

The marble-floor bathrooms have a tub, fixed showerhead (not as hygienic as a hand-held unit), single washbasin, and plenty of high-quality towels. Personalized stationery, an eight-pillow menu from soft down to memory foam, bathrobes, and a range of Acqua di Parma bathroom amenities are provided in all suites.

All suites have televisions and VCR or DVD players, and top grade suites also have CD players. However, the walk-in closets don't actually provide much hanging space, particularly for such items as full-length dresses, and it would be better for the door to open outward instead of inward. The drawers themselves are poorly positioned, but several other drawers and storage areas are provided in the living area.

Although the cabin insulation above and below each cabin is good, the insulation between cabins is not – a privacy curtain installed between entry door and sleeping area would be most useful. Light from the passageway leaks into the cabin, making it hard to achieve a dark room.

The top-grade suites have teak balcony furniture, while other suites do not – but all balconies have teak floors. Suites with balconies on the lowest deck can suffer from sticky salt spray when the ship is moving, so the balconies need lots of cleaning. Each evening, the stewardesses bring plates of canapés to your suite – just right for a light bite with cocktails. In the Grand, Royal, Rossellini or Owner's Suites, you get unobtrusive butler service from butlers certified by London's Guild of Professional Butlers.

CUISINE. *The Restaurant* provides open-seating dining in elegant surroundings. It has an attractive arched gazebo center and a wavy ceiling design as its focal point, and is set with fine Eschenbach china and well-balanced Christofle silverware. Meals are served in an open seating, which means you can eat when you like within the given dining room opening times, and with whom you like.

The dining is good throughout the ship, with a choice of three dining salons, and both the cuisine and its presentation have improved substantially in the past few years. Standard table wines are included for lunch and dinner, and there is a "connoisseur list" of premium wines at extra charge. All meals are prepared as à la carte items, with almost none of the pre-preparation that used to exist.

La Saletta, adjacent to the main dining room, is an alternative, intimate 24-seat dining salon. Dégustation menus include dishes designed for Silversea Cruises by chefs from Relais Châteaux Gourmands, the cuisine-oriented division of Relais & Châteaux, paired with selected wines. Reservations are required, and there's a cover charge.

For more informal dining, *La Terrazza* provides self-serve breakfast and lunch buffets and informal evening dining with different regional Italian dishes nightly. Both indoor and outdoor seating is at teakwood tables and chairs.

Theere is a 24-hour in-cabin dining service. Full course-by-course dinners are available, although the balcony tables in the standard suites are rather low for dining outdoors.

ENTERTAINMENT. The Showlounge hosts all entertainment events and some social functions. The room spans two decks and has a sloping floor; banquette and individual seating are provided, with good sightlines.

Although Silversea Cruises places more emphasis on food than entertainment, what is provided is quite tasteful and not overbearing, as aboard some larger ships. A decent array of cabaret acts does the Silversea circuit and small colorful production shows have been reintroduced.

Most of the cabaret acts provide intelligent entertainment that is generally appreciated by the well-traveled international clientele. Also, more emphasis is now placed on classical music ensembles. A band, as well as several small musical units, provide live music in the evenings in The Bar, and Panorama Lounge.

SPA/FITNESS. Although "The Spa at Silversea" facility is not large, it underwent a sea change in 2007 with redesigned, more welcoming decor, and an updated range of treatments and spa packages for both men and women. Massage and other body pampering treatments, facials, pedicures, and beauty salon treatments cost extra.

Facilities include a separate sauna for men and women, several treatment rooms, and a beauty salon. A separate gymnasium (formerly an observation lounge), located atop the ship, provides sea views.

Silver Explorer
★★★★ +

Size:...................... Boutique Ship	Propulsion/Propellers: .... diesel (4,500kw)/2	Cabins (with private balcony):............ 6
Tonnage:........................... 6,072	Passenger Decks: 5	+ 14 French balconies
Lifestyle: .... Premium	Total Crew: 111	Cabins (wheelchair accessible): 0
Cruise Line: .... Silversea Cruises	Passengers:	Wheelchair accessibility: .... .None
Former Names: .... *Prince Albert II,*	(lower beds/all berths): 132/158	Cabin Current: .... 110/220 volts
World Discoverer, Dream 21, Baltic Clipper,	Passenger Space Ratio	Elevators:............................. 2
Sally Clipper, Delfin Star, Delfin Clipper,	(lower beds/all berths): 46.0/38.4	Casino (gaming tables): .... No
World Adventurer, Delfin Clipper	Crew/Passenger Ratio:	Slot Machines: .... No
Builder:........... Rauma-Repola (Finland)	(lower beds/all berths): 1.1/1.4	Swimming Pools (outdoors): 0
Original Cost: .... $50 million	Cabins (total): 66	Swimming Pools (indoors): 0
Entered Service: .... Jul 1989/Jun 2008	Size Range (sq.ft./m.): 172.2–785.7/	Whirlpools: 2
Registry: .... The Bahamas	16.0–73.0	Self-Service Launderette: .... No
Length (ft/m): 354.9/108.20	Cabins (outside view): 66	Movie Theater/Seats: .... No
Beam (ft/m): 51.1/15.60	Cabins (interior/no view): 0	Library:.............................. No
Draft (ft/m): 13.1/4.00	Cabins (for one person): 0	Onboard currency:................... US$

A small "soft" expedition ship with premium style.

OVERVIEW. *Silver Explorer* is best suited to adventurous couples and single travelers of mature years who enjoy seeing nature at close range, but want an extremely comfortable setting, plus good food and service in a small ship setting. The ship, which carries an expedition leaderand wildlife lecturers, specializes in Polar itineraries.

THE SHIP. Twin swept-back outboard funnels highlight the semi-smart exterior design of this small specialist 22-year-old expedition cruise ship. It has a dark ice-hardened hull, carries a fleet of eight Zodiac inflatable landing craft for shore landings and exploration, and has one boot washing station, the "Mud Room," with six bays. There is no walk-around promenade deck outdoors.

Silversea Cruises bought the ship in 2007, towed it to Italy from Singapore, where it had been laid up for four years, and completely refitted it at Genoa's Mariotti shipyard. The idea behind the conversion is to take Silversea Cruises passengers to more remote regions, but in style.

The accommodation is located forward, with all public rooms aft, an arrangement that helps keep noise to a minimum in accommodation areas. The interior has many European design elements, including warm color combinations. Public rooms include an observation lounge, large lecture room/cinema with bar, and library/internet center.

This small expedition cruise vessel has many of the creature comforts of much larger vessels. It will provide a very comfortable expedition-style cruise experience in tasteful and elegant surroundings. All passengers receive a pre-cruise amenities package that typically includes a field guide, backpack, carry-on travel bag, and luggage tags.

ACCOMMODATION. There are six types of accommodation, and 11 price grades. The cabins – quite large for such a small ship – are fitted out to a fairly high standard, with ample closet and drawer space. All cabins have outside views and have twin beds that can convert to a queen-size bed, TV/DVD unit, telephone, hairdryer, refrigerator, and lockable drawer for valuables.

Although only six suites have a large private balcony (they really are not needed in cold-weather regions), another 14 cabins have glass doors that open onto a few inches of space outdoors. The suites have whirlpool bathtubs. The owner's suite has two rooms, linked by an interconnecting door, to provide a separate lounge, bedroom, and two bathrooms.

The sizes are: Owners Suites 538 sq.ft. (50 sq.meters); Medallion Suites 358 sq.ft. (33.2 sq.meters); Grand Suites 650 sq.ft. (60.3 sq.meters); Silver Suites 430.5 sq.ft. (40 sq.meters); Veranda Suites 215 sq.ft. (20 sq.meters); Explorer Class 190 sq.ft. (27.5 sq.meters); Expedition Suites 430.5 sq.ft. (40 sq.meters).

CUISINE. The spacious dining room, with pastel-colored decor, accommodates all passengers in one seating. Casual al-fresco bites can be had at the outdoor grill.

ENTERTAINMENT. Daily recaps; after-dinner conversation.

SPA/FITNESS. Facilities include a small gymnasium, sauna, and treatment room for massage.

BERLITZ'S RATINGS

	Possible	Achieved
Ship	500	411
Accommodation	200	174
Food	400	334
Service	400	334
Entertainment	n/a	n/a
Cruise	500	431

OVERALL SCORE
1,684 points out of 2,000

Silver Shadow
★★★★★

Size: . . . . .Small Ship	Passenger Decks: 7	Cabins (with private balcony): 166
Tonnage: 28,258	Total Crew: 295	Cabins (wheelchair accessible): 2
Lifestyle: .Luxury	Passengers	Wheelchair accessibility: . . . . .Good
Cruise Line: . . . . .Silversea Cruises	(lower beds/all berths): 388/429	Cabin Current: . . . . .110 and 220 volts
Former Names: . . . . .none	Passenger Space Ratio	Elevators: 5
Builder: . . . . .Visentini/Mariotti	(lower beds/all berths): 72.8/65.8	Casino (gaming tables): . . . . .Yes
(Italy)	Crew/Passenger Ratio	Slot Machines: . . . . .Yes
Original Cost: . . . .$150 million	(lower beds/all berths): 1.3/1.3	Swimming Pools (outdoors): 1
Entered Service: . . . . .Sep 2000	Cabins (total): .194	Swimming Pools (indoors): 0
Registry: . . . . .The Bahamas	Size Range (sq ft/m): 287.0–1,435.0/	Whirlpools: 2
Length (ft/m): 610.2/186.0	26.6–133.3	Self-Service Launderette: . . . . .Yes
Beam (ft/m): 81.8/24.8	Cabins (outside view): 194	Dedicated Cinema/Seats: . . . . .No
Draft (ft/m): 19.6/6.0	Cabins (interior/no view): 0	Library: . . . . .Yes
Propulsion/Propellers: diesel/2	Cabins (for one person): 0	Onboard currency: . . . . .US$

An all-inclusive premium ship for mature-age cruisers.

OVERVIEW. This ship is best suited to discerning, well-traveled couples, typically over 50, who seek a small ship setting, with excellent food that approaches gourmet standards, and fine European-style service in surroundings bordering on the elegant and luxurious. Few ships make it to a five-star Berlitz rating, but Silversea Cruises has earned an enviable reputation for high quality.

THE SHIP. *Silver Shadow* is one of the second generation of vessels in the six-ship Silversea Cruises fleet. It is slightly larger than the first two ships, *Silver Cloud* and *Silver Wind*, with a more streamlined forward profile and large, sleek single funnel. However, the stern section is not particularly handsome. There is a generous amount of open deck and sunbathing space, and aluminum/teak deck furniture is provided.

The company's many international passengers react well to the ambience, food, service and the helpful staff. The cruise line has "all-inclusive" fares, including gratuities and many things that cost extra aboard many rivals' ships, but the fares don't include vintage wines, massage, or other personal services. The passenger mix includes many nationalities, which makes for a more interesting experience, although the majority of passengers are North American. Children are sometimes seen aboard, although they are not really welcomed by most passengers, who enjoy cruising without them.

Although the ship shows signs of wear, the onboard product is very good, particularly the cuisine and its presentation. Shuttle buses are provided in most ports of call, and all the little extras that passengers receive make this an extremely pleasant experience, in surroundings that are comfortable and contemporary without being extravagant, with open

BERLITZ'S RATINGS

	Possible	Achieved
Ship	500	452
Accommodation	200	181
Food	400	341
Service	400	347
Entertainment	100	85
Cruise	400	344

OVERALL SCORE
1,750 points out of 2,000

seating dining and drinks included, cold canapés and hot hors d'oeuvres served in the bars in the pre-dinner cocktail hour, a captain's welcome aboard and farewell cocktail party.

The swimming pool is surprisingly small, as is the fitness room, although it was expanded in 2007. The Humidor, by Davidoff, the cigar lounge, has 25 seats and the style of an English smoking club. There is a champagne bar and a four-terminal computer learning center (wi-fi costs extra).

"Personalized Voyages" enable you choose the port of embarkation and disembarkation and the length of cruise you want (minimum five days). While this adds flexibility, the onboard programming is already set, so you may be joining and leaving in the middle of a "normal" cruise.

ACCOMMODATION. There are eight price grades in this all-suite ship. All suites have double vanities in the marble-floored bathrooms, which also have a tub and separate shower enclosure. All grades receive Silversea monogrammed Frette bed linen, an eight-pillow menu (from soft down to memory foam), 100% cotton bathrobes, a range of Acqua di Parma bathroom amenities, and personalized stationery. Stay in the Grand, Royal, Rossellini or Owner's Suite and you get unobtrusive service from butlers certified by London's Guild of Professional Butlers.

Vista Suites: These 287-sq.-ft (27-sq.-meter) suites do not have a private balcony. Instead there is a large window, twin beds that convert to a queen-size bed, sitting area, TV set and video player, refrigerator, writing desk, personal safe, cocktail cabinet, dressing table with hairdryer, and walk-in closet. The bathroom is marble-clad in gentle colors, and has two washbasins, a full-size tub, separate shower enclosure, and toilet.

Veranda Suites: Each of these suites (really Vista Suites plus a veranda) measures 345 sq. ft (33 sq. meters) and has convertible twin-to-queen beds. They are well fitted out with just about everything you would need, including large floor-to-ceiling windows, large walk-in closet, dressing table, writing desk, stocked mini-bar/refrigerator with all drinks are included in the fare, and fresh flowers. The marble-clad bathrooms have two washbasins, full-size tub, separate shower enclosure, and toilet.

Silver Suites: These measure 701 sq. ft (65 sq. meters). These are much wider than the Vista Suites or Veranda Suites and have a separate bedroom, an entertainment center with CD player, TV/video player in both bedroom and living room, and much more living space that includes a large dining area with table and four chairs. The marble-clad bathrooms have two washbasins, full size tub, separate shower enclosure, and toilet.

Owner's Suites: These two suites, each measuring 1,208 sq. ft (112 sq. meters), are much larger and include an extra powder room/toilet for guests, as well as more living space. There is a 200 sq.-ft (18 sq.-meter) veranda, two bedrooms with queen-size beds, two walk-in closets, two living rooms, two sitting areas, separate dining area, an entertainment center with flat-screen plasma television in the living room and a TV set/video player player in each bedroom, telephones, refrigerators, cocktail cabinet, writing desk, dressing tables with hairdryers. There are two marble-clad bathrooms, one with a full-size whirlpool tub and two washbasins, separate toilet, and separate shower, as well as a powder room for guests. Owner's Suites can be configured as one or two bedrooms.

Royal Suites: Stately accommodation can be found in two Royal Suites measuring either 1,312 sq. ft (122 sq. meters) or 1,352 sq. ft (126 sq. meters). These are two-bedroom suites, with two teakwood verandas, two living rooms, sitting areas, dining area, queen-size beds, an entertainment center with flat-screen plasma television in the living room and a TV/video player player in each bedroom, telephones, refrigerators, cocktail cabinet, writing desk, two closets, dressing tables with hairdryers. There are two marble-clad bathrooms, one with a full-size whirlpool tub and two washbasins, separate toilet, and separate shower, as well as a powder room for guests. Royal Suites can be either a one- or two-bedroom configuration.

Grand Suites: There are two of these, one measuring 1,286 sq. ft (119 sq. meters), and the other (including an adjoining suite with interconnecting door) 1,435 sq. ft (133 sq. meters). These have two bedrooms, two large walk-in closets, two living rooms, Bang & Olufsen entertainment centers, and large, forward-facing, private verandas. These really are sumptuous apartments that have all the comforts of home, and then some.

Disabled Suites: There are two suites for the physically disabled (535 and 537), both adjacent to an elevator and next to each other. Measuring a generous 398 sq. ft (37 sq. meters), they are well equipped with an accessible hanging rail, and roll-in bathroom with roll-in shower unit.

CUISINE. The main dining room, *The Restaurant* has open-seating in elegant surroundings. Three grand chandeliers provide an upward focal point, while you can dine when you want, and with whom you wish. Meals can also be served, course-by-course, in your suite, although the balcony tables are rather low for dining outdoors. The cuisine is very good, with a choice of formal and informal areas. Standard table wines are included for lunch and dinner, with an extra-cost "connoisseur list" of premium wines. Once each cruise, there's a "Galley Brunch" when the galley is transformed into a large "chef's kitchen." There's dinner dancing with a live band on some nights.

As an alternative, *Le Champagne* is a more intimate extra-cost venue that allows diners to sample highly specialized dégustation menus marrying international cuisine with vintage wines selection by Relais et Châteaux sommeliers. Reservations are needed, and the wines also cost extra.

For more informal meals, *La Terrazza* provides self-serve breakfast and lunch buffets; outdoor seating is at teakwood tables and chairs. The buffet design and set-up presents flow problems during breakfast, and "active" stations for cooking eggs or pasta to order would help. In the evening, La Terrazza serves regional Italian cuisine, and softer lighting creates a more intimate atmosphere.

Adjacent to La Terazza is a wine bar and a cigar smoking room. A poolside grill provides a casual alternative daytime bistro-style eatery, for grilled and fast-food items, and becomes *The Grill* for evening dining, with food cooked on hot stones.

ENTERTAINMENT. The Showlounge, the venue for entertainment and some social functions, spans two decks and has a sloping floor; both banquette and individual seating are provided, with good sightlines from almost all seats.

Although Silversea Cruises places more emphasis on food than entertainment, what is provided is quite tasteful. A decent array of cabaret acts does the Silversea circuit, and small, colorful production shows have been reintroduced. More emphasis is placed on classical music ensembles. There is a band, and several small musical units for live music in the evenings in The Bar, and the Panorama Lounge.

SPA/FITNESS. "The Spa at Silversea" health/fitness facility, just behind the Observation Lounge, high atop the ship. had a complete make-over in 2007. It includes a gymnasium, beauty salon, and separate saunas and steam rooms for men and women, plus several personal treatment rooms. A new range of body-pampering services was introduced for men and women. Massage and other treatments, facials, pedicures, and beauty salon treatments cost extra.

Silver Spirit
★★★★★

Size: ....Small Ship	Passenger Decks: 8	Cabins (with private balcony): 258
Tonnage: 36,009	Total Crew: 370	Cabins (wheelchair accessible): 4
Lifestyle: ....Luxury	Passengers	Wheelchair accessibility: ....Best
Cruise Line: ....Silversea Cruises	(lower beds/all berths): 540/608	Cabin Voltage: ....110 volts
Former Names: ....none	Passenger Space Ratio	Elevators: 6
Builder: ....Fincantieri (Italy)	(lower beds/all berths): 66.6/59.2	Casino (gaming tables): ....Yes
Original Cost: ....$250 million	Crew/Passenger Ratio	Slot Machines: ....Yes
Entered Service: ....Dec 2009	(lower beds/all berths): 1.4/1.6	Swimming Pools (outdoors): 1
Registry: ....The Bahamas	Cabins (total): 270	Swimming Pools (indoors): 0
Length (ft/m): 642.3/195.8	Size Range (sq ft/m): 312.1–1,614.6/	Whirlpools: 4
Beam (ft/m): 86.9/26.5	29–150	Self-Service Launderette: ....Yes
Draft (ft/m): 20.9/6.4	Cabins (outside view): 270	Dedicated Cinema/Seats: ....No
Propulsion/Propellers: ....diesel-electric/	Cabins (interior/no view): 0	Library: ....Yes
(26,100kW)/2	Cabins (for one person): 0	Onboard currency: ....US$

An upper-class, stylish ship for mature-age cruisers.

OVERVIEW. This ship suits discerning, well-traveled couples, typically over 50, who are looking for a smaller ship setting with fine food and European-style service in surroundings bordering on the elegant and luxurious without being extravagant. Shuttle buses are provided in most ports of call, and all the little extras passengers receive make a cruise an extremely pleasant experience.

THE SHIP. *Silver Spirit*, larger than *Silver Shadow* and *Silver Whisper*, is the newest "all-inclusive" addition to the Silversea Cruises fleet – although "all-inclusive" doesn't include the two alternative dining venues . It represents a substantial investment in new tonnage. Sharing its name with a famous Rolls-Royce car, *Silver Spirit* has a similar profile to the smaller *Silver Shadow* and *Silver Whisper*, with a nicely shaped stern with tiered aft decks, but exudes more style and provides more choice than the line's other ships.

Although there's a main pool and hot tub deck, there's little shade, and no hot tubs on any other deck. Also, because there are so many balcony suites/cabins, there's no walk-around outdoor promenade deck.

The interior layout has a cake-layer stacking of almost all the public rooms in the aft section, and the accommodation located forward, so there is minimal noise in passenger accommodation, although it means there are more stairs and no "flow-through" horizontal deck where passengers can parade. But regular Silversea Cruises passengers are used to this arrangement, and it's good exercise. The decor is elegant and understated, but bland (muted colors), a mix of art deco and modern, but not contemporary.

The Observation Lounge, at the front of the ship with

BERLITZ'S RATINGS

	Possible	Achieved
Ship	500	458
Accommodation	200	182
Food	400	343
Service	400	349
Entertainment	100	87
Cruise	400	353

OVERALL SCORE
1,772 points out of 2,000

access from a central passageway, has fine ocean views, and is a very comfortable place to relax and read. A Panorama Lounge, at the stern, is a comfortable multi-function room. Non-smokers should note that smoking is allowed on the port side. A cigar lounge, with doors that open in to the casino, has a pleasing list of cigars. The casino has five blackjack tables, American Roulette table, and 52 slot machines.

Silversea Cruises' "all-inclusive" fares include gratuities, drinks with meals, and many things that cost extra on rivals' ships. Vintage wines, massage, and other personal services do cost extra, though. Passengers appreciate open-seating dining, cold canapés and hot hors d'oeuvres served in the bars in the pre-dinner cocktail hour, a captain's welcome aboard and a farewell cocktail party.

The passenger mix includes many nationalities, which makes for a more interesting experience, although most passengers are North American. Children are sometimes seen aboard, but are not really welcomed by most people.

Passenger niggles include the lack of electrical sockets in the cabins; there are almost no shaded outdoor areas; the "butler" service is sometimes poor, not least because each butler has about 15 cabins to look after.

ACCOMMODATION. *Silver Spirit*, like other Silversea Cruises ships, has "all-suite" accommodation. Some suites can accommodate a third person. Eight have interconnecting doors, so families and friends can be adjacent.

Accommodation consists of: two Owner's suites, approx. 1,291.7 sq. ft (120 sq. meters) for one bedroom and 1,614 sq.ft (150 sq. meters) for two bedrooms; six Grand suites in the front of the ship (990 sq.ft/ 92 sq. meters for one bedroom and 1,302 sq.ft/117 sq. meters for two bedrooms); 26 Silver suites (742 sq.ft/ 69 sq. meters); Midship Veranda suites (376 sq.ft/35 sq. meters); 222 Verandah suites (376 sq.ft/35 sq. meters); and 14 Vista suites (312 sq.ft/29 sq. meters).

All provide personalized stationery, a menu with a choice of eight pillows from soft down to memory foam, bathrobes, and an array of Bulgari bathroom amenities. All have walk-in closets with personal safe, TV set, DVD unit, and vanity desk with hairdryer. Suite bathrooms are marble-clad, with marble and wood floors, and contain a toilet, one or two washbasins, a full-size tub, and a shower enclosure with a fixed "rainshower" and a separate hand-held hose). Occupants of the Owner's Suites or Grand Suites receive unobtrusive service from 21 butlers certified by London's Guild of Professional Butlers.

The suites have recessed lighting in the ceiling – a nice touch that allows a little diffused mood lighting when needed. Balconies have sliding doors that can move if not securely locked when not in use. Non-smokers should be aware that Silversea Cruises allows smoking in cabins.

CUISINE. There are certainly plenty of dining choices. *The Restaurant* is the name of the ship's main dining room – a light, airy venue, although its design is quite disappointing – in particular because of its low ceiling height. It seats up to 456, and has an integral dance floor. This is all about open-seating dining in elegant surroundings, with unhurried, unobtrusive service. It is open for breakfast, lunch and dinner; tables are set with fine china, silverware, and Riedel wine glasses. For complete privacy, meals can also be served, course-by-course, in your suite.

● *Le Champagne*, adjacent to The Restaurant, is an extra-cost, reservations-required, dinner-only venue offering a six-course mini-dégustation menu based on Relais & Châteaux menus. Sadly, the banquette seating along the outer walls detracts from the otherwise very comfortable, uncluttered, intimate dining spot, which has a small walk-in wine room as its central, focal point.

● *Seishin* Restaurant, also adjacent to The Restaurant, is an extra-cost reservations-required venue, with just 24 seats. It serves Kobe beef, sushi items, and Asian seafood, and an octagonal display counter is the focal point to the venue. It is open for dinner only, and there's a cover charge.

● *La Terrazza* is the venue for self-serve buffet-style items for breakfast and lunch. Each evening, it turns into an Italian-themed dining spot, with waiter service and regional Italian cuisine cooked to order. Reservations are required for dinner (not open for lunch).

● *Stars Supper Club,* with 58 seats and a dance floor, is designed in the manner of an English supper club of the 1920s to provide an intimate, club-like ambience and all-night entertainment – which means volume-intrusive. Reservations are required for dinner (not open for lunch).

● *The Pool Grill* is a casual outside eatery serving steaks, seafood, and pizza. Pizza cannot possibly be considered a luxury food item, but then, this *is* a ship with Italian connections. Meals are served on hot stones that act as plates, so you can't touch them, but this is more a casual eating novelty than proper dining.

Additionally, a lobby bar serves Lavazza Italian coffees, wines, spirits, and pastries.

ENTERTAINMENT. The Showlounge, in the aft section, has a main stage and two ancillary side stages. It seats about 320 passengers, and there are good sightlines from all seats but no beverage service. It's a lovely room, and seating consists of two-person love seats, and each has a small table for personal items such as ladies' clutch purses for formal evenings. Production shows have been re-introduced, and these, together with cabaret acts, provide a balanced entertainment program.

SPA/FITNESS. The Spa at Silversea, with 8,300 sq.ft (770 sq. meters) of space, is quite large for this size of ship, and includes a sanctuary for total relaxation and detox. Located at the stern of the ship, above La Terrazza, it is a haven for me-time and personal treatments.

Silver Whisper
★★★★★

Size: ....Small Ship	Passengers	Wheelchair accessibility: ....Good
Tonnage: 28,258	(lower beds/all berths): 388/429	Cabin Current: ....110 and 220 volts
Lifestyle: ....Luxury	Passenger Space Ratio	Elevators: 5
Cruise Line: ....Silversea Cruises	(lower beds/all berths): 72.8/65.8	Casino (gaming tables): ....Yes
Former Names: ....none	Crew/Passenger Ratio	Slot Machines: ....Yes
Builder: ....Visentini/Mariotti(Italy)	(lower beds/all berths): 1.3/1.3	Swimming Pools (outdoors): 1
Original Cost: ....$150 million	Cabins (total): 194	Swimming Pools (indoors): 0
Entered Service: ....Jul 2001	Size Range (sq ft/m): 287.0–1,435.0/	Whirlpools: 2
Registry: ....The Bahamas	26.6–133.3	Fitness Center: ....Yes
Length (ft/m): 610.2/186.0	Cabins (outside view): 194	Sauna/Steam Room: ....Yes/Yes
Beam (ft/m): 81.8/24.8	Cabins (interior/no view): 0	Massage: ....Yes
Draft (ft/m): 19.6/6.0	Cabins (for one person): 0	Self-Service Launderette: ....Yes
Propulsion/Propellers: diesel/2	Cabins (with private balcony): 166	Dedicated Cinema/Seats: ....No
Passenger Decks: 7	Cabins (with private balcony): 157	Library: ....Yes
Total Crew: 295	Cabins (wheelchair accessible): 2	Onboard currency: ....US$

All-inclusive cruising with space, style, and good food.

OVERVIEW. This ship suits discerning, well-traveled couples who like a small ship that provides excellent food and fine European-style service in elegant, highly comfortable surroundings. Silversea Cruises promotes its Italian Heritage theme, and its many international passengers respond well to the ambience, food, and the staff, most of whom go out of their way to please.

THE SHIP. *Silver Whisper*, which Russia's Vladimir Putin chartered in 2003 to host guests for the three-day celebrations of St Petersburg's 300th anniversary, is the second generation of vessels in the Silversea Cruises fleet. It is sister to *Silver Shadow*, and is slightly larger than the line's first two ships, *Silver Cloud* and *Silver Wind*, but with a more streamlined profile and a large, sleek single funnel.

The cruise line has "all-inclusive" fares, including gratuities (although additional tips are not expected, they are not prohibited). The fares do not include vintage wines, or massage, or other personal services, but they do include many things that are at extra cost compared aboard the ships of many other cruise lines. The passenger mix includes many nationalities, although the majority of passengers are North American. Children are sometimes seen aboard, although they are not really welcomed by most passengers.

Only a few ships make it to a five-star Berlitz rating, but Silversea Cruises' emphasis on quality has earned it an enviable reputation, particularly for cuisine. Shuttle buses are provided in most ports of call, and all the little extras that passengers receive makes this ship an extremely pleasant cruise experience. The surroundings are very comfortable

BERLITZ'S RATINGS

	Possible	Achieved
Ship	500	452
Accommodation	200	181
Food	400	341
Service	400	349
Entertainment	100	85
Cruise	400	345

OVERALL SCORE
1,753 points out of 2,000

and contemporary without being extravagant, there is open-seating dining with drinks included, cold canapés and hot hors d'oeuvres are served in the bars in the pre-dinner cocktail hour, and there's a captain's welcome aboard and farewell cocktail party.

Aluminum/teak deck furniture is provided around the swimming pool, although the pool itself is quite small. The Humidor, by Davidoff, a 25-seat cigar smoking lounge, has been styled like an English smoking club. There's a wine bar and computer learning center.

ACCOMMODATION. This "all-suite" ship has eight cabin price categories. All grades have double vanities in the marble-floored bathrooms, plus tub and separate shower enclosure. Silversea-monogrammed Frette bed linen is provided in all grades, as is an eight-pillow menu from soft down to memory foam, 100% cotton bathrobes, a fine array of Acqua di Parma bathroom amenities, and personalized stationery. In the Grand, Royal, Rossellini or Owner's Suites, you get unobtrusive service from butlers certified by London's Guild of Professional Butlers.

Vista Suites: These suites measure 287 sq. ft (27 sq. meters), and do not have a private balcony. Instead there is a large window, twin beds that convert to a queen-size bed, sitting area, TV and video player, refrigerator, writing desk, personal safe, cocktail cabinet, dressing table with hairdryer, and walk-in closet. The bathroom is marble-clad in gentle colors, and has two washbasins, full-size tub, separate shower enclosure, and toilet.

Veranda Suites: Each of the Veranda Suites – which are

really Vista Suites plus a veranda – measures 345 sq. ft (32 sq. meters) and has convertible twin-to-queen beds. They are well fitted-out, and have large floor-to-ceiling windows, large walk-in closet, dressing table, writing desk, stocked mini-bar/refrigerator (drinks included in the fare), and fresh flowers. The marble-clad bathrooms have two washbasins, full-size tub, separate shower enclosure, and toilet.

Silver Suites: The Silver Suites measure 701 sq. ft. (65 sq. meters). Much wider than the Vista Suites or Veranda Suites, they have a separate bedroom, an audio-visual entertainment center in both bedroom and living room, and much more living space, including a large dining area with table and four chairs. The marble-clad bathrooms have two washbasins, full-size tub, separate shower enclosure, and toilet.

Owner's Suites: The two Owner's Suites, each 1,208 sq. ft (112 sq. meters), are much larger units and include an extra bathroom for guests, plus more living space. There is a 200-sq.-ft (18-sq.-meter) veranda, two bedrooms with queen-size beds, two walk-in closets, two living rooms, two sitting areas, separate dining area, an entertainment center with flat-screen plasma television in the living room and TV/DVD player in each bedroom, telephones, refrigerators, cocktail cabinet, writing desk, dressing tables with hairdryers. There are two marble-clad bathrooms, one with a full-size whirlpool tub and two washbasins, separate toilet, and separate shower, plus a powder room for guests. Owner's Suites can be a one- or two-bedroom configuration.

Royal Suites: Stately accommodation can be found in two Royal Suites, measuring 1,312 sq. ft (122 sq. meters) and 1,352 sq. ft (126 sq. meters). These are two-bedroom suites, with two teakwood verandas, two living rooms, sitting areas, dining area, queen-size beds, an entertainment center with flat-screen plasma television in the living room and TV/DVD player in each bedroom, telephones, refrigerators, cocktail cabinet, writing desk, two closets, dressing tables with hairdryers. There are two marble-clad bathrooms, one with a full-size whirlpool tub and two washbasins, separate toilet, and separate shower, as well as a powder room for guests. Royal Suites can be either a one- or two-bedroom configuration.

Grand Suites: There are two, one 1,286 sq. ft (119 sq. meters) and the other, including an adjoining suite with interconnecting door, 1,435 sq. ft (133 sq. meters). These have two bedrooms, two large walk-in closets, two living rooms, Bang & Olufsen entertainment centers, and large, forward-facing, private verandas. These are sumptuous apartments with all the comforts of home, and then some.

Disabled Suites: There are two adjacent suites for the physically disabled (535 and 537), both beside an elevator. They measure a generous 398 sq. ft (37 sq. meters) and are well-equipped with an accessible hanging rail, and roll-in bathroom with roll-in shower unit.

CUISINE. The main dining room, called *The Restaurant*, offers open-seating dining in elegant surroundings. Three grand chandeliers provide an upward focal point, while you can dine when you want, and with whom you wish within the given opening times. Meals can also be served, course-by-course, in your suite, although the balcony tables are rather low for dining outdoors. The dining is good throughout the ship, with a choice of formal and informal areas, although the cuisine and presentation don't quite match up to that of vessels such as the smaller Seabourn Cruise Line ships. Cristofle silverware is provided. Standard table wines are included for lunch and dinner, and there is an extra-cost "connoisseur list" of premium wines.

Once each cruise, there's a "Galley Brunch" when the galley is transformed into a large "chef's kitchen."

As an alternative to the main restaurant, the extra-cost *Le Champagne* offers a more intimate, reservation-only dining spot that enables diners to dine from highly specialized dégustation menus marrying international cuisine with vintage wines selected by Relais et Châteaux sommeliers.

La Terrazza has self-serve breakfast and lunch buffets. The buffet design and set-up presents flow problems during breakfast, however, and "active" stations for cooking eggs or pasta to order would help. In the evening this room serves regional Italian cuisine, and has softer lighting to create a more intimate atmosphere.

Adjacent to the café is a wine bar and a cigar smoking room. A poolside grill provides a casual alternative daytime dining spot; in the evening it turns into *The Grill*, with food cooked using the Black Rock (hot stone) method.

ENTERTAINMENT. The Showlounge spans two decks and has a sloping floor; both banquette and individual seating are provided, with good sightlines from almost all seats.

A decent array of cabaret acts does the Silversea circuit, most providing intelligent entertainment, and colorful production shows are back. More emphasis is placed on classical music ensembles. A band and small musical units provide music in the evenings in The Bar and the Panorama Lounge.

SPA/FITNESS. "The Spa at Silversea" health/fitness facility, just behind the Observation Lounge, high atop the ship, includes a gymnasium, beauty salon, and separate saunas and steam rooms for men and women, plus several treatment rooms. A range of body-pampering services is offered to men and women. Massage and other treatments, facials, pedicures, and beauty salon treatments cost extra.

Silver Wind
★★★★+

Size ....Small Ship	Total Crew: 222	Cabins (wheelchair accessible): 2
Tonnage: 16,927	Passengers	Wheelchair accessibility: ....Fair
Lifestyle: ....Luxury	(lower beds/all berths): 298/332	Cabin Current: ....110 and 220 volts
Cruise Line: ....Silversea Cruises	Passenger Space Ratio	Elevators: 4
Former Names: ....none	(lower beds/all berths): 56.8/50.9	Casino (gaming tables): ....Yes
Builder: ....Visentini/Mariotti (Italy)	Crew/Passenger Ratio	Slot Machines: ....Yes
Original Cost: ....$125 million	(lower beds/all berths): 1.3/1.4	Swimming Pools (outdoors): 1
Entered Service: ....Jan 1995	Cabins (total): 149	Swimming Pools (indoors): 0
Registry: ....Italy	Size Range (sq ft/m): 240.0–1,314.0/	Whirlpools: 2
Length (ft/m): 514.4/155.8	22.2–122.0	Self-Service Launderette: ....Yes
Beam (ft/m): 70.62/21.4	Cabins (outside view): 149	Dedicated Cinema/Seats: Yes/306
Draft (ft/m): 17.3/5.3	Cabins (interior/no view): 0	Library: ....Yes
Propulsion/Propellers: diesel (11,700kW)/2	Cabins (for one person): 0	Onboard currency: ....US$
Passenger Decks: 6	Cabins (with private balcony): 119	

An all-inclusive small ship for mature-age cruisers.

OVERVIEW. This ship is best suited to discerning, well-traveled couples, typically over 50, who seek a small ship with fine cuisine, European-style service and surroundings that border on the elegant. An announcement-free ambience prevails, and there is no pressure or hype, and an enthusiastic staff knows how to pamper you.

THE SHIP. *Silver Wind* has a quite handsome profile, with a sloping stern reminiscent of an Airstream trailer. The size is just about ideal for personalized cruising in an elegant environment. The vertical cake-layer stacking of public rooms aft and the location of accommodation units forward ensures quiet cabins. There is a synthetic turf-covered walk-around promenade deck outdoors – which should be upgraded to teak or Bolidt – and a fairly spacious swimming pool and sunbathing deck with teak/aluminum deck furniture. Little Silversea touches such as cold towels, water sprays and fresh fruit provide poolside pampering on hot days.

The ship had a multi-million dollar makeover in 2003, and a further refit in 2009 made it more user-friendly by adding a proper observation lounge and covered walkway to access it. The spacious interior is well-planned, with elegant decor and fine-quality soft furnishings throughout, accented by brass fittings – some of sub-standard quality and showing blotchy patches in several places – fine woods and creative ceilings. There is an excellent amount of space per passenger and no hint of a line anywhere. There is a useful internet center, a 24-hour library with hardback books and DVDs, and a cigar lounge.

Before your cruise, good documentation is provided in a high-quality document wallet and presentation box. Insur-

BERLITZ'S RATINGS

	Possible	Achieved
Ship	500	413
Accommodation	200	177
Food	400	333
Service	400	335
Entertainment	100	74
Cruise	400	337

OVERALL SCORE
1,669 points out of 2,000

ance, once included in the fare, now costs extra. All drinks, gratuities and port taxes are included, and no further tipping anywhere on board is necessary, though it is not prohibited. It would be hard not to have good cruise aboard this ship, albeit at a fairly high price. The company's many international passengers like the ambience, food, service and the staff, most of whom go out of their way to please.

Silversea Cruises' "all-inclusive" fares include gratuities and many things that cost extra aboard the ships of some rivals. Not included, however, are vintage wines, massage, and other personal services. Shuttle buses are provided in most ports of call, and all the little extras that passengers receive aboard this ship makes it an extremely pleasant experience, in surroundings that are very comfortable and contemporary without being extravagant, with open seating dining and drinks included, cold canapés and hot hors d'oeuvres served in the bars in the pre-dinner cocktail hour, a captain's welcome aboard and a farewell cocktail party.

After 10 years, Silversea Cruises re-invented itself with a more defined and refined product based on an Italian Heritage theme. The past few years sometimes saw the delivery of a tarnished service, but this has been recognized and Silversea Cruises is now polishing the silver again.

The passenger mix includes many nationalities, although most passengers are North American. Children are sometimes seen aboard, although they are not really welcomed by most passengers.

Passenger niggles include the fact that some vibration is evident when bow thrusters or the anchors are used, particularly in the forward-most suites. The self-service launderette is poor and not large enough for longer cruises, when passengers like to wash their own small items. Crew facilities are minimal, so crew turnover is quite high, making it difficult to maintaining consistency.

ACCOMMODATION. There are seven price grades. The all-outside suites, 75% with fine private teakwood-floor balconies, have convertible queen-to-twin beds and are nicely fitted out. They include large floor-to-ceiling windows, large walk-in closets, dressing table, writing desk, stocked mini-bar/refrigerator (no charge), and fresh flowers. The marble floor bathrooms have a tub, fixed shower head – not as hygienic as a hand-held unit – single washbasin, and plenty of high-quality towels. Personalized stationery, an eight-pillow menu from soft down to memory foam, bathrobes, and an array of Acqua di Parma bathroom amenities are provided in all suites.

In the Grand, Royal, Rossellini or Owner's Suites, you get unobtrusive service from butlers certified by London's Guild of Professional Butlers.

All suites have TV and DVD players (top-grade suites also have CD players). However, the walk-in closets don't actually provide much hanging space, particularly for such items as full-length dresses, and it would be better for the door to open outward instead of inward. The drawers themselves are poorly positioned, although several other drawers and storage areas are provided in the living area. Although the cabin insulation above and below each suite is good, the insulation between them is not – a privacy curtain installed between entry door and sleeping area would be useful – and light from the passageway leaks into the suite, making it hard to achieve a dark room.

The top grades of suites have teak balcony furniture, while others don't – but all balconies have teak floors. Suites with balconies on the lowest deck can suffer from sticky salt spray when the ship is moving, so the balconies need lots of cleaning. Each evening, the stewardesses bring plates of canapés to your suite – just right for a light bite with cocktails.

CUISINE. The main dining room, called simply *The Restaurant*, provides open-seating dining in elegant surroundings. It has an attractive arched gazebo center and a wavy ceiling design as its focal point, and is set with fine Limoges china and well-balanced Christofle silverware. Meals are served in an open seating, which means you can eat when you like within the given dining room opening times, and with whom you like.

The cuisine/dining experience is good, with a choice of three dining salons. Standard table wines are included for lunch and dinner, but there is also a "connoisseur list" of premium wines at extra charge. All meals are prepared as à la carte items, with almost none of the pre-preparation that used to exist. Special orders are also possible.

An alternative dining salon, the intimate 24-seat *La Saletta*, adjacent to the main dining room, has dégustation menus that include dishes designed for Silversea Cruises by chefs from Relais et Châteaux Gourmands, the cuisine-oriented division of Relais et Châteaux, paired with selected wines. Reservations are required, and there's a cover charge.

For more informal dining, *La Terrazza* offers self-serve breakfast and lunch buffets. In the evening it serves Italian regional dishes and has softer lighting, with both indoor and outdoors seating at teakwood tables and chairs.

There is a 24-hour in-cabin dining service; full course-by-course dinners are available, although the balcony tables in the standard suites are rather low for dining outdoors.

ENTERTAINMENT. The Showlounge is the venue for all entertainment events and some social functions. The room spans two decks and has a sloping floor; both banquette and individual seating are provided, with good sightlines from almost all seats.

Although Silversea Cruises places more emphasis on food than entertainment, what is provided is quite tasteful and not overbearing, as aboard some larger ships. A decent array of cabaret acts does the Silversea circuit, and small, colorful production shows have been reintroduced. Most of the cabaret acts provide intelligent entertainment.

Also, more emphasis is now placed on classical music ensembles. There is also a band, as well as several small musical units for live music in the evenings in The Bar, and the Panorama Lounge.

SPA/FITNESS. Although The Spa at Silversea facility isn't large, it underwent a sea change in 2007 with redesigned, more welcoming decor, and an updated range of treatments and spa packages for both men and women. Massage and other body pampering treatments, facials, pedicures, and beauty salon treatments cost extra.

Facilities include a separate sauna for men and women, several treatment rooms, and a beauty salon. A separate gymnasium, formerly an observation lounge, located atop the ship, provides sea views.

Sovereign
★★★

Size: . . . . .Large Resort Ship	Passenger Decks: 11	Cabins (with private balcony): 62
Tonnage: .73,192	Total Crew: 825	Cabins (wheelchair accessible): 6
Lifestyle: . . . . .Standard	Passengers	Wheelchair accessibility: . . . . .Fair
Cruise Line: . . . . .Pullmantur Cruises	(lower beds/all berths): 2,306/2,882	Cabin Current: . . . . .110 volts
Former Names: . . . .Sovereign of the Seas	Passenger Space Ratio	Elevators: 13
Builder: Chantiers de l'Atlantique (France)	(lower beds/all berths): 31.7/25.3	Casino (gaming tables): . . . . .Yes
Original Cost: . . . .$183.5 million	Crew/Passenger Ratio	Slot Machines: . . . . .Yes
Entered Service: . . . . . . .Jan 1988/2008	(lower beds/all berths): 2.7/3.4	Swimming Pools (outdoors): 2
Registry: . . . . .The Bahamas	Cabins (total): 1,153	Swimming Pools (indoors): 0
Length (ft/m): 879.9/268.2	Size Range (sq ft/m): 118.4–670.0/	Whirlpools: 2
Beam (ft/m): 105.9/32.3	11.0–62.2	Self-Service Launderette: . . . . .No
Draft (ft/m): 24.9/7.6	Cabins (outside view): 722	Dedicated Cinema/Seats: . . . . .No
Propulsion/Propellers: . . . . .diesel	Cabins (interior/no view): 431	Library: . . . . .Yes
(21,844kW)/2	Cabins (for one person): 0	Onboard currency: . . . . .Euros

A busy big ship for casual, Spanish family cruising.

OVERVIEW. This ship is best suited to Spanish-speaking families, young couples, and singles seeking a first cruise at an all-inclusive price that even includes drinks. The high-density ship is well-run, highly programmed, and is geared to families with children.

THE SHIP. Pullmantur Cruises bought *Sovereign* (formerly *Sovereign of the Seas*) from Royal Caribbean International in 2008. It has a smart, contemporary profile and nicely rounded lines. Open deck space isn't generous, but outdoors there's a wide walk-around polished wood promenade deck.

The interior layout is unusual for a large resort ship in that most of the public rooms are located aft in a sort of cake-layer stacking, with the accommodation located forward, as this helps to keep down the noise level in cabins.

There is a good array of spacious, fairly smart public rooms, with lots of wood paneling and fairly elegant decor that also has some bright color splashes. The ship has a range of rooms for children and teens, including a chill-out lounge and an open aft sundeck with open-air dance floor.

The dress code is very casual. Gratuities are included.

ACCOMMODATION. There are 16 cabin price grades. Some cabins have interconnecting doors – useful for families. **Suites:** Thirteen suites on Bridge Deck, the largest of which is the Royal Suite, are reasonably large and nicely furnished, with separate living and sleeping spaces. **Standard Cabins**: The standard outside-view and interior cabins are very small, although an arched window treat-

BERLITZ'S RATINGS		
	Possible	Achieved
Ship	500	327
Accommodation	200	119
Food	400	229
Service	400	254
Entertainment	100	63
Cruise	400	250
OVERALL SCORE		
1,242 points out of 2,000		

ment and colorful soft furnishings give the illusion of more space. Almost all cabins have twin beds that convert to a queen-size or double-bed configuration. There is little closet and drawer space. All cabins have a private bathroom, with shower enclosure, toilet and wash-basin.

CUISINE. *El Guardiana* and *El Duero*, two dining rooms off the Centrum (lobby), have tables for four, six, or eight persons but none for two. Both have two seatings, with table wines included in the fare. An à la carte restaurant offers better menus at an extra cost. For casual meals and snacks, the two-level *Buffet Panorama* is open almost 24 hours a day, although it is usually congested at peak times. Several food islands provide pasta and deli sections and a carving station. Asian fusion and Asian tapas are available on the venue's upper level.

ENTERTAINMENT. The Follies Lounge has both main and balcony levels, with banquette seating. On the stage is a video wall with 50 screens. A smaller venue, Finian's Rainbow Lounge, is where cabaret acts, including late-night adult comedy, are presented, as well as music for dancing.

SPA/FITNESS. There is a gymnasium with fine ocean views, full of muscle-pumping cardio-vascular equipment. There's also an aerobics studio, a hair and nails salon, and a sauna, as well as 11 treatment rooms, including one for couples' massages – all of which form The Spa. An outdoors rock-climbing wall has several climbing tracks.

Spirit of Adventure
★★★

Size: ....Small Ship	Propulsion/Propellers: ..diesel (7,060kW)/2	Cabins (with private balcony): 0
Tonnage: 9,570	Passenger Decks: 8	Cabins (wheelchair accessible): 1
Lifestyle: ....Standard	Total Crew: 168	Wheelchair accessibility: ....None
Cruise Line: ....Spirit of Adventure/	Passengers	Cabin Current: ....220 volts
Saga Cruises	(lower beds/all berths): 352/352	Elevators: 1
Former Names:*Berlin, Princess Mahsuri, Berlin*	Passenger Space Ratio	Casino (gaming tables): ....No
Builder: .....Howaldtswerke Deutsche Werft	(lower beds/all berths): 27.1/27.1	Slot Machines: ....No
(Germany)	Crew/Passenger Ratio	Swimming Pools (outdoors): 1
Original Cost: ....n/a	(lower beds/all berths): 2.0/2.0	Swimming Pools (indoors): 1
Entered Service: .....Jun 1980/Mar 2006	Cabins (total): 206	Whirlpools: 0
Registry: ....The Bahamas	Size Range (sq ft/m): ..92.5–191.6/8.6–17.8	Self-Service Launderette: ....Yes
Length (ft/m): 457.0/139.3	Cabins (outside view): 174	Dedicated Cinema/Seats: ....No
Beam (ft/m): 57.5/17.52	Cabins (interior/no view): 32	Library: ....Yes
Draft (ft/m): 15.7/4.8	Cabins (for one person): 60	Onboard currency: ....UK£

A small ship for "soft" discovery cruising in comfort.

OVERVIEW. This soft-adventure ship is best suited to couples and solo travelers over 21 who want a holiday in a traditional ship that is unpretentious yet provides a decent standard of accommodation, food and friendly service, as well as interesting itineraries. Despite its small size, it is a good sea ship and rides well. Itineraries include Europe, the Aegean and Black Seas, the Indian Ocean, Southeast Asia, and Antarctica.

BERLITZ'S RATINGS		
	Possible	Achieved
Ship	500	275
Accommodation	200	109
Food	400	276
Service	400	251
Entertainment	n/a	n/a
Cruise	500	338
OVERALL SCORE		
1,249 points out of 2,000		

THE SHIP. *Spirit of Adventure,* a somewhat angular ship, has an all-white hull with a blue line between hull and superstructure, a balanced profile with buff-colored funnel and black top, and an ice-strengthened hull. As *Berlin,* it starred for many years in the long-running German TV show *Traumschiff* (Dream Ship). In 1986 it was "chopped and stretched" with the addition of a 66-ft (20-meter) mid-section. Saga Holidays bought it in April 2005, refurbished it for warm-weather cruising, and assigned it to a sister company, Spirit of Adventure.

The interiors are crisp, contemporary and well-appointed, with tasteful European decor and furnishings. The Library is a fine room, with a 3,000-book library/DVD collection (open 24 hours), plus internet access at four computer stations.

The swimming pool, located aft, is tiny – it's really just a "dip" pool. The surrounding open-deck and sunbathing space is cramped, because it's in the same area as the outdoor seating for The Verandah dining venue. However, there's a reasonable amount of open-deck sunbathing space on the uppermost deck, forward of the mast.

This well-run ship provides a destination-intensive fly-cruise in a comfortable, well maintained, and intimate environment for those who seek to explore and learn about less visited places, and who don't need constant entertainment.

While the ship is not the latest, and doesn't have any cabins with balconies, its attention to passenger care, and the company's meet-and-greet and transfer services are extremely good. Shuttle buses are provided in many ports of call. Onboard wines and drinks prices are very low in comparison with almost all other cruise lines.

Value for money is good. Insurance and staff gratuities are included in the fare, as are scheduled or charter flights (plus all airport fees and taxes), visas for full UK-resident British citizens, port taxes, luggage handling, some shore excursions (others are available at extra cost), and lectures. Mountain bikes are available for anyone wanting to explore independently or on escorted rides.

There is only one elevator and it doesn't go to the two topmost decks or to the Spa Aquarius on the lowermost deck. The passenger accommodation hallways are rather narrow. However, it's the Filippino hotel crew that makes this ship so popular with passengers. It's also the manner in which Saga's meet-and-greet and passenger handling systems work, supplying the kind of care and attention many cruise lines seem to have forgotten about.

ACCOMMODATION. There are four types: Superior Suite, Junior Suite, Standard outside-view and interior cabins, in 20 price categories (12 for double occupancy and eight for single occupancy – a wide range). Most of the cabins are small by today's standards, but they are comfortable enough for short cruises. There are no balcony cabins. While most cabins have fixed twin beds that can't be moved together (over

60 cabins do have a double bed), there are also many cabins for single occupancy. The bathrooms have showers but no tubs, and storage space for toiletries is quite limited. All cabins have a refrigerator, TV/DVD player and a pair of binoculars. A range of Molton Brown toiletries is provided for all accommodation grades. Cabins nearest the engine room do suffer from more noise, otherwise the cabins are quiet, although the insulation is actually rather poor.

The largest accommodation is in two Owner's Suites (Rhapsody and Sonata); both have a double bed, lounge area, more closet and drawer space, and larger bathroom.

The 220-volt electricity system uses European-style two-pin round sockets, so UK passengers will need to bring converters.

CUISINE. The charming dining room has large, ocean-view picture windows and dark wood accents. There are tables for four, six, and dining is open seating. Regional specialties are served, plus an international cuisine that includes many traditional British favorites. The chef often goes ashore in ports of call to buy fresh fish and produce.

Casual breakfasts, lunches and dinners) can be taken in *The Verandah*, a self-serve buffet-style venue with both indoor and outdoor seating areas; a self-help beverage station is open 24 hours a day. A good variety of well prepared and presented items is the norm. There's also an extensive 24-hour room service menu.

ENTERTAINMENT. The Sirocco Lounge is a single-level venue designed for cabaret performances, but used mainly for concerts, destination and specialist subject lectures and guest speakers, and other social gatherings. The Yacht Club Lounge/Bar is the evening/late-night gathering place for pub-style entertainment and passenger participation events.

SPA/FITNESS. Spa Aquarius is an indoor health spa, including a shallow swimming pool, small fitness area, massage room, sauna and relaxation room – deep inside the ship on a lower deck with no elevator access. A beauty salon is in a separate location, adjacent to the Library. Some fitness classes are free, while others, such as Pilates and yoga, cost extra.

STEERING

Two different methods can be used to steer a ship: **Electrohydraulic steering** uses automatic (telemotor-type) transmission from the wheel itself to the steering gear aft. This is generally used when traffic is heavy, during maneuvers into and out of ports, or when there is poor visibility. **Automatic steering** (gyropilot) is used only in the open sea. This system does not require anyone at the wheel because it is controlled by computer. However, aboard all ships, a quartermaster is always at the wheel, for extra safety, and just in case a need should arise to switch from one steering system to another.

Satellite Navigator
Using this latest high-tech piece of equipment, ship's officers can read, on a small television

screen, the ship's position in the open ocean anywhere in the world, any time, and in any weather with pinpoint accuracy.

Satellite navigation systems use the information transmitted by a constellation of orbiting satellites. Each is in a normal circular polar orbit at an altitude of 450 to 700 nautical miles, and orbits the Earth in about 108 minutes.

Data from each gives the current orbital position every two minutes. Apart from telling the ship where it is, it continuously provides the distance from any given point, calculates the drift caused by currents and so on, and tells the ship when the next satellite will pass.

The basis of the satellite navigation is the US Navy Satellite System (NNSS). This first became operational in January

1964 as the precision guidance system for the Polaris submarine fleet and was made available for commercial use in 1967.

The latest (and more accurate) system is the GPS (Global Positioning System), which is now fitted to an increasing number of ships. This uses 24 satellites (18 of which are on-line at any given time) that provide accuracy in estimating a ship's position to plus or minus 6 ft. Another variation is the NACOS (Navigational Command System), which collects information from a variety of sources: satellites, radar, gyroscopic compass, speed log, and surface navigational systems as well as engines, thrusters, rudders, and human input. It then displays relevant computations and information on one screen, controlled by a single keyboard.

Splendour of the Seas
★★★★

Size: . . . . .Large Resort Ship	Total Crew: 720	Cabins (wheelchair accessible): 17
Tonnage: .69,130	Passengers	Wheelchair accessibility: . . . . .Good
Lifestyle: . . . . .Standard	(lower beds/all berths): 1,804/2,064	Cabin Current: . . . . . . .110 and 220 volts
Cruise Line: Royal Caribbean International	Passenger Space Ratio	Elevators: 11
Former Names: . . . . .none	(lower beds/all berths): 38.3/33.4	Casino (gaming tables): . . . . .Yes
Builder: .Chantiers de l'Atlantique (France)	Crew/Passenger Ratio	Slot Machines: . . . . .Yes
Original Cost: . . . .$325 million	(lower beds/all berths): 2.5/2.8	Swimming Pools (outdoors): 2
Entered Service: . . . . .Mar 1996	Cabins (total): .902	(1 with sliding roof)
Registry: . . . . .The Bahamas	Size Range (sq ft/m): 137.7–1,147.4/	Swimming Pools (indoors): 0
Length (ft/m): 867.0/264.2	12.8–106.6	Whirlpools: 4
Beam (ft/m): 105.0/32.0	Cabins (outside view): 575	Self-Service Launderette: . . . . .No
Draft (ft/m): 24.5/7.3	Cabins (interior/no view): 327	Dedicated Cinema/Seats: . . . . .No
Propulsion/Propellers: diesel(40,200kW)/2	Cabins (for one person): 0	Library: . . . . .Yes
Passenger Decks: 11	Cabins (with private balcony): 231	Onboard currency: . . . . .US$

A large, lively ship for family-friendly cruising.

OVERVIEW. Realizing that small cabins don't please passengers, Royal Caribbean International set about designing a ship with much larger standard cabins than in any of its previous vessels except for sister ship *Legend of the Seas*. The interior decor is very colorful, but a little too glitzy for European tastes.

THE SHIP. *Splendour of the Seas* has a contemporary profile that looks somewhat unbalanced – although it grows on you – and does have a nicely tiered stern. The pool deck amidships overhangs the hull to provide an extremely wide deck, while still allowing the ship to navigate the Panama Canal. With engines placed amidships, there is little noise and no noticeable vibration, and the ship has an operating speed of up to 24 knots.

The outside light is brought inside in many places, with more than 2 acres/8,000 sq. meters of glass that provides contact with sea and air. There's an innovative single-level sliding glass roof (not a magrodome) over the more formal setting of one of two swimming pools, providing a large, multi-activity, all-weather indoor/outdoor area, called the Solarium. The glass roof provides shelter for the Roman-style pool and the superb health and fitness facilities and slides aft to cover the miniature golf course when required – though both can't be covered at the same time.

For golfers, there's an 18-hole, 6,000 sq.-ft (557 sq.-meter) miniature course with the topography of a real golf course, complete with trees, foliage, grass, bridges, water hazards, and lighting for play at night. The holes are 155–230 sq. ft. (14–21 sq. meters).

Inside, two full entertainment decks are sandwiched

BERLITZ'S RATINGS		
	Possible	Achieved
Ship	500	401
Accommodation	200	153
Food	400	227
Service	400	274
Entertainment	100	76
Cruise	400	284

OVERALL SCORE
1,415 points out of 2,000

between five decks full of cabins. The tiered and balconied showlounge, which covers two decks, is expansive and has excellent sightlines and very comfortable seats. Large-scale production shows are presented here, and the orchestra pit can be raised or lowered as required.

A multi-tiered seven-deck-high atrium lobby, complete with a huge stainless steel sculpture, connects with the impressive Viking Crown Lounge via glass-walled elevators. The casino, which has mirrored walls and lights flashing everywhere, is really expansive, overly glitzy and absolutely packed. The library, outside of which is a bust of Shakespeare, is a fine facility with more than 2,000 books.

As with any large ship, you can expect to find yourself standing in lines for embarkation, disembarkation, buffets and shore excursions, although the company does its best to minimize such lines.

ACCOMMODATION. There are 17 cabin price grades, which is far too many. All cabins have a sitting area and beds that convert to double configuration, and there is ample closet and drawer space, although there is not much space around the bed. Also, the showers could have been better designed.

Cabins with balconies have glass railings rather than steel/wood to provide less intrusive sightlines.

The largest accommodation, the Royal Suite, is a superb living space for those who can afford the best. It is beautifully designed, finely decorated, and has a baby grand piano and whirlpool bathtub. Quiet sitting areas are located adjacent to the best cabins amidships. There are no cabins for singles.

Some cabins on Deck 8 have a larger door for wheelchair access in addition to the 17 cabins for the disabled, and the ship is very accessible, with ample ramped areas and sloping decks.

CUISINE. The two-deck-high *King and I* dining room has dramatic two-deck-high glass side walls, so many passengers both upstairs and downstairs can see both the ocean and each other in reflection. It would, perhaps, have been even better located at the stern, and it is quite noisy when full – call it atmosphere. When you book, choose one of two seatings, or "My Time Dining" which allows you to eat when you want during dining room hours.

For casual meals, there are two informal options: a cavernous indoor-outdoor cafe, located towards the bow and above the bridge, and a good-sized snack area.

ENTERTAINMENT. The 42nd Street Theater seats 802 and is a single-level showlounge with tiered seating levels. The sightlines are generally good from almost all seats. Strong cabaret acts are also presented here.

Other cabaret acts are featured in the Top Hat Lounge, and these include late-night adult comedy, as well as live music for dancing. A number of other bars and lounges have live music of differing types.

SPA/FITNESS. The ShipShape Fitness Center has a gymnasium, located on the port side of the ship, aft of the funnel, with a small selection of high-tech muscle-pumping equipment. There is also an aerobics studio that runs classes in a variety of keep-fit regimes, a beauty salon, and a sauna, as well as rooms for such pampering treatments as massages, facials, etc.

While the facilities are quite small when compared with those aboard the company's newer ships, they are adequate for the short cruises this ship operates. The spa is operated by Steiner, a specialist concession.

For the more sporting, there is activity galore – including a rock-climbing wall, with several separate climbing tracks. It is outdoors at the aft end of the funnel.

● **For more extensive general information about the Royal Caribbean cruise experience, see pages 152–6.**

A PASSENGER'S PRAYER

"Heavenly Father, look down on us, Your humble, obedient passengers who are doomed to travel the seas and waterways of this earth, taking photographs, mailing postcards, buying useless souvenirs, and walking around in ill-fitting swimwear.

"We beseech You, oh Lord, to see that our plane is not hijacked, our luggage is not lost, and that our oversized carry-ons go unnoticed.

"Protect us from surly and unscrupulous taxi drivers, avaricious porters, and unlicensed, English-speaking guides in foreign places.

"Give us this day Divine guidance in the selection of our cruise ships and our travel agents — so that we may find our bookings and dining room reservations honored, our cabins of generous proportions, that our luggage arrives before the first evening meal, and that our beds are made up.

"We humbly ask that our shower curtains and personal safes do not provoke us into meaningless frustration and destructive thoughts.

"We pray for art auction-free cruise ships, duty-free-free zones, and mobile phone-free restaurants and open decks.

"We pray that our cabin telephones work, the operator (human or electrical) speaks our tongue, and that there are no phone calls from our children forcing us to abandon our cruise early.

"Lead us, dear Lord, to good, affordable restaurants in the world ashore, where the food is superb, the waiters friendly, and the wine included in the price of a meal.

"Please grant us a cruise director who does not "cream" excessively from the spoils of bingo or horse racing, or does not stress only those jewelry stores from which he accepts an offering.

"Grant us the strength to take shore excursions – to visit the museums, cathedrals, spice stalls, and gift shops listed in Berlitz Pocket Guides.

"And if on our return journey by non-air-conditioned buses we slip into slumber, have mercy on us for our flesh is weak, hot, and tired.

"Give us the wisdom to tip correctly at the end of our voyage. Forgive us for under-tipping out of ignorance, and over-tipping out of fear. Please make the chief purser and ship's staff loves us for what we are and not for what we can contribute to their worldly goods or company comment forms.

"Dear God, keep our wives from shopping sprees and protect them from bargains they do not need or cannot afford. Lead them not into temptation in St. Thomas or Hong Kong for they know not what they do.

"Almighty Father, keep our husbands from looking at foreign women and comparing them to us. Save them from making fools of themselves in cafés and nightclubs. Above all, please do not forgive them their trespasses for they know exactly what they do.

"And when our voyage is over and we return home to our loved ones, grant us the favor of finding someone who will look at our home videos and listen to our stories, so our lives as tourists will not have been in vain. This we ask you in the name of our chosen cruise line, and in the name of American Express, Visa, MasterCard, and our banks. Amen."

Star Clipper
★★★★

Size: . . . . .Boutique Ship	Sail Area (sq. ft/sq.m): 36,221/3,365/	Cabins (outside view): 79
Tonnage: .2,298	16 manually furled sails	Cabins (interior/no view): 6
Lifestyle: . . . . .Standard	Main Propulsion: . . . . .sail power	Cabins (for one person): 0
Cruise Line: . . . . .Star Clippers	Propulsion/Propellers: . . . . .diesel	Cabins (with private balcony): 0
Former Names: . . . . .none	(1,030kW)/1	Cabins (wheelchair accessible): 0
Builder: . . . . .Scheepswerven van	Passenger Decks: 4	Wheelchair accessibility: . . . . .None
Langerbrugge (Belgium)	Total Crew: 72	Cabin Current: . . . . .110 volts
Original Cost: . . . .$30 million	Passengers	Elevators: 0
Entered Service: . . . . .May 1992	(lower beds/all berths): 170/182	Casino (gaming tables): . . . . .No
Registry: . . . . .Luxembourg	Passenger Space Ratio	Slot Machines: .No
Length (ft/m): 378.9/115.5	(lower beds/all berths): 13.5/12.6	Swimming Pools (outdoors): 2
Beam (ft/m): 49.2/15.0	Crew/Passenger Ratio	Whirlpools: 0
Draft (ft/m): 17.7/5.6	(lower beds/all berths): 2.3/2.5	Self-Service Launderette: . . . . .No
Type of Vessel: . . . . .barkentine schooner	Cabins (total): .85	Library: . . . . .Yes
Number of Masts: . . . . .4 (208 ft)	Size Range (sq ft/m): .95.0–225.0/8.8–21.0	Onboard currency: . . . . .Euros

> **A real tall ship experience to put wind in your sails.**

OVERVIEW: This ship suits couples and singles who would probably never even consider a "normal" cruise ship, but who enjoy sailing and the thrill of ocean and wind, with everything packaged to include accommodation, decent food, like-minded companions, interesting destinations, and an almost unstructured lifestyle. Some amenities found aboard large cruise vessels are provided, such as air conditioning, cashless cruising, occasional live music, a small shop, and two pools to "dip" in.

BERLITZ'S RATINGS		
	Possible	Achieved
Ship	500	382
Accommodation	200	134
Food	400	249
Service	400	271
Entertainment	n/a	n/a
Cruise	500	366
OVERALL SCORE		
1,402 points out of 2,000		

THE SHIP. *Star Clipper* is one of a pair of almost identical tall ships – its sister ship is *Star Flyer*, which was the first clipper sailing ship to be built for 140 years and became the first commercial sailing vessel to cross the North Atlantic in 90 years. It is, first and foremost a sailing vessel with cruise accommodation that evokes memories of the 19th-century clipper sailing ships. This is an accurate four-mast, barkentine-rigged vessel with graceful lines, a finely shaped hull and masts that are 206 ft (63 meters) tall.

Breathtaking when under full sail, the ship displays excellent sea manners – heeling is kept to a very comfortable 6%. This working sailing ship relies on the wind about 80% of the time. During a typical cruise, you'll be able to climb the main mast to a platform 75 ft (25 meters) above the sea and help with the ropes and sails at appropriate times – this could be an unnerving experience if you're not used to heights, but it is exhilarating when the ship is moving under sail. One really neat chill-out pleasure is to lie in the netting at the front of the ship's bows, watching the bow wake as it streams along the ship's sides.

Engine room visits are offered. A diesel engine is used as the main propulsion engine when the ship is not under sail (in poor wind conditions), and two generators supply electrical power and help desalinate 40 or so tons of seawater each day for shipboard needs. The crew performs almost every task, including hoisting, trimming, winching and repairing the sails, helped by electric winches. Water sports facilities include a water ski boat, sunfish, scuba and snorkel equipment, and eight Zodiac inflatables. Sports directors provide basic dive instruction for a fee.

Inside the vessel, classic Edwardian nautical decor throughout is clean, warm, intimate, and inviting. The paneled library has a fireplace and comfortable chairs. There are no lines and no hassle. "Sailing a Square Rigger" and other nautical classes are a part of every cruise, as is stargazing at night.

Depending on the itinerary and region, passengers may gather for "captain's story time," normally held on an open deck area adjacent to the bridge, or bar – which, incidentally, has a collection of single malt whiskies. The captain may explain sailing maneuvers when changing the rigging or directing the ship as it sails into port, and notes the important events of the day.

The vessel promotes total informality and provides a carefree sailing experience in a totally unstructured and relaxed setting at a reasonable price. Take minimal clothing: short-sleeved shirts and shorts for men, shorts and tops for women are the order of the day (smart casual at night). No jackets, ties, high-heeled shoes, cocktail dresses, or formal wear are needed. Take flat shoes because there are lots of ropes and sailing rig to negotiate on deck, not to mention the high thresholds to climb over and steps to negotiate – this is, after all a tall ship, not a cruise ship. The deck crew consists of real sailors, brought up with yachts and tall ships – most wouldn't set foot aboard a "normal" cruise ship.

The steps of the internal stairways are short and steep, as in all sailing vessels, and so this ship cannot be recommended for anyone with walking disabilities. Also, there is no doctor on board, although there is a nurse.

For yachting enthusiasts, sailing aboard either *Star Clipper* or *Star Flyer* is like finding themselves in heaven, as there is plenty of sailing during a typical one-week cruise. The whole experience evokes the feeling of sailing aboard some famous private yacht, and even the most jaded passenger should enjoy the feel of the wind and sea close at hand. Just don't expect fine food to go with what is decidedly a fine sailing experience – which is what Star Clipper is all about. Note that 12.5% is added to all beverage purchases.

For the nautically-minded, the sailing rig consists of 16 sails. These include: fore staysail, inner jib, outer jib, flying jib, fore course, lower topsail, upper topsail, lower topgallant, upper topgallant, main staysail, upper main staysail, mizzen staysail, main fisherman, jigger staysail, mizzen fisherman, and spanker. The square sails are furled electronically by custom-made winches.

ACCOMMODATION. There are six cabin price grades plus one owner's suite. Generally, the higher the deck, the more expensive a cabin. The cabins are quite well equipped and comfortable; they have rosewood-trimmed cabinetry and wall-to-wall carpeting, two-channel audio, color TV and DVD player, personal safe and full-length mirrors. The bathrooms are very compact but practical units, and have gray marble tiling, glazed rosewood toiletries cabinet and paneling, some under-shelf storage space, washbasin, shower stall and toilet. There is no "lip" to prevent water from the shower from moving onto the bathroom floor.

Individual European 100% individual cotton duvets are provided. There is no cabin food or beverage service.

The deluxe cabins (called "deck cabins") are larger, and additional features include a full-size Jacuzzi tub or corner tub, flat-screen television and DVD player, and minibar/refrigerator. However, these cabins are subject to noise pollution from the same-deck Tropical Bar's music at night (typically until midnight), from the electric winches during sail maneuvers, and from noisy walkabout exercisers in the early morning.

The cabins in the lowest price grade are interior cabins with upper and lower berths, and not two lower beds – so someone will need to be agile to climb a ladder to the upper berth. A handful of cabins have a third, upper Pullman-style berth – good for families with children, but closet and drawer space will be at a premium with three persons in a cabin, so take only the minimal amount of clothing. Luggage can be stored under the bed, where extra large drawers are also provided.

CUISINE. The dining room is quite attractive, and has lots of wood and brass accenting and nautical decor. There are self-serve buffet breakfasts and lunches, together with a mix of buffet and à la carte dinners, generally with a choice of three entrées, in an open-seating environment.

The seating, mostly at tables of six, adjacent to a porthole or inboard, makes it difficult for waiters to serve properly – food is passed along the tables that occupy a porthole position. However, you can dine with whomever you wish, and this is supposed to be a casual experience, after all.

While cuisine aboard the Star Clippers ships is perhaps less than the advertised "gourmet" excellence as far as presentation and choice are concerned, it is fairly creative – and there's plenty of it. Also, one has to take into account the small galley – changed to a better layout in a recent refurbishment. Passenger niggles include repetitious breakfasts and lunchtime salad items, because lack of space prevents more choices. But most passengers are happy with the dinners, which tend to be good, although there is a lack of green vegetables.

Perhaps fewer passenger cabins and more room in the galley would have enabled the chefs to provide a better dining experience than the present arrangement. There is a good choice of bread rolls, pastry items, and fruit.

Tea and coffee is available 24 hours a day in the lounge – mugs, tea cups and saucers are provided. There is no cabin food service. Drinks prices include a service charge, currently 12.5%.

ENTERTAINMENT. There are no shows as such, except for an occasional local folklore show from ashore, nor are any expected by passengers aboard a tall ship such as this. Live music is typically provided by a solo lounge pianist/singer. Otherwise, dinner is the main evening event, as well as "captain's story-time" recapping the day's events, and conversation with fellow passengers.

During the day, when the ship is sailing, passengers can learn about the sails and their repair, and the captain or chief officer will give briefings as the sails are being furled and unfurled. The closest this tall ship comes to any kind of "show" is perhaps on provided by members of the crew, plus a few traditional sea shanties.

SPA/FITNESS. There are no fitness facilities, or beauty salon, although a masseuse provides Oriental massage. For recreation, the ship does have a water sports program. Facilities include kayaks, a water ski boat, sunfish, scuba and snorkel equipment, and eight Zodiac inflatable craft. The use of scuba facilities costs extra.

Star Flyer
★★★★

Size:	.Boutique Ship	Sail Area (sq. ft/sq.m):	....36,221/3,365/	Cabins (outside view):	.79
Tonnage:	.2,298		16 manually furled sails	Cabins (interior/no view):	.6
Lifestyle:	.Standard	Main Propulsion:	.sail power	Cabins (for one person):	.0
Cruise Line:	.Star Clippers	Propulsion/Propellers:	.diesel	Cabins (with private balcony):	.0
Former Names:	.none		(1,030kW)/1	Cabins (wheelchair accessible):	.0
Builder:	.Sheepswerven van	Passenger Decks:	.4	Wheelchair accessibility:	.None
	Langerbrugge (Belgium)	Total Crew:	.72	Cabin Current:	.110 volts
Original Cost:	.$25 million	Passengers		Elevators:	.0
Entered Service:	.July 1991	(lower beds/all berths):	.170/182	Casino (gaming tables):	.No
Registry:	.Luxembourg	Passenger Space Ratio		Slot Machines:	.No
Length (ft/m):	.378.9/115.5	(lower beds/all berths):	.13.5/12.6	Swimming Pools (outdoors):	.2
Beam (ft/m):	.49.2/15.0	Crew/Passenger Ratio		Whirlpools:	.0
Draft (ft/m):	.17.7/5.6	(lower beds/all berths):	.2.3/2.5	Self-Service Launderette:	.No
Type of Vessel:	.barkentine schooner	Cabins (total):	.85	Library:	.Yes
No. of Masts:	.4 (208 ft)	Size Range (sq ft/m):	.95.0–225.9/8.8–21.0	Onboard currency:	.Euros

---

This proper sailing ship provides an antidote to cruise ships.

OVERVIEW: The first clipper sailing ship to be built for 140 years, *Star Flyer* became the first commercial sailing vessel to cross the North Atlantic in 90 years. It suits couples and singles who would probably never even consider a "normal" cruise ship, but who enjoy sailing and the thrill of ocean and wind and don't want the bother of owning or chartering their own yacht. The ship sails year-round from Papeete, Tahiti.

THE SHIP. *Star Flyer*, sister to the almost identical *Star Clipper*, is first and foremost a sailing vessel with cruise accommodation that evokes memories of the 19th-century clipper sailing ships. This is an accurate four-mast, barkentine-rigged vessel with graceful lines, a finely shaped hull and masts 206 ft (63 meters) tall.

Breathtaking when under full sail, the ship displays excellent sea manners and relies on the wind about 80% of the time. A diesel engine is used as backup in emergencies, for generating electrical power and for desalinating the approximately 40 tons of seawater each day for shipboard needs. The crew performs almost every task – including, with the help of electric winches, hoisting, trimming, winching and repairing the sails.

The whole experience evokes the feeling of sailing aboard a famous private yacht a century ago. Tips are pooled (the suggested amount is $8 per passenger, per day) and 12.5% is added to all beverage purchases.

For details of facilities, ambience and activities aboard, see the preceding entry for *Star Clipper*

BERLITZ'S RATINGS

	Possible	Achieved
Ship	500	382
Accommodation	200	134
Food	400	249
Service	400	271
Entertainment	n/a	n/a
Cruise	500	366

OVERALL SCORE
1,402 points out of 2,000

ACCOMMODATION. There are six cabin price grades plus one owner's suite. Generally, the higher the deck, the more expensive your cabin will be. For full details of the facilities, see the entry for *Star Clipper* on page 616.

CUISINE. The dining room is quite attractive, with lots of wood and brass accenting and nautical decor. For details of menus, seating arrangements and gratuities, see the entry for *Star Clipper*.

ENTERTAINMENT. There are no entertainment shows, nor are any expected since sailing is the main purpose of a cruise aboard *Star Flyer*. Live music, which is provided by a single lounge pianist/singer. Otherwise, dinner is the main evening event, as well as talks by the captain. Conversation with fellow passengers in the lounge or on deck under the stars provides engaging entertainment.

During the daytime, when the ship is sailing, passengers can learn about the sails, and the captain or chief officer will give briefings as the sails are being furled and unfurled. The closest this tall ship comes to any kind of "show" is when, one evening towards the end of each cruise, the crew presents a nautical performance of sea songs, sea shanties, and other light diversions.

SPA/FITNESS. Water sports facilities include a water ski boat, sunfish, scuba and snorkel equipment, and eight Zodiac inflatable craft. Water sports directors provide basic dive instruction, for a fee.

Star Princess
★★★★

Size: ....Large Resort Ship	Total Crew: 1,200	Cabins (wheelchair accessible): 28
Tonnage: 108,977	Passengers	(18 outside/10 interior)
Lifestyle: ....Standard	(lower beds/all berths): 2,602/3,102	Wheelchair accessibility: ....Best
Cruise Line: ....Princess Cruises	Passenger Space Ratio	Cabin Current: ....110 volts
Former Names: ....none	(lower beds/all berths):........41.8/35.1	Elevators: 14
Builder: ....Fincantieri (Italy)	Crew/Passenger Ratio	Casino (gaming tables): ....Yes
Original Cost: ....$460 million	(lower beds/all berths): 2.3/2.8	Slot Machines: ....Yes
Entered Service: ....Feb 2002	Cabins (total): 1,301	Swimming Pools (outdoors): 4
Registry: ....Bermuda	Size Range (sq ft/m): 161.4–1,314.0/	Swimming Pools (indoors): 0
Length (ft/m): 951.4/290.0	15.0–122.0	Whirlpools: 9
Beam (ft/m): 118.1/36.0	Cabins (outside view): 935	Self-Service Launderette: ....Yes
Draft (ft/m): 26.2/8.0	Cabins (interior/no view): 366	Dedicated Cinema/Seats: ....No
Propulsion/Propellers: .....diesel-electric	Cabins (for one person): 0	Library: ....Yes
(42,000kW)/2	Cabins (with private balcony): 711	Onboard currency: ....US$
Passenger Decks: 13		

A large resort ship cruising for the whole family.

OVERVIEW. *Star Princess* is quite a ship – a stunning, grand resort playground – but whether it provides a genuinely relaxing holiday is a moot point. With so many choices and "small" rooms to enjoy, however, it has been extremely well designed and is competitively priced. The odds are that you'll have a fine time, in a controlled, well-packaged way. The ship is full of revenue centers, designed to help you part with more money.

THE SHIP. The design for this large cruise ship, whose sister ships are *Golden Princess* and *Grand Princess* (and slightly larger half-sister *Caribbean Princess)*, presents a bold, forthright profile, with a racy "spoiler" effect at its galleon-like transom stern that I don't consider handsome – the "spoiler" acts as a stern observation lounge by day, and a stunning discotheque by night. With a beam of 118 ft/36 meters, including the navigation bridge wings and with many balcony cabins overhanging the ship's hull, it is too wide – by more than 13 ft/3.9 meters – to transit the Panama Canal.

A few changes – compared with *Golden Princess* and *Grand Princess* – have been incorporated, including a much enlarged and improved children's area (the Fun Zone) at the stern. Also improved is the layout of the Lotus Spa, particularly the placement of the saunas/changing rooms.

There is a good sheltered faux teak promenade deck – it's actually painted steel – which almost wraps around (three times round is equal to one mile) and a walkway which goes right to the ship's enclosed bow. The outdoor pools have various beach-like surroundings. One lap pool

BERLITZ'S RATINGS

	Possible	Achieved
Ship	500	414
Accommodation	200	163
Food	400	252
Service	400	289
Entertainment	100	79
Cruise	400	299

OVERALL SCORE
1,496 points out of 2,000

has a pumped "current" to swim against.

Unlike the outside decks, there is plenty of space inside the ship – but there are also plenty of passengers – and a wide array of public rooms, with many "intimate" (this being a relative word) spaces and places to play. The passenger flow has been well thought-out, and works with little congestion. The decor is attractive, with lots of earth tones, well suited to both American and European tastes.

Four areas center on swimming pools, one of which is two decks high and is covered by a glass dome, itself an extension of the funnel housing.

An extensive collection of art works complements the interior design and colors well. If you see something you like, you can buy it on board – it's almost all for sale.

Like its sister ships, *Star Princess* has a Wedding Chapel; a live web-cam can relay ceremonies via the internet. The ship's captain can legally marry American couples, thanks to the ship's Bermuda registry and a special dispensation – which should be verified when in the planning stage, according to where you reside. There are three wedding packages – Pearl, Emerald, Diamond. The fee includes registration and official marriage certificate. The "Hearts & Minds" chapel is also useful for "renewal of vows" ceremonies.

The Grand Casino has more than 260 slot machines; there are blackjack, craps and roulette tables, plus other games. But the highlight could well be the specially linked slot machines that provide a combined payout.

Other facilities include a decent library/computer room, and a separate card room. Ship lovers should enjoy the wood-paneled Wheelhouse Bar, finely decorated with memorabilia and ship models tracing part of the history of sister company P&O; this ship highlights the 1950-built cargo ship *Ganges*. A sports bar, Shooters, has two billiard tables, as well as eight television screens.

A high-tech hospital has a live SeaMed tele-medicine link-up to the Cedars-Sinai Medical Center in Los Angeles, with specialists available for emergency help.

The dress code has been simplified to formal or smart casual, the latter interpreted by many as jeans and trainers. Gratuities are added to your account, at $10 per person, per day for both adults and children. To have these charges adjusted, you'll need to line up at the reception desk.

Passenger niggles? The cabin bath towels are small, and drawer space is very limited. There are no butlers – even for top-grade suites. Cabin attendants have too many cabins to look after – typically 20 – which doesn't translate to fine personal service. The automated telephone system is frustrating, and luggage delivery is inefficient.

FAMILIES. For children, there is a two-deck-high playroom, teen room, and a host of specially trained counselors. Children have their own pools, hot tubs, and open deck area at the stern, thankfully away from adult areas. There are good netted-in areas; one section has a dip pool, while another has a mini-basketball court.

ACCOMMODATION. There are six principal types of cabins and configurations: (a) grand suite, (b) suite, (c) mini-suite, (d) outside-view double cabins with balcony, (e) outside-view double cabins, and (f) interior double cabins. These come in 35 different price categories. The choice is quite bewildering for both travel agents and passengers. (a) The largest, most lavish suite is the Grand Suite (B748, located at the ship's stern – a different position to the two Grand Suites aboard *Grand Princess*. It has a large bedroom with queen-size bed, huge walk-in closets, two bathrooms, a lounge with fireplace and sofa bed, plus wet bar and refrigerator, and a large private balcony with a hot tub that can be accessed from both balcony and bedroom. (b/c) Suites, with a semi-private balcony, have a separate living room with sofa bed and bedroom, and a TV set in each. The bathroom is quite large and has both a tub and shower stall. The mini-suites also have a private balcony, and a separate living and sleeping area, with a TV set in each. The differences between the suites and mini-suites are basically that the suite is more of a square shape while mini-suites are more rectangular and have few drawers. Both have plush bathrobes, and fully tiled bathrooms with ample open shelf storage space. Suite and mini-suite passengers receive greater attention, including priority embarkation and disembarkation privileges. What is not good is that the most expensive accommodation has only semi-private balconies that can be seen from above and so there is little privacy. (d/e/f). Both interior (no view) and outside-view (with or without private balcony) cabins are of a functional design, although almost no drawers are provided. They are quite

attractive, with warm, pleasing decor and fine soft furnishing fabrics; 80 percent of the outside-view cabins have a private balcony. Interior cabins measure 160 sq. ft (14.4 sq. meters), while the standard outside-view cabins measure 228 sq. ft (21 sq. meters).

The 28 wheelchair-accessible cabins measure 250–385 sq. ft (23.2–35.7 sq. meters). Surprisingly, there is no mirror for dressing, and no full-length hanging space for long dresses – yes, some passengers in wheelchairs do also use mirrors and full-length clothing. Additionally, two family suites consist of two suites with an interconnecting door, plus a large balcony. These can sleep up to 10 if at least four are children or up to eight adults.

All passengers receive turndown service and chocolates on pillows each night, bathrobes on request, and toiletry kits (larger for suite/mini-suite occupants). A hairdryer is provided in all cabins, sensibly located at the vanity desk unit in the living area. All bathrooms have tiled floors, and there is a decent amount of open shelf storage space for toiletries, although the plain beige decor is very basic and unappealing. Princess Cruises typically carries CNN, CNBC, ESPN and TNT, when available, on the in-cabin television system.

Lifeboats obstruct most outside cabins on Emerald Deck. There are no cabins for singles. Your name is placed outside your suite or cabin in a documents holder – making it simple for delivery service personnel but also making it intrusive as far as privacy is concerned. There is 24-hour room service, though some items on the menu are not available during early morning hours.

Some cabins can accommodate a third and fourth person in upper berths. However, in such cabins, the lower beds cannot then be pushed together to make queen-size bed.

Almost all balcony suites and cabins can be overlooked both from the navigation bridge wing, as well as from the port and starboard sections of the ship's discotheque – located high above the ship at the stern. Cabins with balconies on Dolphin, Caribe and Baja decks are also overlooked by passengers on balconies on the deck above. They are, therefore, not at all private. However, perhaps the least desirable balcony cabins are eight balcony cabins located forward on Emerald Deck, as the balconies do not extend to the side of the ship and can be passed by walkers and gawkers on the adjacent Upper Promenade walkway, so occupants need to keep their curtains closed most of the time. Also, passengers in some the most expensive suites with balconies at the stern may experience considerable vibration during certain ship maneuvers.

CUISINE. For formal meals there are three principal dining rooms: *Amalfi*, with 504 seats; *Capri*, with 486 seats; and *Portofino*, with 486 seats. Seating is assigned according to the location of your cabin. There are two seatings in Amalfi, while the other two typically offer "anytime dining" where you choose when and with whom you want to eat. All three are split into multi-tier sections in a non-symmetrical design that breaks the large spaces into smaller sections, for better ambience. Each dining room has its own galley.

While four elevators go to Fiesta Deck where the Amalfi

and Portofino restaurants are located, only two elevators go to Plaza Deck 5 where the Capri Restaurant is located; this can cause long wait problems at peak times, particularly for anyone in a wheelchair.

Specially designed dinnerware and high-quality linens and silverware are used in the main dining rooms; by Dudson of England (dinnerware), Frette Egyptian cotton table linens, and silverware by Hepp of Germany. Note that 15% is added to all beverage bills, including wines.

Alternative Dining Options: There are two extra-charge restaurants: *Sabatini's* and *Tequila's*, both open for lunch and dinner on days at sea. Sabatini's, with colorful tiled Mediterranean-style decor, serves Italian-style pizzas and pastas, with a variety of sauces, plus Italian-style entrées including tiger prawns and lobster tail. All provided with flair and entertainment from by the staff of waiters. Reservations are required.

Tequila's has "southwestern American" food, with a cover charge for lunch or dinner on sea days only. It is spread over the ship's entire width and two walkways intersect it, which means that it's a very open area, with people walking through it as you eat – not a very comfortable arrangement. Reservations are needed.

The cuisine in both of these spots is decidedly better than in the three main dining rooms, with superior ingredients and more attention to presentation and taste.

A poolside hamburger grill and pizza bar (no additional charge) are dining spots for casual bites. But it costs extra to eat at either the coffee bar/patisserie, or the caviar/champagne bar.

Other casual meals can be taken in the *Horizon Court*, open 24 hours a day. It has large ocean-view on port and starboard sides and direct access to the two main swimming pools and lido deck. There is no real finesse in presentation, however, as plastic plates are provided.

ENTERTAINMENT. The Princess Theater is the main entertainment venue; it spans two decks and has comfortable seating on both main and balcony levels. It has $3 million in sound and light equipment, plus a nine-piece orchestra.

The Vista Lounge, a second entertainment lounge, has cabaret acts such as magicians, comedy jugglers, and ventriloquists at night, and lectures, bingo and horse racing during the day. Explorers, a third lounge, can also host cabaret acts and dance bands. Various other lounges and bars have live music, and Princess Cruises has a number of male dance hosts as partners for women traveling alone.

SPA/FITNESS. The Lotus Spa has Japanese-style decor, and surrounds one of the swimming pools. You can have a massage or other spa treatment in an ocean-view treatment room. It is unfortunate, however – perhaps a lack of knowledge on the part of the interior designer – that the Japanese symbol on the door of the steam inhalation rooms means insect, not a prudent thing to call passengers. Some of the massage treatment rooms are located directly underneath the jogging track.

● **For more extensive general information about the Princess Cruises experience, see pages 149–52.**

Statendam
★★★★

Size: . . . . .Mid-Size Ship	Total Crew: 557	Wheelchair accessibility: . . . . .Good
Tonnage: .55,819	Passengers	Cabin Current: . . . . . . .110 and 220 volts
Lifestyle: . . . . .Premium	(lower beds/all berths): 1,266/1,627	Elevators: 8
Cruise Line: . . . . . . .Holland America Line	Passenger Space Ratio	Casino (gaming tables): . . . . .Yes
Former Names: . . . . .none	(lower beds/all berths): 44.0/34.3	Slot Machines: . . . . .Yes
Builder: . . . . .Fincantieri (Italy)	Crew/Passenger Ratio	Swimming Pools (outdoors): 1
Original Cost: . . . .$215 million	(lower beds/all berths): 2.2/2.9	Swimming Pools (indoors): 1
Entered Service: . . . . .Jan 1993	Cabins (total): .633	(sliding glass dome)
Registry: . . . . .The Netherlands	Size Range (sq ft/m): 186.2–1,124.8/	Whirlpools: 2
Length (ft/m): 719.4/219.3	17.3–104.5	Self-Service Launderette: . . . . .Yes
Beam (ft/m): 101.0/30.8	Cabins (outside view): 502	Dedicated Cinema/Seats: Yes/249
Draft (ft/m): 24.6/7.5	Cabins (interior/no view): 131	Library: . . . . .Yes
Propulsion/Propellers: . . . . .diesel-electric	Cabins (for one person): 0	Onboard currency: . . . . .US$
(34,560kW)/2	Cabins (with private balcony): 150	
Passenger Decks: 10	Cabins (wheelchair accessible): 6	

Dutch decor and artifacts for senior-age cruisers.

OVERVIEW. This ship has fairly decent interior fit and finish. Holland America Line constantly fine-tunes its performance as a cruise operator and regular passengers, almost all of whom are North American, find its ships very comfortable and well-run, even though the current food and service let down the rest of the cruise experience. HAL keeps its ships clean and tidy, and there is good passenger flow in public areas.

THE SHIP. *Statendam* was the first of a series of four almost identical ships, the others being *Maasdam*, *Ryndam* and *Veendam*. The exterior styling is rather angular, although it is softened and balanced somewhat by the fact that the hull is painted black. There is a full walk-around teakwood promenade deck outdoors – excellent for strolling, and, thankfully, there's no sign of synthetic turf. The sunloungers on the exterior promenade deck are wood, and come with comfortable cushioned pads, while those at the swimming pool on Lido Deck are of white plastic.

In the interiors of this "S" -class ship, an asymmetrical layout helps to reduce bottlenecks and congestion. Most public rooms are concentrated on two decks, Promenade Deck, and Upper Promenade Deck, which creates a spacious feel to the ship's interiors. A restrained approach to interior styling is taken, using a mixture of contemporary materials combined with traditional woods and ceramics. There is little "glitz" anywhere.

What is outstanding is the array of artworks, costing about $2 million, assembled and nicely displayed to represent the fine Dutch heritage of Holland America Line. Also noticeable are the fine flower arrangements in public areas.

BERLITZ'S RATINGS

	Possible	Achieved
Ship	500	372
Accommodation	200	150
Food	400	247
Service	400	280
Entertainment	100	72
Cruise	400	282

OVERALL SCORE
1,403 points out of 2,000

Atop the ship, with forward-facing views that wrap around the sides, is the Crow's Nest Lounge. By day it's a fine observation lounge with large ocean-view windows, while by night it turns into a nightclub with extremely variable lighting. The atrium foyer is three decks high, although its sculptured center-piece – *Fountain of the Sirens*, a late 17th-century bronze piece by Willem de Groat – makes it look a little crowded, and leaves little room in front of the Front Office. A hydraulic glass roof covers the reasonably sized swimming pool and whirlpools and central Lido area, whose focal point is a large dolphin sculpture, so that this can be used in fine or poor weather.

The ship has a large, relaxing library. There's also a room for card games, an Explorer's Lounge (good for relaxing in, for afternoon tea, and after-dinner coffees), an intimate Piano Bar, and, of course, a casino.

As part of HAL's "Signature of Excellence" program, the ships have received a new "Mix" lifestyle area. The trendy, upbeat space combines three specialty theme bars: Champagne (serving champagne and sparkling wines), Martinis (in individual shakers), and Spirits & Ales (a sports bar – beer and baseball/ basketball). Microsoft Surface touch-screen technology is available for playing checkers and chess, air hockey, and other sports games

Statendam is a fairly well-built ship, and has reasonably decent interior fit and finish. HAL is constantly fine-tuning its performance as a cruise operator and its regular passengers find the company's ships very comfortable and well-run. Almost all the regulars are North American – there are few international passengers. The company continues its strong maritime traditions, although the present food and service components let down the rest of the cruise experience. Perhaps the ship's best asset is its friendly and personable Filipino and Indonesian crew, although communication can be frustrating.

An escalator travels between two of the lower decks, one of which was originally planned to be the embarkation point, but it is almost worthless. The charge to use the washing machines and dryers in the self-service launderette is petty, particularly for occupants of expensive suites. The men's urinals in public restrooms are unusually high.

ACCOMMODATION. There are 17 cabin price grades. Cabins range from small interior cabins to a large penthouse suite with ocean views. All cabin televisions carry CNN.

The interior and outside-view standard cabins have twin beds that convert to a queen-size bed, and there is a separate living space with sofa and coffee table. Although the drawer space is generally good, the closet space is very tight, particularly for long cruises – although more than adequate for a seven-night cruise. The tiled bathrooms are compact but practical. Bathrobes are provided for all suites/cabins, as are hairdryers, and a small range of toiletries. The bathrooms are quite well laid out, but the tubs are small units better described as shower tubs.

On Navigation Deck, 28 suites have accommodation for up to four people. These also have in-suite dining as an alternative to the dining room. These are very spacious, tastefully decorated and well laid-out, and have a separate living room, bedroom with two lower beds (convertible to a king-size bed), a good size living area, dressing room, plenty of closet and drawer space, and a marble bathroom with whirlpool tub.

The largest accommodation is a penthouse suite, located on the starboard side of Navigation Deck at the forward staircase. It has a king-size bed, television and video player, and vanity desk. A large walk-in closet has superb drawer space. There is an oversize whirlpool bath that could seat four, a separate shower enclosure, and a separate washroom with toilet, bidet and washbasin. The living room has a writing desk, a large TV set and a full set of audio equipment. The dressing room has a large private balcony with teak lounge chairs and drinks tables, dining table and four chairs. The pantry has a large refrigerator, toaster unit, and full coffee/tea making facilities and food preparation area, and a separate entrance from the hallway.

There's a mini-bar/refrigerator, a guest toilet and floor to ceiling windows. There is no bell push.

Passengers in accommodation designated as suites and mini-suites have the use of a private concierge club called the Neptune Lounge, where light breakfast and snacks throughout the day can be taken.

CUISINE. The *Rotterdam Dining Room* spans two decks at the stern of the ship, and is quite dramatic. It has two grand staircases to connect the two levels, panoramic views on three sides, and a music balcony. Both open seating and fixed (assigned tables and times) seating are available, while breakfast and lunch are open-seating – you'll be seated by restaurant staff when you enter. There are tables for two, four, six and eight, but the waiter stations are very noisy for anyone seated adjacent to them. Fine Rosenthal china and cutlery are used.

Alternative Dining Option: A small restaurant, the 66-seat *Pinnacle Grill*, is located just forward of the balcony level of the main dining room on the starboard side. It has Pacific Northwest cuisine such as Alaska salmon, halibut and other regional specialities, plus a selection of premium steaks. Reservations are necessary, and there's a cover charge. A Bulgari show plate, Rosenthal china, Reidel wine glasses, and Frette table linen are used. The Pinnacle Grill is a better dining experience than the main dining room, and worth it for that special celebration.

For more casual evening eating, the *Lido Buffet* is open for dinners on all except the last night of each cruise, in an open-seating arrangement. Tables are set with crisp linens, flatware and stemware. A set menu includes a choice of four entrées. Breakfasts and lunches are also served here. There is much use of canned fruits and packets of items, although there are several commercial low-calorie salad dressings. The choice of cheeses and accompanying crackers is poor. The beverage station also lets it down, being no better than those in family outlets ashore in the USA. Each night, a section of the venue is transformed into *Canaletto* using glass screens; the cuisine is Italian-flavored, but the Italian wine list is poor. There's no additional charge, although reservations are requested.

Passengers will need to eat in the Lido Buffet on days when the dining room is closed for lunch – typically once or twice per cruise, depending on the itinerary. A poolside grill provides basic hamburgers and hot dogs.

ENTERTAINMENT. The Showlounge at Sea, at the forward part of the ship, spans two decks, with banquette seating on both main and upper levels. It is basically a well-designed room, but the ceiling is low and the sightlines from the balcony level are quite poor.

SPA/FITNESS. The Ocean Spa is one deck below the navigation bridge at the very forward part of the ship. It includes a gymnasium with all the latest muscle-pumping exercise machines, including an abundance of treadmills. It has ocean views, an aerobics exercise area, a large beauty salon, several treatment rooms, and men's and women's sauna, steam room and changing areas.

● **For more extensive general information on what a Holland America Line cruise is like, see pages 140–3.**

Sun Princess
★★★★

Size: ....Large Resort Ship	Passenger Decks: 10	Cabins (with private balcony): 410
Tonnage: 77,499	Total Crew: 900	Cabins (wheelchair accessible): 19
Lifestyle: ....Standard	Passengers	Wheelchair accessibility: ....Good
Cruise Line: ....Princess Cruises	(lower beds/all berths): 1,950/2,250	Cabin Current: ....110 and 220 volts
Former Names: ....none	Passenger Space Ratio	Elevators: 11
Builder: ....Fincantieri (Italy)	(lower beds/all berths): 39.7/34.4	Casino (gaming tables): ....Yes
Original Cost: ....$300 million	Crew/Passenger Ratio	Slot Machines: ....Yes
Entered Service: ....Dec 1995	(lower beds/all berths): 2.0/2.5	Swimming Pools (outdoors): 4
Registry: ....Great Britain	Cabins (total): 975	Swimming Pools (indoors): 0
Length (ft/m): 857.2/261.3	Size Range (sq ft/m): 134.5–753.4/	Whirlpools: 5
Beam (ft/m): 105.6/32.2	12.5–70.0	Self-Service Launderette: ....Yes
Draft (ft/m): 26.5/8.1	Cabins (outside view): 603	Dedicated Cinema/Seats: ....No
Propulsion/Propellers: .....diesel-electric	Cabins (interior/no view): 372	Library: ....Yes
(28,000kW)/2	Cabins (for one person): 0	Onboard currency: ....Australian $

A large, family-friendly ship with modern decor.

OVERVIEW. The ship, while large, absorbs passengers well, and has an almost intimate feel to it. The interiors are very pretty and warm, with attractive colors and welcoming decor that includes some very attractive murals and other artwork. As aboard most large ships today, you will be well attended if you live in the top suites; otherwise, you'll be just one of a very large number of passengers.

THE SHIP. In November 2007, *Sun Princess* moved its permanent base to Australia, operating cruises from Sydney, Melbourne, and Freemantle. The onboard currency became the Australian dollar, the entertainment was geared to Australian tastes, and other aspects of the cruise operation modified accordingly. Note that, for long voyages such as a Grand Circle Pacific cruise, the cabin closet space is extremely small.

Although large, this all-white ship has a good profile, and is well balanced by its large funnel, which contains a deck tennis/basketball/volleyball court in its sheltered aft base. There is a wide, teakwood wrap-around promenade deck outdoors, some real teak steamer-style deck chairs with royal blue cushioned pads, and 93,000 sq. ft (8,600 sq. meters) of space outdoors. An extensive glass area on the upper decks provides plenty of light and connection with the outside world.

The signs around the ship could be improved, however. A wide range of public rooms includes several intimate rooms and spaces so that you don't feel overwhelmed by large spaces. The interior focal point is a huge four-deck-high atrium lobby with winding, double stairways, complete with two panoramic glass-walled elevators.

BERLITZ'S RATINGS		
	Possible	Achieved
Ship	500	415
Accommodation	200	162
Food	400	257
Service	400	278
Entertainment	100	80
Cruise	400	297

OVERALL SCORE
1,489 points out of 2,000

The main entertainment rooms are located under three decks of cabins. There is plenty of space, the traffic flow is good, and the ship absorbs people well. There are two showlounges, one at each end of the ship; one is a superb 550-seat, theater-style showlounge where movies are also shown, and the other is a 480-seat cabaret-style lounge, complete with bar.

The library is a very warm room with ocean-view windows, and has six large buttery leather chairs for listening to audio CDs. There is a conference center for up to 300, as well as a business center, with computers, photocopiers and fax machines. The collection of artwork is good, particularly on the stairways, and helps make the ship feel smaller than it is, although in places it doesn't always seem co-coordinated. The casino, while large, is not really in the main passenger flow and so it doesn't generate the "walk-through" factor found aboard so many ships.

The most traditional room aboard is the Wheelhouse Lounge/Bar, decorated in the style of a late 19th-century gentleman's club, complete with wood paneling and comfortable seating. Its focal point is a large ship model from the P&O archives.

One nice feature is the captain's cocktail party; it is held in the four-deck-high main atrium so you can come and go as you please – and there's no standing in line to have your photograph taken with the captain if you don't want to.

There are a number of dead ends in the interior layout, so it's not as user-friendly as a ship this size should be. The cabin numbering system is extremely illogical, with numbers going through several hundred series on the same deck. The walls of the passenger accommodation decks are very plain (some artwork would be a distinct improvement).

The swimming pools are quite small for so many passengers, and the pool deck is cluttered with white, plastic sun-loungers that don't have cushioned pads.

ACCOMMODATION. There are 28 different cabin grades: 20 outside-view and eight interior. Although the standard outside-view and interior cabins are a little small, they are well designed and functional in layout, and have earth tone colors accentuated by splashes of color from the bedspreads. Proportionately, there are quite a lot of interior cabins. Many of the outside-view cabins have private balconies, and all seem to be quite well soundproofed, although the balcony partition is not floor to ceiling type, so you can hear your neighbors clearly or smell their smoke. The balconies are very narrow, just large enough for two small chairs, and there is balcony light.

A reasonable amount of closet and abundant drawer and other storage space is provided in all cabins – adequate for a seven-night cruise, as are a TV set and refrigerator. Each night a chocolate will appear on your pillow. The cabin bathrooms are practical, and come complete with all the details one needs, although they really are tight spaces, one person at-a-time units. They do have a decent shower enclosure, real glasses, a hairdryer and bathrobe, and a small amount of shelving for toiletries.

The largest accommodation is in six suites, two on each of three decks at the stern, with large private balcony (536–754 sq. ft./49.8–21.3 sq. meters, including balcony). They are well laid-out, and have large bathrooms with two basins, a Jacuzzi tub, and a separate shower enclosure. The bedroom has generous amounts of wood accenting and detailing, TV sets in both bedroom and lounge areas. The suites also have a dining room table and four chairs.

The 32 mini-suites (374–536 sq. ft./34.7–49.7 sq. meters) typically have two lower beds that convert to a queen-size bed. There is a separate bedroom/sleeping area with vanity desk, and a lounge with sofa and coffee table, indented ceilings with generous amounts of wood accenting and detailing, walk-in closet, and larger bathroom with Jacuzzi tub and separate shower enclosure.

There are 19 wheelchair-accessible cabins, which measure 213–305 sq. ft (19.7–28.2 sq. meters.), and are a mix of seven outside-view and 12 interior cabins.

CUISINE. There are two main dining rooms of asymmetrical design: *Marquis* and *Regency*, located adjacent to the two lower levels of the four-deck-high atrium lobby. Each seats around 500, has its own galley, and is split into multi-tier sections that help create a feeling of intimacy, although there is a lot of noise from the waiter stations adjacent to many tables. Breakfast and lunch are provided in an open-seating arrangement, while dinner is in two seatings.

On any given seven-day cruise, a typical menu cycle will include a Sailaway Dinner, Captain's Welcome Dinner, Chef's Dinner, Italian Dinner, French Dinner, Captain's Gala Dinner, and Landfall Dinner. The wine list is reasonable but not good, and the company has, sadly, dispensed with wine waiters. Note that 15% is added to all beverage bills, including wines.

Alternative Dining Option: For some really good meat, however, consider the extra-cost *Sterling Steakhouse*; it's for those who want to taste four different cuts of Angus beef from the popular "Sterling Silver" brand of USDA prime meats – Filet Mignon, New York Strip, Porterhouse, and Rib-Eye, all presented on a silver tray. There is also a barbecue chicken option, plus the usual baked potato or French fries as accompaniments. This is available as an alternative to the dining rooms between 6.30pm and 9.30pm but, instead of being a separate, intimate room as you might expect, it is located in a section of the *Horizon Buffet*, with its own portable bar and some decorative touches to set it apart from the regular Horizon Buffet.

The Horizon Buffet is open 24 hours a day, and, at night, has an informal dinner setting with sit-down waiter service; a small bistro menu is also available. The buffet displays are, for the most part, quite repetitious, but better than they have been in the past few years. There is no real finesse in presentation, however, as plastic plates are provided, instead of trays. The cabin service menu is very limited, and presentation of the food items featured is poor.

There is also a pâtisserie (for cappuccino/espresso coffees and pastries), a wine/caviar bar, and a pizzeria (complete with cobblestone floors and wrought-iron decorative features), and a choice of six excellent pizzas.

ENTERTAINMENT. There are two showlounges, both theater and cabaret style. The main one, the Princess Theater, has a sloping floor, with aisle-style seating that is well-tiered, and with good sightlines to the raised stage from most of the 500 seats.

The Vista Lounge, at the aft end, has cabaret entertainment, and acts as a lecture and presentation room. Princess Cruises has a good stable of regular cabaret acts to draw from, so there should be something for most tastes.

SPA/FITNESS. A glass-walled Lotus Spa complex is located high atop ship and includes a gymnasium with high-tech machines. One swimming pool is "suspended" aft between two decks. There are two other pools, although they are not large for the size of the ship.

Sports facilities are located in an open-air sports deck positioned inside the funnel and adaptable for basketball, volleyball, badminton or paddle tennis. Joggers can exercise on the walk-around open Promenade Deck.

● **For more extensive general information about the Princess Cruises experience, see pages 149–52.**

Superstar Aquarius
★★★

Size: ....Mid-Size Ship	Total Crew: 889	Cabins (wheelchair accessible): ......11)
Tonnage: 50,760	Passengers	Wheelchair accessibility: ....Fair
Lifestyle: ....Standard	(lower beds/all berths): 1,529/1,607	Cabin Current: ....110 volts
Cruise Line: ....Star Cruises	Passenger Space Ratio	Elevators: 10
Former Names: *Norwegian Wind, Windward*	(lower beds/all berths): 33.1/31.5	Casino (gaming tables): ....Yes
Builder: .Chantiers de l'Atlantique (France)	Crew/Passenger Ratio	Slot Machines: ....Yes
Original Cost: ....$240 million	(lower beds/all berths): 1.7/1.8	Swimming Pools (outdoors): 1
Entered Service: ....Jun 1993/May 2007	Cabins (total): 765	Swimming Pools (indoors): 0
Registry: ....The Bahamas	Size Range (sq ft/m): 139.9–349.8/	Whirlpools: 2
Length (ft/m): 754.0/229.8	13.0–32.5	Self-Service Launderette: ....No
Beam (ft/m): 93.5/28.5	Cabins (outside view): 611	Dedicated Cinema/Seats: ....No
Draft (ft/m): 22.3/6.8	Cabins (interior/no view): 154	Library: ....Yes
Propulsion/Propellers: diesel (18,480 kW)/2	Cabins (for one person): 0	Onboard currency: ....Hong Kong $
Passenger Decks: 10	Cabins (with private balcony): 74	

Family-friendly casual cruising that's good for gamblers.

OVERVIEW. This ship was transferred from Norwegian Cruise Line to the Star Cruises fleet in 2007 to operate overnight and short cruises from Hong Kong. The dress code is strictly casual. Some lounges were converted into a large Star Club, for casino gamers. Several cabins are specially equipped for the hearing-impaired. All gratuities for staff are included.

THE SHIP. The exterior design emphasizes a clever and extensive use of large windows that help create a sense of open spaces, but the interior design has many smaller public rooms. There is no big atrium lobby, as one might expect, and the ceiling height is low.

Public rooms include several bars and lounges, including Skyline Karaoke, which occupies five private karaoke rooms. There's a mahjong/card room, childcare center, video arcade, Genting Club for invited gaming guests, three small business meeting rooms, an internet-connect center/library, cigar lounge, and a small boutique. There is a blue rubber-covered walk-around promenade deck outdoors.

Outdoor stairways are numerous and confusing, while the carpeted steel interior stairwell steps are tinny. Standing in line for embarkation, disembarkation, and for buffet meals is inevitable aspect when cruising aboard large ships.

ACCOMMODATION. There are 16 cabin price grades. Most cabins have outside views and wood-trimmed cabinetry and warm decor with multi-colored soft furnishings, but there is almost no drawer space (although the closets have open shelves), so take minimal clothing. All cabins have a

BERLITZ'S RATINGS		
	Possible	Achieved
Ship	500	331
Accommodation	200	124
Food	400	216
Service	400	249
Entertainment	100	64
Cruise	400	248
OVERALL SCORE		
1,232 points out of 2,000		

sitting area. The bathrooms are small but practical, but there is little space for storage of toiletries.

There are 18 suites (12 with a private entrance and a small, private balcony), each with separate living room and bedroom, and plenty of closet and drawer space. Occupants of suites receive "concierge" service. In addition, 16 suites and 70 cabins have interconnecting doors.

CUISINE. Freestyle Dining venues include the 280-seat *Dynasty Restaurant*, for Chinese family-style food. The largest sit-down dining spot, it has some prime tables at ocean-view window seats in a section that extends from the ship's port and starboard sides in half-moon shapes.

There's also *Spices Restaurant*, an Asian specialty buffet venue with 180 seats; *Oceana Barbeque*, an outdoor buffet venue; *Blue Lagoon*, a 24-hour bistro, with 80 seats; and *Mariner's Buffet*, an international self-service buffet.

ENTERTAINMENT. The 700-seat Stardust Lounge, almost in the center of the ship, is two decks high, but the banquette and individual tub chair seating is only on the main level. There is no live showband, only recorded music. High-volume razzle-dazzle shows are presented to a pre-recorded track, as well as special individual cabaret acts.

SPA/FITNESS. A gymnasium has high-tech muscle-toning equipment, reflexology lounge, and Oscar Hair and Beauty Salon. There's a ping pong table, basketball/volleyball court, golf driving range, and a jogging track.

SuperStar Libra
★★★

Size:	Mid-Size Ship	Passenger Decks: 9	Cabins (with private balcony): 0

Size: .... Mid-Size Ship	Passenger Decks: 9	Cabins (with private balcony): 0
Tonnage: 42,276	Total Crew: 700	Cabins (wheelchair accessible): 4
Lifestyle: ....Standard	Passengers	Wheelchair accessibility: ....Fair
Cruise Line: ....Star Cruises	(lower beds/all berths): 1,472/1,800	Cabin Current: ....110 volts
Former Names: ...Norwegian Sea, Seaward	Passenger Space Ratio	Elevators: 6
Builder: ....Wartsila (Finland)	(lower beds/all berths): 28.0/23.5	Casino (gaming tables): ....Yes
Original Cost: ....$120 million	Crew/Passenger Ratio	Slot Machines: ....Yes
Entered Service: ....Jun 1988/Oct 2005	(lower beds/all berths): 2.1/2.5	Swimming Pools (outdoors): 2
Registry: ....The Bahamas	Cabins (total): 732	Swimming Pools (indoors): 0
Length (ft/m): 708.6/216.0	Size Range (sq ft/m): 109.7–269.1/	Whirlpools: 2
Beam (ft/m): 95.1/29.0	10.2–25.0	Self-Service Launderette: ....No
Draft (ft/m): 22.9/7.0	Cabins (outside view): 501	Dedicated Cinema/Seats: ....No
Propulsion/Propellers: ....diesel	Cabins (interior/no view): 231	Library: ....No
(21,120 kW)/2	Cabins (for one person): 0	Onboard currency: ....Hong Kong $

A casual, family-friendly Asian ship for gambling.

OVERVIEW. This ship, now based at Penang in Malaysia, is suited for couples and solo travellers seeking a short cruise experience in surroundings tailored specifically for them. It was built before balcony cabins came into vogue – so there aren't any.

THE SHIP. This is an angular yet reasonably attractive ship that has a contemporary European cruise-ferry profile with a sharply raked bow and sleek mast and funnel added. It is quite well designed, with generally sound passenger flow. The interior decor, stressing corals, blues and mauves, reminds you of sea and sky.

The lobby, two decks high, is pleasing without being overwhelming. There is a decent selection of public rooms, bars and lounges, including an inviting wood-paneled Admiral's Lounge, a Star Club casino, a discotheque (Boomer's), and The Bollywood karaoke lounge. Gratuities are included in the cruise fare.

The open decks are cluttered, and badly dented and scuffed panels in the accommodation hallways are unattractive. The steps on the stairways are quite tinny. The constant background music in the hallways is irritating. There is too much use of synthetic turf on the upper outdoors decks – this gets soggy when wet.

ACCOMMODATION. There are 16 suite/cabin price categories. The cabins are of average size – meaning "a bit cramped for two" – although they are tastefully appointed and comfortable, with warm, pastel colors, bright soft furnishings and a touch of art deco styling. However, the walls and ceilings are plain and simple. Audio channels are avail-

BERLITZ'S RATINGS

	Possible	Achieved
Ship	500	324
Accommodation	200	123
Food	400	238
Service	400	250
Entertainment	100	61
Cruise	400	250

OVERALL SCORE
1,246 points out of 2,000

able via the TV set, although the picture cannot be turned off. The bathrooms are efficient units that are well designed but basic; weakly-powered hairdryers are included.

If you book a suite or one of two upper-grade cabins, you'll get a little more space, a lounge area with table and sofa that converts into another bed – good for families – European duvets, and a refrigerator (top categories only). The bathrooms also have a tub, shower and retractable clothesline.

CUISINE. There are no assigned dining rooms, tables or seats, but some eateries cost extra. All restaurants and eateries are non-smoking. They include: *Four Seasons Restaurant*, the principal dining room, serving Continental Cuisine; *The Saffron* (Indian vegetarian and Jain buffet, located aft with fine ocean views); *Two Trees Restaurant* (exclusive lounge/restaurant); *Taj by the Bay* (Indian family-style restaurant, with aft-facing ocean views); *Blue Lagoon* for 24-hour casual refreshments; and *Coconut Willy's*, a poolside refreshment center.

ENTERTAINMENT. The 770-seat Stardust Lounge is the venue for shows and major cabaret acts, although 12 thick pillars obstruct many sightlines. The Galaxy of the Stars Lounge, located aft, is for cabaret acts. A number of bands and solo entertaining musicians provide live music for listening and dancing in several lounges and bars.

SPA/FITNESS. There's a good gymnasium/fitness center, located around the mast and accessible only from the outside deck – not good when it rains.

SuperStar Virgo
★★★★

Size: . . . . .Large Resort Ship	Total Crew: 1,225	Cabins (wheelchair accessible): 4
Tonnage: 75,338	Passengers	Wheelchair accessibility: . . . . .Good
Lifestyle: . . . . .Standard	(lower beds/all berths): 1,804/2,800	Cabin Current: . . . . .240 volts
Cruise Line: . . . . .Star Cruises	Passenger Space Ratio	Elevators: 9
Former Names: . . . . .none	(lower beds/all berths): 41.7/26.9	Casino (gaming tables): . . . . .Yes
Builder: . . . . .Meyer Werft (Germany)	Crew/Passenger Ratio	Slot Machines: . . . . .Yes
Original Cost: . . . .$350 million	(lower beds/all berths): 1.4/2.2	Swimming Pools (outdoors): 2
Entered Service: . . . . .Aug 1999	Cabins (total): 902	Swimming Pools (indoors): 0
Registry: . . . . .Panama	Size Range (sq ft/m): 150.6–638.3/	Whirlpools: 4
Length (ft/m): 879.2/268.0	14.0–59.3	Self-Service Launderette: . . . . .No
Beam (ft/m): 105.6/32.2	Cabins (outside view): 575	Dedicated Cinema/Seats: . . . . .No
Draft (ft/m): 25.9/7.9	Cabins (interior/no view): 327	Library: . . . . .Yes
Propulsion/Propellers: diesel (50,400kW)/2	Cabins (for one person): 0	Onboard currency: . . . . .Hong Kong $
Passenger Decks: 10	Cabins (with private balcony): 390	

A large, family-friendly ship for casual-style cruising.

OVERVIEW. This ship is best suited to couples, singles, and families with children who want to cruise aboard a real contemporary floating resort with decent facilities and many dining spots dedicated to Asians, at a very attractive price. The decor mixes east and west, and public room names have been chosen to appeal to a mixture of Australian, European and Asian passengers.

THE SHIP. *SuperStar Virgo* was the second new ship ordered for the Asian market. The all-white vessel has a distinctive red/blue funnel with gold star logo. There are three distinct classes of passengers. As you check-in, you will be issued with a colored boarding card to denote Admiral Class passengers (yellow), Balcony Class (red), or World Cruisers (blue).

There is a walk-around promenade deck outdoors, good for strolling. Inside are two boulevards, and a stunning, larger two-deck-high central atrium lobby with three glass-walled elevators and ample space to peruse the shops and cafés that line its inner sanctum.

The casino complex is at the forward end of the atrium boulevard on Deck 7. This includes a large general-purpose, brightly lit casino, called Oasis, with gaming tables and slot machines. There's a smaller "members only" gaming club, as well as VIP gaming rooms, one of which has its own access to the upper level of the showlounge. The 450-seat Galaxy of the Stars Lounge is an observation lounge by day and a nightclub at night, with live music.

The interior decor has some distinctly European touches in its design, taste and color combinations. The lobby, for example, has become an Italian Piazza, with a stunning *trompe l'oeil* and multi-colored stained-glass ceiling. Three

BERLITZ'S RATINGS

	Possible	Achieved
Ship	500	417
Accommodation	200	156
Food	400	289
Service	400	284
Entertainment	100	66
Cruise	400	290

OVERALL SCORE
1,502 points out of 2,000

stairways are each carpeted in a different color, which helps new cruise passengers find their way around easily.

Other facilities include a business center with six meeting rooms, a large library and writing room, plus private mahjong and karaoke rooms, and a smoking room. A shopping concourse includes a wine shop.

Star Cruises has established a Southeast Asian regional cruise audience for its diverse fleet. *SuperStar Virgo* is good for the active local market, and is the most comprehensive ship sailing year-round in this popular region. The passenger mix is international, although the local market is now developed, so expect to find lots of families with children, who are allowed to roam around the ship uncontrolled – particularly on the weekend cruise.

Lots of choices, more dining options, and Asian hospitality all add up to a very attractive holiday package particularly suitable for families with children, in a very contemporary floating resort that operates from Hong Kong (Apr–Nov) and Singapore (Nov–Mar). The dress code is ultra-casual (no jacket and tie needed), and the ship operates a "no tipping" policy. While the initial cruise fare seems very reasonable, the extra costs and charges soon mount up if you want to indulge in more than the basics. Although service levels and finesse are inconsistent, hospitality is very good.

There are many extra-cost items in addition to the à la carte dining spots, such as for morning tea, afternoon tea, most cabaret shows (except a crew show), and childcare. Finding your way around many areas blocked by portable "crowd containment" ribbon barriers can prove frustrating.

FAMILIES. Teens have their own huge video arcade, while

younger children get to play in a wet 'n' wild aft pool (complete with pirate ship and caves) and two whirlpool tubs. Plus there's all the fun and facilities of Charlie's 24-hours-a-day childcare center, which includes a painting room, computer learning center, and small cinema. There's a room full of cots for toddlers to use for sleepovers, and even the toilets are at a special low height. About 15,000 sq. ft (1,400 sq. meters) is devoted to children's facilities. On deck is the world's first stainless-steel water slide. Installed in 2009, it cost $550,000, and is 330ft (100 meters) long. You can zoom along at up to 22 ft (6.7 meters) a second due to its steep incline, from 35 ft (10.7 meters) above the deck.

ACCOMMODATION. There are seven types, in 15 price categories. Three entire decks of cabins have private balconies, while two-thirds of all cabins have an outside view. Both the standard outside-view and interior cabins really are very small, particularly since all cabins have extra berths for a third/fourth person. So take the smallest amount of clothing you can – there's almost no storage space for luggage.

All cabins have a personal safe, 100% cotton towels and duvets or sheets. Bathrooms have a good-sized shower enclosure, and include toiletries such as Burberry soap, conditioning shampoo and body lotion.

For more space, choose one of 13 suites. Each has a separate lounge/dining room, bedroom, and bathroom, and an interconnecting door to an ocean-view cabin with private lit balcony. All cabinetry has richly lacquered woods, large (stocked) wet bar with refrigerator, dining table with a top that flips over to reveal a card table, and four chairs, sofa, drinks table, and trouser press.

The bedroom is small, completely filled by its queen-size bed; there is a reasonable amount of drawer space, but the drawers are very small. The closet space is rather tight – it contains two personal safes. A large ensuite bathroom is part of the bedroom and open to it – as is the trend in high-cost, interior architect-designed bathrooms ashore, and has a gorgeous mosaic tiled floor, kidney bean-shaped whirlpool tub, two basins, separate shower enclosure with floor-to-ceiling ocean-view window, and separate toilet with glass door. There are TV sets in the lounge, bedroom and bathroom.

For even more space, choose one of the six largest suites (Boracay, Nicobar, Langkawi, Majorca, Phuket, and Sentosa) and you'll have a generous amount of private living space, with a separate lounge, dining area, bedroom, large bathroom, and private lit balcony. The facilities are similar to those in the suites already described. There are TV sets in the lounge, bedroom and bathroom.

A small room service menu is available, with a 15% service charge plus a gratuity.

CUISINE. There's certainly no lack of choice, with eight venues and a café:

● *Bella Vista* seats over 600 in an open-seating arrangement, although in effect it operates two seatings. The aft section is two decks high, and huge cathedral-style windows are set in three sections overlooking the stern.

● *Mediterranean Buffet:* this is a large self-serve buffet restaurant with indoor/outdoor seating for 400.

● *The Pavilion Room* has traditional Cantonese Chinese cuisine, including dim sum at lunchtime.

The following are à la carte (extra-cost) dining spots:

● *Noble House:* a Chinese Restaurant, with traditional Hong Kong-themed decor and items such as dim sum, There are also two small private dining rooms.

● *Palazzo:* a beautiful, if slightly ostentatious Italian restaurant. It has fine food, and a genuine Renoir painting well protected by cameras and alarms.

● *Samurai:* a Japanese restaurant and sushi bar (for sashimi and sushi). There are two teppanyaki grills, each with 10 seats, where the chef cooks in front of you.

● *The Taj:* an Indian/vegetarian dining spot that offers a range of food in a self-serve buffet setup.

● *Blue Lagoon:* a casual 24-hour street café with noodle dishes, fried rice and other Southeast Asian dishes.

● *Out of Africa:* a casual karaoke café and bar, where coffees, teas and pastries are available.

ENTERTAINMENT. The Lido showlounge, with 934 seats, is two decks high. It has a main and balcony levels, with the balcony level reserved for "gaming club" members. The room has almost no support columns to obstruct the sightlines, and a revolving stage for revues and other production shows, typically to recorded music – there is no live showband. "Kingdom of Kung-Fu," with a cast of 30, features the power and form of the Shaolin Masters in an action-packed martial arts show. The showlounge can also be used as a large-screen cinema, with superb surround sound.

In addition, local specialty cabaret acts are brought on board, as are revue-style shows complete with topless dancers. Bands and small musical units provide plenty of live music for dancing and listening in the various lounges.

SPA/FITNESS. The Roman Spa and Fitness Center is on one of the uppermost decks, just forward of the Tivoli Pool. It has a gymnasium full of high-tech muscle-toning equipment, plus an aerobics exercise room, hair and beauty salon, and saunas, steam rooms, changing rooms for men and women, several treatment rooms, and aqua-swim pools that provide counter-flow jets. There is an extra charge for use of the sauna and steam rooms.

Although there are several types of massages available, Thai massage is a specialty – you can have it in the spa, outdoors on deck, in your cabin or on your private balcony, space permitting. Sports facilities include a jogging track, golf driving range, basketball and tennis courts, and there are four levels of sunbathing decks.

The Calypso
★★+

Size:	Small Ship	Passenger Decks:	8	Cabins (wheelchair accessible):	2
Tonnage:	11,162	Total Crew:	220	Wheelchair accessibility:	None
Lifestyle:	Standard	Passengers		Cabin Current:	110 volts
Cruise Line:	Louis Cruises	(lower beds/all berths):	486/740	Elevators:	2
Former Names:	*Regent Jewel, Sun*	Passenger Space Ratio		Casino (gaming tables):	Yes
Fiesta, Ionian Harmony, Canguro Verde		(lower beds/all berths):	22.9/15.0	Slot Machines:	Yes
Builder:	Fincantieri (Italy)	Crew/Passenger Ratio		Swimming Pools (outdoors):	1
Original Cost:	n/a	(lower beds/all berths):	2.2/3.3	Swimming Pools (indoors):	0
Entered Service:	1968/Jul 2000	Cabins (total):	243	Whirlpools:	0
Registry:	Malta	Size Range (sq ft/m):	135–244/12.5–22.6	Self-Service Launderette:	No
Length (ft/m):	444.2/135.4	Cabins (outside view):	158	Dedicated Cinema/Seats:	No
Beam (ft/m):	62.9/19.2	Cabins (interior/no view):	85	Library:	Yes
Draft (ft/m):	20.6/6.3	Cabins (for one person):	0	Onboard currency:	Euros
Propulsion/Propellers:	diesel (9,000kW)/2	Cabins (with private balcony):	0		

A friendly, small ship for casual, frugal cruisers.

OVERVIEW. This ship suits adult couples seeking a low-priced, but comfortable ship for a first short cruise, with unpretentious, unstuffy surroundings and acceptable food and service. The interior decor is very pleasant. There's a cozy ambience, and the dress code is totally casual.

THE SHIP. *The Calypso*, a former Mediterranean ferry, was extensively reconstructed in 1999. Although its profile is a little bit unusual, one nice aspect is its enclosed wooden promenade deck – good for strolling, or just sitting and reading. There's a decent selection of public rooms, bars and lounges, considering the ship's size.

This is a high-density ship, so it is very crowded when full, and there may be a large number of smokers. There are very steep, narrow stairways on the outer decks.

ACCOMMODATION. There are four suites, seven semi-deluxe, 147 outside-view cabins and 85 interior cabins. Cabins on higher decks command higher prices. All cabins have double or twin beds, TV set, telephone, personal safe, and bathrooms have a shower enclosure, toilet and washbasin.

The cabins have warm pastel decor, although the artwork is minimal, and the fabrics and other soft furnishings could be of better quality. Some cabins have a third and fourth

BERLITZ'S RATINGS		
	Possible	Achieved
Ship	500	195
Accommodation	200	95
Food	400	209
Service	400	241
Entertainment	100	55
Cruise	400	195
OVERALL SCORE		
990 points out of 2,000		

upper berth (though only one personal safe), and drawer and storage space is very limited – in other words, take as little clothing as possible. Those designated as suites have a refrigerator/minibar. There's a limited cabin service menu.

CUISINE. *L'Orchidée* dining room, in the aft section, is reasonably attractive and decorated, although its layout is somewhat awkward, as it is positioned on two slightly different levels. There are two seatings, and tables are for four, six or eight persons. The menu choice, including a vegetarian option is quite good, and the food has plenty of taste. The service comes with a smile. Breakfast and lunch buffets are quite attractive, with plenty of variety. The wine list is very small and non-vintage, but prices are reasonable.

ENTERTAINMENT. The showlounge is a single-level room, and several pillars obstruct the sightlines from many seats. The entertainment consists mainly of cabaret acts. Several bands and musical units provide live music for dancing and listening.

SPA/FITNESS. Apart from a small gymnasium and sauna, there is little else. Massage, however, is available in a tiny room, and there are beauty/hair treatments.

The Emerald
★★ +

Size:	Mid-Size Ship
Tonnage:	26,428
Lifestyle:	Standard
Cruise Line:	Louis Cruises
Former Names:	*Regent Rainbow,*
	Diamond Island, Santa Rosa
Builder:	Newport News Shipbuilding (USA)
Original Cost:	$25 million
Entered Service:	Jun 1958/Apr 1997
Registry:	Cyprus
Length (ft/m):	599.0/182.57
Beam (ft/m):	84.0/25.60
Draft (ft/m):	27.5/8.38
Propulsion/Propellers:	steam turbine
	(16,400kW)/2

Passenger Decks:	10
Total Crew:	412
Passengers	
(lower beds/all berths):	990/1,198
Passenger Space Ratio	
(lower beds/all berths):	26.6/22.0
Crew/Passenger Ratio	
(lower beds/all berths):	2.4/2.9
Cabins (total):	500
Size Range (sq ft/m):	124.8–304.6/
	11.6–28.3
Cabins (outside view):	338
Cabins (interior/no view):	162
Cabins (for one person):	10
Cabins (with private balcony):	0

Cabins (wheelchair accessible):	2
Wheelchair accessibility:	None
Cabin Current:	110 and 220 volts
Elevators:	3
Casino (gaming tables):	Yes
Slot Machines:	Yes
Swimming Pools (outdoors):	1
Swimming Pools (indoors):	0
Whirlpools:	2
Self-Service Launderette:	No
Dedicated Cinema/Seats:	No
Library:	Yes
Onboard currency:	Euros

A friendly ship for casual, low-budget cruisers.

OVERVIEW. This ship is suited to adult couples and singles who want a first cruise providing a very good value-for-money vacation in unpretentious, old-style surroundings. Typically, 80% of passengers are over 45. For its short cruises from Cyprus, it provides a range of public spaces that, in turn, promote good ambience and include no fewer than five bars.

THE SHIP. This solid, American-built, former ocean liner benefits from a strong, riveted hull; all new ships are seam-welded. The open deck and sunbathing space is quite limited when the ship is full, although there are a good number of sunloungers. There's a good outdoor promenade deck, with plenty of chairs.

The interiors are quite pleasant and surprisingly comfortable, with warm decor that is contemporary without being at all brash. Many public rooms have high ceilings, and the ship has a spacious ocean-liner feel. There are some fine wrought-iron railings on the stairways. The artwork is low-budget stuff. The casino, quite large, has a high ceiling.

ACCOMMODATION. There are six main categories: Premier, Superior Outside Plus, Superior Outside, Superior Inside, Standard Outside, and Standard Inside.

Cabins are assigned at embarkation check-in unless you pay a supplement to pre-book, choosing your cabin from the deck plan. This method of assigning cabins means that those who pre-book first and those who arrive first at the embarkation port will probably get the best cabins.

BERLITZ'S RATINGS

	Possible	Achieved
Ship	500	243
Accommodation	200	107
Food	400	210
Service	400	238
Entertainment	100	50
Cruise	400	215

OVERALL SCORE
1,063 points out of 2,000

Many of the original cabins are quite spacious, with good closet and drawer space, but newer ones are a little more compact, with poor insulation. Continental breakfast in your cabin will cost about $7.50 (£4.50) extra per person per day. A 24-hour cabin service menu offers extra-cost snacks.

CUISINE. The *Chanterelle Dining Room*, in the center of the ship, has large ocean-view windows. A second restaurant, *Le Bistro*, is also in the center of the ship, but two decks above the Chanterelle. While it won't win any awards, the food quality and its variety and presentation are actually quite decent considering the cost of a cruise. That there is always a vegetarian entrée for lunch and dinner, as well as vegetarian appetizers and soups. The service is friendly and quite attentive, but don't expect grand hotel-style service.

ENTERTAINMENT. The sightlines in the showlounge are poor, particularly from port and starboard side seating areas. The shows, although not of top professional quality, are fun and entertaining for the whole family. In addition, there is plenty of music for dancing, both live and recorded.

SPA/FITNESS. A small, windowless fitness center is located low down in the ship. There's also a sauna, while the beauty salon is located on another deck – again in an interior position. There is no natural light, which makes tinting and coloring difficult.

Thomson Celebration
★★★ +

Size: . . . . .Mid-Size Ship	Passenger Decks: 10	Cabins (with private balcony): 0
Tonnage: 33,930	Total Crew: 520	Cabins (wheelchair accessible): 4
Lifestyle: . . . . .Standard	Passengers	Wheelchair accessibility: . . . . .Fair
Cruise Line: . . . . .Thomson Cruises	(lower beds/all berths): 1,254/1,350	Cabin Current: . . . . . . .110 and 220 volts
Former Names: . . . . .Noordam	Passenger Space Ratio	Elevators: 7
Builder: .Chantiers de l'Atlantique (France)	(lower beds/all berths): 27.0/25.1	Casino (gaming tables): . . . . .Yes
Original Cost: . . . .$160 million	Crew/Passenger Ratio	Slot Machines: . . . . .Yes
Entered Service: . . . . .Apr 1984/May 2005	(lower beds/all berths): 2.4/2.6	Swimming Pools (outdoors): 2
Registry: . . . . .Dutch Antilles	Cabins (total): 627	Swimming Pools (indoors): 0
Length (ft/m): 704.2/214.66	Size Range (sq ft/m): 150.6–296.0/	Whirlpools: 1
Beam (ft/m): 89.4/27.26	14.0–27.5	Self-Service Launderette: . . . . .Yes
Draft (ft/m): 24.2/7.40	Cabins (outside view): 413	Dedicated Cinema/Seats: Yes/230
Propulsion/Propellers: . . . . .diesel	Cabins (interior/no view): 194	Library: . . . . .Yes
(21,600 kW)/2	Cabins (for one person): 0	Onboard currency: . . . . .UK£

A family-friendly ship for a low-budget first cruise.

OVERVIEW. This ship suits adult couples and singles taking their first or second cruise, seeking a modern but not glitzy ship with a wide array of public lounges and bars, a middle-of-the-road lifestyle, and food and entertainment that is acceptable rather than fancy. It is exclusively chartered by Thomson Cruises, so your fellow passengers are likely to be mostly British, and typically about 90% of them will be over 55.

THE SHIP. *Thomson Celebration* (formerly Holland America Line's *Noordam*) and sister to *Thomson Spirit*, has a nicely raked bow and a contemporary transom stern, but overall the ship's angular exterior superstructure design makes it look rather squat. There is a good amount of open deck space, and the traditional teakwood decks outdoors include a wrap-around promenade deck. The ship, however, is quite dated and occasionally suffers from some vibration. Perhaps its best asset is its friendly and personable international crew.

The ship has a spacious interior design and layout, with most public rooms located aft in a vertical arrangement, while accommodation is positioned in the forward section, which keeps noise away from the accommodation areas. The soothing color combinations do not jar the senses; although they are rather dark and somber, with some new color splashes added during the ship's refurbishment in 2005. There is much polished teakwood and rosewood paneling throughout the interiors. Horizon's observation lounge, atop the ship, is a pleasant retreat, with fine views forward. The main lounge, which has a small balcony level, is reminiscent of those found on former ocean liners, and is really

BERLITZ'S RATINGS

	Possible	Achieved
Ship	500	332
Accommodation	200	137
Food	400	235
Service	400	261
Entertainment	100	64
Cruise	400	278

OVERALL SCORE
1,307 points out of 2,000

more suited to cabaret entertainment, and not full production shows. While children are also catered to, with their own play areas and hosts, the majority of passengers are adults.

The ship operates a wide variety of cruises, and, for part of the year, is based in the UK. There are many interior cabins, and standing in line for embarkation, disembarkation, shore tenders and for self-serve buffet meals is an inevitable aspect of cruising aboard all large ships.

ACCOMMODATION. There is one suite grade, four grades of outside-view cabins (one designated Deluxe), and two grades of interior cabins. Four cabins with great forward-facing views are for the disabled. You can pre-book your preferred cabin for an extra per-cabin fee.

In general, most cabins have a reasonable amount of space, although they are small when compared with those of many other ships. In general, they are adequately appointed and practically laid out, with some wood furniture and fittings, wood paneling, good counter and storage space (although there is very little drawer space), a large mirror, and a private bathroom very modest in size.

The top three categories of cabins – which are only marginally larger and should not really be called suites or mini-suites – have bathtubs while all others have shower enclosures only. Several cabins have king- or queen-size beds, although most have twin beds, some but not all of which can be pushed together. In many cabins, particularly those that are interior, the bed configuration is L-shaped, and the beds cannot be pushed together.

A number of cabins also have additional upper berths

for a third/fourth person. Room service is provided 24 hours a day. All cabin TV sets receive live news via satellite. The cabin insulation is really quite poor, and bathroom towels are small. Some cabins on Mariner and Bridge Decks have lifeboat-obstructed views.

CUISINE. The *Meridian Restaurant*, in the center of the ship, is a reasonably large and attractive room, with warm decor, and ample space. Breakfast and lunch and dinner (6pm–10.30pm) are served in an open-seating arrangement, so you may get a different table and different waiters for each meal. Although there are a few tables for two, most are for four, six, or eight. Dinners typically include a choice of four entrées and a daily vegetarian entrée.

Children have their own menu, with "home-from-home" dishes and small portions. Dessert and pastry items will usually be of good quality, and made specifically for British tastes, although there is much use of canned fruits and jellies.

A small à la carte restaurant, called *Zilli's* after celebrity chef Aldo Zilli, is an alternative dining spot; reservations are required and there's a per-person cover charge. It seats up to 45 and has superior food and service plus a quieter, more refined atmosphere. It is adjacent to the Meridian Restaurant, but is best entered from the aft stairway.

The Lido Restaurant has a more casual setting and is active 24 hours a day in an open-seating arrangement. Tables are set with crisp linens, flatware and stemware for dinner, when a set menu includes a choice of four entrées. Each week a themed buffet (Chinese, Indian or Mexican, depending on the cruise itinerary) may be offered for dinner. However, self-serve buffets are quite repetitive and not as creative as aboard *Thomson Destiny* or *Thomson Spirit*. On Lido Deck, the outdoor *Terrace Grill* provides fast-food grilled items and pizza during the day.

ENTERTAINMENT. The two-decks-high 600-seat Broadway Showlounge, with a main and balcony level, is the main venue for production shows and cabaret entertainment. The many pillars in the showlounge obstruct sightlines from some seats. *Thomson Celebration* presents an array of production shows that are colorful, lively, and entertaining, while cabaret acts provide entertainment on evenings when there are no production shows.

A second entertainment venue, Hemingway's, is a multifunctional room for quizzes, dancing, and for use as a late-night discotheque. A number of bands and musical units provide live music for dancing and listening in several lounges and bars.

SPA/FITNESS. Oceans Health Club is atop the ship at the aft end. It has good ocean views, and overlooks the aft pool. Facilities include an aerobics exercise room, a decent size gymnasium with plenty of treadmills, exercycles, and other body-toning and muscle-pumping equipment, sauna but no steam room, and four body treatment rooms. You can have massages, aromatherapy facials, body wraps, manicures, pedicures, and hair beautifying treatments.

The beauty salon is located in a completely different area to the health and fitness facilities – it's close to the Reception Desk on the port side.

Thomson Destiny
★★★ +

Size: . . . . .Mid-Size Ship	Total Crew: 540	Cabins (wheelchair accessible): 0
Tonnage: .37,773	Passengers	Wheelchair accessibility: . . . . .Fair
Lifestyle: . . . . .Standard	(lower beds/all berths): 1,450/1,611	Cabin Current: . . . . .110 volts
Cruise Line: . . . . .Thomson Cruises	Passenger Space Ratio	Elevators: 7
Former Names: *Sunbird, Song of America*	(lower beds/all berths): 26.0/23.4	Casino (gaming tables): . . . . .Yes
Builder: . . . . .Wartsila (Finland)	Crew/Passenger Ratio	Slot Machines: . . . . .Yes
Original Cost: . . . .$140 million	(lower beds/all berths): 2.6/2.9	Swimming Pools (outdoors): 2
Entered Service: . . . .Dec 1982/May 2005	Cabins (total): .725	Swimming Pools (indoors): 0
Registry: . . . . .The Bahamas	Size Range (sq ft/m): 118.4–425.1/	Whirlpools: 0
Length (ft/m): 705.0/214.88	11.0–39.5	Self-Service Launderette: . . . . .No
Beam (ft/m): 93.1/28.40	Cabins (outside view): 425	Dedicated Cinema/Seats: . . . . .No
Draft (ft/m): 22.3/6.80	Cabins (interior/no view): 300	Library: . . . . .Yes
Propulsion/Propellers: diesel (16,480kW)/2	Cabins (for one person): 0	Onboard currency: . . . . .UK£
Passenger Decks: 11	Cabins (with private balcony): 9	

A large family-friendly ship for casual cruising.

OVERVIEW. This ship is best suited to adult couples and singles taking their first or second cruise, and families with children, all seeking a modern but not glitzy ship with a wide array of public lounges and bars, a middle-of-the-road lifestyle, food and entertainment that is acceptable rather than fancy, and a British ambience. Like other vessels in the Thomson Cruises fleet, the space per passenger, especially on the open decks, is very tight when the ship is full.

BERLITZ'S RATINGS		
	Possible	Achieved
Ship	500	340
Accommodation	200	125
Food	400	241
Service	400	261
Entertainment	100	66
Cruise	400	270
OVERALL SCORE		
1,303 points out of 2,000		

THE SHIP. Originally built for Royal Caribbean International, the ship was sold in 1999 to My Travel/Sun Cruises, which pulled out of cruise vacations in 2004. The all-white ship is smart-looking, with nicely rounded lines, sharply raked bow, and a single funnel with a cantilevered, wraparound lounge called the Chart Room – a fine place from which to observe the world around and below you.

There is a decent amount of open deck and sunbathing space – but it will be crowded when the ship sails full, which is most of the time. There are some nicely polished wooden decks and rails and two swimming pools – the aft one designated for children, the forward one for adults.

The interior decor is bright and breezy. There is a good array of public rooms, most with high ceilings, and are located one deck above the dining room. These include the main show lounge, casino and nightclub. There is also a small conference center for meetings, as well as an internet café which has six computer terminals – but no café.

Thomson Cruises provides a consistent, well-tuned and well-packaged, fun product, in comfortable surroundings. As part of Thomson Holidays, it uses its own Thomson Airways and is therefore able to offer complete cruise-air-stay

packages at such attractive rates. The company does a good job of getting you and your luggage from aircraft to ship without having to go through immigration (depending on itinerary) in foreign countries whenever possible – so your cruise holiday is relatively seamless. The company offers airlift from almost a score of UK airports via Britannia Airlines. You can pre-book a window seat for an extra cost, including a premium seat (more space than standard seats), and pre-booked meals also cost extra.

Thomson's brochures tell it like it is – so you know before you go exactly what you will get for your money. There is little choice of tea and coffee. There are no cushioned pads for the sunloungers. Standing in line for embarkation, disembarkation, shore tenders and for self-serve buffet meals is an inevitable aspect of cruising aboard all large ships.

Your fellow passengers are likely to be British, and typically about 80 percent will be over 45. In summer a lot of families with children go cruising, so you can expect to find them everywhere. Perhaps the best part of cruising aboard *Thomson Destiny* lies in the destinations, and not the ship – although it is perfectly comfortable. Hotel add-ons can extend a cruise vacation, and Thomson has a fine collection, depending on your needs, budget, and whether you are traveling with children or grandchildren.

Passenger niggles include some serious vibration in the Clipper Bar, and the tired look of the ship's interiors.

ACCOMMODATION. This is provided in five categories and nine price bands: Interior Cabins (parallel or L-shaped bed arrangement), Outside View Cabins (parallel or L-shaped bed arrangement), Deluxe Cabins (with parallel twin beds that can convert to a queen-size bed), Suites and Grand Suites. You can pre-book an exact cabin and location if you pay an extra per-cabin charge, which also lets you choose whether to dine at the early or late evening seating.

Most cabins are of a similar size – actually very small compared to today's newer ships – and insulation between them is quite poor. The cabins also have mediocre closets and very little storage space, yet somehow everyone seems to manage. They are just about adequate for a one-week cruise, as you will need only a small selection of mainly casual clothes. You'll probably have to store your shoes and luggage under the bed.

Most bathrooms typically contain a washbasin, toilet, and shower, with very little space for toiletries. Although they are reasonably cheerful, the shower enclosure is small, and has a curtain that you will probably end up dancing with. Towels are 100% cotton.

In some cabins, twin beds are fixed in a parallel mode – some are moveable and can be made into a queen-size bed – while others may be in an L-shape. In almost all cabins there is a "lip" or threshold of about 9 inches (23 cm) at the bathroom door to step over.

You can get more space and a larger cabin if you book one of the 21 slightly more expensive deluxe-grade cabins on Promenade Deck. These have twin beds that convert to a queen-size bed, set diagonally into a sleeping area adjacent to outside-view windows. There is more drawer space, more closet space, and the bathroom has a half-size tub and shower combination. Bathrobes are also provided. The largest of these deluxe-grade cabins is Cabin 7000.

For even more exclusivity, you can book one of nine suites. All are located in a private area, have fine wood paneling and trim, and come with additional space and better, more personalized service.

The additional space includes a lounge area with sofa (this converts to a double bed – making it ideal for families with children), coffee table and two chairs, a vanity desk, combination TV/VCR, an abundance of drawers, illuminated closets with both hanging space and several shelves, excellent storage space, king-size bed, and bathrobes. The bathroom is fully tiled, and has a full-size enamel tub (rare in ships today) with shower, pink granite-look washbasin, and plenty of storage space for toiletries.

Suite occupants also get a semi-private balcony – whose door is extremely heavy and hard to open – with drinks table and two teak chairs. Book one of the two Grand Suites, and you'll get even more room – plus views over the bows and a larger balcony (these can be overlooked from the open deck above), more floor space, and a walk-in closet. Missing are a bedside telephone and a bathroom telephone.

The cabin voltage is 110 volts, so British passengers will need to take a US-style adapter for electrical appliances such as a hairdryer. Note that the accommodation deck hallways are also very narrow on some decks.

CUISINE. The *Seven Seas Restaurant*, a large room, consists of a central main section and two long, narrow wings – the Magellan Room and Galileo Room – with large, ocean-view windows. The low ceiling creates a high level of ambient noise. There are two seatings. There are tables for two (but only 14), four, six, or eight, and window tables are for two or six. The service is average.

There is plenty of food – indeed, quantity, not quality, prevails – but do remember that it is all provided at a low cost. Presentation is weak, and there are no fish knives. If you enjoy eating out adventurously, you could be disappointed. The menus are standard and deviation is difficult. Bottled water is offered, and costs extra; the ship's drinking water (at no charge) is adequate. There is an adequate, but limited, wine list, and the wines are almost all very young – typical of supermarket bottles. Wine prices are quite modest, as are the prices for most alcoholic drinks.

For casual, self-serve breakfasts and lunches, the *Veranda Café* is the alternative choice, although the tables and seats outdoors are of metal and plastic, and the buffets are basic and old-fashioned. The low cruise fare dictates the use of plastic cups and plastic stirrers – teaspoons are unheard of. At night you can "dine" under the steel and canvas canopy, where the café becomes a pleasant, outdoors alternative to the dining room – and includes waiter service.

ENTERTAINMENT. The Can Can Lounge, the venue for all entertainment events and social functions, has a stage and hardwood dance floor. It is a single-level room, designed more for cabaret acts than for large-scale production shows. The revue-style shows are typically of the end-of-pier variety type, with an energetic, well-meaning cast of young people who also double as cruise staff during the day, together with some professional cabaret acts.

Another, smaller room, the Oklahoma Lounge, has a stage and dance floor, and is often used to present late-night comedy and other acts.

SPA/FITNESS. Although the spa facilities are not exactly generous, there is a gymnasium, sauna but no steam room, changing rooms for men and women, and a beauty salon. Spa and beauty services are provided by Harding Brothers, which operates similar services for a number of cruise lines. You can book a massage, an aromatherapy facial, manicure and pedicure, among other treatments.

Thomson Dream
★★★

Size: ....Mid-Size Ship	Total Crew: 650	Wheelchair accessibility: ....Fair
Tonnage: 53,872	Passengers	Cabin Current: ....110/220 volts
Lifestyle: ....Standard	(lower beds/all berths): ...1,506/1,756	Elevators: 7
Cruise Line: ....Thomson Cruises	Passenger Space Ratio	Casino (gaming tables): ....Yes
Former Names: .... Costa Europa,	(lower beds/all berths): 35.7/30.6	Slot Machines: ....Yes
Westerdam, Homeric	Crew/Passenger Ratio	Swimming Pools (outdoors): 2
Builder: ....Meyer Werft (Germany)	(lower beds/all berths): 2.4/2.7	(1 with glass dome)
Original Cost: ....$150 million	Cabins (total): 753	Swimming Pools (indoors): 0
Entered Service: ....May 1986/Dec 2010	Size Range (sq ft/m):	Whirlpools: 2
Registry: ....Italy	129.1–425.1/12.0–39.5	Self-Service Launderette: ....Yes (5)
Length (ft/m): 797.9/243.23	Cabins (outside view): 501	Dedicated Cinema/Seats: Yes/237
Beam (ft/m): 95.1/29.00	Cabins (interior/no view): 252	Library: ....Yes
Draft (ft/m): 23.6/7.20	Cabins (for one person): 18	Onboard currency: ....UK£
Propulsion/Propellers: diesel (23,830kW)/2	Cabins (with private balcony): 6	
Passenger Decks: 9	Cabins (wheelchair accessible): 4	

A dated mid-size ship for frugal, family-friendly cruises.

OVERVIEW. *Thomson Dream,* the largest ship in the Thomson fleet, suits adult couples and singles taking their first or second cruise, and families with children of all ages, all seeking a modern but not glitzy ship with a wide array of public lounges and bars, and a middle-of-the-road lifestyle, with food and entertainment that is no-frills basic.

THE SHIP. *Thomson Dream* was originally *Homeric* for the long-defunct Home Lines, and was given an $84 million "chop and stretch" operation in 1990 when bought by Holland America Line. You don't even have to look closely to tell where the mid-section was inserted, because the windows are larger than the fore and aft sections. The ship was moved to Costa Cruises (owned by Carnival Corporation) in 2002, and then acquired by Thomson Cruises in 2009, when it was sent for an extensive refurbishment to cater to Thomson's mainly British passengers.

The ship has good teak outside decks and a walk-around promenade deck, plus a decent amount of open deck space for sunbathing. There is also a swimming pool deck, which can be covered by a sliding glass dome, although it is rather small for the number of passengers carried.

The ship has a functional, restful interior decor, mainly with pastel tones and some added color accents. It absorbs people well, and the passenger flow is good, although the layout is a little awkward to learn at first. But many of the public entertainment rooms are located on one deck, which makes access simple.

There are several bars and lounges, some small and intimate, others larger and noisier. There are lots of nooks and

BERLITZ'S RATINGS		
	Possible	Achieved
Ship	500	330
Accommodation	200	124
Food	400	239
Service	400	252
Entertainment	100	63
Cruise	400	240
OVERALL SCORE		
1,248 points out of 2,000		

crannies – much nicer than the warehouse-style public rooms of the latest ships. Other facilities include an internet lounge, library, card room and shops.

Passenger niggles include irritating, repetitious announcements, expensive shore excursions, and noticeable vibration in some areas.

FAMILIES. *Thomson Dream* allots a good amount of space to children's facilities, suiting the increased number of families who will choose this ship. Some larger cabins have a sofa that turns into a bed – good for families with small children.

ACCOMMODATION. There are several cabin price grades, including suites, mini-suites, outside-view cabins, and inside cabins, priced according to grade, size and location. You can pre-book your preference for a per cabin fee of £39 (around US$60).

Except for five suite category cabins, each with king-size beds, separate lounge area and bathroom with full size tub, almost all other cabins are of a similar size. In general, they are generously proportioned and well equipped. Facilities include ample closet, drawer and storage space, hairdryer, and good-size bathrooms, but the towels are quite small. There are far too many interior cabins – over 50 percent of all cabins – and soundproofing is rather poor, so you can hear your neighbors brushing their hair. All cabin TV sets receive European news channels.

Most cabins have twin beds, but some have the old-style upper and lower berths, so make sure when you book that you request – and get – a cabin with the sleeping arrangements you want. There are four cabins for the disabled, suitably located, on higher decks, close to elevators.

CUISINE. There are several eateries to choose from, depending on your taste and budget.

The *Orion Restaurant*, enlarged by 345 sq.ft/32 sq. meters in 2006, is a traditional dining room with a raised central, cupola-style dome, and port and starboard side portholes are highlighted at night by pleasing lighting. Open-seating dining is the norm. The tables are extremely close together, and, except for the center section, the ceiling is just one deck high, so the noise level can be extremely loud. The service is decent enough, but communication can sometimes be frustrating, and smiles from the waiters and assistants can do only so much. The cuisine is British-Continental in nature, but, although there is plenty of food, its quality and presentation are disappointing when compared to other cruise products on the market. The restaurant is open for breakfast, lunch and dinner.

The Grill is an extra-cost steak and seafood (including surf 'n' turf) restaurant, with food cooked to order. Reservations are required.

The 24-hour *Andromeda Restaurant* and a smaller *Sirens Restaurant*, both in the aft section, provide breakfast, lunch and dinner in a self-serve buffet style, but lines and a crowded environment make these noisy eateries. Twice during each cruise, there's a theme night.

The Terrace Grill, open for lunch, serves fast-food such as BBQ items, pizzas and salads.

ENTERTAINMENT. Facilities include the Atlante Theater, the ship's two-decks-high show lounge, with seating on both main and balcony levels. Pillars obstruct sightlines from some seats. A resident troupe of singers and dancers presents colorful, high-energy production shows. For nights when there's no production show, the show lounge presents cabaret acts such as singers, comedy jugglers, magicians and ventriloquists.

A number of bands and small musical units provide live music in many lounges and bars – so there is always plenty of music to dance to or listen to, from light classical in the Argo Lounge to jazz to pop, dance and rap. There's also a discotheque.

SPA/FITNESS. The Nereidi Fitness Center, on an upper deck aft of the mast, includes a gymnasium, saunas and massage rooms, but there is no steam room. The facility is really small, given the number of passengers carried – although, to be fair, such facilities weren't very popular when the ship was built.

The spa is operated by Harding Brothers, a specialist concession. Some fitness classes are free, while some, such as yoga, cost extra.

Being aboard will give you an opportunity to try some of the more exotic treatments, particularly Aroma Stone massage and Chakra Balancing massage. These plus facials, pedicures, and beauty salon treatments cost extra. Make appointments early – aboard a ship of this size, time slots go quickly, so the day you board is the best time to book your treatments.

Thomson Spirit
★★★ +

Size: . . . . .Mid-Size Ship	Passenger Decks: 10	Cabins (with private balcony): 0
Tonnage: .33,930	Total Crew: 520	Cabins (wheelchair accessible): 4
Lifestyle: . . . . .Standard	Passengers	Wheelchair accessibility: . . . . .Fair
Cruise Line: . . . . .Thomson Cruises	(lower beds/all berths): 1,254/1,350	Cabin Current: . . . . .110 and 220 volts
Former Names: . . . . . .Nieuw Amsterdam,	Passenger Space Ratio	Elevators: 7
Patriot, Nieuw Amsterdam	(lower beds/all berths): 27.0/25.1	Casino (gaming tables): . . . . .Yes
Builder: .Chantiers de l'Atlantique (France)	Crew/Passenger Ratio	Slot Machines: . . . . .Yes
Original Cost: . . . .$150 million	(lower beds/all berths): 2.4/2.6	Swimming Pools (outdoors): 2
Entered Service: . . . . .Jul 1983/May 2002	Cabins (total): 627	Swimming Pools (indoors): 0
Registry: . . . . .The Bahamas	Size Range (sq ft/m): 150.6–296.0/	Whirlpools: 1
Length (ft/m): 704.2/214.66	14.0–27.5	Self-Service Launderette: . . . . .Yes (3)
Beam (ft/m): 89.4/27.26	Cabins (outside view): 413	Dedicated Cinema/Seats: Yes/230
Draft (ft/m): 24.6/7.52	Cabins (interior/no view): 194	Library: . . . . .Yes
Propulsion/Propellers: diesel (21,600 kW)/2	Cabins (for one person): 0	Onboard currency: . . . . .UK£

A family-friendly ship with decent food and service.

OVERVIEW. This ship is best suited to adult couples and singles taking their first or second cruise, and families with children of all ages, all seeking a modern, non-glitzy ship with a decent array of public lounges and bars, and a mid-dle-of-the-road lifestyle, with food and entertainment that is acceptable rather than fancy. Perhaps the best part of cruising aboard *Thomson Spirit* lies in the destinations and not the ship – although it is perfectly comfortable.

BERLITZ'S RATINGS		
	Possible	Achieved
Ship	500	330
Accommodation	200	137
Food	400	245
Service	400	262
Entertainment	100	64
Cruise	400	278
OVERALL SCORE		
1,316 points out of 2,000		

has been a highly successful venture, offering extremely good value for money, particularly for adult couples, and occasionally families with children.

Thomson Spirit has quite a spacious interior design and layout, with little crowding and almost no points of congestion, and most public rooms are on a single deck. The color combinations do not jar the senses – most are pretty nondescript, though there are many splashes of color – and the decor was greatly changed and brightened by its new owners. There is much polished teakwood and rosewood paneling throughout the interiors. For quieter moments, try the Horizon Lounge, atop the ship; it has a wooden dance floor. The main lounge, with a small balcony level, is reminiscent of the ocean liners of yesteryear.

THE SHIP. *Thomson Spirit,* originally built for Holland America Line, has a nicely raked bow and a contemporary transom stern, but overall the ship's angular exterior super-structure design makes it look squat and quite boxy. The exterior has an all-white hull and superstructure. There is a good amount of open teakwood deck space, particularly at the aft section of the ship, and the traditional outdoors teak-wood decks include a walk-around promenade deck. Unfortunately, the French-built ship has always suffered from poor build quality and excessive vibration, particularly at the stern.

Holland America Line sold the ship to the publicly funded United States Lines in 2000, but that company sank in a sea of debt the following year. Carnival Corporation, which owns Holland America Line, bought back the ship and chartered it to Louis Cruises, which in turn has sub-chartered it to Thom-son Cruises. *Thomson Spirit* has a sister ship in the slightly newer, 1984-built *Thomson Celebration* (formerly Holland America Line's *Noordam*).

Thomson first operated cruises in the 1970s, then aban-doned them, only to start cruises operations again in the mid-1990s using chartered, rather than wholly-owned ships. It

It's good to see a tour operator like Thomson Cruises charter and operate this vessel, especially since competi-tion in the cruise industry is increasing. This ship is quite acceptable for passengers wanting pleasant surroundings and an all-British ambience. However, many newer ships have more space, better facilities and more options, and that means this ship loses a few points in relation to the increased competition in the international marketplace.

Hotel add-ons can extend a cruise vacation, and Thom-son has a fine collection, depending on your needs, budget, and whether you are traveling with children or grand-children. Because the ship is exclusive to Thomson Cruises, your fellow passengers are likely to be British, with typically about 80 percent of them over 45.

Thomson owns its own airline, Thomson Airways, and has much experience in operating fly-cruises to the Mediter-ranean – the company offers airlift from almost a score of

UK airports. With Thomson, you pay only for what you want. You can pre-book a window seat or a premium seat with more space than standard seats for an extra fee.

All Thomson Cruises' ships are non-smoking, although smoking areas are provided in most public rooms. Standing in line for embarkation, disembarkation, shore tenders and for self-serve buffet meals is inevitable aboard all large ships.

FAMILIES. Children have their own play areas at the aft of Bridge Deck. There are several children's clubs: Tots is for 3–5-year-olds, Team is for 6–8-year-olds, while Tribe is for 9–12-year-olds. The clubs operate five days a week (not on embarkation or disembarkation days), and are supervised by qualified "Children's Hosts."

ACCOMMODATION. There is one suite grade, four grades of outside-view cabins (one designated Deluxe), and two grades of interior cabins. There are four large cabins, great forward-facing views, for the disabled. You can pre-book your preference for an extra per-cabin fee.

Most of the cabins are quite small – below the industry standard of 170 sq. ft (15.7 sq. meters). They are reasonably well appointed and practically laid out. Some have wood furniture, fittings, or accenting, good counter and storage space but little drawer space, a large dressing mirror, and private bathrooms that are adequate, but no more. The top cabin categories – which are only marginally larger and should not really be called suites – have full-size bathtubs while all others have showers. Several cabins have king- or queen-size beds, although most have twin beds.

The largest accommodation is in the Presidential Suite. Small by comparison to suites aboard many other ships, it measures 464 sq. ft (43.1 sq. meters) and is on Eagle Deck, the uppermost accommodation deck. There is a king-size bed, walk-in closet, wet bar, study and dining areas, TV set, video player, and stereo system. The bathroom includes a whirlpool tub, double sink unit, and a powder room.

A number of cabins also have additional berths for a third/fourth person. Room service is provided 24 hours a day. All cabin TVs carry live news channels, when available). The cabin insulation is extremely poor, and the bathroom towels are small.

CUISINE. The *Compass Rose Restaurant* is reasonably large and attractive, with warm decor and ample space. Breakfast, lunch and dinner (6pm–10.30pm) are served in an open-seating arrangement, so you may get a different table and different waiters for each meal. Although there are a few tables for two, most are for four, six or eight. Dinners typically include a choice of four entrées; a vegetarian entrée is also available daily. Children have their own menu, with "home-from-home" dishes and small portions.

Dessert and pastry items will typically be of good quality, and made specifically for British tastes, although there is much use of canned fruits and jellies.

Sirocco's A La Carte Restaurant is the ship's alternative dining spot; reservations are required and there's a per-person cover charge. It seats only 45 and has superior food and service as well as a more refined, quieter atmosphere. It is adjacent to the Compass Rose Restaurant, but is best entered from the aft stairway.

Instead of the more formal dining room, there is a more casual *Lido Restaurant*. This is open 24 hours a day, with open-seating. Tables are set with crisp linens, flatware and stemware for dinner, when the set menu includes a choice of four entrées. Each week a themed buffet – Chinese, Indian or Mexican, depending on the cruise itinerary – may be offered for dinner. On Lido Deck, the outdoor *Terrace Grill* provides fast-food grilled items and pizza during the day.

ENTERTAINMENT. The 600-seat Broadway Showlounge is two decks high (main and balcony levels) and is the principal venue for production shows and cabaret entertainment. Although Thomson is not generally known for high-quality shows, they are, in fact, good fun, and are professionally produced, while cabaret acts provide entertainment on evenings when there is no production show.

A second entertainment venue, High Spirits, is a multi-functional room for quizzes, dancing, and late-night discotheque. A number of bands and musical units provide live music for dancing and listening in several lounges and bars.

SPA/FITNESS. Oceans Health Club is atop the ship at the aft end. It has good ocean views, and overlooks the aft pool and hot tub, on Bridge Deck. Facilities include an aerobics exercise room, a decent size gymnasium with plenty of treadmills, exercycles, and other body-toning and muscle-pumping equipment, a sauna but no steam room, and several treatment rooms.

You can have massages, aromatherapy facials, body wraps, manicures, pedicures, and hair beautifying treatments. The beauty salon is located close to the Reception Desk on the port side, in a completely different area to the health and fitness facilities.

Veendam
★★★★

Size: ....Mid-Size Ship	Passenger Decks: 10	Cabins (with private balcony): 182
Tonnage: 57,092	Total Crew: 561	Cabins (wheelchair accessible): 8
Lifestyle: ....Premium	Passengers	Wheelchair accessibility: ....Fair
Cruise Line: ....Holland America Line	(lower beds/all berths): 1,346/1,719	Cabin Current: ....110 and 220 volts
Former Names: ....none	Passenger Space Ratio	Elevators: 8
Builder: ....Fincantieri (Italy)	(lower beds/all berths): 42.4/33.2	Casino (gaming tables): ....Yes
Original Cost: ....$215 million	Crew/Passenger Ratio	Slot Machines: ....Yes
Entered Service: ....May 1996	(lower beds/all berths): 2.2/2.9	Swimming Pools (outdoors): 1
Registry: ....The Bahamas	Cabins (total): 674	Swimming Pools (indoors): ..1 (glass dome)
Length (ft/m): 719.3/219.3	Size Range (sq ft/m): 186.2–1,124.8/	Whirlpools: 2
Beam (ft/m): 101.0/30.8	........................17.3–104.5	Self-Service Launderette: ....Yes
Draft (ft/m): 24.6/7.5	Cabins (outside view): 534	Dedicated Cinema/Seats: Yes/249
Propulsion/Propellers:......diesel-electric	Cabins (interior/no view): 140	Library: ....Yes
(34,560kW)/2	Cabins (for one person): 0	Onboard currency: ....US$

Dutch heritage and decor for mature-age cruisers.

OVERVIEW. This ship is fairly well-built, with decent interior fit and finish quality. Holland America Line is constantly fine-tuning its performance, and its regular passengers, almost all North American, find its ships very comfortable and well-run. The company continues its strong maritime traditions, although the present food and service components still let the rest of the cruise experience down.

THE SHIP. *Veendam* is one of four almost identical ships, the others being *Maasdam, Statendam,* and *Ryndam.* The exterior styling is rather angular (some would say boxy – the funnel certainly is), although it is softened and balanced somewhat by the hull being painted black. A ducktail sponson stern was added in 2009 for better stability and ride characteristics. There is a full walk-around teakwood promenade deck outdoors – excellent for strolling, and there's no sign of synthetic turf anywhere. The sunloungers one the exterior promenade deck are wood, with comfortable cushioned pads, while those at the swimming pool on Lido Deck are white plastic.

In the interiors of this "S" -class ship, an asymmetrical layout helps to reduce bottlenecks and congestion. Most public rooms are concentrated on two decks, Promenade Deck, and Upper Promenade Deck, which creates a spacious feel to the interiors. In general, there's a restrained approach to interior styling, using a mixture of contemporary materials combined with traditional woods and ceramics. There is little glitz anywhere.

What is pleasing is the $2 million of artworks, assembled and displayed to represent Holland America Line's fine Dutch heritage and to present a balance between standard

BERLITZ'S RATINGS		
	Possible	Achieved
Ship	500	372
Accommodation	200	150
Food	400	254
Service	400	287
Entertainment	100	72
Cruise	400	285

OVERALL SCORE
1,420 points out of 2,000

itineraries and onboard creature comforts. Also noticeable are the fine flower arrangements,used to good effect to brighten up the dull decor.

Atop the ship is the Crow's Nest Lounge. By day it makes a fine observation lounge, with large ocean-view windows; in the evening it is a nightclub with extremely variable lighting.

A three-deck high atrium foyer is quite appealing, although its sculpted centerpiece makes it look a little crowded, and leaves little room in front of the reception office. A hydraulic glass roof covers the reasonably sized swimming pool/whirlpools and central Lido area so that it can be used in good or bad weather. The focal point here is a large dolphin sculpture.

There is a large, relaxing reference library. The company keeps its ships very clean and tidy, and there is good passenger flow throughout. As part of its "Signature of Excellence" program, the ships have received a new "Mix" lifestyle area. Mix is a trendy, upbeat space combining three specialty theme bars in one central space: Champagne (serving champagne and sparkling wines), Martinis (in individual shakers), and Spirits & Ales (a sports bar with beer and baseball/basketball). Microsoft Surface touch-screen technology is available for playing checkers and chess, air hockey, and other sports game.

The service staff is Indonesian. Although they are mostly quite charming, communication often proves frustrating, and service is spotty and inconsistent.

An escalator travels between two of the lower decks, one of which was originally planned to be the embarkation point, but it is almost redundant. The charge to use the washing machines and dryers in the self-service launderette is petty, particularly for suite occupants who pay high prices for their cruises. The men's urinals in public restrooms are unusually high.

ACCOMMODATION. The accommodation ranges from small interior cabins to a large penthouse suite, in 17 price categories. All cabin TV sets normally carry CNN and TNT programming.

The interior and outside-view standard cabins have twin beds that convert to a queen-size bed, and there is a separate living space with sofa and coffee table. Although the drawer space is generally good, the closet space is very tight, particularly for long cruises – although more than adequate for seven nights. The tiled bathrooms are compact but practical. Bathrobes, hairdryers and a small range of toiletries are provided for all suites/cabins. The bathrooms are quite well laid out, but the tubs are small units better described as shower tubs. Some cabins have interconnecting doors.

On Navigation Deck, 28 suites have accommodation for up to four and offer in-suite dining as an alternative to the dining room, for private meals. They are very spacious, tastefully decorated and well laid-out, with a separate living room, bedroom with two lower beds that convert to a king-size bed, a good-sized living area, dressing room, plenty of closet and drawer space, and marble bathroom with a Jacuzzi tub.

The largest accommodation is the single penthouse suite, located on the starboard side of Navigation Deck at the forward staircase. It has a king-size bed and vanity desk; large walk-in closet with superb drawer space; TV and video player; an oversize whirlpool bath that could seat four and separate shower enclosure, separate washroom with toilet, bidet and washbasin; a living room with writing desk, large TV and full set of audio equipment; dressing room, large private balcony with teak lounge chairs and drinks tables, dining table and four chairs; a pantry with large refrigerator, toaster unit, full coffee/tea-making facilities, and food preparation area and a separate entrance from the hallway; a mini-bar/refrigerator, and a guest toilet and floor-to-ceiling windows. There is no bell push.

CUISINE/DINING. The dramatic *Rotterdam Dining Room* spans two decks at the stern of the ship, and has two grand staircases to connect the two levels, panoramic views on three sides, and a music balcony. Both open-seating and assigned-tables seating are available, while breakfast and lunch are open-seating, though you'll be seated by restaurant staff when you enter. There are tables for two, four, six or eight. The waiter stations are very noisy for those seated

near them. Fine Rosenthal china and good-quality cutlery are provided.

Alternative Dining Option: The intimate *Pinnacle Grill* is located just forward of the balcony level of the main dining room on the starboard side. The 66-seat dining spot has Pacific Northwest cuisine such as fresh Alaskan salmon and halibut, and other regional specialties, plus a selection of premium steaks such as filet mignon from Black Angus beef. Reservations are needed, and a service charge applies. A Bulgari show plate, Rosenthal china, Reidel wine glasses, and Frette table linen are used. The Pinnacle Grill is a better dining experience than the main dining room and worth it for that special celebration.

For more casual evening eating, the dual-line, self-serve *Lido Buffet* is open for casual dinners on all except the last night of each cruise, in an open-seating arrangement. Tables are set with crisp linens, flatware and stemware. A set menu is featured, and this includes a choice of four entreés. It is also the place for casual breakfasts and lunches. At night, a section is transformed into *Canaletto* for casual Italian meals. It is open 5.30–9pm and reservations are requested.

There is much use of canned fruits and packeted items, although there are several commercial low-calorie salad dressings. The choice of cheeses and crackers is poor. The beverage station also lets it down, being no better than those found in family outlets ashore in the USA.

Passengers will need to eat in the Lido Buffet on days when the dining room is closed for lunch – typically once or twice per cruise, depending on the itinerary.

In addition, a poolside grill provides basic American hamburgers and hot dogs.

ENTERTAINMENT. The Showlounge at Sea, at the forward part of the ship, spans two decks, with banquette seating on both main and upper levels. It is basically a well-designed room, but the ceiling is low and sightlines from the balcony level are quite poor.

SPA/FITNESS. The Ocean Spa is one deck below the navigation bridge at the very forward part of the ship. It includes a gymnasium with all the latest muscle-pumping exercise machines, including an abundance of treadmills. It has ocean views, an aerobics exercise area, a large beauty salon with ocean-view windows to the port side, several treatment rooms, and men's and women's sauna, steam room, and changing areas.

● **For more extensive general information on what a Holland America Line cruise is like, see pages 140–3.**

Ventura
★★★★

Size:	.Large Resort Ship	Passenger Decks:	.15	Cabins (with private balcony):	.880
Tonnage:	.116,017	Total Crew:	.1,239	Cabins (wheelchair accessible):	.25
Lifestyle:	.Standard	Passengers		Wheelchair accessibility:	.Good
Cruise Line:	.P&O Cruises	(lower beds/all berths):	.3,092/3,574	Cabin Voltage:	.220 volts
Former Names:	.none	Passenger Space Ratio		Elevators:	.12
Builder:	.Fincantieri (Italy)	(lower beds/all berths):	.37.5/32.4	Casino (gaming tables):	.Yes
Original Cost:	.€535 million	Crew/Passenger Ratio		Slot Machines:	.Yes
Entered Service:	.Apr 2008	(lower beds/all berths):	.2.4/2.8	Swimming Pools (outdoors):	.3
Registry:	.Bermuda	Cabins (total):	.1,546	Swimming Pools (indoors):	.0
Length (ft/m):	.951.4/290.0	Size Range (sq ft/m):	.134.5–534.0/	Whirlpools:	.6
Beam (ft/m):	.118.1/36.0		12.5–49.6	Self-Service Launderette:	.Yes
Draft (ft/m):	.27.8/8.5	Cabins (outside view):	.1,101	Dedicated Cinema/Seats:	.No
Propulsion/Propellers:	.diesel-electric	Cabins (interior/no view):	.445	Library:	.Yes
	(42,000kW)/2	Cabins (for one person):	.0	Onboard currency:	.UK£

Family-friendly cruising to suit British family tastes.

OVERVIEW. *Ventura* is targeted at families with children as well as adult couples who are looking for a big-ship environment with comfortable but unstuffy surroundings and lots of options. Active types can take instruction in Cirque Ventura's activities, including juggling, acro-balancing, tight-wire walking, stilt walking, and clowning.

THE SHIP. *Ventura* is the P&O version of Princess Cruises' Grand-class ships, and, along with sister ship *Azura*, is the largest cruise ship yet built specifically for UK passengers. With its flat stern, it looks a bit like a giant hatchback, but the ship's side profile is softer and more balanced. There are promenade walking decks to port and starboard sides, underneath the lifeboats. You can't walk completely around, however; it's narrow in some places, and you have to weave past a number of deck lounge chairs. There are three pools: two on the pool deck, one of which can be covered by a glass-roofed skydome, and one at the stern. If your cabin is towards the front of the ship, it's a long walk to get to the pool at the stern. Considering the number of passengers carried, there's not a lot of outdoor deck space.

Inside, a three-deck atrium is the focal point. Designed on a gateway theme, central to which are four towering black granite archways sourced from India, it's the place to see and be seen, and the best location to arrange to meet friends. The upper-deck public room layout is challenging because you can't go from one end of the ship to the other without first going down, along and up – not so good for those with mobility problems. In other words, you'll need to plan your journey and use the most appropriate of three elevator banks.

Public rooms include a surprisingly small, rather open-plan library (Chapter One) that's not at all intimate, a Cyb@center for internet connections, an overly large Cruise Sales Centre, Fortunes Casino, and several bars, including The Exchange (an urban warehouse bar), and Metropolis (set high atop the ship with great aft views and views along the ship's sides – over everyone's balcony), a Cuban bar, and a Spanish tapas bar. It's all rather multi-cultural and not so British. But check out the train that runs around the upper part of the upper bar of The Exchange.

The Cirque Ventura area has four bungee trampolines and a flying trapeze – all up high on Deck 19. There are 7,000 pieces of art on board from 55 British artists, and you can buy "artwork" in an art gallery.

Passenger niggles include the constant push for onboard revenue; low passenger space ratio; mediocre self-service buffet food; and a charge for shuttle buses in many ports.

Smoking is permitted on cabin balconies and in designated spots on the open decks. Gratuities are at your discretion, but recommended at £3.75 per person, per day.

FAMILIES. Children will be pleased to find that, for 2–4-year olds, Noddy is on board. There are children's clubs for the under-twos up to 17 years, plus a rock 'n' roll school. Youngsters can also enjoy Scalextric at sea with Grand Prix-style track, 3D cinema, and interactive art classes. Family shore programs feature aqua and "theme parks." There's a useful Night Nursery for the under-fives. It's possible to get married on board, with the captain officiating.

ACCOMMODATION. There are 31 accommodation price grades, according to size and location chosen, although there

BERLITZ'S RATINGS

	Possible	Achieved
Ship	500	425
Accommodation	200	166
Food	400	249
Service	400	286
Entertainment	100	77
Cruise	400	306

OVERALL SCORE
1,509 points out of 2,000

are really just five types of accommodation: suite with balcony; family suite with balcony; outside-view twin/queen with balcony; outside-view twin/queen; interior no-view cabin. More than one-third of all cabins are of the interior variety. Some have extra third/fourth berths that fold down from the ceiling. While the suites are quite spacious, they are quite small when compared to suites aboard some other cruise lines, such as Celebrity Cruises or NCL.

Standard in all cabins: bed runners, 10.5 tog duvets, Slumberland eight-inch sprung mattresses, Egyptian cotton towels and robes, and extensive Nick Munro-designed stainless steel tea/coffee making facilities including water kettle, coffee pot, proper teapot, and mugs, all on a bespoke silver tray. The tea-making set-up is excellent, but getting fresh milk can sometimes be a problem.

Open closets are new for P&O Cruises, however (no doors = save money), and actually provide easier access. Balcony cabins have teak patio furniture, and an outside light. Decent-quality personal toiletries are by Temple Spa.

Wheelchair-accessible cabins have a shower enclosure, except one (R415) that has a bathtub with integral shower. They are mostly in the front section, but the Bay Tree restaurant is aft – so be prepared for lots of waiting time at elevators. Wheelchair users should note that breakfast in the three main restaurants typically ends at 9.30am on sea days (9am on port days). To take breakfast in the self-serve Waterside casual eatery, wheelchair users need to wheel across the decks containing the Beachcomber and Laguna pools and lots of deck chairs – not easy. Alternatively, they can order room service breakfast – typically cold items only. There is no room service breakfast on disembarkation day, when the company wants you out of your cabin by 8am.

CUISINE. P&O's marketing blurb claims that there are 10 restaurants. There aren't. There are five genuine restaurants (Bay Tree, Cinnnamon, Saffron, The White Room, and East); the rest are eateries.

The three principal dining rooms, *Bay Tree, Cinnamon,* and *Saffron,* have standard à la carte menus. The Bay Tree offers fixed seating dining, with assigned tables and typical seating times of 6:30pm or 8:30pm. In the other two, you can dine when you want, with whom you want, between 6pm and 10pm – P&O calls it "Freedom Dining" – although at peak times there can be long waiting times for a table.

Once or twice per cruise, additional special dinners are served in the main dining rooms, one being a Chaîne des Rôtisseurs event. The ship's wine list is ho-hum average.

Alternative dining venues include the following:
● *The White Room* is located high up on the ship, above the children's play area, with a quarter of the tables on deck. It serves modern European dishes by celebrity chef Marco Pierre White in an environment which is intimate and atten-

tive but not stuffy and is particularly suitable for families. Reservations are necessary, and there's a cover charge. The food is good because it's cooked to order, unlike in the main dining rooms. Occasionally, Marco Pierre White will sail aboard the ship, and hold cooking classes for up to eight participants in one of the ship's galleys; the extra cost is high, but worth it, and includes a tasting of the finished product.
● For complete privacy, private balcony dining, with selections from the Marco Pierre White menu, is also available as a rather pricey (but perhaps worthwhile) extra-cost option.
● *The Waterside* is a large, self-serve buffet "seaside chic" dining spot, with indoor-outdoor seating, but the seating is rather poorly designed and cramped.
● On the same deck, adjacent to the forward pool, are *Frankie's Grill* and *Frankie's Pizzeria.*
● *Tazzine,* a coffee lounge by day, turns into a cocktail bar in the evening.
● *The Beach House* is a casual dining spot for families, open 24 hours. Marco's roof-side café serves gourmet pizzas, grills and original ice cream flavors, such as chocolate truffle and prune and Armagnac. Children's cutlery, bibs, and beakers are available.
● *Ramblas* is a tapas and wine bar (some items at extra cost).
● *East,* an Asian fusion eatery on the main indoor promenade.
In addition, 24-hour room service is available in cabins.

ENTERTAINMENT. P&O claims the 785-seat Arena Theatre, at the front of the ship and spanning two decks, is the largest showlounge aboard a UK-based cruise ship, but in fact the showlounge aboard *Queen Mary 2* is bigger, with 1,094 seats, as is the Showlounge aboard *Independence of the Seas.* Havana, the main nightclub and entertainment venue, where movies are sometimes shown, is an activities room by day and a sultry Cuba-inspired club by night, but sightlines are extremely poor from many seats.

A video wall in the Cosmopolitan club lounge screens real-time footage of the world's seven most famous city skylines – Sydney, Paris, New York, Rio de Janeiro, Las Vegas, Hong Kong and London. It's neat.

SPA/FITNESS. The Oasis Spa is located forward, almost atop the ship. It includes a gymnasium, aerobics room, beauty salon, separate male and female sauna and steam rooms, and 11 treatment rooms. An internal stairway connects to the deck below, which contains an extra-charge Thermal Suite. Harding Brothers provide the spa staff and services. Treatments include special packages for couples, and the SilverSpa Generation, as well as a whole range of individual treatments.

● **For more extensive general information on what a P&O cruise is like, see pages 148–9.**
see pages 148–9.

Vision of the Seas
★★★★

Size: . . . . .Large Resort Ship	Total Crew: 765	Wheelchair accessibility: . . . . .Good
Tonnage: 78,491	Passengers	Cabin Current: . . . . . . .110 and 220 volts
Lifestyle: . . . . .Standard	(lower beds/all berths): 2,000/2,435	Elevators: 9
Cruise Line: Royal Caribbean International	Passenger Space Ratio	Casino (gaming tables): . . . . .Yes
Former Names: . . . . .none	(lower beds/all berths): 39.2/32.2	Slot Machines: . . . . .Yes
Builder: Chantiers de l'Atlantique (France)	Crew/Passenger Ratio	Swimming Pools (outdoors): 1
Original Cost: . . . .$275 million	(lower beds/all berths): 3.0/3.6	Swimming Pools (indoors): 1
Entered Service: . . . . .May 1998	Cabins (total): 1,000	(inside/outside)
Registry: . . . . .The Bahamas	Size Range (sq ft/m): 135.0–1,270.1/	Whirlpools: 6
Length (ft/m): 915.3/279.0	12.5–118.0	Self-Service Launderette: . . . . .No
Beam (ft/m): 105.6/32.2	Cabins (outside view): 593	Dedicated Cinema/Seats: . . . . .No
Draft (ft/m): 24.9/7.6	Cabins (interior/no view): 407	Library: . . . . .Yes
Propulsion/Propellers: . . . . .diesel-electric	Cabins (for one person): 0	Onboard currency: . . . . .US$
(50,400kW)2	Cabins (with private balcony): 229	
Passenger Decks: 11	Cabins (wheelchair accessible): 14	

Pleasant decor for casual, family-friendly cruising.

OVERVIEW. This ship represents Royal Caribbean International's interpretation of a floating contemporary hotel, and has the nicest mix of colors and decor of any of the Vision-class ships, with lots of warm beige and pink tones, particularly in the expansive atrium. There are plenty of public rooms, bars and lounges, as well as a large, well-lit casino.

THE SHIP. This sister to *Rhapsody of the Seas* shares design features that make all Royal Caribbean International ships identifiable, including a Viking Crown Lounge that's also the ship's multi-level disco. The lounge is just aft of the center of the ship, above the central atrium lobby, with the funnel located well aft. The ship's stern is beautifully rounded. There is a reasonable amount of open-air walking space, although this can become cluttered with sunloungers that would benefit from having cushioned pads.

The $6 million-worth of artwork is colorful and very creative, with more previously blank wall space covered with interesting artworks of differing shapes and sizes. Most noticeable is the extensive use of glass. Two beautiful glass sculptures stand out: one in the atrium, at the entrance to a Champagne Bar, and one on the upper level of the Viking Crown Lounge. The music in this nightspot can be loud and overbearing, and so can cigarette smoke around the bar – one of few places smokers can light up.

The best atmosphere is in the nautical-theme Schooner Bar. The Library has an excellent array of hardbacks, and a neat wooden sculpture of something that looks like the Tin Man from *The Wizard of Oz*.

BERLITZ'S RATINGS		
	Possible	Achieved
Ship	500	425
Accommodation	200	166
Food	400	240
Service	400	287
Entertainment	100	81
Cruise	400	292

OVERALL SCORE
1,491 points out of 2,000

ACCOMMODATION. There are 18 cabin categories, at 11 price points. The standard interior and exterior view cabins are of an adequate size, and have just enough functional facilities to make them comfortable for a one-week cruise, but longer might prove confining. The decor is bright and cheerful, although the ceilings are plain; colorful soft furnishings make one's home away from home look like the inside of a modern Scandinavian hotel – minimalist yet colorful. Twin lower beds convert to queen-size beds, and there is a reasonable amount of closet and drawer space, but there is little room to maneuver between the bed and desk/television unit.

The bathrooms are small but functional, and the shower units are small. There is no cabinet for toiletries. The towels could be larger and thicker.

Choose a "C" grade suite for spacious accommodation that includes a curtained-off sleeping area, a good-sized outside balcony with part-partition, lounge with sofa, two chairs and coffee table, three closets, plenty of drawer and storage space, TV set and video player. The bathroom is large and has a full-size tub, integral shower, and two washbasins/two toiletries cabinets.

For the ultimate accommodation, choose the Royal Suite, which resembles a Palm Beach apartment and has a white baby grand piano. It has a separate bedroom with king-size bed, living room with queen-size sofa bed, refrigerator/minibar, dining table, entertainment center, and vanity dressing area. The decor is simple and elegant, with pastel colors. Located just under the starboard-side navigation bridge wing, it has its own private balcony.

CUISINE. The *Aquarius Dining Room* is set on two levels with large ocean-view picture windows on two sides – rectangular windows on the upper level, large circular windows on the lower level – and a large connecting stairway. Choose one of two seatings, or "My Time Dining" where you can eat when you want, during dining room hours.

The *Windjammer Café* is the casual dining spot for self-serve buffets. The area is well-designed, with contemporary decor and colors, but the food is really basic fare and disappointing and the four-sided self-service buffet area is small for the number of passengers that use it. More money needs to be spent for better-quality ingredients and more variety is needed. Each evening, the room offers an alternative to the dressier dining room. The evening buffets typically feature a different theme, something this company has been doing for more than 25 years – perhaps the time has come for more creativity.

A hamburger/hot dog grill counter in the Solarium, but you don't usually get a choice of how you like your hamburgers cooked – everything seems to be well done.

The company has introduced a drinks package, available at all bars in the form of cards or stickers, that enables you to pre-pay for a selection of standard soft drinks and alcoholic drinks. The packages are not easy to understand.

ENTERTAINMENT. The Masquerade Theatre, the ship's principal showlounge, is located in the forward section of the ship and presents production shows and other major cabaret shows. It is a large, but a well-designed room with main and balcony levels, and good sightlines from most of the banquette seats.

Other cabaret acts are presented in the Some Enchanted Evening Lounge, located aft, and these include late-night adult comedy, as well as live music for dancing. A number of other bars and lounges have live music of differing types.

The entertainment throughout is upbeat – in fact, it's difficult to get away from music and noise. There's even background music in all corridors and elevators, and constant music outdoors on the pool deck. If you want a quiet relaxing holiday, choose another ship.

SPA/FITNESS. The spa, with its solarium and indoor/outdoor dome-covered pool, Inca- and Mayan-theme decor, sauna/steam rooms and gymnasium, provides a haven for health-conscious and fitness buffs, if they can resist a pizza bar forward of the pool area. A lovely "Mayan Serpent" sculpture is displayed in the solarium.

For more sporting passengers, there is activity galore – including a rock-climbing wall with several separate climbing tracks. It is located outdoors at the aft end of the funnel.

● **For more extensive general information about the Royal Caribbean cruise experience, see pages 152–6.**

WATERTIGHT CONTRACTS

Cruise lines are masters of small print when it comes to contracts. A clause in the ticket typically reads: "The Carrier's legal responsibility for death, injury, illness, damage, delay, or other loss or detriment of person or property of whatever kind suffered by the Passenger will, in the first instance, be governed by the Athens Convention relating to the Carriage of Passengers and their Luggage by Sea, 1974, with protocols and amendments, together with the further provisions of the International Convention on Limitation of Liability for Maritime Claims, 1976, with revisions and amendments (hereinafter collectively referred to as the "Convention"). The Carrier shall not be liable for any such death, injury, illness, damage, delay, loss, or detriment caused by Act of God, war or warlike operations, civil commotions, labor trouble, interference by Authorities, perils of the sea, or any other cause beyond the control of the Carrier, fire, thefts or any other crime, errors in the navigation or management of the Vessel, or defect in, or unseaworthiness of hull, machinery, appurtenances, equipment, furnishings, or supplies of the Vessel, fault or neglect of pilot, tugs, agents, independent contractors, such as ship's Physician, Passengers or other persons on board not in the Carrier's employ or for any other cause of whatsoever nature except and unless it is proven that such death, injury, illness, damage, delay, loss resulting from Carrier's act or omission was committed with the intent to cause such loss or with knowledge that such loss would probably result therefrom and in that event the Carrier's liability therefore shall not exceed the specified limitations per Passenger in Special Drawing Rights (S.D.R.) as defined in the applicable conventions or in any further revision and/or amendment thereto as shall become applicable."

Vistamar
★★ +

Size: ....Small Ship	Passenger Decks: 6	Cabins (with private balcony): 11
Tonnage: 7,478	Total Crew: 114	Cabins (wheelchair accessible): 0
Lifestyle: ....Standard	Passengers	Wheelchair accessibility: ....None
Cruise Line: ....Plein Cap	(lower beds/all berths): 299/320	Cabin Current: ....220 volts
Former Names: ...Santa Cruz de Tenerife	Passenger Space Ratio	Elevators: 1
Builder: ....Union Navale de Levante	(lower beds/all berths): 25.3/23.3	Casino (gaming tables): ....No
(Spain)	Crew/Passenger Ratio	Slot Machines: ....No
Original Cost: ....$45 million	(lower beds/all berths): 2.7/2.9	Swimming Pools (outdoors): 1
Entered Service: ....Sep 1989/2011	Cabins (total): 152	Swimming Pools (indoors): 0
Registry: ....Italy	Size Range (sq ft/m): 129.1–150.6/	Whirlpools: 0
Length (ft/m): 396.9/121.00	12.0–14.0	Self-Service Launderette: ....No
Beam (ft/m): 55.1/16.82	Cabins (outside view): 126	Dedicated Cinema/Seats: ....No
Draft (ft/m): 14.9/4.55	Cabins (interior/no view): 26	Library: ....Yes
Propulsion/Propellers: .diesel (3,900kW)/2	Cabins (for one person): 5	Onboard currency: ....Euros

Casual small ship cruising for budget-minded adults.

OVERVIEW. This ship operates under charter to French Riviera-based Plein Cap for the French-speaking market. It suits couples and single travelers looking for a first cruise in the comfortable, contemporary, but not luxurious or pretentious surroundings of a small ship offering interesting itineraries, and all at a low price.

THE SHIP. *Vistamar* has a moderately smart, reasonably contemporary, but rather squat small ship profile. The ship, which has an ice-hardened hull, also carries six inflatable rubber landing craft for close-up landings during certain itineraries that include the Amazon, Arctic and Antarctic.

An "open bridge" policy means you can join the captain and other navigation officers at almost any time except during difficult maneuvers. There is a good open observation deck at the forward-most part of the ship atop the navigation bridge. But the other open deck and sunbathing space is a little limited, particularly on the aft open deck around the small outdoor pool – really only a "dip" pool, though it has a large splash surround.

The interior layout has all the public rooms located aft in a "cake-layer" stacking, with a single, central staircase that takes up most of the space in a three-deck-high atrium lobby with a glass elevator shaped like half a cable car. Features include wood-trimmed interior decor, which is quite jazzy, attractive and warm, although the mirrored metallic ceilings are somewhat irritating.

A four-deck high atrium with a "sky dome" has a glass-walled elevator and a wrap-around staircase, and is the focal point of the interior. The library has comfortable high wing-back chairs but not many books. There is a Card Room,

BERLITZ'S RATINGS		
	Possible	Achieved
Ship	500	232
Accommodation	200	107
Food	400	210
Service	400	237
Entertainment	100	56
Cruise	400	219
OVERALL SCORE		
1,061 points out of 2,000		

and board games are available. The main lounge, Don Fernando, is named after Señor Don Fernando Abril Martorell, the president of the Union Navale de Levante shipyard that constructed *Vistamar* in 444 days (perhaps if more time had been taken, the ship would have been built better). For the late-night set, there is a rather jazzy nightclub/disco, with acres of glass, set around the base of the funnel, with a long bar, and dance floor.

The product is aimed at the inexpensive end of the market. The dress code is ultra-casual – no tuxedos, no ties. There is an abundance of greenery, which provides a warm, comfortable and less clinical ambience.

The ship is quite small, enabling passengers to enjoy interesting destination-intensive cruises, with many port calls that larger ships can't access. Plein Cap's focus is on its lecture and enrichment programs, and its convivial staff and atmosphere. Its cruises include drinks, table wines, and mineral water with meals. Tipping is recommended at €5–€6 per person, per day.

The downside? The tiny "dip" swimming pool is virtually useless. There is a distinct odor of diesel fuel at the upper level of the lobby, where there is no air-conditioning. The hotel operation is rather sloppy and needs streamlining. There is no walking track or walk-around promenade deck outdoors. The fit, finish and maintenance are all quite poor. Sightlines in the single-level showlounge are awful, and there is a lack of good stage lighting.

ACCOMMODATION. Cabins are located forward, while the public rooms are positioned aft, which means there is a minimal amount of noise in cabins – good if you're having an early night. There are 11 grades, but in just two sizes: suites with private (covered) balcony and queen-size bed; outside-view or interior cabins for two, three or four persons, all with fixed, wide single beds. All cabins are reasonably comfortable, although bathrooms are extremely small and tight (there's a considerable "lip" to step over to access the bathroom). Closet and drawer space is limited.

Cabins have twin beds with wooden headboard, small vanity/writing desk, TV set, climate-control, telephone, and hairdryer. Most cabinetry is made with a wood finish.

There are 11 suites, each with a small, narrow, private, covered balcony outdoors. The suites are: Alboran, Algarve, Almeria, Armador, Cadiz, Cordoba, Granada, Huelva, Jaen, Malaga, Seville – all regions of Andalucia. They also have a more spacious bathroom, with a large tub and integral shower. The living area is also larger, and comes with a sofa, coffee table, vanity/writing desk, and a larger TV set. Armador is the owner's suite, and has a circular bathtub with integral shower, set against large picture windows – wonderful for the Arctic and Antarctic cruises that this company operates in the appropriate season. Petit fours and mineral water are provided for suite occupants.

All passengers get personal amenities that include soap, shampoo, body lotion and bath/shower gel, and shoeshine mitt. Accommodation hallways are provided either in hospital green, powder blue, or hot pink.

CUISINE. The *Andalucia Restaurant* is quite warm and inviting, with contemporary colors and decor, and large picture windows, although the six pillars detract from the otherwise attractive room. Its focal point is a model of a sailing vessel with an emerald green hull – about the same color as the fabrics on the dining room chairs. There is one seating for all passengers, so meals are leisurely, with assigned tables for four, six or eight – but none for two. Window-side tables are for six, and chairs have armrests. Some dinners are themed.

The food is reasonably adequate and quite sound, and dinners typically come with a choice of three entrées plus a vegetarian selection. The selection of cooked green vegetables, breads, cheeses and fruits is limited, and the overall cuisine really is of quite a low standard. The service is adequate, no more, as is the wine list. Sekt (sweet sparkling wine) is provided for breakfast, while white and red table wines are provided for lunch and dinner. Breakfast and lunch buffets are available on the Lido deck.

ENTERTAINMENT. There is little entertainment apart from some cabaret acts and live music for dancing and listening.

SPA/FITNESS. There is no spa to speak of, although there is a fitness room, a sauna, a massage treatment room, and a small beauty salon.

Volendam
★★★★

Size:	Mid-Size Ship	Total Crew:	561	Wheelchair accessibility:	Good

Size: ....Mid-Size Ship
Tonnage: 61,396
Lifestyle: ....Premium
Cruise Line: ......Holland America Line
Former Names: ....none
Builder: ....Fincantieri (Italy)
Original Cost: ....$300 million
Entered Service: ....Nov 1999
Registry: ....The Netherlands
Length (ft/m): 781.0/238.00
Beam (ft/m): 105.8/32.25
Draft (ft/m): 25.5/7.80
Propulsion/Propellers: .....diesel-electric
(37,500kW)/2
Passenger Decks: 10

Total Crew: 561
Passengers
(lower beds/all berths): 1,440/1,850
Passenger Space Ratio
(lower beds/all berths): 42.6/33.1
Crew/Passenger Ratio
(lower beds/all berths): 2.5/2.5
Cabins (total): 720
Size Range (sq ft/m): 113.0–1,126.0/
10.5–104.6
Cabins (outside view): 581
Cabins (interior/no view): 139
Cabins (for one person): 0
Cabins (with private balcony): 197
Cabins (wheelchair accessible): 23

Wheelchair accessibility: ....Good
Cabin Current: ....110 volts
Elevators: 12
Casino (gaming tables): ....Yes
Slot Machines: ....Yes
Swimming Pools (outdoors): 2
Swimming Pools (indoors): 1
(glass dome cover)
Whirlpools: 2
Self-Service Launderette: ....Yes (2)
Dedicated Cinema/Seats: Yes/205
Library: ....Yes
Onboard currency: ....US$

Dutch decor and heritage for mature-age cruisers.

OVERVIEW. Having been built to approximately the same size as the company's newest *Rotterdam*, the same layout and public rooms have been incorporated into the interiors. This carries on the same flow and comfortable feeling so that repeat passengers will quickly feel at home aboard almost any ship in the Holland America Line fleet.

THE SHIP. The ship's name is taken from the fishing village of Volendam, north of Amsterdam, Holland. The hull is dark blue, in keeping with all Holland America Line ships.

Volendam has three main passenger stairways, which is so much better than two, from the viewpoints of safety, accessibility and passenger flow. There is a glass dome-covered pool on the Lido Deck between the mast and the funnel. The main interior design theme is flowers, from the 17th to the 21st centuries. The interior focal point is a huge crystal sculpture, *Caleido*, in the three-deck-high atrium, by one of Italy's leading contemporary glass artists, Luciano Vistosi. Health spa facilities include more treatment rooms.

In the casino bar, also known as the sports bar, a cinematic theme presents visions of Hollywood, and includes a collection of costumes, props, photos and posters of movies and the actors who starred in them.

At the Lido Deck swimming pool, leaping dolphins are the focal point. The pool itself is also one deck higher than the Statendam-class ships, with the positive result being the fact that there is now direct access between the aft and midships pools (not so aboard the S-class ships).

There is a charge to use the washing machines and dryers in the self-service launderette, although it really should

BERLITZ'S RATINGS

	Possible	Achieved
Ship	500	429
Accommodation	200	165
Food	400	282
Service	400	276
Entertainment	100	77
Cruise	400	311

OVERALL SCORE
1,540 points out of 2,000

be included for the occupants of high-priced suites. Although room service is adequate, it remains a weak point.

ACCOMMODATION. The range is similar to that found aboard the similarly sized *Rotterdam*, and has 17 categories. There is one penthouse suite, and 28 suites, with the rest of the accommodation a mix of outside-view and interior cabins, and many more balcony cabins ("mini-suites") than aboard the slightly smaller *Statendam*-class ships. All standard interior and outside cabins are tastefully furnished, and have twin beds that convert to a queen-size bed, but space is tight for walking between beds and vanity unit. The fully tiled bathrooms are disappointingly small, particularly for long cruises, and have small shower tubs, utilitarian toiletries cupboards, and exposed under-sink plumbing. Storage space is also small for long cruises.

There are 28 full Verandah Suites on Navigation Deck, and one Penthouse Suite. All suite occupants share a private Concierge Lounge, with a concierge to handle such things as special dining arrangements, shore excursions, private parties and special requests. Strangely, there are no butlers for these suites. Each Verandah Suite has a separate bedroom, dressing and living areas. Suite passengers get personal stationery, complimentary laundry and ironing, cocktail hour hors d'oeuvres and other goodies, as well as priority embarkation and disembarkation.

For the ultimate in accommodation and living space aboard this ship, choose the Penthouse Suite. It has a separate steward's entrance, a large bedroom with king-size bed, separate living room with baby grand piano, and a dining room, dressing room, walk-in closet, butler's pantry, and private balcony – though the balcony is no larger than that of any other suite. Other facilities include an audio-visual center with TV set and DVD player, wet bar with refrigerator, large bathroom with Jacuzzi tub, separate toilet with bidet, and a guest bathroom with toilet and washbasin.

Except for the penthouse suite, located forward on the starboard side, the bathrooms in suites and "mini-suites" are a little disappointing – neither as spacious nor as opulent as one would expect. All outside-view suites and cabin bathrooms have a tub/shower while interior cabins have a shower only.

The 23 cabins for the mobility-limited have a roll-in shower enclosure for wheelchair users – none have bathtubs, no matter what the category.

CUISINE. There is one main dining room, and one alternative dining spot (dinner only). The 747-seat *Rotterdam Dining Room* is a traditional, grand room spread over two decks, with ocean views on three sides and an imposing staircase connecting upper and lower levels.

Both open seating and fixed seating with assigned tables and times are available, while breakfast and lunch are open-seating where you'll be seated by restaurant staff on entry. Fine Rosenthal china and good-quality cutlery are provided, but no fish knives. Tables are four two, four, six or eight.

Alternative Dining Option: The casual-dress *Marco Polo Restaurant* seats 88, and there is no charge, although reservations are required. Created in the style of a California artists' bistro, it provides Italian cuisine with a set menu and nightly specials. So passengers have more choice and an occasional change of venue; anyone booking suite-grade accommodation get priority reservations.

The *Lido Buffet* is a self-serve café for casual breakfasts and luncheons. There is also an outdoor grill for those who enjoy hamburgers, hot dogs and other fast-food items. The Lido Buffet is also open for casual dinners on each night except for the last one, in an open-seating arrangement. Tables are set with crisp linens, flatware and stemware. A set menu includes a choice of four entrées.

ENTERTAINMENT. The Frans Hals Showlounge spans two decks, with banquette seating on both main and upper levels. It is basically a well-designed room, but the ceiling is low and the sight lines from the balcony level are poor.

SPA/FITNESS. The health spa facilities are quite decent, and include a gymnasium with muscle-toning equipment, separate saunas and steam rooms for men and women, and several treatment rooms, each with a shower and toilet. There are practice tennis courts outdoors, as well as the traditional shuffleboard courts, jogging track, and a full walk-around teakwood promenade deck for strolling.

The Ocean Spa and onboard fitness classes are operated by Steiner, a specialist concession.

● **For more extensive general information on what a Holland America Line cruise is like, see pages 140–3.**

Voyager of the Seas
★★★★

Size: . . . . .Large Resort Ship	Passenger Decks: 14	Cabins (with private balcony): 757
Tonnage: 137,280	Total Crew: 1,176	Cabins (wheelchair accessible): 26
Lifestyle: . . . . .Standard	Passengers	Wheelchair accessibility: . . . . .Best
Cruise Line: Royal Caribbean International	(lower beds/all berths): 3,114/3,838	Cabin Current: . . . . .110 volts
Former Names: . . . . .none	Passenger Space Ratio	Elevators: . . . . .14 (6 glass-enclosed)
Builder: . . .Kvaerner Masa-Yards (Finland)	(lower beds/all berths): 44.0/35.7	Casino (gaming tables): . . . . .Yes
Original Cost: . . . .$500 million	Crew/Passenger Ratio	Slot Machines: . . . . .Yes
Entered Service: . . . . .Nov 1999	(lower beds/all berths): 2.6/3.2	Swimming Pools (outdoors): 3
Registry: . . . . .The Bahamas	Cabins (total): 1,557	Swimming Pools (indoors): 0
Length (ft/m): 1,020.6/311.1	Size Range (sq ft/m): 151.0–1,358.0/	Whirlpools: 6
Beam (ft/m): 155.5/47.4	14.0–126.1	Self-Service Launderette: . . . . .No
Draft (ft/m): 28.8/8.8	Cabins (outside view): 939	Dedicated Cinema/Seats: . . . . .No
Propulsion/Propellers: . . . . .diesel-electric	Cabins (interior/no view): 618	Library: . . . . .Yes
(2 azimuthing, 1 fixed/14 MW each)	Cabins (for one person): 0	Onboard currency: . . . . .US$

A large, family-friendly ship with multiple eating venues.

OVERVIEW. In terms of sheer size, this ship presently dwarfs many others in the cruise industry, but in terms of personal service, the reverse is the case, unless you happen to reside in one of the top suites. This is impersonal city life at sea, and a superb, well-designed alternative to a land-based resort. Take lots of extra pennies – you'll need them to pay for all the additional-cost items.

THE SHIP. The exterior design of *Voyager of the Seas* is not unlike an enlarged version of the Royal Caribbean International's Vision-class ships. With its large proportions, it provides more facilities and options, yet manages to have a healthy passenger space ratio (the amount of space per passenger). It's too large to go through the Panama Canal, thus limiting itineraries almost exclusively to the Caribbean, where few islands have decent enough sized facilities to service it, or for use as a floating island resort. When you step aboard, spend the first few hours exploring all the many facilities and public spaces aboard this vessel; you'll find it to be time well spent.

Although the ship is large, the cabin hallways have an extremely warm and attractive feel, with artwork cabinets and wavy lines to lead you along and break up the monotony. In fact, there are plenty of colorful, even whimsical, decorative touches to help brighten up what would otherwise be a very clinical environment.

At certain times, passengers may be allowed to stand right at the bows of the ship on an observation platform, perhaps with arms spread in an "eagle-like" position like the stars in the movie *Titanic*. What a photo opportunity! However, for the best ones, as in the film, you'll need to

BERLITZ'S RATINGS		
	Possible	Achieved
Ship	500	414
Accommodation	200	150
Food	400	222
Service	400	272
Entertainment	100	83
Cruise	400	304
OVERALL SCORE		
1,445 points out of 2,000		

bring a helicopter. But just looking up at the cake-layer stacking of the decks towards the bridge gives you an idea of the size of the ship.

Embarkation and disembarkation take place through two access points, designed to minimize the inevitable lines at the start and end of the cruise – more than 1,500 people for each access point. Once inside the ship, you'll need good walking shoes, particularly when you need to go from one end to the other – it really is quite a long way.

A four-deck-high Royal Promenade, the interior focal point, is a good place to arrange to meet someone. It is 393.7 ft (120 meters) long – the length of two American football fields, and has two internal lobbies that rise through 11 decks, one at each end. There are 16 elevators in four banks of four.

The entrance to one of three levels of the main restaurant, together with shops and entertainment locations are spun off from this "boulevard", while interior "interior promenade-view" cabins, with bay windows, look into it from above. It houses a traditional English "pub" (the "Pig 'n' Whistle, with draft beer and "street-front" seating), a Promenade Café (for continental breakfast, all-day pizzas, sandwiches and coffees), Ben & Jerry's Ice Cream (at extra cost), Sprinkles (for round-the-clock ice-cream and yoghurt), and Scoreboard (a sports bar).

Several shops complete the picture: a jewelry shop, gift shop, perfume shop, liquor shop and a logo souvenir shop. A bright red telephone kiosk houses an ATM cash machine. Altogether, it's a nice place to see and be seen, and street performers provide a diversion. It really is a cross between a shopping arcade and an amusement park – Florida's

Aventura meets New York's Coney Island. The chairman of Royal Caribbean International even donated his own treasured Morgan sports car to grace the Royal Promenade, which is supposedly designed in the image of London's fashionable Burlington Arcade. Actually, by far the best view of the whole promenade is from one of the 138 premium-price cabins that look into it, or from a "captain's bridge" that crosses above it. At the forward end is the showlounge. A Connoisseur's Club cigar lounge is on the starboard side between the showlounge and the main section of the Royal Promenade.

Arched across the grand promenade is a captain's balcony, and in the center of the promenade a stairway connects you to the deck below, where you'll find the Schooner Bar (a piano lounge that's a feature of all RCI ships) and the colorful Casino Royale (large and full of flashing lights and noises). Gaming includes blackjack, Caribbean stud poker, and craps, as well as 300 slot machines and the world's largest interactive roulette wheel, activated by a roulette ball tower four decks high.

A second showlounge – Studio B, a regulation-size ice-skating rink that has real, not fake, ice – has arena seating for up to 900 and the latest in broadcast facilities. A number of slim pillars obstruct the clear-view arena stage sight-lines, however. An Ice Follies show is presented by a professional ice-skating show team each cruise. If ice-skating in the Caribbean doesn't particularly appeal, you might like to visit the stunning two-deck library; it's the first aboard any cruise ship, and is open 24 hours a day. A total of $12 million was spent on permanent artwork.

Drinking places include a neat Aquarium Bar, with 50 tons of glass and water in four large aquariums worth over $1 million, the small and intimate Champagne Bar, and the Connoisseur Club – for cigars and cognacs. Jazz fans might appreciate High Notes, an intimate room for cool music atop the ship within the Viking Crown Lounge, and the Schooner Bar piano lounge. For golfers, there's the 19th Hole, a golf bar.

A large TV studio, part of Studio "B", is adjacent to rooms that can be used for trade show exhibit space, with a 400-seat conference center and a 60-seat multi-media screening room. Many decks above, couples can tie the knot in a "wedding chapel in the sky," the Skylight Chapel, which is located on the upper level of the Viking Crown Lounge and even has wheelchair access via an electric stairway elevator. Outdoors, the pool and open deck areas on Deck 11 provide a resort-like environment.

Expect lines at the reception desk, elevators, particularly at peak meal times, as well as for embarkation and disembarkation. If you arrange to meet someone, be very specific about the location – this really is a large ship. My advice is to arrange to meet somewhere along the Royal Promenade.

The theme-park, banquet-style regimentation is well organized, but it's hard to find better value for money, particularly for families with children. You will, however, need to plan your time aboard, otherwise you'll miss out on some of the things that you might like to include in your vacation.

Because the cruise fares are so reasonable, you can expect a big push aboard the ship for extra revenue items, drinks packages, extra-cost dining options, etc. In the end, however, you should have a decent floating vacation. The same comments apply to the other sister ships (*Adventure of the Seas, Explorer of the Seas, Mariner of the Seas*, and *Navigator of the Seas*); their layout and flow are the same, and, although there may be some slight differences, it's mainly in the decor and trimmings.

FAMILIES. Facilities for children and teenagers are quite extensive. "Aquanauts" is for 3–5-year-olds. "Explorers" is for 6–8-year-olds. "Voyagers" is for 9–12-year-olds. Optix, a dedicated area for teenagers, includes a daytime club with computers, soda bar, disk jockey and dance floor. Challenger's Arcade has the latest video games. Virtual Submarine is a virtual reality underwater center for all ages. Computer Lab has 14 computer stations loaded with fun and games. Paint and Clay is an arts and crafts center for younger children. Adjacent to these indoor areas is Adventure Beach, an area for all the family: it includes swimming pools, a water slide and game areas outdoors.

ACCOMMODATION. There is a wide range of 22 cabin price grades, in four major groupings: Premium ocean-view suites and cabins, interior (atrium-view) cabins, Ocean-view cabins, and Interior (no view) cabins. Many cabins are of a similar size – good for incentives and large groups – and 300 have interconnecting doors (good for families).

A total of 138 interior cabins have bay windows that look into an interior horizontal atrium – a cruise industry first when the ship debuted. Regardless of what cabin grade you choose, all except for the Royal Suite and Owner's Suite have twin beds that convert to a queen-size unit, TV set, radio and telephone, personal safe, vanity unit, hairdryer and private bathroom. However, you'll need to keep the curtains closed in the bay windows if you wear little clothing, because you can be seen easily from adjacent bay windows (Bay Watch?).

Royal Suite (Deck 10): At around 1,146 sq. ft (106.5 sq. meters), the Royal Suite is the largest private living space, located almost at the top of the Centrum lobby on the port side. It is a nicely appointed penthouse suite, whose occupants, sadly, must share the rest of the ship with everyone else, except for access to their own exclusive concierge club. It has a king-size circular bed in a separate large bedroom that can be fully closed off; a living room with an additional queen-size sofa bed, baby grand piano, refrigerator/wet bar, dining table and four chairs, expansive entertainment center, and a reasonably large bathroom.

Royal Family Suite: The four Royal Family suites (two aft on Deck 9, two aft on Deck 8, each measuring approximately 574 sq. ft/53 sq. meters), have two separate bedrooms. The main bedroom has a large vanity desk; the second, smaller bedroom also includes two beds and third/fourth upper Pullman berths. There's a lounge with dining table and four chairs, wet bar, walk-in closet; and large bathroom with Jacuzzi tub, washbasin, and separate shower enclosure. The suites, at the stern, have large balconies with views out over the ship's wash.

Owner's Suites: Ten slightly smaller but desirable Owner's Suites (approximately 468 sq. ft/43 sq. meters) are in the center of the ship, on both port and starboard sides, adjacent to the Centrum lobby on Deck 10. Each has a bedroom with queen-size bed or twin beds; lounge with large sofa; wet bar; bathroom with Jacuzzi tub, washbasin and separate shower enclosure. There's also a private balcony, although it is not very large.

Standard Outside-View and Interior Cabins: All cabins have a private bathroom, as well as interactive TV and pay-per-view movies, including an X-rated channel. Cabin bathrooms really are compact, but at least they have a proper shower enclosure instead of a shower curtain.

Some accommodation grades have a refrigerator/mini-bar, although there is no space left because it is crammed with "take-and-pay" items. If you take anything from the mini-bar/refrigerator on the day of embarkation in Miami, Florida sales tax will be added to your bill.

Cabins with "private balconies" are not so private. The balcony decking is made of Bolidt – a sort of rubberized sand – and not wood, though the balcony rail is of wood. If you have a cabin with a connecting door to another cabin, be aware that you'll probably be able to hear everything your next-door neighbors say and do. Bathroom toilets are explosively noisy, based on the vacuum system. Cabin bath towels are small and skimpy. Room service food menus are very basic.

CUISINE. The main dining room is extremely large and is set on three levels, each with an operatic name and theme: *Carmen, La Bohème* and *Magic Flute*. A dramatic staircase connects all three levels, and huge, fat support pillars obstruct sight lines from many seats. All three have exactly the same menus and food. Choose one of two seatings, or "My Time Dining" which allows you to eat when you want during dining room hours.

Alternative Dining Options: Casual and informal meals at all hours can be taken at:

● *Promenade Café:* for continental breakfast, all-day pizzas, sandwiches and coffees in paper cups.

● *Windjammer Café:* for casual buffet-style breakfast, lunch and light dinner (except for the cruise's last night).

● *Island Grill* – actually a section inside the Windjammer Café – has a grill and open kitchen, and serves casual dinners, with no reservations necessary.

● *Portofino:* this is the ship's "upscale" Euro-Italian restaurant, open for dinner only. Reservations are required, and there's a cover charge. The food and its presentation are better than the food in the dining room, although the restaurant isn't large enough for all passengers to try even once during a cruise. Choices include antipasti, soup, salad, pasta, main dish, dessert, cheese and coffee.

● *Johnny Rockets*, a retro 1950s all-day, all-night diner-style eatery that has hamburgers, malt shakes, and jukebox hits, with both indoor and outdoor seating. All indoor tables have a mini-jukebox with dimes are provided for you to make your selection of vintage records, and there are all-singing, all-dancing waitresses. There's a cover charge, whether you eat in or take out.

● *Sprinkles:* for round-the-clock ice cream and free yoghurt, pastries and coffee.

ENTERTAINMENT. The 1,350-seat Lyric Theater, a really stunning showlounge, is located at the forward end of the ship and spans the height of five decks, with only a few slim pillars and almost no disruption of sightlines from any seat. The room has a hydraulic orchestra pit and huge stage areas, together with sonic-boom loud sound, and some superb lighting equipment.

In addition, the ship has an array of cabaret acts. Although many are not what you would call headliners, they regularly travel the cruise ship circuit. The strongest cabaret acts are presented in the main showlounge, while others appear in the Cleopatra's Needle Lounge, also the venue for late-night adults-only comedy, The best shows are the Ice Spectaculars.

There is also a TV studio that can be used, for example, for trade show exhibit space – good for conventions at sea.

SPA/FITNESS. The large ShipShape health spa includes a large aerobics room, a fitness center with the usual stairmasters, treadmills, stationary bikes, and weight machines, treatment rooms, and men's and women's sauna/ steam rooms. There is also a substantial Solarium with a sliding glass roof.

For the more sporting, there is activity galore – including a 33-ft (10-meter) rock-climbing wall with five separate climbing tracks. Other sports facilities include a roller-blading track, a dive-and-snorkel shop, a full-size basketball court and nine-hole, par 26 golf course.

● **For more extensive general information about a Royal Caribbean cruise experience, see pages 152–6.**

Westerdam
★★★★

Size:	Large Resort Ship	Passenger Decks:	11	Cabins (wheelchair accessible):	28	
Tonnage:	81,811	Total Crew:	817	Wheelchair accessibility:	Good	
Lifestyle:	Premium	Passengers		Cabin Current:	110 volts	
Cruise Line:	Holland America Line	(lower beds/all berths):	1,916/2,455	Elevators:	14	
Former Names:	none	Passenger Space Ratio		Casino (gaming tables):	Yes	
Builder:	Fincantieri (Italy)	(lower beds/all berths):	42.6/33.3	Slot Machines:	Yes	
Original Cost:	$400 million	Crew/Passenger Ratio		Swimming Pools (outdoors):	2	
Entered Service:	Apr 2004	(lower beds/all berths):	2.3/3.0		+1 children's pool	
Registry:	The Netherlands	Cabins (total):	958	Swimming Pools (indoor/outdoor):	1	
Length (ft/m):	935.0/285.0	Size Range (sq ft/m):	170.0–1,318.6/	Whirlpools:	5	
Beam (ft/m):	105.6/32.2		15.7–122.5	Self-Service Launderette:	No	
Draft (ft/m):	25.5/7.80	Cabins (outside view):	804	Dedicated Cinema/Seats	Yes/170	
Propulsion/Propellers	diesel-electric	Cabins (interior/no view):	154	Library:	Yes	
(34,000 kW)/2 azimuthing pods		Cabins (for one person):	0	Onboard currency:	US$	
(17.6 MW each)		Cabins (with private balcony):	641			

A contemporary ship with Dutch decor and crafts.

OVERVIEW. With this large resort ship, Holland America Line tries hard to be all things to all people, but this formula may not work well for the many loyal repeat passengers used to the smaller ships. However, *Westerdam* does offer a range of public rooms that have a reasonably intimate ambience. Also, the overall feel of the ship, relative to its size, and its eclectic decor are quite homely.

THE SHIP. *Westerdam* is another in the series of Vista-class vessels (sister ships: *Eurodam, Nieuw Amsterdam, Noordam, Oosterdam* and *Zuiderdam*) designed to appeal to younger, active vacationers. It has two funnels, placed close together, one in front of the other, the result of the slightly unusual machinery configuration. The ship has, in effect, two engine rooms – one with three diesels, and one with two diesels and a gas turbine. Pod propulsion *(see page 191 for explanation)* is provided, powered by a diesel-electric system, and a small gas turbine in the funnel helps reduce emissions.

There's a complete walk-around exterior teak promenade deck, with teak "steamer" style sunloungers. A jogging track is located around the mast and the forward third of the ship. Exterior glass elevators, mounted midships on both port and starboard sides, provide ocean views. There are two centrally located swimming pools outdoors, one of which can be used in poor weather because it has a retractable sliding glass roof. Two whirlpool tubs, adjacent to the swimming pools, are abridged by a bar. Another smaller pool is for children; it incorporates a winding water slide that spans two decks in height. There is an additional whirlpool tub outdoors.

You enter the ship through an intimate lobby that spans three decks, and is topped by a beautiful, rotating, Water-

BERLITZ'S RATINGS

	Possible	Achieved
Ship	500	428
Accommodation	200	162
Food	400	269
Service	400	278
Entertainment	100	77
Cruise	400	308

OVERALL SCORE
1,522 points out of 2,000

ford crystal globe of the world. The interior decor is interesting; the ceilings are particularly noticeable in the public decor, the colours are muted and warm. Maintaining its traditions, HAL provides a large collection of artwork, including Dutch exploration, maritime history and art. The ship's focal point is its soothing midnight blue atrium lobby containing a glass replica of a sailing ship.

There are two whole entertainment/public room decks. The most dramatic room is the showlounge, spanning four decks in the forward section.

Other facilities include a winding shopping street with boutique stores and logo shops, an internet center, a fine library, card room, an art gallery, photo gallery, and several small meeting rooms. The casino is large – one has to walk through it to get from the restaurant to the showlounge on one of the entertainments decks – and has the usual gaming tables and slot machines.

The information desk in the lobby is small and somewhat removed from the main passenger flow on the two decks above it. Many pillars obstruct the passenger flow and lines of sight throughout the ship.

There are no self-service launderettes – something families with children might miss, although special laundry packages *are* available. The air conditioning cannot be turned off in cabins or bathrooms.

FAMILIES. Club HAL's KidZone is dedicated to children's facilities and extensive programming for different age groups (5–17), with one counselor for every 30 youngsters.

ACCOMMODATION. There are 24 price categories – 16

outside-view and eight interior. Lifeboats obstruct the view from some cabins on the lowest accommodation deck, Main Deck. Some cabins that can accommodate a third and fourth person have very little closet space and only one personal safe. Some cabins have interconnecting doors – good for families with children.

Occupants of suites also get exclusive use of a Neptune Lounge and concierge service, priority embarkation and disembarkation, and other benefits – thus, in effect, making this a two-class ship. In many suites and cabins with private balconies the balconies aren't really very private, as many can be overlooked from public locations. **Penthouse Verandah Suites** (2): These measure 1,318 sq. ft (122.5 sq. meters), including balcony. They have a separate bedroom with a king-size bed; there's also a walk-in closet, dressing room, living room, dining room, butler's pantry, mini-bar and refrigerator, and private balcony. The main bathroom has a large whirlpool tub, two washbasins, toilet, and plenty of storage space for toiletries. Personalized stationery and complimentary dry cleaning are included, as are hot hors d'oeuvres daily.

DeLuxe Verandah Suites (60): These measure 563 sq. ft (52.3 sq. meters). They have twin beds that convert to a king-size bed, vanity desk, lounge area, walk-in closet, mini-bar and refrigerator, and bathroom with full-size tub, washbasin and toilet. Personalized stationery, complimentary dry cleaning, and hot hors d'oeuvres are included.

Verandah Suites (100): Actually, these are really cabins, not proper suites, and measure 284 sq. ft (26.3 sq. meters). Twin beds convert to a queen-size bed; there is a lounge area, mini-bar and refrigerator, while the bathroom has a tub, washbasin and toilet. Floor-to-ceiling windows open onto a private balcony.

Outside-view Cabins: Standard outside cabins (197 sq. ft/18.3 sq. meters) have twin beds that convert to a queen-size bed. There's also a small sitting area, while the bathroom has a tub/shower combination. The interior cabins are slightly smaller (182.9 sq. ft/17 sq. meters).

CUISINE. Dining options range from full-service meals in the main dining room and à la carte restaurant to casual, self-serve buffet-style meals and fast-food outlets.

The 1,045-seat *Vista Dining Room* is two decks high, with seating provided on both main and balcony levels, and is at the stern. It provides a traditional Holland America Line dining experience, with friendly service from smiling Indonesian and Filipino stewards. Both open seating and fixed (assigned tables and times) seating are available, while breakfast and lunch are open-seating where you'll be seated by restaurant staff when you enter.

There are tables for two, four, six or eight. The waiter stations can be noisy for anyone seated adjacent to them. Fine Rosenthal china and decent cutlery are used, but there are no fish knives. Live music is provided for dinner each evening.

Once each cruise, a Dutch Dinner is held (hats are provided), as is an Indonesian Lunch. "Lighter option" meals are available for the nutrition-conscious. HAL can provide Kosher meals, although these are prepared ashore, frozen, and brought to the table sealed in their original containers.

Alternative Dining Option: The 130-seat *Pinnacle Grill* is a more upscale dining spot with higher quality ingredients and smarter presentation than in the larger main dining room. It is on Lower Promenade Deck, and fronts onto the second level of the atrium lobby; a Pinnacle Bar was added in a 2007 refit. Pacific Northwest cuisine is served, plus an array of premium-quality steaks from hand-selected cuts of beef, shown to you at tableside. Fine table settings, china and silverware, and leather-bound menus are provided. The wine bar offers mostly American wines. Reservations are required and there is a cover charge.

Informal Eateries: For casual eating, there is an extensive *Lido Café*, which wraps around the funnel housing and extends aft. It includes a pizzeria counter, a salad bar, Asian stir-fry counter, deli sandwiches, and a dessert buffet. Warm green vegetables are hard to come by – as are warm plates. Movement around the buffet area can be very slow.

An outdoor self-serve buffet, adjacent to the fantail pool, serves fast-food such as hamburgers and hot dogs, chicken and fries. There are also two smaller buffets adjacent to the midships swimming pool area, and an extra-cost *Windsurf Café* in the atrium lobby, open 20 hours a day for coffee, pastries, snack foods, deli sandwiches and, in the evening, liqueur coffees.

An *Explorations Café* was added to the Crow's Nest (a HAL trademark observation lounge atop ship) in a 2007 refit.

ENTERTAINMENT. The 867-seat Vista Lounge is the main venue for Las Vegas-style revue shows and major cabaret presentations. It spans three decks in the forward section. The main floor level has a bar in its starboard aft section. Spiral stairways at the back of the lounge connect all levels. The upper levels have better sightlines.

SPA/FITNESS. The Greenhouse Spa, a large, two-decks-high health spa, is directly above the navigation bridge. Facilities include a solarium, hydrotherapy pool, and a unisex thermal suite – an area incorporating a Laconium (gentle sauna), Hammam (mild steam), and Camomile Grotto (small aromatic steam room). There's also a beauty parlor, 11 massage/therapy rooms, including one for couples, and a large gymnasium with floor-to-ceiling windows on three sides and forward-facing ocean views, and the latest high-tech muscle-toning equipment.

Sports facilities include a basketball court, volleyball court, and golf simulator.

● **For more extensive general information on what a Holland America Line cruise is like, see pages 140–3.**

Wilderness Adventurer
★★

Boutique Ship: . . . . .89.5 tons	Total Crew: 20	Cabin Current: . . . . .110 volts
Lifestyle: . . . . .Standard	Passengers (lower beds/all berths): 57/ 61	Elevators: 0
Cruise Line: . . . . . . .InnerSea Discoveries	Passenger Space Ratio	Casino (gaming tables): . . . . .No
Former Names: . . . . .Caribbean Prince	(lower beds/all berths): 1.5/ 1.4	Slot Machines: .No
Builder: . . . . .Blount Shipyards (USA)	Crew/Passenger Ratio:	Swimming Pools (outdoors): 0
Original Cost: . . . .$6 million	(lower beds/all berths): 2.8/ 3.0	Swimming Pools (indoors): 0
Entered Service: 1983/May 2011	Cabins (total): .30	Whirlpools: 2
Registry: . . . . .USA	Size (sq ft/m.): 70.0–88.0/6.5–8.1	Self-Service Launderette: . . . . .No
Length (ft/m): 156.6/47.7	Cabins (outside view): 30	Movie Theater/Seats: . . . . .No
Beam (ft/m): 38.0/11.0	Cabins (interior/no view): 0	Library: . . . . .Yes
Draft (ft/m): 6.5/1.8	Cabins (for one person): 3	Onboard currency: . . . . .US$
Propulsion/Propellers: diesel (1,472kw)/1	Cabins (with private balcony): 0	
Passenger Decks: 3	Cabins (wheelchair accessible): 0	

A tiny but expensive ship for up-close nature cruising.

OVERVIEW. This ship is best suited to couples and single travelers who enjoy nature and wildlife at close range, and who wouldn't dream of cruising aboard a large resort ship. This is for hardy, outdoors types who don't need entertainment or vapid parlor games, but who prefer an all-American crew. InnerSea Discovery Cruises is the parent company of American Safari Cruises.

THE SHIP. *Wilderness Adventurer* was originally built for the American Canadian Caribbean Line, and provides a platform for in-depth, up-close cruising along the coastline and inlets of Alaska. Essentially, it's a sport utility vessel, with a platform at the stern. A fleet of 28 kayaks, 10 stand-up paddle boards, and a limited supply of wetsuits, rain gear, binoculars, trekking poles, daypacks, and snorkeling equipment is carried. The fare includes guided excursions, with an emphasis on hiking and kayaking. Do take comfortable walking shoes, as well as a camera for wildlife photography.

The cruises are very expensive when compared with most other ships operating in the area. Tips are pooled and shared among all the staff, using the amounts recommended in the cruise line's brochure. The dress code is ultra-casual – men don't even need a jacket.

You can expect some dull throbbing from the diesel engines/generator. There is no doctor on board, and so any-

BERLITZ'S RATINGS

	Possible	Achieved
Ship	500	181
Accommodation	200	76
Food	400	201
Service	400	205
Entertainment	n/a	n/a
Cruise	500	245

OVERALL SCORE
908 points out of 2,000

one with medical problems shouldn't consider this vessel.

ACCOMMODATION. There are only three types of cabin, one on each of three decks, and they really are utilitarian, ultra-tiny, no-frills units that are just about adequate if you aren't used to, or don't want, anything better. While cabins have a double bed, others have two lower beds with memory foam mattresses. Each cabin has a private bathroom, although these are small and basic. There is no room service for food or snacks, but a hairdryer is provided, as is an iPod docking station.

CUISINE. The dining room has an open-seating policy, so you can eat with whomever you wish, in a single seating. The all-American cuisine is plain and simple, as is the cutlery. Ingredients are all as fresh as possible, with lots of fish and seafood – but no fish knives. A full-service bar provides wines and other alcoholic drinks.

ENTERTAINMENT. There is no formal entertainment. Dinner and after-dinner conversation with fellow passengers in the ship's lounge/bar constitutes the entertainment each evening.

SPA/FITNESS. There is a sauna, and massage is available.

Wind Spirit
★★★ +

Size: ....Boutique Ship	Sail Area (sq ft/m2): 21,489/1,996.4	Cabins (outside view): 74
Tonnage: 5,350	Main Propulsion: .....(a) engines (b) sails	Cabins (interior/no view): 0
Lifestyle: ....Premium	Propulsion/Propellers: .....diesel-electric	Cabins (for one person): 0
Cruise Line: ....Windstar Cruises	(1,400kW)/1	Cabins (with private balcony): 0
Former Names: ....none	Passenger Decks: 5	Cabins (wheelchair accessible): 0
Builder: ....Ateliers et Chantiers du Havre	Total Crew: 88	Wheelchair accessibility: ....None
Original Cost: ....$34.2 million	Passengers	Cabin Current: ....110 volts
Entered Service: .... Apr 1988	(lower beds/all berths): 148/159	Casino (gaming tables): ....Yes
Registry: ....The Bahamas	Passenger Space Ratio	Slot Machines: ....Yes
Length (ft/m): 439.6/134.0	(lower beds/all berths): 36.1/33.6	Swimming Pools (outdoors): ..1 (dip pool)
Beam (ft/m): 51.8/15.8	Crew/Passenger Ratio	Whirlpools: 1
Draft (ft/m): 13.4/4.1	(lower beds/all berths): 1.6/1.8	Self-Service Launderette: ....No
Type of Vessel: .....computer-controlled	Cabins (total): 74	Library: ....Yes
sail-cruiser	Size Range (sq ft/m): 185.0–220.0/	Onboard currency: ....US$
Number of Masts: ...4/6 self-furling sails	17.0–22.5	

A modern sail-cruise ship with an unstructured lifestyle.

OVERVIEW. This ship is suited to youthful couples and singles who want contemporary facilities and some watersports in a very relaxed but chic setting that is different to "normal" cruise ships, with good food and service, but with no entertainment, silly parlour games, structured activities, or ship's photographers. You will probably be under sail for less than 40% of the time, conditions and cruise area winds permitting.

THE SHIP. *Wind Spirit*, an identical twin to *Wind Star*, is a long, sleek-looking craft that is part-yacht, part-cruise ship, with four giant masts that tower 170ft (52 meters) above the deck, and is fitted with computer-controlled sails. The masts, sails and rigging alone cost $5 million. The computer keeps the ship on an even keel via the movement of a water hydraulic ballast system of 142,653 gallons (540,000 liters), so there is no rolling over 6°.

Because of the amount of complex sail machinery, there is little open deck space when the ship is full. At the stern is a small water sports platform that can be used when at anchor and only in really calm sea conditions. Water sports facilities include a banana boat, kayaks, sunfish sailboats, windsurf boards, water ski boat, scuba and snorkel equipment, and four Zodiacs. You will be asked to sign a waiver if you wish to use the water sports equipment.

The ship has a finely crafted interior with pleasing, blond woods, together with soft, complementary colors and decor that is chic, even elegant, but a little cold. Note that the main lounge aboard this ship is of a slightly different design to that aboard *Wind Star*.

BERLITZ'S RATINGS		
	Possible	Achieved
Ship	500	361
Accommodation	200	160
Food	400	265
Service	400	270
Entertainment	n/a	n/a
Cruise	500	338

OVERALL SCORE
1,394 points out of 2,000

No scheduled activities help to make this a real relaxing, unregimented "get away from it all" vacation. The Windstar ships help you to cruise in very comfortable, contemporary surroundings bordering on the luxurious, yet in an unstructured environment. They are just right for seven idyllic nights in sheltered areas, but can be disturbing when a Windstar vessel is in small ports alongside several gigantic cruise ships.

The swimming pool is really only a tiny "dip" pool. Be prepared for the "whine" of the vessel's generators, which are needed to run the air-conditioning and lighting systems 24 hours a day. You will hear it at night in your cabin, and it takes most passengers a day or two to get used to.

Beverage prices are high. The library is small, and needs more hardback fiction. The staff, though friendly, is casual and a little sloppy at times in the finer points of service.

The dress code is casual, with no jackets and ties, even for dinner – the brochure states casual elegance. There are no formal nights or theme nights. Gratuities are charged at about $12 per person, per day, and 15% is added to bar and wine accounts.

ACCOMMODATION. All cabins are nicely equipped, have crisp, inviting decor and a mini-bar/refrigerator (stocked when you embark, but all drinks cost extra), 24-hour room service, personal safe, and plenty of storage space. A TV set, with CNN when available, rotates so that it is viewable from the bed and the bathroom. There's a video player and compact disc player. All cabins all have two portholes with outside views, and deadlights (steel covers that provide a complete blackout at night and can be closed in inclement weather conditions). The decor is a pleasant mix of rich woods, natural fabrics and colorful soft furnishings, and hi-tech yacht-style amenities. Some of the cabinetry is looking a little tired, and has that "I've been varnished many times" look. A basket of fruit is replenished daily.

The bathrooms are compact units, designed in a figure of eight, with a teakwood floor in the central section. There is a good amount of storage space for toiletries in two cabinets, as well as under-sink cupboard space. A wall-mounted hairdryer is also provided. The shower enclosure (no cabins have bathtubs) is circular – like many of today's passengers – and has both a hand-held as well as a fixed shower so you can wash your hair without getting the rest of your body wet. L'Occitane bathroom amenities are provided, as are a vanity kit and shower cap.

The lighting is not strong enough for women to apply make-up – this is better applied at the vanity desk in the cabin, which has stronger overhead (halogen) lighting. Bathrobes and towels are 100% cotton.

CUISINE. There is one rather chic and elegant dining room, *The Restaurant*, with ocean views from large, picture windows, a lovely wood ceiling and wood paneling on the walls. California-style nouvelle cuisine is served, with dishes that are attractively presented. Additionally, "signature" dishes, created by master chefs Joachim Splichal and Jeanne Jones, are offered daily. Open seating means you dine when you want and with whomever you wish to.

When the company first started, European waiters provided service with practiced European finesse. However, they have been replaced by Indonesians and Filipinos, whose communication skills at times can prove inadequate, although their service is pleasant enough. The selection of breads, cheeses, and fruits could be better. There is a big push to sell wines, although the prices are extremely high, as they are for most alcoholic drinks – even bottled water is the highest in the industry, at $7 per liter bottle.

There is often casual dinner on the open deck under the stars, with grilled seafood and steaks. At the bars, hot and cold hors d'oeuvres appear at cocktail times.

Fancy something quiet and romantic? At no extra charge, a "Cuisine de l'Amour" romantic dinner for two can be served to you in your cabin, complete with candle. The menu, with seductive sounding selections, offers a choice of appetizer, a set soup, choice of salad, and two entrée options, and a set dessert to finish.

ENTERTAINMENT. There is no showlounge, shows or cabaret. However, none are really needed, because a cruise aboard this high-tech sailing ship provides an opportunity to get away from all that noise and "entertainment". The main lounge, a corner of which houses a small casino, has a small dance floor, and, typically, a trio is there to play.

The main lounge is also used for cocktail parties and other social functions. Otherwise, it's down to more personal entertainment, such as a video in your cabin late at night – or, much more romantic, after-dinner hours spent outside strolling or simply lounging on deck.

SPA/FITNESS. A gymnasium (with a modicum of muscle-toning equipment, treadmills and exercycles) and sauna are located at the aft of the ship, adjacent to the Watersports platform. Special spa packages can be pre-booked through your travel agent before you arrive at the ship. Well-being massages, aromatherapy facials, manicures, pedicures, and hair beautifying treatments all cost extra. The spa is operated by Steiner Leisure, a specialist concession.

Wind Star
★★★ +

Size: . . . . .Boutique Ship	Sail Area (sq ft/m2): 21,489/1,996.4	Cabins (outside view): 74
Tonnage: 5,350	Main Propulsion: . . . . .(a) engines (b) sails	Cabins (interior/no view): 0
Lifestyle: . . . . .Premium	Propulsion/Propellers: . . . . .diesel-electric	Cabins (for one person): 0
Cruise Line: . . . . .Windstar Cruises	(1,400kW)/1	Cabins (with private balcony): 0
Former Names: . . . . .none	Passenger Decks: 5	Cabins (wheelchair accessible): 0
Builder: . . . .Ateliers et Chantiers du Havre	Total Crew: 88	Wheelchair accessibility: . . . . .None
Original Cost: . . . .$34.2 million	Passengers	Cabin Current: . . . . .110 volts
Entered Service: . . . . Dec 1986	(lower beds/all berths): 148/168	Casino (gaming tables): . . . . .Yes
Registry: . . . . .The Bahamas	Passenger Space Ratio	Slot Machines: . . . . .Yes
Length (ft/m): 439.6/134.0	(lower beds/all berths): 36.1/33.6	Swimming Pools (outdoors): . .1 (dip pool)
Beam (ft/m): 51.8/15.8	Crew/Passenger Ratio	Whirlpools: 1
Draft (ft/m): 13.4/4.1	(lower beds/all berths): 1.6/1.8	Self-Service Launderette: . . . . .No
Type of Vessel: . . . . . .computer-controlled	Cabins (total): .74	Library: . . . . .Yes
sail-cruiser	Size Range (sq ft/m): 185.0–220.0/	Onboard currency: . . . . .US$
Number of Masts: . . .4/6 self-furling sails	17.0–22.5	

A contemporary sail-cruise ship for casual cruising.

OVERVIEW. This ship is suited to youthful couples and singles who want contemporary facilities and some watersports in a very relaxed but chic setting that is different to "normal" cruise ships, with good food and service. The absence of scheduled activities help make this an unregimented "get away from it all" vacation.

THE SHIP. *Wind Star,* an identical twin to *Wind Spirit,* is a long, sleek-looking craft that is part-yacht, part-cruise ship, with four giant masts that tower 170ft (52 meters) above the deck, and is fitted with computer-controlled sails. When the masts were lowered into position, a US silver dollar, dated 1889, was placed under the main mast.

For a full description of the ship's facilities and ambience, plus details of beverage pricing and gratuities, see the preceding entry for *Wind Spirit.* The only significant difference is that the main lounge aboard *Wind Star* is of a different design to that aboard *Wind Spirit.*

BERLITZ'S RATINGS		
	Possible	Achieved
Ship	500	359
Accommodation	200	160
Food	400	265
Service	400	270
Entertainment	n/a	n/a
Cruise	500	339

OVERALL SCORE
1,393 points out of 2,000

ACCOMMODATION. For a full description of cabin facilities, see the entry for *Wind Spirit* on page 656.

CUISINE. For a full description of *The Restaurant* and its atmosphere and cuisine, see the preceding entry for *Wind Spirit.* As on its sister ship, a "Cuisine de l'Amour" romantic dinner for two can be served to you in your cabin, complete with candle.

ENTERTAINMENT. There is no showlounge, shows or cabaret. The main lounge contains a small casino and has a small dance floor. Otherwise, you can watch a video in your cabin late at night or, more romantically, spend after-dinner hours strolling or simply lounging on deck.

SPA/FITNESS. For details of the gymnasium's facilities and the spa treatments available, see the preceding entry for *Wind Spirit.*

Wind Surf
★★★★

Size: ....Small Ship	Sail Area (sq ft/m2): 26,910/2,500	Cabins (interior/no view): 0
Tonnage: 14,745	Main Propulsion: ......a) engines/b) sails	Cabins (for one person): 0
Lifestyle: ....Premium	Propulsion/Propellers: diesel (9,120kW)/2	Cabins (with private balcony): 0
Cruise Line: ....Windstar Cruises	Passenger Decks: 8	Cabins (wheelchair accessible): 0
Former Names: ....*Club Med I*	Total Crew: 163	Wheelchair accessibility: ....None
Builder: ....Ateliers et Chantiers du Havre	Passengers	Cabin Current: ....220 volts
Original Cost: ....$140 million	(lower beds/all berths): 312/347	Elevators: 2
Entered Service: ....Feb 1990/May 1998	Passenger Space Ratio	Casino (gaming tables): ....Yes
Registry: ....The Bahamas	(lower beds/all berths): 47.2/42.4	Slot Machines: ....Yes
Length (ft/m): 613.5/187.0	Crew/Passenger Ratio	Swimming Pools (outdoors): 2
Beam (ft/m): 65.6/20.0	(lower beds/all berths): 1.9/2.1	Whirlpools: 2
Draft (ft/m): 16.4/5.0	Cabins (total): 156	Self-Service Launderette: ....No
Type of Vessel: .....high-tech sail-cruiser	Size Range (sq ft/m): 188.0–500.5/	Library: ....Yes
Number of Masts: ....5/7 computer-	17.5–46.5	Onboard currency: ....US$
controlled sails	Cabins (outside view): 156	

Elegant decor for casual, chic cruising in comfort.

OVERVIEW. This ship is a good choice for couples seeking informality (no jackets or ties), but who don't want the inconvenience of the workings of a real tall ship. It cruises from Barbados (November–March) and in the Mediterranean (May–October). The European itineraries are really port-intensive, which means you sail each night and are in port each day – so there seems little point to having the sails, as passengers don't get to experience them.

BERLITZ'S RATINGS		
	Possible	Achieved
Ship	500	374
Accommodation	200	160
Food	400	282
Service	400	281
Entertainment	n/a	n/a
Cruise	500	374
OVERALL SCORE		
1,471 points out of 2,000		

THE SHIP. *Wind Surf*, one of a pair of the world's largest sail-cruisers, is part-cruise ship, part-yacht – its sister ship operates as *Club Med II*. This is a larger, grander sister to the original three Windstar Cruises vessels. Five huge masts of 164 ft/50 meters (rising 221 ft/67.5 meters above sea level) carry seven triangular, self-furling Dacron sails, with a total surface area of 26,881 sq. ft (2,497 sq. meters). No human hands touch the sails, as everything is handled electronically by computer control from the bridge – which makes it a little boring for real "yachties."

A computer keeps the ship on an even keel via the movement of a water hydraulic ballast system of 266,800 gallons (1 million liters), so there is no heeling over 6 degrees. When the ship isn't using the sails, four diesel-electric motors propel it at up to approximately 12 knots. The ship is very quiet – almost serene – when moving.

Swimming from the watersports platform at the stern isn't allowed. But extensive water sports facilities include windsurfers, sailboats, water-ski boats, single scuba tanks, snorkels, fins and masks, and inflatable Zodiac motorized boats for water-skiing – all at no extra charge, except for the scuba tanks. You must sign an "Assumption of Risk" waiver to use the water sports equipment.

There are two saltwater swimming pools – little more than dip pools. One is amidships on the uppermost deck of the ship, while the other is aft, together with two hot tubs, and an adjacent bar. There are no showers at either of the pools, so passengers get into the pools or hot tubs while covered in oil or lotion, an unhygienic arrangement.

A meeting room can accommodate 30–60 people. The casino/main lounge has four blackjack and one roulette table, and 21 slot machines). It has an unusually high ceiling for the size of the ship.

A Yacht Club includes books and a DVDs for in-cabin use and provides comfortable seating for relaxation or listening to music loaded for you on iPods available from reception. An espresso bar offers extra-cost Lavazza coffee drinks and deli sandwiches. There are eight computers with internet access, and wi-fi access for laptops.

Hotel service is provided mostly by Filipino and Indonesian staff. Gratuities are charged at about $12 per person, per day, and 15% is added to bar and wine accounts, and to all spa treatments and services. The quality of food and its presentation is a definite plus, as is the policy of no music in passenger hallways or elevators. In other words, it's a delightful, fairly peaceful environment.

ACCOMMODATION. There are just three price categories. Unusually, the cabin numbers (port side even numbers, odd number starboard side) are sequenced with lower numbers aft, while higher numbers are forward. All cabins are very nicely equipped, with crisp, inviting decor. They have a mini-bar/refrigerator (stocked when you embark, but all drinks are at extra cost), 24-hour room service, personal safe, a flat-screen TV set viewable from the bed (or sofa, depending on cabin configuration), DVD/CD player, plenty of storage space, and two portholes. DVDs and CDs are available from the library. There are six four-person cabins; 35 doubles are fitted with an extra Pullman berth, and several cabins have an interconnecting door – good for families. "Spa Suite" packages are available at extra cost. All cabins have wi-fi access, at extra cost.

The bathrooms are compact, designed in a figure of eight, with a teakwood floor in the central section. There is a good amount of storage space for toiletries in two cabinets, as well as under-sink cupboard space, and a wall-mounted hairdryer. The shower enclosure is circular, and has both a hand-held and a fixed shower, enabling you to wash your hair without getting the rest of your body wet. The lighting is not strong enough for women to apply make-up – this is better applied at the cabin's vanity desk.

All but one of the 31 suites have two bathrooms, a separate living/dining area, sleeping area that can be curtained off, two vanity/writing desks, and four portholes instead of two. There are two TV sets (one in the lounge, one in the sleeping area), video player and CD player, and Bose SoundDock for iPods. Popcorn for movie viewing is available from room service. Bathrooms have granite countertops, open shelving, new cabinets, and magnifying mirror.

A further two Bridge Deck suites (approximately 495 sq.ft/ 46 sq. meters) would be delightful for a honeymoon; each has a bedroom, separate living/dining room, and marble bathroom with Jacuzzi tub, two washbasins, and separate toilet, plus a walk-in closet.

New "Spa Suite" packages, introduced in 2010, take an existing cabin and provide extras such as a queen-size bed with microfiber bed linen, bathrobes, an orchid flower arrangement, two bathrooms, a flat-screen TV with DVD player, and Bose SoundDock speakers for iPods. Also, a pillow menu provides several choices, including a "snore-no-more" hypoallergenic pillow.

Tea collections include well-being, herbal, or exotic teas. Brewing service includes contemporary, porcelain teaware and is available from room service 24 hours a day. Berlitz tip: ask for it to be made with mineral water, not the standard chlorinated ship's water.

CUISINE. *The Restaurant* seats 272 and has tables for two, four or six. It has open seating with no pre-assigned tables, and is open only for dinner, typically between 7.30pm and 9.30pm. California-style nouvelle cuisine is served, with dishes attractively presented.

A 124-seat *Degrees Restaurant*, an alternative dinner venue, serves Mediterranean cuisine. Located atop the ship, on Star Deck, it has picture windows on port and starboard sides, an open kitchen, and tables for two, four or six. Reservations are required for dinner, although there is no extra charge.

The Veranda, amidships on Star Deck, has its own open "terrace" for informal, self-serve breakfast and lunch buffets. It really is very pleasant to be outside, eating an informal breakfast or lunch. Do try the bread pudding, available daily at lunch – the ship is famous for it and each day has a variation on the theme.

The *Compass Rose*, an indoor/outdoor bar, provides snack items plus some pastries and coffee for breakfast, lunch, afternoon tea. At night, it turns into *Candles* for al fresco dining around the aft pool. A permanent outdoor barbecue offers fresh grilled items for breakfast and lunch.

Windstar Cruises food is generally very good, although highly geared toward American tastes. Europeans and other nationals should note that items such as bacon may be fried to death, and the choice of cheeses and teas is limited. Service in the dining room is also quite fast, geared towards those who haven't yet learned to unwind.

A nice addition is a "Cuisine de l'Amour" romantic candlelight dinner for two served to you in your cabin at no extra charge. The menu, with its seductive sounding selections, offers a choice of appetizer, a set soup, choice of salad, two entrée options, and a set dessert to finish.

Finally, there's an extensive room service menu.

ENTERTAINMENT. There is no showlounge as such, although the main lounge, part of which is a small casino, serves as an occasional cabaret room. It has a small dance floor, with music provided by a house band. The room is also used for cocktail parties and other social functions.

SPA/FITNESS. The Health Spa has a unisex sauna (bathing suits required), beauty salon, and several treatment rooms for massage, facials and body wraps. There is a decent gymnasium – on a separate deck, with ocean views – and an aerobics workout room. Unfortunately, the spa facilities are split on three separate decks, making them rather disjointed. Special spa packages can be pre-booked through your travel agent. The spa is operated by the UK's Onboard Spa Company.

Zaandam
★★★★

Size: . . . . .Mid-Size Ship	Total Crew: 561	Wheelchair accessibility: . . . . .Good
Tonnage: .60,906	Passengers	Cabin Current: . . . . .110 volts
Lifestyle: . . . . .Premium	(lower beds/all berths): 1,440/1,850	Elevators: 12
Cruise Line: . . . . . . .Holland America Line	Passenger Space Ratio	Casino (gaming tables): . . . . .Yes
Former Names: . . . . .none	(lower beds/all berths): 42.3/32.9	Slot Machines: . . . . .Yes
Builder: . . . . .Fincantieri (Italy)	Crew/Passenger Ratio	Swimming Pools (outdoors): 2
Original Cost: . . . .$300 million	(lower beds/all berths): 2.5/2.5	Swimming Pools (indoors): 1
Entered Service: . . . . .May 2000	Cabins (total): 720	(glass dome cover)
Registry: . . . . .The Netherlands	Size Range (sq ft/m): 113.0–1,126.3/	Whirlpools: 2
Length (ft/m): 777.5/237.00	10.5–104.6	Self-Service Launderette: . . . . .Yes
Beam (ft/m): 105.8/32.25	Cabins (outside view): 581	Dedicated Cinema/Seats: Yes/205
Draft (ft/m): 25.5/7.80	Cabins (interior/no view): 139	Library: . . . . .Yes
Propulsion/Propellers: . . . . .diesel-electric	Cabins (for one person): 0	Onboard currency: . . . . .US$
(37,500kW)/2	Cabins (with private balcony): 197	
Passenger Decks: 10	Cabins (wheelchair accessible): 23	

Dutch-style decor for mature-age cruisers.

OVERVIEW. Holland America Line's "Signature of Excellence" program provides passengers with more choice. Music memorabilia scattered throughout the ship includes instruments used by such diverse players as the Rolling Stones, David Bowie and Bill Clinton. There's also a huge Dutch pipe organ complete with puppets that move in time with the music.

THE SHIP. *Zaandam*'s hull is dark blue, in keeping with all Holland America Line ships. Although similar in size to *Rotterdam*, this ship has a single funnel, and is a sister ship to *Volendam*.

It has three principal passenger stairways, which is so much better than two stairways from the viewpoints of safety, accessibility and passenger flow. A magrodome-covered pool is located on the Lido Deck between the mast and the funnel.

The interior decor is restrained, with much traditional ocean liner detailing and wood accenting. The design theme of music includes fabrics, posters, and – believe it or not – real instruments. Most of this memorabilia was acquired from the "Pop and Guitars" auction at Christie's in London in 1997. It includes a Fender Squire Telecaster guitar signed by Mick Jagger, Keith Richards, Charlie Watts, Ronnie Wood and Bill Wyman of the Rolling Stones; a Conn Saxophone signed on the mouthpiece by former US President Bill Clinton; an Ariana acoustic guitar signed by David Bowie and Iggy Pop; a Fender Stratocaster guitar signed in silver ink by the members of the rock band Queen; a Bently "Les Paul" style guitar signed by artists including Carlos Santana, Eric Clapton, B.B. King, Robert Cray, Keith

BERLITZ'S RATINGS

	Possible	Achieved
Ship	500	430
Accommodation	200	165
Food	400	282
Service	400	276
Entertainment	100	77
Cruise	400	311

OVERALL SCORE
1,541 points out of 2,000

Richards and Les Paul. Perhaps the ship should be called *Rockerdam*.

The Oasis outdoor relaxation areas aft of the funnel include a waterfall and family gathering areas. Explorations is an excellent combination coffee/tea café, internet connection center, and library. There are children's and teens' play areas. Popcorn is provided at the Wajang Theater for moviegoers, and this location incorporates a fully equipped kitchen for HAL's "Culinary Arts" program, which involves visiting chefs and interactive cooking and tasting demonstrations. The casino has blackjack, roulette, stud poker and dice tables, and the requisite rows of slot machines. Adjacent is a sports bar.

The ship's focal point is a three-deck-high atrium, with the reception desk, shore excursions desk, photo shop, and photo gallery grouped around it. It also houses a real showpiece – a fancy 22-ft (6.7-meter) high pipe organ with puppets that move with the music. One of the largest such Dutch band organs ever built, it was custom-made for Holland America Line in Hilversum in the Netherlands.

As in *Volendam*, the Lido Deck swimming pool is located one deck higher than the Statendam-class ships, so that you can have direct access between the aft and midships pools (not so aboard the S-class ships). This provided more space for extra cabins on the Navigation Deck below.

With one whole deck of suites and a dedicated, private concierge lounge, the company has in effect created a two-class ship. The charge to use the washing machines and dryers in the self-service launderette is petty and irritating, particularly for the occupants of suites who pay high prices for their cruises.

Communication in English with many of the staff, particularly in the dining room and buffet areas, can be frustrating. Room service is poor. Standing in line for embarkation, disembarkation, shore tenders and for self-serve buffet meals is inevitable aboard large ships.

ACCOMMODATION. The range is comparable to that found aboard the similarly sized *Rotterdam*, and comprises 17 different categories. There is one penthouse suite, 28 suites, and 168 mini-suites, with the rest of the accommodation a mixture of outside-view and interior cabins. There are many more balcony cabins (called "mini-suites") than aboard the slightly smaller *Statendam*-class ships (*Maasdam, Ryndam, Statendam*, and *Veendam*). All passenger hallways now include pleasing artwork.

All standard interior and outside cabins are tastefully furnished, with twin beds that convert to a queen-size bed, though space is tight for walking between beds and vanity unit. There is a decent amount of closet and drawer space, but this will be tight for longer voyages. The fully tiled bathrooms are disappointingly small, particularly for long cruises, and have small shower tubs, utilitarian toiletries cupboards, and exposed under-sink plumbing. There is no detailing to distinguish them from bathrooms aboard the Statendam-class ships.

There are 28 full Verandah Suites on Navigation Deck, and one penthouse suite. All suite occupants share a private concierge lounge, called the Neptune Lounge; the concierge handles such things as special dining arrangements, shore excursions and special requests. Strangely, there are no butlers for these suites, as aboard many other ships with similar facilities.

Each Verandah Suite has a separate bedroom, dressing and living areas. Suite passengers get personal stationery, complimentary laundry and ironing, cocktail hour hors d'oeuvres and other goodies, as well as priority embarkation and disembarkation. The concierge lounge, with its latticework teak detailing and private library, is accessible only by private key-card.

The ultimate in living space is the Penthouse Suite. It has a separate steward's entrance, and has a large bedroom with king-size bed, separate living room with baby grand piano, and a dining room, dressing room, walk-in closet, butler's pantry, private balcony – though the balcony is no larger than the balcony of any of the other suites.

Other facilities include an audio-visual center with television and video player, wet bar with refrigerator, large bathroom with Jacuzzi tub, separate toilet with bidet, and a guest bathroom with toilet and washbasin.

Except for the penthouse suite, located forward on the starboard side, the bathrooms in the other suites and "mini-suites" are a little disappointing – not as spacious or opulent as one might expect. All outside-view suites and cabin bathrooms have a tub/shower while interior cabins have only a shower. The 23 cabins for the mobility-limited are very spacious and have a large roll-in shower enclosure for wheelchair users (some also have a bathtub), and ramped access to the balcony.

CUISINE. The *Rotterdam Dining Room*, a grand, traditional room, is spread over two decks, with ocean views on three sides and a grand staircase connecting the upper and lower levels. Both open seating and fixed (assigned tables and times) seating are available, while breakfast and lunch are open-seating where you'll be seated by restaurant staff when you enter. There are tables for two, four, six, or eight. The waiter stations are very noisy for anyone seated adjacent to them.

Live music is provided for dinner each evening; once each cruise, a Dutch Dinner is featured (hats are provided), as is an Indonesian Lunch. "Lighter option" meals are available for the nutrition- and weight-conscious. Fine Rosenthal china and cutlery are used, but there are no fish knives.

Alternative Dining Option: The *Pinnacle Grill* serves Pacific Northwest cuisine and seats 88. There's a cover charge and reservations are required, although suite-grade occupants qualify for priority reservations.

The *Lido Buffet* is a casual, self-serve café for casual breakfasts and luncheons. A poolside grill, *Terrace Café*, has hamburgers, hot dogs and other fast-food items. The Lido Buffet is also open for casual dinners on several nights each cruise – typically three nights on a seven-night cruise – in an open-seating arrangement. Tables are set with crisp linens, flatware and stemware. The set menu includes a choice of four entrées.

ENTERTAINMENT. The Mondriaan Showlounge, at the forward part of the ship, spans two decks, with banquette seating on both main and upper levels. It is basically a well-designed room, but the ceiling is low and the sightlines from the balcony level are quite poor.

SPA/FITNESS. The Greenhouse Spa facilities are quite extensive, and include a gymnasium with good muscle-toning equipment, separate saunas and steam rooms for men and women, and several treatment rooms, each with a shower and toilet. Outdoor facilities include basketball and shuffleboard courts, a jogging track, and a full walk-around teakwood promenade deck for strolling.

● **For more extensive general information on what a Holland America Line cruise is like, see pages 140–3.**

Zenith
★★★+

Size:	Mid-Size Ship	Total Crew:	670
Tonnage:	47,255	Passengers	
Lifestyle:	Standard	(lower beds/all berths):	1,378/1,800
Cruise Line:	Pullmantur Cruises	Passenger Space Ratio	
Former Names:	none	(lower beds/all berths):	34.2 /26.2
Builder:	Meyer Werft (Germany)	Crew/Passenger Ratio	
Original Cost:	$210 million	(lower beds/all berths):	2.0/2.6
Entered Service:	Apr 1992/Jun 2007	Cabins (total):	720
Registry:	Malta	Size Range (sq ft/m):	172.2–500.5/
Length (ft/m):	681.0/207.59		16.0–46.50
Beam (ft/m):	95.1/29.00	Cabins (outside view):	572
Draft (ft/m):	23.6/7.20	Cabins (interior/no view):	148
Propulsion/Propellers: diesel (19,960kW)/2		Cabins (for one person):	0
Passenger Decks:	10	Cabins (with private balcony):	110

Cabins (wheelchair accessible):	4
Wheelchair accessibility:	Good
Cabin Current:	110/220 volts
Elevators:	7
Casino (gaming tables):	Yes
Slot Machines:	Yes
Swimming Pools (outdoors):	2
Swimming Pools (indoors):	0
Whirlpools:	3
Self-Service Launderette:	No
Dedicated Cinema/Seats:	No
Library:	Yes
Onboard currency:	Euros

A family-friendly casual ship for Spanish speakers.

OVERVIEW. This ship is best suited to young (and young at heart) Spanish-speaking couples, singles, and families with children of all ages who want a first cruise experience in an elegant ship, with plenty of public rooms and a lively atmosphere, and food that is quantity rather than quality, at low cost.

THE SHIP. Zenith was formerly owned and operated by Celebrity Cruises. Although now 20 years old, it still has a contemporary, though rather sharp, angular profile that gives the impression of power and speed thanks to its blue paint striping along the sides, separating the hull from the superstructure (the hull was designed by mega-yacht designer Jon Bannenberg). Pullmantur Cruises took over the ship in 2007, and installed 220-volt European outlets in all cabins.

Inside, there is a similar interior layout to its sister ship, Island Cruises' *Island Star* (formerly *Horizon),* with elegant and restrained decor. The feeling is one of uncluttered surroundings, and the ship has some interesting artwork. Soothing, pastel colors and high-quality soft furnishings are used throughout the interiors.

The art deco-style hotel-like lobby, reminiscent of hotels in Miami Beach, has a two-deck-high ceiling and a spacious feel, and is the contact point for the reception desk, shore excursions, and onboard accounts.

The principal deck that houses many of the public entertainment rooms has a double-width indoor promenade. There is a good-sized library. Other facilities include Harry's Bar, a cigar-smoking lounge complete with fireplace and bookshelves containing leather-bound volumes; a library and internet-connect center; and a Plaza Café for coffee and

BERLITZ'S RATINGS

	Possible	Achieved
Ship	500	371
Accommodation	200	147
Food	400	234
Service	400	263
Entertainment	100	63
Cruise	400	265

OVERALL SCORE
1,343 points out of 2,000

loud chat. A large, elegantly appointed casino has its own bar.

Pullmantur Cruises has changed some of the public rooms and open areas, and has added splashes of bright colors, motifs, and new signage. The hospitality and the range and variety of food have been tailored to its Spanish-speaking family clientele. You will typically find a lot of smokers aboard.

Passenger niggles? Standing in line for embarkation, disembarkation, shore tenders and for self-serve buffet meals is inevitable aboard large ships. The doors to the public restrooms and the outdoor decks are rather heavy. The public restrooms are clinical and need some softer decor. There are no cushioned pads for poolside sunloungers.

FAMILIES. Pullmantur Cruises has a good program for children and teenagers, with specially trained youth counsellors, and lots of activities. All drinks are included, which makes things simpler for families with children.

ACCOMMODATION. There are 15 price grades, including outside-view suites and cabins, and interior cabins, but even Many outside-view cabins on Fantasy Deck have lifeboat-obstructed views.

Standard Cabins: The outside-view and interior cabins have good-quality fittings with lots of wood accenting, are tastefully decorated and of an above-average size, with an excellent amount of closet and drawer space and reasonable insulation between cabins. All have twin beds that convert to a queen-size bed, and a good amount of closet and drawer space. The cabin soundproofing is quite good although this depends on location – some cabins are located opposite crew access doors, which can be busy and noisy. The bathrooms have a generous shower area, and a small range of toiletries is provided, although towels are a little small, as is storage space for toiletries. The lowest-grade outside-view cabins have a porthole, but all others have picture windows.

Royal Suites: The largest accommodation is in two Royal Suites midships on Atlantic Deck (Deck 10), and forward on Marina Deck. These have a large private balcony and a separate bedroom and lounge, a dining area with glass dining table, plus CD and DVD players in addition to the large TV set. The bathroom is also larger and has a whirlpool tub with integral shower.

Another 20 suites, also on Atlantic Deck, are very tastefully furnished, although they are really just larger cabins rather than suites. They do have a generous amount of drawer and other storage space, however, and a sleeping area with European duvets on the beds instead of sheets and blankets, plus a lounge area. They also have good bathrooms. Butler service is standard.

All accommodation designated as suites suffers from noise generated on the swimming pool deck directly above. No suites or cabins have private balconies – they weren't in vogue when this ship was built.

In early 2005, *Zenith* had a major refit and reconstruction that moved the navigation bridge forward and added cabins. Balconies were added to many cabins on Atlantic and Marina Decks, while the spa/fitness area was expanded, the observation lounge was enlarged forwards, a new "alternative" restaurant was added, and public rooms and foyers were redecorated. All cabins were refurbished, new furniture was introduced, and bathrooms were renewed.

CUISINE. The *Caravelle Dining Room*, with a raised section in its center, has several tables for two, as well as for four, six or eight (in banquettes), although the chairs do not have armrests. There are two seatings for dinner, and open seating for breakfast and lunch, at tables for two, four, six, eight or 10. The cuisine, its presentation and service are more notable for quantity than quality, and green vegetables are hard to come by.

For informal meals, the *Windsurf Buffet* has a traditional single-line self-service buffet for breakfast and lunch, and includes a pasta station, rotisserie and pizza ovens. At peak times, the buffet is simply too small, too crowded, and very noisy. The Grill, located outdoors adjacent to the Windsurf Buffet, serves typical fast-food such as pizzas.

ENTERTAINMENT. The two-level Celebrity Showlounge, with main and balcony levels, has good sightlines from almost all seats, though the railing at the front of the balcony level does impede sightlines. It has a large stage for this size of ship, and decent lighting and sound equipment.

The shows consist of a troupe of showgirl dancers, whose routines are reminiscent of high-school shows. Cabaret acts are the main feature; these include singers, magicians, and comedians, among others, and very much geared to the family audience that this ship carries on most cruises. There is also plenty of live – and loud – music for dancing to in various bars and lounges, plus the inevitable discotheque. Participation activities tend to be quite amateurish.

SPA/FITNESS. The Belleza Spa is high in the ship, aft of the funnel. It has a gymnasium with ocean-view windows and high-tech muscle-pump equipment, an exercise area, several therapy treatment rooms including a rasul room, and men's/women's saunas.

Zuiderdam
★★★★

Size: . . . . .Large Resort Ship	Passenger Decks: 11	Cabins (wheelchair accessible): 28
Tonnage: .81,679	Total Crew: 800	Wheelchair accessibility: . . . . .Good
Lifestyle: . . . . .Premium	Passengers	Cabin Current: . . . . .110 volts
Cruise Line: . . . . . . .Holland America Line	(lower beds/all berths): 1,848/2,387	Elevators: 14
Former Names: . . . . .none	Passenger Space Ratio	Casino (gaming tables): . . . . .Yes
Builder: . . . . .Fincantieri (Italy)	(lower beds/all berths): 43.6/34.2	Slot Machines: . . . . .Yes
Original Cost: . . . .$400 million	Crew/Passenger Ratio	Swimming Pools (outdoors): . . . . .2+1
Entered Service: . . . . .Dec 2002	(lower beds/all berths): 2.3/2.9	children's pool
Registry: . . . . .The Netherlands	Cabins (total): 924	Swimming Pools (indoors): 1
Length (ft/m): 935.0/285.00	Size Range (sq ft/m): 185.0–1,318.6/	(indoor/outdoor)
Beam (ft/m): 105.6/32.25	17.1–122.5	Whirlpools: 5
Draft (ft/m): 25.5/7.80	Cabins (outside view): 788	Self-Service Launderette: . . . . .Yes
Propulsion/Propellers: . . . . .diesel-electric	Cabins (interior/no view): 136	Dedicated Cinema/Seats: Yes/170
(34,000 kW)/2 azimuthing pods	Cabins (for one person): 0	Library: . . . . .Yes
(17.6 MW each)	Cabins (with private balcony): 623	Onboard currency: . . . . .US$

Dutch heritage and decor for family-friendly cruising.

OVERVIEW. This ship is designed to appeal to younger, more vibrant, multi-generational family-oriented passengers. In keeping with the traditions of Holland America Line, there is a large collection of artwork. A winding shopping street includes boutique stores.

THE SHIP. *Zuiderdam*, pronounced Zider-dam, is sister to *Eurodam, Noordam, Oosterdam* and *Westerdam*, and shares a common platform and hull shape. There are two funnels, placed close together, one in front of the other, and not side by side as aboard the smaller *Amsterdam* and *Rotterdam*. This placement is the result of the slightly unusual machinery configuration. The ship has, in effect, two engine rooms – one with three diesels, and one with two diesels and a gas turbine. Pod propulsion *(see page 191 for definition)* is provided, powered by a diesel-electric system, with a small gas turbine located in the funnel for the reduction of emissions.

A complete walk-around exterior promenade deck is enjoyed by many. Exterior glass elevators, mounted midships on both port and starboard sides, provide fine ocean views. There are two centrally located swimming pools outdoors, and one of the pools can be used in poor weather due to its retractable glass-domed cover. Two whirlpool tubs, adjacent to the swimming pools, are abridged by a bar. Another smaller pool is provided for children.

When you first walk into the ship's interior, you'll be greeted by the small size of the lobby space that spans just three decks. It has a stairway, and its focal point is a large, 10-ft-high (3-meter) transparent seahorse. The decor is extremely bright for a Holland America Line ship, with an

BERLITZ'S RATINGS

	Possible	Achieved
Ship	500	426
Accommodation	200	162
Food	400	269
Service	400	277
Entertainment	100	77
Cruise	400	306

OVERALL SCORE
1,517 points out of 2,000

eclectic color and pattern mix that assails you from all directions.

There are two entertainment/public room decks, the upper of which has an exterior promenade deck – something new for this traditional cruise line. Although it doesn't go around the whole ship, it's long enough for some serious walking. There is also a jogging track outdoors, around the mast and the forward third of the ship.

The most dramatic public room is the Vista Lounge, the ship's showlounge; it spans three decks in the forward section of the ship. The main floor level has a bar in its starboard aft section. The casino is equipped with all the gaming paraphernalia and slot machines you can think of, and is so large that you have to walk through it to get from the restaurant to the showlounge.

The information desk in the lobby is small in comparison to the size of the lobby. Many of the private balconies are not so private, and can be overlooked from various public locations. Many pillars obstruct the passenger flow and lines of sight throughout the ship.

Communication in English with many of the staff, particularly in the dining room and buffet areas, can prove very frustrating. It may be difficult to escape from smokers, and people walking around in unsuitable clothing, clutching plastic sport drinks bottles.

FAMILIES. Children have KidZone, an indoor/outdoor facility, and Cub Hal for ages 5–12 (sleepovers aren't allowed, though), with dedicated youth counselors. Teenagers get to use WaveRunner, which includes a dance floor, special lighting effects, and a booming sound system. There's also a video game room, and big-screen television for movies.

ACCOMMODATION. There are 19 price grades.

Penthouse Verandah Suites: The largest accommodation (1,318 sq. ft/122.5 sq. meters, including balcony) is in two of these suites. These have a separate bedroom with a king-size bed; there's also a walk-in closet, dressing room, living room, dining room, butler's pantry, mini-bar and refrigerator, and private balcony. The main bathroom has a large whirlpool tub, two washbasins, toilet, and plenty of storage space for toiletries. Personalized stationery and complimentary dry cleaning are included, as are hot hors d'oeuvres and other goodies daily.

DeLuxe Verandah Suites (60): Measuring 563 sq. ft (52.3 sq. meters), these have twin beds that convert to a king-size bed, vanity desk, lounge area, walk-in closet, mini-bar and refrigerator, and bathroom with full-size tub, washbasin and toilet. Personalized stationery and complimentary dry cleaning are included, as are hot hors d'oeuvres daily and other goodies.

Verandah Suites (100): These are better described as cabins rather than suites, and measure 284 sq. ft (26.3 sq. meters). Twin beds convert to a queen-size bed. There is also a lounge area, mini-bar and refrigerator, while the bathroom has a tub, washbasin and toilet. Floor-to-ceiling windows open onto a private balcony.

Outside-view Cabins: Standard outside cabins, measuring 197 sq. ft (18.3 sq. meters), have twin beds that convert to a queen-size bed. There's a small sitting area, while the bathroom has a tub/shower combination. The interior cabins are slightly smaller, at 182.9 sq ft (17 sq. meters).

A number of cabins on the lowest accommodation deck, Main Deck, have views obstructed by lifeboats. Some cabins that can accommodate a third and fourth person have very little closet space, and there's only one personal safe. There is no separate radio in each cabin – instead, audio channels are provided on the in-cabin TV system.

Each morning, an eight-page *New York Times* (Times Fax) is provided for each cabin. Fresh fruit is available on request. Shoe shine service and evening turndown service are also provided, as is a small range of toiletries including shampoo, bath and facial soaps, and body lotion.

Niggles include noisy cabin air-conditioning – the flow can't be regulated or turned off in cabins or bathrooms, the only regulation being for temperature control.

CUISINE. The stunning 1,045-seat *Vista Dining Room*, at the stern, is two decks high. Both open seating and fixed (assigned tables and times) seating are available, while breakfast and lunch are open-seating where you'll be seated by restaurant staff when you enter. It is traditional Holland America Line in its operation, with friendly service from smiling Indonesian stewards. There are tables for two, four, six or eight. The waiter stations in the dining room can be noisy for anyone seated adjacent to them. Live music is provided for dinner each evening. Once each cruise, there's a Dutch Dinner (hats are provided), and an Indonesian Lunch. "Lighter option" meals are always available for the nutrition-conscious and the weight-conscious.

Alternative Dining Option: The 130-seat *Pinnacle Grill* is a more upscale dining spot with higher-quality ingredients and better presentation than in the larger main dining room. Located on Lower Promenade Deck, it fronts onto the second level of the atrium lobby. The cuisine is Pacific Northwest, plus premium quality steaks from hand-selected cuts of beef. Fine table settings, china and silverware and leather-bound menus are provided. The wine bar offers mostly American wines. Reservations are needed and there's a cover charge.

Informal Eateries: For casual eating, there is an extensive *Lido Café*, which forms an eatery that wraps around the funnel housing and extends aft. It includes a pizzeria counter, a salad bar, Asian stir-fry counter, deli sandwiches, and a separate dessert buffet, although movement around the buffet area is very slow – particularly at peak times, such as in the mornings in port before shore excursions – and requires you to stand in line for everything.

Additionally, there is an outdoor self-serve buffet adjacent to the fantail pool that serves fast-food such as hamburgers and hot dogs, chicken and fries. There are two smaller buffets adjacent to the midships swimming pool area, and a *Windsurf Café* open 20 hours a day in the atrium lobby for pastries, snack foods, deli sandwiches and, in the evenings, liqueur coffees.

ENTERTAINMENT. The 867-seat Vista Lounge is the principal venue for Las Vegas-style revue shows and major cabaret presentations. It spans three decks in the forward section. The main floor level has a bar in its starboard aft section. Spiral stairways at the back of the lounge connect all levels. Stage shows are best seen from the upper levels, from where the sightlines are quite good.

SPA/FITNESS. The Greenhouse Spa is a large, two-decks-high health spa, located directly above the navigation bridge. Facilities include a solarium, and a thermal suite – a unisex area incorporating a Laconium (gentle sauna), Hammam (mild steam), and Camomile Grotto (small aromatic steam room). There's also a beauty parlor, 11 massage and therapy rooms, including one for couples.

A large gymnasium with floor-to-ceiling windows on three sides and forward-facing ocean views has the latest high-tech muscle-toning equipment.

● **For more extensive general information on what a Holland America Line cruise is like, see pages 140–3.**

SHIPS RATED BY SCORE

Ship	Score	Rating	Ship	Score	Rating
LARGE (RESORT) SHIPS			SuperStar Virgo	1,502	4
(over 1,600 passengers)			Golden Princess	1,499	4
			Oriana	1,497	4
Queen Mary 2 (Grill Class)	1,702	5	Grand Princess	1,496	4
Queen Elizabeth (Grill Class)	1,690	4+	Star Princess	1,496	4
Queen Victoria (Grill Class)	1,671	4+	Oceana	1,494	4
Celebrity Eclipse	1,612	4+	Queen Elizabeth (Britannia Class)	1,493	4
Celebrity Silhouette	1,612	4 +	Disney Wonder	1,491	4
Celebrity Equinox	1,611	4+	Serenade of the Seas	1,491	4
Celebrity Solstice	1,611	4+	Vision of the Seas	1,491	4
MSC Fantasia (Yacht Club)	1,570	4+	AIDAsol	1,490	4
MSC Splendida (Yacht Club)	1,570	4+	Arcadia	1,490	4
Celebrity Constellation	1,568	4+	Disney Magic	1,490	4
Celebrity Millennium	1,568	4+	Rhapsody of the Seas	1,490	4
Celebrity Summit	1,568	4+	Sun Princess	1,489	4
Celebrity Infinity	1,566	4+	AIDAblu	1,487	4
Disney Dream	1,555	4+	Norwegian Dawn	1,487	4
Mein Schiff 2	1,548	4	Norwegian Gem	1,487	4
Ruby Princess	1,547	4	Sea Princess	1,487	4
Emerald Princess	1,546	4	Norwegian Jewel	1,486	4
Mein Schiff 1	1,546	4	AIDAbella	1,485	4
Celebrity Century	1,545	4	AIDAluna	1,485	4
Coral Princess	1,544	4	Norwegian Pearl	1,485	4
Diamond Princess	1,544	4	Norwegian Spirit	1,485	4
Sapphire Princess	1,544	4	Norwegian Star	1,485	4
Norwegian Epic	1,543	4	AIDAdiva	1,484	4
Island Princess	1,542	4	Queen Victoria (Britannia Class)	1,483	4
Crown Princess	1,541	4	Norwegian Jade	1,481	4
Queen Mary 2 (Britannia Class)	1,541	4	MSC Magnifica	1,467	4
Zaandam	1,541	4	MSC Poesia	1,467	4
Volendam	1,540	4	MSC Orchestra	1,465	4
Caribbean Princess	1,539	4	MSC Musica	1,462	4
Rotterdam	1,539	4	Explorer of the Seas	1,461	4
Amsterdam	1,537	4	Mariner of the Seas	1,457	4
Nieuw Amsterdam	1,535	4	Navigator of the Seas	1,456	4
Eurodam	1,534	4	Adventure of the Seas	1,454	4
Allure of the Seas	1,528	4	Costa Favolosa	1,447	4
MSC Fantasia (standard cabins)	1,528	4	Brilliance of the Seas	1,446	4
MSC Splendida (standard cabins)	1,528	4	Costa Deliziosa	1,446	4
Dawn Princess	1,527	4	Radiance of the Seas	1,446	4
Oasis of the Seas	1,526	4	Costa Luminosa	1,445	4
Westerdam	1,522	4	Costa Magica	1,445	4
Jewel of the Seas	1,520	4	MSC Opera	1,445	4
Oosterdam	1,520	4	Voyager of the Seas	1,445	4
Noordam	1,519	4	Costa Fortuna	1,444	4
Zuiderdam	1,517	4	Costa Pacifica	1,443	4
Azura	1,514	4	Costa Serena	1,442	4
Freedom of the Seas	1,510	4	Costa Concordia	1,440	4
Independence of the Seas	1,510	4	MSC Lirica	1,439	4
Liberty of the Seas	1,510	4	Costa Mediterranea	1,437	4
Ventura	1,509	4	Costa Atlantica	1,436	4
Aurora	1,503	4	Splendour of the Seas	1,415	4

Ship	Score	Rating	Ship	Score	Rating
Legend of the Seas	1,414	4	Seven Seas Voyager	1,654	4+
Enchantment of the Seas	1,407	4	Seven Seas Mariner	1,651	4+
Grandeur of the Seas	1,407	4	Prinsendam	1,642	4+
Carnival Magic	1,396	3+	Amadea	1,600	4+
MSC Sinfonia	1,396	3+	Nautica	1,575	4+
Carnival Dream	1,395	3+	Insignia	1,574	4+
Carnival Splendor	1,393	3+	Regatta	1,572	4+
MSC Armonia	1,393	3+	Artania	1,568	4+
Norwegian Sun	1,393	3+	Azamara Quest	1,562	4+
Carnival Freedom	1,390	3+	Azamara Journey	1,561	4+
Carnival Spirit	1,390	3+	Pacific Venus	1,548	4
Carnival Legend	1,388	3+	Adonia	1,540	4
Norwegian Sky	1,388	3+	Ocean Princess	1,487	4
Carnival Miracle	1,387	3+	Pacific Princess	1,487	4
Carnival Pride	1,386	3+	Saga Ruby	1,421	4
Carnival Conquest	1,385	3+	Ryndam	1,420	4
Carnival Liberty	1,383	3+	Veendam	1,420	4
Costa Victoria	1,382	3+	Maasdam	1,412	4
Carnival Glory	1,380	3+	Statendam	1,403	4
Carnival Valor	1,380	3+	Balmoral	1,402	4
Carnival Triumph	1,379	3+	Bleu de France	1,396	3+
Carnival Victory	1,369	3+	AIDAvita	1,381	3+
Pacific Jewel	1,365	3+	AIDAaura	1,380	3+
Pacific Pearl	1,364	3+	Astor	1,379	3+
Carnival Destiny	1,361	3+	AIDAcara	1,367	3+
Pride of America	1,268	3+	Boudicca	1,357	3+
Monarch of the Seas	1,248	3	Pacific Dream	1,344	3+
Carnival Ecstasy	1,248	3	Zenith	1,343	3+
Carnival Fantasy	1,247	3	Black Watch	1,339	3+
Carnival Fascination	1,247	3	Thomson Spirit	1,316	3+
Costa Romantica	1,247	3	Braemar	1,315	3+
Majesty of the Seas	1,246	3	Grand Mistral	1,315	3+
Costa Classica	1,245	3	Grand Voyager	1,314	3+
Carnival Sensation	1,244	3	Thomson Celebration	1,307	3+
Sovereign	1,242	3	Thomson Destiny	1,303	3+
Carnival Imagination	1,226	3	Louis Majesty	1,294	3+
Empress	1,226	3	Gemini	1,252	3+
Carnival Elation	1,225	3	Thomson Dream	1,248	3
Carnival Inspiration	1,223	3	SuperStar Libra	1,246	3
Carnival Paradise	1,222	3	Happy Dolphin	1,243	3
Grand Celebration	1,182	3	Louis Cristal	1,236	3
Pacific Dawn	1,181	3	SuperStar Aquarius	1,232	3
Grand Holiday	1,160	3	Albatros	1,194	3
AIDAmar	NYR	NYR	MSC Melody	1,175	3
Celebrity Reflection	NYR	NYR	Ocean Countess	1,178	3
Costa Fascinosa	NYR	NYR	Pacific Sun	1,167	3
			Discovery	1,111	3
MID-SIZE SHIPS			Ocean Dream	1,110	3
(600–1,600 passengers)			Island Escape	1,109	3
			Orient Queen	1,103	3
Crystal Serenity	1,717	5	Costa Allegra	1,092	2+
Crystal Symphony	1,701	5	Costa Marina	1,090	2+
Marina	1,701	5	Marco Polo	1,082	2+
Asuka II	1,685	4+	Ocean Pearl	1,080	2+

Ship	Score	Rating	Ship	Score	Rating
The Emerald	1,063	2+	Arion	902	2
Bahamas Celebration	1,035	2+	Alexander von Humboldt	NYR	NYR
Ocean Star Pacific	1,014	2+	Deutschland	NYR	NYR
Pacific	1,013	2+			
Coral	944	2	**BOUTIQUE SHIPS**		
Columbus 2	NYR	NYR	(50–200 passengers)		
Riviera	NYR	NYR			
Saga Sapphire	NYR	NYR	SeaDream II	1,788	5
			SeaDream I	1,786	5
			Hanseatic	1,746	5
SMALL SHIPS			Sea Cloud	1,704	5
(201–600 passengers)			Sea Cloud II	1,702	5
Europa	1,852	5+	Silver Explorer	1,684	4+
Seabourn Quest	1,787	5	Hebridean Princess	1,680	4+
Seabourn Odyssey	1,786	5	Orion	1,612	4+
Seabourn Sojourn	1,783	5	Island Sky	1,562	4+
Seabourn Legend	1,774	5	Bremen	1,553	4+
Silver Spirit	1,772	5	Corinthian II	1,546	4
Seabourn Spirit	1,770	5	Le Levant	1,415	4
Seabourn Pride	1,769	5	50 Years of Victory	1,411	4
Silver Whisper	1,753	5	Celebrity Xpedition	1,404	4
Silver Shadow	1,750	5	Orion II	1,404	4
Silver Wind	1,669	4+	Star Clipper	1,402	4
Silver Cloud	1,664	4+	Star Flyer	1,402	4
Seven Seas Navigator	1,595	4+	Wind Spirit	1,394	3+
Paul Gauguin	1,547	4	Wind Star	1,393	3+
L'Austral	1,543	4	Le Ponant	1,385	3+
Le Boreal	1,543	4	Clipper Odyssey	1,245	3
Royal Clipper	1,540	4	Galapagos Explorer II	1,244	3
Nippon Maru	1,503	4	Sea Spirit	1,222	3
Wind Surf	1,471	4	Le Diamant	1,219	3
Club Med 2	1,459	4	Kapitan Khlebnikov	1,144	3
Hamburg	1,398	3+	Independence	962	2+
Saga Pearl II	1,350	3+	Clipper Adventurer	947	2
Aegean Odyssey	1,341	3+	Professor Multanovskiy	947	2
Minerva	1,324	3+	National Geographic Endeavour	945	2
Fram	1,321	3	National Geographic Polaris	943	2
Spirit of Adventure	1,249	3	Admiralty Dream	930	2
Fuji Maru	1,186	3	American Star	925	2
Funchal	1,144	3	American Spirit	922	2
Princess Danae	1,135	3	Wilderness Adventurer	908	2
Princess Daphne	1,128	3	American Glory	868	2
Athena	1,092	2+	National Geographic Explorer	856	1+
The Emerald	1,063	2+	Grande Caribe	756	1+
Vistamar	1,061	2+	Grande Mariner	747	1+
Sapphire	1,030	2+	National Geographic Sea Bird	743	1+
The Calypso	990	2+	National Geographic Sea Lion	743	1+

NYR = Not Yet Rated

BOOKING AND BUDGETING

Is it better to book a cruise directly with the operator or through a travel agent? And what hidden extras should you look for when calculating costs?

Booking direct

In the 1960s, about 90% of all cruises were booked by passengers directly with cruise lines and about 10% were booked by travel agents. Then along came some enterprising travel agents. They saw a golden opportunity and started to act on behalf of the cruise lines, which were happy to accept such bookings because they could then reduce staff and overheads in their sales offices.

Established companies such as American Express and Thomas Cook booked cruises, as did many others, and received a commission. Today, about 80% of all cruises are booked by travel agents, and about 20% are booked direct (including internet bookings).

When you see newspaper adverts for cruises, check what's included in any heavily discounted offers. Make sure that all port charges, government fees, and any additional fuel surcharges are included in the quote.

The internet

While the Internet may be a good *resource* tool, it is not the place to book your cruise, unless you know *exactly* what you want. You can't ask questions, and most of the information provided by the cruise companies is strictly marketing hype. Most sites providing cruise ship reviews have something to sell, and the sound-byte information can be misleading or outdated. Also, many discounts for senior citizens, military personnel, and alumni groups, or special discounts for various regions and locales are typically not available on the web, but only through cruise-booking agencies

If you do book with an internet-based cruise agency or wholesaler, you should confirm with the cruise line that the booking has been made and that final payment has been received. Be aware that many internet booking agents are unlicensed and unregulated. Some add a "booking fee" – which can be substantial.

The internet vs travel agents

So, you've found a discounted rate for your cruise on the net. That's fine. But, if a cruise line suddenly offers special discounts for your sailing, or cabin upgrades, or if things go wrong with your booking, your internet booking service may prove unfriendly or may even have disappeared. Your travel agent, however, can probably make special discounts work for *you* and perhaps even provide upgrades. It's called personal service.

Large travel agency groups and consortiums, such as American Express, often reserve huge blocks of cabins,

LEFT: accessing the internet, *Carnival Miracle.*

and smaller independent agencies can access extensive discounts not available on the internet. Furthermore, the cruise lines consider travel agents as their distribution system, and provide special discounts and value-added amenities that are not provided over the internet.

Travel agents

Travel agents do not charge for their services, although they earn a commission from cruise lines. Consider a travel agent as your business advisor, not just a ticket agent. He/she will handle all matters relevant to your booking and should have the latest information on changes of itinerary, cruise fares, fuel surcharges, discounts, and any other related items, including insurance in case you have to cancel prior to sailing. Most travel agents are linked into cruise line computer systems and have access to most shipboard information.

Your travel agent should find exactly the right ship for your needs and lifestyle. Some sell only a limited number of cruises and are known as "preferred suppliers," because they receive special "overrides" on top of their normal commission (they probably know their limited number of ships well, however).

If *you* have chosen a ship and cruise, be firm and book exactly what you want, or change agencies. In the UK, look for a member of the Guild of Professional Cruise Agents. ACE (Association for Cruise Education), part of the UK's Passenger Shipping Association, provides in-depth agent training, as well as a full "bonding" scheme to protect passengers from failed cruise lines. In the US, look for a CLIA (Cruise Lines International Association) affiliated agency, or one belonging to the National Association of Cruise Oriented Agencies (NACOA), or the National Association of Commissioned Travel Agents (NACTA).

Questions to ask a travel agent

● Is air transportation included in the cabin rate quoted? If not, what will be the extra cost?

● What other extra costs will be involved? These can include port charges, insurance, gratuities, shore excursions, laundry, and drinks.

● What is the cruise line's cancellation policy?

● If I want to make changes to my flight, routing, dates, and so on, will the insurance policy cover everything in case of missed or canceled flights?

● Does your agency deal with only one, or several different insurance companies?

● Does the cruise line offer advance booking discounts or other incentives?

● Do you have preferred suppliers, or do you book any cruise on any cruise ship?
● Have you sailed aboard the ship I want to book or that you are recommending?
● Is your agency bonded and insured? If so, by whom?
● If you book the shore excursions offered by the cruise line, is insurance coverage provided?
● Can I occupy my cabin on the day of disembarkation until I am ready to disembark?

Reservations

Plan ahead and book early. After choosing a ship, cruise, date, and cabin, you pay a deposit that is roughly 10% for long cruises, 20% for short cruises. The balance is normally payable 45 to 60 days before departure. For a late reservation, you pay in full when space is confirmed (when booking via the internet, for example). Cruise lines reserve the right to change prices in the event of tax increases, fluctuating exchange rates, fuel surcharges, or other costs beyond their control.

When you make your reservation, also make special dining requests known, and any seating preferences. It's useful to keep a note of them.

After the line has received full payment, your cruise ticket will be sent by mail, or as an e-document. Check all documents. Make sure the ship, date, and cruise details are correct. Verify connecting flight times that seem suspiciously short.

Extra costs

Cruise brochures boldly proclaim that "almost everything's included," but in most cases you will find this is not true. In fact, for some cruises "all-exclusive" would be a more appropriate term. In the recent credit crisis, many cruise lines cut their fares dramatically in order to attract business. At the same time, the cost of many onboard items went up. So allow for extra onboard costs.

Your fare covers the ship as transportation, your cabin, meals, entertainment, activities, and service on board; it typically does not include alcoholic drinks, laundry, dry cleaning or valet services, shore excursions, meals ashore, spa treatments, wine/martini tasting seminars, gratuities, port charges, cancellation insurance, optional onboard activities such as gambling.

Expect to spend at least $25 a day per person on extras, plus $10–$12 a day per person in gratuities. Exceptions can be found in some small ships (those with fewer than 600 passengers) where more is included.

Calculate the total cost of your cruise (not including any extra-cost services you might decide you want once on board) with the help of your travel agent. Here are the approximate prices per person for a typical seven-day cruise aboard a well-rated mid-size or large cruise ship, based on an outside-view two-bed cabin:

Cruise fare	*$1,000*
Port charges	*$100 (if not included)*
Gratuities	*$50*
Total per person	*$1,150*

The cost of cocktails can quickly add up.

This is less than $165 per person per day. For this price, you wouldn't get a decent hotel room, without meals, in London, Miami, New York, Tokyo, or Venice.

However, your seven-day cruise can become expensive when you start adding on any extras. For example, add two flight-seeing excursions in Alaska (at about $250 each), two cappuccinos each a day ($25), a scotch and soda each a day ($35), a massage ($125), 7 mineral waters ($28), 30 minutes' access to the internet for emails ($15), three other assorted excursions ($150), and gratuities ($50). That's an extra $928 – without even one bottle of wine with dinner! So a couple will need to add an extra $1,856 for a seven-day cruise, plus the cruise fare, of course, and the cost of getting to and from your local airport, or ship port.
● *For a list of 30 typical extra-cost items with their current prices, see the chart on page 13.*

Discounts and incentives

Book ahead to get the best discounts (they decrease closer to the cruise date). You may be able to reserve a cabin grade, but not a specific cabin – "tba" (to be assigned). Some lines will accept this arrangement and may even upgrade you. The first cabins to be sold out are usually those at minimum and maximum rates. Note: Premium rates apply to Christmas/New Year cruises.

Cancellations and refunds

Do take out full cancellation insurance (if it is not included), as cruises (and air transportation to/from them) must be paid in full before your tickets are issued. Otherwise, if you cancel at the last minute – even for medical reasons – you could lose the whole fare. Insurance coverage can be obtained from your travel agent or from an independent company, and paying by credit card makes sense (you'll probably get your money back if the agency goes bust) or through the internet.

Note that cancellation insurance offered by a cruise line is a "one-size-fits-all" product, so personalization is impossible. It covers only the cruise itself but not any add-ons that you may have arranged on your own – such as non-refundable air tickets.

Cruise lines usually accept cancellations more than 30 days before sailing, but all charge full fare if you don't

Insurance may exclude sports such as horse riding.

turn up on sailing day. Other cancellation fees depend on the cruise and length of trip. Many lines do not return port taxes, which are not part of the cruise fare.

If your cruise company appears to have gone out of business, some insurance policies will not cover you unless the cruise company declares bankruptcy.

Medical insurance

Whether you intend to travel overseas or cruise down a local river, and your present medical insurance does not cover you, you should look into extra coverage for your cruise. The cruise line may offer a "passenger protection program," the charge for which will appear on your final invoice, unless you decline. It is worth every penny, and typically covers such things as evacuation at sea by air ambulance (Medivac), high-limit baggage, baggage transfers, personal liability, and missed departure.

Port taxes/Handling charges

These are assessed by individual port authorities and are usually shown in the brochure. Port charges form part of the final payment, although they can be changed right up to the day of embarkation.

Fuel surcharges

Cruise lines publish their brochures a year ahead. If oil and other fuel costs rise in the interim, a fuel surcharge may be imposed, in addition to the quoted fare.

Air/Sea packages

If your cruise fare includes air transportation (as in a one-way or round-trip air ticket), then airline arrangements usually cannot be changed without paying a premium, as cruise lines often book group space on aircraft to obtain the lowest rates. If you do make changes, remember that, if the airline cancels your flight, the cruise line is under no obligation to help you or return your cruise fare if you don't reach the ship on time. If flying to a foreign country, allow extra time (particularly in winter) for flight delays and cancellations.

Airlines often use a "hub-and-spoke" system, which can prove frustrating. Because of changes to air schedules, cruise and air tickets may not be sent to passengers until a few days before the cruise.

In Europe, air/sea packages generally start at a major metropolitan airport; some include first-class rail travel from outlying districts. In the US, many cruise lines include connecting flights from suburban airports convenient to the traveler. If you fly and want to lock your check-in baggage, use a TSA (Transportation Security Administration)-approved security lock.

Most cruise lines allow you to fly out to join a ship in one port and fly home from another. An advantage is that you only have to check your baggage once at the departure airport and its transfer from plane to ship is handled for you. This doesn't include intercontinental fly/cruises, where you must claim your baggage at the airport on arrival to clear it though customs.

Travel insurance

Note that cruise lines and travel agents routinely sell travel cover policies that, on close inspection, appear to wriggle out of payment due to a litany of exclusion clauses, most of which are never explained. Examples:
● "Pre-existing" medical conditions – ignoring this little gem could cost you dearly.
● "Valuables" left unattended on a tour bus, even if the guide says it is safe and that the driver will lock the door.

Getting the best travel insurance deal:

● Allow time to shop around and don't accept the first travel insurance policy you are offered.
● Read the contract carefully and make sure you know exactly what you are covered for.
● If you purchase your own air transportation, it may not cover you if the airline fails, or if bad weather prevents you from joining your ship on time.
● Beware of the "box ticking" approach to travel cover, which is often done quickly at the travel agent's office in lieu of providing expert advice. Insurers should not, in reality, be allowed to apply exclusions that have not been clearly pointed out to the policyholder.
● Ask for a detailed explanation of all exclusions, excesses, and limitations.
● Check out the procedure you need to follow if you are the victim of a crime, such as your wallet or camera being stolen while on a shore excursion. If anything does happen, *always* obtain a police report as soon as possible. Many insurance policies will reimburse you only for the secondhand value of any lost or stolen item, rather than the full cost of replacement, and you may have to produce the original receipt for any such items claimed.
● Watch out for exclusions for "hazardous sports." These could include things typically offered as shore excursions aboard ships. Examples: horse riding (there goes that horse riding on the beach excursion in Jamaica) or cycling (mountain biking excursions), jet skiing (most beaches), or ziplining.
● If you purchase travel cover over the internet, check the credentials of the company underwriting the scheme. It is best to deal with well-established names, and not to take what appears to be the cheapest deal offered. ❏

DON'T LEAVE HOME WITHOUT...

Cruise ships are well stocked for most people's
everyday needs, but there are certain things
you need to take with you

Baggage

There is generally no limit to the amount of personal
baggage you can take on your cruise (most ships provide towels, soap, shampoo, and shower caps), but airlines do have weight limits. Do allow extra space for
purchases on the cruise.

Tag all baggage with your name, ship, cabin number, sailing date, and port of embarkation (tags are provided with your tickets). Baggage transfers from airport
to ship are generally smooth and problem-free when
handled by the cruise line.

Liability for loss or damage to baggage is contained
in the passenger contract (part of your ticket). Do take
out insurance; the policy should extend from the date of
departure until two or three days after your return home.

Some cruise lines offer fee-based luggage courier
services that collect your luggage from your home and
the next time you see your luggage, it will be in your
cabin (and vice versa at the end of the cruise).

Clothing

Closet space aboard many ships is at a premium. So,
unless you are on an extended cruise, keep your baggage to a minimum. It's a good idea to choose four or
five interchangeable outfits to wear throughout the
week, in two or three color groups and mix-and-match
clothing that can be layered. Black is always a good
neutral color to team with other colors.

For cruises to tropical areas, casual wear should
include plenty of lightweight cottons and other natural
fibers. Synthetic materials do not "breathe" as well and
often retain heat. Clothes should be as opaque as possible to counteract the sun's ultraviolet rays. Take a lightweight cotton sweater or windbreaker for the evenings,
when the ship's air-conditioning will seem even more
powerful after a day in the sun. Pack sunglasses and a
hat. Rainstorms in the tropics don't last long, but they
can give you a good soaking, so take inexpensive, lightweight rainwear for excursions.

The same is true for cruises to the Mediterranean,
Greek Isles, or North Africa, although there will be little or no humidity for most of the year. Certain areas
may be dusty as well as dry. In these latitudes, the
weather can be cool in the evenings from October to
March, so take extra sweaters and a windbreaker.

For cruises to Alaska, the North Cape, or the Norwegian fjords, pack warm comfortable clothing layers,
plus a raincoat or parka for the northernmost port calls.
Cruises to Alaska and the Land of the Midnight Sun

are operated in summer, when temperatures are pleasant. Unless you are going to northern ports such as St.
Petersburg in winter, you will not need thermal underwear. However, you will need thermal underwear, thick
socks – and heavy sweaters – if you take an expedition
cruise to the Antarctic Peninsula or through the Northwest Passage.

In destinations with a strong religious tradition, like
Venezuela, Haiti, the Dominican Republic, Colombia,
and countries in the Middle East and Far East, shorts or
bare shoulders may cause offense, so cover up.

Aboard ship, dress rules are relaxed by day, but in the
evening what you wear should be tasteful. Men should
take a blazer or sports jacket and ties for the dining
room and for any "informal" occasions. Transatlantic
crossings are normally more elegant and require formal attire.

For formal nights (usually two out of seven), women
can wear a long evening gown, elegant cocktail dress, or
a smart pants suit. Gentlemen are expected to wear
either a tuxedo or dark business suit and tie. These
"rules" are less rigid on short and moderately priced
cruises. If you are the athletic type, pack sportswear
and gym shoes for the gymnasium or aerobics classes.

No matter where you are going, comfortable low- or
flat-heeled shoes are a must for women, except for formal nights. Light, airy walking shoes are best for walking. If you are in the Caribbean or Pan-Pacific region
and you are not used to heat and humidity, your ankles
may swell, so tight shoes are not recommended. Rubber
soles are best for walking on the open deck of a ship.
Formal: Tuxedo, dinner jacket or dark suit and tie for
men; evening gown or other appropriate formal attire
for women.
Informal: Jacket and tie for men; cocktail dress, dressy
pantsuit, or the like for women.
Casual (Elegant/Smart): While this is an oxymoron, it
generally means long trousers (no shorts or jeans),
proper collared and sleeved shirt (gentlemen); skirt or
slacks and top for women.
Casual (Relaxed): Slacks over sweater or open shirt
(no tie) for men (no beach wear or muscle shirts); a
blouse with skirt, slacks, or similar comfortable attire
for women. Shoes are required.

Documents

A passport is the most practical proof of your citizen-
ship and identification. Visas are required for some
countries (allow time to obtain these). On most cruises,

you will hand in your passport to the company at embarkation (it would be wise to keep a copy of the main pages with you). This helps the ship to clear customs and immigration inspection on arrival in ports of call. It will be returned before you reach the port of disembarkation.

Flying... and airports

If you purchase anything in Duty Free outlets such as a camera or electronic goods (from a well known high-street chain, for example), note that if the item goes wrong, and you cannot return it to the airport store concerned, any high-street branch store may refuse to help, because the item was not purchased "in the country."

Flying... and jet lag

Several cruise lines have "air deviation" desks that allow you to change your flights and connections, for a fee (typically $25–$50 per person).

Air travel today is fast and efficient. But even experienced travelers find that the stress of international travel can persist long after the flight is over (for long international flights, I recommend the flat beds in Club Class on British Airways or in Upper Class on Virgin Atlantic aircraft). Eastbound flights tend to cause more pronounced jet lag than westbound flights. Jet aircraft are generally pressurized to some 8,000 ft (2,400 meters) in altitude, causing discomfort in the ears and the stomach, and swollen feet.

A few precautions should help. Plan as far in advance of your cruise as possible. Take a daytime flight, so that you can arrive at, or close to, your normal bedtime. Try to be as quiet as possible before flying, and allow for another five hours of rest after any flight that crosses more than five time zones.

Medication

Take any medicine and other medical supplies that you need, plus spare eyeglasses or contact lenses. In many countries it may be difficult to find certain medicines.

FIVE FIRSTS

● In 1903 the British liner *Lucania* acquired wireless equipment which enabled it to keep in touch with both sides of the Atlantic Ocean at the same time.

● The first ship-to-shore wireless telegraphy took place on the American passenger ship *St. Paul* in 1899.

● The first twin-screw passenger ship was the Compagnie Générale Transatlantique's 3,200-ton *Washington*, built in 1863 and converted in 1868.

● The first floating eclipse expedition was led by the US astronomer Ted Pedas in 1972, when 800 passengers sailed to a spectacular rendezvous with a total sun eclipse in the North Atlantic.

● The first passenger ship to exceed 80,000 gross tonnage was the Compagnie Générale Transatlantique's *Normandie* (82,799 gross tonnage in 1936).

Others may be sold under different names. If taking a long cruise, ask your doctor to name alternatives.

The ship's pharmacy will stock certain standard remedies, but do not expect a supply of the more unusual medicines. Remember to take along a doctor's prescription for any medication (required if you join a cruise in Dubai). Also, be advised that if you run out of your medication and you need to get a supply aboard ship, most ships will require that you see the doctor, even if you have a prescription. There is a charge for each visit, plus the cost of any medication.

Let spouses/companions carry a supply of your medicine and medical supplies. Do not pack medicine or medical information in luggage to be checked in when flying; take it in your carry-on.

Money matters

Most ships operate primarily in US dollars, euros or UK pounds, but a few use other currencies (check with your travel agent or supplier). Major credit cards and traveler's checks are accepted on board but not personal checks. You sign for drinks and other services, as part of "cashless cruising." Some large resort ships have ATM cash machines, although a "transaction fee" is assessed.

Pets

Pets are not allowed aboard cruise ships, with one exception: the regular transatlantic crossings aboard Cunard Line's *Queen Mary 2* ocean liner, which has air-conditioned kennels, plus a genuine British lamp-post, New York fire hydrant, and cat containers.

Photography

Users of digital cameras should pack a spare memory card unless they are carrying a laptop onto which they can transfer pictures. Users of film should bring low-speed film for tropical areas such as the Caribbean or South Pacific – heat can damage high-speed film.

Sun protection

Take suncream/sunlotion with a minimum SPF 15 or higher protection factor. Keep reapplying it after you take a dip in the pool or hot tub, and allow for the fact that if you perspire, the suncream/sunlotion dissolves. If you wear a tee-shirt over your swimsuit, its SPF protection factor is between 7 (white tee-shirt), and 10 (dark tee-shirt).

While cotton tee-shirts allow more "breathing," unbleached cotton has special pigments that can actually absorb UV rays vs polyester/other synthetic or silk tee-shirts that reflect radiation.

Clothing designated as sun-protective, including swimwear, carries a UPF number. This is similar to the SPF factor, except that the UPT number shows how much UVA and UVB is blocked. Companies specializing in outdoor sports clothing and swimwear now make sun-protective clothing from special microfibers that have a very tight weave to block out the sun. ❏

WHAT TO EXPECT

Your first cruise? Here is what you need to know about a typical initial embarkation process

Taking your first cruise? Make sure you have your passport and any visas required (in some countries – such as China or Russia – you might go ashore on organized excursions under a group visa. Pack any medication you may need (in original, labeled containers) in your carry-on hand luggage.

You already have been sent your cruise tickets and documents by the cruise line or your travel agent. Increasingly, e-documents are provided. A typical document package might include:

- Air ticket (or e-ticket boarding pass or reference code)
- Cruise ticket and e-boarding pass (not all lines)
- Luggage tags
- Embarkation/Immigration card (to fill out before you get to the ship)
- Discount coupons for the shops on board
- Bon Voyage gift selection form
- Shore excursion brochure
- Onboard credit account form
- Guide to services on board (including e-mail)
- Ship's telephone and fax contact numbers
- Coupon for tuxedo rental

Assume that you've arrived at the airport closest to your ship's embarkation point, and retrieved your luggage. It is likely that there will be a representative from the cruise line waiting, holding aloft the company's name. You will be asked to place your luggage in a cluster together with those of other passengers. The next time you see your luggage should be in your cabin.

You'll find check-in desks in the passenger terminal. If your accommodation is designated as a "suite," there should be a separate check-in facility.

If you are cruising from a US port and you are a non-US citizen or "resident alien," you will go to a separate desk to check in (*Note*: Do not buy duty-free liquor to take on board – it will not be allowed by the cruise line and will be confiscated until the last day of the cruise). You will leave your passport with the check-in personnel. Ask for a receipt – it is a valuable document – and preferably have a photocopy of the main pages to keep with you. If you are cruising from any other port in the world that is not a US port, be aware that each country has its own check-in requirements.

Getting aboard

You will then proceed through a security-screening device, for both your body and hand luggage, as at airports. Next, you'll walk a few paces towards the gangway. This may be a covered, airport-type gangway, or an open one (hopefully with a net underneath it in case you drop something over the side). The gangway could be flat, or you may have to walk up (or down) an incline, depending on the location of the gangway, the tide, or other local conditions. As you approach the gangway you will probably be greeted by the ship's photographers, a snap-happy team ready to take your photograph, bedraggled as you may appear after having traveled for hours. If you don't want your photograph taken, say "no" firmly.

At the ship end of the gangway, you will find a decorated (hopefully) entrance and the comfortable feel of air-

HOW TO CHECK IN ONLINE

Most major cruise lines now insist that you check-in online. This helps reduce staff numbers – usually locally sourced part-time retirees – at check-in desks in embarkation cruise terminals. This could be smooth if you are computer-literate or a frustrating nightmare if you are not.

The truth is that the old paper cruise tickets and other documents of most of the major cruise lines have become collectors' items, because these companies have gone to paperless ticketing (at least in their offices), although you will need to print your boarding pass at your own cost. Expect more cruise lines to follow suit in an effort to cut costs. It typically takes about 15–20 minutes to complete the online check-in process, assuming that you have all your personal details to hand.

Pretty soon there'll be self-serve cruising, where you wait your own tables, and...? Wait a moment, didn't easyCruise try the no-frills style of cruising – and failed? Warning to cruise line accountants: you may soon not be needed.

Depending on the cruise line, there are usually four major steps to complete, each step requesting information before you can actually reach the stage where you can print out your "boarding pass." Before you start the online check-in procedure, however, you'll need to put in your name, reservation number, and any other pertinent personal information requested.

- **Step 1:** Passenger information.
- **Step 2:** Your onboard expense account information (pre-register your credit card).
- **Step 3:** Cruise ticket contract (you'll need to have 20/20 eyesight to read this, or take it to your local optician).
- **Step 4:** Print your boarding pass.

Offer to do the online check-in for your whole family or group, and you could end up spending hours and hours at your computer.

conditioning if the weather is hot. The ship's cruise staff will welcome you aboard.

Things to check

The door to your cabin should be open. If it is locked, ask the steward to obtain the key to open the door. Aboard the newest ships, you will probably be handed an electronically coded key card. Once inside the cabin, take a good look around. Is it clean? Is it tidy? Are the beds properly made? Make sure there is ice in the ice container. Check the bathroom, bathtub (if there is one), or shower. Make sure there are towels and soap.

If there are problems, bring them to the attention of your cabin steward immediately. Or call the reception desk, explain the problem, and establish how it will be resolved and by whom.

Memorize the telephone number for the ship's hospital, doctor, or for medical emergencies, just so you know how to call for help should an emergency arise.

Your luggage probably will not have arrived yet – especially if it is a large resort ship carrying more than 1,600 passengers – but there's no need to sit in the cabin waiting for it. Put your hand luggage away somewhere, and, deck plan in hand, take a walk. If you're hungry, you may want to head to the self-serve buffet – but, be warned that aboard the large resort ships, it'll probably be a bit of a free-for-all.

Familiarize yourself with the layout of the ship.

Learn which way is forward, which way is aft, and how to reach your cabin from the main stairways. This is also a good time to learn how to get from your cabin to the outside decks in an emergency (these are rare, but they do happen).

Control that thirst

You're thirsty when you arrive in your cabin. You notice a bottle of water with a tab around its neck. Be sure to read the notice on the tab: "This bottle is provided for your convenience. If you open it, your account will be charged $4.50."

On deck, you are greeted by a smilingwaiter offering you a colorful, cool drink. But, put your fingers on the glass as he hands it to you and he'll also ask for your cruise card. Bang, you've just paid $6.95 for a drink full of ice worth 5 cents.

Drinks costs soon add up. Aboard ships operated by Europe-based companies, mixers such as tonic for gin are usually charged separately.

The safety drill

Regulations dictate that a Passenger Lifeboat Drill must take place within 24 hours after the ship sails from the embarkation port, but typically it takes place before the ship sails. You'll find your lifejacket in the cabin and directions to your assembly station will be posted on the back of the cabin door. After the drill, you can take off the lifejacket and relax. By now, your luggage probably will have arrived. ❑

CRUISE LINES BY MARKET CLASSIFICATION

Although there are three fairly distinctive divisions of cruise lines and their ships, some blurring between these divisions has occurred as companies have responded to more demanding passenger tastes and to the market conditions created by the threat of international terrorism and a harsher economic climate.

LUXURY
Crystal Cruises **
Cunard Line **
Hapag-Lloyd Cruises *
Sea Cloud Cruises
Seabourn
SeaDream Yacht Club
Silversea Cruises

PREMIUM
Asuka Cruise (NYK)
Azamara Club Cruises
Celebrity Cruises
Hebridean Island
   Cruises
Holland America Line
Oceania Cruises
Orion Expedition Cruises
Peter Deilmann Cruises
Paul Gauguin Cruises

Ponant Cruises (CIP)
Regent Seven Seas
   Cruises **
Saga Cruises
Venus Cruise
Voyages to Antiquity
Windstar Cruises

STANDARD
Abercrombie & Kent
AIDA Cruises
American Canadian
   Caribbean Line
American Cruise Lines
CDF Croisières de
   France **
Canodros
Carnival Cruise Lines
Classic International
   Cruises

Club Mediterranée
   Cruises
Costa Cruises
Cruise and Maritime
   Voyages
Cruise West
Disney Cruise Line
Fred Olsen Cruise Lines
Galapagos Cruises
Hapag-Lloyd Cruises *
Happy Cruises
Hurtigruten
Iberocruceros
Island Cruises (part of
   Thomson Cruises)
Kristina Cruises
Lindblad Expeditions
Louis Cruises
MSC Cruises ***
Mano Cruises

Mediterranean Classic
   Cruises
Mitsui OSK Passenger
   Line ***
Noble Caledonia
Norwegian Cruise Line
P&O Cruises
P&O Cruises (Australia)
Page & Moy Cruises
Phoenix Reisen
Plantours & Partner
Plein Cap Cruises
Princess Cruises
Pullmantur Cruises
Quark Expeditions
Royal Caribbean
   International
Star Cruises
Star Clippers
Swan Hellenic Cruises

Thomson Cruises
Transocean Tours
TUI Cruises
Voyages of Discovery

NICHE MARKET OPERATORS
These small expedition-
market companies
charter ships for specific
voyages or seasons:
Antarctic Shipping
Antarpply Expeditions
Arcturus Expeditions (Far
   Frontiers Travel Ltd)
Aurora Expeditions
GAP Expeditions
Heritage Expeditions
Oceanwide Expeditions
OneOcean Expeditions
Zegrahm Expeditions

* Europa only   ** This company operates ships that straddle the line between Luxury and Premium.   *** Some of this company's ships straddle the line between Premium and Standard.

WHAT TO DO IF...

Twenty practical tips for a good cruise experience

❶ Your luggage does not arrive at the ship.
If you are part of the cruise line's air/sea package, the airline is responsible for locating your luggage and delivering it to the next port. If you arranged your own air transportation it is wholly *your* problem. Always have easy-to-read name and address tags both *inside* as well as *outside* your luggage. Keep track of claim documents and give the airline a detailed itinerary and list of port agents (usually included with your documents).

❷ *You* miss the ship.
If you miss the ship's departure at the port of embarkation (due to late or non-performing flight connections, etc), and you are traveling on an air/sea package, the airline will arrange to get you to the ship, possibly at the next port of call. If you are traveling "cruise-only," however, and have arranged your own air transportation, then *you* are responsible for onward flights, hotel stays, and transfers. If you arrive at the port just as your ship is pulling away, see the ship's port agent immediately (contact details will be included in your documents).

You miss the ship in a port of call. The onus is on you to get back to the ship before its appointed sailing time, unless you are participating in a ship-organized shore excursion. Miss the ship and you'll need to get to its next port at your own cost. It could prove difficult if the ship is going to a different country, and your passport is on board, and it's a Sunday, for example. So, *always* take a copy of your passport with you, just in case. Ships have also been known to leave port early because of impending inclement weather conditions or some impending natural disaster. However, if you do miss your ship, the ship's port agent should be close by to assist you. In case he's not, always take the name and telephone contact details with you – they are normally provided on the daily program for each port. Your plastic electronic card should also have the ship's phone number on it.

❸ Your cabin is too small.
Almost all cruise ship cabins are too small (I am convinced that some are designed for packages rather than people). When you book a cruise, you pay for a certain category and type of cabin but have little or no control over which one you actually get. Go to the reception desk as soon as possible and explain what is wrong with the cabin (noisy, too hot, etc). If the ship is full (most are nowadays), it will be difficult to change. However, staff may try to move you from known problem cabins, although they are not required to do so.

❹ Your cabin has no air-conditioning, it is noisy, or there are plumbing problems.
If there is anything wrong in your cabin, or if there is something wrong with the plumbing in your bathroom, tell your cabin steward immediately. If nothing gets better, complain at the reception desk. Some cabins, for example, are located above the ship's laundry, generator, or galley (hot); others may be above the disco (noisy). If the ship is full, it may be difficult to change.

❺ You have noisy cabin neighbors.
First, politely tell your neighbors that you can hear them brushing their hair as the cabin walls are so thin, and would they please not bang the drawers shut at 2am! If that does not work, complain to the purser or hotel manager, and ask them to attend to the problem.

❻ You have a problem with a crew member.
Go to the hotel manager or chief purser and explain the problem; for single women this could be a persistent cabin steward who has a master door key. No one will do anything unless you complain. Cruise ships try to hire decent staff, but, with so many crew, there are bound to be a few bad apples. Insist on a full written report of the incident, which must be entered into the ship's daily log by the staff captain (deputy captain).

❼ You have small children and the brochure implied that the ship has special programs for them, but when on board you find out it is not an all-year-round program.
In this instance, either the brochure was misleading, or your travel agent did not know enough about the ship or did not bother to ask the right questions. If you have genuine cause for complaint, then see your travel agent when you get home. Most ships generally will try to accommodate your young ones (the large resort ships – those carrying more than 1,600 passengers – have more facilities), but may not be covered by their insurance for "looking after" them throughout the day, as the brochure seemed to promise. Again, check thoroughly with your travel agent *before* you book.

❽ You do not like your dining room seating.
Some "standard" market ships (particularly the large "resort" ships) operate two seatings for dinner (sometimes this applies to all meals). When you book your cruise, you are asked whether you want the first or second seating. The line will make every attempt to please you. But if you want second seating and are

given first seating (perhaps a large group has taken over the entire second seating, or the ship is full), there may be little the restaurant manager can do.

❾ You want a table for two and are put at a table for eight.
Again, see the restaurant manager (maître d') and explain why you are not satisfied. A little gratuity should prove helpful.

❿ You cannot communicate with your dining room waiter.
Dining room waiters are probably of a nationality and tongue completely foreign to yours, and all they can do is smile. This could prove frustrating for a whole cruise, especially if you need something out of the ordinary. See the restaurant manager, and tell him you want a waiter with whom you can communicate. If he does not solve the problem, see the hotel manager.

⓫ The food is definitely not "gourmet" cuisine as portrayed in the brochure.
If the food is not as described (for example, whole lobster in the brochure, but only cold lobster salad once during the cruise, or the "fresh squeezed" orange juice on the breakfast menu is anything but), inform the maître d' of the problem.

⓬ A large group has taken over the ship.
Sometimes, large groups have blocked (pre-booked) several public rooms for meetings (seemingly every hour on the hour in the rooms you want to use). This means the individual passenger (that is you) becomes a second-class citizen. Make your displeasure known to the hotel manager immediately, tell your travel agent, and write a follow-up letter to the line when you get home.

⓭ A port of call is deleted from the itinerary.
If you only took the cruise because the ship goes to the place you have wanted to go for years, then read the fine print in the brochure *before* you book. A cruise line is under *no* obligation to perform the stated itinerary. For whatever reason (political unrest, weather, mechanical problems, no berth space, safety, etc.), the ship's captain has the ultimate say.

⓮ You leave personal belongings on a tour bus.
If you find you have left something on a tour bus, and you are back on board your ship, the first thing to do is advise the shore excursion manager or the purser's office. The tour operator ashore will then be contacted to ascertain whether any items have been handed in to their office.

⓯ You are unwell aboard ship.
There will be a qualified doctor (who generally oper-ates as a concession, and therefore charges) and medical facilities, including a small pharmacy. You will be well taken care of. Although there are charges for medical services, almost all cruise lines offer insurance packages that include medical coverage for most eventualities. It is wise to take out this insurance when you book.

⓰ The cruise line's air arrangements have you flying from Los Angeles via Timbuktu to get to your cruise ship.
Fine if your cruise ship is in Timbuktu (difficult, as it is inland). Most cruise lines with low rates also use the cheapest air routing to get you to your ship. That could mean flights from a central hub. Be warned: you get what you pay for. Ask questions *before* you book.

⓱ You fly internationally to take a cruise.
If your cruise is a long distance away from your home, then it usually makes good sense to fly to your cruise embarkation point and stay for at least a day or two before the cruise. Why? Because you will be better rested and able to adjust to any time changes. You will step aboard your ship already relaxed and ready for a real vacation. As a bonus, you will get to know the port of departure.

⓲ The ship's laundry ruins your clothes.
If any of your clothing is ruined or discolored by the ship's laundry, first tell your cabin steward(ess), and then follow up by going to the purser's office and getting it registered as a proper complaint. Take a copy of the complaint with you, so you can follow up when you get home. Unfortunately, you will probably find a disclaimer on the laundry list saying something to the effect that liability is limited to about $1 per item, which is not a lot. So, although the laundry and dry cleaning facilities generally work well, things can occasionally go wrong just like ashore.

⓳ You have extra charges on your bill.
Check your itemized bill carefully. Then talk to the purser's office and ask them to show you the charge slips. Finally, make sure you are given a copy of your bill, *after* any modifications have been made.

⓴ You're unhappy with your cruise experience.
You (or your travel agent) ultimately choose the ship and cruise. But if your ship does not meet your specific lifestyle and interests, or the ship performs less well than the brochure promises, then let your travel agent and the cruise line know as soon as possible. If your grievance is valid, many cruise lines will offer a credit, good towards a future cruise. But do be sure to read the fine print on the ticket. ❑

HOW SAFE ARE CRUISE SHIPS?

How likely is an accident at sea? What if there's a fire? Can you
fall overboard? How good are are medical facilities aboard?

You can't always stop passengers having too much to drink and falling over balconies. But, for maritime accidents, cruising has the travel industry's best safety record, with fewer than 20 passenger fatalities during the past 20 years. Of those, 11 happened when the *Royal Pacific* sank off Malaysia in 1992 after colliding with a Taiwanese trawler.

International regulations require all crew to undergo basic safety training *before* they are allowed to work aboard any cruise ship. On-the-job training is no longer enough. And safety regulations are getting more stringent all the time, governed by an international convention called SOLAS (Safety of Life at Sea), introduced in 1914 in the aftermath of *Titanic*'s sinking in 1912.

Can you accidentally fall overboard?

No. All cruise ships have sufficient railings to protect you and your children. You simply can't go overboard unless you really, really want to.

Safety measures

All cruise ships built since 1986 must have either totally or partially enclosed lifeboats with diesel engines that will operate even if the lifeboat is inverted.

Since October 1997, cruise ships have had:
● All stairways enclosed in self-contained fire zones.
● Smoke detectors and smoke alarms fitted in all passenger cabins and all public spaces.
● Low-level lighting showing routes of escape (such as in corridors and stairways).
● All fire doors throughout the ship controllable from the ship's navigation bridge.
● All fire doors that are held open by hinges capable of release from a remote location.
● Emergency alarms audible in all cabins.

Since 2002, ocean-going cruise ships on international voyages have had to carry voyage data recorders (VDRs), similar to black boxes carried by aircraft). Since October 2010, new SOLAS regulations have prohibited the use of combustible materials in all new cruise ships.

Crew members attend frequent emergency drills, the lifeboat equipment is regularly tested, and the fire-detecting devices, and alarm and fire-fighting systems are checked. Any passenger spotting fire or smoke is encouraged to use the nearest fire alarm box, alert a member of staff, or contact the bridge.

Lifeboat drill

Few recent incidents have required the evacuation of passengers, although two cruise ships were lost following collisions (*Jupiter* in 1988, and *Royal Pacific* in 1992), one after striking an iceberg near Antarctica (*Explorer* in 2007) and one after foundering on a reef off the Greek island of Santorini (*Sea Diamond* in 2007).

A passenger lifeboat drill, announced publicly by the captain, must be held within 24 hours of leaving the embarkation port. Attendance is compulsory. Learn your boat station or assembly point and how to get to it in an emergency. If other passengers are lighthearted about the drill, don't be distracted. Note your exit and escape pathways and learn how to put on your lifejacket correctly. The drill takes no more than 20 minutes and is a good investment in playing safe – the *Royal Pacific* took less than 20 minutes to sink after its collision in 1992.

Medical services

Except for ships registered in the UK or Norway, there are no mandatory international maritime requirements for cruise lines to carry a licensed physician or to have hospital facilities aboard. However, in general, all ships carrying over 50 passengers do have medical facilities and at least one doctor.

The standard of medical practice and of the doctors themselves may vary from line to line. Most shipboard doctors are generalists; there are no cardiologists or neurosurgeons. Doctors are typically employed as outside contractors and will charge for use of their services, including seasickness shots.

Regrettably, many cruise lines make medical services a low priority. Most shipboard physicians are not certified

---

IS SECURITY GOOD ENOUGH?

Cruise lines are subject to stringent international safety and security regulations. Passengers and crew can embark or disembark only by passing through a security checkpoint. Cruise ships maintain zero tolerance for onboard crime or offences against the person. Trained security professionals are employed aboard all cruise ships. In the case of the USA, where more than 60 percent of cruise passengers reside, you will be far more secure aboard a cruise ship than almost anywhere on land.

It is recommended that you keep your cabin locked at all times when you are not there. All new ships have encoded plastic key cards that operate a lock electronically; older ships have metal keys. Cruise lines do not accept responsibility for any money or valuables left in cabins and suggest that you store them in a safety deposit box at the purser's office, or, if one is provided, in your in-cabin personal safe.

You will be issued a personal boarding pass when you embark. This typically includes your photo, lifeboat station, restaurant seating, and other pertinent information, and serves as identification to be shown at the gangway each time you board. You may also be asked for a government-issued photo ID, such as a passport.

PIRACY IN THE GULF OF ADEN

The UN Security Council has renewed its authorization for countries to use military force against the pirates operating off Somalia who have been sabotaging one of the world's busiest shipping lanes. There were scores of pirate attacks in Somali waters in 2010, with nearly 40 cargo ships, several fishing vessels, one yacht and one cruise ship attacked or hijacked.

The pirates rarely harm people – their aim is to take hostages and demand a ransom from a ship's owners. Cruise ships are not immune from attack, particularly smaller ones. But *MSC Melody*, carrying 1,500 passengers, was attacked in 2009; its crew repelled the pirates by firing in the air and spraying water on them. *Oceanic*, the Maltese-flagged educational cruise ship attacked with grenades in 2010, escaped by blasting the pirates with high-pressure water hoses.

In 2008, the US Navy created a special unit, called Combined Task Force 150, to combat piracy in the Gulf of Aden.

In February 2009 the Maritime Security Patrol Area, introduced by coalition navies in 2008 as a safe passage corridor, was replaced by two separate five-mile wide eastbound and westbound, separated by a two-mile buffer.

in trauma treatment or medical evacuation procedures, for example. However, some medical organizations, such as the American College of Emergency Physicians, have a special division for cruise medicine. Most ships catering to North American passengers carry doctors licensed in the United States, Canada, or Britain, but doctors aboard many other ships come from a variety of countries and disciplines.

Cunard Line's *QM2*, with 4,344 passengers and crew, has a fully equipped hospital with one surgeon, one doctor, a staff of six nurses, and two medical orderlies; contrast this with *Carnival Paradise*, which carries up to 3,514 passengers and crew, with just one doctor and two nurses.

Any ship operating long-distance cruises, with several days at sea should have better medical facilities than one engaged in a standard 7-day Caribbean cruise, with a port of call almost every day.

Ideally, a ship's medical staff should be certified in advanced cardiac life support. The equipment should include an examination room, isolation ward/bed, X-ray machine (to verify fractures), cardiac monitor (EKG) and defibrillator, oxygen-saturation monitor, external pacemaker, oxygen, suction and ventilators, hematology analyzer, culture incubator, and a mobile trolley intensive care unit.

Existing health problems requiring treatment on board must be reported when you book. Aboard some ships, you may be charged for filling a prescription as well as for the cost of prescribed drugs. There may also be a charge if you have to cancel a shore excursion and need a doctor's letter to prove that you are ill.

Shipboard injury

Slipping, tripping, and falling are the major sources of shipboard injury. There are things you can do to minimize the chance of injury.

● Aboard many ships, raised thresholds separate a cabin's bathroom from its sleeping area.

● Don't hang anything from the fire sprinkler heads on the cabin ceilings.

● On older ships, note how the door lock works. Some require a key on the inside in order to unlock the door. Leave the key in the lock, so that in the event of a real emergency, you don't have to hunt for the key.

● Aboard older ships, take care not to trip over raised thresholds in doorways leading to the open deck.

● Walk with caution when the outer decks are wet after being washed, or if they are wet after rain. This applies especially to solid steel decks – falling onto them is really painful.

● Do not throw a lighted cigarette or cigar butt, or knock out your pipe, over the ship's side. They can easily be sucked into an opening in the ship's side or onto an aft open deck area, and cause a fire.

Surviving a shipboard fire

Shipboard fires can generate an incredible amount of heat, smoke, and often panic. In the unlikely event that you are in one, try to remain calm and think logically and clearly.

When you board the ship and get to your cabin, check the way to the nearest emergency exits fore and aft. Count the number of cabin doorways and other distinguishing features to the exits in case you have to escape without the benefit of lighting, or in case the passageway is filled with smoke. All ships use "low location" lighting systems.

Exit signs are normally located just above your head – this is virtually useless, as smoke and flames rise. Note the nearest fire alarm location and know how to use it in case of dense smoke. In future, it is likely that directional sound evacuation beacons will be mandated; these will direct passengers to exits, escape-ways and other safe areas and may be better than the present inadequate visual aids.

If you are in your cabin and there is fire in the passageway outside, put on your lifejacket. If the cabin's door handle is hot, soak a towel in water and use it to turn the handle. If a fire is raging in the passageway, cover yourself in wet towels and go through the flames.

Check the passageway. If there are no flames, or if everything looks clear, walk to the nearest emergency exit or stairway. If there is smoke in the passageway, crawl to the nearest exit. If the exit is blocked, go to an alternate one. It may take considerable effort to open a heavy fire door to the exit. Don't use the elevators: they may stop at a deck that's on fire, or they may stop working.

If there's a fire in your cabin or on the balcony, report it immediately by telephone. Then get out of your cabin, close the door behind you, sound the alarm, and alert your neighbors. ❑

ECO CRUISING AND EMISSIONS

The good news: sea travel produces an estimated 36 times less carbon dioxide than flying. The bad news: that's still not good enough

Although marine vessels are responsible for almost 3% of the world's greenhouse gases, the world's fleet of around 350 ocean-going cruise ships produces just 0.1% of those emissions. But can the cruise industry achieve the proposed international sulphur emissions (NOx) reduction to 0.5%, set to be introduced in 2020?

Eco diligence

Cruise companies are trying to achieve an integrated, industry-wide approach to reduce air emissions, to provide more fuel-efficient ships, and to retrofit some older ships with more efficient replacement machinery. New ships also benefit from better hydrodynamic hull design and advanced hull coatings can also improve efficiency. Careful handling of solid and liquid waste results in lower fuel consumption, and, therefore, CO_2 emissions. Further, flue gas from shipboard incinerators is controlled and ozone-depleting substances are prohibited. Advanced Water Treatment (AWT) systems recycle and treat waste water according to the toughest legal and eco-friendly standards.

MSC Fantasia and *MSC Splendida*, for example, use only low-sulphur fuels worldwide. *Celebrity Solstice*-class ships have 80 solar panels that help power elevators. Some ships have their hulls painted with "foul release" paint with fluor-polymers, non-toxic substances that help reduce CO_2 emissions through reduced fuel use.

The large resort ship operators exited Antarctica in 2011 due to a ban on carrying or burning heavy fuel oil below 60° south latitude, leaving travel to the white continent in the hands of specialist expedition ship operators. Antarctic fuel is now the highest cost fuel in the world, which adds to the expense of operating expedition ships.

Other eco-friendly measures include the use of LED lighting rather than fuel-guzzling halogen lighting; cabin lights and other electrical devices that function only when

a cabin key card is in the cabin door; water flow reducers fitted to faucets (taps) and showers; use of darkness-activated sensors that switch on the ship's external lights at dusk; the use of chilled river rocks that retain low temperatures well for buffet items, rather than ice; heat-deflecting window coatings; and the latest wastewater treatment technology. While all these measures help, they must be weighed against the costs of implementing them.

Emissions control areas

In 2009 the British Isles introduced the first Emissions Control Areas (ECA) around its shores and in the English Channel. This was followed by 10 countries in the Baltic and North Sea region. The International Maritime Organization (IMO) formally established a North American Emission Control Area, an area ringing the USA/Canada coast with a 200-mile (320-km) exclusion zone, coming into force in August 2012 (the US Virgin Islands may have its own ECA). IMO's global air emissions standards called for a progressive reduction of SOx emissions from 4.5% to 3.5% by January 2012, then to 0.5% by January 2020, subject to a review to be completed by 2018. The stricter ECA sulphur limits were reduced from 1.5% to 1% in 2010 and will be reduced further to 0.1% by 2015.

Fuels

Blended fuels and even some residual fuels have 1.5% sulphur content, but meeting the 0.1% limit will necessitate a shift to costlier distillate. This means passengers will probably be paying more for cruises, particularly for Alaska and Canada/New England itineraries, regions entirely within the new ECA, as operators switch to distillate in 2015. While most cruise ship burn heavy fuel oil (HFO), the smaller expedition-style ships burn the more expensive Marine Gas Oil (MGO).

Wastewater discharge

The IMO also introduced an International Convention on the Management of Ballast Water and Sediments (wastewater discharge) in 2010. By the end of 2010, MSC Cruises, for example, had almost eliminated the use of plastics, and no chemical detergents were being used in its shipboard laundries.

Cold ironing

This means plugging a ship into a land-based energy supply capable of running its essential functions while in port. The procedure makes sense in areas where electricity can be generated from renewable sources through a national grid, and allows the cruise ship to turn off its engines, thus reducing emissions. So far, cold ironing has been introduced in Juneau, Los Angeles, San Diego, Seattle, San

Francisco, and Vancouver, and other ports are looking at the possibilities. Because the power requirements of a large resort ship are high, any such hook-ups must be able to cope with demand. It is not cost-effective or practical for ships to convert to cold-ironing until more ports offer it.

The Port of San Francisco calculated that the provision of shoreside power supply prevents 140 pounds of diesel soot emissions and 1.3 tons of airborne nitrogen oxide emissions for each 10-hour ship call. It also reduces carbon dioxide by 19.7 tons. More city ports are expected to build this option into their infrastructure, but while shore power delivers excellent local air quality benefits, it costs about $5 million to install. ❑

THE LAST WORD: TELL-TALE SIGNS THAT YOU'VE CHOSEN THE WRONG SHIP

● When, as you embark, a waiter hands you a drink in a tall plastic glass from a tray of drinks of identical color and froth, then gives you a bill to sign without even saying "Welcome Aboard."

● When you wanted a quiet, restful cruise, but your travel agent booked you aboard a ship with 300 baseball fans and provided them all with signed baseball bats and boom boxes for their use on deck.

● When your "luxury" cabin has walls so thin you can hear your neighbors combing their hair.

● When the brochure's "full bathtub" turns out to be "a large washbasin" located at floor level.

● When you packed your tuxedo, but other passengers take "formal" attire to mean clean cut-off jeans and a less stained T-shirt.

● When you have a cabin with an "obstructed view" (usually there is a lifeboat hanging outside it), and it is next to or below the disco. Or the laundry. Or the garbage disposal facility. Or the anchor.

● When the "medical facility" is located in the purser's office and consists of a box of adhesive bandages with instructions in a foreign language.

● When the gymnasium equipment is kept in the restaurant manager's office.

● When "fresh selected greens" means a sprig of parsley on the entrée plate, at every lunch and dinner seating (boring even on a three-day cruise).

● When the cruise director tries to sell passengers a watch or an artwork over the public address system.

● When front-row seats at a rock concert would be quieter than a poolside deck chair at midday.

● When you hear the same rap tracks 10 times during the first morning.

● When you need shin pads to prevent injury caused by 600 children noisily chasing through passageways.

● When the cruise brochure shows your cabin with flowers and champagne, but you get neither.

● When the bottled water on your dining room table incurs a bill as soon as you open the bottle.

● When the brochure says "Butler Service," but you have to clean your own shoes, get your own ice, and still tip twice the amount you would for an "ordinary" cabin steward.

● When the Beer Drinking or Hog Calling Contest, Knobby Knees Contest, and Pajama Bingo are listed as "enrichment lectures."

● When the so-called "fresh-squeezed orange juice" you just ordered means fresh-squeezed, but last week, on land, and poured into industrial-size containers before being transferred to your polystyrene or plastic cup on deck.

● When the brochure says tipping is not required, but your waiter and cabin steward insist otherwise.

● When the cruise director telephones you at 2.30am to let you know that the bingo jackpot is up to $1,000 and that an exciting art auction is about to start.

● When, on the final day, the words "early breakfast" means 5am, and "vacate your cabin by 7.30am" means you face the dismal prospect of spending three hours sitting in the showlounge waiting for disembarkation, with 500 available seats, your hand luggage, and up to 5,000 other passengers, probably playing bingo.

● When on deck, you notice a large hole in the bottom of one or more of the ship's lifeboats.

● When the cabin steward tries to sell you a cut-price time-share in his uncle's coal mine.

● When the proclaimed "five-course gourmet meal" is four courses of salty chicken soup and a potato.

● When the "Deck Buffet" means that there are no tables and chairs, only the deck, to eat off.

● When the brochure shows photos of smiling young couples, but you and your spouse/partner are the only passengers under 80.

● When the library is located in the engine room.

● When the captain tells you he is really a concert pianist and his professional diploma is really for the piano, not navigation.

Index

Numbers in **bold** refer to pages containing cruise ship reviews

Credits

Photography:
4Corners Images cover
A1A Vista Cruises 106
ABB Group 191
AIDA Cruises 7
American Safari Cruises 10B, 100, 159T
Antigua & Barbuda Tourism 35
Apa Publications 112 (both), 113 (all)
Blount Small Ship Adventures 99B, 161
Brimberg & Coulson/Lindblad 85
Captain Cook Cruises 11B, 97, 98, 110B
Carnival Cruise Lines 6, 18B, 21B, 22T, 27, 30, 55T, 59T, 60, 65, 67T, 74, 78–79, 86, 88, 92, 124, 127T, 127B, 128T, 128B, 129, 130T, 130B, 131, 157(7), 185, 188T, 670, 673
Celebrity Cruises 95B, 123T, 132, 133T, 133B, 134T, 134B
Corbis 1, 4–5, 17T, 46, 95T, 111, 118, 159B
Costa Cruises 68–69, 114, 135T, 135B, 137T, 137B, 157(5), 178
CPTM (Danee Hazama, Julien Aurial) 104, 105B,
Cruceros Australis 160–161
Cruise People, The 105

Crystal Cruises 28–29, 41, 54, 76T, 79B, 117B, 162B, 175
Cunard Line 25T, 64T, 89T, 101, 121, 125, 138, 139T, 139B, 157(2), 183, 190
Disney Cruise Line 8T, 14L, 14C, 14–15, 15T, 15BL, 17B, 73, 75T, 80–81, 162–163
Fred Olsen Cruise Line 22B, 25B, 120, 163B, 672
Glyn Genin/Apa 108B, 109B
Getty Images 48B, 89B, 126
Hapag Lloyd 9B, 29B, 31T, 55B, 184
Hebridean Island Cruises 58T
Holland America Line 16, 47, 72, 140, 141T, 141B, 142T, 142B
Hurtigruten 99T, 164
iStockphoto 81
Sven-Olof Lindblad 96B
Louis Cruises 143
Meyer Werft 192 (all)
Henny Miltenburg/Quark Expeditions 93
MSC Cruises 49B, 51, 66, 67B, 70, 82, 87T, 116B, 119, 144, 145, 157(3), 179B
Michael S. Nolan/Lindblad 94
Norwegian Cruise Line 57T, 58B, 116–117, 123B(2), 146T, 146B, 147, 180
P&O Cruises 148, 149, 157(4)
Ponant Cruises 96T, 168

Princess Cruises 52B, 87B, 150B, 150T, 151T, 151B, 157(6), 181, 186
Puerto Rico Tourist Company 52T
Regent Seven Seas Cruises 13, 23, 53, 71B, 169B
Royal Caribbean International 3, 8B, 12, 18–19, 26, 28B, 32T, 49T, 56T, 56B, 62, 63T, 63B, 64B, 68, 71T, 75B, 76B, 77, 83, 84, 115, 122 (all), 123B(3), 152B, 152–153, 153B, 154B, 154–155, 155B, 156T, 156B, 157(1), 187
Seabourn 176–7, 189
SeaDream Yacht Cruises 174
Silversea Cruises 57B, 123B(1)
Ayako Ward 2, 90, 103T, 109T, 172B, 188B
Douglas Ward 9T, 10–11, 15BR, 20, 21T, 24T, 24B, 31B, 32B, 33, 48T, 50T, 50B, 61, 78B, 91, 102, 107, 108T, 110T, 136, 158, 160, 165, 166B, 166–167, 167B, 170–171T, 170–171B, 172T, 173, 182
Peter Stuckings/Apa 179T
John Weller/Quark Expeditions 169T

Cover design: Richard Cooke
Cartography Editor: Zoë Goodwin
Map Production Apa Cartography Dept.
Maps © 2011 Apa Publications (UK) Ltd